Criminal Investigation

SEVENTH EDITION

Charles R. Swanson
UNIVERSITY OF GEORGIA

Neil C. Chamelin
FLORIDA DIVISION OF MOTOR VEHICLES

Leonard Territo
UNIVERSITY OF SOUTH FLORIDA

Boston, MA   Burr Ridge, IL   Dubuque, IA   Madison, WI
New York, NY   San Francisco, CA   St. Louis, MO
Bangkok   Bogotá   Caracas   Lisbon   London   Madrid   Mexico City
Milan   New Delhi   Seoul   Singapore   Sydney   Taipei   Toronto

McGraw-Hill Higher Education

*A Division of The **McGraw-Hill** Companies*

Criminal Investigation

Copyright © 2000, 1996, 1992, 1988, 1984, 1981, 1977 by The McGraw-Hill Companies, Inc. All rights reserved. Printed in the United States of America. Except as permitted under the United States Copyright Act of 1976, no part of this publication may be reproduced or distributed in any form or by any means, or stored in a data base or retrieval system, without the prior written permission of the publisher.

This book is printed on acid-free paper.

1 2 3 4 5 6 7 8 9 0 DOW/DOW 9 0 9 8 7 6 5 4 3 2 1 0 9

ISBN 0-07-228594-X

Editorial director: *Phillip A. Butcher*
Senior sponsoring editor: *Alan McClare*
Developmental editor: *Jennie Katsaros*
Marketing manager: *Leslie A. Kraham*
Project manager: *Christine Parker*
Production supervisor: *Kari Geltemeyer*
Director of design: *Keith J. McPherson*
Photo research coordinator: *Sharon Miller*
Supplement coordinator: *Carol Loreth*
Compositor: *GAC Indianapolis*
Typeface: *10.5/12 Goudy*
Printer: *R. R. Donnelley & Sons Company*

Library of Congress Cataloging-in-Publication Data

Swanson, Charles R. (date)
    Criminal investigation / Charles R. Swanson, Neil C. Chamelin,
Leonard Territo. — 7th ed.
      p. cm.
    Includes bibliographical references and index.
    ISBN 0-07-228594-X
    1. Criminal investigation. 2. Criminal investigation—United
States. I. Chamelin, Neil C., 1942– . II. Territo, Leonard.
III. Title.
HV8073.S84 2000
363.25—dc21   99-15560

http://www.mhhe.com

Charles R. "Mike" Swanson received his bachelor's and master's degrees in criminology from Florida State University and a doctorate in public administration from the University of Georgia, where he is Associate Director of the Carl Vinson Institute of Government. His primary responsibilities are to direct applied research, technical assistance, and training to Georgia units of state and local government. He has extensive experience in designing police promotional systems, conducting job task analyses, preparing written promotional tests, developing assessment center exercises, training assessors, and administering the assessment center process. The clients with whom he has worked include state police, patrol, and investigative agencies, sheriff's offices, and county and municipal police departments. Mike has testified in federal district court as an expert on promotional issues and in employee grievance hearings. He has designed and led training programs for over 10,000 police officers from throughout the country. A former patrol officer and detective with the Tampa Police Department, he also served as Senior Police Planner and Acting Deputy Director of the Florida Governor's Law Enforcement Council. Mike has coauthored five books and is the author or coauthor of a number of monographs, articles, and conference papers.

Neil C. Chamelin, an attorney, is a Hearing Officer in the Florida Division of Motor Vehicles. He previously served as Director of Criminal Justice Programs for Troy State University—European Region; Director of the Florida Police Standards and Training Commission; Division Director, Standards and Training Division, Florida Department of Law Enforcement; Administrator of the Police Science Division, Institute of Government at the University of Georgia; and Director of the Florida Institute for Law Enforcement. He has also served as a police officer in Sarasota, Florida. Chamelin is coauthor of *Criminal Law for Police Officers, Introduction to Criminal Justice,* and *Police Personnel Selection Process.*

Leonard Territo is Professor of Criminology at the University of South Florida, Tampa. Previously he was Chief Deputy (Undersheriff) of the Leon County, Florida, Sheriff's Office, and served for nine years in the patrol, traffic, detective, and personnel and training divisions of the Tampa Police Department. He is former Chairperson of the Department of Police Administration at St. Petersburg Junior College, where he also directed specialized continuing education programs for police officers through the Florida Institute for Law Enforcement. In addition to numerous articles, book chapters and technical reports, he has authored or coauthored nine books, the most recent of which are *Stress Management in Law Enforcement; Police Administration: Structures, Processes and Behavior;* and *Crime and Justice in America.* His books have been used in over 1,000 colleges and universities in all 50 states.

For Vicki and Paige; our children Traci, Kellie, Ben, Cole; Todd and Chris; Lorraine; and our grandchildren Kathleen, Bryan, and Tucker; Matthew and Branden.

For reasons that we can all articulate, crime is a terrible burden on society. The men and women who will, or presently, investigate crime play a crucial role in combating it. This book is intended as a tool with which to educate those trying to make life safer for all of us. There is much that is new in the seventh edition.

This book continues to differ from traditional investigation texts; it is important to understand these differences as they are again reflected throughout this edition. The distinctions made in the first edition between this and other investigative texts still apply.

First, investigation generally has been conceived of, and touted as, an art. This approach depreciates the precision required to conduct inquiries; it denies the existence of, and adherence to, rigorous methods; and it associates investigation with unneeded mysticism. Investigation is in large part a science. The fact that criminals are not always apprehended does not make it less so. The rational scientific method will, of necessity, be supplemented by initiative and occasional fortuitous circumstances, but it is the application of the method rather than shrewd hunches that most frequently produce results. This book unfolds along the same logical continuum as an investigation.

A second major difference arises from our judgment that writing about techniques takes on more substance if one understands something of the nature of the event being investigated. Thus, we have discussed typologies—including offenses, offenders, and victims. The treatment of these has not been equal in the crime-specific chapters because of the literature available. Collateral approaches have been the extensive use of illustrations, primary citations, and the judicious use of case studies.

Third, because crime prevention technology has been a significant milestone for both the police and the public, we have inserted short sections on prevention in the crime-specific chapters. The complexity of crime prevention dictates it as a specialization within police departments. Yet, at the scene of a crime, the investigator may be in a unique position to make a few helpful, if only rudimentary, suggestions to a victim on how to avoid further loss.

Finally, most investigative books in the past have blurred the distinction between the roles of the uniformed officer and the detective. While everyone may not agree with our dichotomizing, it is essential that the uniformed officer's role be properly recognized for the contribution it makes to the ultimate success of an investigation.

Criminal investigation is always in the process of evolving due to scientific, legal, and social developments, as well as changes in the behavior of criminals. While many investigative techniques are fundamental and remain basically the same over time, there are also significant changes that occur on a continuing basis. We hope that this edition captures both the ongoing and the changing dimensions of criminal investigation.

ACKNOWLEDGMENTS

Without the kindness of many people from throughout the country—literally from Alaska to Maine—this book could not have been written. They have contributed case histories; reviewed portions of the manuscript within their area of expertise; written a few sections; contributed photographs, forms, and other illustrations; and otherwise gone out of their way to be helpful. Our continuing concern in writing these acknowledgements is that, inadvertently, we may have omitted someone. If this is so, let us know so that we may correct this oversight, and also please accept our apologies. Our acknowledgments include both those who have contributed to this edition and those who helped with earlier editions. Some of the people identified have retired or taken on new responsibilities since assisting us. Unless otherwise requested, we show their organizational affiliation and status at the time of their original contributions. We feel that the agencies then employing them are also deserving of some continuing recognition.

Photographs in this book are credited as requested by the individual or organization submitting them. In this regard we note that photographs and other material were provided by William Cooper, Kern County, California, Sheriff's Department; Dr. B. G. Brogdon, University of South Alabama; John Ott and Brian Parnell, Federal Bureau of Investigation; Kathy L. Morrison, freelance photographer; Chief Thomas Coe and Sergeant Jack Adkins, Tallahassee, Florida, Police Department; Sheriff Cal Henderson and Detective Herb Metzgar, Hillsborough County, Florida, Sheriff's Office; Sergeant Christopher McKissick and Detective Tyler Parks, Port Orange, Florida, Police Department, James McGivney, Terry Parham, Michael Cashman, and Bob Quinn, DEA; Michael Gonzalez, Tampa Fire Department; Ronald Battelle and Mark Gartland, St. Louis County Police Department; Juliann Willey, Delaware State Police Crime Laboratory; Jack Dietz, Santa Fe Police Department; Pete Riley, Forensic Document Laboratory, Immigration and Naturalization Service; Kathy Saviers, Lightning Powder Company, Salem, Oregon; Bill Darby, Tennessee Bureau of Investigation; George Reis, Newport Beach, California, Police Department; Barry Carver, Texas Rangers, Austin; Joe Bubonic, Illinois State Police; Gerald Baril and R. Mailhot, Lewiston, Maine, Police Department; Cris Pardo and Derry Upshaw; Westminster, Colorado, Police Department; Robert Hicks, Oklahoma Bureau of Investigation; David Rosegrant, Arkansas State Police; Marilyn Lee, Frank Jensen, and Jill Marks, Tampa Police Department; Turner Pippin, Alaska Crime Laboratory; Donald Kane, Paul Tully, James Granelle, Ken Duffy, John Auletta, and Cheroxie Marks, Nassau County, New York, Police Department; Charlie Norton, Don Walsh, and Al Tamala, Maracopa County, Arizona, Sheriff's Office; Greg Stryker, National Insurance Crime Bureau; Bob Smith, ATF; Law Dow, ODV Equipment, South Paris, Maine; Rita Hall, Nursing Program Specialist, Pinellas County Public Health Unit, St. Petersburg, Florida; William Celester and Jon Shane, Newark Police Department; Michael Snowden, Cincinnati Police Department; Jack Ellis, Sarasota County, Florida, Sheriff's Office; Dr. Timothy Helentjaris, Department of Plant Sciences, University of Arizona; A. C. Stewart, Jr., Greensboro, North Carolina, Police Department; John Eck, Police Executive Research Forum; Thomas Deakin, retired editor, *FBI Law Enforcement Bulletin;* Dave MacGillis, Florida Marine Patrol; Dick Waldbauer, National Park Service; Superior Court Judge Sherry Hutt, Phoenix, Arizona; Woody Jones, Federal Law Enforcement Training Center, Glynco, Georgia; Martin McAllester, Archeological Research Investigation, Rolla, Missouri; Jim Kundell, University of Georgia; Charles Dreveskracht, Northeast State University, Oklahoma; Bruce Mirkin and Phillip Andrew, Environmental Protection Agency; James Dunn, John Reynolds, Dr. William Mooney, Frank Sass, Charles Steinmetz, Roger F. Depue, and Robert R. Hazelwood, FBI; Wayne Hopkins, United States Chamber of Commerce; Bruce Boart, American Insurance Institute; retired Sgt. Bill Bacon of the Los Angeles County Sheriff's Office; Charles Higgenbotham, editor, *The Police Chief;* Robert J. Roberton, Division of Drug Programs, State of California; Dr. William Rodriguez, Forensic Anthropologist and Director of Laboratories, Caddo Parish Coroner's Office, Shreveport, Louisiana; William M. Bass; former Sheriff Ken Katsaris, Leon County, Florida; Melodie Wilson-Hobbick and John Barracato, Aetna Casualty and Surety Company; R. Keppel, New Scotland Yard, London, England; Jim Besonen, Michigan State Police; John Steward, Austin, Texas, Police Department; Robert Edmons, Los Angeles County Sheriff's Office; W. W. Pope, Atlanta Police Department; Ruben Ortega, Tim Black, and Ken Johnson, Phoenix, Arizona, Police Department; George O'Neil, Pinkerton, New York; James Todd and David Easthon, Geauga County, Ohio, Sheriff's Department; Mike Cox, Texas Department of Public Safety; Rodney Snedeker, U.S. Forest Service; Dan Dowd, Wisconsin State Crime Laboratory; Ken Zercle and Roland Carignan, Connecticut State Police; Tom Streed, San Diego County Sheriff's Department; Douglas Knight, Jr.,

Questar Corporation; William Grube, Night Vision Equipment Company; Charlie Midkiff, ATF; Eddie McNelley, Boston Police Department; Elizabeth Watson and Don Kruger, Houston Police Department; Don Hiebert and Jim Whitehead, Idaho Bureau of Investigation; Tom Osberg and Steve Delaney, EPA; R. A. Bergman, Royal Canadian Mounted Police; Dick Waldbauer and Peter Baril, National Park Service; Victor Kovacic, Cleveland Police Department; Kevin Lothridge, National Forensic Science Technology Center; Dr. Deanne Dabbs, Virginia Division of Forensic Science; Ray Rice, Jose Alentado, and Patsy Andrew, FLETC, Glynco; Kevin Curry, 3M Company; Deborah Hewitt, Iowa Division of Criminal Investigation; Roland Lascola, Baltimore County Police Department; Donald Ghostlaw, Aetna Casualty and Surety Company; Dorothy Knox, Detroit Police Department; Bob Collins, Aviation Crime Prevention Institute; Andrew P. Johnson and John E. Granfield, Loudon County Sheriff's Department; Rick Buckner, Clark County, Washington, Sheriff's Office; Julia Cartwright, National Center for Missing and Exploited Children; Robert Farley, Cook County, Illinois, Sheriff's Department; Phil Dacey, Pittsburgh Police Department; Gary Barbour, Lakewood, Colorado, Police Department; Steve Reynolds, Tuscon Video Systems; Randy Desilet, Florida Department of Law Enforce-ment; Tom Pertierra, Havis Shields Equipment Company; Bill Hartner, Metro-Dade Police Department; Dennis Keener, FBI National Academy; Raymond Davis, Santa Ana, California, Police Department; John Donaldson and Robert Lane, Oregon Department of Public Safety; Robert Dempsey and Dale Heidman, Florida Department of Law Enforcement; Tom Evans, Pinellas County; Tom Carbone, Maine Department of Inland Fisheries and Wildlife; Barbara Carlsen, Wyoming Game and Fish Department; Barry Glover and Sandy Stevens, Clearwater, Florida, Police Department; Craig Carnevale, Gemprint, Ltd., Chicago, Illinois; Steve Munday, Texas and Southwestern Cattle Raisers Association, Fort Worth, Texas; Mario Alberti, Robert Jordan, and Charles Otero, retired, Tampa Police Department; William Barker and Jay Cochran, FBI; Joseph McNamara and Lester Harris, Kansas City Police; Department; Truett Ricks, formerly with the Kentucky State Police; Dick Mellard, retired, Wichita Police Department; and Frank Flanagan, Marsh Considine, and Art Paholke, formerly with the Chicago Police Department. Art and Marsh also made themselves available to answer questions and added immeasurably to the book with their patience and thoroughness.

In addition to those professionals who helped us with photographs, there was another group who helped out in a variety of ways. Bob Hopkins, Hillsborough County, Florida, Sheriff's Office, gave us information to strengthen the section on follow-up investigations; Michael Marksman, New York City Police Department, provided material which was used in the crimes against the elderly chapter; Commander Michael Frazier, Phoenix, Arizona, Police Department, was helpful with information on arson and explosives, as were Chief Richard Pennington and Officer R. Bonelli from the New Orleans Police Department; Chief Lee Donahue and Major William Gulledge, Honalulu, Hawaii Police Department; Kenneth V. Lanning, Supervising Special Agent of the Federal Bureau of Investigation and the National Center for Missing and Exploited Children, allowed us to reprint in Chapter 12—Crimes Against Children—from his previously published material on the topics of child molestation and child pornography. Major Andy Garrison and Frank Broadrick, Northeast Georgia Police Academy reviewed the chapter on report writing and made good suggestions for its revision.

Gene Lazarus, Florida State Fire College, Ocala, and Steve Mraz, formerly with the Pinellas County, Florida, Fire Academy, reviewed and contributed to the arson chapter. Bob Quinn, Tom Costigan, Mike Rendina, Jim Wilder, and Richard Frank, presently or formerly with the Drug Enforcement Administration; Tom Matthews, Temple Terrace, Florida, Police Department; and Mike Sciales, formerly with the Hillsborough County, Florida, Sheriff's Office, reviewed and contributed to the chapter on drug abuse. Richard Souviron, Chief Forensic Odontologist, Dade County Florida, Medical Examiners Office, was the principal author of the material dealing with bite marks and dental evidence. Dr. Wally Graves, Medical Examiner for Lee, Henry, and Glades Counties, Florida, provided information on dental evidence. John Valor, forensic artist and photographer, provided illustrations for the dental section. Dick

Williams, FBI Crime Laboratory, read the questioned documents section and made a number of suggestions to clarify and strengthen it. Don Hampton, Springfield, Missouri, Police Department, did the same for parts of the crime scene chapter. Bob Taylor, University of North Texas, who has yet to master the nuances of steelhead fishing, authored the chapter on computer crime. We continue to benefit from the reviews and research materials provided by Jim Halligan, formerly with the Florida Department of Law Enforcement, and more recently, a professor in Florida State University's School of Criminology. He is a superb teacher and a real friend.

Maryellin Territo devoted long hours to researching sources for the most current information relating to all facets of criminal investigation. Manuscript typing and revisions were handled by Marianne Bell, Carol Rennick, and Sally Phillips who worked hard and were patient with our changes and deadlines. Thanks to all of you.

This seventh edition of the book benefited from the counsel of reviewers; thanks to James M. Adcock, University of New Haven; William J. Vizzard, California State University, Sacramento; Anthony C. Trevelino, Camden County College; Norman J. Raasch, Lakeland Community College; Dennis M. Payne, Michigan State University; Richard H. DeLung, Wayland Baptist University; C. Wayne Johnston, Arkansas State University; Michael J. McCrystle, California State University, Sacramento; Daniel K. Maxwell, University of New Haven; and Steven Brandl, University of Wisconsin, Milwaukee.

Finally, a few words about the hard-working people at McGraw-Hill who helped make this a better book. We would also like to thank our McGraw-Hill Editors, Alan McClare and Jennie Katsaros; Project Manager Christine Parker; Designer Keith McPherson; Production Supervisor Kari Geltemeyer; Leslie Kraham in Marketing; and Carol Loreth who coordinated supplements. Finally, we acknowledge Wayne Moquin for his assistance with the Index.

Charles R. "Mike" Swanson
Neil C. Chamelin
Leonard Territo

BRIEF CONTENTS

Preface   xi

1   The Evolution of Criminal Investigation and
        Criminalistics   1

2   Crime and Its Investigation   21

3   The Crime Scene and Its Associated
        Procedures   33

4   Physical Evidence   67

5   Interviews   123

6   Field Notes and Reporting   139

7   Follow-Up Investigation   155

8   Interrogation   177

9   The Crime Laboratory and the Criminal
        Investigation Process   205

10 Injury and Death Investigation   225

11 Sex-Related Offenses   287

12 Crimes against Children   313

13 Crimes against the Elderly   353

14 Robbery   365

15 Burglary Investigation   391

16 Larceny Offenses   423

17 Vehicle Thefts and Related
        Offenses   465

18 Computer Crime   511

19 Agricultural, Wildlife, and Environmental
        Crimes   537

20 Arson and Explosives Investigations   563

21 Recognition, Control, and Investigation of
        Drug Abuse   605

22 The Decision to Initiate the Criminal
        Process   647

23 The Rules of Evidence   657

24 The Investigator as Witness   669

Index   679

CONTENTS

Chapter 1   The Evolution of Criminal Investigation and Criminalistics   1

The Evolution of Criminal Investigation   2
Historical Milestones of Criminalistics   10
A Parting View   18

Questions   18
Notes   19

Chapter 2   Crime and Its Investigation   21

The Investigation of Crime   22
Organization of the Investigative
   Function   24

Questions   31
Notes   31

Chapter 3   The Crime Scene and Its Associated Procedures   33

Organization of the Crime Scene
   Investigation   34
Typical Crime Scene Problems   35
Rules for the Crime Scene Investigator   36
Types of Evidence and Their
   Usefulness   47
The Crime Scene Search   48

The Collection and Care of Evidence   52
Visually Documenting the Crime
   Scene   53
Submission of Evidence to the
   Laboratory   60
Questions   63
Notes   64

Chapter 4 Physical Evidence   **67**

Class versus Individual
 Characteristics   68

Soil   69

Paint   74

Glass   75

Fibers, Cloth Fragments, and
 Impressions   77

String, Cord, and Rope   79

Fingerprints   81

Dental Evidence   92

Hair   97

Blood   99

Human Excretions and Secretions   104

Lipstick and Lip-Print Evidence   105

Firearms   106

Tool Marks   111

Questioned Documents   113

Questions   **118**

Notes   **119**

Chapter 5 Interviews   **123**

Witnesses: Motivations and
 Perceptions   124

Reliability of Eyewitness Identification   126

Hypnosis as an Investigative Tool   128

Qualifications of the Interviewer   130

Time, Place, and Setting of the
 Interview   130

Interviewing: Processes and
 Techniques   132

Documenting the Interview   135

Questions   **137**

Notes   **137**

Chapter 6 Field Notes and Reporting   **139**

Field Notes   140

The Importance and Use of Reports   141

Writing Effective Reports   143

Aids to Information Gathering during the
 Original Investigation   149

The Follow-Up Investigation and
 Supplemental Reports   149

Questions   **154**

Notes   **154**

Chapter 7 Follow-Up Investigation   **155**

The Decision to Initiate a Follow-Up
 Report   156

Crime Analysis   160

The National Crime Information
 Center   164

Neighborhood Canvass   165

Informants   165

Surveillance   167

Mechanical Lie Detection   169

Relationships with Victims and
 Witnesses   171

Guidelines for Conducting Lineups   172

Questions   **175**

Notes   **175**

Chapter 8 Interrogation   177

    Objectives of Interrogation   178

    Interviews and Interrogations: Similarities and Differences   178

    Preinterrogation Legal Requirements   179

    In-Custody Interrogation Defined   183

    Planning for Interrogation   188

    Beginning the Interrogation   192

    The Interrogation   193

    Interrogation Techniques and Approaches   197

    The Importance of Listening   198

    Documenting the Interrogation   199

    Admissibility of Confessions and Admissions   202

    Questions   203

    Notes   203

Chapter 9 The Crime Laboratory and the Criminal Investigation Process   205

    Forensic Science and Criminalistics Defined   206

    Crime Laboratories: Programs and Personnel Distribution   206

    Measures of Effectiveness of Crime Laboratories   207

    Technologies   211

    Handling Evidence in the Laboratory   217

    ATF Forensic Science Laboratories   219

    The FBI Crime Laboratory   220

    Questions   223

    Notes   223

Chapter 10 Injury and Death Investigation   225

    The Law   226

    Motivational Models for Classification of Homicide   226

    Responding to the Scene   227

    Arrival at the Scene of a Homicide   227

    Establishing a Chain of Custody   227

    Investigative Tools and Equipment   228

    The Medico-Legal Examination   229

    The Autopsy   229

    Identification of the Dead Person   230

    The Search for Buried Bodies   233

    Estimating Time of Death   239

    Evidence from Wounds   246

    The Uncooperative Victim   258

    Suicide   259

    Vehicle Homicides   270

    Fire Deaths   272

    Family/Domestic Violence   276

    Stalking   278

    Serial Murder and the NCAVC   280

    Criminal Investigative Analysis   282

    Questions   284

    Notes   284

Chapter 11 Sex-Related Offenses   287

    Classification of Sex-Related Offenses   288

    Typology of Rape   288

    Sex-Related Investigations   294

    Why Women Do Not Report Rape to the Police   298

    False Rape Allegations   298

    The Victim and Physical Evidence   300

Condom Trace Evidence   304

Record of Injuries   306

Autoerotic Deaths   306

Questions   310

Notes   310

Chapter 12   Crimes against Children   313

Assaults against Children   314

Burn Injuries and Child Abuse   314

Shaken-Baby Syndrome   319

Munchausen Syndrome by Proxy   321

Child Molestation   323

Child Pornography   336

Incest   339

Sudden Infant Death Syndrome   343

Infant Abduction   346

Use of Age Progression Technology to Search for Missing Children   348

Questions   349

Notes   350

Chapter 13   Crime against the Elderly   353

The Process of Aging   354

Categories of Mistreatment   356

Crimes Affecting the Elderly   358

Triads–Preventing Crimes against the Elderly   362

Questions   364

Notes   364

Chapter 14   Robbery   365

Elements of the Crime   366

Overview: The Offense, the Victim, and the Offender   368

Typology of Robberies   371

Arrest Probabilities   375

Investigative Techniques   376

The Crime Scene Technician and the Laboratory   385

"Three-Strikes" Laws   385

The Investigator's Educative Responsibility   386

Questions   388

Notes   388

Chapter 15   Burglary Investigation   391

Offenders   392

The Law   395

Approaching the Scene and Initial Actions   396

Investigative Considerations at the Scene   397

Safe Burglaries   401

Residential Burglary   414

Tracing and Recovering Stolen Property   416

The Investigator's Crime Prevention Role   417

Questions   419

Notes   420

Chapter 16   Larceny Offenses   423

Investigative Procedure   424
Credit Card Fraud   425
Check Fraud   427
Cellular Phone Cloning   431
Receiving Stolen Property   434
Shoplifting   437

Confidence Games   440
White-Collar Crime   442
Fraudulent Use of Social Security
  Numbers   451
The Looting of Archaeological Sites   453
Questions   461
Notes   462

Chapter 17   Vehicle Thefts and Related Offenses   465

Auto Theft   466
Theft of Heavy Equipment and Farm
  Equipment   473
Investigative Tools and Techniques   474
Prevention Programs   497

Odometer Fraud   501
Marine Theft   502
Aircraft and Avionics Theft   506
Questions   509
Notes   509

Chapter 18   Computer Crime   511

Types of Computer Crime   512
The Hacker Profile   526
The Insider Profile   528
Investigating Computer Crime   529

Preventing Computer Crime   531
Questions   534
Notes   534

Chapter 19   Agricultural, Wildlife, and Environmental Crimes   537

Agricultural Crime and Its City
  Connection   538
Some Dimensions of Agricultural, Wildlife,
  and Environmental Crimes   538
Timber Theft   539
Theft of Agrichemicals   540
Livestock and Tack Theft   541

Livestock Identification   546
Physical Evidence   547
Crime Prevention Measures   549
Wildlife Crimes   550
Environmental Crime   553
Questions   561
Notes   561

Chapter 20   Arson and Explosives Investigations   563

Preliminary Investigation   564
Where and How Did the Fire Start?   564
Burn Indicators   567
Fire Setting and Related Mechanisms   568

Arson for Profit   573
Other Motives for Arson   579
Detection and Recovery of Fire-Accelerant
  Residues   583

Scientific Methods in Arson
Investigation   585

Interviews   588

The Arson Suspect   591

Photographing the Arson Scene   592

Explosives Investigation   592

Bomb Threats   597

Suspicious Packages and Letters   600

Questions   601
Notes   602

Chapter 21   Recognition, Control, and Investigation of Drug Abuse   605

The Opium Poppy   606

Synthetic Narcotics   608

Recognizing an Addict   609

Stimulants   610

Depressants   619

Speedballing   622

Hallucinogens   622

Field Testing for Controlled
Substances   628

Investigative Procedures   628

Drug Informants: Motives, Methods,
and Management   629

The Investigator's Prevention
Responsibility   633

Drug Abuse by Practitioners   634

Clandestine Drug Laboratories   635

Search Warrants and Probable
Cause   638

Evidence Handling and Security
Problems   639

Questions   641
Notes   641
Drug Glossary   643

Chapter 22   The Decision to Initiate the Criminal Process   647

Arrest Defined   648

Arrest Procedures   649

The Arrest Warrant   650

The Probable-Cause Requirement   651

Evaluating the Case   653

Questions   655
Notes   655

Chapter 23   The Rules of Evidence   657

Evidentiary Concepts   658

Judicial Notice   662

Types of Evidence   663

The Hearsay Rule   665

Evidentiary Privileges   667

Witnesses   668

Questions   668

Chapter 24   The Investigator as Witness   669

The Role of the Police Witness   670

Credibility   670

Characteristics of a Good Witness   670

Understanding the Jury   671

Appearance and Demeanor   671

Trial Process   671

Taking the Witness Stand   672

Answering Questions   673

Cross-Examination   674

Use of Notes on the Stand   675

Leaving the Witness Stand   676

Questions   677

Index   679

The Evolution of Criminal Investigation and Criminalistics

CHAPTER OUTLINE

The Evolution of Criminal Investigation 2
Historical Milestones of Criminalistcs 10
A Parting View 18
Questions 18
Notes 19

INTRODUCTION

Writing about two separate but entwined fields–criminal investigation and criminalistics–is a difficult task. Many volumes have been written on each of these two fields, but the space that can be devoted to them here is limited. However, sufficient broad perspectives and supporting details are provided in this chapter to allow those intrigued by these subjects to independently pursue their interest with a basic working knowledge.

THE EVOLUTION OF CRIMINAL INVESTIGATION

For present purposes, the evolution of criminal investigation began in eighteenth-century England, when massive changes were being unleashed. To fully appreciate the development of criminal investigation, you should first understand the social, economic, political, and legal contexts in which it evolved. Thus, the balance of this section provides this background under four major headings: (1) "The Impact of the Agricultural and Industrial Revolutions," (2) "The Fieldings: Crime Information and the Bow Street Runners," (3) "The Metropolitan Police Act of 1829," and (4) "American Initiatives."

THE IMPACT OF THE AGRICULTURAL AND INDUSTRIAL REVOLUTIONS

During the eighteenth century two events—an agricultural revolution and an industrial revolution—began a process of change that profoundly affected how police services were delivered and investigations conducted. Improved agricultural methods, such as the introduction in 1730 of Charles Townshend's crop rotation system and Jethro Tull's four-bladed plow, gave England increased agricultural productivity in the first half of the eighteenth century.[1] Improvements in agriculture were essential preconditions to the Industrial Revolution, in the second half of the eighteenth century, because they freed people from farmwork for city jobs. As the population of England's cities grew, slums also grew, crime increased, and disorders became more frequent. Consequently, public demands for government to control crime grew louder.

THE FIELDINGS: CRIME INFORMATION AND THE BOW STREET RUNNERS

In 1748, Henry Fielding became chief magistrate of Bow Street and set out to improve the administration of justice. In 1750, he established a small group of volunteer, nonuniformed homeowners to "take thieves." Known as the "Bow Street Runners," these Londoners hurried to the scenes of reported crimes and began investigations, thus becoming the first modern detective force. By 1752, Fielding began publishing *The Covent Garden Journal* as a means of circulating the descriptions of wanted persons. Upon his death in 1754, Henry Fielding was succeeded by his blind half-brother, John Fielding, who carried on Henry's ideas for another 25 years.[2] Under John Fielding, Bow Street became a clearinghouse for information on crime, and by 1785 at least four of the Bow Street Runners were no longer volunteers but paid government detectives.[3]

THE METROPOLITAN POLICE ACT OF 1829

In 1816, 1818, and again in 1822, England's Parliament rejected proposals for a centralized professional police force for London. Highly different political philosophies were at odds. One group argued that such a force was a direct threat to personal liberty. The other group—composed of reformers such as Jeremy Bentham and Patrick Colquhoun—argued that the absence, rather than the presence, of social control was the greater danger to personal liberty. Finally, in 1829, due in large measure to the efforts of Sir Robert Peel, Parliament created a metropolitan police force for London. Police headquarters became known as "Scotland Yard," because the building formerly had housed Scottish royalty. Police constables were referred to as "bobbies," a play on Peel's first name, Robert. Peel selected Charles Rowan and Richard Mayne as police commissioners, responsible for the development of this new force, and important new principles governing police work were stated:

1. The police must be stable, efficient, and organized along military lines.
2. The police must be under government control.
3. The absence of crime best proves the efficiency of police.
4. The distribution of crime news is essential.
5. The development of police strength both over time and by area is essential.
6. No quality is more indispensable to a police officer than a perfect command of temper; a

quiet, determined manner has more effect than violent action.

7. Good appearance commands respect.

8. The securing and training of the proper people is at the root of efficiency.

9. Public security demands that every police officer be given a number.

10. Police headquarters should be centrally located and easily accessible to the people.

11. Police should be hired on a probationary basis.

12. Police records are necessary to the correct distribution of police strength.[4]

Because French citizens had experienced oppression under centralized police, the British public was suspicious of and at times even hostile to the new force. In response to the high standards set for the police force, there were 5,000 dismissals and 6,000 forced resignations from the force during the first three years of operations.[5] This record was a clear indication to the public that police administrators were requiring officers to maintain high standards of conduct. Within a few years, the London Metropolitan Police had won a reputation for fairness, and it became the international model of professional policing. Despite the growing popularity of the uniformed bobbies, however, there was fear that the use of "police spies"—detectives in plain clothes—would reduce civil liberties.

In the years immediately following 1829, some Metropolitan Police constables were temporarily relieved from patrolling in uniform to investigate crimes on their beats.[6] As the distinction between the use of uniformed constables to prevent crime and the use of plainclothes detectives for investigation and surveillance became clear, the public became uneasy. Illustratively, in 1833, a Sergeant Popay was dismissed following a parliamentary investigation which revealed that he had infiltrated a radical group, acquired a leadership position, and argued for the use of violence. Until 1842, Metropolitan Police constables assigned to investigate crimes competed with the Bow Street Runners; in that year, a regular detective branch was opened at Scotland Yard, superseding the Bow Street forces.[7] Under Commissioner Mayne, the detective force was limited to no more than 16 investigators, and its operations were restricted because of his distrust of "clandestine methods."[8]

Following a scandal in which three of four chief inspectors of detectives were convicted of taking bribes,[9] a separate, centralized Criminal Investigation Department (CID) was established in 1878 at Scotland Yard. It was headed by an attorney, Howard Vincent.[10] Uniformed constables who had shown an aptitude for investigation were recruited to become CID detectives.[11] Interestingly, at least since Vincent's time, the use of strong central control has been a recurrent theme in the reform of police organizations to correct for abuses. (See Figure 1–1.)

AMERICAN INITIATIVES

The success of Peel's reform in England did not go unnoticed in the United States. Stephen Girard bequeathed $33,190 to Philadelphia to develop a competent police force. In 1833, Philadelphia passed an ordinance creating America's first paid, daylight police force. Although the ordinance was repealed just three years later, the concept of a paid police force would reappear as American cities staggered under the burdens of tremendous population growth, poverty, and massive crime. In 1836, New York City rejected the notion of a police force organized along the lines advocated by Peel. The committee studying the idea concluded:

> Though it might be necessary, at some future period, to adopt a system of police similar to that of London . . . the nature of our institution is such that more reliance may be placed upon the people for aid, in case of any emergency, than in despotic governments.[12]

Thus, before midcentury, few American cities had police service, and what existed was inadequate. Many cities had paid police service only at night or treated day and night police services as entirely separate organizations. Finally, in 1844, the New York state legislature created the first unified police force in the country, although New York City did not actually implement the measure until a year later. Other cities rapidly followed New York's lead: Chicago in 1851, New Orleans and Cincinnati in 1852, and Baltimore and Newark in 1857. By 1880, virtually every major American city had a police

Figure 1–1
New Scotland Yard
In 1890, the Metropolitan Police left their original quarters and were housed in New Scotland Yard, which is pictured here circa 1895. Subsequently, in 1967, the Metropolitan Police moved again, to their present facilities, which are also referred to as New Scotland Yard.

(Courtesy London Metropolitan Police)

force based on England's Peelian reforms of 1829 and pioneered in this country by New York City.

If one of the problems of the London Metropolitan Police had been getting the public to accept some constables' working out of uniform as detectives, in this country the problem was getting the police to wear uniforms in the first place. American officers felt that a uniform made them easy targets for public harassment and made them look like servants. Only after the Civil War did the wearing of a uniform—invariably blue—become widely accepted by American police officers.

Pinkerton's National Detective Agency

American cities needed reliable detectives for several reasons. First, graft and corruption were common among America's big-city police officers. Second, police jurisdiction was limited. Third, there was little communication of information among departments in different cities. Thus, offenders often fled from one jurisdiction to another with impunity.

In 1846, seeing the need for reliable investigators, two former St. Louis police officers formed the first recorded private detective agency.[13] But the major private detective agency of the nineteenth century was formed by Allan Pinkerton (1819–1884). In 1849, Chicago's Mayor Boone appointed Pinkerton as the city's first detective. Pinkerton enjoyed great success, but he resigned due to political interference and took a job as a special U.S. mail agent to solve a series of post office thefts and robberies in the Chicago area.[14] In 1850, after succeeding in this job, Pinkerton, by then a well-known public figure, formed a private detective agency with a Chicago attorney, Edward Rucker.[15] Pinkerton's trademark was an open eye above the slogan "We never sleep."[16] The trademark gave rise to the use of the term "private eye" in reference to any private investigator.[17] The Pinkertons enjoyed such enormous success in the United States and throughout the world that some people thought "Pinkerton" was a nickname for any American government detective.[18]

The list of achievements by Pinkerton and his operatives is impressive. Pinkerton reportedly discovered and foiled an assassination attempt on President-elect Lincoln in Baltimore as Lincoln traveled to his inauguration in Washington, D.C.[19] At the outbreak of the Civil War in 1861, Pinkerton organized a Secret Service Division within the army (not to be confused with the U.S. Secret Service, which was organized after that war) and worked closely with Union General George McClellan until 1862, when McClellan was dismissed (see Figure 1–2).[20] Although Pinkerton infiltrated

Figure 1–2
Pinkerton at Work
Allan Pinkerton, President Lincoln, and
General McClellan at Antietam, Maryland,
about October 3, 1862.

(Courtesy Pinkerton's Archives)

Confederate lines in disguise on several occasions, he usually functioned as a military analyst.[21]

Following the Civil War, the Pinkertons were primarily engaged in two broad areas: (1) controlling a discontented working class, which was pushing for better wages and working conditions, and (2) pursuing bank and railroad robbers.[22] Unrestricted by jurisdictional limits, Pinkerton agents roamed far and wide pursuing lawbreakers. In a violent time, they sometimes used harsh and unwise methods. For instance, suspecting that they had found the hideout of Jesse James's gang, Pinkerton agents lobbed in a 32-pound bomb, killing a boy and injuring a woman.[23]

Pinkerton understood the importance of information, records, and publicity and made good use of all of them. For example, in 1868, Pinkerton agent Dick Winscott was assigned responsibility for smashing a group of bandits known as the Reno gang. Taking a camera with him, Winscott located Fred and John Reno and, after a drinking bout persuaded them to let him photograph them.[24] He sent the photographs to Pinkerton files, and within a year the Reno gang was smashed.[25] Pinkerton also collected photographs of jewel thieves and other types of criminals and photographed horses to prevent illegal substitutions before races.[26] The Pinkertons also pushed Butch Cassidy (Robert Parker)

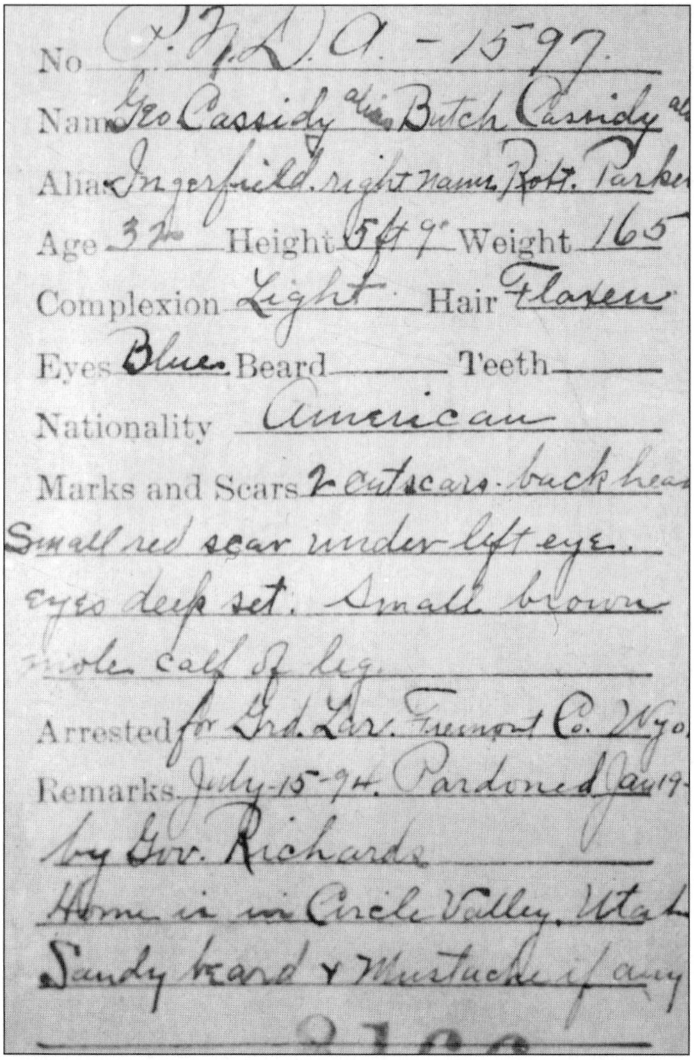

No P.N.D.A. - 1597.
Name Geo Cassidy alias Butch Cassidy al
Alias Ingerfield. right name Robt. Parker
Age 32 Height 5 ft 9" Weight 165
Complexion Light Hair Flaxen
Eyes Blue Beard ____ Teeth ____
Nationality American
Marks and Scars 2 cut scars. back head
Small red scar under left eye.
eyes deep set. Small brown
mole calf of leg.
Arrested for Grd. Lar. Fremont Co. Wyo.
Remarks July-15-94. Pardoned Jan 19-
by Gov. Richards
Home is in Circle Valley, Utah
Sandy beard & Mustache if any

(Courtesy Wyoming State Archives and Historical Department)

Figure 1–3
Butch Cassidy's Pinkerton Record
Butch Cassidy's Pinkerton record; note the "P.N.D.A." initials on the first line, which stand for Pinkerton National Detective Agency.

and the Sun Dance Kid (Harry Longabaugh) into leaving the United States for South America, where they were reportedly killed by Bolivian soldiers at San Vincente in 1909 (see Figure 1–3).

The Pinkertons investigated other major types of crimes as well. They caught two safecrackers who stole $1,250,000 from a Massachusetts bank and a state treasurer of South Dakota who had embezzled $300,000.[27] Because of their better-known antilabor activities, the Pinkertons' other work often is overlooked. But they were the only consistently competent detectives available in this country for over 50 years[28] and provided a good model for government detectives.

The Emergence of Municipal Detectives

As early as 1845, New York City had 800 plainclothes officers,[29] although not until 1857 were the police authorized to designate 20 patrol officers as detectives.[30] In November 1857, the New York City Police Department set up a rogues' gallery—photographs of known offenders arranged by criminal specialty and height—and by June 1858, it had over 700 photographs for detectives to study so that they might recognize criminals on the street (see Figure 1–4).[31] Photographs from rogues' galleries of that era reveal that some offenders grimaced, puffed their cheeks, rolled their eyes, and otherwise tried to distort

Figure 1–4
NYPD Rogues' Gallery
Uniformed officers of the New York City Police Department maintaining a rogues' gallery in the detective bureau, circa 1896.

(Courtesy Library of Congress)

their appearance to lessen the chance of later recognition.

To assist detectives, in 1884 Chicago established this country's first municipal Criminal Identification Bureau.[32] The Atlanta Police Department's Detective Bureau was organized in 1885 with a staff of one captain, one sergeant, and eight detectives.[33] In 1886, Thomas Byrnes, the dynamic chief detective of New York City, published *Professional Criminals in America,* which included pictures, descriptions, and the methods of all criminals known to him.[34] Byrnes thereby contributed to information sharing among police departments. To supplement the rogues' gallery, Byrnes instituted the "Mulberry Street Morning Parade." At 9

o'clock every morning, all criminals arrested in the past 24 hours were marched before his detectives, who were expected to make notes and to recognize the criminals later.[35] Despite such innovations, Byrnes was tragically flawed; in 1894 he was forced to leave the department when he admitted that he had grown wealthy by tolerating gambling dens and brothels. In spite of such setbacks, by the turn of the century many municipal police departments used detectives.

State and Federal Developments

From its earliest days, the federal government employed investigators to detect revenue violations, but their responsibilities were narrow and their numbers few.[36] In 1865, Congress created the U.S. Secret Service to combat counterfeiting. In 1903—two years after President McKinley was assassinated by Leon Czolgosz in Buffalo—the previously informal arrangement of guarding the president was made a permanent Secret Service responsibility.[37]

In 1905, the California Bureau of Criminal Identification was set up to share information about criminal activity, and Pennsylvania governor Samuel Pennypacker signed legislation creating a state police force. Widely regarded then by labor as "strikebusters on management's side," the Pennsylvania State Police nevertheless was the prototype for modern state police organizations (see Figure 1–5). New York and Michigan in 1917 and Delaware in 1919 adopted the state police concept. One function that state police forces since have assumed is providing local police with help in investigations.

After Prohibition was adopted nationally in 1920, the Bureau of Internal Revenue was responsible for its enforcement. Eventually the ranks of the bureau's agents swelled to a massive 4,000.[38] Because the Bureau of Internal Revenue was lodged in the Department of the Treasury, these federal agents were referred to as "T-men."

In 1908, U.S. Attorney General Charles Bonaparte created the embryo of what was later to become the Federal Bureau of Investigation (FBI) when he ordered that investigations were to be handled by a special group. In 1924, J. Edgar Hoover (1895–1972) assumed leadership of the Bureau of Investigation; 11 years later Congress passed a measure giving the FBI its present designation. When Prohibition was repealed by the Eighteenth Amendment to the U.S. Constitution in 1933, many former bootleggers and other criminals turned to bank robbery and kidnapping.[39] During the Depression, some people saw John Dillinger, "Pretty Boy" Floyd, Bonnie and Clyde, and Ma Barker and her boys as "plain folks" and did not grieve over a bank robbery or the "snatching" of a millionaire (see Figure 1–6).[40] Given the restricted roles of other federal investigative agencies, it became the FBI's role to deal with these criminals.

Under Hoover, who understood the importance and uses of information, records, and publicity as well as Allan Pinkerton had, the FBI became known for investigative efficiency.

In 1932, the FBI established a crime laboratory and made its services available free to state and

Figure 1–5
The Pennsylvania State Police

Troop D, Pennsylvania State Police, Punxsutawney, Pennsylvania, 1906. Note that both plainclothes and uniformed personnel are represented.

(Courtesy Pennsylvania State Police)

Figure 1–6
FBI Director Hoover

J. Edgar Hoover (foreground, wearing a dark suit and light-colored hat) with Alvin "Old Creepy" Karpis (in handcuffs) in New Orleans on May 1, 1936. Nicknamed "Old Creepy" because of his cold stare and his precision in carrying out crimes, Karpis was personally arrested by Director Hoover. Karpis was a key member of Ma Barker's gang, which included her four sons, and he participated in a number of bank robberies and kidnappings. By the late 1930s, all the members of the notorious Barker-Karpis gang had been killed in gun battles or imprisoned, marking the end of the "gangster era."

(Courtesy Federal Bureau of Investigation)

local police. In 1935, it opened the National Academy, a training course for state and local police. In 1967, the National Crime Information Center (NCIC) was made operational by the FBI, providing data on wanted persons and property stolen from all 50 states. Altogether, these developments gave the FBI considerable influence over law enforcement throughout the country. Although some people argue that such federal influence is undesirable, others point out that Hoover and the FBI strengthened police practices in this country, from keeping crime statistics to improving investigation.

The Hague Conference in 1914 called for international action against illicit drugs. Subsequently, Congress passed the Harrison Act, making the distribution of nonmedical drugs a federal crime. Enforcement responsibility was initially given to the Internal Revenue Service, although by 1930 a separate Narcotics Bureau was established in the Treasury Department. In 1949, a

federal commission noted that federal narcotics enforcement was fragmented among several agencies, resulting in duplication of effort and other ills. In 1968, some consolidation of effort was achieved with the creation of the Bureau of Narcotics and Dangerous Drugs in the Department of Justice, and in 1973, with the creation of its successor, the Drug Enforcement Administration (DEA). Today the DEA devotes many of its resources to fighting international drug traffic. Like the FBI, the DEA trains state and local police in investigative work. The training focuses on recognition of illegal drugs, control of drug purchases, surveillance methods, and handling of informants.

The Police and the Supreme Court: The Due Process Revolution

From 1961 to 1966—a period frequently referred to as the "due process revolution"—the United States Supreme Court took an activist role, becoming quite literally makers of the law rather than interpreters of it.[41] Under Chief Justice Earl Warren (1891–1974), the Court used the due process clause of the Fourteenth Amendment to extend the provisions of the Bill of Rights to criminal proceedings in the various states.[42]

The Supreme Court could scarcely have picked a worse time to police the police. A burgeoning crime rate far outstripped population increases. Many politicians campaigned on "law and order" platforms. The problem of crime increasingly came to public notice through the mass media. In effect, the court extended procedural safeguards to defendants in criminal cases just when public fear of crime and social pressure to combat crime were becoming intense. The reaction of the country was swift: "Impeach Warren" billboards dotted the landscape.

Why did the Supreme Court undertake its activist role? What decisions so aroused public ire? How did the decisions affect police work, and how did police react? Fundamentally, the Supreme Court's role in the due process revolution was a response to a vacuum created when the police themselves failed to provide necessary leadership. The era of strong social activism by special-interest groups was not yet at hand, and neither state courts nor legislatures had displayed any broad interest in reforming the criminal law. What institution was better positioned to undertake this responsibility? The Court may even have felt obligated by the inaction of others. The high court did not move into this arena until after it had issued warnings that, to responsive and responsible leaders, would have been a mandate for reform. It thus became the Warren Court's lot to provide the reforms so genuinely needed but so unpopularly received.

Among the key decisions in the due process revolution were *Mapp* v. *Ohio* (1961), *Gideon* v. *Wainwright* (1963), *Escobedo* v. *Illinois* (1964), and *Miranda* v. *Arizona* (1966). For present purposes, the facts of these and related cases are less important than their focus and effect. Their focus was on the two vital areas of search and seizure and the right to counsel; their effect was a marked extension of the rights of defendants. Their effect on police work was staggering: they greatly reduced the use of questionable and improper tactics, thereby creating the need for new procedures in interrogations, lineups, and seizure of physical evidence. In general, police reacted to this whirlwind of due process with wariness tinged with outcries that they were being "handcuffed" and could not adequately perform their jobs. Many people felt that the decisions went beyond seeking a fair trial in quest of a perfect one.

By the early 1970s, many police executives had recognized that, although these Supreme Court decisions had placed new demands on policing, the decisions also had subtly hastened the development of professional policing, because the police had been forced to abandon improper tactics and to engage in virtually continuous, sophisticated training in order to conduct interrogations and searches that would be legal under Supreme Court guidelines. Another important side effect of the due process revolution was to reinforce the importance of the police's gathering and using physical evidence and obtaining criminalistical analysis of such evidence.

HISTORICAL MILESTONES OF CRIMINALISTICS

The origins of criminalistics are largely European. *Criminalistics* draws from diverse disciplines, such as geology, physics, chemistry, biology, and mathematics, to study physical evidence related to crime. The first major book describing the application of scientific disciplines to criminal investigation was written in 1893 by Hans Gross, a public prosecutor and later a judge from Graz, Austria.[43] Translated into English in 1906 under the title *Criminal Investigation,* it remains highly respected today as the seminal work in the field.

Criminalistics, like other scientific disciplines, enjoys periods of stability, but on the whole it is dynamic and in constant progress. To illustrate this principle of dynamic change, the histories of two commonly used services—personal identification and firearms identification—are traced in the following sections.

PERSONAL IDENTIFICATION

There are three major scientific systems for personal identification of criminals: anthropometry, dactylography, and deoxyribonucleic acid

(DNA) typing. The first was relatively short-lived. The second, dactylography, or fingerprint identification, remains in use today throughout the world. The third, DNA typing, is a contemporary development.

Anthropometry

Anthropometry was developed by Alphonse Bertillon (1853–1914), who is rightly regarded as the father of criminal identification (see Figure 1–7). The first method of criminal identification that was thought to be reliable, *anthropometry* "was based on the fact that every human being differs from every other one in the exact measurements of their body, and that the sum of these measurements yields a characteristic formula for each individual."[44] Figure 1–8 depicts a New York City police detective taking one type of measurement used in the "Bertillon system."

There was little in Alphonse Bertillon's early life to suggest that he would later make significant contributions. The grandson of a well-known naturalist and mathematician and the son of a distinguished French physician and statistician, who was also the vice president of the Anthropological Society of Paris,[45] Bertillon came from a family with a strong scientific tradition.[46] Moreover, in the late nineteenth century, there was a basic belief that all of life's problems could be solved by scientific knowledge, precise thinking, and scholarly deductions.[47] Yet Bertillon's early life reflected several failures and suggested little ability. He was expelled from several schools for poor grades, dismissed from an apprenticeship in a bank after only a few weeks, performed poorly as a tutor in England, and while in the army had difficulty telling the difference between the bugle signals for reveille and roll call.[48]

Figure 1–7
Bertillon
Alphonse Bertillon, the father of personal identification.

Figure 1–8
Taking a Bertillon Measurement
A New York Police Department detective taking Bertillon measurements circa 1896.

(Courtesy Jacques Genthial)

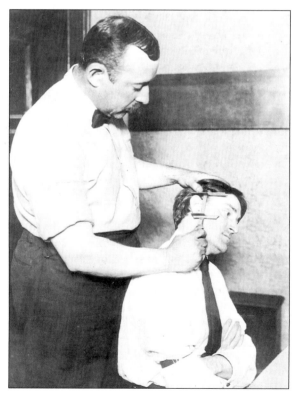

(Courtesy of the Library of Congress)

He was, therefore, able to obtain only a minor position in 1879, filing cards on criminals for the Paris police, because of his father's good connections.[49] The cards described criminals so vaguely that they might have fit almost anyone: "stature: average . . . face: ordinary."[50]

With growing resentment over the dreariness and senselessness of his work, Bertillon asked himself why so much time, money, and human energy were wasted on a useless system of identifying criminals.[51] Bertillon became a source of jokes and popular amusement as he began comparing photographs of criminals and taking measurements of those who had been arrested.[52] Bertillon concluded that if 11 physical measurements of a person were taken, the chances of finding another person with the same 11 measurements were 4,191,304 to 1.[53] His report outlining his criminal identification system was not warmly received. After reading it, the chief said:

> Bertillon? If I am not mistaken, you are a clerk of the twentieth grade and have been with us for only eight months, right? And already you are getting ideas? . . . Your report sounds like a joke.[54]

Yet in 1883, the "joke" received worldwide attention, because within 90 days of its implementation on an experimental basis, Bertillon correctly made his first criminal identification. Soon almost all European countries adopted Bertillon's system of anthropometry. In 1888, Bertillon's fertile mind produced yet another innovation, the *portrait parlé* or "speaking picture," which combines full-face and profile photographs of each criminal with his or her exact body measurements and other descriptive data onto a single card (see Figure 1–9).

After the turn of the century, many countries abandoned anthropometry and adopted the simpler and more reliable system of fingerprints instead. Bertillon himself was not insensitive to the potential of fingerprints. In 1902, he solved the murder of Joseph Riebel when he discovered the prints of Henri Scheffer on the pane of a glass cupboard.[55] Yet Bertillon's rigid personality would not allow him to acknowledge the clear superiority of dactylography to anthropometry. In 1906, Bertillon testified as an expert in handwriting—although he was unqualified—and his testimony helped to convict Captain Alfred Dreyfus of spying for Germany. Although the French government later admitted that the Dreyfus conviction had been an injustice,

Figure 1–9
Early Identification Card

A Bertillon-style identification card, combining both personal measurements and photographs, prepared on February 28, 1917, by the Chicago Police Department.

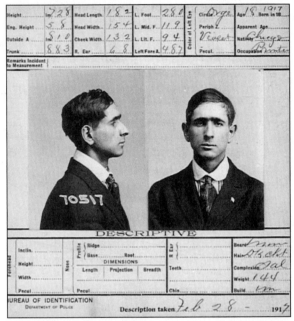

(Courtesy Chicago Police Department)

Bertillon refused to admit his error.[56] The Dreyfus incident tarnished Bertillon's reputation on two counts: (1) acting as an expert out of one's field and (2) refusing to admit error. It also illustrates from another perspective his rigid character.

Even so, Bertillon's place in history is secure as the father of criminal identification. His portrait parlé—an ancestor of the "mug shot"—was a significant innovation, to which Bertillon reluctantly added fingerprints, at first only four from the left hand but later all ten fingerprints from both hands.[57] Bertillon was also a pioneer in police photography beyond its application in the portrait parlé; when Bertillon found the fingerprint in the 1902 Riebel murder, his primary interest was in how to best photograph it. Ironically, his success in photographing this fingerprint found at the crime scene not only underscored the practical use of photography in criminal investigation; it also illustrated the value of dactylography, which even then was quickly gaining favor over Bertillon's anthropometry. Upon Bertillon's death in 1914, France became the last major country to replace anthropometry with dactylography as its system of criminal identification.

Dactylography

Early Discoveries Although in 1900 England became the first country to use dactylography as a system of criminal identification, fingerprints have a long legal and scientific history. In a legal context, in the first century, the Roman lawyer Quintilianus introduced a bloody fingerprint in a murder trial, successfully defending a child against the charge of murdering his father.[58] Fingerprints also were used on contracts during China's T'ang Dynasty in the eighth century as well as on official papers in fourteenth-century Persia and seventeenth-century England.[59]

In a scientific context, in 1684 in England, Dr. Nehemiah Grew first called attention to the system of pores and ridges in the hands and feet.[60] Just two years later, Marcello Malpighi made similar observations.[61] In 1823, John Perkinje, a professor at the University of Breslau, named nine standard types of fingerprint patterns and outlined a broad method of classification.[62] Despite these early stirrings, dactylography as a system of criminal identification took nearly another 75 years to emerge.

The Herschel-Faulds Controversy Beginning in 1858, William Herschel, a British official in India, requested the palm prints and fingerprints of those with whom he did business, thinking that it might awe people into keeping agreements.[63] Over the next 20 years, Herschel noted from his records that the patterns of the lines on the fingerprints never changed for an individual; a person might grow and undergo other physical changes, yet the fingerprints remained the same. Excited by the prospects of applying this knowledge to the identification of criminals, Herschel wrote in 1877 to the inspector general of the prisons of Bengal. The reply was kindly in tone, but it was clear that the inspector general thought that Herschel's letter was the product of delirium. Herschel was so dispirited by the reply that he made no further efforts to pursue his discovery. Meanwhile, Henry Faulds, a Scottish physician teaching physiology in Tsukiji Hospital in Tokyo, had been interested in fingerprints for several years before 1880. When a thief

left a sooty print on a whitewashed wall, Faulds was able to tell that the person in police custody was not the thief[64] and to match another suspect's fingerprints with those on the wall.[65] Faulds reported his findings in the journal *Nature* in 1880. Herschel read the account and published a reply, claiming credit for the discovery over 20 years before. A controversy broke out that was never resolved to anyone's satisfaction. Because there was also no official interest in using fingerprints, both Herschel and Faulds were even further frustrated.

Galton's and Vucetich's Systems In 1888, Sir Francis Galton (1822–1911), a cousin of Charles Darwin, turned his attention to criminal identification.[66] When the thorough Galton contacted the editor of *Nature* for both Herschel's and Faulds's addresses, he was by chance sent only Herschel's. Contacted by Galton, Herschel unselfishly turned over all of his files in the hopes that this revived interest would lead to practical uses of fingerprints.[67] In 1892, Galton published the first definitive book on dactylography, *Finger Prints*. It presented statistical proof of the uniqueness of fingerprints and outlined many principles of identification by fingerprints.[68] In Argentina, in 1894, Juan Vucetich (1858–1925) published *Dactiloscopia Comparada*, outlining his method of fingerprint classification. In 1892, a disciple of Vucetich's, an Inspector Alvarez, obtained South America's first criminal conviction based on fingerprints by using Vucetich's system to convict a woman of beating her two children to death.[69]

The Henry System The final breakthrough for the fingerprint method of personal identification was made by Edward Henry. At the age of 23 he went to India and by 1891 had become the inspector general of police of Nepal, the same province in which Herschel had worked some 15 years earlier.[70] Subject to many of the same influences as Herschel, but apparently working independently, Henry developed an interest in fingerprints[71] and instituted Bertillon's system with the addition of fingerprints to the cards. In 1893, Henry obtained a copy of Galton's book and began working on a simple, reliable method of classification. The governor general of India received a report from Henry in 1897 recommending that anthropometry be dropped in favor of Henry's fingerprint classification system. It was adopted throughout British

Figure 1–10
The Two Wests
Photographs and Bertillon measurements of William West and Will West.

	William West	Will West
Bertillon Measurements (in centimeters)		
Height	177.5	178.5
Outstretched arms	188.0	187.0
Trunk	91.3	91.2
Head length	19.8	19.7
Head width	15.9	15.8
Cheek width	14.8	14.8
Right ear	6.5	6.6
Left foot	27.5	28.2
Left middle finger	12.2	12.3
Left little finger	9.6	9.7
Left forearm	50.3	50.2

(Compiled from Federal Bureau of Investigation records)

India just six months later.[72] In 1900, Henry's system was adopted in England. The next year, Henry enjoyed two personal triumphs, the publication of his *Classification and Use of Finger Prints* and his appointment as assistant police commissioner of London,[73] rising to the post of commissioner two years later.

Faurot and "James Jones" In 1904, New York City Detective Sergeant Joseph Faurot was sent to England to study fingerprints, becoming the first foreigner trained in the use of the Henry classification system. Upon Faurot's return, the new police commissioner told him to forget about such "scientific notions" and transferred him to walking a beat.[74] In 1906, Faurot arrested a man dressed in formal evening wear, but not wearing shoes, as the man crept out of a suite in the Waldorf-Astoria Hotel.[75] Claiming to be a respectable citizen named "James Jones," the man demanded to see the British consul and threatened Faurot with nasty consequences.[76] Faurot sent the man's fingerprints to Scotland Yard[77] and got back a reply that "James Jones" was actually Daniel Nolan, who had 12 prior convictions of hotel thefts and who was wanted for burglarizing a home in England. Confronted with this evidence, Nolan confessed to several thefts in the Waldorf-Astoria and received a sentence of seven years.[78] Newspaper stories about the case brought Faurot appropriate credit and advanced the use of fingerprints in this country.

The West Case Despite the fame achieved by Faurot, the most important incident to advance the use of fingerprints in this country was the West case. In 1903, Will West arrived at the U.S. penitentiary at Leavenworth, Kansas. While West was being processed in through identification, a staff member said that there were already a photograph and Bertillon measurements for him on file. But a comparison of fingerprints showed that despite identical appearances and nearly identical Bertillon measurements, the identification card on file belonged to a William West, who had been in Leavenworth since 1901 (see Figure 1–10). The incident accelerated the recognition that fingerprints were superior to anthropometry as a system of identification.

Rivalry of Vucetich's and Henry's Systems
Vucetich's book on fingerprint classification was published in 1894, seven years before Henry's, but Henry's system has become much more widely used. To this day, however, some experts prefer Vucetich's system.[79] The rivalry between partisans of the two classification systems deserves attention.

In 1911, the provincial government of Buenos Aires passed a law requiring fingerprint registration for all adults subject to military service and eligible to vote.[80] By 1913 Vucetich had completed the task and decided to travel. In his travels, he was showered with decorations for his classification system. But when he visited Bertillon to pay his respects to the father of criminal identification,[81] Bertillon kept Vucetich waiting and finally opened the door just long enough to yell, "Sir, you have done me great harm," before slamming it shut again.[82] They were never to meet again. Upon his return to Argentina, Vucetich was to face further humiliation. When Buenos Aires planned an expansion of fingerprint registration, there were strong protests. In 1917 the Argentine government canceled registrations, seized Vucetich's records, and forbade him to continue his work.[83] In 1925, much as Bertillon had in 1914, Vucetich died a disappointed man. Although Vucetich's system is in use in South America today, Vucetich did not live long enough to see the vindication of his life's work.

In contrast, Henry became the head of what was then the world's most prestigious police organization and enjoyed the support of his government. These advantages, coupled with Vucetich's loss of support in his own country, meant that the Henry classification would become adopted virtually throughout the world.

DNA Typing

DNA as "Blueprint" Although *deoxyribonucleic acid (DNA)* was discovered in 1868, scientists were slow to understand its role in heredity.[84] During the early 1950s, James Watson and Francis Crick deduced the structure of DNA, ushering in a new era in the study of genetics.[85] Such developments were seemingly of peripheral interest to forensic scientists until 1985, when research into the structure of the human gene by Alec Jeffreys and his colleagues at Leicester University, England, led to the discovery that portions of the DNA structure of certain genes can be as unique to individuals as are fingerprints.[86] In fact, according to Jeffreys, the chance of two persons having identical DNA patterns is between 30 billion and 100 billion to 1.[87]

In all life forms—with the exception of a few viruses—the basis for variation lies in genetic material called DNA.[88] This DNA is a chemical "blueprint," which determines everything from our hair color to our susceptibility to diseases.[89] In every cell of the same human that contains DNA, this blueprint is identical, whether the material is blood, tissue, spermatozoa, bone marrow, tooth pulp, or a hair root cell.[90] Thus, with the exception of identical twins, each person has distinctive DNA. Initially, the process of isolating and reading this genetic material was referred to as "DNA fingerprinting," but currently the term *DNA typing* is used to describe this practice.

The Enderby Cases The first use of DNA typing in a criminal case was in 1987 in England.[91] In 1983, Lynda Mann, age 15, was raped and murdered near the village of Enderby. This case was unsolved. Three years later, another 15-year-old, Dawn Ashworth, was a victim in a similar offense. Comparing the DNA "fingerprints" derived from semen recovered from both victims' bodies, investigators realized that the same man had raped and killed both women. A 17-year-old man was initially arrested and a sample of his blood was subjected to DNA typing. This man's innocence, however, was clearly established by the lack of a DNA match, and he was released. Subsequently, all males in the Enderby area between 13 and 30 years of age were asked by the police to voluntarily provide blood samples for DNA typing. Of 5,500 men living in the area, all but 2 complied with the request. A man then came forward and told the police that he had used false identification to supply a blood sample in the name of a friend. This friend, Colin Pitchfork, was subsequently arrested and convicted of Ashworth's murder, with DNA evidence playing a crucial role in the prosecution's case.

The Orlando Cases During 1986, a series of rapes and assaults occurred in Orlando, Florida, which set the stage for the first use of DNA typing in the United States.[92] The crimes shared a common pattern: the attacks occurred after midnight, in the victims' homes, by a knife-wielding perpetrator. The perpetrator was quick to cover the eyes of the victims with a sheet or blanket, so none of them could give detailed descriptions of their assailant. During early 1987, investigators staking out a neighborhood in which it was believed the rapist might strike saw a blue 1979 Ford speeding out of the area. They followed the car for a short distance before it crashed into a utility pole while making a turn. The suspect, Tommie Lee Andrews, lived just 3 miles from the home of the first victim, who identified him at a photographic lineup the next morning. The prosecutor's case was certainly not ironclad. The identification rested on the victim's having seen the defendant for six seconds in a well-lit bathroom nearly a year prior to the photo lineup. Standard forensic tests comparing characteristics of the suspect's blood with characteristics derived from the semen found on the victim suggested only that Andrews *could* have committed the offense; but 30 percent of the male population of the United States shared these same characteristics. In short, there was enough evidence to prosecute, but a conviction was by no means a certainty. However, upon learning about the Enderby cases, the prosecutor secured DNA processing of the evidence and Andrews was convicted.

DNA Analysis In 1988, the FBI became the first public sector crime laboratory in the United States to accept cases for DNA analysis.[93] Since that time, there has been a substantial increase in the number of crime laboratories providing this type of service. Private firms also offer DNA typing, including Cellmark Diagnostics in Germantown, Maryland.

While DNA analysis of blood and other evidence from humans in criminal investigation cases is widely understood and used, there was no application of "genetic fingerprinting" to plant evidence in criminal cases until 1992 in Phoenix, Arizona.[94] Joggers found the body of a female who had been strangled. At the scene, investigators found a beeper, which led them to a suspect. The suspect admitted that (1) he had been with the victim the evening she disappeared, (2) the victim had been in his vehicle, (3) he and the victim had had sex, and (4) he and the victim had struggled. However, the suspect also maintained that the victim had run off with his beeper when he refused to help her get drugs and that he had not been anywhere near the place the body was found in 15 years. Investigators had found two seedpods from a palo verde tree in the bed of the suspect's truck. A University of Arizona plant geneticist was asked to determine if the seedpods came from a palo verde tree at the scene. The Maricopa County Sheriff's Office collected a total of 41 samples of palo verde seedpods from the crime scene and the surrounding region. The geneticist was able to exactly match the seedpods from the bed of the suspect's truck with those seized from the crime scene as part of the sample of 41 seedpods (see Figures 1–11 and 1–12). Additionally, none of the 41 seedpods exactly matched each other. This evidence was admitted at the trial. The defense attacked the evidence, properly arguing that the findings from a study based on 41 trees had substantial limitations and did not establish conclusively that the suspect could have gotten the seedpods only at the crime scene. However, along with other evidence, the testimony given by the geneticist had sufficient weight for the jury to convict the suspect.

The use of DNA evidence from humans continues to evolve. However, it has very rapidly achieved a high level of acceptance by the courts. Although it is difficult to forecast the future of DNA evidence from plants, the Phoenix case represents a promising new application of this technology.

Figure 1–11
Palo Verde Seedpods
A palo verde tree with seedpods.

(Courtesy Al Tamala, Maricopa County Sheriff's Office, Phoenix, Arizona)

**Figure 1–12
Location of seedpods in
defendent's vehicle**
The back of the defendant's truck,
where the palo verde seedpods
were found.

(Courtesy Dan Walsh, Maricopa County Sheriff's Office, Phoenix, Arizona)

FIREARMS IDENTIFICATION

Personal identification grew as several rival systems, with one of them finally predominating. In contrast, firearms identification moved forward in a series of successive steps. In this country, the frequency of shootings has made firearms identification extremely important.[95] As a specialty within criminalistics, firearms identification extends far beyond the comparison of two fired bullets. It includes identification of types of ammunition, knowledge of the design and functioning of firearms, the restoration of obliterated serial numbers on weapons, and estimation of the distance between a gun's muzzle and a victim[96] when the weapon was fired.

In 1835, Henry Goddard, one of the last of the Bow Street Runners, made the first successful attempt to identify a murderer from a bullet recovered from the body of a victim.[97] Goddard noticed that the bullet had a distinctive blemish on it, a slight gouge. At the home of one suspect, Goddard seized a bullet mold with a defect whose location corresponded exactly to the gouge on the bullet. The owner of the mold confessed to the crime when confronted with this evidence.[98]

Professor Lacassagne removed a bullet in 1889 from a corpse in France; upon examining it closely, he found seven grooves made as the bullet passed through the barrel of a gun.[99] Shown the guns of a number of suspects, Lacassagne identified the one that could have left seven grooves. On the basis of this evidence, a man was convicted of the murder.[100] However, any number of guns manufactured at that time could have produced seven grooves. There is no way of knowing whether the right person was found guilty.[101]

In 1898, a German chemist named Paul Jeserich was given a bullet taken from the body of a man murdered near Berlin. After firing a test bullet from the defendant's revolver, Jeserich took microphotographs of the fatal and test bullets and, on the basis of the agreement between both their respective normalities and abnormalities, testified that the defendant's revolver fired the fatal bullet, contributing materially to the conviction obtained.[102] Unknowingly at the doorstep of scientific greatness, Jeserich did not pursue this discovery any further, choosing instead to return to his other interests.

Gradually, attention began to shift from just bullets to other aspects of firearms. In 1913, Professor Balthazard published perhaps the single most important article on firearms identification. In it, he noted that the firing pin, breechblock, extractor, and ejector all leave marks on cartridges and that these vary among different types of weapons. With World War I looming, Balthazard's article was not widely read for some years.

Calvin Goddard (1858–1946), a U.S. physician who had served in the army during World War I, is the person considered most responsible for raising firearms identification to a science and for perfecting the bullet-comparison microscope. To no small degree, Goddard's accomplishments were contributed to heavily by three other Americans—Charles Waite, John Fisher, and Phillip Gravelle—working as a team on firearms identification. In 1925, Goddard joined Waite's team and upon Waite's death a year later, Goddard became its undisputed driving force and leader.[103] Like many pioneers, Waite's contributions are often overlooked. He had been interested in firearms since 1917, and from 1920 on he visited firearms manufacturers to get data on those manufactured since 1850. Because of Waite, the first significant cataloged firearms collection in this country was assembled. Nonetheless, ultimately it was Goddard who raised firearms identification to the status of a science.

A PARTING VIEW

There are many other contributors to the evolution of investigation and criminalistics. For example, in 1910 Albert Osborn (1858–1946) wrote *Questioned Documents*, still regarded as a definitive work. From at least 1911 onward, Edmond Locard (1877–1966) maintained a central interest in locating microscope evidence; all crime scenes processed today are based on the presumed validity of Locard's principle: There is something to be found. Leone Lattes (1887–1954) developed a procedure in 1915 that permitted blood typing from a dried bloodstain, a key event in forensic serology. Although more an administrator and innovator than a criminalist, August Vollmer (1876–1955), through his support, helped John Larson produce the first workable polygraph in 1921, and Vollmer established America's first full forensic laboratory in Los Angeles in 1923. In 1935, Harry Soderman and John O'Connell coauthored *Modern Criminal Investigation,* the standard work for the field for decades until the publication of Paul Kirk's *Crime Investigation* in 1953. A biochemist, educator, and criminalist, Kirk helped develop the careers of many criminalists.

Questions

1. Who were the Bow Street Runners, and of what historical importance are they?
2. Why did the British public object to the use of detectives after enactment of the Metropolitan Police Act of 1829?
3. Why did the profession of detective in this country basically evolve in the private sector?
4. What assessment can be made of the work of Pinkerton and his National Detective Agency?
5. What is a rogues' gallery?
6. What parallels can be drawn between Allan Pinkerton and J. Edgar Hoover?
7. What is anthropometry, and why was it abandoned in favor of dactylography?
8. What are the milestones in the development of dactylography?
9. Why does the Henry classification system enjoy greater use than Vucetich's system?
10. What are the different human sources of DNA material identified in this chapter?
11. Of what significance is the palo verde case?
12. What are the milestones in the development of firearms identification?

Notes

1. Material on the evolution of criminal investigation is drawn, in part, from Thomas R. Phelps, Charles R. Swanson, Jr., and Kenneth Evans, *Introduction to Criminal Justice* (New York: Random House, 1979), pp. 42–55.

2. T. A. Critchley, *A History of Police in England and Wales,* 2nd ed. (Montclair, N.J.: Patterson Smith, 1972), p. 34.

3. Ibid.

4. A. C. Germann, Frank D. Day, and Robert J. Gallati, *Introduction to Law Enforcement and Criminal Justice* (Springfield, Ill.: Charles C. Thomas, 1970), pp. 54–55.

5. Melville Lee, *A History of Police in England* (Montclair, N.J.: Patterson Smith reprint, 1971), p. 240.

6. Thomas A. Reppetto, *The Blue Parade* (New York: Free Press, 1978), p. 26.

7. Ibid., pp. 26–28.

8. Ibid., p. 29.

9. Ibid., p. 29, states three of four; John Coatman, *Police* (New York: Oxford, 1959), pp. 98–99, notes only one such conviction. Vincent's CID was based on his study of the Paris centralized detective system.

10. Coatman, *Police,* pp. 98–99.

11. Ibid., p. 99.

12. James F. Richardson, *The New York Police* (New York: Oxford, 1970), p. 37.

13. James D. Horan, *The Pinkertons* (New York: Bonanza Books, 1967), p. 25.

14. Ibid., p. 23.

15. Ibid., p. 25.

16. Jurgen Thorwald, *The Marks of Cain* (London: Thames and Hudson, 1965), p. 129.

17. Reppetto, *The Blue Parade,* p. 258.

18. Thorwald, *The Marks of Cain,* p. 129.

19. Reppetto, *The Blue Parade,* p. 257. There seems to be some dispute over whether there was ever any real threat and, if so, whether Pinkerton or New York City Police actually discovered it.

20. Ibid., pp. 257–258.

21. Ibid., p. 258. Reppetto asserts that as a military analyst Pinkerton was a failure and that his overestimates of enemy strength made General McClellan too cautious, contributing to McClellan's dismissal as head of the Union army.

22. Ibid.

23. William J. Bopp and Donald Shultz, *Principles of American Law Enforcement and Criminal Justice* (Springfield, Ill.: Charles C. Thomas, 1972), pp. 70–71.

24. Thorwald, *The Marks of Cain,* p. 131.

25. Reppetto, *The Blue Parade,* p. 259, notes that in two separate instances a total of eight Reno gang members arrested by the Pinkertons were subsequently lynched. In the first instance, three gang members reportedly were taken from Pinkerton custody.

26. Thorwald, *The Marks of Cain,* p. 131.

27. Reppetto, *The Blue Parade,* p. 261.

28. Ibid., p. 263.

29. Clive Emsley, *Policing and Its Context 1750–1870* (New York: Schocken Books, 1983), p. 106.

30. Augustine E. Costello, *Our Police Protectors* (Montclair, N.J.: Patterson Smith, 1972 reprint of an 1885 edition), p. 402.

31. Richardson, *The New York Police,* p. 122.

32. Bopp and Shultz, *Principles of American Law Enforcement and Criminal Justice,* p. 66.

33. William J. Mathias and Stuart Anderson, *Horse to Helicopter* (Atlanta: Community Life Publications, Georgia State University, 1973), p. 22.

34. Thorwald, *The Marks of Cain,* p. 136.

35. Ibid.

36. Reppetto, *The Blue Parade,* p. 263.

37. Ibid., p. 267.

38. Ibid., p. 278.

39. Ibid., p. 282.

40. Ibid., p. 283.

41. Material in this section is drawn from Phelps, Swanson, and Evans, *Introduction to Criminal Justice,* pp. 128–131.

42. The Supreme Court opted for piecemeal application when it rejected the "shorthand doctrine," that is, rejected making a blanket application of the Bill of Rights binding on the states, in its consideration of *Hurtado* v. *California* (110 U.S. 516 [1884]).

43. Richard Saferstein, *Criminalistics* (Englewood Cliffs, N.J.: Prentice-Hall, 1977), p. 5.

44. Jurgen Thorwald, *Crime and Science* (New York: Harcourt, Brace & World, 1967), p. 4.

45. Jurgen Thorwald, *The Century of the Detective* (New York: Harcourt, Brace & World, 1965), p. 6.

46. Thorwald, *Crime and Science*, p. 233.

47. Ibid.

48. Thorwald, *The Century of the Detective*, p. 6.

49. Ibid.

50. Ibid., p. 7.

51. Ibid., p. 9.

52. Ibid.

53. Ibid., p. 10.

54. Ibid., p. 12.

55. Ibid., pp. 83–84.

56. Ibid., p. 89.

57. Raymond D. Fosdick, *European Police Systems* (Montclair, N.J.: Patterson Smith, 1969 reprint of the 1915 original), p. 323.

58. Anthony L. Califana and Jerome S. Levkov, *Criminalistics for the Law Enforcement Officer* (New York: McGraw-Hill, 1978), p. 20.

59. Ibid.; also see Frederick R. Cherrill, *The Finger Print System at Scotland Yard* (London: Her Majesty's Stationery Office, 1954), p. 3.

60. Cherrill, *The Finger Print System at Scotland Yard*, p. 2.

61. Califana and Levkov, *Criminalistics for the Law Enforcement Officer*, p. 20.

62. Cherrill, *The Finger Print System at Scotland Yard*, p. 4.

63. Thorwald, *The Century of the Detective*, pp. 14–16.

64. Ibid., p. 18.

65. Ibid.

66. Ibid., p. 32.

67. Ibid., p. 33.

68. Saferstein, *Criminalistics*, p. 4.

69. Thorwald, *The Marks of Cain*, p. 81.

70. Thorwald, *The Century of the Detective*, p. 58.

71. Ibid.

72. Ibid., p. 60.

73. Ibid., p. 62.

74. Thorwald, *The Marks of Cain*, p. 138.

75. Ibid.

76. Ibid.

77. Ibid., p. 139.

78. Ibid.

79. Saferstein, *Criminalistics*, p. 281.

80. Thorwald, *The Century of the Detective*, p. 88.

81. Ibid.

82. Ibid., p. 87.

83. Ibid., p. 88.

84. Richard Saferstein, *Criminalistics: An Introduction to Forensic Science*, 4th ed. (Englewood Cliffs, N.J.: Prentice-Hall, 1990), p. 334.

85. Tod W. Burke and Walter F. Row, "DNA Analysis: The Challenge for Police," *The Police Chief*, October 1989, p. 92.

86. Saferstein, *Criminalistics*, 4th ed., p. 343.

87. "British Police Use Genetic Technique in Murder Arrest," *The Atlanta Constitution*, September 22, 1987, p. A3.

88. David Bigbee et al., "Implementation of DNA Analysis in American Crime Laboratories," *The Police Chief*, October 1989, p. 86.

89. Saferstein, *Criminalistics*, 4th ed., p. 344.

90. Bigbee et al., "Implementation of DNA Analysis," p. 86.

91. The account of the role of DNA in solving the Mann-Ashworth murders is drawn, in part, from Clare M. Tande, "DNA Typing: A New Investigatory Tool," *Duke Law Journal*, April 1989, p. 474.

92. This information is from Ricki Lewis, "DNA Fingerprints: Witness for the Prosecution," *Discover*, June 1988, pp. 44, 46.

93. Bigbee et al., "Implementation of DNA Analysis," p. 88.

94. This account is drawn from several sources: Jim Erickson, "Tree Genes: UA Professor's DNA Work Helps Convict Killer," *The Arizona Daily Star*, May 28, 1993, Metro/Region Section, p. 1; and Tim Henderson, "Report on Analysis of Palo Verde Samples," University of Arizona, April 14, 1993.

95. Saferstein, *Criminalistics*, 1st ed., p. 300.

96. Ibid., p. 30.

97. Thorwald, *The Marks of Cain*, p. 161.

98. Ibid.

99. Thorwald, *The Century of the Detective*, pp. 418–419.

100. Ibid., p. 419.

101. Thorwald, *The Marks of Cain*, p. 164.

102. Ibid.

103. Thorwald, *The Century of the Detective*, p. 434.

TWO

Crime and Its Investigation

CHAPTER OUTLINE

The Investigation of Crime 22

Organization of the Investigative Function 24

Questions 31

Notes 31

INTRODUCTION

Although crime is a national problem, its control is primarily the responsibility of local government. When officials fail to prevent or cannot deal effectively with crime, there are negative consequences. First, when individuals commit crimes and escape prosecution, future illegal acts are encouraged. Second, an escalating crime rate requires that resources which could be devoted to other social problems be diverted to crime control, resulting in further entrenchment of such ills as poverty, substandard housing, and inadequate medical care. Third, as crime increases, our system of government faces the real possibility of a crisis of confidence in its ability to maintain public welfare. Finally, crime tears the fabric of social relations and living patterns. People become fearful of strangers and of being on the streets after dark, homes become fortresses, and families move to new locations in search of a secure life. A terrible reality is that until significant inroads are made in controlling crime, the overall quality of life is lower than it could be.

THE INVESTIGATION OF CRIME

A *crime* is the commission of an act prohibited or the omission of an act required by the penal code of an organized political state. There can be no crime unless there is advance notice of the behavior prohibited or required. Legislatures enact criminal codes that distinguish between felonies and misdemeanors. In most states a *felony* is an act punishable by incarceration for a term of one or more years in a penitentiary or by death. The test to determine whether a person was convicted of a felony is not whether imprisonment actually took place for such a period of time but, rather, whether the sentence was possible. Generally, violations of the criminal code not deemed to be felonies are *misdemeanors*, lesser offenses often punishable by a fine not to exceed $500 and/or imprisonment of not more than one year. Some states have added a third crime category called a *violation* (e.g., criminal littering). Violations are punishable not by imprisonment but, instead, typically by a fine not to exceed $250.

An *investigator* is an individual who gathers, documents, and evaluates facts about a crime; *investigation* is the process through which these are accomplished. The purposes of the investigator's actions are several:

1. To establish that, in fact, a crime was committed.
2. To identify and apprehend the suspect.
3. To recover stolen property.
4. To assist the state in prosecuting the party charged with the offense.

The achievement of these objectives requires that the investigator have certain knowledge concepts and techniques as well as particular skills. Among the most important skills is the ability to converse equally well with a wide range of people. This is particularly critical because investigation essentially is working with people. Thus, investigators must be as adroit in talking with bartenders, elevator operators, and prostitutes as they are with art gallery owners, corporate heads, and attorneys. Other knowledge and skills needed by the investigator include the recognition, collection, marking, and preservation of evidence; crime scene sketching and photography; note taking and report preparation; appreciation of the potential contributions to be made to an investigation by psychologists, crime laboratory personnel, and medical examiners; interrogation; the elements needed to prove specific crimes were committed; the rules under which evidence will be admitted into court; and how to testify effectively.

Knowledge and skills will not in and of themselves make a successful investigator. A hallmark of the competent investigator is the clarity with which he or she sees the relationship between knowing and doing; they are very different, yet they are inexorably bound together. Investigation is fraught with challenges and complexities. These will be most successfully met when investigators consistently translate their knowledge into actual behaviors.

THE IMPORTANCE OF INVESTIGATION

The investigation of any crime imposes heavy responsibilities on the individual assigned that function. This burden is greater in the investigation of felonies because of the latitude of police discretionary judgment involved and the possible consequences. In order to make a legal arrest, an officer, unless in possession of a warrant, generally must personally witness a misdemeanor. In a number of states there is an exception to this general rule: When spouses are beaten, the offense is typically not commited in front of a police officer, and in the past it was not categorized as a felony assault. Thus, despite its being distasteful to police officers, they could only advise the victimized spouse to take out a misdemeanor warrant. This often did not happen, because abused spouses were too frightened about what would happen to them if they did so. Recognizing this dilemma, many states have made spouse abuse/assault a misdemeanor for which an officer may make a warrantless arrest even if it is not committed in his or her presence. In some states a second or any subsequent incident results in a felony charge being filed against the aggressor. Furthermore, at least one state—California—has made any act of spouse abuse a felony.

In felony cases an arrest may be made on the basis of probable cause, which, however, often requires a subjective evaluation of both the event and the intent of the suspect. While deadly force cannot be invoked as a last resort in effecting a misdemeanor arrest, its application in a felony apprehension is a possibility necessitating the exercise of sound discretionary judgment within a critically limited time frame. The consequences in felony investigations are of the utmost seriousness. An individual arrested, let alone convicted of a felony, is often socially stigmatized to a significant degree. If convicted, such a person stands to lose his or her freedom for a period of years or perhaps even to forfeit his or her life.

If an individual is to meet the responsibilities associated with the criminal investigation function successfully, certain personal qualities are essential.

ESSENTIAL QUALITIES OF THE INVESTIGATOR

The investigator who consistently solves the most difficult and bizarre cases is often said to be lucky. While good fortune occasionally plays a key role in successful investigations, no one is constantly lucky. The investigator referred to as being lucky is, instead, an individual who possesses—in addition to adequate professional preparation—an abundance of certain qualities.

Successful investigators will invariably possess a high degree of self-discipline; it is not the presence or absence of others that regulates their behavior but, rather, internalized control. Such individuals have knowledge of, and practice, methods that are legally acceptable. Patience and thoroughness are indispensable; successful investigators approach each case with alert, fastidious attention to detail, leaving nothing to chance. In so doing, they forfeit no opportunities to develop evidence, while creating many. The fact that a particular step or steps of an investigation are only rarely productive does not mean they should be omitted; the opposite is true. Investigation is a systematic method of inquiry that is more science than art. The logic of the scientific method must, however, be supplemented by the investigator's initiative and resourcefulness. Investigations cannot always be performed successfully by rote application of procedures outlined in texts. Rather, the sequences of investigation should be

regarded as a scientific, operating framework that, when applied to a particular case, may require improvisation on the investigator's part.

The successful investigator is also characterized by objectivity and freedom from preconceived notions or predispositions. An officer makes an arrest in the belief that the actual perpetrator has been identified; while personally certain of that individual's guilt, he or she recognizes that the legal condition of guilt arises only out of a judicial proceeding. Investigators, therefore, never disregard or fail to document anything that might tend to weaken the state's case. However unsavory the character of a suspect, the investigator must be steadfast in the role of fact finder. This behavior is crucial if we are to be a nation of laws and the investigator is to be ethical.

Criminal investigation may be likened to a series of gates at each of which certain evaluations and judgments must be made before advancing to the next. The investigator must possess keen decision-making capabilities, drawing on deductive or inductive reasoning when a course of action is not immediately apparent. *Inductive reasoning* involves examination of the evidence and particulars of a case and the use of this information as a basis for formulating a unifying and internally consistent explanation of the event. *Deductive reasoning* begins with the formulation of an explanation of the crime, which is then tested against the available information. The use of either process requires considerable ability, as both are fraught with the dangers of untenable inferences, logical fallacies, the failure to consider all alternatives, persuasive but false analogies, and the distortion of personal bias. Despite these dangers, however, deductive reasoning and inductive reasoning are important elements in the repertoire of the complete investigator.

In dealing with both suspects and complainants, a high degree of sensitivity and compassion is important. For example, in attempting to solve a rape case, the investigator must conduct the interview of the victim in such a fashion as to elicit available information without causing unnecessary anguish. Because of constant association with the criminal element and its fringe, the investigator will find abundant opportunity to become calloused and cynical. Investigators must constantly bear in mind that while they will frequently come into contact with unsavory characters in the performance of their duties, such individuals do not represent the population as a whole. The failure to maintain this distinction results in a cynicism that may be the precursor of unethical behavior.

As a final note, successful investigators lose no opportunity to learn something from every person with whom they have contact, for they recognize that the wider their understanding of occupations, lifestyles, vocabularies, and related topics, the more effective they will be.

ORGANIZATION OF THE INVESTIGATIVE FUNCTION

The major events in the investigation of crime are depicted in Figure 2–1. A discussion of these and their subelements will provide an overview of the investigative process and introduce concepts covered in greater detail in subsequent chapters.

Once a criminal offense has been committed, three immediate outcomes are possible. It may go

Figure 2–1
Major Events in the Investigation of a Crime

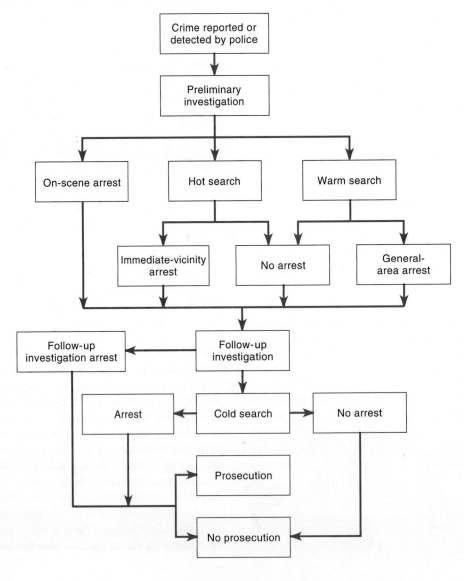

Figure 2-2
The Scene of the
False Report of a
Murder/Robbery

Mortally wounded wife and wounded husband, who used his car phone to describe the incident as a robbery, being helped by emergency personnel.

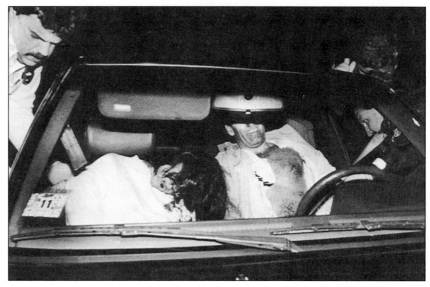

(Photograph © 1989 by Evan Richman—The Boston Herald)

undetected, as in the case of a carefully planned and conducted murder by organized-crime figures, in which the body is disposed of in such a way that it will remain undiscovered. If a violation is detected, it may not be reported, such as when a proprietor finds that his or her business premises have been burglarized but does not contact the police because the loss is minor or because the insurance coverage would be adversely affected. Finally, the crime may come to the attention of the police through their observation or a complaint by the victim or witnesses.

Regardless of the outcome, a crime has occurred in each of the three preceding instances. However, only in the last case, when it is both detected and reported, is the offense of concern to the investigator, because only at that time does it become subject to formal processing.

THE PRELIMINARY INVESTIGATION

The actions taken at the scene of a crime immediately following its detection and reporting constitute what is termed the *preliminary investigation.* It is desirable to vest the uniformed officer with the responsibility of conducting the preliminary investigation. This should be the case even when departmental size permits some degree of specialization, which ordinarily occurs where personnel with the

power of arrest total approximately 20 or more. The following list outlines the key elements of this preliminary phase of investigation:

1. There should be an immediate request for medical services in instances where the victim or suspect has sustained a serious injury.
2. A determination must be made as to whether a crime was committed and, if so, what the specific type of offense was. Occasionally this can be a difficult problem, as the following case histories suggest:

A 911 dispatcher received a frantic call from a man using his car phone. The dispatcher was told that the man and his wife had been on their way home from childbirth classes at a hospital when a black male jumped into their car and robbed them at gunpoint. The subject shot the wife and then the husband and ran from the scene. In intense pain and passing out periodically, the husband for 13 long minutes could not identify his location or any identifiable landmarks for the dispatcher. When they were finally located through the efforts of a state police trooper who happened to be in the city, the wife was found to have been mortally wounded (see Figure 2–2). The 7-month fetus delivered by caesarean section died 17 days later. The husband's abdomen wound was so severe that he spent 6 weeks in the hospital, including 10 days in intensive care. Numerous mourners, including the governor, attended the wife's funeral. Many of them wept when a letter composed by the hospitalized husband to express his love for his wife was read.

The entire nation was stunned by the vicious nature of the crime, and local police launched an aggressive search for the "shooter." Investigative tactics included numerous field stops of black males. An apparent break in the case came when the police learned that a black male in custody on another robbery charge had bragged to his 15-year-old nephew that he had committed the crime. This subject was identified by the husband at a lineup as being the shooter.

Despite such developments, there were some doubts about the case. Why had the husband driven into the area in which the crime was committed when his home was in the opposite direction from the hospital? What motivated the suspect to shoot the presumably less threatening wife first? Where was the jewelry and the wife's Gucci bag, which had been taken by the suspect? Why had the husband not inquired at the scene and in the ambulance about his wife's wound instead of only about the severity of his own wound? How could a man who had lived all of his life in this city not be able to provide the emergency dispatcher with any information that would be helpful in locating him and his wife during the 13 minutes that the police searched for them?

When some weeks later the husband committed suicide by jumping from a bridge into an icy river, it seemed to be the act of a man overcome by grief. Yet the truth was that the case was beginning to unravel. It is now believed that the man shot both his wife and himself, handed the gun, jewelry, and the Gucci bag to his brother, and made up the account of the black male shooter. Not only had the husband's account misdirected the investigation for weeks, but when the truth was finally established, there was an outcry from the black community about the willingness of the police to believe that a black had committed the crime and about the use of police investigative tactics in the black community. This development created strong tensions in police-community relations, as evidenced by several demonstrations.

The husband had committed suicide after learning that his brother was going to the police to give them information about the case. On the basis of the brother's statement, the police recovered the Gucci bag and a .38-caliber revolver from a river. The husband's motivations appear to have been the desire to collect on the wife's life insurance, a fantasy about another woman, and a desire not be tied to a family so that he could pursue a new career as a restaurant owner.[1]

For four years, a 47-year-old woman was terrorized in a series of incidents by a mysterious individual identified as the "Poet" due to the verse form used in threatening letters sent to her. She reported receiving a butcher knife at Christmas, having her telephone line cut, having chunks of concrete thrown at her home, and being kidnapped and stabbed in the lower back. When the woman was discovered mailing letters from the Poet along with her bills and normal correspondence, she admitted that there was no Poet and that she had even stabbed herself to lend credence to her stories. A psychologist working on the case speculated that an assault on the woman when she was 16 years old had been the motivating force behind the Poet episode. In that assault, an unknown assailant had drugged her and branded her on both thighs.[2]

The police found an adult male, approximately 30 years old, wandering in the woods. The man presented himself as a 4-year-old who had been abandoned. The police couldn't find any identification, there were no matching fingerprints on file, and the person didn't correspond to any of the descriptions on missing-persons reports. A psychologist became convinced that he was working with someone with multiple personalities when the subject suddenly started snarling, growling, and sounding diabolical. Medical personnel later discovered that the man had up to 27 different personalities, none of which was aware of the other. His IQ ranged from 88 to 128, depending on which personality took the test. Among the personalities were a punk rocker who went to concerts with his hair dyed purple and got into fights; blind Jeffrey; Robert, the intellectual; the sinister T. K.; Mark, the angry enforcer; and three women, including Tina, the prostitute, Maria, the 48-year-old housekeeper, and a lesbian named Rachel. The psychologist said that it made the hair on the back of his head stand up because it was almost like a scene from *The Exorcist*, a story of demonic possession. The break came when the sinister T. K. committed suicide in the man's mind, setting the other characters free. Thus, the real character of who the person was awoke one morning with no memory of what had happened to him during the nine months that T. K. had dominated his life.[3]

Clearly these are unusual cases. The first case, if it unfolded as is presently believed, reflects a heinous betrayal. The second case is unusual in the duration of the deception and the lengths to which the "victim" went to maintain it. The third case is an excellent example of the complexity of the human mind and how specialists trained in fields other than law enforcement are an absolutely essential adjunct to the investigative effort from time to time. There are, however, examples of deception by "victims" that are not quite as unusual. First, an individual may become intoxicated, be involved as a driver in a hit-and-run accident, abandon the car, walk to another location, and report the car stolen in an attempt to escape culpability for the violation. A variation on this is that the individual, after abandoning the car, goes home and "falls asleep." The police find the abandoned vehicle and trace it to the person's residence. "Awakened from sleep" by the police, the person admits to having been drinking but claims to have made it home and parked the car in the driveway, from which it "has been stolen." A second example is the man who cashes his paycheck and stops by a bar to have a few drinks. An attractive woman finds him "fascinating," and they agree to go to her place. In the process the man is, by prior plans, robbed by the female's accomplice. The victim, knowing that this explanation will cause conflict with his wife, decides the only way out is to fabricate a story of being robbed.

Although the majority of complaints are made honestly, the investigator must be alert for indications of a false complaint. Included in these indications are possible motivations for the crime or the concealment of the crime on the victim's part, inconsistencies in accounts of the incident, illogical relationships between the account of the incident given by the victim and the available physical evidence, and sufficient time, opportunity, and motive to have been involved with the incident in ways other than that which the victim reports.

It is sometimes difficult to distinguish between a frightened victim and a person attempting to file a false crime report. Many times, through skillful and apparently innocuous questioning, the reality of the situation will finally emerge. In other situations the suspicions of the investigator cannot be resolved through questioning alone and other means will prove useful:

A cashier at a loan company reported a robbery of $400 cash and $1,600 in checks. An investigator responded to the crime scene and spoke with the victim. The victim's statement was very vague and at times inconsistent. She stated that two males had approached her, pulled a gun, and demanded all the money. There were no witnesses to the crime, and the victim said she was too shaken to notice any of the physical features of the perpetrators.

The investigator interviewed the victim further and was suspicious about the circumstances of the robbery. He asked the woman to take a polygraph test, which she submitted to and failed. The "victim" subsequently confessed that the robber was not real, and that she had conspired with the two men she was living with to falsify the report.[4]

A doctor in a small town created a stir when he announced that he had diagnosed an unusually high number of cancer cases. He speculated that a river apparently polluted by a local plant was among the possible explanations for the cancer rate. Subsequently, the doctor's home was set on fire as he and his family slept in it, and the doctor was attacked while fishing. He was stabbed four times and wounded in the abdomen by a 5-inch knife, which miraculously missed all vital parts. The doctor expressed the belief that his announcement might have led to the attacks. Investigators became suspicious when the laboratory found traces of pain-killing medication on the blade of the knife that had inflicted the wounds. After failing a lie detector test, the doctor admitted that he had set fire to his own home and stabbed himself.[5]

The receipt of a radio message to proceed to a particular location to handle a specific type of call does not ensure that any particular type of offense has occurred. While every effort is made to properly screen and classify calls for service, errors will be made. Sometimes the results are harmless and at other times tragic:

A marked unit was dispatched to the Red and Black Grocery Store on a call designated as a robbery with two juvenile white males as perpetrators. Legally, robbery is a felony defined as the taking of something of value from the control, custody, or person of another by threatening, putting in fear, or using force. Upon arrival at the scene, officers found that the proprietor had reported a robbery but had used the term in a loose sense, meaning that property had been taken. An interview of the complainant revealed that she had discovered the two youths removing cartons of empty bottles from the rear of the store in order to present them for a deposit refund elsewhere. Thus, the specific offense was petty larceny, a misdemeanor.

A 13-year-old girl called the emergency dispatcher and stated, "There is someone trying to break into my house right now." The radio dispatcher classified the call as a "34"—a routine disturbance in which no one's life is in imminent danger. The girl, either before or after calling the police, also called her mother at work; the mother rushed home to find her daughter raped and stabbed to death. Only then were the police dispatched to the scene, some 40 minutes after the girl's original call to the police.[6]

3. To the maximum extent possible, and simultaneous with executing the two preceding steps, the investigator must also preserve the integrity of the crime scene to ensure that evidence is not lost, destroyed, or altered in such a manner as to eliminate its value in court (see Figure 2–3).

4. In those instances where witnesses to the offense exist and the perpetrator has escaped arrest at the scene, certain immediate actions are necessary. The witnesses should be separated to avoid a discussion of their perceptions of the event being investigated. Each must then be individually interviewed to gain sufficient details and descriptions for

Figure 2–3
Technician Collecting Blood Evidence

A technician collecting blood at the scene of a crime. The evidence/crime cone has been placed both to mark the location of the blood and to prevent its accidental loss, destruction, or alteration. Small flags, which can either be stuck in the ground or mounted on tripods, are also available for this purpose.

(Courtesy Nassau County, New York, Police Department)

placing a *preliminary pickup order* with the radio dispatcher, who, in turn, will transmit it to all units. To maximize the likelihood of apprehension, this order must be placed as rapidly as possible following the confirmation of the offense and the gathering of sufficient descriptive data. While the officer assigned to the call conducts the preliminary investigation, other units should be available to assist, in cases where the suspect has fled the scene, by conducting "hot" and "warm" searches. A *hot search* is an examination of the immediate vicinity of the crime scene when the perpetrator is known or believed to be there. A *warm search* is a check of the general area beyond the immediate vicinity of the crime scene when it is believed that the perpetrator may still be there. A swift issuance of the preliminary pickup order, or

BOLO ("be on lookout"), is also necessary to minimize the chance that an unsuspecting officer may stop what appears to be an ordinary traffic violator and be suddenly assailed because he or she has unknowingly stopped the perpetrator of a major offense. The temporary pickup order should minimally include the following points: the number of suspects; their age, race, sex, height, weight, build, coloration; clothing, scars, marks, tattoos, jewelry worn; names and nicknames applicable to each suspect, which may have been overheard; whether the suspects were unarmed or armed and, where used, the numbers, types, and descriptions of weapons; and the method and direction of flight, including a full description of any vehicle involved. The description of the vehicle should include not only the year, make, model, and color but also other distinguishing factors such as damage to the vehicle, stickers, articles and markings on and within the vehicle, and unusual conditions, such as the existence of loud motor noise. A case history illustrates the importance of complete descriptions:

An armed robbery of a convenience store was committed in Tampa, Florida. At the scene it was determined that a toy pistol may have been employed and the suspect's vehicle had a construction worker's hard hat on its rear shelf. A vehicle matching the description broadcast was found parked behind a tavern, with a box for a toy gun on the rear floorboard and a hard hat on the rear seat. Interviews with personnel operating the tavern established that a person of the suspect's description had entered hurriedly, made a phone call, had a drink, and left. A check with a cab company revealed that a pickup near that location had been taken to the airport. A check of the airline counters revealed that the suspect had been ticketed and had departed for Miami, where an apprehension was made as he left the plane.

5. The case must be documented and evidence gathered. This requires in-depth interviews of witnesses and the complainant, along with the collection, marking, and preservation of evidence. Additional tasks include photographing the scene and, where warranted, preparing a crime scene sketch. The investigator must be particularly alert to search for evidence not only at the immediate scene of the crime but also, where discernible, along the perpetrator's lines of approach to and flight from the scene. Ordinarily, the suspect will approach the scene with care, but in haste to flee the scene, he or she may drop something that will be of significant evidentiary value.

6. An *offense report* must be prepared that includes the facts known to the investigator, all actions taken, and the listing of all items of evidence seized. Another term for an offense report is *incident report*.

7. Ordinarily in the detailed interviews that follow the placement of the preliminary pickup order, the investigator will obtain additional information from witnesses concerning the description of the suspect and any vehicle involved. Thus, a second pickup order, termed the *permanent pickup,* must be placed. This is accomplished by calling a central point, often called the pickup desk, where the information is recorded and then relayed to the radio dispatcher for rebroadcast to all units. A copy of this second order is also posted for the information of officers coming on duty, who will record it in their notebooks and refer to it as may be required during their tour of duty. After a permanent pickup order is placed, it continues to be in effect until it is canceled by an arrest, by a determination that the offense was "unfounded" (i.e., without a factual basis), or for other reasons. A cancellation of the permanent pickup order is formally placed and processed in the same manner as the placement of the permanent pickup order.

8. All evidence seized must be transmitted to the police station, where it will be stored in the central depository to which access is limited in order to ensure the integrity of materials. Upon receipt of the evidence, the evidence custodian will issue a receipt, a copy of which should be appended to the offense report. At this point the supervisor of the officer

conducting the preliminary investigation will review the report for completeness, accuracy, and conformity to reporting standards and regulations. Ordinarily in major-case investigations the report is immediately referred to the unit of the police department responsible for the latent or follow-up investigation, which most frequently is conducted by a plainclothes officer.[7]

THE FOLLOW-UP INVESTIGATION

Follow-up investigation is the effort expended by the police in gathering information subsequent to the initiation of the original report until the case is ready for prosecution.

Upon receipt of a major-case offense report, a supervisor in the investigative unit will assign it to a particular individual who will be responsible for the latent or follow-up work, which often involves a cold search for the perpetrator. When the suspect is not already in custody as a result of an on-scene arrest or the hot or warm search, the follow-up investigator must:

1. Read and become thoroughly conversant with the offense report in order to follow up leads and begin to consider what activities might produce additional leads.
2. View all evidence seized and arrange to have it submitted to a crime laboratory for analysis.
3. Effect a liaison with the officer initiating the report, reinterviewing witnesses and the complainant as necessary in an attempt to develop further information and to clarify aspects of the case. In many instances the officer originating the report may not have been able to locate any witnesses, requiring an effort in this phase to determine whether they exist and, if so, to locate them.
4. Evaluate the legal significance of statements, evidence, and laboratory findings.
5. Employ, where appropriate, specialized techniques such as physical or electronic surveillance and polygraph examinations.
6. Identify, locate, and arrest the suspect.
7. Conduct an in-custody interrogation in conformity with legal requirements.
8. Recover stolen property.
9. Arrange to meet with the prosecuting attorney.

A final note is required with respect to various perceptions of what constitutes a successful investigation. In the public's mind that status is attained when the perpetrator is arrested, property is recovered, and the person charged subsequently is convicted. In administrative terms success is achieved when the offense is accorded one of two classifications: it may be "exceptionally cleared," in that a factor external to the investigation, such as a complainant's refusal to testify, results in no charge being filed against a suspect; or it may be "cleared by arrest," when the perpetrator has been arrested and there is sufficient evidence to file a formal charge. Here it must be observed that not every arrest will result in prosecution; the police can and do make mistakes, or the evidence may be found to be legally insufficient.

An examination of the data in Table 2–1 leads to the conclusion that in many types of major case offenses the investigator will not experience success as defined by the public or administrative classifications. What, then, should be the investigator's attitude? How can feelings of frustration be avoided? The investigator knows that many crimes are highly resistant to clearance and some crimes are simply insoluble because of insufficient evidence or legal restrictions. Therefore, success for the investigator must rest in the knowledge that the case was vigorously pursued and all avenues leading to clearance were examined.

Table 2–1

National Clearance Rates, by Percentage, for Selected Major Cities

Offense	Cleared	Not Cleared
Murder	66	34
Rape	51	49
Aggravated assult	58	42
Robbery	26	74
Burglary	14	86
Larceny	20	80
Auto theft	14	86

Source: Federal Bureau of Investigation, *Crime in the United States–1997* (Washington, D.C.: Government Printing Office, 1998), p. 211.

Questions

1. What is the definition of *crime*?
2. How are felonies and misdemeanors distinguished?
3. What are the four major aims of an investigator's action?
4. The investigator must have certain essential qualities. What are they?
5. Contrast inductive reasoning and deductive reasoning.
6. What are the major steps in preliminary and follow-up investigations?
7. Identify the varying definitions of what constitutes a successful investigation.

Notes

1. This account is drawn from *Time,* January 22, 1990, Vol. 135, No. 4, pp. 10–14.
2. "Mysterious 'Poet' Assailant Proves to Be Victim Herself," *The Atlanta Journal Weekend, Atlanta Constitution,* October 3, 1981, p. A3. For a similar case, see B. Kava, "Police Arrest Woman Who Reported Family Was Being Harassed," *The Kansas City Times,* April 10, 1985, pp. A1, A10.
3. "Man Troubled by Having Up to 27 Personalities," *Miami* (Florida) *Herald,* October 4, 1982, pp. B1, B2.
4. Peter W. Greenwood et al., *The Criminal Investigation Process, Vol. III: Observations and Analysis* (Santa Monica, Calif.: Rand Corporation, 1975), p. 138.
5. "Doctor Confesses to Self-Stabbing, Setting Fire," *The Atlanta Journal Weekend, Atlanta Constitution,* October 2, 1982, p. A2; Hal Clarendon, "Altha Doctor's Confession Is Talk of Town," *Florida Times-Union* (Jacksonville), October 4, 1982, p. A2.
6. "Girl Slain as Help Call Handled as Routine," *The Atlanta Journal,* December 2, 1980, p. A16.
7. See Paul N. Conner and Clinton H. Richards, "Evaluating Detectives' Performance," *The Police Chief,* September 1991, Vol. 58, No. 9, pp. 51–55.

THREE

The Crime Scene and Its Associated Procedures

CHAPTER OUTLINE

Organization of the Crime Scene Investigation 34

Typical Crime Scene Problems 35

Rules for the Crime Scene Investigator 36

Types of Evidence and Their Usefulness 47

The Crime Scene Search 48

The Collection and Care of Evidence 52

Visually Documenting the Crime Scene 53

Submission of Evidence to the Laboratory 60

Questions 63

Notes 64

INTRODUCTION

Unlike eyewitness testimony or the innocent individual who confesses to a crime because of some personality disorder, physical evidence can never be intrinsically wrong.[1] The contributions of physical evidence to an investigation are diminished primarily by the inability, unwillingness, or failure to locate, properly collect, mark, and preserve it and by the drawing of improper conclusions from its analysis. Also, because evidence cannot speak for itself, its proper value can be altered by incomplete or inaccurate testimony.[2]

A *crime scene* may be defined as the location at which the offense was committed; the search of the crime scene for physical evidence must, however, involve a wider area, including the perpetrator's lines of approach and flight. Thus, a crime scene search must include the specific setting of the crime and its general environs. Crimes vary by type with respect to their propensity to yield physical evidence. For example, examination of the counter of a business at which a worthless check was passed is highly unlikely to produce any physical evidence. On the other hand, the scene of a criminal homicide may be expected to produce an abundance of items of considerable importance to the investigation. Regardless of the type of offense involved, the fundamental assumption that underlies the crime scene search is Locard's principle: There is something to be found.

ORGANIZATION OF THE CRIME SCENE INVESTIGATION

There are three major functions to be executed at the scene of an offense: coordination, technical services, and investigative services (see Figure 3–1). The first function is vested in the crime scene coordinator, who has overall responsibility for the investigation at that time, including technical and investigative services. This individual will make or approve all major decisions as they relate to the case. Technical services are concerned with processing the scene; they encompass the identification, collection, marking, and preservation of evidence, along with scene documentation, including sketching and photography. Technical services also involve transmitting the evidence to the evidence depository or to the laboratory, according to departmental procedure. Those providing technical services will be specially trained technicians whose sole function is the processing of crime scenes (see Figures 3–2, 3–3, and 3–4). The investigative service function includes interviewing witnesses and the complainant; if the suspect is in custody, conducting the field interrogation; and conducting a neighborhood canvass to identify additional witnesses. While investigative services at the scene are usually performed by uniformed officers, the officers will occasionally be complemented by plainclothes personnel. In smaller departments where there is no specialization, these three functions will generally be accomplished by a patrol officer. The larger the department, the more certain it is that one or more persons will be working in each of the technical and investigative service areas under the scene coordinator. In such situations the scene coordinator will often be a supervisor with at least the rank of sergeant.

Figure 3–1
Crime Scene Van
A van containing the equipment and materials needed to process a crime scene. The crime scene technician has seized a hatchet as evidence. It is held firmly in place on a peg board by wooden dowels which have been inserted around the hatchet.

(Courtesy Nassau County, New York, Police Department)

Figure 3–2
Compact or Basic Crime Scene Kit

A Compact Crime Scene Kit, containing such items as latex gloves, a fingerprint brush, several types of fingerprint powders, a magnifying glass, and a measuring tape.

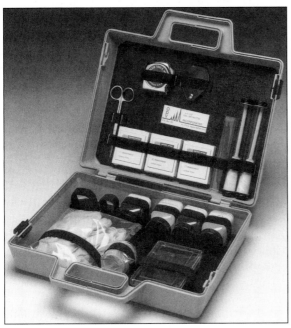

(Courtesy ODV Incorporated, South Paris, Maine)

Figure 3–3
Universal Crime Scene Kit

A Universal Crime Scene Investigation Kit, the contents of which go well beyond those of a compact kit, adding such features as the materials for casting toolmarks.

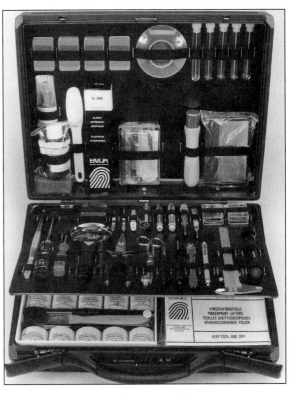

(Courtesy ODV Incorporated, South Paris, Maine)

TYPICAL CRIME SCENE PROBLEMS

Although the procedures to be followed at a crime scene investigation may be neatly delineated in theory, any number of conditions may render their accomplishment a good bit less orderly than the ideal. The resources of a police department are finite, and considerable demands are made upon them. Ideally, every crime scene should be fastidiously processed. In reality, the scenes of misdemeanor offenses receive at best a cursory examination, and even the thoroughness with which felony crime scenes are processed will frequently be affected by the severity of the offense. To the person victimized, the situation is of considerable importance, possibly even traumatically so, and may have brought him or her into direct contact with the police for the first time. From the police standpoint, the offense committed may be a nonpriority crime that—due to limitations of

personnel and time—does not warrant employing the full range of technical and investigative services. For example, in some of our nation's largest cities it is a practice not to conduct any investigation beyond the preliminary stage when the property loss in a burglary is less than $5,000, unless there are promising leads. However, even when investigating a nonpriority case, officers must display a genuine interest in their work.

At the scenes of violent crimes, especially when they are interracial, emotions may run high. Even a small crowd may add considerable confusion to the process of ascertaining what has happened and along what lines the investigation should proceed. In such situations it is not unusual for witnesses to be lost, for their versions and perceptions of what occurred to be altered by contamination through contact with the crowd, or even for so-called

Figure 3–4
Post Mortem Crime Scene Kit
A Post Mortem Investigation Kit, especially put together for taking fingerprints and teeth impressions from dead persons.

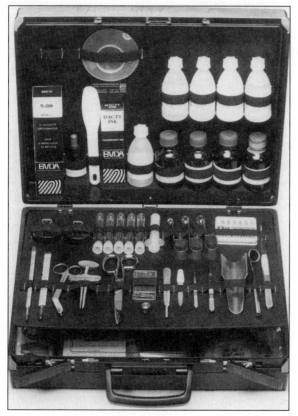

(Courtesy ODV Incorporated, South Paris, Maine)

witnesses to be added. In this last circumstance, an individual standing in the crowd may have been at, or very near to, the scene when the crime occurred, without actually viewing the offense. However, in the emotionally charged atmosphere, hearing the comments and descriptions of people standing nearby, the person suddenly and earnestly believes that he or she has something of value to share with the investigative team.

Limitations on the availability of equipment may force an investigator to use less desirable procedures or to eliminate a particular step. Police officers and supervisors occasionally make investigations more difficult when they "drop by" to see if they can be of help when in reality they are simply curious. Too many people at the scene may lead to confusion of assignments or accidental alteration or destruction of evidence. Finally, at the scenes of major crimes, such as bank robberies and criminal homicides, members of the press typically arrive shortly after the investigation and immediately attempt to obtain information from any police officer or witness, creating no small amount of confusion and sometimes producing erroneous reports.

RULES FOR THE CRIME SCENE INVESTIGATOR

Regardless of the type of crime involved, certain fundamentals must be observed.

MAINTENANCE OF CONTROL

Without control a life might be lost, evidence destroyed, assignments overlooked, or the investigation conducted in a generally slovenly manner. Control begins with the arrival of the first responder—the first officer—at the scene, whose immediate responsibility is to rope off or otherwise secure the area, positioning personnel to prevent unauthorized access to the scene and covering areas or individual pieces of evidence that might be adversely affected by inclement weather. The values of life and proper investigative procedure may occasionally be at odds. The inadvertent or deliberate destruction of evidence by an officer seeking to render first aid to a victim or checking for the presence of life is, under all circumstances, to be regarded as a necessary cost of fulfilling a higher duty.

At the scene of sensational crimes, particularly those involving well-known figures, the crime scene coordinator will be approached by members of the press who want to photograph or videotape the scene as well as obtain information for their newspapers or television stations. Properly responding to such individuals is an essential aspect of control. The person in charge of the crime scene should cooperate with the press, but the scope of cooperation is limited by the need to avoid interference with the investigation, to protect the legal rights of a suspect, and to avoid placing a witness in danger, as well as other good reasons. Although some states have enacted "shield laws" so that news media personnel are not required to divulge their sources, as a general matter reporters have no legal rights beyond those granted each citizen. Although news officials may be permitted to enter a crime scene, they do so at their own risk; if their presence in any way jeopardizes police operations, it should not be allowed. It is not the responsibility of the police to provide security for news media personnel who voluntarily choose to subject themselves to danger. The arrest of a news media worker at a crime scene should be made only upon the most serious provocation and with full awareness of the adverse publicity for the police department that is certain to follow.

News media personnel may photograph or report anything that they observe while legally at a crime scene or covering any other incident involving the police. If in this process they obtain information that could endanger people or adversely affect the investigative process, both they and their supervisors should be notified of the possible consequences.

When suspects have been interviewed but not arrested, their identities should not be disclosed. It is appropriate for the crime scene coordinator to generally describe to reporters the physical evidence found at the scene, proceeds of the crime, weapons, and the issuance and service of search warrants. However, detailed descriptions of evidence, proceeds, or weapons should not be disclosed, nor should information pertaining to how physical evidence, proceeds of the crime, or weapons were located.

In some investigations it may be appropriate to withhold certain details about the crime scene, such as how a victim was mutilated, messages left at the scene by the perpetrator, particular types of evidence seized, or the exact words spoken to a rape victim. Such information could be vital in solving the case, evaluating informants' tips, or determining the authenticity of statements or confessions made by subsequently identified suspects. If a suspect has been identified and an identity established or a likeness generated by use of an artist's sketch or by an Identi-kit or a Compusketch computer program (see Chapter 14, Robbery), it may be advantageous to widely publicize this information if it is not likely to hinder apprehension of the suspect.

Relevant information can be supplied to the news media if it cannot be characterized as being prejudicial to a fair trial for the defendant. Among the actions and statements that are impermissible under the policies of many departments are the following:

1. Requiring the suspect to pose for photographers.
2. Reenacting the crime.
3. Disclosing that the suspect told where weapons, proceeds of the crime, or other materials were located.
4. Referring to the suspect as a "depraved character," "a real no-good," "a sexual monster," or similar terms.
5. Revealing that the suspect declined to take certain types of tests or that the suspect did take certain tests, for example, a blood alcohol test to determine the degree, if any, to which the suspect was under the influence of drugs or alcohol.
6. Telling the press the results of any tests to which the suspect submitted.
7. Making statements as to the guilt or innocence of a suspect.
8. Releasing the identities of prospective witnesses or commenting on the nature of their anticipated testimony or credibility.
9. Making statements of a purely speculative nature about any aspect of the case.

If a suspect is arrested, it is permissible in most states to release the following types of information:

1. The defendant's name, age, sex, residence, employment, marital status, and similar background information, unless the defendent is a juvenile.
2. The nature of the crime for which the arrest was made and the identity of the complainant, if disclosing this information does not create a danger for the complainant and will not result in serious embarrassment to him or her, (as can be the case for the victims of sexual offenses) or does not run counter to other reasons of good judgment or applicable laws.
3. The identities of any other agencies participating in the investigation and/or making the arrest, as well as those of the individual officers involved.

4. The circumstances surrounding the arrest, such as the time and place, extent of any pursuit, amount of resistance, possession and use of weapons, injuries (notification to the family should precede disclosing an individual officer's identity), and a general description of items seized at the time of arrest.

The person in charge of the crime scene should never allow the press, the presence of superior officers, or other factors to distract him or her from doing a deliberate and thorough job. In addition to the importance of control, this is necessary because the investigator is personally responsible for the operation.[3] Additional aspects of maintaining control include ensuring that there is no unnecessary walking about the crime scene; that items or surfaces likely to yield latent fingerprints are not indiscriminately picked up; and that evidence to be removed from the scene is properly inventoried and taken with the knowledge and permission of the crime scene coordinator.[4]

CONCEPTUALIZATION

Inexperienced investigators sometimes jump to conclusions after taking a brief look at a crime scene. This can result in their looking for evidence that supports their "theory" or conceptualization of the crime and ignoring evidence that does not fit into their explanation—a dangerous and potentially disastrous practice. In processing the crime scene, it is necessary to keep both known facts and inferences in mind. This facilitates the reconstruction of the offense and identification of the perpetrator's method of operation, suggests the possible existence of certain types of physical evidence, and assists in establishing appropriate lines of inquiry:

Multiple female murder victims were found strangled and stabbed in an apartment. The lead investigator studied the crime scene very carefully. One of the victims was lying near the doorway to one of the bedrooms with a pillow under her head. The investigator concluded that the perpetrator may have touched the very lowest portion of the door to steady himself as he stood up after killing that victim. The crime scene technician processed that portion of the door and located the only fingerprint of the suspect found at the crime scene. The suspect was identified by this print and subsequently convicted of the murders.

Without the investigator's thoughtful examination of the crime and reconstruction of how the perpetrator may have acted, that lower portion of the door would not have been dusted for fingerprints because it would have been so illogical to expect to find a fingerprint there. Consequently, the single most important piece of evidence would never have been located.

Assumptions that are made must be checked for accuracy as quickly as possible. The failure to do so may result in an offender's escaping prosecution and in embarrassment for the investigator and the department. It may also produce confusion in, or misdirect, the investigation. For example, a woman in a large city was murdered in her apartment. The investigators assumed that the woman's husband had thoroughly searched the apartment for their missing infant child when he first arrived and found his wife's body. Thus, they further assumed that the baby had been kidnapped. Some four days later the baby's body was found by the grandmother in the apartment under a sofa cushion.[5]

Human behavior is rich in its variety; in reconstructing the crime, investigators must be alert to the danger of imparting their own probable motives or actions to the perpetrator unless there are solid grounds for so doing. Alternatively stated, this proposition dictates that simply because, under the same or a similar set of circumstances, we would not have acted in a particular fashion does not preclude the possibility that the perpetrator may have acted in that way. Two cases illustrate the importance of this point: In Woodbridge, New Jersey, a series of burglaries was cleared when it was established that two inmates had been breaking out of a correctional facility to commit the offenses, returning nightly to the facility.[6] In Palm Beach, Florida, a guard at a bank was surprised one night by an intruder who took $50,000 in gold coins. Unable to find a point of entry, investigators were puzzled until they received an anonymous tip that the intruder had shipped himself into the bank in a crate and broken out of it after the regular employees had gone home.[7]

Large physical evidence, such as a handgun used in a criminal homicide, is often easily found at the crime scene and requires little in the way of conceptualization. However, there is the possibility that much smaller types of evidence are also present; these will be located only if the investigator is able to conceptualize events:

A university student claimed that several hours ago her date had raped her at his apartment. This had been their second date. In addition to being able to identify her assailant, the victim gave the investigator a Polaroid photograph taken of the two of them earlier in the evening. In examining the photograph, the investigator noticed that the victim was wearing a sorority pin in the photograph, but the victim's pin was now missing. Believing that the pin could have been lost at the crime scene, the investigator went to the suspect's apartment. The suspect's version of events was that he told the victim he no longer wanted to date her and she swore to get even for "being dumped." The suspect also said that the woman had never been in his apartment and consented to a search. The investigator found the missing sorority pin in the perpetrator's bedroom, and the suspect subsequently gave her a confession.

Investigators must also be able to conceptualize the scene in order to locate extremely small pieces of evidence, called *trace evidence*. Trace evidence is small evidence, which is often—but not exclusively—microscopic in size.[8] Examples of trace evidence include hair, semen, fibers, drugs, paint chips, soil, and blood. Three important means by which crime scene investigators can locate trace and other types of evidence are through the use of (1) an alternative light source (brand names for alternative light sources include BlueMaxx, Polilight, Omnichrome, and Luma-Lite; they are designated "alternative light sources" because they are alternatives to laser illumination); (2) ultraviolet illumination; and (3) a trace-evidence vacuum system.

Although lasers have been used to examine and locate evidence, such as fingerprints, in crime laboratories for more than 15 years, large lasers have a number of disadvantages, including being very expensive and nonportable.[9] However, an alternative light source—such as a Luma-Lite—overcomes these shortcomings.[10] As the beam from a handheld Luma-Lite is swept over a darkened crime scene, it causes many types of evidence to fluoresce, or glow (see Figure 3–5). Typical crime scene evidence that

Figure 3–5
Use of Luma-Lite
A Texas Ranger demonstrating the use of the Luma-Lite at a simulated crime scene. Note the use of special goggles.

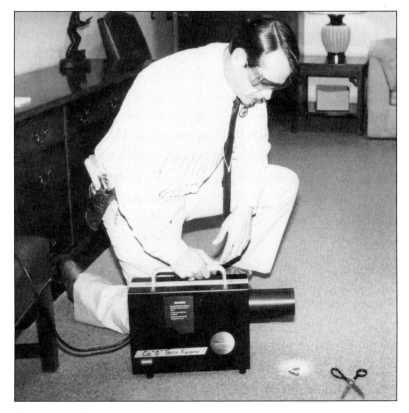

(Courtesy Texas Department of Public Safety)

will fluoresce under an alternative light source includes clothing fibers; body fluids such as semen, urine, and saliva; footprints; and fingerprints. Sometimes hair will fluoresce, especially if it has been dyed; undyed hair can be located with lights such as the Luma-Lite simply due to its reflectance.[11] Blood will not fluoresce, but it will appear as a darker spot if the background is slightly fluorescent.[12] The following case illustrates the successful use of fluorescent illumination at crime scene:

A small leaf was found on a window sill where a burglar had entered. He had been bare-footed, and investigators were able to locate his footprint on the leaf with the Luma-Lite. This print was then developed, and the suspect was subsequently convicted of burglary.[13]

Ultraviolet (UV) simply means "beyond violet."[14] At the top of the color spectrum is violet; the next tint would be ultraviolet, but our unassisted eyes cannot see it.[15] However, when a crime scene is flooded with UV light, hard-to-locate evidence, such as footprints and fingerprints, body fluids, and metal fragments, becomes visible. It is also advisable to scan a crime scene for fibers using a UV light source, because it will detect white-colored fibers, which fluoresce blue in the UV light.[16]

Luma-Lite and UV lighting—both of which should be used with protective goggles—can locate injuries, bite marks, scars, bruising, and other marks of forensic interest on the body that might otherwise be overlooked. In addition to the value of such lighting in processing crime scenes, some hospitals are using it to combat child abuse. In one case, a child was brought to an emergency room for treatment. Suspecting physical abuse, hospital personnel examined the child under fluorescent lighting. A series of L-shaped bruises, which were not otherwise visible, were detected. The child's father admitted to investigators that he struck the child from time to time with a tire iron to discipline him. In another case, a woman was blindfolded, beaten, and raped in her home. During the assault, she managed to bite one of her attackers on the arm. In the investigation that followed, the victim's husband became a suspect. Under UV light, a bite mark was found on the husband, who tried to pass it off as an old scar. However, a forensic dentist compared photographs of the bite mark on the husband with a bite mark made by the victim on an anatomically correct arm, establishing that the victim was the source of both bite marks. The husband was subsequently convicted of participating in the attack.[17]

Trace-evidence collection vacuum systems are highly compact and therefore portable (see Figure 3–6). In order to prevent the accidental

Figure 3–6
Trace Evidence Vacuum
A trace-evidence vacuum used on a sofa where a sexual assault took place.

(Courtesy Westminster, Colorado, Police Department)

contamination of evidence, the nozzle and evidence filter unit (which sits on top of the vacuum's nozzle) is packaged and sealed at the factory's "clean room." At the crime scene, as each different area is vacuumed, such as the sofa in Figure 3-6, the nozzle and the filter are detached. A lid is snapped onto the filter, and then nozzle and filter are sealed in a clear plastic envelope. After the appropriate identifying information is placed on the plastic envelope, it is sent to the crime laboratory, where the material caught in the filter is analyzed. These systems are particularly effective in gathering hairs, fibers, and certain types of drug evidence, such as cocaine. Thus, trace-evidence vacuum systems can often be effectively used in assault, rape, and some drug cases. However, if clothing is seized as evidence and fiber, hair, or other evidence from the suspect or victim may be on it, crime laboratories generally prefer that the clothing not be vacuumed but be sent to the laboratory for processing to prevent the possibility that other valuable evidence may be lost during the vacuuming.

CAUTION

Many crime scenes provide an immediate focus; in criminal homicide, for example, there is a tendency to move directly to the body. Such action, when the person is obviously deceased, has a number of disadvantages. In approaching the point of focus, minute but extremely important evidence may be altered or destroyed; the area to be searched may be too rapidly defined; and other areas that might be fruitfully explored are overlooked or given only a cursory examination.

INCLUSIVENESS

The rule of *inclusiveness* dictates that every available piece of evidence be obtained and, where there is a question as to whether a particular item constitutes evidence, be defined as such. The rationale is that mistakes made in excluding potential evidence often cannot be rectified. One cannot always return to the crime scene and recover evidence. The rule of inclusiveness also requires that standard samples and elimination prints always be obtained when appropriate. If, for example, a burglary has been committed and a safe inside the building successfully attacked, exposing the insulation of the safe, then standard samples of the insulation should be obtained. This will ensure that if at some future time a suspect is identified, comparisons can be made between the standard sample of safe insulation and any traces of safe insulation that might be recovered from the soles of the suspect's shoes or car floormat. Elimination prints are useful in determining whether a latent fingerprint found at a crime scene belongs to the suspect. To use the hypothetical case of a residential burglary, if a latent print was developed inside the house on the window ledge where the perpetrator entered, the residents of the household should be fingerprinted and a comparison made between the latent fingerprint and those of the residents. If the latent fingerprint does not belong to any of the residents, there is a good possibility that it belongs to the perpetrator. In some instances, the fingerprint might belong to someone having authorized access to the dwelling. In cases where this is found to be true, however, the possibility cannot be overlooked that the person with authorized access may be the perpetrator. An example of this possibility is the case of a licensed real estate dealer operating in the Washington, D.C., area who may have entered more than 100 homes that were being offered for sale, stealing furs, tape recorders, silverware, and other valuables worth between $200,000 and $300,000.[18]

PROTECTION FROM INFECTIOUS DISEASE

In the normal course of performing their duties, patrol officers, crime scene technicians, and follow-up investigators have opportunity for contact with pathogenic (disease-causing) microorganisms. Of particular concern are the disease-causing organisms responsible for acquired immune deficiency syndrome (AIDS), hepatitus B,[19] and tuberculosis. Officers need basic information about these diseases and the precautionary measures that are considered appropriate in light of current information.

AIDS

As many as 1.2 million Americans are HIV-positive; of this number roughly 20 percent are women.[20] It is estimated that 10 percent of all diagnosed AIDS cases are not reported.[21] AIDS is not a single disease but a range of health problems whose presence is facilitated by the presence of the AIDS virus, which weakens the body's defense system. These health problems are one or more "opportunistic infections or diseases" and include a particular type of pneumonia, certain malignancies, a type of skin cancer, and some eye infections. Even with treatment, the eye infections can result in blindness in 9 to 18 months. People die from the opportunistic infections and not from AIDS itself. Other symptoms of AIDS includes weight loss, fever, diarrhea, and persistently swollen lymph nodes.

Although some police officers believe "it could never happen to me" and fail to take appropriate precautions, officers have contracted AIDS while working and are dying from AIDS. The following incidents illustrate this point:

An officer received a needle-stick while conducting a prisoner search following an arrest. This officer is HIV-positive. An officer with open sores on his hands fingerprinted prostitutes who were bleeding; because of his subsequent HIV infection, he was medically retired. A 25-year-old deputy sheriff investigated a homicide that took place in the AIDS ward of a correctional facility. The officer subsequently died of AIDS. It is believed that he became infected through cracks in his hands while handling HIV-infected evidence. An intravenous drug user stuck an officer with a hypodermic needle. The officer first developed hepatitis B and later AIDS, from which he died.[22]

In general, the most likely means of HIV transmittal is through contact between an infected body fluid and a person's own blood. Illustrative situations include movement into the bloodstream by sexual contact between an infected person and a partner who has or develops a slight cut or abrasion, resulting in transfer of the HIV through infected semen, vaginal secretions, or blood-to-blood contact, and the sharing of contaminated hypodermic needles by intravenous (IV) drug users. If one person is infected and the other is not, then the likelihood of developing HIV from a single episode of unprotected vaginal intercourse is approximately 1 in 600.[23] Approximately 85 percent of the 28 million HIV cases worldwide have occured as the result of sexual contact.[24] Presently, the greatest HIV danger to on-duty police officers occurs in handling drug-related evidence and in processing crime and accident scenes where body fluids are exposed.

HIV is not an airborne disease. There is no evidence that casual contact, sneezing, sharing the same work space, hugging, using the same toilet, touching, handshaking, or similar nonsexual activities are sources of transmission.[25] It is highly unlikely that an officer could be infected if spit upon. The virus is isolated in only low concentrations in urine and not at all in feces; there have been no HIV infections or AIDS cases associated with these sources. Because the person who does the biting is usually the one who gets the blood, transmission of the virus to an officer through this means is unlikely, unless the biter has open sores or bleeding in or around the mouth.

When it was first identified in 1983, the groups at high risk for contracting AIDS were homosexuals and bisexuals and hemophiliacs receiving transfusions prior to the use of pertinent blood-screening precautions in 1985. Up to 80 percent of the hemophiliacs receiving blood-bank transfusions before 1985 may have become HIV-infected. It was estimated that by 1996 a patient receiving 1 pint from a blood bank had about a 1 in 493,000 chance of contracting HIV from that source, and the likelihood increases with the number of pints of blood used by the patient.[26] In 1986, there was a sharp increase in AIDS cases among IV drug users as a result of sharing contaminated hypodermic needles; the following year, reports of heterosexually acquired AIDS cases accelerated dramatically. This increase was associated with increased numbers of "shooting galleries," where IV drug users rent or borrow injection equipment, and the transmission of HIV to non-drug-injecting sexual partners by IV drug users.[27] To a lesser degree, some HIV infection has resulted from drug-using prostitutes who share IV hypodermic needles.

The AIDS virus is not easily transmitted. For example, even if an officer is accidentally stuck with a needle used by an IV drug user known to be HIV-infected, it is believed that the chance of the officer's developing HIV is about 1 in 300.[28] Outside of the human body, HIV is fragile and will survive only minutes to hours on a flat surface. Tap water at 103 degrees kills the virus, as do many types of disinfectants. (See Figure 3–7.) When using bleach or alcohol as a disinfectant, officers should never mix them and especially should not mix them with ammonia, which will produce toxic fumes.[29] Despite the fact that HIV is not easily transmitted, the

**Figure 3–7
Disinfectant Types**

TYPES OF DISINFECTANTS USED FOR THE AIDS VIRUS

Applications of a disinfectant must be done on clean surfaces. The greater the amount of blood and dirt, the less effective the disinfectant.

1. Bleach–1:10 dilution. This is 1 cup of bleach to 9 cups of water (slightly more than ½ gallon). Contact time is 10–30 minutes for high-level disinfection. Bleach is a powerful antimicrobial (germ-killing) agent and is therefore recommended to clean up fresh (un-dried) blood spills. It does have some disadvantages: it is corrosive to metal; it can hamper the function of electronic and electrical equipment; and it can decolorize fabrics.

2. Alcohol–70 percent isopropyl. Contact time is 5–30 minutes for high-level disinfection. This leaves no ionic residue, does not corrode metal, and can be used around electrical and electronic equipment. It is a good skin antiseptic. The disadvantages are that it is flammable, evaporates quickly, and is inactivated by the presence of blood and dirt.

3. Hydrogen peroxide–3 percent. Commercially available hydrogen peroxide is good for dissolving blood and body fluids from the surfaces of equipment. However, if this is used on heavily soiled equipment, cleaning and decontamination are still required.

(Courtesy Federal Law Enforcement Training Center, Glynco, Georgia)

potentially lethal consequence of developing AIDS requires that officers employ self-protection techniques, including the following:

1. Do not try to bend or recap hypodermic needles seized as evidence, and use caution at a crime scene when handling sharp objects such as razor blades, glass, and knives. For example, place needles, using pliers, forceps, or similar tools, into plastic or metal tubes with screw-on tops.[30] Among health workers exposed to HIV, 14 percent of all exposures resulted from the improper handling or disposal of needles and other sharp objects.[31]

2. Although HIV is most commonly communicated by blood-to-blood exposure, semen, and vaginal secretions, consider all body fluids—whether wet or dry—from everyone as potentially infected. For example, 20 percent of all AIDS patients will develop raised, purplish colored lesions. There is no pattern as to where these lesions may appear; they may be on the face, arms, hands, or other parts of the body. In a limited number of cases, the AIDS patient may develop so-called weeping lesions, which emit HIV-carrying body fluid.

3. Wear latex gloves when contact with blood or body fluids, eye, nose, or mouth membranes, or nonintact skin of any person is likely.[32] Be

constantly aware of the possibility that something you have touched, such as a rough piece of wood, may have pierced your gloves. If you have any doubts about the protection provided by your gloves, replace them immediately. Although latex gloves provide a better sense of touch than vinyl gloves, petroleum products will eat away latex gloves. Therefore, vinyl gloves are preferred when at the scene of a hit-and-run or automobile accident with injuries when gasoline or other petroleum products are exposed. At scenes where potential HIV-carrying fluids are present and/or on evidence that will also be processed for latent fingerprints, wear cotton gloves over latex gloves when collecting the evidence.[33]

4. In addition to wearing appropriate gloves, officers should wear disposable boots, gowns, masks, and protective eyewear with side shields where gross amounts of blood or blood splatters are present at the crime scene. Similar precautions should be taken by officers who attend autopsies. (See Figure 3–8.)

5. "Intact skin is the most important barrier against potential infection and is a fundamental part of the body's immune system."[34] HIV can enter the body not only through cuts but also through small abrasions;

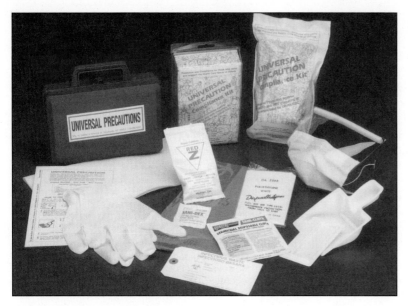

Figure 3–8
Universal Precaution Kit
A Universal Precaution Kit containing combination safety shield/mask, an apron to protect clothing, identification tag for infectious waste, hand wipe, germicidal disinfectant wipe, gloves, Red Z™ pouch, and pickup scoop and scraper. Red Z is used to clean up body fluid spills, such as blood at crime scenes or vomit in jails. Its grains are simply sprinkled on the spill, which very quickly turns into a gel that can easily be scooped up.

(Courtesy Safetec, Buffalo, New York)

there is also a reported case of a health worker whose probable point of entry for the virus was through a small patch of chafed skin on her ear, which she reached up and touched while wearing contaminated gloves. Six percent of the health care workers who became HIV infected had some type of skin opening.[35] Therefore, officers responsible for collecting evidence that is regarded as potentially contaminated and for processing scenes where blood and other body fluids are present must carefully seal all cuts, abrasions, rashes, acne, skin breaks, and similar areas with a 360-degree impermeable bandage. Eating, drinking, smoking, or application of makeup should never be allowed at potential HIV scenes.[36] Officers must become acutely aware of their movements and avoid all hand-to-mouth, hand-to-eye, hand-to-nose, and related movements.[37]

6. If practical, use only disposable items when processing crime scenes. Avoid using or touching your own personal items whenever possible.[38]

7. Any reports, forms, evidence tags, or labels exposed to contaminated blood or other body fluids should be replaced with clean ones at the scene after any needed information is copied.[39]

8. If it is necessary to scrape dried blood loose, it is particularly important to wear a mask and protective eyewear. These will not hinder an individual virus, which is submicroscopic, but the mask will protect the wearer from very small flakes of blood.[40]

9. It is reasonable to assume that all persons and areas to be searched possess sharp objects. Officers should conduct a light pat-type search, as opposed to crushing the clothing of the subject being searched. On the basis of officer's discretion, subjects arrested at a crime scene may be directed to remove the contents of their pockets, to turn their pockets inside out, or to remove bulky outer clothing to facilitate the pat-down. Purses, bags, eyeglass holders, or other containers should be emptied and the contents visibly examined before they are handled. If the searching officer finds or an individual admits to the possession of a hypodermic needle or other sharp object, the person should be restrained before the officer attempts to remove the item. Officers should not run their hands around hatbands or between or under car or sofa seats or other areas that they have not already personally inspected visually. The area underneath a car seat can be searched using a long-handled mirror and

a flashlight, and a wooden paint stirrer can be run between car seats.[41]

10. If it is necessary to provide cardiopulmonary resuscitation (CPR), officers should use a face shield and CPR device. These relatively inexpensive devices are equipped with a one-way valve that is fitted into the "patient's" mouth and a disposable or reusable (after decontamination) plastic shield that will cover the patient's face or mouth, depending on which type is used. The one-way valve prevents blood, saliva, or vomit from entering the caregiver's mouth. Some of these devices cannot be used on children because of their size. Therefore, officers should be sure to follow the directions of the manufacturer.[42]

11. If bitten, the officer should squeeze the area around the wound to encourage bleeding, wash the area thoroughly with soap and hot water, and seek medical attention as soon as possible.[43] Whenever possible, officers should carry small, sealed alcohol sponge packets. These contain 70 percent isopropyl alcohol, which will inactivate HIV within a minute. The alcohol should be placed on, but not wiped from, any wound site and allowed to air-dry.[44] If an alcohol pack is available, it should be used and the wound allowed to air-dry before washing and seeking medical treatment.

12. A bag must be maintained at the crime scene in which all disposable items, such as gloves and shoe covers, will be placed and disposed of according to applicable state laws, health regulations, and departmental policies and procedures. Officers should use a soap dispenser when washing their hands as opposed to sharing a bar of soap. Uniforms that are contaminated may be washed in hot water using ordinary detergent and, if appropriate, bleach; blood-soaked wool uniforms should be soaked in cold water and dry-cleaned. The dry-cleaning process will kill HIV. Even though bloody garments have been removed, the officer should be sure to take a hot shower and use soap to clean his or her body. Items such as handcuffs, eye shields, shoe bottoms, night-sticks, or personal pens should be disinfected using either a bleach or an alcohol solution. Any

potentially contaminated fluids in a police car should be cleaned and decontaminated using bleach, alcohol, or a commercial disinfectant.[45] As a rule of thumb, equipment and environmental surfaces should be treated with an approved disinfectant and left wet for ten or more minutes.[46] Leather items such as gunbelts and shoes should be professionally cleaned and decontaminated or replaced, as indicated by the facts of the situation.[47]

13. The bag used at the crime scene to collect disposable items which may have been contaminated should be clearly marked so that it is disposed of in a proper and timely manner. Some departments use orange bags specially constructed for this purpose.

14. All evidence that may be contaminated should be placed into an appropriate container, sealed, properly identified, and marked "Biological Hazard" or "Bio-Hazard." Garments soaked with wet blood should be placed into a doubled plastic bag and transported to a secure place where they can dry naturally.

Officers who learn that someone is HIV-positive or has AIDS must be aware of the conditions under which such information can be disclosed. In the event of an improper disclosure, an officer may be individually liable and his or her department may also be liable if it failed to train the officer in the applicable laws pertaining to the confidentiality of medical information and constitutional right to privacy. In one case, "John Doe," his wife "Jane Doe," and a friend were traveling in a pickup truck when they were stopped and questioned by the police. John was arrested for unlawful possession of a hypodermic needle. At the time of his arrest, John advised the officers to be careful searching him because he had tested positive for HIV and had weeping lesions. Later that same day, Jane Doe and friend drove to a neighboring jurisdiction where the Does maintained their residence. The friend's car, which had been left in gear, somehow rolled into a neighbor's fence and the police were called. While two officers were investigating the accident, an officer from the jurisdiction that had arrested John Doe arrived. This officer informed one of the officers investigating the accident that John Doe had been arrested earlier and had AIDS. In turn, the officer receiving this information told his partner. After Jane Doe and the friend had left the area, the partner told a neighbor of the Does that John Doe had AIDS and that to protect herself, she should wash with disinfectant. This neighbor, who was a local school employee, became upset, in part because her daughter attended the same school as the four Doe children. The neighbor also contacted other parents with children in the same school, and the next day 11 parents removed their children from the school in a panic over attendance by the Doe children. The story was covered by local newspaper and television stations and at least one report mentioned the Doe family by name. While the federal courts have struggled with whether there is a constitutional right to privacy, the federal district court had no such difficulty in *Doe* v. *Borough of Barrington*,[48] holding that the department which had sent the two officers to investigate the accident was liable for damages, as was the officer at the accident scene who told a neighbor of the Does that John had AIDS. In so doing, the court held that the Fourteenth Amendment protects against unauthorized disclosure by government officials of sensitive personal matters, including medical records and medical information. In the case of the Does, the unauthorized disclosure had resulted in harassment, discrimination, humiliation, and shunning by the community.[49]

Hepatitis B

An estimated 750,000 to 1 million Americans carry the hepatitis B (HBV) virus.[50] The disease can result in jaundice, cirrhosis, dark urine, nausea, extreme fatigue, flulike symptoms, rashes, fevers, anorexia, abdominal pain, and sometimes cancer of the liver.[51] Approximately 90 percent of pregnant women with the disease pass it along to their unborn children.[52] Officers are most likely to contract HBV under the same conditions as they would HIV. HBV is much more hardy than HIV and is therefore easier to contract in the absence of precautions. The incubation period for hepatitis B averages about 120 days versus up to 42 months for HIV, although HIV can often be detected in 6 weeks to 6 months.[53] Unlike AIDS, for which there is no present inoculation, a vaccine has been available for HBV protection since 1982 and provides 90 percent protection for seven years.[54] Under federal Occupational Safety and Health Administration (OSHA) regulations, employers are required to offer all vulnerable employees free hepatitis-B vaccinations and to provide them with protective equipment, such as gloves, to protect them from blood-borne diseases.[55] These requirements became effective July 6, 1992; noncompliance can result in a fine of $70,000 per occurrence, and continued noncompliance can produce fines of up to $7,000 per day.[56]

Tuberculosis

Although tuberculosis (TB) caused 1 death in 500 in the early 1900s, that number dropped to 1 in 30,000 with improved living conditions and the introduction of new drugs.[57] Approximately 15 million people are infected with TB, but only 10 percent of them will ever become ill from the disease.[58] TB usually develops only after the immune systems of victims have been impaired by other diseases, such as cancer or AIDS.[59] Because the bacteria that cause TB most often attack the lungs, airborne transmission of saliva and sputum from infected people is almost the only way by which the disease is spread.[60] When people with TB cough, they produce tiny droplets that can remain suspended in air for long periods of time; anyone who breathes this contaminated air can become infected, although a person with a healthy immune system usually does not.[61] Those who do become infected—especially with the multidrug-resistant strain—usually die from respiratory failure.[62]

The federal Americans with Disabilities Act (ADA) makes it illegal to discriminate against an otherwise-qualified individual in employment practices—such as assignments and promotions—solely on the basis that he or she has, or is merely thought to have, a disability. Thus, if a police officer who either is actually HIV-positive or is inaccurately believed to be so is refused a promotion only on that basis, he or she could invoke the protection of the ADA. "Disability" means a physical or mental impairment that limits one or more major life activities of an individual. Illustrations of "major life activities" include walking, breathing, seeing, hearing, learning, working, and the ability to care for oneself. Employees must make a reasonable accommodation to an otherwise-qualified person with a disability, unless the employer can demonstrate that such an accommodation actually works an undue hardship on the employer. "Reasonable accommodations" include redesigning jobs, allowing part-time hours, and making modifications to facilities and equipment. Thus, otherwise-qualified police officers who have contracted infectious diseases—on or off the job—or otherwise experience a disability covered by the ADA cannot be subject to discriminatory employment practices, such as being assigned to less desirable shifts or assignments or being refused promotions.

✓DOCUMENTATION

Documentation of the crime scene should be a constant activity and often consists of seven important categories in major offenses:

1. *The administrative worksheet*, recording the managment steps taken to ensure that a thorough crime scene search was conducted.
2. *The narrative description*, detailing what the general appearance of the crime scene was when the first responder arrived. It does not include extreme detail concerning evidence or the collection thereof.
3. *The video log*, disclosing what taping was done by whom of what areas in what sequence.
4. *The photographic log*, itemizing the technical and descriptive information for each shot taken.
5. *The diagram or sketch*, illustrating the location of significant crime scene features and the points at which each piece of evidence was recovered.
6. *The evidence recovery log*, identifying who recognized, collected, marked, and packaged each item of physical evidence for administrative and chain-of-custody purposes.
7. *The latent-print lift log*, containing the same type of information as does the evidence recovery log.

At the scenes of crimes of lesser legal importance, the first responder's notes and the incident report he or she subsequently writes may be the only documentation of the scene. Thus, the responsibility of the lone investigator at a scene is especially important because he or she provides all that may ever be known about it in an official sense. Whether the investigator is working as part of a team or alone, it is vitally important that he or she record all steps taken and whether they yielded results or were unproductive. Even steps which do not reveal any useful information are important to record because they document investigative thoroughness. Additionally, documentation also ensures that investigative resources will not later be used to repeat work already completed.[63]

A subseqent section of this chapter deals in greater detail with the three major methods of visually documenting the crime scene—videotaping, photographing, and sketching.

TYPES OF EVIDENCE AND THEIR USEFULNESS

The search of the crime scene forms the main focus of the preliminary investigation. Its importance lies in the fact that ordinarily its fruits, or the lack thereof, will shape much of what occurs in the latent investigation. It can uncover several types of evidence.

CORPUS DELICTI EVIDENCE

Each criminal offense contains a distinct set of elements whose commission or omission must be demonstrated to have occurred in order to prove a case; *corpus delicti evidence* substantiates these elements. Thus, at each crime scene the investigator must keep in mind the unique requirements of proof required and attempt to locate related evidence.

ASSOCIATIVE EVIDENCE

Associative evidence is bidirectional in that it connects the perpetrator to the scene or victim, or connects the scene or victim with the suspect. A case history illustrates this:

A silent burglary alarm was triggered at a bar in a high-crime area. Officers responding to the scene found a point of forced entry at a rear window of the building. An individual was detected hiding in a small shed attached to the building. His statement was that when walking up the alley, he suddenly saw police cars, panicked, and hid in the shed. The search of this person following his arrest revealed the presence of valuables and materials taken from the burglarized premises, connecting the suspect with the scene.

TRACING EVIDENCE

The identification and location of the suspect are the goals of *tracing evidence*; corpus delicti and associative evidence may also serve these purposes:

A 20-year-old female was at a laundromat washing her clothes. A male loitered nearby, observing her. When the woman was alone, he walked rapidly to the laundromat and entered the men's room. A few minutes later, with his pants and underwear around his ankles, he approached the woman, shook his genitals at her, pulled up his clothing, and ran off. The officer who responded to the call found a man's wallet on the floor of the men's restroom. A records check on the identification contained in it revealed that the owner of the wallet had a history of sex offenses and lived in the neighborhood of the laundromat. When the victim identified the suspect from a series of photographs, a warrant for the suspect's arrest was obtained.

THE CRIME SCENE SEARCH

The purpose of the crime scene search is to obtain physical evidence useful in establishing that, in fact, an offense has been committed; identify the method of operation employed by the perpetrator; reduce the number of suspects; and identify the perpetrator. Five major considerations dominate the crime scene search.

BOUNDARY DETERMINATION

The crime scene coordinator must make a decision concerning what the perimeters of the search will be. In buildings the boundary determination is defined by the structure and is, therefore, easily established. In addition, the perpetrator must have approached the crime scene and fled from it, and these avenues must be established and searched.

Here the most vexing decision is how far along the lines of approach and flight the search might profitably extend. Crimes committed in the open may require a considerable amount of attention and thought as to what the boundaries of the search pattern should be. For example, if an individual was taken into a field and murdered, that situation is far different than would be the case if the same crime had been committed in a house. As a rule, when examining an outdoor scene, it is better to define the limits of the search in very broad terms. While this might result in some possible waste of effort due to searching a larger area than is absolutely necessary, it is an acceptable trade-off because more than occasionally evidence is unexpectedly encountered.

CHOICE OF SEARCH PATTERN

There are five fundamental search patterns from which the crime scene coordinator may select. The *spiral*, depicted in Figure 3–9, is usually employed in outdoor scenes and is normally executed by a single person. It involves the searcher's walking in slightly ever-decreasing, less-than-concentric circles from the outermost boundary determination

Figure 3–9
The Spiral Search Pattern

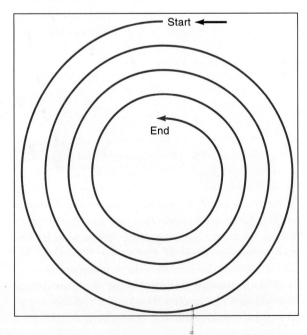

Figure 3–10
The Strip Search Pattern

toward a central point. This pattern should not be operated in the reverse, that is, beginning at some central point and working toward the perimeter of the crime scene in ever-increasing, less-than-concentric circles, as there is a real danger that some evidence may be inadvertently destroyed while walking to the central point to initiate the search. Use of the *strip* search, shown in Figure 3–10, involves the demarcation of a series of lanes down which one or more persons proceed. Upon reaching the starting point, the searchers proceed down their respective lanes, reverse their direction, and continue in this fashion until the area has been thoroughly examined. If multiple searchers are being used in this method, then whenever physical evidence is encountered, all searchers should stop until it is properly handled and they have received information with respect to its nature. The search is then resumed in the fashion previously described. Figure 3–11 shows a single searcher using a metal detector to look for a bullet casing while conducting a strip search in lanes established by landmarks. A variation of the strip search is the *grid*, depicted in Figure 3–12. After having completed the strip pattern, the searchers double back perpendicularly across the area being examined. While more time-consuming than the strip search, the grid offers the advantage of being more methodical and thorough; examined from two different viewpoints, an area is more likely to yield evidence that might otherwise have been overlooked.

Figure 3–13 shows the *zone* search pattern, which requires that an area be divided into four large quadrants, each of which is then examined using any of the methods previously described. Where the area to be searched is particularly large, a variation of the zone method would be to subdivide the larger quadrants into four smaller quadrants. The *pie* search pattern, also referred to as the *wheel*, is shown in Figure 3–14. It entails dividing the area into a number of pie-shaped sections, usually six, which are then searched, usually by a variation of the strip method.

In actual practice, both the spiral and pie search, or wheel, patterns are rarely employed. Where the area to be searched is not excessively large, the strip or grid pattern is normally used. When the crime scene is of significant size, the zone search pattern is normally employed.

INSTRUCTION OF PERSONNEL

Even when the same type of criminal offense has been committed, the variation among crime scenes may be enormous. These variations are due to such factors as the physical setting, the manner and means that the perpetrators used to execute the offense, and the lengths to which they may have gone to eliminate or destroy evidence. Thus, it is of paramount importance that the crime scene coordinator call together all those individuals who will be, in various capacities, processing the scene and share

Figure 3–11
Conducting a Strip Search
Officer conducting a strip search for a bullet casing using a metal detector.

(Courtesy Houston Police Department)

with them all of the available information concerning the case. This serves to minimize the possibility of excluding any available evidence. On receipt of this information, the members of the crime scene processing team may then begin their work.

COORDINATION

One of the most important responsibilities of the person in charge of the crime scene is to integrate the efforts of those assigned to the technical and investigative service functions, along with ensuring the timely flow of pertinent information. For example, if a suspect is in custody and the interrogation yields information concerning the weapon or tool that may have been used, or where it may be located, then the crime scene coordinator should rapidly relay this information to those involved in technical services at the scene so that they will be alert to specific possibilities for the recovery of physical evidence. Conversely, as significant physical evidence is recovered, the information should be conveyed to the crime scene coordinator, who can then transmit it to the investigators so that they can move toward apprehending a suspect or be assisted in the interrogation of a possible perpetrator already in custody.

TERMINATION OF THE CRIME SCENE SEARCH

The amount of time required to process a crime scene varies considerably, depending on such variables as the extent and nature of the area to be examined, the complexity of a case, the abundance or scarcity of physical evidence, and available personnel. Once it has been established that a crime has been committed, under no circumstances should the search be terminated until all possible fruitful avenues for developing physical evidence

Figure 3–12
The Grid Search Pattern

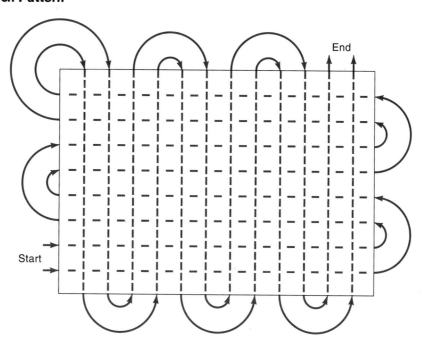

Figure 3–13
The Zone Search Pattern

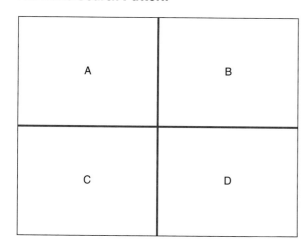

Figure 3–14
The Pie Search, or Wheel, Pattern

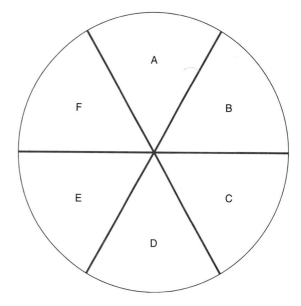

have been thoroughly explored. Occasionally it may be necessary to suspend an operation temporarily; one of the most common situations would be one in which a priority crime with evidence subject to decay requires the temporary diversion of personnel from a scene where delayed processing would not result in any loss of physical evidence. If it becomes necessary to stop the examination of one scene for a time, that scene should be secured in such a fashion that there is no possibility of contamination, alteration, or accidental destruction of any evidence that may exist.

THE COLLECTION AND CARE OF EVIDENCE

The location of physical evidence during the crime scene search merely marks the first step in its long journey toward presentation in court. To satisfy legal requirements related to its introduction in a judicial proceeding, the investigator must be able to:

1. Identify each piece of evidence, even years after it was collected.
2. Describe the location and condition of the item at the time it was collected.
3. Assist in establishing that, from the time of its collection until presentation in court, the evidence was continuously in proper custody.
4. Assist in describing any changes that may have occurred in the evidence between the time of collection and the subsequent introduction as evidence in court.[64]

Where photography is employed, shots should be taken of each piece of evidence prior to its examination. After the photograph has been taken, or when this service is not used, the investigator may then handle and examine the article. At this time the evidence is marked; the standard practice is to place the officer's initials, shield number, and date on the article. When the article is too small to permit this or of such a character as to prohibit it (such as narcotics evidence), or when doing this would alter its evidentiary value (for example, dislodging blood from a murder weapon), the material should be placed in a container and tape-sealed, with the necessary information written across the tape in such a fashion that any opening of the container would be immediately apparent.

Very small pieces of evidence are normally placed in test tubes or pill boxes, while evidence envelopes are used for larger articles. Two common types of evidence envelopes are the gum-sealed (Figure 3–15) and the clear plastic (Figure 3–16) varieties. The gum-sealed envelope has printed lines on which the investigator fills in information about the current case, such as when and where the evidence was seized. Clear plastic pouches are heat-sealed so that the evidence can be viewed without opening the pouch and any tampering with the evidence is immediately apparent, providing major advantages over the gum-sealed envelopes. Identifying information about a case can be placed into the plastic evidence pouch before sealing, or can be stuck onto it. There is also an evidence envelope that falls in between the gum-sealed and the clear plastic pouch: paper bags with a clear plastic window that allows one to view the contents without having to open the bag. This type of envelope is excellent for clothing that may contain moist semen or other nondried organic stains, because the paper bag breathes—thus reducing the likelihood of putrefaction or partial decomposition of the organic evidence. As discussed more fully in Chapter 4, Physical Evidence, bloodstained clothing seized as evidence should be allowed to air-dry before it is packaged and sent to the crime laboratory. Because there is always the possibility that some undetected moisture may remain, a paper bag, with or without a plastic window, should always be used for this type of evidence.

Administratively, the chain of custody is the witnessed, written record of all individuals who have maintained unbroken control over the evidence since its acquisition by a police agency. It begins when an item of evidence is collected and is maintained until final disposition of that item. Continuous accountability is secured by maintaining this chain of custody. Each individual in the chain of custody has personal responsibility for an item of evidence, including its care and safekeeping.

Record-keeping systems and the attendant forms vary from one police agency to another. A good evidence control system will, however, meet the following standards:

1. Prevent loss or unauthorized release of evidence.
2. Establish and maintain a continuous chain of custody.
3. Establish custodial responsibility for evidence
4. List, identify, and indicate the location of items held in custody.
5. Require a supervisor's approval before evidence is released.

Figure 3–15
Gum-Sealed Evidence Envelope
Evidence in gum-sealed envelope being transferred from one investigator to another.

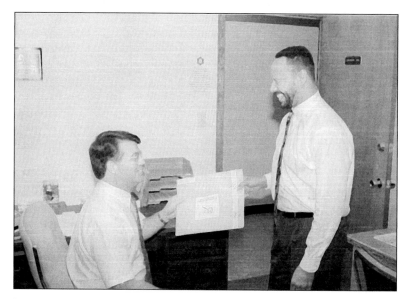

(Courtesy Arkansas State Police)

Figure 3–16
Clear Plastic Evidence Envelope
Heat-sealed clear plastic envelope with crime laboratory evidence tag.

(Courtesy St. Louis County, Missouri, Police Department)

6. Identify the individual to whom evidence is released.

7. Indicate the reasons for any release of evidence.

8. Provide documented proof that the evidence release is authorized, and indicate its final disposition.[65]

Investigators should not regard such requirements as administrative decisions beyond the purview of their concern; being in an excellent position to observe the inner workings of the system, they can help identify actual or potential deficiencies and recommend improvements. In the absence of a workable records system supported by uncomplicated forms, the security of evidence is considerably weakened, the chain of custody is in danger of being severed, and the opportunity is created for mishandling, tampering, stealing, or accidentally losing physical evidence.

VISUALLY DOCUMENTING THE CRIME SCENE

Much like the sports adage, "Many a good game has been left on the practice field," the value of many excellent investigations has been reduced considerably by the failure to visually document them. People process information differently. The more ways a crime scene is visually documented, the greater the likelihood that the method or methods used will help others understand it accurately. In general, scenes should be visually documented in the following sequence: videotaping, photographing, and sketching.

VIDEOTAPING

Video cameras are relatively inexpensive, easy to operate, and provide immediate playback capability; moreover, the motion captured on tape holds the viewer's attention and imparts a sense of actually being present.[66] Additionally, crime scene videotapes are a powerful tool for training investigators.

Quality crime scene videos start with the proper equipment. Most departments do not have the internal resources to evaluate the technical capabilities of video cameras. It is well worth the effort to check with other departments as to their experience with ease of operations, portability, any useful auxiliary equipment, picture quality, and durability of equipment they use. Publications such as *Consumer Reports* provide additional information.

Keeping the camera lens and heads clean will assist in providing crisp, sharp images. Batteries should be kept charged, technicians should periodically check the equipment, and personnel who are to use the camera must be trained. All manuals should be kept with the equipment so that they can be consulted if need be. Each crime scene should be documented with a separate, new, good-quality tape. As a practical matter, most scenes can be recorded on 30-minute tapes, although a small supply of 2-hour tapes should be kept on hand for more complicated cases. Previously used tapes that have been erased should not be used; they can produce streaks and other flaws that cannot be removed. Moreover, in some instances images from a used tape that has been erased can appear on a new recording made with that tape.

Proper lighting will enhance the quality of a videotape. The need for lights at night is apparent; they are also useful under lower light conditions during the day. Proper lighting is important because it speeds up the focusing of the camera, truer colors are produced, and greater detail is recorded. Various terms are used to refer to a light mounted on a video camera, including fill light, color-enhancement light, and, more simply, video light. Battery-operated fill lights eliminate the need to pull cords through the scene and allow free movement through it.

Videotaping should be used not as a substitute for conventional still photography of the crime scene but, instead, as an adjunct. Because video is a low-resolution medium even in its most technologically advanced form, it is no match for a 35-millimeter photograph. and neither are individual photographs made from a videotape. (See Figure 3–17.)

Figure 3–17
Documenting the Crime Scene
Police officer documenting the location of a shotgun found at a crime scene.

(Courtesy Lewiston, Maine, Police Department)

Videotape should provide a continuous flow of visual information to the viewer; when shot without adequate planning, videos provide insufficient information and are confusing. Gaps in the chronology of a tape may also raise questions at trial regarding possible alterations of evidence. Once taping is started, it should continue uninterrupted until completion. Although walking from one area to another may result in a tape with some "bouncing" in it, this is more easily explained than a tape that is turned off and on as the camera operator repositions himself or herself. There are two distinctly different views with respect to narrating observations about the scene as it is taped. The first view is that the moment-by-moment narrative of the particulars of a scene is highly useful in recording details that may otherwise be lost. The second view is that the camera's sound recorder should be off at all times, eliminating the possibility of making erroneous statements or picking up extraneous comments, which can be embarrassing.

Videotaping should follow the same basic principles as still photography, that is, movement from the general to the specific. A tripod or monopod will help steady the camera and provide a smooth pan. The mistake made most frequently in panning an area is too rapid movement, which produces a "jumpy," coarse picture. As a rule of thumb, the camera operator should pan at a speed that is half of what he or she thinks it should be—and then reduce that by about 50 to 75 percent. This helps keep the autofocus working and images sharp. Another common mistake is overuse of the camera's zoom feature, which if done rapidly only confuses the viewer.

Immediately after completing the taping session, rewind the tape and remove it from the recorder. Initial, date, and preserve it just as with any other type of physical evidence. Cassette tapes that have a tab can be punched out to prevent rerecording on the tape. Tapes to be used for evidence must be stored in a place free of dust and machinery producing magnetic fields, which can reduce the quality of or even destroy the tape. If the original crime scene tape is to be viewed more than once or twice, it should be preserved by making a working copy for frequent viewing.

Videotapes have been widely accepted by the courts as long as they represent the crime scene accurately. The courts do not expect to see a polished Hollywood studio production. They recognize the limitations under which police departments operate. Some courts have objected to the use of videos on the basis that the color might inflame the jury in particularly gruesome cases where the victim is depicted, but this has been overcome by showing such scenes in monochrome. In general, poor execution, rambling narratives and/or extraneous comments, and similar flaws that reflect the lack of a serious effort are the greatest barriers to admissibility of videotapes.

When used in court, videotapes typically require separate monitors for the judge, the jury, the defense, and the prosecution. No effort should be spared in obtaining the proper equipment with which to show a tape. All equipment should be set up well ahead of time and carefully checked out, including ensuring that the color, contrast, and brightness are consistent on all monitors.

PHOTOGRAPHING

The statement "One picture is worth a thousand words" may or may not be true; it is certain, however, that good photography is an invaluable asset in documenting crime scenes. Investigative photographs are those that are made to record an object or event or to clarify a point that is related to a particular investigation. A number of pictures are taken in crime laboratories and constitute investigative photographs; for the purposes at hand, treatment is limited to those taken at the crime scene. Comprehensive photographic coverage of a crime scene is possible without great expertise; the handling and use of cameras and associated equipment is not a topic of this section. Instead, the purpose is to provide an overview of the matters relating to photographic coverage of a crime scene and the use of photographs.

General Considerations

Time is an essential factor, and photography may preempt other aspects of the investigation. Objects must not be moved until they have been photographed from all necessary angles. As there are situations in which the object of interest undergoes significant change with the passage of time, photographic equipment must be in a constant state of readiness.

The camera position for all exposures may be recorded on the crime scene sketches or in the offense report from notes made at the scene. Photographs of interior scenes, intended to depict the area as a whole, should be taken as overlapping segments moving in one direction around the room or area. In making such photographs, it is best to have the camera at about eye level unless a tripod is used.

The most important element in crime scene photography is maintaining perspective. Proper photographic perspective produces the same impression of relative position and size of objects as when they are viewed with the naked eye. Any significant distortion in the perspective will reduce, or destroy altogether, the evidentiary value of a photograph.

✓ Critical Photographic Requirements

Using a criminal homicide committed in a house as an example, the following represent the essential photographs that must be taken:

1. The line of approach to, and flight from, the scene.

2. Significant adjacent areas, such as the yard of the house in which the homicide occurred.

3. Close-up photographs of the entrance and exit to the house used by the suspect or those most likely to have been used if these are not obvious.

4. A general scenario photograph showing the location of the body and its position in relation to the room in which it was found.

5. A least two photographs of the body, at 90-degree angles to each other, with the camera positioned as high as possible, pointing downward toward the body.

6. As many close-ups of the body as needed to show wounds or injuries, weapons lying near the body, and the immediate surroundings.

7. The area underneath the body and under each item of evidence immediately after its removal, if there is any mark, stain, or other apparent alteration produced by the presence of the body or evidence.

8. All blood stains, preferably in color film.

9. All latent fingerprints before they are lifted and the weapon on which the prints were found, showing its relationship to the general surroundings. (Latent fingerprints likely to be destroyed by lifting always must be photographed, even when it is not standard practice to shoot all fingerprints before handling.)

ADMISSIBILITY OF PHOTOGRAPHS AS EVIDENCE

Photographs are admissible in court if testimony can establish that they accurately depict the scene. The accuracy of the photograph always relates to the degree to which it represents the appearance of the subject matter as to form, tone, color, and scale. The use of a lens that will record objects and areas in focus may not always portray correct distances between objects or reproduce them with the proper perspective. In such situations, the crime scene sketch and field notes take on added importance.

Usually the negative is considered sufficient proof to refute any allegation that a photograph has been altered. However, if enlarged photographs are made for presentation in court, a contact print without borders should also be made. Because of the importance of scale, distances, and perspective in interpreting the photographs taken at crime scenes, it is good procedure to include a ruler or other scale measurement in the photograph, when this is practical. However, because some courts have not allowed even this minor modification of the scene, an identical photograph without the scale indicator should also be taken.

If the photograph is to have the highest quality as evidence, it must depict the scene, persons, or objects precisely as they were found. Therefore, the photograph must depict the crime scene exclusively. No people should be working within the scene at the time, nor should extraneous objects, such as police equipment, be included.

SKETCHING

Sketches are useful during questioning, in preparing the offense report, and in presenting information in court.[67] The sketch complements the photographs and notes taken during the crime scene search. It has the communication value of any illustration with the additional advantage that unnecessary detail can be eliminated to portray the essential elements of the scene and their relationships. Several techniques may be used to establish the location of evidence and other important items on a sketch. It is important to remember that the purpose of the sketch is to portray the information accurately, but not necessarily artistically; the investigator need not have any artistic ability to draft an adequate sketch.

Basic Equipment

Although any type of paper may be used in preparing a crime scene sketch, plain, unlined paper is adequate, and graph paper is best. The following basic equipment should be available for producing the sketch:

1. One 50-foot steel tape.
2. Several thumbtacks to hold one end of the tape when an investigator is working alone.
3. One straightedge, preferably 18 inches long.
4. One 8- or 12-foot steel tape for ancillary measurements.

Additional equipment that is useful, but not essential, includes a T-square, several templates for easy drawing of curves, special symbols and related figures, two plastic triangles of different angles, and a compass for making circles. An infrequently used but occasionally helpful item is a magnetic compass.

Information to Be Included in the Sketch

The items of information that are essential in a crime scene sketch are listed below. The list is not comprehensive in the sense that it restricts the investigating officer's judgment as to what might be included. The major constraint on detail in sketching is that the result must be easily intelligible to the viewer without detailed study. If too much detail is included, a major advantage of the sketch over the photograph is lost. The sketch should include at least the following information:

1. The investigator's full name, rank, and shield number.
2. The date, time, crime classification, and case number.
3. The full name of any person assisting in taking measurements.

4. The address of the crime scene, its location within a building, landmarks, and compass direction.
5. The scale of the drawing, if a scale drawing has been made. When a scale drawing has not been made, the sketch should include a notation: "Not to scale, dimensions and distances tape-measured."
6. The major items of physical evidence and the critical features of the crime scene along with the location of such items, indicated by accurate measurements from at least two fixed points, or by other methods discussed later in this chapter.
7. A legend of the symbols used to identify objects or points of interest on the sketch. Color may be used to distinguish objects or features; however, the use of large numbers of colors may be confusing and eliminates the ability to reproduce the sketch rapidly.

General Considerations

It is critical that measurements shown on the sketch be as accurate as possible and that they be made and recorded uniformly; if one aspect is inaccurate, such as the dimensions of a field in which a body was found, the distortion introduced renders the sketch relatively useless. The coordinate distances of an item in the sketch must be measured in the same manner; one coordinate leg should not be paced and the other measured. It is also a poor practice to pace off a distance and then show it on the sketch expressed in feet and inches. Such an indication connotes a greater degree of accuracy than actually exists. If the point arose in court, such an inconsistency would significantly detract from the value of the sketch. An erroneous measurement in a drawing, once discovered, is difficult to explain and frequently introduces doubt as to the competency of the entire investigation.

Sketching Methods

This section deals with various techniques employed to prepare sketches, particularly the methods that can be used to establish the location of evidence and other important items.

Coordinate This technique involves measuring the distance of an object from two fixed points. One form of the coordinate method uses a baseline drawn between two known points. The baseline may also be a wall or be drawn as the mathematical center of a room, the exact dimensions of which are known. The measurements of a given object are then taken from left to right along the baseline to a point at right angles to the object that is to be plotted. The object is indicated on the sketch by a number, and the object is identified by a corresponding number in the legend. Figure 3–18 illustrates this method, which is the simplest form of a sketch, namely, the two-dimensional presentation of the scene as if viewed directly from above, using a number keyed to description of the item located in it. Figure 3–18 incorporates the full range of information essential to a proper sketch; however, this is omitted from subsequent diagrams to avoid needless repetition.

Triangulation This method, illustrated in Figure 3–19, is particularly useful in an outdoor situation where there are no easily identifiable edges of fields or roads for use as baselines. Two or more widely separated reference points are located, and the item of interest is located by measuring along a straight line from each of the reference points. The reference points must be ones that are not likely to disappear. Note in Figure 3–19 that a metal light pole, the corner of a brick house, and a fire hydrant were used.

Cross-Projection Depicted in Figure 3–20, the cross-projection method is useful when the items or locations of interest are on or in the walls as well as elsewhere in an enclosed space. The walls, windows, and doors in a cross-projection sketch are drawn as though the walls had been folded flat on the floor. The measurements

Figure 3–18
Baseline, or Coordinate, Method of Sketching

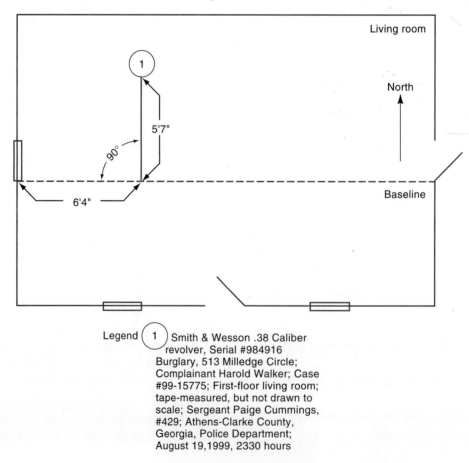

Legend (1) Smith & Wesson .38 Caliber revolver, Serial #984916 Burglary, 513 Milledge Circle; Complainant Harold Walker; Case #99-15775; First-floor living room; tape-measured, but not drawn to scale; Sergeant Paige Cummings, #429; Athens-Clarke County, Georgia, Police Department; August 19, 1999, 2330 hours

Figure 3–19
Triangulation Method of Sketching

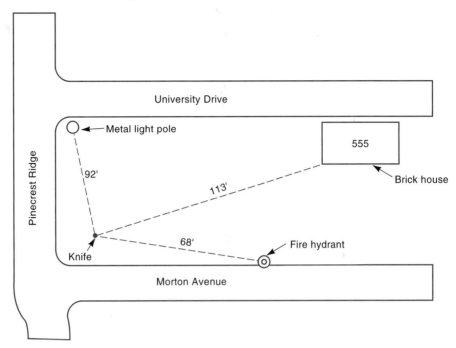

Figure 3–20
The Cross-Projection Sketch Method

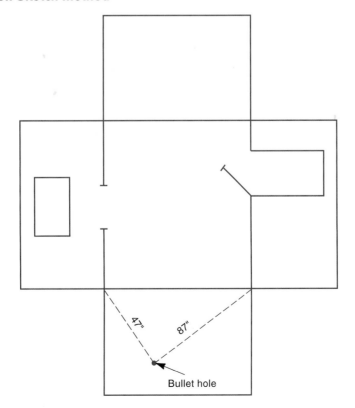

from a given point on the floor to the wall are then indicated.

Rough and Smooth Sketches A *rough sketch* is one drawn by the investigator at the scene of the crime. Changes should not be made after the investigator leaves the scene. The rough is not drawn to scale but indicates accurate distances and dimensions. To eliminate excessive detail, it may be necessary to prepare more than one sketch. For example, one sketch may be devoted to the position of the victim's body and a limited number of critical evidence items. Additional sketches might depict the location of other evidence with respect to the point of entry or other critical areas.

A *smooth sketch* is simply one that is finished, frequently being drawn to scale using information contained in the rough sketch. In a scaled diagram, the numbers concerning distances can be eliminated; if the smooth sketch is not drawn to scale, these distances must be shown. The person preparing the rough sketch must verify the accuracy of the final product whenever the smooth sketch is drafted by someone else.

While many law enforcement agencies continue to make crime scene sketches by hand, other agencies have chosen to take advantage of computer technology to produce them. Several software programs are used for this purpose, including Compuscene (Figure 3–21) and Autosketch (Figure 3–22). Compuscene is more specifically intended for crime scene sketching, while Autosketch is a general drafting program. Once the measurements and other data for the crime scene sketch are assembled, Compuscene or Autosketch can prepare the diagrams at the scene on a laptop computer or in the office on a desktop computer. Additionally, by using a color printer, it is possible to quickly reproduce diagrams that use color, thus overcoming one of the limitations of using hand-drawn sketches that incorporate this feature.

SUBMISSION OF EVIDENCE TO THE LABORATORY

Evidence for examination is most often transmitted to the crime laboratory by courier, air express, registered mail, or railway express. Ideally, however, a member of the investigative team intimately familiar with the details of the case personally conveys the evidence to the laboratory. As a practical matter, the method of transmittal is determined by two factors: the nature of the evidence and the urgency with which results must be obtained. Certain types of materials cannot be transmitted through the mail. For example, Interstate Commerce Commission regulations and various state and local provisions shape the conditions under which explosive or flammable materials may be transported. When chemicals, blasting caps, or similar materials are to be sent to the laboratory, it is sound procedure to get instructions from the laboratory before the actual transmittal.

The laboratory must be provided with certain information if it is to make an intelligent and complete examination. Ordinarily this includes:

- *Administrative data:*
  1. The identity of the subject under investigation.
  2. The name of the victim or complainant.
  3. The nature of the offense and its date of commission.
  4. The location at which the offense occurred.
  5. The case number assigned by the agency submitting the material for examination.

- *Summary of facts:* This information includes a synopsis of the case; often a copy of the crime report is included.

- *List of articles submitted and examinations requested:* So that the laboratory examiners can perform their work rapidly and return the results to the requesting agency, a list of requested examinations should be included. For example, the agency may ask whether the bullet contained in the submission as Exhibit A was fired from the revolver labeled Exhibit B.

- *Miscellaneous information:* Such matters as the identity of the officer to whom the laboratory report should be directed, to whom the evidence should be returned, the inclusion of pertinent photographs, and, where applicable, the degree of urgency for rapid processing, as in the case of a suspect's being held in custody pending findings in the report—all are miscellaneous information.

Figure 3–21
Compuscene Software

A crime scene drawing made using the Compuscene software program.

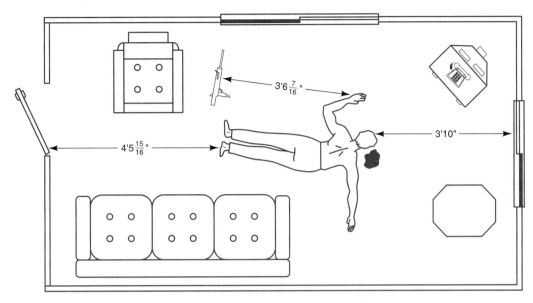

(Courtesy Visatex Corporation, Campbell, California)

Figure 3–22
Autosketch Software

With the use of symbols from a shapes library, Autosketch was used to generate this drawing of a crime scene.

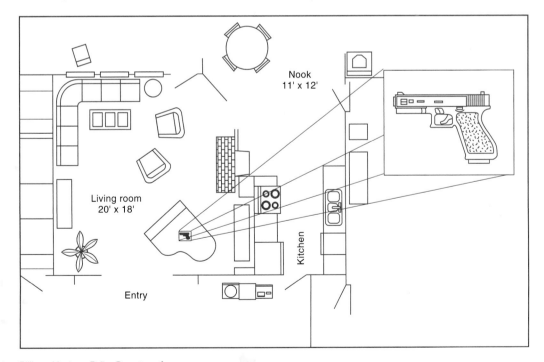

(Courtesy Billings, Montana, Police Department)

A sample letter of request from a local police department to the FBI is depicted in Figure 3–23.

The proper packaging of evidence is depicted in Figure 3–24. Great care must be exercised in the packaging of evidence in order to prevent breakage or other accidental destruction while in transit and to avoid the contamination of one piece of evidence by another. Also, it should be noted that evidence pertaining to several different cases should not be included in the same package; each case should always be submitted separately.

Figure 3–23
Sample Request for Examination of Physical Evidence

Police Headquarters
Right City, State (Zip Code)
March 17, 20--

Director
Federal Bureau of Investigation
10th Street and Pennsylvania Avenue, N.W.
Washington, D. C. 20535

ATTENTION: FBI LABORATORY

Dear Sir:

RE: GUY PIDGIN, SUSPECT
EMPALL MERCHANDISE MART
BURGLARY

Sometime during the early morning of March16, 20--, someone entered the Empall Merchandise Mart through an unlocked side window and made an unsuccessful attempt to rip open the safe. The outer layer of metal on the safe door had been pried loose from the upper right corner and bent outward ripping the metal along the top and down the side of the safe about 12" each way. The burglar my have been scared away because the job was not completed. Investigation led us to one Guy Pidgin who denies involvement. He voluntarily let us take his shoes and trousers and a crowbar that was under his bed in his rooming house.

I am sending by registered mail a package containing the following evidence in this case:

1. One pair of shoes obtained from Guy Pidgin.
2. A pair of gray flannel trousers obtained from Guy Pidgin.
3. One 28" crowbar obtained from Guy Pidgin.
4. Safe insulation taken from door of safe at Empall Merchandise Mart.
5. Piece of bent metal approximately 12" x 12" taken from door of safe at Empall Merchandise Mart. In order to differentiate the two sides cut by us we have placed adhesive tape on them.
6. Chips of paint taken from front and side of safe.
7. One fingerprint card for Guy Pidgin, FBI # 213762J9.
8. Ten transparent lifts taken from the crime scene.

It would be appreciated if you would examine the shoes and trousers to see if there is any safe insulation or paint chips on them and match the paint taken from the safe. Also, we would be interested to know whether it is possible to determine if the crowbar was used to open the safe. Please compare the transparent lifts to the fingerprints of Guy Pidgin, FBI # 213762J9.

This evidence, which should be returned to us, has not been examined by any other expert.

Very truly yours,

James T. Wixling
Chief of Police

(Courtesy Federal Bureau of Investigation)

Figure 3–24
Proper Sealing of Evidence

The method shown permits access to the invoice letter without breaking the inner seal. This allows the person entitled to receive the evidence to receive it in a sealed condition just as it was packed by the sender.

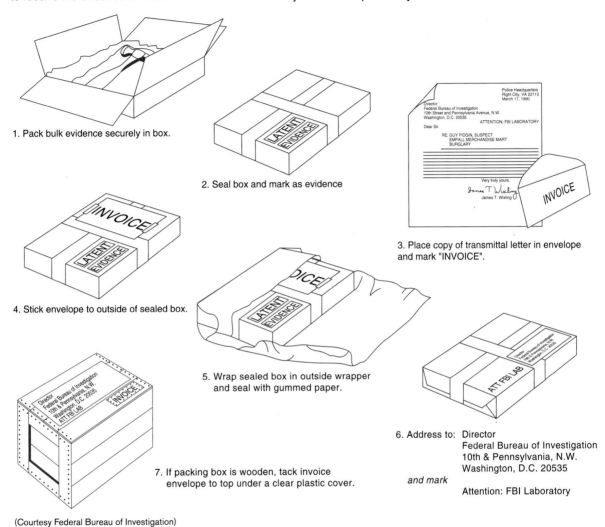

1. Pack bulk evidence securely in box.

2. Seal box and mark as evidence

3. Place copy of transmittal letter in envelope and mark "INVOICE".

4. Stick envelope to outside of sealed box.

5. Wrap sealed box in outside wrapper and seal with gummed paper.

6. Address to: Director
Federal Bureau of Investigation
10th & Pennsylvania, N.W.
Washington, D.C. 20535

and mark

Attention: FBI Laboratory

7. If packing box is wooden, tack invoice envelope to top under a clear plastic cover.

(Courtesy Federal Bureau of Investigation)

Questions

1. What is a crime scene?

2. What are the major crime scene functions?

3. At the scene of a crime, what are some typical problems that may be encountered?

4. Of what importance is crime scene control?

5. What does the rule of inclusiveness dictate?

6. Identify and give examples of the three types of evidence.

7. What are the purposes of a crime scene search?

8. The police may release relevant information about a defendant if it is not of a nature that is prejudicial to the defendant's right to a fair

trial. Identify at least seven statements and actions that are generally regarded as being impermissible in this regard.

9. What considerations dominate the crime scene search?

10. Define *trace evidence* and give two examples of it from among those given in this chapter.

11. Identify two alternative light sources and discuss their use at a crime scene.

12. Define and discuss AIDS, HBV, and TB.

13. Describe the major provisions of the Americans with Disabilities Act, and explain how they relate to police officers.

14. State three beliefs about the means of transmittal of HIV that are false and give three likely scenarios for actually communicating it.

15. Of what importance are intact skin and the wearing of protective gear at a crime scene with considerable blood?

16. Identify the five crime scene search patterns.

17. What are the characteristics of a good evidence control system?

18. By what means may evidence be submitted to a crime laboratory, and which two factors shape the choice of which method to use?

19. What information should accompany evidence submitted for laboratory examination?

20. Distinguish between rough and smooth sketches.

21. Immediately after completing a videotaping session of a crime scene, what actions should be taken to preserve the video for use as evidence?

22. Identify two software programs discussed in this chapter that can be used to make crime scene drawings.

23. What is the major advantage of a clear plastic evidence pouch over a gum-sealed evidence envelope?

Notes

1. A number of texts contain similar statements; for example, see Paul I. Kirk, *Crime Investigation* (New York: Interscience, 1960), p. 4.

2. For example, see Mark Hansen, "Laboratory Evidence Questioned," *ABA Journal,* July 1994, Vol. 80, No. 16(2); "Forensic Expert Charged with Perjury," *The New York Times,* July 23, 1994, p. 9.

3. Arne Svensson and Otto Wendel, *Techniques of Crime Scene Investigation* (New York: American Elsevier, 1965), p. 15.

4. Richard H. Fox and Carl L. Cunningham, *Crime Scene Search and Physical Evidence Handbook* (Washington, D.C.: Government Printing Office, 1985), pp. 12–13.

5. Bill Berkeley, "Wrong Assumptions Ruined Probe," *The Atlanta Journal,* February 17, 1982, pp. A1, A13.

6. "But Some Have Ins and Outs," *St. Petersburg* (Florida) *Times,* February 24, 1979, p. A1.

7. "Man Accused of Shipping Self to Bank," *The Atlanta Journal,* May 10, 1979, p. A18.

8. Barry A. J. Fisher, *Techniques of Crime Scene Investigation,* 5th ed. (New York: Elsevier, 1992), p. 163.

9. Dr. J. E. Watkin and Sgt. A. H. Misner, "Fluorescence and Crime Scenes in the 90s," *RCMP Gazette,* 1990,

Vol. 52, No. 9, p. 1. Large lasers at the time of this writing cost approximately $100,000.

10. The prototype for the Luma-Lite was developed by Canada's National Research Council. This prototype was then actually produced and marketed by Payton Scientific, now Ion Trace of Toronto.

11. Watkin and Misner, "Fluorescence and Crime Scenes," p. 4.

12. Ibid.

13. John Lester, "Forensic Expert Uses Tiny Clues to Solve Crimes," *The Tampa Tribune,* September 9, 1992, pp. 1–2.

14. Michael H. West and Robert E. Barsley, "Ultraviolet Forensic Imaging," *FBI Law Enforcement Bulletin,* May 1992, Vol. 61, No. 5, p. 14.

15. Ibid.

16. Watkin and Misner, "Fluorescence and Crime Scenes," p. 4.

17. West and Barsley, "Ultraviolet Forensic Imaging," p. 15.

18. "Real Estate Agent Pleads Guilty to 5 'Lock Box' Thefts," *The Washington Post,* September 12, 1978, p. B5.

19. Paul D. Bigbee, "Collecting and Handling Evidence Infected with Human Disease-Causing Organisms." *FBI Law Enforcement Bulletin,* July 1987, Vol. 56, No. 7, p. 1. Also see David Bigbee, "Pathogenic Microorganisms: Law Enforcement's Silent Enemies," *FBI Law Enforcement Bulletin,* May 1993, Vol. 62, No. 5, pp. 1–4; Lois Pilant, "Preventing Infectious Disease," *The Police Chief,* July 1993, pp. 32–42; Jerry D. Stewart, "Bloodborne Diseases: Developing a Training Curriculum," *FBI Law Enforcement Bulletin,* May 1993, Vol. 62, No. 5, pp. 11–15; Daniel B. Kennedy, Robert J. Homant, and George L. Emery, "AIDS Concerns among Crime Scene Investigators," *Journal of Police Science and Administration,* 1990, Vol. 17, No. 1, pp. 12–19.

20. John M. Karon et al., "Prevalence of HIV Infection in the United States, 1984 to 1992," *Journal of the American Medical Association,* July 10, 1996, Vol. 276, No. 2, p. 126. The estimate is 900,000 cases in 1992, which has remained relatively flat as compared to the 1986 estimate of 750,000 cases. The 1.2 million figure cited herein is a projection by the authors from the 1992 estimate.

21. Ibid., p. 127.

22. Bigbee, "Pathogenic Microorganisms," p. 3.

23. Mitchell H. Katz and Julie Louise Gerberding, "Post Exposure Treatment of People Exposed to the HIV Virus through Sexual Contact or Injection-Drug Use," *New England Journal of Medicine,* April 10, 1997, Vol. 336, No. 15, p. 1097.

24. Rachel A. Royce et al., "Sexual Transmission of HIV," *New England Journal of Medicine,* April 10, 1997, Vol. 336, No. 15, p. 1072.

25. David Kennedy, Robert Homant, and George Emery, "AIDS and the Crime Scene Investigator," *The Police Chief,* December 1989, p. 19.

26. George B. Schreiber et al., "The Risk of Transfusion Transmitted Viral Infection," *New England Journal of Medicine,* June 27, 1996, Vol. 334, No. 26, p. 1686.

27. On this point, see Don Des Jarlais and Dana Hunt, *AIDS and Intravenous Drug Use* (Washington D.C.: National Institute of Justice, February 1988), pp. 2–4.

28. Katz and Gerberding, p. 1097.

29. David Bigbee, *The Law Enforcement Officer and AIDS,* 3rd ed. (Washington, D.C.: Government Printing Office, 1989), p. 10.

30. Ibid., p. 19.

31. Presentation by Dr. Macdonell, Director, Northwestern University Hospital AIDS Clinic, Federal Law Enforcement Training Center, Glynco, Georgia, June 12, 1990.

32. San Francisco Police Department, Training Bulletin 88–04, *Infectious Disease Control,* February 18, 1988, p. 2. Some authorities recommend using double latex gloves; see William G. Eckert and Stuart H. James, *Interpretation of Bloodstain Evidence at Crime Scenes* (New York: Elsevier, 1989), p. 301.

33. Bigbee, *The Law Enforcement Officer and AIDS,* p. 19.

34. San Francisco Police Department, Training Bulletin 88–04, p. 1.

35. Macdonell, June 12, 1990.

36. Bigbee, *The Law Enforcement Officer and AIDS,* p. 18.

37. Theodore M. Hammett, *Precautionary Measures and Protective Equipment* (Washington, D.C.: National Institute of Justice, 1988), p. 2.

38. Eckert and James, *Interpretation of Bloodstains,* p. 302.

39. Ibid.

40. Bigbee, *The Law Enforcement Officer and AIDS,* p. 18.

41. The points in this paragraph are drawn from San Francisco Police Department, Training Bulletin 88–04, unnumbered page in Chapter 11.

42. Bigbee, *The Law Enforcement Officer and AIDS,* pp. 15–16.

43. Hammett, *Precautionary Measures and Protective Equipment,* p. 2.

44. Bigbee, *The Law Enforcement Officer and AIDS,* p. 36.

45. This is standard advice. However, there is no evidence that such actions further reduce the risk of HIV transmission. See "Public Health Service Guidelines for the Management of Health Care Worker Exposures to HIV and Recommendations for Postexposure Prophylaxis," *Morbidity and Morality Weekly Report,* U.S. Department of Health and Human Services, Centers for Disease Control and Prevention, Atlanta, Georgia, May, 15, 1998, Vol. 47, No. RR-7, p. 12.

46. San Francisco Police Department, Training Bulletin 88–04, p. 2.

47. Ibid.

48. See *Doe v. Borough of Barrington,* 729 F. Supp. 376 (D.N.J. 1990).

49. Presentation and handout from Michael R. Smith, *Liability for Failure to Provide AIDS Training,* Federal Law Enforcement Training Center, Glynn County, Georgia, June 12, 1990, is the source of information for this paragraph.

50. Bigbee, "Pathogenic Microorganisms," p. 2.

51. Pilant, "Preventing Infectious Disease," p. 35.

52. Bigbee, "Pathogenic Microorganisms," p. 2.

53. Pilant, "Preventing Infectious Disease," p. 35; Bigbee, "Pathogenic Microorganisms," p. 2.

54. Pilant, "Preventing Infectious Disease," p. 35.

55. Stewart, "Bloodborne Diseases," p. 12.

56. Pilant, "Preventing Infectious Disease," p. 41.

57. Pilant, "Preventing Infectious Disease," p. 35.

58. Bigbee, "Pathogenic Microorganisms," p. 2.

59. Ibid.

60. Ibid.

61. Ibid.

62. Ibid.

63. The information in this section was adapted from "Forensic Technology for Law Enforcement," a telecourse presented May 13, 1993, by the California Commission on Peace Officers Standards and Training.

64. Fox and Cunningham, *Crime Scene Search and Physical Evidence Handbook,* p. 14.

65. The description of the various evidence envelopes is taken from Drug Enforcement Administration and International Association of Chiefs of Police, *Guidelines for Narcotic and Dangerous Drug Evidence Handling and Security Procedures* (1975), pp. 57–58.

66. Information in this section is drawn from unpublished information provided by the FBI National Academy, Quantico, Virginia, in November 1990.

67. The material on sketching and photography is taken, with modification, from *Crime Scene Search and Physical Evidence Handbook,* pp. 35–43, by permission.

FOUR

Physical Evidence

CHAPTER OUTLINE

Class versus Individual Characteristics 68

Soil 69

Paint 74

Glass 75

Fibers, Cloth Fragments, and Impressions 77

String, Cord, and Rope 79

Fingerprints 81

Dental Evidence 92

Hair 97

Blood 99

Human Excretions and Secretions 104

Lipstick and Lip-Print Evidence 105

Firearms 106

Tool Marks 111

Questioned Documents 113

Questions 118

Notes 119

INTRODUCTION

Physical evidence plays a crucial role in criminal investigation. Investigation must understand how to identify, collect, and preserve various types of physical evidence. They must also know the various determinations which can and cannot be made from such evidence. This chapter covers these and related matters.

CLASS VERSUS INDIVIDUAL CHARACTERISTICS

To fully appreciate the potential value of physical evidence, the investigator must understand the difference between class and individual characteristics. When the characteristics of physical evidence are common to a group of objects or persons, they may be termed *class*. Regardless of how thoroughly examined, such evidence can be placed only into a broad category; an individual identification cannot be made because there is a possibility of more than one source for the evidence.[1] Examples of this type of evidence include glass fragments too small to be matched to broken edges and tool marks or shoeprints in instances where microscopic or accidental markings are insufficient for positive individual identification.[2] Evidence with *individual characteristics* can be identified as originating with a particular person or source. The ability to establish individuality distinguishes this type of physical evidence from that possessing only class characteristics. Some examples of evidence with individual characteristics are fingerprints, palmprints, and footprints.

Conceptually, the distinction between class and individual characteristics is clear. But as a practical matter, the crime scene technician or investigator often may not be able to make this differentiation and must rely on the results yielded by crime laboratory examination. For example, a shoeprint collected at one scene may yield only class characteristics: left by a man's shoe of a particular brand from the left foot and of such newness as to yield no individual markings. However, Figure 4–1 illustrates a situation in which a heelprint yielded not only class characteristics but also individual ones. Thus, while the investigator must recognize that physical evidence that allows for individualization is of more value, for no reason should he or she disdain evidence that appears to offer only class characteristics, as these may show individual characteristics through laboratory examination.

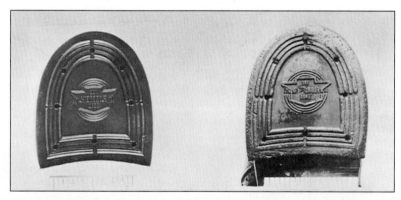

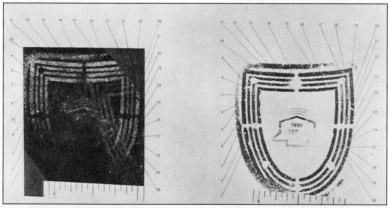

Figure 4–1
Class versus Individual Characteristics
The upper left is a new Florsheim shoe heel representing class characteristics; the upper right is a shoe heel of a suspect, incorporating both class and individual characteristics. The lower left is a shoe-heel print left on a piece of carbon paper at the scene of a burglary; the lower right is an inked print of the suspect's shoe heel, indicating positive identification as the print on the carbon paper.

(Courtesy Chicago Crime Laboratory)

Furthermore, a preponderance of class-characteristic evidence tying a suspect or tools in the suspect's possession to the scene strengthens the case for prosecution; it should also be noted that occasionally class-characteristic evidence may be of such an unusual nature that it has much greater value than that ordinarily associated with evidence of this type. In an Alaska case a suspect was apprehended in the general area where a burglary had been committed; the pry bar found in his possession contained white stucco, which was of considerable importance, as the building burglarized was the only white stucco building in that town.[3] Finally, class-characteristic evidence can be useful in excluding suspects in a crime, resulting in a more effective use of investigative effort.

SOIL

Combinations of particles of earth materials—soils, rocks, minerals, and fossils—occurring by themselves or in conjunction with contamination by other types of minute debris may serve a variety of critical functions.[4] For example, although soil is class-characteristic evidence, it may be useful in destroying an alibi:

A man was arrested and charged with the beating of a young girl. The scene of the crime was a construction site adjacent to a newly poured concrete wall. The soil was sand, which had been transported to the scene for construction purposes. As such, it had received additional mixing during the moving and construction process and was quite distinctive. The glove of the suspect contained sand that was similar to that found at the scene and significantly different in composition and particle size from that in the area of the suspect's home. This was important because the suspect claimed the soil on the gloves came from his garden.[5]

An elderly woman was robbed and murdered in a Washington, D.C., park, and her body was found under a park bench. Within a short time, a suspect was apprehended as a result of a description given by a witness who had seen the person leaving the park on the night of the murder. It was obvious that the suspect had been involved in a struggle and had soil adhering to his clothing and inside his trouser cuffs. He claimed to have been in a fight in another part of the city and gave the location of the fight. Study of the soil near the park bench and of that collected from the scene of the alleged fight revealed that the soil from the suspect's clothing was similar to soil near the park bench but did not compare favorably with samples from the area of the described fight. These comparisons strongly suggested that the suspect had been in contact with the ground in that area and cast strong doubt on his statement that he had not been in the park for years. Furthermore, the lack of similarity between the clothing soil samples and those from the area in which he claimed to have been fighting questioned the validity of his alibi.[6]

Thus, although soil is class-characteristic evidence, its specificity can approach the level of individual characterization:

In a rape case, the knees of the suspect's trousers contained encrusted soil samples; the sample from the right knee was different from that collected from the left. In examining the crime scene, two impressions were found in the soil corresponding to a right and left knee; samples taken from these two impressions were different. The soil sample from the left-knee impression compared with that removed from the left trouser knee of the suspect, as did the right-knee impression and the right trouser knee soils. The significant difference in soil type between the two knee impressions and their consistency with samples obtained from the suspect's trousers strongly indicated his presence at the scene.[7]

LOCATING AND HANDLING SOIL EVIDENCE

"Soil and rock evidence is most likely to be obtained when the crime is committed out of doors or when the suspect was required to drive or to walk on unpaved areas."[8] Offenders may pick up soil or rock particles from crime scenes and retain them in the cracks or heels of their shoes or cuffs. Suspects also may deposit on floors or paved areas soil particles that were picked up outside of the area of the crime.

It is important to collect soil samples that may have been dislodged from the undercarriage of a vehicle at the scene of a crime. Such evidence may be particularly valuable when the clothing of a victim of a hit-and-run accident retains particles from the striking vehicle. In an unusual case, a solid soil crust approximately the shape of a triangle, about 3 inches on each side, was recovered at the scene. Subsequently, when the suspect and the vehicle were identified, it was found that the triangular piece fitted exactly into an area on the underside of the vehicle.

Once shoe or tire impressions have been photographed and a cast has been made, samples of the soil should be collected from the impression.[9] Then additional samples should be systematically obtained from the area around the first sample; the areas chosen for these additional samples should be measured with respect to their relationship to the impression

and the information documented in a sketch (see Figure 4–2).[10] Ordinarily soil samples are gathered from the first quarter inch of soil in an amount of about 3 tablespoons.[11] The spoon or other similar item used to collect the samples must be carefully cleaned between each gathering to eliminate the likelihood of contamination. If there is to be any delay in transmitting moist soil samples to the crime laboratory, they should be spread on separate pieces of nonabsorbent paper and allowed to air-dry to avoid the formation of mold. Subsequently, they should be placed in separate pill boxes, mason-type jars, or 35-millimeter canisters and sealed.[12]

Where soil samples have been gathered at the scene of the crime and a suspect subsequently has been identified, the suspect's shoes and garments should be seized and forwarded to the laboratory for examination, ensuring in the packaging that there is no possibility of cross-contamination. Additionally, it is desirable to process the floor of the interior of the suspect's vehicle, if any, in an attempt

Figure 4–2
Collecting Soil Samples
Method of collecting soil samples from foot and tire impressions and from the surrounding area. The numbers in the figure suggest the sampling sequence.

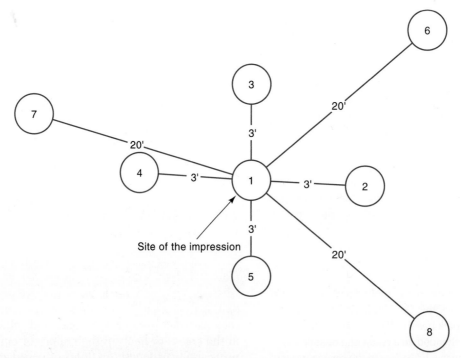

Source: Based on Richard H. Fox and Carl Cunningham, *Crime Scene Search and Physical Evidence Handbook* (Washington, D.C.: Government Printing Office, 1985), p. 82, with modification.

to locate samples. If, however, the floorboard of the vehicle has not been cleaned in some time and represents an accumulation of material, then the results are not likely to be conclusive. The comparison of soil materials obtained at the scene of a crime with material collected from a dirty floorboard is roughly analogous to the attempted comparison of the fibers of a jacket found at the scene of a crime with the floor sweepings from a clothing store.[13] Despite limitations such as this, the investigator must never fail to realize the potential importance of soil as evidence.

PRESERVING SHOEPRINTS AND SHOE IMPRESSION EVIDENCE

Preserving Shoeprints

For the purposes of this section, the term "shoeprints" also includes foot and tire-tread prints. Shoeprints are created when—after being contaminated by some matter such as dust, dirt, or blood—shoes are pressed on a firm surface such as a floor, a sheet of paper, a desktop or countertop, a file folder, or even clothing (see Figure 4–3).[14] Shoeprints may also be referred to as *dust prints* or *residue prints*. Such prints may be completely visible or only partially so. If shoeprints are not imme-

diately seen, all lights should be turned off and prints searched for by holding a strong flashlight or floodlight parallel to the ground.

When such a print is found, it should first be photographed using a light source that is held parallel to the impression and obliquely grazing the print. The camera is placed directly over the print and parallel to its plane; as a minimum, one rigid photo evidence scale is placed next to the print before photographing it. Alternatively, two rigid photo evidence scales or adhesive evidence scales can be placed next to the print at right angles. These are available in different colors to contrast with whatever background the print is found on. The use of a rigid L-shaped scale serves the same purpose. The base of the L is located at the base of the print, with its long side running roughly parallel to the print.

Whenever possible, the original item should be submitted to the laboratory. In no case should the print be transported or stored in plastic or in any manner that might lead to its accidental erasure. To lift a print, an appropriately sized rubber-gelatin lifter—which is coated with a thin film of very sensitive gelatin—is carefully placed over the print and then removed (see Figure 4–4). Transparent, black, and white lifters are available. Transparent and white lifters can be used for dark prints, while a

Figure 4–3
Tire Print on Fabric
Tire print left on the trousers of the victim struck by an automobile in a hit-and-run offense.

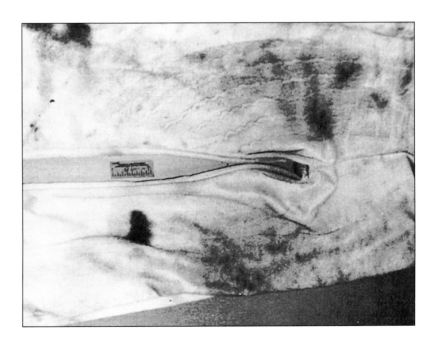

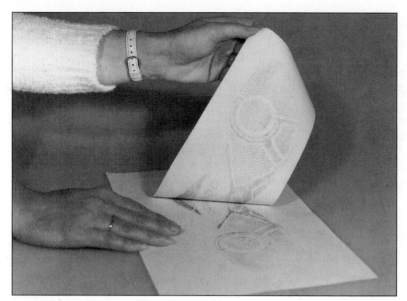

Figure 4–4
Rubber-Gelatin Lifter

A rubber-gelatin lifter being used to lift a shoeprint. Because such lifters are elastic, they are often bought in sheets and then cut into smaller sections to lift fingerprints and palmprints from rounded surfaces.

black lifter should be used for light prints. Dust prints can also be lifted through the use of an electrostatic device. These devices use static electricity to attract the dust particles of the print onto a dark-colored lift film. The special film is taped over the dust print, an electrical probe is touched to the film to charge it with electricity, and a roller is then used on the top surface of the film to ensure maximum contact between the film and the dust print (see Figure 4–5). The resulting image must be photographed as soon as possible as it is in dust and therefore not permanent.

Preserving Shoe Impressions in Soil

In contrast to dust or residue prints, shoe or foot or tire-tread impressions occur when any of these objects are placed in some moldable material, such as earth or clay.[15] As in the case of prints, these impressions should first be photographed (see Figure 4–6). These photographs should be taken from directly overhead and from three different sides with the use of oblique lighting. A flat, rigid ruler laid on the same plane as the impression should be in every photograph (see Figure 4–7).

Plaster of paris is no longer recommended for use in casting impressions. Dental stone is the preferred medium because of its greater strength,

Figure 4–5
Use of Electrostatic Lifter

A charged electrostatic lifter being rolled (*top*) and the image which was lifted (*bottom*)

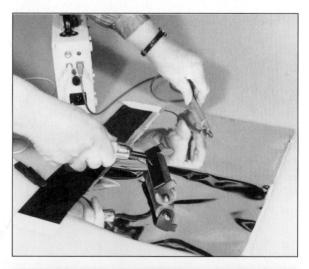

Figure 4–6
Shoe Impressions

Shoe impressions left in the safe insulation at the scene of a burglary.

(Courtesy Tampa, Florida, Police Department)

Figure 4–7
Shoe Impression Photography

Photographing a shoe impression prior to making a cast of it.

quicker setting time, and ease of use and because it provides more detailed impressions.

The first step in casting is the preparation of the impression. The rule is that the impression itself should not be disturbed. Thus, if twigs, leaves, or other materials are stuck *in* the impression, they should remain there. Loose water lying in the impression should be allowed to remain there. Only loose material lying *on* the impression, such as leaves, should be moved. The impression does not need to be sprayed to "fix" it in place before the casting begins. There is no need to use a casting form around the impression unless it is on a hill or on uneven ground.[16] If a casting form is used, there should be a 2-inch space around the impression and it should be of sufficient height to allow a 2-inch-thick cast to be made.

About 2 pounds of dental stone and 12 ounces of water are needed to cast a shoe impression. To facilitate the casting process, 2-pound bags of dental stone can be premeasured into 8-by-12-inch zip-lock bags. Initially, 9 to 10 ounces of water should be added to the zip-lock bag and the mixture massaged thoroughly through the closed bag. Several ounces of water may be added to adjust the mixture until it has the consistency of pancake batter. The dental

(Courtesy Nassau County, New York, Police Department)

stone is then poured alongside the impression and allowed to flow into it, or it can be gently laid onto the impression. To prevent the accidental destruction of detail, the fall of the dental stone into the impression can be broken by using a spoon or tongue depressor. The impression should be filled until the dental stone overflows from the impression.

Dental stone sets fairly rapidly. In warm weather it can be moved within 20 minutes, but a longer time should be allowed when the weather is colder. When the cast is firm, but still soft, basic identifying information should be scratched on its back. Moving the cast requires that it be packed carefully, but without the use of plastic materials. The laboratory examiner will clean the cast and examine it in the laboratory after it has dried for at least 48 hours (see Figure 4–8).

If there is standing water in the impression, the following procedure should be used: (1) Sift dental stone that has not been mixed with water directly into the impression to a depth of about 1 inch; (2)

Figure 4–8
Forensic Comparison
Evidence technician making a comparison between a plaster cast made at a crime scene and the suspect's shoe.

(Courtesy Fairfax County, Virginia, Police Department)

add enough mixed dental stone to form a second 1-inch layer; and (3) allow the cast to set in place for at least 1 hour.[17]

Preserving Shoe Impressions in Snow

Dental stone is also the preferred material for casting impressions in snow, replacing the more difficult and time-consuming process of using sulfur, which has to be heated. Impressions in snow should first be photographed in the manner previously described. A red-colored product called Snow Print Wax, is sprayed on the impression until it is lightly tinted. A dark-colored spray paint will also serve the same purpose. In either case, the spray can must be held far enough away so that the force of the aerosol does not disturb the details of the impression. The impression is then rephotographed (see Figure 4–9). The casting process is continued, with the impression being sprayed with enough Snow Print Wax to form a layer of wax, followed by the dental-stone casting process. Because some heat is generated when dental stone is mixed, use snow or cold water instead of water to form a consistency somewhat thinner than pancake batter.[18] A box should be placed over the cast as it dries for at least 1 hour before it is moved.

PAINT

Ordinarily, paint is class-characteristic evidence, although circumstances may combine to make it individual. It will be encountered in one of three different states: chips from dried paint, smears from fresh or "chalking" paint, or either of the two previous states intact on objects of evidence.[19] Examination of paint evidence is conducted chemically, spectrographically, and microscopically, with the important factors in identification being shade of color, chemical composition, number of coats and their characteristics, weathering, and texture.[20]

While paint evidence may be found in a variety of crimes, it is most commonly encountered in breaking-and-entering and hit-and-run offenses. Of particular evidentiary value are samples that have received several different coats of paint and those recovered in chip form, allowing for the possibility of a fracture match. The Federal Bureau of Investigation maintains the National Automotive Paint File, consisting of paint panels from automobile

Figure 4–9
Snow Print Wax Use
Having already photographed the shoe impression in the snow, the officer sprays red-colored Snow Print Wax on the impression (*top*); the impression is rephotographed (*middle*); and the dental-stone mix is poured from a plastic pouch onto the impression (*bottom*).

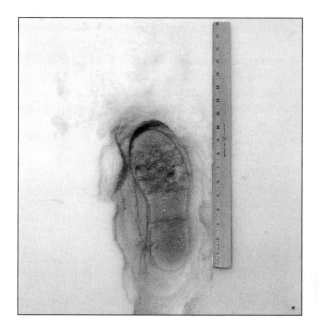

(Courtesy Lewiston, Maine, Police Department)

manufacturers that are representative of the original finishes on cars at the time of manufacture. Thus, paint recovered from the victim or at the scene of a hit-and-run may be particularly useful in the investigative process because the year and make of the car involved may be determinable. Samples of paint at the point of forced entry in a breaking and entering should be recovered because there is the possibility that matching layered paint or fracture matches may be obtained from samples recovered from a suspect's trouser cuffs, shoes, or tools.

In no case should paint chips or particles be collected with transparent tape or mounted on a card using this material, because it makes separation in the laboratory difficult without damage. Similarly, small particles should not be placed in cotton because it is difficult to separate them. Paint evidence should not be placed in envelopes because the chips may slip out or be broken; small plastic bags should be avoided because they have a static electrical charge that makes it extremely difficult to remove the chips in the crime laboratory.[21] Clear plastic containers are ideal because the paint evidence can be seen, and if the container is accidentally dropped, it will not break. Where it is particularly difficult to gather paint samples, a small portion of the surface to which the paint has adhered should be cut or chipped off.

GLASS

"One of the most important types of physical evidence, which is frequently overlooked by the investigator, is glass; its evidentiary value lies in the fact that there are thousands of different formulas used in the manufacturing of glass."[22] Although it is ordinarily class-characteristic evidence, glass has high evidentiary value because of its variations in density, refractive index, and light-dispersion characteristics. Additionally, where the fragments are sufficiently large to allow for a fracture match, glass may assume individuality. Most commonly this will occur in hit-and-run cases where a piece of the headlight lens found at the scene or embedded in the victim's body or clothing matches a missing portion of lens from a suspect's vehicle (see Figure 4–10). Before the accident, cleaning or other actions may have created surface striations on the headlight lens. Along with a fracture match, these further strengthen the condition of individuality.

Glass is a common form of evidence, particularly at the scenes of burglaries where a window has been the point of entry. When a suspect is apprehended soon after the commission of an offense,

his or her clothing should be carefully examined for minute traces of glass evidence. Although they may be so small as to permit only the conclusion that they are consistent with samples obtained at the scene, this conclusion can strengthen the case for the prosecution. At other times, the clothing of a burglary suspect may contain pieces of glass large enough to provide for fracture matches. A case history illustrates this possibility:

Walking a beat in a downtown business section in the late evening hours, a uniformed officer heard an alarm go off and saw an individual round the corner and run toward him at full speed. Upon seeing the officer, the individual started to double back the other way and then stopped. As the officer approached, the man started to flee, but stopped upon being commanded to do so. The man then told the officer that he had observed two people standing in front of a jewelry store window take a brick from a shopping bag and throw it

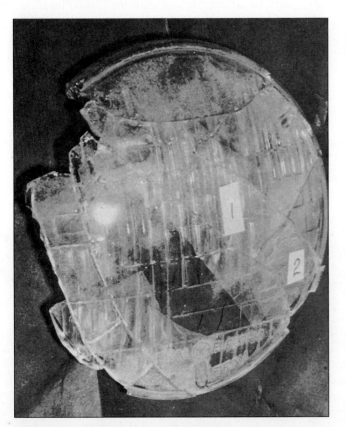

Figure 4–10
Glass Fracture Match of Headlight Lens
Pieces 1 and 2 were recovered at the scene of a hit-and-run automobile accident. The remaining pieces were obtained from the grille and light housing of the suspect's vehicle.

(Courtesy Regional Criminalistics Laboratory, Metropolitan Kansas City, Missouri)

through the window. The person said that, upon seeing this, he became frightened and ran. Subsequent investigation revealed that the person who had rounded the corner was in fact the perpetrator of the offense and that he had fled before obtaining any material from the display window because a lookout had seen a police car responding to a call in an adjacent block and had given warning. Processing of the perpetrator's clothing revealed pieces of glass in the cuff of his pants sufficiently large to make fracture matches with glass at the scene.

Larger pieces of glass evidence should be packed in cotton and in a rigid container to prevent breakage. Smaller particles can be placed in pillboxes or plastic tubes to prevent breakage. Glass evidence found in separate areas should be packaged separately. For example, in a burglary where a window has been the point of attack, the glass found on the floor inside the broken window should be packaged separately from that found on the ground outside, and that, in turn, should be kept separate from any glass remaining in the frame of the broken window.[23]

It is essential that the crime scene technician and investigator understand the ways in which glass reacts to force. Often this knowledge is critical in determining whether a crime has been committed and in establishing the credibility of statements given by parties at the scene. A case history illustrates this:

Police were called to a residence where the occupant alleged that while standing in his living room he was suddenly fired on by someone standing outside the window. The occupant further related that he immediately fell to the floor and crawled to a desk in which a handgun was kept and after a short period of time stood up, when second and third shots were fired from outside the building. The complainant stated he could clearly see the person and, in turn, fired one shot. The perpetrator identified by the complainant lived a short distance away and was at home when contacted by the police. The alleged suspect maintained that he was walking by the home of the complainant, with whom there had been a history of ill feelings, and was suddenly fired on three times, but he admitted firing one shot in return.

Figure 4–11 illustrates the four bullet holes found in the window by the police. When a glass window is broken by a shot, both radial and concentric fracture lines may develop. *Radial fractures* move away from the point of impact, while *concentric fracture* lines more or less circle the same point. From Figure 4–11 we know that shot B came before shot A, because the radial and concentric fracture lines of shot B stop those of shot A. From examination, we know nothing of the relationship of holes C and D. However, as suggested in Figure 4–12, it is possible to determine the direction from which a bullet penetrated glass: on the side opposite the surface of initial impact, there will be a characteristic cone-shaped area. In the case being illustrated, shots A, B, and D all contained a cone-shaped characteristic on the inside of the window, indicating that these three shots had been fired from the outside. Shot C had the cone-shaped area on the outside, revealing that it had been fired from inside the house. Thus the physical evidence substantiated the complainant's statement.

Before any glass or window pane is moved at all, it should be photographed in detail to reflect the exact nature of the existent glass fractures. Moving the evidence may cause fracture extensions that could confuse or reverse the findings of the investigator and laboratory examiner. This same principle applies to fractures of automobile glass when a vehicle is pulled to the side of the road by a wrecker operator. Such examples underscore the importance of the investigator's paying particular attention to what has occurred between the time of the crime and the time that he or she arrives at the scene. In this light, a key question that the investigator must attempt to answer with all types of evidence is whether the characteristics could have been caused by someone other than the suspect, such as a witness, the victim, emergency medical personnel, or another officer.[24]

FIBERS, CLOTH FRAGMENTS, AND IMPRESSIONS

Fibers are of greater value as evidence than are rootless hairs because they incorporate such variables as number of fibers per strand, number of

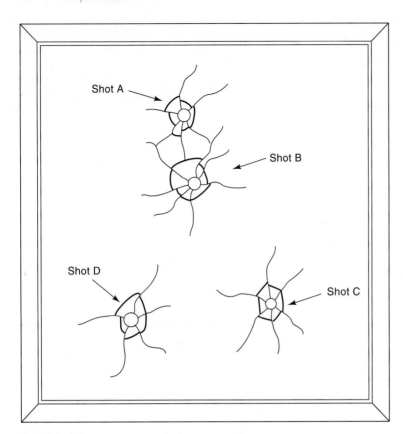

Figure 4–11
Bullet Holes Found in Window

Figure 4–12
Determining the Direction of a Bullet's Penetration of Glass

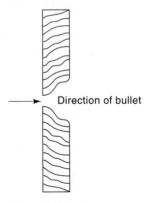

Direction of bullet

strands, the thickness of fibers and strands, the amount and direction of twists, dye content, type of weave, and the possible presence of foreign matter embedded in them (see Figures 4–13, 4–14, and 4–15). When something composed of fibers, such as clothing, comes into contact with other clothing or objects, there is the opportunity for the exchange

or transfer of fibers. Fibers may also be located on the body of the victim or the suspect, serving to connect one to the other.

Cloth fragments may be found at the scene of violent crimes or along the perpetrator's point of approach to or exit from a crime scene. They may be found on such diverse points as a chain fence, the splintered edge of a wooden building, or protruding nails. In hit-and-run offenses, cloth fragments may be found in the grille or undercarriage of the striking vehicle (see Figure 4–16). Cloth impressions are found infrequently in investigations, usually on wet paint or some surface of a vehicle involved in striking a pedestrian (see Figure 4–17).

Both fibers and cloth fragments should be packaged in a pillbox or folded paper that is taped shut. Only on rare occasions will it be possible to obtain a cast of a cloth impression. This effort, however, should invariably be preceded by the taking of several photographs; at least one of these photos should show a ruler to allow for comparisons at some future date.

Figure 4–13
Comparison of Questioned and Known Cotton-Fiber Samples

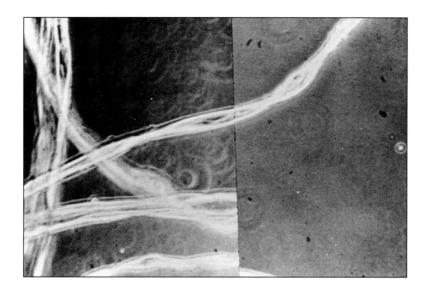

Figure 4–14
Comparison of Wool Fibers
Photomicrographic comparison of wool fiber from the victim's sweater (*right*) versus wool fiber recovered from the trousers of the suspect who sexually assaulted her, resulting in a finding that the two fibers matched in all characteristics.

(Courtesy Royal Canadian Mounted Police)

STRING, CORD, AND ROPE

String, cord, and rope evidence is usually found in robbery, criminal homicide, rape, and abduction cases. Less frequently it is found in accidental hangings by children and accidental sexual asphyxiations.

String can be identified by its fibers and the method of its manufacture. The following synopsis of a case processed by the Kansas City Police

(Courtesy Federal Bureau of Investigation)

Figure 4–15
Scanning Electron Micrograph
Scanning electron micrograph (570 ×) of a nylon fiber removed from a sheet used to transport the body of a murder victim. The fiber, associated with a carpet in the offender's residence, was manufactured only in small quantities about a decade before it was recovered as part of the investigation.

(Courtesy Federal Bureau of Investigation)

Figure 4–16
Fabric Match
The inserted fragment was found in the grille of the suspect's vehicle, which had been involved in a hit-and-run case. The fragment fitted the victim's shirt.

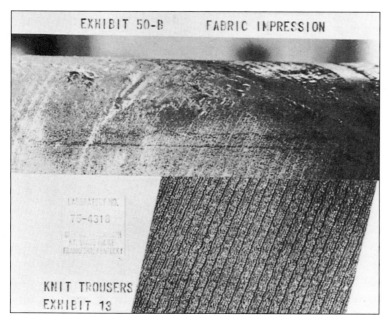

EXHIBIT 50-B   FABRIC IMPRESSION

KNIT TROUSERS
EXHIBIT 13

(Courtesy Kentucky State Police)

Figure 4–17
Fabric Impression
A fabric impression found on the tailpipe of the suspect's car, shown as Exhibit 50-B. Exhibit 13 represents the victim's trousers related to the fabric impression found on the tailpipe. The suspect's car had run over the victim and left the scene of the accident.

Department illustrates the potential evidentiary value of such evidence:

At the scenes of three different arsons, the remains of a cotton wick used to delay the ignition of gasoline were recovered in the debris. The string used for the wicks was examined and found to be of the category 23-strand white cotton. A check with manufacturers of this type of string revealed that it was never intentionally manufactured with 23 strings, but only with 20 or 24. Thus, this particular sample had added value due to its rarity. The string wick gave strong indication that the three wicks were from the same spool of string and suggested that the fires were set by the same individual. This, along with other evidence, led to a successful clearance of the case.[25]

Cord and rope have essentially the same characteristics as string, and all have some characteristics of fibers. "To decide whether two cords or ropes come from one and the same piece is possible only in exceptional cases and then only if characteristic and incontestable agreement is found" (see Figures 4-18 and 4-19).[26] When rope evidence is removed from the victim or some other place, knots should never be severed. Instead, a place away from the knot should be cut and a piece of twine used to loop the two ends together. A tag should be attached to indicate that the investigator has cut the rope. Ordinarily, because of its resilient nature, the packaging of this type of evidence poses no particular problem when standard procedures are followed.

FINGERPRINTS

Several different parts of the body—such as palms, fingers, toes, and the soles of the feet—have friction ridges that can form a "fingerprint." All such prints are collected, preserved, and identified in the same way. Moreover, it may not be immediately apparent which part of a body made the print. As used here, "fingerprint" includes all prints made by friction ridges.[27] Basically, a *fingerprint* is a replica of the friction ridges that touched the surface on which the print was found.

Fingerprints of the offender are found on a wide variety of surfaces and in various states. In all cases, however, the prints are fragile and susceptible to destruction by any careless act. They are also in many instances difficult to locate.

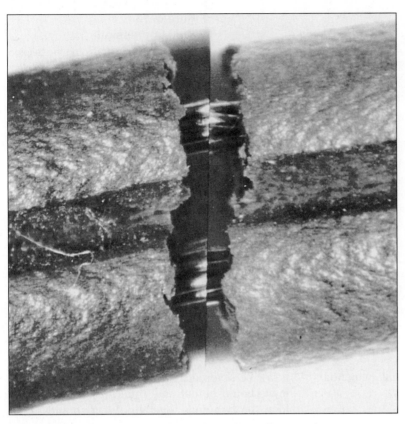

(Courtesy Regional Criminalistics Laboratory, Metropolitan Kansas City, Missouri)

Figure 4–18
Electrical Cord Edge Match
Photomicrograph of electric-cord edge match. The piece on the left was seized in the suspect's custody and matched with the end on the right, which was part of the length used to tie up a homicide victim.

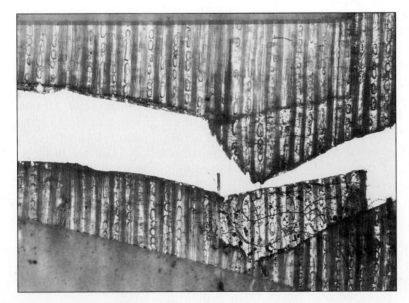

(Courtesy Illinois State Police)

Figure 4–19
Tape Match
In a home-invasion robbery and attempted murder, the suspects used filament strapping tape to tie the victim up. The victim was left for dead, but she managed to crawl out of an open door and hide in nearby bushes. The suspects panicked when they noticed she was gone, and they fled the scene. The lower portion of the photograph is the filament tape recovered from the victim's arms. The top part of the photograph is the end of the filament-tape roll found in the suspects' vehicle when they were arrested. By showing that these two ends of the filament tape match, a physical match is established.

With but a few exceptions—that is, the physically impaired—everyone has fingerprints. This universal characteristic is a prime factor in establishing a standard of identification. Since a print of one finger has never been known to duplicate exactly another fingerprint—even of the same person or an identical twin[28]—it is possible to identify an individual with just one impression. The relative ease with which a set of inked fingerprints can be taken as a means of identification is a further reason for using this standard. Despite such factors as aging and environmental influences, a person's fingerprints do not change. This unaltering pattern is a permanent record of the individual throughout life.

Although there are several different filing systems for fingerprints, each is based on classification of common characteristics. The classification system works to categorize a set of fingerprints readily as well as to provide quick access to a set of prints with a given characteristic.

There are three broad categories of latent fingerprints:

1. *Plastic prints* are created when fingers touch against some material such as a newly painted surface, the gum on envelopes and stamps, oil films, explosives, thick layers of dust, edible fats, putty, and adhesive tape (see Figure 4–20).

2. *Contaminated/visible prints* result after a finger, contaminated with foreign matter such as soot, oils, face powder, ink, and some types of safe insulation, touches a clean surface. The most common type of contaminated print results when a finger is pressed into a

thin layer of dust prior to touching a smooth surface. Fingerprints that result from blood contamination (see Figure 4–21) are sometimes less distinct than those that result from other types of contamination.

3. *Latent/invisible prints* are associated with the small amounts of body perspiration and oil that are normally found on the friction ridges. A latent fingerprint is created when the friction ridges deposit these materials on a surface. While latent prints are easily developed on smooth, nonabsorbent surfaces, under favorable conditions they may also be developed on rough surfaces, such as starched shirts. Latent fingerprints are typically invisible to the unassisted eye. "Developing" a latent fingerprint refers to the process of making it visible.[29]

Note that the term "latent prints" can be used in two different ways: (1) to refer to all three categories of prints identified above, in the sense that they have been found at the scene of the crime or on items of investigative interest, and (2) to refer specifically to latent/invisible prints. Ordinarily, the context in which the term is used helps in understanding which meaning is intended.

BASIS OF IDENTIFICATION OF FINGERPRINTS

The ridge detail of fingerprints—including ends of ridges, their separations, and their relationship to each other—constitutes the basis for identification of fingerprints. The major fingerprint patterns are shown in Figure 4–22. To establish individual identity, some courts require from 10 to 12 points, although no specific number is universally demanded. *Points* are identical characteristics that are found in fingerprints from known and questioned sources. Positive identification cannot be made when an unexplained difference appears, regardless of the points of similarity.

There is no standard requirement of print size for positive identification. It is necessary only that the partial print be large enough to contain the necessary points of individuality. This number may be found in an area as small as the flat end of a pencil. Thus, the rule whenever an investigator develops a partial latent print which appears to have

Figure 4–20
Plastic Print
A plastic print found in windowsill caulking.

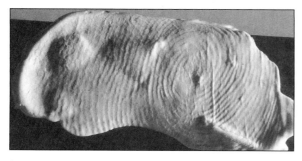

(Courtesy Delaware State Police)

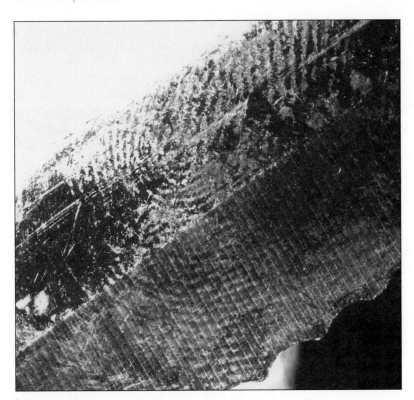

Figure 4–21
Contaminated/Visible Print
A blood contaminated/visible print found on the blade of a knife.

(Courtesy Delaware State Police)

only a few ridges is that it should be submitted to the laboratory.

Some persons, including experienced officers, erroneously believe that the points used for identification of the fingerprint occur only in the pattern area of the finger. In fact, all the different types occur outside of the pattern area on the finger as well as on the first and second joints of the finger and the entire palm of the hand. They are also present on the toes and the entire sole of the foot; they may be found in any area where friction ridges occur.

CONDITIONS AFFECTING THE QUALITY OF LATENT FINGERPRINTS

The quality of latent fingerprints is affected by a number of conditions, including the following:

1. *The surface on which the print is deposited*: Plastic prints can last for years if undisturbed. Latent prints on smooth surfaces, such as porcelain and glass, can be developed after a similar period, while those left on porous material like paper vary more in how long they can survive. Latent prints on documents can fade or deteriorate beyond the point of being useful under conditions of high humidity or if they become wet. Otherwise, latent prints on paper are fairly stable and can be developed even years after they were made.

2. *The nature of the material contaminating the fingerprint*: Latent fingerprints resulting from contamination by soot, safe insulation, and face powder are quickly destroyed, while those made with blood, ink, or oil can last longer periods of time under favorable conditions.[30]

3. *Any physical or occupational defects of the person making the print.*

4. *How the object on which the prints appear was handled*: The distance between friction ridges is very small, and if the finger moves even slightly, that ridge detail can be lost.

Figure 4–22
Major Fingerprint Patterns

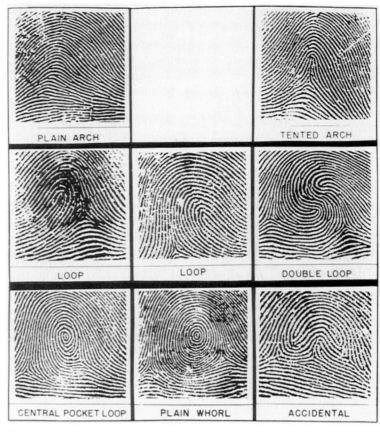

PLAIN ARCH		TENTED ARCH
LOOP	LOOP	DOUBLE LOOP
CENTRAL POCKET LOOP	PLAIN WHORL	ACCIDENTAL

(Courtesy Wichita, Kansas, Police Department)

5. *The amount of the contamination:* When the finger leaving the print is very contaminated, both the ridge surfaces and their "valleys" get filled up, resulting in a smeared appearance with little value as evidence.

LOCATING LATENT FINGERPRINTS

Latent prints are such valuable evidence that extraordinary efforts should be made to recover them. The investigator must adopt a positive attitude about this, regardless of apparent problems or past failures.

It is imperative that the investigator thoroughly search all surface areas in and around the crime scene that might retain prints. Shining a flashlight at an oblique angle to the surface being examined is often helpful in this search. The fact that an individual may have worn gloves in no way lessens the need for a complete search. On occasion, gloves themselves leave impressions as individualized as fingerprints. Moreover, although it is unusual, it may be possible to develop a latent fingerprint on the inside of a glove recovered at a crime scene.[31] Particular attention should be paid to less obvious places, such as the undersides of toilet seats, toilet handles, tabletops, and dresser drawers; the surfaces of dinner plates and filing cabinets; the backs of rear-view mirrors; and the trunk lids of automobiles. Frequently handled objects, such as doorknobs and telephones, ordinarily do not yield good prints. But because they are likely to have been touched, they should always be processed.

It is never safe to assume that the offender took precautions against leaving prints or destroyed those left. The commission of a criminal offense involves stress, and the offender may have made some mistake. If gloves were worn, for example, the suspect may have removed them for some operation.

It helps to attempt to view the scene as the criminal did. Such conditions as time of day, weather, and physical layout may suggest that certain surfaces should be more closely examined. In conducting the examination for latent prints in a burglary case, for example, the search should begin at the point of entry. For other crimes, such as the issuance of worthless checks, the point of entry often takes on less importance. Ordinarily, however, whatever the crime and its attending circumstances, reconstruction by the investigator gives direction to the search.

A person who is familiar with the environment, such as the owner of the building or the occupant of an apartment, may give valuable aid in obtaining latent prints. The person should be allowed to observe the scene so that he or she might indicate items out of place or brought to the scene by the suspect.

The development of latent fingerprints often involves the use of lasers, alternative light, ultraviolet light, powders, and chemicals that can be irritating or toxic. Therefore, appropriate safety precautions should be taken (see Figure 4–23).

METHODS OF DEVELOPING LATENT FINGERPRINTS

Plastic and contaminated prints may require no or little development. However, there are numerous ways to develop latent prints. Five of these with which investigators should be familiar are (1) use of traditional powders, (2) use of fluorescent powders, (3) application of chemicals, (4) cyanoacrylate or superglue fuming, and (5) visualization under laser, alternative light, and ultraviolet illumination. The most common method of developing latent/invisible prints is through the use of traditional powders.

Traditional Powders

Commercially prepared traditional powders come in a number of colors, including black, white, silver, red, and gray. To provide a good contrast between the print and the background on which it has been made, darker powders are used to locate latent/invisible prints on lighter-colored surfaces and lighter ones are used on darker backgrounds. There are also dual-use powders, which will appear black when dusted on a light-colored surface and silver when applied to a dark one. The tip of the

Figure 4–23
Locating Prints
A crime scene technician dusting for fingerprints using protective equipment.

(Courtesy Nassau County, New York, Police Department)

brush is gently placed into the wide-mouthed powder container and then lightly tapped to allow excess powder to drop away. Caution must be used when applying the powder to a latent print. Too much powder creates a print in which the details are difficult to identify (see Figure 4–24). This is why powder is never sprinkled directly on the surface to be dusted. The entire area to be dusted should be covered with smooth and light brush strokes until the ridge detail begins to show. Then, the brush strokes should follow the contours of the ridges until the latent/invisible print is fully visible. Even if the first attempt to develop a print is not successful, a second one may be.

The choices of brushes include squirrel hair, the Zephyr—a fiberglass brush—and feather dusters. There are also applicators that use special magnetic powders (see Figure 4–25). These powders commonly come in black, gray, and white. There are also dual-use magnetic powders. When the magnetic applicator is dipped into the iron powder particles—which are covered with a color pigment—streamers of powder are created that develop a latent print when brought into contact with the surface being examined; the excess powder is then removed from the print by a magnet.[32]

Fluorescent Powders

Low concentrations of some naturally occurring substances will cause a latent print to fluoresce, or glow, under laser, alternative light, or ultraviolet (UV) illumination. However, the intensity of the glow varies considerably, perhaps due to the accidental acquisition of fluorescent materials from the environment.[33] To compensate for the typically low level of naturally occurring fluorescence, the area to be examined can be dusted with a special powder, which chemically enhances the print when viewed under laser, alternative light, or UV illumination. Fluorescent powders are also available in several colors for use with a magnetic applicator.

Chemicals

A variety of chemicals are used to develop and enhance latent prints. These chemicals are applied by spraying or brushing the surface being examined, by fuming, or by dipping the object on which there may be prints in a solution.[34] Because chemicals may interfere with processes like blood typing, a forensic serologist should be consulted before using them.[35] Some of these chemicals will develop prints that are immediately visible, while others—such as DFO, rhodamine 6G, and basic yellow

Figure 4–24
Application of Fingerprint Powder
The photograph on the left illustrates the use of too much fingerprint powder in developing a latent print, resulting in the needless destruction of detail. The photograph on the right shows a latent fingerprint developed by the use of the correct amount of powder.

(Courtesy Wichita, Kansas, Police Department)

Figure 4–25
Magnetic Application
Dusting the metal frame of a screen for fingerprints using a magnetic applicator.

(Courtesy Santa Fe, New Mexico, Police Department)

40—fluoresce under an alternative light source. Among chemicals in use are the following:

- *Amido black:* Amido black is a dye sensitive to properties in blood and may be used with contaminated/visible prints involving blood. It has the capability to turn blood proteins to a blue-black color. As in the case of any procedure aimed at developing prints, a photographic record of the print should be made both prior to and after treatment.

- *Crystal violet:* Crystal violet is used to develop latent prints on the adhesive side of almost any kind of tape. It may also be useful on plastic surfaces. Crystal violet is mixed with water, and the tape is soaked in the solution. The tape is then rinsed with tap water; any latent print that appears is dyed a purple color. The results produced by crystal violet can be enhanced by viewing the treated area under laser illumination.

- *Iodine:* One of the oldest and most proven methods of developing latent prints on both porous—particularly paper—and nonporous surfaces is iodine fuming. If subsequent use of ninhydrin may be required, the iodine fuming should be done first.

- *Ninhydrin:* This chemical is also used to develop latent prints on paper and cardboard, producing purplish prints. It should not be used with money because it turns the entire bill purple.[36] Ninhydrin may be applied by fuming, dipping, or spraying.

- *DFO (1, 8-diazafluren-9-one):* While it functions similarly to ninhydrin, DFO is about three times more effective than it in developing latent prints on paper. These red prints may be immediately visible to the naked eye. DFO prints fluoresce under almost all laser or alternative light sources. DFO and ninhydrin may both be used on paper, but it must be in that sequence to get any fluorescence.

- *Small-particle reagent (SPR):* SPR is used for developing latent prints that have been immersed in water, as when a perpetrator has attempted to dispose of a firearm used in a crime by throwing it into a river or lake. It is also used to develop prints on dew- or rain-soaked cars; on surfaces covered with a residue, such as salt from being on or near the ocean; and on waxed materials, plastics, tile, and glass. Developed prints appear dark gray on a light surface and light gray on a dark surface. Although SPR can be sprayed on an object, immersion of the object for about 30 seconds in an SPR solution produces better results.

- *Rhodamine 6G:* This is an excellent fluorescent chemical dye to use on metal, glass, leather, plastic, wood, and many other types of nonabsorbent surfaces. Rhodamine 6G may enhance latent prints already developed and also reveal others.

- *Basic yellow 40:* Following superglue fuming, basic yellow 40 can be effectively used on surfaces such as cans, leathers, and plastics. After superglue fuming, the article is soaked in the basic-yellow-40 solution for about 1 minute; it will then fluoresce well under alternative lighting.

Cyanoacrylate or Superglue Fuming

In 1978, scientists in the United States and Japan were independently exploring the use of adhesive agents to develop latent prints. The original fuming agent for this was the product Super Glue, which contains the compound cyanoacrylate. In the early years of superglue fuming, a 10-gallon fish tank with a glass top was commonly used as the fuming chamber (see Figure 4–26). A water container was kept in the tank at all times because high humidity was a factor in obtaining good results. A container resembling a coffee can, with holes to allow heat to escape, was placed over a light bulb in the tank. The object to be fumed was hung or placed on a platform in the chamber. One-third of a small tube of Super Glue was placed onto a small piece of aluminum foil (which was curved to prevent the glue from running) and then put on top of the container.

The tank was quickly sealed, and any latent prints were developed within 5 to 15 minutes. These prints appear in white and can be enhanced with powders or washed in dyes that fluoresce under laser, alternative light, or UV illumination. Cyanoacrylate is now supplied as a liquid to crime laboratories; and although Super Glue is no longer used, the process still is referred to as superglue or glue fuming. Another change has been the commercial development of different-size cyanoacrylate chambers that allow fuming conditions to be more closely controlled. Superglue fuming can be done, with appropriate safety precautions, for large areas such as the interiors of cars or even entire rooms. Additionally, superglue fuming wands—developed by the Alaska State Troopers and 3M—are available for examining objects at the crime scene (see Figure 4–27). Some concern has been expressed that hydrogen cyanide may develop if cyanoacrylate or its vapors are exposed to a temperature of 200°C. It is recommended as a precaution that temperatures above 140°C be avoided.

Visualization under Laser, Alternative Light, and Ultraviolet Illumination

The use of alternative light sources—such as the Polilight, BlueMaxx, Omnichrome, and LumaLite—and UV illumination were discussed in Chapter 3. Therefore, the focus of this section is on

Figure 4–26
Early Superglue Fuming Tank

An early superglue fuming tank and a latent print obtained from fuming a clear plastic zip-lock-type bag; the photograph of the fingerprint is enhanced by using a dark background.

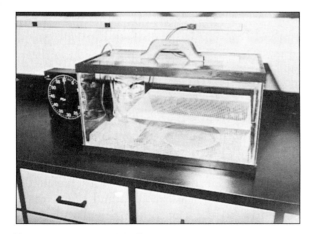

(Courtesy Michigan State Police)

Figure 4–27
Super Glue Wand

Use of a super glue wand, which was developed at the crime laboratory in Anchorage.

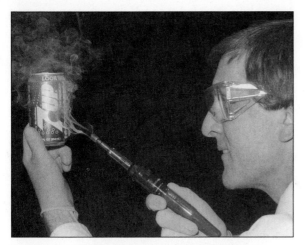

(Courtesy State of Alaska Scientific Crime Detection Laboratory)

lasers. The application of laser-beam technology to the detection of latent prints is a product of work, dating from 1978, by the Ontario Provincial Police Department and the Xerox Research Center in Toronto. Under laser illumination, naturally occurring substances deposited with the latent print fluoresce, or glow, a vivid yellow-orange color when viewed with a special lens. Prints detected in this manner can be photographed. Laser beams are also nondestructive; thus, after their use conventional means of detecting latent prints can still be used, as can fluorescent powders and dyes that may develop and enhance a latent print for laser examination.

Lasers have helped investigators locate prints on a variety of surfaces resistant to traditional detection methods, including Styrofoam (see Figure 4–28) and cloth. In laboratory tests, fingerprints of varying qualities have been found: on paper baked for two weeks at 75° and then soaked in running water for 5 minutes; on the pages of a book that had not been opened for nine years; and on human skin.

MARKING AND IDENTIFYING PRINT LIFTS

When a latent print has been developed, lifted, and placed on a card, it is necessary that the card be properly identified. Information recorded on the card should include the date, title of the case or number, address of the crime scene, name of the officer who made the lift, the exact place of the lift, and the type of object from which it was lifted. Regardless of how well the latent was developed and lifted, if the card is not properly marked with all the data required or if the fingerprint specialist is not furnished with the information required, the entire process may be wasted effort. In describing the exact place the lift was made, it is sometimes helpful to draw a simple sketch of the object. This sketch should be made on the fingerprint card that is sent to the laboratory. The inclusion of corresponding numbers on both the lift and the sketch establishes the placement of the latent print.

DEVELOPING LATENT FINGERPRINTS ON BODIES

For the most part, the history of trying to locate and develop latent fingerprints on the bodies of deceased victims is one of failure. There have been occasional success stories but no methods that regularly produced results. Once in a great while, the application of powder directly on the deceased's skin developed usable prints.

However, a new method, which involves glue fuming of the deceased's body, followed by the application of magnetic powders, shows great promise in producing results—so much so that it is now recommended that homicide victims be examined for latent prints whenever it is believed that the perpetrator may have touched the victim.[37] If possible, a body at the crime scene should be processed immediately after the medical examiner has completed the initial examination and released the body. At a minimum, the body should be fumed at the scene to preserve the prints and to prevent their obliteration when the body is moved. Ideally, bodies should not be refrigerated before they are fumed. Condensation from refrigeration can wash away prints and interfere with the proper functioning of glue fuming and application of magnetic powder. Refrigerated bodies should not be processed until all moisture has evaporated naturally, a matter of several minutes. A test area of the body, where it is least likely to find latent prints, should be used to make a trial application and make sure that the moisture isn't reacting to the glue and washing possible prints away and that the

Figure 4–28
Laser Illumination of Prints

Following unsuccessful conventional processing of a Styrofoam cup for prints (*left*), the laser was used and produced identifiable latent prints on the cup (*right*).

 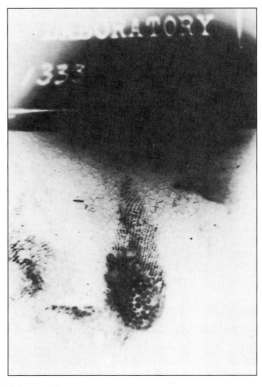

(Courtesy Tallahassee Regional Crime Laboratory, Florida Department of Law Enforcement)

powder can be used without its caking and destroying the prints. Skin that is warm or near normal body temperature should be glue-fumed for 5 to 10 seconds. Colder skin should be fumed for not more than 15 seconds.

COLLECTING AND PRESERVING LATENT PRINTS

Occasionally items such as beer cans or glasses that have condensation on them need to be processed for prints. Heat lamps or any other source of artificial heat should not be used to dry the object quickly. Such objects should be allowed to air-dry naturally. Similarly, articles that have been frozen and must be processed for prints must be allowed to thaw and dry naturally.

Once a print is found—regardless of whether it is plastic, contaminated/visible, or a latent that has been developed with powders—it should be pho-

tographed immediately with a rigid scale in view. The ruler allows a one-to-one, or actual-size, picture of the print to be made. This provides a permanent record of the print in the event that collecting the print, attempting to further develop and enhance it, or transporting it results in its accidental alteration or destruction. Some law enforcement agencies are using digital cameras to record important crime scene evidence such as latent fingerprints[38] (see Figure 4–29). This type of camera digitizes the image, which can then be put into a computer and enhanced through a software package such as Adobe Photoshop. In years past, every aspect of fingerprint examination was labor-intensive. However, computerized Automated Fingerprint Identification Systems (AFISs; see Chapter 9 for more information on this subject) have speeded up the process of fingerprint identification and comparison enormously. An AFIS can supply a list of potential matches for the latent prints submitted

Figure 4–29
Digital Camera
Use of a digital camera to document latent fingerprints.

(Courtesy Newport Beach, California, Police Department)

from the records on file. At that point, however, an experienced examiner then personally makes the comparison to see if there is indeed a match.

When latent prints are submitted to California's AFIS, potential matches with prints on file are ranked by score, with the highest being 9,999. In one instance, the Newport Beach Police Department had submitted a conventionally developed print to the AFIS and received a top score of 2,595. This same print was later photographed with a digital camera, enhanced, and resubmitted, with a resulting top score of 5,422 points. Such capabilities may make a critical difference in convicting or clearing a suspect.

Whenever possible, a plastic print should be taken to the laboratory on the object on which it was found. When this is not practical, the photographic record of it may be supplemented by a cast of the print made of a material such as silicone.

Most latent prints are lifted with a clear strip of tape or clear flap lifter after they have been developed with powders (see Figure 4–30). One end of the clear tape is placed on the surface just before the latent print appears. Pressure is then applied to progressively lay the tape over the print, taking care not to leave air bubbles. If air bubbles are accidentally created, the tape should be carefully smoothed over to eliminate them. The tape may be left on the object if the object is to be submitted to the laboratory. Alternatively, the pattern of the print is lifted by pulling up the tape, starting at one end and moving progressively to the other end. Now the powder that shows the print pattern is stuck to the sticky side of the tape. This tape is then laid back down on an appropriately colored backing card. For example, assume that a latent print is developed with dark powder on a clear window. The clear tape used to lift it would then be placed on a white card for maximum contrast. Occasionally prints are found in uneven or curved places, such as light bulbs, clothes hangers, and doorknobs. In these cases a rubber-gelatin lifter, described earlier in this chapter, can be used to lift the print. Such prints can first be photographed with a Rotorgraph, a device invented in 1992 by Turner Pippin of the State of Alaska Crime Laboratory. The Rotorgraph makes it possible to accurately take photographs of developed latent prints on rounded surfaces (see Figure 4–31).

DENTAL EVIDENCE

Forensic dentistry is a specialty that relates dental evidence to investigation.[39] The dental apparatus, including teeth, prosthetic appliances, and morphological (shape and form) peculiarities, is of primary importance in the identification of mutilated, decomposed, or otherwise visually unrecognizable human remains. Teeth themselves leave patterns in the skin, and analysis of bite marks has played a major role in many criminal cases. Teeth marks left in food (Figure 4–32), pencils, Styrofoam cups, and other objects at crime scenes can be analyzed for the bite record; in addition, they can be the source of saliva samples for comparison of blood-type groups. Analysis of a bite mark in and of itself can be of great value in helping investigators to eliminate suspects as well as to identify a suspect.

Figure 4–30
Clear Flap Lifter
Lifting a latent fingerprint using a clear flap lifter. Flap lifters are made with the lifting surface permanently attached to the backing card onto which the lifted print is laid.

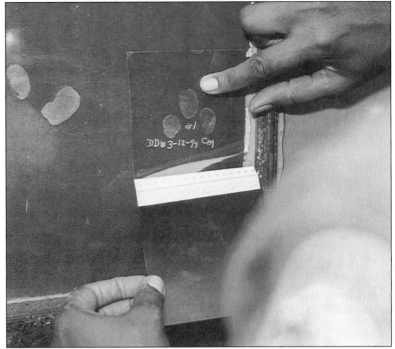

(Courtesy Nassau County, New York, Police Department)

Figure 4–31
Fingerprint from Rounded Surface
Fingerprint on a 9-mm cartridge photographed with the Rotorgraph invented by Turner Pippin.

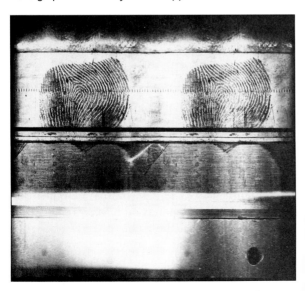

(Courtesy State of Alaska Scientific Crime Detection Laboratory)

HISTORY

The teeth and facial bones are a major means of identifying skeletal remains and have been used by anthropologists for many years. It is interesting to speculate that the first forensic dentist in the United States may have been Paul Revere. In 1775, he constructed a silver bridge for his friend General Joseph Warren, who was later killed by the British during the Battle of Bunker Hill. Warren was buried in a mass grave, and Revere later identified his remains by the bridgework he had constructed for Warren—the earliest-known dental identification in the United States.

Nearly 100 years after Revere's identification, the body of President Lincoln's assassin, John Wilkes Booth, was identified by a gold "plug tooth" on the right side of his jaw. Probably the most publicized bite-mark case involved Ted Bundy, who allegedly committed homicides in Washington, California, Utah, Colorado, and Florida. He was arrested for murdering several women in a sorority house in 1978. At trial, the positive relationship between bite-mark evidence obtained from one of the victims and the teeth of the accused contributed to his successful prosecution.

Figure 4–32
Bite Mark in Food

A partially eaten "Moon Pie" bitten by one of the suspects in a double homicide. From the bite marks it can be determined that the individual making them had two nonequally protruding upper front teeth. Such information can play an important role in determining probable cause for arrest and/or search warrants.

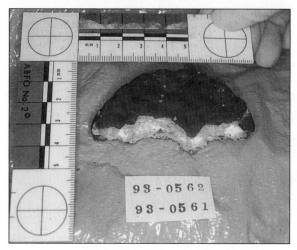

(Courtesy Dr. Richard R. Souviron, D.D.S., A.B.F.O., Chief Forensic Odontologist, Dade County Medical Examiner Department, Miami, Florida)

DENTAL IDENTIFICATION

Dental records include, but are not limited to, dental X-rays, dentagrams, dental charts, prosthetic molds, and dental casts. The forensic dentist compares antemortem (before death) records with postmortem (after death) findings to determine if there is a positive match. No set number of points are required for a positive match. Sometimes one unique feature of the teeth can be enough for a positive identification. This usually includes some type of human-made anomaly, such as a root canal, a post, a crown, pins in the tooth, or a unique cavity or crown preparation form.

Like human fingerprints, human dentitions (teeth) are unique. The average adult has 32 teeth. A combination of tooth form and arrangement, missing teeth, and mechanical alterations from dental fillings or accidents produce hundreds of thousands of possible combinations. It is important that the crime scene search not overlook dental evidence that appears to be useless. A single tooth with unusual anatomy may provide a basis for

identification of the individual. On the basis of skull and jaw formations, a forensic dentist may be able to give investigators valuable opinions and information as to the victim's age, race, sex, and possibly unusual habits. A forensic dentist can state with reasonable certainty the approximate age within six months of an individual through age 13. From age 14 through 25, a one-year plus-or-minus estimate is possible. After age 25, certain sophisticated tests can be performed to approximate age.

Certain groups—Orientals and Indians—have deep grooves in the inner aspect of the upper front teeth. These are referred to as *shovel-shaped incisors*. Functioning third molars (wisdom teeth) are common among blacks but are found in less than 20 percent of whites, who are likely to have had their wisdom teeth extracted to prevent crowding of their remaining teeth. Crowding of the teeth is common among whites but not among blacks or Native Americans. The absence of certain teeth may help identify age and race. For example, the first premolars, like the wisdom teeth, are usually extracted for orthodontic reasons (crowding) among whites. Anterior wear will suggest habits such as pipe smoking or nail biting. Fractured upper incisors are very useful not only in visual identification and photographic comparisons but also in bite-mark analysis. The jaws will also show evidence of previous injuries as well as past or present disease. In discussing these and other aspects of the case with a forensic dentist, investigators must be sure that they understand any distinctions made between scientific fact and investigative opinion.

Dental records are hard to obtain, and searches for them are not always productive because (1) many individuals under the age of 30 have had no dental decay and (2) individuals with decayed or missing teeth may never have sought treatment. In either case, there are no records of antemortem dental restorations that can be compared with the postmortem dental features of a victim. For these reasons, "smiling-photograph" comparisons have become important in making dental identifications (see Figure 4–33). The technique is quick and cost-effective but depends on having a reasonably good photograph of the front teeth. Several such photographs showing the front teeth will enhance the weight of the evidence. However, comparison with dental records such as X-rays and dentagrams is far more accurate.

Figure 4-33
Dental Comparison

Left photo shows upper and lower jaws of an unknown white male. Some bone loss (pyorrhea) and tobacco staining are evident. There were no fillings, decay, or missing teeth and no evidence of any dental treatment. Right photo is enhancement and enlargement of the victim, pictured at his son's birthday party. His kidnappers/killers were sentenced to life terms.

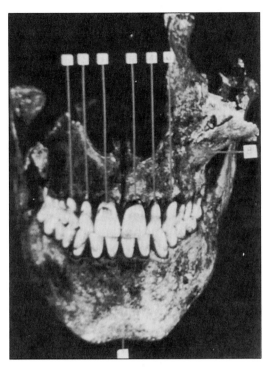 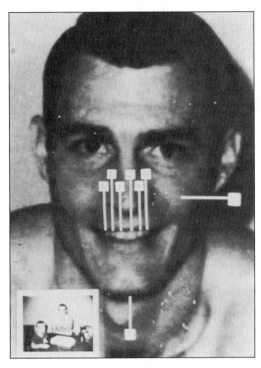

(Courtesy Dr. Richard R. Souviron, DDS, ABFO, Chief Forensic Odontologist, Dade County Medical Examiner Department, Miami, Florida)

BITE-MARK EVIDENCE

Investigators must be particularly alert to the possibility that bite-mark evidence exists whenever they are working violent-crime and child-abuse cases. Aggressive bites are left by attackers and defensive bites are by victims. While some bite marks are fairly obvious, others are less so. In Figure 4–34, two classic "donut" bites are immediately evident. However, on the left of the photograph there are other, smaller bites that could easily be mistaken for bruises left by a beating or injuries caused by blunt-force trauma. Sometimes bites are less distinct, as in Figure 4–35, because they were made through clothing. Occasionally, what appears to be a bite mark is actually a pseudo, or false, bite mark. The injuries shown in Figure 4–36, for example, were caused by striking the victim with the open end of a pipe.

All suspected or actual bites should be photographed, using both black-and-white and color film if feasible. A color scale should always be included in color photographs because it will be of use in determining the approximate time the victim was bitten. A ruler should be placed next to the bite area (see Figures 4–36 and 4–37). This documentation helps the forensic dentist make an exact replica of the bite, which can later be compared with that of a suspect. The ideal ruler to use is the ABFO scale, shown in Figure 4–38, which corrects for curvature of the skin surface. The first set of photographs should be taken before the wound is cleaned. Qualified medical personnel should then swab the bites and save each swab for laboratory analysis of any saliva or blood. Each time a new bite area is swabbed, a new swab should be used. As with other types of evidence, swabs should be packaged individually to avoid cross-contamination. After this

Figure 4–34
Two Forms of Bite Marks
Two forms of bite marks on the same victim.

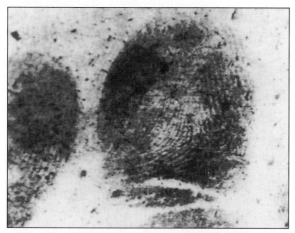

(Courtesy Norman D. Sperber, DDS, San Diego County Coroner's Office)

procedure is complete, a second set of photgraphs should be taken. If feasible, follow-up photographs should be taken in 12 to 24 hours. Photographs of bites on live victims may actually be clearer when photographed several days later, as blood seeping into the wound will be lessened. If the victim is dead, embalming will bleach out the color of the

wound and make photographs of it less instructive. Bite marks should also be documented by lifting them like latent prints and by making a cast of them using some suitable material, such as silicone.

The records needed from the suspect for comparison are photographs and impressions of the teeth, wax bite records, X-rays, and saliva and blood samples. All may be obtained quickly and with little or no discomfort to the suspect. Duplicates of everything should be taken to safeguard against loss or breakage. A suspect may voluntarily bite into a Styrofoam cup or into a block of beeswax. From this "impression," a duplicate or cast can quickly be made of the biting, or incisal, edges of the suspect's teeth. This can be extremely helpful in eliminating multiple suspects. However, care should be taken that a suspect is not forced to bite into an object but does so with his or her full consent. It is best that the forensic dentist making the comparisons get the evidence from the victim and the records from the suspect. Teeth can be altered, broken off, or removed by a suspect. If a suspect does this before dental impressions are taken, the bite-mark comparison becomes more difficult or even impossible to make. Therefore, bite-mark evidence should not be publicized.

If the suspect does not give informed consent, the courts provide two methods of obtaining these

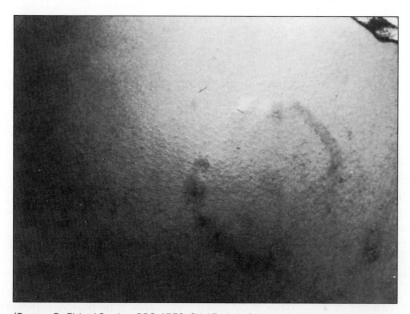

(Courtesy Dr. Richard Souviron, DDS, ABFO, Chief Forensic Odontologist, Dade County Medical Examiner Department, Miami, Florida)

Figure 4–35
Lack of Detail in Bite Mark
Bite mark on shoulder of rape victim. The lack of detail is due to the bite's having been made through clothing.

Figure 4-36
False Bite Marks

Pseudo, or false, bite marks on the stomach of a victim. Although thought at first to resemble human bite marks, closer examination revealed that the injuries were caused by the end of a pipe.

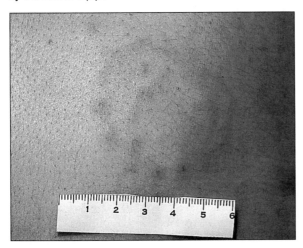

(Courtesy Dr. Richard Souviron, DDS, ABFO, Chief Forensic Odontologist, Dade County Medical Examiner Department, Miami, Florida)

Figure 4-37
Hand Abrasion

Abrasion caused by striking victim in the mouth.

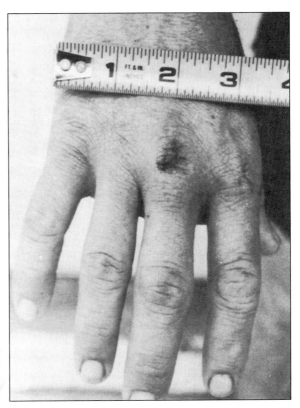

(Courtesy Dr. Richard Souviron, DDS, ABFO, Chief Forensic Odontologist, Dade County Medical Examiner Department, Miami, Florida)

records from the suspect—a court order or a search warrant. A court order is often used, but it has the disadvantage of informing the suspect, and in some cases his or her attorney, of the pending examination and permits sufficient time for the teeth to be altered. Thus, a search warrant is a safer method if the alteration of teeth is a distinct possibility. In this way, the suspect is prevented from knowing of the impending examination ahead of time. It is important that the dentist taking these records have a signed copy of the court order or search warrant before he or she examines the suspect. Proceeding on any other basis will jeopardize the admissibility of any evidence obtained. The presence of the prosecutor or his or her representative is desirable but not a requirement.

HAIR

An initial step in the forensic examination of hair is to determine whether or not it is of human origin. Human hair has unique characteristics, and ordinarily this determination is not difficult unless the hair has been subject to gross destruction. When the hair is not human, it is possible to establish the species involved, such as dog, cat, or horse.

Human hair evidence is most frequently found in violent crimes. If the hair root is attached, it may be possible to establish individuality.[40]

Even when there are no roots attached to the hair, there are a number of useful conclusions that can be established:

1. The area of the body from which the hair came, as well as the race of the donor.[41]

2. The manner in which the hair was removed, such as having been cut or forcibly pulled out.

3. Differentiations between hair samples based on shampoo residues.[42]

4. Whether the hair has been bleached or dyed.[43]

Figure 4–38
The ABFO Scale

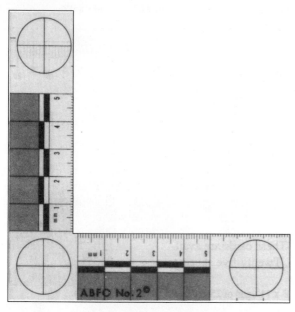

(Courtesy of Lightning Powder Company, Salem, Oregon)

5. What contaminants are in the hair, such as blood, semen, soil, paint, pet hair, or fibers.

6. Whether the hair has been subject to some force, such as burning or blunt-instrument trauma.

7. Identification of drugs ingested, as well as how long ago they were taken based on a hair-growth rate of 1 millimeter per day.[44]

Although distinctions between the hair of infants and adults can be made, examiners cannot conclusively determine the age of a hair donor. Even when the condition of hair evidence is not sufficiently good to permit all these determinations to be made, the remaining conclusions that can be reached may be of considerable assistance in eliminating suspects or focusing the investigation. Additionally, these conclusions may have more than their ordinary value when combined with other evidence, or they may be useful in destroying an alibi. To illustrate, a rape suspect maintained that he had never had contact with the victim, and his mother stated that he was watching television with her when the crime occurred. An eyewitness maintained that she had seen the victim and the suspect in the parking lot of a mall. The suspect maintained

that the eyewitness was mistaken. However, the suspect confessed when confronted with the fact that hairs consistent with the victim's were found in his car, as well as fibers consistent with the victim's sweater and skirt.

Upon completing the examination of hair evidence without any roots attached, the laboratory will normally issue one of three findings: the hair could have originated from the suspect, the hair is dissimilar to that of the suspect, or no meaningful conclusion could be reached.[45]

Hair recovered at the scene of the crime should be carefully gathered, using a pair of tweezers.[46] Samples recovered at different locations, as in the case of other types of evidence, should be individually packaged. Hair evidence may be placed in a pillbox that is fully sealed with tape or placed in a folded piece of paper that is also fully taped shut. Some laboratories, such as the FBI's, request that hair evidence not be packaged in an envelope. In all cases the container used should be marked with the appropriate identifying information.

Because most examinations of hair are comparative in nature, a collection of standards from both the victim and the suspect, where the latter is known, is critical. The collection of hair standards is a function for medical personnel. When hair standards are collected from a deceased victim, representative samples should be obtained from throughout the body areas that are pertinent to the investigation; ordinarily, the collection of approximately 30 to 40 hairs from each area is sufficient, taking care to package the samples from each body area separately. Where hair surrounds wounds on the body of a victim, special notation should be made of this point on the container in which the hair is placed.

In collecting hair samples, combing is used to gather hair left on the victim by the suspect or on the suspect by the victim. For comparison purposes, standard hair samples must be plucked from the individual to ensure that the hair was indeed attached to that person. If this proves to be too painful, then the hair needed may be cut, but the person doing the cutting must be able to substantiate that the hair was attached to the person. The hair should be cut as close to the skin as possible. Approximately 20 hairs from each area of concern are sufficient for a standard hair sample from a living donor.

It is desirable that the investigator be present at the time the hair samples are obtained by medical personnel; if the latter are unfamiliar with investigative procedures, they might fail to clean the tweezers, comb, or scissors after each area is sampled, thereby introducing contamination.

BLOOD

In a healthy person, blood accounts for less than 8 percent of body weight; adults have somewhat more than 9 pints of blood.[47] Blood is one of the most common forms of evidence found at the scenes of serious crimes. It is encountered in small trace amounts, drops, smears, splatters, and pools of various sizes; in liquid and dry states; on clothing; in soil;, on knives, guns, clubs, and other weapons; and in other forms.

Because of the frequency with which blood evidence will be encountered and the fact that DNA analysis can yield individual identification from drops of wet- or dry-blood evidence, investigators must have a strong working knowledge of the proper methods of collecting and preserving such evidence. Moreover, officers must take the precautions outlined in Chapter 3, The Crime Scene and Its Associated Procedures, when collecting blood or other types of potential biohazard evidence, including semen. As discussed in Chapter 3, these precautions extend to collecting other forms of evidence on which potentially infectious matter may be located, such as hypodermic needles.

In addition to potentially yielding individual identification, the examination of blood can answer a number of questions useful to investigators:[48]

1. *Is this stain blood?* On the surface this would appear to be a relatively easy question to answer. However, dried blood stains have a variety of appearances, including gray, blue, and greenish hues, and apparent blood samples may be a variety of other things, such as rust combined with some liquid or paint. Moreover, blood mixed with something else, such as grease or earth, may take on an appearance very unlike a blood stain. When there is any suspicion that blood might be present, the investigator should take a sample and submit it to the laboratory for a determination rather than attempting to arrive at this decision on the basis of nonscientific judgment. Ordinarily, whether the stain is in a solid or liquid state, the laboratory will be able to make a determination as to whether or not it is blood. Alternatively, a presumptive or preliminary field test using Hemident can be performed (see Figure 4–39). Such presumptive tests must be confirmed by more advanced

Figure 4–39
Hemident
The use of Hemident as a presumptive or preliminary field test for blood.

1. Wear protective gloves. Rub the stain with a clean cotton swab.

2. Insert the swab into the test unit and break off the excess handle.

3. Put the cap back on the tube and break the bottom ampoule.

4. Tap the tube to make sure the swab is wet. Wait about 20 to 30 seconds.

5. Break the top ampoule in the lid.

6. Observe the color change on the point where the swab has the suspect stain.

(Courtesy Lightning Powder Company, Salem, Oregon)

laboratory techniques because they have little value as evidence in court. Hemident cannot distinguish between human and animal blood, which is ordinarily done through serological testing. Depending on which Hemident chemical reagent is used to conduct the test, a vivid pink or blue-green color is produced if the stain or fluid being tested is blood. Hemident is nondestructive and will not interfere with subsequent serological testing.

2. *What is the origin of the blood?* Regardless of whether the stain is in a liquid or dried state, if it has not been subject to gross deterioration, whether it is of human or animal origin can be determined. Furthermore, if the blood is nonhuman, it is frequently possible to determine the species of animal from which it originated. After the disappearance of labor leader James Hoffa, it was thought that an individual close to the victim may have been involved because blood stains were found in his car; however, laboratory examination corroborated the statement of the person in question that the stains had originated from a fish. If the blood is human, under certain circumstances it may be possible to determine what part of the body it came from. If the blood was recovered in a liquid state, it may be possible to determine whether it was venous, fetal, or menstrual in origin.[49] Additionally, there may be rare instances in which the blood contains impurities—secretions and hairs—that might allow it to be identified as having come from the nose.[50]

3. *How old are these blood stains?* It is difficult to determine the age of blood stains. A variety of factors affect the rapidity with which blood dries; among these are presence or absence of wind or a draft, temperature, and humidity. Wind and higher temperatures accelerate the drying process; increased humidity retards it. "Blood begins to clot within three to five minutes after it is exposed to air; as it dries, the clot darkens in color, becoming reddish brown or dark brown when completely dry . . . an old dried blood clot may appear black."[51] On a smooth surface at room temperature a drop of blood, depending on the size and thickness of the stain, will take about an hour to dry fully; the process begins at the edges, working toward the center. Under the same conditions, small pools will take some 2 to 3 hours to reach a dry state. If the blood is between the fluid state and the dry state, due to the formation of fibrin, it may be termed *gelatinous*. "On further drying, the stain will contract and finally pucker and crack around the edges."[52]

4. *What was the condition of the donor of this sample of blood?* If the blood sample is recovered in liquid form and there is a sufficiently large quantity, it may be possible to determine whether the person leaving the stain was under the influence of alcohol or drugs. Additionally, it may be possible to detect such conditions as the presence of carbon monoxide or the existence of venereal disease. In attempting to make these determinations, it is essential not only that the blood not be dried out, but that it not have undergone any degree of decomposition or contamination by foreign materials.

5. *What contributions can blood stains make to the reconstruction of the crime?* The study of blood drops or splashes, along with their direction and placement, occasionally makes it possible to determine where an assault occurred, the position of the injured portion of the body at the time of the assault, where the perpetrator was positioned at that particular time, whether the victim was attempting to evade blows, the number of blows struck, and related factors.[53] In general, the size and shape of a blood stain indicates the height from which the blood has fallen (see Figure 4–40), but the type of surface onto which it falls affects this outcome considerably (see Figure 4–41). Moreover, if the person or object that released the blood was in motion, it will fall downward obliquely in the direction in which the person or object was moving (see Figure 4–42).

LOCATING BLOOD EVIDENCE

The places at which the investigator will find blood stains are virtually unlimited. For example, if a

Figure 4-40
Basic Blood Shapes and Sizes
The effect on shape and size of average-size (0.05-milliliter) blood drops falling onto hard, smooth cardboard.

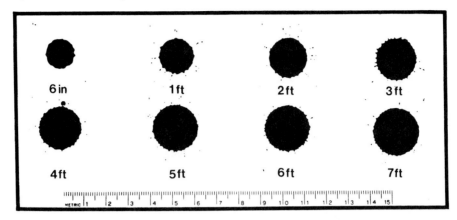

Source: William G. Eckert and Stuart H. James, *Interpretation of Bloodstain Evidence at Crime Scenes* (New York: Elsevier, 1989), Fig. 2-3, p. 17, by permission.

criminal homicide occurred indoors, blood might be found not only on the floor but perhaps on the walls or even the ceiling. Ordinarily when perpetrators of violent crime get blood on their bodies or clothing, they will attempt to rid themselves of it immediately. In some instances, they may be so repelled by the sight of blood on their hands that they will impulsively wipe it on a piece of furniture, such as a stuffed chair; if the fabric is multicolored or sufficiently dark, the stain may escape detection by the unobservant investigator. They may also attempt to clean bloodied hands prior to leaving the scene by using such places as the reverse side of a small throw rug or the undersides of cushions on a couch. Occasionally, a criminal homicide will occur indoors, but the perpetrator will remove the body to an outdoor area to avoid discovery, return to the scene, and attempt to eliminate all traces of the crime. Typically, this would involve washing hands and scrubbing or mopping the floor on which the body had lain. A case illustrates these types of behaviors and the actions required by the investigator:

An aggravated assault occurred between two friends who mutually agreed to misrepresent the crime and claim the cutting was an accident. When the victim appeared at the local hospital for treatment, the police were summoned due to the nature of the several wounds and their locations, which suggested to the doctor that they were not accidentally inflicted. Subsequent examination of the scene revealed blood traces under the faucet handles in the kitchen, where the perpetrator had turned on the water to wash his hands, and in the trap of the sink; and although the perpetrator had washed portions of his shirt on which the victim's blood had fallen, he had done so in hot water, which merely set the stain, making it fairly readily observable to the naked eye. Additionally, although the floor at the scene had been mopped, traces of the same-type blood as the victim's were also recovered. The location of the blood evidence was particularly pertinent because the people involved alleged that the incident had happened outside the house while they were barbecuing and that they had gone directly to the hospital.

The investigator must also be alert to the fact that although there are no apparent blood stains, laboratory examinations may be able to detect their existence. For example, blood from a victim may be on the perpetrator's clothes. A suspect may initially attempt to wipe the blood away with a washcloth and then later wash both it and his or her clothes. The retention of blood stains on cloth after washing is variable; it is dependent on several

Figure 4–41
Surface Type and Blood Shapes and Sizes
Effect of surface type on the shape and size of average-sized blood drops falling from 12 inches.

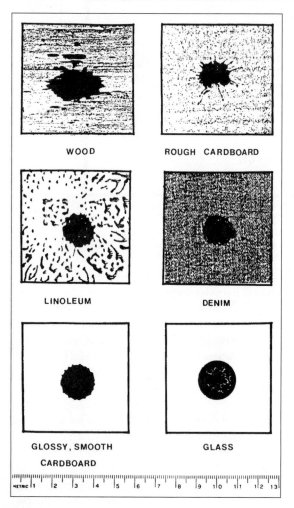

Source: William G. Eckert and Stuart H. James, *Interpretation of Bloodstain Evidence at Crime Scenes* (New York: Elsevier, 1989), Fig. 2-2, p. 16, by permission.

factors, such as the type of fiber and the conditions under which the cloth was washed.[54]

Furthermore, if the perpetrator has walked through blood stains at the scene and collected samples on the soles of the shoes, even though these may have been scrubbed or rubbed by walking some distance, minute traces may still be available up inside the nail holes, cracks in the soles, or other such crevices.[55] Very often, it will be possible

to detect smaller drops of blood under daylight conditions if the investigator crouches close to the floor, viewing the surface at an angle. From the same position under conditions of darkness, the use of a flashlight held at an oblique angle to the floor will often allow otherwise-unobservable stains to be seen.

HANDLING BLOOD EVIDENCE

Prior to the actual handling of blood evidence, the investigator should make notes concerning such aspects as the physical state of the stain, the amount present, the shape, the exact location of the stain in relationship to fixed objects, the pattern of the stain, temperature, humidity, and other pertinent details.[56] Naturally, as part of processing the crime scene, photographs should be taken. In criminal homicide cases the recording of the amount of blood found at the crime scene may be particularly important; the existence of severe wounds or numerous wounds coupled with the absence of any significant amount of blood at the scene may suggest that the actual killing took place elsewhere and the body was removed to its present location.

If blood is found in a liquid state at the crime scene, there are several methods of collection. Some laboratories recommend buying white, 100 percent–cotton sheets, washing them in hot water using light detergent to remove the sizing, and then rinsing them several times. The sheets are then cut into small sections that can be separately placed onto different blood pools as needed. The strips are then allowed to air-dry naturally, placed in separate paper bags, taped shut, and marked "Blood Evidence—Potential Biohazard," along with the appropriate identifying information. Other laboratories recommend the same process but substitute the use of a gauze pad for the section of a cotton sheet. In the event that neither a section of a properly prepared cotton sheet nor a gauze pad is available, then the blood can be put into a "red-stoppered" blood collection tube, which has no preservatives, or any clean and suitable container and also allowed to air-dry naturally. A clean medicine dropper or disposable plastic spoon can be used to place the blood into the tube.

Figure 4–42
Parent and Wave Cast-Off Patterns
The formation of parent and wave cast-off patterns from a blood drop striking a floor.

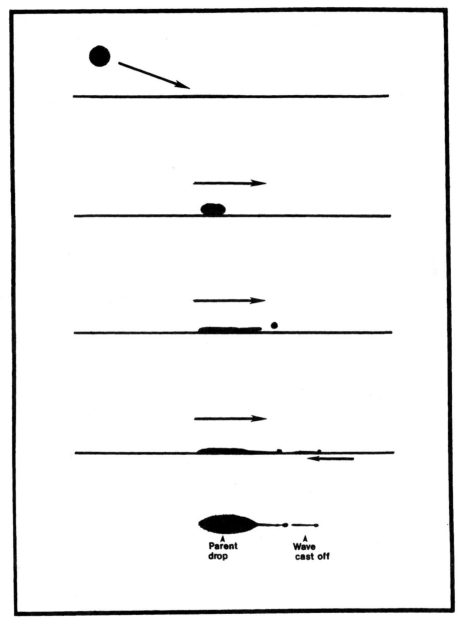

Parent
drop

Wave
cast off

Source: William G. Eckert and Stuart H. James. *Interpretation of Bloodstain Evidence at Crime Scenes* (New York: Elsevier, 1989), Fig. 2-17, p. 30, by permission.

In contrast, when blood is collected for DNA analysis under clinical conditions from a suspect and/or a victim, approximately 5 milliliters of blood should be drawn and placed into a "purple-stoppered" tube, the inside of which is treated with the preservative EDTA. If various serological tests are also going to be requested, then second blood samples must be drawn from the suspect and/or victim and placed into a red-stoppered or untreated blood collection tube.

On immovable objects, blood stains that are dried and in crust form may be gathered using one of several methods. A clean razor blade will free the crust, which is then placed into a container, or a piece of clean paper can be slid under the crust, freeing it. Dried blood stains should be placed in a pillbox or a plastic tube; the use of envelopes should be avoided because the crust may break, complicating the examination process. Whether the blood is recovered in liquid or solid state, it is a good practice to obtain an unstained sample of the surface from which it was gathered in order to allow the laboratory to demonstrate that the result of the tests performed was not affected by the surface on which the blood stain was deposited.[57] When fresh blood stains appear on a weapon, they should be allowed to air-dry and then be packaged with the dry crust still on the weapon for transmittal to the laboratory. When dried blood crusts appear on a movable object or weapon, they should not be removed; rather, the object should be carefully packaged with these stains intact. In violent crimes it is not unusual for the investigator to recover, either at the scene of the crime or at the hospital, articles of clothing that contain wet blood stains. Such garments should be hung and allowed to air-dry. In no case should they be subject to accelerated drying by hanging them close to a heat source; this could produce decomposition, thereby reducing the evidentiary value of the blood stain. Once blood-stained garments have dried, they should be folded so that none of the creases are in the same areas as the encrusted blood stains, since this could dislodge the blood crusts. Moreover, in packaging such garments, tissue paper should be used to separate the various portions of the garment in order to lessen the possibility of dislodging blood crusts. After it is arranged in this fashion, the clothing is placed into a paper bag and sealed and marked in the same manner described for gauze pads with dried blood stains on them.

During warm weather and especially during daylight hours, blood evidence should not be placed in car trunks or left in locked cars while the investigator handles other tasks. Heat extremes can rapidly degrade the determinations that might otherwise be provided by the laboratory.

If there is going to be a delay of more than 24 hours in submitting dried blood evidence to the laboratory—including both individual stains as well as those dried on garments or objects—it should be kept refrigerated or be frozen. Samples of fresh blood drawn under laboratory conditions from the suspect or victim should be kept refrigerated, but not frozen, until they are transmitted to the laboratory overnight or faster. As a rule of thumb, there should be no more than a 30-day lapse from the time that blood is drawn until its arrival at the laboratory.

HUMAN EXCRETIONS AND SECRETIONS

Evidence falling into this category includes saliva, urine, semen, perspiration, vaginal secretions, feces, and vomitus.[58] With the exception of semen and vaginal secretions, this type of evidence will only rarely be encountered. However, the investigator must be prepared to take advantage of the opportunities presented. Historically, the principal value of this category of evidence has been that approximately 75 percent of all people are secretors, meaning that body materials produce a substance that makes it possible to identify their blood group. However, through DNA analysis we are now able to establish individual identification from semen and also vaginal secretions, even if the woman is not menstruating. Therefore, these two types of evidence have assumed even greater importance to investigators.

Saliva may be found on cigarette butts, gags, cups, toothpicks, and related items. In addition to the possibility of determining the blood type of the donor, if sufficient quantity is available, it may also be possible to determine any alcohol content. A saliva sample is gathered by having a suspect expectorate on a piece of filter paper. The saliva should be clean and undiluted and form a stain of about 1½ inches in diameter. This sample is then circled in pencil before it dries. After the filter paper dries, it can be placed in a paper envelope and sealed properly. Liquid saliva samples should never be submitted to the laboratory. Saliva samples should be obtained from both the victim and the suspect in all sexual assault cases.[59]

Urine is ordinarily associated with sex offenses and breaking and enterings. It may be possible with urine evidence to determine the alcohol content in the donor's blood. However, unless there is a fairly large sample, it may be difficult to distinguish between animal and human samples.

Semen is found as evidence in sexual offenses, in autoerotic deaths (sexual asphyxiations), occasionally in burglaries, and on rare occasions in criminal homicides. Semen is grayish-white in color, and in liquid form it has a chlorinelike odor. When dried, it is stiff and starchlike in consistency.

Semen is subject to contamination by foreign agents, such as blood; it may be virtually invisible to the eye but can be detected by an alternative light source or laboratory examination. Semen may also be located on material such as the victim's sheets or clothes. In these cases, it should be allowed to dry naturally on the material, placed into a breathable container such as a paper bag, and kept frozen until submission to the laboratory.[60] Semen that is on some immovable object should be dissolved with water and then gathered with an eye dropper. The collection of semen evidence from a victim is discussed in Chapter 12.

Perspiration will only rarely be encountered due to the rapidity with which it evaporates. It will ordinarily be found on handkerchiefs, gloves, or similar items left at the crime scene.

Feces are occasionally encountered at the scenes of burglaries, particularly those involving attacks on money chests or safes. Opinion varies as to whether defecation occurs because of nervousness, as a matter of convenience, or as an indication of contempt toward the police or owners of the property. If the person is a secretor, this type of evidence might help to establish the blood type of the donor, and the paper or other material used by the person for self-cleaning may yield useful information, including fingerprints.

Vomitus is highly unusual evidence and is often associated with violent personal crimes or burglaries; it is possible from examination of this type of evidence to make some determination about the content and time of the last meal, along with an occasional indication as to the medical condition of the suspect.

LIPSTICK AND LIP-PRINT EVIDENCE

A forensic study of 117 types of common lipsticks from 15 manufacturers showed that each type could be separately identified by laboratory testing.[61] Lipstick evidence is occasionally encountered in a variety of offenses, but it is often not appreciated for the contributions it can make to an investigation, particularly its potential to connect the offender with the scene and/or victim and to help evaluate a suspect's alibi. For example, lipstick may be transferred from the victim to her assailant's clothing during rape. If a suspect is stopped in the general area shortly thereafter with lipstick on the collar or shoulder of his shirt, he may claim that it is that of his girlfriend. Comparisons of the victim's lipstick, the lipstick on the suspect's clothing, and that of the girlfriend could reveal that only the victim's lipstick and that on the suspect's clothing are consistent. Other types of crimes in which lipstick may be encountered as evidence include ritualistic slayings, armed robberies, and other crimes of violence. Even in property offenses, where there has been no victim-suspect contact, obscene messages may be left, with lipstick used to write on mirrors, walls, or other places. Lipstick evidence should be photographed before disturbing it. When it is on clothing, the entire garment should be submitted to the laboratory, and care should be taken to pack it in such a fashion that the affected area is well protected. Where there are sufficient quantities on other surfaces, a sample should be collected with a clean razor blade or similar instrument and placed in a clean pillbox. Lipstick evidence encountered at several different locations of a crime scene should be collected and packaged separately. Dry cotton should not be used to protect lipstick evidence because it creates problems in handling the evidence in the laboratory. Nor should lipstick evidence be allowed to sit in the sun or to remain in the trunks of cars where it may be subject to extreme heat. In all cases a generous sample of the victim's or other donor's lipstick should also be obtained.

Lip prints are found under many of the same circumstances as is lipstick evidence. Every individual has unique lip prints that do not change with age. As with fingerprints, technicians can lift these prints from objects at the crime scene, such as a glass, and compare them with the suspect's lip pattern. Lip prints are also found elsewhere, such as on the starched collar of a shirt.[62]

FIREARMS

Firearms evidence is one of the most common types to be encountered, consisting of such items as revolvers, pistols, rifles, shotguns, loaded cartridges, misfired cartridges, bullets, shell cases, powder residues, magazines, clips, shot pellets, and the wads used in older shotgun ammunition.

The investigator must develop a familiarity with firearms in order to answer important questions: Is the weapon a pistol or a revolver? Is it a rifle or a shotgun? Of what shot construction is the weapon—that is, single shot, tubular fed, semiautomatic, automatic, or rotating cylinder? How many shots does the weapon hold? How are expended cartridges ejected? Does the weapon chamber-load, or is it fed by a magazine or clip? Is the weapon intended for rimfire or centerfire ammunition? What caliber is the weapon? What are lands and grooves? Is the barrel of the weapon rifled, and, if so, does it have left- or right-handed twist?[63]

As in the case of blood and other types of evidence, certain determinations can be made from the examination of firearms evidence. These are presented in response to typical questions facing the investigator:

1. *Was this bullet fired from this particular weapon?* Figure 4–43 depicts one view of the interior of the rifled barrel of a firearm and Figure 4–44 the comparison of two bullets. In contrast, the barrel of a shotgun is smooth. *Bore* is the correct term to apply to the diameter of the interior of a weapon's barrel; in a rifled barrel, it is measured between two opposing lands, or ridges. Technically, *caliber* refers to the diameter of the bullet intended for use in the weapon. Generally, a bullet is somewhat larger than the diameter of the bore, so that as it passes through the barrel, the lands grip it, causing it to rotate, usually in a right-hand direction.[64] It is this process of movement that creates the highly individualized striations on the bullet. Occasionally, distinctive markings may also be

left on bullets by the loading action or a flash suppressor. Additionally, in defective revolvers, where the barrel and the chamber containing the loaded cartridge do not align properly, there will be a sheering effect, which is observable on the recovered bullet. In order to determine whether a particular firearm fired a particular bullet, it is necessary to compare the bullet recovered at the scene with a test bullet fired through the gun that is suspected of having fired the bullet in question. Whether or not it is possible to make a positive identification is affected by the condition of the recovered bullet and the condition of the gun at the time it is finally located. For example, there is evidence that the part of the body from which a bullet is recovered in a 90 percent–decomposed body can affect the striations. This is due to a reaction between the bullet material and body tissue.[65]

2. *What findings are possible by examination of a bullet?* A fired bullet yields evidence of the class characteristics of the weapon that fired it with respect to the number of lands and grooves and their height, depth, and width. The class characteristics of a firearm are those design specifications to which it was manufactured; weapons of a given make and

Figure 4–43
Rifled Barrel
Important features of a rifled firearm's barrel.

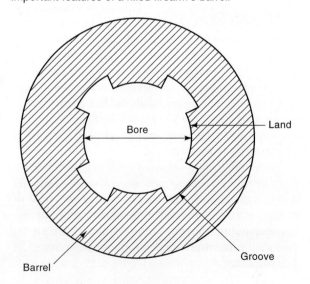

Figure 4–44
Bullet Comparison
A drug user murdered his supplier in order to "cancel" his debt and obtain additional drugs. Photomicrograph of the bullet recovered from the body (*left*) compared to the bullet fired from the murder gun (*right*) after the revolver was recovered from a river by police divers.

(Courtesy Royal Canadian Mounted Police)

model will have the same class characteristics. The individual characteristics of the bore are found in the striae along the fired bullet. Examination of a fired bullet will suggest the type of weapon from which it was fired, whether the bullet is a hard-nose or soft-nose projectile, and the pitch and direction of twist within the barrel. Additionally, if the fired bullet is recovered in sufficient size, it may be possible, through weighing and measurement, to determine its caliber. Since bullets are often recovered as fragments, the caliber may only be implied by the weight's ruling out smaller calibers. While it is possible to determine the caliber of the bullet, some caution must be taken with respect to determining the bore of the weapon from which it was fired, as it is possible to fire a smaller-caliber bullet through a larger-bored weapon.

Fired bullets ordinarily will have experienced some damage as a result of their impacting. In some cases it will be possible to see fabric impressions on the bullet's nose, the impression having been made as it passed through the victim's outer garment. Additionally, there may be minute traces of blood, tissue, bone, or other such materials. Great care must be taken by the investigator not to destroy or in any way alter such evidence. Where the fired bullet is recovered from the person or body of the victim, the investigator should alert the attending medical personnel, if there is any doubt about their familiarity with proper handling procedure, as to the irreparable damage that can be wrought by the careless application of forceps or other such instruments in removing the bullet.

It should be noted that it is ordinarily not possible to make a positive identification as to whether pellets were fired from a particular shotgun. However, in extraordinarily rare circumstances involving smooth-bore firearms, it may be possible to make an individual identification due to gross defects in the barrel.[66]

3. *What findings can be made by examining fired cartridge cases?* While the fired bullet is marked by the barrel only, the fired cartridge

case is marked by several parts of the weapon in the actions of loading, firing, and extracting.[67] When the firing pin strikes the weapon, its impression is recorded; this is true in both centerfire and rimfire ammunition.[68] Subsequent to the firing pin's striking the primer, the burning gases inside the casing begin to expand, forcing the cartridge outward against the walls of the chamber and back against the breach face of the weapon. Any striations present on the breach face and any damage in the chamber will thereby be recorded on the cartridge case. In semiautomatic and automatic weapons, extractor and ejector markings are left on the rim of the casing, even if the cartridge is merely run through the action of the weapon and not actually fired. Additionally, in the case of semiautomatic pistols, the cartridge case may be marked by the magazine. Other markings may appear on the cartridge casing due to a particular type of action by a firearm (see Figures 4–45, 4–46, and 4–47).

4. *What miscellaneous determinations can be made by examination of firearms evidence?* If a firearm is received at a crime laboratory, its general mechanical condition can be assessed, which will lend credence to or discredit statements that the shooting was accidental. For example, if the trigger pull on a weapon is of the "hair" nature, requiring only the slightest pressure to pull it, this would indicate that an accidental shooting was possible. Laboratory examination might reveal that a firearm is constructed—or malfunctioning—in such a way that it could discharge by being dropped on its hammer, thereby giving more credibility to a claim that a shooting was accidental. Furthermore, even though invisible to the naked eye, obliterated serial numbers can sometimes be restored by the laboratory, thus providing an additional investigative lead. Proximity of the gun to the

Figure 4–45
Firing Pin Impressions
Photomicrograph showing comparison of questioned and known firing-pin impressions on a .22-caliber rimfire cartridge case.

(Courtesy Regional Criminalistics Laboratory, Metropolitan Kansas City, Missouri)

victim at the time of discharge may be established by an examination of powder residues on the victim's clothing or skin. A close shot with black powder shows burning at 4 to 6 inches from the surface; a distinctive powder deposit is created at a range from 10 to 12 inches, while dispersed grains of powder may be found even when the weapon is fired at a distance of up to 3 feet.[69] The absence or presence of powder residues might be an important factor in assessing whether a shooting was a criminal homicide or a suicide.[70] Additionally, even though there is no apparent presence of powder residues, the victim's clothing should be processed by the laboratory. Finally, by assessing the amount of dust or other debris inside the barrel of a seized weapon, the expert can come to a conclusion with respect to how recently the weapon was fired.

COLLECTING FIREARMS EVIDENCE

A cardinal rule in handling weapons at the scene of a crime is that they should never be picked up or moved until they have been photographed and measurements made for the crime scene sketch. As in the case of many rules for criminal investigations, there are several exceptions to this. First, if the weapon is found outdoors and there is any likelihood that inclement weather may destroy the possibility of obtaining latent fingerprints, it should be immediately removed to a protected area. Second, at the scenes of aggravated assaults and murders, feelings run high and there is a danger that an emotionally charged person may suddenly attempt to pick up the weapon and shoot another party. Third, there may be some compelling safety need, such as uncocking the weapon. Ordinarily, however, the first handling of a weapon should be to process it for fingerprints. The investigator must pick up a firearm with great care, despite familiarity with weapons, as many weapons have individual peculiarities that may produce an accidental discharge through careless or indiscriminate handling.

In no case should a pencil or similar object be placed into the barrel of the gun to pick it up; this can dislodge evidence that may be in the barrel,

Figure 4–46
Breach-Face Markings

Photomicrograph of the breach-face markings on two Winchester 9-mm cartridge cases that were recovered at different locations at the scene of a murder. The victim was scheduled to testify in the trial of a drug dealer the next day. The murder is unsolved and under active investigation.

(Courtesy Tennessee Bureau of Investigation)

such as tissue, blood, hair, or other trace evidence, and it can contaminate the barrel, thereby confusing the laboratory examiner. The proper method of packaging a handgun—once unloaded—is to suspend it in a small box by a ring that passes through the trigger guard. As bullets, cartridge cases, and related firearms evidence are gathered, they should be packaged separately. The practice of putting a handgun in a coat or pants pocket until transferred to an evidence envelope at some later time is to be strictly avoided.

MARKING FIREARMS EVIDENCE

When bullets, fragments, cartridges, and live ammunition are collected, they should be packed

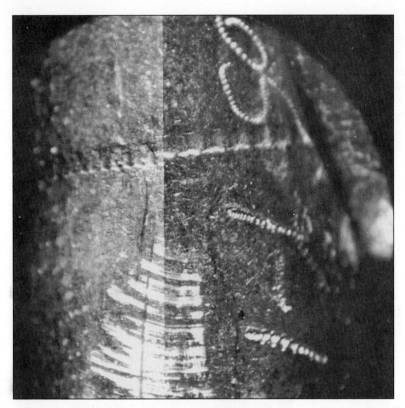

Figure 4–47
Striations Made by Slide Action

Photomicrograph of striated marks made on questioned and known cartridge cases. The marks were made as a slide acted on the mouths of cartridge cases in a Colt .45-caliber semiautomatic pistol.

(Courtesy Regional Criminalistics Laboratory, Metropolitan Kansas City, Missouri)

tightly in cotton or soft paper and sealed in a plastic tube or small box.[71] By doing so, the possibility of damage to such evidence is avoided, trace evidence is not disturbed, and the possibility of destroying possible latent fingerprints is reduced, as is potential contamination of the evidence.[72] If a bullet passes through a person and is lying loose on the floor, it can be picked up by sliding a clean sheet of white paper under it and then packaged in the normal way. Shotgun pellets and wads should be gathered in the manner just described for bullets.[73] Once the evidence is placed into an appropriate container, it should be sealed with tape and the necessary identifying information should be written on the tape.

Guns themselves should be marked in a place that is a permanent part of the weapon, for example, on the frame if the weapon is an automatic or semiautomatic; the clip or magazine should also be marked. Care should be taken in marking firearms to avoid unnecessary defacement. There are certain permanent places that can be marked unobtrusively: inside the frame of a revolver that has been broken open; on the magazine of a pump-action gun, after moving the slide to the rear; and inside the handle of semiautomatic pistols. Additionally, a string tag, marked with the essential information, should be attached to a firearm.

In all cases involving firearms, the number of shells or rounds remaining in a weapon should be noted, as should any misfeeds or other blockages to the proper functioning of the gun. Additionally, with revolvers there is the possibility of some mixture of unfired bullets, cartridge cases of fired rounds, and empty chambers. The numbers and locations of all these should be noted. The proper procedure is to designate the chamber aligned with the barrel as "1" and to continue numbering the chambers in a clockwise manner until all of them are accounted for. Afterward, each round should be placed in a rigid container.

TOOL MARKS

For forensic purposes, a *tool mark* is any impression, cut, gouge, or abrasion made when a tool comes into contact with another object. Most often tool marks are found at the scenes of burglaries because the perpetrators have forced their way into a building and then forced open such things as locked filing cabinets and safes.[74] To illustrate, a pry bar may be used to force a door open, leaving an indented impression of the tool action on the doorframe. In this process, the pry bar may also scrape across the door, its hinges, its screws (see Figure 4–48), its edge, or the doorframe, cutting tiny furrows called *striae*.[75] As different types of tools are used in burglaries, other marks of investigative interest may also be produced, such as the action of pliers (see Figure 4–49) or channel locks on a doorknob. As burglars force their way into buildings and their contents, they also break tools. When a broken tool part is recovered at the scene of a burglary, it is possible to align it with a broken tool in the perpetrator's possession, which is called a *fracture match* (see Figure 4–50).

The examination of a tool mark may yield a great deal of useful information, such as the type, size, and action employed when the instrument was operated. For example, a clear impression may suggest the use of a hammer or punch; scrape marks may indicate the use of some flat-bladed tool such as a crowbar or screwdriver; a shearing instrument—where the blades pass one another, as in the case of scissors and tin snips—may be suggested; or a pinching-type tool—where the blades butt against each other, as in wire cutters—may seem to have been used.

Additionally, by examining the manner in which the tool was employed, it is often possible to make a determination with some degree of reliability with respect to the skill of the perpetrator. Perhaps most important in the examination of a tool mark is whether it offers sufficient characteristics to allow for individual identification should a tool be located in a suspect's possession.

Figure 4–48
Screwdriver Marks
Photomicrograph on left depicts microscopic striae left on the head of a woodscrew by a burglar attacking a door. The right side is a known or test impression made by the laboratory examiner using the screwdriver seized in the suspect's custody.

Figure 4–49
Pliar Marks
Photomicrograph on left reveals striae left by a burglar using pliers to attack a doorknob. At right is a test impression made with the suspect's pliers in the laboratory.

Figure 4–50
Fracture Match Tool
Fracture match of claws of hammer, found at the scene of a burglary, with remainder of tool.

In those instances where a tool is found in a suspect's possession, the examination of it may yield foreign deposits, such as paint or metal, which may have either class or individual characteristics. The comparison of the tool with the tool mark may establish whether they have consistent class characteristics and, when sufficient microscopic marks are present, whether there are sufficient individual characteristics to say with certainty that this particular tool made this particular mark.

In collecting evidence of tool marks, every effort should be made to obtain and submit the actual area for direct comparison. Where this is not possible, a cast should be made. There are several good choices for casting tool marks, including a silicone plastic putty, Duplicast. While photographs are useful in establishing the overall location of the mark, they are ordinarily of no value for identification purposes.[76] In no event should the investigator place a tool against a tool mark for size evaluation, as it may lead to accidental cross-contamination or result in the accidental destruction of evidence.

When a tool is to be submitted to the crime laboratory for examination, the actual tool should be submitted; the making of test impressions or cuts is a function of qualified technicians in the laboratory. The importance of this last point is illustrated by the fact that under test conditions in the laboratory it was found that when there was more than a 15-degree difference between the vertical angle at which a screwdriver was actually used and the comparison mark made in the laboratory, an improper finding of no identity from the same tool could result.[77]

QUESTIONED DOCUMENTS

There are numerous illustrations of questioned documents: Pensioners sued a corporation, alleging that $21 million was missing due to forged signatures[78]; a check made payable to the "IRS" can be altered to "MRS" followed by a name for whom the forger has false identification;[79] six "newly discovered" piano sonatas by the famous composer Haydn turned out to be complete forgeries;[80] and counterfeiters have made bogus items such as automobile inspection stickers, coupons, ski-lift tickets, driver's licenses, gift certificates, baseball cards, and car and real estate titles (see Figures 4-51, 4-52, and 4-53).[81]

Loosely defined, a *document* is anything on which a mark is made for the purpose of transmitting a message. A disputed or questioned document is one whose source or authenticity is in doubt (see Figure 4–54).[82] Examples of questions that document examiners may help answer are these: Is this the deceased's handwriting on the suicide note? Did the suspect handwrite or print this holdup note or harassing letter? Is the signature on this collector's item, credit application, jail release order, or other document genuine? Was the typewriter seized from the suspect's apartment used to prepare this letter?

Because of the important contributions that can be made, investigators must have a basic familiarity with the different types of document examination.

DOCUMENT EXAMININATION

Handwriting and Handprinting Examinations
Because handwriting identification is based on the characteristics found in a person's normal writing,

Figure 4–51
A Counterfeit Marriage License

Note the differences between the "M" in "Robert M. Webster" and the "Ms" in "May," "March," and "Minister." Also, notice the differences between the "34" listed as Webster's age and the "3s" and "4s" elsewhere in the document. The differences in these fonts as well as the gaps in the lines under the letters changed, left by whiting out the original entry, indicate a counterfeit document.

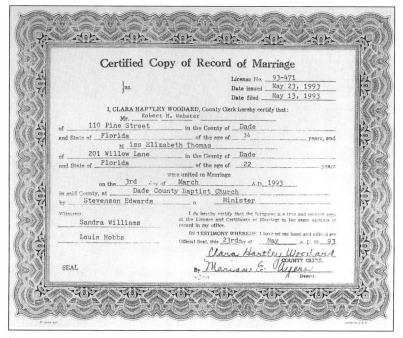

(Courtesy Immigration and Naturalization Service, Forensic Document Laboratory)

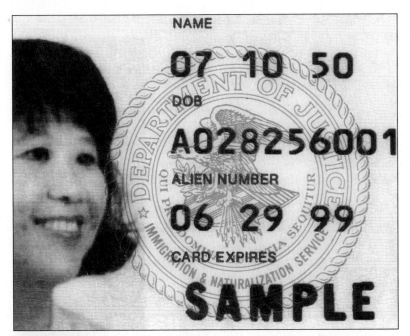

Figure 4-52
A Genuine Alien Registration Card *(top)* and a Counterfeit One *(bottom)*

A comparison of these two photographs illustrates a basic principle: In general, the difference between a genuine and a counterfeit document is found in the quality of printing, especially in the area with the most fine detail. In this figure that area is the INS seal.

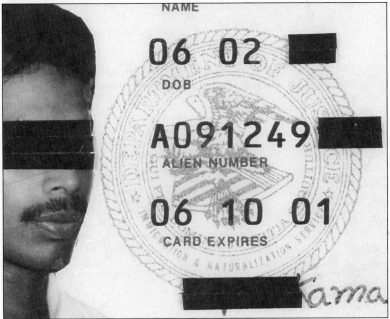

(Courtesy Immigration and Naturalization Service, Forensic Documents Laboratory)

writers of a document can often be positively and reliably identified.[83] However, it is not always possible to reach a definite conclusion. Some of the reasons for inconclusive results are a limited amount of the writing in question and/or an inadequate sample from a known source, disguised handwriting, and insufficient identifying characteristics. There are three types of forgery:

1. *A traced forgery* is created by tracing over a genuine signature. A forgery of this type can be tied to the original, or master, signature if that original signature can be located.[84]

Figure 4–53
A Counterfeit Social Security Card

Notice the lack of sharpness in areas of fine detail.

(Courtesy Immigration and Naturalization Service, Forensic Documents Laboratory)

2. A *simulated forgery* is produced by the writer who learns to mimic a genuine signature. It may or may not be possible to identify the forger, depending on the extent to which the suspect's normal handwriting characteristics remain in the signature.

3. A *freehand forgery* represents the suspect's normal handwriting, with no attempt to mimic the style of the genuine signature.

In addition, it is possible under certain conditions for offenders to lift an actual signature made with certain types of erasable pens for about 1 hour after the signature was affixed to the paper. The lift is done using a Scotch frosted tape; the tape is then laid back down on the signature block of a contract or other document and photocopied. The signature on the actual document remains intact, and the signature on the forged document looks right. This procedure can be detected by document examiners.

When obtaining a handwriting sample from a known source, such as a suspect, the following guidelines should be followed:

1. Provide the person with the same type of paper and writing instrument as were used in the questioned document.

2. Direct the person to use the same writing style—cursive or printed—as was used in the questioned document, to write the same words, and to execute the same signature.

Figure 4–54
Forged Passport

The original photograph on this Venezuelan passport was removed and the photograph of a different person has been substituted for it. Examine the lower left-hand corner of the person's photograph. A counterfeit stamp was used to mark the substituted photograph. Note that the stamp print is misaligned, the stamp print is much sharper on the substituted photograph, and there are inconsistencies in the thickness of stamp lines where the substituted photograph meets the genuine stamp lines on the passport itself.

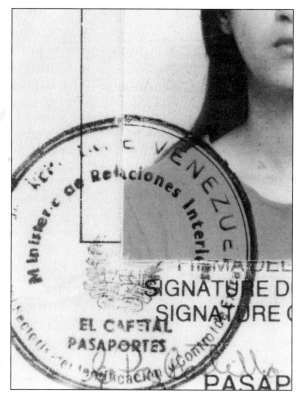

(Courtesy Immigration and Naturalization Service, Forensic Documents Laboratory)

3. Remove each page of writing from the person's sight as soon as it is completed.

4. Provide no instructions as to format, spelling, or punctuation.

5. Where the writing in question is short—such as a forged check—have the person repeat it 10 to 20 times; for longer documents—such as death threats—dictate the entire text word for word and get at least three full copies.

6. In forgery cases, get at least 10 samples of the victim's signature.

7. If the person does not appear to be writing normally, have him or her speed up, slow down, or alter the slant of the writing. Another technique is to have the person provide some writing with the other hand.

8. Obtain samples of nondictated writing from employment records or correspondence.

9. At the end of the session have the writer and a witness initial and date each page.

Photocopier Examinations

This involves splicing two documents together by photocopying them to form a totally new and illegitimate, but legal-appearing, document. This method can be detected by the appearance of faint lines where the documents were joined, as well as by slight variations in font size, typeface, and line spacing. It is possible to link a photocopied document with the machine that produced it if the document whose source is questioned and the samples taken from the machine are made relatively contemporaneously.[85] In collecting samples, the following actions are recommended: (1) Make nine copies of a paper with some writing or typewriting on it; (2) make nine copies of a blank sheet of paper; and (3) place no paper on the glass, close the cover, and make another nine copies. When a questioned photocopy is examined, it may be possible to determine the brand or manufacturer of the photocopier. Among the conditions that can help link a copy to a machine are striations on the glass, distinctive indentation marks on the paper from passing over rollers, and "trash marks"—the spots that can appear on a copied document.[86]

Paper Examinations

This type of examination can yield several different results. It is possible to positively match the torn edges of paper.[87] For example, if a single paper match is found at a crime scene, it can be tied to the stub from which it originated in the matchbook recovered from a suspect. If there is a watermark on paper, the manufacturer can be determined; in addition, some watermarks include information indicating the date the paper was made. Paper can also be examined for indented writing impressions. It is important to realize that indentations not visible to the eye can be made readable by qualified examiners. Investigators should not attempt to develop any page that may have indented writing on

it. The paper should not be folded or handled, and caution must be exercised so that additional indentations are not accidentally created by writing on a page that is on top of the evidence.

Age of Documents

The age of a document is often difficult to establish. It may, however, be possible to determine the earliest date at which a document could have been prepared through examination of watermarks, indented writing, printing, and typewriting.[88] Chemical analysis of the writing ink used may yield some useful information, as inks vary by manufacturer and even production lots.[89] A genuine document could not have been prepared any earlier than the date on which the ink was available. Examiners may also conclude that documents were treated in some manner, such as baking, to make them look older than they actually are.[90] The trash marks produced on copied documents may also be useful in determining the age of a document. By examining months or even years of documents copied and on file in a business, examiners may be able to conclude that a questioned document was produced during a certain time frame on the basis of the similarity between its trash marks and the trash marks of file documents.

Burned or Charred Paper

Illegal gambling operations, like other businesses, must maintain records. In order to prevent these records from falling into the hands of investigators, they may be chemically treated so that they will burn instantly when touched with a lighted cigarette or match in the event of a raid. Burned and charred documents are also encountered in other types of investigations. For example, a person who has committed a simulated forgery on a check may have attempted to burn the pages on which he or she practiced mimicking the genuine signature in order to destroy evidence related to the crime. Also, a kidnapper may have prepared several drafts of a written ransom demand and tried to destroy unused versions of the note by burning them. Entries on such burned and charred evidence may be revealed when examined. The handling of this type of evidence should be kept to an absolute minimum to avoid its crumbling. It is desirable to ship burned and charred evidence to the laboratory in the container in which it was burned, such as an ashtray.[91]

Altered or Obliterated Writing

Many types of documents are easily altered. For example, bank deposit slips commonly have a line "less cash received." A dishonest teller could raise the figure in this line, pocket the difference, and still be in balance. Ways to obliterate an entry include the use of crayons, correction fluid to white it out, ink, and mechanical or chemical erasures. All of these are detectable under laboratory examination by such means as alternative light sources.

Writing Instruments

It is possible to compare the ink in which a message involved in a crime was written with the ink in a pen recovered from a suspect. This type of examination cannot identify a specific pen but can determine whether or not the inks are of the same formulation.[92]

Mechanical-Impression Examination

A questioned document that is produced by mechanical impression can be compared with genuine printed documents to determine if it is counterfeit.[93] Two or more printed documents can be associated with the same printing source. It is possible to match a printed document with the source printing paraphernalia, such as negatives and plates. The examination of a checkwriter impression can determine the brand of the checkwriter that produced it, and this type of impression can then be matched with the individual checkwriter that produced it. If it is not possible to send a checkwriter to the laboratory for examination, make at least five copies of the questioned numbers and submit these instead. Both rubber stamps and embossers or seal impressions can be matched with the instruments that produced them. When seized as evidence, an embosser or seal or a rubber stamp should be sent to the laboratory for testing without cleaning or altering it in any way.

Typewriting

The first commercially successful typewriter was made by Remington in 1873, and there has been a slow but steady improvement in that technology since then. Despite the availability of personal computers, many agencies and people prefer or continue to have a need for a typewriter. The possible brands or manufacturers may be determined from a typewritten document. It is also possible to identify the individual typewriter that produced a questioned document. The following are guidelines investigators should follow in collecting this type of evidence:

1. The ribbon should be removed and submitted to the laboratory, as the text of the material in question may be on it; the correction tape should also be included.
2. All samples of printing should be prepared with a fresh ribbon.
3. The entire text of the questioned document should be reproduced unless it is unusually long, in which case a representative sample will be sufficient.
4. After the ribbon is removed or the machine is placed in the stencil position, samples of each character should be obtained by typing through carbon paper onto a piece of white bond paper.
5. It is usually not necessary to submit the machine to the laboratory, although the document examiner may subsequently request it if comparisons of the questioned and known documents reveal questions about matters such as alignment, which can be satisfactorily determined only by examining the machine itself.
6. It must be determined when the machine was last cleaned, maintained, and repaired, as all of these could affect the examiner's conclusion. Whenever possible, the machine should be maintained in its current condition until the document examiner submits his or her findings in the event that the machine may have to be sent to the laboratory.
7. All specimens obtained by the investigator should include the machine's make, model, and serial number in addition to the investigator's usual identifying marks.[94]

Computer Printers: Dot-Matrix, Laser, Ink-Jet, and Wax-Jet

Instead of completing an image in one single stroke, a dot-matrix printer produces an image that is built up by individual dots.[95] These dots are made by pins; in 9-pin printers the dots are more apparent, while in 24-pin printers they are less so. Some dot-matrix printers have a color-ribbon option. Laser printers also produce dots; the laser projects a light against a spinning mirror, which flashes light to a rotating drum; the printing toner adheres electrostatically to the charged areas of the drum and is then fused to the paper, creating characters.[96] Color laser printers are also available. Dot-matrix printers are quickly losing market share to ink-jet printers, which can print in multiple colors. Ink-jet printers approach, but fall short of, laser quality; basically, ink jets fire droplets of ink at a page to make the dots that form the characters. Although there is no generally accepted name for printers that melt wax and then spray it on paper, they are often called wax jets; these are high-end printers that produce outstanding color.

Because computer technology requires such precision in producing parts, making useful distinctions for purposes of document examination is very difficult and simply is not happening on a routine basis in laboratories. Neither the brand nor the manufacturer of a dot-matrix printer can be determined from examining a computer-printed page. In unusual circumstances it may be possible to identify a particular dot-matrix printer as having produced the writing on a page. When this does occur, the conclusion can be reached because of some characteristic defects in the pins making the dots.[97] The same conclusions may be reached with laser printers in unusual cases due to defects on the drum.[98] Based on present conditions and technologies, the likelihood of an examiner's concluding that a specific printer of any type is the source of a particular document is remote.

There are, however, indirect ways of associating a questioned computer document with particular locations. For example, the message may have been saved to a computer's hard disk or to a floppy disk. Collecting computer-related evidence is covered more fully in Chapter 18, Computer Crime.

Questions

1. Define and give two examples of *class-characteristics* and *individual-characteristic* evidence.
2. What is the proper method of collecting soil evidence?
3. What is the difference between shoeprints and shoe impressions?
4. Describe the steps involved in using dental stone to cast a shoe impression in soil.
5. How is Snow Print Wax used?
6. What are the important considerations in collecting and packaging glass evidence?
7. How are friction ridges and fingerprints related?
8. What are the three broad categories of latent fingerprints?
9. How do you develop latent fingerprints with a traditional dust and brush?
10. How would you use a magnetic applicator?
11. What are dual-use powders?
12. Can you describe the use of at least five of the following: Amido black, crystal violet, iodine, ninhydrin, DFO, SPR, rhodamine 6G, and basic yellow 40?
13. What is the superglue fuming process?
14. What advantage does a digital camera offer?
15. What are antemortem and postmortem records?
16. Identify and discuss the two methods of obtaining dental evidence from a suspect.
17. Name seven determinations that can be made from the examination of hair evidence.
18. What is Hemident, and why is it called a presumptive or preliminary field test?
19. What is Duplicast?
20. Define *document*.
21. What are the three types of forgery, and how are they different?
22. Discuss the proper procedure for collecting samples from a photocopier.

Notes

1. Federal Bureau of Investigation, *Handbook of Forensic Science* (Washington, D.C.: Government Printing Office, 1984), p. 2.

2. Ibid.

3. Federal Bureau of Investigation, *Handbook of Forensic Science* (Washington, D.C.: Government Printing Office, 1978), p. 2.

4. Raymond C. Murray and John C. F. Tedrow, *Forensic Geology* (New Brunswick, N.J.: Rutgers University Press, 1975), p. 22.

5. Murray and Tedrow, *Forensic Geology,* pp. 17–19.

6. Ibid., p. 23.

7. Ibid., p. 25.

8. Richard H. Fox and Carl L. Cunningham, *Crime Scene Search and Physical Evidence Handbook* (Washington, D.C.: Government Printing Office, 1985), p. 80.

9. Ibid., p. 81.

10. Ibid.

11. Crime Laboratory Division, *Criminal Investigation and Physical Evidence Handbook* (Madison: State of Wisconsin, 1969), p. 105.

12. Bruce Wayne Hall, "The Forensic Utility of Soil," *FBI Law Enforcement Bulletin,* September 1993, Vol. 62, No. 9, pp. 16, 17.

13. Murray and Tedrow, *Forensic Geology,* p. 26.

14. Arne Svensson and Otto Wendel, *Techniques of Crime Scene Investigation* (New York: American Elsevier, 1965), p. 75. The information on preserving dust and residue prints is drawn from the Federal Bureau of Investigation, *Handbook of Forensic Science* (Washington, D.C.: Government Printing Office, 1992), pp. 86-87.

15. Unless otherwise indicated, the information on preserving shoe impressions is drawn from FBI, *Handbook on Forensic Science,* 1992, pp. 84–86.

16. Ibid., p. 85.

17. Barry A. J. Fisher, *Techniques of Crime Scene Investigation* (New York: Elsevier Science Publishing, 1992), p. 248.

18. Ibid., p. 249.

19. Paul L. Kirk, *Crime Investigation* (New York: Interscience, 1960), p. 257.

20. Fisher, *Techniques of Crime Scene Investigation,* pp. 175-176.

21. Ibid., p. 175.

22. Crime Laboratory Division, *Criminal Investigation and Physical Evidence Handbook,* p. 110.

23. Ibid., p. 11.

24. Zug Standing Bear, "Glass Examinations in Old and New Reflections," a paper presented at the 1983 meeting of the American Academy of Forensic Sciences.

25. Fox and Cunningham, *Crime Scene Search and Physical Evidence Handbook,* p. 79.

26. Svensson and Wendel, *Techniques of Crime Scene Investigation,* p. 165.

27. The thoughts in this paragraph are drawn from Fisher, *Techniques of Crime Scene Investigation,* p. 90.

28. Although the fingerprints of twins may have a high degree of similarity, variations still occur that permit their differentiation. See C. H. Lin, J. H. Liu, J. W. Osterburg, and J. D. Nicol, "Fingerprint Comparison I: Similarity of Fingerprints," *Journal of Forensic Sciences,* 1982, Vol. 27, No. 2, pp. 290–304.

29. Fisher, *Techniques of Crime Scene Investigation,* pp. 99–101.

30. Ibid., p. 115.

31. A. J. Brooks, "The Search for Latent Prints When an Offender Wears Gloves," *Fingerprint and Identification Magazine,* 1972, Vol. 53, No. 12, pp. 3–7, 15–16.

32. Fisher, *Techniques of Crime Scene Investigation,* p. 104.

33. J. E. Watkin and A. H. Misner, "Fluorescence and Crime Scenes in the 90s," *The RCMP Gazette,* 1990, Vol. 52, No. 9, p. 1.

34. James Osterburg and Richard H. Ward, *Criminal Investigation* (Cincinnati, Ohio: Anderson Publishing Company, 1992), p. 109. For general information on the subject, see S. Clark, "Chemical-Detection of Latent Fingerprints," *Journal of Chemical Education,* July 1993, Vol. 70, No. 7, pp. 593–595.

35. Richard Saferstein, *Criminalistics,* 4th ed. (Englewood Cliffs, N.J.: Prentice-Hall, 1990), p. 378.

36. Osterberg and Ward, *Criminal Investigation,* p. 110.

37. Ivan Ross Futrell, "Hidden Evidence: Latent Prints on Human Skin," *FBI Law Enforcement Bulletin,* April 1996, pp. 21–24. This section is drawn from that source.

38. The information about digital cameras is drawn from George Reis's excellent "Digital Cameras Raid California Crime Scenes," *Photo Electronic Imaging,* October 1993, pp. 22–27.

39. The author of this section on dental evidence is Dr. Richard R. Souviron, Chief Forensic Odontologist, Dade County Medical Examiner Department, One Bob Hope Road, Miami, Florida 33136-1133, (305/545-2400). Dr. Souviron submitted more material than could be used in a book of this type. His portion of the manuscript was, therefore, subject to editing. Any editing that may have unintentionally changed the meaning intended by him is the responsibility of the present authors.

40. FBI, *Handbook of Forensic Science*, 1992, p. 37. Also see H. Pfitzinger, B. Ludes, and P. Mangin, "Sex Determination of Forensic Samples," *International Journal of Legal Medicine*, 1993, Vol. 105, No. 4, pp. 213–216.

41. FBI, *Handbook of Forensic Science*, 1992, p. 37.

42. J. Andrasko and B. Stocklassa, "Shampoo Residue Profiles in Human Head Hair," *Journal of Forensic Sciences*, May 1990, Vol. 35, No. 3, pp. 569–579.

43. N. Tanada et al., "Identification of Human Hair Stained with Oxidation Hair Dyes by Gas Chromatographic–Mass Spectrometric Analysis," *Forensic Science International*, December 1991, Vol. 52, No. 1, pp. 5–11.

44. Tom Mieczkowski et al., *Testing Hair for Illicit Drug Use* (Washington, D.C.: National Institute of Justice, U.S. Department of Justice, 1993).

45. Fox and Cunningham, *Crime Scene Search and Physical Evidence Handbook*, pp. 75–76.

46. The procedures for gathering hair were taken from Fox and Cunningham, *Crime Scene Search and Physical Evidence Handbook*, p. 77.

47. Svensson and Wendel, *Techniques of Crime Scene Investigation*, p. 117.

48. In addition to the specific citations, a number of sources were generally useful in preparing this section. See R. O. Arthur, *The Scientific Investigator* (Springfield, Ill.: Charles C. Thomas, 1970), pp. 40–49; Svensson and Wendel, *Techniques of Crime Scene Investigation*, pp. 118–120; and Fox and Cunningham, *Crime Scene Search and Physical Evidence Handbook*, p. 62.

49. Fox and Cunningham, *Crime Scene Search and Physical Evidence Handbook*, p. 62.

50. Svensson and Wendel, *Techniques of Crime Scene Investigation*, p. 119.

51. Fox and Cunningham, *Crime Scene Search and Physical Evidence Handbook*, p. 63.

52. Svensson and Wendel, *Techniques of Crime Scene Investigation*, p. 120.

53. Ibid., pp. 127-129. Also see William G. Eckert and Stuart H. James, *Interpretation of Bloodstain Evidence at Crime Scenes* (New York: Elsevier, 1989).

54. M. Cox, "Effect of Fabric Washing on the Presumptive Identification of Bloodstains," *Journal of Forensic Sciences*, November 1990, Vol. 35, No. 6, pp. 1335–1341.

55. Arthur, *The Scientific Investigator*, pp. 50–51.

56. Crime Laboratory Division, *Criminal Investigation and Physical Evidence Handbook*, p. 16.

57. Fox and Cunningham, *Crime Scene Search and Physical Evidence Handbook*, p. 65.

58. See Fred E. Inbau et al., *Scientific Police Investigation* (New York: Chilton Books, 1972), p. 125; Svensson and Wendel, *Techniques of Crime Scene Investigation*, pp. 134-140; William W. Turner, ed., *Criminalistics* (San Francisco: Bancroft-Whitney, 1965), pp. 319–348.

59. FBI, *Handbook of Forensic Science*, 1992, pp. 32, 34.

60. Ibid., p. 32.

61. J. Andrasko, "Forensic Analysis of Lipsticks," *Forensic Science International*, 1981, Vol. 17, No. 3, pp. 235–251.

62. Mary Lee Schnuth, "Focus on Forensics: Lip Prints," *FBI Law Enforcement Bulletin*, November 1992, Vol. 61, No. 11, pp. 18–19.

63. Svensson and Wendel, *Techniques of Crime Scene Investigation*, p. 210. Also see V. "Jack" Krema, *The Identification and Registration of Firearms* (Springfield, Ill.: Charles C. Thomas, 1971).

64. Svensson and Wendel, *Techniques of Crime Scene Investigation*, pp. 212-213. See also Frederick C. Kerr and Walter F. Rowe, "Effects of Range, Caliber, Barrel Length, and Rifling on Pellet Patterns," *Journal of Forensic Sciences*, 1985, Vol. 30, No. 2, pp. 405–419. Kerr and Rowe note that shotgun ammunition for .22-caliber handguns and rifles, and .38- and .44-caliber magnum handguns is also available. What appear to be wounds inflicted by a long shotgun may have been inflicted by a handgun, although experienced homicide investigators could tell the difference by visual inspection of the wounds.

65. O. C. Smith, L. Jantz, H. E. Berryman, and S. A. Symes, "Effects of Human Decomposition on Striations," *Journal of Forensic Sciences*, 1993, Vol. 38, No. 3, pp. 593-598.

66. This was reported in a 1972 case. See R. Thomas, "Contribution to the Identification of Smooth Bore Firearms," *International Criminal Police Review*, 1974, Vol. 28, No. 280, pp. 190-193.

67. The material in this section is drawn from Fox and Cunningham, *Crime Scene Search and Physical Evidence Handbook,* p. 91.

68. The firing-pin impression may be found at different places due to secondary impacts. See Basalo J. Martiney, "Study of Spent Cartridge Cases," *International Criminal Police Review,* 1973, Vol. 28, No. 270, pp. 220–222.

69. Fisher, *Techniques of Crime Scene Investigation,* p. 457.

70. There are some unique exceptions to determining proximity by gunpowder residues. At one time a compressed-air explosive-propellant .22 caliber was commercially available and used caseless ammunition; as no nitrates were present in the discharge residues, this method was voided. See H. L. MacDonell and V. J. Fusco, "An Unusual Firearm Suicide Case," *Canadian Society of Forensic Science Journal,* 1975, Vol. 8, No. 2, pp. 53–55.

71. FBI, *Handbook of Forensic Science,* 1992, p. 107.

72. Crime Laboratory Division, *Criminal Investigation and Physical Evidence Handbook,* p. 154.

73. Ibid., p. 155.

74. Saferstein, *Criminalistics,* p. 406.

75. FBI, *Handbook of Forensic Science,* 1984, p. 60.

76. Ibid., p. 61.

77. H. S. Maheshwari, "Influence of Vertical Angle of a Tool on Its Tool Mark," *Forensic Science International,* 1981, Vol. 18, No. 1, pp. 5–12.

78. Michael Davis, "Pensioners Suing Texas Gas Claim Signatures Faked," *Houston Post,* May 8, 1994, p. D1.

79. "Tax Report: Warning," *The Wall Street Journal,* May 25, 1994, p. A1. Reprinted by permission of Dow Jones, Inc., via Copyright Clearance Center, Inc. © (1994) Dow Jones and Company, Inc. All Rights Reserved Worldwide.

80. Michael Beckerman, "All Right, So Maybe Haydn Didn't Write Them. So What?" *New York Times,* May 15, 1994, p. 33.

81. See Ethan Michaeli, "Cops Put End to Fake ID Operation," *Chicago Defender,* January 28, 1993, p. 3; "Business Bulletin: Cunning Copiers," *Wall Street Journal,* December 31, 1992, p. A1; Alexandra Peers, "Your Money Matters: Forgeries Are Coming to Bat More Often as Sports Memorabilia Prices Hit Homer," *Wall Street Journal,* August 14, 1992, p. C1; Beth Potter, "2 Brothers Arrested in Lift-Ticket Forgeries," *Denver Post,* February 20, 1992, p. B1; Michael A. Smith, "Bogus Auto Inspection Stickers Increase," *Houston Post,* January 3, 1992, p. A14; Peter Mantius, "High-Tech Forgeries Easy, Hard to Detect," *Atlanta Journal and Constitution,* November 26, 1993, p. D8.

82. Saferstein, *Criminalistics,* p. 417.

83. Unless otherwise noted, the information in this section is from FBI, *Handbook of Forensic Science,* 1992, pp. 75–76.

84. See S. C. Leung, H. T. Fung, Y. S. Cheng, and N. L. Poon, "Forgery. 1 Simulation," *Journal of Forensic Sciences,* March 1993, Vol. 38, No. 2, pp. 402–412.

85. Unless otherwise noted, the information in this section is from FBI, *Handbook of Forensic Science,* 1992, p. 77.

86. F. J. Gerhart, "Identification of Photocopiers from Fusing Roller Defects," *Journal of Forensic Sciences,* January 1992, Vol. 37, No. 1, pp. 130-139.

87. Unless otherwise noted, the information in this section is from FBI, *Handbook of Forensic Science,* 1992, p. 79.

88. Ibid., p. 78.

89. A. Lofgren and J. Andrasko, "HPLC Analysis of Printing Inks," *Journal of Forensic Sciences,* May 1993, Vol. 38, No. 5, pp. 1151–1160.

90. L. F. Stewart, "Artificial Aging of Documents," *Journal of Forensic Sciences,* February 1982, Vol. 27, No. 2, pp. 450–453.

91. FBI, *Handbook of Forensic Science,* 1992, p. 79.

92. Ibid., pp. 78-79.

93. Ibid., pp. 77-78.

94. Ibid., pp. 76-77.

95. David Allen, *The Scientific Examination of Documents: Methods and Techniques* (New York: Wiley, 1989), p. 84.

96. Alfred Poor, "Resolution Game: What's in a Dot?" *PC Magazine,* November 22, 1994, Vol. 13, No. 20, p. 128.

97. J. A. Blanco, "Identifying Documents Printed by Dot Matrix Computer Printers," *Journal of Forensic Sciences,* April 1993, Vol. 38, No. 1, pp. 35–47.

98. M. W. Arbouine and S. P. Day, "The Use of Drum Defects to Link Laser-Printed Documents to Individual Laser Printers," *Journal of the Forensic Science Society,* April-June 1994, Vol. 34, No. 2, pp. 99–104.

F I V E

Interviews

CHAPTER OUTLINE

Witnesses: Motivations and Perceptions 124
Reliability of Eyewitness Identification 126
Hypnosis as an Investigative Tool 128
Qualifications of the Interviewer 130
Time, Place, and Setting of the Interview 130
Interviewing: Processes and Techniques 132
Documenting the Interview 135
Questions 137
Notes 137

INTRODUCTION

The business of the police is people. Every facet of police work is concerned with the problems of people. The job of the criminal investigator is no exception. People and the information they supply help accomplish investigative tasks; collecting information is the key investigative task of police work. Roughly 90 percent of an investigator's activity involves gathering, sorting, compiling, and evaluating information. The investigator cannot function without information, and information cannot be obtained without help from people.

Interviewing is both an art and a skill that must be cultivated and practiced. Not all people who possess information needed by the investigator are willing to share it. The successful interviewer must fully understand the techniques of interviewing and have the ability to evaluate the psychological reasons why people are willing or reluctant to impart information. The interviewer-investigator's own capabilities and limitations must be recognized. Personality and the manner in which interpersonal communications are handled can greatly influence the quality and quantity of information obtained. Above all, the successful interviewer, like the successful investigator, must have an insatiable curiosity.

Interviews are conducted in criminal cases for the purpose of gathering information from people who have or may have knowledge needed in the investigation. The information may come from a victim or from a person who has no other relationship to the criminal activity other than being where he or she was. But interviewing is not a haphazard process; it is a planned converstion with a specific goal.

The job of the investigator-interviewer is to extract from the witness information actually perceived through one or more of the witness's five senses—sight, hearing, smell, taste, and touch. In any given case, any or all of a witness's senses may be involved. For example, in a case involving a drug-related killing, a witness may see the perpetrator pull the trigger, hear the victim scream, smell the pungent odor of marijuana burning, taste the white powdery substance later identified as heroin, and touch the victim to feel for a pulse.

Because witnesses report perceptions based on their own interests, priorities, and biases, extracting information from witnesses is not as easy as it may first appear. Investigators must always be sensitive to any and all psychological influences and motivations affecting witness perceptions, the specifics of which are discussed in the next section.

At the outset of the interview, the person to be interviewed must satisfy three requirements of being a witness: presence, consciousness, and attentiveness to what was happening.[1] Presence and consciousness are relatively easy to establish in the interview process; attentiveness is more difficult. Yet all three elements are important to establishing the accuracy of a witness's perception.

WITNESSES: MOTIVATIONS AND PERCEPTIONS

There are many types of witnesses, and each has different motivations and perceptions that influence his or her responses during an interview. Those motivations and perceptions may be based on either conscious choices or subconscious stimuli. The interviewer must learn to recognize, overcome, and compensate for these factors.

There is no way to categorize all personalities, attitudes, and other character traits. The variables are too numerous and individualized; the combinations are as complex as the human mind. Nevertheless, there are some basic groupings that can be mentioned:

- Some witnesses may be honest and cooperative and desire to impart information in their possession to the investigator. Despite these admirable qualities, however, the information may still be affected by other factors that influence all witnesses, such as age, physical characteristics, and emotions. It may be wise in

most circumstances to interview this type of witness first to obtain basic information which can then be compared with later-acquired stories.
- Some witnesses may desire not to give any information in an interview regardless of what they may know. Some of these witnesses simply may not want to get involved, others may fear any contact with a law enforcement agency, some may not understand the significance of any information they may have, and others may not want to do anything that would aide the police.
- Some witnesses may be reluctant or suspicious of the motives of the interviewer until such time as a rapport can be established and the investigator can assure the witness of his or her good intentions.

Because there are some witnesses who may be deceitful and provide incorrect information, it is a basic principle that an investigator should never take a witness's explanation totally at face value, without obtaining other supporting information or evidence.

There may be other barriers which must be overcome in order to successfully interview someone who has knowledge of the circumstances under which a crime was committed. Language barriers, which may not initially be recognized as being significant, may prevent the interviewer from obtaining any useful information; on the other hand, some people may be so talkative and provide so much information that their motives should be questioned, along with the information they provide. A potential witness who may be under the influence of alcohol or drugs may or may not have information that could be used at trial, but the condition of the witness is a major factor to be considered in assessing the value of any information obtained.

In evaluating information provided by juveniles, consideration needs to be given not only to chronological age but also to the level of schooling. In preschool juveniles, generally under 5 or 6 years of age, verbal ability is still being developed as the primary means of communication and recall ability tends to be underdeveloped. Hence, accounts of an event may be rambling and disjointed as well as accompanied by poor distinction between relevant and irrelevant data and by a limited ability to comprehend abstract concepts. A child at this age generally can focus only on one thought at a time and cannot combine thoughts into an integrated whole. The child may have a short attention span, occasional problems in differentiating between what was seen and what was heard, and difficulty distinguishing between fact and fantasy.

Verbal ability improves with the growth of vocabulary and is strongly influenced by peer groups. These are, of course, products (or by-products) of schooling, affecting juveniles between 6 and 18 years of age. Abstract concepts are learned through trial-and-error evaluations rather than an understanding of cause-and-effect relationships. Recall ability improves with age and maturity but develops differently for males and females. For example, males can recall the make and model of an automobile more accurately, while females can generally recall colors and clothing more accurately. (For a more detailed discussion of interviewing children, see Chapter 12, Crimes against Children.)

Because the witness's information also must be evaluated in light of its potential value in court, the interviewer must evaluate the witness's competency and credibility. (These concepts are treated in more detail in Chapter 23, The Rules of Evidence.)

COMPETENCY OF A WITNESS

Competency describes a witness's personal qualifications to testify in court. It must be determined before he or she is permitted to give any testimony. The witness's personal qualifications depend on circumstances that affect his or her legal ability to function as a sworn witness in court. Competency has nothing to do with the believability of a witness's information.

Among the factors an investigator must evaluate in determining the competency of a witness are age, level of intelligence, mental state, relationship to individuals involved in the case, and background characteristics that might preclude the testimony of the witness from being heard in court. For example, in many jurisdictions, a young child cannot be a witness unless it can be shown that the child knows the difference between truth and imagination and understands the importance of telling the truth. Chronological age is not the determining factor. Similarly, any person whose intelligence or mental state prevents him or her from understanding the obligation of telling the truth is not permitted to testify, regardless of the information he or she may possess.

Relationships among individuals involved in a case may also affect a witness's competency. Husbands and wives need not testify against each other, nor may attorneys testify against clients, doctors against patients, or ministers against penitents. Privileges vary by state (see Chapter 23, The Rules of Evidence). Background characteristics also may preclude a witness's testimony from being accepted in court. For example, some state laws forbid a convicted perjurer from testifying in court.

Possibilities like those described in the preceding paragraphs mean that the investigator must learn as much as possible about the witness before and during the interview.

CREDIBILITY

Credibility is distinguished from competency in that the latter is based on the assumption that a witness is qualified and will be permitted to testify.

Credibility relates to that quality of a witness that renders his or her testimony worthy of belief. Credibility in this sense is the same as weight or believability. The credibility of a witness is established in terms of presence, consciousness, and attentiveness during the interviewing process. An investigator must examine each of these requirements carefully and in detail. Among the questions to which the interviewer must receive satisfactory answers in evaluating the credibility of a witness are:

- Was the witness conscious at the time of the event?
- Was the witness under the influence of alcohol or drugs?
- How did the witness happen to be in a position of seeing, hearing, or otherwise perceiving the crime?
- Where was the witness coming from or going to?
- What was the witness doing at the exact moment that the crime occurred?
- What else was going on at the time that might have distracted the witness's attention?

The rules of evidence, which guide the admissibility and use of witnesses and their testimony in court, also guide the impeachment or attack by the opposing side on cross-examination of a witness's testimony (see Chapter 24, The Investigator as Witness). The investigator-interviewer must be aware of these factors to prevent the witnesses who appear for the state from being impeached. To do this, the investigator must ascertain the truth of the following:

- Does the witness have any particular bias, prejudice, or personal interest in the case?
- Does the witness have any physical or mental impairments that may affect his or her ability to observe, recollect, or recount the events? (Does the witness normally wear glasses? Was the witness wearing them at the time? Does the witness have a hearing problem?)
- What physical conditions, such as weather, lighting, and visibility, existed at the crime scene?
- What is the witness's reputation for being a truthful person?

The effective interviewer cannot accept any witness's account at face value. The interviewer must question and requestion, check and recheck. The investigator must recognize and gauge the effects that physical and emotional characteristics, external influences, and attitudinal and behavioral factors have on the witness's perception and on the reliability of the information possessed.

RELIABILITY OF EYEWITNESS IDENTIFICATION

Information provided by eyewitnesses to a criminal event is relied on heavily by both the police and courts in the investigative and adjudication stages of our system of justice,[2] yet research indicates that eyewitness testimony may be unreliable:[3]

> Eyewitness identification and description is regarded as the most unreliable form of evidence and causes more miscarriages of justice than any other method of proof.[4]

> Research and courtroom experience provide ample evidence that an eyewitness to a crime is being asked to be something and do something that a normal human being was not created to be or do. Human perception is sloppy and uneven.[5]

> Existing research does not permit precise conclusions about the overall accuracy of the eyewitness identifications that are a common feature of criminal prosecutions, but research does lead us to conclude that identification errors are not infrequent.[6]

Many factors influence an individual's ability to accurately recognize and identify persons and all of them are dependent on the circumstances under which the information is initally perceived and encoded, stored, and retreived.[7] Eyewitness identifications take place in a social context[8] in which the witness's own personality and characteristics along with those of the target observed are as critical as factors relating to the situation or environment in which the action takes place.

The gender, age, expectations, intelligence, race, and facial recognition skills of the witness are factors that individually may or may not influence the eyewitness identification process but collectively or in combination with other variables may likely have a bearing.[9] Facial attractiveness and distinctiveness, disguises, facial transformations, and gender and race of the target (the person identified) are factors likely to influence identification.[10] Situational factors include such things as the presence of a weapon, exposure duration, and significance of the event in relation to all surrounding circumstances.[11]

Thus, human perception and memory are selective and constructive functions, not exact copiers of the event perceived—constructive in that gaps will be filled to produce a logical and complete sequence of events.

> Perception and memory are decision-making processes affected by the totality of a person's abilities, background, attitudes, motives and beliefs, by the environment and the way his recollection is eventually tested. The observer is an active rather than a passive perceiver and recorder; he reaches conclusions on what he has seen by evaluating fragments of information and reconstructing them. He is motivated by a desire to be accurate as he imposes meaning on the overabundance of information that impinges on his senses, but also by a desire to live up to the expectations of other people and to stay in their good graces. The eye, the ear, and other sense organs are, therefore, social organs as well as physical ones.[12]

Loftus also agrees with this theory of eyewitness perception. She notes:

> Studies of memory for sentences and pictures indicate that when we experience an event, we do not simply file a memory, and then on some later occasion retrieve it and read off what we've stored. Rather, at the time of recall or recognition we reconstruct the event, using information from many sources. These include both the original perception of the event and inferences drawn later, after the fact. Over a period of time, information from these sources may integrate, so that a witness becomes unable to say how he knows a specific detail. He has only a single, unified memory.[13]

Experts distinguish a number of factors that limit a person's ability to give a complete account of events or to identify people accurately. The following are among those factors:

- *The significance or insignificance of the event:* When an insignificant event occurs in the presence of an individual, it does not generally motivate the individual to bring fully into play the selective process of attention.

- *The length of the period of observation:* If ample opportunity is not provided for observation, the capability of the memory to record that which is perceived is decreased.

- *Lack of ideal conditions:* As previously noted in this chapter, where ideal conditions for observation are absent, the ability of the witness to perceive details is significantly decreased. Distance, poor lighting, fast movement, or the presence of a crowd may significantly interfere with the efficient working of the attention process.

- *Psychological factors internal to the witness:* A witness under stress at the time of observation may find this to be a major source of unreliability in his or her observations.

- *The physical condition of the witness.*

- *Expectancy:* Research has shown that memory recall and judgment are often based on what psychologists term *expectancy*. This means that an individual perceives things in a manner in which he or she expects them to appear. For example, a right-handed eyewitness to a homicide might, in answer to a question and without positive knowledge, state that the assailant held the gun in his right hand, while a left-handed person might say the opposite. Biases or prejudices are also illustrated by the expectancy theory, as is the classic problem associated with stereotyping.[14]

Research shows significant error connected with similar descriptions by two or more eyewitnesses:

> One might expect that two eyewitnesses—or ten or one hundred—who agree are better than one. Similarity of judgment is a two-edged sword, however; people can agree in error as easily as in truth. A large body of research results demonstrates that an observer can be persuaded to conform to the majority opinion even when the majority is completely wrong.[15]

In one test, people were asked to describe a mock crime they had viewed earlier. They first gave individual responses and then met as a group. The group descriptions were more complete and in greater detail than those reported by individual subjects, but group descriptions also gave rise to significantly more errors as well as an assortment of incorrect and stereotyped details.[16]

Eyewitness identifications take place in a social context in which the eyewitness's conduct can be influenced by expectations and inferences, which in turn can be influenced by the verbal and nonverbal behavior of investigators, the structure of the identification process, and the environment in which the identification takes place.[17] Much research has been conducted of lineups, showups, and photographic identifications, with a vast array of results indicating that such processes, by their nature, are suggestive, irrespective of whether the police intended them to be so or not.[18] For example, taking a victim or witness from one place to another to observe a person who has been arrested may be suggestive enough to produce a false identification. The fact that the police spend time putting together a photographic lineup may suggest that they have identified a perpetrator whose picture will be among those presented, regardless of whether such suggestiveness is intended by the police or not. The police may not even have a suspect.[19]

In summary, the problems associated with eyewitness identification can result in errors. Mistaken identifications of people, things, places, times, events, and other facts can result in miscarriages of justice. In some instances, these errors can be corrected. Figure 5–1 is a case in point.

HYPNOSIS AS AN INVESTIGATIVE TOOL

The use of hypnosis as a means of aiding witnesses in recalling facts buried in the subconscious is often thought to overcome many of the difficulties experienced in seeking accurate human memory. Although hypnosis does have the unique capability to elicit many repressed and forgotten memories from witnesses to and victims of crimes, its use is not without problems. Theories suggesting that the human brain is like a videotape recorder—a machine that stores all experiences accurately and, when the right buttons are pushed, can be made to recall an "exact" copy of a prior event—are seriously challenged through research.[20] Moreover, both legal and scientific questions have been raised surrounding the reliability of hypnotically refreshed memory. The problems tend to focus on hypersuggestibility, hypercompliance, and confabulation.[21]

Hypnosis is often erroneously believed to be a form of sleep. In fact, it is the opposite. It is best described as a state of heightened awareness in

Figure 5–1
Look-Alikes
Mistaken identifications led to the arrests of two innocent men: Lawrence Berson (*left*) for several rapes and George Morales (*right*) for a robbery. Both men were picked out of police lineups by victims of the crimes. Berson was cleared when Richard Carbone (*center*) was arrested and implicated in the rapes. Carbone was convicted. Later he confessed to the robbery, clearing Morales.

Source: *Scientific American,* 1974, Vol. 231, No. 6, Reprinted by permission.

which the subconscious is somewhat surfaced and the conscious is somewhat repressed. In this altered state of consciousness, the subject of hypnosis has a heightened degree of suggestibility, or *hypersuggestibility*. This raises perhaps the greatest concern about the admissibility of hypnosis evidence: The hypnotist has the potential to suggest or mislead the subject into giving false information, whether by design or not.[22] There is virtual agreement among hypnosis experts that this can occur unless extreme caution is exercised. Subjects may come to believe such false information after hypnosis, potentially affecting the truthfulness and reliability of any subsequent testimony given in court. Thus, many states refuse to admit testimony developed under hypnosis on the theory that even the witness may not know the truth after being subjected to suggestive influences while hypnotized.

The technique most frequently used in hypnosis is to suggest to the subject that he or she is reliving the event at issue but is doing so in a detached manner, as if watching it on a mental television screen. This is done to avoid a firsthand reinvolvement in a potentially traumatic experience. Nevertheless, a hypnotist may inadvertently suggest a response. Some studies conducted on suggestibility involve cases in which the subject was encouraged to picture a license plate and describe its numbers when, in fact, the witness never saw the car;[23] a witness was asked to describe a suspect's facial features when, in actuality, those features were not seen;[24] and the subject confessed to a crime he did not commit.[25]

Hypercompliance, closely related to hypersuggestibility, is a desire on the part of the hypnotized subject to please the hypnotist or others who have supported the hypnosis effort. Thus, instead of refreshing actual memory, there may be a tendency on the part of the hypnotized subject to provide information or "facts" that are designed to please the listener rather than reflect the subject's actual memory of the event.[26]

The third major area of concern about reliability of hypnotically enhanced memory is referred to as *confabulation*. This is a process of artificially filling in the gaps when the actual memory is not as complete as the subject desires it to be. Thus, a witness who admits to being uncertain of his or her recollection when questioned about a matter prior to

hypnosis may, in fact, become thoroughly convinced of the accuracy of his or her recollections after hypnosis, even though those recollections may be brought about by hypersuggestibility, hypercompliance, and confabulation, resulting in false memories.[27]

All of these concerns have produced various treatments of the subject of admissibility of hypnotically refreshed testimony by the courts of this country.

The forensic use of hypnosis gained popularity in the 1960s, yet courts addressing the issue of admissibility have continually disagreed on whether such testimony should be admissible and, if so, what standards and guidelines are to be followed. There are a variety of judicial positions on the issue of admissibility among the states and the federal judical circuits that have decided on this matter. In a minority of jurisdictions, hypnotically refreshed testimony is not admissible under any circumstances. Many jurisdictions have allowed the admissibility of prehypnosis testimony as long as that testimony is based upon independent recall rather than soley on the product of a hypnosis session. Posthypnotic evidence is not admissible unless it agrees with the prehypnotic statements given by the witness.

Still another group of jurisdictions allow the admissibility of hypnosis evidence provided there are sufficient safeguards and standards, under the law, to ensure that the hypnotically produced testimony was obtained objectively and without a great deal of suggestivity. As research continues to reveal that suggestivity is highly probable and almost impossible to avoid,[28] the legal position of these jurisdictions is becoming more and more questionable. Some jurisdictions admit posthypnotic testimony and allow juries to weigh the evidence and determine its credibilty.

One of the controversies still in existence is whether a hypnotist should be a mental health professional (preferabley a psychiatrist or psychologist) with special training in the use of hypnosis or a trained law enforcement investigator, also with special training in the use of hypnosis. Those who argue for the latter position assume that the trained investigator will best know what questions need to be asked and can best evaluate the information obtained from hypnosis in the context of an ongoing criminal investigation. On the other hand, mental health professionals believe that law enforcement personnel cannot be trained on how to handle a mental health crisis that may occur during a hypnotic session.

As a consequence of all the research, many law enforcement jurisdictions are resorting to the use of hypnosis only as an investigative tool, without seeking to have the results admissible in court. [29] As an investigative tool, hypnosis has proved to be most effective in many cases and continues to be supported.

QUALIFICATIONS OF THE INTERVIEWER

The effective interviewer must be knowledgeable in the art and science of criminal investigation and know how to use psychology, salesmanship, and dramatics. Persuasiveness and perseverance are essential to success. The interviewer must be emphatic, sympathetic, and objective and must establish rapport with witnesses. A positive, firm approach, an ability to inspire confidence, and knowledge of a broad range of topics of general interest all help establish dominance in an interview:

> Behavior, not words, determines dominance. Good interviewers know that an air of confidence and ease typifies the behavior of truly dominant people; they are inclined to do as they please without asking permission and rarely offend others while doing so. On the other hand, arrogance and pomposity, characteristics often intended to pass for dominance, do not create dominance. They sometimes provide amusement, but more often than not, anger the people subjected to such behavior.[30]

A critical element in the interviewer's success is preparation before an interview. Acquiring as much information about the person to be interviewed as possible should be the investigator's first step. The interviewer also must become familiar with the facts of the case under investigation in order to test the information given by witnesses and to establish a baseline along which to direct the interview.

TIME, PLACE, AND SETTING OF THE INTERVIEW

Police officers conduct interviews in a number of situations. The most common is the on-the-scene interview. Whether it is a routine traffic accident investigation or a major felony case, officers who respond to the scene should, at the earliest possible moment, seek out and identify those individuals who may have knowledge of the event and whose information may contribute to the investigation. This, of course, includes victims and other participants as well as uninvolved witnesses. Once witnesses have been identified, they should be separated from one another and, as much as possible, isolated from other people who may be loitering in the area. This prevents the witnesses from seeing or hearing irrelevant matters that may taint their actual knowledge. All witnesses should be interviewed as soon as practical, while their memory is still fresh, but this rule must be flexible in its application to take into account all circumstances.

The physical circumstances under which the interview takes place can be critical to the value of the information obtained. Immediacy may have to be sacrificed in some instances due to lack of privacy, inconvenience, or physical discomfort of the witness. Conditions that tend to decrease the ability or desire of the witness to give full attention to the interview should be avoided. If such conditions exist, investigators may wisely choose to seek only basic preliminary information at the scene, followed by a more detailed interview at a more convenient time and place (see Figure 5–2).

Although convenience of the witness is important to a successful interview, the interviewer need not relinquish the psychological advantage in selecting the time and place of the interview. It is not a good practice, for example, to rouse a witness from bed in the middle of the night. However, there are certain psychological advantages to questioning a witness at police headquarters rather than in the witness's own home or office. A witness may feel in a better position to control the interview in familiar surroundings. The investigator cannot let

Figure 5–2
Inside Interview
Interview of a witness at police headquarters.

(Courtesy New York City Police Department)

Figure 5–3
Outside Interview
Neighborhood canvassing interview.

(Courtesy New York City Police Department)

this happen; he or she must be fair but always in command of the situation.

After taking into account the factors of immediacy, privacy, convenience, and control, and weighing the importance of each in the context of the total circumstances, it may be best to interview witnesses at their homes or places of business. As a matter of courtesy, the investigator should attempt to make an appointment to ensure convenience, particularly for professionals and businesspeople. Others, such as salespeople, office workers, and laborers, may be interviewed during working hours with approval of their supervisors.

Privacy is of the utmost importance in conducting interviews. Distractions, whether in the home, office, or police station, tend to have an adverse effect on the interview and its results. The interviewer should insist on as much privacy as possible, but the circumstances of on-the-scene interviews often have to be recognized as a fact of life for the investigator, who can only be expected to perform to the best of his or her ability in the given case. Similarly, investigators are often called on to canvass neighborhoods and interview residents. In these instances, investigators often are in no

position to influence the conditions under which the interview takes place. Noisy children, blaring television sets, nosy neighbors, and similar factors must be accepted (see Figure 5–3).

The physical and emotional states of the witnesses are important in conducting or in determining whether to conduct an interview. "Cold, sleepy, hungry, or physically uncomfortable people generally prove to be unsatisfactory witnesses."[31] Similarly, persons suffering noticeable emotional problems can give, at the most, highly questionable information. Most investigators can recognize this state and wisely prefer to wait until the witness becomes lucid before conducting the interview.

Particular caution must be exercised in interviewing juveniles. In many jurisdictions parents must be notified of the purpose of the interview and the nature of the information sought from the juvenile. In other jurisdictions, notification may be recommended but not required. In some instances the presence of the parent during the interview is required or possibly desirable. Even when their presence is required, parents should not be allowed to distract or in any way influence the juvenile's responses. Local law should be consulted.

Reinterviewing witnesses should be avoided if the reinterview is likely to produce nothing beyond the information given in the initial statement. Reinterviewing tends to become less and less convenient for witnesses, even though they may be friendly and cooperative. There may also be a tendency for reinterviewed witnesses to feel that the investigator does not know his or her job or was not prepared during the initial interview. To avoid this problem, the investigator should first tell the witness that the purpose of the interview is not to rehash old information and then explain what new information is being sought. The investigator should ask for the information in a manner that does not elicit a repetition of the previous interview. But investigators should not hesitate to conduct follow-up interviews when necessary, whether because there was lack of skill in obtaining an initial statement, new information has developed, or the time or setting of the initial interview did not elicit the full attention of the witnesses.

INTERVIEWING: PROCESSES AND TECHNIQUES

Regardless of the time, place, or setting of the interview, or ultimately the type of witness or victim interviewed, there exists some standardization in technique. "An interview . . . has a beginning, a middle—its main segment—and an end."[32] The beginning is the warm-up period, the time when the interviewer must establish rapport. The main segment is devoted to acquiring the desired information. The end occurs when the investigator has accomplished certain goals and shows appreciation to the witness.

The investigator must remember that the mission is to gather all relevant information possessed by the witness about a particular occurrence. Regardless of the attitude of a particular witness, the interviewer must establish rapport. The warm-up period allows the interviewer to provide identification, state the purpose of the interview, and put the witness at ease with small talk. Matters of common interest may be discussed, such as children, sports,

military service, or membership in civic organizations. Friendly conversation can convey interest in the witness, get the witness talking, and provide the interviewer with an opportunity to evaluate the witness.

Although topics of mutual interest do not guarantee rapport, the purpose of the warm-up period is to attempt to reduce anxiety on the part of the person being interviewed. Sometimes flattery may also work to accomplish this objective.[33] Now the investigator can determine the type of witness being interviewed, the appropriate techniques and approaches to use, and, in general, the tone to be taken in the interview. The length of the warm-up period depends on a number of variables, including the attitude of the witness, the level of cooperation, and the degree to which the witness can be motivated to provide useful information. The warm-up is time well spent if it helps to ensure a successful interview.

When leading into the main body of the interview, the investigator should remember that his or her role is to direct the flow of the interview and to do so in a nonsuggestive manner. That is, care should be taken not to lead the witness by asking questions that imply the answer.

Questions should always be phrased positively so that the response is also positive. Questions such as "You don't really believe that, do you?" imply that anything other than a negative answer will be unacceptable. "Do you believe that?" allows the witness more freedom to respond.

Studies substantiate that the exact manner in which interview questions are asked is critical to the response. The choice of a single word and its use in a sentence can dramatically affect the nature of a response. In laboratory studies in which subjects were shown a film of a traffic accident, portions of the study group were later asked if they had seen *the* broken headlight; others were asked if they had seen *a* broken headlight. The group presented with the question using "the" said yes significantly more often than did the group presented with the question containing "a." These results were consistent whether witnesses had or had not seen a broken headlight. The significance of this illustration is that use of "the" by the questioner implies the existence of a broken headlight, causing the witness to assume its existence and potentially influencing the answer given by the witness.

Further studies attempted to determine if word substitutions could affect quantitative judgments as well as a simple yes or no answer. Seven films of traffic accidents were shown to a group of subjects. Later, they were all asked *substantially* the same question: "About how fast were the cars going when they hit each other?" The only difference was in the verb used in the question. When various subjects were asked the question, the words "smashed," "collided," "bumped," or "contacted" were substituted for "hit." Although any of the words could be used properly in the question, each tends to imply a difference in speed and force of impact. Results showed that estimates of the speed of vehicles involved tended to increase as a more forceful verb was used in the question.[34]

To avoid such problems, interviewers should begin by asking witnesses to relate in their own words the events of which they have knowledge. Witnesses should be allowed to continue this narrative uninterrupted, unless the amount of superfluous or irrelevant material becomes excessive. Interviewers must remain attentive to what is and is not said and must prepare questions that separate facts from inferences and implications.

When beginning the questioning process, investigators should recall that their objective is to gather information so that they may picture the occurrence with the same clarity and in the same order as the witness. Questions should be asked in systematic and chronological order. They should be stated simply and clearly so that the witness understands them. Concise questions should be asked one at a time. Long, complex questions must be avoided, because they tend to produce disorganized and confused answers. For example, take the question, "Was the man you saw with the scar on his face walking south from where you saw the other man lying near the curb, or did he have the gun in his hand, and was he going the other way, toward the hill, and about how old would you say he was?" This question certainly looks ridiculous on paper. But many people utter questions like these—run-on, complicated, and disorganized.

In developing the chronology of events through questioning, the interviewer should first establish where the witness was positioned and related facts. The interviewer must keep the witness talking and discourage digressions as much as possible. Perhaps the most successful technique for keeping the witness talking is the use of open-ended, nondirectional questions, such as "What happened next?" They are designed to compel the witness to elaborate on the issue rather than merely respond in a yes-or-no fashion.

The interviewer should always permit witnesses to save face if errors in their statements become apparent. Provided the interviewer is satisfied that the mistake is an honest one and not the result of deliberate misrepresentations, he or she should attempt to assist the witness in clarifying the statement without seeming judgmental.

Often, what the interviewee said was not what the interviewer heard, and when such differences arise in a courtroom situation much later, the discrepency can be embarrassing for the investigator. Consequently, it is always advisable to verify the information presented by the witness. To do this, interviewers should simply rephrase what they think they have heard and ask the witness to verify its accuracy. Although this is often not done, it can overcome a major stumbling block to proceeding with an effective investigation and a successful prosecution, where warranted. Also, verifying what was heard can cause the witness to recall additional information that was not told during the basic part of the interview.[35]

Occasionally the interviewer misses or fails to ask questions on some points simply because there was a lack of information that would have caused a question to be asked. Therefore, it is also advisable for the interviewer to ask a final "catch-all" question, such as "Is there anything I have not asked that you think I should have asked?" This way, if there were any gaps in the questioning, the witness has the opportunity to provide the missing information to the investigator. This method ensures that if a relevant issue crops up later, the investigator will not have to ask, "Why didn't you tell me this during the interview," only to have the witness reply, "You didn't ask."[36]

The complexity of the case and the amount of information possessed by the witness are critical variables in the amount of time required for the interview. When satisfied that all relevant information has been obtained, the interviewer has reached the primary goal and may terminate the interview, preferably with a thank-you and a short statement of appreciation for the witness's time and efforts to cooperate with the police in the investigation.

THE COGNITIVE INTERVIEW TECHNIQUE

To this point we have discovered that eyewitness reports of crime are known to be incomplete, often unreliable, and at least partially incorrect. During the normal police interview an "eyewitness" is generally asked what happened. After a 10- or 15-minute narrative by the witness, the interviewer then asks specific questions to clarify certain points. None of this improves the memory of the witness, largely because many eyewitnesses are so preoccupied with the shocking reality of the event that has occurred that they don't have time to learn or memorize details about the suspect or about the crime at the time it occurs. In a typical situation the events occur so rapidly and are so emotionally charged that the eyewitness has trouble concentrating on those things that should be remembered, even if the eyewitness is a trained observer, such as an off-duty police officer.[37] On the other hand, the concern about the inherent unreliability of the hypnosis interview and the legal questions it raises for the purposes of determining admissibility in court makes its use in many cases less than desirable.

The inherent problems of these two types of interviews are further complicated by the traditional type of questioning used by police investigators to ascertain who, what, where, when, why, and how. This process hardly encourages careful disclosure of the facts. The cognitive interview technique was developed in the hope of improving the completeness and accuracy of eyewitness accounts while avoiding some of the legal pitfalls that surround the use of hypnosis.

The cognitive interview technique is deceptively simple. At first glance it does not appear to be unique or particularly useful. However, the four general methods for jogging memory, used along with several specific techniques, become a very powerful and effective means of obtaining a complete and accurate picture of the events recalled.[38] The four techniques used to elicit information are explained to the witness beforehand and are designed to allow the witness to approach memory recall and retrieval from several different avenues.

The first step is to ask the witness to reconstruct the general circumstances surrounding the incident. The witness is asked to think about and recall what the surrounding environment looked like at the scene: rooms, arrangement of furniture, lighting, the presence of vehicles, weather conditions, smells, nearby objects or people, and any other details. In addition, the witness is asked how he or she was feeling at the time and what his or her reaction was to the incident. The purpose of this line of inquiry is to return the witness deeply into the scene.

Second, the investigator asks the witness to report everything remembered about the incident and all surrounding circumstances. The investigator explains that some people hold back information they don't think is relevant or important. The witness is asked not to edit any information or make any determination as to the importance of that material. In addition to the possibility that a tidbit of information may be of extreme importance, the mere act of relaying all information may cause the witness to remember something that had been forgotten.

An example of how obtaining all the details can work occurred when federal drug agents were debriefing an informant who had been to Central America about what he had seen at a remote airstrip used by drug smugglers. The informant recalled that there were mango trees around the airstrip and that he had eaten one of the mangoes. The answers given by the informant when he was asked to relive the experience of eating the mango and describe the taste, the smell, and the reactions of his other senses elicited some other memories of important details that enabled the drug agents to identify and locate the airstrip.[39]

Step three is to have the witness recall the events in a different order. For example, the witness may be asked to begin with the thing that most impressed him or her and work backward and forward from that point. Too often a witness asked to begin at the beginning will fill in gaps and tell a "complete" and logical story that makes sense but may not be entirely accurate. Starting at a different point forces the witness to recall events that actually occurred.

The fourth technique is to have the witness change perspectives. The witness is asked to look at the incident from a different point of view or to put himself or herself in the position of some other person who was present and describe the incident from that other person's point of view.

Several other specific techniques may be used by an investigator to help strengthen the ability of the witness to retrieve stored memory. For example, in an attempt to obtain a physical description, the investigator may ask if the suspect reminded the witness of anyone. If so, who? Or why? Did anything about the person's appearance or clothing bring back any memories? How about names? Go through the alphabet to try to recall the first letter of a name. Did the person's voice remind the witness of anyone else's voice? Were any unusual words used? Any accent?

Many parts of the cognitive interview technique have been used for years. The parts are old, but using them together in a systematic method seems to be proving successful. Investigators can be trained in the technique easily, and, from the studies and experiments conducted thus far, it appears to be efficient and effective as a workable memory enhancement technique.[40]

THE IMPORTANCE OF LISTENING

Regardless of the amount of their preparation and experience, interviewers can conduct a fully successful interview only if they are good listeners. There never was and never will be a completely successful interview if the interviewer *hears* but does not *listen*. Hearing without listening, without concentrating, without comprehending that which is being communicated by the other party, provides little useful information.

Listening is as valuable in interviewing as is questioning. Interviewers first should listen to witnesses' full stories and then ask specific questions triggered by that careful listening. The resulting information is likely to be complete and accurate.

Being a good listener is not easy. To be effective, one must be an active listener, too. It has been estimated that 65 percent of communication is nonverbal. Active listening requires listeners to be conscious of their own body movements, eye contact, hand gestures, facial expressions, head nodding, and tones of voice. All of these nonverbal forms of communication must convey interest in a witness and what the witness is saying. Even a slight movement, such as leaning toward a witness while listening, conveys interest and enthusiasm. Discouraging nonverbal messages may adversely affect the interview and cause an otherwise cooperative witness to become evasive or defensive. In such an instance, a witness might wonder, "Why should I try to help if this investigator isn't interested enough to care what I'm saying?"

Another tactic in good listening is for interviewers to repeat or paraphrase witnesses' stories. This tactic, refered to earlier as verification, provides the opportunity to check the stories and ensure the quality of communication in the interview.

Every communication has two components—the verbal, consisting of the content, and the nonverbal, the emotional or attitudinal component. Both are critical to listening and, hence, to effective communication.

Notes or other methods of documenting the interview should, when possible, reflect the emotional as well as factual content of the interview.

DOCUMENTING THE INTERVIEW

In the majority of routine cases involving interviews, handwritten notes made by the investigator during and immediately following the interview generally serve as sufficient documentation. Investigators should not rely on memory for the storage of investigative information. The human mind can absorb and recount only a limited amount of information at one time, and most of the information is soon lost if notes are not taken.

Note taking during the interview raises two primary concerns for the interviewer. First, it may occasionally be distracting or suspicious to a witness; witnesses may be reluctant to give information knowing that it is being documented. Consequently, the investigator should tell witnesses that notes will prevent the need for subsequent interviews due to lapses of the investigator's memory. This will usually ease the reluctance of the witness. Second, the interviewer should avoid becoming preoccupied with taking notes, for it creates the appearance of inattentiveness. As important as notes may be, the interviewer should treat them as less important than conversation with the witness. Note taking during the interview should be kept to a minimum, recording only salient details. As soon as possible after the interview, the investigator should complete the notes, before memory wanes.

In some instances, it is desirable for witnesses to write or sign statements concerning the events of which they have knowledge. Statements generally are not necessary in routine cases. However, in important cases, when there is a likelihood that the witness may change statements in the courtroom or may not be available to testify, a signed statement, in the witness's handwriting, can be extremely valuable.

The best form of documentation is a sound recording or a sound and visual recording of the interview. Visual recordings are generally not practical when the interview is held anywhere other than a police station, where equipment can be permanently situated. Cassette tape recorders, however, are inexpensive, portable, and helpful in the majority of cases. The recorded interview has many significant advantages: all information is recorded in the witness's own words, details are not left to be recalled by human memory, concerns about detracting from the interview by note taking are absent, interviewers may listen to the verbatim conversations over and over at a later time to be sure that they have understood completely and accurately, and the taped interview might avoid unnecessary reinterviews. The advantages and disadvantages of each method of documentation are shown in Table 5-1.

At the conclusion of an interview, it is wise for investigators to review and evaluate their performance. The checklist in Table 5-2 may serve as a good review and basis for self-evaluation. Such a self-critique can serve as an excellent learning tool for improving one's ability as an interviewer. Experience is the best teacher only if you learn from your mistakes.[41]

Table 5–1 Comparison of Interview Documentation Methods

Method	Advantages	Disadvantages
Memory	Quick and easy	Limited absorption and recall Most information lost shortly afterward
Note taking by interviewer	Sufficient in most cases Captures salient details Prevents need for reinterviewing	May distract or offend witness May preoccupy interviewer, creating appearance of inattentiveness May cause interviewer to miss nonverbal messages
Handwritten or signed statements by witness	Useful if witness cannot testify Can be used to impeach if witness changes story in court	Request may be offensive to witness Not necessary in routine cases
Sound or sound visual recordings	Relatively inexpensive Some equipment portable All information recorded in witnesses' own words Does not rely on inaccuracies of memory or another's notes Does not distract Prevents unnecessary reinterviews	Not necessary except in the most important cases Generally not practical

Table 5–2 Postinterview Self-Evaluation Checklist

WITH THIS WITNESS, DID I:

1	Conduct the interview as quickly, privately, yet conveniently as possible?
2	Establish good rapport with the witness?
3	Listen?
4	Ask good questions?
5	Control the interview?
6	Establish the witness's presence, consciousness, and attentiveness?
7	Determine any factors that now would affect the witness's competency in court?
8	Evaluate the witness's potential credibility in court?
9	Use the right approach in seeking information?
10	Get complete and accurate information?
11	Document the interview well?

Questions

1. What is the importance of information to the criminal investigator? How is information obtained?

2. What criteria will affect the competency of a witness?

3. In evaluating the credibility of a witness, with what factors must the investigator be concerned?

4. Despite the amount of reliance placed on information supplied by eyewitnesses, how reliable are they? Why?

5. What criteria motivate witnesses to give or withhold information?

6. What are the qualifications for an effective interviewer?

7. Assuming the setting for an interview is not ideal, what conditions should be established for conducting the interview?

8. Describe the steps in the interview process.

9. Describe the cognitive interview technique.

10. How can the investigator best document an interview?

11. Why is listening important to a successful interview?

Notes

1. Marshall Houts, *From Evidence to Proof* (Springfield, Ill:. Charles C. Thomas, 1956), pp. 10–11.

2. Brian L. Cutler and Steven D. Penrod, *Mistaken Identification: The Eyewitness, Psychology, and the Law* (New York: Cambridge University Press, 1995), p. 6.

3. Ibid., p. 7.

4. Robert L. Donigan, Edward C. Fisher, et al., *The Evidence Handbook*, 4th ed. (Evanston, Ill.: The Traffic Institute, Northwestern University, 1980), p. 205.

5. Robert Buckhout, "Eyewitness Testimony," *Scientific American,* December 1974, Vol. 231, No. 6, p. 23. Also see Elizabeth F. Loftus, Edith L. Greene, and James M. Doyle, "The Psychology of Eyewitness Testimony," in *Psychological Methods in Criminal Investigation and Evidence,* David C. Raskin, ed. (New York: Springer, 1989), pp. 3–45; Hunter A. McAllister, Robert H. I. Dale, and Cynthia E. Hunt, "Effects of Lineup Modality on Witness Creditability," *Journal of Social Psychology,* June 1993, Vol. 133, No. 3, p. 365.

6. Cutler and Penrod, *Mistaken Identification*, p. 112.

7. Siegried Ludwig Sporer, Roy S. Malpass, and Guenter Koehnken, *Psychological Issues in Eyewitness Identification* (Mahwah, N.J.: Lawrence Erlbaum, 1996), p. 23.

8. Cutler and Penrod, *Mistaken Identification*, p. 113.

9. Sporer, Malpass, and Koehnken, *Psychological Issues in Eyewitness Identification*, pp. 26–29.

10. Ibid., pp. 34–35.

11. Ibid., pp. 36–39.

12. Buckhout, "Eyewitness Testimony," p. 24.

13. Elizabeth Loftus, "Incredible Eyewitness," *Psychology Today,* December 1974, Vol. 8, No. 7, p. 118.

14. Buckhout, "Eyewitness Testimony," pp. 24–26.

15. Ibid., p. 28.

16. Ibid.

17. Cutler and Penrod, *Mistaken Identification*, p. 113.

18. Ibid., p. 135.

19. Ibid., p. 113.

20. Bill Putnam, "Some Precautions Regarding the Use of Hypnosis in Criminal Investigations," *The Police Chief,* May 1979, p. 62. Also see G. D. Burrows, "Forensic Aspects of Hypnosis," *Australian Journal of Forensic Sciences,* 1981, Vol. 13, No. 4, pp. 120–125.

21. Kimberly A. Kingston, "Admissibility of Post-Hypnotic Testimony," *FBI Law Enforcement Bulletin,* April 1986, pp. 23–24.

22. Ibid., p. 23.

23. Fred Graham, "Should Our Courts Reject Hypnosis?" *Parade Magazine,* October 25, 1981, p. 10.

24. Ibid.

25. Ephram Margolin, "Hypnosis Enhanced Testimony: Valid Evidence or Prosecutor's Tool?" *Trial,* 1981, Vol. 17, No. 110, p. 43.

26. Kingston, "Admissibility of Post-Hypnotic Testimony," p. 23.

27. Ibid., p. 24.

28. Kevin M. McConkey and Peter W. Sheehan, *Hypnosis, Memory, and Behavior in Criminal Investigation* (New York: Guilford, 1995), pp. 4–6.

29. John E. Hess, *Interviewing and Interrogation for Law Enforcement* (Cincinnati: Anderson, 1997), p. 19.

30. Ibid., p. 33.

31. Paul B. Weston and Kenneth M. Wells, *Criminal Investigation: Basic Perspectives* (Englewood Cliffs, N.J.: Prentice-Hall, 1970), p. 151.

32. Charles C. Vanderbosch, *Criminal Investigation* (Washington, D.C.: International Association of Chiefs of Police, 1968), p. 196.

33. Hess, *Interviewing and Interrogation for Law Enforcement*, pp. 13–14.

34. Loftus, "Incredible Eyewitness," p. 119.

35. Hess, *Interviewing and Interrogation for Law Enforcement*, pp. 24–25.

36. Ibid., p. 25.

37. R. Edward Geiselman and Ronald P. Fisher, "Interviewing Victims and Witnesses of Crime," National Institute of Justice, *Research in Brief*, December 1985, p. 1. See also Ronald P. Fisher and Edward Geiselman, *Memory Enhancing Techniques for Investigative Interviewing: The Cognitive Interview* (Springfield, Ill.: Charles C. Thomas, 1992).

38. Irwin W. Fisk, *Hypnotic Transition*, Police, June 1990, p. 94; Geiselman and Fisher, "Interviewing Victims and Witnesses," p. 2.

39. Geiselman and Fisher, "Interviewing Victims and Witnesses," p. 2.

40. Ibid., p. 3. For an exhaustive treatment of the cognitive interview technique and experiments that have been conducted, see R. Edward Geiselman and Ronald P. Fisher, "The Cognitive Interview Technique for Victims and Witnesses of Crime," in *Psychological Methods in Criminal Investigation and Evidence,* David C. Raskin (ed.) (New York: Springer Publishing Company, 1989), pp. 191–215.

41. Hess, *Interviewing and Interrogation for Law Enforcement*, p. 26.

SIX

Field Notes and Reporting

CHAPTER OUTLINE

Field Notes 140

The Importance and Use of Reports 141

Writing Effective Reports 143

Aids to Information Gathering during the
Original Investigation 149

The Follow-Up Investigation and Supplemental
Reports 149

Questions 154

Notes 154

INTRODUCTION

From the time of arrival at the scene of an offense, the police officer is constantly engaged in obtaining, assessing, and correlating information. The crime scene is observed, witnesses are interviewed, evidence is collected, and other functions are performed. It is impossible—except for those rare individuals blessed with extraordinary memories—to remember all of the details necessary to prepare a report immediately following an investigation, let alone months or years later when the case comes to trial. Therefore, a continuous written record must be made as the inquiry progresses; the product of this process is termed *field notes* (see Figure 6–1).

FIELD NOTES

There are two main reasons why field notes are of importance: They represent the basic source of information that will be drawn on in writing the offense report, and they are often of assistance when the officer testifies in court.

A small looseleaf notebook lends itself best to field note taking. The identity of its owner and related pertinent information should be entered on the inside cover; this is best accomplished by the use of the business card that many police departments supply their officers. In no case should an officer's home address and telephone number be entered; this merely provides easy opportunity for harassment should the notebook ever be lost. Entries should be made on a chronological basis; when the notebook is nearly full, its contents should be removed and placed in an envelope kept in a secure place.

The field notes should include the answers to the following questions, subject to the availability of the information and its relevance to the type of offense involved:

- *Who?*

 Who was the victim?
 Who made the report?

 Who discovered the offense?
 Who saw or heard something of importance?
 Who had a motive for committing the offense?
 Who committed the offense?
 Who helped the offender?
 Who was interviewed?
 Who worked on the case?
 Who marked the evidence?
 Who received the evidence?

- *What?*

 What type of offense was committed?
 What actions were taken by the suspect and using what methods?
 What happened?
 What do the witnesses know about it?
 What evidence was obtained?
 What was done with the evidence?
 What tools or weapons were used?
 What actions did you take?
 What further action is needed?
 What knowledge, skill, or strength was needed to commit the crime?
 What other agencies were notified?

Figure 6–1
Police Officer Taking Field Notes

(Courtesy Georgetown, South Carolina, Police Department)

What witnesses were not contacted?

What time was the offense committed?

What time was the offense reported?

What was the time of your arrival?

What time did you contact witnesses?

- *Where?*

    Where was the offense discovered?

    Where was the offense committed?

    Where were the tools or weapons found?

    Where was the victim?

    Where was the suspect seen?

    Where were the witnesses?

    Where does the perpetrator live or frequently go?

    Where is the perpetrator?

    Where would the perpetrator be most likely to go?

    Where was the perpetrator apprehended?

    Where was the evidence marked?

    Where was the evidence stored?

- *When?*

    When was the perpetrator arrested?

    When was the victim last seen?

    When did help arrive?

- *How?*

    How was the offense committed?

    How did the perpetrator get to and from the scene?

    How did the perpetrator obtain information needed to commit the offense?

    How were the tools or weapons obtained?

    How did you get your information regarding the offense?

    How did you effect the arrest?

- *With what?*

    With what trade or profession are the tools associated?

    With what other offense is this one associated?

- *Why?*

    Why was the offense committed?

    Why were particular tools or weapons used?

    Why was the offense reported?

    Why were witnesses reluctant to talk?

    Why was the witness eager to point out the perpetrator?

    Why was there a delay in reporting the offense?

- *With whom?*

    With whom does the perpetrator associate?

    With whom was the victim last seen?

    With whom are the witnesses connected?

    With whom do you expect to locate the suspect?

- *How much?*

    How much damage was done?

    How much property was taken?

    How much money was taken?

    How much did the victim claim was stolen?

    How much knowledge was necessary to commit the offense?

    How much trouble was it to carry the property away?

    How much information are the witnesses not giving out?

    How much is the victim withholding?

    How much additional information do you need to help clear the offense?[1]

THE IMPORTANCE AND USE OF REPORTS

Among the least popular duties of police officers, reporting is also one of the most important. More than a few excellent investigations have been undone by an officer's failure to document fully in writing the results obtained. By preparing proper reports, investigators also protect themselves from allegations that their investigations were not competent, complete, and professionally correct. A case history illustrates this point:

A burglary in progress was reported at a doctor's office. As two officers moved to cover the building, a suspect was seen leaping from an office window carrying a small flight bag. The suspect ran from the scene, followed by one of the officers. He attempted to scale a fence. In the ensuing struggle, the suspect fell on the far side of the fence, breaking his arm. During treatment at a hospital, the suspect told the officer, in front of medical personnel, that he was going to claim his arm had been broken during questioning. He further indicated this would be an attempt to discredit the police, as he had only recently been released from the state prison and feared that such an immediate second violation would cause the court to invoke a stringent sentence upon conviction. Because many arrested people state that they are going to claim the police violated their civil rights, the officer regarded it as little more than a commonplace occurrence. Even though they did not relate directly to the investigation, the suspect's remarks and the identity of persons witnessing them were included in the report as a matter of thoroughness. Subsequently, when the Federal Bureau of Investigation investigated the matter of a possible violation of the suspect's rights, the allegation was easily refuted by corroborating statements from the medical personnel identified in the police officer's report.

Well-prepared reports based on a thorough investigation of an offense also promote the rapid apprehension of the suspect, thus preventing further crimes and making the recovery of property more likely (see Figure 6–2). The report also serves as the official memory of the department. Offenses may be placed in an inactive status, receiving no further investigative treatment for some time. If officers resign from the force, retire, or get transferred to other duties, resulting in the assignment of another person to the case, the report ensures that complete information will be readily available at future dates to people who may not have been involved in the case originally.

Incomplete or improperly prepared offense reports may, ironically, be associated with complaints that officers often voice about prosecutors and judges. Inadequate reports may contribute to such practices as refusal to prosecute, a weakening of the prosecutor's plea-bargaining position, and lenient sentences. Prosecutors and police agencies serving the same jurisdictions should jointly develop a list of key questions that can be used by the police and the prosecutor as a checklist for investigating and preparing criminal cases.

Police reports also serve important operational and administrative purposes. In the aggregate, individual reports form the records from which

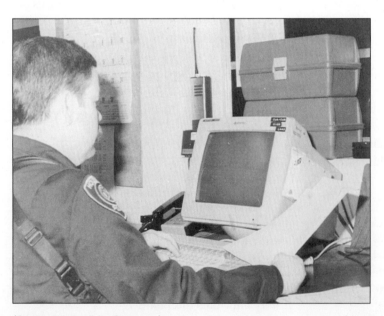

Figure 6–2
Computerized Report Writing
A police officer enters a report into a computer, which also has the capacity to make diagrams.

(Courtesy Houston Police Department)

offense rates are determined and personnel distribution needs established. Additionally, by reviewing the reports of subordinates, supervisors are able to review the work performed and make suggestions to correct any deficiencies.

WRITING EFFECTIVE REPORTS

If reports are to serve the purposes for which they are intended, they must have certain characteristics. Fairly lengthy lists about the traits associated with sound report writing have been developed, such as the following: clear, pertinent, brief, complete, current, accurate, fair, proper classification, informative, objective, correct format, and submission on a timely basis.[2] In addition, various rules for report writing have been formulated:

1. *Fill in all of the blanks* on the report unless the information is not available or it is refused to the officer, which should be explained in the report. It is easier to get the necessary information at the scene than to try to recontact complainants and witnesses for it later.

2. *Write the report in the first person,* using "I arrived at the scene at 1645 hours" as opposed to "Officer Morales arrived at the scene at 1645 hours." The reader of the report knows that Officer Morales wrote the report, and the officer's constant reference to himself or herself in the third person (Officer Morales) is an awkward style. Although some departments require the use of the third person in reports, the trend in report writing is to move away from it.

3. *Avoid unnecessary technical or legalistic jargon* such as "hereinafter," "point of fact," or "thereof," because you may convey a meaning that you do not intend or do not fully understand. Such jargon is a means by which your credibility can be attacked. Avoid writing statements of your own whose meaning you cannot fully explain. Certainly, if a suspect tells you, "I was abducted by aliens who implanted a control box in my head and they sent me commands to rob the pharmacy," you must faithfully record the statment even if you can't explain it—but, the words are not your own.

4. *Write short sentences* because they are less likely to be confusing to or misunderstood by readers, such as the prosecutor. A concise, "punchy" presentation of the facts makes it easier for the reader to "find the beef."

5. *Use shorter paragraphs* for the same reasons as those for writing shorter sentences.

6. *Support any conclusions you express with details*, because others who read the report, such as prosecutors, need to know what facts shaped your thinking. Also, when a trial begins weeks, months, or even years later, you will have forgotten many facts. If you included them in the reports, you will be able to refresh your recollection and provide convincing testimony.

7. *Don't repeat facts more than once,* unless doing so is required by your department's reporting format or policies. Duplication of entries wastes your time, and it creates the possibility that when you are distracted, tired, or in a hurry, your entries may conflict in some way with one another, calling your credibility into question.

8. *Check your spelling.* People who don't know you will form opinions of your capabilities on the basis of the reports you write and they read. Also, you are representing your department, so its reputation is on the line because defense attorneys, judges, members of the news media, juries drawn from the community, and prosecutors read police reports. Misspelled words can change the meaning of a sentence or cause the meaning to be lost. Spell-checker software is an aid to accuracy, but it does not catch words that are spelled correctly but used inappropriately (e.g., "E. Wazolewski took a write turn").

9. *Edit what you write.* Don't miss an opportunity to catch and correct your own errors. Many people do this best when they read slowly and out loud, but you may find a system that works better for you. Taking the time to edit your own report is more important than the system you use. If you are using a computer, editing is far easier than writing several successive handwritten drafts

of a report. Moreover, the software is likely to include a spell checker, thesaurus, and grammar checker.[3]

Officers also have their own rules, such as putting the most effort into reports for important cases and writing other reports—such as those needed solely to make a minor insurance claim— just good enough to be accepted. When all is said and done, there are two indispensable elements of reports: (1) accuracy and (2) communication of the meaning that the writer intended.

Not infrequently the new investigator will, if only at the subconscious level, attempt to impress those who will be reading the report by writing in an elaborate manner in order to display mastery of the English language. However, persons reading the report will learn much, or perhaps all, they will ever know about the investigation from what has been written. Therefore, it is essential to write using a clear and uncluttered style; the report must be written not only so that it can be understood but, more importantly, so that it cannot be misunderstood.

The report must be completely accurate. No detail should be added or deleted; the potential or actual consequences of such deviations, however innocent the motivation, are considerable. For example, at the scene of an armed robbery, a young investigator was conducting interviews necessary to prepare the original report. One of the questions he asked the victim was, "Have you ever seen the perpetrator before this happened?" The response was, "Yes, he works on the loading platform of the grocery on Sixth Avenue." Out of a desire to provide as much detail as possible, the investigator supplemented this statement with information from the telephone directory, writing a portion of the interview in the following manner:

> The victim told the undersigned officer that the suspect works at Blake's Grocery Wholesale, located at 1425 Sixth Avenue, telephone number (813) 223-3291.

Later the following exchange took place between the officer and the defense attorney in court:

Defense Attorney: Officer, do you recognize this report?

Officer: Yes, I do.

Defense Attorney: Did you prepare it?

Officer: Yes, sir, I did.

Defense Attorney: Would it be fair to say that it represents your investigation?

Officer: That is correct, sir.

Defense Attorney: Then, having conducted the investigation and having prepared the report, your testimony would be that it accurately and completely portrays your actions and what you learned?

Officer: Yes, sir.

Defense Attorney: Would you read from page 5 of this report?

Officer: "The victim told the undersigned officer that the suspect works at Blake's Grocery Wholesale, located at 1425 Sixth Avenue, telephone number (813) 223-3291."

Defense Attorney: Officer, the complainant in this case has already testified to the effect that she did not, in fact, tell you this. Why are you prejudiced toward the defendant in this case, and what else have you added to the report or subtracted from it in order to strengthen the state's case?

Thus, a seemingly innocuous addition to a report reduced the credibility of the entire investigation. Clear communication and accuracy are the mainstays of effective reports. The absence of one diminishes the other.

ELEMENTS COMMON TO REPORTS

The content of reports varies according to departmental policy, statistical needs, individual case requirements, and the format in use. Certain crucial elements common to most reports are treated in this section.

Name

The full names of complainants, witnesses, and other parties must always be obtained. In recording proper names, the first time an individual is referred to in a report the sequence of names should be last, first, middle. When a person mentioned in the report is commonly known to acquaintances by some name other than the proper name or an apparent derivation, the nickname should also be provided.

Race and Sex

Race or ethnic extraction should never be documented in such a manner as to cast aspersion on a person. Ordinarily race is indicated by use of one of the following abbreviations:

Race	Abbreviation
White	W
Black	B
Hispanic	H
Asian/Pacific Islander	A
American Indian/Native Alaskan	I
Unknown	U

Sex is always designated by "F" for female and "M" for male. The proper sequence is race/sex, for example, "W/F."

Age

On entries requiring only a person's age, it should be indicated as of the last birthday. However, the first reference to this individual in the narrative portion of the report should give the exact date of birth, if known. Birth dates are recorded in a six-digit sequence of month, day, year. January 10, 1965 should be recorded as "01/10/65."* For certain parties, such as an unidentified deceased person or a suspect whose identity has not been established, age may be approximated or given in a narrow span of years, for example, "approximately 32 years" or "approximately 31-33 years."

Address

This information is particularly important because it helps investigators to find people for additional interviews or related procedures. Each residence and business address should show the street number and, when applicable, the apartment, suite, or room number. If this is not immediately ascertainable, the general location should be described in sufficient detail to make its whereabouts known. When military personnel are involved, the location information should include serial numbers, unit designations, and ship or installation, if applicable. If a person is only visiting a location, both temporary and permanent addresses should be obtained.

Telephone Number

The telephone numbers of an individual should always be obtained, including area code, residence number, and business number, including any extension number. Additionally, officers should inquire about and record any pager or cellular numbers, as well as e-mail addresses.

Personal Description

A model form for gathering personal descriptions is shown and discussed later in this chapter. Minimally, the following points should be included: sex, race, age, complexion, hair and eye color, physical defects, scars, marks, tattoos, build, and the nature and color of clothing worn.

Property Description

Elements useful in describing property are make, model, serial number, color, and type of material from which constructed. Other types of information may also be pertinent. Using the case of a stolen car as an example, the presence of stickers, cracked windows, articles hanging from the mirror, or loud engine noise would be additional information useful in locating the vehicle.

Occupation

The occupation of a person may be of some importance to an investigation. In the case of a suspect it may establish familiarity with the use of certain types of equipment or procedures associated with a particular function, such as banking. It may also lend further credibility to the statement of a witness:

A man exited from a restaurant as two suspects ran about 15 feet from the bank they had just robbed, entered a vehicle, and rapidly drove around the corner. Despite being presented with only a brief view of the car, the witness was able to give the police a fairly detailed description of it. At the trial the defense was unsuccessful in casting doubt upon the accuracy of the description, as the witness operated an automobile repair service.

---

*The Y2K problem is changing this traditional format. As this edition went to press in mid-1999, many departments were still using the traditional six-digit format. There will not be a change over to another format at one specific time. However, some agencies have begun to use a new eight-digit format. In it, January 10, 1965 would be recorded as 19650110 (Year Mo Day).

Occupation is also useful in suggesting times when a person might be successfully and conveniently contacted by the investigator. An unemployed individual's ordinary line of work is to be given along with the notation "currently unemployed." Certain categories of people may be unemployed but not seeking a position in the compensated labor market; in such instances it is more appropriate to give the person's exact status, for example, "college student" or "homemaker." If the individual is employed, the occupation given in a report should be as specific as possible, for example, "brick mason" as opposed to "manual laborer."

Value

The value of property stolen may determine whether the offense is a felony or misdemeanor. For articles subject to depreciation, the fair market value should be used, unless the property is new or almost new, in which case the replacement cost should be used. On goods stolen from retail establishments, the merchant's wholesale cost, which constitutes the actual dollar loss, is the proper value to use. The value placed on nonnegotiable instruments such as traveler's checks or money orders should be the cost of replacing them; negotiable instruments, including bonds payable to the bearer, are valued at the market price at the time of the theft.

When the stolen property is subject to appreciation from the time of its acquisition by the owner—for example, limited-edition prints—the current fair market value is to be indicated.

The value of recovered stolen property ordinarily equals the valuation placed on it at the time of theft unless damaged, in which case it is to be established by the fair market value. In cases where the value of the stolen article is not readily ascertainable, the conservative estimate of the owner may be used.

Date

Like birth dates, dates are documented in the sequence of month, day, year, using two digits for each. For example, December 15, 1999, would be recorded as 12/15/99.*

Time

For all official business, excluding general public and related information, most police agencies use the military system or 24-hour clock, of hundred hours. Time runs from 0001 hours (12:01 A.M.) through 2400 hours (12:00 A.M.).

THE FLOW OF FIELD REPORTS

Figure 6–3 depicts the sequence of events that comprise the flow of field reports. The majority of incidents that result in a police report's being initiated will come about because of a citizen's telephone call to 911 or the complaint desk and the dispatch of an officer to the scene. In a lesser number of situations, officers in the field will be approached by the complainant or a witness or will see a situation requiring investigation. In any of these cases, following work at the scene the officer or officers involved will, when warranted, initiate a report.

If a department uses a word-processing system, the information pertaining to the report is dictated over the telephone and the typed report is subsequently signed by the officers, after reviewing it at the end of their tour of duty. Alternatively, if reports are handwritten, the officers responsible for initiating them may, if time permits, prepare them prior to making themselves available for additional calls, write them later during the shift when work has slowed, or complete them at the police station following the tour of duty. Ordinarily, a supervisor meets with subordinates one or more times during a shift to review and pick up completed reports. The supervisor who approves the report will indicate one of several dispositions (e.g., retained for further investigation by patrol, inactived, referred to detectives or others providing latent or follow-up investigation), and the report is then sent to the records unit, where the original is filed and duplicates are distributed as indicated by the reviewing supervisor and department policy (e.g., to the detectives and to the crime analysis unit).

REPORT FORMAT

The face of a typical police report form is shown in Figure 6–4. Much of the information pertinent to an investigation is so standard that simple one-line entries or checks within boxes corresponding to applicable phrases are sufficient. Such forms offer the

---

*In the new eight-digit format this would be recorded as 19991215.

Figure 6–3
Flow Chart for Field Reports

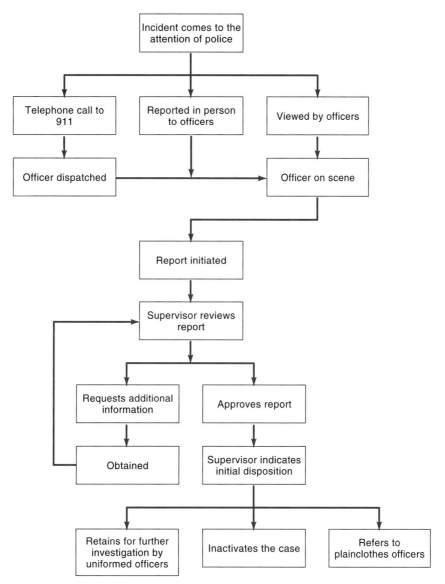

advantages of being rapidly completed and self-coding for high-speed data processing.

The back of the form illustrated is devoted largely to a narrative of the case, based on the following organization of information obtained during the course of the investigation.

Suspects
The listing, description, and, when available, identity of the suspects involved should be provided, along with a notation of whether a pickup order

was placed and, if placed, the time of its initiation and the person receiving it.

Witnesses
All witnesses and pertinent information relating to them, including telephone numbers and addresses, should be listed.

Evidence
The evidence seized, how it was marked, the chain of custody, and numbers assigned by the property or evidence control room must be recorded. If a

Figure 6–4
Face of a Police Report

INCIDENT REPORT - TAMPA POLICE DEPARTMENT		Page 1 of 2

Event

1 ☒ A	Offense/Incident BATTERY (DOMESTIC VIOLENCE)	State Statute 784.03	Location 1710 N. TAMPA St.	1 01	2 01
C A	Offense/Incident	State Statute	Location	1	2
2 A					

Date Occurred 03-01-95	Time Occurred 2130 hrs	Day of Week ☐ Mon ☒ Wed ☐ Fri ☐ Sun / ☐ Tue ☐ Thu ☐ Sat ☐ Unk	Date Reported 03-01-95	Time Reported 2300 HRS	Grid 125

Victim

3 4 01 03	Name: Last DAVIS	First Jo	Middle ANN	Race W	Sex F	D.O.B. 08-18-68	Age 26	5 09	6 01	7 03	8 01
	Home Address 1710 N. TAMPA St.		City TAMPA	County Hills.	State FL	Zip 33601		Home Phone 273-1456			
	Business/School Address NONE		City	County	Zip		Business Phone		Hrs.		

3 4	Name: Last	First	Middle	Race	Sex	D.O.B.	Age	5	6	7	8
	Home Address		City	County	State	Zip		Home Phone			
	Business/School Address		City	County	Zip		Business Phone		Hrs.		

Property

Codes W/U=Weapon/Instrument Used S=Stolen R=Recovered L=Lost F=Found K=Safekeeping RJ=Recovered for Other Jurisdiction

Property Receipt No.

Code	Item	Description/Serial Number/Identification No., etc.	Value	Rec. Val.
WU		FIST AND FEET USED TO PUNCH AND KICK THE VICTIM		

Vehicle

Codes SL=Stolen/Leased Z=Seized E=Evidence SV=Suspect Vehicle VA=Vehicle Attacked   Evidence No

Code	Type	YR	Make	Model/Style	Color	Tag/State/Year	VIN No.	Value

Further Description		Impound/Repo Check ☐ Yes ☐ No	
9	Rec. Value	Finance and Insurance Co.	P/U ☐ Yes ☐ No	With/Time

Arrests

Name: Last DAVIS,	First LUKE	Middle ANTON	Race W	Sex M	D.O.B. 07-20-50	Age 44	OBTS No 00056179
Home Address 1710 N. TAMPA St.		City TAMPA	County Hillsb.	State FL US	10 Influence Drugs/Alcohol ☐ Yes ☐ No ☒ Unk		
Charges BATTERY (DOMESTIC VIOLENCE)		11 01	State Statute 784.03	CTS 01	State Statute	CTS	
Name: Last	First	Middle	Race	Sex	D.O.B.	Age	OBTS No
Home Address		City	County	State	10 Influence Drugs/Alcohol ☐ Yes ☐ No ☐ Unk		
Charges		11	State Statute	CTS	State Statute	CTS	

Reconstruction

THE DEFENDANT AND THE VICTIM BECAME ENGAGED IN A PHYSICAL CONFRONTATION. HE PUNCHED HER SEVERAL TIMES IN the FACE WITH HIS FISTS CAUSING BOTH OF HER EYES TO SWEll SHUT AND KICKED HER IN THE STOMACH WITH HIS FEET. THE DEFENDANT AND VICTIM ARE LEGALLY MARRIED.

Domestic Violence Form Issued ☒ Yes ☐ No	Assault Victim Form Issued ☐ Yes ☒ No

Admin.

Detective Notified	Supervisor Notified	Crime Scene Tech Assigned
Reporting Officer #312/38689 M.L.Lee Div DI	Div./Sqd/ 1/7	Second Officer	Div./Sqd.	Related Reports

Retained To DI By:	☐ Inactive/Admin ☐ Unfounded	☒ Arrest ☐ Notice to Appear	☒ Adult ☐ Juv.
☐ Exceptionally Cleared To: ☐ Adult ☐ Juv. By:	☐ Prosecution Declined ☐ Death of Offender	☐ Extradition Declined ☐ Juv./No Custody	☐ Victim Signed Complaint Withdrawal ☐ Arrested Prior Offense
Edited By Sgt. F. R. Jensen	Div. I	Date 3-1-95	Referred To	Division
Records Section Only: Copies to	Routed By	Data Entry	Pick Up	

Report No. 95-015612

TPD 305 (10/94)

(Courtesy Tampa Police Department)

diagram is made, reference is usually made to it at this point. Original diagrams are placed into the property or evidence control room in the same manner as physical articles seized at the scene. Information pertaining to photographs is also included under this category, as well as other types of evidence, such as latent fingerprints.

Interviews

All persons with whom the investigator talked during the course of the inquiry should be identified, even if they could not provide information at the initial contact. On occasion the perpetrator may remain near the scene, usually in property crimes where no witnesses are involved, in an attempt to determine what the police have established. More rarely, the perpetrator or an accomplice will deliberately provide false information in order to misdirect the investigation. The identification of all witnesses is helpful in ferreting out the rare instances of such occurrences. Moreover, people who have actually seen something of value to the inquiry may be reluctant to discuss it with the police at the scene but will readily reveal it during a follow-up contact.

Investigation

A short description of the crime scene may be given to permit a basic conceptualization of it by persons to whom it is unfamiliar. This element requires the documentation of all actions taken by the investigator at the scene regardless of whether they yielded useful information.

Reconstruction

The reconstruction is a narration of the probable manner in which the crime was committed, based on statements made by the suspect (if in custody and cooperating), interviews of witnesses, the examination of the crime scene, and physical evidence.

AIDS TO INFORMATION GATHERING DURING THE ORIGINAL INVESTIGATION

Whenever there are witnesses to a crime, even the most conscientious investigator may fail to elicit all information available. Certain aids, however, can be of critical importance in preventing this.

One tool, shown in Figure 6–5, is a checklist of all pertinent personal-description information to be acquired by interviewing witnesses. One benefit of such a form is that it enhances efforts to cross-reference information from different cases in which it appears likely that the perpetrator was the same.

One of the most frustrating experiences for investigators occurs when trying to obtain a description of a firearm, as the victim or witnesses are often injured, unfamiliar with firearms, or visibly shaken by their experience. One helpful device in such situations is photographs of some commonly encountered firearms, as shown in Figures 6–6 and 6–7. Very frequently even emotionally upset victims or witnesses can make an identification or at least give a good description of the weapon when these are viewed.

THE FOLLOW-UP INVESTIGATION AND SUPPLEMENTAL REPORTS

Those assigned to the follow-up or latent investigation function also rely on aids to assist them. One such device is the checklist in Figure 6–8, which guides and summarizes the progress of the follow-up investigation. The elements listed are those common to follow-up investigations, although they may occur in a different sequence depending on the particulars of a given case, such as when a suspect has been apprehended at the crime scene and is already in custody. The checklist provides a visual summary of the status of a case and is an adjunct to any supplemental narrative reports initiated rather than a substitute for them. Investigators may choose to simply check the appropriate column associated with each element or to enter in the appropriate column the time and date that an act was accomplished. Additionally, to avoid someone unfamiliar with the case having to read through supplemental reports to find a particular fact, short informational entries can be made; for example, for "Vehicle Released" the notation "to complainant" might be made under the "yes" column.

Periodically during the follow-up investigation supplemental reports must be initiated. Ordinarily, supplemental, or follow-up, reports should be written no less frequently than every 10 days, and the

Figure 6–5
Checklist for Obtaining Person Descriptions

Complainant _____ Nature of offense _____
Address _____ Date _____
Offense # _____ Suspect _____

1. Closest estimate of age _____

2. *Sex*
   Male _____
   Female _____

3. *Race/Nationality*
   White _____
   Black _____
   Hispanic _____
   Asian/Pacific Islander _____
   American Indian/Native Alaskan _
   Unknown _____

4. *Height*
   Less than 5' _____
   5' –5' 2'' _____
   5'3''–5' 5'' _____
   5'6''–5' 8'' _____
   5'9''–5'11'' _____
   6' –6' 3'' _____
   6'4'' or over _____

5. *Eye Color*
   Blue _____
   Brown _____
   Gray _____
   Hazel _____
   Green _____

6. *Weight*
   Less than 100 lbs. _____
   100–120 _____
   121–140 _____
   141–160 _____
   161–180 _____
   181–200 _____
   201–220 _____
   221–240 _____
   240 or more _____

7. *Eye Defects*
   Blind _____
   Crossed _____
   Cockeyed _____
   Deep set _____
   Squints _____
   Bulging _____
   Bloodshot _____
   Oriental _____
   Different colored _____
   Contacts _____
   Glasses _____
   Cataracts _____

8. *Hair Color*
   Blonde or strawberry blonde _____
   Brown (light) _____
   Brown (dark) _____
   Black _____
   Gray or partially gray _____
   White _____
   Red or auburn _____
   Dyed, unusual, or added color ___

9. *Hair type*
   Bald _____
   Partially bald _____
   Long straight _____
   Short straight _____
   Long curly _____
   Short curly _____
   Thinning _____
   Bushy _____
   Wavy _____
   Thin or receding _____
   Kinky _____
   Wig or hairpiece _____
   Afro _____

10. *Complexion*
    Fair _____
    Ruddy _____
    Dark _____
    Medium _____
    Light _____
    Sallow _____

11. *Facial Scars*
    Forehead _____
    Eye (right) _____
    Eye (left) _____
    Nose (including broken) _____
    Ear (right) _____
    Ear (left) _____
    Chin _____
    Lips _____
    Right cheek _____
    Left cheek _____
    Eyebrow (right) _____
    Eyebrow (left) _____

12. *Facial Oddities*
    Pockmarked _____
    Freckled _____
    Pimpled _____
    Birthmark _____
    Protruding chin _____
    Receding chin _____
    Thick lips _____
    Thin lips _____

13. *Torso Scars*
    Chest _____
    Shoulder (right) _____
    Shoulder (left) _____
    Upper back _____
    Lower back _____
    Buttocks _____
    Stomach _____
    Hip (right) _____
    Hip (left) _____

14. *Limb Scars*
    Arm (right) _____
    Arm (left) _____
    Hand (right) _____
    Hand (left) _____
    Leg (right) _____
    Leg (left) _____
    Foot (right) _____
    Foot (left) _____
    Wrist (right) _____
    Wrist (left) _____
    Elbow (right) _____
    Elbow (left) _____
    Pockmarked _____
    Bullet or shrapnel wound _____
    Needle marks _____
    Vaccination (right arm) _____
    Vaccination (left arm) _____
    Multiple scars _____

15. *Mustache or Beard*
    Heavy Mustache _____
    Medium Mustache _____
    Thin Mustache _____
    Full Beard _____
    Goatee _____
    Sideburns _____

16. *Deformities*
    Humpback _____
    Lame leg _____
    Crippled hand (right) _____
    Crippled hand (left) _____
    Crippled fingers (right) _____
    Crippled fingers (left) _____
    Bowlegged _____
    Cauliflower ears _____

17. *Amputations*
    Arm (right) _____
    Arm (left) _____
    Leg (right) _____
    Leg (left) _____
    Foot (right) _____
    Foot (left) _____
    Finger (right) _____
    Finger (left) _____
    Other (specify) _____

18. *Teeth*
    All missing _____
    Missing top _____
    Missing bottom _____
    Irregular _____
    Chipped _____
    Protruding upper (rabbit) _____
    Protruding lower _____
    Visible decay _____
    Stained _____
    Very attractive _____

19. *Accent and Speech Pattern*
    Foreign accent _____
    Southern drawl _____
    Northern accent (if possible, specify.
    Brooklyn, Boston, etc.) _____
    Vulgar language _____
    Beatnik or jive _____
    Spanish accent _____
    Slurred _____
    Stutter _____
    Mute _____
    Soft _____
    Loud _____
    Refined _____
    Used written note _____

20. *Clothing (MEN)*
    Hat (type) _____
    Jacket (color and type, waist,
    length, etc.) _____
    Shirt (color, pattern, short or
    long sleeves) _____
    Trousers (color, style—flared,
    tight fitting) _____
    Sweaters (color, style, sleeves,
    vest, etc.) _____
    Necktie (color and design) _____
    Shoes (color and style—loafers,
    boots, sneakers, etc.) _____
    Gloves (color and type) _____
    Other pertinent information _____
    _____

21. *Clothing (WOMEN)*
    Dress (color, design, length) _____
    _____
    Pants suit (color, design) _____
    _____
    Blouse (color, design) _____
    _____
    Skirt (color, design, length) _____
    _____
    Hat (color, type) _____
    _____
    Gloves (color, type) _____
    _____
    Other pertinent information _____
    _____

22. *Disguises*
    Mask (silk stocking) _____
    Mask (Halloween) _____
    Mask (ski type) _____
    False nose _____
    False beard _____
    False mustache _____
    Sunglasses (color, style) _____

Figure 6–6
Assorted Handguns

9-mm Smith & Wesson Semiautomatic

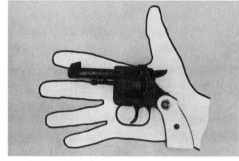

.22 RG-10 Revolver

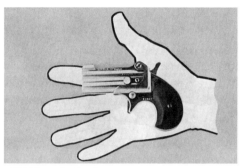

.357 Herter's Derringer

.357 Colt Python Revolver

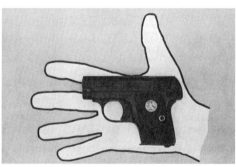

.25 Colt Semiautomatic

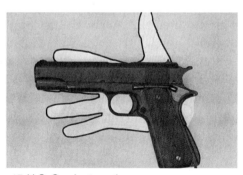

.45 U.S. Semiautomatic

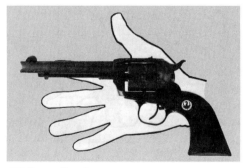

.22 Ruger Revolver

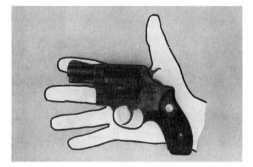

.38 Smith & Wesson Chief's Special Revolver

Source: *A Visual Aid for Firearms Identification*, Federal Bureau of Investigation.

Figure 6–7
Assorted Long Guns

.30-30 Winchester, Model 94, lever action

.30 U.S. M-1 Carbine

9-mm Ingram Model 11, Submachine Gun, with extended folding stock and detached silencer.

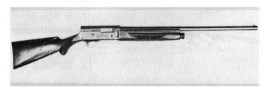

12-Gauge Browning "Automatic 5" Shotgun

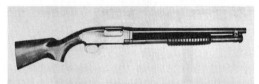

.20-gauge Winchester, Model 12 Shotgun, with chopped stock and barrel.

7.62-mm AK-47 Assault Rifle

.223 Colt AR-15 (M-16) Rifle

.22 Winchester Bolt Action Rifle

Browning Bolt Action Rifle with scope (various calibers)

9-mm Israeli Uzi Submachine Gun with folded stock

Figure 6–8
Checklist for Follow-up Investigations

	YES	NO	NOT APPLICABLE
Reviewed Offense Report			
Evidence: Viewed			
To Laboratory			
Reviewed Technician's Report			
Records Check of Complainant(s)/Witness(s)			
Crime Analysis Information: MO Check			
Field Contacts			
Known Offenders			
Recap Information			
Visited Crime Scene			
Contacted Complainant(s)			
Contacted Witness(s)			
Mugshot File/Likeness Viewed			
Informants Queried			
Pickup Order Placed			
Pickup Order Cancelled			
Interrogated Suspect(s)			
Lineup Conducted			
Conference with Prosecuting Attorney			
Formal Charge Filed			
Final Disposition			
Vehicle Released			
Evidence Disposed of			
Outside Agency Contact: Probation			
Parole			
Other Agencies			
Supplemental Report Made			
Final Supplemental Report Made			

INVESTIGATOR	BADGE #	APPROVING SUPERVISOR	BADGE #

continuance of a particular investigation beyond 30 days should require supervisory approval to ensure proper use of an investigator's time. The purpose of writing follow-up reports is to keep the file current as new or corrected information is gathered. Additionally, specific acts or accomplishments might require individual supplemental reports, such as the activation or cancellation of a pickup order or BOLO, the issuance of a warrant, the arrest of a suspect, the complainant's discovery that additional property was stolen that was not noticed as missing at the time the original report was made, the recovery of all or part of the property taken, or a change in the title of the offense due to improper classification on the original report, for example, a strong-arm robbery reclassified as a purse snatch.

Other circumstances under which supplemental reports are required include (1) when the offense is *unfounded*, that is, when it is established that the offense, in fact, did not occur; (2) when it is *exceptionally cleared*, meaning that the police know who the perpetrator is but are unable to pursue the case further due to circumstances beyond their control, such as the death of the only witness; and (3) when the case is *inactivated*. If the supervi-

sor reviewing the original report inactivates it due to insufficient leads to warrant follow-up investigation, then a supplemental report is not required. However, if some follow-up work is done, no promising leads develop, and the case is then inactivated, the person assigned responsibility for it must complete a supplemental report to substantiate the basis for inactivation.

As a general concluding note, case files inactivated may in later months or years receive further investigative work that is productive. Therefore, it is of considerable importance that at each stage of report writing care is exercised in presenting all available information.

Questions

1. Why are field notes important?
2. Of what importance and use are police reports of crimes?
3. What are the two indispensable elements of an effective report?
4. Why might the occupation of a person be of importance in an investigation?
5. Under what circumstances is a supplemental report required?

Notes

1. Allen Z. Gammage, *Basic Police Report Writing* (Springfield, Ill.: Charles C. Thomas, 1966), pp. 105-108. Also see a special edition on report writing, *Journal of California Law Enforcement,* Winter 1982, Vol. 16, No. 1; Thomas Adams, *Police Field Operations* (Englewood Cliffs, N.J.: Prentice Hall, 1990), pp. 133-175.

2. Gammage, *Basic Police Report Writing*, pp. 13-14.
3. Paul L. Godwin, "Painless Report Writing," *Law and Order*, February 1993, pp. 38–40. The authors have added statements and examples to this work.

SEVEN

Follow-Up Investigation

CHAPTER OUTLINE

The Decision to Initiate a Follow-Up Report 156
Crime Analysis 160
The National Crime Information Center 164
Neighborhood Canvass 165
Informants 165
Surveillance 167

Mechanical Lie Detection 169
Relationships with Victims and Witnesses 171
Guidelines for Conducting Lineups 172
Questions 175
Notes 175

INTRODUCTION

In order to successfully complete a criminal investigation, the investigating officer must be aware of various sources of information available to him or her as well as specific investigative steps that are generally required in order to bring an investigation to a successful conclusion. In this chapter we have tried to identify some of the more valuable resources investigators can utilize in their quest to solve crimes as well as to set forth specific steps that can be followed to assist them in accomplishing this endeavor.

THE DECISION TO INITIATE A FOLLOW-UP INVESTIGATION

Follow-up investigation is the police effort to gather information subsequent to the initiation of the original report and until the case is ready for prosecution. After a uniformed officer initiates a report, his or her immediate supervisor makes an initial disposition. Certain crimes, such as homicides, rapes, and suicides, invariably receive follow-up work. Other offenses receive follow-up investigation depending on department policy. Ordinarily only the most serious offenses and those with potential for conclusive results receive investigative effort beyond that necessary to generate the original report.

INVESTIGATIVE SOLVABILITY FACTORS

The following are some questions that investigative supervisors should answer in determining whether or not to move forward with a follow-up investigation:

- Can the identity of the suspect be established through (1) the discovery of usable fingerprints? (2) the finding of significant physical evidence? (3) victim/witness/informant information? (4) the license number of or a useful description of the vehicle known to have been used in the offense?
- Is there serious physical harm or threat of serious physical harm to the victim? (Generally bomb threats and obscene phone calls would not be assigned for follow-up. However, aggravated circumstances may cause the offense to be so assigned.)
- Did the suspect use a deadly weapon or dangerous ordinance?
- Is there a significant method of operation that will aid in the solution of the offense?
- Is it a sex offense in which the victim and suspect had physical contact?
- Can a suspect be named?
- Can a suspect be identified?
- Can a suspect be described?
- Is there another reason that leads you to believe that the offense should be assigned for a follow-up investigation (e.g., hazardous or dangerous materials stolen or an offense which would raise community concern)?[1]

DECISION MODELS

Some police departments have attempted to develop decision models that are more objective and take away some of the discretion from personnel who decide whether or not to go forward with a follow-up investigation. Figures 7–1 and 7–2 provide examples of two of these models.

RECONTACTING VICTIMS

In many cases, the investigators will recontact victims to verify patrol officers' reports, to find new information, or merely to appease victims. Generally, no new information is forthcoming, and sometimes the public relation attempts backfire.

In the following example the investigator reinterviewed a victim. Because the victim had assumed that nothing would come of the investigation, he was annoyed at being recontacted by the detective.

An investigator visited the victim of a burglary. Earlier that week the victim's home had been broken into and several hundred dollars worth of electronic entertainment and citizens-band radio equipment stolen. The victim expressed surprise at the appearance of the investigator and stated that he had given the patrol officer all the information. The interview of the victim took approximately 20 minutes, provided no new information, and confirmed the lack of substantial leads. The victim seemed bothered by the amount of time the interview was taking. Finally, taking his cue from the victim, the investigator left, having acquired no new leads.

The following example illustrates a case in which recontacting the victim and searching for possible witnesses not only were unsuccessful but also led the investigator to suspect the victim was not being truthful:

Figure 7–1
Police Burglary Screening Decision Model

Weight (circle)	Information Element
	1. Suspect Information
10	A. Positive Identification
8	B. Tentative Identification
6	C. Poor Identification
	2. Vehicle Information
10	A. Positive Identification (tag and/or other)
8	B. Definitive Description
6	C. Poor Description
	3. Estimate Time Between Incident - Report
4	A. Less than one hour
3	B. One to twelve hours
2	C. Twelve hours and over
	4. Method of Reporting
2	A. Witness and/or victim
1	B. Officer on-view
	5. Information Received ⎯⎯⎯⎯⎯⎯➤ SECTION 5 TO BE
	A. Confidential Informant and/or victim USED *ONLY* IF
10	1. Definitive information INFORMATION
8	2. Possible information AVAILABLE AT
6	3. Poor information CODING *OR* TO
	B. Information shared from other ACTIVATE AN
	investigator and/or agency INACTIVE CASE
10	1. Definitive information
8	2. Possible information
6	3. Poor information
	6. Modus Operandi
5	A. Definitive pattern
4	B. Possible pattern
3	C. Poor pattern
	7. Fingerprints
10	A. Identified with suspect
1	B. Without suspect

_____   TOTAL   CUT POINT FOR CASE ACTIVATION IS 10

Case: Active
          Inactive (circle)
Other factors not listed which cause the case to be active.

(Specify) _____

NOTE: *This scale is to be used as a guideline only and is not intended to override nor interfere with the good judgment of a superior in assigning cases where there may be considerations not included in the scale.*

CASE NUMBER_____   INVESTIGATOR_____

DATE_____   SCREENER_____

The victim of a commercial burglary in which an expensive set of power tools was stolen was recontacted by the investigator. The tools were highly specialized and were used in only one type of business, that in which the victim was employed. The investigator was shown the crime scene, and the victim recounted how he had discovered the theft. The victim employed numerous high school students and young adults in low-paying jobs; there was a high turnover of employees. The victim said, however, that he suspected no current or former employee of committing the burglary. After interviewing the victim, the

Figure 7–2
Theft-from-Auto Screening Decision Model

```
POLICE DEPARTMENT
```

DATE OF OFFENSE	NAME OF SCREENING OFFICER		CLASS	DIST. NO.	CENTRAL COMPLAINT NO.

INFORMATION ELEMENT	WEIGHTING FACTOR	INSTRUCTIONS
Can complainant or witness identify the offender by name?	10	(1) Circle the weighting factor for each information element that is present in the Incident Report
Is the stolen property traceable, serial number, etc. ?	7	
Can complainant or witness provide registration of auto used?	7	(2) Total the circled factors.
Will complainant sign a complaint in court if offender is apprehended?	3	(3) If the sum is seven (7) or more, the case is assigned for investigation.
Estimate range of time of occurrence		
Less than 1 hour	5	
1 to12 hours	1	(4) If the sum is less than seven (7), suspend the case.
12 to 24 hours	0.3	
more than 24 hours	0	
Witness's report of offense	7	
On-view report of offense	1	
Usable fingerprints	7	

TOTAL SCORE: _____

DECISION MODEL RULE RECOMMENDATION

_____ ASSIGN CASE   _____   DO NOT ASSIGN CASE _____
                                  OVERRIDE

EXPLAIN OVERRIDE:

SIGNATURE OF SCREEN OFFICER _____

DATE _____

DETECTIVE ASSIGNMENT

CASE ASSIGNED TO: _____ SUSPENSE DATE: _____
                          DETECTIVE

UNIT SUPERVISOR: _____

CASE STATUS

_____ ARREST MADE   _____ _____   OTHER _____
                        PENDING   INACTIVE

DATE _____   SIGNATURE OF CODING OFFICER: _____

investigator canvassed the neighborhood for possible witnesses in the apartments overlooking the crime scene. Although several people had been home at the time, no one had seen or heard anything suspicious. The investigator stated after the canvass that the victim might have reported a false burglary to gain the insurance money. Few people would have had any use

for the items taken. No further investigation was conducted.

But some cases that have no good or apparent leads are not so hopeless as the original report may indicate. In this type of case, recontacting the victim is useful:

An investigator checking the address of a strong-arm robbery victim found that he lived in a halfway house for juvenile delinquents. At the victim's residence, the investigator was introduced to the victim by the adult supervisor. The investigator asked the victim to explain in greater detail than was in the patrol report the circumstances of the robbery. After some hesitation, the victim stated that the suspect was known to him, but not by name, and that the victim and suspect had gone to the location of the incident together. After further inquiries, the victim admitted that he had wanted to purchase some marijuana from the suspect, but the suspect had beaten him and taken his money. The victim had not told this fact to the patrol officer, because the victim had been afraid to incriminate himself. The investigator assured the victim that no charges would be brought against him and confirmed the suspect's description as obtained by the patrol officer. The investigator then continued to investigate the case.

NAMED SUSPECTS

Sometimes a suspect is named in a patrol report assigned for investigation. Investigators then may check department arrest records to see if the named suspect has a criminal record. Since the suspect may not have any record, because he or she either has never been involved with the particular agency or is a juvenile, this activity may not always be useful. Indeed, the identification of a suspect in a patrol report is no guarantee that that person committed or had anything to do with the offense.

Although a named suspect sometimes can be arrested and charged, the testimony of victims and witnesses often leaves much to be desired. For example, the victim may only be theorizing about who committed the offense. Sometimes victims and witnesses see someone they know in the vicinity of an offense, but no other evidence links the suspect to the offense. Thus a named suspect or a description in a patrol report may provide valuable leads, but they often do not make the investigation easy or guarantee a solution. The following example illustrates this point:

While conducting a follow-up investigation to a burglary, an investigator found a juvenile suspect listed in the patrol report. The suspect had been named by the victim, who claimed to have seen the suspect near her house shortly after it was broken into. The suspect's parents were contacted by phone and an appointment made for the next day at the suspect's home. At that time, the investigator interviewed the suspect and discussed the case with his parents in their living room. The suspect claimed not to be involved but was aware of the incident; he also claimed that he could name the people who had committed the burglary. The suspect provided the name of another person who he said could verify that he was not involved. The investigator was aware of the activities (not directly related to the offense under consideration) of some of the people named by the juvenile and felt that this suspect probably had had little or nothing to do with the burglary. After warning the juvenile to stay away from some of his associates because of their links to known offenders, the investigator left. The investigator believed that although the suspect might not have been completely innocent, he certainly was not deeply involved in the offense, and his parents seemed to be the type to keep him in line.

GOOD LEADS

The amount of effort required to follow up a good lead is seldom mentioned in research or investigative work. However, as the following example shows, even when good leads are available, the investigation is not a simple matter of arresting suspects.

A burglary victim called an investigator to explain that she thought the offenders were two employees of a firm that the apartment complex had hired to do some work in her apartment. The described suspects, names unknown, had been given a key to her apartment in order to perform the necessary work. The burglary had been committed eight days later, and there had been no forced entry. The apartment manager, when contacted by the investigator, denied that the suspects could have conducted the burglary but provided the name of the firm that employed them. The owner of the firm testified to the suspects' good employment records and reliability. A message was left for the suspects to contact the investigator. The suspects called back about a half hour later and gave the investigator their full names, dates of birth, and past criminal histories and described the work done on the victim's apartment. The investigator used this information to check his own department's records and also requested a record check on the suspects from a neighboring jurisdiction. The investigator concluded after following up these leads that the suspects were not likely to have been the offenders and closed the investigation.

This example demonstrates that even when apparently good leads are available, additional work is required to check them out, and even then the case still may not be solved.

Although information about a suspect may not be present in a preliminary report, there may be enough evidence to lead to the identification of a suspect. In the following example, the preliminary report included a few tenuous leads that proved very useful. Of particular interest is the fact that at every step of this investigation, the likelihood of identifying the suspect was small.

A patrol report of a robbery included the name and address of a juvenile witness but failed to indicate the nature of the information she might have. The investigator visited the address listed on the patrol report; it was the address of the witness's grandmother. Although the witness had been living there at the time of the robbery, she had just moved back with her parents. The investigator drove to the address provided by the grandmother and interviewed the witness in the company of her parents. The witness thought she recognized the suspect and provided what she thought was the suspect's name. She also stated that she would recognize the suspect if she saw him again.

The investigator returned to the police station and began checking for the suspect's name in department records. Several variations of the name were tried without success. The investigator discussed the case with a youth officer who suggested a different variation on the suspect's name. A recheck of department

records provided a photo, description, name, address, and prior record of a suspect who matched the descriptions given by the victim and witness. Furthermore, and as important to the investigator, the suspect had a prior record of assaults and drug offenses.

The investigator then put together a photo lineup of five color photographs of similar-looking people plus the suspect's photo. When the investigator returned to the witness's home, she easily identified the photo of the suspect. Armed with this information, the investigator drove by the suspect's home but did not stop. He then called the dispatcher and asked that a particular patrol officer meet him nearby. When the officer arrived, the investigator gave the information about the suspect to the officer and directed him to arrest the suspect on sight. Shortly thereafter the suspect was arrested by the officer.

CRIME ANALYSIS

As police departments across the country attempt either to stem increases or maintain decreases in crime rates, many have turned for assistance to the application of information technolgies to conduct crime analysis. *Crime analysis* involves identifying trends and patterns within crime data to attempt to solve crimes or prevent their repeat occurrence. While many officers have been doing some form of informal crime analysis since their careers began, the use of information technology to increase the power and speed of that analysis is now being explored more fully.

THE BASIC FUNTIONS OF CRIME ANALYSIS

The first function of the crime analysis unit is the analysis of crime and other incidents to support resource deployment. This involves detecting patterns in crime or the potential for crime in order to enhance the effectiveness of patrol operations, surveillance, stakeouts, and other police tactics. Tactical analysis also can identify crime "hot spots," those locations characterized by above-normal concentrations of crime. The outcome of these analyses often impacts personnel deployment and resource allocation.

The second function of crime analysis involves identifying crime-suspect correlations to assist investigations. By comparing files that contain *modus operandi* (MO) characteristics with files of new-suspect attributes, more and better arrests may be possible. In addition, the assimilation of numerous investigation leads and information can assist investigators in drawing relationships between suspects and crimes.

Administrative analysis is another of the crime analysis unit's functions and is referred to as *crime reporting*. Included here is the preparation of reports for a variety of requesters, ranging from city agencies, courts, and government offices to community groups and the media. Dissemination of crime information in certain regions is as vital to community relations as it is to community policing purposes; communities must be informed about their local crime situation if they are expected to influence it.

The final function of crime analysis is crime prevention. Analysts focus on identifying locations, times of day, or situations in which crimes appear to cluster so that efforts to harden these potential targets can be initiated. These analyses may lead to recommendations for changes in the physical structure of buildings (e.g., lighting, visibility, security gates) or in the actions of potential victims (e.g., locking doors, parking in illuminated areas of garages, hiding valuables from view) to make them less likely targets of crime.[2]

THE STAGES OF CRIME ANALYSIS

There are five stages of crime analysis: data collection, data collation, analysis, dissemination, and feedback.[3]

Data Collection

Crime analysis begins with the collection of a wide variety of information. The goal of data collection is to gather crime-specific elements that distinguish both one criminal incident from another and one group of offenses, related in one or more ways, from a larger group of similar offenses. This information is compiled largely from a variety of external and internal sources.

External Sources can provide valuable information on adult career criminals and known offenders (see Table 7–1). Parolee information is particularly useful if a department emphasizes apprehension of career offenders. Most agencies probably have few options for obtaining external information, since they have little control over the sources. Still, agreements can be reached so that specific information is provided regularly in a usable format. School disciplinary actions are one example.

In the mid-1980s, after recognizing that a number of serious habitual juvenile offenders were among local students, school officials in Jacksonville, Florida, entered into a partnership with the Duval County Sheriff's Office and the local state attorney to track the "worst of the worst." The ultimate goal was to develop policies and

Table 7–1
External Data Sources and Their Uses

External Sources	Uses
School records	Identify and track problem children; identify potential serious habitual offenders
Bail information	Identify suspects committing crimes while on bail.
Probation information	Provide information to officers about conditions of probation related to associates, places, alcohol use, etc.
Parole information	Provide information to officers about the release of known offenders into the community.
Furloughed prisoners	Track appearances of an old MO over a series of weekends.
Other police agencies	Identify and track crimes and offenders across jurisdictional boundaries.
Census data	Understand the demographics of a given area.

procedures to manage the offenders' impact on classroom order. To assist in this, the partnership created an interagency database that allowed each agency, along with the juvenile courts, probation office, and social service agencies, to share "offender-oriented" information. In a short time, information about truancy, referral rates for absences, tardiness, behavior problems, student-conduct violations, and academic history was made available for the purpose of creating a multiagency supervision and intervention plan. A clear picture of disruptive incidents and trends emerged, along with additional knowledge of how youths interact with other students. From this analysis, troubled youths could be identified more quickly and appropriate interventions applied more broadly. Such efforts had not been previously possible because the participating agencies had long believed that information could not or should not be shared. The result, of course, was the maintenance of separate and usually incomplete files.[4] Fortunately, most jurisdictions have provisions similar to those available in Jacksonville to allow interagency sharing of even juvenile information.[5]

Internal sources Offense reports alone do not provide enough information for analysis purposes. For example, in many crimes against property, an actual time or means of entry is not available from offense reports. Supplemental data sources on tripped alarms, suspicious persons, calls, and field interviews can be used to narrow the time frame within which a burglary occurred. When evidence technicians process a crime scene, their reports may contain more detailed information regarding the types of tools and means used to commit a burglary. Table 7–2 lists various internal sources and examples of their use.

CRIME ANAYLSIS AND TACTICAL ANALYSIS

Crime analysts make a distinction between crime analysis and tactical crime analysis. The differences between the analyses lie in the approach and endproduct of each, rather than in their methodologies.[6] In both instances, crime analysis is a law enforcement agency function whereby data relating to crime are collected, collated, analyzed, and disseminated. *Crime analysis* represents a system utilizing regularly collected information on reported crimes and criminals to prevent and suppress crime and to apprehend criminal offenders. Crime analysis tends to view crime along a longterm continuum for the purpose of departmental strategy and future staffing levels.

Table 7–2
Internal Data Sources and Their Uses

Internal Sources	Uses
Offense-incident reports	Provide information on the crime-specific elements of a particular offense and serve as the basis of crime analysis.
Field-interview cards	Become the primary source of field intelligence about suspicious persons interviewed at specific locations and times and about the activities of known offenders.
Evidence technician reports	Determine the availability of latent fingerprints.
Selected calls for service	Identify the time at which alarms were triggered in specific areas.
Investigative supplements	Provide additional crime-specific elements that result from follow-up investigations and interviews.
Arrest reports	Describe known offenders and the details of how a crime was committed.
Traffic citations	Provide information about vehicle movements in key areas.
Teletypes from local agencies	Track crimes across jurisdictional boundaries.
Confessions from arrestees	Confirm exact MO of offenders.
Intelligence files	Provide information on drug abusers, fences, and organized crime-related activity.

Tactical crime analysis, on the other hand, takes a different approach in that the crime analysis report addresses short-term resource deployment. Unlike crime analysis, tactical crime analysis is more immediate, fluid, and subject to change on a moment's notice. The report not only summarizes the analysis process but also includes a suspect profile, a victim profile, MO factors associated with the perpetrator, area or premise type, day and time preferred by the perpetrator, and other factors that will aid in identifying the perpetrator as he or she enters the area under surveillance. The desired result of tactical analysis is suspect apprehension, through aggressive suspect and victim (either person or business) targeting and surveillance. Tactical crime analysis reports include a section dealing with a suggested tactical response.

When suspects become targets of investigations, it is imperative for the tactical crime analyst to consider all possible information about the suspect. Any additional information collected can only increase the accuracy of the calculations. Tactical crime analysts try to anticipate where the suspect will travel and when he or she is likely to strike again. For example, one researcher presents several methodologies of anticipating when and where the next hit will occur.[7] The result of these computations can be greatly enhanced by factoring in additional information. For example, it is helpful to include the suspect's home and work addresses, any significant other's home and work addresses, and the suspect's favorite haunts, with the locations associated with linked incidents. Tactical crime analysts can also create maps that indicate statistically significant occurrences, or crime hot spots. A wide array of mapping programs can create these maps. By layering a boundary file (a layout of area boundaries), a point file (locations of robberies, burglaries, or recovered vehicles), and an ellipse file (circles of greatest activity), an analyst can produce a map that indicates the hot-spot areas clearly defined by the ellipses. This mapping technique conveys statistically significant areas of high activity; however, there is no "one way" to create a geographic map. Some analysts use pins to mark location; others use adhesive spots or dots. Symbols can also be effective. For example, small pictures of cars are sometimes used to designate the location of auto thefts.

The decision of whether to use pins, dots, or pictures to represent crime occurrences is often dictated by the amount of data one wishes to display on the map. If the crime report number is to be recorded with the location of the offense, colored dots or flags (with colored heads) can be used. The colors indicate the type of crime. The report number is written on the dot or the flag. Similarly, color-coded and marked pins can be employed to identify specific MO patterns.

The length of time a particular map or set of maps should be maintained is also important. No absolute set of rules has been established regarding map maintenance time, but it is recommended that they be maintained for three months to enable quarterly crime comparisons. Two maps may be maintained for each type of crime, one for reflecting weekly or monthly information and the other, year-to-date or quarterly information.

Map data should be stored so that it is easily retrievable. Pin maps can be recorded photographically; taking color slide pictures of the maps and using two projections to superimpose one figure over another is often effective. Acetate overlays marked with color-coded dots are also easily retrievable. This procedure will work well for agencies that use manual mapping techniques. Increasingly, however, agencies have turned to computerized mapping to store and display their data. Among others, programs such as Map Info and Atlas Crime Analysis by Strategic Mapping, Inc., can be used to quickly identify hot spots and patterns of criminal activities. Maps generated by these programs are easily stored and retrieved on a variety of microcomputer systems.

Seven is the minimum number of maps most crime analysis units should maintain. Five crime types are well suited to geographical analysis: burglary, robbery, auto theft, other unique grand- or petty-theft offenses, and sex crimes. Two of these types (burglary and robbery) have logical subclassifications: commercial and residential for burglary and armed and unarmed for robbery.

Four other informational maps are also quite useful. One is designed to support career-criminal apprehension programs by mapping the last-known residences and crime specialties of known suspects. Another supports narcotics operations by indicating locations of crack and crash "pads," street corners where narcotics are sold, and so on. The third map is used to depict locations where stolen property is "fenced." Maps depicting gang "turfs" and the occurrence of gang-related incidents are also beneficial. They aid the field deployment process, help police identify activity patterns existing in emerging criminal groups, and allow officers to forecast locations of future intergang conflicts. The department's ability to "read" spray-painted graffiti often provides the basic data for such maps.[8]

DISSEMINATION OF CRIME ANALYSIS DATA

Once the analysis is completed and a comprehensive report has been prepared, it is time to disseminate the information to all who need it. Dissemination can be carried out in several different ways. Analysts should attend briefings with both investigators and uniformed patrol officers to keep lines of communication open. Also, the analysts can verbally present reports, hear firsthand how the end user used previous information, and solicit suggestions for improved report formats. The importance of face-to-face contact between the analysts and the officers and investigators cannot be overemphasized.

After attending briefings and strategy sessions, analysts should distribute clear, succinct written reports to those who have a need for them. Analysts should have a mechanism for disseminating general information to a large number of individuals. Usually this is achieved by means of written reports directed through normal channels.

Analysts must be able to quickly notify key personnel who are directly involved or directly responsible for deciding if resources will be deployed in response to a situation. Once the analyst has conducted a detailed analysis of an ongoing crime pattern and developed a tactical action plan, key personnel must use the information immediately to determine a course of response action. It is strongly recommended that these types of reports have different names, such as "Special Alerts" or "Special Crime Bulletins" to differentiate them from routine reports.

FEEDBACK

The last aspect of the analysis process is feedback. The analyst should not go blindly forward from day to day without knowing which output products and formats (written reports, charts, graphs, overheads, computer-generated presentations, and maps) work and which do not work. The analyst spends a great deal of time preparing output products so he or she should know how the end user plans to use a final product and should then determine how useful it actually is for the user. Additionally, if the end user views the analyst's output as nonresponsive to a request, he or she may not make additional requests. Such a scenario wastes effort and compromises efficiency.[9]

THE NATIONAL CRIME INFORMATION CENTER

With the advent of computer technology, high-speed retrieval of investigative information has become a reality. The single most important system of this type is the National Crime Information Center (NCIC) located in Washington, D.C., and operated by the FBI. The NCIC was designed to complement, rather than to replace, local and state crime information systems. Local and state computer information systems contain data that should not and cannot be placed into the NCIC. For example, these systems contain data on in-state vehicle registration, outstanding warrants for traffic violations, and subjects wanted for nonextraditable offenses.

The following types of data may be stored and retrieved through the NCIC: stolen, missing, or recovered guns; stolen articles; wanted persons; stolen vehicles; stolen license plates; and stolen, embezzled, or missing securities. To make an entry into the NCIC, one needs a complete description of the item involved, including its manufacturer, brand name, serial number, model, color, and any other applicable information. The NCIC places an individual's name into its wanted-persons file only if a warrant has been issued and the state involved is willing to extradite for the offense for which the warrant was issued.

Whenever entries are to be made into the NCIC, the police agency must also give the date of the offense, the name of the agency initiating the report, and the case number. Agencies entering crime data also are responsible for maintaining the accuracy of records, updating information, and removing old data. Generally, requests to the NCIC are answered within one to five minutes.

NEIGHBORHOOD CANVASS

One fundamental aspect of most investigations is the neighborhood canvass of residents, merchants, and others who may have been in the immediate vicinity of a crime and have useful information. It is estimated that a systematic neighborhood canvass soon after the commission of an offense results in information of investigative value in approximately 20 percent of all cases. The extent of the canvass depends on variables such as the type of offense, time of day, and characteristics of the crime scene. The timing of a neighborhood canvass is an important consideration. People not only move randomly through areas but also ebb and flow on a variety of schedules. To mistime a neighborhood canvass by 30 minutes, for example, may mean eliminating the possibility of locating persons who regularly catch a bus at a particular time and who, on the day of an offense, might have seen something of considerable investigative value.

Before a neighborhood canvass, investigators should be given all information relating to the offense, including a full description of the suspect, any injuries sustained by the suspect, and the type of property taken. The possession of these facts is absolutely essential for two major reasons. First, investigators then can question witnesses intelligently, increasing the probability that all available information will be elicited. Second, it protects the investigator from unknowingly encountering the suspect and thus being placed in jeopardy.

Interviews should be conducted first at businesses or dwellings with a clear view of the crime scene and at the suspect's avenues of approach and flight. When there are substantial numbers of locations involved, several teams of officers canvassing simultaneously are helpful. When merchants or residents are not on site during the canvass, a later contact is necessary. Even when persons interviewed do not provide any useful information, investigators must record the fact that no information was obtained in order to eliminate the possibility of duplicating effort later on. Another reason for recording that no positive information has been provided is shown in the following case study:

On a Sunday morning, a residential burglary of $3,800 in rare coins was reported. The uniformed officer making the original investigation received permission to conduct the neighborhood canvass. Usually the follow-up investigator did the canvass, but the uniformed officer had extra time that day. The victim's home was situated on a cul-de-sac along with four other homes with some view of the victimized premises. There were no homes to the rear of the victim's residence. After interviewing residents of the four neighboring homes, including a teenage boy, the uniformed officer recorded the identities and statements of those with whom he had talked in his report. All indicated they had seen nothing. Because of the value of the property taken, the case was referred for follow-up investigation.

The detective assigned to the case recently had been transferred from the Youth Services Bureau to the Burglary Bureau and recognized the name of the youth identified in the interview section of the uniformed officer's report as an individual with an extensive juvenile record for breaking and entering. Investigation revealed that the youth had committed the offense, and all coins taken were recovered.

Admittedly, this is an unusual case. Although luck played some part, the neighborhood canvass and adherence to sound reporting procedures not only avoided duplication of effort but cleared the case so quickly that the perpetrator had no opportunity to dispose of the stolen property.

INFORMANTS

Information provided by informants often plays a vital role in making an investigation successful. Such information may provide evidence of an unreported crime or constitute the basis for a legal search or an arrest. Whatever the value of information provided by informants, the reality—depending on the motivation of the individual informant involved—is that the informant-investigator transaction is often sordid business. Although relationships with certain informants may approach the genteel, they frequently involve an investigator's finding a point of leverage in the potential informant's values or personal history and applying pressure, ranging from veiled threats to outright coercion.

Not all informants have committed crimes. They come from all walks of life. In dealing with them, investigators often find it useful to determine their motivations. The list of informant types discussed here is not exhaustive, nor are the categories mutually exclusive.

Mercenary informants provide information to the police for financial reward. Foreign police systems, such as the French, historically have placed great reliance on paid informants, but it is less characteristic in this country. It is, nonetheless, not an uncommon occurrence. From time to time, individuals who themselves are engaged in illegal activities may wish to eliminate a competitor. The *rival informant* provides information to establish control over the activity in question, using the police to achieve legally what he or she cannot do alone. An individual arrested for a crime may know of criminal activities by others and, in exchange for telling the police, the *plea-bargaining informant* seeks reduced charges or a lenient sentence. Frequently, police departments receive anonymous information either by telephone or in writing. Because the identity of the *anonymous informant* is unknown, the motivations are not identifiable. Anonymous information should not be discarded but should be pursued, so long as it may be fruitful. Many law-abiding citizens have information about crimes that they will share with the police. In a strict sense, such persons are not informers. But they are designated *legitimate informers* to distinguish them from other types.

The *self-aggrandizing informant* has many contacts in criminal circles and feels important by giving information to the police. When investigators identify this motivation, they should give ample praise each time information is supplied. Otherwise such informants may not continue the relationship. A comparative rarity is the *false informant,* who intentionally provides misleading information to direct attention away from himself or herself, friends, or relatives. *Fearful informants* worry that they will be endangered by the criminal activities of an associate. Fearing for their own well-being, they supply information.

Swap shops and pawnshops, however properly operated, occasionally are places where stolen property is recovered. Shop operators may share information about criminal activities with the police to build credit and reduce the likelihood that they will be formally charged if stolen property is found in their possession.

DEALING WITH INFORMANTS

Investigators must observe certain rules in dealing with informants. Breaking these rules prevents investigators from cultivating and retaining informants and creates a negative image of the police department, thereby reducing the potential flow of information. The following are some of the rules for dealing with informants:

- Investigators must never make promises they cannot or do not intend to keep.
- When talking with a plea-bargaining informant, investigators cannot promise a lenient sentence or reduced charge; they can promise only support in seeking it.
- Meetings with informants should be held not in police facilities but in places where informants will not be identified as having an association with an investigator.
- Investigators should never meet informants by themselves. This can put them in a disadvantageous position, since the informant can allege that promises and threats were make when in fact they have never been made.
- Investigators should corroborate all information provided by informants.
- Investigators should never socialize with informants. This is especially true in regard to female informants. Many a police officer has lost an assignment or a job as a result of having become intimate with a confidential informant. In addtion, confidential informants should not be given the officer's home phone number.
- Investigators should never pay an informant without obtaining a witnessed signed statement. If possible, how much the informant will be paid should be set up in advance and in writing.
- Whenever possible, expenses such as meals and rooms should be reimbursed only on presentation of a receipt or within limits agreed upon by the investigator and the informant.

- Regardless of his or her reliability, no informant should receive payment until the reliability of the information has been verified.
- The proper names of informants should never be used in investigative reports. Instead, informants should be identified by codes, such as A273. The identity should be revealed only to persons designated by the police department, such as investigators and immediate supervisors.
- Access to an informant's file should be limited to the fewest persons possible and be permitted only on a need-to-know basis.
- Regardless of informants' value and reliability, they should never be permitted to act illegally.
- Informants should be fully told the circumstances that constitute entrapment and be advised to avoid them scrupulously.

SURVEILLANCE

Surveillance is defined as the secretive and continuous observation of persons, places, and things to obtain information concerning the activities and identity of individuals. Surveillance, as practiced by law enforcement, is a hidden or secret activity typically designed to be carried on without the subject's knowledge. It is this requirement of secrecy that makes a successful surveillance particularly difficult.[10]

A special jargon, or terminology, is used by surveillance officers. Some of the more commonly used terms are:

Subject or *hare:* The person being observed.

Surveillant: The officer or investigator doing the observing.

Burn: Recognition of the surveillant by the subject.

Covert: Secret or hidden.

Overt: The opposite of covert—an apparent, readily observable surveillance.

Tail: Synonymous with "surveillant."

Visual (eyeball): The officer or investigator can see the subject.

Loose surveillance: Surveillance at a discreet distance from the subject, so that the surveillant avoids being burned.

Tight surveillance: The opposite of loose surveillance; to avoid losing the subject, a minimum distance is maintained between the subject and the surveillant; the risk of being burned is thus high.

USES OF SURVEILLANCE

Surveillance is used for a number of reasons and in varying situations. Primarily, it is used to obtain information. It is used when other information-gathering methods fail or to verify and expand information previously obtained.

In addition to its primary use as an information-gathering method, surveillance is used as a means to prevent crime. An example of this is the open and continuous surveillance of an active criminal by police to discourage any criminal activity. It is also used as a means of apprehending criminals in the act of committing crimes and of providing protection for investigators working under cover.

The methods used to accomplish a surveillance are as varied as the circumstances and imagination will allow. It is accomplished on foot, by vehicle, by aircraft, by boat, and from stationary positions. Binoculars, high-power telescopes, radios, cameras, sophisticated mechanical and electronic tracking and listening devices, and ultraviolet light are used to aid the surveillance officer.

OBJECTIVES OF SURVEILLANCE

A surveillance is initiated when an investigator wants to accomplish a particular investigative objective. For example, the investigator may need to learn a subject's routine in order to make an appropriate undercover approach, to corroborate information given by an informant, or to determine a subject's activities with reference to a conspiracy investigation. The objectives may be single or multiple, or they may change as the surveillance progresses. Whatever the objective, it is important that all surveillants understand what information is being sought.

Surveillance often proves very effective in situations such as those discussed below:

Establishing the Existence of a Violation
Frequently information is received or an allegation is made that an individual is violating the law.

Intelligence concerning the individual's activities might establish that the information or allegation is true, or at least has some basis. Surveillance is one of the more practical approaches in proceeding with the investigation in most of these situations, and in many cases it is the only approach available.

Obtaining Probable Cause for a Search Warrant

If a violation has been established but insufficient probable cause exists for either a search warrant or an arrest warrant, surveillance may be used to find probable cause. Enough probable cause may be obtained after several hours of observation, or several months of prolonged surveillance may be needed to accomplish this objective. The intelligence gained in this manner will not only produce the probable cause needed but may be used as evidence in any subsequent prosecution of the subject.

Apprehending Violators in the Commission of Illegal Acts

Surveillance is especially effective in identifying violators at the scene of a criminal activity and often establishes how each violator is involved. A violation that occurs at a particular location and is repeated over a period of time, such as street-level narcotic sales, is very vulnerable to surveillance.

Identifying Violator Associates

As an investigation develops, the investigator is sometimes surprised at how extensive the violation is and soon realizes that the initial principal has one or more associates in the criminal venture. Surveillance can be the most efficient means of identifying these associates and determining how they are involved with the principal.

Establishing Informant Reliability

Often information received from an informant needs to be expanded or corroborated in order to obtain sufficient probable cause for definite action against the subject of the investigation. Informant reliability, the all-important factor in dealing with informants, can be determined by surveillance. That is, preliminary information may be verified and help establish that a first-time informant's information is reliable even if his or her credibility cannot be established. The informant may even become the subject of a surveillance if the investigator suspects that the informant is using the investigator to entrap a second individual.

Providing Protection for an Undercover Investigator or Informant

At particularly sensitive points in an investigation, both undercover officers and informants may require back-up in the form of investigators in the immediate vicinity to furnish help if needed. This type of security is supplied by surveillance in a very discreet manner. The surveillance investigators must be careful not to reveal their presence to the subject of the investigation; otherwise, the undercover investigator or informant may be compromised. This in turn could jeopardize both the investigators and the success of their investigation.

Locating Persons, Places, or Things

Wanted persons can be located by surveillance when other approaches will not work. If enough information is obtained about the subject's background, a surveillance employed in conjunction with the background information usually will produce results. For example, a surveillance of a person or residence that is closely connected with the subject will likely produce positive results in locating a wanted subject. The locations of contraband stashes and manufacturing sites of illegal products frequently are found through the use of well-executed surveillances.

Preventing Crime

In some situations, law enforcement agencies purposely alert a subject that they are aware of his or her presence in their city, or they make it known to him or her that they are in the subject's area. The U.S. Secret Service, on some protection assignments, will place a high security risk under a tight surveillance with the object being to keep the subject under continuous observation. The surveillance is conducted so tightly that it may evolve from a covert to an overt surveillance, depending on the situation. Its primary objective, however, is to prevent the subject from taking any aggressive action against the protectee. This same type of surveillance has been employed by city and state police when known criminals visit their locality for some illegal purpose. The subject usually is confronted by detectives who establish his or her identity and ask the reason for the visit. Then an almost open surveillance is maintained on the subject for as long as he or she remains in the area. This has the effect of discouraging any criminal activity by that subject.

Gathering Intelligence on Individuals and Premises Prior to the Execution of a Search Warrant

The more current information an agency has about a subject and his or her residence prior to the execution of a search warrant, the more intelligently it can be planned and safely executed. Executing a search warrant with insufficient intelligence about a residence and its occupants is dangerous and foolhardy. Observations of the target of a search warrant should be standard procedure, and surveillance should be carried out over a period of several days and just prior to the execution of the warrant, if possible.

Gathering Intelligence on Illegal Groups' Activities

Militant groups and outlaw gangs present the investigator with unique problems that lend themselves to solution only after sufficient intelligence is gathered. Undercover work is very effective in penetrating these groups, and surveillance is used as a preliminary approach to gain information to determine the jurisdiction of the criminal activity. Once the area of jurisdiction is learned, surveillance is used either to aid in the placing of an undercover agent in the group or to keep the group's activity under observation for intelligence in order to more effectively take enforcement action when needed.

MECHANICAL LIE DETECTION

The *polygraph* can be an invaluable investigative aid. Like any scientific instrument, however, its efficacy is limited by the skill of the operator. It has been demonstrated that there is a significant relation between a person's state of mind and his or her physiological state. Fear and anger, for example, increase the rate of the heartbeat, respiration, and the production of perspiration. The polygraph measures these physiological responses to psychological phenomena. It records physiological changes in breathing, blood pressure, pulse rate and amplitude, and galvanic skin reflex (see Figures 7–3 and 7–4).

It is generally agreed that a polygraph examination should not be undertaken until a thorough investigation has been completed and all physical

Figure 7–3
Typical four-channel polygraph

Records physiological changes in breathing, blood pressure, pulse rate and amplitude, and galvanic response.

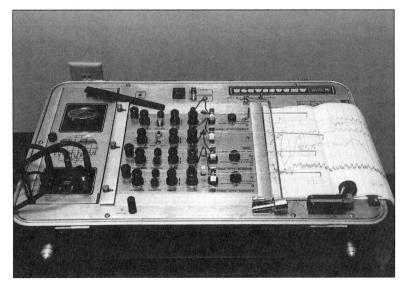

(Courtesy: Sheriff Cal Henderson and Detective Herb Metzgar, Hillsborough County Sheriff's Office, Tampa, Florida)

Figure 7–4
Computerized Polygraph Scoring
Polygraphist using the computer polygraph with automated scoring software.

(Courtesy: Sheriff Cal Henderson and Detective Herb Metzgar, Hillsborough County Sheriff's Office, Tampa, Florida)

evidence processed by the crime laboratory. Without the benefits of such information, it is difficult for the examiner to formulate important questions and to uncover inconsistencies in a subject's statements.

Polygraphs are used for a variety of reasons. Of these, the most important are to free an innocent person from suspicion; to identify deception easily, quickly, and accurately; to make offenders confess under psychological stress; and to promote effective use of investigative time.

The *psychological stress evaluator (PSE)* is an instrument that measures and displays indications of stress in the human voice. When an individual speaks, the voice has two modulations: audible and inaudible to the human ear. Stress may be inaudible to the human ear, but it is both detectable and measurable by the PSE. While to the human ear a person's voice may sound entirely normal, free of tremors or other guilt-suggesting qualities, the PSE would identify the involuntary, inaudible indicators of stress.

The key to the use of the PSE is preparation of simple questions keyed to a specific individual and designed to reveal patterns of truth and deception. Once the voice patterns associated with truthfulness and deception have been established, the questioning proceeds to the area of investigation, and analysis of the subject's voice pattern in this area indicates truthfulness or deception.

Proponents of the PSE maintain that it has two advantages over similar instruments. First, it is simple: it has few moving parts and is relatively easy to operate. Second, it is not necessary to have the PSE in operation at the time of the first interview or interrogation; a recording of the initial interview can be fed into the PSE later. The PSE also may be used on tape recordings of telephone conversations.[11]

COMPUTERIZED "LIE-DETECTOR" SCORING

The Johns Hopkins University Applied Physics Laboratory (APL) has developed a new polygraph technology and incorporated it into a personal-computer program to score polygraph tests automatically and with great reliability, an accomplishment stemming from APL's experience in the complex analysis of submarine-launched missiles.[12]

Called *POLYSCORE*, the APL software uses a highly sophisticated mathematical algorithm to analyze physiological signals recorded during a polygraph examination. The program makes complex statistical comparisons that cannot be made by examiners. After the test, POLYSCORE displays a probability that indicates deception, no deception, or, about 1 time in 20, that the test was inconclusive. The program is designed primarily to score the frequently used "Zone Comparison Test," which asks a number of questions leading up to a single issue, such as "Did you rob the bank?"

Scientists working on the system report that the program's scoring rules deliver consistent, objective results time after time. This allows the software to easily identify the physiological reactions of people who are telling the truth and those who are attempting deception.

A total of 440 cases was used to develop the scoring algorithm. After subtracting a relatively low 5 percent inconclusive findings, the system scored all but one of the remaining cases correctly. Confessions, either by the subject or someone else, were used to identify which subjects attempted deception in 137 of these test cases. The remaining cases were judged by an independent team using traditional scoring methods, and their results matched the program's findings.

Scientists working on the project believe the program makes a highly significant advance in polygraph technology that will affect the whole field.

LEGAL CONSIDERATIONS

No witness, suspect, or defendant can be compelled to take any mechanical lie-detection test, as this would violate the Fifth Amendment privilege. Namely, no one can be required to be a witness against himself or herself. However, a suspect may, subject to the legal requirements discussed more fully in Chapter 8, Interrogation, agree voluntarily to submit to a lie-detector test.

Ordinarily tests are administered after an arrest but before a final decision to lodge formal charges. Frequently police initiate such examinations when evidence is largely circumstantial. Sometimes people under arrest request a lie-detector test in the erroneous belief that they can fool the detection system or in cases where they are earnestly convinced of their innocence.

Occasionally, prosecuting and defense attorneys, after an arrest of a subject but before formal charging, agree to a mechanical lie-detection test pursuant to a stipulated agreement. The prosecuting attorney uses the results to decide whether charges should be made and what they should be. The results of tests taken pursuant to stipulated agreements are generally admissible as evidence in this country. But in general, in those rare instances when trial judges have offered defendants the opportunity to prove their innocence by taking a mechanical lie-detection test, the appellate courts have held this to be improper.[13]

RELATIONSHIPS WITH VICTIMS AND WITNESSES

The cooperation of victims and witnesses—and the same person may play these two roles simultaneously—is frequently the key to successful investigations. But many police departments neglect to consider the adverse effects that the investigative process may have on the investigation itself. Cooperation tends to be reduced when people are unnecessarily inconvenienced, repeat testimony needlessly to different investigators, are not informed of the progress of a case, and are not thanked for their cooperation or extended small courtesies, such as interviews scheduled at times and places most convenient for them.[14]

Some of the preceding obligations clearly belong to the police, others to the prosecutor's office. The distribution of responsibilities should be articulated in a written agreement between the police department head and the prosecutor. However, if the prosecutor's office fails or declines to undertake certain of these responsibilities, they fall to the police.

A Rand Corporation study underscored the importance of providing victims with feedback.[15] Most victims express a very strong desire to learn officially whether the police have solved their case and whether a suspect has been arrested. Most victims also want to be told about progress in the prosecution and adjudication of defendants. Victims are divided in their wish to be informed about when suspects are released from custody. The greater the involvement of a victim in the prosecution of a suspect, the greater the victim's desire to be informed about events in the later stages of proceedings. Most victims prefer to be informed when the police decide to suspend investigation of their case. Victims are divided in wanting to know when a suspect arrested for a crime other than theirs is believed to be responsible for the offense against them. A sizable majority of victims react unfavorably to the police when told of negative developments in the case, for example, that the investigation will be suspended or that their stolen property is unlikely to be recovered, although robbery victims tend to be less troubled about this prospect than do burglary victims. Most victims tend to respect, or at least accept, the exercise of professional judgment by the police or prosecutor's office.

Despite the fact that certain disadvantages may be created for the police, feedback to victims is important to them. Investigators should bear in mind that the study shows that no matter how distressed by the information they get, few victims act unfriendly to police. Although those few instances must be regarded seriously, considerable benefits arise from a system of providing feedback to victims.

GUIDELINES FOR CONDUCTING LINEUPS

With a *lineup*, the victim of a crime can view a suspect along with others of similar physical appearance. In a lineup, those involved must literally line up, side-by-side, usually behind a two-way mirror or similar device, so that the victim can view the suspect without being seen.

With some jurisdictional variations, the following guidelines for conducting lineups have been suggested by law enforcement agencies:[16]

- All persons in the lineup should be of the same general age and race and have similar physical characteristics.
- The clothing worn by each should be similar.
- Statements by persons in the lineup should not be requested unless a witness suggests it. If statements are made, all participants should repeat the same words. However, because many states prohibit a defendant from being forced to say anything during the lineup, investigators should first consult with local prosecutors.
- Front and profile color photographs of the lineup should be taken and developed as soon as possible.

- A witness should be prevented from seeing the defendant in custody prior to the lineup.
- Witnesses should not be shown a photograph of the defendant before the lineup.
- If more than one person is to view a lineup, they should do so one at a time and out of the presence of the other.
- No actions should be taken by investigators or statements made to witnesses to suggest that a suspect is standing in any particular place.
- Before entering the lineup room, the witness should be given a form on which the identification can be made (see Figure 7–5).
- There should be at least six persons in the lineup.
- If the suspect's attorney is present, he or she should be allowed to make suggestions.
- Before the lineup, the witness should give a detailed description of the perpetrator and the description should be put in writing.
- If possible, law enforcement officers should not be used in lineups.
- A suspect has no right to refuse a lineup.

Many police agencies now use police lineup worksheets to create records of suspects, witnesses, attorneys, and officers present at lineups (see Figure 7–6).

In some cases it is virtually impossible to conduct a fair lineup because the suspect's physical appearance and clothing are so distinctive. The following case illustrates this point:

A cab driver reported to the police that he had been robbed by one of his passengers. The cab driver made the report immediately after the suspect had fled on foot with the money. The driver reported that the suspect was a black male, approximately 25 years old, 6'6", 285 pounds, armed with a large chrome-plated semiautomatic pistol. The man was wearing an orange silk shirt, blue jeans, and a cowboy hat. Exactly $52 in cash had been taken. Approximately 1 hour after the crime was reported, the suspect was observed in the vicinity of the robbery by the same two officers who had taken the original report. The suspect was arrested by the police officers. A search produced a chrome-plated .45-caliber semiautomatic pistol and $52.12.

Figure 7–5
Witness Lineup-Identification Form

Offense Number

TO WITNESS: PLEASE READ THESE INSTRUCTIONS CAREFULLY.
The position of the persons in the line-up will be numbered left to right, beginning with the number one (1) on your left. Take as much time as you wish to view the line-up. Examine each of the line-up participants carefully. You will be viewing the line-up in a manner which will enable you to see the participants while they will be unable to see you. PLEASE DO NOT DISCUSS any aspect of the case or line-up with any other witness who may be present.

1. If you can identify any of the persons in the line-up as having participated in the criminal offense to which you were a witness, place a "X" in the appropriate square corresponding to the number of the person in the line-up.

2. If none, place a "X" in the square marked NONE.

| 1 | 2 | 3 | 4 | 5 | 6 |

NONE

3. Then sign your name and fill in the date and time.

4. When completed, hand this sheet to the officer conducting the line-up.

_____
OFFICER CONDUCTING LINE-UP

_____
ATTORNEY FOR THE STATE

_____
LINE-UP ATTORNEY FOR DEFENDANT

_____
WITNESS' SIGNATURE

_____
DATE   TIME

(Courtesy St. Petersburg, Florida, Police Department)

In their effort to conduct a lineup, the officers realized that they could not possibly find five people who approximated the suspect in size, race, age, attire, and so forth. The officers decided to use a photo lineup instead of a live lineup. They had a black-and-white photo taken of the suspect, minus the cowboy hat, and incorporated it into a packet of five other police photos of black males of similar age. The cab driver was able to positively identify the photo of the suspect, who subsequently confessed to the crime.

In addition to conventional lineups, computerized photographic lineups, which operate on personal computers, are also being used. In such systems the investigator types in the characteristics that he or she wants displayed in each of five different panels of photographs. The remaining panel is a photograph of the suspect. The computer automatically makes a record of the lineup, which is similar in nature to the manual one shown in Figure 7–6.

Figure 7–6
Police Lineup Worksheet

						Offense Number

SUBJECT #	1	2	3	4	5	6
NAME						
RACE						
AGE						
HEIGHT						
WEIGHT						
SHIRT						
PANTS						
SHOES						

WITNESS PRESENT AT LINE-UP:

			SUSPECT IDENTIFIED		
NAME	ADDRESS	PHONE	YES	NO	TIME ALLOWED

Did suspect waive right to counsel at line-up?   YES_____   NO_____

NAME OF ATTORNEY PRESENT: _____

ADDRESS: _____ PHONE: _____

OFFICER(S) CONDUCTING LINE-UP: _____

DATE: _____ TIME BEGAN: _____ TIME ENDED: _____ CHARGE: _____

NOTE: All subjects in LINE-UP are numbered from left to right, facing interviewing officer. Officer conducting interview shall fill in description of subjects PRIOR TO LINE-UP BEING CONDUCTED.

REMARKS: _____
_____

(Courtesy St. Petersburg, Florida, Police Department)

Questions

1. What are the questions that should be considered before a follow-up investigation is done on a crime?

2. What are the basic functions of crime analysis?

3. What are some external sources of information for data collection for crime analysis?

4. What are some internal sources of information for data collection for crime analysis?

5. How has the National Crime Information Center (NCIC) improved the crime-fighting capabilities of law enforcement agencies?

6. What type of information should an investigator have before beginning the neighborhood canvass?

7. Describe the major categories of informants.

8. For which situations has surveillance often proved very effective?

9. Discuss the various principles on which the polygraph and psychological stress evaluator work.

10. What are the major legal factors that must be considered when employing any mechanical lie-detection test?

11. Discuss some important steps that can be taken by law enforcement agencies to enhance and ensure victim and witness cooperation in criminal investigations.

Notes

1. The listing of investigative solvability factors was obtained from the Cincinnati Police Department, Cincinnati, Ohio, and the Greensboro Police Department, Greensboro, North Carolina.

2. Melissa Miller Reuland (ed.). *Information Management and Crime Anaylsis: Practitioner's Recipe for Success* (Washington, D.C.: Police Executive Research Forum, 1997), pp. 1–3.

3. John Simmons and Dennis J. Kenney, "The Stages of Crime Analysis," in Melissa Miller Reuland (ed.), *Information Management and Crime Analysis: Practitioner's Recipe for Success* (Washington, D.C.: Police Executive Research Forum, 1997), pp. 7–13.

4. G. Higgins, "Serious Habitual Offenders—the Bad Apples," *School Safety*, Winter 1987, Vol. 11.

5. J. Patterson and K. Houlihan, *Confidentiality of Juvenile Offense Histories: A Statutory Review* (Washington D.C.: Office of Juvenile Justice and Delinquency Prevention, 1983).

6. Melvin B. Knight, "Tactical Crime Analysis," in Melissa Miller Reuland (ed.), *Information Management and Crime Analysis: Practitioner's Recipe for Success* (Washington, D.C.: Police Executive Research Forum, 1997), pp. 30–36.

7. S. Gottlieb, S. Arenberg, and R. Sing, *Crime Analysis: From First Report to Final Arrest* (Upland, Calif.: Alpha, 1994), pp. 440–442.

8. Ibid.

9. Reuland, *Information Managment and Crime Analysis*, pp. 35–37.

10. This discussion of surveillance and the accompanying figures were adapted from materials provided by the Department of Treasury, Federal Law Enforcement Training Center, Glynco, Georgia, 1989.

11. Dektor Counterintelligence and Security, "The Psychological Stress Evaluator" (Springfield, Va., 1975), advertisement cover letter.

12. This discussion of computerized lie-detector scoring was taken from a news release distributed by Johns Hopkins University Applied Physics Laboratory.

13. Thomas J. Gardner and Victor Manian, *Principles and Cases of the Law of Arrest, Search and Seizure* (New York: McGraw-Hill, 1974), p. 133.

14. Block and Weidman, *Managing Criminal Investigations* (Washington, D.C.: Government Printing Office, 1975), p. 15.

15. Peter W. Greenwood et al., *The Criminal Investigation Process*, Vol. III, *Observations and Analysis* (Santa Monica, Calif.: Rand, 1975), p. 15.

16. This discussion and accompanying references were obtained from William W. Daniel, *Georgia Criminal Trial Practice* (Norcross, Ga.: Harrison, 1984), pp. 202-204. Re age: *State* v. *Smith*, 180 S.E. 2d 7 (N.C. 1971); *Bowning* v. *Cox*, 334 F. Supp. 334 (W.D. Va. 1971). Re race: *Young* v. *State*, 243 Ga. 546, 255 S.E. 2d 20;

Smith v. *State,* 239 Ga. 744, 238 S.E. 2d 884 (1977). Re similar physical characteristics: in *Foster* v. *California,* 394 U.S. 440, 89 S. Ct. 1127, 22 L. Ed. 2d 402 (1969), the defendant was about 6 feet tall. The other persons in the lineup were about 5 feet, 6 inches tall. The defendant wore a jacket like that worn by the robber. The court held that the lineup violated due process. Re similar clothing: in *United States* v. *Williams,* 469 F. 2d 540 (D.C. Cir. 1972) only the defendant was hatless; in *La Blanc* v. *People,* 493 P. 2d 1089 (Colo. 1972), only the defendant wore jail overalls; *Arnold* v. *State,* 155 Ga. App. 569, 271 S.E. 2d 702 (1980). Re seeing defendant before lineup: *Bradly* v. *State,* 148 Ga. App. 252 S.E. 2d 648 (1979). Re seeing photo of defendant: *Thornton* v. *State,* 238 Ga. 160, 231 S.E. 2d 729 (1977); appeal after remand, 239 Ga. 693, 238 S.E. 2d 376 (1977) cert. denied, 434 U.S. 1073, 98 S. Ct. 1260, 55 L. Ed. 2d 778 (1978); rehearing denied, 435 U.S. 962, 98 S. Ct. 1595, 55 L. Ed. 2d 812 (1978). Re one witness at a time: *Young* v. *State,* 243 Ga. 546, 255 S.E. 2d 20 (1979). Re attorney: *Moore* v. *Illinois,* 434 U.S. 220, 225, 98 S. Ct. 54 L. Ed. 2d 424 (1977).

EIGHT

Interrogation

CHAPTER OUTLINE

Objectives of Interrogation 178

Interviews and Interrogations: Similarities and
Differences 178

Preinterrogation Legal Requirements 179

In-Custody Interrogation Defined 183

Planning for the Interrogation 188

Beginning the Interrogation 192

The Interrogation 193

Interrogation Techniques and Approaches 197

The Importance of Listening 198

Documenting the Interrogation 199

Admissibility of Confessions and Admissions 202

Questions 203

Notes 203

INTRODUCTION

To many authorities, interrogation is the most important aspect of a criminal investigation, because it offers the possibility of determining, by the statements of suspects themselves, whether the suspects committed particular crimes. Although many of the principles and techniques discussed in this chapter are similar to those presented in Chapter 5, Interviews, there are some significant differences in the objectives of interviewing and interrogation and the relative importance of certain similarities may vary between the two.

OBJECTIVES OF INTERROGATION

Interviewing is the process of obtaining information from people who possess knowledge about a particular offense, as part of the process of investigation. Interrogation is designed to match acquired information to a particular suspect to secure a confession. Another way to describe this difference is that interviewing is primarily for the purpose of gaining information, whereas interrogation is the process of testing that information and its application to a particular suspect.

There are four commonly recognized objectives to the interrogation process. They are:

1. To obtain valuable facts.
2. To eliminate the innocent.
3. To identify the guilty.
4. To obtain a confession.

As the investigator moves from the preliminary task of gathering valuable facts to the concluding task of obtaining a confession, there is an increase in the difficulty of acquiring information. That difficulty, however, is rewarded by an increase in the value of the information. Figure 8–1 illustrates these relationships. It may also be observed that the first three objectives listed above may be equally applied to interviews and interrogations. Thus, in attempting to obtain a confession from a suspect, the interrogator also gains information about the facts and circumstances surrounding the commission of an offense. In seeking such information, the investigator must be concerned with asking the basic questions (as identified in Chapter 6, Field Notes and Reporting) that apply to all aspects of the investigative process: Who? What? Where? When? How? With what? Why? With whom? How much?

INTERVIEWS AND INTERROGATIONS: SIMILARITIES AND DIFFERENCES

As in interviewing, the success of an interrogation depends on a number of personal characteristics and commitments of the investigator. Planning for and controlling the events surrounding both interviews and interrogations are important but are generally viewed as more critical to the success of an interrogation. Establishing rapport, asking good questions, careful listening, and proper documentation are elements common to both forms of obtaining information. Table 8–1 illustrates the similarities between interviews and interrogations.

Besides the difference in purpose between interviewing and interrogation, many other distinctions exist. Of paramount importance are the myriad of legal requirements attendant to interrogations that are absent in interviews. Because of the criticality of confessions and their use in obtaining convictions, it is not surprising that numerous legal guidelines and standards apply in the interrogation that would not be needed in interviewing witnesses or victims. Of course, it is more likely that a hostile and adversary relationship will exist between an interrogator and suspect than between an interviewer and a victim or witness. The differences between interviews and interrogations are noted in Table 8–2.

Table 8–1
Similarities between Interviews and Interrogations

Interviews	Interrogations
Planning important	Planning critical
Controlling surroundings important	Controlling surroundings critical
Privacy or semiprivacy desirable	Absolute privacy essential
Establishing rapport important	Establishing rapport important
Asking good questions important	Asking good questions important
Careful listening	Careful listening
Proper documentation	Proper documentation

Figure 8–1
Objectives of Interrogation

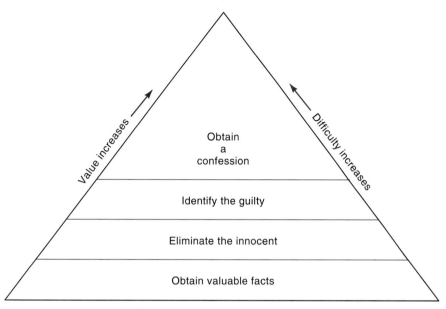

Source: John Fay, unpublished notebook, American Society for Industrial Security, A Workshop in Criminal Interrogation (Jacksonville, Fla.: ASIS, 1981), p. A2-1.

PREINTERROGATION LEGAL REQUIREMENTS

Before delving into the specifics of interrogations, it is important to discuss the legal requirements. This issue became of critical concern during the 1960s, and, as a result, the Supreme Court handed down a landmark decision that has dramatically affected the conditions under which interrogations take place. The issue revolved around the Fifth Amendment protection against self-incrimination and the Sixth Amendment guarantee of the right to counsel, both as made applicable to the states through the due process clause of the Fourteenth Amendment.

MIRANDA V. ARIZONA

The Supreme Court, in a five-to-four decision, spelled out the requirements and procedures to be followed by officers when conducting an in-custody interrogation of a suspect.

In March 1963, Ernest Miranda was arrested for kidnapping and rape. After being identified by the victim, he was questioned by police for several hours and signed a confession that included a statement indicating that the confession was given voluntarily. The confession was admitted into evidence over the objections of Miranda's defense counsel, and the jury found him guilty. The Supreme Court of Arizona affirmed the conviction and held that Miranda's constitutional rights had not been violated in obtaining the conviction because, following the ruling from *Escobedo* v. *Illinois*,[1] the year before, in which Escobedo's confession was ruled to have been improperly admitted because he asked to see his lawyer but was denied that right, Miranda had not specifically requested counsel. The Supreme Court, in reversing the decision, attempted to clarify its intent in the *Escobedo* case by spelling out specific guidelines to be followed by police before they interrogate persons in custody and attempt to use their statements as evidence. In clarifying the requirements of *Escobedo,* the court felt compelled to include the Fifth Amendment requirements against self-incrimination in the decision. The guidelines require that after a person is taken into custody for an offense and prior to any questioning by law

Table 8–2
Differences between Interviews and Interrogations

Interviews	Interrogations
Purpose is to obtain information	Purpose is to test information already obtained
Minimal or no preinterview legal requirements; no rights warning	Extensive preinterrogation legal requirements; rights warning required
Cooperative relationship between interviewer and subject likely	Adversarial or hostile relationship between interrogator and suspect likely
No guilt or guilt uncertain	Guilt suggested or likely
Moderate planning or preparation	Extensive planning and preparation
Private or semiprivate environment desirable	Absolute privacy essential

Source: John Fay, unpublished notebook, American Society for Industrial Security, A Workshop in Criminal Interrogation (Jacksonville, Fla.: ASIS, 1981), p. A1-1.

enforcement officers, if there is any intent to use a suspect's statements in court, the person must first be advised of certain rights. (See Figure 8–2.) These rights include:

1. The right to remain silent.
2. The right to be told that anything said can and will be used in court.
3. The right to consult with an attorney prior to answering any questions and the right to have an attorney present during interrogation.

4. The right to counsel. If the suspect cannot afford an attorney, the court will appoint one.[2]

SUSPECT'S RESPONSE: WAIVER AND ALTERNATIVES

It is common practice for the officer to ask the suspect if he or she understands the rights as they have been explained. If the answer is yes, then the officer may ask if the subject wishes to talk with the

Figure 8–2
Warning Rights Card in English and Spanish

THE EXPLANATION OF THE ADMONITION AND USE OR WAIVER OF YOUR RIGHTS	LA EXPLICACION DEL AVISO Y EL USO O NO DE TUS DERECHOS
1) You have the right to remain silent—you do not have to talk.	1) Tienes el derecho de quedar en silencio—no tienes que hablar.
2) What you say can be used, and shall be used against you in a court of law.	2) Lo que digas se puede usar y se usará en contra de ti en la corte de ley.
3) You have the right to talk with an attorney before you talk with us, and you have the right to have the attorney present during the time we are talking to you.	3) Tienes el derecho de hablar con un abogado antes de hablar con nosotros, y tienes el derecho de tener el abogado presente durante el tiempo que nosotros estamos hablando contigo.
4) If you do not have the funds to employ an attorney, one shall be appointed to represent you free of charge.	4) Si no tienes el dinero para emplear un abogado, uno sere fijado para que te represente, sin pagar.
5) Do you understand these rights as I have explained them to you, yes or no?	5) ¿Comprendes estos derechos como te los expliqué, si o no?
6) Do you want to talk to us about your case now, yes or no?	6) ¿Quieres hablar con nosotros de tu caso ahora, si o no?
7) Do you want an attorney present during the time we are talking to you, yes or no?	7) ¿Quieres un abogado presente durante el tiempo que estamos hablando contigo, si o no?

(Courtesy Los Angeles County Sheriff's Department)

officer. At this point, the alternatives open to the suspect are four:

1. *The suspect may choose to remain silent*, not wishing even to respond to the officer's question. The courts have held that choosing to remain silent does not imply consent to be interrogated.

2. *The suspect may request counsel.* At that point, the investigator must not undertake any questioning of the suspect, for anything said will not be admissible in court. In *Edwards* v. *Arizona* in 1981, the Supreme Court held that no police-initiated interrogation may lawfully take place once the suspect has invoked the right to counsel unless and until an attorney has been provided or unless the defendant voluntarily begins to talk with the officers.[3] In *Minnick* v. *Mississippi* in 1990, the Supreme Court held that once counsel is requested, interrogation must cease; officials may not reinitiate interrogation without counsel being present, whether or not the accused has consulted with his or her attorney. The requirement that counsel be made available to the accused refers not to the opportunity to consult with a lawyer outside the interrogation room, but to the right to have the attorney present during custodial interrogation. This rule is necessary to remove suspects from the coercive pressure of officials who may try to persuade them to waive their rights. The rule also provides a clear and unequivocal guideline to the law enforcement profession.[4] In the 1988 case of *Patterson* v. *Illinois,* the Supreme Court said that a defendant who was indicted but unrepresented could waive the right to counsel after having been given the *Miranda* warnings. No more elaborate warning was required, and it was not deemed necessary that authorities refrain from interrogation until counsel was made available.[5]

3. *The suspect may waive his or her rights and agree to talk with police without the benefit of counsel.* The waiver of rights is a sensitive topic for police, as it is the responsibility of the police and the prosecutor to prove in court that the waiver was validly obtained. A valid waiver must be voluntarily, knowingly, and intelligently given by the suspect. The burden is on the prosecution to prove that the suspect was properly advised of his or her rights, that those rights were understood, and that the suspect voluntarily, knowingly, and intelligently waived those rights before the court will allow the introduction of any incriminating testimony in the form of a confession. The waiver cannot be presumed or inferred. It must be successfully proved by the prosecution. Therefore, it is preferable for the investigator who secures a waiver of rights from a suspect to attempt to get the waiver in writing with sufficient witnesses to substantiate its voluntariness. Figure 8–3 is a sample waiver form. One additional fact should remain under consideration: Even the suspect who has waived his or her rights is free to withdraw that waiver at any time. If this occurs during questioning, the investigator is under a legal obligation to cease the interrogation at that point and either comply with the suspect's request for representation or simply cease the interrogation if the suspect refuses to talk.

4. *The suspect may indicate a desire not to talk with the investigators.* At this point, the police have no choice but to refrain from attempting to interrogate the suspect concerning the events of the crime for which he or she has been arrested. In this event, the case must be based on independent evidence, which may or may not be sufficient to warrant prosecution. The United States Supreme Court's emphatic position on terminating interrogation once a suspect has invoked the right to remain silent was announced in 1975 in the case of *Michigan* v. *Mosley.*[6]

Since the responsibility is on the prosecution, supported by evidence provided by the investigators, to substantiate the voluntariness of the waiver and the propriety of the warnings given the suspect, many police agencies provide printed cards with the exact wording of the required warnings. They further recommend or require that when warnings are given they be read verbatim from the printed card. In this manner the officer, when testifying in court, can positively

Figure 8–3
Rights Waiver Form

YOUR RIGHTS

Date_____

Time_____

WARNING

Before we ask you any questions, you must understand your rights.

You have the right to remain silent.

Anything you say can and will be used against you in court.

You have the right to talk to a lawyer for advice before we ask you any question and to have him with you during questioning.

If you cannot afford a lawyer, one will be appointed for you.

Geauga County has a Public Defender. Before answering any questions, you have a right to talk with the Public Defender.

If you decide to answer questions now, without a lawyer present, you will still have the right to stop answering at any time. You also have the right to stop answering at any time until you talk to a lawyer.

Do you understand these rights? _____

Signed: _____

Witnesses:

_____

_____

WAIVER OF RIGHTS

I have read this statement of my rights and I understand what my rights are. I am willing to make a statement and answer questions. I do not want a lawyer at this time. I understand and know what I am doing. No promises or threats have been made to me and no pressure or coercion of any kind has been used against me.

Signed: _____

Witnesses:

_____

_____

Date: _____

Time: _____

(Courtesy Geauga County, Ohio, Sheriff's Department)

state the exact words used in advising the suspect of his or her constitutional rights. Such a procedure avoids any confrontation with the defense as to the exact wording and contents of the *Miranda* requirements. But in 1989 in *Duckworth* v. *Eagen*, the Supreme Court held that it was not necessary that the warnings be given in the exact form described in the *Miranda* decision, provided that the warnings as a whole fully informed the suspect of his or her rights.[7]

A person being subjected to in-custody interrogation often chooses not to answer any questions posed by the police—or at least not until an attorney is present. When counsel is made available to the suspect prior to or during interrogation, it is almost universal practice for the attorney to advise the client not to say anything to the police. Therefore, the effect of the *Miranda* decision has been to reduce significantly the number of valid interrogations by police agencies in this country today. For the most part, however, confessions obtained in compliance with prescribed rules are of better quality and are more likely to be admissible in court.

It must be impressed upon investigators that the failure to properly advise a suspect of the rights required by *Miranda* does not invalidate an otherwise valid arrest, nor does it necessarily mean that a case cannot be successfully prosecuted. Even in light of the line of court decisions discussed in the next section indicating that *Miranda* warnings may not be required in all interrogation situations, good practice or departmental policy may require that all suspects in custody be advised of their rights.

IN-CUSTODY INTERROGATION DEFINED

For investigators to understand the proper application of *Miranda* requirements, it is essential that they understand the meaning of *in-custody interrogation*. The *Miranda* case involved simultaneous custody and interrogation. Subsequent police actions revealed that all cases were not so nicely defined and that the meanings of "in custody" and "interrogation" required clarification. Although it may be difficult to separate the custody from the interrogation in certain factual situations, the two concepts must be considered separately. The cases cited in the following paragraphs should be examined from the standpoint of the subheading under which each is included.

CUSTODY DEFINED

Analyses of case decisions show that there is not yet a universally accepted definition of custody. Rather, case-by-case analysis is used to determine the applicability of *Miranda* requirements.

In *Beckwith* v. *United States,* agents of the Internal Revenue Service interrogated the defendant, who was the subject of a tax fraud investigation. The defendant was not under arrest at the time but was advised of all the *Miranda* warnings except the right to a court-appointed attorney. He waived his rights, subsequently furnished incriminating evidence, and was convicted. On appeal, the defendant claimed that the complete warnings had not been given and therefore incriminating statements should not have been admitted. On appeal, the Supreme Court held that the agents were not required to apply *Miranda* in those circumstances. *Miranda* application depends on custodial police interrogation, involving questioning in a coercive, police-dominated atmosphere. Those conditions did not exist in this case.[8]

In a 1977 case, the Court again emphasized that something more than suspicion or focus of an investigation is necessary before *Miranda* applies. In *Oregon* v. *Mathiason,* the defendant was asked to come to the state patrol office to be interviewed about a burglary. Mathiason was told that he was not under arrest but was informed that the police believed he had participated in the burglary. No *Miranda* warnings were given. He confessed, was convicted, and appealed. The Oregon Supreme Court reversed the conviction, finding that the defendant was interviewed in a "coercive environment" and that *Miranda* applied.[9] The U.S. Supreme Court disagreed with the state court, pointing out that the defendant had not been formally arrested, his freedom of locomotion had not been restrained in any significant way, and that, without the presence of any of these factors, *Miranda* does not apply. The Court said:

Any interview of one suspected of a crime by a police officer will have coercive aspects to it simply by virtue of the fact that the police officer is part of a law enforcement system which may ultimately cause the suspect to be charged with a crime. But police officers are not required to administer *Miranda* warnings to everyone whom they question. Nor is the requirement of warnings to be imposed simply because the questioning takes place in the station house, or because the questioned person is one whom the police suspect. *Miranda* warnings are required only where there has been such a restriction on a person's freedom as to render him "in custody." It was that sort of coercive environment to which *Miranda* by its terms was made applicable, and to which it is limited.[10]

In 1983, the Supreme Court again addressed the *Miranda* custody issue. In *California v. Beheler,* the defendant and several others had attempted to steal a quantity of hashish from the victim, who was selling the drug in the parking lot of a liquor store. While resisting the robbery, the victim was killed by one of the perpetrators. Shortly afterward, Beheler called the police and told them who had killed the victim. Later the same day, Beheler voluntarily agreed to accompany police to the police station and was specifically told he was not under arrest. During the 30-minute interview, he told police what had happened. He was not advised of his rights under the *Miranda* decision. After the interview, Beheler was permitted to return home. Five days later he was arrested for aiding and abetting first-degree murder. He was advised of his rights, which he waived, and confessed. Both confessions were used against him in his conviction. The California Court of Appeals reversed the decision, holding that the first interview was "in-custody" because it took place in the station, Beheler was a suspect at the time, and the interview was designed to elicit incriminating information.

The U.S. Supreme Court reversed the California appellate court decision and, following its previous holding in *Oregon v. Mathiason,* held that in determining whether custody exists for purposes of *Miranda,* the inquiry is simply whether there is a formal arrest or restraint on freedom of movement usually associated with a formal arrest. Finding that no such restraint existed in this case, the Court added that the amount of information possessed by the police concerning the person to be questioned and the length of time between the commission of the crime and the time of questioning are not relevant to the issue of whether custody exists for purposes of applying *Miranda.*[11]

All interviews do not have to take place in a police station to have a coercive effect. In *Orozco v. Texas,* the Court held inadmissible a confession given after the defendant was questioned in his bed in the middle of the night by four police officers. The Court concluded in this 1969 case that the defendant had been deprived of his freedom in a significant way.[12]

Similarly, the defendant in *United States v. Lee* was questioned by two federal agents in a government car parked in front of his home. The questioning concerned the death of Lee's wife. Lee agreed to answer questions and was told he was free at any time to terminate the interview and leave. The conversation lasted between an hour and an hour and a half, during which time the agents advised Lee of the incriminating evidence they possessed. Lee finally confessed to killing his wife but was not arrested until the next day, when he voluntarily appeared at the police station for further questioning. At no time was he advised of his rights. Using a test called the "totality of the circumstances," a federal appeals court in 1982 upheld the trial court's decision to exclude the statements on the basis that Lee was in custody and was not free to decline the interview under the circumstances, even though he had not been formally arrested.[13]

Other courts using the totality-of-circumstances test have come to conclusions different from those in the *Lee* case, but perhaps because of different factual conditions. In *United States v. Dockery,* a 24-year-old bank employee was questioned by FBI agents concerning the theft of bank funds. She was questioned for just over 15 minutes in a small vacant room in the bank. Dockery was told at the outset that she did not have to answer any questions, that she was not under arrest nor was she going to be arrested, and that she was free to leave at any time. Dockery denied any involvement in the thefts. After the interview ended, Dockery was asked to wait outside the interview room. A few minutes later, she asked to see the agents, who again advised her that she did not have to talk to them and that she was free to leave whenever she desired. Shortly thereafter, Dockery gave a signed statement implicating herself in the thefts. In 1984, the federal appellate court reviewing the conviction ruled that Dockery was not in custody during the interviews, and therefore, her confession was properly admitted at her trial.[14]

To fully comprehend the definition of custody, it is necessary to explore additional case decisions. For example, in *Mathis v. United States,* the defendant was convicted of filing false claims against the government. Part of the evidence used to convict consisted of statements made by the defendant to a federal agent while the defendant was in prison serving a state sentence. At the time of questioning, the government agent did not advise the defendant of his rights. On appeal of the conviction to the Supreme Court, the defendant argued that the statements used against him had been obtained in violation of *Miranda*. The government countered with the argument that *Miranda* did not apply because the defendant had not been put in jail by the agents questioning him, but was there for a much different offense. The Court, in reversing the decision, held in this 1968 case that it was immaterial why a person had been arrested or by whom. It is the coercive aspect of the custody itself, coupled with the police interrogation, that triggers the application of *Miranda*.[15]

But in the 1990 case of *Illinois* v. *Perkins*, an undercover officer was placed in a cell with the defendant, who was in jail on other, unrelated charges. The Supreme Court said, "Conversations between suspects and undercover agents do not implicate the concerns underlying *Miranda*," which "forbids coercion, not mere strategic deception by taking advantage of a suspect's misplaced trust in one he supposes to be a fellow prisoner."[16]

A 1984 decision of the Supreme Court for the first time recognized a "public safety" exception to *Miranda*. The facts in the case of *New York* v. *Quarles* involved an officer who entered a supermarket looking for an alleged rapist who was supposed to be armed. The officer spotted the suspect, Quarles, who, upon seeing the officer, ran toward the rear of the store with the officer in pursuit. The officer lost sight of Quarles for a few seconds. Upon regaining sight of the suspect, the officer ordered him to stop. While frisking Quarles, the officer discovered an empty shoulder holster. After handcuffing him, the officer asked Quarles where the gun was. Quarles nodded in the direction of some empty cartons and stated, "The gun is over there."

After retrieving the gun, the officer formally placed Quarles under arrest and advised him of his rights. Quarles waived his rights and, in answer to questions, admitted ownership of the gun and where he had obtained it. In the prosecution for the criminal possession of the weapon, the trial court suppressed all the statements about the location or ownership of the gun and suppressed evidence of the gun on the grounds that the officer had failed first to advise the suspect of his constitutional rights and that the information acquired after the arrest and subsequent *Miranda* warnings was tainted by the first omission.

In reversing the decision, the Supreme Court agreed that Quarles was subjected to custodial interrogation without proper advisement and waiver of his rights. However, the Court ruled that the statement concerning the location of the gun and the gun itself were admissible under a "public safety" exception to the *Miranda* rule. The Court said that the need for answers to questions in a situation posing a threat to the public safety outweighs the need for protecting the subject's Fifth Amendment privilege against self-incrimination. The Court conceded that this exception lessened the clarity of the *Miranda* rule but that it also would keep police officers from the untenable position of having to consider, often in a matter of seconds, whether it best serves society for them to ask questions without providing the *Miranda* warnings and chance having the evidence excluded or to give the warnings and chance not getting the evidence at all.

The Court further indicated it had confidence that law enforcement officials could easily determine the applicability of the "public safety" exception but cautioned that the burden is on the police later to articulate the specific facts and circumstances justifying the need for questioning, without the warnings, in order to protect themselves, fellow officers, or the public. Furthermore, because this is a very narrow exception to the *Miranda* rule, once the reason for the public safety exception ends, any further questioning should be preceded by the warnings and waiver.[17]

The question of whether *Miranda* applies to misdemeanor arrests has been the subject of controversy for many years. In 1984, the Supreme Court settled this issue. The Court ruled in *Berkemer* v. *McCarty* that *Miranda* applies to the interrogation of an arrested person regardless of whether the offense is a felony or a misdemeanor. The justices found that to make a distinction would cause confusion because many times it is not certain whether the person taken into custody is to be charged with a felony or a misdemeanor.[18]

In 1968, the Supreme Court ruled in the case of *Terry* v. *Ohio* that law enforcement officers may constitutionally detain persons against their will for short periods of time and in a reasonable manner to investigate and resolve suspicious circumstances indicating that a crime has been or is about to be committed. Such "Terry stops" or "stop-and-frisk" situations often require questioning the person detained, because that is often the most effective method of resolving suspicious activities quickly and reasonably.[19] The question has long been asked whether such questioning may be conducted without meeting the requirements of *Miranda*.

Berkemer v. *McCarty* squarely addressed that issue. In this case, a state trooper observed McCarty's car weaving in and out of traffic. The vehicle was stopped and, upon getting out of the car, McCarty had difficulty standing. McCarty was asked to take a "balancing test," which he was unable to complete without falling. His speech was slurred. The trooper asked if he had been using any intoxicants. McCarty replied that he had had two beers and had smoked several marijuana joints. At that point, McCarty was arrested and transported to the police station, where he was administered a test that showed no alcohol in the blood. Upon further questioning by the trooper, who was seeking information to complete his report, McCarty again admitted that he had been drinking and also indicated in writing that the marijuana he had smoked did not contain angel dust (PCP). He was then charged with operating a motor vehicle while under the influence of alcohol and/or drugs. At no time was McCarty advised of his rights. At trial, McCarty moved to have his incriminating statements excluded as violating *Miranda* requirements. The trial court refused. After his conviction and a series of appeals, McCarty's case was heard by the Supreme Court. Two issues were presented. The first was described earlier, in which the court held that *Miranda* applies to misdemeanor arrests as well as to felonies. The second question concerned the application of *Miranda* to roadside questioning. The Court ruled that an investigative detention does not constitute custody if it meets the test of reasonableness. Therefore, *Miranda* does not apply.[20] This decision continues to be followed, as confirmed by the Supreme Court in the 1988 case of *Pennsylvania* v. *Bruder*.[21]

In *United States* v. *J.H.H.*, the Eighth Circuit held that the questioning of a juvenile which occurred in an unlocked room, where the juvenile was told he was not under arrest and was free to leave at any time—and, in fact, he was not arrested after questioning—did not constitute "in custody" for purposes of using these statements against the juvenile in a later proceeding.[22]

A 10-year-old girl disappeared from a playground in California in 1982. Early the next morning, about 10 miles away, a man observed a large man emerge from a turquoise American sedan and throw something into a nearby flood-control channel. He called the police, who later discovered the girl's body in the channel. There was evidence that the girl had been raped and asphyxiated by a blunt-force trauma to the head. A detective learned that the girl had talked to two ice-cream-truck drivers in the hours before her disappearance. One of the drivers was the defendant. The detective's suspicions focused on the other driver. However, at 11:00 P.M. one evening, four uniformed officers arrived at the defendant's mobile home and asked him if he would accompany them to the police station to answer some questions. He agreed and rode in the front seat of the police car. At the police station, the detective questioned him about his whereabouts on the evening the girl had been abducted. Nothing was out of the ordinary until the defendant mentioned that he had left his mobile home about midnight in his housemate's turquoise American-made car. This aroused the detective's suspicion. He terminated the interview, and another officer advised the defendant of his Miranda rights. The defendant refused to make any further statements, requested an attorney, and was taken into custody. A motion to suppress the evidence was denied. He was subsequently convicted of first-degree murder and other crimes. The California Supreme Court affirmed the conviction. The case was heard by the U.S. Supreme Court to determine whether the defendant was in custody at the time he made the statements and thus was entitled to have the statements suppressed. The Court said that in deciding whether the defendant was in custody, the totality of the circumstances is relevant and no one factor alone disposes of the question. The Court went on to say that the most important considerations include where the investigation took place, whether the investigation has focused on the subject, whether the objective bases for making an arrest are present, and the length of questioning. The Court, in reversing the decision, said the California Supreme Court was wrong in considering whether the investigation had focused on the subject to determine the custody issue, primarily because the officers never communicated their feelings so that the defendant was made aware that he was now a suspect in the case. Because the officers did not manifest this view, it could have no bearing on the question of whether the suspect was in custody at the time. The state subsequently acknowleged that the officer's subjective, undisclosed suspicions had no bearing on the question of whether the defendant was in custody for the purposes of *Miranda* during the questioning that occurred in the police station. The state, however, argued that the objective facts and records supported a finding that the defendant was not in custody until the arrest. The defendant, on the other hand, asserted that the objective circumstances showed that he was in custody during the entire time he was questioned. The U.S. Supreme Court reversed and remanded the case back to the California Supreme Court and told the state to consider this question because it had not been considered before.[23]

The cases cited clearly show that the statement offered in the beginning of this section is still correct. There are no universally accepted definitions of custody, and with as much direction as the courts are trying to provide, many decisions are still subject to case-by-case scrutiny.

INTERROGATION DEFINED

For many years following the *Miranda* ruling, there was considerable confusion over what constituted questioning or interrogation. For example, in a 1977 case the Supreme Court found an impermissible interrogation occurred when a detective delivered what has been called the "Christian burial speech" to a man suspected of murdering a young girl. While the suspect was being transported between cities, the detective told the suspect to think about how the weather was turning cold and snow was likely. He pointed out how difficult it would be to find the body later. The detective went on to say that the girl's parents were entitled to have a Christian burial for the little girl, who had been taken from them on Christmas Eve and murdered. Subsequent to this little speech, the suspect led the detectives to the spot where he had disposed of the

body. The Supreme Court held this to be an interrogation within the scope of *Miranda*, even though direct questions had not been asked of the suspect.[24]

The Supreme Court faced the question of what constitutes interrogation for the first time in the 1980 case of *Rhode Island* v. *Innis*. In that instance a robbery suspect was arrested after the victim had identified him from photographs. The prisoner was advised several times of his constitutional rights and was being transported by three officers who had been specifically ordered not to question the suspect. During the trip, two of the officers were having a conversation about the case, and one commented how terrible it would be if some unsuspecting child found the missing shotgun (used in the robbery) and got hurt. The conversation was not directed at the suspect, nor did the officers expect a response from the suspect. However, the suspect interrupted the conversation and, after again being advised of his rights, led the officers to the shotgun. The Supreme Court stated the rule regarding interrogation as follows:

> We conclude that *Miranda* safeguards come into play whenever a person in custody is subjected to either express questioning or its functional equivalent. That is to say, the term "interrogation" under *Miranda* refers not only to express questioning, but also to any words or actions on the part of the police (other than those normally attendant to arrest and custody) that the police should know are reasonably likely to elicit an incriminating response from the suspect. The latter portion of this definition focuses primarily upon the perceptions of the suspect, rather than the intent of the police. This focus reflects the fact that the *Miranda* safeguards were designed to vest a suspect in custody with an added measure of protection against coercive police practices, without regard to objective proof of the underlying intent of the police.[25]

Interrogation, as defined by *Innis*, was found by one federal circuit to have been conducted when officers questioned the defendent about a homicide and showed him physcial evidence linking him to the crime.[26] By applying this rule to the facts of the case, the Court held that the conversation between the officers did not amount to an interrogation and was properly admissible. Consequently, the current rules appear to be that if a suspect is in custody or otherwise deprived of freedom in a significant way, and if the suspect is to be asked pertinent questions, or if an officer uses words or acts in such a way that the officer should know would be reasonably likely to elicit incriminating responses from the suspect, the warnings must be given.[27] It is also fairly clear that volunteered statements, such as those given when a person walks into a police station and confesses to a crime, and general on-the-scene questioning by an investigator—such as "What happened?"—do not fall within the scope of *Miranda* requirements.[28]

The Court's position in the *Innis* case was again supported seven years later in *Arizona* v. *Mauro,* in which the police allowed the defendant's wife to talk with him after he had invoked his right to counsel. The conversation was conducted in the presence of a police officer, who was present for security purposes only, and it was also openly being recorded. The officer asked no questions. Incriminating statements made by the defendant were held to be properly admissible.[29]

As a general rule, *Miranda* warnings need not precede routine booking questions that are asked in order to obtain personal-history data necessary to complete the booking process. As long as the questions are for that purpose and are not a pretext to obtain incriminating information, *Miranda* warnings need not be given.[30]

PLANNING FOR THE INTERROGATION

At the beginning of the chapter, the definition of interrogation made reference to the objective of checking already-acquired information against information that can be gleaned from a suspect. That definition implies that all of the information possessed has been passed on to and is known by the interrogator. The key to the effectiveness of having that aggregate information is in planning for its use during the interrogation. But planning goes beyond just having information about the offense, the victim, and the suspect. Thorough planning also includes understanding why people confess; understanding the interrogator's own personality, including such things as expectations, traits, and biases; and knowing how and where to conduct an interrogation.

WHY PEOPLE CONFESS

It is human nature to talk. Most people cannot keep a secret. It has been estimated that 80 percent of all people will confess to a crime. There are two basic categories of people who tend to confess to crimes. First, there are those guilty parties who psychologically need to "get it off their chest." The second category comprises those who are not guilty but who act under some urge to confess. It is to protect this latter category of people that some procedural safeguards are provided. For example, a conviction cannot be based solely on a confession. There must be some other independent corroborating evidence to support the conviction.

The psychological and physiological pressures that build in a person who has committed a crime or who suffers from guilt feelings concerning any other type of conduct are best alleviated by communicating. Talking is the best means of communicating. Therefore, in spite of having been advised of certain protections guaranteed by the Constitution, some people feel a need to confess. Even most confirmed criminals suffer from the same pangs of conscience as first-time offenders. However, fear of the potential punishments which await them contributes to their silence. Those who confess rarely regret it, for it gives them peace of mind. It permits them to look at themselves and life differently and to live with themselves. Most guilty individuals who confess are, from the outset, looking for the proper opening during an interrogation to communicate their guilt to the interrogator. The good interrogator will seek out and be able to recognize individuals who desire to confess and will approach the interrogation in such a way as to provide the accused with the proper opening and reason for the relief of the psychological and physiological pressures that have built up.[31]

THE INTERROGATOR

If it is human nature to talk and if people cannot generally keep secrets, then the job of the interrogator is to make it easy for a suspect to confess. The interrogator needs to make himself or herself easy to talk to. By the appropriate use of vocal inflection, modulation, and emphasis, even the *Miranda* warnings can be presented to a suspect in such a way as not to cause the suspect to immediately assume a defensive posture. The words can be spoken without creating an adversarial atmosphere.

In the interview, persuasiveness and perseverance are essential. The investigator must have a flexible personality; must be able to convey anger, fear, joy, and sympathy at various times; and must subdue all personal prejudices, keeping an open mind, receptive to all information, regardless of its nature. The investigator must carefully evaluate each development during the interrogation while studiously avoiding the pitfall of underestimating the capabilities of the subject being interrogated. Screaming or shouting, belittling the subject or the information, sneering, and other such unplanned and uncontrolled reactions most often adversely affect the interrogation. The investigator must at all times maintain control of the interrogation without being openly domineering, by being a good active listener, by being serious, by being patient, and most importantly, by being persistent and persuasive.[32] An ability to categorize the psychological and emotional traits being manifested by the suspect helps the investigator react in a manner that increases the possibility of conducting a successful interrogation.

Preparation

The success of both the interrogator and the interrogation will often be determined by the time and dedication committed to preparing for the interrogation. As soon as preparation begins, an evaluation process also begins. The interrogator must evaluate himself or herself and the circumstances surrounding the conduct of the interrogation and must begin to evaluate the suspect. An effective interrogator will understand that a successful interrogation cannot be organized and compartmentalized into a neat, orderly, step-by-step package. Rather, it is a combination of personality, behavior, and interpersonal communication skills between the interrogator and the suspect. It is made up of verbal processes and the way they are communicated, nonverbal actions including body language, and personality characteristics that together might be characterized as a psychological profile.[33] Only by understanding the interaction of all these variables can the interrogator effectively evaluate the interrogation process as it will be initiated and as it will be modified during the interrogation.[34] To begin the preparation, the interrogator should review the offense report, statement of witnesses, laboratory reports, all file information pertaining to the suspect, and other related data. It is also essential that the interrogator know all of the elements of the offense involved. Failure to possess this information may preclude obtaining a complete confession, which, by definition, must contain admissions by the suspect to the commission of each and every element of the crime.

To carry out the four objectives described earlier in the chapter, the interrogator must learn as much as possible about the offense, the victim(s), and the suspect through the process of collecting, assessing, and analyzing data and theorizing about the motivations and thought processes of the suspect. This begins the formulation of a profile which will then dictate the initial approach the interrogator will take upon first contacting the suspect.

The Offense It is necessary that the investigator know specifically what crime or crimes were allegedly committed. This knowledge includes a working familiarity with the elements of each offense and some understanding of the kind of information necessary to prove each. Accurate information on the date, time, place, and method of the crime—including tools used, points of entry and exit, method of travel to and from the scene, complete description of any property involved, weapons used, modus operandi, and physical evidence recovered—are all essential. The investigator should also obtain a full description of the crime scene and the surrounding area. Any and all possible motives should be identified.

The Victim If the victim is a person, the investigator should learn as much as possible about his or her background, the nature of the injury or loss, attitudes toward the investigation, and any other useful information, such as the existence of insurance in a property crime case. If the victim is an organization or business, a determination of any practices that would make the organization a criminal target could be extremely valuable. In addition, the investigator should determine whether the business is insured against losses, if relevant.

The Suspect The investigation should reveal as much personal background information on the suspect as can be obtained. This should include aliases, Social Security number, date and place of birth, education, marital status, employment history, financial history and current circumstances, prior offenses, past and present physical and mental health, any drug or alcohol abuse or addiction, relationship to the victim or crime scene, possible motive, biases and prejudices, home environment, sexual interests (if relevant), and hobbies. Additionally, the investigation and preparation for an interrogation should determine whether the suspect had the capability and opportunity to commit the offense and should confirm or disprove an alibi.

The interrogator should also obtain as much information as possible from other people involved to determine the suspect's attitude. This will enable the interrogator to anticipate levels of hostility or cooperativeness during the interrogation. Figure 8–4 can serve as a review and checklist for the investigator's planning and interrogation.

SETTING: THE INTERROGATION ROOM

Unlike the interview, which may take place in any number of different locations and at various times—which may or may not be advantageous to the investigator—interrogation is a controlled

Figure 8–4
Preinterrogation Checklist

	Do You Have These Facts Regarding the Crime?	Check Here
1	The legal description of the offense	
2	The value and nature of loss	
3	Time, date, and place of occurrence	
4	Description of crime scene and surrounding area	
5	Physical evidence collected	
6	Weather conditions at time of offense	
7	Specific entry/exit points of perpetrator	
8	Approach and departure routes of perpetrator	
9	Methods of travel to and from scene	
10	The modus operandi of the perpetrator	
11	The tools or weapons used	
12	Names of persons having knowledge	
13	Possible motive	
14	Details from other case files that a. point to particular suspects	
	b. show matching modi operandi	
	c. suggest a pattern of criminality	

Source: John Fay, unpublished notebook, American Society for Industrial Security, Workshop in Criminal Interrogation (Jacksonville, Fla.: ASIS, 1981), p. A4-1.

process, controlled by the interrogator. The interrogator is in command of the setting. The interrogator governs the number and kinds of interruptions. The most critical factor in controlling the interrogation is to ensure privacy. Privacy guarantees that any distractions, planned or otherwise, are controlled by the interrogator. In addition, privacy may be used as a psychological tool: the suspect may feel more willing to unload the burden of guilt in front of only one person.

The traditional interrogation room should be sparsely furnished, usually with only two chairs. There should be no physical barriers, such as tables or desks, between the investigator and the suspect. From the officer's standpoint, such barriers may create an unwanted feeling of psychological well-being on the part of the suspect.

Notice the arrangement of the table and chairs in Figure 8–5. They are corner to corner rather than on opposite sides. This arrangement permits the interrogator to move both chairs away from the table and eliminate the barrier.[35]

The two-way mirror, although still a useful tool for allowing others to observe the interrogation, is widely known and may cause some subjects to refuse to cooperate in the interrogation. If a two-way mirror is to be used, it should be small and unobtrusive. As a standard practice, the interrogation room should be equipped with a microphone connected to a recording device located somewhere nearby, unless prohibited by state law.

Although the traditional interrogation room just described is designed to ensure control and domination over the interrogation because of its privacy, security, and aura of authority, this approach does not impress the habitual or experienced offender, who understands the rules and standards of conduct of the classical interrogation room. If the offender is skilled and intelligent, he or she not only can cope with the psychological influences such a setting is designed to foster but perhaps can become the dominant force, or at least be on the same psychological level as the interrogator.

The national trend is to stick with the classical approach. Some experts, though, are attempting to overcome the "orientation" of the experienced offender by using a nontraditional interrogation room. This room is decorated like a fairly plush office or lounge. It is carpeted, paneled, and pleasantly furnished, and it has lighting fixtures capable of being controlled by rheostat for more or less intensity (see Figure 8–6).

The room is "off the beaten path," so that the subject is not led through a larger office where everyone is staring. Soft background music may be piped in and the room may be painted a color that either has a relaxing or calming effect or can increase blood pressure, respiration, perspiration, and brain wave activity. The temperature in the room should be comfortable.

Interrogations of habitual offenders in settings like this have been successful because such a room

Figure 8–5
Traditional Interrogation Room

(Courtesy Dallas Police Department)

Figure 8–6
Nontraditional Interrogation Room

(Courtesy Detective Thomas Streed, San Diego County Sheriff's Department)

is totally unexpected and the interrogation has already begun well before the subject realizes what is happening and before there is an opportunity for the subject's defense mechanisms to take hold and the deception to begin.[36]

BEGINNING THE INTERROGATION

Effective interrogators, like interviewers, must be skilled in psychology, persuasiveness, and acting. Good interrogators must also be good seducers; they must be able to make others do what they want them to do. They must be capable of giving the appearance of empathy, sympathy, and objectivity when those characteristics are most appropriate to accomplishing their objectives. The character one assumes as an interrogator must be determined from the reactions of the suspect and the approach that will obtain the best response. A successful interrogation requires the investigator to sell himself or herself to the subject.

Just as in interviewing, it is important to establish rapport with the person to be questioned. Rapport can be established by showing a sincere interest in the person and his or her personal problems. Complimenting the suspect on some outstanding trait or characteristic often gets the suspect talking. That, of course, is a prime objective—to get the subject talking. Small talk can often accomplish the same objective. Once conversation has started, the objective becomes to keep the suspect talking—about anything.

It is essential that the interrogator be in complete command of the interrogation and that this be made absolutely clear to the suspect at the outset. The interrogator must project competence and self-confidence in making a first impression on the suspect. As an example, if the interrogator perceives that the suspect considers himself or herself superior to the interrogator, the suspect may be addressed by last name only, instructed to sit, instructed not to smoke, and manipulated in other ways.

At this stage, it is important for the interrogator, using personal observations and known facts about the suspect, to evaluate the mental capacity of the suspect. Intelligence is an important aspect of this process. Generally speaking, physiological changes in the suspect's body will be stronger in persons of higher intelligence. This is not always true, however, and often such changes will not be immediately visible. On the other hand, an individual of very low intelligence may be less likely to experience physiological changes due to a lack of understanding of the danger he or she confronts or the inability of the interrogator to communicate the extent of that danger through the conversation. Emotional stability or instability is also important to evaluate. However, caution must be exercised. The emotionally unstable person can often produce reactions completely opposite from that which might be expected. Such unpredictable reactions can make it difficult to assess the emotional stability of the suspect.[37]

In evaluating the suspect, the interrogator also must consider the cultural and ethnic background of the suspect. Often, behavioral signals have cultural roots. What might appear as a deceptiveness signal may, in fact, be quite the opposite. For example, it is not uncommon for Hispanic males to look down when in the presence of a person of authority, rather than directly at that person. Drugs or alcohol can also cause a suspect to produce a deceptive reaction, like delaying answering a question.[38]

Often, an interrogator bombards a suspect with a series of questions, hoping to get satisfactory answers. The interrogator believes that he or she has conducted an interrogation when, in fact, all the interrogator did was try to cross-examine the suspect, which rarely produces a confession. As has been pointed out, a guilty person needs to have an acceptable reason to tell the truth. This does not mean that the interrogator should be noncommittal or anything but firm. It is suggested that at the outset of an interrogation, the interrogator should tell the suspect the exact purpose of the interrogation. Doing so may require initially coming out and accusing the suspect of committing the crime. If the interrogator is confident that the suspect is the offender, showing confidence in that position will often weaken any defenses that the suspect may try to raise and puts the interrogation on a firm footing of understanding as to what is to be accomplished. For example, the interrogator might say, "I know that you have committed this offense, but we need to get beyond that and start talking about why you committed the offense," or "I know there are two sides to every story, and the purpose of this discussion is to find out your version of the truth so that we can get this truth working for you rather than against you."[39]

COMPOSING AND ASKING QUESTIONS: GENERAL PRINCIPLES

There are certain basic rules an interrogator should keep in mind when composing and asking questions.

Questions should not be complex, because they will be difficult to understand; they should be short, direct, and confined to one topic. They must be clear and easily understood. Only words that the suspect can understand should be used. Questions should avoid legal terms—larceny, homicide—and, unless intended, accusatory questions should be avoided. Leading questions (those which are asked in such a manner as to suggest the answer desired, e.g., "You don't mean to tell me that you're actually denying pulling the trigger?") should be avoided unless necessary to facilitate the questioning process. Adherence to these basic rules ensures that interrogator and suspect understand what the other is talking about. As in most processes in criminal investigation, interrogation questions should initially focus on a wide base of general information and then narrow the focus continually to more specific issues.

THE INTERROGATION

Before an interrogator can decide on specific questions to be asked or interrogation techniques and approaches to use, the evaluation process must continue. This includes the ability to recognize and cope with deception.

RECOGNIZING AND COPING WITH DECEPTION

Deception is not always easy to detect, but, in general, there are both verbal and nonverbal cues that can be examined to determine whether a suspect is telling the truth or is being deceptive. In addition, statements can be written or recorded and analyzed to aid in this determination. Human behavior is diverse, and therefore there is no single nonverbal symptom or verbal cue that proves a person is being truthful or deceptive. To believe otherwise is foolish.[40]

To be effective in detecting when a suspect is being deceptive, the investigator who has thoroughly prepared should have some idea of the type of personality of the suspect. All of the factors that are learned about the case and the suspect go into forming some opinion on how to approach the interrogation. In modern terms, this might be a type of "profiling." The interrogator will alter and modify the approaches and techniques used as the interrogation progresses and as he or she learns more about what is being said, how it is being said, and whether or not there are detectable signs of deception.

Verbal Signals

Verbal signals are generally easier for a deceptive subject to control than nonverbal signals. Verbal signals may take the form of changes in voice quality as well as specific statements. Stuttering or slurring words may be an indication of deception, as may a change in the speed of talking. Rapid speech may indicate nervousness, while abnormally slow speech may suggest a careful planning of each word to avoid incriminating statements. An unusually high pitch or cracking of the voice may indicate deception.

Religious statements such as "Honest to God" and qualified answers to questions beginning with such phrases as "to be perfectly honest" are potential indicators of deception and should be pursued by the attentive interrogator.

The content of speech is also important. Guilty suspects often go through a progression of negative responses that include anger, then depression, followed by denial, bargaining, and finally, acceptance.[41] The responses and methods of conducting the interrogation for each one of these states of mind are discussed later, in the section on interrogation techniques.

Nonverbal Signals: Body Language

There are generally far more nonverbal signals and behaviors than there are verbal. The primary reason for this is that suspects are generally not as able to control body language as they are to conceal verbal signals. Individually, nonverbal signals are not as significant as an individual verbal signal. However, when body-language signals appear in clusters, they are generally much larger and much more symptomatic of deception. Body language is best considered as a means of confirming the symptoms and information that are being generated through the questions and answers during the interrogation. Deception is generally taking place, particularly when the verbal cues are inconsistent with the nonverbal cues.[42]

The body of a person who is being deceptive—lying—may experience certain physiological and psychological changes. The changes occur because of an inherent fear of detection. Although not true for all people being interrogated, the deceptive person's fears tend to intensify when questions focus on those investigative details posing the greatest threat to the suspect's personal welfare. Thus, the body language indicating deception tends to become more pronounced the closer the interrogator's questions come to incriminating the suspect. Often the deceptive person who attempts to disguise body language and to create an impression of nonconcern produces the opposite result. When this occurs, the body language is accentuated and more easily interpreted as signs of deception. Although not all persons who act deceptively are in fact deceptive, body language can supplement common sense, experience, and hunches for the investigator who wants to distinguish truth from deception.

Everyone experiences and participates in nonverbal communications with others every day. Most people are capable of making general interpretations of this body language, but the skillful interrogator looks for more—specifically, for signs of deception. The qualified interrogator understands that what may seem to be a sign of deception may in fact be nothing more than natural nervousness or may indicate an emotional illness unrelated to the topic of the interrogation.

Among the more common symptoms that may appear as a result of pressure produced by lying are an increase in sweating; changes of color in the skin; a dry mouth, shown when the subject frequently swallows, wets the lips, or constantly indicates thirst; an increase in the pulse rate; an observable change in the breathing rate; a signifi-

cant increase in the eye-blink rate; and eyes open wider than normal.[43] A good investigator is constantly alert for the manifestation of such symptoms and able to use them to advantage. Such manifestations should be pointed out to the suspect as indications of lying. The interrogator should never allow a suspect to lie and get away with it. If this occurs, the suspect will be in control of the interrogation, an intolerable condition.

Body language is extremely difficult to control. One's body reacts naturally to a situation, and these reactions cannot be fabricated without a great deal of training. Body language indicating deception can be a reaction to a verbal statement, question, remark, photograph, or the sight of evidence. It can occur in response to a body language message sent by the interrogator. The entire body or any part or parts of the body can be involved in body language—the arms, legs, shoulders, lips, eyes, nose, the entire face, posture, and gestures. To illustrate, the sitting posture of a deceptive individual may differ significantly from that of a nondeceptive one. The deceptive individual often slouches rather than sitting upright, sits rigidly instead of relaxedly, does not face the interrogator but looks to the side, sits with arms or legs crossed, and shifts sitting positions often and in a very jerky manner. Gestures indicating tension include wringing the hands, popping knuckles, chewing nails, picking lint from clothes, and clearing the throat, to name but a few.

Facial expressions, including eye movement, can tell much about an individual's thoughts and feelings and can indicate deception if one knows how to properly evaluate those expressions.

The interpretation of neurolinguistic eye movement is based on the understanding that each of us processes information and communicates thoughts on three different levels: visual; auditory, or sound; and kinesic, or touch (see Figure 8–7). The language that a person uses reveals at which level he or she is; by using parallel language, the investigator can more effectively communicate with that person. In the visual mode, a person might say, "I'll *look* back and *see* if I can remember." The auditory level is characterized by statements such as "It *sounds* like I'm really in trouble" or "I can't believe that Carlos did that; it just doesn't *ring* true that he would be involved." At the kinesic, or touch, level, illustrations of the language used include "Can you tell me who my attorney is? I can't keep a *handle* on her name" and "I

Figure 8–7
The Eyes Have It

(*Top left*) Individual is creating visually. (*Top right*) Individual is recalling visually something that he actually experienced. (*Middle left*) Creating an auditory memory. (*Middle right*) Recalling sounds actually experienced. (*Bottom left*) Kinesic or touch position. (*Bottom right*) Internal dialogues, getting in touch with one's feelings.

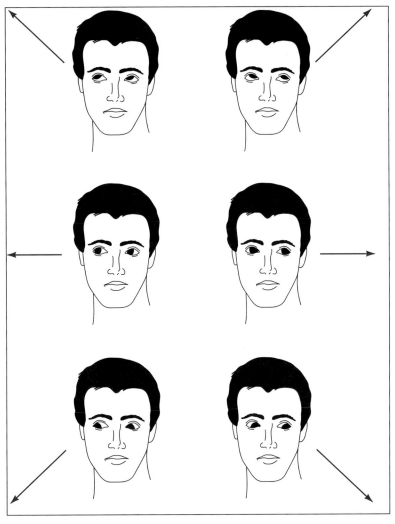

Source: After David E. Zulawski and Douglas E. Wicklander, *Practical Aspects of Interview and Interrogation* (New York: Elsevier, 1992), p. 154.

feel really bad about what happened to Hassan." Referring again to Figure 8–7, if an investigator asked "When was the last time you saw Peggy?" and the person's eye movement was up and to his or her left, the response is likely to be true. Conversely, if the eye movement was up and to his or her right, the response is being created and, therefore, is possibly a lie. For 90 percent of individuals, eye movement to their right indicates creating and to their left indicates recalling something actually experienced. Although neurolinguistic eye movement can be the same for left- and right-handed people, some of the remaining 10 percent is accounted for by left-handed people who simply reverse the cues they give off.[44]

Facial expressions can display fear, anger, confusion, pleasure, and a myriad of other emotions.[45]

Many qualified interrogators have been using body language as part of interviewing and interrogation processes for years. "Body language" may be the current term used to refer to this technique, but its concepts are not new. Rather, closer scientific study has been made of these concepts in more recent years. Some experts now claim that it would take two years to teach a trained social scientist the skills needed to properly evaluate body language.[46]

Proximity in an interrogation can also be important. For years, experts have urged the "knee-to-knee" method of interrogation: close enough to touch without being too close and without any object such as a chair or desk between subject and interrogator. "It seems, for example, that around 27 inches is the limit of proximity for white American middle-class males. . . . If you move closer, people become uncomfortable . . . further away than 27 inches, you can't read a person's face well."[47]

Detecting deception, obviously, is not a science; hence, the phrase "may indicate deception" is frequently used. This is because behavioral actions and reactions must be interpreted in the social and psychological context of a specific situation, which can at times be misleading to even the most skillful interrogator.[48]

Recent research studies, although admittedly not conducted in the real-life law enforcement environment, reveal that many of the beliefs about reading body language can be misinterpreted. For example, vocal pitch may actually decrease during deception. Hand, leg, foot, and other "indicators" of nervousness may decrease and eye contact may actually increase during deception.[49]

Often when the deceiver fails to adequately plan and rehearse the deception beforehand, emotional responses to a skilled interrogation will result in uncontrolled body-language responses, which can be and often are properly interpreted as deceit. Emotional reaction is the key factor. Three emotions closely related to the act of deception are worthy of explanation. The first emotion is the fear of being caught lying. The extent of the fear—mild, moderate, heavy—will, of course, influence the suspect's reaction. A number of determinants will influence the extent of apprehension, including the suspect's belief (or knowledge) about the skill of the interrogator in detecting deception. The greater the interrogator's skills are, or are believed to be, the greater the apprehension on the part of the suspect. In actuality, the interrogator must be able to distinguish between the guilty person's fear of getting caught and the innocent person's fear of not being believed.

Other determinants controlling the degree of apprehension include the level of experiences and successes the suspect has had in deceiving people in the past, the level of fear about the punishment for being detected, and the "acting ability" of the suspect (is he or she a good or bad liar?).[50]

The second type of emotion caused by deception is guilt about lying as distinguished from any feelings about the content of the lie. The greater the guilt about lying, the greater will be the emotional reaction irrespective of the existence or degree of guilt about the criminal act itself.[51]

The third emotion, about which there is not much research, may be classed as a positive feeling for the liar. This applies to subjects who experience some excitement at the challenge of being deceptive or at successfully deceiving the interrogator, especially if the interrogator has a reputation for being hard to deceive.[52]

Thus, physiological changes do occur when a suspect is being deceptive. These changes may be observed when a suspect experiences changes of the position of the head; changes in facial color; and facial expression, including facial tics; changes that occur in the nose, the mouth, and the behavior of lips; changes in smoking behavior; changes in the eyes, including pupillary responses and blinking; changes in the arms, shoulders, and elbows, including the manner and behavior of crossing arms; changes in the use and positioning of the hands; changes in the positioning and movement of the legs, knees and feet; and changes in sitting postures.[53]

In conclusion, Stanley Abrams best describes the emotional triggers of psychological changes:

Fear is the major activator of [these] physical change[s]. The penalty for being caught in a criminal activity is reasonably clear. The threat of imprisonment, financial loss, or personal embarrassment are sufficiently obvious [to the interviewee] so that no life-long conditioning process is necessary to explain the fear response. While fear is the emotion most likely to [surface] during deception. . . conflict and guilt can also alter the physical state of the individual. . . .Conflict causes tension or anxiety that, like guilt and fear, activates the body processes. During interviews, culpable people tend to have more tension and related physiological changes such as blushing, sweating palms, and other reflections of internal turmoil. . . . The autonomic nervous system causes certain behavioral changes which may be evident to the observant investigator as possible signals of deception.

Fear and conflict are inherent responses, but what a person reacts to is learned. Guilt, on the other hand, is a learned response that had its beginnings in early childhood. Parents, church, and important people in a child's life teach a specific set of values, attitudes, and morals. These teachings are begun early and taught so thoroughly that they become very firmly ingrained within the person. Every time he goes against their teachings, he punishes himself through guilt until he, like most people, functions within the bounds of his conscience.[54]

STATEMENT ANALYSIS

Aside from the issues of how to properly document an interrogation, particularly as it relates to obtaining a confession that will later be used in court, a story told by the suspect while being interrogated is more than just facts. How the person says something may reveal far more than what is said. If possible, an experienced interrogator will attempt to have the suspect's statement reduced to a verbatim transcript, which will give the interrogator the opportunity to examine the statement thoroughly. This transcript often provides additional insights into what the suspect intended to convey. For example, honest persons rarely talk about themselves in the third person, but dishonest persons often do so.

Pronoun usage offers a great opportunity for gaining insight into the suspect's thinking. The absence of the word "I" in the later portion of a statement, when questions are more specific about the suspect's involvement in the offense, suggests that the suspect is unwilling to acknowledge involvement. Refusal to use that personal pronoun shows an extremely impersonal approach to the subject about which questions are being asked. However, if the word "I" changes to "we" during the interrogation, the switch often suggests an attempt by the suspect to dilute his or her own responsibility and to imply the involvement of others—in other words, trying to spread the blame.

Verb tense can also be important. Normally when an individual recalls a past event, he or she describes it in the past tense. That is because, when remembering, the mind sees what has occurred. However, if there is no memory, because the event never occurred, the mind must create the occurence as it goes along. Hence, a suspect who is being deceptive may often use descriptive terms in the present tense. When this occurs, there is most likely some deception.

Balance is also a common element of speech. A story usually consists of an introduction, a body, and a closing. A deceptive person will sometimes spend just a short time talking about the important issues concerning the offense and spend a great deal of time describing extraneous information or trivia.[55]

INTERROGATION TECHNIQUES AND APPROACHES

Identical techniques do not work for all interrogations. Approaches and questions differ with the type of suspect being questioned. Questioning a suspect whose guilt is certain requires a different approach from questioning a suspect whose guilt is uncertain. Similarly, different approaches would be used to interrogate an unemotional and an emotional suspect. All of these techniques assume either a logical approach or an emotional approach. The *logical approach* is based on common sense and sound reasoning. It tends to work better with males with past criminal records, educated people, and mature adults. The *emotional approach* appeals to the suspect's sense of honor, morals, righteousness, fair play, justice, family pride, religion, decency, and restitution. This approach tends to work better with women and first-time offenders.

When a suspect's guilt is certain, the interrogator should display confidence in this fact, perhaps by asking the suspect *why* rather than *if* he or she committed the crime, by pointing out the futility of telling lies, and by asking the suspect, "Aren't you sorry to have become involved in this mess?" Warning the suspect to tell the truth and pointing out some of the circumstantial evidence of guilt are also techniques to be used when guilt is certain. Calling attention to psychological and/or physiological symptoms of guilt can also work. A sympathetic approach can often be successful: telling the suspect that anyone would have reacted as he or she did under the same circumstances, minimizing the moral seriousness of the offense, suggesting a less offensive motive than the one known or suspected, or condemning victims, accomplices, or anyone else who might be seen by the suspect as being morally responsible for the crime.

When a suspect's guilt is uncertain, the interrogator should begin with an indirect approach, assuming that the interrogator already possesses all necessary facts. By using all physical evidence, photographs, and sketches, and challenging all lies, the interrogator may make this method extremely productive.

With the emotional suspect, the interrogator may call attention to physiological and psychological symptoms indicating guilt while pointing to the futility of resistance and appealing to the suspect's pride.

The "Mutt-and-Jeff," or good-guy/bad-guy, approach to interrogation works in some cases. One partner plays the bad guy, who rejects and refuses to believe all explanations put forth by the suspect. When that partner finally leaves the room, the good guy makes an emotional appeal and offers friendly assistance so that the suspect will not have to be confronted again by the bad guy.

Playing one person against the other sometimes works when there are at least two suspects, both of whom swear they are telling the truth during separate interrogations. The interrogator asks the first suspect to write on a piece of paper, "I swear I am telling the truth," and sign it. The interrogator then shows the paper to the second suspect, telling this suspect that the first suspect just told the whole story but, before the interrogator totally accepts the story, he or she would like to hear the true story from this suspect.

As a consequence, trickery and deceit are often used in interrogations and the U.S. Supreme Court has not disapproved of these methods as long as they are not forcefully used to encourage an innocent person to incriminate himself or herself.

For suspects who are undergoing the negative reactions of anger, depression, denial, and bargaining before acceptance is achieved, as discussed earlier, there are causes and symptoms that an experienced interrogator can identify and use to prepare the appropriate questions and responses. For example, anger exemplifies frustration of the suspect. The interrogator should not get caught up in the anger but, rather, should allow the anger to burn itself out. If it is not encouraged or the interrogator does not respond to the display of anger, it will generally disintegrate in a short time.

Depression is aggression directed internally rather than externally, as in the case of anger. There may be both verbal and nonverbal symptoms of depression that are fairly obvious, such as a bowed head, downcast eyes, slumped or hunched shoulders, crying, and remarks about being depressed. The interrogator must be able to distinguish between clinical depression, which will clearly indicate that the interrogation will not produce helpful results; feigned depression, in which the interrogator should bargain with the suspect to attempt to overcome the depression; and stress-related depression, which can be caused by the interrogation process. Stress-related depression should be encouraged by the interrogator, as it can result in the suspect's use of additional defensive reserves and thus reduce the energy levels needed to continue resisting the interrogator.

When a suspect whose guilt is certain enters a state of denial, the interrogator must go on the attack. This is an appropriate time to affirmatively accuse the suspect of the commission of the crime and to begin letting the suspect know that there already exists an assumption that he or she committed the crime and that it is time to move on to other issues.

When a suspect enters the state of bargaining, this is indicative that the suspect accepts the reality of his or her involvement, but only to a limited extent. Normally, the suspect will still want to share responsibility. This is a good time to use techniques that will make it easier for the suspect to live with his or her involvement without expecting the suspect to accept full responsiblity.

When the state of acceptance is reached, it is a positive state in which a confession is most likely to occur.[56]

THE IMPORTANCE OF LISTENING

At the risk of being repetitive, the importance of active listening as an essential characteristic of the truly effective interrogator must again be stressed.

In addition to being attuned to the body language of the suspect, the interrogator must listen to the verbal component of a communication in a two-dimensional manner. On the one hand, the content per se is an important outcome of the interrogation. On the other hand, and equally important, is the necessity of understanding the intention and meaning of what is being said. To effectively listen to and evaluate the communication in these two dimensions, it is necessary for the interrogator to follow the basic rule of being a good active listener: Be Quiet! (See Chapter 5, Interviews.)

DOCUMENTING THE INTERROGATION

Documenting an interrogation consists of three main phases: note taking, recording, and obtaining written statements. All three of these phases are geared to accomplishing two basic functions: to retain information for the benefit of the interrogator and the continued investigation and to secure a written statement or confession from the accused for later use as evidence in court.

The three most widely accepted methods of keeping notes during an interrogation are mental notes, written notes, and notes taken by a third party. There are advantages and disadvantages to each. The two advantages of making mental notes are that doing so permits the subject to communicate with the interrogator without being interrupted constantly while the interrogator makes notes and that doing so is not distracting to the subject. The disadvantage is apparent: If the interrogation continues for any period of time, details that might have proved to be of considerable importance are likely to be lost in the maze of information.

Written notes are more advantageous in that they permit the interrogator to document salient information. However, even a well-trained interrogator can record only a certain amount of information during an interrogation, and there is a tendency to concentrate on the major points while disregarding minute but salient details. In addition, making written notes requires thought and concentration. The interrogator may not fully concentrate on what the suspect is saying and thus may miss something

important. Note taking may also distract the subject, who may be hesitant to convey the truth, knowing that the information is being taken down.

Although the presence of a trained third party, such as a stenographer, to take notes during an interrogation has the advantage of allowing for the documentation of a great deal more information and of the suspect's own words (useful for statement analysis), it has the major disadvantage of being a distraction to the subject. Again, the subject may not wish to communicate openly with the interrogator if the subject knows that a third party is present and that complete notes are being taken.

The situation dictates which, if any, of these methods are to be used. The interrogator should keep in mind that the primary objective is to communicate with the subject. If note taking will hinder that function, the advantages and disadvantages must be weighed.

Recording an interrogation is the best means of documentation. Audio, video, or a combination may be used, but, because of the absence of case law to serve as a legal guide, local requirements should be checked. The determination should include consideration of whether it is necessary to inform the suspect that the interrogation is going to be recorded. A videotape with sound that can be shown on a television set that can be introduced into court is best. It can be used to overcome charges of coercion. It permits a jury to see the actual manner in which the interrogation was conducted, to observe the demeanor of the interrogator and the suspect, and to hear any incriminating statements directly from the suspect's own mouth.

Because the law is constantly evolving concerning the use and admissibility of videotaping, many courts allowing its use require testimony of a qualified technician or operator as a condition of admissibility. The technician must be sufficiently knowledgeable and experienced with the equipment and process of videotaping to assure the court that all the equipment was in working order, that the tape was not edited, and that a proper chain of custody was maintained. Despite every effort to ensure fairness and accuracy in the taping process, a court may find other reasons to suppress a tape. Therefore, it has been suggested that, when possible, it is best to obtain a statement first and then have it repeated on tape. Then if the tape is suppressed, the confession may still be admissible.

Quality equipment and tapes should be used to ensure a quality product. It should be remembered that the purpose behind this effort is to convince a jury. The higher the quality, the more convincing it will be. Interrogators and technicians must be aware that little things can affect the message on the tape. For example, it is important to select a location for taping that exudes an atmosphere of fairness and nonhostility. A background filled with handcuffs, firearms, wanted posters, and sounds of blaring sirens is not likely to portray the kind of impression to the jury that the law enforcement agency or prosecutor desires.

Audio documentation is the second-best method for recording. Its introduction in court necessitates establishing the identity of the people involved in the interrogation and what each had to say. One disadvantage arises if the subject does not know that the interrogation is being recorded. The individual is likely to point out things or make statements that an interrogator can see but no one else will be able to identify from the audio recording. For example, the suspect may hold up a knife and say, "I held it like this." The interrogator knows what is meant, but to a third party listening to the recording later, the words may be meaningless.

Documenting information incriminating the accused may take a number of forms. All of them are generally admissible, but the weight they carry with the jury is likely to vary. The most convincing method that can be used is an audiovisual recording of a confession or admission given by a suspect during an interrogation. Barring the use of this technique, the next-best form would be a signed statement written in the first person by the suspect in his or her own handwriting. Frequently, however, it is not possible to convince a suspect to prepare such a statement. Or perhaps the suspect cannot write.

Other forms in which statements may be admitted into evidence, listed in descending order of the credibility that they are likely to have with a jury, are a typed or handwritten statement by someone else that is signed in the accused's own hand; a typed or otherwise prepared statement that the accused does not sign but that is acknowledged in front of witnesses; or the oral testimony of some person who was present and overheard the subject give a confession or admission. In this last case, even though admissible, the testimony is likely to carry little weight with the jury. Table 8–3 shows each of the methods of documentation in descending order of preference and the advantages and disadvantages of each.

The distinction between confessions and admissions is important. A *confession* is defined as an acknowledgment by an accused that he or she has committed a crime. It includes an acknowledgment of the commission of all the elements of the crime and the individual's involvement in their commission. The burden is on the prosecution to prove that a confession was obtained freely and voluntarily. An *admission* is an acknowledgment by the accused of certain facts that tend to incriminate him or her with respect to a particular crime but that are not sufficiently complete to constitute a confession. The burden of proving that an admission was obtained involuntarily is on the defense, should they seek to have it suppressed.

The form and content of a written statement should include a heading, which incorporates the data identifying the circumstances under which the statement was taken, the body of the statement, and a verification. The statement should open with an indication of the place where it was taken, the date, time, city, county, and state, and an identification of the person giving the statement by name, address, and age. The heading must also include a definite statement to the effect that the subject is giving the statement freely and voluntarily after having been appropriately advised of his or her constitutional rights.

The body of the statement, which acknowledges the subject's involvement in the crime under investigation, should, if possible, be phrased in the first person, allowing the suspect to include his or her own ideas in a free-flowing manner. However, if this is not possible or practical, then the question-and-answer format is permissible. The terminology used should include the words, grammar, idioms, and style of the person making the statement. The body of the statement should be arranged so that its content follows the chronological order of the subject's involvement in the case under investigation.

At the end, the statement should indicate that the subject has read the statement or has had it read to him or her, that its contents and implications are understood, and that the subject attests to its accuracy.

Table 8–3
Methods of Documenting a Confession and Their Advantages and Disadvantages
(in descending order of believability to juries)

Method	Advantages	Disadvantages
1. Video/audiotape or movie	Shows all, including fairness, procedures, and treatment Easy to do Can be relatively inexpensive	May be legal constraints Quality equipment may be costly
2. Audio recording	Can hear conversations Can infer fairness	Some words or descriptions may be meaningless without pictorial support Necessitates identifying people and things involved
3. Statement written and signed in suspect's own handwriting	Can be identified as coming directly from suspect	Can't see demeanor or hear voice inflections Suspect may not agree to procedure
4. Typed statement signed by suspect	Signature indicates knowledge of and agreement with contents of statement	Less convincing than methods described above
5. Typed unsigned statement acknowledged by suspect	Contents of confession or admission are present Acknowlegment helps show voluntariness	Reduced believability of volunariness and accuracy of contents
6. Testimony of someone who heard confession or admission given	Contents admissible	Carries little weight with juries

Other suggestions for the interrogator to keep in mind include:

- Each page of the statement should be numbered consecutively with an indication that it is page ____ of ____ pages. If the pages get separated, they can later be easily restored to order.
- The interrogator should ensure that each page is initialed by the subject. If the subject is unwilling to sign, the statement should be acknowledged by him or her. In instances when the subject cannot write, another identifying mark may be used.
- On occasion an interrogator may encounter someone who says, "I'll tell you what I've done, but I'm not writing anything and I'm not signing anything." In these circumstances the interrogator can explain that the suspect just confessed and that the interrogator or other person who heard the confession can go into

court and testify about it. By preparing or signing a statement, the suspect protects himself or herself against the interrogator's testifying to something more damaging by changing the story in court.

- If the suspect cannot read, the statement must be read to him or her, and the interrogator must ensure that the suspect understands its contents before the suspect is allowed to attest to its accuracy.
- All errors in the statement should be corrected on the final copy and initialed by the suspect. The interrogator may accommodate the suspect by allowing small errors if this will help to obtain the suspect's initials on each page of the statement.
- The interrogator should make sure that the suspect understands all the words used in the statement. If some words are confusing, their meanings should be explained to the subject,

and the subject should be required to explain them back in front of witnesses in order to establish understanding.

- During the process of drafting and attesting to a statement derived through interrogation, there should be at least one additional witness who can testify to the authenticity of the statement and the circumstances under which it was obtained. After the suspect signs the statement in ink, the witnesses should sign their names, addresses, and positions.

ADMISSIBILITY OF CONFESSIONS AND ADMISSIONS

Prior to 1936 the only test for the validity and admissibility of a confession or admission was its voluntariness. However, the determination as to whether it was given voluntarily by the suspect was subject to very loose interpretation. There were no rules restricting the method by which police obtained "voluntary" statements. Physical violence, psychological coercion, empty promises, and meaningless guarantees of rewards were not considered objectionable procedures.

THE FREE-AND-VOLUNTARY RULE

The first notable incidence of Supreme Court intervention into interrogation practices came about in *Brown* v. *Mississippi*.[57] In this 1936 case, the Supreme Court held that under no circumstances could a confession be considered freely and voluntarily given when it was obtained as a result of physical brutality and violence inflicted by law enforcement officials on the accused. The reaction to this decision by police was not unexpected. Many threw up their hands and claimed that they could no longer function effectively because "handcuffs had been put on the police." However, as was true with many other decisions placing procedural restrictions on law enforcement agencies, the police found that they were able to compensate by conducting thorough criminal investigations.

Subsequent to the *Brown* decision, the Supreme Court, in a succession of cases, has continued to

reinforce its position that any kind of coercion, whether physical or psychological, would be grounds for making a confession inadmissible as being in violation of the free-and-voluntary rule. This includes such conduct as threatening bodily harm to the suspect or members of the suspect's family,[58] psychological coercion,[59] trickery or deceit, or holding a suspect incommunicado. Investigators are also cautioned about making promises to the suspect that cannot be kept. All these practices were condemned in *Miranda* v. *Arizona*.[60] Despite the appearance that *Miranda* has eliminated all techniques previously used in interrogations, this is not actually the case. What *Miranda* seeks is to abolish techniques that would prompt untrue incriminatory statements by a suspect. Thus, unlike physical coercion, psychological coercion, threats, duress, and some promises, the use of trickery, fraud, falsehood, or other techniques is not absolutely forbidden. If such methods are not likely to cause an individual to make self-incriminating statements or to admit to falsehoods in order to avoid a threatened harm, confessions or admissions so obtained are admissible.[61]

THE DELAY-IN-ARRAIGNMENT RULE

In 1943 the Supreme Court delivered another decision concerning the admissibility of confessions. Even though the free-and-voluntary rule was in effect in both the federal and state courts, another series of statutes seemed to have gone unheeded. Every state and the federal government had legal provisions requiring that after arrest a person must be taken before a committing magistrate "without unnecessary delay." Before 1943, if there was an unnecessary delay in producing the accused before a committing magistrate, the delay was merely one of a number of factors that the courts were required to take into consideration in determining whether the confession was freely and voluntarily given.

The facts of *McNabb* v. *United States* reveal that McNabb and several members of his family were involved in bootlegging. They were arrested following the murder of federal officers who were investigating their operation in Tennessee. McNabb was held incommunicado for several days before he was taken before a committing magistrate. He subsequently confessed, and the confession was admitted into evidence at his trial. He was convicted, and on appeal to the Supreme Court the conviction was reversed. The Court held that the failure of federal officers to take the prisoner before a committing officer without unnecessary delay automatically rendered his confession inadmissible. The significance of this case is that for the first time the Court indicated that failure to comply with this procedural requirement rendered the confession inadmissible regardless of whether it had been obtained freely and voluntarily. Thus, instead of examining the facts of the case to determine the voluntariness of the confession, the Court ruled, as a matter of law, that the procedural violation alone rendered the confession inadmissible.[62] The holding in the *McNabb* case was emphatically reaffirmed in 1957 by the Supreme Court in *Mallory* v. *United States.*[63]

As the mandate of the Supreme Court in the *McNabb* and *Mallory* cases had applicability only to federal prosecutions, the states were free to interpret their own statutes on unnecessary delay as they saw fit. Few chose to follow the *McNabb-Mallory* rule; the majority have continued to require that there must be a connection between the failure of police to produce the accused before a committing magistrate without unnecessary delay and the securing of a confession.

Questions

1. How does interrogation differ from interviewing?
2. What requirements are imposed on the police by *Miranda* v. *Arizona*?
3. Why do some people confess?
4. What are the qualities of an effective interrogator?
5. Describe the importance of planning for the interrogation.
6. How does an interrogator evaluate and thus control a suspect?
7. Describe the conditions under which an interrogation should take place.
8. Of what significance is the investigator's ability to compose proper questions?
9. Why is an understanding of behavioral and physiological principles important to a successful interrogation?
10. Describe the following concepts as they apply to the detection of deception: fear of being caught lying, guilt about lying, and the exhilaration of lying successfully.
11. How may an interrogation be documented?
12. Why is it important to number pages in a statement?
13. What is the evidentiary test for admissibility of confessions and admissions?

Notes

1. *Escobedo* v. *Illinois*, 378 U.S. 478 (1964).
2. *Miranda* v. *Arizona*, 384 U.S. 436 (1966).
3. 451 U.S. 477, 101 S.Ct. 1880 (1981).
4. 498 U.S. 146 (1990).
5. 108 S.Ct. 2389 (1988).
6. 423 U.S. 96, 96 S.Ct. 321 (1975).
7. 492 U.S. 195, 109 S.Ct. 2875 (1989).
8. 425 U.S. 341 (1976).
9. 429 U.S. 492 (1977).
10. 429 U.S. 492, 495 (1977).
11. 103 S.Ct. 3517 (1983).
12. 89 S.Ct. 1095 (1969).
13. 699 F.2d 466 (9th Cir. 1982).
14. 736 F.2d 1232 (8th Cir. 1984).
15. 391 U.S. 1 (1968).
16. 110 S.Ct. 2394 (1990).
17. 104 S.Ct. 2626, 81 L. Ed. 550 (1984).
18. 82 L. Ed. 317 (1984).

19. 392 U.S. 1 (1968). For additional references, see C. E. Riley III, "Finetuning Miranda Policies," *FBI Law Enforcement Bulletin,* January 1985, pp. 23–31; R. Jacobs, "The State of *Miranda," Trial,* January 1985, pp. 45–48.

20. 468 U.S. 420, 104 S.Ct. 3138, 82 L. Ed. 317 (1984). See also *Pennsylvania* v. *Bruder,* 109 S.Ct. 205 (1988).

21. 109 S.Ct. 205 (1988).

22. *United States* v. *J.H.H.,* 22 F.3d 821 (8th Cir. 1994).

23. *Stansbury* v. *California,* 511 U.S. 318 (1994).

24. 430 U.S. 387 (1977).

25. 446 U.S. 291, 100 S.Ct. 1682 (1980).

26. *Pope* v. *Zenon,* 69 F.3d 1018 (9th Cir. 1995).

27. John C. Klotter and Jacqueline R. Kanovitz, *Constitutional Law,* 4th ed. (Cincinnati: Anderson Publishing Co., 1981), p. 343.

28. Robert L. Donigan, Edward C. Fisher, David H. Hugel, Robert H. Reeder, and Richard N. Williams, *The Evidence Handbook,* 4th ed. (Evanston, Ill.: The Traffic Institute, Northwestern University, 1980), p. 44.

29. 107 S.Ct. 1931 (1987).

30. *United States* v. *Clark,* 982 F.2d 965, at 968 (6th Cir. 1993).

31. Fred E. Inbau and John E. Reid, *Criminal Interrogation and Confessions* (Baltimore: Williams & Wilkins, 1962), p. 1.

32. John E. Hess, *Interviewing and Interrogation for Law Enforcement,* (Cincinnati: Anderson, 1997), pp. 81–84; Charles L. Yeschke, *The Art of Investigative Interviewing* (Boston: Butterworth-Heinesmann, 1997), pp. 56–68.

33. Stan B. Walters, *Principles of Kenesic Interview and Interrogation* (New York: CRC Press, 1996), p. 1.

34. Yeschke, *The Art of Investigative Interviewing,* pp. 25–40, 113–134.

35. Hess, *Interviewing and Interrogation for Law Enforcement,* p. 84.

36. Thomas Streed, "The Psychology of Interviewing and Interrogation," unpublished document copyright by Thomas Streed, 1986, pp. 21–22, and used with permission of the author. Portions of this material were obtained in a telephone interview with Detective Thomas Streed, San Diego, California, County Sheriff's Department, October and November 1990.

37. Paul Eckman and Maureen O'Sullivan, "Hazards in Detecting Deceit," in *Psychological Methods in Criminal Investigation and Evidence,* David C. Raskin, ed. (New York: Springer Publishing Company, 1989), p. 297.

38. John Fay, unpublished notebook from a Workshop in Criminal Interrogation, November 17–18, 1981, sponsored by the Jacksonville, Florida, Chapter, American Society for Industrial Security, pp. A5-1–A5-2.

39. Hess, *Interviewing and Interrogation for Law Enforcement,* pp. 66–69.

40. Walters, *Principles of Kenesic Interview and Interrogation,* p. 9.

41. Yeschke, *The Art of Investigative Interviewing,* pp. 13–14.

42. Walters, *Principles of Kenesic Interview and Interrogation,* p. 73.

43. Charles G. Brougham, "Nonverbal Communication: Can What They Don't Say Give Them Away?" *FBI Law Enforcement Bulletin,* July 1992, pp. 15–18.

44. All of the information in this paragraph is drawn, with restatement, from David E. Zulawski and Douglas E. Wicklander, *Practical Aspects of Interview and Interrogation* (New York: Elsevier, 1992), pp. 146–147.

45. See Daniel Goleman, "People Who Read People," *Psychology Today,* July 1979. See also Daniel Goleman, "The 7000 Faces of Dr. Ekman," *Psychology Today,* February 1981, p. 43; John Leo, "The Fine Art of Catching Liars," *Time,* April 22, 1985, p. 59.

46. Forest E. Kay, Jr., "Detecting Deceptions during the Criminal Interview," *The Police Chief,* May 1979, p. 57.

47. William Hart, "The Subtle Art of Persuasion," *Police Magazine,* January 1981, p. 10.

48. Eckman and O'Sullivan, "Hazards in Detecting Deceit," p. 297.

49. Ibid., pp. 297–299.

50. Ibid., pp. 302–306.

51. Ibid., pp. 306–310.

52. Ibid., pp. 310–312.

53. Stan B. Walters, *Principles of Kenesic Interview and Interrogation,* pp. 73–138.

54. Stanley A. Abrams, *Polygraph Handbook for Attorneys* (Lexington, Mass.: Lexington Books, 1977), as reported in Yeschke, *The Art of Investigative Interviewing,* pp. 16–17.

55. Hess, *Interviewing and Interrogation for Law Enforcement,* pp. 59–64.

56. Walters, *Principles of Kenesic Interview and Interrogation,* pp. 141–158.

57. 297 U.S. 278 (1936).

58. *Payne* v. *Arkansas,* 356 U.S. 560 (1958).

59. *Miranda* v. *Arizona,* 384 U.S. 436 (1966).

60. Ibid.

61. Donigan et al., *The Evidence Handbook,* pp. 47–48. See also *Frazier* v. *Cupp,* 394 U.S. 731 (1969); *Oregon* v. *Mathiason,* 429 U.S. 492 (1977).

62. 318 U.S. 332 (1943).

63. 354 U.S. 449 (1957).

N I N E

The Crime Laboratory and the Criminal Investigation Process

CHAPTER OUTLINE

Forensic Science and Criminalistics Defined 206

Crime Laboratories: Programs and Personnel
Distribution 206

Measures of Effectiveness of Crime
Laboratories 208

Technologies 211

Handling Evidence in the Laboratory 217

ATF Forensic Science Laboratories 219

The FBI Crime Laboratory 220

Questions 223

Notes 223

INTRODUCTION

A crime laboratory is a scientific organization with a closely dedicated mission of aiding the process of criminal justice. It provides this aid by answering, or helping to answer, the vital question of whether a crime has been committed, how and when it was committed, who committed it, and, just as important, who could not have committed it. The crime laboratory seeks answers such as these through the scientific analysis of physical material collected primarily from the scene of crimes or from suspects.[1]

To understand the role of crime laboratories, one must understand their relationship to the scientific community and to the functions of the criminal justice system. There are two distinct activities involved in laboratory work. One is the gathering of evidence at the scene of the crime by evidence technicians or investigators. The second function is the scientific analysis of evidence, which occurs in the laboratory. The effectiveness of the latter activity often depends on the efficiency with which the first operation is performed.

FORENSIC SCIENCE AND CRIMINALISTICS DEFINED

The terms "forensic science" and "criminalistics" are often used interchangeably. *Forensic science* is that part of science applied to answering legal questions. It is the examination, evaluation, and explanation of physical evidence in law. Forensic science encompasses pathology, toxicology, physical anthropology, odontology (dental structure, development, and diseases), psychiatry, questioned documents, firearms, tool mark comparison, and serology, among other fields. Recent technological advances have added molecular biology and genetics to this list.

One of the branches of forensic science, *criminalistics*, deals with the study of physical evidence related to a crime. From such a study, a crime may be reconstructed. Criminalistics too is interdisciplinary, drawing on mathematics, physics, chemistry, biology, anthropology, and many other scientific endeavors. The late Paul L. Kirk, a leader in the criminalistics movement in the United States, once remarked, "Criminalistics is an occupation that has all of the responsibilities of medicine, the intricacy of the law, and the universality of science."[2]

CRIME LABORATORIES: PROGRAMS AND PERSONNEL DISTRIBUTION

There are approximately 350 federal, state, and local crime laboratories in this country. The oldest crime laboratory in the United States was established in 1923. Fifty-five percent of the labs were established between 1968 and 1978, just after Supreme Court decisions limited police interrogations and while funds were available from the now defunct Law Enforcement Assistance Administration. Seventy-nine percent of the laboratories are within public safety and law enforcement agencies; the remainder are distributed in medical examiners' offices, prosecutors' offices, scientific and health agencies, and other private and public institutions.[3]

Most crime laboratories have developed in response to a particular need in a community or region. The areas of scientific concentration in particular laboratories are based on those needs and also on the interests and skills of the people available:

> Not all crime laboratories have the same capabilities. Some can do much more than others. Laboratories also tend to emphasize and build up expertise in particular areas. The manner of collection of some types of physical evidence . . . will vary according to the type of test procedures the laboratory applies. Therefore, it is important that police investigators familiarize themselves with the capabilities of the crime laboratories supporting their jurisdictions, as well as with the requirements of the national forensic science laboratories.[4]

As can be expected, almost all laboratories originated or were expanded to examine drugs, but the percentage of crime laboratories with the capability to examine other categories of physical evidence varies from 5 to 81 percent. In an effort to overcome some of the problems caused by varying specializations and concerns, and because of the absence of agreement on what should be the purpose, function, and services of crime laboratories, the American Society of Crime Laboratory Directors (ASCLD) was formed. This organization is a nonprofit professional society of more than 400 crime laboratory directors, managers, and supervisors from the United States and 17 foreign countries, who have backgrounds as biologists, chemists, document examiners, physicists, toxicologists, and law enforcement officers. The ASCLD is devoted to the improvement of crime laboratory operations through sound management practices. Its purpose includes fostering common professional interests, management practices, information, and communication among its members and to promote, encourage, and maintain the highest standards of practice for crime laboratories. To carry out its purpose, ASCLD has established two additional entities.[5]

ASCLD/LAB, the crime laboratory accreditation program, is a voluntary program in which any crime laboratory may participate to demonstrate that its management, operations, personnel, procedures, instruments, physical plant, security, and personnel safety procedures meet certain standards. At the federal level, the ATF laboratory system was the first to be accredited, and, as of this writing, the FBI laboratory, perhaps the most comprehensive crime laboratory in the world, just received its accreditation. This is not to imply that a laboratory is inadequate or untrustworthy if it chooses not to undertake this voluntary accreditation process.[6] Accreditation can be very time-consuming and expensive.

The National Forensic Science Technology Center (NFSTC) was established by ASCLD in 1995 and began operating in 1996. Its two primary functions are to help crime laboratories prepare for accreditation, especially laboratories whose primary focus is on DNA analysis, and to offer continuing education programs for crime laboratory personnel, including the support of college and university degree programs.[7]

THE MORGUE

One type of crime lab often forgotten is the morgue. A *morgue* is not just a place that houses the bodies of deceased persons but is critical on the forensic scene as the place where cause of death is determined. Experienced forensic pathologists conduct autopsies and analyze body fluids, tissues, and organs to produce information useful in an investigation when cause of death is questionable or when death has been caused by something other than a known disease.

EXPECTATIONS

It is not unusual to find situations in which investigators not acquainted with the services of the crime laboratory expect too much from scientific analysis. Some expect the crime laboratory to be able to provide a solution in every criminal case. When investigators do not receive answers to the questions they pose through the submission of physical evidence, they are not only disappointed but more than occasionally reluctant to use the technical assistance of the laboratory again.

To some extent, investigators must be selective in collecting and preserving evidence that they believe can be profitably submitted for scientific analysis to a crime laboratory. It should always be kept in mind that the laboratory was never intended to replace a complete field investigation. The function of the laboratory is to support the investigator and the primary line units of the police agency. The laboratory is sometimes capable of lightening the burden of the investigator, but it can never completely assume that burden. Too often personnel collect evidence at

the scene, send it to the laboratory, and then allow the investigation to stall until the laboratory report is received, expecting the laboratory to come up with some magical solution. This is an unrealistic expectation and largely results because the investigator does not understand what is and is not evidence subject to laboratory examination. The analysis of evidence can be no better than the samples submitted. The investigator therefore has a vital role to play in the success of laboratory examinations. James Osterburg, another criminalistics leader, summarizes why there is underutilization or total neglect of crime laboratories. What he said in 1968 is still largely true:

1. Lack of knowledge about how the laboratory can aid the criminal investigator.

2. Unfamiliarity with the more esoteric varieties of clue material, resulting in evidence not being preserved for examination.

3. Failure to collect physical evidence. This may be caused by a fear of cross-examination on some technical, legal, or scientific requirement that may be overlooked. It may be due to inadequate training or experience or to the overcautiousness of field investigators and the fear of destroying evidence.

4. Overrepresentation of laboratory capabilities.

5. Inconvenience to the investigator when there is no local laboratory available or backlogs are so great as to prohibit timely reports of laboratory results.[8]

This list is accurate and complete. The second and fourth points are especially important. If investigators do not know how the most minute or insignificant-looking item can be processed at a properly equipped laboratory, critical pieces of material go uncollected, unprocessed, and unused in substantiating guilt or innocence. In addition, if the capabilities of a crime laboratory are overrepresented so that investigators, uniformed officers, prosecutors, and judges all believe it can produce results that it, in fact, cannot produce, these people eventually will underuse the laboratory. Too often scientists fail to keep justice personnel informed of the state of the art in forensic work.[9]

The laboratory can be an extremely valuable investigative tool if the field investigator uses it intelligently and understands its capabilities and limitations. The investigator must also assume responsibility for providing the laboratory with evidence that is properly collected, marked, and preserved so that laboratory analysis, to the effective limits of present technology, can be successful.[10]

MEASURES OF EFFECTIVENESS OF CRIME LABORATORIES

The effectiveness of crime laboratory services can be measured in terms of three criteria: quality, proximity, and timeliness.[11]

QUALITY

Quality is judged largely on the technical capabilities of the laboratory and the abilities of the personnel who staff the laboratory.

The technical capabilities of the scientific community affect how fully laboratories answer the questions posed by investigators. Although technical advances are developing rapidly, there are still limits on what science can do in analyzing and individualizing evidence. Unfortunately, because of these inherent technological limitations of crime laboratories, they may not receive the needed resources to expand or even deliver basic services.

Budget considerations largely determine the level of services that a crime laboratory can deliver. A lack of understanding of the extent to which efficient crime laboratory programs can contribute to the effectiveness of a law enforcement agency has led many administrators to channel financial resources into more traditional kinds of law enforcement operations.

"The most important resource in any crime laboratory is the scientific staff. Without an ade-

Figure 9–1
Laboratory Personnel at Work

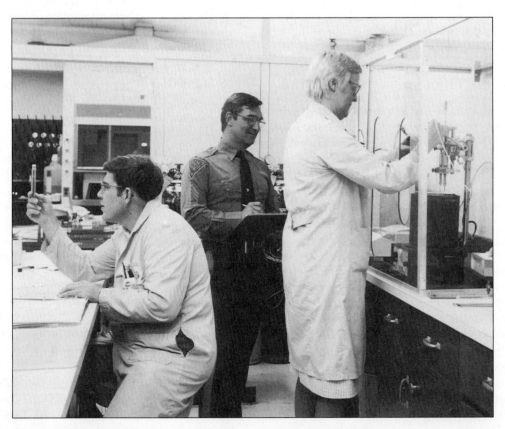

(Courtesy New Jersey State Police)

quately trained, competent staff, the best organized and equipped laboratory will not be efficient."[12] Historically, there has been a shortage of qualified personnel with scientific backgrounds interested in working in a criminalistics laboratory. Many who are qualified shun police laboratory work, particularly on a local level, because private industry can offer much more attractive salaries.[13] (See Figure 9–1.)

PROXIMITY

It is understood, if not accepted, that most law enforcement agencies cannot afford to staff and maintain a crime laboratory. In light of this fact, however, police agencies that desire and will utilize the facilities of a crime laboratory should not be denied the opportunity to have such services at their disposal. Past experience indicates that police investigators rarely seek laboratory assistance when the facility is inconvenient. There are areas where the technician or investigator must travel an unreasonable distance to obtain laboratory services. Studies have shown that evidence submission decreased sharply as the distance from the crime scene to the laboratory increased.[14] The solution to this dilemma lies in adequate planning on the state level to provide needed laboratory services.

Studies have indicated that a unified state system can best serve the needs of the law enforcement community by providing a parent, or core, laboratory on the state level capable of delivering most laboratory services and strategically located regional laboratories that respond to immediate, less sophisticated analytical needs and funnel evidence when more sophisticated analysis is required. Texas, for example, has its headquarters laboratory located under the auspices of the Texas Department of Public Safety in Austin, with field laboratories in Dallas, Tyler, Houston, Corpus Christi, Midland, El Paso, Lubbock, and Waco. The Division of Consolidated Laboratory Services in Richmond, Virginia, serves as a parent laboratory with regional facilities located in Norfolk, Roanoke, and Fairfax. Other states adopting the regionalized concept include Alabama, California, Florida, Georgia, and Illinois. Figure 9–2 shows the location in one state of regional and state-subsidized local crime laboratories joined into a regional network.

Several studies have addressed the issue of proximity of crime labs. One recommended that a regional crime laboratory should be established to serve each population group of 500,000 to 1,000,000 in an area where at least 5,000 Part I crimes are committed each year. (Part I crimes are serious offenses categorized by the FBI's *Uniform Crime Reports* into the following eight categories: murder, forcible rape, robbery, aggravated assault, burglary, larceny, arson, and auto theft.) Another study recommended that regional laboratories be located within a 20-mile radius of 90 percent of the law enforcement agencies' sworn personnel who would use the facilities. A third recommendation is that a regional laboratory be located within 50 miles of any agency that it routinely serves.[15] Local laboratories, such as those serving large cities, continue to provide the level of services within their capabilities and also serve as regional laboratories for surrounding agencies.

Even in law enforcement agencies that have a crime laboratory, the organization of the lab and its placement within the organizational structure may reveal much about the importance and priority the criminalistics function carries within the agency. In turn, that decision affects budget considerations and the quality of services provided. It is highly unlikely that an administrator who has fought for and was instrumental in establishing a crime lab would give it anything other than high priority and provide for adequate funding. But what about the next administrator? Or the one after that? Priorities in a law enforcement agency, just as in any other organization, can and do change.

If the crime lab or forensic sciences program has any importance to the chief executive, that function will not be buried within the organization; rather, it will be accessible to the operations functions and "within sight" of the administration in case assistance is needed. The committed chief executive will also ensure that the supervisory chain of command understands and appreciates the scientific roles and responsibilities of the laboratory. In fact, it is in the agency's and the laboratory's best interests for the entire supervising and command staff of the laboratory to be scientists who happen to have supervisory or command capabilities. In this manner, when resource allocation and criticality-of-function issues arise in the agency, the people representing the laboratory are knowledgeable about the scientific mission.

Figure 9–2
Location of Crime Laboratories in Florida

● Regional laboratories–state system

    Escambia (Pensacola)
    Leon (Tallahassee)
    Duval (Jacksonville)
    Orange (Orlando)
    Hillsborough (Tampa)
    Lee (Fort Myers)

★ Local laboratories–state subsidized

    Dade (Miami)
    Broward (Fort Lauderdale)
    Palm Beach (West Palm Beach)
    Indian River (Fort Pierce)
    Pinellas (Clearwater)

◆ State satellite laboratories

    Volusia (Daytona Beach)
    Monroe (Key West)

TIMELINESS

Timeliness, also extremely important to the investigator, is the third measure of effectiveness of a crime laboratory. A major portion of the caseload of most laboratories today results from requests from investigators for analysis of suspected or known samples of narcotics or dangerous drugs.[16] Even in areas where officers carry and are trained to use presumptive test kits that are available on the commercial market, the results of laboratory analysis provide conclusive evidence necessary to the success of cases. Unlike the case

with many other articles or items submitted to a laboratory for examination, which only corroborate evidence possessed by the investigator, the analysis of suspected narcotics or dangerous drugs can be a key to a successful prosecution. Their identification can significantly affect early stages of the judicial proceedings, such as the probable-cause hearing; and very often this is an essential piece of corpus delicti evidence. Hence, it is necessary that the results of laboratory examinations be made available to the investigator as quickly as possible. Such a prompt turnaround requires an appropriate allocation of money and personnel to the process by those who control the purse strings and make the decisions.

Timeliness is occasionally affected by the length of the examination or the processing time necessary for accurate and reliable test results. Early DNA analysis, for example took weeks before conclusions could be properly drawn. This lack of timeliness, in large measure, caused further research that has resulted in faster, easier, and more reliable DNA testing methods.

ADMISSIBILITY OF EXAMINATION RESULTS

In 1923, a federal court rendered a decision in the case of *Frye* v. *United States*, that ruled inadmissible the results of a "deception test," an early version of the polygraph, and established a standard which provided that, for the results of a scientific technique to be admissible, the technique must be sufficiently established to have gained general acceptance in its particular field.[17]

Half a century later, the federal rules of evidence were adopted, which provide that if scientific, technical, or other specialized knowledge will assist the trier of fact to understand the evidence or to determine a fact in issue, such evidence is admissible. The federal rules of evidence do not apply to the states, and several circuits continued to follow *Frye* rather than the federal rules. In 1993, the U.S. Supreme Court decided the case of *Daubert* v. *Merrell Dow Pharmaceuticals, Inc.* In that case, the Court said that the "general acceptance" test of *Frye* is not part of the federal rules and, in fact, was superceded by the rules' adoption. The Court went on to say that the trial judge must make a preliminary assessment of whether the testimony of an expert provides an underlying reasoning or methodology that is scientifically valid and can properly be applied to the facts of the case. Many considerations will bear on the inquiry, including whether the theory or technique in question can be (and has been) tested, whether it has been subjected to peer review and publication, its known or potential error rate, the existence and maintenance of standards controlling its operation, and whether it has attracted widespread acceptance within a relevant scientific community. The Court went on to say that the inquiry is a flexible one and that its focus must be solely on principles and methodology, not on conclusions that they generate.[18]

The application of *Daubert* and its aftermath has presented a challenge to crime laboratories to ensure that the standards imposed by the Court are followed in forensic examinations so that expert testimony and the results of examinations by crime laboratory personnel will be admissible, in both state and federal courts.

TECHNOLOGIES

The speed at which technological advances with forensic applications are developing, expanding, and evolving makes their description immediately obsolete. Computerization has increased speed and reliability of many of the processes formerly manually performed. Computer software is available to identify and track serial killers; produce aging progression, facial imaging, and other data to aid in the search for missing children; analyze hair to improve the detection of drug abuse, particularly after a long period of time has elapsed since the use of specified drugs; highlight fingerprints with laser technology that were previously unrecognizable or undetectable on smooth surfaces; and digitally enhance photographs.

DNA ANALYSIS

Advances in technology have helpd DNA testing to become an established part of criminal justice procedure. Despite early controversies and challenges by defense attorneys, the admissibility of DNA test results in the courtroom has become routine. In 1996, there were more than 17,000 cases involving forensic DNA in the United States alone. In a 1996 survey, almost half of the more than 2,300 prosecuting officers reporting indicated that they had used DNA evidence either in plea bargaining or in the trial of felony cases. It was primarily used in cases involving sex offenses, followed by a lesser number of murder and manslaughter cases and aggravated-assault cases.[19]

Questions about the validity and reliability of forensic DNA test methods have been addressed, and for the most part validity and reliability are established. As a result of DNA testing, traditional blood testing and saliva testing have been rendered obsolete because DNA is found in these substances and, in fact, is found in all body tissues and fluids.

Deoxyribonucleic acid (DNA) consists of molecules that carry the body's genetic information and establish each person as separate and distinct. Until recently, DNA was found primarily within the nuclei of cells in the chromosomes. DNA can now be extracted and processed from blood, tissue, spermatozoa, bone marrow, hair (with or without roots), saliva, skin cells, bone, teeth, urine, feces, and a host of other biological specimens, all of which may be found at crime scenes. DNA has been recovered from fingerprints, cigarette butts, drinking cups, and hatbands and other articles of clothing (e.g., Monica Lewinsky's dress).

Because of recent developments, there are two places in a cell where DNA is found. They are used for different crime detection purposes. *Nuclear DNA* is found in the nucleus, and *mitochondrial DNA* is found in the mitochondria, which are in the body of the cell. Nuclear DNA is the product of the DNA of a person's mother and father. When a sperm and an egg join at conception, the new individual gets half of his or her nuclear genetic information from each parent. Conversely, mitochondrial DNA is inherited only from the mother. At conception, all of the new person's mitochondria come from the mother. Since mitochondrial DNA (mtDNA) is passed directly through maternal relatives, it serves as a perfect identity marker for those relatives.[20]

Of the DNA evidence collected at a large number of crime scenes, only a small percentage is ever submitted to a crime lab for analysis and even a smaller percentage of that which is submitted is ever analyzed. The backlog of cases, as noted, is caused by limited resources. However, there have been some successes in both identifying offenders and clearing those who had been suspects. Ten years ago, a woman informed the FBI that she had overheard a man talking on a pay phone. The man said that he had killed a woman and buried her in the woods of a local park reserve. The local police were notified, and they located the badly decomposed skeletal remains of a person but could not find the victim's teeth. Since the medical examiner could not visually identify the person or use dental records for identification, she sent the remains to the FBI laboratory, where examiners removed DNA from the victim's bones and performed mitochondrial DNA analysis. The results were compared to the DNA of missing persons in a national database. Law enforcement authorities were able to identify the victim and later convicted her killer—the man on the pay phone (see, for example, the positive match in Figure 9–3.)[21] Another example involved a threatening letter that was sent to a newspaper editor. The FBI swabbed the envelope flap and recovered some saliva cells, which were then typed using a DNA marker. The result was compared to a known suspect and was found to match.[22]

DNA can be extracted and analyzed from specimens that may be years or even decades old. In a case involving Kirk Bloodworth, who was found guilty of sexually assaulting and murdering a young girl, the verdict was based upon an anonymous tip, identification from a police artist's sketch, eyewitness statements, and other evidence. He was later retried and again found guilty. But in 1993, more than eight years after his arrest, prosecutors compared DNA evidence from the victim's clothing to Bloodworth's DNA and found that the two did not match. He was subsequently released and then pardoned (see, for example, the negative match in Figure 9–3.)[23]

Initially, DNA analysis was hampered by the need for a large-enough sample and by the fact that manual processing took from 4 to 14 weeks, on the average. Technological developments, however, have made it possible for small samples to be reproduced into large quantities for easier processing, and recently introduced automated typing methods now permit much greater use of DNA evidence.

Today, almost all U.S. jurisdictions have legislation that allows for the data banking of DNA evidence of convicted offenders. In some jurisdictions, DNA can be collected only from offenders convicted of sex-related crimes and homicides. In others, legislation has been expanded to allow for the collection of DNA specimens from all convicted offenders, and this has dramatically increased the workload of laboratories in processing the material to establish the data banks. In addition to individual-jurisdiction data banking, there is a national investigation support database, developed by the FBI, called CODIS (Combined DNA Index System). CODIS is used in the national, state, and local index-system networks to link typing results from unresolved crimes with cases in multiple jurisdictions or persons convicted of offenses specified in the data-banking laws passed by the jurisdictions. By alerting investigators to similarities among unsolved crimes, CODIS can aid in

Figure 9–3
Forensic Identity Test

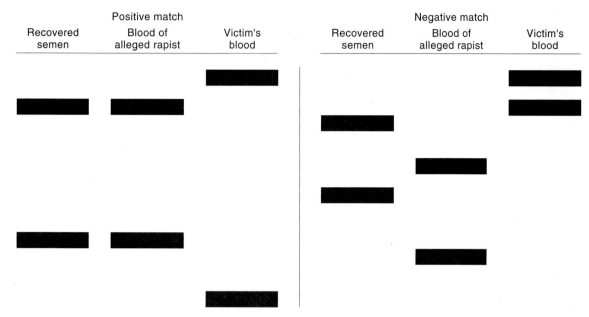

(Courtesy Lifecodes Corporation, Tarrytown, New York)

apprehending perpetrators who commit a series of crimes. There are over 83 laboratories in more than 38 states participating in CODIS, and, as of December 1997, they had produced 126 hits relating cases to one another and 76 hits relating cases to offenders.[24]

According to statistics released by the FBI, in about one-third of the cases in which DNA testing is done, suspects have been cleared.[25]

As rapidly as technologies are evolving, current DNA testing has hit only the tip of the iceberg both for forensic and nonforensic purposes. It is anticipated that, within a decade, genetics laboratories will be able to determine an individual's personalized DNA sequence from his or her blood sample. From that data, a physician will be able to ascertain if the person has any of some 5,000 known genetic diseases and will be able to evaluate the patient's probability of contracting any number of specific diseases, perhaps months, years, or decades in advance. What will make this revolution a reality is the $20 billion international Human Genome Program (HGP), which is attempting to map, by the year 2005, the 50,000 to 100,000 genes found in the human body. Once this mapping is done, many medical as well

as forensic developments will be possible.[26] (See Figure 9–4.)

AUTOMATED FINGERPRINT IDENTIFICATION SYSTEM

In the mid-1970s, in San Francisco, Miriam Slamovich, a concentration camp survivor, was shot point-blank in the face. She died a month later. On the bedroom window, her killer left a full, perfect fingerprint that became the object of thousands of hours of manual fingerprint comparisons over a 10-year period. When San Francisco installed an Automated Fingerprint Identification System (AFIS), the latent print from the Slamovich case was the first such search made, and a hit was recorded in less than 6 minutes. The killer was in custody that same day.[27]

In August 1991, two pieces of paper allegedly handled by an unknown suspect in a Jacksonville, Florida, sexual-assault case were submitted to the Florida Department of Law Enforcement regional crime lab for analysis. A number of latent prints were developed on the paper and searched in the Automated Fingerprint Identification System (AFIS) without success. The unidentified latent

Figure 9–4
DNA Evidence Being Processed in a Laboratory

(Courtesy: San Bernardino County, California Sheriff's Department)

prints were entered into the AFIS Unsolved Latent Fingerprint File (ULF) so that they could be searched against incoming fingerprint cards from current arrests throughout the state. In April 1994, an individual was arrested for auto theft and released. The fingerprint card taken at the time of the arrest was submitted to the department and searched against the ULF. On May 16, 1994, as a result of the reverse search (current fingerprint cards searched against the ULF), an identification was made. The offender was eventually located in New York and extradited to Florida. As a result of the AFIS search, blood was drawn from the suspect for comparison with semen samples obtained from the victim at the time of the offense almost three years earlier. There was a DNA match. In April 1995, the offender pled guilty to the sexual assault and was sentenced to 10 years in prision.[28]

Traditionally, fingerprints have been classified, filed, and searched according to the Henry Classification System. Technical searches of newly fingerprinted persons, conducted to determine if they have any prior criminal record, are labor-intensive but have been fairly productive. On the other hand, searches of latent fingerprints collected from crime scenes against a Henry system file have been so labor-intensive and unproductive that some jurisdictions don't even attempt them. Certainly, the larger the agency, the greater the problem is.

In the early 1970s, the FBI and the National Bureau of Standards conducted feasibility research for establishing an automated fingerprint identification process. After a successful pilot study, the computers hit the market and one of the most beneficial high-tech tools for law enforcement use in this century became a reality.[29] (See Figures 9–5 and 9–6.)

AFIS allows law enforcement agencies to conduct comparisons of applicant and suspect fingerprints with literally thousands or millions of file prints in a matter of minutes. A manual search of this nature would take hundreds of hours with little hope for and less chance of success. The heart of AFIS technology is the ability of the computer equipment to scan and digitize fingerprints by

Figure 9–5
AFIS System
A general view of an AFIS computer system.

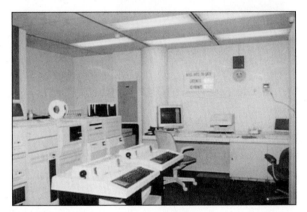

(Courtesy Iowa Division of Criminal Investigation)

Figure 9–6
AFIS Workstation
An individual AFIS workstation.

(Courtesy St. Louis Police Department)

reading spacing and ridge patterns and translating them into the appropriate computer language coding. The computer is capable of making extremely fine distinctions among prints, which lends further accuracy and reliability to the system.

The computer can map 90 or more minutia points (ridge endings, bifurcations, directions, and contours) for each finger. This is a number high enough to individualize a fingerprint and distinguish it from all others. Latent prints normally do not have 90 minutia points, but matches usually can be made with as few as 15 or 20 minutia points. One agency reported a hit on 8 minutia points.

Technicians can computer-enhance fingerprints when preparing them for a search. This process enables an experienced technician to fill in missing or blurred portions of print fragments or to correct for breaks in patterns or ridges caused by burns or scars.

As noted, the computer translates patterns into mathematical computer codes. Thus, the computer is not comparing images of a suspect's prints against images of known prints; rather, it is conducting a mathematical search that can compare a subject print against file prints at a rate of up to 600 prints per second. Search time will vary depending on such factors as preparation time, demographic data that are entered to limit the prints required to be searched, the size of the file, and the number of key factors, or matchers, being used to seek a match. A latent print can be searched against a file of 500,000 prints in about half an hour.

Although the accuracy of the AFIS system is 98 to 100 percent, this does not mean that the computer makes positive matches that percentage of the time. In fact, the system never makes a final decision on identity. The system produces a list of possibles, called a *candidate list*. It is from this list that further determinations are made by a qualified fingerprint examiner.

The computer uses a scoring system that assigns points to each criterion used in the match. The technician sets a threshold score above which a hit is fairly well assured. The technician also sets the size of the candidate list. If any of the scores are high above the threshold, a hit may be likely. If all the scores on the candidate list are low, a hit is unlikely. Policy of the agency may dictate the placement of the threshold, thus limiting or enlarging the number of candidates. Time constraints and resources may be controlling factors in these determinations.

AFIS makes no final decisions on identity. A technician must make the final verification as to whether the system has obtained a hit. The computer assists but does not replace the fingerprint expert.

AFIS has two major duties. First is performing the functions of classifying, searching, and matching prints. Second is the storage and retrieval of fingerprint data. Data are stored on optical disks, which permits side-by-side comparisons of search prints and file prints. Such comparisons are useful for verifying the data found in an AFIS search (see Figure 9–7).[30]

The Integrated Automated Fingerprint Identification System (IAFIS) is a new-generation system being developed by the FBI to support the electronic capture, submission, processing, matching, and storage of fingerprints. Scheduled to be implemented in 1999, IAFIS will provide enhanced system capabilities, improved reliability, and rapid response times. When fully operational, there will be a 2-hour turnaround on electronically submitted criminal print search requests and a 24-hour turnaround on all other criminal and civil submissions. The IAFIS system will support a paperless environment. Users will be able to submit requests electronically, and requests submitted by paper will be converted into digital images before processing. The ultimate goal is to put all fingerprint processing into an electronic environment as soon as possible. The system will be able to process 10-print-based identifications based on arrests (or fingerprints taken for employment and licensing purposes). The system will also process latent fingerprints. It will respond to requests for criminal-history searches of both known and unknown subjects and associated criminal-history information based on an individual's name, date of birth, and other descriptive information. Searches of a criminal-history file will determine whether one or more subjects meeting the search criteria have criminal records. This information will be returned to the requesting agency. IAFIS will also be able to update and purge data from an individual's criminal history.

CEASEFIRE AND DRUGFIRE

Computerized law enforcement technology has spread beyond fingerprints to the identification, analysis, and comparison of spent bullets and cartridge cases.

Figure 9-7
AFIS Fingerprint Comparison
This is an actual AFIS print. On the left is a file print several years old. On the right is a latent print left at the scene of a burglary. Even though a new scar is seen on the fingerprint on the right, AFIS was still able to match the prints.

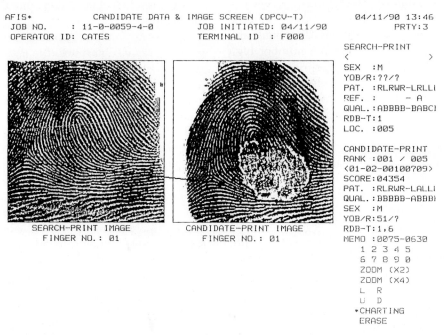

(Courtesy Dallas Police Department)

Ceasefire is a system developed by and being used by the Bureau of Alcohol, Tobacco and Firearms. It has two parts. One of these, Bullet-proof, is a system for identifying bullets by using a video camera, laser photography, and a highly sophisticated computer to identify the striations and other marks created on bullets by the rifling of a gun's barrel. These marks and striations are found on the land surfaces between the grooves of the bullet. Fourteen microscopic pictures are needed to form one land picture. The overlapping images are then digitized into a bar code that is read and stored by the computer. The other part of the Ceasefire system is "Brasscatcher," a database module that examines shell casings. In fiscal year 1996, Ceasefire had 22,179 bullets entered into the system, with 55 matches made; 26,390 shell casings were entered, with 188 matches made. Ceasefire was expanded to 10 new sites during the 1996 fiscal year.[31]

The FBI has a similar program called *Drugfire*, which uses automated computer technology to make links between firearm-related evidence such as cartridge cases, bullets, and guns. Drugfire is operational in 115 laboratories in the United States, and another 80 laboratories were to install the system by the end of 1998. (See Figure 9–8.) Nationwide, over 65,000 criminal investigations, represented by over 100,000 images, have been entered into Drugfire. Drugfire has linked nearly 2,400 cartridge cases, matching one of every eight cartridge cases entered from crime scenes and providing law enforcement with investigative leads that would otherwise have gone undetected.

These computerized systems are able to accomplish the workload equivalent of many firearms examiners and process thousands of hours of examinations that would have otherwise been processed manually.[32]

Figure 9–8
Forensic Chemist Conducting Examination

(Courtesy Indiana State Police)

HANDLING EVIDENCE IN THE LABORATORY

HUMAN FACTORS

In handling evidentiary materials, laboratory personnel—scientists and technicians alike—have always been cautious not to disturb or ruin the viability of the materials for any possible examination that would later prove to be useful. Today, because of concerns over the transmission of hepatitis and the AIDS virus, the handling of evidence is of even greater concern.

Although a few laboratories may autoclave specimens, such sterilization with heat may tend to decrease the usefulness of the specimen for analysis purposes. Most laboratories, including the FBI, are merely extra careful in handling evidence involving tissue or body fluids. The procedure followed normally is to ask the agency sending the specimen for any factual information available on the subject so that a determination can be made as to whether the evidence was obtained from a person who may have been infected. In addition, scientists and technicians are instructed to keep their work areas clean, to clean those areas between conducting examinations, and to change and clean lab coats frequently.

INSTRUMENTAL ANALYSIS

As noted in Chapter 4, Physical Evidence, the kinds of evidence subject to laboratory examinations are many and varied. For laboratory purposes, examinations generally fall into the following categories: chemical examinations, biological examinations, physical examinations, personal identification, firearms identification, documentary examinations, and photography.

In a textbook of this nature it is not practical to present a detailed discussion of the technical intricacies of various scientific instruments. However, it is appropriate to acquaint readers with some of the capabilities of instruments used in scientific analysis of evidence.

The first, and perhaps most important, instrument that needs to be mentioned is the computer. The advances that have been made in laboratory analyses can largely be credited to computerization and its continued refinement. A majority of the instruments discussed in this section and many others used in laboratories depend on computers for rapid and accurate analysis.

Emission Spectrograph

Each element, such as tin, iron, and copper, when properly burned, will give off light that is characteristic of itself and different from the light produced by all other elements. *Emission spectrography* is capable of identifying elements from the light that is produced. Its uses include rapid analysis of all metallic constituents in an unknown substance; detection of traces of metallic impurities in residues such as oils, ashes, glasses, or metals; testing the purity of a substance; detection of rare metals; and the examination of paint specimens. Emission spectrography has the advantage of allowing a complete analysis of metallic elements in an unknown substance through one operation. In addition, analysis requires only a relatively small sample, and it provides positive identification of the elements present in the substance.[33]

Mass Spectrometer

This instrument is used in analyzing a wide range of forensic specimens, including drugs, poisons, accelerants, explosive residues, and biological samples, by breaking the samples down into chemical "building blocks" and creating profiles of the molecules (see Figure 9–9).

Visible Spectrophotometer

This instrument is used for studying color and coloring agents such as dyes and pigments. For

Figure 9–9
Mass Spectrometer

A mass spectrometer being used to analyze a hair sample for drugs. To the left is a gas chromatograph used to introduce volatile samples.

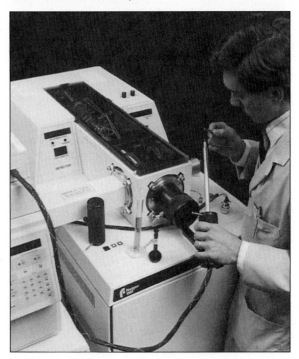

(Courtesy Federal Bureau of Investigation)

example, all the colors of the rainbow are paraded through a dye in solution. The instrument records the percentages of each color that pass through the solution. The variation in the amount of each color that can pass through the solution is characteristic of the dye. The instrument can also be used to measure the amount of each color reflected from a colored surface. The visible spectrophotometer is often used in comparing dyes and coloring agents in materials such as cloth, paint, and glass. The instrumental analysis of colors can eliminate personal error in color comparisons. Small samples can be examined and studied and the instrumentation provides a rapid analysis.

Infrared Spectrophotometer

This instrument passes a narrow beam of infrared energy through a thin film of the substance being studied. As the wavelengths change, the amount of energy transmitted by the specimen is measured and recorded on a chart. The chart is a "fingerprint" of the material being subjected to study. Infrared spectrophotometry is a primary means for the identification and comparisons of plastics, rubber, paint, and other organic compounds, as well as for inorganic minerals. It has the advantage of being able to detect slight differences in composition and molecular arrangements of minute amounts of material.

Atomic Absorption Spectrophotometer

Atomic absorption spectroscopy is a quantitative technique whereby elements in a sample are placed in a vapor state, which allows them to be analyzed by means of a flame. It is used to determine concentrations of specific elements in a sample. This procedure is used not for a survey-type analysis to establish which elements may be present but, rather, to determine proportional concentration of each known element in the sample. The advantage of atomic absorption spectroscopy is that it is a very accurate and sensitive method of determining elemental concentration, especially when many samples are involved and when a sample can be readily placed in solution. It also provides a relatively economical and normally rapid procedure for determining the concentrations of elements (see Figure 9–10).

Gas Chromatograph

Essentially used as an analytical method for separation and identification of gases or liquids from com-

Figure 9–10
Atomic Absorption

Flameless atomic absorption is used to analyze the level of poison in hair, blood, tissue, and the like, as well as gunshot residues, water analysis, and bullet lead.

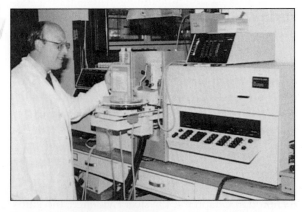

(Courtesy Federal Bureau of Investigation)

plex mixtures or solutions, the *gas chromatograph* can analyze organic material such as narcotics, explosives, paints, plastics, inks, or petroleum products (see Figure 9–11). Since the crime laboratory rarely will receive evidence of a chemical nature that is pure, separation methods are essential to the proper identification of constituent components, liquids, or gases. The gas chromatograph can separate and indicate the composition by retention time and relative amounts of components. It can also be used for solving a wide variety of analytical tasks through the analysis of volatile solids, high-boiling liquids, or gases. The recording and evaluation of the analytical results of the testing are not time-consuming. The gas chromatograph frequently is used in conjunction with the mass spectrometer.

X-Ray Diffraction Spectrophotometer

This instrument is used to identify and compare unknown crystalline substances. Crystals that differ in chemical composition also differ in size and shape and will diffract X-rays differently, thus permitting the identification of crystalline material in comparison with known standards. Only small samples are required, and the sample is not consumed in using this technique.

This listing defines some of the more sophisticated equipment currently being used in full-service crime laboratories. It excludes some of the more obvious or technical examination methods, such as many chemical analyses, fingerprint identi-

Figure 9–11
Gas Chromatograph Operated by a Forensic Chemist

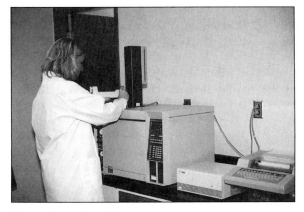

(Courtesy Indiana State Police)

fication, firearm identification, physical and chemical documentary examinations, photographic techniques and equipment, and microscopy.

ATF FORENSIC SCIENCE LABORATORIES

The Bureau of Alcohol, Tobacco and Firearms (ATF) of the U.S. Department of the Treasury maintains three forensic science laboratories located in Rockville, Maryland; San Francisco, California; and Atlanta, Georgia. The ATF National Laboratory was created by Congress in 1886. These laboratories, in addition to analyzing alcohol and tobacco samples, conduct forensic examinations in support of the bureau's explosives, bombing and arson, and illegal-firearm-trafficking investigations, along with major case investigations of state and local authorities. In 1996, the laboratories analyzed over 8,400 alcohol and tobacco samples and processed over 3,134 forensic cases.

The laboratories hold the distinction of being the first federal laboratory system accredited by the ASCLD.[34] The majority of the examinations conducted by the laboratories involve chemical and physical examinations of explosives, firearms, and arson evidence, and the document, tool mark, and latent fingerprint examinations associated with those investigations.

The forensic laboratories are staffed by over 90 employees, most of whom are chemists, physical scientists, document analysts, latent print specialists, and firearms and tool mark examiners. The remainder are evidence technicians and clerical personnel.

Evidence collected at crime scenes of suspected arsons is examined to identify accelerants, incendiaries, and incendiary-device components. Evidence collected at explosion scenes is examined to identify explosives used, blasting caps, leg wires, fuses, timing mechanisms, energy sources, containers, wires, tapes, and various other component parts used to make the bomb. The laboratory system maintains liaison with explosive manufacturers, who provide exemplars of new explosives products on the market.

Comparative trace-evidence examinations are conducted on materials including tapes, wires, glass, metals, soil, hair, paint, fibers, ink, paper, and wood to determine whether the materials could have a common origin and thereby associate a suspect with a crime.

Questioned document examinations are conducted to identify handwriting on firearm transaction forms. In addition, examinations are performed to identify typewriters, copy machines, and cigarette tax stamps. Attempts are also made to decipher indented and obliterated writings.

The laboratories also perform a full range of fingerprint, firearms, and tool-mark examinations in support of agency investigations.

Firearms examinations involve primarily serial number restoration, determination of the operability of weapons, comparison of metals in sawed-off barrels, and determination of the possible common origin of silencers seized from different suspects or locations. Gunshot-residue tests are conducted in shootings that involve law enforcement officers. In addition, special tests to evaluate the performance of ammunition and weapons are occasionally done.

Tool-mark examinations generally involve evidence associated with bombings and arson. This includes examination of cut wires, torn tapes, drill holes, pipe wrench marks, saw marks on wood and metal, and numerous other marks made by tools.

The bureau has four National Response Teams that respond to major bombings and arson disasters, nationally and internationally. The teams consist of highly trained investigators, forensic chemists, and explosive technology experts. The teams respond within 24 hours, collect evidence, and complete most laboratory examinations before leaving the crime scene.[35]

THE FBI CRIME LABORATORY

The FBI Crime Laboratory is one of the largest and most comprehensive forensic laboratories, and it is the only full-service forensic laboratory. It was established in 1932. Of importance to the investigator is the fact that the facilities of the FBI laboratory are available without charge to all state, county, and municipal law enforcement agencies of the United States.[36] There are, however, some provisos concerning the submission of evidence for examination to the laboratory. The laboratory will not make examinations if any evidence in the case has been or will be subjected to the same type of technical examination by another laboratory or other experts. This policy is designed to eliminate duplication of effort and to ensure that evidence is received in its original condition, thereby allowing laboratory personnel to interpret their findings properly and ensure meaningful testimony and presentation of evidence in subsequent court cases.

In order to more effectively and efficiently use its current resources, the FBI laboratory has a policy not to accept cases from other crime laboratories that have the capability of conducting the requested examination. In the event such cases are submitted by other crime laboratories, in the absence of special circumstances, the cases will be returned unopened and unexamined. This policy should not be construed as lessening the FBI laboratory's continuing commitment to the scientific training of state and local crime laboratory personnel, and it does not limit the laboratory's acceptance of cases from other crime laboratories when special circumstances prevail.

In addition, the FBI laboratory no longer accepts evidence from state and local law enforcement agencies regarding property crime investigations unless the cases involve personal injury or the offenses were designed to cause personal injury.

In addition to analysis, the FBI furnishes experts necessary to testify in connection with the results of their examination in either state or federal courts. Again, there is no charge to local law enforcement agencies for this service.

The laboratory provides a comprehensive array of forensic services. Laboratory personnel also conduct microscopic examinations of hair and fiber, fabric, tape, rope, and wool (see Figure 9–12). Chemical examinations are conducted on many substances, often to supplement examinations conducted by other sections. Examinations are conducted on poisons (toxicology), paint, ink, tear gas, dyes, flash and watersoluble paper, among others.

Mineralogy examinations are conducted on soils and combinations of mineral substances such as safe insulation, concrete, plaster, mortar, glass, ore, abrasives, gems, industrial dusts, and building materials.

Firearms examiners may be asked to determine if firearms are operating properly or to conduct gunpowder shot pattern tests (see Figure 9–13). Using the same basic principles of firearm examination, the identification of telltale marks left at crime scenes by punches, hammers, axes, pliers, screwdrivers, chisels, wrenches, and other objects can be made. The explosives specialist can analyze fragments of explosives to determine their original composition and possible sources of raw materials.

The metallurgy unit is called on to restore obliterated or altered numbers on such things as firearms, sewing machines, watches, outboard motors, slot machines, automobiles, tools, and other metallic items. Tests can show whether two or more pieces of metal are related, the possible cause of metal separation, and whether production specifications for metals have been met.

Handwriting examiners agree that no two individuals write exactly alike. Even though there may be superficial resemblances in the writing of two or more persons as a result of similar training, the complexity of writing is such that individual peculiarities and characteristics appear. These characteristics can be detected by a documents expert, who then can arrive at a scientific opinion.

The FBI laboratory has also developed the ability to conduct forensic examinations on chemical, biological, and nuclear hazards. In 1996, the Hazardous Materials Response Unit was established in response to the threat of terrorism involving chemical, biological, and nuclear weapons and to an ex-

Figure 9–13
Forensic Examiner Conducting Firearms Examination

(Courtesy Indiana State Police)

Figure 9–12
Forensic Examiner Conducting Examination with a Scanning Electron Microscope

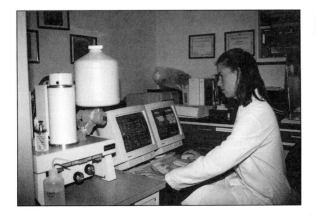

(Courtesy Indiana State Police)

panding caseload of environmental crimes. The laboratory has also developed the Computer Analysis and Response Team (CART) program, capable of conducting examinations in which information is extracted from magnetic, optical, and similar storage media and converted into a form usable to investigators or prosecutors. The FBI's laboratory is leading the research and development efforts to improve and expedite DNA analysis methods and is currently the only laboratory conducting mitochondrial DNA testing.

In 1997, the FBI laboratory received almost 150,000 specimens. There were over 500,000 examinations and over 1.7 million latent-fingerprint comparisons performed by the laboratory in 1997.

REFERENCE FILES

To aid examiners in their work, the FBI laboratory in 1932 established what is now one of the largest reference collections for helping solve cases. These files are of two types: *standard reference files and collections*, which contain known samples of items, generally of manufactured products; and *reference files of questioned materials*, which are composed of items actually arising from cases worked and which may form the basis for subsequent identification of individuals or their method of operation (MOs). Many of these collections and reference files have been computerized to provide better and faster analyses and comparisons.

A Standard Ammunition File contains over 13,000 specimens of domestic and foreign manufacturers' samples. The Firearms Reference Collection contains over 2,900 handguns and 1,600 shoulder weapons and is used for identifying gun parts and locating serial numbers. The Reference Fired Specimen File contains test bullets and cartridge cases from weapons that have been in the laboratory.

The National Automobile Altered Numbers File is composed of selected specimens, including replica plastic impressions of altered vehicle identification numbers (VINs) found on stolen cars, trucks, and heavy equipment. The file helps investigators to identify recovered stolen cars and link them with commercialized theft rings nationwide or other FBI-investigated cases. The National Vehicle Identification Number Standard File maintains standards of VIN plates from each factory of the major manufacturers of American automobiles. The file allows laboratory personnel to determine if a submitted VIN plate is authentic. In the event that bogus VIN plates are being prepared in an automobile factory, the factory as well as the particular machine used can be identified.

The Typewriter Standards File consists of original samples of typewriting from numerous styles of type made in this country as well as in foreign countries. The file permits classification of questioned typewriting on the basis of make and model. The Watermark Standards File is an index of watermarks and brands used by paper manufacturers and aids in tracing the source or origin of paper.

Original samples of safety paper used for checks are the contents of the Safety Paper Standards File. These can be used to determine manufacturers. The Checkwriter Standards File is a collection of original checkwriter impressions and permits classification of questioned checkwriter impressions as to make and model. As an aid in determining the manufacturers of office copying machines (either photocopy or duplicator), the laboratory maintains an Office Copier Standards File.

The Shoe Print File contains photographs of designs used in soles and heels made by major U.S. manufacturers. The Tire Tread File, including wheelbase and tire-stance information, is now in a database against which comparisons can be made. This replaces the blueprints, drawings, and photographs of tire-tread patterns, furnished by tire manufacturers, that used to form the basis of the reference file.

The National Motor Vehicle Certificate of Title File consists of original state motor vehicle certificates of title, manufacturers' certificates of origin, and vehicle emission stickers. This file also contains photographic copies of fraudulent titles, statements, and stickers. The National Fraudulent Check File contains over 100,000 samples of checks, writings, and other documents. More than half of all checks examined are identified with other material in this file. The Anonymous Letter File consists of photographic copies of kidnap notes and extortion and threatening letters. The Bank Robbery Note File contains photocopies of writings of known bank robbers and holdup notes. A Pornographic Materials File is kept of materials submitted to the laboratory; it assists in determining the production and distribution sources of the material. The Explosive Reference Files contain technical data, known standards of explosive items, and bomb components of commercial and military explosives and improvised explosive devices or homemade bombs.

Other files maintained by the FBI are the Automotive Paint File (which can identify makes and models involved in hit-and-run cases), Hair and Fiber File, the National Stolen Coin File, Blood Serum Files, Safe Insulation Files, and the National Stolen Art File.

Questions

1. Define *forensic science*.
2. What difficulties are caused by an investigator's not understanding the capabilities and limitations of crime laboratories?
3. Define *criminalistics*.
4. Describe the most important resource in a crime laboratory.
5. Describe the measures of effectiveness of crime laboratories.
6. Describe the role and importance of DNA analysis in criminal investigation.
7. Describe AFIS.
8. How are body fluids submitted for analysis handled in a laboratory, in light of concerns about the transmittal of hepatitis and AIDS?
9. What are the main areas of responsibility of the ATF laboratories?
10. What limitations are placed on the submission of evidence to the FBI laboratory?

Notes

1. Florida Bureau of Law Enforcement, *Crime Laboratory*, unpublished document, p. 2.
2. Paul L. Kirk, "The Ontogeny of Criminalistics," *Journal of Criminology and Police Science*, 1963, Vol. 54, p. 238.
3. Joseph L. Peterson, Steven Mihajlovic, and Joanne L. Bedrosian, "The Capabilities, Uses, and Effects of the Nation's Criminalistics Laboratories," *Journal of Forensic Sciences*, 1985, Vol. 30, No. 1, p. 11.
4. Richard Fox and Carl L. Cunningham, *Crime Scene Search and Physical Evidence Handbook* (Washington, D.C.: U.S. Department of Justice, 1985), p. 1.
5. Statement of Kevin L. Lothridge, president, American Society of Crime Laboratory Directors, National Forensic Science Technology Center, before the House Judiciary Committee, Subcommittee on Crime, May 13, 1997.
6. Ibid.
7. www.nfstc.org/aboutus.htm (graciously supplied by NFSTC).
8. James W. Osterburg, *The Crime Laboratory* (Bloomington: Indiana University Press, 1968), p. 3.
9. Marc H. Caplan and Joe Holt Anderson, *Forensics: When Science Bears Witness*, National Institute of Justice (Washington, D.C.: Government Printing Office, October 1984), p. 2.
10. For a discussion of working relationships between police investigators and crime laboratory personnel, see Joseph L. Peterson, *The Utilization of Criminalistics Services by the Police, An Analysis of the Physical Evidence Recovery Process*, Law Enforcement Assistance Administration, National Institute of Law Enforcement and Criminal Justice (Washington, D.C.: Government Printing Office, March 1974).
11. The President's Commission on Law Enforcement and the Administration of Justice, Task Force Report: *The Police* (Washington, D.C.: Government Printing Office, 1967), p. 90.
12. National Advisory Commission on Criminal Justice Standards and Goals, *Police* (Washington, D.C.: Government Printing Office, 1973), p. 303.
13. See Kenneth S. Field, Oliver Schroeder, Jr., Ina J. Curtis, Ellen L. Fabricant, and Beth Ann Lipskin, *Assessment of the Forensic Sciences Profession: Assessment of the Personnel of the Forensic Sciences Profession*, Vol. II, National Institute of Law Enforcement and Criminal Justice, Law Enforcement Assistance Administration, U.S. Department of Justice (Washington, D.C.: Government Printing Office, March 1977), pp. I–4–I–9.
14. National Advisory Commission, *Police*, p. 302.
15. Ibid.
16. Peterson, *Utilization of Criminalistics Services*, p. 6.
17. 293 Fed. 1013 (D.C. Cir. 1923).
18. 507 U.S. 904 (1993).
19. Prosecutors in State Courts, 1996, (Washington, D.C.: U.S. Department of Justice, 1996), p. 6.
20. www.fbi.gov/kids/dna/dna.htm (7/17/98).
21. www.fbi.gov/kids/dna/dnastory.htm (7/17/98).
22. Ibid.
23. *National Institute of Justice Journal*, U.S. Department of Justice, Office of Justice Programs, December 1997, pp. 17–19.
24. Federal Bureau of Investigation, *FBI Laboratory Annual Report 97*, p. 7.
25. *National Institute of Justice Journal*, p. 23.

26. *"Solutions"* (Publication for policyholders, General American Life Insurance Company), Spring–Summer 1998, Vol. 5, No. 1, pp. 5–7.

27. Thomas F. Wilson, "Automated Fingerprint Identification Systems," *Law Enforcement Technology*, August–September 1986, p. 17.

28. Florida Department of Law Enforcement, *Criminal Justice Information Systems Newsletter,* May 1995, p. 1.

29. Kenneth R. Moses, "A Consumer's Guide to Fingerprint Computers," *Identification News*, June 1986, p. 6.

30. Much of the material in this section is drawn from Thomas F. Wilson and Paul L. Woodward, *Automated Fingerprint Identification Systems: Technology and Policy Issues* (Washington, D.C.: U.S. Department of Justice, 1987).

31. Department of the Treasury, Bureau of Alcohol, Tobacco and Firearms, *1996 Highlights of the Bureau of Alcohol, Tobacco and Firearms*, p. 22.

32. *FBI Laboratory Annual Report 97* p. 7.

33. Federal Bureau of Investigation, *Handbook of Forensic Science,* rev. ed. (Washington, D.C.: Government Printing Office), October 1978). This discussion of the equipment used by crime laboratories was taken with permission from pp. 63–64 of this source.

34. www.atf.treas.gov/cor/explarson.htm.

35. www.atf.treas.gov/cor/labs/hist.htm.

36. www.fbi.gov/lab/report/labhome.htm.

Injury and Death Investigation

CHAPTER OUTLINE

The Law 226

Motivational Models for Classification of
Homicide 226

Responding to the Scene 227

Arrival at the Scene of a Homicide 227

Establishing a Chain of Custody 228

Investigative Tools and Equipment 229

The Medico-Legal Examination 229

The Autopsy 229

Identification of the Dead Person 230

The Search for Buried Bodies 233

Estimating Time of Death 239

Evidence from Wounds 246

The Uncooperative Victim 258

Suicide 259

Vehicle Homicides 270

Fire Deaths 272

Family/Domestic Violence 276

Stalking 278

Serial Murder and the NCAVC 280

Criminal Investigative Analysis 282

Questions 284

Notes 284

INTRODUCTION

Felonious injuries and criminal homicides are viewed as among the most serious offenses committed in our society. The seriousness is reflected in all state statutes, which impose severe penalties for acts resulting in the grave bodily injury or death of a human being. It is therefore appropriate that all available resources be employed in their investigation.

THE LAW

The various state statutes contain different names for felonious assaults, such as *aggravated assault, assault with intent to commit murder, felonious battery*, and so forth, but all have certain common legal elements, namely, that the assault was committed for the purpose of inflicting severe bodily harm or death. In most such assaults, a deadly weapon is employed.

Police officials and members of the public often use the terms "homicide" and "murder" interchangeably. In fact, murder is only a part of the broad category of homicide, and *homicide*, defined as the killing of a human being by another human being, is divided into two broad classifications of homicides: nonfelonious homicides and felonious homicides.

NONFELONIOUS HOMICIDES

Nonfelonious homicides may be justifiable or excusable. *Justifiable homicide* is the necessary killing of another person in performance of a legal duty or the exercise of a legal right when the slayer was not at fault.

Excusable homicide differs from justifiable homicide in that one who commits an excusable homicide is to some degree at fault but the degree of fault is not enough to constitute a criminal homicide. There are two fundamental types of excusable homicide. The first involves death that results from misadventure. This is similar to what may be termed "accidental" death at the hands of another. *Misadventure* is death occurring during the commission of a lawful or an unlawful act when the slayer has no intent to hurt and there is no criminal negligence. An example of misadventure would include the death of a person who runs in front of a moving automobile whose driver is unable to avoid the collision.

The second type of excusable homicide involves death that results from self-defense when the slayer is not totally without fault, such as someone who gets in a sudden brawl and has to kill to preserve his or her life.[1]

FELONIOUS HOMICIDES

Felonious homicides are treated and punished as crimes and typically fall into two categories:

murder and manslaughter. *Murder* is defined by common law as the killing of any human being by another with malice aforethought. Most states now provide for varying degrees of murder. *Manslaughter* is a criminal homicide committed under circumstances not severe enough to constitute murder, yet it cannot be classified as either justifiable or excusable homicide.[2]

MOTIVATIONAL MODELS FOR CLASSIFICATION OF HOMICIDE

The identification of a criminal's motives has both legal and investigative implications. By identifying the motive for a crime, investigators can begin to focus investigative efforts in a specific direction. If a motive cannot be identified, the range of possible suspects is broad and the investigation therefore more difficult.

In the late 1980s the agents from the Investigative Support Unit at the FBI Academy joined with the Behavioral Science Unit to begin working on a crime classifiction manual (CCM). In the CCM,[3] classification of homicide by motive includes four major categories: the criminal enterprise, the personal cause, the sexual homicide, and the group cause.[4]

CRIMINAL ENTERPRISE HOMICIDE

Criminal enterprise homicide entails murder committed for material gain. The material gain takes many forms, for example, money, goods, territory, or favors. This category has eight subcategories: contract killing (third party), gang-motivated murder, criminal competition, kidnap murder, product tampering, drug murder, insurance-motivated murder (individual profit or commercial profit), and felony murder (indiscriminate or situational).

PERSONAL-CAUSE HOMICIDE

Personal-cause homicide is motivated by a personal cause and ensues from interpersonal aggression; the slayer and the victim(s) may not be known to each other. This type of homicide is not motivated by material gain or sex and is not sanctioned by a group. It is the result of an underlying emotional conflict that propels the offender to kill. The victim targeted is very often a person with high mass-media visibility of local, national, or international scope, but victims also include superiors at work or even complete strangers. The victim is almost always perceived by the offender as someone of higher status. Personal-cause homicide has 11 subcategories: erotomania-motivated killing, domestic killing (spontaneous or staged), argument murder, conflict murder, authority killing, revenge killing, nonspecific motive killing, extremist murder (political, religious, or socioeconomic), mercy killing, hero killing, and hostage murder.

SEXUAL HOMICIDE

In *sexual homicide*, a sexual element (activity) is the basis for the sequence of acts leading to death. Performance and meaning of this sexual element vary with the offender. The act may range from actual rape involving penetration (either before or after death) to a symbolic sexual assault, such as insertion of foreign objects into a victim's body orifices. Sexual homicide has four subcategories: organized crime-scene murder, disorganized crime-scene murder, mixed crime-scene murder, and sadistic murder.

GROUP-CAUSE HOMICIDE

In *group-cause homicide*, two or more people with a common ideology sanction an act, committed by one or more of the group's members, that results in death. This category has three subcategories: cult murder, extremist (political, religious, or socioeconomic) murder (paramilitary or hostage), and group-excitement murder.

RESPONDING TO THE SCENE

In responding to the scene of a suspected homicide or assault, fundamental rules must be followed. The officer should proceed with deliberate but not reckless speed. As the officer approaches the scene, he or she should be observant for a suspect fleeing either on foot or by vehicle. The dispatcher may have been able to obtain and relate specific details to the responding officer about the offense and suspect. If not, the officer has to rely on discriminating observations, training, and past experience. The officer should be suspicious of a vehicle being driven away from the crime scene at a high rate of speed or in an erratic manner, an individual who attempts to hide from view, or a person whose clothing indicates recent involvement in a struggle.

ARRIVAL AT THE SCENE OF A HOMICIDE

When the investigator arrives at the scene, formal contact should be established with other official agency representatives. The investigator must identify the first respondent to ascertain if any artifacts or contamination may have been introduced to the death scene. The investigator must work with all people to ensure the scene's safety before entering the scene. The investigator must take the initiative to introduce himself or herself, identify essential personnel, and establish rapport. Before entering the scene, the investigator should identify other essential officials at the scene (e.g., fire, EMS, social or child protective services), explain his or her role in the investigation, and identify and document the identity of the first essential official(s) to the scene (first "professional" arrival at the scene for investigative follow-up).

SCENE SAFETY

Determining scene safety for all investigative personnel is essential to the investigative process. The risk of environmental and physical injury must be removed prior to initiating a scene investigation. Risks can include hostile crowds, collapsing structures, traffic, and environmental and chemical threats. To prevent injury or loss of life, the investigator must attempt to establish scene safety before entering the scene and should contact appropriate agencies for assistance with particular scene-safety issues.

Upon arrival at the scene the investigator should assess and/or establish physical boundaries; secure his or her vehicle and park as safely as possible; use personal safety devices (physical, biochemical safety); arrange for removal of animals or secure them, if present, and if possible; and obtain clearance/authorization at the scene from the individual responsible for scene safety (e.g., fire marshall, disaster coordinator).

While exercising scene safety, the investigator must protect the integrity of the scene and evidence, to the extent possible, from contamination by people, animals, and the elements. Due to the potential scene hazards, the body may have to be removed before the scene investigation can continue.

CONFIRM OR PRONOUNCE DEATH

Appropriate medically trained personnel must make a determination of death prior to the initiation of the death investigation. The confirmation or pronouncement of death determines jurisdictional responsibilites. The investigator must be certain that appropriate personnel have viewed the body and that death has been confirmed. The investigator should also identify and document the name and organizational affiliation of the individual who made the official determination of death, as well as the time of determination.

Once death has been determined and rescue/resuscitative efforts have ceased, medical and legal jurisdiction can be established.

PARTICIPATE IN SCENE BRIEFING WITH ATTENDING AGENCY REPRESENTATIVES

Scene investigators must recognize the varying jurisdictional and statutory responsibilities that apply to individual agency representatives (e.g., law enforcement, fire, EMT, judicial, legal). Determining each agency's responsibility at the scene is essential in planning the scope and depth of each scene investigation and the release of information to the public. Investigators must identify specific responsibilties, share appropriate preliminary information, and establish investigative goals with each agency that is present at the scene. When participating in scene briefing, the investigator should locate the staging area (entry point to the scene, command post, etc.), document the scene location (address, mile marker, building name), determine the nature and scope of the investigation

by obtaining preliminary investigative results (e.g., suspicious versus nonsuspicious death), and ensure that initial accounts have been obtained from the first witness(es).

CONDUCT A SCENE WALK-THROUGH

Conducting a scene "walk-through" provides the investigator with an overview of the entire scene. The walk-through is the investigator's first opportunity to locate and view the body, identify valuable and/or fragile evidence, and determine the initial investigative procedures for a systematic examination and documentation of the scene and body. The investigator can also conduct a scene walk-through to establish pertinency and perimeters. Upon arrival at the scene the investigator should reassess scene boundaries and adjust as appropriate; establish a path of entry and exit; identify visible physical and fragile evidence; document and photograph fragile evidence immediately and collect it, if appropriate; and locate and view the body. An initial scene walk-through is essential for minimizing scene disturbance and preventing the loss and/or contamination of physical and fragile evidence.

ESTABLISHING A CHAIN OF CUSTODY

Ensuring the integrity of the evidence by establishing and maintaining a chain of custody is vital to the investigation. This will save the investigator from subsequent allegations of tampering, theft, planting, and contamination of evidence. Before the removal of any evidence the custodian(s) of evidence should be designated and should generate and maintain a chain of custody for all evidence collected. Throughout the investigation those responsible for preserving the chain of custody should document the location of the scene and the time of the death investigator's arrival at the scene; determine the custodian(s) of evidence, determine which agencies are responsible for the collection of specific types of evidence, and determine evidence-collection priority; identify, secure, and preserve evidence, using proper containers, labels, and preservatives; document the collection of evidence by recording its location at the scene, time of collection, and time and location of disposition; and develop personnel lists, witness lists, and documentation of times of arrival and departure of personnel. It is essential to maintain a proper chain of custody for evidence. Through proper documentation, collection, and preservation, the integrity of the evidence can be ensured. A properly maintained chain of custody and prompt transport of the evidence will reduce the likelihood of a challenge to the integrity of the evidence.

INVESTIGATIVE TOOLS AND EQUIPMENT

Following are the tools and equipment necessary for conducting an appropriate crime scene investigation in homicide cases: gloves; writing implements (pens, pencils, markers); body bags; communication equipment (cell phone, pager, radio); flashlight; body ID tags; camera (35-millimeter camera, video camera, Polaroid), with extra batteries, film, tapes, etc.; investigative notebook (for scene notes, etc.); measurement instruments (tape measure, ruler, rolling measuring tape, etc.); official identification (for yourself); watch; paper bags (for hands, feet, etc); specimen containers (for evidence items and toxicology specimens); disinfectant; departmental scene forms; blood collection tubes (syringes and needles); inventory lists (clothes, drugs, etc.); paper envelopes; clean white linen sheet (stored in plastic bag); evidence tape; business cards or office cards with phone numbers; foul-weather gear (raincoat, umbrella, etc.); medical equipment kit (scissors, forceps, tweezers, exposure suit, scalpel handle, blades, disposable syringe, large-gauge needles, cotton-tipped swabs, etc); phone listing (important phone numbers); tape or rubber bands; disposable (paper) jumpsuits, hair covers, face shield, etc.; evidence seal (use with body bags and locks); pocketknife; shoe covers; trace-evidence kit (tape, etc.); waterless hand wash; thermometer; crime scene tape; first-aid kit; latent-print kit; local maps; plastic trash bags; gunshot-residue analysis kits; boots (for wet conditions, construction sites, etc.); hand lens (magnifying glass); portable electric area lighting; barrier sheeting (to shield body or a specific area from public view); purification mask (disposable); reflective vest; tape recorder; basic hand tools (bolt cutter, screwdrivers, hammer, shovel, trowel, paintbrushes, etc.); body-bag locks (to secure body inside bag); personal comfort supplies (insect spray, sunscreen, hat, etc.); and presumptive blood test kit.[5]

THE MEDICAO-LEGAL EXAMINATION

The medico-legal examination brings medical skill to bear upon injury and death investigations. The medical specialist frequently called upon to assist in such cases is the forensic pathologist. *Forensic pathology*, a subspecialty of pathology, is the study of how and why people die. To become a forensic pathologist, a physician first attends an approved pathology residency program and then attends three years in a strictly anatomic program or five years in a combined anatomic and clinical program. One or two additional years are devoted to studying the pathology of sudden, unexpected, natural death, as well as violent death, in an approved forensic fellowship training program (there are approximately 30 throughout the country). Most programs are centered in major cities that have a large number of deaths from various causes. The most important area of study for a forensic pathologist is death investigation, but some forensic pathology programs also include examination of the living to determine physical and sexual abuse. Physicians specializing in forensic pathology are ordinarily employed by some unit of government and are not in private practice.[6]

THE AUTOPSY

All violent and suspicious deaths require an autopsy to determine the time and precise cause of death.[7] The autopsy may also answer the following questions:

- What type of weapon was employed?

- If multiple wounds were inflicted, which wound was fatal?
- How long did the victim live after the injury?
- What position was the victim in at the time of the assault?
- From what direction was the force applied?
- Is there any evidence of a struggle or self-defense?
- Is there any evidence of rape or other sex-related acts?
- Was the deceased under the influence of alcohol or any type of drug?[8] (The actual analysis will be done by the toxicologist.)

Answers to all or even some of these questions increase the possibility of bringing the death investigation to a successful conclusion.

If any of the victim's clothing is damaged, the investigator should determine whether the damage was related to the assault or was caused by hospital or emergency personnel giving emergency treatment. When a determination is made of the cause of the damage, it should be recorded in the investigation report.

The victim should be fingerprinted, even if there is positive proof of identification. If circumstances dictate, palmprints and footprints should also be obtained. They may prove useful if later found in the suspect's home, business, car, or some other location. In those instances of possible physical contact by the victim with the assailant or contact with some object employed in the attack by the assailant, standard specimens of hair should be removed by medical personnel from the victim's head, eyebrows, pubic area, anus, armpits, legs, and chest.

IDENTIFICATION OF THE DEAD PERSON

Personal identification is one of the most important functions of an investigation. The inability to identify a deceased person greatly complicates the investigative process. The major problem attending the failure to identify a deceased person is the difficulty in focusing the investigation toward, for example, the victim's enemies or those who would most stand to gain from the death. These and other important questions cannot be answered until the victim's identity is established.

A number of techniques contribute to establishing the deceased person's identity, including fingerprinting, forensic odontology, DNA, physical description, surgical history, viewing by possible identifiers, occupational trademarks, and personal belongings. On any unidentified body, fingerprints should be obtained if the hands are in such condition to yield diagnostic prints.[9]

Identification based on examination of teeth, fillings, inlays, crowns, bridgework, and dentures is valuable inasmuch as the teeth are probably the most durable part of the human body.[10] Physical-description data—sex, age, weight, height, build, color of hair, color of eyes, race, amputations, deformities, birthmarks, or tattoos—help in the checking of missing-persons reports in an effort to locate individuals who fit the description of the victim.

The medical examiner should search for the presence of evidence of surgery on the victim. In some cases, scars are readily visible, as in the case of an appendix operation. However, in other instances, surgical scars may be completely internal. The medical examiner should also note the surgical removal of any internal organs.

Visual inspection leaves much to be desired for two reasons. First, if the victim has sustained severe facial injuries, they may cause gross distortion of the face. This is also true if decomposition has begun and the face is swollen. Second, this method of identification results in a certain amount of psychological trauma for relatives and friends called on to view the body. Sometimes there is no choice but to use this method, but if other options are available, they should be used.

Valuable indicators may be obtained by close examination of the victim's body, especially the hands. For example, the occupational trademarks of a bricklayer's hands will be distinctly different from those of a clerk. Also, one frequently finds that an auto mechanic has hard-to-remove grease stains under the fingernails. An examination of personal belongings may prove to be of value in establishing where they were purchased or, in the case of clothing, where they were dry cleaned. If the victim was wearing a watch, the internal portion of the watch may possess the unique markings left by the watchmaker who repaired it. In some instances, the victim's jewelry, such as rings or watches, may have the victim's initials or personal inscriptions inscribed.[11]

PERSONALITY RECONSTRUCTION FROM UNIDENTIFIED REMAINS

The identification of deceased persons takes on additional difficulty when the body is badly decomposed. However, remarkable work has been done in recent years by scientists in identifying such victims. The following case, investigated by an East Coast police department, provides an excellent example of the state of the art.

The badly decomposed remains of a human were found in an isolated wooded area adjacent to an industrial park. The crime scene investigation disclosed that the skeletal remains had been dragged a few feet from the location, and it was suspected that this dislocation of the remains resulted from animal activities. An intensive search produced only a few strands of hair, a medium-size sweater, and a few pieces of women's jewelry. The physical remains were taken to the medical examiner's office, where the time of death was estimated to be three to six weeks prior to the discovery of the body. A subsequent review of missing-persons reports for the pertinent time period produced no additional clues.

With the question of the victim's identity still unresolved, the remains were forwarded to the curator of physical anthropology at the Smithsonian Institution in Washington, D.C. Based on an examination of the skeletal remains (see Figure 10–1), it was concluded that the skeleton was that of a Caucasian female, approximately 17 to 22 years of age, who was of less-than-average stature. She had broader-than-average shoulders and hips and was believed to be right-handed. Her head and face were long, the nose was high-bridged. Also noted was the subcartilage damage to the right hip joint, a condition that had probably caused occasional pain and suggested occupational stress. An irregularity of the left clavicle (collarbone) revealed a healed childhood fracture.

Local police officials then began a social and personality profile of the deceased based on an analysis of the physical evidence obtained through the crime scene search and related photographs, medical examiner's reports, and reports from the FBI laboratory. In addition, aided by a physical anthropologist from the Smithsonian Institution, a police artist was able to provide a sketch (see Figure 10–2). The sketch was then published in a local newspaper, and police officials immediately received calls from three different readers who all supplied the same name of a female whom they all knew. They advised that she resembled the sketch, and they further advised that she had been missing for approximately four months.

A search of the local police files disclosed that the individual with this name had been previously photographed (see Figure 10–3) and fingerprinted. These prints were compared with the badly decomposed prints from one of the victim's fingers, and a positive identification was made.

Further investigation by the police determined the victim was 20 years of age. Associates related that when she had worked as a nightclub dancer, she occasionally had favored one leg. It was further determined that she had suffered a fracture of the left clavicle at age 6.[12]

Figure 10–1
Skull of Murder Victim

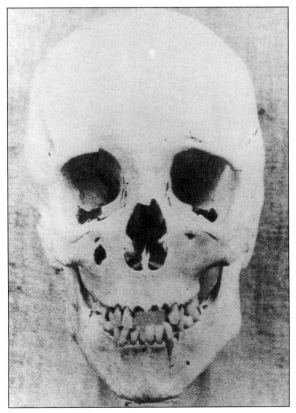

(Courtesy Federal Bureau of Investigation)

Figure 10–2
Police Artist Sketch Based on Information Provided by the Physical Anthropologist

(Courtesy Federal Bureau of Investigation)

Figure 10–3
Police Photograph of Victim

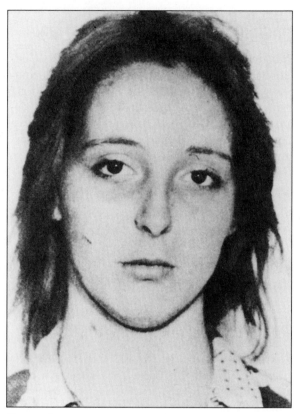

(Courtesy Federal Bureau of Investigation)

The lessons learned from this case have significantly contributed to forensic anthropology and crime scene technology. When police investigate a crime scene where skeletal remains are located, extreme caution should be exercised in the search. Because animals may have disturbed parts of the body, the search should be conducted over a fairly large area. It may be significant to know that dogs, coyotes, and hogs consume bones and that rodents gnaw or nibble on skeletal remains. Although murderers may scatter or burn parts of victims, enough bone fragments may survive to be useful for identification. A victim's facial features, however, can be reconstructed only when the skull is virtually complete, with lower jaw and teeth.

Depending on the composition of the ground beneath the remains, there may be an outline of the body. If so, this area should be recorded with precise measurements and photographs, and if possible, plaster casts of the site should be considered. Through the use of such techniques, valuable clues to tissue thickness may be found, indicating whether the deceased was heavy or thin. Clothing sizes are helpful, too. If a skeleton is situated on an incline, a very careful search should be conducted downhill from the original site because the action of rain, wind, animals, and even gravity may have caused some parts to separate from the main skeleton.

The skeletal remains themselves must, of course, be carefully measured and photographed. After the bones have been recovered, the ground under them should be sifted for additional bits of evidence.

The artistic team, having made a thorough analysis of all physical evidence, must then strive to recreate a living likeness.

This case provides an excellent example of what can be accomplished when the police artist, scientist, and investigator pool their talents to reconstruct a face, life style, and personal history—a personality—from skeletal remains.

THE SEARCH FOR BURIED BODIES

The multitude of problems an investigator faces at the scene of a murder case is compounded when the victim has been buried.[13] These cases are not common, but they are common enough to warrant training in their proper handling.

PREPLANNING

One important facet of major case investigations is administrative preplanning, an area that is frequently and unfortunately neglected.

The case supervisor usually is confronted with a series of problems in the initial stage of the investigation, most of them requiring immediate decisions and actions. Often the result is confusion, which can hinder the successful completion of an investigation. However, on-scene confusion can be avoided by good planning of details, from how to run a command post in a wooded area to establishing written policy dealing with written confessions.

DISCOVERY

Many buried bodies come to light accidentally. Occasionally, information is received that a body is buried at a particular location; these cases will be considered later.

The first duty of an officer responsible for such a case is to establish a list of priority items, despite pressures from both within and outside the department. Officers should not allow themselves to be rushed or misdirected from orderly procedures. On notification of a body's discovery, efforts should be made to safeguard the entire scene before the arrival of law enforcement officials. Generally, a hunter, passer-by, or construction worker will find the buried body and notify a police agency. The entire area should be cordoned off, as with any scene, and access refused to *anyone* prior to the arrival of

the investigator in charge, who can appraise the situation before any damage is done.

If the body has already been removed from the burial site, an archaeologist as well as a forensic pathologist and evidence technician should be called to the scene. This example of preplanning is critical: these experts should have been contacted previously and contingency plans formulated so that they are on call when the need arises. Generally, they are enthusiastic about such an opportunity, especially when the crime scene remains undisturbed.

The archaeologist is proficient in the careful and systematic excavation of a burial site. Most of the excavation phase of the investigation should be left to the archaeologist's direction, while others of the team assist as necessary.[14]

Forensic pathologists are the experts most familiar to law enforcement officers, and their work is becoming more prevalent throughout the country as a replacement for the coroner. They can provide valuable and impartial expertise when investigating the various forms of death.

Unless some extremely unusual circumstances exist, there is generally no need to hurry at this stage. If, for example, the weather is inclement, guards should be posted about the area until the weather improves. If there is need for immediate excavation, the erection of a tent over the site should be adequate. (This item should be included in preplanning equipment.) The same rule would apply during hours of darkness. Nothing is to be gained, and all may be lost, by a premature excavation. After the area is secured, all team members are assembled, and plans have been completed, the actual work may commence. The golden rule of homicide investigation is never move, touch, or alter anything until it has been noted, sketched, and photographed. This is especially applicable in this type of case.

Prior to a thorough search and processing of the area, the entire site should be mapped. Then the search may continue, both visually and with mechanical assistance (metal detectors and the like), and any items noted, sketched, and photographed.

Photographs should be taken of the entire area, including aerial views if possible. The team can then move in slowly to the actual site. Photographs, both black-and-white and color, are to be taken at intervals up to and including the actual burial site.

If possible, as with any discovered body, determine the path taken to the site by the finding party, mark it, and then use *only* this way in for the initial investigation in order to preserve as much of the general area as possible. The photographer should be accompanied by the crime scene technician or investigator, who can note and preserve any item of evidentiary nature on the way to the site—tire tracks, articles of clothing, possible weapons, or anything that might possibly be connected to the crime.

Photographs should not include any persons standing around the scene or any items not originally located there. At the same time, any item of evidence that has been moved, even accidentally, must never be replaced for purposes of photographing. It can never be put back exactly as found, and the fact that it was moved and replaced for photographing could be damaging in subsequent court testimony. Items should be photographed with and without identifying numbers, a scale, and an arrow pointing to magnetic north.

The definition of *site* is important in the buried-body case. When a grave is dug and the excavated soil is placed near the grave, the surface of the soil is disturbed, so the grave site is considered to be the entire disturbed area. If an average-size body had been buried, the entire site of grave and disturbed section would easily measure 6 feet wide and 8 feet long. The depth of the excavation generally depends on soil composition and the amount of time the subject spent burying the body.

When the excavated soil is placed on the surface, vegetation may be compressed or broken off. When the grave is refilled, some of this surface vegetation goes back into the grave (see Figure 10–4). Here another expert may be of value—a botanist, who can estimate when the vegetation was damaged by observing the height, distribution, and depth of root systems. If a botanist is not available, measurements and samples should be taken for later study. Damage done by digging and refilling a grave may be visible and measurable for years. If any dead insects are recovered from the grave, an entomologist may give information about them. (An expanded discussion of the role of the entomologist is presented later in this chapter.)

EXCAVATION

The surface of the grave should now be carefully cleared of extraneous material with a flat-bladed

Figure 10–4
Excavation Site

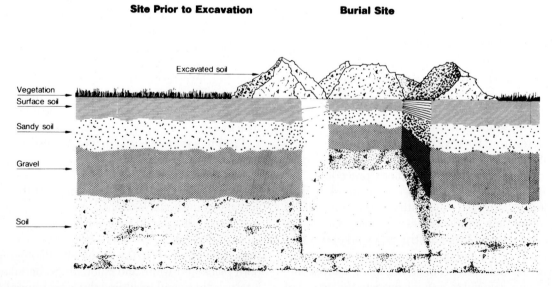

(Courtesy Federal Bureau of Investigation)

spade or hand trowel so that the boundary of the actual grave may be visible. Then the dimensions should be recorded on the map and excavation begun.

Extreme care should be taken to preserve the exact limits of the original grave or the undisturbed remains, if part of the site has been damaged during the discovery. When the soil was originally removed and then thrown back into the grave, the various layers and compositions of soil and vegetation may have become mixed or mottled. Slow and careful removal of this material may reveal the tool marks made on the outside edges; it may even show the type of blade involved, whether curved or straight, with enough definitions to make tool mark identification later on.

Before actual excavation and after the photographs have been taken of the burial site in its original condition, additional maps should be made of the site to show both plane and elevation views of the grave and to tie in items found both by horizontal location and depth (see Figure 10–5 and 10–6). Expert help may be available through a county or state highway department engineer or surveyor, who would have the tools necessary to do the job properly. (Items such as a compass, plumb bob, string, protractor, and string level are necessities.)

The soil should be removed in even layers of 4 to 6 inches and all material sifted through two screens. The first screen should have ¼-inch mesh; the second should be standard window screen. As items are located and recovered, they should be plotted on the elevation or side view of the drawings. The completed drawing then accurately reflects the various vertical levels of items in the grave, and the plane view indicates their horizontal distances apart. For comparison, soil samples should be taken where each item is recovered, and each should be accurately documented. Recovered items may still bear latent fingerprints.

THE BODY

When the body is uncovered and has tissue remaining on it, the forensic pathologist may make an on-scene cursory examination. When this examination is completed and photographs taken, a freshly laundered or new sheet should be available and the remains carefully placed in it so as to preserve any evidence that is not immediately visible but might be lost in transit. Next, the sheet's edges should be

Figure 10–4 (continued)

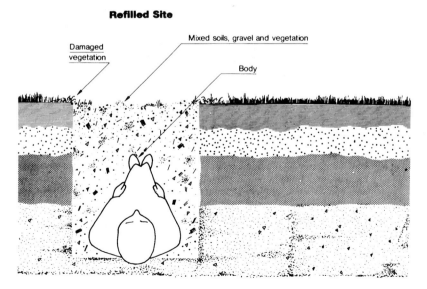

(Courtesy Federal Bureau of Investigation)

Figure 10–5
Plane View of Site

Illustration of lanes laid out in north-south direction. Then a cross-grid is laid out when the body is located. Smaller grids may be used when small objects are found in the grave.

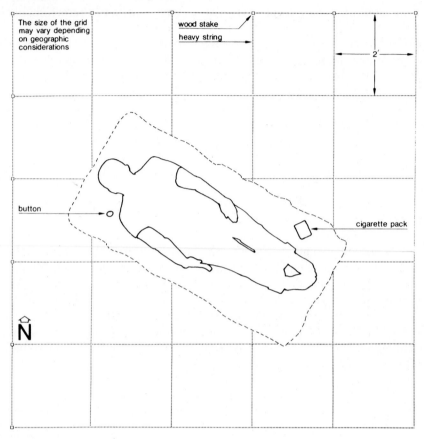

(Courtesy Federal Bureau of Investigation)

folded over and placed with the remains in a body bag or container for removal to a proper place of autopsy. The sheet and physical evidence should be separately marked for identification and carefully packaged.

After removal of the body, the grave should again be photographed and the area under the body carefully searched and excavated to a depth of several more inches. A metal detector is useful if bullets were fired into the body after it was placed in the grave or to find other metal objects.

SEARCH FOR A BURIED BODY

In some cases, information is received through an informant, a citizen, or a confession that a body has been buried, and an approximate location is given.

The grave site may be identified precisely or as in an area as small as a city lot or as large as several hundred acres. In all cases, it is critical to establish security quickly around the entire suspected area to prevent access by unauthorized persons.

Good planning is vital. The more that is known about the circumstances of the crime and burial, the greater the chances for locating the site. For example, if it is known or believed the victim was killed and then buried elsewhere, the grave may not be too far from a road. However, if the killing was alleged to have taken place at the site, then the victim could have been made to walk a considerable distance. The time since the killing affects vegetation around the site and the grave itself; the grave may have sunk, or the surplus dirt may still be in a mound. A botanist can give approximations

Figure 10–6
Elevation View of Site
Photograph items of evidence with ruler and north indicator.

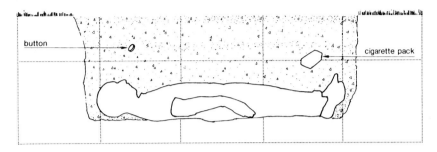

(Courtesy Federal Bureau of Investigation)

on damaged plant life that started growing again. Areas of sparse vegetation offer little to go on. Buried insects may be useful. When the surface has been cultivated, the only remaining visual indicator of a grave may be a depression in the surface.

An aircraft, especially a helicopter, may be used before a foot search to spot soil or vegetation disturbance. Thermal infrared photography may be of help. Infrared film detects heat, and a decomposing body emits heat. However, heat ceases to be generated very soon after a body has been buried, and nothing will show on infrared film. Aerial photographs should be taken of the area before a search and, if the search is successful, after it.

When it becomes necessary to conduct a foot search in a suspected area, mechanical aids become essential, especially if a visual search has been negative. Probing is the first step. Before probing begins, the coordinator of the search must formulate the plans carefully by having a map of the area, making a grid overlay tied into known landmarks, and preparing lanes with stakes and string for the searchers. In areas of woods or heavy underbrush, the establishing of grids is more difficult, and the case coordinator will have to be especially watchful to ensure that locations are checked properly. The area should be probed in not more than 2-foot squares and in a staggered pattern. Coordinators must also keep their maps posted on areas where the search has been completed. As probing is difficult and requires the use of generally unused muscles, care should be taken to plan for shifts of searchers and frequent rest periods.

Probing is done with a steel rod, preferably stainless steel, approximately 5⁄16 inch in diameter and 4½ to 5 feet long. A "tee" handle is welded to one end; the other end is sharply pointed. Probing works by detecting differences in disturbed and undisturbed subsurface soil. Investigators need to practice in the immediate area to get a feel for the soil.

When a soft spot is located, indicating a possible grave, the probe should be left in the ground and no further probing done to the area. At that point a second mechanical aid is employed, an instrument to verify the presence of a body without the need of excavating. One such instrument uses methane gas as a primary source of verification. Gases are formed by a decomposing body. The gas formation is minimal at low temperatures, 32° to 35°F, but at these low temperatures the ground also would likely be frozen, and probing would not be attempted. At warmer temperatures, gas forms.

After a suspected site is located, a temperature-sensing probe is inserted and a reading is taken to adjust the gas instrument to the correct sensitivity. Gases from a buried body penetrate the soil upward in a V shape, with the greatest concentration directly over the body. A probe inserted beside a body or too deeply could therefore miss the gas area. Consequently, several probings are made at different depths to ensure complete coverage (see Figure 10–7). This probe can be an invaluable aid in checking suspected areas without an excavation at each one. It can also be used to check under concrete—roadways, patios, floors—after a small

Figure 10–7
Vapor Detector
(a) Missed vapors–too deep. (b) Not directly over body, but shallow vapors. (c) Directly over body–strongest vapors.

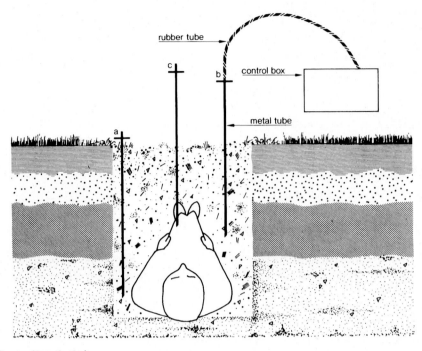

(Courtesy Federal Bureau of Investigation)

hole is drilled through the concrete. This instrument or one like it should be a part of a crime lab's equipment, especially where rural areas are included in the jurisdiction.

USE OF CADAVER DOGS

Dogs have been used in a variety of forensic contexts because of their superior sense of smell.[15] It is estimated that their ability to smell some scents, particularly fatty acids, is as much as a million times more sensitive than that of humans. Around 1985, a number of police departments in the United States started using specially trained dogs to assist in locating bodies that were either buried in the ground or submerged in water. These dogs, which are also often used as canine patrol dogs, are trained to become sensitive to the odor of decomposing human remains. There are typically two methods employed to train the dogs. One method is exposing the dogs to decomposing human tissues and bones. Specimens of decomposing human flesh and bone are usually provided by the local

medical examiner's office. A second method is exposing the dogs to artifical chemical combinations that mimic the scent well enough for training purposes.[16] Once a geographic area has been identified where a body might be either buried in the ground or submerged in water, the dogs are brought into the area to begin tracking. If the body is submerged in water, a dog is typically placed at the bow of a small boat while the handler sets up a systematic search pattern in order to cover the water area where the body is most likely to be submerged (see Figure 10–8). Even though the body may be submerged in many feet of water, the gases from the decomposing tissue will still come to the surface, and it is these gases that the dogs detect. When these gases are detected, whether on land or in the water, the dogs will signal by barking, scratching at the surface, or doing a combination of these actions. Once a suspicious area has been located on the water surface, divers can be called in to search for the body. Officers who have utilized cadaver dogs for water searches report that such searches are easier to conduct in freshwater than in

Figure 10-8
Use of a Cadaver Dog
Cadaver dog with two law enforcement officers searching a lake for a missing child.

(Courtesy Bob Westenhouser, *Tampa Tribune*)

salty tidal water. However, in spite of this, dogs have been successful in locating bodies in both types of water.

ESTIMATING TIME OF DEATH

Determination of the time of death or the interval between the time of death and the time that a body is found (i.e., the *postmortem interval*) can be difficult. A forensic pathologist attempts to determine the time of death as accurately as possible, realizing, however, that such a determination is only a best estimate. Unless a death is witnessed, or a watch breaks during a traumatic incident, the exact time of death cannot be determined. The longer the time since death, the greater the chance for error in determining the postmortem interval. There are numerous individual observations that, when used together, provide the best estimate of the time

of death. These include body temperature, rigor mortis, livor mortis, decompositional changes, and stomach contents. A thorough scene investigation must also be performed, and environmental conditions should be documented. The environment is the single most important factor in determining the postmortem interval.[17]

BODY COOLING (ALGOR MORTIS)

After death, the body cools from its normal internal temperature of 98.6°F to the surrounding environmental temperature. Many studies have examined this decrease in body temperature to determine formulas that could predict its consistency. Unfortunately, because of numerous variables, body cooling is an inaccurate method of predicing postmortem interval. In general, however, evaluating a decrease in body temperature is most helpful within the first 10 hours after death. During this time, with a normal body temperature and at an ideal environmental temperature of 70 to 75°F, the body cools at approximately 1.5°F per hour.

However, the problem with using the 1.5°F-per-hour calculation is the assumptions that the internal temperature is 98.6°F and the environmental temperature is 70 to75°F. If a decedent's body temperature is higher than normal because of infection or physical exercise, the body temperature of 98.6°F cannot be used. Furthermore, the outside environment is rarely in the 70 to 75°F range. For example, a body may actually gain heat if an individual expires outdoors in July, when temperatures may be greater than 100°F. Conversely, if a person expires in a 25°F environment, rapid cooling will take place.

Nonetheless, if body temperature is measured at a scene, it should be taken by the attending physician on at least two separate occasions before the body is moved. A rectal or liver temperature is the most accurate measurement. The environmental temperature should also be recorded. If these relatively simple procedures are followed, a very crude estimate of the postmortem interval can be made.[18]

RIGOR MORTIS

After death, the muscles of the body initially become flaccid. Within 1 to 3 hours they become increasingly rigid and the joints freeze by a process called *rigor mortis* (or *postmortem rigidity* or *rigor*).

Rigor mortis is affected by body temperature and metabolic rate: the higher the body temperature, the more lactic acid is produced, and rigor occurs sooner. For example, a person dying with pneumonia and a fever will develop rigor sooner than a person with normal body temperature. Similarly, if a person's muscles were involved in strenuous physical activity just before death, rigor develops much more quickly. The process is also retarded in cooler environmental temperatures and accelerated in warmer ones.

All muscles of the body begin to stiffen at the same time after death. Muscle groups appear to stiffen at different rates because of their different sizes. For example, stiffness is apparent sooner in the jaw than in the knees. Thus, an examiner must check to see if joints are movable in the jaws, arms, and legs.

A body is said to be in complete rigor when the jaw, elbow, and knee joints are immovable. This takes approximately 10 to 15 hours at an environmental temperature of 70 to 75°F. A body remains rigid for 24 to 36 hours before the muscles begin to loosen, apparently in the same order they stiffened.

A body remains rigid until rigor passes or until a joint is physically moved and rigor is broken. Consequently, in addition to indicating an approximate time of death, body position in full rigor can indicate whether or not a body has been moved after death.[19]

LIVOR MORTIS

A purplish color that appears under the skin on those portions of the body closest to the ground denotes *livor mortis*. The discoloration is caused by the settling of the blood. It may begin as early as a half hour after death and is pronounced 4 hours after death. The officer who is unfamiliar with this condition could erroneously conclude that the discoloration resulted from an assault. However, there are certain differences between the discoloration caused by lividity and that caused by bruising: A bruise may have swelling or abrasions around the wound, whereas lividity does not; the coloring of bruises may vary, being black, blue, yellowish green, and so forth, but lividity color remains uniform; and finally, bruises may appear on numerous parts of the body, while lividity appears only on the portions of the body closest to the ground, unless the body was removed before the blood completely clotted.

Livor mortis is extremely important for three reasons:

1. When considered with other factors, it may help estimate the time of death.
2. Because the skin must be relaxed and not lying flush against any surface, object, or even clothing folds for the lividity coloration to develop, it may indicate whether the body has been moved or even slightly disturbed after death. It is for this reason that exact measurements, sketches, and photographs must be made at the scene before and as a body is being recovered.
3. The actual coloration of the skin may indicate the cause of death, as in the case of carbon

monoxide poisoning, certain forms of cyanide poisoning, or extreme cold, when the color of the lividity is not purplish but a cherry red color.[20]

The following case illustrates that in some instances livor mortis and rigor mortis can provide valuable clues in determining if a body has been moved after death:

A young woman failed to report to work one morning, and a female coworker and close friend became concerned after telephoning the victim's home and receiving no answer. The friend left work and went directly to the victim's apartment. She knocked on the door several times, and when no one answered she tried the doorknob and discovered that the door was unlocked. She entered the apartment, went through the living room and into the bedroom, where she discovered the victim clad in her nightgown lying in bed on her back. She tried to revive the victim but could not. She then called for the police and an ambulance. When the medical personnel arrived, they examined the victim and pronounced her dead. There were no signs of foul play, but the police did discover some barbiturates on the nightstand and suspected, quite correctly as it turned out, that the victim had died of an overdose of drugs. There was a small amount of blood approximately 2 inches in diameter on the front of the victim's nightgown in the pubic area, and as would later be determined, it was blood from her menstrual period.

The body was removed and taken to the morgue, where a visual examination revealed the presence of livor mortis on both the front and back of the victim's body. In addition, rigor mortis had begun and the victim's left foot was extending straight out (see Figure 10–9). The position of the foot was not consistent with the rigor mortis patterns that would normally result when someone was lying on her back but rather would be consistent with someone who was lying on her stomach. These inconsistencies, along with the presence of the menstrual blood on the front of the victim's nightgown rather than on the back, strongly suggested that the victim had likely been lying face down for several hours after death and that someone had moved the body.

The autopsy revealed no signs of foul play; however, semen was found in the victim's vagina. The cause of death was determined to be from an overdose of drugs used in combination with liquor.

The subsequent investigation and interviews of her friends revealed that the victim was last seen alive in a nearby bar the evening before. She was drinking quite heavily and was also taking some barbiturates. During the course of the evening she met a man who bought her several drinks. Around midnight she left the bar with the male companion. The witnesses who were at the bar were able to

Figure 10–9
Rigor Mortis Clues
Rigor mortis pattern in left foot not consistent with the position of the body when discovered.

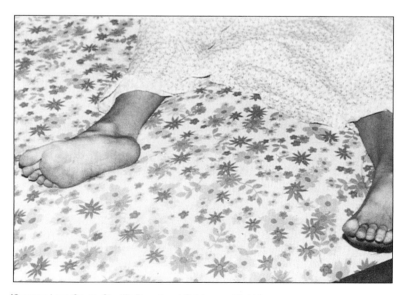

(Courtesy Leon County Sheriff's Department, Tallahassee, Florida)

provide the police with the name and address of the man. The male companion, who was married and from out-of-town, provided the police with the following information.

After leaving the bar, he and the woman had gone directly to her apartment. They went to her bedroom, disrobed, and had sexual intercourse in her bed. The man fell asleep and was awakened when the alarm clock went off at 7:30 A.M. When he woke up, the woman was lying face down on the floor next to the bed in her nightgown. He picked her up and put her back in bed. When he realized that she was dead, he became frightened about having to explain what he was doing there, got dressed, and left the apartment.

The fact that this woman's body was moved is really inconsequential in this specific case, but in other instances the knowledge that a body was moved, especially from one location to another, can be profoundly important. This is so because important physical evidence available at the first location may be totally absent from the second location. On occasion, postmortem conditions may provide important clues to determine if in fact the body was moved after death.

CADAVERIC SPASM

Although firm statements are frequently made concerning the instantaneous tightening of an extrem-

ity or other part of the body at the time of death (commonly called a "death grip"), there seems to be a general failure to explain its mechanism. The literature typically describes a decedent's hand tightly clutching a weapon, usually a gun, knife, or razor at the moment of death (see Figure 10–10). However, the actual cases of cadaveric spasm are few and far between. To date, the precise physiological mechanism of cadaveric spasm remains unknown.[21]

DECOMPOSITION

In general, as rigor passes, skin first turns green at the abdomen. As discoloration spreads to the rest of the trunk, the body begins to swell due to bacterial methane-gas formation. These bacteria are normal inhabitants of the body. They proliferate after death, and their overgrowth is promoted in warm weather and retarded in cold weather.

The different rates and types of decomposition a body undergoes depend upon the environment. Bodies buried in earth, submerged in water, left in the hot sun, or placed in a cool basement appear different after the same postmortem interval. When a body is bloated, epidermal sloughing and hemoglobin degradation begin. Moreover, as bloating continues, hair is forced from the skin. The increased internal pressure, caused by bacterial gas production, forces decomposed blood and body

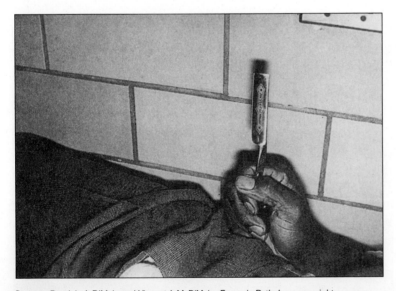

Figure 10–10
Cadaveric Spasm
Cadaveric spasm in 43-year-old male with razor in right hand.

Source: Dominic J. DiMaio and Vincent J. M. DiMaio, *Forensic Pathology*, copyright 1989, reproduced with permission of copyright owner, CRC Press, Boca Raton, Florida

Figure 10–11
Decomposition
This white female was a victim of suicide by an overdose of drugs. She was dead for approximately one week in an unventilated hot room before her body was discovered. Note that her skin has turned black, there is thickening of the features, liquid and gas blisters appear on the skin, and body fluids have been secreted through the body cavities.

fluids out of body orifices by a process called *purging*. (See Figure 10–11.) As the body undergoes skeletonization, the rate of tissue deterioration is dependent on environmental temperature. For example, a body exposed to a 100°F environmental temperature may completely decompose to a skeleton within a few weeks. In contrast, a body in a temperature of 65°F may not skeletonize for many months or years. In general, a body decomposing above ground for a week looks similar to a body that has been under water for two weeks or has been buried for six weeks. This generalization should serve as a reminder that an uncovered or naked body decomposes more rapidly than a covered or clothed one.

After a body is found, it is usually refrigerated until an autopsy is performed or a final disposition is made. Decomposition slows down or ceases if a body is refrigerated. When the body is exposed to room temperature, decomposition occurs rapidly. Recognition of this accelerated decomposition is particularly important if a person dies in a cold environment and is then moved to a warmer one.

Decomposition may not occur evenly throughout the body. For example, decomposition occurs more rapidly in injured areas. If a person is struck on the head, and bleeding occurs only in that area, decomposition may be much more advanced on the head than on the remainer of the body. Fly larvae proliferate during summer, spring, and fall in warm, moist areas of the body such as the eyes, nose, and mouth. Larvae are attracted to injured areas, where they feed on exposed blood proteins and cause accelerated decomposition. Due to the

uneven decomposition, it is common to see skeletonization in only part of the body.[22]

DETERMINATION OF TIME OF DEATH BY MEANS OF CARRION INSECTS

The forensic entomologist can help in estimating the time of death by examining the various carrion insects, because different carrion insects successfully attack the body at various stages of decomposition and under certain environmental conditions.[23]

The following case illustrates how a qualified entomologist can assist investigations in death cases.

Dr. Bernard Greenberg, of the University of Illinois (Chicago), helped to solve a double murder that had occurred in the basement of an apartment house. The only evidence he had to work with was a photograph of the bodies at the scene. He examined the photograph, which clearly depicted the advanced pupae (the developmental stage immediately before full maturity) of flies, under a microscope. He then obtained National Weather Service information for the period when the murders took place and determined how long it would have taken the flies to develop to the stage shown in the photograph. His estimate of the time of death came within two days of the actual murders, and this evidence linked the suspect to the murders. The suspect was eventually convicted.

Collection of Carrion Insects from a Clothed and Decomposing Body

When an entomologist is to assist, the investigator must, before examining the body, take several photographs of the body, including close-ups of the areas of insect activity. Then the investigator should record the present air temperature, relative humidity, and environmental setting (shaded wooded area, open field, and the like).

Collection of the insects should begin in the facial area of the decomposing body, because it is the first to undergo degradation by insects. Only an open wound attracts insects more readily. The investigator must be sure to collect as many different insect forms as possible and all life stages (egg, larvae, pupae, and adult).

If time or other complications limit insect collection, the investigator should collect at least fly larvae. With fly larvae the largest specimens should be obtained, because they represent the earliest attacking insects. Examination of the folds in the clothing and underlying soil for pupating larvae or pupae cases is very important. If there is no evidence of hatched pupae cases, one may assume that the fly larvae collected represent the first life cycle.

Collected insect specimens should be placed in a container of preservative solution of 85-percent alcohol. Duplicate samples should be placed in aerated containers with small amounts of soil. Each specimen container should be labeled with the date, time, and area of the body from which it was collected.

As the clothing is removed from the body, many more insects are observable. Efforts should be made to collect samples from within the folds of the clothing. If the decomposed body has been placed in a disaster bag and transported to a morgue, insects still can be easily collected. Some insects drop off the body before it is placed in the disaster bag, but most continue feeding on the body. On opening the disaster bag, the investigator will observe many beetle forms. The darkness in the disaster bag causes the fly larvae to migrate into the various body orifices and the beetles to surface from the clothing and body orifices. The same procedure as described above for collecting insects should be followed after the body is removed from the disaster bag. (See Figure 10–12 for areas of the body from which to collect insects.)

Figure 10–12
Body Areas from Which to Collect Insects

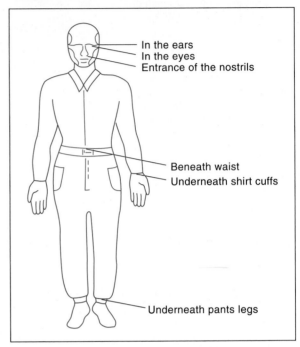

After a complete examination of the body, collected insects should be taken immediately to an entomologist for identification and determination of how long the insects have been feeding on the human remains.

Collection of Carrion Insects from Human Skeletal Remains

As a body decomposes, it is attacked by many insect forms. Most belong to the insect orders Diptera (flies) and Coleoptera (beetles). These insects feed on decomposing tissue or on other carrion insects.

Some of the carrion insects that attack a body shortly after death themselves die after laying eggs or after being caught in the viscous and putrefying liquids of the decaying corpse. The remains (exoskeletons) of these insects, however, stay intact for long periods in the many skeletal cavities or underlying soil. Close examination of the cavities of a skeleton (before it is removed from the crime scene) usually produces numerous insect remains.

The best area in which to find these remains is the skull, particularly inside the cranial vault (see

Figure 10–13
**Areas of Skeleton Most Likely
to Harbor Insects**

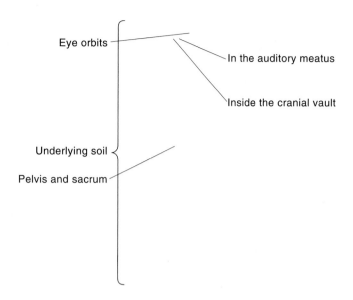

Figure 10–13). The examination can begin when the skull is placed carefully on a white sheet or on a large piece of paper. Then with forceps and a penlight, the investigator probes the eye orbits, nasal opening, and external auditory meatus for insect remains. The remains most commonly belong to carrion and rove beetles and blowflies. Sometimes the remains are obscured by mud or dried debris within the skull. In this case, the skull should be carefully placed into a plastic bag to avoid the loss of any insect remains. Later the skull should be removed from the bag and washed over a fine screen tray. The mud and debris along with the insect remains will become separated and caught on the screen. After recovery of the insect remains, they should be air-dried, placed in cotton in a small container, and taken to an entomologist for identification. The entomologist can also provide information on the developmental timing of the insects, from which can be inferred a fairly accurate estimation of time since death.

In certain instances, when a consulting entomologist is not available, an investigator must rely on taxonomic and entomological texts for identification of the insect remains. Many states publish entomological bulletins with good information on seasonality, developmental rates, and geographical ranges.

Entomologists may also be able to assist investigators in other types of criminal investigations. The following case illustrates this:

In a case referred to as the "Cocklebur Caper," a woman was raped near her apartment by a man wearing a ski mask. Investigators found such a mask in the apartment of a suspect, who said he had not worn it since the previous winter. A small cocklebur was embedded in the mask, and inside it was a beetle. It was determined that a beetle larva in the cocklebur could not possibly have survived from the previous winter, and therefore the mask had been worn outside during the current summer. The cocklebur was of the same species as others found near the rape scene. The suspect was ultimately convicted of the rape.

USE OF AQUATIC INSECTS IN DETERMINING SUBMERSION INTERVAL

Although potentially valuable, the use of aquatic insects in determining submersion intervals at death scene investigations has not been exploited. Aquatic environments have no known true specific indicator species, as do terrestrial habitats. The aquatic environment is a new frontier for forensic entomology. The primary problem in aquatic environments, however, is that there are no purely sarcophagous aquatic insects to compare with the common terrestrial indicator species such as blowflies or carrion beetles. Aquatic insects feed primarily on algae, decaying plant matter, and other insects. They do not commonly have access to submerged carrion of large animals; therefore, aquatic insect species have no specialized sarcophagous feeding habits.

In spite of lack of specific indicator species in the aquatic environment, there is tremendous potential for determining the submersion interval for a human body. Some factors that may help determine submersion intervals are progression and development, on the corpse, of algae and aquatic insect "communities"; deposition of silt; presence of specific life stages of aquatic insects; presence of specific structures built by aquatic insects; and presence of species known to inhabit certain microhabitats. The majority of these factors, however, will involve some speculation. The development of an aquatic insect community on a corpse is highly dependent on available colonizers, location of introduced colonizers, geographic location, seasonality, temperature, and current speed. It is recommended that if a body is recovered from the water and some insect colonization is found, the forensic entomologist be called on for assistance.[24]

EVIDENCE FROM WOUNDS

A basic knowledge of wounds is of great assistance to officers who are responsible for injury and death investigations. It helps them reach preliminary conclusions. The five most common types of wounds encountered by police officers in injury and death investigations are firearm wounds, incised wounds, stab wounds, puncture wounds, and lacerations.

FIREARM WOUNDS

When a bullet strikes a body, the skin is first pushed in and then perforated while in the stretched state. After the bullet has passed, the skin partially returns to its original position, and the entry opening is drawn together and is thus smaller than the diameter of the bullet. The slower the speed of the bullet, the smaller the entry opening. The bullet passing through the stretched skin forms a so-called contusion ring around the entrance opening as the bullet slips against the skin that is pressed inward and scrapes the external epithelial layers. The skin itself, in the contusion ring, becomes conspicuous by drying after some hours. In a favorable case, rifling marks on the bullet leave such a distinct mark in the contusion ring that the number of grooves in the rifling can be counted. The combined section of the contusion ring and entrance opening corresponds to the caliber of the bullet or exceeds it slightly. When a bullet strikes the body squarely, the contusion ring is round; when a bullet strikes at an angle, the ring is oval.

Along with the contusion ring there is another black-colored ring, the "smudge ring," which often entirely covers the contusion ring. It does not contain any powder residues or contamination from the bore of the firearm but consists wholly of small particles originating from the surface of the bullet. The smudge ring may be absent in the case of clean-jacketed bullets or when the bullet has passed through clothing.

A bullet passing through the body forms a track that is usually straight but can also be bent at an angle in an unpredictable manner if the bullet meets or passes through a bone. Thus it is not possible to determine with certainty, from observation of the entrance and exit openings, the direction of the weapon when the shot was fired. The direction must be calculated by the pathologist from the results of the autopsy. The velocity of the bullet has a great influence on the appearance of the track: straight tracks indicate a high velocity, and bent or angular ones indicate a low velocity.

In gunshot injuries in soft parts of the body, especially in the brain, the bullet can produce a considerable explosive effect, which is greatest with unjacketed or soft-nosed bullets from large-caliber firearms. Such a bullet may split into several parts, each of which forms its own track, and thus there may be *several exit wounds*. When such a bullet strikes the head, large parts of the cranium can be blown away and the brain scattered around. A soft-nosed bullet that, before hitting the body, is split by striking against a tree branch can produce a number of regular entrance holes.

A shot through the head is not always fatal. To be immediately fatal, the bullet must either produce a bursting effect or injure an artery of the brain or a vital brain center. A shot through the brain that is not immediately fatal does not always produce unconsciousness. Even when the heart has been perforated by a bullet, it occasionally happens that the injured person lives for several hours retaining some capacity for movement.

It is often difficult to distinguish the exit wound from the entrance wound, especially from a shot at long range with a metal-jacketed bullet, assuming, of course, that the bullet passes through the body intact. In a favorable case, the exit wound may have a ragged appearance with flaps directed outward. To determine the direction of the shot with certainty in such a case, an autopsy is necessary. If the bullet was damaged by its passage through the body or if there was a bursting effect, it is generally easy to determine the exit wound, which is then considerabley larger than the entrance wound and shows a star-shaped, ragged character, with flaps directed outward. Note, however, that in contact shots the entrance wound may be ragged and star-shaped. A bullet that ricochets may strike with its side or obliquely and produce a large and characteristic entrance wound.

Close and Distant Shots

It is very important to be able to estimate the distance from which a shot was fired. In many cases this fact is the only evidence available that can distinguish between suicide, a self-defense killing, manslaughter, or murder.

In practice, a distinction is made between contact, close, and distant shots. A *contact shot* is one in which the muzzle of the weapon is pressed against the body when the shot is fired. In a *close shot*, the distance of the muzzle is less than about 18 inches from the body, whereas a *distant shot* is one fired at a distance greater than 18 inches (see Figures 10–16 through 10–20).

In the case of a contact shot against an exposed part of the body, soot, metallic particles, and powder residues are driven into the body and can be found there during the autopsy. Blackening, caused by soot and powder, around the entry opening is often absent. A contact shot against a part of the body protected by clothing often produces a powder zone on the skin or in the clothes, and soot, powder residue, and fragments of clothing are driven into the track. In a contact discharge, the entrance

Figure 10–14
A Bullet Penetrating the Skin
Representation of a bullet prenetrating the skin. The skin is pressed inward, stretched, and perforated in the stretched condition, after which it returns to its original position. The entry opening is smaller than the diameter of the bullet. Immediately around the opening is the contusion ring, caused by the bullet's rubbing against this part of the skin and scraping off the external layer of epithelial cells.

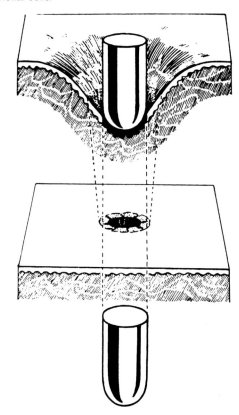

Source: Barry A. J. Fisher, *Techniques of Crime Scene Investigation*, copyright 1992, reproduced with permission of copyright owner, CRC Press, Boca Raton, Florida.

wound differs considerably from an entrance wound in a close shot or distant shot. When a contact shot is fired, the gases of the explosion are driven into the track but they are forced out again and produce a bursting effect on the skin and clothes. The entrance wound is often star-shaped with flaps directed outward (see Figures 10–16 and 10–17). It is also possible, in a contact shot, for the muzzle of the weapon to mark the skin, causing an impression that reproduces the shape of the muzzle of the weapon.

Figure 10–15
Marks Around an Entry Opening of a Bullet Wound
A diagram showing the marks that may be found around the entry opening of a bullet in a close shot: (*a*) contusion ring, (*b*) smudge ring, (*c*) grains of powder, and (*c*) deposit of powder residue.

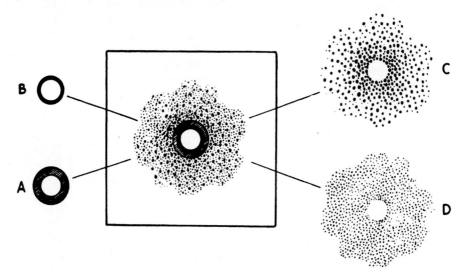

A close shot produces a zone of blackening around the entrance wound of the track, either on the skin or on the clothes. Sometimes the flame from the muzzle has a singeing action around this opening, with hair and textile fibers curled up. The zone of blackening is formed of substances carried along with the explosion gases. When a cartridge is fired, the bullet is forced through the barrel of the weapon by the explosion gases. Only a small amount of the gas passes in front of the bullet. The combustion of the powder is never complete, even with smokeless powder and still less with black powder, and the explosion gases therefore carry with them incompletely burned powder residues, the amount of which decreases as the distance increases. Thus, in a close shot, a considerable amount of incompletely burned powder residue is found on the target. In addition to carrying this residue, the gases also carry along impurities from the inside of the barrel, consisting of rust (iron), oil, and particles rubbed off the bullet. Metallic residues from the percussion cap and cartridge case also occur in the gases of the explosion. If the shot is fired at a right angle to the body, the zone of blackening is practially circular; if fired

obliquely, the zone is oval. The extent of the zone of blackening is often difficult to determine by direct observation, and it is often better to photograph it, using infrared-sensitive material, which intensifies the zone of blackening so that its extent is more easily determined. The zone of blackening gives valuable information for determining the distance from which a shot was fired, which may be an important factor in deciding between murder and suicide. It is important that comparative test shots be fired with the *same weapon* and *same type of ammunition* as those used in the actual crime.

Close shots with black powder show marks of burning up to a distance of 4 to 6 inches and a distinct deposit of powder smoke up to 10 or 12 inches. Dispersed grains of powder embedded in the target may be detected even at a distance of 3 feet. In distant shots, none of the characteristics of a close shot can be detected.

Powder residues occur on the object fired at in the form of incompletely and completely burned particles. A careful microscopic examination should precede any chemical examination, as it is often possible to establish in this way the shape and color of

Figure 10–16
Contact Bullet Wound
Homicidal contact bullet wound of forehead. Notice the charring of the edges and the star-shaped tears of the skin due to undermining of the scalp.

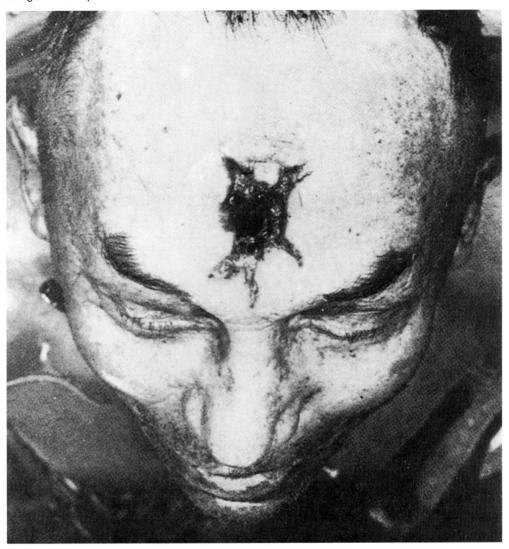

(Courtesy Santa Ana, California, Police Department)

unburned powder particles and to distinguish many kinds of powder (see Figures 10–18 and 10–19).

Black powder, which consists of potassium nitrate, sulfur, and charcoal, is identified by the presence of potassium and nitrate in the entrance wound. Smokeless powder consists chiefly of nitrocellulose or of nitrocellulose with nigroglycerine and is identified by the presence of nitrite, which can be detected by various microreactions. The grains of smokeless powder are generally coated with graphite and occur in many forms (e.g., round or angular discs, pellets, and cylinders).[25]

Shotgun Wounds

A shotgun is a smoothbore, shoulder-fired firearm and is usually used to fire multiple pellets, rather than a single slug. The most common gauges with their corresponding bore diameters are:[26]

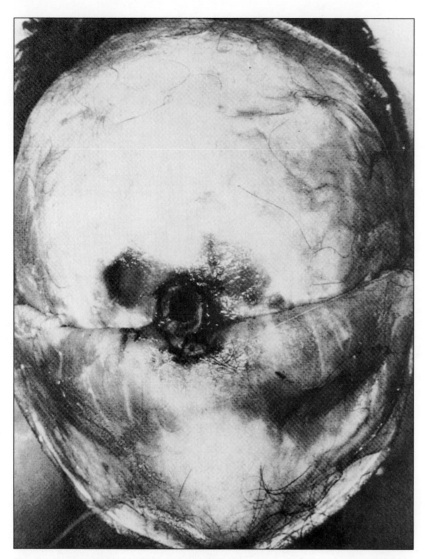

Figure 10–17
Contact Bullet Wound Damage to Underlying Scalp Tissue and Skull
The same bullet wound shown in Figure 10–16, but with the scalp reflected forward over the face. Notice how the blast has undermined the scalp, singeing and blackening the surface of the skull.

(Courtesy Santa Ana, California, Police Department)

Gauge	Diameter (Inches)
12	.729
16	.662
20	.615
410	.410

The pellets fired range in size from 0.08 inch for No. 9 shot to 0.33 inch for 00 Buck. A "wad," which may be either paper or plastic, lies between the shot pellets and the powder. Most modern shells use plastic wads. A shotgun shell can contain any-where from a couple of hundred pellets to nine for 00 Buck, to one large lead slug.

Entrance Wounds   From contact to 12 inches, there is a single round entrance 0.75 to 1 inch in diameter. The edge of the wound shows an abrasion ring. As the distance between muzzle and skin increases, powder tattooing appears. Powder blackening is most prominent at less than 12 inches. Powder tattooing is considerably less dense than in pistol wounds (see Figure 10–20).

When pellets are discharged at between 3 and 6 feet of range, the single entrance wound widens to 1.5 to 2 inches in diameter and shows "scalloping"

Figure 10–18
Firearm Discharged at Close Range

Close shot, short distance. The diagram shows both incompletely burner powder grains and smoke deposits in the zone of blackening. The powder grains are concentrated immediately around the entrance hole.

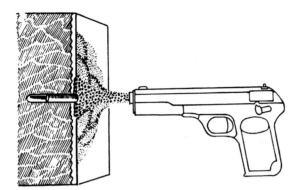

Source: Barry A. J. Fisher, *Techniques of Crime Scene Investigation*, copyright 1992, reproduced with permission of copyright owner, CRC Press, Boca Raton, Florida

Figure 10–19
Firearm Discharged from a Distance

Close shot, greater distance than in Figure 10–18. The diagram shows unburned powder grains, but no smoke deposits, in the zone of blackening.

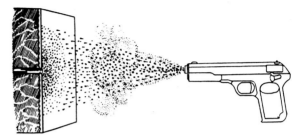

Source: Barry A. J. Fisher, *Techniques of Crime Scene Investigation*, copyright 1992, reproduced with permission of copyright owner, CRC Press, Boca Raton, Florida.

of the edges. At about 6 feet, the pellets begin to separate from the main mass of pellets. Beyond 10 to 12 feet, there is great variation in the spread of the pellets.

The Wad At close ranges, the wad will be propelled into the body through the large single entrance wound. Beyond 10 to 15 feet, the wad will have separated from the pellets and will not enter. However, it may mark the body. The gauge of the shotgun and the size of the pellets can be obtained from the wad and pellets, respectively. On occasion, a plastic wad may be marked by the choke or irregularities at the end of the barrel, making ballistic comparison possible.

Range Determination Range determinations can be made later if the size of the shotgun pattern

Figure 10–20
Close-Range Wound from a 12-Gauge Shotgun

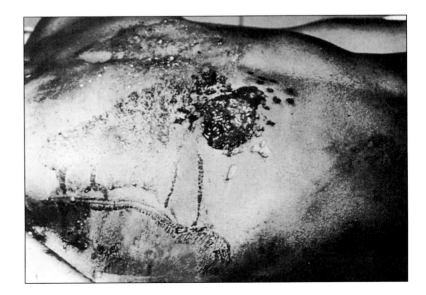

was described at autopsy and duplicated on paper. The same weapon with the same type of ammunition must be used in duplication of the pattern if accurate results are desired. Range formulas do *not* work.

X-ray patterns of the shot in the body are useless for range determinations, as are patterns on the body in which the shot first struck the target.

The size of the shot pattern on the body depends primarily on the choke of the gun. The type of ammunition and barrel length are secondary factors. The size of the pellet pattern is independent of the gauge of the shotgun, and an increase in gauge just increases the density of the pattern.

Exit Wounds   Shotgun pellets very rarely exit except when used as instruments of suicide in the region of the head.

Firearm Residues

Detecting firearm residues on the hands of an individual may be of great importance in evaluating deaths due to gunshot wounds. Detection of such residues on the hands of a deceased individual is often confirmatory evidence of a suspected suicide.[27]

One of the earliest methods of determining whether an individual discharged a weapon, the paraffin test or dermal nitrate test, was based on the detection of nitrates on the surfaces of the hands. Paraffin was employed for the removal of powder residues from the hands. Diphenylamine was the reagent used to detect the nitrates picked up by the paraffin. This test is no longer considered valid, because no distinction can be made between nitrates of gunpowder origin and those from other sources, which are quite commonly encountered in day-to-day living.

Several years ago, a series of chemical spot tests for detection of metallic components of firearm discharge residues was developed. Such metallic substances originate mainly from the primer, though they can also come from the bullet or cartridge case. Spot tests were developed for the presence of antimony, barium, and lead, substances found in most primers. These tests are inconclusive because they are essentially qualitative rather than quantitative.[28]

The concept of detecting metallic primer components led to more sophisticated approaches now in general use. Compounds of antimony, bar-

ium, and lead are used in modern noncorrosive primers. When a handgun is discharged, discrete particulate matter containing these elements is deposited on the thumb, forefinger, and connecting web (the back of the hand holding the weapon). The metallic compounds are removed from the hand, either with paraffin or, more commonly, with cotton swabs saturated with a dilute solution of acid. This material is then submitted for analysis.

Atomic Absorption Analysis and Neutron Activation Analysis   The two methods for the detection of firearm discharge residue that have received the greatest attention in recent years are atomic absorption analysis and neutron activation analysis. However, atomic absorption analysis has emerged as the test of choice, in part because the necessary equipment is less expensive. Most modern crime laboratories now offer atomic absorption analysis. Both methods of analysis have been employed to detect the trace elements of antimony and barium deposited on the hands when a gun is discharged. Atomic absorption analysis, however, is also able to detect lead deposits in gunshot residue, thus giving it one more advantage over neutron activation analysis.[29]

Removal of Gunshot Residue   Whatever the system of analysis to which the pathologist has access, the procedures for removal of firearm discharge residues from the hand are the same. The solution most commonly used is of dilute acid. Four cotton swabs are used to remove the firearm discharge residues from the hands. Two swabs are used on each hand; one for the palm, the other for the "back" of the hand. The swabs of the nonfiring hand and the palm of the hand suspected of discharging the weapon act as controls. A control swab dipped in the acid also should be submitted as a blank. Cotton swabs with plastic shafts should be used. Those with wood shafts should not be used because the wood may be contaminated with metallic elements. Because wood shows great variation in the concentration of such elements, no blank can be used.

If a person has discharged the handgun, firearm discharge residues should appear only on the back of the hand that fired the weapon, not on the palm of that hand or on the other hand. Some people, because of their occupations, may have high levels of barium, antimony, or lead on their hands. Thus if the back of the hand were the only area submitted for examination, a misleadingly positive report would come back. If analysis reveals firearm discharge residues only on the palms, it strongly suggests that the individual's hands were around the weapon at the time of the discharge or were trying to ward off the weapon. However, in suicide, high levels of residue often show up on the nonfiring palm when that hand is used to steady the weapon by grasping the barrel and receiving the muzzle or cylinder discharge.

It must be realized that determining whether an individual fired a gun cannot be based on absolute quantities of primer residue on the hands. Rather, it is based on contrast of the levels of these compounds from right to left and from palm to back.

INCISED AND STAB WOUNDS

The *incised wound*—more commonly referred to as the "cutting wound"—is inflicted with a sharp-edged instrument such as a knife or razor. The weapon typically employed in inflicting both incised and stab wounds is a pocketknife, although kitchen knives are also common. In comparison with shootings, fewer cutting assaults result in death, largely because the perpetrator's intention was to injure or disfigure rather than kill the victim. Cutting wounds are often found on the arms, face, and legs. Even in these "friendly" cuttings, as they are sometimes referred to, death may occur. When the victim does die from a cutting wound, it generally is found around the throat. The severity of most incised wounds is directly related to the shape and sharpness of the weapon, the part of the body being cut, and the amount of force used in striking the victim. The incised wound is typically narrow at the edges and gaping at the center, with considerable bleeding (see Figure 10–21). The inexperienced investigator may conclude that a gaping incised wound was inflicted by a large cutting instrument. However, a small knife with a honed blade is capable of causing very severe wounds.

Most frequently, death is caused after a stab results in severe damage to a vital organ, internal bleeding, shock, or fatal secondary infections that develop several days after the attack. Any of these factors may itself be fatal; they often occur in combination. The shape, size, and keenness of the

Figure 10–21
Incised Wound Inflicted with a Knife
Note the wound is narrow at the edges and gaping in the middle. Such wounds also typically bleed a lot.

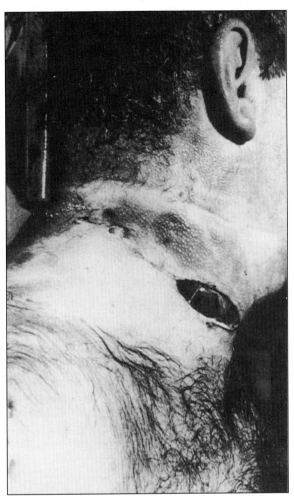

(Courtesy Federal Bureau of Investigation)

blade all determine a wound's shape and depth, as does the manner in which the knife is thrust into and pulled out of the body. One noticeable aspect of multiple stab wounds is their different shapes when made with the same knife. The proximity of the wounds in a multiple stabbing assault may be helpful in determining the actions of the victim prior to death. If the wounds are concentrated within a small region of the body, then there is a good possibility that the victim was immobilized at the time of the assault, that is, held down, asleep, or intoxicated.

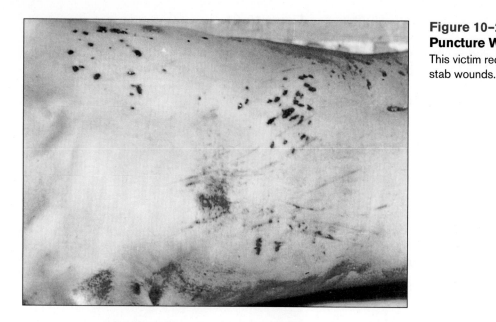

Figure 10–22
Puncture Wound
This victim received multiple ice-pick stab wounds.

PUNCTURE WOUNDS

The weapon most frequently used in assaults resulting in puncture wounds once was the ice pick. It is less common today. Leather punches and screwdrivers also are capable of producing puncture wounds, which are normally small and have little or no bleeding (see Figure 10–22). Such wounds can be easily overlooked, particularly if they are in hairy parts of the body. Infliction of a

puncture wound produces death in the same way as do stab wounds.

LACERATIONS

When used in an assault, clubs, pipes, pistols, or other such blunt objects can produce open, irregularly shaped wounds termed *lacerations*. Such wounds bleed freely and characteristically are accompanied by bruising around the edges. There is no necessary relationship between the shape of the wound and that of the weapon employed. Occasionally, such force will be used in an attack that an impression of the weapon is left on the victim's skin. Most frequently, when death results from an assault in which lacerations were inflicted, the cause is severe head injuries (see Figure 10–23). Laceration wounds may be inflicted accidentally, as in the case of an intoxicated person who falls and strikes his or her head against a curb or step. In other instances, circumstances may appear more suspicious.

Figure 10–23
Laceration Wounds
Lacerations inflicted on top of this victim's head resulting from a pistol whipping by a robber.

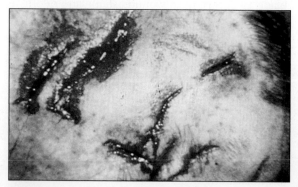

Checking the back doors of businesses at about 9:30 P.M., an officer found the proprietor of a jewelry store dead at the open rear entrance to his store. He had sustained a large laceration on his forehead and had bled considerably. It appeared that a murder had taken place during a robbery or burglary. Careful processing of the scene yielded traces of blood and one small skin fragment from the brick wall near the rear entrance.

Nothing was established as missing from the business. The medical examiner found the cause of death to be a heart attack. The head laceration contained minute traces of brick. Thus a reconstruction of events showed that as the owner was closing his business, he suffered a heart attack and convulsions, striking his head against the brick wall. The lacerations he suffered made it look as though he had suffered a fatal head wound.

The severity, extent, and appearance of injuries due to blunt trauma depend on the amount of force delivered to the body, the amount of time over which the force is delivered, the region struck, the amount (extent) of body surface over which the force is delivered, and the nature of the weapon. If a weapon deforms and/or breaks on impacting the body, less energy is delivered to the body to produce injury, since some of the energy is used to deform and/or break the weapon. Thus, the resultant injury is less severe than would have been the case if the weapon did not deform and/or break. If the body moves with the blow, this increases the period of time over which the energy is delivered and decreases the severity of the injury.[30]

For any given amount of force, the greater the area over which it is delivered, the less severe the wound, because the force is dissipated. The size of the area affected by a blow depends on the nature of the weapon and the region of the body. For a weapon with a flat surface, such as a board, there is a diffusion of the energy and a less severe injury than that due to a narrow object, for example, a steel rod, delivered with the same amount of energy. If an object projects from the surface of the weapon, then all the force will be delivered to the end of the projection and a much more severe wound will be produced. If a blow is delivered to a rounded portion of the body, such as the top of the head, the wound will be much more severe than if the same force is delivered to a flat portion of the body, such as the back, where there will be a greater area of contact and more dispersion of force.[31]

DEFENSE WOUNDS

Defense wounds are suffered by victims attempting to protect themselves from an assault, often by a knife or club. These wounds are commonly found on the palms of the hands, the fingers, or the forearms (see Figure 10–24). In the most aggravated

Figure 10–24
Defense Wounds
This victim received severe defense knife wounds on the hands while trying to stop his assailant from stabbing him to death.

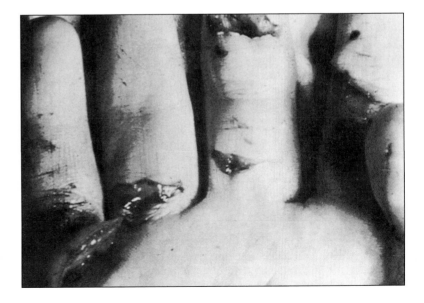

form, the defense wound may sever one or more fingers.

STRANGULATION WOUNDS

Ligature Strangulation

In *ligature strangulation*, the pressure on the neck is applied by a constricting band that is tightened by a force other than the body weight. Virtually all cases of ligature strangulation are homicides. Females predominate as victims. Suicides and accidents are rare. The mechanism of death is the same as in hanging, occlusion of the vessels supplying blood and thus oxygen to the brain. Consciousness is lost in 10 to 15 seconds.[32]

Ligatures used range from electric cords, neckties, ropes, and telephone cords to sheets, hose, and undergarments (see Figures 10–26 and 10–27). The appearance of a ligature mark on the neck is subject to considerable variation, depending upon the nature of the ligature, the amount of resistance offered by the victim, and the amount of force used

Figure 10–25
Death by Ligature Strangulation
Victim strangled with (*a*) Telephone cord and (*b*) boot lace. Face congested with numerous petechiae. Horizonally oriented ligature mark overlying larynx, encircling neck.

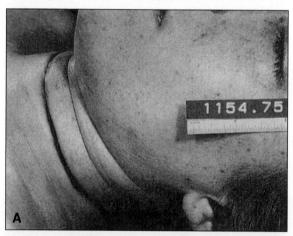

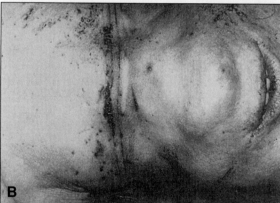

Figure 10–26
Death by Ligature Strangulation
(*a*) Ligature strangulation with cloth band. Ligature marks on anterior and lateral aspects of neck. (*b*) Close-up showing vertically oriented pattern to cloth.

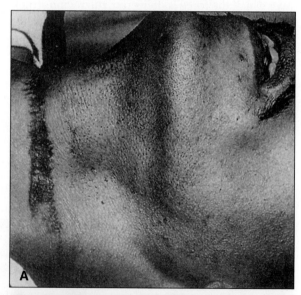

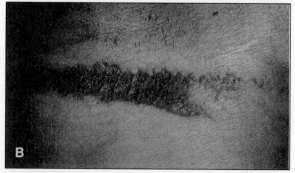

by the assailant. The ligature mark may be faint, barely visible, or absent in young children or incapacitated adults, especially if the ligature is soft (e.g., a towel) and removed immediately after death. If a thin ligature is used, there will be a very prominent deep mark encircling the neck. Initially, it has a yellow parchmentlike appearance that later turns dark brown.

In ligature strangulation, in contrast to hangings, the ligature mark usually encircles the neck in a horizontal plane often overlying the larynx or upper trachea. When a wire or cord is used, it often completely encircles the neck. There may be a break in the furrow, however, usually at the back of the neck, where a hand has grasped the ligature and tightened it at that point. Aside from the ligature mark, abrasions and contusions of the skin of the neck are usually not present. They may occur, however, if the assailant places his or her hands beneath and around the ligature and twists it, tightening it around the neck, or if the victim claws at the neck in an attempt to remove the ligature or relieve the pressure. If there is more than one loop of the ligature around the neck, there may be bruising of the skin if the ligature pinches the skin between two loops.

Manual Strangulation

Manual strangulation is produced by pressure of the hand, forearm, or other limb against the neck, compressing the internal structures of the neck. The mechanism of death is occlusion of the blood vessels supplying blood to the brain. Occlusion of the airway probably plays a minor, if any, role in causing death.

Virtually all manual strangulations are homicides. One cannot commit suicide by manual strangulation since as soon as consciousness is lost, pressure would be released and consciousness would be regained.

In most cases of manual strangulation, the assailant uses more force than is necessary to subdue and kill the victim. Hence, marks of violence are frequently present on the skin of the neck. Usually, there are abrasions, contusions, and fingernail marks on the skin (see Figure 10–28).

While in most manual strangulations, there is evidence of both external and internal injury to the neck, in some cases there is no injury, either externally or internally. For example, one medical examiner reports seeing three women in a three-month period who had been manually strangled. The first woman showed absolutely no evidence either externally or internally; the second showed congestion of the face with fine petechiae of the conjunctivae and skin of the face, but no evidence of injury to the neck, either externally or internally; and the third victim showed the classic evidence of injury: abrasions and scratches of the skin with extensive hemorrhage into the muscles of the neck. All three women were killed by the same individual. All three had blood alcohol levels above 0.30.

Figure 10–27
Death by Manual Strangulation
(*a and b*) Manual strangulation with fingernail marks and scratches on side of neck.

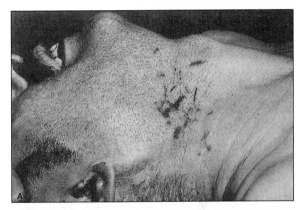

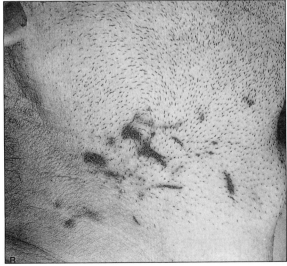

Source: Dominic J. DiMaio and Vincent J. M. DiMaio, *Forensic Pathology*, copyright 1989, reproduced with permission of copyright owner, CRC Press, Boca Raton, Florida.

The modus operandi of the perpetrator was to meet a woman in a bar, buy her liquor until she was extremely intoxicated, and then go off with her and have intercourse. He would then strangle her. At the time he strangled them, the women were unconscious due to acute alcohol intoxication, so a very minimal amount of pressure was necessary. He would place his hand over their necks and push downward, compressing the vessels of the neck. In the last case, the individual regained consciousness and struggled, with the resultant injuries. The perpetrator admitted having killed a number of other women the same way over the past years in a number of states.

In manual strangulation, the victims are usually female. When they are male, they are often highly intoxicated. It is suggested that in all manual strangulations, a complete toxicological screen be performed.

THE UNCOOPERATIVE VICTIM

Officers sometimes find victims uncooperative in identifying assailants and in providing details about offenses. When the victim is uncooperative, it is often for one of the following reasons:

- The assailant is a husband or boyfriend, wife or girlfriend, whose arrest would undo an arrangement from which the victim benefits.
- The victim wants to settle the dispute personally.
- The victim believes that he or she deserved the assault and therefore does not want the assailant punished.
- The victim fears revenge if charges are pursued.

The uncooperative victim creates both legal and investigative difficulties. All states consider felony assaults to be crimes against the people of the state; thus the state is legally considered the aggrieved party. Technically, the victim has no legal right to decide whether the offense will or will not be prosecuted. This decision is the prosecutor's. However, many prosecutors are reluctant to pursue the prosecution of a felony assault when the victim is going to be uncooperative, especially when the victim's injuries are not critical and when the parties involved are related. Because victims often do not know that the usual practice is not to prosecute such cases, they may be uncooperative or even fabricate a story about how the offense occurred. The officer's concern is to get the uncooperative victim to provide facts about the crime. There are a number of ways in which this may be done, but they generally revolve around convincing the victim that no legal action will be taken against the assailant. The laws vary from state to state, but in some jurisdictions informal arrangements have been worked out between the prosecutor's office or the courts and the police department, and under carefully controlled conditions the police may be given authority to have the victim sign a complaint-withdrawal affidavit, which includes the following:

- The name of the assailant.
- The victim's total satisfaction with the investigation by the police department.
- The victim's desire not to have the state pursue prosecution.

There are those who object to these practices because they believe such approaches tend to encourage assault offenses. They base their objection on the assumption that persons who commit assaults and are not punished will be encouraged to commit other assaults. Nevertheless, overcrowded court dockets and the difficulties associated with prosecuting cases with reluctant victims obviate any benefits that might derive from the full prosecution of such cases.

Many state and local governments have statutes and ordinances that make it unlawful either to withhold information relating to a crime intentionally or to provide false and misleading information about it. The victim who is uncooperative or who is suspected of not being completely truthful should be advised of such laws and of the penalties associated with them.

Incapacity may also be the cause of noncooperation. If the victim is intoxicated at the time of the initial interview, then it may be necessary to wait until he or she is sober before continuing. Naturally, if the severity of the injury makes any delay in interviewing unwise, then the investigator must proceed with the interview, while recognizing the inherent limitations.

SUICIDE

For the investigator, a major concern in an apparent suicide case is to make certain that the death was self-induced and not the result of a homicide. In some cases, the investigator finds overwhelming evidence to this effect at the scene. In other cases, important information about the victim's behavior before death can be obtained from relatives, friends, coworkers, and employers. Suicide is often committed for the following reasons:

- Ill health or considerable pain.
- Severe marital strife.
- A recent emotionally damaging experience, such as an unhappy love affair, separation, or divorce.
- Financial difficulties, including the threat of a much lower standard of living or failure to meet some significant and past-due financial commitments.
- Perceived or actual humiliation.
- Remorse over the loss of a loved one or over an act of one's own.
- Revenge, a frequent motive for adolescents who have serious difficulties with parents and for spurned lovers.[33]

These factors are far from all-inclusive, but the investigator will find a significant number of suicides associated with them. Conversely, if there is an apparent suicide and thorough scrutiny fails to produce a solid motive, then the investigator's suspicion should be aroused. Thus, in all apparent suicides the possibility of a criminal homicide should never be lightly discarded.

METHODS AND EVIDENCE OF SUICIDE

Nine methods are most commonly employed in suicides: shooting, hanging, ingestion of sleeping pills and other pharmaceuticals, drowning, cutting and piercing, ingestion of poisons, inhalation of gases, jumping from high places, and intentionally crashing an automobile.[34]

Although all of these can be simulated in the commission of murders, there are important differences in physical evidence that distinguish suicides from murders.

Gunshot Wounds

It is sometimes difficult to determine whether a gunshot wound was self-inflicted or resulted from the actions of an assailant. However, there are certain indicators that may be helpful in reaching a conclusion. One of these is the location of the wound and the trajectory of the projectile on entering the body. The most common method of committing suicide with a firearm involves the victim's placing a handgun to the temple and firing a shot into his or her head. Frequently, there is no exit wound, and it will be impossible for the investigator to determine the precise angle at which the projectile entered. This information is obtained during the autopsy, but it may be several days before this is performed. The investigator must therefore make some preliminary determination. The following case illustrates some of the points discussed thus far:

A man telephoned the police hysterically, reporting that his wife had just shot and killed herself. When the police and an ambulance arrived, the victim was dead of a bullet wound in her upper left temple. The husband was holding the gun with which he alleged his wife had shot herself. He stated that he had arrived home from work just before the incident but that neither his wife nor their three preschool-age children had been there. His wife had arrived home a short while later, and she had been drinking heavily. When he questioned her about the whereabouts of their three children, she had told him they were at his mother's home. A heated argument then followed about her neglect of their children, her drinking, and her seeing other men. According to the husband, his wife then slapped him in his face, and he slapped her back. At that point, she walked over to a nearby desk drawer, where he kept a revolver. She removed the revolver from the desk drawer, placed the barrel against her head, fired a single shot, and fell to the floor. No one else was home at the time this incident occurred.

The following set of facts was revealed by the medical examiner's autopsy report:

- The bullet entered the upper left portion of the head, traveled downward through the brain, and continued downward through the victim's body, coming to rest in her chest.
- There were no powder burns present around the gunshot wound.

- Death occurred immediately.

- If the wound had been self-inflicted, the victim would have been holding the weapon in her left hand, at least two feet from her head, and would have used her thumb to pull the trigger.

The relatives of both the victim and her husband provided the police with the following information:

- To their knowledge, the victim had not been despondent, nor had she ever previously attempted or discussed suicide.

- The victim and her husband had been having serious domestic difficulties because she was seeing other men, spending the house money on liquor, and not properly caring for their three young children.

- Both parties were known to have assaulted each other in domestic disputes in the past.

These facts tended to indicate that the victim's death was perhaps not a suicide but a criminal homicide. An interrogation of the husband established what the facts suggested. The husband related that he had been truthful about the events leading up to the argument but that after his wife slapped him, he had angrily knocked her to the floor, removed the revolver from the desk drawer, and gone back to his wife, who was now on her knees. Standing over her, he fired a single shot into her head. After shooting her, he became frightened and fabricated the story of his wife's suicide.

This case demonstrates the importance of two factors in the investigation of an alleged suicide. The first is the importance of the location of the wound on the body and its trajectory on entering the body. Second is the presence or absence of evidence indicating that the victim was predisposed to committing suicide.

In certain rare instances there may be more than one self-inflicted gunshot wound in the body. In an investigation conducted by one police department, a suicide victim was found with three gunshot wounds in the right temple, but the handgun reviewed at the scene had only two spent shells. Although there was considerable physical evidence at the scene, along with supporting historical data to suggest that the death was a suicide, the presence of the three wounds was an apparent contradiction of this evidence. The medical examiner's autopsy report revealed that two of the wounds were gunshot entrance wounds and that one wound was a gunshot exit wound. After establishing the nature of the three wounds, the medical examiner concluded that the victim first fired a single shot into his right temple. The bullet had failed to penetrate the skull, but instead slid under the scalp for a distance of approximately two inches and then exited. The victim's second shot into his head penetrated the skull and lodged in the brain. Death resulted as soon as the second shot was fired. The medical examiner hypothesized that the first shot did not penetrate the skull because of the angle at which the victim was holding the gun (see Figure 10–28).

Hammer-spur impressions can provide important physical evidence, as was the case several years ago when a homicide investigator and a police officer from the Identification Section of the Fairfax County, Virginia, Police Department were dispatched to an alleged suicide scene. On arriving, they were met by a patrol officer, who was conducting the preliminary investigation. The victim was a white male, 61 years of age, who had apparently died of a self-inflicted gunshot wound to the head; the weapon was still in the decedent's right hand. The victim's daughter, who discovered the body when she returned home from work, advised the investigating officer that her father had given her no indication that he was contemplating suicide.[35]

The decedent, found in the master bedroom, was clad in pajamas, lying on his back on the right side of the bed. There was a penetrating gunshot wound to the right side of the head; a 9-millimeter Walther pistol was located in the deceased's right hand. The hammer was cocked, with a 9-millimeter Winchester Western cartridge chambered. On the right thumb of the deceased was a hammer spur impression that contained class characteristics similar to the hammer spur on the pistol.

The impression was photographed and cast. The impression of the hammer spur of the pistol was found only to be similar in size and shape to the contours of the weapon's hammer. Yet it was one more piece of evidence supplied to the medical examiner to aid in determining whether the cause of the man's death was a self-inflicted gunshot wound (see Figure 10–29).

Figure 10–28
Self-Inflicted Gunshot Wounds
The medical examiner's autopsy revealed that the wound in the upper right portion of the head was the first gunshot entrance wound. The wound in the center was an exit wound resulting from the first gunshot, and the entry in the lower left portion of the photograph represents the second and fatal self-inflicted wound.

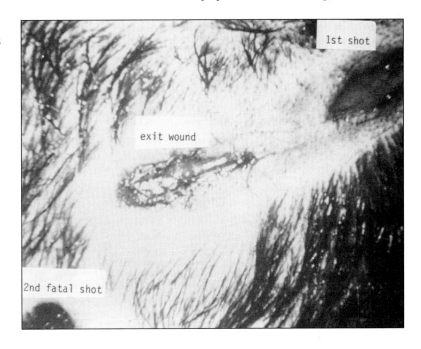

Figure 10–29
Comparison Microscope Used in a Suicide Investigation
Comparison microscope photograph of a hammer-spur impression and the actual hammer spur.

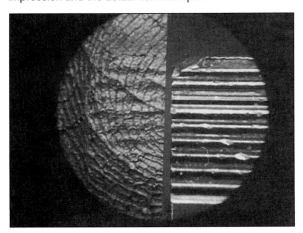

(Courtesy Federal Bureau of Investigation)

While examining the scene, investigators look for the usual physical evidence associated with gunshots to be present on the deceased. This includes a contact entrance wound, blood spattered on the hand or hands, and gunshot residue on the hand that held the gun. An item of physical evidence often overlooked is the presence of a hammer-spur impression on the decedent's finger or fingers; this enhances the probability that death was caused by a self-inflicted gunshot wound. These impressions often are obliterated and subsequently overlooked when inked fingerprint impressions are taken for comparison and identification purposes.

The hammer-spur impression is caused when the firearm is cocked in the single-action phase, causing the principal identifying features of the hammer—for example, machine marks, outline of the hammer size and shape, and contours formed through wear and accidental damage—to be impressed into the skin of the finger. If blood circulation stops soon after the fatal wound is inflicted, some or all of the characteristics revealed in the impression may remain on the finger that cocked the weapon for several hours after death.

Hanging
Certain misconceptions associated with suicidal hangings can lead to erroneous conclusions. The first is that the victim's neck gets broken; the second, that the feet are off the floor. Although both of these conditions *may* occur, they are exceptions rather than the rule. The first misconception is related to the circumstances of legal executions by

hanging. In legal executions the procedures involved in inflicting death are intended to result in the neck being broken. This is accomplished by the use of a specific type of noose and a gallows with a trap door through which the person will drop some distance before being abruptly stopped. However, in a suicidal hanging, even when the feet are suspended, the neck is rarely broken, because the fall is not long enough to cause the jolt necessary to break the neck.

It is also common in suicidal hangings for the victim's feet or even the knees to be touching the ground. Occasionally, the victim is found in a sitting position (see Figure 10–30). Finding victims in these positions often creates suspicion because it is

difficult for inexperienced investigators to understand how anyone could remain in these positions while slowly choking to death. They might improperly conclude that the victim first was rendered unconscious or was killed and placed in the hanging position. It is more likely, however, that the victim did not slowly choke to death, but rather first tied the rope around some supporting device and then around his or her neck. Pressure was then applied by the victim either by crouching down, if in a standing position, or leaning forward, if in a sitting position. This initial pressure painlessly cuts off the flow of blood to the brain, which results in unconsciousness. When unconsciousness does occur, the full weight of the body is then applied to the noose,

Figure 10–30
Various Positions in Hanging

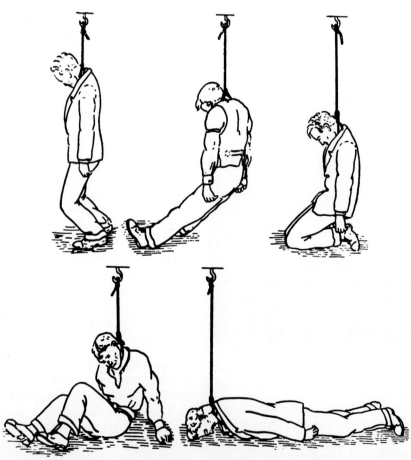

Source: Arne Svensson and Otto Wendel, *Techniques of Crime Scene Investigation* (New York: Elsevier-North Holland, 1973) p. 352. Reprinted by permission of the publisher.

whereupon all oxygen is cut off to the brain and death follows. There is very little physical pain associated with suicides of this type. If one considers that many suicidal hangings occur in victims' homes, then it is logical to expect the feet not to be suspended above the floor because few household objects are strong enough to hold the weight of a fully suspended body or one that has fallen several feet from a chair or table.

Livor mortis is most pronounced in the lower portion of the arms and legs and around the face, lips, and jaw. There may be some variations in the location of the discoloration, depending on the position of the body. When death occurs in this manner, one frequently finds petechial hemorrhaging in the eyes, caused when small blood vessels in the eye bleed because blood pressure increases in response to compression around the neck (see Figure 10–31).

Occasionally, hangings are accidental, not suicidal. The individual may have himself in a modified hanging position while masturbating and accidentally fall, slip, and knock over the object on which he is standing, resulting in an accidental death, known as autoerotic death or sexual asphyxia; the intent is sexual rather than suicidal. In these cases, the genitals are exposed and semen may be present. Chapter 11, Sex-Related Offenses, provides an in-depth explanation of autoerotic death. The presence of feces and urine is common because of the total relaxation of the bladder and bowel muscles at the time of death.

Figure 10–31
Petechial Hemorrhaging in the Eye
Victim of suicidal hanging.

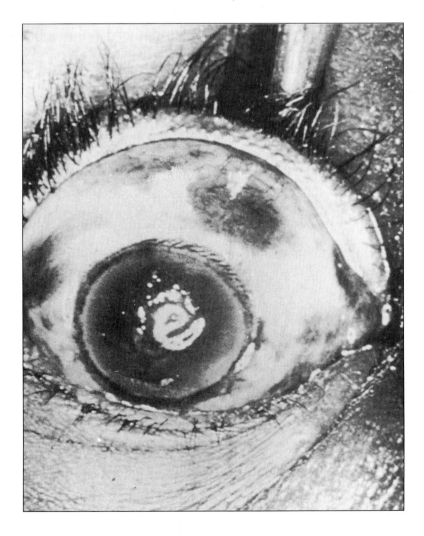

Sleeping Pills and Other Pharmaceuticals

Sleeping pills and other pharmaceuticals have for many years been a common means of committing suicide. However, some deaths resulting from the ingestion of sleeping pills or tranquilizing drugs may be accidental, not suicidal. The investigator has an obligation to determine whether the death was accidental or suicidal. Certain types of medication, such as barbiturates, when mixed with alcohol have a synergistic effect, which increases the potency of the drug beyond its normal strength. One should not be too quick to decide that the death is a suicide until the investigation is completed and some evidence is available to support this conclusion. In these cases, the investigator should seize as evidence any remaining medication and its container. Frequently, the container identifies the medication, the drugstore dispensing it, and the physician prescribing it. There is always the possibility that the medication was purchased or obtained illegally, thus complicating the investigative process. As in all apparent suicides, the investigator should conduct interviews of relatives, friends, or neighbors who may be able to provide background information about the victim.

Drowning

The majority of drowning incidents are either accidental or suicidal, but some are homicidal. Three questions must be answered in apparent drowning cases before any final conclusions can be reached: Was the cause of death drowning, or was the victim first killed and then placed in water? If the cause of death was drowning, did it take place in the water where the body was recovered, or was the victim drowned elsewhere and then placed in the water where found? Was the victim conscious when placed in the water? Answers to these questions can be obtained by external examination of the body by the investigator. External signs to indicate that the victim was alive and conscious when entering the water include:

- Objects clutched in the hand, such as grass or bottom soil commonly found in water.
- Fingernail marks on the palms of the hands.
- White, pink, or red foam extruding from the nose and open mouth.

- Livor mortis most marked in the head and neck because the body settled with these parts in a dependent position.[36]

An internal examination by a physician serves to establish whether death occurred by drowning. The following may be found in drowning cases:

- The chest cavity and the lungs are distended and soggy, with fine foam in the trachea and bronchi.
- The heart is flabby, with its right side dilated and filled with dark red fluid. The blood is unclotted and usually hemolyzed due to the absorption of the drowning fluid into the system.
- The mastoid cells of the ear have hemorrhaged.
- Air embolisms may have formed in the blood in deep-water drownings.
- There may be water in the stomach and duodenum.
- Algae and other marine particles may be found in the stomach and adhering to the sides of the air passages.

In removing the body from the water, the investigator may notice considerable damage to portions of the victim's body, especially around the head and face. This should not cause the investigator to conclude prematurely that the victim was the object of foul play. Some bodies of water contain many rocks and shells; a free-floating body that is subject to strong currents can be repeatedly slammed into and dragged across such objects, causing severe damage, especially to the forehead, knees, tops of the feet, and backs of the hands. In addition, if the water is rich with fish, crabs, and other marine life, these too can cause damage. It is not unusual for the lips, ears, and nose to be at least partially eaten away (see Figure 10–32). The extent of damage from the objects or marine life in the water varies; understanding what can result from their presence minimizes the possibility of premature conclusions. But the investigator must not prematurely conclude either that all damage resulted after the body was placed in the water. The medical examiner can help draw conclusions about the actual nature of wounds.

Figure 10–32
Decomposition and Marine Life Damage to an Immersed Body

Damage sustained by the victim in this photograph occurred while immersed in water. Note that the ears and eyelids are completely missing and there is extensive damage to the nostrils and lips. These are areas that are among the first attacked by marine life.

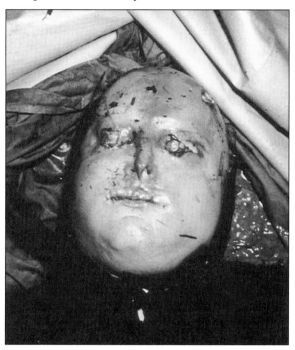

Cutting and Piercing Instruments

The instruments ordinarily employed in suicides by cutting are razor blades, knives, and occasionally glass. One of the common characteristics of suicides inflicted by these instruments is the presence of hesitation marks. Hesitation marks are a series of lesser wounds inflicted by the victim in the general region of the fatal wound, often the wrists, forearms, or throat. In certain throat cuttings, it may be possible to reach a conclusion about whether the injury was self-inflicted or resulted from an assault. If a wound is self-inflicted, it tends to be deep at the point of entry and to shallow out at its terminus, which is near, or slightly past, the midline of the throat. In homicidal throat cutting, the wound appears deep from the start to the terminus. It is not unusual for a victim to inflict a series of severe cuts on different parts of the body to ensure death. The reasons vary, sometimes involving the influence of alcohol or hallucinogenic drugs. The ingestion of drugs may have been a planned prelude to the act of self-destruction. Self-inflicted wounds can be surprisingly brutal and tend to make people disbelieve that they were self-imposed, particularly when mutilation of the sexual parts is involved. In one case, a 28-year-old man used a single-edged razor blade to cut off his penis. When questioned by paramedics, the man said: "Its just been eating away at me for so long and when I thought about it, I heard voices saying 'Do it, do it.' I was just angry at myself. I had it all planned out and I did it."[37]

Poisons

The ingestion of liquid poisons is sometimes clear from outward signs on the body. Powerful caustic lyes or acids may produce vomiting once the liquid reaches the digestive tract. There is considerable damage to lips, tongue, and mouth, and there may be blood in the vomitus, along with pieces of the esophagus and stomach (see Figure 10–33). Usually, death does not occur rapidly, and victims may employ another means of suicide to stop the excruciating pain.

Cases of suspected poisoning frequently pose very difficult problems to the police investigator and to the medical examiner. Many poisons produce symptoms similar to those of certain diseases, a fact that can complicate determination of whether a crime has been committed. However, if there is any reason to suspect poisoning, the investigation must proceed along the lines of a possible homicide, suicide, or accidental death, until death due to natural causes is established.[38] To compound the problem, suicides and accidental deaths by poisoning are sometimes very difficult to distinguish from homicide. Alcohol, when consumed with certain medications, may result in an accidental (possibly suicidal) death by respiratory failure. An example is the combination of barbiturates and alcohol. When the alcohol level in the blood reaches about half the lethal dose, most individuals lose consciousness and thus stop drinking. But with the addition of a stimulant, such as an amphetamine, this effect may not occur, and individuals may drink a lethal dose of alcohol before they fall into a coma.

Actually, poisoning is now rarely used in homicides because modern laboratory techniques can

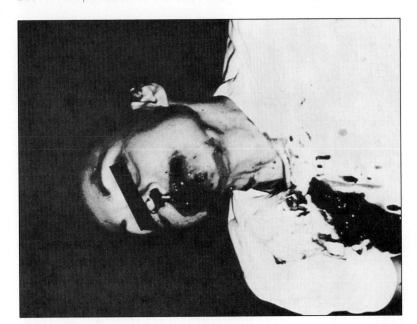

Figure 10–33
Ingestion of a Caustic Drain Cleaner
This victim committed suicide by ingesting a strong caustic drain cleaner. On ingestion, vomiting was induced, thereby causing severe burns to the nose, chin, and chest area.

readily detect most poisons, thus unmasking an intended homicide. But when it is the method, a wide variety of poisons may be used.

Even though the crime scene investigators seldom can identify the chemical compound that-caused the death, they should be alert to the general range of possibilities and the potentially hazardous environmental factors that may be connected with a poisoning.

Regardless of the nature of the incident—homicide, suicide, or accident—the symptoms of death by poison are the same. The field investigator should attempt to determine if the victim had any of the symptoms—vomiting, convulsions, diarrhea, paralysis, rapid or slow breathing, contracted or dilated pupils, changes in skin color, or difficulty in swallowing just prior to death. These symptoms are general manifestations of systemic poisoning. They do not provide proof of poisoning but can be meaningful in relation to other evidence. Someone who observed the victim just before death provides the best source of information concerning his or her symptoms. If no witness is available, the investigator must rely all the more on physical evidence from the crime scene. Table 10-1 lists common poisons and their associated physical manifestations.

The investigator should collect all available information concerning the activities of the victim during the last three days of life. Information on types of medication taken, when the last meal was eaten, and where it was eaten can be very important in determining the type of poison involved. Medical history may indicate that death was due to natural causes.

The *toxicologist* is concerned with the identification and recognition of poisons, with their physiological effects on humans and animals, and with their antidotes. Crime laboratories usually provide some toxicological support but vary considerably in the amount and type that they can furnish. However, full toxicological support is always available through a combination of hospital, medical examiner's, coroner's, and criminalistics laboratories. Crime laboratories can direct police to local facilities.

If the investigator suspects that poison was ingested, a diligent search should be conducted for the container. In suicides and accidental poisonings, the container frequently is close at hand. Even though a container appears empty, it should be processed for fingerprints, packaged, marked, and forwarded to the laboratory for examination. Additionally, any other object that could reasonably

Table 10–1
Poisons and Associated Physical Manifestations

Type of Poison	Symptom or Evidence
Caustic poison (lye)	Characteristic burns around lips and mouth of victim
Carbon monoxide	Victim's skin takes on an abnormally bright cherry red color
Sulfuric acid	Black vomit
Hydrochloric acid	Greenish-brown vomit
Nitric acid	Yellow vomit
Silver salts	White vomit turning black in daylight
Copper sulfate	Blue-green vomit
Phosphorus	Coffee-brown vomit, onion or garlic odor
Cyanide	Burnt almond odor in air, cherry red lividity color
Ammonia, vinegar, Lysol, etc.	Characteristic odors
Arsenic, mercury, lead salts	Pronounced diarrhea
Methyl (wood) alcohol, isopropyl (rubbing) alcohol	Nausea and vomiting, unconsciousness, possibly blindness

Source: Richard H. Fox and Carl L. Cunningham, *Crime Scene Search and Physical Evidence Handbook* (Washington, D.C.: Government Printing Office, 1985), p. 126.

relate to the poisoning should be collected, such as unwashed dishes and glasses, wastebasket contents, envelopes, and medicine containers.

Gases
The gas most frequently involved in medico-legal investigations is carbon monoxide. When a death does result from this gas, it is generally accidental or suicidal. Carbon monoxide is found in automobile exhaust fumes and improperly ventilated space heaters in homes. In a death caused by auto emissions, the individual may have started the engine of the vehicle in the garage after closing the garage door or may have extended a flexible hose from the exhaust pipe into the vehicle and then closed the windows.

When death occurs from carbon monoxide poisoning, the victim's skin takes on an abnormally bright cherry red color because of the reaction of the red blood cells to the gas. The red blood cells have a very high affinity for carbon monoxide molecules (approximately 210 times greater than for oxygen), absorbing them rapidly, making them incapable of absorbing oxygen, and rendering them

dysfunctional in the life-sustaining process. Death generally occurs when the red blood cells have reached a saturation level usually above 40 percent, although this varies, the level sometimes going higher before death results if the victim is asleep, due to the body's reduced oxygen needs.

Jumping from High Places
The major question to be answered in death resulting from jumping is whether the victim voluntarily leaped or was thrown or pushed. Often, there are witnesses who can provide this information, suicide notes, or background information that indicates previous suicide attempts or a predisposition toward suicide.

Vehicle Suicide
The motor vehicle as a means of suicide, although not as common as the means previously discussed, is one that police officers should be sensitive to. Usually a vehicle suicide entails a single occupant speeding into an off-road obstacle. Physical evidence to look for in these accidents includes a lack of skid marks, indications that the person did not

attempt to stop or avoid the obstacle, and shoe-sole imprints.

Shoe-sole imprints can provide information regarding the position of a driver's feet and thus his or her action. Most imprints are found on soft-soled shoes, but some are found on hard leather soles. These shoe imprints are clear and indisputable impressions; they are not simply dust marks that may be easily erased by rubbing the sole with a finger or cloth. A word of caution to the police officers—these marks are evidence and must be handled properly. For laboratory personnel to properly examine the sole imprint, control pedals from the car need to be removed. Routinely officers should examine the brake, clutch, and accelerator. These pedals, as well as other floor-mounted controls such as the dimmer switch, should be collected as evidence. Figure 10–34

shows an accelerator pattern imprinted on a tennis-shoe sole. The driver and only occupant committed suicide by crashing the motor vehicle against a concrete support next to a highway. The imprint comparison provided evidence that it had been a suicide, and follow-up investigation revealed the suicidal tendencies of the deceased.

All of the deceased's clothing should be retained as evidence. Officers need to alert the personnel in the hospital emergency room that the person's clothing must not be discarded, regardless of its condition. Additionally, officers at the crash scene must find any shoes that may have been torn off during the force of the crash and strewn about the area. At the laboratory, the clothing is examined. Marks on shoe soles are compared with patterns on the control pedals.

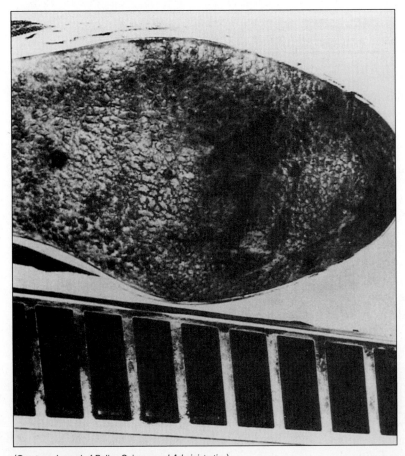

Figure 10–34
Accelerator Pattern Clearly Imprinted on Tennis-Shoe Sole
The driver and only occupant successfully committed suicide by crashing her motor vehicle against a concrete support of an elevated highway.

(Courtesy *Journal of Police Science and Administration*)

It is only after painstaking investigation that a death is determined to be a suicide. By recognizing some of the important evidence of self-inflicted wounds, investigators contribute to the successful solution of the death investigation.[39]

THE SUICIDE NOTE

Research indicates that suicide notes are not left in most suicides. One study revealed certain facts about those who do and do not leave notes. Generally there are no differences between the two groups in age, race, sex, employment, marital status, history of mental illness, place of suicide, reported causes or unusual circumstances preceding the act, medical care and supervision, or history of previous suicidal attempts or threats. However, the note writers differed from the non-note writers in the methods used to kill themselves. The note writers used poisons, firearms, and hanging more often as a means of death than did the non-note writers.[40]

GENDER DIFFERENCES IN SUICIDAL BEHAVIOR

Studies of suicide in the United States indicate that the suicide rate is higher for men than for women, whereas the attempted suicide rate is higher for women than men. There is some evidence to suggest that there are often differences between men and women in the methods employed to commit suicide, women preferring barbiturates and poisons. If women do use a firearm, the fatal wound is frequently in the body rather than the head. It has been suggested that these methods are used because they are not disfiguring and that women appear to be concerned more often about their appearance after death than are men. It is not uncommon for a female to leave a note to her female friends or relatives specifying in detail the clothes she wishes to be buried in along with details relating to facial cosmetics.[41]

In contrast, some males kill themselves where their body will not be discovered by family members, such as in the woods. These types of suicides can create investigative problems, especially if a note is not written. For example, if a passer-by is tempted to steal a gun and valuables from a suicide victim, the police may think that the death was a murder and robbery rather than suicide.

SUICIDE-INSURANCE SCHEMES

Sometimes individuals take their own lives and try to convey the impression that the death was accidental or even homicidal. Generally, they try to create this impression because they have invested in insurance policies that will not pay out money to the beneficiary if a death is self-inflicted. The following case illustrates such an instance:

Several years ago an Armenian man from Iran died in the Marina del Rey area of Los Angeles, California, when a bomb blew up his car. At first investigators believed that it might have been a terrorist killing. However, after a long investigation, the investigators concluded that the man had killed himself in a way that looked like a terrorist attack to allow his father to collect more than $1 million from newly secured insurance policies.

Victor R. Galustian, 42, had lived in Los Angeles since 1950, when his father returned to Iran. His father had sent him money illegally from Iran for safekeeping against the day when the father would come to the United States. Galustian used the money to entertain acquaintances at lavish restaurant dinners, passing himself off as a real estate businessman or sometimes an engineer.

Because the money entered this country illegally, it is impossible to know just how much Galustian received, but investigators estimate that he spent at least $600,000 of the money his father had sent. Desperate when he learned that his father was planning to return to this country, Galustian began planning how to regain the money he had spent. He took out numerous insurance policies shortly before he died, with his father as beneficiary. All the policies had double-indemnity clauses, which double the benefits if the policyholder dies an unnatural death. The policies prohibit payoff if the policyholder commits suicide.

Early one morning, Galustian was driving his car near his apartment when a powerful explosive under his front seat went off, propelling Galustian's body 25 feet from the demolished auto and spewing debris for 600 feet. The explosion occurred after an outbreak of violence involving local Armenian and Iranian families. Authorities initially believed that the explosion, too, might be political. A few days before his death, Galustian had told a security guard in his apartment building that he had found a bomb in his car. That and other clues, including his lack of political activity in the

Armenian community, convinced investigators that Galustian's death was not the result of a political attack. It took investigators several months to piece it together, but they eventually concluded that it was a suicide.[42]

VEHICLE HOMICIDES

Few drivers in fatal hit-and-run accidents intended the accident to occur. The driver generally fails to stop for one or more of the following reasons:

- The driver had been drinking.
- The vehicle was stolen.
- The driver had a suspended or revoked operator's license.
- There was someone in the car whose presence, if discovered, could cause additional problems (for instance, someone else's spouse).
- The driver had no liability insurance.
- The driver or a passenger was injured, thus requiring a trip to the nearest emergency room.
- The driver did not realize that he or she had hit anyone.
- The driver had committed a crime before the accident and still had evidence of it in the vehicle.

PHYSICAL EVIDENCE FROM HIT-AND-RUN ACCIDENTS

The physical evidence created by hit-and-run accidents is located at the scene, on the victim's body, and on the hit-and-run vehicle. The physical evidence left by the vehicle typically is broken glass from headlights, paint fragments, and underbody debris. Chapter 4, Physical Evidence, provides an in-depth explanation of the potential of these items as physical evidence. The investigator may also find broken equipment, which can provide extremely valuable clues in identifying the make, model, and year of the hit-and-run vehicle, especially if the equipment was manufactured for a specific model. Broken equipment at the scene can often be matched to parts on the hit-and-run vehicle.

Tire marks typically are found in mud, clay, dirt, snow, warm tar, and sometimes on the body of the

Figure 10–35
Hit-and-Run Victim

Tire tread marks across arm and chest on a 42-year-old man who, while asleep in a parking lot, was run over by a truck.

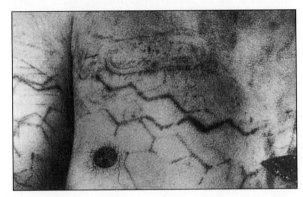

Source: Dominic J. DiMaio and Vincent J. DiMaio, *Forensic Pathology* (New York: Elsevier, 1990).

victim (see Figure 10–35). If a good negative impression is left and the hit-and-run vehicle is recovered, it can often lead to a positive identification. As with all other physical evidence, the tire prints should be protected, photographed, and measured before any efforts are made to make a cast.

Skid marks show the direction of travel before the accident and allow for estimates of the speed of the vehicle. Skid marks, unlike tire marks, provide clues regarding direction of travel prior to the accident and the estimated speed of the vehicle. The absence of skid marks at the point of impact suggests a variety of things. The driver may not have seen the victim ahead of time, possibly because the driver fell asleep at the wheel or was intoxicated or because visibility was poor. This would also be the case if the skid marks appear only after the point of impact. If there are no skid marks at all, the investigator should consider the possibility of planned vehicular assault. However, most modern vehicles are equipped with antiskid braking systems, which is another possibility to consider in the absence of skid marks.

The investigator is looking for complementary physical evidence between the hit-and-run vehicle and the victim. Because the physical evidence may be quite small, such as paint fragments or a few fibers from the victim's clothing, the investigator must take painstaking efforts in searching for, collecting, and preserving such evidence. If the accident involved a pedestrian, his or her clothing may be of value in two ways. First, fibers from the victim's clothing may adhere to the vehicle, and these can be compared and matched. They are likely to be found on or near the part of the vehicle first striking the victim. If the victim was rolled under the vehicle, pieces of cloth, blood, hair, and skin may adhere to the undercarriage. Second, fiber marks from the victim's clothing may be embedded in the paint of the hit-and-run vehicle.

The medical examiner should obtain blood samples from the victim for possible comparison with blood found on the hit-and-run vehicle. In addition, the victim's blood should be analyzed for the presence of alcohol or drugs, because the victim's condition at the time of the accident may have contributed to the accident.

On occasion, it may be important to determine if the headlights of a hit-and-run vehicle were on or off at the time of the accident. For example, a driver suspected of being involved in a nighttime hit-and-run collision claimed that the damage to his car was done in a previous daytime accident. Examination of the damaged headlight showed that the headlights were on at the time of the collision. This finding by the investigator suggested that the damage to the suspect's vehicle was done during the evening hours and not during the daytime, as stated by the driver.

Determining whether a vehicle's headlights were on or off at the time of impact is done by examining the filament. The effect of a crack on a filament is quite different when the filament is incandescent and when it is cold. This fact gives two bases for judging whether the lamp was on or off. First, if the glass breaks and air replaces the nitrogen surrounding the filament, oxygen in the air has no effect on a cold filament but quickly blackens an incandescent one. Second, if the glass does not break, collision shock may sharply fracture a cold, brittle filament but it will stretch out and uncoil an incandescent filament, which is quite elastic in this condition.[43] Investigators therefore should be certain to preserve not only the external glass lens of the lamp but its internal components as well, especially when there is a question of whether the headlights were on or off at the time of the accident.

SEARCH FOR THE VEHICLE

The steps to be taken in searching for a hit-and-run vehicle depend mainly on information provided by witnesses and victim and by physical evidence located at the scene. In the absence of eyewitnesses or physical evidence that readily identifies the suspect or the vehicle, the investigator may have to use logic and deductive reasoning. For example, the investigator may often safely assume that the driver of the vehicle was at the scene of the accident because the driver was coming from someplace and going to another place by apparently the best route. But in some cases drivers are lost or otherwise unaware of where they are and what they are doing. These cases are exceptions.

Three significant facts should be determined by the investigator in seeking to discover the driver's objective: first, the time of the accident; second, the direction of travel; and third, if it can be learned, the direction of travel after the accident.[44] Every area has certain features that investigators must consider in making tentative assumptions. For example, let us assume that a hit-and-run vehicle was described by witnesses as a flashy sports car driven by a man approximately 20 years old. The accident occurred on a weekday at 9:00 A.M. Before the accident, the vehicle was traveling in the direction of a nearby college. In the absence of other evidence, the investigator might assume that the vehicle was being driven by a student to the college. Of course, this assumption could be totally erroneous, but when there are no solid leads, then the only initial course of action may be to apply logical and deductive reasoning.

If the investigator can locate physical evidence or a witness who can identify the make, model, year, and color of the vehicle, a detailed notice should be sent out to area repair shops, garages, and parts stores. If the damage to the vehicle is severe, the driver generally does one of several things. First, the driver may try to keep the car concealed in a private garage. Second, the driver may take the vehicle to a repair shop. Third, the driver may try to purchase the replacement parts from a dealer or junkyard.

In some situations, investigators ask for help from the news media and, through them, help from the public. They may do so when existing clues are sparse.

FIRE DEATHS

Frequently, human remains are found at the scene of a fire. Properly examined, these remains may provide important data to the investigator about the facts surrounding the fire and the cause of death. Investigators should ask these questions:

- Was the decedent accidentally killed by the fire (whether or not the fire was caused by arson)?
- Was the decedent deliberately killed by the fire?
- Was the decedent already dead when the fire occurred?

To answer these questions, investigators should determine certain facts. These facts are outlined in the remainder of this section.[45]

COORDINATION AND COOPERATION

Coordination of and cooperation between police and fire investigators are of paramount importance in the successful investigation of any questioned fire. As with other forms of physical evidence at a fire scene, a body should never be moved until fully examined at the scene unless there is some possibility that the person is still alive or there is danger of further destruction of the body if it remains where it is. Also, because a dead human being is probably the most complex and rapidly changing type of physical evidence at a crime scene, cooperation between medical personnel (preferably forensic pathologists) and investigators is essential. This coordination should extend from the scene of the fire to the medical facility where the postmortem examination is conducted.

DEGREES OF BURNING

Burns are medically classified into four types. The extent of burns may provide information about the proximity of the body to the point of origin of the fire, the length of time the body was exposed to the fire, and the intensity of the fire.

First-degree burns are superficial and limited to the outer layers of skin. Although the burned area is red and swollen, blisters do not form and peeling may follow. Second-degree burns involve blistering and the destruction of the upper layers of skin.

Scarring occasionally results in living victims. In third-degree burns, the entire thickness of the skin (epidermis and dermis) is destroyed. In living victims with third-degree burns, pain is usually absent as nerve endings are destroyed; scarring results and skin grafting is usually necessary. Fourth-degree burns completely destroy (char) the skin and underlying tissue (see Figure 10–36).

The degree of incineration of the body should be considered in comparison with other facts and circumstances of the fire. Are the burns of the decedent consistent with the nature of the fire and other burned areas? Body mass should be considered, keeping in mind that faster and greater destruction occurs to smaller, lighter bodies. Less destruction may be expected in ordinary house fires (usually of 1,200°F or less) than in fires accelerated, for example, by certain chemicals. Complete incineration of a body, as in cremation, usually takes 1½ hours at temperatures of 1,600° to 1,800°F, resulting in an ash weight of 2 to 3 pounds for an adult.

IDENTIFICATION OF REMAINS

Because fire destroys human tissue, identification of the remains may be especially difficult. Yet because identification of a decedent is a key factor in any questioned death investigation, an orderly, sequential approach must be used in the identification process. The six methods that follow should be considered in sequence, from the "best" identification means to the "worst."

Fingerprints
Although considered the best means of identification because of centralized files of fingerprints, fingerprint identification may not be possible in fire death cases due to the destruction of the skin.

Dentition
Being the hardest substance in the human body, teeth are frequently the best form of identification for fire victims. The only drawback is that in order to make a dental comparison, one must have something to compare the decedent's teeth with. The investigator must have some idea of who the decedent was.

DNA Printing
Following recent advances, identification using DNA printing (described in Chapter 4, Physical

Evidence) has emerged as a viable tool in identifying fire death victims. As with dental records, the investigator must have some indication of the identity of the deceased before DNA printing can yield results.

Scars, Marks, or Tattoos on the Exterior of the Body

These abnormalities on the skin, like fingerprints, are frequently obscured or destroyed by the fire.

Scars, Marks, Abnormalities, or Appliances inside the Body

Bone abnormalities, surgical appliances, or operative scars may be helpful, but the investigator must have some idea of who the victim was so that appropriate medical records may be examined.

Identification, Jewelry, and Clothing on the Body

The least desirable method is a last resort due to the possibility of substitution. Indeed, in some arson and/or murder cases, the body is disguised to look like someone else.

SCENE CONSIDERATIONS

As with any physical evidence, burned bodies must be sketched, measured, and photographed in place and in relation to other evidence at the scene of the fire. The actual location of the bodies may be crucial to the investigation. Determination as to whether the decedent was a smoker is important for establishing the cause of the fire and whether he or she was alive at the time of the fire.

EXAMINATION OF THE EXTERNAL BODY

The body of the deceased should be examined in detail both at the scene and again at the morgue. Significant areas for examination include those discussed below.

Signs of Trauma

Any sign of injury to the external body should be carefully noted, sketched, and photographed. The use of a five-power magnifying glass (as a minimum) is required, because fire obscures signs of injury.

Skull Fracture

Another factor that may be misconstrued is the discovery that the victim's skull is fractured. Care must be taken to determine whether the fracture is implosive or explosive. An implosive fracture may have been caused by a fall, may be evidence of a prior felonious assault or homicide, or may result from a collapsed structural member. The exact cause will be determined at autopsy and evaluated during the follow-up investigation. An explosive fracture, however, is usually a natural consequence of fire. The extreme heat may cause the fluids in and around the brain to boil and expand. The resulting steam produces pressure sufficient to cause an explosive (pressure-release) reaction (see Figure 10–36). The fracture(s) that result usually follow the natural suture lines of the skull. In extreme cases, the cranium may burst, causing the expelled brain and skull matter to form a circular pattern around the head. This is more common in children than in adults: the fontanel, or membrane-covered opening between the uncompleted parietal bones, is the weakest point in a fetal or young skull. The resulting circular pattern (0 to 12 inches from the skull) is significant when compared with the type of splattering that might result from a shotgun blast or high-order explosion.[46]

Blistering and Splitting Skin

The inexperienced investigator may be somewhat apprehensive in attempting to evaluate the effects of heat and flame on the skin of the victim. The medical investigator is in the best position to render a judgment in this area.

The formation of blisters (vesicles) is part of the body's natural defense system. The exact distinction between antemortem and postmortem blistering can be made only at autopsy. There are, however, certain signs that a medical investigator can use in developing a hypothesis. Postmortem blisters are generally limited in size and may contain only air or air mixed with a small amount of body fluid. Antemortem blisters are larger in size and contain a complex mix of body fluids. The precise determination of the fluids requires microscopic analysis. A blister surrounded by a pink or red ring can be considered to have occurred before death; the reddish ring is the result of an antemortem inflammatory reaction.

In some instances, temperatures may not have been sufficiently high to produce blistering. Likewise, if the skin is burned off or otherwise heavily damaged, blistering will not be evident.

The heat and flames of the fire also cause the skin to shrink or tighten and ultimately split. The splitting or lesions may be seen on the arms, legs, and torso. At first glance this condition, coupled with pugilistic attitude (see below), could be misinterpreted as indicating defense wounds.

In some cases, a seriously burned person survives the fire and is removed to a burn center. In an effort to save the person, the medical staff at the center may attempt to duplicate the natural splitting of the skin with a surgical technique known as an *escharotomy*. This technique is used to help foster circulation and to prevent the onset of gangrene. Should the burn victim die some time after the fire, these splits should not be misinterpreted as fire-induced.[47]

Noncranial Fractures

If enough heat is applied, bones shrink, warp, and fracture. Determining whether fractures were caused by a trauma or heat requires painstaking examination.

Pugilistic Attitude

The so-called pugilistic attitude of the body is a natural result of the dehydrating effect caused by the heat from the fire and is not related to the cause or manner of death. The arms and legs will be drawn into a posture resembling that of a boxer (see Figure 10–36).

More often than not in these cases, a forensic pathologist who is an expert on burned bodies may have to be summoned.

EXAMINATION OF THE INTERNAL BODY

After the body has been closely examined, sketched, and photographed, an internal examination of the body should be conducted by a forensic pathologist. Investigators should attend this procedure to get information about the facts, to correct discrepancies in data (such as measurements), and to recover evidence from the body. Significant areas for examination are as follows:

Figure 10–36
Pugilistic Attitude
Victim of vehicle fire, showing pugilistic attitude of arms and hands and separation of the skull from the top of the head resulting from the intense heat of the fire. This is also an example of fourth-degree burns, in which the skin and underlying tissues are completely destroyed.

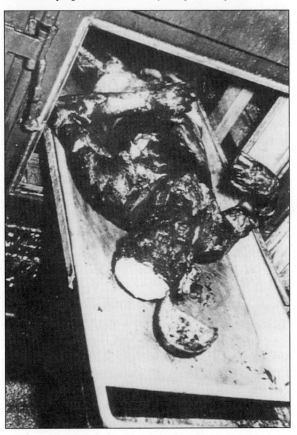

Soot, Other Debris, or Burning in the Air Passages

These findings may indicate that the decedent was breathing while the fire was burning.

Pulmonary Edema

Frothy substance in the lungs may result from irritants breathed in during a fire.

Epidural Hemorrhages

Hemorrhages above the tough membrane covering the brain (the dura mater) and under the skull may occur at the rear of the head due to heat. These hemorrhages should not be mistaken for the hemorrhages associated with blunt force injuries.[48]

Internal Injuries

All internal injuries should be closely examined, measured, and photographed, with samples taken by the pathologist for later microscopic examination.

Foreign Objects

Any foreign objects found in the body, such as bullets, should be recovered as evidence by the investigator. Because these objects are frequently small and difficult to locate, X-ray examination of the body before internal examination is recommended.

TOXICOLOGIC EXAMINATION

The pathologist should take samples for later examination by a toxicologist. Toxicologic results may be of extreme importance to the investigation.

Alcohol

Alcohol in blood indicates whether the decedent was incapacitated at the time of the fire and thus unable to escape. A finding of high levels of alcohol raises questions for the investigator about the decedent's habits.

Other Drugs

Indications of other possibly incapacitating drugs may provide new leads. The possibility of drug interactions—barbiturates with alcohol, for example—should also be considered.

Carboxyhemoglobin

Carbon monoxide (CO) is an odorless, colorless gas present at hazardous levels in all structural fires. Carbon monoxide asphyxiation (usually about 40 percent saturation) is probably the single most common cause of death in fires. As previously discussed, CO causes the cherry red color of postmortem lividity (as well as that of internal organs and muscle tissue).

At autopsy, the pathologist will test the victim's blood for the level of carboxyhemoglobin–carbon monoxide present in the pigment of the red blood cells. The concentration of carbon monoxide in the blood is a very important element in determining whether the victim was alive before and during the fire. Its concentration is quantified in terms of a percentage of saturation. Because carbon monoxide in the blood is generally due to the inhalation of CO during the fire, the absence of CO in the red blood cells (less than a 10 percent saturation) would be rather conclusive evidence that the victim was dead prior to the fire.[49]

Presence of Other Chemicals

Chemicals given off by burning materials may indicate the accelerant of the fire and that the decedent was breathing them in at the time of the fire. Hydrogen cyanide or hydrogen sulfide found in the blood may contribute to death. Nitrous oxides may indicate the presence of nitrogen-containing fuels; acrolein may indicate the destructive distillation of fats and oils. Refrigerants and other chemicals such as ammonia, Freon, or methyl chloride may indicate the nature of the fire.

HISTOLOGIC EXAMINATION

Microscopic examination of tissues is also an important part of the postmortem examination and is carried out by the pathologist after selected tissues from the victim have been placed in a fixative, usually for 10 to 14 days. Frequently, injury sites are microscopically examined for signs of white blood cells at the injury. White blood cells may indicate that the injury was inflicted at least several hours before death.

"FLASH" FIRES

Concentrated burns in one area of a body may indicate the nature and cause of death. Examples include a spray of burning fuel, as in a motorcycle accident, or the application of a device such as a blowtorch to a particular area of the body (face or hands) to obscure identification.

MOTIVES OF FIRE DEATHS

In fire deaths, the following motives should be kept in mind by investigators:

- Destruction or mutilation of the body to conceal the identity of the decedent.
- Destruction or mutilation of the body to conceal the true cause or manner of death.
- Incineration of the body with homicidal intent.

- Insurance fraud—the incineration of a body to collect on an insurance policy. For example, a decedent may have committed suicide but have an insurance policy prohibiting collection after death by suicide. Beneficiaries may burn the body to indicate accidental death by fire.
- Suicide with an accelerant.
- An attempt by a suicide victim to hide the cause of death.
- Victim trapped in building burned by an arsonist or by accident.

RECORDING THE SCENE

Photographs of the body in its original position and of the room or area in which it is found will prove to be very valuable later in the investigation. These photographs, along with investigative notes and any rough sketches prepared at the scene, serve the following purposes:

- To provide an overview of the body and its surroundings so that its relative position can later be established.
- To provide close-up photographs (including a ruler for true size comparison) of any evidence that indicates the identity of the victim; a circumvented alarm or fire-suppression system; point(s) of forced entry or exit; another (underlying) crime or signs of a struggle; the presence of gas cans, trailers, plants, and so on.
- To clarify the condition of the body regarding the extent of burning or cremation; the flow of fire patterns on the body and whether they are consistent with the extent of damages to the surroundings (e.g., was a victim who died on the second floor found buried in an ash-filled basement because of the collapse of interior structural members?); whether the body was found face up or face down, and the degree to which it insulated the floor below it (or failed to do so).
- To identify furnishings (e.g., bed, coffee table, desk) in the area where the body was found.
- To indicate the relative position of the body in relation to the point(s) of origin.
- To identify any other factors of importance to technical or forensic procedures.

In some cases, especially when the victim is found quite a distance from the point of origin of the fire, it is necessary to trace the connection between the fire and the resultant death. The connection may seem obvious when the investigator is at the scene, but while on the witness stand some 12 or 15 months later, the connection may not be as clear. To illustrate this problem, let us examine the particulars of a fire that occurred in the Bronx, New York, several years ago:

At 5 A.M., a fire started in the basement of an abandoned five-story walkup. The adjoining buildings were fully occupied and were evacuated by the responding fire units. One of the evacuees was a 9-year-old, mentally retarded boy. During the ensuing confusion, the boy was separated from his parents; apparently frightened by the crowd, he reentered his residence to seek the safety of his room. The boy's father, searching for his son, found him under his bed. The boy had died from carbon monoxide asphyxiation.

The fire damage to the abandoned building was extensive, but the fire did not extend to the adjoining buildings. The boy's body was found one building away and four stories above the source of the carbon monoxide that caused his death. The investigators involved in the case traced and (wisely) photographically documented the path that the billowing smoke and gases took between the source and the boy's room.

On occasion, the medical examiner will, after autopsy, refer a case to the police for further investigation. The autopsy may have revealed insufficient and/or contradictory data or may have raised additional questions that the medical examiner wants to have clarified before signing a death certificate. These cases are referred to as *CUPPIs* (circumstances undetermined pending police investigation). If the crime scene was processed and recorded accurately, the investigator, in many cases, should be able to review the crime scene data and provide the medical examiner with satisfactory answers.[50]

FAMILY/DOMESTIC VIOLENCE

This type of violence is unquestionably underreported, even by victimization studies. It often happens in private, and many victims are reluctant to report it because they are ashamed, they are afraid of reprisals if they do speak out,[51] they suffer from such low self-esteem that they think they "deserve what they got," or they were raised in violent families where abuse was "normal." As was discussed in Chapter 2, Crime and Its Investigation, acts constituting domestic/family violence are exceptions in most states to the general rule that an officer must personally view the commission of a misdemeanor in order to make an arrest. And because the bulk of these crimes do not rise to the level of felonious acts, in years past officers could only tell the victim to take out a warrant. However, as can be seen by the following laws from one state, not only is it possible for officers to now take immediate action in nonfelony situations, but there are specific requirements as to what investigative actions must be taken:

19-13-1 "Family Violence" . . . "means the occurrence of one or more of the following acts between past or present spouses, persons who are parents of the same child, parents and children, stepparents and stepchildren, foster parents and foster children, or other persons living or formerly living in the same household:

(1) any felony; or

(2) commission of offenses of battery, simple battery, simple assault, assault, stalking, criminal damage to property, unlawful restraint, or criminal trespass."

As used in 19-13-1, the term "family violence" does not include reasonable discipline administered by a parent to a child in the form of corporal punishment, restraint, or detention.[52]

17-4-20 "Arrest by Law Enforcement Officers Generally" provides that "an arrest for a crime may be made by a law enforcement officer either under a warrant or without a warrant if the offense is committed in his presence or within his immediate knowledge; if the offender is endeavoring to escape; if the officer has probable cause to believe that an act of family violence, as defined in Code Section 19-13-1, has been committed; or for other cause if there is likely to be a failure of justice for want of a judicial officer to issue a warrant."[53]

17-4-20.1 "Investigation of Family Violence" imposes the following requirements for law enforcement officers conducting an investigation into an act of family violence:

1. an officer may not base a decision of whether to arrest and charge a person on the specific consent of the victim or on a request by the victim solely or on consideration of the relationship of the parties;

2. no officer investigating an incident of family violence shall threaten, suggest, or otherwise indicate the arrest of all parties for the purpose of discouraging requests for law enforcement intervention;

3. when family violence complaints are received from two or more opposing parties, the officer shall evaluate each complaint separately to attempt to determine who was the primary aggressor. If the officer determines that one of the parties was the primary physical aggressor, the officer shall not be required to arrest any other person believed to have committed an act of family violence during the incident. In determining whether a person is a primary physical aggressor, an officer shall consider:

a) prior family violence involving either party;

b) the relative severity of the injuries inflicted on each person;

c) the potential for future injury; and

d) whether one of the parties acted in self-defense.

If the officer concludes that an act of family violence has occurred, regardless if an arrest is made, the officer must prepare a Family Violence offense or incident report and address the following matters:

a) names of the parties;

b) relationship of the parties;

c) sex of the parties;

d) time, date, and place of the incident;

e) whether children were involved or whether the incident was committed in the presence of children;

f) type and extent of the alleged abuse;

g) existence of substance abuse;

h) number and types of weapons involved;

i) existence of any prior court orders;

j) number of complaints involving persons who have previously filed complaints;

k) type of police action taken to dispose of the case, the reasons for the officer's determination that one party was the primary physical aggressor, and mitigating circumstances if an arrest is not made;

l) whether the victim was advised of available remedies and services; and

m) any other pertinent information.[54]

STALKING

Stalking is harrassing or threatening behavior that an individual engages in repeatedly, such as following a person, appearing at a person's home or place of business, making harrassing phone calls, leaving written messages or objects, or vandalizing a person's property. These actions may or may not be accompanied by a credible threat of serious harm, and they may or may not be precursors to an assault or murder.[55]

Legal definitions of stalking vary widely from state to state. Though most states define stalking as the willful, malicious, and repeated following and harrassing of another person, some states include in their definition such activities as lying in wait, surveillance, nonconsensual communication, telephone harassment, and vandalism.[56] While most states require that the alleged stalker engage in a course of conduct showing that the crime was not an isolated event, some states specify how many acts (usually two or more) must occur before the conduct can be considered stalking.[57] State stalking laws also vary in their threat and fear requirements. Most stalking laws require that to be deemed a stalker the perpetrator must make a credible threat of violence against the victim; others include in their requirements threats against the victim's immediate family; and still others require only that the alleged stalker's course of conduct constitute an implied threat.[58]

The definition of stalking used in the National Violence against Women (NVAW) survey closely resembles the definition used in the model antistalking code developed for states by the National Institute of Justice.[59] The survey defines stalking as "a course of conduct directed at a specific person that involves repeated visual or physical proximity, non-consensual communication, or verbal, written or implied threats, or a combination thereof, that would cause a reasonable person fear," with "repeated" meaning two or more occasions. The model antistalking code does not require, as a criterion of stalking, that stalkers make a credible threat of violence against victims, but it does require that victims feel a high level of fear ("fear of bodily harm"). Similarly, the definition of stalking used in the NVAW survey does not require that stalkers make a credible threat against victims, but it does require that victims feel a high level of fear.[60]

THREE CATAGORIES OF STALKERS

Relationship Stalkers, Type 1

Most stalking cases arise out of past intimate relationships or work. The offender and the victim are known to each other, although the identity of the stalker may not necessarily be known initially.[61] Relationship stalkers prefer direct, confrontational contact. Most of these stalkers are men, though a large minority are women. Relationship stalkers make the most threats and actual attacks; this category has the highest potential for violence, especially if it is allowed to escalate to the point of being overtly threatening.[62] Illustrations of this type include subordinates who stalk a supervisor because they believe the supervisor has not given them a fair raise or has blocked their promotion, married persons who have separated pending a divorce, and college students rejected for dates by a person to whom they are powerfully attracted. Indirect relational stalking may also take place; for example, a couple who had been living together separates, and the one who was left stalks the person who succeeded him or her in the relationship.

Stranger Stalking, Type 2

In stranger stalking, the victim is usually a male and the suspect a female.[63] Often rich or famous, the victim is beyond the offender's social circle and is known only from a distance. Despite any evidence to the contrary, the suspect is convinced that the victim loves her and attempts to be close to him by writing letters or watching his home. Direct personal contact is rare, and despite the relatively high frequency of threats by these stalkers, actual action is unusual—but it does occur.

Stranger Stalking, Type 3

This stalker is usually an older, unmarried man who does not necessarily believe that the victim loves him.[64] Typically the victim is a younger, attractive woman in the entertainment industry. He goes to great lengths to make himself known to her, writing letters and, less frequently, making visits to her home. But the offender rarely makes personal contact, rarely threatens, and rarely takes violent action.

Pseudo Stalking

It is important that investigators also be alert to instances of pseudo, or false, stalking. Offenders may simulate a stalking incident in order to mask the real reasons for an assault on a celebrity and thereby misdirect the investigation. Persons associated with Olympic skating hopeful Tonya Harding attacked her competitor, Nancy Kerrigan, in an attempt to increase Harding's chances of winning the gold medal at the 1994 Winter Games in Lillehammer. In other instances, what appears to be a stalking case is simply grotesque fan support, as in the case of the tennis fan who stabbed Monica Seles at a tournament in front of thousands of fans in order to increase the chances of winning by the competitor he supported.

THREAT MANAGEMENT

A study of only 74 cases conducted by the Los Angeles Police Department's Threat Management Unit attempted to create a profile of the dangerous stalker and developed the following factors:[65]

1. Not all stalkers threatened their victims, and not all who did actually attempted violence. However, all who committed a dangerous act did first threaten their victims.

2. The more dangerous offenders engaged in more personal contact, such as confrontations at the victim's home.

3. The dangerous group comprised men and women in about equal numbers, but women and homosexuals were overrepresented in relationship to the general population.

4. The relationship offenders committed 75 percent of the dangerous acts.

Another study found that communications with references to obsessive love, weapons, death, suicide, and religion were common indicators of a forthcoming dangerous act.[66] However, it is important to remember that not all violent acts are preceded by such communications and that even seemingly minor stalking behavior can turn very dangerous without any apparent reason.

Because so little is known about stalkers and their behavior and because the studies cited here are based on small samples, the information here cannot be considered as an authoritative guide for managing threats from stalkers. Investigators should seek qualified assistance from fields such as psychiatry, psychology, and psychiatric social work.

PROTECTIVE ORDERS

Most states have laws authorizing civil orders of protection in domestic abuse cases.[67] Such statutes limit in some way the eligibility for protection under such orders; in some states the applicant must be presently or formerly married to the person against whom the protective order is sought.[68] There is a need for each state to review its protective order statutes to determine if under the present provisions such orders are available to all stalking victims.[69]

Protective orders can serve as the first line of defense against stalkers: such orders put them on notice that their behavior is unwanted and that future acts will be dealt with more severely; in most states investigators can immediately make a warrantless arrest if they have probable cause to believe an order was violated.[70] All states allow temporary protective orders to be issued on an emergency basis and without the defendant's being present.[71] If an emergency or temporary order is issued, then a hearing on a permanent order is subsequently held. Among the things that protective orders prohibit a defendant from doing is communicating with the victim and entering the residence, workplace, school, or property of the victim, as well as any place frequented by the victim.[72] In some cases, mental illness and use of drugs or alcohol may be major factors in the behavior of a stalker; officers should be alert to documenting this possibility when conducting their investigation and coordinate with appropriate officials so that judges can incorporate mental health and substance-abuse counseling and monitoring into restraining orders.[73]

To be effective, protective orders must be rigorously enforced and violators dealt with in a manner that ensures their strict accountability. This requires that victims promptly report all violations. While victims may initially be satisfied with the response of the police to their original complaint, they are often disappointed with the lack of responsiveness to later complaints of a violation of the protective order.[74] Investigators must rapidly respond to such complaints and take enforcement action whenever the defendant's conduct warrants it. To do otherwise may make a defendant bolder and can result in serious injury or death.

PSYCHOLOGICAL AND SOCIAL CONSEQUENCES OF STALKING

The NVAW survey produced strong confirmation of the negative mental health impact of stalking. Of the respondents, about one-third of the women (30 percent) and one-fifth of the men (20 percent) said they sought psychological counseling as a result of their stalking victimization. In addition, stalking victims were significantly more likely than nonstalking victims to be very concerned about their personal safety and about being stalked, to carry something on their person to defend themselves, and to think personal safety for men and women had gotten worse in recent years.

Over one-quarter (26 percent) of the stalking victims said their victimization caused them to lose time from work. While the survey did not query victims about why they lost time from work, it can be assumed they missed work for a variety of reasons—to attend court hearings, to meet with a psychologist or other mental health professional, to avoid contact with their assailant, and to consult with an attorney. On average, victims who lost time from and returned to work missed 11 days.

Stalking victims were asked whether they took any measures (other than reporting their victimization to the police or obtaining a protective order) to protect themselves from their stalker. Fifty-six percent of the women and 51 percent of the men reported taking some type of self-protective measure.[75]

SERIAL MURDER AND THE NCAVC

If a serial murderer confines his or her activities to a single community or a small region, local police are in a good position to see emerging patterns. But because many serial murderers cover many miles in a short period of time, the FBI has developed the National Center for the Analysis of Violent Crime (NCAVC). It is designed to form a partnership among federal, state, and local law enforcement agencies in the investigation of potentially related, unsolved violent crimes. NCAVC combines law enforcement techniques, behavioral science principles, and data processing to help any law enforcement agency confronted with unusual, bizarre, particularly vicious, or repetitive crimes.

The following are the types of offenses and incidents that are reported to NCAVC for analysis:

- Sexually oriented murder or assault by mutilation or torture, dismemberment, violent sexual trauma, or asphyxiation.
- Spree murder (a series of indiscriminate murders or assaults, all committed within hours or days; e.g., a series of sniper murders or the Chicago cyanide murders).
- Mass murder (four or more murders in a single incident).
- Robbery murder and nonfatal robbery with extreme violence.
- Murder committed during the commission of another felony.
- Kidnapping: fatal, with injury, or for ransom
- Murder of a hostage.
- Murder for hire, contract murder, syndicate execution.
- Murder of a law enforcement officer.
- Political or other assassination.
- Terrorist or nationalistic murder.
- Drug-related murder.
- Gang murder.
- Missing person with evidence of foul play.
- Unidentified dead body when the manner of death is classified as a homicide.[76]

NCAVC can analyze every unsolved murder in the United States, identify the existence of serial patterns, and link cases together. It then notifies the individual local agencies that have similar murders, and they in turn may establish investigative contact among themselves. NCAVC emphasizes that the primary responsibility for investigative cases lies with the state and local authorities.

NCAVC also conducts research in violent crimes and trains local officers in analytic techniques. It is located at the FBI Academy in Quantico, Virginia, where it is administered by the Behavioral Science Unit. The FBI Academy was chosen as the site because it is a national law enforcement training center with vast resources for research and many capabilities for providing investigative support.

VI-CAP CRIME REPORT

When a violent crime remains unsolved for a period of time, the local law enforcement agency provides details about it on a special violent-criminal apprehension program (VI-CAP) reporting form.[77] This form is submitted to the nearest FBI field office, which reviews and forwards it to NCAVC.

The form has been organized into the following categories:

- *Part I: Administration:*
  Case administration
  Crime classification
  Date and time parameters
- *Part II: Victim information:*
  Victim status
  Victim identification
  Physical description
  Scars and /or birthmarks
  Tattoos
  Outstanding physical features
  Clothing of victim
  Miscellaneous
- *Part III: Offender information:*
  Offender defined
  Offender status
  Offender identification
  Physical description
  Scars and/or birthmarks
  Tattoos
  Outstanding physical features

- *Part IV: Identified-offender information:*
  Offender background
  Property of others
  Offender admissions
- *Part V: Vehicle description:*
  Vehicles used in the incident
  Offender's approach to the victim at time of incident
  Exact geographic location
  Location of events, body recovery site
  Site of offender's initial contact with victim
  Victim's last-known location
  Events at assault site
  Offender's writing or carving on body of victim
  Offender's writing or drawing at the scene
  Symbolic artifacts at crime scene
  Offender's communications
  Body disposition
  Restraints used on victim
  Clothing and property of victim
- *Part VI: Cause of death and/or trauma:*
  Cause of death
  Bite marks on victim
  Elements of torture or unusual assault
  Sexual assault
- *Part VII: Forensic evidence:*
  Weapons
  Blood
- *Part VIII: Request for profile*
- *Part IX: Other related cases*
- *Part X: Narrative summary*

FLOW OF INFORMATION

Information flow in the VI-CAP process is outlined in the following hypothetical case:

January –Los Angeles County: The body of a young female is found near Interstate 10 east of La Puente. The victim has blunt-force skull fractures and a number of mutilation knife wounds, several of which are unique. Two days later, the Los Angeles homicide detectives forward a VI-CAP offense report to VI-CAP. This report includes coroner protocol information and the identity of the victim, a 14-year-old runaway from a small northern California town. All information is entered in the VI-CAP computer and analyzed to compare MO and physical-evidence characteristics with those in other reported homicides. Los Angeles detectives are advised that the VI-CAP search reveals no similar-pattern cases on file.

February—San Bernardino, California: Detectives respond to a "found body" call on the southern edge of the city. The victim is a 16-year-old female from Hollywood. Injuries are similar to those of the January homicide in Los Angeles County. Regardless of the proximity of the two departments and the cooperation that exists between the detectives, a VI-CAP analysis confirms that a simiar pattern does exist, and both agencies are notified.

April—Marshall, Texas: Detectives forward VI-CAP information of the mutilation murder of a 19-year-old female college student whose vehicle, with a flat tire, was located on I-20 east of Dallas. After a pattern analysis, VI-CAP alerts Los Angeles, San Bernardino, and Marshall detectives that MO and physical evidence in the three murder cases are similar. It is also apparent that the killer is traveling east on the I-10, I-20 interstate system.

VI-CAP, after a request from the three police departments, prepares and transmits an information all-points bulletin (APB) directed to the special attention of all law enforcement agencies on or near the I-10, I-20 route. The APB requests that any department with information related in any way to the MO of the three murders contact the VI-CAP center. The following day, the police in Las Cruces, New Mexico, respond. In March, in that city, a 15-year-old female, hitchhiking to a friend's house, escaped after being assaulted by a male subject who had identified himself as a juvenile officer "working runaway cases." A description of the suspect, suspect vehicle, and MO of the assault is forwarded to VI-CAP. VI-CAP alerts the departments working on the three murder cases. VI-CAP is asked to transmit an APB of the suspect and vehicle description.

The VI-CAP center also conducts a computer search on its known-offender (profile and MO) file using the MO, physical evidence, and victim information from the murders in California and Texas and the assault MO and suspect description from New Mexico. Two possible names are produced. VI-CAP alerts the case investigators, who send for and receive mug photos from two state prisons.

One subject is positively identified by the Las Cruces victim. Arrest warrants are issued, and a supplemental APB is transmitted. Two days later the suspect, a parolee from a northwestern state, is arrested after picking up a young hitchhiker in Jackson, Mississippi.[78]

CRIMINAL INVESTIGATIVE ANALYSIS

Criminal investigative analysis, formally referred to as *psychological profiling*, is the analysis of crime scene patterns in order to identify the personality and behavioral characteristics of offenders who commit serial crimes of rape and homicide.

Criminal investigative analysis is not a new concept. During World War II, the Office of Strategic Services (OSS) employed a psychiatrist, William Langer, to profile Adolf Hitler. Langer assembled all that was known about Hitler at the time; he then attempted a long-range "diagnosis" and offered predictions on how Hitler might react to defeat.[79]

The concept of criminal investigative analysis works in tandem with the search for physical evidence. Behavioral scientists research nonphysical items of evidence, such as rage, hatred, fear, and love. Their results are applied in teaching police officers to recognize signs of these emotions or personality traits at a crime scene. Thus, police can construct a profile of the type of person who might possess the emotions or personality traits indicated by the nonphysical evidence at a crime scene. Behavioral scientists try to classify human behavior. The American Psychiatric Association's *Diagnostic and Statistical Manual of Mental Disorders* (DSM), used by mental health professionals, is an example of such a classification.[80] Many types of "normal" and "abnormal" behavior are labeled by behavioral scientists, with the labels serving as abbreviated ways of describing behavior patterns.[81]

Symptoms of behavior patterns are revealed in the way an individual "acts out" and in the responses that the individual may make to a professional. A *symptom* is the "visible evidence of a disease or disturbance"[82] and a crime, particularly a bizarre crime, is as much a symptom as any other type of acting out by an individual. A crime may reflect the personality characteristics of the perpetrator in much the same way that the decor of a person's home reflects something about the homeowner's personality.[83]

A crime scene is usually considered the area in which a crime was committed. In criminal investigative analysis, the crime scene includes not only the scene of the crime, but also the victim of the crime, as in the case of rape, and all locations involved in the crime, including such areas as the recovery site of the body of a person killed in one location and deposited in another.

The victim is one of the most important aspects of criminal investigative analysis. In cases involving a surviving victim, particularly a rape victim, the perpetrator's exact conversation with the victim is of utmost importance and can play a very large role in the construction of an accurate profile.

One criminal investigative analysis does not provide the same information as another. Each is based on what was or was not left at the crime scene. Psychological evidence, like physical evidence, varies, and so the profile may also vary. The profile information may include the perpetrator's:

- Race.
- Sex.
- Age range.
- Marital status.
- General employment.
- Reaction to questioning by police.
- Degree of sexual maturity.
- Likelihood of striking again or of having struck before.
- Likelihood of having a police record.

Profilers need wide exposure to crime scenes to discern patterns and some exposure to criminals who have committed similar crimes.[84] Items necessary for a psychological profile include:

- Complete photographs of the crime scene, including photographs of the victim if the crime is homicide. Also helpful is some means of determining the angle from which the photographs were taken and a general description of the immediate area. One enterprising police officer developed the excellent technique of photocopying his crime scene sketch, attaching one copy to each photo, and then outlining in red the area that was included in the photograph.
- The completed autopsy protocol, including, if possible, results of lab tests on the victim.

- A complete report of the incident, including date and time of the offense, location (by town as well as by actual site of incident), weapon used (if known), investigative officers' reconstruction of the sequence of events (if any), and detailed interviews of surviving victims or witnesses.

These items are usually part of all investigations, and most investigative reports also include background information on the victims. However, this information often is only scantily available to the person doing the criminal investigative analysis because the investigating officers cannot possibly write down all the details about victims that they collect. When investigators provide information about victims to a profiler, they should include:

- Occupation (former and present).
- Residence (former and present).
- Reputation at work and in the neighborhood.
- Physical description, including dress at the time of the incident.
- Marital status, including children and close family members.
- Educational level.
- Financial status, past and present.
- Information and background on victim's family and parents, including victim's relationship with parents.
- Medical history, both phycial and mental.
- Fears.
- Personal habits.
- Social habits.
- Use of alcohol and drugs.
- Hobbies.
- Friends and enemies.
- Recent changes in lifestyle.
- Recent court actions.

The primary psychological evidence being sought is motive. After a survey of the evidence, a rule known as "Ockham's razor" can be applied: "What can be done with fewer assumptions is done in vain with more."[85] This fourteenth-century philosophy has, in investigative circles, come to mean that, given a problem with several alternative solutions, the most obvious answer is usually correct. An aid to the application of Ockham's razor is the intangible evidence that the observer gathers from the crime scene to determine such things as whether the crime appears to have been planned or is the result of an irrational thought process.

Questions

1. Briefly discuss the differences between felonious and nonfelonious homicides.
2. What are the four major categories of homicide set forth in the *Crime Classification Manual*?
3. What should the investigator do when responding to a death scene?
4. What are the purposes of an autopsy?
5. Why is the personal identification of a victim so important in homicide investigation?
6. What roles can be played by archaeologists, forensic pathologists, entomologists, and botanists in the search for and discovery of buried bodies?
7. What two methods are typically employed to train cadaver dogs to become sensitive to the smell of decomposing human remains?
8. What role can be played by entomologists in estimating time of death?
9. Briefly describe the typical entrance and exit gunshot wound.
10. What are the basic differences between neutron activation analysis and atomic absorption analysis in testing for firearm residues?
11. Describe an incised wound, stab wound, and laceration.
12. What are defense wounds, and where are they most commonly found?
13. What are the mechanisms of death in ligature strangulation?
14. How is death produced by manual strangulation?
15. Which misconceptions are associated with suicidal hangings?
16. Why are poisons rarely used in homicides?
17. Discuss the differences in suicidal behavior between men and women.
18. What are the most common reasons that hit-and-run drivers fail to stop?
19. In regard to human remains at a fire, what three broad questions should investigators keep in mind?
20. What are the common motives in fire deaths?
21. In determining whether a person is a primary physical aggressor in a family violence complaint, an officer should consider certain factors. What are these factors?
22. What is stalking?
23. What are three categories of stalkers?
24. What types of offenses and incidents are reported to the National Center for the Analysis of Violent Crime for analysis?
25. What items are necessary for a psychological profile?

Notes

1. Neil C. Chamelin and Kenneth R. Evans, *Criminal Law for Policemen* (Englewood Cliffs, N.J.: Prentice-Hall, 1995), pp. 116–130.
2. Ibid.
3. John E. Douglas, W. Burgess, Allen G. Burgess, and Robert K. Ressler, *Crime Classification Manual* (New York: Lexington Books, 1992), pp. 22–123.
4. Readers interested in the topic should refer to the most recent *Crime Classification Manual* for a more detailed treatment of the subject.
5. Steven C. Clark, *National Guidelines for Death Investigation*, (Washington, D.C.: U.S. Department of Justice, December 1997), pp. 13–20.
6. Jay Dix and Robert Calaluce, *Guide to Forensic Pathology* (Columbia: University of Missouri, 1998), p. 3.
7. Wisconsin Crime Laboratory, *Criminal Investigation and Physical Evidence Handbook* (Madison: Department of Justice, State of Wisconsin, 1968), p. 10.
8. John J. Horgan, *Criminal Investigation* (New York: McGraw-Hill, 1974), p. 292.

9. Lemoyne Snyder, *Homicide Investigation* (Springfield, Ill.: Charles C. Thomas, 1973), p. 62.

10. Horgan, *Criminal Investigation*, p. 294.

11. Wisconsin Crime Laboratory, *Criminal Investigation and Physical Evidence Handbook*, p. 11.

12. Donald G. Cherry and J. Lawrence Angel, "Personality Reconstruction from Unidentified Remains," *FBI Law Enforcement Bulletin*, 1977, Vol. 46, No. 48, pp. 12–15. Much of the information dealing with personality reconstruction was obtained from this article.

13. R. M. Boyd, "Buried Bodies," *FBI Law Enforcement Bulletin*, 1979, Vol. 48, No. 2, pp. 1–7. Much of the information dealing with the search for buried bodies was obtained from this article.

14. William M. Bass and Walter H. Birkby, "Exhumation: The Method Could Make the Difference," *FBI Law Enforcement Bulletin*, 1978, Vol. 47, No. 7, pp. 6--11.

15. Marcella H. Sorg, Edward David, and Andrew J. Rebmann, "Cadaver Dogs, Taphonmy, and Post-Mortem Interval in the Northeast,"in *Forensic Osteology*, Kathleen J. Reichs (ed.) (Springfield, Ill.: Charles C. Thomas, 1998), p. 121.

16. J.S. Sachs, "Fake Smell of Death," *Discover: The World of Science*, 1996, Vol. 17, No. 3, pp. 87–94.

17. Dix and Calaluce, *Guide to Forensic Pathology*, p. 32.

18. Ibid., pp. 35–36.

19. Ibid., pp. 33–34.

20. Francis E. Camps (ed.), *Gradwohl's Legal Medicine*, 3rd ed. (Bristol: John Wright and Sons, 1976), p. 83.

21. There is no mention of cadaveric spasm in the voluminous and comprehensive work of Werner V. Spitz and Russell S. Fisher (eds.), *Medicolegal Investigation of Death*, 2nd ed. (Springfield, Ill.: Charles C. Thomas, 1980).

22. Dix and Calaluce, *Guide to Forensic Pathology*, pp. 38–40.

23. W. C. Rodriguez and William C. Bass, *Determination of Time of Death by Means of Carrion Insects*, paper presented at the 35th annual meeting of the American Academy of Forensic Sciences, February 15–19, 1983, Cincinnati, Ohio. (This discussion and accompanying figures were taken, with modification, from pp. 1–6.)

24. N. H. Haskell, David G. McShaffrey, D. A. Hawley, R. E. Williams, and J. E. Pless, "Use of Aquatic Insects in Determining Submersion Interval," *Journal of Forensic Sciences*, May 1989, Vol. 34, No. 3, pp. 622, 623.

25. Barry A. J. Fisher, *Techniques of Crime Scene Investigation* (New York: Elsevier, 1992), pp. 452–458. (This discussion was adapted with permission from this source.)

26. The information on shotgun wounds was obtained from material developed by Vincent J. M. DiMaio, M.D., medical examiner, Dallas County, Texas.

27. The information on firearm residue included in this chapter was developed by the Southwestern Institute of Forensic Sciences at Dallas, Texas.

28. R. C. Harrison and R. Gilroy, "Firearms Discharge Residues," *Journal of Forensic Sciences*, 1959, No. 4, pp. 184–199.

29. S. S. Krishman, K. A. Gillespie, and E. J. Anderson, "Rapid Detection of Firearm Discharge Residues by Atomic Absorption and Neutron Activation Analysis," *Journal of Forensic Sciences*, 1977, No. 16, pp. 144–151. Also see I. C. Stone and C. S. Petty, "Examination of Gunshot Residues," *Journal of Forensic Sciences*, 1974, No. 19, pp. 784–788.

30. Dominic J. DiMaio and Vincent J. M. DiMaio, *Forensic Pathology* (New York: Elsevier, 1989), p. 87.

31. Ibid.

32. DiMaio and DiMaio, *Forensic Pathology*, pp. 231–243.

33. Jacques Charon, *Suicide* (New York: Scribner's, 1972), p. 56.

34. Ibid., p. 39.

35. Andrew P. Johnson, "Hammer Spur Impressions: Physical Evidence in Suicides," *FBI Law Enforcement Bulletin*, September 1988, pp. 11-14. This discussion was adapted from this article.

36. Lemoyne Snyder, *Homicide Investigation* (Springfield, Ill.: Charles C. Thomas, 1973), p. 228.

37. Donna Newson, "Doctors Perform Rare Surgery," *Tampa Tribune*, July 25, 1980, pp. A1, A10.

38. Richard H. Fox and Carl L. Cunningham, *Crime Scene Search and Physical Evidence Handbook* (Washington, D.C.: Government Printing Office, 1973), pp. 124, 126. This discussion of poisons was taken from this source.

39. *Suicide Investigation, Part II: Training Key 196* (Gaithersburg, Md.: International Association of Chiefs of Police, 1973), pp. 4–5.

40. J. Tuckman et al., "Credibility of Suicide Notes," *American Journal of Psychiatry*, June 1960, No. 65, pp. 1104–1106.

41. David Lester, *Why People Kill Themselves* (Springfield, Ill.: Charles C. Thomas, 1972), p. 36.

42. D. Hastings, "Long Investigation Uncovers Suicide Scheme," *Tampa Tribune-Times*, January 22, 1984, p. A24.

43. J. Stannard Baker and Thomas Lindquist, *Lamp Examination for On or Off in Traffic Accidents*, 3rd ed. (Evanston, Ill.: Traffic Institute, Northwestern University, 1983).

44. *Hit and Run Investigation: Training Key 7* (Washington, D.C.: International Association of Chiefs of Police, 1967), pp. 2–3.

45. Z. G. Standing Bear, *The Investigation of Questioned Deaths and Injuries—Conference Notes and Outline* (Valdosta, Ga.: Valdosta State College Press, 1988), pp. 78–82.

46. John J. O'Conner, *Practical Fire and Arson Investigation* (Boca Raton, Fla.: CRC Press, 1993), pp. 160–161.

47. Ibid.

48. Camps, *Gradwohl's Legal Medicine*, p. 358; Lester Adelson, *The Pathology of Homicide* (Springfield, Ill.: Charles C. Thomas, 1974), p. 610; Richard Lindenberg, "Mechanical Injuries of the Brain and Meninges," in Spitz and Fisher, *Medicolegal Investigation of Death*, pp. 447–456.

49. O'Conner, *Practical Fire and Arson Investigation*, pp. 165–166.

50. Ibid., pp. 152-153. (This discussion is taken with permission from this source.)

51. Ronet Bachman, *Violence against Women* (Washington, D.C.: National Institute of Justice, Department of Justice, 1994), p. 6.

52. *Official Code of Georgia Annotated*, Vol. 16 Cumulative Supplement (Charlottesville, Va: The Michie Company, 1994), p. 89.

53. *Official Code of Georgia Annotated*, Vol. 15 Cumulative Supplement (Charlottesville, Va.: The Michie Company, 1994), p. 8.

54. Ibid., pp. 11–12.

55. Patricia Tjaden and Nancy Thoennes, *Stalking in America: Finding from the National Violence against Women Survey*, National Institute of Justice, Center for Disease Control and Prevention, U.S. Department of Justice (Washington, D.C.: Government Printing Office, April 1998), pp. 1–3.

56. Kenneth R. Thomas, "How to Stop the Stalker: State Anti-Stalking Laws," *Criminal Law Bulletin*, Vol. 29, No. 2, pp. 124–136.

57. "Stalking Laws," *State Legislative Report*, Denver, Col., National Conference of State Legislatures, Vol. 17, No. 19, October 1992, pp. 1–6.

58. National Institute of Justice, *Domestic Violence, Stalking and Anti-Stalking Legislation: An Annual Report to Congress under the Violence against Women Act*, (Washington, D.C.: U. S. Department of Justice, April 1996).

59. Ibid.

60. National Criminal Justice Association, *Project to Develop a Model Anti-Stalking Code for States* (Washington, D.C.: U.S. Department of Justice, October 1993).

61. Benson, "Stalking: Stopped in Its Tracks," *Police*, September 1994, p. 38.

62. Ibid., p. 39.

63. The description of this type of stalker is drawn from Ibid., pp. 38-39.

64. Ibid., p. 39.

65. Ibid.

66. Mike Tharp, "In the Mind of a Stalker," *U.S. News & World Report*, February 17, 1992, p. 28.

67. National Criminal Justice Association (NCJA), *Project to Develop a Model Anti-Stalking Code for States* (Washington, D.C.: National Institute of Justice, Department of Justice, 1993), p. 75.

68. Ibid., p. 76.

69. Ibid., p. 75.

70. Ibid.

71. Ibid., p. 76.

72. Ibid.

73. Ibid.

74. Ibid., p. 77.

75. Tjaden and Thoennes, *Stalking in America*, p. 11.

76. National Center for the Analysis of Violent Crime, Behavioral Science Unit, FBI Academy (Quantico, Va.: 1985), p. 5.

77. VI-CAP Crime Analysis Report Form used by the FBI for profiling, 1999.

78. National Center for the Analysis of Violent Crime, p. 7.

79. Richard L. Ault, Jr., and James T. Reese, "A Psychological Assessment of Crime Profiling," *FBI Law Enforcement Bulletin*, March 1980, pp. 22–25.

80. American Psychiatric Association, *Diagnostic and Statistical Manual of Mental Disorders*, 4th ed. (Washington, D.C.: American Psychiatric Association, 1994).

81. James C. Coleman, *Abnormal Psychology and Modern Life*, 6th ed. (Glenview, Ill.: Scott, Foresman, 1980).

82. J. V. McConnell, *Understanding Human Behavior* (New York: Holt, Rinehart and Winston, 1974), p. 25.

83. Sherrill Whitson, *Elements of Interior Design and Decoration* (New York: Lippincott, 1963), p. 751.

84. For a further discussion, see R. Brittain, "The Sadistic Murder," *Medical Science and the Law*, 1970, Vol. 10, pp. 198–204; Donald Lunde, *Murder and Madness* (San Francisco: San Francisco Book Company, 1976).

85. *The Encyclopedia of Philosphy*, Vol. 8 (New York: Macmillan, 1967), p. 307.

ELEVEN

Sex-Related Offenses

CHAPTER OUTLINE

Classification of Sex-Related Offenses 288

Typology of Rape 288

Sex-Related Investigations 294

Why Women Do Not Report Rape to the Police 298

False Rape Allegations 298

The Victim and Physical Evidence 300

Condom Trace Evidence 304

Record of Injuries 306

Autoerotic Deaths 306

Questions 310

Notes 310

INTRODUCTION

The term sex-related offenses covers a broad category of specific acts against adults, children, males, and females. However, in this chapter we will focus primarily on those sexual assaults which are typically directed towards postpubescent and adult females. We will examine various types of sex offenses as well as the different categoris of rapists. Further, we will provide very specific recommendations on how to conduct criminal investigations which are sexual in nature. We will also outline and discuss the considerable amount of physical evidence that is often available when sex crimes are committed. Lastly, we will discuss sexual asphyxia/autoerotic deaths as well as psychological autopsies.

CLASSIFICATION OF SEX OFFENSES

Sex offenses may be grouped into three classifications: serious, nuisance, and mutually consenting. With the exception of murder, few crimes generate greater public concern and interest than serious sex offenses.

SERIOUS SEX OFFENSES

The term "serious" is used because not all sex offenses are a significant threat to the individual or to the public. Sex offenses of this type, such as rape or sexual battery as it is also called, are high-priority offenses because they constitute the greatest physical and psychological injury to the victim.

In this chapter, we will focus primarily on the crime of rape and the physical evidence associated with this crime.

NUISANCE SEX OFFENSES

Included in this classification are such acts as voyeurism and exhibitionism. Usually such acts present no personal danger to anyone except the offender, who may fall prey to an angry father, husband, or boyfriend. Few perpetrators of nuisance sex offenses physically injure anyone. But such instances do sometimes occur:

The police were called to an apartment complex by tenants who had become concerned after not having seen their next-door neighbor for two days. The neighbor was an attractive 25-year-old woman. The police entered the apartment of the woman and discovered her dismembered body stuffed in a clothes trunk in her bedroom.

The investigation resulted in the arrest of a suspect. He stated that a few days before the murder, he had seen the victim hanging some undergarments on a clothesline. The suspect returned a few hours later at dark and stole two of the victim's panties and bras off the clothesline.

The victim mentioned the incident to a neighbor but not to the police. Later, the suspect returned to the victim's home and saw her, through a bedroom window, disrobe and put on a nightgown. He became sexually aroused and entered the house through an unlocked, rear kitchen door. He picked up a knife from a table in the kitchen and went directly to the victim's bedroom. When she saw him she became frightened. The perpetrator told her not to scream or he would kill her. He ordered her to take off her nightgown and get into bed. He got into bed with her, still clutching the knife. While having sexual intercourse with her, for some reason he could not explain, he started choking her. When she started to resist, he plunged the knife into her heart, killing her instantly. He then dressed the victim in undergarments and a dress, propped her in a chair in the bedroom, and talked to the deceased victim for approximately 45 minutes. Then he disrobed and dismembered the body and stuffed it into the clothes trunk. The suspect admitted to the police that he had acted as a voyeur on other occasions but had never before assaulted any woman.

SEX OFFENSES INVOLVING MUTUAL CONSENT

Sex offenses of this nature involve consenting adults whose behavior is deemed illegal by various state and local laws; examples include adultery, fornication, prostitution, and certain homosexual activities. Except for commercial prostitution and public solicitation by homosexuals, many police agencies assign these acts low investigative priority. When enforcement action is taken, it is generally because of a citizen complaint or because the act was performed in a public place and observed by the police or a private citizen.

TYPOLOGY OF RAPE

Extensive interviews with 133 convicted rapists of adult females and rape victims raised three major factors in understanding the rapists' behavior. These three factors—power, anger, and sexuality—seemed to operate in all rapes, but the proportion varied. In any given rape, one factor seemed to dominate. By ranking each offender and each victim's account for the dominant issue, the following typology of rape emerged:

1. Power rape—sexuality used in the service of power.
2. Anger rape—sexuality used in the service of anger.

3. There were *no* rapes in which sex was the dominant issue; sexuality was instead always used for other motives.[1]

POWER RAPE

In power rape, the offender achieves power over his victim through intimidation with a weapon, physical force, or threat of bodily harm. Physical aggression is used to subdue the victim. To effect sexual intercourse, many power rapists kidnap or tie up their victims.

This type of offender shows little skill in negotiating personal relationships and feels inadequate in both sexual and nonsexual areas of his life. With few other avenues of personal expression, sexuality becomes the core of his self-image and self-esteem. Rape becomes the means by which he reassures himself of his sexual adequacy and identity. In that it is a test of his adequacy, the rape fills the rapist with anxiety, excitement, and anticipated pleasure. The assault is premeditated and preceded by an obsessional fantasy in which, although his victim may initially resist him, she submits gratefully to his sexual embrace and responds with wild abandon. In reality, many power rapists are handicapped by failure to achieve or sustain an erection or by premature ejaculation and find little sexual satisfaction in rape. The assault never lives up to the fantasy. Further, they do not feel reassured by their own performance or their victims' response and, therefore, look for another victim—this time the "right one."

Power rapes become repetitive and compulsive. The amount of force used in the assault may vary, and there may be an increase in aggression over time as the offender becomes more desperate to achieve what continues to elude him. Usually there is no conscious intent on the part of this offender to hurt or degrade his victim.

The victim is typically near the age of the offender or younger. Hospital examination generally shows minimum or inconclusive evidence of physical or sexual injury. Clinical evidence of intercourse—presence of active sperm—may be absent. Victims often report being questioned by the offender about their sexual lives, their reactions to the rapist's sexual performance, and their identities with the implication of expected further contact.

Power rapists are subdivided into two groups according to whether the major goal in the offense is assertion or reassurance.

The Power-Assertive Rapist

This type regards rape as an expression of his virility, mastery, and dominance. He feels entitled to "take it" or sees sexual domination as a way of keeping "his" women in line. The rape is a reflection of an inadequate sense of identity and effectiveness. The following are examples of power-assertive rapes:

Warren is a 20-year-old single male. While at home on leave from the Coast Guard, he picked up an 18-year-old hitchhiker and drove her to a secluded beach. She begged to be let go, but he grabbed her, saying, "You don't want to get hurt, baby. You want to get laid. You want it as much as I do." He forced her to submit to intercourse and then offered to buy her dinner. Arrested and convicted for this rape, while out on bail, he committed an identical offense. As an adolescent Warren had been involved in a number of sexual incidents involving exhibitionism and sexual play with children. He was treated at a local mental health clinic. As an adult he had no steady girlfriends. In the service, he lived with and was supported by a 30-year-old man in exchange for sexual favors, although he did not regard himself as homosexual. Apart from his two rape offenses (and two earlier ones for which he was never apprehended), he had been arrested for driving without a license, driving under the influence, and speeding. Although of above-average intelligence, his academic and vocational accomplishments were mediocre. The only activity he had pursued diligently was body-building.

Nancy is a 45-year-old divorced woman. While at home on a Friday evening, she was visited by a former boyfriend, who arrived with a bottle of gin. He asked her to share drinks with him and Nancy agreed. Later in the evening, she refused to have sex with him and her account of what happened follows: "He messed me over the street way. I'm not supposed to tell. He said he'd beat me if I told and he gave me a sample tonight to show me. They work you over to control you so they can have you sexually anytime they want. He hit me on the ear, pulled my hair, hit me in the back by my kidneys–very strategic. But it's not the physical part that's the thing. It's mental—to control you. They project onto you. Violence and sex—they think you want that—they project onto you what they want." On follow-up, Nancy reported that she had dropped the rape charge, saying, "He knows I mean business. As long as he doesn't put his hands on me is all I care about. I reported it and have pointed him out to people so that they know him."[2]

The Power-Reassurance Rapist

This type commits the offense to resolve disturbing doubts about his sexual adequacy and masculinity. He aims to place a woman in a helpless position so that she cannot refuse or reject him:

Steve is a 24-year-old married man who pleaded guilty to six charges of rape. In every case, he approached the victim in a shopping mall with a gun. His fantasy was that the woman would say, "You don't need a gun. You're just what I've been waiting for," and then "rape" him. He would kidnap them, force them to submit to intercourse, and then ask them whether they had enjoyed the sex and whether he was as good as other sex partners they had had. In every case, he tied up his victims. Steve had no other criminal history. His background was unremarkable, but Steve felt that he had never done particularly well in any area of life (academic, social, vocational, marital) with the exception of his military service, which had been the most satisfying area of his life. He had dated actively as a teenager and indulged in sexual play but stopped short of intercourse. He finds intercourse unsatisfying, partly because of premature ejaculation and partly because it never lived up to his expectations. He saw marriage as a solution, but because he could not be attentive to anyone else's needs, his marriage floundered. Just before his offense, Steve discovered that he was sterile and began to have disturbing homosexual thoughts. He described the offense as a compulsion. Although he realized the consequences of what he was doing, he found that he could not control himself.

Arlene, a 21-year-old single woman, had just stepped off a bus and was walking down a well-lit street. A man approached her from behind, held a knife to her back, pushed her into some bushes, and pulled her sweater over her head so that she would not see him. He raped her, asking her questions such as: "How does it feel? Am I as good as your boyfriend?" Arlene said, "He seemed as if he needed to be reassured, and so I tried to reassure him. I was lying on my back in the gravel. He was odd saying those things, and then I had to bargain with him to get my clothes back. He also wanted my address and to know if he could come and do it again. I felt that if I could convince him I was being honest, he would let me go. He had my pocketbook and would know who I was, so I told him where I lived but not the right apartment."

The medical record indicated abrasions on lower and upper back but no other signs of bleeding or trauma.

ANGER RAPE

In this type of sexual assault, the offender expresses anger, rage, contempt, and hatred of his victim by physically beating her, sexually assaulting her, and forcing her to perform or submit to additional degrading acts. The rapist assaults all parts of the victim's body. The rapist often approaches his victim by striking and beating her; he tears her clothing; and he uses profane and abusive language. The rapist vents his rage on his victim to retaliate for perceived wrongs he has suffered at the hands of women. His relationship to important women in his life is fraught with conflict, irritation, and irrational jealousy, and he is often physically assaultive toward them. His offenses tend to be episodic and sporadic, triggered by conflicts in his relationships to significant women in his life (mother, girlfriend, wife) but frequently displaced onto other individuals. Sex becomes a weapon, and rape is a means of hurting and degrading.

This kind of offender considers women unloving, ungiving "whores and bitches." Sex is regarded as base and degrading; this offender finds little sexual satisfaction in the rape. He frequently feels revulsion and disgust and often has difficulty in achieving erection or ejaculation.

Because the rape is one of conscious anger or sadistic excitement, the assault is brutal, violent, sometimes homicidal.

The anger rapist finds it difficult to explain his rapes and often rationalizes them by saying that he was under the influence of alcohol or drugs. Often the details of the assault are vague to the rapist because during the attack he was blind with rage. His satisfaction and relief result from the discharge of anger rather than from sexual gratification.

Older women may be particular targets for this type of rapist, although victims may be of any age. Medical examination generally reveals considerable physical trauma to all areas of the body, often requiring X-rays and consultation with other medical specialists. Victims report experiencing the rape as life-threatening; symptoms following rape are disruptive to physical, social, psychological, and sexual life.

Victims indicate that initial contact with the assailant generally is cordial and nonthreatening. For example, the rapist may pick up a woman hitchhiking, or vice versa; or the rapist may use some confidence ploy to gain access to the victim's home (pretends to need to use the phone, poses as a salesman, and so forth). However, once the rapist feels confident that the victim is under his control, he lashes out suddenly and violently. The victim is often physically immobilized and unable to fight back. The offender may use humiliating language, and perverted acts may become a major aspect of the assault.

The rapists who fall into the anger-assault category are subdivided into two groups according to whether the major goal in the offense is retaliation or excitation.

The Anger-Retaliation Rapist

This type commits rape as an expression of his hostility and rage toward women. His motive is revenge, and his aims are degradation and humiliation:

Derek is a white, 25-year-old married man and father of four. His mother abandoned the family shortly after his birth. Throughout his life, Derek's father reminded him that his mother was "a whore, and never to trust any woman; they are no good." During his adolescence, Derek became acquainted with his mother. Once, while she was drunk, she exposed herself to him and asked him to fondle her. He fled, terrified. In a vain effort to win his father's recognition and approval, Derek put a premium on physical toughness. In high school, he played sports "like a savage" and then entered the Marine Corps. He had an outstanding service record and after dis-

charge got married and attended college. One day he got into a dispute with his female history teacher over the merits of the Vietnam War and felt that she was ridiculing and humiliating him in front of the class. He stormed out of the room, thinking "women are dirty, rotten bastards" and went to a bar to drink. On his way to his car, he spotted a 40-year-old woman (whom he thought was older) in the parking lot. He grabbed her by the throat, hit her in the mouth, ripped off her clothes, and raped her. Before this offense, Derek had been arrested for gambling, loitering, and drunkenness.

Shortly after midnight, Catherine, a 33-year-old mother of two, was in bed reading and waiting for her husband to return from work. A man known to the family for 10 years knocked at the door. The 14-year-old son let him in. He said that he was leaving town the next day and wanted to say good-bye. Catherine talked to him from the bedroom and wished him well on his trip. Suddenly the man ordered the son to his room, grabbed Catherine, and forced her to go outside with him to another building. He beat her, choked her, and sexually assaulted her. It was only after the man fell asleep that Catherine was able to escape and return home.

On follow-up, Catherine reported considerable physical pain from the beatings. She had pain and swelling to her face, neck, arms, and legs; she also reported loss of appetite, insomnia, nightmares, crying spells, restlessness, and a fear of being followed as she walked home from work. She was unable to carry out usual household tasks. Her relationship with her husband suffered, and she had flashbacks to the assault.

Charges were pressed against the offender, who "copped a plea" for the charges of rape, unnatural acts, and kidnapping. The judge sentenced him to three years on probation. One year later, the offender committed two rapes on teenage girls.

The Anger-Excitation Rapist (Criminal Sexual Sadist)

This type of offender finds pleasure, thrills, and excitation in the suffering of his victim. He is a criminal sexual sadist, and his aim is to punish, hurt, and torture his victims.

Sexual sadism is a persistent pattern of becoming sexually excited in response to another's suffering. Granted, sexual excitement can occur at odd times even in normal people. But to the sexually sadistic offender, it is the suffering of the victim that is sexually arousing.[3]

The writings of two sexual sadists graphically convey their desires. One writes: "the most important radical aim is to make her suffer since there is no greater power over another person than that of inflicting pain on her to force her to undergo suffering without her being able to defend herself. The pleasure in the complete domination over another person is the very essence of the sadistic drive." Of his sexually sadistic activities with a victim he killed, another offender writes: "she was writhering [*sic*] in pain and I loved it. I was now combining my sexual high of rape and my power high of fear to make a total sum that is now beyond explaining. . . . I was alive for the sole purpose of causing pain and receiving sexual gratification. . . . I was relishing the pain just as much as the sex. . ."

Each offender's account confirms that it is the suffering of the victim, not the infliction of physical or psychological pain, that is sexually arousing. In fact, one of these men resuscitated his victim from unconsciousness so that he could continue to savor her suffering. Inflicting pain is a means of creating suffering and of eliciting the desired responses of obedience, submission, humiliation, fear, and terror.

Specific findings uncovered during an investigation determine if the crime committed involves sexual sadism. The critical issues are whether the victim suffered, whether the suffering was intentionally elicited, and whether the suffering sexually aroused the offender. This is why neither a sexual nor a cruel act committed on an unconscious or dead victim is necessarily evidence of sexual sadism: such a victim cannot experience suffering. For this reason, postmortem injuries alone do not indicate sexual sadism.

Rapists cause their victims to suffer, but only sexual sadists intentionally inflict that suffering, whether physical or psychological, to enhance their own arousal. Neither the severity of an offender's cruelty nor the extent of a victim's suffering is evidence of sexual sadism. Acts of extreme cruelty or those that cause great suffering are often performed for nonsexual purposes, even during sexual assaults.

The behavior of sexual sadists, like that of other sexual deviants, extends along a wide spectrum.

Sexual sadists can be law-abiding citizens who fantasize but do not act or who fulfill these fantasies with freely consenting partners. Only when sexual sadists commit crimes do their fantasies become relevant to law enforcement.

All sexual acts and sexual crimes begin with fantasy. However, in contrast to normal sexual fantasies, those of the sexual sadist center on domination, control, humiliation, pain, injury, and violence—or a combination of these—as a means of causing suffering. As the fantasies of the sexual sadist vary, so does the degree of violence.

The fantasies discerned from the personal records of offenders are complex, elaborate, and involve detailed scenarios that include specific methods of capture and control, location, scripts to be followed by the victim, sequence of sexual acts, and desired victim responses. Sexual sadists dwell frequently on these fantasies, which often involve multiple victims and sometimes include partners:

One offender, who is believed to have kidnapped, tortured, and murdered more than 20 women and young girls, wrote extensively about his sexually sadistic fantasies involving women. These writings included descriptions of his victims' capture, torment, and death by hanging. At the time of his arrest, photographs were found depicting the subject in female attire and participating in autoerotic asphyxia. The offender apparently acted out his fantasies on both himself and others.

Some individuals act out their sadistic desires against inanimate objects, most often dolls, pictures, and clothing, but sometimes corpses. As in the case of fantasy, the suffering in such activity is imagined:

A female doll was found hanging outside an emergency room of a hospital. Around its neck was a hangman's noose, and its hands were bound behind its back. Needles penetrated one eye and one ear. Burn marks were present on the doll, and cotton protruded from its mouth. Drawn on the chest of the doll were what appeared to be sutures. An incision had been made between the legs, creating an orifice to which hair had been glued and into which a pencil had been inserted. Nothing indicated that a crime had occurred.

Although it is commonly believed that sexual sadists are cruel toward animals, it has not been determined that such cruelty is related to sexual sadism. Violent men were often cruel to animals during childhood, but without sexual excitement. Cruel acts toward animals may reflect nonsexual aggressive and sadistic motives or may be sacrifices demanded by religious rituals or delusional beliefs. Someone who is sexually excited by an animal's suffering is probably both a sexual sadist and a zoophile (one attracted to animals).

Sexual sadism may also be acted out with freely consenting or paid partners, such as prostitutes who specialize in role playing the "submissive" for sexually sadistic clients. The nature of the acts varies from simulations of discomfort to actions that result in severe injury. A consenting partner turns into a victim when her withdrawal of consent goes unheeded or when an act results in unexpected injury or death. This is when such acts come to the attention of law enforcement.

Some sexual sadists cultivate compliant victims, that is, those who enter into a relationship voluntarily but are manipulated into sadomasochistic activities for an extended time. These victims are wives or girlfriends who underwent extreme emotional, physical, and sexual abuse over months or years of a relationship that began as an ordinary courtship. In these instances, the offenders shaped the behavior of the women into gradual acceptance of progressively deviant sexual acts and then, through social isolation and repeated abuse, battered their self-images until the women believed they deserved the punishments meted out by their "lovers."

One woman in her thirties advised authorities that she had been coerced into an emotionally, physically, and sexually abusive relationship over an 18-month period. At first, she considered her offender to be the most loving and caring man she had ever known, and she fell deeply in love. Having occasionally used cocaine in the past, she was receptive to his suggestion that they use cocaine to enhance their sexual relations. Eventually, she became

addicted. After six months together, he began to abuse her sexually. This abuse included forced anal sex, whipping, painful sexual bondage, anal rape by other males, and the insertion of large objects into her rectum. This abusive behavior continued for a full year before she made her initial complaint to the police.

These cases pose special problems to investigators and prosecutors because it appears as if the complainant "consented" to the abuse. However, the transformation of the vulnerable partner into a compliant victim resembles the process by which other abusive men batter women and intimidate them into remaining in the relationship.

While many crimes contain elements of cruelty, these acts are not necessarily sexually sadistic in nature:

Two men, escaped from a state prison, captured a young couple and took them to an isolated area. After repeatedly raping the woman, they severely beat the couple and locked them in the trunk of their car. They then set the car on fire and left the couple to burn to death.

Although these men intentionally inflicted physical and psychological suffering on their victims, there was no indication that they did so for sexual excitement. They beat the couple after the rape and left as the victims were screaming and begging for mercy. Sexual sadists would have been sexually stimulated by the victims' torment and would have remained at the scene until the suffering ended.

Cruelty often arises in offenses committed by a group, even when the individuals involved have no history of cruelty:

A group of adolescents attacked a mother of six as she walked through her neighborhood. They dragged her into a shed, where they beat her and repeatedly inserted a long steel rod into her rectum, causing her death. Some of her attackers were friends of her children.

Most likely, the participants in this attack tried to prove themselves to the others by intensifying the acts of cruelty.

SEX-RELATED INVESTIGATIONS

Rape, or *sexual battery*, is a legal term defining the crime of a person having sexual relations with another person under the following circumstances: (1) against the person's consent, (2) while the person is unconscious, (3) while the person is under the influence of alcohol or drugs, (4) with a person who is feeble-minded or insane, and (5) with a child who is under the age of consent as fixed by statute. A number of state statutes include men as victims of rape. However in cases when men are the rape victims the assailant is almost always another male.

When the police and medical examiner are dealing with a dead body, obviously they can elicit no story from the victim that can be confirmed or denied. Investigators often must rely on their initial impression of the scene, such as the state of the clothing, items found, and the presence or absence of injuries related to sexual intercourse (fingernail scratches, bite marks, hickeys, direct genital injury, etc.), in deciding whether sexual intercourse (or attempted intercourse) was related to death. But investigators must be careful, because the victim might have had sexual intercourse with another person before death, and the intercourse might not be related to the death.

When investigating a homicide and the victim is a female, the question frequently arises of whether rape also has been committed. But the question should also arise when the victim is a male, and especially if a child. Sex is a major motivator and modifier of human behavior. Therefore, a determination of sexual activity may be of great value not only in the classic rape-murder case but also in natural, suicidal, or accidental deaths. Careful observation of the scene and the body may indicate a need for a rape investigation. Even if sexual intercourse does not seem to have any direct bearing on the cause of death, it may explain motives or timing of death, or simply provide a check on the veracity of a suspect or witness. The following cases illustrate these points:

A 53-year-old businessman was found dead in a motel room. There was no evidence of foul play. The bed was in slight disarray, with one of the pillows on the floor. The bed covers were bunched in an unusual position. The body on the floor was dressed in a shirt, loosened tie, trousers, underclothes, and socks. Shoes were neatly laid out next to a chair, and a jacket was on the back of a chair. Examination of the contents of the deceased's trouser pockets revealed the usual items, except for a pair of female panties. Autopsy revealed a massive heart attack and no vaginal cells on the penis. A logical reconstruction of the events preceding death suggested sexual foreplay with a female, in the course of which a wrestling match ensued during which the man took the woman's panties and then suffered a heart attack.

Although establishing the absence of sexual intercourse in this case did not significantly add to the medical solution of the problem, it did explain why the victim was found at a motel when he was supposedly having lunch.

A furnace repairman was found dead, slumped over the front seat of his van. There was no evidence of foul play, and the medical examiner was not called to the scene. Observation at the morgue revealed that there were peculiar parallel linear abrasions over the victim's knees, tearing of the overalls at the same region, and no underwear. His boots were reversed and loosely laced. Penile washings were positive for vaginal cells. Further investigation disclosed that he had visited a woman at 7 in the morning under the pretext of cleaning her furnace and had been stricken by a heart attack during intercourse. The woman hastily dressed him and dragged him across the back alley to his truck, not realizing that his underwear was neatly tucked under her bed.

A 15-year-old girl's body was found in a vacant lot. The absence of clothing on the lower body suggested sexual intercourse immediately before or at the time of death. Faint abrasions were present on the back of the neck, and marked hemorrhages were present in the eye. The medical examiner believed that this was a case of rape-murder. Autopsy confirmed recent sexual intercourse. The scratch on the back of the neck, however, proved to be superficial, and there were no deeper injuries. Reconstruction of the events immediately preceding death confirmed that the girl had had sexual intercourse with her boyfriend (who lived nearby), in the course of which (according to the boyfriend's testimony) the girl started making choking noises. She reported pain in her chest but said that it was going away. The boyfriend resumed intercourse. The girl started making even more violent noises. He assumed these to be related to orgasm. After intercourse, he noticed that the girl was motionless and unresponsive. After a few minutes, he decided that she was dead and became very scared. He escaped from the scene and told investigators that he had not seen his girlfriend on the night of her death.

The body of a missing preadolescent boy was found in the woods, face down, with his hands tied behind his back by laces removed from his sneakers and his belt. His trousers and jockey shorts were pulled down below the buttocks. The ligature on the hands consisted of laces removed from the boy's sneakers and the boy's own belt. He had been tied around the neck with a torn piece of his shirt. The scene suggested homosexual rape-murder. However, the investigation revealed no evidence of sexual assault. Although there was a depressed groove under the ligature, no subcutaneous hemorrhages were associated with it. A contusion on the back of the neck was associated with deep hemorrhages in the muscles and around the base of the skull and cervical spine. Reconstruction of the case directed suspicion to the boy's stepfather, who had discovered the body. The subsequent investigation revealed that after finding the boy, who frequently played hooky from school, wandering through the woods, the stepfather had hit him with a karate chop to the neck, killing him. The stepfather then tied and disrobed the child to convey the impression of homosexual assault.

INTERVIEW OF THE RAPE VICTIM

The interview requires intimate communication between a police officer and a victim who has been physically and psychologically assaulted. As such, the investigative nature of the interview represents only one dimension of the officer's responsibility. By conducting the interview tactfully and compassionately, the officer can avoid intensifying emotional suffering. At the same time, the cooperation of the victim is gained and the investigative process is thereby made easier.[4]

The psychological reactions of rape victims vary. For many, the psychological trauma is worse than the physical injury. One psychiatrist believes that victims of rape experience depression, shock, and anxiety, which may last only an hour or may persist for several months or even years.[5]

A psychotherapist notes that submitting to rape does "something to a woman, you have no sense of self; once you are used and raped you are a thing, an object, a non-person . . . the victim feels shock, feelings of being apart, split from humanity."[6] Thus, the investigator must be sensitive to the psychological state of the victim. Insensitivity can have two ill effects. First, from a practical standpoint, it might diminish the ability or the willingness of the victim to cooperate in the investigation. Second, it might cause serious psychological aftereffects. Certain steps make the interview less painful for the victim and more effective for the investigator.

INTERVIEW PROCEDURES AND INVESTIGATIVE QUESTIONS

The attitude of the officer is extremely important and makes a lasting impression on the victim. The initial interview of the victim should not be excessively thorough. It is frequently best to obtain only a brief account of events and a description of the perpetrator for the pickup order. Rapid placement of the pickup order is essential. Unless the circumstances of the offense make it unwise to delay the investigation, the detailed interview should be conducted the following day, when the victim has calmed down. When threats have been made against the victim, protection should be provided. The interview should be conducted in a comfortable environment with absolute privacy from everyone, including husbands, boyfriends, parents, children, friends, or anyone else personally associated with the victim. Without privacy the victim's reluctance to discuss the details may be magnified greatly.[7]

There is some question about whether the investigator interviewing the victim should be male or female. Some argue that a female victim feels more at ease in discussing the details of the assault with another woman. Others argue that an understanding male may help the victim to overcome a possibly aversive reaction to men, especially if the victim is relatively young or sexually inexperienced. The major criterion, regardless of whether the investigator is male or female, is that the person have the ability to elicit trust and confidence from the victim, while possessing considerable investigative ability. Many police departments have moved toward male-female teams in rape investigation.[8]

In interviewing the victim, the investigator may find that the victim uses slang terms to describe the sex act or parts of the body. This may be done because the victim does not know the proper terminology. It is possible that at some point the investigator may find it necessary to use slang terms to interview the victim; however, in today's world investigators must protect themselves from allegations of insensitivity or professional misconduct. Delicately employed proper terms can be used immediately after a victim's slang usage. This in no way demeans the victim's intellect but, rather, conveys an image of professionalism to which most victims respond positively.

When the victim has had an opportunity to compose herself, the investigator should make inquiries into the following areas.

Type and Sequence of Sexual Acts during an Assault

To determine the motivation behind a rape, it is imperative to ascertain the type and sequence of the rape.[9] This task may be made difficult because of the victim's reluctance to discuss certain aspects of the crime out of fear, shame, or humiliation. Often, however, investigators can overcome victims' reluctance with a professional and empathic approach. It has been found that although interviewers are likely to ask about vaginal, oral, and anal acts, they often do not ask about kissing, fondling, use of foreign objects, digital manipulation of the vagina or anus, fetishism, voyeurism, or exhibitionism by the offender.[10] In a sample of 115 adult, teenage, and child rape victims, researchers have reported vaginal sex as the most frequent act, but they also reported 18 other sexual acts. Repetition and sequence of acts are infrequently reported. Most reports state, "the victim was raped," "vaginally assaulted," or "raped repeatedly."

By analyzing the sequence of acts during the assault, the investigator may determine whether the offender was acting out a fantasy, experimenting, or committing the sexual acts to punish or degrade the victim. For example, if anal sex were followed by fellatio (oral sex—mouth to penis), the motivation to punish and degrade would be strongly suggested. In acting out a fantasy, the offender normally engages in kissing, fondling, or cunnilingus (oral sex—mouth to female genitals). If fellatio occurs, it generally precedes anal sex. If a rapist is experimenting sexually, he is moderately forceful and verbally profane and derogatory. Fellatio may precede or follow anal sex.[11]

Verbal Activity of Rapist

A rapist reveals a good deal about himself and the motivation behind the assault through what he says to the victim. For this reason, it is important to elicit from the victim everything the rapist said and the tone and attitude in which he said it.

A study of 115 rape victims revealed several themes in rapists' conversations, including "threats, orders, confidence lines, personal inquiries of the victim, personal revelations by the rapist, obscene names and racial epithets, inquiries about the victim's sexual 'enjoyment,' soft-sell departures, sexual put-downs, possession of women, and taking property from another male."[12]

Preciseness is important. For example, a rapist who states, "I'm going to hurt you if you don't do what I say," has threatened the victim, whereas the rapist who says, "Do what I say, and I won't hurt you," may be trying to reassure the victim and gain her compliance without force. A rapist who states, "I want to make love to you," has used a passive and affectionate phrase, and may not want to harm the victim physically. But a statement such as, "I'm going to fuck you," is much more aggressive, hostile, and angry. Compliments to the victim, politeness, expressions of concern, apologies, and discussions of the offender's personal life, whether fact or fiction, indicate low self-esteem in the offender. In contrast, derogatory, profane, threatening, or abusive language suggests anger and the use of sex to punish or degrade the victim.

When analyzing a rape victim's statement, the interviewer is advised to write down an adjective that accurately describes each of the offender's statements. For example, the interviewer might record, "You're a beautiful person" (complimentary); "Shut up, bitch" (hostility); "Am I hurting you?" (concern). The interviewer then has better insight into the offender's motivation and personality.

Verbal Activity of Victim

The rapist may make the victim say certain words or phrases that enhance the rape for him. By determining what, if anything, the victim was forced to say, the interviewer learns about the rapist's motivation and about what gratifies him. For example, a rapist who demands such phrases as "I love you," "Make love to me," or "You're better than my husband" suggests the need for affection or ego-building. One who demands that the victim plead or scream suggests sadism and a need for total domination. If the victim is forced to demean herself, the offender may be motivated by anger and hostility.

Sudden Change in Rapist's Attitude during Attack

The victim should be specifically asked whether she observed any change in the attitude of the rapist during the time he was with her. She should be asked whether he became angry, contrite, physically abusive, or apologetic, and whether this was a departure from his previous attitude. If the victim reports such a change, she should be asked to recall what immediately preceded the change. A sudden behavioral change may reflect weakness or fear. Factors that may cause such sudden behavioral changes include a rapist's sexual dysfunction, external disruptions (a phone ringing, noise, or a knock on the door), the victim's resistance or lack of fear, ridicule or scorn, or even completion of the rape. An attitudinal change may be signaled verbally, physically, or sexually. Because the rape is stressful for the rapist, how he reacts to stress may become important in future interrogations, and knowing what caused the change can be a valuable psychological tool to the investigator.

In attempting to determine the experience of the rapist, the investigator should ask the victim what actions the offender took to protect his identity, remove physical or trace evidence, or facilitate his escape. It may be possible to conclude from the offender's actions whether he is a novice or an experienced offender who may have been arrested previously for rape or similar offenses. Most rapists take some action, such as wearing a mask or telling the victim not to look at them, to protect their identity. But some go to great lengths to protect themselves from future prosecution. As in any criminal act, the more rapes a person commits, the more proficient he becomes in eluding detection. If a person is arrested because of a mistake and later repeats the crime, he is not likely to repeat the same costly mistake.

The offender's experience level can sometimes be determined from the protective actions he takes. Novice rapists are not familiar with modern medical or police technology and take minimal actions to protect their identity. Some wear a ski mask and gloves, change their voice, affect an accent, or blindfold and bind their victims. The experienced rapist's modus operandi can indicate a more than common knowledge of police and medical developments. The rapist may walk through the victim's residence or prepare an escape route prior to the sexual assault, disable the victim's telephone, order the victim to shower or douche, bring bindings or gags rather than using those available at the scene, wear surgical gloves during the assault, or take or force the victim to wash items the rapist touched or ejaculated on, such as bedding and the victim's clothing.

Theft during Rape

Almost without exception, police record the theft of items from rape victims. All too often, however, investigators fail to probe the matter unless it involves articles of value. But knowing about the items stolen may provide information about the criminal and aid in the investigative process. In some cases, the victim initially may not realize that something has been taken. For this reason, the victim should be asked to inventory items.

Missing items fall into one of three categories: evidentiary, valuables, and personal. The rapist who takes evidentiary items—those he has touched or ejaculated on—suggests prior rape experience or an arrest history. One who takes items of value may be unemployed or working at a job providing little income. The type of missing items may also provide a clue as to the age of the rapist. Younger rapists have been noted to steal items such as stereos or televisions; older rapists tend to take jewelry or items more easily concealed and transported. Personal items taken sometimes include photographs of the victim, lingerie, driver's licenses, and the like. These items have no intrinsic value but remind the rapist of the rape and the victim. A final factor to consider is whether the offender later returns the items to the victim, and if so, why. Some do so to maintain power over the victim by intimidation. Others wish to convince the victim that they meant her no harm and wish to convince themselves that they are not bad people.

Rapists often target their victims beforehand. A series of rapes involving victims who were either alone or in the company of small children is a strong indication that the offender had engaged in peeping or surveillance. He may have entered the residence or communicated with the victim earlier. For this reason, the investigator should determine whether the victim or her neighbors experienced any of the following before the rape:

1. Calls or notes from unidentified persons.
2. Residential or automobile break-in.
3. Prowlers or peeping toms.
4. Feelings of being watched or followed.

Frequently, rapists who target their victims have prior arrests for breaking and entering, prowling, peeping, or theft of women's clothing.

Delayed Reporting

If the victim has delayed making a complaint, the investigator should establish the reason. It may be that the victim was frightened, confused, or apprehensive. However, delays of several weeks or several months reduce the likelihood of apprehending the suspect and tend to weaken the state's case should a trial be held. Nevertheless, such a complaint must be investigated in the same way as all other similar complaints, until or unless it is substantiated or considered unfounded. An unfounded case does not go forward for prosecution for such reasons as lack of medical evidence, delay in reporting, intoxication of the victim, previous relationships between victim and offender, or because the victim is too embarrassed or too upset to cooperate.[13]

WHY WOMEN DO NOT REPORT RAPE TO THE POLICE

Studies have shown that there is considerable reluctance on the part of many women to report rape to their local police. Victims do not report the crime because of:

- Lack of belief in the ability of the police to apprehend the suspect.
- Worries about unsympathetic treatment from police and discomforting procedures.
- Apprehension, a result of television programs or newspaper reports, of being further victimized by court proceedings.
- Embarrassment about publicity, however limited.
- Fear of reprisal by the rapist.[14]

Unfortunately, some complaints about the criminal justice system's treatment of rape victims are justified. In many jurisdictions, efforts are being made to correct deficiencies. Many corrections have come about through legislative changes.[15] In other instances, women's groups have worked with local police departments to educate the public, especially women, about the crime of rape and to correct much of the misinformation that may be transmitted via television programs and other news media.

The failure of victims to report rapes has serious implications, because without such information, the effectiveness of the police in protecting other women is considerably diminished. A case in point occurred a few years ago in San Francisco.

A young woman who was raped turned first to her friends for help and comfort, then sought aid from a local Women Against Rape group. No one encouraged her to make a police report; she was indecisive and did nothing. Several days later, she read a news account describing a rape similar to her own. She immediately notified the police and learned that the rapist had attacked three other women. With the additional information that she provided, the police located and arrested the rapist by the end of the day.[16]

FALSE RAPE ALLEGATIONS

During the past several years, police agencies have been more selective in assigning personnel to rape investigations. They are now more sensitive to the emotional trauma experienced by victims. However, although the vast majority of rape complaints are legitimate, investigators must remain alert to the possibility of false rape complaints.

In the rape investigation, officers have a responsibility both to the legitimate victims of rape and to men who are falsely accused of rape. There are no hard-and-fast rules to guide the investigator to the truth, but experienced investigators generally find it by carefully questioning all parties involved and scrutinizing the circumstantial and physical evidence. Investigators should conduct a complete check on the background of the victim and all suspects. If the victim is a prostitute or promiscuous, these facts should be considered in the search for the truth. But once it is evident that the legal elements for rape are present, the victim's character should be disregarded. The following case shows the importance of the victim's background in rape complaints:

An 18-year-old woman reported that she had been walking past a vacant house at night when three young men who she knew casually leaped from behind some bushes and dragged her, kicking and screaming, into the house. She claimed that she resisted. But while two men held her down, each of the three had sexual intercourse with her. When the last one had finished, they fled. She went to a nearby store and called the police.

The officer assigned to the case had reservations about the validity of the victim's complaint for the following reasons:

- The occupant of the house next to the vacant house said that he had heard no scream even though his house was only 20 feet away and his windows were open.

- Sand examined in the area where the men supposedly had leaped from behind the bushes was undisturbed, although there were a number of shoe impressions in the sandy patch leading into the house.

- The woman's clothing showed no indications of struggle.

- The interior of the house was examined and a large piece of cardboard found on the floor in a back room. The woman stated that she had been forced to lie on this while the men raped her. There was a considerable amount of dirt in the room and near the cardboard, but, except for some shoe

impressions, there were no tracks that would indicate that a person had been dragged through the house and to the cardboard.

- Physical examination indicated that the victim had recently had sexual intercourse, but there were no injuries or other traumas. The investigator assigned to the case went to the suspects' hangout, a pool hall. The pool hall manager reported that the victim had voluntarily left the pool hall with the three suspects earlier in the evening.

The manager said that the girl frequently came into the pool hall to pick up men; he said that he had been told by patrons that she was a prostitute who took her customers to an abandoned house nearby to have sexual intercourse. The manager was asked to call the police if any of the men returned. The following day one of the young men, who had heard that the police were looking for him, voluntarily came to police headquarters. He said that he and two other young men had agreed to pay the girl $1 each for her sexual services, to which she agreed. They were directed by her to a nearby abandoned house, and each had sexual intercourse with her. When they finished, they refused to pay her and one of the men stole her brand-new shoes to give to his girlfriend. The victim was reinterviewed and admitted that she had lied to the police because she was angry with the men for cheating her out of the money they had agreed to pay her and because they also had stolen her shoes.

Had the victim actually been sexually assaulted, her background would have been immaterial.

Occasionally women will report that they have been raped as an attention-getting device. The following case illustrates this point:

A woman whose husband was a long-distance truck driver and frequently away from home reported to police that a house painter, who had responded to her home to apply for a painting job she had advertised in a local paper, had raped her. Because of the detailed information she gave the police, they were able to arrest the man. A lineup was conducted at police headquarters, and she positively identified the painter as the man who raped her. He was then charged with rape and bound over to the local district court. He spent three days in jail before being bonded out. Several days later the woman had second thoughts, contacted the prosecutors, and confessed that she had fabricated the rape story in order to get her husband to stay home and pay more attention to her. She was subsequently charged with and convicted of perjury.

She was sentenced to 180 days in jail and two years probation. Further, she was ordered by the court to apologize to the man in the local newspaper and in radio advertisements. The man who was arrested lost his job and had to employ a lawyer; his children in school were confronted by other children who said, "Your dad's a rapist." His wife was too embarrassed to go to town, and his 18-year-old daughter quit high school because of the way she was treated. The accused man was also fired from his primary job as a driver after being arrested. Even though he has been cleared of the charges, there was still a stigma associated with his arrest.[17]

Some inexperienced investigators are not suspicious of false allegations because of the victim's age. This complacency is an error, as the following case illustrates:

A 65-year-old great-grandmother reported that a 19-year-old neighbor had raped and robbed her in her home. The woman advised police that she had invited the young man over for a cup of coffee. After a while, he told her that he wanted to have sexual intercourse with her. She refused his request, whereupon he slapped her in the face and told her he would kill her great-grandson, who was asleep in a nearby bedroom, unless she had sexual intercourse with him. The woman said she agreed because of her concern for her great-grandson's safety. She went into her bedroom, disrobed, and had sexual intercourse with the man. When they were finished, he demanded that she give him some money and again threatened to injure the child if she failed to comply with his wishes. She gave him money, and he left.

The police pickup order was broadcast for the man. The woman was questioned and admitted that she had invited the young man to her home and had suggested that they have sexual intercourse; he had agreed. When they were finished, he demanded money from her. She refused, and he threatened her great-grandson. The woman said that she became frightened and gave the man the rent money. Because she now had to explain to her husband why the rent

money was gone, she made up the rape complaint. Although the rape complaint was unfounded, a robbery had occurred.

Conversely, at least occasionally, legitimate rape allegations are not deemed credible by the police:

On arriving home late one evening and prior to going to bed, a 30-year-old woman living alone checked all of the windows and doors to be certain that they were locked. After checking them, she went to bed. Shortly thereafter she was awakened by a man in her bed; he held a knife to her throat and warned her not to make any noise or attempt to resist or he would kill her. The man then proceeded to rape the woman. After raping her, he ordered her to go to the bathroom and to douche. After douching, she was instructed to flush the toilet. The suspect then fled by the front door. When the police arrived, they could find no signs of forced entry into the home. When the woman was examined at the hospital, there was no evidence of sexual intercourse or the presence of semen. The police thought the woman had fabricated the incident because of the absence of forcible entry into the home or any physical evidence of sexual intercourse. Two months later the man was arrested for another rape in the same general area where this first rape had occurred. The police found in his possession a number of keys; with the cooperation of his family members, it was determined that one of the keys was for a home the family had been renting several months before. This was the same home in which the first victim had been raped. The owners of the home had failed to rekey the lock after the family moved out and the new tenant moved in. The rapist merely retained the key and used it to enter through the front door, whereupon he committed the rape.

THE VICTIM AND PHYSICAL EVIDENCE

Victims of sex offenses provide important investigative details and ordinarily are a major source of physical evidence. Certain investigative procedures must be followed to ensure that physical evidence is not lost or accidentally destroyed.

INSTRUCTIONS TO THE VICTIM

The victim of a rape attack should be instructed not to douche, because douching could result in the loss of valuable physical evidence, such as semen and pubic hairs.

SEMEN AND HAIR AS EVIDENCE

As was discussed in considerable detail in Chapter 4, Physical Evidence, semen that contains sperm and hair with the root attached can now be identified as coming from a specific individual as a result of DNA typing. Thus, it is absolutely essential that appropriate samples of both be collected and preserved from both the victim and suspect. It should be noted that the presence of semen is not evidence that a rape occurred, nor does its absence mean that a rape did not occur. For example, because rapists sometimes experience sexual dysfunction, the examining physician may find no semen during the pelvic examination. In the interviews of the 133 convicted rapists previously discussed, 50 (30 percent) admitted some sexual dysfunction. Twenty-three of the rapists stated that they were unable to achieve an orgasm during the sex act; 22 experienced difficulty in achieving and sustaining an erection (impotency); and 5 experienced premature ejaculation.[18]

It must be pointed out that the terms "semen" and "sperm" are not synonymous. *Semen* is a grayish-white fluid, produced in the male reproductive organs, ejaculated during orgasm. In liquid form, it has a chlorinelike odor; when dried, it has a starchlike consistency. *Sperm* are the tadpolelike organisms that are contained in and travel through semen to fertilize the female egg. This distinction is important because the laboratory examinations and tests that are employed to search for each are quite different. Thus, if a rape were committed by a male who was sterile (having no sperm in his ejaculate), then semen but not sperm may be present. It should be noted that DNA typing is conducted on the sperm, not the semen. The physician examining the victim for sperm in the vagina therefore aspirates the vagina—removes fluids with a suction device—and microscopically examines them for sperm. The motility of sperm in the vagina is short, measured in hours rather than days; motility decreases to zero in about 3 hours. Menstruation may prolong motility to 4 hours. If large numbers of highly motile sperm are aspirated from the vagina, one may conclude that sexual intercourse had occurred 1 to 2 hours before the examination. If a few motile sperm remain, one may conclude that sexual intercourse had occurred within 3 hours of the examination. Nonmotile sperm may be found in a living female in small numbers up to 48 hours after sexual intercourse. Nonmotile sperm have been found in dead bodies for up to several hours after death.[19]

When sperm cannot be found, a second test may be employed to identify the presence of acid phosphatase. Acid phosphatase, an enzyme, is a component in the liquid portion of semen. The test should be conducted by experienced crime laboratory personnel and interpreted with care. Routine hospital laboratory techniques are not applicable to this type of examination and may be erroneously interpreted as significant. Only strong reactions should be considered evidence of semen, as mild positive reactions have been noted with vegetable matter, feces, and many other types of organic substances. Experiments have been conducted to determine the persistence of a significantly positive reaction to the acid phosphatase test over variable lengths of time following sexual intercourse. In the living, acid phosphatase may be lost from the vagina after 12 to 40 hours.

INFORMATION FOR THE EXAMINING PHYSICIAN

The physician responsible for examining the victim should be provided with all of the available facts before the physical examination. Frequently, a gynecologist is called in to examine a living victim; a forensic pathologist should examine a deceased victim.

Usually certain hospitals in a community are designated as the ones to which rape victims are taken for a physical examination. These hospitals frequently have both specially trained staffs and the necessary technical facilities. Under no circumstances should a male investigator be present in the hospital room when a physical examination is being made of a female victim. If a male investigator believes that some physical evidence may be adhering to the victim's body, he should instruct the examining physician to collect such evidence and turn it over to him. The collection of physical evidence in this manner must conform to all guidelines for preserving the chain of custody.

COLLECTION OF THE VICTIM'S CLOTHING

The victim's clothing should be collected as soon as possible. Even if the victim was forced to disrobe prior to the sexual attack, it is possible that hair, semen, or fibers from the suspect's clothing have been deposited on her undergarments. Great care should be employed in collecting and packaging the victim's clothing because the physical evidence adhering to it may be minute and fragile. Underpants should not be the only item of a victim's clothing recovered, because they often offer only limited physical evidence and are likely to be con-taminated with other stains, such as vaginal secretions or urine, that interfere with the laboratory examination. Other garments, such as the dress, slip, or coat, may be of greater value in providing physical evidence. The evidence most frequently obtained from the victim's clothing are fibers from a suspect's clothing and loose pubic hairs. If the assault occurred in a wooded or grassy area, there will often be soil, seeds, weeds, and other vegetation adhering to the victim's clothing.[20]

The following actual case, which occurred before the advent of DNA fingerprinting, illustrates the importance of a careful search for physical evidence:

The partly dressed body of a 16-year-old female was discovered by two young boys traveling through a wooded area. The victim's slacks and underpants were pulled down around her ankles, and her brassiere was pulled up around her head. A check of the missing-persons file revealed that a female fitting her description had been reported missing by her parents 18 hours earlier. The body was later identified as the missing female.

The victim's body was removed from the scene in a clean white sheet and transported to a local hospital. The medical examination of the victim revealed that she had died from brain damage after being struck repeatedly with a blunt object. In addition, she had a large bruise on her right cheek, also caused by

a blow from a blunt object, possibly a fist. The examination of the deceased's person and clothing yielded the following:

- Her clothing.
- Pubic-hair samples.
- Blood samples for typing.
- Grease stains on the inside of her thighs. The grease was initially deposited on the suspect's hands after he used an automobile master cylinder which had been on the floor board of his car to batter the victim unconscious.
- A single human hair clutched in her hand, mixed with considerable dirt, leaves, twigs, and so forth.
- No semen either in or on her body, clothing, or the immediate area.

Physical evidence also was obtained from the crime scene:

- Tire impressions.
- Samples of soil, leaves, weeds, and other vegetation.

A suspect who had been the last person seen with the victim and who also had an arrest record for a similar offense was taken into custody and his vehicle was impounded. The vehicle's entire interior, including steering wheel, dashboard, door panels, seats, floor mats, and visor, was removed, as were all four wheels. These items were transported to the FBI laboratory along with all of the evidence collected from the victim and the crime scene. A pair of blood-stained trousers and hair samples were obtained from the suspect. The results of the laboratory examination revealed the following:

- The victim's brassiere had several fibers caught in the hooks, which were identical to those of the terrycloth seat covers in the suspect's car.
- The grease stain on the victim's thighs was compared with the grease found under the dashboard and near the ignition switch in the suspect's vehicle and found to be identical. An examination of the ignition switch revealed that the car could be started only if someone reached under the dash and crossed the ignition wires, thus when the suspect tried to start his car he deposited grease from the master cylinder on to the ignition switch.
- The single hair found in the victim's hand was similar in all characteristics to that of the suspect.

- Samples collected from the victim's hair at the morgue were similar to those recovered from the floorboard of the suspect's vehicle.
- Fibers from the victim's underpants were identical to fibers recovered from the suspect's vehicle.
- A tire impression at the scene matched a tire on the suspect's vehicle.
- Debris collected from the scene matched debris recovered from the interior of the suspect's car and dirt extracted from the rims of the wheels of the suspect's car.
- Human blood was found on the steering wheel of the suspect's car, but the presence of various contaminants prevented the blood from being typed accurately.
- Because the suspect had soaked his trousers in cold water overnight, blood typing was impossible.

The suspect confessed to murdering the victim after abducting her from a teenage dance, although his confession was not needed in view of the physical evidence. As previously indicated, he identified the murder weapon as an automobile master cylinder, which he had disposed of after the crime. It was never located. He had killed the victim after she violently resisted his efforts to assault her sexually.

This case clearly illustrates the importance of recognizing, collecting, and preserving even the smallest piece of physical evidence. Except for the tire impression, the evidence had only class characteristics (discussed in considerable detail in Chapter 4, Physical Evidence). However, the preponderance of it, coupled with the particulars of the case, made a compelling case against the suspect.

ERRORS MOST COMMONLY MADE IN COLLECTING EVIDENCE

The importance of identifying, collecting, and preserving physical evidence in sex-related offenses cannot be overstated. Yet evidence continues to be mishandled or not recovered. The FBI crime laboratory indicates a number of common errors in collecting physical evidence. It cites the failure to:

- Obtain fingernail scrapings from the victim.
- Obtain all of the victim's and suspect's clothing worn at the time of the offense.
- Obtain samples of soil and other vegetation at the crime scene.

- Mark each item of evidence properly for future identification purposes.
- Obtain saliva and blood samples.
- Remove obvious, visible hair and package it properly when the location of the hair may be germane to the investigation.
- Obtain hair samples from the suspect and the victim. Hair samples are extremely important because in rape-murder cases the victim is soon buried, and obtaining samples after the burial presents serious problems.[21]

The FBI also cites faulty handling and packaging of evidence, which results in contamination during shipment.

SEXUAL-BATTERY EXAMINATION

Most hospitals or crisis centers responsible for the collection of evidence from sex-offense victims have developed sexual-battery examination kits. Such kits generally include the following components:

1. A large envelope containing all the appropriate forms and specific items needed for the collection of evidence. This envelope is also used for the storage of evidence once it is collected. It is then forwarded to the crime laboratory for analysis.

2. Sexual-assault victim examination consent form, sexual-assault victim exam summary for the patient, and victim confidential evaluation.

3. Blood vials used for collecting blood from the victim for blood typing; paper bag used to collect victim's panties, bra, blouse, pants, and other items; sterile Dacron-tipped applicator used in obtaining oral swabs, vaginal swabs, and anal swabs; holder for glass slide containing vaginal smears; envelope for holding oral swabs; envelope for holding possible perspiration; envelope for holding possible saliva samples; envelope for holding vaginal swabs; envelope for holding possible semen; envelope for holding anal swab; and envelope for holding fingernail scrapings. (See Figure 11–1).

4. Tissue paper for collecting hair samples; envelope for storage of pubic-hair pluckings;

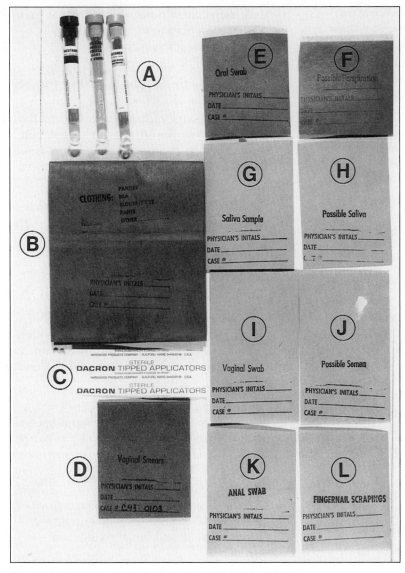

Figure 11–1
Sexual Battery Examination Kit

Partial contents of a sexual battery examination kit. (A) Blood vials: left vial, which has a red top, is used for collecting blood from the victim for blood typing; center vial, which has a purple top is used for collecting blood from the victim used in the DNA fingerprinting; right vial, which has a gray top is used for collecting blood from the victim for drug screening. (B) Paper bag used to collect victim's panties, bra, blouse, pants, and other items. (C) Sterile dacron-tipped applicators used in obtaining oral swabs, vaginal swabs, and anal swabs. (D) Holder for glass slide containing vaginal smears. (E) Envelope for holding oral swabs. (F) Envelope for holding possible perspiration. (G) Envelope for holding saliva samples. (H) Envelope for holding possible saliva. (I) Envelope for holding vaginal swabs. (J) Envelope for holding possible semen. (K) Envelope for holding anal swab. (L) Envelope for holding fingernail scrapings.

(Courtesy Pinellas County Florida, Public Health Unit, Sexual Assault Victim Examination Program)

envelope for storage of public-hair cuttings; envelope for storage of scalp-hair cuttings; and envelope for storage of scalp-hair pluckings.

CONDOM TRACE EVIDENCE

Manufacturers produce condoms using a variety of materials, both natural and synthetic. Each manu-facturer has its own formula, which may vary even among its different brands.[22] Some condoms are made from lamb membranes, and one manufac-turer recently introduced a model made from polyurethane plastic. Still, latex rubber condoms have, by far, the largest share of the market, per-haps because they cost considerably less. In addi-tion to the basic materials they use to produce condoms, manufacturers also add other substances, known as *exchangeable traces,* which comprise par-ticulates, lubricants, and spermicide.

EXCHANGEABLE TRACES

Particulates

Condom manufacturers add finely powdered particulates to prevent a rolled-up latex condom from sticking to itself. Particulates found in different brands include cornstarch, potato starch, and lycopodium (a powder found in plants), as well as amorphous silica, talc, or other minerals. In the laboratory, forensic scientists use several different techniques to characterize these particles and compare them with those obtained from other condom brands.

Lubricants

Sexual assailants prefer lubricated condoms, probably for the same reason they use petroleum jelly, that is, to facilitate their crimes.[23] Many condom brands contain a liquid lubricant, which may be classified as either "wet" or "dry." Both types of condom lubricant have an oil-like consistency, but wet lubricants are water-based and/or water-soluble, while dry lubricants are not. Although many different manufacturers use the same dry lubricant, the viscosity grades sometimes differ. The forensic laboratory can recover these silicone oils easily from items of evidence and possibly associate them with a condom manufacturer. Wet lubricants may contain either polyethylene glycol or a gel made from a combination of ingredients similar to those found in vaginal lubricants. Despite similarities to other products on the market, forensic examination can associate specific formulations with particular condom brands.

Spermicide

Both wet- and dry-lubricated condoms also may contain the spermicide nonoxynol-9. Its recovery and detection, along with lubricant ingredients and particulates, can help show condom use and indicate the specific brand.

THE VALUE OF CONDOM TRACE EVIDENCE

Condom trace evidence can assist investigators in several ways. It can help prove corpus delicti, provide evidence of penetration, produce associative evidence, and link the acts of serial rapists.

In Proving Corpus Delicti

Traces associated with condoms can help prove corpus delicti, the fact that a crime has occurred.

This evidence can support the claims of either the victim or the accused. For example, the U.S. military can prosecute personnel diagnosed as HIV-positive for aggravated assault if they engage in unprotected sex, even if it is consensual. If servicemen accused of aggravated assault claim that they did in fact wear a condom but it broke or slipped off, condom trace evidence can support that claim.

In Providing Evidence of Penetration

Condom traces found inside a victim can provide evidence of penetration. In many jurisdictions, this evidence raises the charge to a higher degree of sexual assault.

In Producing Associative Evidence

Recovered condom traces may correspond to those found in a certain brand or used by a certain manufacturer. An empty packet of this particular brand found near the crime scene, especially if it bears the suspect's fingerprints, provides a strong association between the suspect and the crime. Unopened condom packages of the same brand found on the suspect, in his car, or at his residence also would help tie the suspect to the crime.

In Linking the Acts of Serial Rapists

People tend to be creatures of habit, and sexual criminals are no exception. A serial rapist likely will use the same brand of condom to commit repeated acts. Moreover, repeat offenders whose DNA profiles have been stored in a computer data bank may be likely to use a condom when committing subsequent crimes. Along with other aspects of his modus operandi, traces from the same condom brand or manufacturer found during several different investigations can help connect a suspect to an entire series of assaults.

GUIDELINES FOR EVIDENCE COLLECTION

Investigators need not make any drastic changes in their usual procedures in order to include the possibility of condom trace evidence. The following guidelines will assist criminal investigators and medical examiners in collecting this valuable evidence.[24]

At the Crime Scene

First and foremost, investigators must wear *powder-free* gloves to protect themselves from blood-borne pathogens and to avoid leaving particulates that may be similar to those contained in some condom brands. After collecting the evidence, they should package the gloves separately and submit them with the evidence so that the forensic laboratory can verify that the gloves did not leave behind any particulates.

At the crime scene, investigators should make every effort to locate any used condom and its foil package. If a condom is recovered, the traces from the victim on the outside and the seminal fluids from the assailant on the inside would have the greatest evidentiary value.

If investigators find an empty packet, they first should try to recover any latent prints from the outside. The inside of the package will probably not contain prints, but it may contain lubricant, spermicide, and particulate residues. Investigators should wipe the inside with a clean cotton swab. The traces on this swab will serve as a standard for comparison with traces recovered from the victim and the suspect.

With the Victim

In addition to providing general information about the crime, victims may be able to supply valuable details about the condom and its wrapper. They may recall the brand itself or other important details, including the condom's color, shape, texture, odor, taste, and lubrication.

After obtaining facts about the condom, investigators should ask victims about their sexual and hygienic habits, which might account for traces not attributable to the crime. A comprehensive interview would include the following questions:

- Has the victim recently engaged in consensual sex?
- If so, was a condom used? A vaginal lubricant? What brand?
- Does the victim use any external or internal vaginal products (anti-itch medications, deodorants, douches, suppositories, etc.)?
- If so, what brands?

These questions assume an adult female victim. Investigators must modify the interview to accommodate male or child sexual-assault victims.

With the Suspect(s)

Investigators also should question the suspect about the condom. A cooperative suspect will reveal the brand, tell where he purchased it, and describe how and where he disposed of both the condom and the empty packet. An uncooperative or deceitful suspect may claim he does not know or cannot remember, or he may name a popular brand but will not be able to describe the condom or the packet in detail.

Legal Considerations

When investigators know or suspect that a sexual offender used a condom, they must remember to list condoms on the warrant obtained to search the suspect's possessions. The search of a suspect's home may reveal intact condom packets, but if investigators have not listed condoms on the search warrant, they will not be able to seize this valuable evidence.

RECORD OF INJURIES

A careful record should be made of the victim's injuries and included in the report. Photographs of the victim's injuries serve two purposes. First, if a suspect is arrested and tried for the offense, the photographs tend to corroborate the victim's account of the attack. Second, the injuries may be of an unusual nature—bite marks, scratches, or burns from cigarettes—and may provide data valuable for developing the suspect's MO. In some cases, the injuries are readily visible to the investigator. In other cases, the injuries are concealed by the victim's clothing. The examining physician can provide details of injuries not readily noticeable. Color photographs should be taken if the victim has sustained visible severe injuries. If the injuries are in a location that requires the victim to disrobe partially or completely to be photographed, then it is essential that a female nurse, female police officer, or some other female officially associated with the police department or the hospital be present. If possible, a female police photographer should photograph the victim.

AUTOEROTIC DEATHS

Death from accidental asphyxiation occasionally occurs as a result of masochistic activities of the deceased. This manner of death has been described as *autoerotic death,* or *sexual asphyxia.*

Typically, a white male is found partially suspended and nude, dressed in women's clothing or women's undergarments (see Figure 11–2) or with his penis exposed. A ligature, suspended from a point within his reach, is affixed to his neck; it is padded to prevent bruising and visible evidence of his activity. There is no indication of suicidal intent, and the death surprises friends, relatives, and associates. Usually, the deceased has no history of mental or sexual disorder.[25]

The death is attributable to asphyxia. The most common method is neck compression; more exotic forms involve chest compression, airway obstruction, and oxygen exclusion with gas or chemical replacement. Neck compression is illustrated in the first and chest compression in the second of the cases that follow:

A 38-year-old government employee was found in a rented motel room. He was in an upright position, and his feet were resting on the floor. A T-shirt around his neck suspended him from a room divider. He was attired in a skirt, sweater, brassiere padded with socks, panties, panty hose, and high heels. In the room were two suitcases. One contained men's trousers, shirts, socks, and undergarments. The second contained a knit sweater, skirt, slip, panties, bra, panty hose, and high heels. Investigators determined that he was married, had two preschool children, had recently been promoted in his job, and was well thought of by his associates.

The victim was a 40-year-old commercial airline pilot who was married and the father of two small children. On his day off, he left home, telling his wife that he was going to target practice. A fisherman discovered him a short time later, crushed against the left rear fender of his 1968 Volkswagen in a large turnaround area at the end of a secluded road. The left door was open and the motor was running. The steering wheel was fixed in an extreme left-turn position and the automatic transmission was in low gear. Tire tracks indicated that the automobile had been moving in concentric circles. The body was held against the car by heavy link chain and was totally nude except for a chain harness. The harness had a moderately tight loop around the neck and was bolted

Figure 11–2
Autoerotic Death
Note female undergarments being worn by male victim with oranges stuffed into the cups of the brassiere. A towel was wrapped around the rope to keep it from bruising his neck.

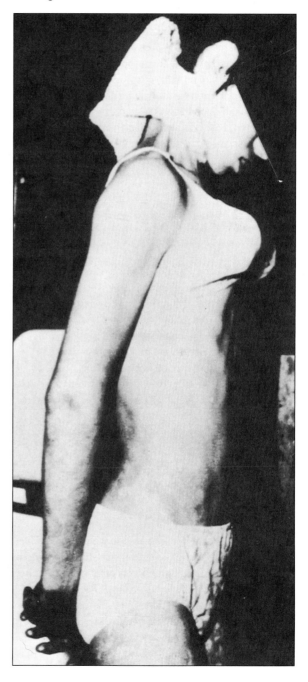

in front. The chain passed down the sternum and abdomen and around the waist to form a second loop. From the waist loop, strands of chain passed on each side of the testicles and into the gluteal fold and were secured to the waist loop in the small of the back. A 10-foot length of chain was attached from the waist loop to the rear bumper and had become wound around the rear axle five times. It is not known whether he jogged behind the car or was dragged; however, when he tired of the exercise, he approached the car intending to turn off the motor. In doing so, the chain became slack and the back tire rolled over it, causing the chain to become wound onto the rear axle. The trunk of the car contained his clothing, a zippered bag holding locks, bolts, chains, and wrenches. A lock and key were on the ground beside the body and another lock was found 20 feet from the body.[26]

Airway obstruction is illustrated in the following case:

The victim, a middle-aged male, was discovered dead in his apartment. He was totally nude and held to a pole that had been fitted into his apartment floor. Several black leather belts had been permanently affixed to the pole. These belts supported the victim from the neck, waist, and legs. Leg irons connected his ankles, handcuffs dangled from one wrist, and a gag was over his mouth. The belt around his neck was so tightly buckled that it lacerated his neck. On removal of the gag, it was found that he had placed so much paper in his mouth that he had been asphyxiated. Evidence of masturbation was also present.

The following is a case of oxygen exclusion with gas replacement:

A 50-year-old dentist was discovered dead in his office by an assistant. He was lying on his stomach, and over his face was a mask that he used to administer nitrous oxide to his patients. The mask was connected to a nitrous oxide container and was operational. His pants were unzipped, and he was thought to have been fondling himself while inhaling the gas.

Each of these cases was ruled accidental, and each occurred while the victim was involved in autoerotic activities. Although the motivation for such

activity is not completely understood, asphyxia appears to be the cardinal feature of the act: "A disruption of the arterial blood supply resulting in a diminished oxygenation of the brain . . . will heighten sensations through diminished ego controls that will be subjectively perceived as giddiness, light-headedness, and exhilaration. This reinforces masturbatory sensations."[27] In autoerotic deaths, there does not appear to be a conscious intent to die, although the danger of death may well play a role. The masochistic aspect of this activity is evidenced by the elaborate bondage employed. Another masochistic practice associated with sexual asphyxia is the practice of *infibulation*, or masochism involving the genitals. The fantasies of the individuals who engage in sexual asphyxiation are heavily masochistic, involving such thoughts as one's own "penis being skewered with pins; being tied up in an initiation rite; being the leader of an imperiled group; and being raped by cowboys."[28] Evidence of the fantasy involvement may be found in the form of diaries, erotic literature, pornography, films or photographs of the individual's activities, or other such paraphernalia.

It appears that this phenomenon is quite rare among females, but the following case illustrates that it certainly does occur.[29]

This case involved a 35-year-old woman, a divorcée with a 9-year-old daughter. The mother was found by the daughter deceased in the morning after the child arose from a night's sleep in an adjoining room.

The child had gone to bed at 10 P.M. the night before and upon awakening noticed a strange humming noise coming from her mother's room. After entering the room she found her mother hanging dead in a small closet off the bedroom.

The victim was found completely nude lying on a small shelved space at the rear of the closet. Her feet were against the wall and her body was extended in a prone position, head downward, thus placing her legs and thighs in a horizontal position, resting on the shelved area from her feet to her waist. There was a folded quilt placed on the front portion of the shelf that was immediately under her abdomen and upper thighs. Behind the quilt and toward the rear of the shelf area was a broken cardboard box containing numerous books and other personal or family items. Her lower legs and feet were lying on these boxes, causing them to be at a slight upward angle from her waist.

It was estimated that the victim had been dead 10 to 12 hours, as there was evidence of scattered livor mortis on the body. She died of strangulation. An electric vibrator connected to an extension cord was found running. The vibrator was positioned between her thighs with the hard rubber massaging head in contact with the victim's vulva. There was a string-type clothespin on the nipple of her right breast, compressing the nipple, and another clothespin of the same type was found in a basket, immediately below her left breast.

In front of the shelved area, on the floor of the closet, was a laundry basket containing dirty clothes, and another quilt was folded and placed on top of the dirty clothes. The victim's hands were resting on this folded quilt in an arms-down position. The palms were facing upward. Over the place where the body was

lying on this shelved area was a small narrow shelf 66 inches above the floor. This was attached to the wall by two steel brackets, and the one closest to the shelved area had a nylon hose tied around it that formed a long loop. The victim had placed her head in the loop and placed a hand towel between her neck and the nylon hose. Her face was turned toward the wall and lying against it.

The investigating officer made several important observations based on the body's position and condition at the time of discovery.

1. Because of the position of the clothespin on the nipple of her right breast and the depressed or flattened nipple on the left breast, it appeared that this second clothespin had fallen off and dropped into the basket.
2. It was felt that the hand towel beneath the nylon stocking served as a padding to prevent

Figure 11–3
Sexual Asphyxiation
Accidental Death
Victim of sexual asphyxiation.

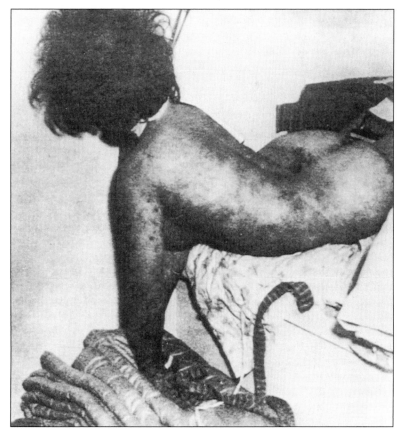

(Courtesy of *Journal of Forensic Science*)

injury to the neck. The padding in the form of the quilt on the shelved area in the closet was probably placed there to make the deceased more comfortable.

3. The victim placed herself in this position, placed clothespins on her nipples to cause discomfort, and used the electric vibrator for additional sexual gratification. The victim intended to support part of her weight with her arms, as in a push-up, but passed out. This relaxed her arms, and the full weight of her body then came to rest on the nylon stocking around her neck, causing the strangulation (see Figure 11–3).[30]

THE PSYCHOLOGICAL AUTOPSY

Occasionally the medical examiner or police investigator is confronted with a death that may be the result of autoerotic or suicidal intent on the part of the deceased. For resolving questions about the death, there is a technique employed called the *psychological autopsy*, described as follows:

Resolution of unexplained death has long been of concern within law enforcement activities and for the past quarter century, an object of inquiry within the mental health specialties. The term "autopsy" is usually associated with postmortem examination of human remains to determine the cause of death. The psychological autopsy is an analytical statement prepared by a mental health professional based upon the deceased's thoughts, feelings, and behavior.

Its specific purpose, therefore, is to form a logical understanding of death from tangible physical evidence, documented life events, and intangible, often illusive, emotional factors. To accomplish its purpose, the psychological autopsy is structured to address three questions: What was the deceased like? What occurred in his/her life that could have been stressful? What were his/her reactions to those stresses? To accomplish this, structured interviews are conducted with friends, relatives, and associates of the deceased in the hope of developing psychological motivation for the death and pinpointing patterns of life-threatening behavior.[31]

Questions

1. Briefly discuss the major characteristics of men who are classified as power rapists and anger rapists.
2. What is sexual sadism?
3. Briefly discuss the major factors that should be considered in interviewing rape victims.
4. What are some of the major reasons that women do not report rape?
5. Why do women sometimes make false rape allegations?
6. Why is the discovery of semen, sperm, and hair valuable in rape investigations?
7. Why is the absence of semen fairly common in rape cases?
8. What errors are most commonly made in collecting evidence on rape investigations?
9. In addition to the basic materials that condom manufacturers use, they also add other substances known as exchangeable traces. What are these composed of?
10. How can condom trace evidence be of value in linking acts of serial rapists?
11. What factors should indicate to the investigator that a death may have resulted from accidental sexual asphyxiation?
12. What is a psychological autopsy?

Notes

1. A. N. Groth, A. W. Burgess, and L. L. Holmstrom, *Rape, Power, Anger, and Sexuality,* paper presented at the LEAA Conference on Rape, Atlanta, Georgia, March 1977. The information from this study was collected from a random sample of 133 convicted rapists of adult victims. The rapists were committed to the

Massachusetts Treatment Center for Clinical Assessment. The victim sample population was derived from a one-year counseling and research study conducted at Boston City Hospital, which included all persons admitted to the emergency service with the chief complaint, "I've been raped." This discussion of the typology of rape has been derived from this paper. In 1971, Menachem Amir published the results of a study similar to the one more recently conducted by Groth et al., 1977. The Amir study, titled *Patterns in Forcible Rape* (Chicago: University of Chicago Press, 1971), served to dispel some of the most erroneous beliefs and myths about rapists, the most common of which was that they were sexually unfulfilled men carried away by a sudden uncontrollable surge of desire. Data collected by Amir showed that 90 percent of group rapes were planned in advance and 58 percent of the rapes committed by a single man were planned. As for the belief that rapists were sexually unfulfilled, 60 percent of the men in Amir's study were married and led normal lives. Another popular myth is that rapes occur in dark back alleys or to women who hitchhike; however, Amir's study showed that one-third of all rapes are committed by a man who forces his way into the victim's home, and over half of all rapes occur in a residence. Further results of Amir's study showed that in fully 48 percent of the cases, the rapists knew their victims either as casual friends or close relatives. Rapes also tend to be overwhelmingly intraracial. This was so in 93.2 percent of the cases studied by Amir.

2. The information discussed in this section of the chapter was obtained from material developed by Peter Lipkovic, M.D., medical examiner, Jacksonville, Florida.

3. Robert Hazelwood, Park Elliott Dietz, and Janet Warren, "The Criminal Sexual Sadist," *FBI Law Enforcement Bulletin*, February 1992, Vol. 61, No. 2, pp. 12–20. (This discussion of the criminal sexual sadist was taken with modification from this article.)

4. *Interviewing the Rape Victim: Training Key 210* (Gaithersburg, Md.: International Association of Chiefs of Police, 1974), p. 1.

5. *Rape and the Treatment of Rape Victims in Georgia* (Atlanta: Georgia Commission on the Status of Women, 1974), p. 5.

6. Ibid.

7. Ibid., p. 13.

8. Morton Bard and Katherine Ellison, "Crisis Intervention and Investigation of Forcible Rape," *The Police Chief*, May 1974, Vol. 41, No. 5, pp. 68–74.

9. This discussion and accompanying references came from R. R. Hazelwood, "The Behavior-Oriented Interview of Rape Victims: The Key to Profiling," *FBI Law Enforcement Bulletin*, September 1983, pp. 13–15.

10. L. L. Holmstrom and A. W. Burgess, "Sexual Behavior of Assailants during Rape," *Archives of Sexual Behavior,* 1980, Vol. 9, No. 5, p. 437.

11. Ibid., p. 427.

12. L. L. Holmstrom and A. W. Burgess, "Rapist's Talk: Linguistic Strategies to Control the Victim," *Deviant Behavior,* 1979, Vol. 1, p. 101.

13. C. LeGrande, "Rape and Rape Laws: Sexism in Society and Law," *California Law Review,* 1973, p. 929.

14. Queens Bench Foundation, *Rape Victimization Study* (San Francisco, 1975), pp. 81–87; E. L. Willoughby and James A. Inciardi, "Estimating the Incidence of Crime," *The Police Chief*, 1975, Vol. 42, No. 8, pp. 69–70; President's Commission on Law Enforcement and the Administration of Justice, *Task Force Report: Crime and Its Impact* (Washington, D.C.: Government Printing Office, 1967), p. 80.

15. The state of Florida several years ago repealed its previous statute on Forcible Rape and Carnal Knowledge 794, with a new statue, titled Sexual Battery 794. The new law provides for various penalties for sexual battery depending on the amount of force used and the injuries sustained by the victim. In addition, the statute provides that specific instances of prior sexual activity between the victim and any person other than the defendant cannot be admitted into evidence.

16. Queens Bench Foundation, *Rape Victimization Study,* p. 86.

17. "Vicious Lies and Apologies," *St. Petersburg Times,* July 30, 1990, pp. A1, A4.

18. A. N. Groth and A. W. Burgess, *Rape, A Sexual Deviation,* paper presented to the American Psychological Association Meeting, September 5, 1976, Washington, D.C., p. 4. This deals with the same group of rapists discussed earlier by Groth, Burgess, and Holmstrom.

19. J H. Davis, "Examination of Victims of Sexual Assault and Murder," material developed for a homicide seminar offered by the Florida Institute for Law Enforcement, St. Petersburg, Florida, 1965.

20. Arne Svensson and Otto Wendel, *Techniques of Crime Scene Investigation* (New York: American Elsevier, 1973).

21. FBI National Academy, *Collection of Physical Evidence in Sex Crimes* (Quantico, Va.: 1975), p. 2.

22. Robert D. Blackledge, "Condom Trace Evidence: A New Factor in Sexual Assault Investigations," *FBI Bulletin,* May 1996, pp. 12–16. (This discussion was adapted from this article.)

23. R. D. Blackledge and L. R. Cabiness, "Examination for Petroleum Based Lubricants in Evidence from Rapes and Sodomies," *Journal of Forensic Sciences,* 1983, Vol. 28, pp. 451–462.

24. R. D. Blackledge, "Collection and Identification Guidelines for Traces from Latex Condoms in Sexual Assault Cases," *Crime Laboratory Digest,* 1994, Vol. 21, pp. 57–61.

25. R. R. Hazelwood, *Autoerotic Deaths* (Quantico, Va.: Behavioral Science Unit, FBI Academy, 1984.)

26. J. Rupp, "The Love Bug," *Journal of Forensic Science,* 1973, pp. 259–262.

27. H. L. P. Resnick, "Eroticized Repetitive Hangings: A Form of Self-Destructive Behavior," *American Journal of Psychotherapy,* January 1972, p. 10.

28. R. Litman and C. Swearingen, "Bondage and Suicide," *Archives of General Psychiatry,* July 1972, Vol. 27, p. 82.

29. R. D. Henry, *Medical Legal Bulletin,* Office of the Chief Medical Examiner, Department of Health, State of Virginia, 1971, Vol. 20, No. 2, Bulletin 214.

30. E. A. Sass, "Sexual Asphyxia in the Female," *Journal of Forensic Science,* 1975, pp. 182–184.

31. N. Hibbler, "The Psychological Autopsy," *Forensic Science Digest,* September 1978, Vol. 5, pp. 42–44.

TWELVE

Crimes against Children

CHAPTER OUTLINE

Assaults against Children 314
Burn Injuries and Child Abuse 314
Shaken-Baby Syndrome 319
Munchausen Syndrome by Proxy 321
Child Molestation 323
Child Pornography 336

Incest 339
Sudden Infant Death Syndrome 343
Infant Abduction 346
Use of Age Progression Technology to Search for Missing Children 348
Questions 349
Notes 350

INTRODUCTION

There is no question that reports of crimes against children have increased dramatically during the past decade. As a matter of fact, it seems as though they have reached epidemic proportions. As a result, increasing numbers of police departments have investigators who are assigned exclusively to investigate crimes against children. For this reason, we have chosen to devote a separate chapter to this ongoing problem and focus on some of the unique investigative techniques and problems associated with the investigation of crimes against children.

ASSAULTS AGAINST CHILDREN

The most common cause of children's death is physical abuse, often by their own parents. The clinical term commonly used to describe physically abused children is the *battered-child syndrome*. This possibility should be considered in any child exhibiting evidence of bone fracture, subdermal hematoma, failure to thrive, soft-tissue swelling, or skin bruising; in any child who dies suddenly; or in any child when the degree and type of injury is at variance with the history given regarding the occurrence of the trauma.[1]

Abuse of children takes various forms, from minor assaults to flagrant physical torture. Many times these injuries cannot or will not be explained by the parents or the story seems inconsistent with the injuries received. For example, bruises in various stages of healing generally vary in color. Thus, one should be suspicious of an explanation of such injuries as being from a fall from a bike. Intentional injuries tend to occur most frequently on the face, back, ribs, buttocks, genitals, palms, or soles of the feet. Although abusers use a wide variety of instruments, the two most common are the belt (see Figure 12–1) and electric cord.

BURN INJURIES AND CHILD ABUSE

Although general awareness of the magnitude of child abuse is increasing, deliberate injury by burning is often unrecognized. Burn injuries make up about 10 percent of all child-abuse cases, and about 10 percent of hospital admissions of children to burn units are the result of child abuse. In comparison with accidentally burned children, abused children are significantly younger and have longer hospital stays and higher mortality rates. The child burn victim is almost always under the age of 10, with the majority under the age of 2.[2]

Children are burned for different reasons. Immersion burns may occur during toilet training, with the perpetrator immersing the child in scalding water for cleaning or punishment. Hands may be immersed in pots of water for playing near the stove. A person may place a child in an oven for punishment or with homicidal intentions.

Inflicted burns often leave characteristic patterns of injury that fortunately cannot be concealed. Along with the history of the burn incident, these patterns are primary indicators of inflicted burns versus accidental ones. Finds in response to the following questions can raise or lower the index of suspicion, helping to determine whether a burn was deliberately inflicted:

- Is the explanation of what happened consistent with the injury? Are there contradictory or varying accounts of the method or time of the "accident" or other discrepancies in the witnesses' descriptions of what happened?
- Does the injury have a clean line of demarcation, parts within or immediately around the injured area that are not burned, a burn pattern inconsistent with the injury

Figure 12–1
Boy Beaten with the Buckle End of a Belt

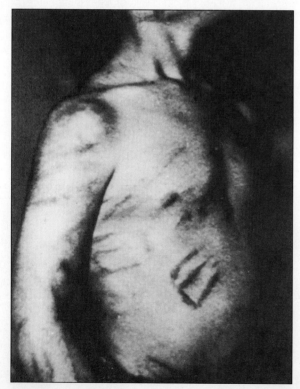

(Courtesy Tampa Police Department)

314

account, or any other of the typical characteristics of an inflicted burn? Are the burns located on the buttocks, the area betweeen the child's legs, or the ankles, wrists, palms, or soles?

- Are other injuries present, such as fractures, healed burns, or bruises?
- Are the child's age and level of development compatible with the caretaker's and witnesses' account of the injury?
- Was there a delay in seeking medical attention? Less serious burns may have been treated at home.
- Does the caretaker insist there were no witnesses to the injury incident, including the caretaker?
- Do those who were present seem to be angry or resentful toward the child or each other?

A detailed history, including previous trauma, presence of recent illnesses, immunization status, and the status of routine medical care, is critical, as is careful documentation of the scene of the injury, including photographs and drawings. To investigate a burn injury, the investigator should do the following:

- Stay focused on the facts, and proceed slowly and methodically.
- Ask questions, be objective, and reenact the incident.
- Treat each case individually.

The incidence of further injury and death is so high in deliberate burn cases that it is critical for all concerned persons to be aware of the indicators of this form of child abuse. The following descriptions provide information about various types of accidental and nonaccidental burns children may incur:

- *Scald burns* are the most common type. They may be caused by any hot liquid—hot tap water, boiling water, waterlike liquids such as tea or coffee, and thicker liquids such as soup and grease. Scald burns may be either a spill/splash type of burn or an immersion burn, the most common of the liquid burn injuries. Most deliberate burns are caused by tap water.
- *Contact burns* are usually of the branding type and will mirror the object used to cause the

injury—curling iron, steam iron, cigarette lighter, fireplace or hibachi grill, and heated kitchen tool or other implement.

Young children have thinner skin than adults; therefore, a child's skin will be destroyed more rapidly and by less heat. Thicker-skinned areas of the body include the palms, soles, back, scalp, and the back of the neck. Thinner-skinned areas are the front of the trunk, inner thighs, bottom of forearms, and inner-arm area.

It is important to work with the emergency medical personnel, who were probably the first persons to see the child's injuries, hospital personnel, and social service investigators.

CLASSIFICATION OF BURNS

The preferred classification of burns used by most physicians is "partial" or "full thickness" (see Table 12–1). Only an experienced medical practitioner can make a determination of how deep a burn is, but there are some features of partial- and full-thickness burns that can be observed immediately after the incident:

- Patches of reddened skin that blanch with fingertip pressure and then refill are shallow partial-thickness burns. Blisters usually indicate deeper partial-thickness burning, especially if the blisters increase in size just after the burn occurs.
- A leathery or dry surface with a color of white, tan, brown, red, or black represents a full-thickness burn. The child feels no pain because the nerve endings have been destroyed. Small blisters may be present but will not increase in size.

SPILL/SPLASH INJURIES

These injuries occur when a hot liquid falls from a height onto the victim. The burn pattern is characterized by irregular margins and nonuniform depth. A key indicator to look for is where the scalding liquid first came into contact with the victim. Water travels downward and cools as it moves away from the initial contact point. When a pan of water is spilled or thrown on a person's chest, the initial contact point shows a splash pattern. The area below this

Table 12–1
Classification of Burns

Classification	Characteristics
First degree	Partial-thickness burns: • Characterized by erythema (localized redness) • Appear sunburnlike • Are not included when calculating burn size • Usually heal by themselves
Second degree	Partial-thickness burns: • Part of skin damaged • Have blisters containing clear fluid • Pink underlying tissue • Often heal by themselves
Third degree	Full-thickness burns: • Full skin destroyed • Deep red tissue underlying blister • Presence of bloody blister fluid • Muscle and bone possibly destroyed • Require professional treatment
Fouth degree	Full-thickness burns: • Penetrate deep tissue to fat, muscle, bone • Require immediate professional treatment

point tapers down, creating what is called an "arrow-down" pattern. This pattern is more commonly seen in assaults on adults than in assaults on children.

If the child was wearing clothing at the time of injury, the pattern may be altered. This is why it is important to determine whether clothing was worn and, if possible, to retain the actual clothing. Depending on the material, the water may have been against the skin longer, which would result in a deeper injury and pattern. A fleece sleeper, for instance, will change the course of the water and hold the temperature longer in one area as opposed to a thin, cotton T-shirt.

Questions to ask in a scalding-injury investigation include the following:

• Where were the caretakers at the time of the accident?
• How many persons were home at the time?
• How tall is the child? How far can he or she reach?
• Can the child walk, and are the child's coordination and development consistent with his or her age?

• How much water was in the pan, and how much does it weigh?
• What is the height to the handle of the pan when it is sitting on the stove (or counter or table)?
• Was the oven on at the time (thus making it unlikely that the child could have climbed onto the stove)?
• Does the child habitually play in the kitchen or near the stove? Does the child usually climb on the cabinets or table?
• Has the child been scolded for playing in the kitchen? For touching the stove?

It is unusual for a child to incur an accidental scald burn on his or her back, but it has happened. As in all burn investigations, factors other than location of the burn must be considered before concluding that the injury was nonaccidental. Deliberate burning by throwing a hot liquid on a child is usually done either as punishment for playing near a hot object or in anger. However, the child may have been caught in the crossfire between two fighting adults and then been accused of having spilled the liquid accidentally.

IMMERSION BURNS

Immersion burns result from the child's falling into or being placed into a tub or other container of hot liquid. In a deliberate immersion burn, the depth of the burn is uniform. The wound borders are very distinct, sharply defined "waterlines" with little tapering of depth at the edges, and there is little evidence that the child thrashed about during the immersion, indicating that the child was held in place. Occasionally there may be bruising in the area of the soft tissue where the child was being forcibly held.

Only children with deliberate immersion burns sustain deep burns of the buttocks and/or the area between the anus and the genitals. The motivation for this type of injury generally involves punishment for failing to toilet train or for soiling of clothing. Dirty diapers or soiled clothing may be found in the bathroom. The water in the bathtub may be deeper than what is normal for bathing an infant or child and may be so hot that the first responding adult at the scene is unable to immerse his or her own hand in it.

Several key variables must be observed in investigating immersion burns:

- *The temperature of the water:* Variables that must be taken into account include the temperature of the water heater, the ease with which it can be reset, and recent prior usage of water.
- *The time of exposure:* This is an unknown that can sometimes be estimated from the burn pattern and its depth.
- *The depth of the burn:* Several days may need to pass before the true depth of the burn can be determined.
- *The occurrence of "sparing":* These may be areas within or immediately around the burn site that were not burned.

An adult will experience a significant injury of the skin after 1 minute of exposure to water at 127°F, 30 seconds of exposure at 130°F, and 2 seconds of exposure at 150°F. A child, however, will suffer a significant burn in less time than an adult.

When a child's hand is forced into hot water, the child will make a fist, thus "sparing" the palm and discounting the statement that the child reached into the pan of hot water for something. A child whose body is immersed in hot water will attempt to fold up, and there will be sparing in creases in the abdomen. Curling up the toes when the foot is forced into a hot liquid will spare part of the soles of the feet or the area between the toes. The area where the child was held by the perpetrator will also be spared. These flexing actions prevent burning within the body's creases, causing a striped configuration of burned and unburned zones, or a "zebra" pattern.

Deliberate immersion burns can often be recognized by one of the following characteristic patterns:

- *Doughnut pattern in the buttocks:* When a child falls or steps into a hot liquid, the immediate reaction is to thrash about, try to get out, and jump up and down. When a child is held in scalding hot bathwater, the buttocks are pressed against the bottom of the tub so forcibly that the water will not come into contact with the center of the buttocks, sparing this part of the buttocks and causing the burn injury to have a doughnut pattern.
- *Sparing the soles of the feet:* Another instance of sparing occurs in a child whose buttocks and feet are burned but whose soles have been spared. If a caretaker's account is that the child was left in the bathroom and told not to get into the tub, and that the caretaker then heard screaming and returned to find the child jumping up and down in the water, the absence of burns on the soles of the child's feet is evidence that the account is not true. A child cannot jump up and down in hot water without burning the bottoms of the feet.
- *Stocking- or glove-pattern burns:* Stocking and glove patterns are seen when feet or hands are held in the water. The line of demaracation is possible evidence that the injury was not accidental.
- *Waterlines:* A sharp line on the lower back or in some cases the legs indicates that the child was held still in the water. A child falling into the water would show splash and irregular line patterns. The waterline on a child's torso indicates how deep the water was. (see Figure 12–2)

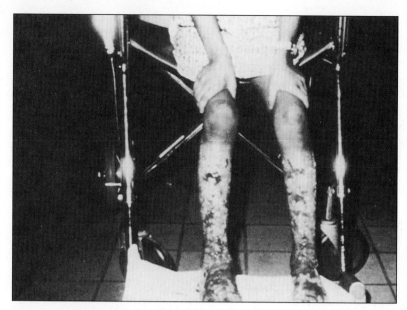

Figure 12–2
Wet Burn
A child forcibly immersed in a tub of hot water. Note the end of the immersion line near the knees.

(Courtesy Tampa Police Department)

CONTACT BURNS

Contact burns may be caused by flames or hot solid objects. Flame burns are a much less common cause of deliberate injury. When they do occur, they are characterized by extreme depth and are relatively well defined as compared with accidental flame burns.

When a child accidently touches a hot object or the object falls on the child, there is usually a lack of pattern in the burn injury, since the child quickly moves away from the object. However, even brief accidental contact, such as falling against a hot radiator or grate, can cause a second-degree burn with the pattern of the object.

Distinguishing Nonaccidental from Accidental Contact Burns

Nonaccidental burns caused by a hot solid object are the most difficult to distinguish from accidental injuries. Cigarette and iron burns are the most frequent types of these injuries (see Figures 12–3 and 12–4). Cigarette burns, especially multiple burns on the child's feet, back, or buttocks, are unlikely to have been caused by an accident; therefore, they are more suspect than individual burns about the face and eyes, which can occur accidentally if the child walks or runs into the adult's lighted cigarette held at waist height. Accidental burns are usually more shallow, irregular, and less well defined than deliberate burns.

Purposely inflicted "branding" injuries usually mirror the objects that caused the burn (such as cigarette lighters and curling irons) and are much deeper than the superficial and random burns caused by accidentally touching these objects. Most accidental injuries with hot steam or curling irons occur when the hot item is grasped or falls. These are usually second-degree injuries that are randomly placed, as might happen when a hot iron strikes the skin in multiple places as it falls. It is important to know where the iron was—for example, on an ironing board or a coffee table at the child's height?

Another source of accidental burns is contact with items that have been exposed for prolonged periods to hot sun. Pavement in hot sun, which can reach a temperature of 176°F, can burn a child's bare feet; however, such burns are not likely to be deep. A child placed in a carseat that has been in a car in the sun can receive second- and even third-degree burns. Full-thickness burns have also resulted from contact with a hot seat-belt buckle.

Key questions in this area are:

- Where is the burn injury, and could the child reach the area unassisted?

Figure 12–3
Contact Burns

Intentional burns inflicted to this child's hands by use of a hot iron.

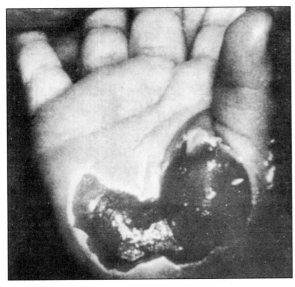

(Courtesy Milwaukee County Department of Social Service)

Figure 12–4
Cigarette Burns

Burn injuries to the soles of this child's feet by use of a lit cigarette.

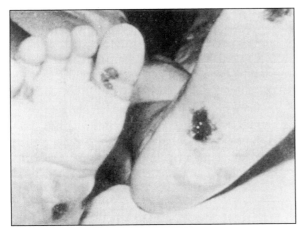

(Courtesy Milwaukee County Department of Social Service)

- Does the child normally have access to the item (such as a cigarette lighter) that caused the injury?
- How heavy is the item, and how strong is the child? For instance, is the steam iron a compact, travel-size one that a small child could lift or a full-size home model that might be too heavy?
- Is there any sparing that would be significant to the injury?
- How was the item heated, and how long did it take for the item to become hot enough to cause the injury?
- Is the injury clean and crisp, with a distinctive pattern of the object, or is it shallow or irregular, as from a glancing blow? Several cleanly defined injuries, especially on an older child, could indicate that the child was held motionless by a second perpetrator while the first perpetrator carefully branded the child.
- Are there multiple burns or other healed burns?
- Has the child been punished before for playing with or being too close to the hot object?

SHAKEN-BABY SYNDROME

The phrase "shaken-baby syndrome" was coined to explain instances in which severe intracranial trauma occurs in the absence of signs of external head trauma. Shaken-baby syndrome (SBS) is the severe intentional application of violent force (shaking), in one or more episodes, that results in intracranial injuries to the child. Physical abuse of children by shaking usually is not an isolated event. Many shaken infants show evidence of previous trauma. Frequently, the shaking has been preceeded by other types of abuse.[3]

MECHANISM OF INJURY

The mechanism of injury in SBS is thought to result from a combination of physical factors, including the proportionately large cranial size of infants, the laxity of their neck muscles, and the vulnerability of their intracranial bridging veins. However, the primary factor is the proportionately large size of the adult relative to the child. Shaking by admitted assailants has produced remarkably similar injury patterns:

- The infant is held by the chest, facing the assailant, and is shaken violently back and forth.

- The shaking causes the infant's head to whip forward and backward from chest to the back.
- The infant's chest is compressed, and the arms and legs move about with a whiplash action.
- At the completion of the assault, the infant may be limp and either not breathing or breathing shallowly.
- During the assault, the infant's head may strike a solid object.
- After the shaking, the infant may be dropped, thrown, or slammed onto a solid surface.

The last two events likely explain the many cases of blunt injury, including skull fractures, found in shaken infants. However, although blunt injury may be seen at autopsy in shaken infants, research data suggest that shaking in and of itself is often sufficient to cause serious intracranial injury or death.

INDICATORS AND SYMPTOMS

Crying has come under increasing scrutiny as a stimulus for abusive activity. Because shaking is generally a response to crying, a previous illness causing irritability may increase the likelihood that the infant will be shaken. The occurrence of infant abuse is a product of a delicate balance between the severity of the stimulus of crying and the threshold for violent action by potential abusers. The effects of drugs, alcohol, and environmental conditions may trigger this interaction.

The average age of infants abused by shaking is 6 months. The physical alterations characteristic of SBS are uncommon in children older than 1 year. Many symptomatic shaken infants have seizures, are lethargic, or are in a coma. Many are resuscitated at home or en route to the hospital and arrive there in serious condition. Some children have milder changes in consciousness or a history of choking, vomiting, or poor feeding. Although gross evidence of trauma is usually absent, careful inspection may reveal sites of bruising.

Most infants in whom shaking has been documented have retinal hemorrhage (bleeding along the back inside layer of the eyeball). Other intracranial injuries ascribed to shaking trauma are fluid between the skull and brain, tearing of brain tissue, and swelling of the brain.

INVESTIGATIVE GUIDELINES

- The use of MRI has helped detect old and new intracranial injuries and has aided recognition of subtle instances of repetitive shaking.
- Repetitive abuse has important legal and clinical implications. If abuse is repetitive, the child is at high risk for further injury unless legal action is taken. Establishing that there has been a pattern of abuse can also help in identifying potential perpetrators and may lead to increased legal penalties.
- The fact that shaken children, and possibly their siblings, often have been previously abused should dispel the notion that shaking is an isolated and somewhat "unintentional" event.
- From the perspective of the protection of the child or the criminal prosecution of the abuser, it is not as important to distinguish the precise mechanism of injury as it is to be certain that the event was nonaccidental.
- Pediatricians should not be deterred from testifying when the cause of the nonaccidental injury is not entirely clear.
- Shaking a child creates an imminent risk for an acute injury.
- Injuries that appear to be caused by shaking create a high index of suspicion of child abuse and should be followed by intensive efforts (e.g., skeletal survey, CT scan, and MRI) to identify concurrent and previous abuse of the patient and any siblings.
- If an infant's injuries are fatal, an autopsy should be performed by a forensic pathologist. Autopsies of all infants who die of causes other than known natural illness should include thorough skeletal imaging.

THE ROLE OF THE PHYSICIAN IN CHILD-ABUSE CASES

The problem the investigator often encounters is that the victim is either too young to explain what has occurred or is too intimidated to cooperate. In injuries or deaths of young children, investigators find radiologists, physicians who specialize in the interpretation of X-rays, especially helpful. It is common for those abused to be brought to the hospital emergency room by their parents or relatives, who tell hospital personnel that the child was injured in a fall or some other accident. When there is a discrepancy between the characteristics of the injury and the explanation, X-rays can be useful in determining whether the injuries were accidental. X-rays of the entire body reveal not only the presence of fractures and other injuries to joints and bones but also the existence of older injuries in various stages of healing.

Careful questioning of those bringing the child to the hospital may be sufficient to confirm the need for a complete investigation. The following facts about child abuse are helpful in such questioning:

- In many cases, only one of a number of children in the family is chosen as the target of abuse, and frequently that child was conceived or born extramaritally or premaritally.

- The marital partner tends to protect the abusive parent through denial of the facts.

- Occasionally, an abusing father also assaults his wife, but more frequently he restricts the gross abuse to a child.

- In over half the cases in which child abuse results in hospitalization, there was a preceding incident of abuse of equal severity.

- Not infrequently the battered child is taken to a different hospital after each abuse in order to conceal the recurrence of injuries.[4]

The families of battered children range across the entire socioeconomic spectrum. The investigator cannot assume that the injured child who comes from what appears to be a "good home" is not the victim of child abuse.

In cases where medical examination is inconclusive but abuse is strongly suspected, interviewing becomes even more significant. The rule is to leave no source unexamined. To fail to do so places the abused child back into a defenseless position in which death could occur. The interviewing of babysitters, neighbors, teachers, and others must be conducted sensibly and sensitively. The aim is not to "get the person who did it," because there may not in fact have been an abuse incident. The primary objective is to get the information so that if there has been abuse, the child can be protected.

MUNCHAUSEN SYNDROME BY PROXY

Munchausen syndrome is a psychological disorder in which the patient fabricates the symptoms of disease or injury in order to undergo medical tests, hospitalization, or even medical or surgical treatment. To command medical attention, patients with Munchausen syndrome may intentionally injure themselves or induce illness in themselves. In cases of *Munchausen syndrome by proxy (MSBP)*, a parent or caretaker suffering from Munchausen syndrome attempts to bring medical attention to himself or herself by injuring or inducing illness in a child. The parent then may try to resuscitate the child or to have paramedics or hospital personnel save the child.[5] The following actual cases are examples of MSBP:

M.A., a 9-month-old boy, had been repeatedly admitted to Children's Hospital because of recurrent life-threatening apnea (cessation of breathing). At 7 weeks of age, he experienced his first apneic event, and his mother administered mouth-to-mouth ventilation. Spontaneous respiration returned, and M.A. was hospitalized, treated, and discharged with a home monitor.

During the next 9 months, M.A. experienced 10 similar events and 7 more hospitalizations. Eight of the events required mouth-to-mouth ventilation. All of these episodes occurred while mother and child were alone, so only M.A.'s mother witnessed the actual events. Two episodes occurred in the hospital.

Unfortunately, despite many tests and surgical procedures, M.A.'s apnea persisted and his growth slowed. Because of his persistent apnea and failure to thrive, M.A. received home nursing care. During these home visits, several nurses observed that M.A. would refuse to eat in his mother's presence. If she left the room, however, he would eat.

In time, both medical and nursing staffs became increasingly suspicious that Mrs. A. was somehow responsible for her child's apnea. To better observe mother-child interaction, M.A. was moved to a hospital room equipped for covert audiovisual surveillance.

On the sixth day, the video clearly recorded Mrs. A. bringing on the apnea by forcing the child against her chest, which caused him to lose consciousness. M.A.

became limp and experienced a falling heart rate. Mrs. A. then placed the baby back on the bed, called for help, and began mouth-to-mouth resuscitation.

The hospital immediately informed child protection services and police authorities, who reviewed the recording. Shortly thereafter, a team consisting of a physician, nurse, social worker, and police officer confronted her. At first, Mrs. A. expressed disbelief at the suggestion that she had smothered M.A., but when she was informed of the video, she made no comment. She was then arrested.

Mrs. A. was a 36-year-old occupational therapist and the mother of three boys. Late into her pregnancy with M.A., she worked in an early intervention program for developmentally delayed children. During many of M.A.'s hospitalizations, she appeared caring and concerned, but emotionally distant. Clearly, Mrs. A. was the dominant parent, who made all decisions regarding medical treatment.

Mrs. A. subsequently pled guilty to felonious, third-degree assault. At the time, she stated: "The only time I ever caused M.A. to stop breathing was in the hospital." She received three years' probation, during which she was to receive psychotherapy. If she successfully completed psychotherapy, the felony charge would be reduced to a misdemeanor. She also had to live apart from her children and could visit them only in the presence of two other adults.

M.A. had no further apnea, and at 24 months of age he appeared vigorous, healthy, and normal. Eventually, the family was reunited.

C.B.,

a 10-month-old girl, was admitted to a hospital because of recurrent life-threatening apnea. C.B. had been born in another state and had been sexually assaulted at the age of 3 months by an acquaintance of her father. After the assault, local child protection services closely monitored the family.

At 6 months of age, C.B. experienced her first apneic episode. Her father shook her vigorously, then administered mouth-to-mouth ventilation. She was subsequently admitted to a local hospital. After examination and treatment, she was discharged with a home monitor. During the next two months, C.B. experienced six apneic events and three hospitalizations. The family then moved to Minnesota.

During her first month in Minnesota, C.B. experienced four apneic episodes and three more hospital-izations. All required vigorous stimulations to restore spontaneous breathing. Other family members observed the child immediately following the events. However, only C.B.'s father had witnessed all the actual events. C.B. was eventually referred to Children's Hospital.

While in the hospital, C.B. had no clinical apnea or monitor alarms. And most of the time, she appeared happy and playful. However, when anyone attempted to touch her face, she became hysterical and combative. Over time, both the medical and nursing staffs began to suspect that C.B.'s parents were responsible for her apnea.

Local police and child protection services were notified, and C.B. was placed in a room with covert audiovisual surveillance. On the third day of monitoring, the video recording clearly showed C.B.'s father producing an apneic event by smothering her. Mr. B. was seen picking up the sleeping child, placing her prone on the bed, and forcing her face into the mattress. C.B. awoke and struggled to escape, wildly kicking her legs. Mr. B. continued until C.B.'s struggling stopped and she appeared limp and unconscious. Then he repositioned her on the bed and called for help. A nurse entered the room, stimulated her, and administered supplemental oxygen.

C.B.'s parents were confronted by a physician, nurse, and police officer. Mr. B. adamantly denied smothering C.B. He was subsequently arrested and removed from the hospital.

Mr. B. was a 27-year-old, unemployed, semiliterate laborer in good health. He was actively involved in C.B.'s day-to-day medical care and was clearly the dominant parent. He also became very knowledgeable about the mechanics of the various county and hospital welfare systems. Officials described him as "demanding and manipulative." During C.B.'s hospitalizations, the family lived in a hotel adjacent to the hospital with room, board, and radio pagers provided by the hospital. Throughout C.B.'s hospitalization, Mrs. B. was passive and deferred all medical decisions to her husband.

When they first arrived in Minnesota, the family had received emergency financial assistance and was closely monitored by local social service agencies. Four years earlier, Mrs. B. had allegedly been assaulted and raped. Two months prior to C.B.'s monitored episode, Mrs. B. was evaluated at a local emergency room for a "hysterical conversion reaction."

Following the incident at Children's Hospital, Mr. B. was taken to the county jail, and upon viewing the video, he admitted to smothering C.B. He also was charged with felonious, third-degree assault. The judge ordered a psychiatric examination. Mr. B. also received a 10-month sentence in a local workhouse and 5 years' probation. Also, he was to have no contact with his daughter and no unsupervised contact with any child in the future.

J.C., a 2½-year-old boy, suffered from asthma, severe pneumonia, mysterious infections, and sudden fevers. He was hospitalized 20 times during an 18-month period. Doctors were even concerned that he might have AIDS. However, they soon began to suspect that the mother may have caused the child's problems. Finally, when the boy complained to his mother's friend that his thigh was sore because "mommy gave me shots," the authorities were called.

On searching the residence, investigators seized medical charts and information and hypodermic needles. It was believed that material had also entered the boy through a catheter doctors surgically inserted in the arteries near his heart to give him constant medication.

J.C.'s mother was a 24-year-old homemaker and part-time worker in a fast-food restaurant. When the mother was 7 years old, an older sister had died of a brain tumor at Children's Hospital. During her sister's prolonged illness, J.C.'s mother, of necessity, spent long periods of time at the hospital. Although this had occurred long ago, J.C.'s mother remembered the experience vividly.

During J.C.'s many hospitalizations, the mother seemed almost obsessively involved in medical matters and hospital routines. She spent hours in the hospital library reading medical texts. She had few friends outside the hospital, and the medical and nursing staff described her as an isolated person.

J.C.'s father was a 24-year-old church janitor afflicted with many health problems, the most notable being severe insulin-dependent diabetes. During J.C.'s many hospitalizations, his father appeared distant and only marginally involved. J.C.'s 7-year-old sister was in good health and was named after her mother's deceased sister.

Since J.C. was removed from his home, he has been healthy. As in previous cases, only Mrs. C. was present when the boy became ill, and until investigators showed evidence linking her to her child's illnesses, she denied any wrongdoing. Assault charges were filed, and Mrs. C.'s case is pending.[6]

INVESTIGATIVE GUIDELINES

- Consult with all experts possible, including psychologists.
- Exhaust every possible explanation of the cause of the child's illness or death.
- Find out who had exclusive control over the child when the symptoms of the illness began or at the time of the child's death.
- Find out if there is a history of abusive conduct toward the child.
- Find out if the nature of the child's illness or injury allows medical professionals to express an opinion that the child's illness or death was neither accidental nor the result of a natural cause or disease.
- In cases of hospitalization, utilize covert video surveillance to monitor the suspect.
- Determine whether the caretaker had any medical training or a history of seeking medical treatment needlessly. MSBP is often a multigenerational condition.

CHILD MOLESTATION

For purposes of discussion, Kenneth V. Lanning, Supervisory Special Agent of the Federal Bureau of Investigation, divides child molesters into two categories, namely, situational and preferential.[7]

SITUATIONAL CHILD MOLESTERS

The *situational child molester* does not have a true sexual preference for children but engages in sex with children for varied and sometimes complex reasons. For such a child molester, sex with children may range from a "once-in-a-lifetime" act to a long-term pattern of behavior. The more long term the pattern is, the harder it is to distinguish from preferential molesting. The situational child molester usually has fewer numbers of different child victims. Other vulnerable individuals, such as the elderly, sick, or disabled, may also be at risk of sexual victimization by him or her. For example, the situational child molester who sexually abuses children in a day-care center might leave that job and begin to sexually abuse elderly people in a nursing home. The number of situational child molesters is larger and increasing faster than that of preferential child molesters. Members of lower socioeconomic groups tend to be overrepresented among situational child molesters. Within this category the following four major patterns of behavior emerge, namely: regressed, morally indiscriminate, sexually indiscriminate, and inadequate. (see Table 12–2).

Regressed

Such an offender usually has low self-esteem and poor coping skills; he turns to children as a sexual substitute for the preferred peer sex partner. Precipitating stress may play a bigger role in his molesting behavior. His main victim criterion seems to be availability, which is why many of these offenders molest their own children. His principle method of operation is to coerce the child into having sex. This type of situational child molester may or may not collect child or adult pornography. If he does have child pornography, it will usually be the best kind of evidence from an investigative point of view; and will often include homemade photographs or videos of the child he is molesting.

Morally Indiscriminate

This is a growing category of child molesters. For this individual, the sexual abuse of children is simply part of a general pattern of abuse in his life. He is a user and abuser of people. He abuses his wife, friends, coworkers. He lies, cheats, or steals whenever he thinks he can get away with it. His primary victim criteria are vulnerability and opportunity. He has the urge, a child is there, and so he acts. He typically uses force, lures, or manipulation to obtain his victims. He may violently or nonviolently abduct his victims. Although his victims frequently are strangers or acquaintances, it is important for the investigator to realize his victims can also be the offender's own children. The incestuous father or mother might be this morally indiscriminate offender. He frequently collects detective magazines or adult pornography of a sadomasochistic nature. He may collect some child pornography, especially that which depicts pubescent children. Because he is an impulsive person who lacks conscience, he is an especially high risk to molest pubescent children. Such acts may be criminal but not necessarily sexually deviant.

Table 12–2
Situational Child Molester

	Regressed	Morally Indiscriminate	Sexually Indiscriminate	Inadequate
Basic characteristics	Poor coping skills	User of people	Sexual experimentation	Social misfit
Motivation	Substitution	Why not?	Boredom	Insecurity and curiosity
Victim criteria	Availability	Vulnerability and opportunity	New and different	Nonthreatening
Method of operation	Coercion	Lure, force or manipulation	Involve in existing activity	Exploits size, advantage
Pornography collection	Possible	Sadomasochistic; detective magazines	Highly likely, varied nature	Likely

Source: Kenneth V. Lanning, *Child Molesters: A Behavioral Analysis for Law Enforcement Officers Investigating Cases of Child Sexual Exploitation*, 3rd ed. (Arlington: Va.: National Center for Missing and Exploited Children, 1992). p. 10. Reprinted with permission of the National Center for Missing and Exploited Children (NCMEC). Copyright 1986, 1987, and 1992, NCMEC. All rights reserved.

Sexually Indiscriminate

This pattern of behavior is the most difficult to define. Although the previously described morally indiscriminate offender often is a sexual experimenter, this individual differs in that he appears to be discriminating in his behavior except when it comes to sex. He is the "try-sexual"—willing to try anything sexual. Much of his behavior is similar to and is most often confused with the preferential child molester. While he may have clearly defined sexual preferences—such as bondage or sadomasochism, and so forth—however, he has no real sexual preference for children. His basic motivation is sexual experimentation, and he appears to have sex with children out of boredom. His main criteria for such children are that they are new and different, and he involves children in previously existing sexual activity. Again, it is important to realize these children may be his own. Although much of his sexual activity with adults may not be criminal, such an individual may also provide his children to other adults as part of group sex, spouse-swapping activity, or even some bizarre ritual. Of all situational child molesters, he is by far the most likely to have multiple victims, be from a higher socioeconomic background, and collect pornography and erotica. Child pornography will only be a small portion of his potentially large and varied collection, however.

Inadequate

This pattern of behavior is also difficult to define and includes those suffering from psychoses, eccentric personality disorders, mental retardation, and senility. In layperson's terms he is the social misfit, the withdrawn, the unusual. He might be the shy teenager who has no friends of his own age or the eccentric loner who still lives with his parents. Although most such individuals are harmless, some can be child molesters and, in a few cases, even child killers. This offender seems to become sexually involved with children out of insecurity or curiosity. He finds children to be nonthreatening objects with whom he can explore his sexual fantasies. The child victim could be someone he knows or a random stranger. In some cases the victim might be a specific "stranger" selected as a substitute for a specific adult (possibly a relative of the child) whom the offender is afraid of approaching directly. Often his sexual activity with children is the result of built-up impulses. Some of these individuals find it difficult to express anger and hostility, which then builds until it explodes—possibly against their child victims. Because of mental or emotional problems, some might take out their frustration in cruel sexual torture. His victims, however, could be among the elderly as well as children—anyone who appears helpless at first sight. He might collect pornography, but it will most likely be of adults.

PREFERENTIAL CHILD MOLESTERS

The *preferential child molesters* have a definite sexual preference for children. Their sexual fantasies and erotic imagery focus on children. They have sex with children not because of some situational stress or insecurity but because they are sexually attracted to and prefer children. They can possess a wide variety of character traits but engage in highly predictable sexual behavior. These highly predictable sexual behavior patterns are called *sexual ritual* and are frequently engaged in even when they are counterproductive to getting away with the criminal activity. Although they may be smaller in number than the situational child molesters, they have the potential to molest large numbers of victims. For many of them, their problem is not only the nature of the sex drive (attraction to children) but also the quantity (need for frequent and repeated sex with children). They usually have age and gender preferences for their victims. Members of higher socioeconomic groups tend to be overrepresented among preferential child molesters. More preferential child molesters seem to prefer boys rather than girls. Within this category at least three major patterns of behavior emerge, namely: seductive, introverted, and sadistic. (see Table 12–3).

Seduction

This pattern characterizes the offender who engages children in sexual activity by "seducing" them—courting them with attention, affection, and gifts. Just as one adult courts another, the pedophile seduces children over a period of time by gradually lowering their sexual inhibitions. Frequently his victims arrive at the point where they are willing to trade sex for the attention, affection, and other benefits they receive from the offender.

Table 12-3
Preferential Child Molester

	Seduction	Introverted	Sadistic
Common characteristics	1. Sexual preference for children 2. Collects child pornography or erotica		
Motivation	Identification	Fear of communication	Need to inflict pain
Victim criteria	Age and gender preferences	Strangers or very young	Age and gender preferences
Method of operation	Seduction process	Nonverbal sexual contact	Lure or force

Source: Kenneth V. Lanning, *Child Molesters: A Behavioral Analysis for Law Enforcement Officers Investigating Cases of Child Sexual Exploitation,* 3rd ed. (Arlington: Va.: National Center for Missing and Exploited Children, 1992). p. 10. Reprinted with permission of the National Center for Missing and Exploited Children (NCMEC). Copyright 1986, 1987, and 1992, NCMEC. All rights reserved.

Many of these offenders are simultaneously involved with multiple victims, operating what has come to be called a *child sex ring*. This may include a group of children in the same class at school, in the same scout troop, or in the same neighborhood. The characteristic that seems to make this individual a master seducer of children is his ability to identify with them. He knows how to talk to children—but, more important, he knows how to listen to them. His adult status and authority is also an important part of the seduction process. In addition, he frequently selects as targets children who are victims of emotional or physical neglect. The biggest problem for this child molester is not how to obtain child victims but how to get them to leave after they are too old. This must be done without the disclosure of the "secret." Victim disclosure often occurs when the offender is attempting to terminate the relationship. This child molester is most likely to use threats and physical violence to avoid identification and disclosure or to prevent a victim from leaving before he is ready to "dump" the victim.

Introverted

This pattern of behavior characterizes the offender who has a preference for children but lacks the interpersonal skills necessary to seduce them. Therefore, he typically engages in a minimal amount of verbal communication with his victims and usually molests strangers or very young children. He is like the old stereotype of the child molester in that he is more likely to hang around playgrounds and other areas where children congregate, watching them or engaging them in brief sexual encounters. He may expose himself to children or make obscene phone calls to children. He may utilize the services of a child prostitute. Unable to figure out any other way to gain access to a child, he might even marry a woman and have his own children, very likely molesting them from the time they are infants. He is similar to the inadequate situational child molester, except that he has a definite sexual preference for children and his selection of only children as victims is more predictable.

Sadistic

This pattern of behavior characterizes the offender who has a sexual preference for children but who, in order to be aroused or gratified, must inflict psychological or physical pain or suffering on the child victim. He is aroused by his victim's response to the infliction of pain or suffering. They typically use lures or force to gain access to their victims. They are more likely than other preferential child molesters to abduct and even murder their victims. There have been some cases where seduction molesters have become sadistic molesters. It is not known whether the sadistic needs developed late or were always there and surfaced for some reason. In any case, it is fortunate that sadistic child molesters do not appear to be large in number.[8]

INTERVIEWING MOLESTED CHILDREN

Common sense and formal research would agree that children are not merely miniature adults. We know, for example, that children develop in stages during which they acquire capacities for new functions and understanding. We do not, generally speaking, read Shakespeare to 2-year-olds, nor do we expect adult commentary on political issues from them. Adults, for the most part, attempt to speak to and treat children in accordance with their capabilities. We do not ordinarily expect children to understand or function on a par with adults.[9]

When children become victims or witnesses of violence or sexual abuse, however, they are thrust into an adult system that traditionally does not differentiate between children and adults. As one attorney has said:

> Child victims of crime are specially handicapped. First, the criminal justice system distrusts them and puts special barriers in the path of prosecuting their claims to justice. Second, the criminal justice system seems indifferent to the legitimate special needs that arise from their participation.[10]

What are some of the reasons for the problems that arise when children are called to participate in criminal proceedings? The first reason is the children's immaturity with regard to physical, cognitive, and emotional development. The second reason involves unique attributes of the offense of child sexual abuse, particularly when the perpetrator is a parent, parent substitute, or other adult having a trusting or loving relationship with the child. The third reason is our limited understanding of children's capabilities as witnesses. These three factors affect children's ability to comply with the expectations of our judicial system and inform our entire discussion of interviewing molested children.

Developmental Issues

Waterman has identified three types of developmental issues that are important when allegations of sexual abuse arise.[11]

First is the child's developmental level relative to other children in his or her age group. Knowing this information will dictate the nature of questioning to which the child can reasonably be expected to respond. It will also help to place the child's observable reactions to victimization in an appropriate context.

Second is the child's developmental level with regard to sexuality. Normal preschoolers, for example, express curiosity about the origin of babies and mild interest in physical differences between the sexes. While it is not unusual for young children to engage in self-stimulatory behavior or exhibition-

ism, intercourse or other adult sexual behaviors are quite rare.[12]

Third is the child's ability to respond adequately to interviews and to testify in court. Those who work with young children should be aware of the following:

- Children think in concrete terms.
- Children do not organize their thoughts logically. They often include extraneous information, and they have trouble generalizing to new situations.
- Children have limited understanding of space, distance, and time. A child may not be able to say at "what time" or in "what month" something occurred but may be able to say whether it was before or after school, what was on television, or whether there was snow on the ground.
- Children have a complex understanding of truth and lying.
- Children see the world egocentrically. Because they believe that adults are omniscient, they may expect to be understood even when they have only answered questions partially.[13]
- Children have a limited attention span.
- Children may have varying degrees of comfort with strangers.

These kinds of cognitive limitations are common among young children.

Older children tend to exhibit different, yet equally challenging, developmental patterns.[14] For example, although preadolescents have fairly sophisticated language capabilities, they may use words or phrases they do not fully understand. The emergence of sexuality and concern with sexual identities during preadolescence make these youngsters particularly vulnerable to disruption when they are sexually abused. As they enter adolescence, they tend to become very self-centered and have strong needs for privacy and secrecy. It is common for preteens and teenagers to express their feelings through the arts or physical activity or by acting out in inappropriate or socially unacceptable ways.

Some researchers have specifically explored developmental aspects of children's understanding of the legal system.[15] Not surprisingly, they have found that older children have more accurate and complete knowledge of legal terminology (e.g., court, lawyer, jury, judge, and witness) as well as a

328 .... Chapter **Twelve**

better grasp of certain basic concepts of American justice. The researchers caution that children's understanding of the legal system is not only limited but sometimes faulty, so that child witnesses may behave in ways that appear counterintuitive or inappropriate to the context.

For example, an interview with a child may begin by requesting identifying information: name, age, school, grade, home address. But young children may misinterpret these initial questions to mean they are under suspicion or arrest.[16] Also, because they do not understand the different roles and obligations of all the people who interview them, children do not understand why they must tell their stories for police, social workers, doctors, prosecutors, and, ultimately, the court. While this repetition may be simply exasperating for some children, others may relive the traumatic event each time; still others may assume the story is already known and proceed to omit important details in subsequent interviews. Some children may feel protected by the presence of the judge, but others may be intimidated by the big stranger in the dark, scary robe who yells at people in the courtroom and sits towering above the witness stand. One therapist tells of a child witness who was afraid that the judge would hit her with the gavel, which she referred to as a hammer. Children perceive the judge's power to punish and may not understand that they are not the potential object of that punishment.

To correct these problems, researchers recommend that attorneys, judges, and investigators choose their words with care when questioning child witnesses.[17] Some believe that targeted instruction for children who may serve as witnesses, possibly in the form of a "court school," would be helpful as well.[18] Many prosecutors and victim advocates take children for a tour of the courtroom and introduce them to some of the key players before their scheduled court date. Critics contend, however, that such precautions may induce unnecessary apprehension for children who ultimately are not called to testify. At a minimum, interviewers would be wise to explain thoroughly the nature and purpose of each interview or court appearance before the child is questioned.

A further problem in interviewing children who may be victims of sexual molestation centers on the delicate issue of body parts and techniques for achieving accurate communication. The two major techniques involve the use of anatomically detailed dolls and the alternative method of asking children to create their own drawings.

Anatomically Detailed Dolls

When anatomically detailed dolls (male and female dolls with all body parts, including genitals; see Figure 12–5) were first introduced in the late 1970s,[19] they were widely hailed and almost universally adopted by child-serving professionals as an important advance in techniques for communicating with troubled children. The U.S. Congress (in the Victims of Child Abuse Act of 1990) and eight states[20] have enacted legislation expressly permitting children to use anatomically detailed dolls as demonstrative aids when they testify in court, and many appellate courts have upheld this use of such dolls.[21] The actual use of dolls at trial appears limited, however: courtroom observations of child sexual-abuse trials in eight jurisdictions revealed only one use of dolls per jurisdiction over the course of a year, with one exception where dolls were used in three of four cases observed.[22]

Yet, even as the dolls' value as demonstrative aids in court has gained widespread acceptance, their use in investigative interviews to arrive at a finding, or "diagnosis," of sexual abuse that is later presented in court as expert opinion has been sharply criticized. At the core of the controversy is the extent to which anatomically detailed dolls may suggest sexual behaviors even among children with no history of abuse. Improper use of the dolls, and unsupported inferences about children's behavior with them, can imperil the search for truth.

Proponents of anatomically detailed dolls maintain that, when properly used, the dolls can facilitate and enhance interviews with children.[23] Dolls can help in the following ways:

- They can help to establish rapport and reduce stress. Most children relate well to dolls. They can have a calming effect and make the interview room appear less formal and more child-oriented.
- They can reduce vocabulary problems. Interviewers can use the dolls to learn a child's sexual vocabulary before questioning the child about the alleged abuse.

Figure 12–5
Anatomically Detailed Dolls

(Courtesy Eymann Anatomically Correct Dolls, Sacramento, California)

- They allow the child to show what may be difficult or embarrassing to say. Anatomically detailed dolls can be an invaluable aid to children who are unable or unwilling to verbalize what happened to them.
- They can enhance the quality of information. Dolls may help interviewers gather information without resorting to leading or protracted questioning to overcome children's reluctance to describe sexual acts.
- They can establish competency. Interviewers can use the dolls in a general way to demonstrate the child's mental capacity and ability to communicate.

Many critics fear, however, that anatomically detailed dolls could have adverse effects, whether by provoking horror or alarm at the sight of genitalia or by eliciting apparently sexualized responses, even among children who have not been sexually abused. Even some appellate courts have raised the issue that interviewing children with anatomically detailed dolls may contaminate their memory.[24] Research offers little support for these contentions, however. For example, one study of "nonreferred" children (i.e., children with no history or current allegation of sexual abuse) found that they did play more with undressed dolls than with dressed dolls;

the children's primary activity was, in fact, dressing the dolls.[25] Others report that nonreferred children do examine the genitalia and orifices of anatomically detailed dolls, but only rarely do they enact sexual behaviors.[26] It should be recognized, of course, that some proportion of nonreferred children may have experienced some form of undetected sexual abuse.

Related to this controversy is the fact that professionals in this field have yet to reach consensus on "proper" use of anatomically detailed dolls. A number of questions remain unanswered:[27]

- How "correct" in their appearance must the dolls be? Some respondents to a survey by Boat and Everson[28] revealed using Barbie dolls, Cabbage Patch dolls, and homemade stuffed dolls with varying degrees of accuracy in their representation of genitalia. Does the presence or absence of certain details influence children's behavior with the dolls? Must the dolls also be matched by age and racial features to the child and alleged perpetrator?
- When and how should the dolls be used to assist an investigation? Should the dolls be available to children at the start of the interview, or should they be introduced only after the child falters in responding to

traditional questioning? Who should undress the dolls, and how should this activity be incorporated into the interview?

- How many sessions with a child are necessary before drawing conclusions about the child's behavior with the dolls?
- Should other adults be present during the interview?
- How many dolls should be available?

The answers to these questions vary with the professional orientations of the people who are asked. Clinicians' responses are more likely to reflect concerns for the children's well-being; legal professionals, on the other hand, express concern for the potential effects of certain practices when revealed in court. From the courts' perspective, it is probably least objectionable to:

- Introduce the dolls only after the child has verbally disclosed, or as a last resort to assist reluctant children.[29]
- Allow children to choose from a variety of dolls (rather than present only two to represent child and perpetrator).[30]
- Offer the child minimal or no instruction in use of the dolls.
- Incorporate information gathered from doll interviews with other data to provide a complete assessment.[31]

Similar recommendations would apply to use of other props, such as puppets or artwork.

"Drawing Interviews"

One alternative that is being used by some police agencies either in connection with or instead of an anatomically detailed doll is to have the child draw his or her own picture. It is believed by investigators using this technique that in many cases using the child's own drawings rather than the dolls will provide a more productive interview with the child abuse victim.[32]

The drawing interview should begin with the interviewer asking the victim to write or print his or her name on a sheet of paper, which, depending on the victim's age, is either lined or unlined and colored. This step of the interview will provide the police officer with some idea of the educational and developmental stages of the victim.

The second step is to ask the child to draw a picture of himself or herself. Children may object at this point, telling the interviewer that they can't draw, but they should simply be encouraged to do the best they can.

When the child has finished the drawing, the interviewer can use it to go over the child's name and locations of the different body parts. The interviewer should begin this portion of the interview by asking the child to color the hair on the drawing and to locate the eyes, the mouth, and body parts, and so on. The last question asked should be the location and names of the sexual body parts. In some cases, the interviewer may wish to have the child label the body part locations on the drawing. It is important to realize that children often have their own terms for body parts; the interviewer should learn what their words are and use them. For

Figure 12–6
"Draw Yourself"

Drawing completed by a 14-year-old boy who had been anally and orally sodomized by his stepfather for over six years.

(Courtesy Robert Hugh Farley, Cook County, Illinois, Sheriff's Department)

example, in Figure 12–6, the drawing was done by a 14-year-old boy who had been anally and orally sodomized by his stepfather for over six years. When questioned by the investigators about the object depicted in his mouth, the boy said that it was a "wanger." Further questioning established that the wanger was the stepfather's penis.

In the third step, the child should be provided with another sheet of paper and asked to draw a picture of the "family." This step is important; it may provide the interviewer with important information concerning an outsider, such as a boyfriend or grandfather, who is living in the family residence or has daily access to the family. When the family drawing is completed, the child is asked to label all the people in the drawing, including the family pet. The interviewer can ask such questions as where the various people sleep in the house, which person the child likes the least or the best, and so forth. For example, in Figure 12–7 a 10-year-old girl who was asked to draw all members of the family depicted two friends between Mom and stepdad. When later questioned by the interviewer, she identified them as Mom's two boyfriends, who visit the house when stepdad is out driving his truck on the road.

In the final step of the drawing interview, the child is provided with another sheet of paper and asked to "draw what happened." When the drawing is completed, the child is asked to explain the circumstances of the abuse portrayed in the picture, to label the name of the abuser and victim, and in cases of physical abuse to identify the instrument of abuse and where it was stored. For example, in Figure 12–8 the drawing was done by an 8-year-old boy who had suffered a history of physical abuse from his stepfather. In the drawing, the boy had knocked over a bag of feed in the basement of the family's home. The boy's 6-foot 5-inch stepfather grabbed him by the neck and, while holding him in the air, choked the breath out of him. Going over the drawing with the interviewer, the boy explained that the shading on his face was from when he had turned red and the tear was from when he was crying. Note the heavy black mouth depicting the anger on the stepfather's face.

As the child completes each drawing, the interviewer must take the time to go over it in detail with the child. The interviewer who observes some portion of the drawing that is unusual, exaggerated, or overemphasized, such as the mouth in Figure 12–8, should ask the child for an explanation rather than making assumptions of any kind. Of course the police officer–interviewer, who is typically untrained in art therapy, must remember not to fall into the trap of playing amateur psychologist and attempt to analyze the drawings. This job must be left to professional art therapists.

Figure 12–7
"Draw Your Family"
Drawing by a 10-year-old girl identifying members of her family unit. The two "friends" were her mother's boyfriends, who visited the house when her stepfather was away.

(Courtesy Robert Hugh Farley, Cook County, Illinois, Sheriff's Department)

Figure 12-8
"Draw What Happened"
This drawing was done by an 8-year-old boy who had suffered a history of physical abuse from his stepfather.

(Courtesy Robert Hugh Farley, Cook County, Illinois, Sheriff's Department)

Asking Leading Questions

Professionals who interview children who are suspected of having been sexually abused are caught in a perilous dilemma. In the words of two leading clinicians:

> In the best of all possible worlds, it would be advisable not to ask children leading questions. . . . But in the best of all possible worlds, children are not sexually assaulted in secrecy, and then bribed, threatened, or intimidated not to talk about it. In the real world, where such things do happen, leading questions may sometimes be necessary.[33]

As with the anatomical dolls, leading questions are widely used as a courtroom technique to assist child witnesses,[34] but they are seriously challenged when used in investigative interviews. There is, however, a grain of truth to the argument that children can be led, coached, or even "brainwashed" by the interview process, and interviewers would be wise to reexamine their methods in light of our growing experience in the courts.

Briefly, the defense argument rests on the social psychological theory of social influence. In essence, as it applies to child sexual-abuse cases, this theory holds that children's responses to questioning are heavily influenced by the perceived authority or power of the adult interviewers. When they are praised or otherwise "rewarded" for disclosing elements of abuse, children learn what the interviewers want to hear. In other words, children answer to please adults.[35]

Furthermore, to continue this argument, the effect of social influence is magnified in child sexual-abuse cases because the children are typically interviewed repeatedly by several different adults, each of whom contributes to the child's expanding story by infusing—and reinforcing—new information. Ultimately, according to one of the leading defense experts,

> In situations where a child will eventually testify, the memory will consist of a combination of recall and reconstruction influenced by all of the interrogations, conversations, and sexual abuse therapy that have occurred during the delay. The longer the delay, the greater the possibility of social influence and the more the memory may consist of reconstruction rather than recall.[36]

Challenges based on this theory have successfully undermined prosecution of several highly publicized cases, including the well-known Jordan, Minnesota, case and the McMartin Preschool case.

In one study, 72 children age 5 to 7 underwent physical examinations. Half received external examinations of their genital and anal areas; the other half were examined for scoliosis (curvature of the spine). Within one month of the exam, the children were interviewed about the event using open-ended questions, anatomically detailed dolls, and specific and misleading questions. The results of this study were both illuminating and provocative. Specifically:

- The majority of children who experienced genital and anal touching did not report it, either in response to open-ended questions or when asked to demonstrate with the dolls.
- All but 5 (of 36) disclosed touching in response to specific questions (e.g., "Did the doctor touch you here?").
- Only 3 (of 36) girls who received scoliosis examinations incorrectly reported genital/anal touching; only 1 of those provided additional (incorrect) details.

In sum, based on the total number of questions asked, "When all of the chances to reveal genital/anal contact were considered, children failed to disclose it 64 percent of the time, whereas the chance of obtaining a false report of genital/anal touching was only 1 percent, even when leading questions were asked.[37]

CHILDREN'S REACTIONS TO VICTIMIZATION

There are few in our society who would argue that child sexual abuse does not cause serious problems for its victims. The burgeoning research on this subject suggests that the effects of victimization on children can be far-reaching, negative, and complex. In their review of the literature, Lusk and Waterman found seven "clusters" of effects on children:[38]

- *Affective problems:* guilt, shame, anxiety, fear, depression, anger.
- *Physical effects:* genital injuries, pregnancy, sexually transmitted diseases, somatic complaints (e.g., headaches, stomachaches, bed-wetting, hypochondria), changes in appetite or sleep patterns.
- *Cognitive effects:* concentration problems, short attention spans.
- *Behavioral Symptoms:* acting out (hostile-aggressive behaviors, antisocial behaviors, delinquency, stealing, tantrums, substance abuse), withdrawal, repetition of the abusive relationship.
- *Self-destructive behaviors:* self-mutilation, suicidal thoughts and attempts.
- *Psychopathology:* neuroses, character disorders, multiple personalities, psychotic features.
- *Sexualized behavior:* excessive masturbation, repetition of sexual acts with others, atypical sexual knowledge.

Other commonly cited effects were low self-esteem and problems with interpersonal relationships.

Many of the early studies in this area were flawed because they relied on populations of clinical samples of sexually abused children or on retrospective findings from adults who had been sexually abused as children. Neither approach allows comparisons to "normal" populations. But in one study that compared 369 sexually abused children to 318 nonabused children, eight factors emerged to distinguish the two groups.[39] The sexually abused children were significantly more likely to demonstrate the following:

- Poor self-esteem
- Aggressive behaviors
- Fearfulness
- Concentration problems
- Withdrawal
- Acting out
- Need to please others

Another study compared sexually abused children to two groups of nonabused children: one from a psychiatric outpatient clinic and the other from a well-child clinic. The researchers found that the sexually abused children were more similar to the psychiatric outpatients than to the normal children.[40] Sexually abused children displayed significantly more behavior problems (and particularly sexual behaviors) and fewer social competencies than did normal children.

Sexually Abused Child Syndrome

Early attempts to describe a "sexually abused child syndrome" were quickly discarded as lacking a foundation in empirical research. Today, however, some of the leading researchers and clinicians in this field are moving toward consensus on behavioral indicators of child sexual abuse. The results of a nationwide survey of professionals experienced in evaluating suspected child sexual abuse revealed high levels of agreement around the following factors:[41]

- The child possesses age-inappropriate sexual knowledge.
- The child engages in sexualized play.
- The child displays precocious behavior.
- The child engages in excessive masturbation.
- The child is preoccupied with his or her genitals.
- There are indications that pressure or coercion was exerted on the child.
- The child's story remains consistent over time.
- The child's report indicates an escalating progression of sexual abuse over time.
- The child describes idiosyncratic details of the abuse.
- There is physical evidence of abuse.

It is important to recognize, however, that these indicators represent a broad constellation of behaviors that are frequently seen among sexually abused children as a group. Because sexual abuse takes many forms (e.g., a long-term incestuous relationship or a single event), each child will exhibit a different set of behaviors. Thus, a child who experienced a single abusive incident may well be consistent with her story over time. Conversely, a child who experienced several years of abuse by a close relative may seem to contradict her story over time, depending on the attitudes expressed by family members or the manner in which she is questioned. In other words, there is no single array of behavioral indicators that will definitively identify a sexually abused child.

THE RISK OF FALSE ALLEGATIONS

A recent spate of highly publicized sexual-abuse allegations has caused the public to recoil and question the limits of credulity. These allegations tend to fall into two categories: alleged sexual abuse of preschool children in day-care facilities, sometimes including bizarre and ritualistic elements; and sexual abuse allegations arising in the context of divorce and custody or visitation disputes. Such cases have caused many observers to question the veracity of child sexual abuse reports.[42]

Researchers have attempted to determine the percentage of unsubstantiated cases that can actually be attributed to false reports. The most comprehensive of these studies analyzed all reports of suspected sexual abuse filed with the Denver Department of Social Services (DSS) several years ago. All 576 reports had been investigated by the DSS Sexual Abuse Team and designated either "founded" (53 percent) or "unfounded" (47 percent). With the assistance of DSS caseworkers, the researchers applied clinical judgments to the case files and reclassified these reports, using the following categories:

- *Founded Cases*
  Reliable accounts
  Recantations of reliable accounts
- *Unfounded Cases*
  Unsubstantiated suspicions
  Insufficient information
  Fictitious reports by adults
  Fictitious reports by children

The latter two categories, "fictitious reports by adults" and "fictitious reports by children," included deliberate falsifications, misperceptions, confused interpretations of nonsexual events, and children who had been coached by adults. On reclassification by the researchers, 6 percent of the total cases (34 allegations) were found to be fictitious. Of those, only 8 allegations had been made by five children, four of whom had been substantiated victims of abuse in the past.[43]

In a second phase of this study, the researchers examined 21 fictitious cases that had been referred to a sexual-abuse clinic for evaluation over a 5-year period. Of these allegations, 5 had been initiated by the child and 9 by an adult; in 7 cases the researchers could not determine who had initiated the charge. Custody/visitation disputes were ongoing in 15 of these cases: in 1 child-initiated case, in 7 adult-initiated cases, and in all of the "mixed" cases.[44]

Another study examined 162 consecutive sexual-abuse cases seen at a children's hospital over a

10-month period. Twenty-five of those cases involved allegations against a parent, and seven of those (28 percent) involved a custody or visitation dispute. The disputed cases were less likely to be substantiated than cases without such conflict, but they were nevertheless substantiated more than half of the time.[45]

Other studies have approached the relationship between custody disputes and false allegations from a different perspective, beginning with cases that are referred to clinicians for custody evaluations (rather than sexual-abuse diagnosis). These studies have found that a relatively high proportion of custody disputes involve false sexual-abuse allegations.[46] It is important to note, however, that these studies depend on clinical populations (i.e., troublesome cases that had been referred to a specialist for evaluation or diagnosis). Findings are based on a small number of cases, and, furthermore, the decision to label a report "fictitious" is based on clinical judgment: there is no objective, definitive measure of "truth." Because of these limitations, such studies cannot generalize to a conclusion that sexual-abuse allegations associated with custody disputes are necessarily false.[47]

In fact, sexual-abuse allegations arising from divorce and custody disputes appear to be quite rare. One study that attempted to quantify this phenomenon found that in most courts, about 2 to 10 percent of all family court cases involving custody and/or visitation disputes also involved a charge of sexual abuse. As an alternative way of framing the magnitude of this problem, sexual-abuse allegations occurred in the range of approximately 2 to 15 per 1,000 divorce filings among the courts that were studied. Based on data from seven jurisdictions, 105 of 6,100 cases (or less than 2 percent) of custody or visitation disputes involved sexual-abuse allegations.[48]

Research also suggests that sexual abuse in day care is no more common than it is within families. Extrapolating from 270 substantiated cases in 35 states over a three-year period, researchers estimate that 500 to 550 actual cases occurred in that period, involving more than 2,500 children. Based on the total of 7 million children attending day-care facilities nationwide, the researchers calculate that 5.5 of every 10,000 children enrolled in day care are sexually abused. This compares to an estimated 8.9 of every 10,000 children who are sexually abused in their homes. The conclusion: The apparently large number of sexual-abuse cases reported in day care "is simply a reflection of the large number of children in day care and the relatively high risk of sexual abuse to children everywhere.[49]

EMOTIONAL REACTION TO THE PEDOPHILE

Because many investigators themselves are parents, they react strongly to the pedophile. However, for legal and pragmatic reasons, such feelings must never be translated into physical or verbal abuse. Physical abuse by police is unlawful and should result in criminal and civil charges. Verbal abuse or open expressions of revulsion minimize the possibility of obtaining the suspect's cooperation and, perhaps, of obtaining a much-needed voluntary statement. The following case illustrates this point.

A 5-year-old girl told her mother that the man next door had taken her into his home, removed her underpants, placed his penis between her legs, and rubbed her vagina with it. After putting her underpants back on, he had sent her home. The mother called the police, but when they arrived the child was very hesitant to repeat the story.

Careful handling of the interview by the officer provided enough information to justify probable cause for an arrest, although the suspect denied the offense. Supplementing the child's statements were those of neighbors who had seen the man taking the child into his house, where she had remained for about 10 minutes.

The child was taken to the hospital and given an examination. The examining physician could find no injuries, semen, or pubic hair. The victim's clothing was normal in appearance. The situation at this juncture was a shy young child who probably would not be a good witness, an absence of physical evidence, a suspect who denied the charges, and witnesses who saw the child enter the suspect's house but saw no molestation. A voluntary statement was imperative if a successful prosecution was to result.

The suspect was interrogated and at first denied the charges. But when confronted with the child's and the neighbors' statements, he admitted molesting the child in the manner she described. He said that he had been drinking heavily at the time and attributed his actions to intoxication. The suspect agreed to give a full statement under oath to the state prosecutor.

Before the suspect was sworn in, the prosecutor was advised, outside the presence of the suspect, of the facts in the case. The prosecutor requested that the suspect be brought into his office. And in an angry voice, told the suspect, "If that had been my little girl, you son of a bitch, I would have broken your god-damned neck." The prosecutor then asked the suspect if he would like to make a statement. The suspect replied, "I have nothing to say to you." Subsequently, he pleaded guilty to contributing to the delinquency of a minor, a misdemeanor.

The reason for this misdemeanor rather than the felony charge was insufficient evidence. The prosecutor was not new to this job, and he had an excellent reputation. Unfortunately, what he had done was to identify the victim with his own daughter, who was about the same age as the molested child.

CHILD PORNOGRAPHY

Kenneth V. Lanning, Supervisory Special Agent of the Federal Bureau of Investigation, divides what the pedophile collects into two categories: child pornography and child erotica.[50] *Child pornography* can be behaviorally (not legally) defined as the sexually explicit reproduction of a child's image, including sexually explicit photographs, negatives, slides, magazines, movies, videotapes, and computer disks. In essence, it is the permanent record of the sexual abuse or exploitation of an actual child. In order to legally be child pornography, it must be a visual depiction (not the written word) of a minor (as defined by statute) which is sexually explicit (not necessarily obscene, unless required by state law). Child pornography can be divided into two subcategories: commercial and homemade.

COMMERCIAL CHILD PORNOGRAPHY

Commerical child pornography is that which is produced and intended for commercial sale. Because of strict federal and state laws today, there is no place in the United States where commerical "child" pornography is knowingly openly sold. In the United States it is primarily a cottage industry run by pedophiles and child molesters. The commercial child pornography still being distributed in the United States is smuggled in from foreign countries—primarily by pedophiles. The risks are usually too high for the strictly commercial dealer. Because of their sexual and personal interest, however, pedophiles are more willing to take those risks. Their motive goes beyond just profit. Commercial child pornography is still assembled and is much more readily available in foreign countries. United States citizens, however, seem to be the main customers for this material. Some offenders collect their commercial child pornography in ways (e.g., photographs of pictures in magazines, pictures cut up and mounted in photo albums, names and descriptive information written below, homemade labels on commercial videotapes) that make it appear to be homemade child pornography. If necessary highly experienced investigators and forensic laboratories could be of assistance in making distinctions between homemade and commercially produced child pornography.

HOMEMADE CHILD PORNOGRAPHY

Contrary to what its name implies, the quality of homemade child pornography can be as good if not better than the quality of any commercial pornography. The pedophile has a personal interest in the product. *Homemade* simply means it was not originally produced primarily for commercial sale. Although commercial child pornography is not openly sold anywhere in this country, homemade child pornography is continually produced, swapped, and traded in almost every community in America. Although rarely found in "adult" bookstores, child pornography is frequently found in the homes and offices of doctors, lawyers, teachers, ministers, and other apparent pillars of the community. There is, however, a connection between commerical and homemade child pornography. Sometimes homemade child pornography is sold or winds up in commercial child pornography magazines, movies, or videos. The same pictures are reproduced and circulated again and again. With rapidly increasing frequency, more and more of both commercial and homemade child pornography is in the videotape format. This actually increases the odds of finding child pornography in any investigation.

It is important for the law enforcement investigator to realize that most of the children in prepubescent child pornography were not abducted into sexual slavery. They were seduced into posing for these pictures or videos by a pedophile they probably know. They were never missing children. The children in child pornography are frequently smiling or have neutral expressions on their faces because they have been seduced into the activity after having had their inhibitions lowered by clever offenders. In some cases their own parents took the pictures or made them available for others to take the pictures. Children in pubescent or technical child pornography, however, are more likely to be missing children—especially runaways or thrownaways being exploited by morally indiscriminate pimps or profiteers. In contrast to adult pornography, but consistent with the gender preference of most preferential child molesters, there are more boys than girls in child pornography.

In understanding the nature of child pornography, the law enforcement officer must recognize the distinction between *technical* and *simulated* child pornography. The Child Protection Act of 1984 defines a *child* as anyone under the age of 18. Therefore, a sexually explicit photograph of a 15-, 16-, or 17-year-old girl or boy is *technical* child pornography. Technical child pornography does not look like child pornography, but it is. The production, distribution, and in some cases, possession of this child pornography could and should be investigated under appropriate child pornography statutes. Technical child pornography is an exception to much of what we say about child pornography. It often is produced, distributed, and consumed by individuals who are not child molesters or pedophiles; it is openly sold around the United States; and it more often portrays females than males. Because it looks like adult pornography, it is more like adult pornography.

USE OF COLLECTION

Although the reasons why pedophiles collect child pornography and erotica are conjecture, we can be more certain as to how this material is used. Study and police investigations have identified certain criminal uses of the material.

Child pornography and child erotica are used for the sexual arousal and gratification of pedophiles. They use child pornography the same way other people use adult pornography—to feed sexual fantasies. Some pedophiles only collect and fantasize about the material without acting out the fantasies, but in most cases the arousal and fantasy fueled by the pornography is only a prelude to actual sexual activity with children.

A second use of child pornography and erotica is to lower children's inhibitions. A child who is reluctant to engage in sexual activity with an adult or to pose for sexually explicit photos can sometimes be convinced by viewing other children having "fun" participating in the activity. Peer pressure can have a tremendous effect on children; if other children are involved, the child might be led to believe the activity is acceptable. When the pornography is used to lower inhibitions, the children portrayed will usually *appear* to be having a good time.

Books on human sexuality, sex education, and sex manuals are also used to lower inhibitions. Children accept what they see in books, and many pedophiles have used sex education books to prove to children that such sexual behavior is acceptable. Adult pornography is also used, particularly with adolescent boy victims, to arouse them or to lower inhibitions.

A third major use of child pornography collections is blackmail. If a pedophile already has a relationship with a child, seducing the child into sexual activity is only part of the plan. The pedophile must also ensure that the child keep the secret. Children are most afraid of pictures being shown to their friends. Pedophiles use many techniques to blackmail; one of them is through photographs taken of the child. If the child threatens to tell his or her parents or the authorities, the existence of sexually explicit photographs can be an effective silencer.

A fourth use of child pornography and erotica is a medium of exchange. Some pedophiles exchange photographs of children for access to or phone numbers of other children. The quality and theme of the material determine its value as an exchange medium. Rather than paying cash for access to a child, the pedophile may exchange a small part (usually duplicates) of his collection. The younger the child and the more bizarre the acts, the greater the value of the pornography.

A fifth use of the collected material is profit. Some people involved in the sale and distribution of child pornography are not pedophiles; they are profiteers. In contrast, most pedophiles seem to collect child erotica and pornography for reasons other than profit. Some pedophiles may begin non-profit trading, which they pursue until they accumulate certain amounts or types of photographs, which are then sold to commercial dealers for reproduction in commercial child pornography magazines. Others combine their pedophilic interest with their profit motive. Some collectors even have their own photographic reproduction equipment. Thus, the photograph of a child taken with or without parental knowledge by a neighborhood pedophile in any American community can wind up in a commercial child pornography magazine with worldwide distribution.

USE OF THE COMPUTER IN CHILD PORNOGRAPHY

Computers are increasingly being used by pedophiles to assist them in locating more potential victims. It could be a large computer system at his place of business or a small personal computer at his home. It is simply a matter of modern technology catching up with long-known personality traits. The computer helps fill their need for organization, for validation, for souvenir records, and to find victims.

Law enforcement investigations have determined that pedophiles use computers to organize their collections and correspondence. Many pedophiles seem to be compulsive record keepers. A computer makes it much easier to store and retrieve names and addresses of victims and other pedophiles. Innumerable characteristics of victims and sexual acts can be easily recorded and analyzed. An extensive pornography collection can be cataloged by subject matter. Even fantasy writings and other narrative descriptions can be stored and retrieved for future use.

Many pedophiles communicate with other pedophiles. Now, instead of putting a stamp on a letter or package, they can use their computers to exchange information. Pedophiles can use their computers to locate individuals with similar interests.

The computer may enable them to obtain active validation with less risk of identification or discovery. Like advertisements in "swinger magazines," electronic bulletin boards are used to identify individuals of mutual interest concerning age, gender, and sexual preference. For example, several years ago in an issue of the North American Man-Boy Love Association (NAMBLA) bulletin, a member from Michigan proposed that NAMBLA establish its own electronic bulletin board. The pedophile may use an electronic bulletin board to which he has authorized access, or he may illegally enter a system. The pedophile can also set up his own or participate in other surreptitious or underground bulletin boards.

The pedophile can also use the computer to troll for and communicate with potential victims with minimal risk of being identified. Adolescent boys who spend many hours "hacking" on their computers are at particularly high risk of such contacts. The child can be indirectly "victimized" through the transfer of sexually explicit information and material or the child can be evaluated for future face-to-face contact and direct victimization.

Pedophiles who have turned their child pornography into a profit-making business use computers the same way any business uses them. Lists of customers, dollar amounts of transactions, descriptions of inventory, and so on, can all be recorded on the computer. The pedophile can now use a computer to transfer, manipulate, and even create child pornography. This is a small problem that will soon be a big problem. Computer software and hardware is being developed so rapidly that the potential of this problem is almost unlimited. The ability to manipulate digital visual images may make it difficult to believe your eyes when viewing child pornography. Recent television commercials show Elton John singing with a visual image of Louis Armstrong and Paula Abdul dancing with a visual image of Gene Kelly. Soon visual images of computer-generated "children" engaging in sexually explicit conduct may call into question the basis for highly restrictive (*i.e.,* possession, advertising, etc.) child pornography laws. It would be hard to argue that child pornography is the permanent record of the abuse or exploitation of an actual child if no real child is involved. Only obscenity laws may apply to such material.

Police must be alert to the fact that any pedophile with the intelligence, economic means, or employment access might be using a computer in any or all of the above ways. As computers become less expensive, more sophisticated, and easier to operate, the potential for abuse will grow rapidly. If the risks of trafficking in child pornography do not remain high, the pure profiteers may even return.[51]

INCEST

THE DEFINITIONS OF INCEST

Almost every state has some mention of incest in its statutes. However, the focus of these statutes varies broadly. Many states describe the biological relationship and the kind of sexual contact that occurred (e.g., intercourse); other states refer only to the prohibition of marriage between biologically related persons, with no mention of sexual activity with a minor child. These statutes appear to have two purposes: to prevent marriage and sexual relations between people who are too closely related and to protect children from sexual abuse by adult relatives. Some state laws do not recognize stepparents, foster parents, or adoptive parents in their incest statutes and handle these cases of sexual abuse under their sexual-assault or rape statutes.[52]

In this chapter we define *incest* broadly, to include any sexual abuse of a minor child by an adult perceived by the child to be a family member. The sexual behaviors include genital fondling, indecent exposure, oral and anal sexual contact, finger insertion, and intercourse. The perpetrator may be a biological parent, stepparent, foster parent, adoptive parent, mother's boyfriend, other parent surrogate, or relative in a caretaking relationship to the child, including extended family members such as grandparents or uncles. Sibling relationships are included when there is exploitation, assault, or a large age gap between parties. We do not discuss incest between consenting adults.

Because the most frequently reported form of sexual abuse is between father and daughter, we use the pronouns "he" to refer to the perpetrator and "she" to the victim. However, it is important to be aware that the child may be male and the adult, female.

SOME CHARACTERISTICS OF INCESTUOUS FAMILIES

What kinds of families are involved in incest? All kinds. There are many kinds of incestuous families, and there is much discussion in the professional literature about how the family members got the way they are. In this section, we briefly describe some of the common behavior and attitudes of incestuous families.

The incestuous family is often reclusive. The child victim lives in a secretive home environment and frequently cannot have friends in, especially as overnight guests. Further, she is discouraged from mingling with neighbors, developing close relationships, or taking part in outside activities or events. The family may be zealously religious. There may be heavy dependency on the closeness of the family relationships, with extreme authority residing in the father figure. The family may have strong beliefs about right and wrong, good and evil, and these beliefs may be imposed on the children by the authoritarian parent. Fear is often used to control the child's behavior.

Overt incest is an example of tension-reducing acting out in a dysfunctional family. Yet the family maintains a facade to outsiders. Many factors can contribute to the incest: family breakdown due to some sort of stress, such as unemployment, alcoholism, or the physical or mental illness of one parent; an emotionally immature parent or parents; and a lack of understanding of adult nurturing roles within the family. The parents may come from poor family backgrounds.

Serious disorganization in family roles often occurs before the beginning of the incestuous relationship. Usually the mother becomes passive or absent. The victimized daughter becomes the mother substitute, supporting the mother in her housework but giving in to the father, whom she perceives as having been turned away by her own mother. In turn, the father, unrelieved in his sexual drives, turns to the daughter to maintain the family unit. The incest may be reported only after some outsider notes evidence of it or of other maltreatment of the children in the family.

It is not uncommon for more than one child to be sexually exploited in the same family. When a series of children are being abused, disclosure may occur when the oldest child becomes aware that her younger siblings are also being victimized. In one such case, the eldest daughter had kept her own abuse a secret in exchange for her father's promise that he would not touch her younger sisters. When she discovered that they, too, were being abused, she reported her father to the authorities out of her desire to protect them.

PROFILE OF INCESTUOUS FATHERS

David Finkelhor and Linda Meyer Williams, sociologists at the Family Research Laboratory of the University of New Hampshire, have recently completed the most thorough study to date of men who have sexually abused their daughters. The sample consisted of 118 incestuous fathers—55 men in the U.S. Navy and 63 civilians from treatment centers around the country—and a carefully matched control group of nonincestuous fathers.[53]

In this landmark study on the characteristics of incest offenders, Finkelhor and Williams set out to determine whether men are socialized to see all intimacy and dominance as sexual, whether fathers separated from their daughters for long periods soon after birth are more likely to molest them than fathers who have not been absent, and whether incestuous men were more likely than nonoffenders to have themselves been abused as children. The researchers also sought to learn each man's feelings about his daughter, his outlook on sex, and his attitudes toward incest.

Many theories have been posited about why fathers molest their daughters. Everything from alcoholism to a frigid wife has been blamed. With this study, Finkelhor and Williams have shed new light on the subject and produced much new insight. They have established, for example, that there are distinct differences in the onset of abuse: daughters ranged in age from 4 weeks to 15 years old when the incest began. "Fathers were more likely to start abuse when their daughter was four to six years old or ten to twelve years old," the study reveals, "than to initiate abuse when she was seven, eight, or nine years old." Men reported various behaviors leading up to the abuse. Some of the fathers said they had masturbated while thinking of their daughters, had exposed themselves to the daughter, or had made her touch their genitals before they began touching

hers. A substantial percentage of the men—63 percent—had been sexually attracted to their daughters for a period of years before the abuse began. Most significantly, the findings reveal that there are many paths to incestuous behavior and that there is not just one type of man who commits such abuse.

Each man was interviewed for at least 6 hours and was asked hundreds of questions. The results dispel some common myths and prompt the following typology:

- *Type 1—The sexually preoccupied:* Twenty-six percent of the fathers studied fell into this category. These men had "a clear and conscious (often obsessive) sexual interest in their daughters." When they told what attracted them to the daughter, they talked in detail about her physical qualities—the feel of her skin, for example, or the smell of her body.

- *Type 1 subcategory—Early sexualizers:* Among the sexually preoccupied fathers, many regarded their daughters as a sex object almost from birth. "One father reported that he had been stimulated by the sight of his daughter nursing and that he could never remember a time when he did not have sexual feelings for her. . . . He began sexually abusing her when she was four weeks old." Many of the offenders had themselves been sexually abused as children. "These men are so sexualized that they may simply project their sexual needs onto everybody and everything. . . . The children may be those who are most easily manipulated to satisfy the preoccupations."

- *Type 2—Adolescent regressives:* About one third of the fathers—33 percent—became sexually interested in their daughters when the girls entered puberty. They said they were "transfixed" by the daughter's body's changes. For some the attraction began when the daughter started to act more grown up, but before her body changed. Some of the fathers in this group became aroused by a daughter after having been away from her for a long time. Her new maturity and developing body caught them by surprise. Sometimes the fathers let the attraction build for years, masturbating to fantasies of the daughter, before they acted. These men acted and sounded like young adolescents themselves when they talked about their daughters. One said, "I started to wonder what it would be like to touch her breasts and touch between her legs and wondered how she would react if I did." "The father-adult in me shut down," said another offender, "and I was like a kid again."

- *Type 3—Instrumental self-gratifiers:* These fathers accounted for 20 percent of the sample. They described their daughters in terms that were nonerotic. When they abused the daughter, they thought about someone else— the wife, even the daughter as an adult. In contrast to the sexually preoccupied and adolescent-regressive fathers who focused on their daughters, the instrumental self-gratifiers blocked what they were doing from their minds: "They used their daughter's body as a receptacle." The fact that they were abusing a daughter or that a daughter was so young was actually "a distracting element" that these fathers had to work to ignore. While one man was giving his 7-year-old a bath, she rubbed against his penis. "I realized that I could take advantage of the situation," he said. "She wasn't a person to me." Another man said, "I abused her from behind so I wouldn't see her face." Instrumental self-gratifiers abused sporadically, worried about the harm they were causing, and felt great guilt. To alleviate the guilt, some convinced themselves that the daughter was aroused.

- *Type 4—The emotionally dependent:* Just over 10 percent of the sample fit this category. These fathers were emotionally needy, lonely, depressed. They thought of themselves as failures and looked to their daughters for "close, exclusive, emotionally dependent relationships," including sexual gratification, which they linked to intimacy and not to the daughter's real or imagined sexual qualities. One man, separated from his wife, saw his 5-year-old daughter only on weekends. "It was companionship," he said. "I had been alone for six months. We slept together and would fondle each other. The closeness was very good and loving. Then oral sex began." The average age of the daughters when the incest began was 6 to 7 years. But it happened with older

daughters as well. The fathers of older daughters described the girls as their "best friends," and the relationships had a more romantic quality: the men described their daughters as they might have described an adult lover.

- *Type 5—Angry retaliators:* About 10 percent of the men were in this category. These fathers were the most likely to have criminal histories of assault and rape. They abused a daughter out of anger at her or, more often, at her mother for neglecting or deserting them. Some denied any sexual feelings for the daughter. One father of a 3-year-old said, "My daughter has no sex appeal for me at all. What I did was just an opportunity to get back at my daughter for being the center of my wife's life. There was no room for me." Sometimes the daughter was abused because she resembled her mother, sometimes because of the father's desire to desecrate her or to possess her out of an angry sense of entitlement. Some angry retaliators tied up, gagged, beat, and raped their daughters and were aroused by the violence.

While 33 percent of the men reported being under the influence of alcohol when the abuse occurred, and 10 percent reported that they were using drugs, only 9 percent held alcohol or drugs responsible. "Preliminary analysis indicates that the incestuous fathers are not more likely than the comparison fathers to have drug or alcohol abuse problems, although they may use alcohol or drugs to lower their inhibitions to abuse."

Forty-three percent of the men felt that their relationship with their wives was part of the reason for the incest. "However, the wife was rarely the only factor mentioned. . . . Different men probably come to incestuous acts as a result of different needs, motives, and impairments."

Significantly, 70 percent of the men said that they themselves had been sexually abused in their childhood. Half were physically abused by their fathers and almost half—44 percent—had been physically abused by their mothers. "Although not all who are abused go on to become perpetrators, it is critical that we learn more about how child sexual victimization affects male sexual development and male sexual socialization."

Considering the "intergenerational transmission of sexual abuse," Finkelhor and Williams suggest that men be given more opportunities for positive fathering—including paternity leave and more liberal visitation in cases of divorce or separation. They also suggest that males be encouraged to be intimate in nonsexual ways, beginning in boyhood. The study argues that, based on the evidence, it is very likely that people can become more aware of the precursory signs of incest. "It is conceivable," Finkelhor and Williams conclude, "that the sequence of events that leads to abuse can be interrupted."

THE MOTHER'S ROLE

The role of the mother in incestuous families has been a controversial subject. Mothers have been accused of setting up opportunities for the incest to occur and of working against authorities attempting to end it. For effective intervention to occur, it is important for investigators to realize the difficulties a woman confronts when she must cope with these behaviors in her family. It is very easy to judge a mother's lack of support for the child victim as indicating a lack of love or caring. However, this judgmental attitude merely alienates the mother further from helping systems. It is important to recognize that the mother is often emotionally and financially dependent on the abuser. She fears public disclosure and embarrassment, loss of economic support, loss of partnership, disruption of the family, and incarceration of her partner or spouse.

Even when a mother reports the abuse, she will have ambivalent feelings, and her support for the child may waver over time. It is helpful to have some understanding of what precipitated the mother's report. It may surface that she made the report in the heat of anger without considering the consequences. It is possible that she had been aware of the sexual abuse for some time and reported it out of anger because of other events in the relationship. It is also possible that she genuinely had no idea that abuse was taking place. She may start out very supportive of the child and yet, as her anger dissipates, her support may waver.

Often the mother experiences the disclosure of the information as a reflection on her adequacy as a wife, sexual partner, and mother. She may feel guilty, ashamed, and inadequate. She may begin to place pressure on the child to drop the charges or may give overt or covert messages to the child until the child decides on her own to end cooperation with the authorities. In some cases, mothers have taken extreme measures to avoid cooperation with authorities, including taking the child out of the state, providing negative information about the child to discredit her statements, or expressing a willingness to testify against the child.

THE POLICE OFFICER'S ROLE

A police officer and protective service worker may interview a child jointly. In such an interview, the role of the police officer is to investigate the suspected incest and to compile evidence for a case against the abuser. The role of the protective service worker is to assess the validity of the abuse complaint and the needs of the family. It is also important to be aware that people working on cases of childhood sexual abuse often have strong feelings about the information they receive from the children. Many express anger, discomfort, and embarrassment when they first encounter sexual abuse. To intervene effectively in these cases, they must be aware of their feelings and keep them in check during the interview.

Before the interview with the child, it is important to obtain answers to the following questions: Who reported it? What is that person's relationship to the child? How did he or she come to know? Information about the child's personality is helpful. Is this child very verbal and expressive, readily showing her feelings, or is she controlled and closed? It is an advantage when a child makes a self-report, because it indicates that she looks at the police officer as a helping resource and that she has decided to take action to end the sexual abuse. Other children may interpret the presence of a police officer to mean that they are the ones who are in trouble. The police should reassure the child that telling about the abuse, in the long run, will do good, for her and her family.

Because it is extremely important not to make the child confront the abuser during the interview, it is best if the social worker and police officer can interview the child alone, in a place that is comfortable for her. Tape-recording the interview can be a very efficient way of gathering information without distracting the child. If a child has first gone to a trusted person, such as a school counselor or pastor, she may request that person's presence during the initial interview to allay her fears and provide emotional support. A child who is extremely frightened and fearful of strangers may be unwilling to communicate without such support.

The earlier section "Child Molestation" addresses in depth the topic of interviewing molested children. Since incest is a special instance of child molestation, the reader is referred back to that section for guidelines in conducting such an interview. But there are also two further considerations to bear in mind when interviewing a victim of incest.

First, it is important to be aware of how the child may be viewing the sexual experience(s) and her interview. Some children have no idea that the behavior was wrong or inappropriate. Consequently, it is important not to convey, by attitude or words, negative judgments about what happened. The incestuous activity may have been the only affection the child has known, and she may have very strong positive feelings about the abuser.

Second, if the incest has been undetected for a long time, the child may have built up catastrophic expectations about what will happen when she tells. The interviewer can find out what she has been told will happen to her if she tells. Frequently children have been threatened with physical harm or harm to their family. They may have been told that telling will destroy the family, put Daddy in jail, cause Mother to have a nervous breakdown, and send the children to a foster home. They also may have been bribed to keep silent through special favors, presents, or money. For other children, the authority of the adult involved, plus assurances that there is nothing wrong with the sexual behavior, may have been enough to have ensured the child's silence.

SUDDEN INFANT DEATH SYNDROME

Although sudden infant death syndrome (SIDS) is a medical phenomenon, not a crime, a lack of knowlege about its elements can cause individuals involved in its investigation to erroneously conclude they have a criminal homicide.

Health professionals in the past had limited contact with SIDS families because SIDS rarely occurs outside of the home. A few babies have died of SIDS while hospitalized, but the usual case involves a baby who is brought to the hospital emergency room and is pronounced dead on arrival. As a result, many physicians and nurses have had little knowledge of SIDS.[54]

WHAT IS SUDDEN INFANT DEATH SYNDROME?

Simply defined, *SIDS* is the sudden and unexpected death of an apparently healthy infant that remains unexplained after the performance of a complete autopsy. On the average, 2 of every 1,000 infants born alive succumb to SIDS, and it is the leading cause of death among infants 1 week to 1 year of age.

In the majority of instances, the baby is apparently in good health prior to death and feeds without difficulty. Although there may be evidence of a slight cold or stuffy nose, there is usually no history of serious upper respiratory infection. In most cases, the infant is placed in a crib to sleep and is found dead several hours later.

Most SIDS deaths occur between November and March. Sudden changes in temperature may trigger SIDS. The risk of SIDS appears to be highest in crowded dwellings; in infants of young mothers; in males; in nonwhites regardless of socioeconomic status; in families of lower socioeconomic status regardless of race; and in premature infants. Twins have an increased risk of SIDS, likely a consequence of their low birthweight and premature birth. SIDS occurs in both breast-fed and bottle-fed babies. Most victims are between the ages of 1 and 6 months, with the highest frequency of occurrence between 2 and 4 months.

Characteristics of SIDS Victims' Appearance

- Usually normal state of nutrition and hydration.
- Blood-tinged, frothy fluids around mouth and nostrils, indicative of pulmonary edema.
- Vomitus on the face.
- Diaper wet and full of stool.
- Bruiselike marks on head or body limbs (postmortem pooling or settling of blood in dependent body parts).

Autopsy Findings

- Some congestion and edema of the lungs.
- Petechial hemorrhages in thymus, heart, and lungs.
- Minor evidence of respiratory tract inflammation.

MISCONCEPTIONS ABOUT SIDS

Aspiration, Choking

These babies do not inhale or choke on their feeding.

Unsuspected Illness

Particularly if the baby had a cold, the parents may feel guilty about not having taken the child to the doctor. If the baby was checked by the doctor, the parents (and the doctor) may wonder what the doctor missed. In any case, neither is at fault.

Freezing

Although the body may be cold when discovered, this is a postmortem change.

Accidental Injury, Neglect, or Abuse

Law enforcement officers should not jump to the wrong conclusions because of the appearance of the infant. The results of accusations of wrongdoing have been tragic. A few innocent and grief-stricken parents have been accused of murdering their babies and put in jail. Appearances can be deceiving.

SIDS RESEARCH

Currently, the most widely recognized theory about the mechanism of SIDS is spontaneous, protracted apnea, or cessation of breathing. Considerable progress in understanding SIDS has been made by the SIDS Institute at the University of Maryland. In comprehensive tests of 1,000 babies, it was found that fully 10 percent stopped breathing for periods longer than 15 to 20 seconds or their heart rate dropped below 80 beats per minute. Detected in time, such infants are considered at risk for SIDS and are monitored with an electronic device that sets off an alarm if the child's breathing or heart rate drops below a certain level (see Figure 12–9).

Perhaps the most significant research supporting the apnea theory is the work of Dr. Richard Naeye of the Pennsylvania State University College of Medicine. Dr. Naeye began to look for structural changes in the infant's body at autopsy that would indicate chronic lack of oxygen attributable to repeated and relatively long periods of apnea. He found the following changes in a large group of SIDS victims:

1. The walls of the small arteries in the lungs were thicker than normal.
2. The wall of the right ventricle of the heart was thicker than normal.
3. The relative retention of brown fat around the adrenal gland was greater than normal.
4. There was abnormal retention of fetal capacity for the production of red blood cells in the liver.

Dr. Marie Valdes-Dapena, of the University of Miami School of Medicine, has confirmed Naeye's observations with respect to the two latter changes and is currently working on the first two.

In a study conducted several years ago and reported in the *New England Journal of Medicine*, it was found that infants who usually slept in the prone position had a significantly higher risk of SIDS than those who slept on their backs.[55] The respiratory obstruction in relation to the position of infants was also studied by Emery and Thornton.[56] It was concluded that the air passage of an infant is impaired when the body is placed face down on any type of mattress or pillow. Another study, conducted by Kemp and Thach[57] described 25 infants with SIDS discovered prone on polystyrene cushions. The studies in animals have suggested that the accidental suffocation results from the rebreathing of carbon dioxide.[58]

THE POLICE OFFICER'S ROLE

The law enforcement officer serves a key role in the SIDS case and is often the first person to encounter the shock, grief, and guilt experienced by the parents.

It may be an experience such as this: The officer responds to a call, entering a house where an infant has just died. The mother is hysterical, incoherent, and unable to clarify what happened. The father is dazed yet tearless; he is confused and responding evasively. As the officer proceeds, the mother

Figure 12–9
Electronic Monitoring Device Used to Prevent SIDS

Electronic device attached to this child is used to monitor the heart and respiration rates. If the heart rate drops below 80 beats per minute or the child stops breathing for 15 to 20 seconds, a red light comes on and an audible alarm is sounded by the monitor depicted in the upper right corner of the figure.

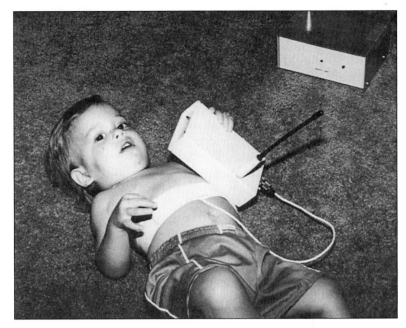

(Courtesy Joseph and Karin Venero)

continues to sob, blaming herself. The infant is in the cradle, its head covered with a blanket. When the blanket is removed, the officer notes a small amount of blood-tinged fluid in and around the mouth and nose and bruiselike marks on the body where the blood settled after death.

Was the death a result of illness, abuse, neglect, or unexplained causes? The officer will make a preliminary assessment based on the information obtained at the scene.

If the circumstances are unclear, an autopsy may establish the need for criminal investigation. If the death is unexplainable, the officer can do a great service to the family by telling them that their baby was possibly a victim of SIDS. The officer can explain that it is the leading cause of death in infants after the first month of life and can tell them that there are organizations to provide them with information and assistance. By knowing about this disease and being able to provide sympathy and information to parents, the law enforcement officer serves a key role in the management of a SIDS case.

CRIMINAL HOMICIDE AS A POSSIBILITY

Nevertheless, in spite of the findings just discussed, the police must be sensitive to the possibility of an intentional suffocation. Some recent studies raise the specter that in recent years there may have been cases in which children had actually been murdered but the deaths were incorrectly classified as SIDS. Every year in the United States more than 3,000 infant deaths are listed as SIDS, while 300 or more are identified as infanticides. Now two scientific studies suggest that some of the deaths in the first category belong in the second:

- Dr. David Southall of City General Hospital in Stoke-on-Trent, England, set up video cameras in the hospital rooms of children brought in after parents reported that the children had stopped breathing and nearly died. The cameras captured 39 instances of mothers trying to smother their babies. Fully one-third of these "near-miss SIDS" cases, it is estimated, are actually cases of Munchausen syndrome by proxy. Overall, Dr. Southall concludes that 5 to 10 percent of SIDS deaths are in fact infanticides.[59]

- In an unpublished study, Dr. Thomas Truman concluded that as many as one-third of the repeated near-SIDS cases at what may be the most prestigious SIDS center in the United States may be cases of Munchausen syndrome by proxy. While serving a fellowship at

Massachusetts General Hospital from 1993 to 1996, Truman analyzed the medical records of 155 children treated at the hospital. In 56 of these cases the child's chart contained circumstantial evidence of possible abuse. One baby suffered repeated breathing crises at home, turning blue and limp, but only when the mother and no one else was present. Another one had no breathing problems during the six-months he spent in a local hospital, but the day he went home alone with his mother he had a life-threatening breathing emergency. The authorities were alerted to the possiblity of the case, but no action was taken. The child died 1 year after being sent home.[60]

It should be noted that if death has been induced by intentional suffocation, there may be petechial hemorrhaging of the eye and surrounding areas (see Chapter 10, Injury and Death Investigation, for a more detailed discussion of this condition).

INFANT ABDUCTION

Infant abduction is the taking of a child less than 1 year old by a nonfamily member. Although the FBI classifies such cases as kidnappings, infant abductions occur, by definition, for reasons not typically associated with kidnappings. For the most part, infant abductions do not appear to be motivated by a desire for money, sex, revenge, or custody, which are considered traditional motives in kidnapping cases.[61]

Since 1987, an average of 14 infants have been abducted annually. These abductions had no boundaries in terms of location or size of the hospital or of race, sex, or socioeconomic background of the infant.

PROFILE OF THE ABDUCTOR

The data from these cases bring to light certain offender characteristics. Investigators can use these traits to profile and apprehend suspects.

By way of general background, infant abductors usually are women, accounting for 141 of the 145 cases analyzed. Offenders whose ages were verified ranged from 14 to 48 years old, with an average age of 28. Race was determined in 142 cases:

63 offenders were white, 54 were black, and 25 were Hispanic. The typical abductor may not have a criminal record. If a criminal record does exist, it likely will consist of nonviolent offenses, such as check fraud or shoplifting. To gain further insight into infant abductors and the crimes they commit, members of the FBI's National Center for the Analysis of Violent Crime (NCAVC) interviewed 16 abductors.[62] Offenders included whites, blacks, and Hispanics and ranged in age (at the time of the abduction) from 19 to 42. They had abducted infants in 10 different states. Nine of the abductors targeted hospitals directly; five approached the infant's residence; and two chose other locations. Although none had commited a violent crime before, four killed the infant's mother before stealing her baby.

Five of the abductors were single, seven were married, and four were either separated or divorced. Ten had no children. Though 13 offenders said they were involved in a significant relationship at the time of the abduction, many described it as "rocky," stressful, and lacking in communication.

Motivation

Although little research exists on the topic of infant abductors' motivation, the cases outlined here illustrate that the need to present their partners with a baby often drives the female offender. Ten of the women interviewed admitted they had faked pregnancy. One of them recalled crying in the parking lot of a hospital, wondering if she should tell her husband she was not pregnant. Though she knew in her heart that she should tell him the truth, she thought he would leave her if she did. She chose to remain silent. Later, she followed a mother home and stole her baby.

Another woman had feigned pregnancy successfully with her husband before they were married, but her second attempt proved unsuccessful. Following her conviction for infant abduction, her husband admitted that he would not have married her had he known she was not pregnant.

Five other women claimed to have miscarried without telling their partners, although no evidence existed to confirm their pregnancies. One said she had miscarried 4 months into her prgnancy but had countinued living the lie, rationalizing that the stress placed on her by her husband's desire to have a baby had prompted her to deceive him.

Thus, as these cases illustrate, the infant abductor frequently attempts to prevent her husband or boyfriend from deserting her or tries to win back his affection by claiming pregnancy and, later, the birth of a child.[63] She may view a baby as the only way to salvage the relationship with her partner.[64]

According to the National Center for Missing and Exploited Children (NCMEC), sometimes the infant abductor is driven by a desire to experience vicariously the birth of a child she is "unable to conceive" or carry to term.[65] She is desperate to "bask in the rapture of baby love—to feel adored and needed.[66] Just as many expectant mothers tell others the "good news," the typical infant abductor truly believes that "she is about to give birth, and she fully expects everyone to accept the reality she has attempted to create.[67]

Planning

Some abductors spent a great deal of time planning their crimes; others apparently acted on impulse. Their efforts ranged from a few hours to over nine months before the abduction. Eleven of the abductors interviewed gained weight prior to the abduction: one gained 61 pounds. Eleven purchased baby goods, and 12 told others they were pregnant. Then, when it came time to "deliver," the abductors employed such tactics as surveilling hospitals, monitoring birth announcements in the newspaper, following mothers home, and posing as hospital employees, baby-sitters, or social workers.

One abductor drove over 300 miles to steal an infant from an area where she had once resided. She also admitted to "checking out the security" of at least two area hospitals. While her actions appear premeditated, when asked to explain them, she responded, "I knew I was going somewhere, but I didn't know where. It was like I escaped into this little dream."

In fact, though most women planned events leading up to the abduction, many seemed to have not prepared for the act itself. They also could not, or would not, recall the mechanics of how they had carried out the abduction. One woman, who had entered a residence and murdered the mother before stealing her baby, remembered, "I had no plan of action, you know, it just was whatever happened, happened." The same woman had visited at least three hospitals, while wearing maternity clothes, prior to committing her crime.

Following the abduction, 14 of the 16 offenders openly displayed the stolen infant to others. Six claimed to have given birth in an area hospital; four, out of town; and two, at home. Only three of the abductors altered the baby's appearance. According to one abductor, she cut the baby's hair to make him look younger.

THE SCENE OF THE CRIME

Location

Traditionally, the hospital setting has been the primary target for infant abductions. In the analysis discussed above, 83 of the 145 infants were taken from within a hospital: 49 from the mother's room, 14 from the nursery, 13 from pediatric hospital rooms, and 7 from other hospital locations.

Bolder criminals try locations outside the hospital. Three babies were stolen from a clinic or doctor's office; two from day-care centers. One quick-thinking abductor snatched a baby from the hospital curb. Forty brazen abductors targeted the residence of the infant or a baby-sitter.

Time of Day

Even in these emotion-driven crimes, the perpetrators showed signs of logic. In the majority of these cases the abductors chose to act during normal business hours: of the 145 cases, 121 occurred on a weekday, and in the 124 cases where the time of the abduction was recorded, 95 occured between 8 A.M. and 6 P.M. The reason for this appears to be ease of movement. That is, in a hospital during normal working hours, abductors could disguise themselves as employees and slip in and out virtually undetected. Similarly, at a residence, there would be less likelihood of confronting a spouse during the workday.

Month

From January 1983 through December 1994, abductions occurred more frequently between May and October and less frequently between November and April, with the exception of December. More infant abductions occurred in December (20 total) and May (19 total) than in any other month. Historically, November has shown the lowest number of abductions (a total of 8). Although a pattern seems to exist here, it simply could be coincidence:

Most of the 16 abductors interviewed had feigned pregnancy. They had to "deliver" a baby 9 months later, regardless of the time of year.

Method

Whether they steal babies from a hospital or from another location, abductors usually gain access through a con or ruse, as did 101 of the 145 subjects studied. Methods vary but have included posing as hospital employees, baby-sitters, or social workers. Some abductors have asked to use the telephone to get into the victim's home.

While cons help abductors gain access, they do not always make the abduction itself easier. As a result, abductors have used force either alone or in combination with a con in 16 cases, leading to the deaths of seven mothers and one father. Of these forcible abductions, 10 occurred in the victim's home, and the abductors used guns in 11 cases.

Abductions away from the hospital pose access difficulties for the offender and may account for the need to exercise force. In these cases, the degree of force ranged from threatening or binding the mother to shooting and stabbing the parents. In one of the most gruesome cases, the abductor strangled the mother and removed her unborn child from her womb, performing a crude caesarean section with car keys. Miraculously, the infant survived. Unfortunately, the mother did not. In 25 cases, the abductor stole the infant without having direct contact with another person at the moment of abduction.

INVESTIGATIVE STRATEGIES

Successful resolution of any case depends on several factors, including the efforts of law enforcement. In 135 of the 136 resolved cases, the amount of time the infants remained missing ranged from mere hours to just over 300 days. Ninety three of the babies were recovered in two days or less. Overall, law enforcement has a 94 percent rate of resolution.

One of the primary investigative strategies in infant abduction cases has been using the media to activate community awareness. Friends, relatives, and/or neighbors identified the abductor following media reports in approximately 53 out of 129 cases where researchers knew how the crime was solved.

Anonymous phone tips resulted in the capture of 20 abductors following media exposure of the 16 abductors interviewed by researchers; four admitted to following the media reports, but none altered her plans on the basis of the coverage. In short, the media played a significant role in identifying the offenders but did not affect their actions. Accordingly, investigators probably need not fear that publicizing a case will bring harm to the infant.

USE OF AGE-PROGRESSION TECHNOLOGY TO SEARCH FOR MISSING CHILDREN

One of the serious difficulties encountered by authorities in attempting to locate children who have been missing for a number of years is that their appearances can be dramatically changed during the normal aging process.[68] However, in recent years, computer technology has been used to age-enhance photographs of missing children. The Sony Corporation of America and QMA Corporation of Reston, Virginia, recently collaborated with the National Center for Missing and Exploited Children to assist in searching for missing and unidentified youth. Through their collective efforts, they installed a Video Imaging Laboratory at the NCMEC headquarters in Arlington, Virginia. The system was built using the expertise and techniques of the Federal Bureau of Investigation and experienced police artists, and this technology will help to breathe new life into cases of abducted children who have remained missing for long periods of time. NCMEC's Video Imaging Laboratory represents a potentially dramatic breakthrough in law enforcement technology, speeding the process by which these pictures are enhanced.

The process is accomplished by collecting information on the missing child, including full frontal photographs of the child; videotapes of the child, if available; and any information regarding identifying marks, hair color and style, and traditional information. Photographs of the parents and siblings at the comparable age of enhancement are also valuable. Computerized records of these photographs and details are then created and stored (see Figures 12–10 and 12–11).

Figure 12–10

A photograph of Marjorie C. (Christy) Luna at 8 years of age. A facial image was stretched for merging with her sister's photograph, which appears in the insert, lower right corner.

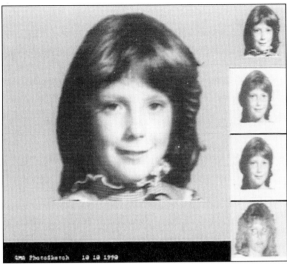

(Courtesy National Center for Missing and Exploited Children)

Figure 12–11

Completed age progression of Marjorie C. Luna. Her age has been progressed from 8 to 14 years of age.

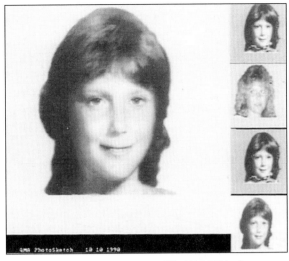

(Courtesy National Center for Missing and Exploited Children)

Dissemination of photographs of missing children has proved to be a successful tool in their location, but in long-term cases the age enhancement of the photograph plays a vital role in the search for the child as he or she might currently look.

Questions

1. What are the two most common instruments used in child abuse?

2. What are some of the ways that intentional immersion burns are distinguished from accidental immersion burns?

3. Why was the phrase "shaken-baby syndrome" coined?

4. What is the mechanism of injuries in shaken-baby syndrome?

5. What role does the physician play in child-abuse cases?

6. What is Munchausen syndrome by proxy (MSBP)?

7. What are some of the major behavioral characteristics of the situational and preferential child molester?

8. Waterman has identified three types of developmental issues that are important when allegations of sexual abuse arise. What are they?

9. What are some of the benefits of using an anatomically detailed doll in interviewing children?

10. How is child pornography behaviorally defined?

11. Five different categories of incestuous fathers were discussed in the text. What are these categories?

12. Describe the appearance of a SIDS victim.

13. What are typically *not* the motivations involved in infant abduction?

14. What appears to be the major motivating factor that drives female offenders to abduct infants?

15. How is the process of age progression technologically accomplished?

Notes

1. C. J. Flammang, *The Police and the Unprotected Child* (Springfield, Ill.: Charles C. Thomas, 1970), p. 90; Harold E. Simmons, *Protective Services for Children* (Sacramento, Calif.: General Welfare Publications, 1968), p. 45.

2. Phylip J. Peltier, Gary Purdue, and Jack R. Shepherd, *Burn Injuries in Child Abuse* (Washington, D.C.: U.S. Department of Justice, 1997), pp. 1–9.

3. Randell Alexander and K. Kleinmann, *Diagnostic Imaging of Child Abuse* (Washington, D.C.: U.S. Department of Justice, 1996), pp. 6–9.

4. James D. Regis, "The Battered Child," *Police Work*, April 1980, pp. 41–42.

5. Rob Parrish, *Battered Child Syndrome: Investigating Physical Abuse* (Washington, D.C.: U.S. Department of Justice, 1996), pp.9–10.

6. Stephen J. Boros and Larry C. Brubaker, "Munchausen Syndrome by Proxy: Case Accounts," *FBI Law Enforcement Bulletin,* 1992, Vol. 61, No. 6, pp. 16-20. These case reports were taken from this article.

7. Kenneth V. Lanning, *Child Molesters: A Behavioral Analysis for Law Enforcement Officers Investigating Cases of Child Sexual Exploitation*, 3rd ed. (Arlington, Va.: National Center for Missing and Exploited Children, 1992), pp. 6–10. This entire discussion of child molesters has been reproduced with permission. No part of this may be reproduced without the express written permission of the National Center for Missing and Exploited Children, 1-800-843-5678.

8. Ibid.

9. Debra Whitcomb, *When the Victim Is a Child* (Washington D.C.: National Institute of Justice, 1992), pp. 15-20.

10. D. Floyd, testimony before President's Task Force on Victims of Crime, Final Report, December 1982, p. 51.

11. J. Waterman, "Development Considerations," in *Sexual Abuse of Young Children,* K. MacFarlane and J. Waterman (eds.) (New York: Guilford Press, 1986), pp. 15-29.

12. W. M. Friedrich, J. Fischer, D. Broughton, D. Houston, and C. R. Shafran, "Normative Sexual Behavior in Children: A Contemporary Sample," *Pediatrics*, Vol. 101, No. 4, April P.E. 9.

13. A. Warren-Leubecker et al., "What Do Children Know about the Legal System and When Do They Know It? First Steps down a Less-Traveled Path in Child Witness Research," in *Perspectives on Children's Testimony*, S. J. Ceci, D. F. Ross, and M. P. Toglia (eds.), (New York: Springer-Verlag, 1989), pp. 158-183.

14. M. A. Young, "Working with Victims Who Are Children or Adolescents: Using the Lessons of Child Development with Young Trauma Victims," *NOVA Newsletter,* 1989, Vol. 13.

15. Warren-Leubecker et al., "What Do Children Know about the Legal System"; K. J. Saywitz, "Children's Conceptions of the Legal System: 'Court Is a Place to Play Basketball,'" in Ceci et al., *Perspectives on Children's Testimony*, pp. 131-157. Also see S. P. Limber, G. B. Melton, and S. J. Rahe, "Legal Knowledge, Attitudes, and Reasoning Abilities of Witnesses," paper presented at AP-LS Division 41 Biennial Convention, Williamsburg, Va., March 1990.

16. R. Pynoos and S. Eth, "The Child Witness to Homicide," *Journal of Social Issues*, 1984, Vol. 40, p. 98.

17. K. J. Saywitz and C. Jaenicke, "Children's Understanding of Legal Terms: A Preliminary Report of Grade-Related Trends," paper presented at the Society for Research on Child Development Biennial Meeting, Baltimore, Md., April 1987.

18. A. Warren-Leubecker et al., "What Do Children Know about the Legal System."

19. Whitcomb, *When the Victim Is a Child*, pp. 33-38. This discussion was adapted from this source.

20. Alabama, Connecticut, Michigan, New Jersey, New York, Pennsylvania, West Virginia, and Wyoming.

21. See, for example, *Cleveland* v. *State,* 490 N.R. 2nd 1140 (Ind. App. 1986); *People* v. *Garvie*, 148 Mich. App. 444, 384 N.W. 2d 796 (1986); *State* v. *Jenkins*, 326 N.W. 2d 67 (N.D. 1982).

22. E. Gray, "Children as Witnesses in Child Sexual Abuse Cases Study," Final Report submitted to the National Center on Child Abuse and Neglect under Grant No. 90-CA-1273, by the National Council of Jewish Women, New York, New York, 1990, p. 51. (Henceforth referred to as NCJW Study.)

23. K. R. Freemand and T. Estrada-Mullany, "Using Dolls to Interview Child Victims: Legal Concerns and Interview Procedures," *Research in Action* (National Institute of Justice), January/February 1988, p. 2.

24. White, pp. 472-473.

25. S. White and G. Santilli, "A Review of Clinical Practices and Research Data on Anatomical Dolls," *Journal of Interpersonal Violence*, December 1988, Vol. 3, pp. 437-439.

26. L. Berliner, "Anatomical Dolls," *Journal of Interpersonal Violence,* December 1988, Vol. 3, pp. 468-470; also see B. W. Boat and M. D. Everson, "Normative

Data: How Non-Referred Young Children Interact with Anatomical Dolls," paper presented at the Symposium of Interviewing Children, cited in Berliner, "Anatomical Dolls," p. 469.

27. White and Santilli, "A Review of Clinical Practices," p. 431.

28. B. Boat and M. Everson, "Use of Anatomical Dolls among Professionals in Sexual Abuse Evaluations," *Child Abuse and Neglect,* 1988, Vol. 12, pp. 171-179.

29. K. MacFarlane and S. Krebs, "Techniques for Interviewing and Evidence Gathering," in MacFarlane and Waterman, *Sexual Abuse of Young Children,* pp. 74-75.

30. Ibid.

31. White and Santilli, "A Review of Clinical Practices," pp. 439-440.

32. Robert H. Farley, "Drawing Interviews: An Alternative Technique," *The Police Chief,* 1987, pp. 37-38. Copyright held by the International Association of Chiefs of Police, Inc., 1110 North Glebe Road, Suite 200, Arlington, Virginia 22201, U.S.A. Further reproduction without express written permission from the IACP is strictly prohibited.

33. MacFarlane and Krebs, "Techniques for Interviewing and Evidence Gathering," p. 87.

34. NCJW Study, pp. 439-440.

35. S. J. Ceci, D. Ross, and M. Toglia, "Age Differences in Suggestibility: Narrowing the Uncertainties," in *Children's Eyewitness Memory,* S. J. Ceci, M. P. Toglia, and D. F. Ross (eds.) (New York: Springer-Verlag, 1987), pp. 79-91.

36. H. Wakefield and R. Underwager, "Techniques for Interviewing Children in Sexual Abuse Cases," *VOCAL Perspective,* Summer 1989, pp. 7-15.

37. K. Saywitz et al., "Children's Memories of Genital Examinations: Implications for Cases of Child Sexual Assault," paper presented at the Society for Research in Child Development Meetings, Kansas City, Mo., 1989.

38. R. Lusk and J. Waterman, "Effects of Sexual Abuse on Children," in MacFarlane and Waterman, *Sexual Abuse of Young Children,* pp. 15-29. Also see A. Browne and D. Finkelhor, "Initial and Long-Term Effects: A Review of the Research," in *A Sourcebook on Child Sexual Abuse,* D. Finkelhor et al. (eds.) (Beverly Hills: Sage, 1986), pp. 143-152.

39. J. R. Conte and J. R. Schuerman, "The Effects of Sexual Abuse on Children: A Multidimensional View," *Journal of Interpersonal Violence,* December 1987, Vol. 2, pp. 380-390.

40. W. N. Freidrich, R. L. Beilke, and A. J. Urquiza, "Children from Sexually Abusive Families: A Behavioral Comparison," *Journal of Interpersonal Violence,* December 1987, Vol. 2, pp. 391-402.

41. J. Conte et al., "Evaluating Children's Report of Sexual Abuse: Results from a Survey of Professionals," unpublished manuscript, University of Chicago, undated; cited in J. E. B. Myers et al., "Expert Testimony in Child Sexual Abuse Litigation," *Nebraska Law Review,* 1989, Vol. 68, p. 75.

42. Whitcomb, *When the Victim Is a Child,* pp. 6-11

43. D. Jones and J. McGraw, "Reliable and Fictitious Accounts of Sexual Abuse to Children," *Journal of Interpersonal Violence,* March 1987, Vol. 2, pp. 27-45.

44. Ibid.

45. J. Paradise, A. Rostain, and M. Nathanson, "Substantiation of Sexual Abuse Charges When Parents Dispute Custody or Visitation," *Pediatrics,* June 1988, Vol. 81, pp. 835-839.

46. See, for example, E. P. Benedek and D. H. Schetky, "Allegations of Sexual Abuse in Child Custody and Visitation Disputes," in *Emerging Issues in Child Psychiatry and the Law,* D. H. Schetky and E. P. Benedek (eds.) (New York: Brunner/Mazel, 1985), pp. 145-158; A. H. Green, "True and False Allegations of Sexual Abuse in Child Custody Disputes," *Journal of the American Academy of Child Psychiatry,* 1986, Vol. 25, pp. 449-456.

47. For an excellent summary of the drawbacks of such studies, see D. Corwin et al., "Child Sexual Abuse and Custody Disputes: No Easy Answers," *Journal of Interpersonal Violence,* March 1987, Vol. 2, pp. 91-105; also see Berliner, "Deciding Whether a Child Has Been Sexually Abused," in *Sexual Abuse Allegations in Custody and Visitation Cases,* E. B. Nicholson (ed.) (Washington, D.C.: American Bar Association, 1988), pp. 48-69.

48. N. Thoennes and J. Pearson, "Summary of Findings from the Sexual Abuse Allegations Project," in Nicholson, *Sexual Abuse Allegations,* pp. 1-21.

49. D. Finkelhor, L. M. Williams, and N. Burns, *Nursery Crimes: Sexual Abuse in Day Care* (Newbury Park, Calif.: Sage, 1988).

50. Kenneth V. Lanning, *Child Molesters: A Behavioral Analysis for Law Enforcement Officers Investigating Cases of Child Sexual Exploitation* 3rd ed. (Arlington, Va.: National Center for Missing and Exploited Children, 1992), pp. 24–31. This entire discussion of child pornography has been reproduced with permission. No part of this may be reproduced without the express written permission of the National Center for Missing and Exploited Children, 1-800-843-5678.

51. Ibid.

52. Marianne Ewig, Lynne Ketchum, and Carolyn Kott Washburne, "Incest," *Police Work*, April 1980, pp. 11-18. The discussion was taken with modifications from this source.

53. Heidi Vanderbilt, "Incest—A Chilling Report," *Lear's*, February 1992, pp. 49-64. For a more detailed discussion of the results of this study, see David Finkelhor and Linda Meyer Williams, University of New Hampshire, Family Research Laboratory, Durham, N.H., 1992.

54. *A Resource Handbook: Sudden Infant Death Syndrome* (Tallahassee, Fla.: Department of Health and Rehabilitative Services, 1978), pp. 1-2. Much of the information dealing with SIDS was taken from this source.

55. Ann L. Ponsonby, Terrence Dwyer, Laura E. Gibbons, Jennifer A. Cochrane, and You-gan Wang, "Factors Potentiating the Risk of Sudden Infant Death Syndrome Associated with the Prone Position," *New England Journal of Medicine*, August 1993, Vol. 329, No. 6, p. 378. The scientists conducting this study analyzed data from a case-controlled study (58 infants with SIDS and 120 controlled infants) and perspective cohort study (22 infants with SIDS and 233 control infants) in Tasmania. Interactions were examined and math analyses done with a multiplicative model of interaction.

56. J. L. Emery and J. A. Thornton, "Affects of Obstruction to Respiration in Infants with Particular Reference to Mattresses, Pillows, and Their Coverings," *BMJ*, 1968, Vol. 3, pp. 309-313.

57. J. S. Kemp and B. T. Thach, "Sudden Infant Deaths in Sleeping on Polystyrene Filled Cushions," *New England Journal of Medicine*, 1991, Vol. 324, pp. 1858-1864.

58. J. A. Corbyn and P. Matthews, *Environmental Causes of Sudden Infant Death* (Freemantle, Australia: Western Technical Press, 1992); E. L. Ryan, "Distribution of Expired Air in Carrying Cots—A Possible Explanation for Some Sudden Infant Deaths," *Australias Phys. Eng. Sci. Med.*, 1991, Vol. 14, pp. 112-118.

59. David P. Southall, "Covert Video Recording of Life-Threatening Child Abuse: Lessons for Child Protection," *Pediatrics*, November 1997, Vol. 100, No. 5, pp. 735–760; Sharon Begley, "The Nursery's Littlest Victim," *Newsweek*, September 22, 1997, p. 72.

60. Begley, "The Nursery's Littlest Victim," p. 72.

61. L. G. Ankrom and C. J. Lent, "Cradle Robbers: A Study of the Infant Abductor," *FBI Law Enforcement Bulletin*, September 1995, pp. 12–17.

62. These interviews were conducted with funds provided by Interagency Agreement #91–MC-004, issued through the cooperation of the Office of Juvenile Justice and Deliquency Prevention.

63. P. Beachy and J. Deacon, "Preventing Neonatal Kidnapping," *Journal of GN*, 1991, Vol. 21, No. 1, pp. 12–16.

64. Ibid.

65. Ibid.

66. R. Grant, "The New Babysnatchers, *Redbook*, May 1990, p. 153.

67. Ibid, p. 152.

68. This discussion of age-progression technology was adapted from a news release distributed by the National Center for Missing and Exploited Children, June 18, 1990.

THIRTEEN

Crimes against the Elderly

CHAPTER OUTLINE

The Process of Aging 354
Categories of Mistreatment 356
Crimes Affecting the Elderly 358
Triads—Preventing Crimes against the Elderly 362
Questions 364
Notes 364

INTRODUCTION

As of the year 2000 nearly one of every five Americans will be age 65 or older. Today, more than 2 million Americans exceed the age of 85. The quality of life enjoyed by many of these older persons has been unequaled in previous decades. However, as individuals age, they can develop chronic diseases and disabilities that impair their ability to function independently and can eventually become dependent on the care of others. In the future, more than 60 percent of dependent persons will live with family members. Most of these family members will provide adequately for the elderly person. However, some might be reluctant, ill prepared, or incapable of providing necessary care. Such circumstances may lead to situations in which the aged individual becomes a victim, suffering neglect and abuse at the hands of the caregivers.[1]

In the last two decades abuse of the elderly has attracted the attention of the public and the medical establishment, but it is not a new phenomenon. It had merely gone unnoticed until a letter on "granny-battering" appeared in the *British Medical Journal* in 1975.[2] This was followed closely by the book *"Why Survive? Growing Old in America."*[3] Considerable interest in the problem has been stimulated, and all 50 states now have some form of elder-abuse law.[4]

Elderly abuse is almost as common as child abuse, affecting as many as 10 percent of the elderly in some form and about 2 percent in the form of physical abuse. These numbers are "soft" because large epidemiological studies are lacking, and both the victim and the perpetrators tend to deny the existence of elderly abuse or belittle its seriousness.[5]

In this chapter we focus on the process of aging, categories of mistreatment, crimes affecting the elderly, and the prevention of crimes against the elderly. Lastly, we discuss the concept of Triads, which are formed when the local police and sheriff's departments agree to work cooperatively with senior citizens to prevent the victimization of the elderly in the community.

THE PROCESS OF AGING

In order for law enforcement officers to be effective in the investigation of crimes against the elderly, it is important that they understand both the physical and psychological changes that may occur with aging, as well as how to deal with them. Whether the officer is interviewing an older person, offering safety and security advice, or assisting an older crime victim, having a knowledge of the physical changes that may occur with aging and being able to deal with these changes can make all the difference in providing good service.[6] (See Figure 13–1.)

VISION

Changes in vision that are related to aging vary widely from person to person. These changes are not strictly dependent upon chronological age or general health. The eye is so constructed that excellent vision without glasses is sometimes maintained even in extreme old age. However, this is an exception. About three-fourths of all older

Figure 13–1
Senior Citizens Engaging in Exercise Routine
Senior citizens in a local park engage in a daily exercise routine. A police officer (upper right-hand corner) is standing by to be certain there are no disruptions by local youngsters who also frequent the park.

(Courtesy Federal Bureau of Investigation; photographer, Kathy L. Morrison)

women and over half of all older men experience moderate to severe changes in visual functions. Those 65 or older account for half of all legally blind persons in the United States. The simple statistical probabilities are that an older person will have vision difficulties of one kind or another.

There are many ways in which police officers help people with poor vision. In any written communications—letters, memos, or signs—large lettering should be used, and the focus should be on conveying important information rather than including too many details.

Farsightedness is a condition that facilitates the ability to see distant objects clearly but makes it more difficult to focus on objects at close range. Because of farsightedness problems, the identification of a purse snatcher, for example, may be a problem, since the only opportunity the elderly person may have to recognize the suspect is when the thief is at a very close proximity. In contrast, when the elderly are *nearsighted*, they may need to hold objects closely to see them clearly.

Older persons are twice as likely as the rest of the population to wear glasses to facilitate reading. However, the fact that an older person is wearing glasses does not necessarily mean that he or she has adequately compensated for vision changes. For example, the eyeglass prescription may be outdated, or dirty glasses may be interfering with clear

vision. Therefore, when the police officer is assisting an older person who is nearsighted or farsighted, positioning is important. The most suitable distance will vary from individual to individual. (See Figure 13–2.)

HEARING

Hearing loss resulting in a distortion of sounds generally is caused by changes in the inner ear. A person who suffers from a hearing loss must take advantage of every opportunity to use other skills in communicating, such as speech reading. *Speech reading*, often thought of as "lip reading," is the process of visually receiving cues from all lip movements, facial expressions, body posture, gestures, and the environment. Speech reading is a skill everyone has to a certain degree. It is only when hearing becomes impaired that this skill becomes important.

Officers will be able to communicate most effectively and patiently with hearing-impaired people by following these suggestions:

- *Gain attention:* The police officer should wait until he or she is visible to the older person before speaking. The officer should attract the older person's attention by facing the person and looking straight into his or her eyes or by touching the person's hands or shoulders lightly. The environment should be arranged so that the speaker's face and body can be seen

Figure 13–2
Arts and Craft Activities for the Elderly
Elderly couple involved in arts and crafts activities at a recreation center.

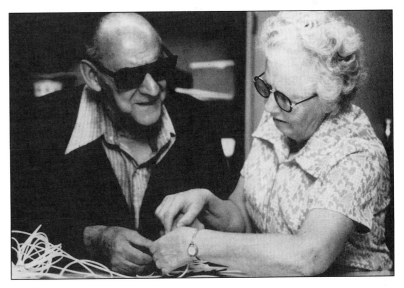

(Courtesy Federal Bureau of Investigation; photographer, Kathy L. Morrison)

easily and clearly. Good lighting on the speaker's face is important. Facial expressions, gestures, and lip and body movements serve to illustrate the verbal message. Chewing, eating, or covering the mouth with a hand or a piece of paper minimizes effective communication.

- *Be at the right distance:* When speaking to an older person, the police officer should be between 3 and 6 feet from the person.

- *Speak clearly:* The police officer should carefully monitor his or her speaking voice for volume, pitch, pace, and enunciation and should speak slightly louder than normal if necessary. A low-pitched voice is often easier to hear; older persons may have difficulty understanding the higher-pitched voices of women and children. The officer should speak at a moderate pace, but if there is to be a change in subject, a new name, a number, or an unusual word, it should be communicated at a slower rate. Sounds should not be exaggerated when speaking because this tends to distort the message and makes visual cues from the face difficult to understand.

- *Reinforce and rephrase:* Whenever possible, the officer should give a clue to the topic of the conversation. If the older person does not appear to understand what is being said, the statement should be rephrased in short, simple sentences. The officer should not repeat the whole sentence. Some persons with hearing loss are unduly sensitive about the handicap and pretend to understand when they do not. An officer who detects this situation should tactfully repeat the communication using different words until he or she is certain the person understood. The officer should use gestures and objects to reinforce messages.

- *Control noises:* Communication with a hearing-impaired older person is much more difficult when there is a great deal of environmental noise.

- *Encourage participation:* The older person should be encouraged to communicate. Because a hearing-impaired person takes longer to respond, the officer should allow an appropriate amount of time for the person to answer a question.

In many ways a hearing loss can have a greater impact than a loss of vision. Many people seem to have less patience and sympathy for those who cannot hear well than they do for those with vision impairments. Because of this, people with hearing losses may pretend to understand. Hearing loss is very strongly related to feelings of depression and suspicion. The isolation that can result from a declining ability to communicate detracts from the quality of life. By using the skills that help offset hearing impairments, an officer can communicate more effectively with anyone who needs to understand and be understood.

CATEGORIES OF MISTREATMENT

Since 1977, when the problem of mistreatment of the elderly began to attract attention, researchers have suggested different ways to classify "mistreatment." The classification offered here is consistent with most recent approaches.[7]

The principal forms of mistreatment all involve the personal needs of elderly people, particularly the needs that must be filled by others who are close to the victim. These needs may be physical, emotional, psychological, or financial. Researchers have provided what may become the commonly accepted bases for defining different types of mistreatment. These are:

Passive neglect: The unintentional failure to fulfill a caretaking obligation. There is no conscious or willful attempt to inflict physical or emotional distress on the older person. An example is the nonprovision of food or health-related services because of the caregiver's infirmity, laziness, or inadequate skills, knowledge, or understanding of the necessity of prescribed or other essential services.

Psychological abuse: The infliction of mental anguish. Examples are name-calling; demeaning, insulting, ignoring, frightening, humiliating, intimidating, threatening, or isolating the elderly person; or treating him or her as a child.

Active neglect: The intentional failure to fulfill a caretaking obligation, including a conscious and willful attempt to inflict physical or emotional stress or injury on the older person. Examples are deliberately denying the person food or health-related services or depriving him or her of dentures or eyeglasses.

Physical abuse: The infliction of physical pain or injury or physical coercion. Physical abuse of the elderly is perpetrated most often by the victim's spouse (50 percent), less often by the victim's child or children (23 percent); contrary to popular opinion, only in 17 percent of the cases is the physical violence at the hands of nonfamily caregivers.[8] While the reported incidents of physical abuse are almost gender-neutral, the abuse is proportionately higher in males because fewer females live alone. The actual act of physical violence can range from a push or a shake to an assault with a deadly weapon. In a survey taken in Boston several years ago,[9] the most common act of physical violence was pushing, grabbing, or shoving (63 percent), followed by throwing something at the victim (46 percent) and slapping (42 percent); 10 percent of the physically abused in this survey had been hit with a fist, kicked, or bitten.[10] However, one must be cautious: The mere presence of injury in an elderly person receiving home care or domiciled in a nursing facility is not proof of abuse. An elderly person with chronic disease, malnutrition, senile osteoporosis, or disuse atrophy can be extremely fragile and incur injuries naturally. Investigators must be vigilant in watching for signs of abuse or neglect and must be alert to injuries inappropriate to the patient's level of activity. (See Figure 13–3.)

SOME SIGNS AND SYMPTOMS OF MISTREATMENT OR ABUSE

In Caregivers

- New self-neglect
- Conflicting stories
- Mounting resentment
- Excusing failure
- Shifting blame
- Aggressive/defensive behavior
- Substance abuse

Figure 13–3
Victim of Assault
An elderly victim struck on the side of the jaw. Note the black eye at the edge of the photograph.

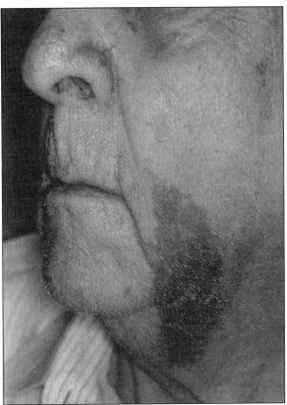

(Courtesy CRC Press, LLC, and B. G. Brogdon, MD, University of South Alabama, Mobile)

- Unusual fatigue
- New affluence
- New health problems
- Preoccupation/depression
- Withholding food or medicine

In Older Persons

- Increasing depression
- Anxiety
- Withdrawn/timid
- Hostile
- Unresponsive
- Confused
- Physically injured
- New poverty

- Longing for death
- Vague health complaints
- Anxious to please
- Shopping for physicians

There are other signs and symptoms, and not all of those listed by themselves indicate mistreatment, neglect, or abuse. But if any seem to increase in number or severity in a domestic setting, the increase may indicate mistreatment or abuse.[11]

CRIMES AFFECTING THE ELDERLY

Older persons fall victim to certain crimes at a greater rate than the rest of the population. Among these crimes are robbery, purse snatching, burglary, vandalism, telemarketing fraud, and financial abuse. The effects of these crimes upon elderly victims are often more serious and longer-lasting than they are on younger persons.

ROBBERY AND PURSE SNATCHING

For elderly persons, robbery and purse snatching are among the most fear-provoking crimes because they involve a high possibility of injury. Robbery through the use of physical force without weapons is committed most often against older persons because there is little fear of resistance or retaliation. The physical force used demonstrates the intent of the perpetrator and shows that he or she is in command of the situation.

Older persons are, in general, more easily victimized by robbers than are younger persons because of certain behavioral and psychological traits that tend to be associated with the aging process. For example:

- The ability of older persons to defend themselves declines with age.
- The elderly are less likely to resist or retaliate.
- The elderly tend not to carry weapons.
- The ability of the elderly to identify dangerous situations decreases with age.
- Older women tend to carry more items of value in their purses, including cash rather than checks or credit cards, than do younger women.

- The elderly are less likely to adequately identify perpetrators.
- The behavioral patterns of the elderly are more predictable (e.g., a monthly trip to the bank to cash a Social Security check).
- The elderly are often dependent upon public transportation, which further regulates travel schedules and requires extended periods of waiting on sidewalks and subway platforms.
- The elderly often fail to report crime to the police for fear of reprisal.

A purse snatching usually is committed in the following manner: The assailant approaches the victim from the rear and makes an immediate escape after seizing the purse. Usually little contact with the victim is made. The main advantages of this approach for the perpetrator are speed of escape and inadequate or no identification by the victim. The chance of bodily harm still exists, however, since the assailant usually will not hesitate to use force to seize the purse.

BURGLARY

Burglary is a national crime problem that does not seem to be directed toward older persons to a greater extent than toward anyone else. However, one characteristic about older persons does make them attractive targets for burglars: While they may not necessarily own more expensive possessions, it is believed that they keep larger sums of cash in the house—and cash is easy to remove from the scene. Also, the older victim has usually followed a distinguishable schedule of travel for a long period of time and this makes it relatively easy for a burglar to determine the most opportune time to break into the house.

VANDALISM

Adolescents are almost exclusively the perpetrators of vandalism. They choose their targets for a variety of reasons; in the case of older victims, one of those reasons is increased social isolation. Many older persons in a mixed community will withdraw from social contacts in their neighborhood more than the average resident would. Whether by choice or fear, this withdrawal tends to make them "outsiders" in the eye of the vandal and thus a choice target for destruction of property. (See Figure 13–4.)

Figure 13–4
Victim of Crime
Police officer taking a crime report from
a victim.

(Courtesy Federal Bureau of Investigation; photographer, Kathy L. Morrison)

TELEMARKETING FRAUDS

The following represent some of the more common
types of telemarketing frauds targeted at the
elderly.

Phantom Sweepstakes

In the most common form of telemarketing fraud,
the caller tells the intended victim he or she has
won a prize but first must send money to cover
shipping and handling, taxes, customs duties, au-
dits, bonding, or other expenses. Legally, there is
no such thing as a "free" prize for which the "win-
ner" must send money. Usually the victim receives
nothing in return for the payment. Occasionally,
there may be a prize but one worth far less than the
victim had been led to believe: the "luxury cruise"

in a recent case turned out to be a ferry ride, and a
"solar clothes dryer" was only a wire coat hanger.[13]

Make-Believe Lotteries

Thousands of U.S. citizens engage in illegal lottery
schemes promoted by criminals who claim to have
a system that will bring big winnings with no risk.
In reality, it is illegal to sell or buy lottery tickets or
even promote lotteries through the mail or by telephone—with the sole exception of a state-run lottery mailing to citizens within the state's own
borders.

Can't-Miss Investments

Exploiting people's hopes of getting rich quick,
telemarketers often sell questionable and even illegal securities, stocks in gold mines or oil wells,

gemstones, precious metals, or shares in unseen "new" inventions or high-technology ventures such as broadcast licenses, cellular telephone projects, and wireless cable television.

Something for Nothing

Even the most routine-sounding transactions may be fraudulent. Sometimes, people collect money for magazine subscriptions, tropical cruises, or dream vacations that do not exist or are not worth the price they ask. In one case reported by the National Fraud Information Center, an older person agreed over the phone to a magazine subscription program and learned later that she had authorized the company to take $60 per month from her savings account for a period of 10 years.

Sham Charities

Older Americans tend to be very generous, and this is a characteristic that scam artists count on. If there is a flood in the Midwest, a hurricane in Florida, or an earthquake in California, they get on the phone and solicit donations to aid the victims— and then keep any money they collect. Criminals who pretend to be raising money for police or fire-fighter charities and activities are particularly brazen; some victims are afraid to turn down a request from someone they think is a public safety officer. Legitimate fundraisers will not be reluctant to show or send proof that they are who they say they are and that the cause is legitimate.

"Get Rich at Home" Schemes

One of the most popular scams promises that big profits can be made by working at home stringing beads, licking stamps, and so on. These schemes always involve up-front payments for supplies, franchise rights, starter kits, and other things. The fact of the matter is that there is no market for the homemade trinkets and any real business will have machines that can seal, address, and stamp envelopes faster than an army of home workers.

Double Trouble

A particularly shameless sting is the *recovery scam.* A person who has already been bilked gets a call offering help in recovering the stolen money. The caller may even claim to be connected with or endorsed by the police or some other government agency. He or she is not. The caller probably knows the victim has been bilked because he or she either was the one who bilked the victim in the first place or bought the victim's name from the first crook. After most scams, money is recovered only if the government seizes it from the crooks and returns it to the victims through court-appointed trustees. The trustees do not ask for payment of any kind.

"I'm Calling Where?"

One of the newer scams involves messages that tell people to return calls placed from certain area codes. Messages are left on answering machines, flashed to beepers, and sent by e-mail. They may claim that a bill is overdue or a relative is ill or may use any other lure that would prompt a person to return a call quickly. The phone numbers look like any ordinary number, with an area code followed by seven digits. But they are, in fact, codes for calling foreign countries. The one most often used is 809, which is the code for the Virgin Islands and various other Caribbean locations. Once the call is placed, the party at the other end tries to keep the caller talking as long as possible to run up the phone bill. Not until the bill comes does the caller know he or she made a very expensive overseas call. Typically, the overseas phone company involved splits the excessive charges with the scam artist with whom the victim spoke.

Phony Customs Agents

Con artists have begun impersonating customs officials of the United States and Canada. A crook telephones and says there is a large check or other fabulous prize being held at the border but, before it can be released, the intended recipient must first pay the taxes or customs duties, or both. In reality, the U.S. Customs Service never asks anyone for money over the phone. If someone has a letter or other shipment coming to him or her with duties owed, the money will be collected at the post office when the item is picked up. There are several variations on this scheme, with the callers saying they represent a Canadian law firm, bonding company, or delivery service. Some callers suggest that for some cash they can help the person avoid some of the taxes. Even if the caller had a prize and could lower the taxes on it, this would be a crime.

FINANCIAL ABUSE

Ironically, the elderly often are financially abused by their own legally appointed conservators or guardians. *Conservatorship,* a court-appointed position, involves involuntary removal of an elderly person's civil rights, including the right to handle his or her own finances. Conservatorship usually is limited to financial decisions, as opposed to *guardianship,* which gives the guardian control of every aspect of the elder's personal life.[14] Some conservators and guardians abuse older persons by using an elder's financial assets for their own personal gain.

A survey of various financial institutions with elderly clients revealed that 83 percent suspected that some of their elderly clients were victims of financial abuse. Forms of suspected abuse included exploitation of the elders' finances by substance-abusing relatives, roommates, or boarders; misappropriation of cash or belongings; and abuse of power of attorney.[15]

A *power of attorney* authorizes a person to act on someone else's behalf in legal or financial matters for a specific period of time.[16] The power of attorney becomes void should the person it pertains to be ruled mentally incapacitated. A related legal construct, the *durable power of attorney,* remains in effect even if the person becomes mentally incapacitated. Both types are often abused. In fact, in a survey conducted several years ago among attorneys and service providers for the elderly, two-thirds of the 410 respondents reported cases of abuse of the durable power of attorney, and 38 percent had knowledge of five or more cases.[17]

A survey of a small number of banks in the New York City area is particularly revealing. The banks reported that the most common forms of financial exploitation their elderly customers encountered were forgery, misappropriation of funds, abuse of joint accounts, and abuse of powers of attorney. The respondents listed the most common abuser as a relative of the victim. Unfortunately, only 43 percent of banks said they always reported the abuse to Adult Protective Services. In fact, 43 percent never reported the abuse, and 14 percent only reported it sometimes.[18] Yet bank employees may stand the best chance of recognizing the signs of financial abuse.

Clues to Financial Abuse of the Elderly

Law enforcement officers investigating suspected financial abuse can look for certain indicators of criminal activity. These include:

- Unusual activity in a bank account, including activity inconsistent with the victim's ability, such as the use of an automatic teller machine on an account of a bedridden elder.
- New acquaintances of the elder expressing a desire to reside with the elder.
- Loss of amenities, such as the disconnection of utilities, when the elder is known to be able to afford such amenities.
- New signees or unusual activity on credit cards.
- Suspicious signatures on documents, particularly if the elder is incapable of writing.[19]

Cases can come to an investigator's attention from a variety of sources, including social service agencies, medical personnel (such as home health-care nurses or emergency medical technicians), and neighbors, acquaintances, and relatives of current victims, as well as from victims themselves. Unfortunately, many of these sources can also be possible offenders.

The scant amount of research on traits of offenders and victims suggests a certain profile for each. A slight majority of victims (over 60 percent) are likely to be white females over age 70. Offenders are often relatives, many of whom depend on the elderly victim for housing or other forms of assistance.[20] Many offenders have substance-abuse problems that factor into their crimes. Perpetrators are represented almost equally from both sexes and are often the children or grandchildren of the victim.

Proof of the Offense

Suspects usually gain access to their victim's bank accounts by presenting a power of attorney to the bank or by having their victims agree to have a second signature on the accounts in case of emergency. Therefore, proving financial exploitation usually requires accessing checking and savings accounts by subpoena or search warrant; retrieving canceled checks, statements, and items of deposit; and determining the flow of the alleged victim's funds.[21]

If a suspect clearly profits from using a victim's funds, and the victim meets the state's definition of aged or disabled, the issue becomes one of intent. That is, the investigator must determine whether the suspect intended to exploit the victim or whether the suspect believed, in good faith, that he or she had the right to use the victim's funds for that particular purpose. In most jurisdictions, if any evidence, however minimal, exists to prove the exploitation was intentional, the court will allow a jury trial.

As noted, case law relating to power-of-attorney fraud places a higher burden of responsibility on guardians. They have the right and the obligation to serve their charges' needs, not their own. Therefore, prosecutors who present a power of attorney as evidence will actually help the state's case because victims, in conveying those powers, placed trust in the defendants to act in their best interest.

Use of Theft Statutes

In order to apply theft or theft-related statutes to guardianship and power-of-attorney cases, the prosecution must prove that the defendants did not have the victims' consent to use the funds in the manner indicated. One difficulty prosecutors often face is the inability of victims to provide testimony. Victims may be deceased or physically or mentally unable to testify.

In *Gainer* v. *the State of Alabama*,[22] the Alabama Court of Criminal Appeals upheld a conviction for theft in a case in which the victim was deceased at the time the matter went to trial. The court determined that a victim's consent or nonconsent can be established through circumstantial evidence as in any other crime and, therefore, that the victim's testimony is not required.

In *Gainer*, the defendant was a beautician at a nursing home where the victim was a patient. For a period of approximately 14 months, the defendant befriended the victim—a childless widow with no relatives living in the state—and obtained $111,000 of her money. The defendant began taking the victim on outings and eventually opened a joint checking account in both their names. She also changed the victim's old account to a joint account. Then she purchased a Corvette, a boat, a home computer, a tanning bed, furniture, a refrigerator, a dishwasher, and gold jewelry, in addition to paying her own utility bills.

Even though the victim was deceased at the time of the trial, friends and acquaintances described her as "tight," a "miser," and a person who "kept close to her money," wore old clothes, and drove a 12-year-old automobile. They also testified that the defendant had not allowed the victim to see the financial records from the joint accounts.

In its decision, the court noted that while proving nonconsent to the taking of property is a necessary element in a theft case, the lack of consent may be proved by circumstantial evidence. Further, even when victims apparently agree to allow others to control their finances, that consent is not effective unless, as a factual matter, it is voluntary and intelligent. The court found that the victim was not mentally competent to understand the nature of the joint-bank-account arrangements she had with the defendant and was not capable of giving valid consent and, therefore, that the defendant had gained unauthorized control over the victim's property.

Undue Influence

Gainer points to another problem that prosecutors face in financial-exploitation cases. At times, evidence exists showing that victims consented to the arrangement; however, they lacked an understanding of the nature of the transaction, the meaning of the expenditures, or other circumstances which, had they known or understood, would have caused them to act differently.

While undue influence has been carefully explored in civil cases relating to financial transactions, it has rarely been applied in the criminal context, especially in theft cases. The closest analogy has been in states that use instances of coercion, undue influence, or victims' lack of fully understanding transactions as evidence in exploitation cases. Under such circumstances, most states require proof of the victims' limited capacity or ability to care for their own needs for them to meet the definition of aged adults. Further, there is often an age requirement, usually 60 or 65 years.[23]

TRIADS—PREVENTING CRIMES AGAINST THE ELDERLY

Triads are formed when the local police and sheriff's departments agree to work cooperatively with senior citizens to prevent the victimization of the elderly in the community. The three groups share ideas and resources to provide programs and training for vulnerable and often-fearful elderly citizens. In addition, the groups work to expand and renew interest in existing programs and develop cooperative strategies to address needs and concerns identified by older citizens.[24]

The Triad concept emerged in 1987, when several members of the International Association of Chiefs of Police (IACP), National Sheriffs' Association (NSA), and members of the American Association of Retired Persons (AARP) met to consider mutual crime prevention concerns and to plan for the future. The group recognized that the rapidly growing number of elderly persons in the United States required that the law enforcement community begin to address ways to combat the problems confronted by this segment of the population.

The chiefs and sheriffs who met believed it was important to develop a strategy to enhance law enforcement services to older persons and to expand efforts to prevent their victimization. Further, it was clear that the problems senior citizens were encountering could best be combated through a cooperative effort between law enforcement and the senior-citizen community. This effort was quickly dubbed "Triad," representing the three-way cooperative effort between sheriffs, police chiefs, and the AARP, which represents the senior-citizen population.

FORMING TRIADS

A Triad usually begins when a police chief, a sheriff, or a leader in the senior-citizen community contacts the other two essential participants to discuss a combined effort. Although each entity may already have programs to reduce the victimization rate among the elderly, the three-way involvement of a Triad adds strength, resources, and greater credibility.

Most Triads include representatives from agencies that serve older persons, such as the Agency of Aging, senior centers, the health department, and adult protective services. Law enforcement leaders then invite seniors and those working with the seniors to serve on an advisory council, often called Seniors and Lawmen Together (SALT).

At the initial SALT council meetings, members of the council discuss the involvement and goals of their agencies, as well as the role they hope to play with the seniors. Typically, the first task of the council is to conduct a preliminary survey to determine the needs and concerns of seniors throughout the jurisdiction.

Once established, SALT councils generally meet monthly. Police chiefs and sheriffs often join the group to hear discussions firsthand and to respond to any questions or concerns. Many times, the group's preliminary strategies focus on crime prevention and victim assistance for seniors or on seniors' need for security and reassurance. Strategies implemented early on are usually in response to survey results.

The SALT council is often the first collaborative effort between seniors and law enforcement. For this reason, seniors serving on the council acquire basic criminal justice information by attending a citizen police academy or rookie school to learn about the criminal justice system and the workings of the various law enforcement agencies.

TRIAD VOLUNTEERS

If the SALT council provides the starter and the fuel for a Triad, older volunteers serve as the motor and wheels. Mature individuals often have the experience and skills to guide Triad endeavors. Among these volunteers may be retired teachers, truck drivers, or law enforcement officers—the volunteers represent all segments of the community.

Volunteers may staff reception desks in law enforcement agencies, present programs to senior organizations, conduct informal home-security surveys, and become leaders in new or rejuvenated neighborhood watch groups. They may also provide information and support to crime victims, call citizens concerning civil warrants, or assist law enforcement agencies in maintaining records or property rooms at substations or in other areas.

Most senior volunteers derive great satisfaction from working with Triads. In fact, some volunteers enjoy their duties so much that they work as many as 40 hours a week on various Triad programs.

Questions

1. Why is it important for law enforcement officers to understand the process of aging?
2. What are the categories of mistreatment against the elderly?
3. What are some of the signs and symptoms of abuse in caregivers and in the older person?
4. Older persons are in general more easily victimized by robbers and younger persons. Why is this so?
5. What are some of the more common types of telemarketing fraud that target the elderly?
6. What are some clues to the financial abuse of the elderly?
7. How does the Triad concept work in regard to prevention of crimes against the elderly?

Notes

1. J. D. McDowell and B. G. Brogdon, "Spousal Abuse and Abuse of the Elderly," in *Forensic Radiology*, B. G. Brogdon (ed.) (Boca Raton, Fla.: 1998), p. 321; J. D. McDowell, "Elder Abuse, the Presenting Signs and Symptoms in the Dental Practice," *Texas Dental Journal*, 1990, Vol. 107, No. 2, p. 29.
2. G. R. Burston, "Granny-Battering," *British Medical Journal*, 1975, Vol. 3, p. 592.
3. R. N. Butler, *Why Survive? Growing Old in America* (New York: Harper & Row, 1975).
4. R. S. Wolf, "Elderly Abuse: Ten Years Later," *Journal of the American Geriatric Society*, 1988, Vol. 36, p. 758.
5. American Medical Association, "Council on Scientific Affairs Report: Elder Abuse and Neglect," *Journal of the American Medical Association*, 1987, Vol. 257, p. 966.
6. New York City Police Department *Student's Guide—Social Science 1998*, pp. 4–7. This discussion of the process of aging was provided by the New York City Police Department.
7. R. L. Douglas, *Domestic Mistreatment of the Elderly—Toward Prevention* (Washington, D.C.: American Association of Retired Persons, 1995), pp. 3–4.
8. K. Pillemer and D. Finkelhor, "The Prevalence of Elder Abuse: A Random Sample Survey," *Gerontologist*, 1988, Vol. 28, p. 51.
9. Wolf, *Elder Abuse.*
10. Pillemer and Finkelhor, "The Prevalence of Elder Abuse."
11. Ibid.
12. New York City Police Department, *Student's Guide*, p. 13.
13. "Protect Yourself from the Scam," *AARP Bulletin*, December 1997, Vol. 38, No. 11, pp. 10–11.
14. Johnny Koker and Bobby Little, "Investigating in the Future—Protecting the Elderly from Financial Abuse," *FBI Law Enforcement Bulletin*, December 1997, pp. 1–5; William H. Overman, "Preventing Elder Abuse and Neglect through Advance Legal Planning," *Journal of Elder Abuse and Neglect*, 1991, Vol. 3, pp. 5–21.
15. Candace J. Heisler and Jane E. Tewksbury, "Fiduciary Abuse of the Elderly: A Prosecutor's Perspective," *Journal of Elder Abuse and Neglect*, 1992, Vol. 3, pp. 23–40.
16. Richard L. Douglass, *Domestic Mistreatment of the Elderly—Towards Prevention* (Washington, D.C.: American Association of Retired Persons, 1995), pp. 22–23.
17. Debra Sacks, "Prevention of Financial Abuse Focus of New Institute at the Brookdale Center on Aging," *Aging Magazine*, 1996, No. 367, pp. 86–89.
18. Ibid.
19. Ibid.
20. Karl A. Pillemer and David Finkelhor, "Causes of Elder Abuse: Caregiver Stress versus Problem Relatives," *American Journal of Orthopsychiatry*, 1989, Vol. 59, pp. 179–187.
21. E. McRae Mathis, "Policing the Guardians—Combating Guardianship and Power of Attorney Fraud," *FBI Law Enforcement Bulletin*, February 1994, pp. 3–4.
22. *Gainer v. State*, 553 So.2d 673 (ALA. CR. APP. 1989).
23. See, e.g., FLA. STAT. Sec 415.102(3)(1963).
24. Betsy Cantrell, "Triad—Reducing Criminal Victimization of the Elderly," *FBI Law Enforcement Bulletin*, February 1994, pp. 19–21.

FOURTEEN

Robbery

CHAPTER OUTLINE

Elements of the Crime 366
Overview: The Offense, the Victim, and the Offender 368
Typology of Robberies 371
Arrest Probabilities 375
Investigative Techniques 376

The Crime Scene Technician and the Laboratory 385
"Three-Strikes" Law 385
The Investigator's Educative Responsibility 386
Questions 388
Notes 388

INTRODUCTION

Robbery is defined as the illegal taking of something of value from the control, custody, or person of another by threatening, putting in fear, or using force. Because of this face-to-face confrontation between perpetrator and victim, the potential for violence is always present and, when it does occur, may range from minor injury to loss of life. Because of its personal and often violent nature, robbery is one of the crimes most feared by the public, a fear that may be heightened by perceptions of police inability to deal effectively with these offenses. Police solve about one in four reported robberies. The importance of robbery resides in economics, its frequency, the fear created, the potential for violence, and its frequent resistance to investigative efforts.

ELEMENTS OF THE CRIME

Robbery consists of the following elements: the (1) taking and (2) carrying away of (3) personal property of (4) another, with (5) the intent to deprive permanently, by (6) the use of force, fear, or threat of force.

TAKING

The property taken in a robbery must be taken illegally by the robber. Someone who has the right to take such property cannot properly be convicted of robbery. This illegal taking is called *trespassory*. The property must be taken from the custody, control, or possession of the victim and, as will be seen later, from the victim's presence. This element of the crime is satisfied once the robber has possession of the property; until possession has occurred, only an attempt has taken place (see Figure 14–1).

CARRYING AWAY

Once the element of taking has been satisfied, the robber must then have carried away the property. As is true in the crime of larceny, this element can be satisfied simply by showing that the accused totally removed the article from the position that it formerly occupied. It is not necessary to show that any great distance was involved in the carrying away.

Figure 14–1
A Bank Robbery in Progress
The man in the foreground glances over his shoulder at the entrance while he keeps bank employees and patrons covered. His female accomplice is stuffing money into a briefcase held in front of her. Note the bills that have dropped to the floor.

(Courtesy Atlanta Police Department)

PERSONAL PROPERTY

The object of the robbery must be personal property as opposed to real estate or things attached to the land. Again as in larceny, any tangible property and some forms of intangible property represented by tangible items, such as stocks and bonds, gas, electricity, minerals, and other such commodities, can be objects of robbery.

ANOTHER

The property taken must belong to another, not to the accused. This again relates to the first element of taking. If the taking is trespassory—illegal—then the property must be the rightful property of someone other than the robber.

THE INTENT TO DEPRIVE PERMANENTLY

Robbery is a crime of specific intent and requires that the prosecution establish, in court, that the defendant, at the time of taking the property by force or threat of force from the victim or the victim's presence, did, in fact, intend to deprive the victim of the use and enjoyment of that property permanently. In most cases this can be concluded from the facts and circumstances surrounding the case, but in specific-intent crime cases juries are not permitted to assume this particular fact. Thus, the police officer's investigation must be geared to establishing this as an essential element of the crime. The fact that force or the threat of force was used to secure the property from the victim is often enough to convince a jury of the accused's intent to deprive permanently.

THE USE OF FORCE, FEAR, OR THREAT OF FORCE

This element of the crime requires that the force or threat of force was directed against the physical safety of the victim rather than his or her social well-being. Thus, threats to expose the victim as a homosexual or an embezzler do not satisfy this element of the crime. Proof that force was used or, at the very least, that threats were made such that the victim feared imminent bodily harm is essential for successful prosecutions of robbery cases. The taking of property without force is simply a theft. However, the force used to separate the victim from his or her property in robbery need not be great.

When the victim of a robbery is seriously injured, there is usually little difficulty in convincing the investigator or the jury that force was used. However, difficulties may arise in the case of a victim who claims to have been robbed under the threat of force when no actual injury occurred. In this case, the skill of the investigator in determining the facts of the case becomes crucial to successful prosecution.

There are also more subtle situations in which the investigator must know legal requirements as well as investigative techniques. The typical purse-snatching case is an illustration. Often, the force element of the crime of robbery can be satisfied only by determining whether the victim attempted to resist the force used and, if so, the extent of that resistance. It is generally accepted by courts that a woman who puts her purse next to her on the seat of a bus without keeping her hand on it or loosely holds it in her hand is not the victim of robbery if someone quickly grabs the purse and runs. In these cases, the woman has not resisted. However, if she were clutching the bag tightly and someone managed to grab it from her after even a slight struggle, sufficient force and resistance would have occurred to constitute robbery. A good rule for the investigator to follow in cases of uncertainty is that the removal of an article without more force than is absolutely necessary to remove it from its original resting place constitutes larceny. If any additional force, no matter how slight, is used, it is then robbery, provided the object is taken from the presence or person of the victim. The property does not have to be held by the victim physically or be on his or her person. It merely has to be under the victim's control. "Control" in this sense means the right or privilege to use the property as the victim sees fit. Neither is it necessary or essential that the property be visible to the victim when the crime is committed.

The force or threat of force must precede or accompany the taking. Force applied after the taking does not constitute robbery. Thus a victim who realizes that his or her property has been stolen and attempts to recover that property, at which time force ensues, is not the victim of a robbery if the property was originally taken surreptitiously and without force.

When force is not used but a threat to the physical well-being of the victim is indeed made, it is not necessary that the victim actually be frightened to the point of panic. It is enough that the victim is reasonably apprehensive and aware of the potential for injury.

OVERVIEW: THE OFFENSE, THE VICTIM, AND THE OFFENDER

When generalizing about offenses, victims, and offenders, certain limitations must be acknowledged. Research findings are occasionally inconclusive and conflicting. A variety of factors account for this. For example, a study of the various aspects of robbery in one city has limited generalization power because, while cities may share certain characteristics, such factors are not precisely duplicated from city to city or perhaps not even in the same city over time. If we attempt to compensate for this factor by using national data, a general picture emerges and individual differences disappear. If we use an intensive scrutiny of a smaller number of cases, their profile may not be like that of other intensive studies or the general profile. Additionally, a limitation common to most studies of criminals is that we are focusing on those who "failed," that is, those who were caught and whose resemblance to those not apprehended is a matter of conjecture. Despite such issues, information concerning offenses, victims, and offenders is useful in providing a qualified frame of reference.

Robbery is essentially a problem of our large cities. In metropolitan areas the robbery rate per 100,000 people is 223.[1] However, in cities outside of metro areas the robbery rate is only 72 and in rural areas it is 18.[2] Regionally, the most populous southern states registered 32 percent of all reported robberies.[3] Table 14–1 indicates the settings of reported robberies nationally.

In terms of weapons used, a firearm is used in 40 percent of the incidents, a knife or other cutting instrument in 9 percent of the cases, and "some other weapon" in another 13 percent of reported robberies; the remaining 38 percent of the incidents are "strong-armed," meaning no weapon was used.[4] An illustration of the use of "some other weapon" is the robbery of a convenience store by a man using a hypodermic needle filled with what he claimed was AIDS-contaminated blood. Together

Table 14–1

Settings of Robberies as Reported Nationally

Setting	Percent of Total
Street or highway	50.0
Commercial house	13.8
Gas or service station	2.4
Convenience store	5.7
Residence	11.6
Bank	1.9
Miscellaneous	14.6
Total	100.0

Source: Federal Bureau of Investigation, *Crime in the United States–1997* (Washington, D.C.: Government Printing Office, 1998), p. 29.

these data reveal that approximately 6 of every 10 robberies are armed and the balance strong-armed. Armed robbers often carry two or more weapons. Because of this, officers must continue to exercise great caution when approaching a suspect who has thrown a weapon down.

About one-third of all robberies result in a physical injury to the victim.[5] Females are about 5 percent more likely to be injured than are males, while Caucasians and African Americans face nearly the same prospects for being injured.[6] Robbery is basically a stranger-to-stranger crime: 78 percent of the time the robber and victim do not know each other.[7] However, African Americans are nearly 50 percent more likely to be robbed by nonstrangers than are Caucasians.[8] Robbers are about equally inclined to work alone as they are to commit their crimes with two or more accomplices.[9] When violence does occur, the robber initiates it 95 percent of the time.[10]

The objective of the confrontation between robber and victim is to get the victim's immediate compliance. In most situations, the mere showing of a gun will accomplish this. One offender reports, "Sometimes I don't even touch them; I just point the gun right in front of their face. I don't even have to say nothing half the time. When they see that pistol, they know what time it is."[11] A victim who hesitates or is seen as uncooperative, may or may not get a warning:

"If I run up to you with a revolver like this and then you hesitate, I'm gonna cock it back and that will be your warning right there."[12]

"If they think I'm bullshitting, I'll smack them up in the M____ F____ head. You'd be surprised how cooperative a person will be once he has been smashed across the face with a .357 Magnum."[13]

Other robbers are less "tolerant," and when faced with uncooperative victims, they will shoot them in the leg or foot. However, for some offenders injuring the victim is part of the thrill, the "kick" of "pulling a job." What type of violence is used and when it is used may form part of an identifiable modus operandi. Such an MO can tie together several robberies, and the combined information from various investigations often produces significant investigative leads.

There is not a great deal of variation in robberies by month, although December is the highest.[14] Forty-one percent of robberies take place between 6 A.M. and 6 P.M. and another 42 percent between 6 P.M. and midnight.[15] The average dollar loss nationally per robbery is $995, with an average loss of $576 for convenience stores and $4,802 for banks.[16]

There is no question that being under the influence and committing robberies are intimately related. Victims believe that 25 percent of those robbing them are high on drugs and/or alcohol.[17] Some offenders use alcohol to lessen their apprehension about getting caught:

> When you get it in your head to do a stickup and you get high, you ain't gonna care no more about getting caught . . . that's why me and my partners get high so much. We get high and stupid . . . whatever happens, happens . . . you don't care at the time.[18]

Robbery is basically an intraracial crime; in one study, blacks said that they were robbed by blacks 76 percent of the time, and whites said that they were robbed by whites 72 percent of the time.[19] Nationally, among those apprehended for robbery, 90 percent are males, 57 percent are blacks, and 65 percent are under 25 years of age.[20] Although gas stations and convenience, liquor, grocery, and other stores are often the targets of robbery, such incidents take place in a variety of settings, including buses,[21] bridal shops,[22] novelty stores,[23] cabs, and sidewalks and streets, as in the case of carjackings or when pedestrians are victimized—as were four priests in their own driveway.[24] Other illustrations of robberies include the following:

At 3:40 in the afternoon armed subjects in three cars forced a stretch limo off an expressway and robbed two German gem dealers of more than $1 million in jewelry, cash, and gems.

A 15-member robbery ring pulled more than 50 jobs over several months, referring to their crimes as "going out on a mission." Their method of operation was to cruise "high-class" neighborhoods in pairs. When they spotted an expensive car, they would follow the driver home and take cash, furs, and jewelry.[25]

Two robbers, one of them armed with a club, threatened a female Salvation Army "bell ringer" and took both the collections kettle and the $40 it contained.[26]

An armed man wearing a Nazi helmet and a bulletproof vest shot a wrecker driver and drove off in the victim's vehicle.[27]

A shotgun-carrying bandit, with one or more accomplices, robbed a remote mine of 1 ton of silver valued at $204,000. Before leaving, they disabled all telephones, two-way radios, and vehicles, giving them hours of head start before the crime was detected.[28]

Two men wearing masks of Jason—a character in the *Friday the 13th* horror movies—went on a robbery spree in southern San Francisco. The two committed four robberies in less than an hour. At the TJ Market one robber was holding a gun to the clerk's head when his accomplice began urging him to shoot, yelling "Kill him! Kill him!" Just as the gunman fired, the clerk managed to grab the gun and the bandits ran from the store.[29]

Despite these variations, three styles of robberies—the ambush, the selective raid, and the planned operation—can be classified according to the amount of planning conducted by the perpetrators. The *ambush* involves virtually no planning and depends almost entirely on the element of surprise. A prime example is robberies in which victims are physically overpowered by sudden, crude force and in which "scores" are generally small.[30] The lack of planning does not mean, however, that there is no premeditation, a distinction made by one offender:

> I never really did any planning, as you see it. I pulled robberies at random . . . without disguises or anything. . . . But you must understand one thing, just because I didn't do "planning" as you describe it doesn't mean I didn't think about crime a lot. I had to get myself mentally ready to do crimes. This doesn't mean I planned . . . but . . . I was thinking and preparing for crime constantly; I simply waited for the right circumstances to occur. When I saw the time was right, I would pull the job.[31]

The *selective raid* is characterized by a minimal amount of casual planning. Sites are tentatively selected and very briefly cased, and possible routes of approach are formulated. "Scores" vary from low to moderate, and several robberies may be committed in rapid succession:

> When I get ready to fall in for one, I visit the place a couple of times in one day. I want to see how it's laid out, how to get away as quick as possible and what kind of people work there . . . women are bad to rob because they get all emotional . . . if the man there looks hard, I might not even mess with the place. You can tell what people are like by the way they present themselves. . . . I wouldn't want to just blow a family man away, but if it's me or him, that's business. I like to do pharmacies because besides the money, there's drugs and on the streets that's the same as cash. You can't even worry about being caught because that is negative thinking. . . . I don't mess with no disguises, I just go to someplace like about 25 or 30 miles away where nobody knows me and do it, sometimes a couple real quick if I'm on a roll. Before I go out to do one, I try to relax and fish or make love a lot. You want your head to be right because it could be your life or someone else's. I don't do no pills or drink until after the work for the same reason . . . but if I need the money and have

> been doing some of that shit, I'll just go ahead and pull one, but working that way is dangerous.[32]

The *planned operation* is characterized by larger "scores," no force, less likelihood of apprehension, and careful planning:

> The reason I was never apprehended in five years was because I never had any partners, I worked alone, kept my own counsel, I wasn't on an ego trip— I wasn't shooting my mouth off to the girls I went around with, I changed my name like I changed my socks. I had four different aliases during that period— legitimate aliases where I would go down and get a driver's license in a different name and tell them that I was retired military or had just gotten discharged after thirteen years and didn't have a current license, and the only license I had was a military license. With the driver's license, I opened up savings accounts, checking accounts, and so forth. As far as the friends I had at the time, I never knew a thief in my life. Not even when I was robbing banks. I never knew a thief until I went to prison.
>
> I would go into the bank well dressed—suit and so forth, dyed hair and moustache, a couple of sweatshirts under the suit to make me look heavier, a hat to make me look taller . . . never sunglasses . . . and an attaché case and so forth. And I would go into the manager's outer office where his secretary was by saying I had an appointment or something like this. To make an impression on her, I [would show her my pistol]. I wanted [the manager] to call his chief teller or whoever he considered the most reliable and tell him to take my attaché case into the vault and come out with all the larger bills—no ones, fives, or tens—which, incidentally, led to my downfall, that little old line, because I may just as well have signed my name to every bank I ever robbed. So the guy would go out and bring the money back, and then I would have him open the attaché [so I could check it and see] how much money was in it. If it looked like a considerable sum of money, then I had transacted my business. Very rarely was anyone in the bank aware of what was going on. I wanted to be in and out of there in three minutes flat.
>
> The way I left the bank is—I never stole a car in my life—I'd buy a clunker for a few hundred dollars two weeks before I robbed the bank. This guy advertised in the paper, and you go, give him the money, sign the slip, and that's all there is to it. You

never reregister it; you use it two times—driving it from where you bought it and the next time when you rob the bank. Then you ditch it within one minute, however far you can get. I used to pick a shopping center within a mile or whatever of the bank, and there I'd have my other car, and I'd switch cars. And I would be wearing these dishwashing type gloves so there would be no fingerprints. Sometimes I'd let the car be running with the key in it, hoping some kid would steal it. I'd be tickled to death if he'd run off with it! And then of course I would change clothes and sometimes take the old clothes and throw them in a convenient garbage can, Goodwill box, or whatever. Then I'd take cover, more or less, whether it be a local hotel, motel, crowded part of town, and I'd just stay inside.[33]

TYPOLOGY OF ROBBERIES

In addition to knowing the broad profile of the offense, the investigator must also be familiar with various types of robberies.

VISIBLE STREET ROBBERIES

Approximately five of every 10 robberies happen on the street.[34] In 95 percent of the cases, the victim is alone[35] and typically on the way to or from a leisure activity within 5 miles of his or her home,[36] such as patronizing a nightclub or restaurant:[37]

> I'd watch people in bars and follow them. One time, I followed this guy and grabbed his tie and swung it down to the ground. And, uh, he hit his head and that's when I took the money and ran.[38]

The victim is 10 percent more likely to be confronted by a single perpetrator than by multiple perpetrators.[39] Youthful robbers are particularly likely to commit strong-armed robberies—also referred to as "muggings"—in which no weapons are involved and in which they suddenly physically attack and beat the victim, taking cash, jewelry, wallets, purses, and other valuables. Purse snatching may or may not be a robbery. If a woman is carrying a purse loosely on her open fingers and someone grabs it and runs and she then experiences fear, robbery is not an appropriate charge because the fear did not precede the taking. But, if we change the facts of the situation slightly and the same woman sees or hears someone running toward her and in

fear clutches her purse, which is then ripped from her by the perpetrator, a robbery has occurred.

Street robberies usually involve little or no planning by the perpetrators. They may have been waiting in one place for a potential victim to appear, or they may walk around looking for someone to rob on the spur of the moment:

> You know, we knew we was going . . . to stick somebody up, but we wasn't gonna be like, let's rob her . . . we just did it, just you know, whoever we saw.[40]

Another perpetrator expressed a similar view about the amount of planning he did prior to a robbery:

> Well, once the gun was bought you might say it was planned, but, you know as far as who or where, no. That was kind of spontaneous. You have to have an eye open for that type of thing.[41]

Because street robberies happen so quickly and often occur at night in areas that are not well lighted, victims often have difficulty providing anything more than a basic physical description. The description may be even more limited if the victim is injured either by a weapon or by a beating in a sudden, overpowering mugging.

Spontaneous street robbers may "graduate" to jobs that involve a certain amount of planning. For example, they may stake out automatic teller machines (ATMs) or banks. In the case of ATMs, they may have decided that they are going to rob the first "soft-looking" person who is alone and driving an expensive car. In the case of banks, they may rob someone on the street whom they have watched long enough to know the person is going to the bank to make a cash deposit or to use the night depository. Although people sometimes commit robberies for excitement or to be "one of the guys," for the most part they do it to get the money, which often goes to pay for drugs:

> When I first started it was for fun. I was 15. I wanted to be down with the group. We'd just take things . . . chains, jewelry, stuff like that. Now, it is to take care of my habit. It is money for drugs.[42]

CARJACKINGS

Until the 1960s, the vast majority of stolen cars were traced to joyriders who simply sought transportation or were taken for use as getaways from crimes that were subsequently committed.[43] Beginning in the late 1960s, increasing numbers of cars were stolen for profit and disposed of through a variety of schemes, including chop shops, insurance scams, and domestic and foreign resale (see Chapter 17, Vehicle Thefts and Related Offenses). Until 1990, any danger to the public largely resulted from joyriders without driving skills or from efforts to elude the police.[44] Until that time, roughly 95 percent of the vehicles stolen were taken surreptitiously. However, in 1990, a violent method of vehicle theft called *carjacking* achieved national prominence. This term, which originated in Detroit,[45] is defined as "the taking of a motor vehicle from the person or presence of another by force, violence or intimidation."[46] Thus, carjacking is essentially an armed robbery in which the victim's vehicle is taken. It is the face-to-face confrontation between the vehicle operator and the perpetrator that creates the high potential for violence. In 77 percent of carjackings the perpetrator is armed with some kind of a firearm, typically a handgun.[47] Most carjacking victims escape without injury; still, 24 percent of victims of completed carjackings and 18 percent of victims in attempted offenses suffer some injury.[48] To put the risk of being carjacked into context, you are just as likely to be a victim of this crime as you are to die in a motor vehicle accident.[49]

There have always been a certain number of what are now called carjackings: Bonnie and Clyde used to carjack.[50] Previously they were reported as armed robberies with the property taken being the vehicles. Although these types of robberies previously occurred, their number constituted only a small percentage of the total number of robberies, there was no special term to distinguish them from other types of robberies, and incidents were not well publicized. But in 1992 "carjacking" became a household word nationally as a result of the Pamela Basu case. Two men carjacked Mrs. Basu's BMW by pushing her out of the vehicle at a stop sign. Entangled in her seat beat, Mrs. Basu was dragged by the car for more than 1 mile and died as a result of her injuries. Her 22-month-old daughter, strapped in a car seat, survived after being thrown from the vehicle a few blocks after it was seized.[51]

One explanation for the increase in carjackings is that such crimes are the result of too much success in the "anti-theft device" field. Owners can now protect their vehicles with "The Club," alarm/locking devices, motion sensors, and sophisticated tracking systems such as "Lojack" (see Chapter 17, Vehicle Thefts and Related Offenses).[52] Car manufacturers are also making keys that cannot be easily duplicated because the automaker is the only source of them; other car producers embed computer chips into the ignition key, which means that only a key with that computer chip can start the vehicle.[53] Such developments make carjacking an attractive alternative to the traditional surreptitious method of vehicle theft. Other explanations for the increase in carjackings include the facts that there is a widespread availability of potential victims, that no inside information or elaborate advance planning is required, and that the mere use of the term "carjacking" hypes the problem and may create some incentive to "do one." For example, shortly after a San Diego newspaper ran a front-page story about carjacking, such incidents leaped from an average of 10 per month to 22 per month.[54]

The thought of being carjacked frightens people in two major ways. First is the possibility of a violent confrontation with an armed subject who may injure or kill the victim. In fact, such violent episodes, although highly publicized, are presently infrequent. Second is the realization by the public that cars are no longer "bubbles of safety," that simply going to or being in your vehicle can be dangerous.[55]

There are 35,000 carjackings per year, a figure which represents about 2 percent of all vehicle thefts and 3 percent of all robberies.[56] Of this number, about two-thirds happen after dark; men commit nearly 9 out of every 10 offenses.[57] About half of all carjackings are carried out by males between 21 and 29 years of age.[58] Carjackings can take place wherever people and their cars are together; such incidents have been reported at apartment parking lots, self-service car washes, parking decks, gas stations, convenience stores, shopping center parking lots, pay telephones, red lights, ATMs, and fast food drive-though lanes.[59] Others occur when robbers tail expensive cars to the victims' homes, where they may also loot the residence of valuables and commit other crimes, such as rape. One method of carjacking involves "accidentally" bumping the victim's car from the rear; when the victim gets out to investigate, one subject pulls a gun, jumps into the bumped vehicle, and leaves the scene accompanied by the "bumper" car—which itself may have been stolen earlier and will be quickly abandoned. Although many carjacking victims are alone, there have also been numerous reports of parents with children being preyed on[60] because threatening to do violence to a child will quickly gain the compliance of the accompanying adult. Another modus operandi of carjackers is to box the moving target vehicle in with one or more vehicles and force it to the curb or simply to slow down gradually until it is brought to a stop and then quickly overpower the victim. Victims have also been robbed of their cars after going into high-crime areas to buy drugs.

According to the FBI, the primary motives for carjacking appear to be to acquire transportation away from the scene after robbing the driver, to get to and from another crime—including bank robberies and drive-by shootings—to joyride, to obtain temporary transportation, and, to a lesser degree, to sell the vehicle itself or its parts for cash or to trade the car or parts for drugs.[61] Whenever a vehicle is carjacked for temporary transportation, the potential for tragedy exists:

> A woman had taken the railroad from downtown to a heavily used stop where her husband was waiting for her in their car. As she exited the train, she heard shots and rushed to the street to find her husband dying from gunshot wounds. The perpetrators, who were later arrested, said that they were waiting for the train, but when they saw the victim in the car, they decided to carjack so they could drive downtown instead.

Presently, about 90 percent of carjacked vehicles are recovered, often within 24 hours, as compared to a recovery rate for surreptitiously stolen vehicles of about 62 percent.[62] Carjackers seldom operate alone, instead tending to work in groups of two to five. Their accomplices often provide the initial transportation to the scene and/or assist in the actual robbery.

HOME INVASION ROBBERIES

Robberies in which one or more perpetrators actually enter the home make up about 12 percent of reported robberies.[63] Although deliberate *home invasion robberies* (HIRs) are thought to be a recent development, their roots can be traced to the "cocaine cowboys" operating in South Florida in the late 1970s and early 1980s.[64] Rival drug dealers and drug bandits saw HIRs as a quick and effective means of obtaining large amounts of drugs and cash.[65] Subsequently, this very violent modus operandi was copied by other criminals.

Home invaders typically target the person, rather than the residence, often selecting women, senior citizens, and others.[66] Invaders often follow potential targets from shopping centers to their homes. They may enter the residence through an unlocked door or window, talk an unsuspecting victim into opening the door, or simply smash the door down. Occasionally targets turn out to be much more difficult than the offenders could possibly imagine: two intruders got more than they bargained for when, after knocking a farmhouse door down, they were attacked by the couple living there. The woman threw scalding water on them, giving the husband time to start his chain saw.[67] When the police arrived, one invader was laying on the lawn bleeding profusely and the other one was apprehended nearby.

In some cases, the targets are "fingered," or identified, by others who pass information on to the invaders for drugs or money. This type of offender will also use deceit to gain entry into a residence. Home invaders pose as police officers, water department employees, florists delivering bouquets, motorists who have "just struck your parked car," natural gas and electric company representatives, and "supervisors checking on your newspaper delivery service," to name just a few, to get people to initially open their doors.

Invaders tend to work in "crews" of two to seven men who may work in a single city or travel nationally to commit their crimes. In some instances, these crews are ethnically based, such as Asians, who specialize on preying on those who share their heritage. Whatever their composition, the gangs carry firearms, handcuffs, tape, masks, and clubs, which they employ to strike terror in their victims and to achieve maximum control over the victims. Gangs burst into houses shouting and striking people, often forcing them to lay face-down on the floor. In additon to making family members easier to control, this tactic also makes it harder for victims to give good descriptions of the invaders to the police. The offenders may also threaten to shoot children, strip and fondle females, break plates over victims' heads, and fire warning shots, all of which are intended to ensure swift and total compliance to their commands.[68] In some cities juvenile invaders have quickly struck a room or two at a motel and then vanished back into the security of their neighborhoods knowing that the victims are usually from out of town, which will hinder prosecutorial efforts if gang members are apprehended.

AUTOMATIC-TELLER-MACHINE ROBBERIES

ATMs are attractive places for robberies because both customers and bank teams servicing the site can be robbed.[69] Additionally, there are many different ATM locations from which to choose, they operate 24 hours a day, a person can be seized at one location and forced to use an ATM at another, victims can be compelled to make several withdrawals, victims can be robbed of other valuables such as jewelry, and vehicles may be carjacked to leave the scene.

Forty-nine percent of all ATM cases take place between 7 P.M. and midnight. The robbery site is overwhelmingly a walk-up ATM that is visible to other persons on the street. Men and women—usually in the 20-to-39 age range—are equally likely to be robbery victims at ATMs. Most commonly, customers are robbed after making a withdrawal or a forced withdrawal, and their personal valuables may also be taken. The victim is alone in 96 percent of such robberies and is confronted by a lone armed perpetrator in two thirds of all cases.

Banks have been sensitive to the ATM robbery problem and have implemented target-hardening measures, including placing armed guards at some ATM sites and locating ATMs in police buildings.[70]

TAXI-CAB ROBBERIES

Taxi-cab robberies frequently occur during the evening hours. The perpetrators are usually armed and have set out with the intent to commit a robbery. People who rob cabs are ordinarily experienced criminals with police records and are willing to use violence against their victims. According to a study by the National Institute for Occupational Safety and Health, among all occupations, driving a taxi involves the highest risk of being a victim of violent crime.[71] A common method of committing this type of robbery is to use a pay phone to call for a taxi with the instructions to meet the fare at a specific corner. The perpetrator gets into the cab and then asks to be driven to another location, where the driver is robbed. The location at which the cabbie is robbed may be quiet or somewhat secluded, or it may be in a very busy area where the perpetrator can simply slip away into the crowd. Calling a cab implies that the robber does not have his or her own transportation; however, in some instances the cabbie will be robbed near where an accomplice is parked with a getaway vehicle.

CONVENIENCE-STORE ROBBERIES

Although the more spectacular robberies, such as the $1,900,000 one at Tiffany's in New York City, capture the interest of the media and the public, investigators are much more likely to work commercial robberies in which far less is taken, such as those that occur at convenience stores.

As reflected in Table 14–1, convenience stores account for about 5 percent of all reported robberies. Located throughout the country, convenience stores are attractive targets because they are usually open 24 hours a day, there may be only one person on duty, protection for the worker is usually limited or nonexistent, and cash is known to be on hand (see Figure 14–2). Working in a convenience store is second only to driving a taxi in terms of being a victim of on-the-job violence.[72] One clerk said, "You're leery of everyone who walks in the door . . . you're a sitting duck."[73]

In some areas of the country convenience stores have stopped operating 24 hours a day, installed bulletproof glass and security cameras to protect clerks, and have two clerks on duty at all times to combat robberies and to protect workers. These measures have been associated with a reduction in convenience store robberies.[74]

TRUCK-HIJACKING ROBBERIES

Truck-hijacking robberies are a lucrative type of robbery committed by experienced armed robbers acting on inside information. They most often

Figure 14-2
The Robbery of a Convenience Store
Working as a pair, one robber takes the cash from the till while his accomplice controls the clerk by using physical force and holding a weapon in the clerk's back.

(Courtesy Phoenix, Arizona, Police Department)

happen in or near large cities, where the contents can be quickly disposed of. Examples of merchandise that has been taken in this fashion include both predictable things, such as clothing and works of art, and loads such as 42,000 pounds of soap worth $50,000[75] and 1,800 tires valued at $200,000.[76] Arrangements to dispose of the merchandise are made in advance, and the perpetrators may have possession of it for only a few hours before it is sold. The contents of the trucks are sold to a fence or to someone who sells them out of his or her business. In some instances, the merchandise is loaded onto ships bound for foreign ports.

Drivers of the rigs may be confronted at road blocks or "detours" set up by the robbers, just outside of delivery sites, during their coffee or meal breaks, when forced from the road, when tricked

into helping a "disabled motorist," or at a truck stop where they have pulled over to rest or "stretch their legs." Robbers have also invaded truck parks, seized or killed security personnel, and taken the targeted trucks. This type of operation can yield scores worth $1 million or more.[77] The problem of truck hijacking robberies is so severe in southern California that the Los Angeles County Sheriff's Office has established Cargo Criminal Apprehension Teams, or Cargo CATs, to deal with it.[78]

ARREST PROBABILITIES

Robbery bears a comparatively low clearance rate: only 26 percent.[79] The reasons for this are several: physical evidence may not be found; the time of perpetrators at the scene is limited; witnesses are usually shaken, so their information runs from minimal to completely erroneous. Physical descriptions are the most common evidence, but these are of limited use when offenders enjoy geographic mobility.

INVESTIGATIVE TECHNIQUES

The police response to the report of a robbery has these components: responding to the scene, tactical situations at the scene, the original investigation, and latent or follow-up investigation.

RESPONDING TO THE SCENE

En route to the scene of a robbery call, the officer must ensure that all information available from the dispatcher has been obtained, including the answers to the following questions: What is the exact location of the offense, including the type of business? Is the offense in progress? How many suspects are involved? What type of and how many weapons were displayed? What description of the suspect is available? By what method and in what direction did the suspect flee? What is the description of the means of transportation used by the suspect?

In approaching the scene, the officer must be alert for several possibilities:

- The dispatcher may provide information on the suspects' escape, such as their direction in fleeing from the scene and whether they were on foot or in a vehicle.
- If the dispatcher cannot supply any information other than the nature of the call, information about the target, MO, suspects, vehicles, weapons used, and other factors in recent robberies may help the responding officer recognize the suspects if they are moving away from the scene on the street along which the officer approaches.
- The fleeing suspects may, as the officer approaches them on the way to the scene, abruptly turn off, fire at the officer, or otherwise suddenly reveal themselves.

The primary tactical objectives of officers responding to a robbery call are public safety, officer protection, and tactical control of the scene. Secondary objectives include conducting the preliminary investigation, perpetrator apprehension, and property recovery. Arriving at the scene unobserved by the suspects facilitates the achievement of both primary and secondary objectives. It also allows tactical control and the element of surprise to pass from the robbers to the police. Units assigned to a robbery call should plan and coordinate the actions to be taken at the scene. Because the perpetrators may have police scanners, care should be taken with respect to radio transmissions. Arriving officers should not give away their exact positions and should refer to buildings by prearranged letter designations (e.g., "the A building").[80] They can never assume that the robber(s) have left the scene; for example, robbers have been known to hide near or at the scene, seeking to escape detection. Responding units should approach separately on streets parallel to that on which the robbery occurred or is occurring, using emergency lights but not sirens. The use of emergency lights permits more rapid progress through traffic. The reason for not using a siren is that the sound may panic suspects near or at the scene, triggering violence or hostage taking. It is believed that 9 out of 10 hostage situations that develop out of robberies occur because of a too-visible first-responding officer.[81] At a distance of three to five blocks from the scene in an urban area and much farther in rural settings,[82] the emergency lights should be turned off to avoid possible detection by a lookout. The police officer should begin to smoothly decelerate, thus avoiding engine noise, squealing tires, or "emergency" stops that could give away the police car's arrival. The first officer on the scene must quickly "size up" the area to gather any possible intelligence, including location of the robbers, lookouts, and escape vehicles. The locations of the perpetrators are particularly important given the fact that such criminals may have automatic and other weapons—which they are willing to use. Actually identifying the lookouts may be difficult; two officers in New York were killed by a lookout disguised as a nun.[83] The officer should leave his or her car quietly and move—unobserved—to a protected position to watch, where possible, two sides (e.g., north and east) of the building. One of these sides should be the exit most likely to be used by the robbers. Moving unobserved does not necessarily imply moving quickly. Running into position may invite passers-by to "rubberneck," giving away the officer's position.[84] Before moving to any position, the officers should make sure that the background of that position, when viewed from the perpetrators' positions, does not silhouette them.[85]

The officer in the second unit should take the same precautions as the first in moving into position. The second officer's responsibility is to cover the two remaining sides (e.g., the south and west). Both officers should keep their vehicle and portable radios at low volume to avoid being detected. The primary and backup officer should be sure that their positions in the lines of fire do not endanger each other.

It is also of particular importance when moving into their respective unobserved positions that officers not get inside of, that is, between, any possible lookouts and the robbery scene. Such a position would leave them vulnerable to fire from several sides.

Both in approaching the scene and at the scene, officers should avoid action, physical, or situational stereotyping.[86]

Action Stereotyping

Action stereotyping occurs when the officer's expectations are so set to see one thing that he or she fails to perceive the event accurately. For example, the responding officer may expect the suspect to come rushing out of the store, hop into a car, and speed away. Although this may be the case, there are also other possible behaviors:

Two robbers who confessed to over 20 "quick mart" robberies had been apprehended during a police surveillance. While being interrogated, the pair revealed that they had come close to being caught on several occasions when responding units arrived at the scene very quickly. They said they had escaped apprehension at those times by simply walking away in a normal manner. This proved to be an embarrassment for one officer who remembered the pair walking past his car. This officer said they just appeared to be "normal" citizens and that there was nothing extraordinary about them.[87]

In Wilkes-Barre, Pennsylvania, a man walked into one of the busiest branch banks and grabbed a deposit bag from a woman. The bag reportedly contained money from one of the bank's overnight deposit boxes. Running from the bank, the young bandit hopped on a silver performance bike and pedaled rapidly away from the scene.[88]

Officers responding to a robbery call arrived at the scene as several people ran out of the business involved. When the people ignored orders to halt, one officer shot and killed one of them and injured several others. All of them were witnesses or victims running to escape from the robber, who was still inside.

A silent alarm was triggered, and officers were dispatched to the scene of a possible robbery in progress. As the officers got out of their cars, a man calmly walked out and waved at them, stating that the alarm had accidentally been set off. The officers left. Later it was found that the robber had killed a pharmacist and shot a clerk, who survived to identify the robber-murderer as the man who had greeted the police.

Physical Stereotyping

Physical stereotyping is an officer's expectations that the robber will be of a particular description. Such stereotypes may allow the suspect to escape or be fatal to officers:

An officer entered a convenience store in response to an alarm; his gun was drawn, but he started to put it away when he didn't see anything out of the ordinary. As he approached the two clerks behind the counter, the younger one yelled a warning: the other "clerk" was an armed robber whose appearance—he was 60 years old—did not fit with the officer's stereotype of a robber.[89]

Another aspect of physical stereotyping is that investigators may have difficulty believing witnesses' descriptions. For example, we expect bank robbers to be relatively young adults and vigorous. However, in northern Colorado nearly a decade ago, an 82-year-old man known as the "salt-and-pepper bandit" was arrested for a string of bank robberies; in another case, a 105-pound woman just 12 years younger donned a black plastic bag as a disguise and robbed a bank, declaring, "there's a bomb here; give me the money, no bells, no sirens." [90]

Situational Stereotyping

In *situational stereotyping*, the officers' previous experience with and knowledge of a particular location increases their vulnerability:

A silent alarm went off at a bar; the call was dispatched and as the assigned unit drove toward the bar, the two partners joked about the inability of the owner to set the alarm properly as he was continuously tripping it accidentally, creating frequent false alarms. The officer operating the police car parked it in front of the bar, and as the two officers began to saunter casually up to the front door of the bar, two suspects burst out with guns in hand and began shooting. Miraculously, neither officer was hit. One of the suspects was wounded and arrested at the scene; the other one escaped and was not apprehended until several weeks later.

Returning to some earlier points, although the suspects may be observed fleeing the scene or reveal themselves in some manner to the officer assigned to respond to the call, such encounters do not take place with any regularity. In addition, deviating from the assignment to become engaged in a "pursuit," instead of proceeding directly to the call, will often be unproductive. In such instances the "suspect," especially one driving an automobile, may merely be acting in a suspicious manner because he or she may have committed some minor traffic violation and is fearful that the officer is going to write a traffic citation. The officer actually assigned to the robbery call should not normally deviate from the assignment without significant reason; the officer's responsibility is to get to the scene and to get accurate, detailed information for the preliminary pickup order or BOLO as rapidly as possible. By doing so, more resources are then brought to bear on the offense, and the likelihood is reduced that other officers may unknowingly stop armed suspects for what they think is only a traffic violation.

If not assigned to the call as the primary or backup unit, other officers should not respond to the scene. Instead they should patrol along a likely escape route such as entrances to expressways. They should avoid transmitting routine messages, as the primary unit will need to transmit temporary pickup orders or BOLOs concerning the offense.

If available, helicopters have the potential of being helpful in robbery investigations when a good description of the vehicle in which the robbers fled is included in the BOLO. Helicopters can cover territory rapidly. Flying at 500 feet, a helicopter provides observers accompanying the pilot with an excellent observation platform. Approximately 75 percent of all pursuits aided by a helicopter are successful.[91] If ground units are in pursuit of a vehicle containing bandits fleeing the scene, the helicopter can:

1. Direct other units into the area to seal off likely avenues of travel.
2. Make the occupants aware of its presence and induce them to stop and surrender.
3. Keep the bandits' car illuminated at night and —if they stop it and "bail out"—keep one or more of the suspects spotlighted. It can also use its infrared heat-sensing system to locate suspects hiding in yards or fields.
4. Light the road ahead of the vehicle if its lights are turned off, thereby lessening the danger to other motorists.
5. Inform pursuing police units of traffic conditions or special hazards—such as construction equipment actively working on the highway, rush-hour traffic, bridges raised for ships, spectators leaving a sport stadium at the end of an event, and railroad cars blocking an intersection—so that pursuing units can turn off emergency equipment and slow down if necessary to protect the public.
6. Warn ground units if the suspects are setting up ambushes.

TACTICAL SITUATIONS AT THE SCENE

Having arrived undetected at the scene, the first responding officer must make a crucial assessment: Have the suspects fled the scene or are they still inside of the building? The officer's best course of action is to have the dispatcher call the business and have the owner, operator, or an employee come out of the building and approach the officer. When this happens, unless the officer recognizes the person as being connected with the business, he or she should be asked to raise both hands above the head, halt 30 feet away in a position not near cover, raise the coat if he or she is wearing one (so the officer can check for weapons), approach to 15 feet and toss some identification toward the officer, and remain standing there, hands above the head, while the officer examines the identification and shares the information with the dispatcher. In doing so, the officer must be alert as to what is going on at the business, what the subject is doing, and movement on the street generally. It is crucial that the officer not leave protected cover until fully satisfied. An officer who has any suspicions at any time during this process should require the subject to kneel with hands raised above the head and request assistance. Even if the officer recognizes the person who exits the business, he or she must continue to exercise caution. Consider a husband and wife who operate a small neighborhood grocery. A subject in that grocery may have spotted the officer moving into position and ordered the husband out of the store to "get rid of the cop or get him in here or your wife is dead." Thus, any person who comes out of the building should be asked how many people are on the premises. These people should be asked to exit the building individually on the command of the officer, and they should be also checked for weapons. Still, the officer should enter the building with great care only after he or she has appropriate backup in the proper position. Such tactics may occasionally upset the businessperson who has just been robbed if the suspects have already left the scene, but their use is justified by reasons previously noted in this chapter. Moreover, experience has shown that most victims will readily accept their use when given an explanation. While the policy of some departments limits the use of invisible response tactics to robbery-in-progress calls, others use it for all robbery calls, a position that is reflected here.

If a suspect is immediately observed, the investigator should determine the person's most likely avenue of flight and possible locations of any accomplices. If the investigator is fired upon by the perpetrator, he or she should not return the fire unless able to do so without needlessly endangering the victim or passers-by. The dispatcher should immediately be advised of all gunshots so that arriving units will not unknowingly be placed in jeopardy. It is far better to allow the escape of the perpetrator than to kill an innocent person by the premature or careless discharge of a weapon. With a suspect who is not attempting to flee or take aggressive action but who refuses to drop his or her weapon when so directed, the investigator is not authorized to open fire. Instead, the officer should remain alert for some sign that the suspect intends to discharge the weapon or flee. Assistance will arrive rapidly, and at that time the suspect can be disarmed by standard cover-and-disarm techniques. Deadly force must be used only as a last resort.

When the subject is barricaded or holding hostages, the officer assigned to the call should immediately advise the dispatcher of this and proceed as provided by departmental policy. Usually this entails dispatching a supervisor and special tactical units, and sealing off and evacuating the area.

THE ORIGINAL INVESTIGATION

Although a robbery may produce a great variety of physical evidence—hair samples, blood, fingernail scrapings, fibers, buttons, notes, and similar materials—such evidence may be discovered only through diligent effort. Therefore, the investigator must always conduct a thorough crime scene search. The most common type of evidence is produced by careful interviews of victims and witnesses. It usually includes a description of the perpetrator and the weapon, directions given in committing the offense, the direction of approach and flight, and, less frequently, a description of the means of fleeing the scene. Thus, the interview phase of a robbery investigation is critical to a successful conclusion. Because of the availability and importance of this type of evidence in robbery cases, the investigator must be thoroughly familiar with principles of witness perception and identification. The investigator must remember that identifications are made by human beings who perceive things differently. The whole approach to the investigation must be directed toward securing the most accurate identifications and descriptions humanly possible, because no less is acceptable in the courtroom. A number of departments use a checklist for obtaining personal descriptions, such as the one in Chapter 6, Field Notes and Reporting. Even experienced investigators will, on occasion, inadvertently fail to obtain a full description, resulting in lost information and a consequent reduction in opportunity for apprehension. A description report also offers the possibility of computerizing the information so that, by means of periodic "searches" and the correlation of information from offenses involving similar descriptions, the probability of apprehension can be increased.

Typically, robbers approach the scene with care. After the robbery, however, they may flee recklessly (see Figure 14–3). The investigator should take great care to establish and check the avenues of flight and approach to locate dropped articles that might help in the identification of the suspect. The immediate area should be canvassed by a "neighborhood check" to locate witnesses to the offense or to the flight of the perpetrator. In the latter case the investigator is occasionally able to locate persons who observed an individual matching the suspect's description enter a vehicle about which they can provide considerable information.

In addition to obtaining a description of the offense and offender, the interview of the victim should elicit information concerning the exact words spoken by the offender, which may constitute an identifiable MO; the physical condition of the perpetrator, including anything that would suggest the use of alcohol or drugs; the possibility that a disguise was used (see Figure 14–4); any nervous mannerisms of the perpetrator, such as tics or stutters; and the possibility that the perpetrator had recently visited the victimized premises and said, done, or worn something that would assist in

Figure 14–3
Robbers at the Scene
Here is an illustration of an exception to the notion that robbers approach the crime scene with care and flee with abandon: two robbers are calmly counting their "take" while still on the premises. Off camera, two accomplices are standing guard over employees.

(Courtesy Austin, Texas, Police Department)

Figure 14–4
Disguises
The dress of these two bank robbers is intended to hamper the original investigation: the wig, hat, and masks can be readily discarded. Wearing an overcoat, which can also be easily discarded, allows the robber to more easily get weapons into the bank; it also makes it more difficult for witnesses to describe the physical build of the robber.

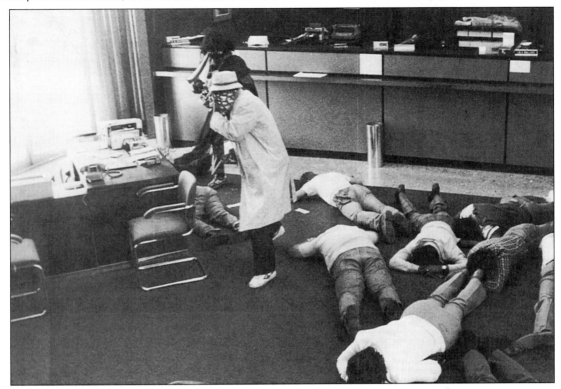

(Courtesy Atlanta Police Department)

identification. Another aspect of an MO is any written note used by bandits to communicate with victims. The threats and demands made, the vocabulary and punctuation used, the manner in which the note was created (e.g., hand printed, letters cut from newspaper, typewritten, type of printer, use of color, or cursive writting) may all be elements of an MO. A classic example of a robbery note as an MO involved a man dubbed the "note bandit," who robbed 23 businesses in 33 days *using the same laminated note*.[92] Whenever possible, the note should be recovered and checked for prints.

A likeness of the suspect should be created as soon as possible. Although some departments rely on artists, investigative agencies usually use one of the manual or computerized "kits." Many police departments use Smith & Wesson's manual Identi-Kit, which relies on a system of over 600 facial transparencies with different features that are "sandwiched" together to form a likeness of the offender. An experienced operator can produce a likeness of a suspect in as little as 20 minutes (see Figure 14–5). Because each overlay has its own designation, the numbers can be transmitted by any means. A trained operator receiving the numbers can quickly assemble the same image. Smith & Wesson also produces a computerized, mouse-operated Identi-Kit with a number of excellent features. It is organized—like its manual counterpart—around features, such as eyes, nose, lips, chin, hair, age lines, facial tones, head gear, glasses, and face hair, all of which can be quickly changed. The "paint brush" command allows the operator to add scars, moles, and other distinguishing features. "Blend brush" provides the capacity to move the hairline back to reduce the height of the suspect's hair. "Reverse" allows the victim to immediately see what the robber would look like if his or her

Figure 14–5
Identi-Kit

Identi-Kit sketch of suspect (*left*) versus photograph of one of two suspects later arrested for the robbery.

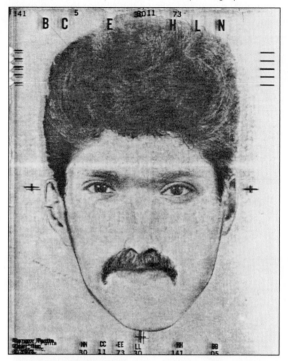 

(Courtesy Clark County Sheriff's Office, Vancouver, Washington)

hair was parted on the opposite side. A notepad function allows the operator to add notes to the file automatically if the witness makes important statements about the suspect while working with the operator. Several different versions of the suspect's likeness can be saved at the bottom of the screen, so the witness can later pick the one that is most like the suspect. All numbers of the specific features that make up the suspect's likeness are automatically generated and saved, so they can be sent in the same manner as the numbers from the manual system. More commonly, the likenesses produced are faxed. The feature-numbering systems in both the manual and computerized Identi-Kits are the same.

Another means of generating a likeness of a suspect is through the use of a computer program such as Compusketch. The process begins with an on-screen interactive interview that includes both multiple-choice and open-ended questions. Upon the completion of the interview, a sketch is automatically assembled from a comprehensive image library of over 40,000 features (see Figure 14–6). This initial sketch can then be further modified to portray unique facial characteristics on the basis of witnesses' reactions. Compusketch can create images of virtually any race, gender, or age beyond approximately 12 years. Compusketch can be used, following an 8-hour course, with appropriately configured Apple or IBM-compatible personal computers. Figure 14–7 presents the results obtained from the use of Compusketch in one case.

FOLLOW-UP INVESTIGATION

The follow-up investigator should review a copy of the original offense report to become familiar with

Figure 14–6
The Visatex Compusketch Feature Library

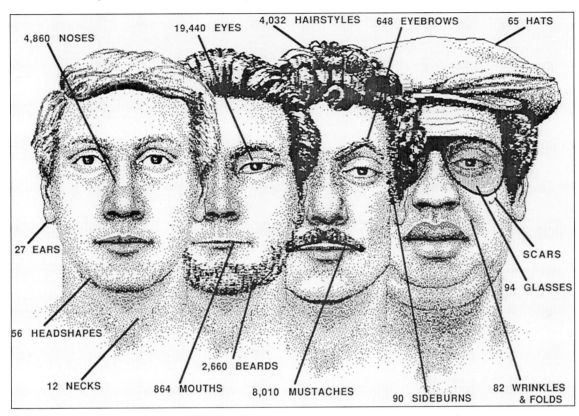

(Courtesy Visatex Corporation)

the case. The investigator should consider facts that suggest an MO, such as the target of the robbery, weapons, type of property taken, the exact words spoken by the perpetrator, the number of suspects and the tasks they performed, needless or vicious force, and similar elements. All physical evidence should be personally examined by the officer assigned to the follow-up investigation. A file check should be made of the victim's name in case the person has a history of making crime reports. For instance, certain types of businesses—such as economy gasoline stations—often do not conduct even a minimal background investigation of employees. Given the availability of cash and long periods of isolation during the night hours, an untrustworthy employee occasionally pockets the cash for his personal gain and covers its absence by claiming a robbery was committed. A file check on the complaining witness may suggest such a pattern.

The investigator should reinterview the victim if there are reasons to believe that a robbery did not actually take place:

Two teenage clerks were shot in a robbery at a Quik-Mart convenience store. Despite these wounds, investigators were suspicious about the incident. Upon further questioning by the police, both "victims" admitted they made up the story about being robbed to conceal their theft of $400 and shot each other to make it look more convincing.[93]

Figure 14–7
Compusketch
Compusketch of suspect (*left*) versus photograph of person subsequently convicted.

 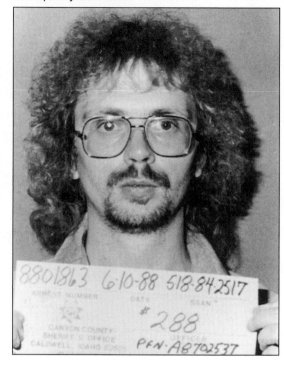

(Courtesy Idaho Bureau of Investigation)

A woman told officers that a laughing man put a gun against her 2-year-old daughter's head and robbed her at an ATM. The victim also reported that no one else was around the ATM when the incident happened at 7:52 A.M. Investigators initially thought it was highly unlikely that nobody else was at that ATM around the time of the alleged robbery. They checked the transactions at the ATM and found that a man had used the ATM just 4 minutes before the robbery and did not see anyone matching the robber's description. Moreover, the man did not immediately leave the ATM after he had finished his transaction. Based on this evidence, it was established that the woman had made up the story because she wanted some attention.[94]

There have been several nationally publicized cases in which black males have been falsely accused of crimes. One of these was discussed in Chapter 2, Crime and Its Investigation; another was the South Carolina case in which Susan Smith subsequently confessed to drowning her two small sons. In this less-noted ATM case, the "laughing man" was also invented as a black male by the "victim."

The investigator should also reinterview the victim and witnesses if it appears that there may be information that was not obtained due to incomplete questioning or insufficient recall of the event. Occasionally witnesses will remember some detail and not go to the "trouble" of looking up the police department's listing. Therefore, the investigator should leave a card with his name and departmental phone number. If a likeness of the suspect has not been made, this should be done immediately. Additionally, the victim and witnesses should review the mug-shot file of known and active robbery perpetrators. The investigator should return to the crime scene at exactly the same time of day that the offense was committed and attempt to locate additional witnesses; at the same time, the neighborhood check should be reconducted. An attempt should be made to tie the offense to other robberies, as the combined information from several offense reports may result in sufficient detail to identify a perpetrator. Reliable informants should be contacted by the investigator. However, this should be done judiciously, as they should not be called on to provide information on every open case regardless of its importance.

THE CRIME SCENE TECHNICIAN AND THE LABORATORY

In many departments, the uniformed officer is responsible for processing the crime scene. Other departments are fortunate enough to have the services of a crime scene technician trained in procuring evidence at the crime scene. It must be borne in mind that such technicians are not miracle workers—they cannot develop evidence that simply does not exist. Likewise, laboratory personnel can contribute little if they have not been given something substantive with which to work. Evidence must be collected, preserved, and identified according to established procedures for the laboratory to process it and for it to be usable in a court proceeding. To ensure the admissibility of physical evidence, responsibility must be firmly fixed for maintaining the chain of custody of each item with a view toward accurate and appropriate identification of the item in court.

FORENSIC PHOTOGRAPHY ANALYSIS

Security surveillance cameras are commonplace. We see them in banks, motels, convenience stores, and other types of businesses. As a result, it is not uncommon to have photographs of an actual robbery. In one case, a police department received reports that police officers were shaking down drug dealers. A "drug den," staffed by undercover investigators, was established. Subsequently, three officers were arrested after they were videotaped breaking into the apartment, beating the undercover investigators, searching for drugs, and stealing cash.[95] In some banks, the number of photographs may be as high as 800 to 1,000, although fewer than a dozen ordinarily yield information of investigative significance. When the robber has not worn a mask, it is possible to compare the forensic photograph with file pictures of suspects. The comparison may involve a simple visual check or laying a photographic transparency over the file pictures to compare the size, shape, and symmetry of the eyes, eyebrows, nose, mouth, ears, facial creases, scars, marks, and head shape.

Even when robbers wear a mask, the analysis of forensic photographs may yield useful information, such as the height of the suspect and defects in clothing. In Figure 14–8, the clothing worn during a robbery is shown next to clothing found in the possession of the suspect. Note that the paint spot on the leg and the crease in the jacket appear in both pictures. Despite the fact that analysis of forensic photographs has already demonstrated their utility on a number of occasions, it is a field from which additional determinations can be expected as the quality of forensic photographs improves and as new methods of analysis are applied.

"THREE-STRIKES" LAWS

In response to the public's demand to "get tough on crime," 24 states and the federal government adopted *"three-strikes" laws* during the mid-1990s which required that those convicted repeatedly of serious crimes be sentenced to lengthy incarcerations or to imprisonment without parole.[96] These laws can be used to remove robbery offenders from the street without having to wait until they can be convicted of yet another robbery.

Most, if not all, states prohibit felons from owning or possessing guns. Such acts are typically felonies in and of themselves. Because weapons are also taken in many crimes, criminals carrying them may be tied to and charged with those crimes. They may have also opened themselves to possession of stolen property or probation- or parole-violation charges. Criminals have a propensity to carry firearms. Fourteen percent of arrestees report that they carry guns most or all of the time.[97] Juveniles do so 20 percent of the time, and for gang members the figure rises to 31 percent.[98] Investigators can legitimately target violent predatory criminals for investigation and use a variety of techniques, including surveillance and sweeps of hot spots, to make arrests of them on firearms and related charges.

Figure 14-8
Forensic Photography Analysis
Comparison of identifying clothing showing common characteristics from bank surveillance photograph and pose with clothing subsequently recovered.

(Courtesy Federal Bureau of Investigation)

THE INVESTIGATOR'S EDUCATIVE RESPONSIBILITY

Investigators and their departments should be prepared not only to identify and locate the perpetrator and recover stolen property but also to prevent as many offenses as possible. Toward this end a number of police departments have undertaken antirobbery campaigns that focus on preventing the offense rather than reacting to its commission. Typically the programs take one of the following forms: seasoned investigators speak before community groups; uniformed patrol and/or crime prevention officers visit businesses in their geographic area of responsibility, offering observations based on the individual premises that will make the businesses less attractive to robbers, coupled with the distrib-

ution of handout materials; or convicted robbery offenders speak to groups about the determinants for selecting a business to be "hit."

Regardless of their form, such presentations usually cover three broad areas: preventive measures, anticipatory strategies, and reactive measures.[99]

PREVENTIVE MEASURES

Business operators can reduce the likelihood of being victimized through basic "target-hardening" and related measures, such as:

- Keeping the interior, exterior, and parking area of the business well lighted.

- Removing from the windows and doors all advertisements that would block a clear view into the store.

- Placing cash registers where they can be seen through the store's front windows.

- Counting the daily receipts out of public view.
- Safeguarding the movement of cash. Armored cars or escort services should be used whenever feasible, but if employees must make cash deposits at a bank, they should vary the routes and times to avoid establishing a pattern.
- Making bank deposits several times each day to minimize the cash on hand.
- Using a "drop safe." A drop safe sits on the floor or is mounted in the floor and has a slot in it through which cash can be deposited. Ordinarily, a drop safe can be opened only by the armored car or escort service with which the business has a contract.
- Writing money orders only after receiving the cash from the customer and placing it in a drop safe.
- Asking customers for the exact change or their smallest bill.
- Using alarms, which are periodically examined to ensure proper functioning.
- Posting prominent notices concerning cash precautions (e.g., "This store keeps less than $100 on hand after 6 P.M.").
- Displaying posters that summarize the state's robbery statute (e.g., "A conviction for armed robbery requires 10 years in prison.").
- Keeping "bait money"—currency whose serial numbers and related information, such as denominations, have been prerecorded—to hand over in the event of a robbery.
- Placing dye packs in stacks of currency. However, even the presence of such paint does not guarantee that people will contact the police:

A man drove his personal car to a branch bank and robbed it. As he was entering his car after the robbery, a dye pack exploded, covering him and his car with bright orange paint. A witness heard him say, "Oh damn!" The suspect drove back to his place of employment, a large manufacturing plant, and went back to work. When the police arrested the man at work a few hours later, they asked his supervisor if he thought it at all odd that the man was covered with bright orange paint. After thinking for a moment, the supervisor replied, "No, a lot of strange people work here."

- Using a surveillance camera, which takes individual photographs when triggered by a remote-control device. Alternatively, a closed-circuit television (CCTV) can be used to continuously record the premises.
- Being alert for suspicious persons on or near the premises. If a vehicle is involved in any such suspicious observation, a full description, including license plate number, should be obtained and all information immediately transmitted to the police.
- Greeting each customer personally so potential robbers know that they have been noted and may be identified later. If an individual enters just ahead of a suspicious person, ask the first individual whether they are together; this will often cause the first person to look at the suspicious person, which creates the attention that robbers want to avoid.
- Keeping opening and closing hours parallel to any other business in the immediate area.
- Using protective glass, if in a high-crime district, to secure the cashier enclosure and register. The glass should be high enough to keep someone from vaulting over the top, and the cash opening should prevent the insertion of anything that could be used to threaten the cashier.

ANTICIPATORY STRATEGIES

All business owners and their employees should recognize that as a matter of statistical probability, they may be victimized at some point. They can, however, reduce the impact of a robbery by planning how they will act when it does occur. This process should lead to all employees being thoroughly trained in their responsibilities in the event of a robbery. As a general guiding principle to behavior in such situations, the primary objective must be protection of life, not of money. This is justified not only by fundamental values but also by the fact that most employers and employees are not properly prepared to resist. Thus, it is generally recognized that during a robbery victims should:

- Have visible near the telephone the number(s) for emergency services—police and emergency medical services.

- Not attempt to reason, negotiate, or argue with the robber; instead, robbers should be given the cash and/or merchandise that is demanded.
- Not fight or attack the robber; trying to overcome an armed robber is not heroic—it is foolhardy.

REACTIVE MEASURES

Because robberies are usually completed within 1 or 2 minutes, reactive measures need to be preestablished. Reactive measures include:

- Concentrating on the robber, if this can be done safely, so as to be able to provide a full description to the police. Although there may be several robbers, it is best to concentrate on one of them. However, if there is more than one employee, there should be preestablished zones of responsibility for each to observe in when multiple robbers are present.
- Calling emergency services to get any needed medical assistance and notifying the police immediately. Once on the telephone with an emergency dispatcher, the victim should not hang up unless instructed to do so. Calling for help first is not an automatic response for some

people. Occasionally victims will call family members to tell them what has happened and that they are all right.

- Not chasing the robber. A chase invites the use of violence; moreover, arriving police units may mistakenly shoot victims or witnesses running out of stores from a perpetrator still inside and/or witnesses in pursuit of the robber.
- Protecting the crime scene. The person in charge of the premises should be prepared to point out things the robbers touched and or left at the crime scene.
- Discontinuing all business until the police complete their investigation. Also, the doors to the business should be locked as soon as it is safe to do so after the robbers leave. This will eliminate the possibility that robbers panicked by arriving police units will retreat back to the crime scene and take hostages.
- Separating witnesses and asking them not to talk. Witnesses should be asked to individually fill out a description checklist on each robber. If witnesses absolutely must leave the premises before the police arrive, an attempt should be made by the person in charge to get their identity and all pertinent locator information.

Questions

1. What are the elements of the crime of robbery?
2. On the basis of the amount of planning involved, describe three robbery styles.
3. Give a profile of visible street robberies.
4. When is purse snatching a robbery?
5. Give four explanations for the increase in carjackings.
6. Discuss how home invaders operate.
7. What are the two occupations with the greatest danger of being the victim of a violent crime on the job?
8. How are drivers confronted in truck hijacking robberies?
9. What are action, physical, and situational stereotyping?
10. What considerations are required as you approach the scene of a robbery?
11. Why is it important to establish the exact words spoken by a robber?
12. What actions must the officer assigned to do the follow-up investigation take?
13. Define and give examples of robbery preventive measures, anticipatory strategies, and reactive measures.

Notes

1. Federal Bureau of Investigation, *Crime in the United States—1997* (Washington, D.C.: Government Printing Office, 1998), p. 29.
2. Ibid.
3. Ibid.
4. Ibid., p. 29.

5. Bureau of Justice Statistics, *Criminal Victimization in the United States—1994* (Washington, D.C.: Bureau of Justice Statistics, 1997), p. 70, table 75.

6. Ibid.

7. Ibid., p. 29, table 27.

8. Ibid., p. 86, table 94.

9. Ibid., p. 38, table 37.

10. Ibid., p. 65, table 67.

11. Jody Miller, "Up It Up: Gender and the Accomplishment of Street Robbery," *Criminology*, 1998, Vol. 36, No. 1, p. 48.

12. Ibid., p. 49

13. Ibid.

14. FBI, *Crime in the United States.*

15. Bureau of Justice Statistics, *Criminal Victimization in the United States*, p. 58, table 59.

16. FBI, *Crime in the United States.*

17. Bureau of Justice Statistics, *Criminal Victimization in the United States*, p. 32, table 32.

18. Richard T. Wright and Scott Decker, *Armed Robbers in Action* (Boston: Northeastern University Press, 1997).

19. Bureau of Justice Statistics, *Criminal Victimization in the United States*, p. 41, table 42.

20. FBI, *Crime in the United States*, p. 31.

21. Arthur Pope, "Teenager Charged in Holdup of Bus Passengers in Queens," *New York Times*, August 2, 1993, p. B12.

22. Clifford Krauss, "Ed Man Arrested in Robbery at an East Side Bridal Shop," *New York Times*, July 15, 1994, p. B3.

23. "Man, 19, Faces Charges after Shooting Incident in Novelty Store," *St. Louis Post-Dispatch*, January 24, 1993, p. D8.

24. Dennis Hevesi, "4 Priests in Queens Are Robbed by Gunman in Their Driveway," *New York Times*, July 12, 1992, Sec. 1, p. 32.

25. Michael Connelly, "Arrests Smash 'Follow Home' Robbery Ring Police Say," *Los Angeles Times*, March 4, 1989, Sec. 2, p. 3.

26. Sebastian Rotella, "Thieves Threaten Salvation Army Bell Ringer," *Los Angeles Times*, November 29, 1989, p. B1.

27. S. K. Bardwell, "Police Wound Man during Chase down Gulf Freeway," *Houston Post*, January 27, 1989, p. A3.

28. Chronicle Staff and Wire Reports, "Nevada Silver Mine Robbed by Methodical Bandits," *San Francisco Chronicle*, August 29, 1989, p. A6.

29. Jim Herron Zamora, "Robbers Wore 'Jason' Masks in 2 of 4 Robberies Saturday," *San Francisco Examiner*, December 7, 1998.

30. See Werner J. Einstadter, "The Social Organization of Armed Robbery," *Social Problems*, 1969, Vol. 17, No. 1, p. 76. The broad categories are those identified by Einstadter; some of the content has been extended by the authors.

31. Joan Petersilia, Peter W. Greenwood, and Marvin Lavin, *Criminal Careers of Habitual Felons* (Washington, D.C.: Government Printing Office, 1978), p. 61.

32. Interview by Charles Swanson with convicted armed robber, January 19, 1983, Clarke County, Georgia, Jail.

33. Petersilia, Greenwood, and Lavin, *Criminal Careers of Habitual Felons*, pp. 60-61.

34. FBI, *Crime in the United States*, p. 29.

35. Bureau of Justice Statistics, *Criminal Victimization in the United States*, p. 37, table 36.

36. Ibid., p. 62, table 64.

37. Ibid., p. 63, table 65.

38. Ira Sommers and Deborah R. Baskin, "The Violent Context of Violent Female Offending," *Journal of Research in Crime and Delinquency*, May 1993, Vol. 30, No. 2, p. 147.

39. Bureau of Justice Statistics, *Criminal Victimization in the United States*, p. 38, table 37,

40. Sommers and Baskin, "The Violent Context of Violent Female Offending," p. 146.

41. Ibid.

42. Ibid., p. 144.

43. Federal Bureau of Investigation, *An Analysis of Carjacking in the United States* (Washington, D.C.: 1992), p. 2.

44. Ibid.

45. Tod W. Burke and Charles E. O'Rear, "Armed Carjacking: A Violent Problem in Need of a Solution," *The Police Chief*, January 1993, Vol. 60, No. 1, p. 18.

46. FBI, *An Analysis of Carjacking in the United States*, p. 1.

47. Michael R. Rand, "Carjacking: National Crime Victimization Survey," *Bureau of Criminal Justice Statistics Crime Data Brief* (Washington, D.C.: Bureau of Justice Statistics, 1994), p. 2.

48. Ibid., p. 1.

49. Ibid.

50. Don Terry, quoting Lawrence W. Sherman, "Carjacking: New Name for an Old Crime," *New York Times*, December 9, 1992, p. A18.

51. Burke and O'Rear, "Armed Carjacking," p. 18.

52. Ibid., p. 21.

53. Mary Ellen Beekman, "Auto Theft: Countering Violent Trends," *FBI Law Enforcement Bulletin*, October 1993, Vol. 62, No. 10, p. 18.

54. FBI, *An Analysis of Carjacking in the United States*, p. 25.

55. Terry, quoting Sherman, "Carjacking," p. A18.

56. Rand, "Carjacking: National Crime Victimization Survey," p. 1.

57. Ibid.

58. Ibid., p. 2.

59. Burke and O'Rear, "Armed Carjacking," p. 18.

60. Ibid.

61. FBI, *An Analysis of Carjacking in the United States*, p. 3.

62. Terry, "Carjacking," p. A18.

63. FBI, *Crime in the United States*, p. 29.

64. James T. Hurley, "Violent Crime Hits Home," *FBI Law Enforcement Bulletin*, June 1995, p. 11.

65. Ibid.

66. Ibid., p. 10.

67. Ron Walton, "Tulsa World On Line," December 8, 1998, http://TULSAWORLD.com

68. Tod W. Burke, "Home Invaders: Gangs of the Future," *The Police Chief*, November 1990, Vol. 57, No. 11, p. 23.

69. The information in this section is drawn, with modification, from Bank Administration Institute, *ATM Security Handbook*, 2nd ed. (Rolling Meadows, Ill.: 1988).

70. Don Terry, "In a Chicago Police Station, Safest Cash Machine Around," *New York Times*, April 1, 1994, p. A12.

71. Peter T. Kilborn, "Convenience Store Jobs: High Risks Alone at Night," *New York Times*, April 7, 1991, p. 1.

72. Kilborn, "Convenience Store Jobs," p. 1.

73. Ibid., p. 27.

74. James D. Calder and John R. Bauer, "Convenience Store Robberies: Security Measures and Store Robbery Incidents," *Journal of Criminal Justice*, November 1992, Vol. 20, No. 6, pp. 553–566.

75. Teresa Wiltz, "The Slickest Soap Heist—Bar None," *Chicago Tribune*, November 27, 1991, p. 2C.

76. Walt Philbin, "2 Booked with Stealing Truck, 1800 Tires," *Times-Picayune* (New Orleans), October 29, 1994, p. B3.

77. Eric Malnic, "Robbers Kill Guard, Steal 2 Big Rigs and $1 Million in Goods," *Los Angeles Times*, September 2, 1993, p. B3.

78. Christina Lima, "CATs Crack Down on Truck Hijackers," *Los Angeles Times*, February 5, 1994, p. B1.

79. FBI, *Crime in the United States*, p. 31.

80. Charles Remsberg, *The Tactical Edge: Surviving High Risk Patrol* (Northbrook, Ill.: Calibre Press, 1986), p. 251.

81. Ibid.

82. Ibid., p. 248.

83. Ibid., p. 253.

84. Ibid., p. 252.

85. Ibid.

86. The distinction between these types of stereotyping is taken from Jerry W. Baker and Carl P. Florez, "Robbery Response," *The Police Chief*, October 1980, Vol. 47, No. 10, pp. 46-47.

87. Ibid., p. 47.

88. Andy Mehalshick, "Bicycle Bank Robber Strikes Busy Branch," http://www.wbre.com, 28 WBRE-TV Home Page, September 25, 1998.

89. Baker and Florez, "Robbery Response," p. 47.

90. Coleman Cornelius, "Police Bag Bank Heist Suspect," *The Denver Post*, December 4, 1998.

91. Geoffrey P. Alpert, *Helicopters in Pursuit Operations* (Washington, D.C.: National Institute of Justice, 1998), p. 3, with some additions by the authors.

92. Erin Emery, "Note Bandit Suspect Arrested, 23 Businesses Robbed in 33 Days," *The Denver Post*, November 4, 1998.

93. Kevin B. O'Leary, "Robbery 'Hoax': Shootings Real," *Boston Globe*, November 19, 1993, p. 1.

94. Richard Perez-Pena, "Teller Machine Robbery Was a Hoax, Police Say," *New York Times*, February 19, 1994, p. A25.

95. Clifford Krauss, "3 Officers Held in New York Police Sting after Robbery Is Taped," *New York Times*, March 19, 1994, p. A1.

96. Jeremy Travis, *Three Strikes and You're Out: A Review of National Legislation* (Washington, D.C.: National Institute of Justice, 1997), pp. 1, 3.

97. Jeremy Travis, *Illegal Firearms: Access and Use by Arrestees*, (Washington, D.C.: National Institute of Justice, 1997), p. 3.

98. Ibid.

99. The information in this section is drawn from the National Crime Prevention Institute, *Understanding Crime Prevention* (Boston: Butterworths Publishing Company, 1986), p. 103; Small Business Reporter, *Crime Prevention for Small Business* (San Francisco: Small Business Reporter, 1984), p. 8; Small Business Administration, *Crime against Small Business* (Washington, D.C.: Government Printing Office, 1969), pp. 242-245.

FIFTEEN

Burglary Investigation

CHAPTER OUTLINE

Offenders 392
The Law 395
Approaching the Scene and Initial Actions 396
Investigative Considerations at the Scene 397
Safe Burglaries 401

Residential Burglary 414
Tracing and Recovering Stolen Propery 416
The Investigator's Crime Prevention Role 417
Questions 419
Notes 420

INTRODUCTION

Two important aspects of burglary are its frequency and its economic impact. Nationally, if reported burglaries were distributed evenly in time, one would occur every 13 seconds.[1] Residential burglaries account for two-thirds of this category of crime, with the rest being attacks on various types of commercial establishments.[2] Despite the fact that in terms of sheer numbers there are more residential than commercial burglaries, the risk of being victimized is greater to a business because there are much fewer of them. The average loss for residential offenses is $1,334; for nonresidential locations, $1,391.[3] In general, property easy to sell is stolen from residences; this includes televisions, tape and compact disc players, speakers, jewelry and furs, clothing, firearms, credit cards, and drugs. In contrast, money and checks that can be forged and cashed are more likely to be taken from businesses. However,

certain types of businesses—for example, men's or women's clothing stores—are targeted because they contain property that is easy to dispose of and hard to trace.

Nationally, among reported burglaries, 66 percent involve a forcible entry in which an instrument such as a pry bar, screwdriver, or axe is employed; 27 percent of the cases involve entries without the use of force, such as by using a master key, opening unlocked doors, and lockpicking; the remaining offenses are made up of attempted entries.[4] Most burglaries are characterized by entry through a door rather than a window. In general, commercial establishments are attacked at the rear, whereas for residences entry tends to be at the front. Although burglars prefer to be invisible, attempts to gain entry at the front of the house have a certain logic to them. Burglary of homes tends to be a daytime crime; neighbors who remain at home are used to seeing salespeople or political workers approach front doors. Thus, to see a pedestrian approaching a door is not an abnormal occurrence, although a stranger going to the rear of a house would be. Further recommending this tactic are the speed with which many doors can be compromised and the fact that doors set back from the main plane of the house's front serve to limit visibility, except to a particularly well-positioned neighbor.

Although national data for reported burglaries vary by month, with July the high and February the low, there is little seasonal fluctuation.[5] Residential burglaries most often occur during working hours on a weekday, when many homes are not occupied; most commercial burglaries are committed on weeknights, when the absence of people can be predicted accurately.

Burglary has a low clearance rate: 14 percent.[6] As a rule of thumb, very low and high losses are associated with a greater clearance rate than are the more frequently reported midrange losses, largely because less sophisticated offenders commit petty burglaries and are more easily identified and burglaries involving high losses receive more attention than do burglaries with midrange losses.

OFFENDERS

From the time people began using even primitive structures, there were thieves who committed the crime which is now called burglary. The elaborate tombs of the Egyptian pharaohs, designed to send the rulers into the next world in splendor, contained magnificent treasures. They also contained elaborate security features to protect those riches. Yet they were often plundered by thieves of that time.

The nature of burglary has stayed the same over time, but *how* it is committed changes, largely as an influence of technological advances and architectural design. For example, now virtually extinct are such specialized methods of burglary as entry through coal chutes—because people in this country heat mainly with electricity, natural gas, and even solar power. As municipalities began requiring the use of fire escapes, they were appended to the outside of apartment buildings. This created a new method of burglary—the "step-over." Although people would place bars or other barriers over apartment windows by the fire escape, they would neglect to protect other windows. The step-over artist would go up a fire escape to the apartment to be hit and then step over from the fire escape to the ledge of a window that was unprotected. As interior fire escapes became more common, the opportunities to be a step-over artist gradually declined, although they certainly still exist. A slight variation on the step-over method is still in practice: parents send children as young as 5 years old to do the step-over and then open the apartment door from the inside to let in the parents, who plunder the premises. In the last 10 years a method of burglary that has gained in popularity is one in which the offenders steal a car and drive it through the front door of a gun, a jewelry, or another type of store. Once inside, they grab what they can in 30 to 45 seconds, exit, get picked up by a confederate (who is often operating another just-stolen car), flee the scene, and then abandon the stolen car. This method is essentially an aggravated case of the well-known "smash-and-grab," in which a perpetrator throws a brick or concrete block through the plate glass window of a jewelry store, seizes what can immediately be reached, and then gets away from the scene as quickly as possible.

Some targets selected for burglaries require more than just crude force; they demand a high level of skill and daring. A former Army paratrooper who stole some $6 million in cash, jewelry, and credit cards was dubbed "Spiderman" by investigators because he specialized in burgarlizing high-rise apartments—a total of 132 of them— before he was apprehended. To reach his targets, Spiderman would climb as many as 30 stories on the outside of the buildings—without any climbing equipment.[7] Initially, investigators had difficulty even considering this method of approaching the target because its use seemed too improbable. Some burglaries require careful planning and coordination. Thieves stole merchandise from parked Susquehanna Railroad freight cars four times in 3 months, netting as much as $100,000. The men used 30-inch bolt cutters to force entry into the cars. Once inside, the merchandise was "selected" and walkie-talkies were used to summon gang members driving gutted vans, which were used to haul the loot off. To stay ahead of the police, the ring monitored a police scanner. After surveillance of the tracks failed to produce any results, officers were pulled off of that assignment and the burglars went back to work. However, a man walking his dog at 9:30 P.M. spotted the men on top of the freight cars and alerted police, who were able to make arrests at the scene.[8]

The purposes and functioning of gangs, ethnically based crime organizations, and crime groups are all well understood by law enforcement agencies. The "players" and the criminal orientation of these entities change over time, and occasionally a major new crime group—such as the YACs (Yugoslavian/Croatian/Serbian)—emerges.

New York City is the center for YACs. Although they operate heavily along the East Coast, YACs have been active as far west as California and into southeastern states as well. This crime group specializes in burglarizing ATMs, especially those in supermarkets and malls and outside of banks, which may have as much as $100,000 in them.[9] They also attack safes in businesses believed to have cash on hand, such as restaurants and bars. For example, in a 2-month period YACs hit 20 restaurants in New York City, steadily bringing in $4,000 to $8,000 a job.

Because YACs operated in different states and most of the burglaries were unsolved, their activity was not understood in the early 1990s. However, as investigators began to develop and share MOs across agencies, states, and regions, a pattern began to emerge. Supermarket operators would arrive to open their stores and find telephone lines slashed

to disable the alarms and holes chopped in roofs— through which the burglars entered and attacked the ATMs. At about the same time, the international association for supermarket corporations— the Food Marketing Institute (FMI)—began to meet with law enforcement officials to advance claims that literally hundreds of supermarket ATM burglaries were likely to have been committed by Yugoslavian or Albanian suspects. This, and the growing number of such suspects being arrested for the burglaries, gave investigators a new investigative avenue to pursue.

In response, the FBI created the YACs Crime Group (YCG) and went to work. FMI security managers developed a partnership with the FBI and began reporting all suspected YAC activities to it within 24 hours of all incidents. The New York field office was selected to lead the investigation because the YAC center was located there. One early initiative was to hold conferences in the areas where YACs had been most active, to alert potential targets to the problems. Many corporations examined their security measures and upgraded to "harden" their stores. Some elected to take special measures whereby slashed telephone lines would register as "telecommunication failures" at central monitoring stations—which meant that armed security guards or the police would be dispatched to investigate.

All available records on known YACs were scrutinized for information and YACs were covertly surveilled to gain additional information. As intelligence piled up, there was a corresponding increase in understanding YAC operations. YACs operated in groups of four to six. Initially, a YAC would be a member of one or more groups; with increased experience, he could become a leader of his own group. Members of a group were selected only hours before going out on a job.

YACs often carried false identification and had a prearranged number to call if they were arrested and needed to be bailed out of jail. This meant that many suspects were released before their true identity was known. Additionally, YACs often supplied other false information when questioned, so written police records were often not reliable. All information, including photographs, was centralized by the FBI, and true identities for suspects began to emerge. Armed with this information, investigators and prosecutors were able to arrest many YACs who were fugitives and to demand higher bails for them because they were likely to flee again.

Many YACs were also caught in the act of burglary because intelligence about their organization, members, and tactics was sufficiently sound to allow investigators to take the offensive. Continuous surveillance of YACs across several state boundaries led to their arrest at burglary scenes; in other instances, arrests were made by covering probable targets more closely.

The YACs have been hurt by law enforcement, but they will continue to operate, perhaps changing the types of crimes they commit or devising new ways to commit them. The significance of this case history, however, is that it highlights the importance of cooperation and information sharing between enforcement agencies and private industry in an era of highly mobile and sophisticated offenders.

Most burglars are poor, and have attained only modest educations. Despite this broad profile, the fact remains that there are many people in well-respected professions who are also burglars:

A former police officer pleaded guilty to 16 felony counts involving a string of residential and commercial burglaries he committed while on duty. Just a month before entering his plea, the 18-year law enforcement veteran was granted a disability pension after experts testified at his retirement hearing that he suffered from an obsessive-compulsive disorder which led to his patholgical gambling.[10]

A former church organist was arrested for committing three burglaries of churches and synagogues in which religious items of gold and silver valued at $25,000 were stolen. Following his arrest, the suspect confessed to having burglarized 500 such places of articles worth $2,500,000. There was little hope that any of the stolen property would ever be recovered, as it was believed to have been melted down and sold. Police were led to the suspect when a drifter was arrested for disorderly conduct. In the drifter's duffel bag, religious articles were found. He admitted having stolen them from the suspect, who had provided him with shelter for the night.[11]

Because so few burglaries are cleared, it is difficult to make sweeping generalizations, but based on arrest statistics, burglary is overwhelmingly a male endeavor involving multiple perpetrators, with females representing only about 12 percent of those arrested for this offense.[12] Of those arrested for burglary, 88 percent are less than 25 years old, 68 percent are Caucasian, and 30 percent are black.[13]

While burglars may be classified according to a number of variables, such as preferences for premises to be attacked and types of property that they will, or will not, take, the most useful classification is skill. Conceived as a continuum, the two extremes would be the amateur and the professional. The largest number of burglars would be clustered toward the less skilled end of the continuum, with progressively fewer toward the skilled end.

Professional burglars may commit only a few offenses per year, going for the "big score":

Burglars in Miami, Florida, were described as "hitting the mother lode" after they successfully circumvented a sophisticated alarm system and removed nearly $8 million worth of gold and silver from one of the nation's largest wholesalers of precious metals. One investigator said that the crime, which resulted in 800 pounds of gold in addition to the silver being stolen, was a "monster hit" and a "masterpiece."[14]

During one weekend, telephone service on Chicago's north side was disrupted for thousands of customers when numerous cables were cut. Police officials speculate that it may have been a diversion for a burglary by highly skilled criminals whose break-in at a jewelry manufacturing firm resulted in the loss of gold and uncut diamonds valued at more than $2 million.[15]

On the other hand, professional burglars can also be quite active, committing a large number of offenses:

Members of a burglary ring were arrested for committing some 1,000 burglaries over a three-year period. They selected shops, businesses, and fast-food restaurants that would have anywhere from several thousand to $75,000 on hand. The targets included McDonald's, Pizza Hut, Burger King, and Dunkin Donuts.[16]

While many professional burglars may commit only a few offenses a year, they are of considerable interest to investigators because of the large value of cash or property taken and their intimate knowledge of sophisticated fencing systems, which are often detected, and therefore investigated, only following the apprehension of a professional. In addition to the "big score," the hallmark of the professional is the thorough planning that precedes each burglary. Professionals refuse to place themselves in jeopardy for anything other than sizable gains and do so only after weeks or even months of painstaking study of the target selected. Knowing exactly what they want in advance, professionals do not ransack premises. Thus, if they have employed surreptitious methods of entry, articles taken may not be missed for some time. Working nationally, or at the very highest professional level, internationally, this type of burglar often operates for long periods of time without being arrested. When arrested, such burglars are often released without being charged due to a lack of physical evidence, coupled with their own adroitness in responding to the questions of investigators. When operating in elegant hotels or apartment buildings, the professional will use a businesslike appearance and manners to talk his way out of a situation. Should an occupant return unexpectedly, the burglar may pull out forged credentials identifying him as the building's security officer and say he found the door ajar and was just beginning his investigation. Or he may pretend to be drunk, ask for directions to some similarly numbered room, and stagger away acting very confused.

However, should these or similar ploys fail or if the burglar's real intent is apparent, the professional will employ violence if necessary to escape:

A well-known cardiologist was shot to death when he walked into the burglary of his home in a fashionable section of Washington, D.C. The police arrested a man who was alleged to be a "superthief" for the crimes. Upon searching the suspect's swank suburban home, the police found some $4 million worth of allegedly stolen property. It took the police 472 manhours and 400 legal-sized pages to count, tag, and describe the property. The eighteen-foot truck in which the seized property was transported away contained fifty-one large boxes and two smelters which were believed to have been used to melt down precious metals.[17]

Amateur burglars often operate on the basis of impulse or react to suddenly presented opportunities. Such burglars tend to work not only in one city but often in a relatively small segment of it. Amateurs may cruise in cars looking for businesses to victimize, prowl hotels seeking unlocked doors, or try to locate doors whose locks can be easily slipped using a credit card. While amateurs may occasionally enjoy a relatively big score, it is the absence of preplanning that sharply differentiates them from professionals. If narcotics addicts, amateurs must often work four or more days per week, committing several offenses each day, in order to support their habits; if not addicts, this may still be necessary to support their lifestyles. Frequently using sheer force to enter, amateurs crudely ransack businesses or residences to find anything of value. Occasionally, unlike their discerning professional counterparts, they take costume jewelry in the belief that they have found something of considerable value. When confronted by an unexpectedly returning business owner or occupant of a residence, amateurs may become immediately violent, and secondary crimes, such as murder or rape, unintended in the original concept of the offense, will occur. Finally, amateur burglars often have lengthy records and are frequently in and out of jail.

THE LAW

The crime of *burglary* generally consists of the following elements: (1) breaking and (2) entering (3) a dwelling house or other building (4) belonging to another, (5) with the intent to commit a crime therein. The common-law crime of burglary necessitates that the act be committed in the nighttime.

This element has been deleted in a number of state statutes.

Burglary and related offenses are classified as crimes against the habitation, dwelling, or building itself; no force need be directed against a person. The breaking element may be satisfied through acts that constitute a breaking into, a breaking out of, or a breaking within. Generally, the slightest force used to remove or put aside something material that makes up a part of the building and is relied on to prevent intrusion, for example, doors or windows, constitutes breaking. This element can be satisfied whether accomplished at the hands of the perpetrator, through the use of some inanimate object like a brick, or by the participation of an innocent third party. Similarly, the element of entry is satisfied once the slightest intrusion has taken place by the perpetrator, an inanimate object, an animal, or an innocent third person.

The character of the building at which the breaking and entering takes place will largely determine the type of offense committed. The most serious offense is breaking and entering of a dwelling house, that is, a place used by another person as a residence. The nature of the dwelling itself is not determinative, but rather the manner in which it is used. Hence, a hotel room can be considered a dwelling house.

The other major ingredient controlling the nature of the crime is the intent with which the perpetrator unlawfully breaks and enters the building. The more serious the crime intended to be committed after entry, the more serious becomes the breaking and entering itself. Thus, the most serious breaking-and-entering offense is that which is done with the intent to commit a felony.

APPROACHING THE SCENE AND INITIAL ACTIONS

When responding to a burglary-in-progress call, uniformed officers should drive rapidly while avoiding excessive noise, such as the dramatic but unnecessary use of the siren. The last several blocks to the scene should be driven at lower speeds for two reasons. It will eliminate the possibility that the squealing tires of the police vehicle will give the perpetrators, if still on the scene, the advantage of crucial seconds of warning. Additionally, it allows opportunity for observation. A vehicle driving away from the vicinity of the scene may be seen and its description and license plate number noted as a possible investigative lead. Under such conditions, late-model, expensive cars, such as Cadillacs or Lincolns, should not be discounted. Burglars often select these, not only because of the large amounts of equipment and stolen property such cars can hold but also because they recognize the fact that the police often act with deference to the occupants of these vehicles because of the implied social status.

When dispatched to a burglary-in-progress call, the uniformed officer working alone should attempt to coordinate his or her arrival time and position with the backup unit. This will enable the officers to secure the building immediately. One unit can arrive positioned so that it can watch two sides of the building, for example, the north and east sides, while the other unit can observe the west and south sides. When a two-officer unit is dispatched to a burglary-in-progress call, the operator of the police vehicle should drop his or her partner off in a position to view two sides of the building and position the vehicle to allow observation of the remaining two sides. When working alone, if it is necessary to begin checking the building immediately, the uniformed officer should drive around the building to determine if there is a readily observable break. If this is not possible, the officer should check rapidly, but cautiously, on foot. When using a flashlight during the hours of darkness, it should be held away from the body, as the suspect is most likely to aim at the light source if firing at the officer. If a point of entry is established, under no circumstances should an officer attempt to enter, as it needlessly exposes him or her to extreme danger. Most burglars prefer to go unarmed because, in many states, breaking and entering while armed is a more serious offense than an unarmed breaking and entering. However, occasionally burglars are armed and willing to use their weapons to avoid apprehension:

A woman whose home overlooked the back of a shopping center saw two people break into a dress shop through the rear door. She called 911, who gave the call out as a burglary-in-progress, subjects on the premises. A motorcycle officer who was returning to the station at the end of his shift heard the call, which was assigned to a patrol unit, and swung by to back them up because he was close to the scene. The woman, still connected to 911, gave a running account of what happened. The motorcycle officer pulled up and pointed his lights at the rear door. Instead of maintaining his position and waiting for assistance, he walked up to the door—fully silhouetted by his own lights. As he stood in the doorway, he was shot three times and collapsed. As the officer lay dying, one of the perpetrators stood over him and emptied his pistol into him. This death should not have occurred. It was caused because the officer used a tactically unsound procedure and because he encountered armed subjects willing to shoot it out with the police. Both subjects were arrested at the scene. Follow-up investigation revealed that they had a major incentive to use deadly force against the police—they were wanted on murder charges in two other states.

The fact that no point of entry is established by riding or walking around the building does not mean that a forcible entry has not occurred; whenever possible, the roof should be checked, particularly vents and skylights.

Even if there is an alarm sounding, there may not be a burglary. Alarms frequently malfunction, particularly during inclement weather. However, officers must never become complacent about checking premises with a reputation for false alarms. If a breaking and entering has occurred, additional cars, if available, should be brought into the general area. Burglars often park their vehicles some blocks from the building to be attacked, and the perpetrator may not yet have had time to flee the area. "Lovers" parked in the general area should not go overlooked by the police. Burglars often use couples as lookouts or have their girlfriends remain in the car while they commit the offense. The perpetrator may have reached the car but have been unable to flee the immediate area; the use of a "just parked lovers" story may allow him to escape detection.

If a burglary has been committed and the police department has a canine unit, the uniformed officer at the scene should request its presence prior to entering the building. The alarm servicing company will ordinarily have a representative at the scene fairly rapidly to provide officers with access to the building. If there is no alarm, then the owner must be contacted either from information usually posted on the door or from other sources. Before beginning the crime scene search, officers must thoroughly check the building to ensure that the burglar is not hidden on the premises. In order to achieve the proper degree of caution, the building check should be conducted as though it were known that the burglar was still there.

INVESTIGATIVE CONSIDERATIONS AT THE SCENE

Caution must be exercised to avoid the accidental destruction of physical evidence while attempting to make a determination of whether the burglar is still in the building. Officers should be sensitive to the possible presence of physical evidence but not act in a manner that might jeopardize the most important thing—the officer's safety. If gross physical force has been used in gaining entry, the point of attack is easily established. However, one cannot assume that it is also the point of exit. Often burglars will break into a building at a particular point and then leave by opening a door. Where gross physical force is used, the point of attack is of particular importance because it may yield the types of physical evidence discussed in Chapter 4, Physical Evidence. In combination, the determination of the points of attack and exit will suggest the avenues of approach and flight traveled by the perpetrator, which also must be explored for the possible presence of physical evidence.

Officers must be particularly attentive for unusual signs that may be of investigative value. Juvenile burglars commonly commit destructive acts of vandalism. Also, age may be suggested from the choices of what is taken and what is left behind:

When I started hustling . . . didn't know much, like what crap be really worth and how to get bills for it . . . at first alotta stuff I just leave back . . . just grabbed things for me . . . like a nice coat or small crap you can just walk with and sell quick for cash . . . like a gun . . . main thing for me was getting some bills so I could high-cat around and get stuff . . . Nike shoes. I couldn't walk around with no stereo or tv . . . had to leave the big stuff.

The sudden removal of trophies or other prized possessions by their owner from a business or residence, followed by a burglary for the purpose of committing an arson, should raise certain questions in the investigator's mind. Further, the weight or dimensions of property taken in a burglary may suggest, if only roughly, the number of people involved in the offense. Articles or tools left behind, combined with other specifics of the crime, may be useful in the identification of an MO.

Many commercial establishments keep check imprinters on their premises. A not uncommon occurrence is for a burglar to gain entry to a commercial building, tear several checks from the company checkbook, imprint them, and cash them the next day. Thus, it is of particular importance to have the proprietor ensure that no checks have been taken. Normally, when a burglar employs this practice the checks will be taken from the very rear of the book or from several different series in order to lessen the likelihood of detection.

RECOGNITION OF BURGLARY TOOLS

Most often when tools used in the commission of a burglary are recovered at the scene, they will not be greatly differentiated from those found in many households. A partial list includes knives, screwdrivers, crowbars, tire irons, pipe wrenches, chisels, sledgehammers, hacksaws, hydraulic jacks, bolt cutters, vise grips, axes, and glass cutters. In the crude "smash-and-grab" burglary, where the display window of a jewelry store is broken and articles immediately available taken, the "tool" may be as unsophisticated as a brick in a paper sack. However, tools left at the scene may have been subject to certain adaptations to facilitate their use in a burglary (see Figure 15–1, for an example). Screwdrivers or crowbars may be carefully sharpened or shaped to increase their effectiveness in attacking doors and windows; nippers can be transformed into lock pullers if they are honed in a manner that permits firmer biting ability on exposed lock edges. Burglars will also apply masking tape in the shape of a cone to the end of a flashlight so that it emits only a very thin light beam.

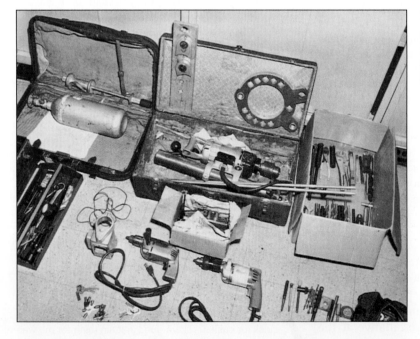

Figure 15–1
An Array of Tools Commonly Employed by a Burglar who Specialized in Attacking Safes

Apprehension of a suspect not in the act of burglary but in possession of lock picks (see Figure 15–2 and 15–3), specially modified tools, or standard tools that can be used in burglaries may permit a felony charge of possession of burglary tools. Some states require that a person have a prior conviction for burglary in order for this charge to be placed. Even where this requirement does not exist, proof of intent to commit burglary is essential for conviction.

SURREPTITIOUS ENTRIES

Occasionally, the investigation of a burglary cannot establish a point of entry or exit. What happens in such instances is in large measure determined by the knowledge and thoroughness of the investigator, who may initiate a report indicating "entrance by unexplained means," decline to take a report due to lack of evidence, or take a report knowing that due to departmental policy it will subsequently be designated "unfounded." Complaints of this nature frequently involve surreptitious entries; that is, a burglary has occurred, but there was no apparent force used. Excluding the case of closed but unlocked doors, the most common explanations are that the door was "loided," the lock picked, or the premises victimized by someone who has unauthorized possession of a key.

"Loiding" is the act of slipping or shimming, by using a strip of celluloid, a spring-bolt lock that does not have an antishim device. Technically, a spring bolt without an antishim device should be considered a privacy, rather than a security, device. Simply stated, picking is a process of manipulating a lock into an unlocked position using picks rather than a key. When picking is suspected as the means used to gain entry, the lock should be submitted to the laboratory for examination. By examining the lock, the laboratory will be able to determine whether or not the lock was picked. From the marks alone on a lock, the laboratory cannot state the type of picking device used, except in general terms. If, however, a pick is seized as evidence, it is possible to make an individual identification by comparing the marks on the lock with test marks made by the seized pick. To facilitate the reassembly of the lock following its examination by laboratory personnel, the key should also be submitted. The laboratory cannot determine whether a lock was loided, due to the lack of physical evidence associated with this technique.

Figure 15–2
A "Ball-Point Pen" Container for Concealing Lock Picks

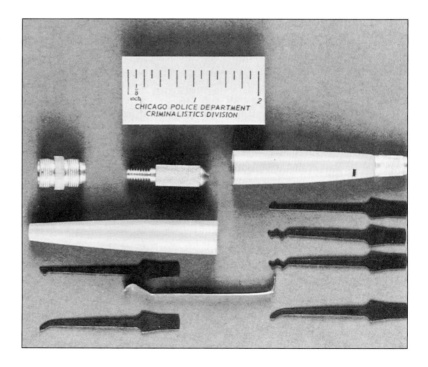

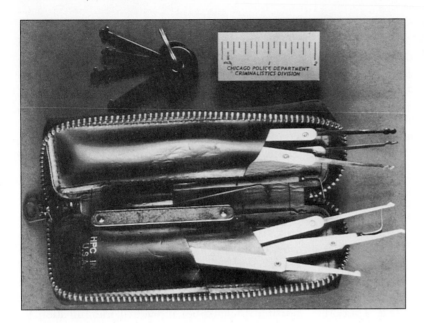

Figure 15–3
Lock Picks Concealed in an Eyeglass-Type Case

Officers must be familiar with privacy and security devices, as this increases their investigative effectiveness and the credibility of their testimony, assists in the construction of MO files, generates data to support crime prevention legislation, and allows them to talk knowledgeably before community groups.

FRAUDULENT AND DISTORTED COMPLAINTS

While most citizens are honest in reporting burglaries, there are others who initiate fake reports. For example, there are situations when a financially troubled individual fabricates an offense, often going so far as to plant physical evidence and create signs of a forced entry. Armed with a police report of large but believable loss, he or she then collects from the insurance company. The fact that an individual does not have insurance should not be automatically taken as an indicator that an offense actually occurred. Schedule A of the Internal Revenue Service's Form 1040 provides for deductions for casualty losses, including thefts.

Perhaps the most widespread and insidious form of distortion involves the legitimately victimized complainant who inflates the value of property taken or overstates the number of things actually taken. False reports, those involving inflation of the value of the property taken, and misrepresentations of the number of articles stolen are not easily detected, although occasionally individuals who seek to create signs of a forced entry on their own homes do so in such a manner as to give themselves away; for example, broken glass at the alleged point of entry will all be on the outside instead of the inside of the residence. Such reports cause the waste of large numbers of investigative hours.

IMPORTANCE OF THE TIME FACTOR

An important aspect of taking burglary reports is attempting to determine when the offense took place. Typically, burglaries are reported from several hours to a number of days after they are committed. Late reporting is largely attributable to the circumstances of businesses closed for the weekend and homeowners away for short trips or extended vacations. Summer communities, populated by people living some distance away who visit their mountain or lakefront vacation homes only intermittently, represent a large problem for the police. Such residences are particularly vulnerable to burglars, who may take all the furniture and dispose of it several months before the offense is even detected. In such instances, the estimate of the time frame in which the offense occurred will of necessity be very broad. Frequently, however, it is possible to identify a range of time during which the perpetrator attacked the premises; this can then be correlated with other data for investigative leads and to include or exclude certain persons as suspects. For example, a person known to employ an MO similar to the one used in a particular offense would be a suspect. If, however, a field interrogation report was initiated on him some distance away from the scene at about the same time as the offense occurred, his presence there would have been virtually impossible, thus excluding him as a suspect. While the example is an unusual occurrence, it is the essence which is important; as the time range in which the offense could have taken place narrows, the more useful other information becomes.

SAFE BURGLARIES

TYPES OF SAFES

Safe burglaries do not occur with any great frequency. Improved designs of commercial buildings have created harder targets, the use of credit and debit cards limit the amount of cash on hand, sophisticated alarm systems are more readily affordable, more stringent employee screening has reduced the flow of information from tipsters, newer safe designs are increasingly "harder nuts to crack," and private police patrols have all contributed to the decline of this type of crime over the past several decades. Yet it is still important for this text to provide information on safe burglaries so that officers can be well-rounded in their knowledge and avoid destroying special types of evidence. Moreover, without such knowledge, officers might take uninformed actions at safe burglary scenes, some of which could be fatal to them.

The term *safe* is often used with little appreciation of the difference between fire-resistant safes and those intended to be burglar-resistant. Victimized business owners will lament, "How could this happen to me, how could they have gotten into my safe?" In fact, what has been compromised is a fire-resistant safe, the construction of which is intended to protect the contents from heat, with a lock system intended for privacy, rather then security.

To the uninitiated, the appearances of safes are very much alike: they are relatively large, have combination locks, and look heavy. Safes, however, can be divided into two distinct classes: the fire-resistant safe and the money chest, which is intended to be burglar-resistant. In general, fire-resistant safes have square or rectangular doors, while money chests have round ones (see Figures 15–4, 15–5, 15–6). There are, however, a few money chests with square or rectangular doors; a check of the manufacturer's label, which is attached to the inside of the door, will resolve any confusion in classifying the safe (see Figure 15–7). The walls of the fire-resistant safe are of comparatively light metal with a thick insulation between the inner and outer walls to protect the contents from heat. The money chest has thick walls and a strong door. Fire-resistant safes are graded by the period of time they can protect their contents from a particular level of heat. In contrast, money chests are classified by the amount of time they can protect their contents from attack by an expert burglar using common hand tools, mechanical tools, torches, and explosives. The fire-resistant safe provides protection from fire but only a minimum amount of security. Security and reasonably good protection from fire are given by the money chest.

ATTACK METHODS FOR SAFES

Knowledge of methods of safe attack is important because it allows the investigator to make judgments about the skill and knowledge of the perpetrator, an important contribution to narrowing the focus of the investigation. The methods covered in this section include the punch, pulling, the peel, the rip, blasting, drilling, burning, manipulation, the pry, and the carry-off. Less commonly encountered methods have been included because in those few instances when they are used, investigators must be prepared to respond properly (see Figure 15–8).

The Punch
Also known as "drifting" and "knob knocking," the *punch* is a popular technique because it requires little skill or knowledge of safe construction. It is used successfully when attacking fire-resistant safes or money chests that do not have relocking devices or spindles constructed to eliminate this approach,

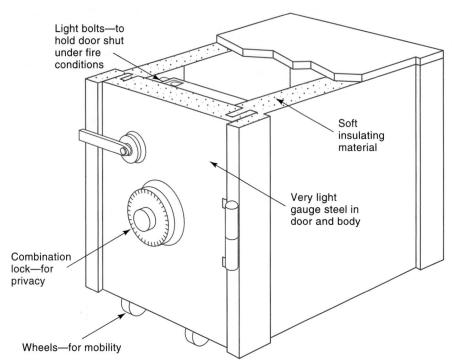

Figure 15–4
Important Features of a Typical Fire-Resistant Safe

Light bolts—to hold door shut under fire conditions

Soft insulating material

Very light gauge steel in door and body

Combination lock—for privacy

Wheels—for mobility

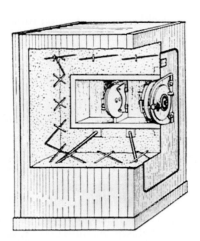

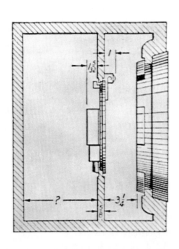

Figure 15–5
Money Chest
The money chest is a burglary-resistant safe; note the round door.

the spindle being an axle that rotates the safe's tumblers or locking wheels to the right or left.[18]

The first step in a punch is removal of the combination dial; this is accomplished by striking it with a heavy hammer, swinging downward parallel to the face of the safe (see Figure 15–9). Alternatively, a cold steel chisel is placed on the top center portion of the combination dial and struck with

a hammer. A drift, or punch, is then placed over the exposed end of the spindle and hit with a hammer (see Figure 15–10), driving the spindle back through the locking case and forcing the locking mechanism out of position so that the door can be opened.[19] The principal disadvantage in using the punch is the noise the hammering makes; occasionally materials such as cloth or strips cut

Figure 15–6
Dual-Unit Money Safe
Round-doored money chest inside of a fire-resistant or records safe. After unexpectedly encountering the interior money chest, the burglars made a minimal, unsuccessful effort to break into it and then fled the premises.

(Courtesy Pittsburgh Police Department)

Figure 15–7
Examples of the Manufacturer's Label
The "TL-15" designation indicates that the safe is burglar-resistant for 15 minutes when attacked by an expert using common hand tools. The Safe Manufacturer's National Association Class C shows that the safe protects records from damage by fire up to 1,700°F for 1 hour.

from inner tubes are used to muffle these sounds; these constitute important physical evidence useful for comparisons, if a suspect is apprehended.

Pulling

The *pull* method is infrequently encountered. The effect of pulling is the same as punching, but the two are differentiated by the direction of force. Punching forces the spindle inward, whereas pulling relies on the use of a type of wheel-puller tool to extract the spindle. Alternatively termed the "drag" or "come along," the pull will work on a few

models of safes with spindles especially constructed to resist punching.

The Peel

The *peel* is a common safe-attack method often employed when a punch attempt fails; it requires a moderate knowledge of safe construction. In general, the amount of damage done to a safe and the perpetrator's skill are inversely correlated: the greater the damage, the less skill possessed. Additionally, if the safe bears evidence of numerous places at which the attacker sought to begin the

Figure 15–8
Safe Recognition Report

The diverse features of a safe are illustrated by this report form; when completed, it provides considerable investigative information.

SAFE RECOGNITION REPORT — CRIME LABORATORY DIVISION/CHICAGO POLICE			DATE OF INVESTIGATION DAY MONTH YEAR	TIME
1. VICTIM	2. ADDRESS OF OCCURRENCE	3. DIST. OCCUR. / 4. R.D. NUMBER	5. CRIME LAB OR P.I. NOTIFIED / 6. PHOTOS TAKEN	7. F.V.I.D. TAKEN

Col A	Col B	Col C	Col D	Col E
8. DRILL SIZE OF HOLE [1]	12. TYPE OF LOCK — COMBINATION [1]	19. LOCATION OF DOOR OPENING — TOP [1]	22C. DIALS (ROUND DOOR) — STANDARD [1]	23C. DIALS — STANDARD [1]
CORE DRILL SIZE OF HOLE [2]	ONE KEY [2]	FRONT [2]	KEY LOCK [2]	KEY LOCK [2]
TORCH SIZE OF HOLE [3]	TWO KEYS [3]	FRONT & BACK [3]	SPY-PROOF [3]	SPY-PROOF [3]
PRY (PRY DOOR OPEN) [4]	COMBINATION AND KEYS [4]	TOP & FRONT [4]	DIAL AND HANDLE COMBINED [4]	DIAL AND HANDLE COMBINED [4]
PEEL (PEEL OFF OUTSIDE METAL) [5]	RELOCKING [5]	OTHER [5]	OTHER [5] (SKETCH ON BACK)	OTHER [5] (SKETCH ON BACK)
PUNCH (DIAL KNOCKED OFF SPINDLE PUNCH OUT OF CASE) [6]	TIME DELAY [6]	20. NUMBER OF DOORS	22D. HANDLES (ROUND DOOR) — ROUND TAPER [1]	23D. HANDLES — ROUND TAPER [1]
CHOP (HOLE CHOPPED IN SAFE) [7]	OTHER [7]	21. NUMBER OPENED	FLAT TAPER [2]	FLAT TAPER [2]
NO FORCE [8]	13. MFR MODEL SERIES	ROUND DOOR SAFE DATA:	RIB TAPER [3]	RIB TAPER [3]
REMOVED [9]	14. UNDERWRITERS LABELS	22. LOCATION OF DOOR*	T-HANDLE [4] — OTHER (SKETCH ON BACK)	T-HANDLE [4]
OTHER [10]	15. INSTALLATION — FREE STANDING [1]	22A. HINGES — RIGHT SIDE [1]	SQUARE OR RECTANGULAR DOOR SAFE DATA:	OTHER [5]
9. POINT OF ATTACK (MEASURE FROM TOP AND FROM LEFT SIDE) ___ X ___	EMBEDDED IN WALL [2]	LEFT SIDE [2]	23. LOCATION OF DOOR*	23E. CORNERS ON SAFE — ROUNDED [1]
10. ALARMS (AREA OF SAFE) YES NO — PROTECTING SAFE	EMBEDDED IN FLOOR [3]	POST HINGE [3]	23A. HINGES — RIGHT SIDE [1]	SQUARE [2]
ON SAFE — YES NO	FASTENED TO WALL [4]	HORSE SHOE HINGE [4]	LEFT SIDE [2]	OTHER [3] (SKETCH ON BACK)
11. TYPE OF SAFE — MONEY CHEST (ROUND DOOR) [1]	FASTENED TO FLOOR [5]	RING HINGE [5]	SURFACE MOUNTED [3]	23F. CORNERS ON DOOR — ROUNDED [1]
FIRE RESISTANT (SQUARE OR RECT. DOOR) [2]	WALL MOUNTED [6]	OTHER [6] (SKETCH ON BACK)	SURFACE MOUNTED ON DOOR PART OF SAFE [4]	SQUARE [2]
COMBINATION (MONEY AND FIRE) (MAKE INDIVIDUAL REPORTS) [3]	OTHER [7]	22B. HINGE PINS HEADS — FLAT [1]	SURFACE MOUNTED ON SAFE PART OF DOOR [5]	OTHER [3] (SKETCH ON BACK)
VAULT (WALK-IN-SAFE) [4]	16. EXTERIOR DIMENSIONS — HIGH / WIDE / DEEP	BALL [2]	OTHER [6] (SKETCHES ON BACK)	23G. WHEELS — FIXED-MOVE LEFT OR RIGHT [1]
INSULATED FILE [5]	17. INTERIOR DIMENSIONS — HIGH / WIDE / THICKNESS	ACORN [3]	23B. HINGE PINS HEADS — FLAT [1]	FIXED-MOVE FRONT OR BACK [2]
ROTARY DEPOSITORY [6]	18. DIMENSIONS OF ROUND DOOR — DIAMETER / THICKNESS	OTHER [4] (SKETCH ON BACK)	BALL [2]	SWIVEL FRONT AND BACK [3]
FLOOR SAFE [7]	DIMENSIONS OF RECT. DOOR — HIGH / WIDE / DEEP		ACORN [3]	OTHER [4]
OTHER [8]		*MEASURE FROM TOP TO TOP OF DOOR AND FROM LEFT SIDE TO LEFT EDGE OF DOOR	OTHER [4] (SKETCH ON BACK)	

peel, then a less knowledgeable perpetrator is suggested (see Figures 15–11 and 15–12).

Typically, the initial move in a peel is to gain some small grip on the door of the safe so the metal sheet can be peeled away to expose the bolt system or locking mechanism, either of which may then be compromised and entry to the safe gained. Often the peel will begin at the upper left-hand corner of the safe, as it is viewed from the front, and the metal face will be curled toward the lower right corner. A sectional jimmy, made from several lengths of automobile axles that are bolted together at the scene, may be used for the peeling.

Several methods may be used to create the opening where the peel begins: the safe door may be crudely pounded; cold steel chisels and metal wedges may be used; a hole may be drilled—ordinarily about ¾ inch in diameter—or an acetylene torch may be employed. When simple pounding is used, the door hinges will often be the attack point, and when they are successfully struck, the torque may force the door to curl. Even if the door does not curl, removal of the hinges exposes the door edge so the peel is still possible. Once the door edge is exposed, a hammer and cold chisel can be used to pop the rivets or spot welds holding the metal plate to the door frame.

Old models of fire-resistant safes are most successfully attacked using this method, but burglar-resistant safes cannot be compromised with a peel. Presently, most safe manufacturers use seam welds to compensate for the inadequacies of rivets or spot welds.

Figure 15–9
An Attempted Punch

Note the dial on the floor. Occasionally a punch will be found in this position when it was slightly too large, indicating an inexperienced safe burglar.

(Courtesy Tampa Police Department)

The Rip

The terms "peel" and "rip" are sometimes erroneously used synonymously. While the peel curls the metal backward to gain access to the bolt system and locking mechanism, the *rip* uses crude force to penetrate the metal face of the safe (see Figure 15–13). The "chop," occasionally viewed as an entirely separate attack method, is actually a rip applied to the bottom of the safe until a hole is made large enough to insert a hand to remove the contents. In its most elementary form, a rip attack on the bottom of a safe—its weakest point, especially in older fire-resistant models—is accomplished with an axe.

Because of the degree of force required, rips often leave a great deal of physical evidence, including shoe impressions in safe insulation and broken edges from tools. The rip or chop attack will not succeed with burglar-resistant safes.

Blasting

Blasting, or "soup jobs"—using explosives to attack a safe—was once popular but has almost disappeared. Its disappearance is attributed to the more severe penalties associated with burglaries committed while carrying explosives, the inherent danger to the safe-man, the noise as compared to other methods, and the stringent federal penalties for the sale, possession, use, transportation, or manufacture of explosives for illegal uses. Blasting can compromise both fire- and burglar-resistant safes.[20]

In those rare instances when the investigator does encounter suspected or known explosives at the scene, extreme caution must be used to avoid accidental detonation. In such situations the following actions should be taken:

- Do not move or touch the material known or believed to be explosives.
- Exclude all persons from the scene until qualified ordnance personnel arrive.
- Evacuate the building and immediate area.
- Open all windows and doors.
- Cease all radio transmissions from portable radios within 300 feet and from mobile radios within 500 feet of the explosives.
- Do not turn lights on or off in the room in which the explosives are located or in adjacent rooms.
- Do not change the settings on thermostats, window air conditioners, or appliances.
- If photographs are necessary, do not use the flash on the camera until the material is examined by ordnance personnel.[21]

Drilling

Burglar-resistant safes are most successfully attacked using a high-torque drill equipped with diamond- or carbide-tipped bits. Successfully employed drilling implies a thorough knowledge of safe construction and considerable skill. Drilling requires precision, and perpetrators, after carefully measuring and marking the appropriate attack points, will often attach the drill to a chain, or bolt-mount onto the safe a drill attached to a jig, to

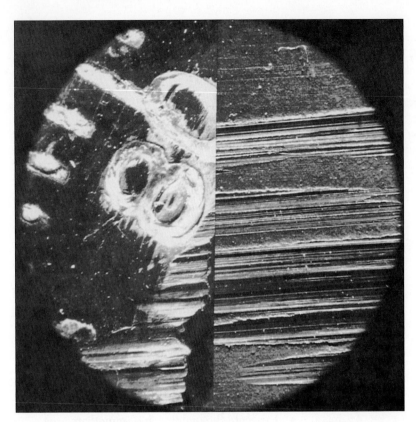

Figure 15-10
Chisel marks
The striae on the left were created when a hammer was used to strike a cold chisel positioned at the center top of the combination dial as the first step in a punch. The striae on the right were made by the laboratory examiner using the chisel after it was seized from the suspect's custody.

steady their aim (see Figure 15–14). Even the most skilled safe-man will occasionally break bits while drilling, and these should be seized as evidence. Moreover, the drill bit, as illustrated in Figure 15–15, will leave microscopic striae on the metal shavings, which must also be collected, as individual class evidence.

A variant of drilling involves the use of a cystoscope. The *cystoscope* is a medical instrument about ⅛ inch in diameter that has its own light source and permits examination of confined areas. Occasionally safe burglars will drill a hole, insert the cystoscope, and manipulate the lock's tumblers.

The *core drill* is a hollow tube that removes a solid plug from the safe of sufficient size for the safe-man to reach inside and take the safe's contents (see Figures 15–16 and 15–17). Most frequently, the door, which is most resistant, will not be attacked, the bottom or sides being preferred. Because of the ease with which core drill bits break, the drill will be attached to the safe in one of the manners previously described. If a safe-man does not have a core drill, but favors that technique, he may repeatedly drill in the same area using a high-torque drill with a large bit until a hand-size hole is made.

Burning

Once on the wane, *burning*—the use of an acetylene torch—is becoming more common and may compromise both fire- and burglar-resistant safes. One reason for the increase in the popularity of burning is the availability of smaller, easily portable, concealable oxygen and acetylene tanks, as illustrated in Figure 15–18. In examining burning jobs, investigators must make two important determinations:

First, how much does the safe-man know about the use of the torch? Second, how much knowledge of safe construction does the attack demonstrate? A skilled torch operator takes pride in his cuts, which are usually straight and clean. Unskilled torch operators may make rough, uneven cuts, start a fire by improper running of the slag, or try to

Figure 15–11
A Peel Preceded by an
Unsuccessful Punch
Note the combination dial on the floor
and the pry marks on the exposed
locking bar.

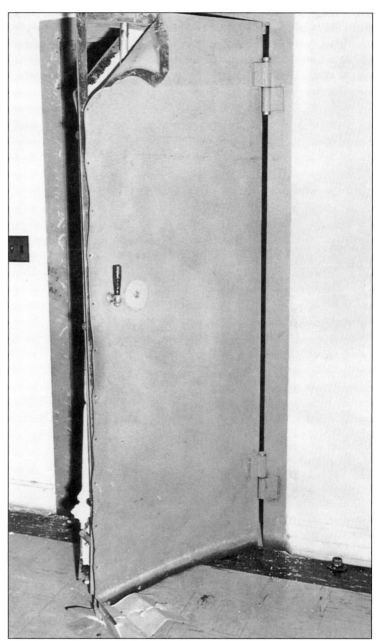

(Courtesy Tampa Police Department)

cut with the improper oxygen-acetylene mixture [see Figure 15–19]. The last is indicated by black soot in the area of the attempted burn.[22]

As a rule, the use of burning on a fire-resistant safe indicates a novice who went to more trouble than was necessary and applied a more advanced technique than was required. Samples of the *slag*—the now-cooled metal that ran off the safe while the burning was in progress—must be seized as evidence for comparison if a suspect is apprehended. While perpetrators almost invariably wear gloves when burning, they occasionally roll their sleeves up and may sustain spot burns from the molten slag. Suspects with such marks should be carefully

Figure 15–12
Indication of a Lack of Skill
The extensive damage created by this peel suggests a lack of skill and knowledge of safe construction by the perpetrator.

(Courtesy Detroit Police Department)

investigated, particularly if their occupation or unverified statements do not explain the presence of the burns.

Manipulation
Combination manipulation involves such extraordinary sensitivity that one can hear or feel the tumblers falling into position, so that the safe can be opened. Genuine manipulation of a safe's combination is such a rarity that few investigators will ever encounter it, although popular depictions give it life in the public's mind. Alleged manipulations usually prove to have involved an unlocked safe, the cooperation of a dishonest employee, the leaving of the combination in a place so obvious that the perpetrator found it, or an employee's dialing two of the three numbers after closing the safe, in order to open it more rapidly next time. In this last instance, to open the safe's door the burglar needs only to turn the dial slowly until the third number is found.

The Pry
An amateurish method that can be used to compromise fire-resistant, but not burglar-resistant,

safes is the *pry*. It simply involves creating a large enough gap so that the door can be pried open by someone employing a jimmy-type tool. The gap may be made by pounding the safe (which may also open it), by tightening a logging chain around the safe using a hydraulic jack, or by any of a number of other methods (see Figure 15–20).

The Carry-Off
The *carry-off* is not strictly a method of attack. Rather, it involves the removal of a safe—most often a fire-resistant one—to a location where it can be compromised at the burglar's leisure using any of the methods previously described. Often carry-offs will be attacked, compromised, and left in isolated wooded areas. In such instances there is an excellent opportunity to locate physical evidence, particularly shoe and tire impressions.

SAFE INSULATION AS EVIDENCE
Whenever an attack on a safe has exposed the safe insulation, samples should be collected as evidence. Depending on circumstances, particles of insulation may be found on perpetrators' tools, adhering to their clothing, under their fingernails, in their shoes, pants cuffs, or pockets, on the floormat of their car, or embedded in their shoes. In a number of cases safe insulation has been found in the nail holes of shoe heels several weeks after the commission of the offense.

It is the variation among insulations that makes them valuable as class evidence. Many safes made prior to 1930 contain an insulation of natural cement made by burning to a powder certain clay-like limestones, used without gravel or cement only as safe insulation. A number of more recently made safes use an insulation of diatomaceous earth, portland cement, and vermiculite mica, a combination used only in safe insulation. Many brands of safes contain distinctive insulation, samples of which are kept in the FBI laboratory files. It is, therefore, possible to compare insulation found on a suspect's tools or person with those in the file and name the make of safe from which it came. Some safe manufacturers use material for insulation, such as gypsum mixed with wood chips, which is not peculiar to safe insulation. In such instances, however, laboratory examination can establish consistency, or the lack thereof, between insulation samples from the scene and the suspect.

Figure 15–13
A Rip Attack
Note the hammer and exposed insulation on the floor.

As a final note on the value of safe insulation as evidence, establishing intent is important in charging a person with possession of burglary tools. Tools found with what can be conclusively established as safe insulation on them may be the basis for providing that intent.

DIALOGUE WITH A SAFE BURGLAR

The following dialogue took place with a 23-year-old convicted safe burglar serving a sentence in a state penitentiary. Although he did not regard his

Figure 15–14
Attempted Drilling with a
Jig-Mounted Drill

particular skill as unusual, he demonstrated it by opening, through the use of a truck tire iron, a large fire-resistant safe in only 6 minutes:

Q: Where do you get your tools?

A: I buy them at stores such as Sears. That way, you have the most suitable tools for the job.

Q: Where do you obtain tanks for burning a safe?

A: We steal them or go to rental companies. By doing it that way we can get the best equipment, and after the job, return it. Obviously, it's best not to use your name.

Q: Do you use your own car for carry-off jobs?

A: No. We buy an old junker, use it on the job, and then sell it a day or two later. We've gotten our money out of it.

Q: How do you identify a business to hit?

A: We try to avoid large shopping centers; they are patrolled more often. We determine the volume of business, the method of transporting money to the bank, look for alarm devices, closing hours, and frequency of patrol. For example, if the business employs an armored car service, we watch the time of pickup, the business volume for the remainder of the day after the pickup, and the business that the store will be prepared to handle on the following day prior to the armored car pickup. We determine if the owner or store manager is bonded for transporting monies to a night deposit box at the bank. We observe the police officer, the time sequence of patrol, whether or not there is a foot officer in the area, and if so, we avoid the business. Casing generally requires ten days to two weeks.

Q: How is entry gained?

A: It depends on the building itself and such things as alarm devices and barred windows. If entry is

Figure 15–15
Marks on Drill Bit Shavings
Comparison of striae on drill-bit shavings found at the scene of a safe burglary with those obtained in the laboratory after the drill and bit were seized from the suspect's custody.

Figure 15–16
Core Drill
A core drill in a specially constructed box to muffle the noise of its operation.

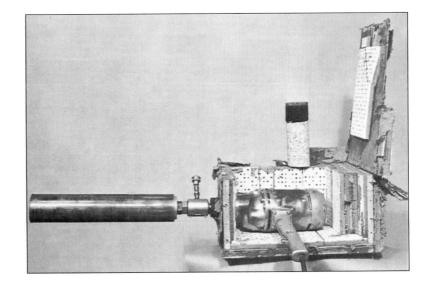

gained through the roof, we attach ropes to exhaust pipes and climb down, generally into a small hallway. On occasion, a building next door is entered, and we break through a wall. If the door is secured by use of a padlock, entry is fairly simple. We take a second padlock, break

Figure 15–17
Core Drill Attack on a Money Chest

Figure 15–18
Portable Oxygen-Acetylene Units

Figure 15-19
A Crude Attempt at Burning a Money Chest

Note the bottom left of the door area, where a peel attempt was abandoned. The techniques and cuts suggest lack of knowledge. The burning unit was taken in a previous burglary of a hardware store.

(Courtesy Tampa Police Department)

the original lock off, enter the building, unlock a window, climb out, replace the lock, climb back through the window, and close it.

Q: How does a lookout system operate?

A: We might have lookouts with cell phones in the area. We use cell phones to . . . except you got to be real careful with them because they keep such good records.

Q: How is the time selected to make a break?

A: Generally, the best times are between 10 and 12 o'clock in the evening, after the business closes. At that time, people are on the street so that we do not attract any unnecessary attention. Also, the on-duty policeman has almost worked a complete tour of duty and is anxious to get off work. He doesn't check the buildings,

Figure 15–20
Express-Type Fire-Resistant Safe Compromised by Pry Attack
Note the bent hinges and the pry marks on the edge of the safe.

(Courtesy Tampa Police Department)

and the first thing the oncoming police officer does is stop for a cup of coffee.

Q: How do you learn about how a safe is constructed?

A: These insurance companies, in describing rates to businesses, list various types of safes, explain their operation, so we just pick up a copy of these books. We also get catalogues from safe companies.

Q: Do you carry a gun?

A: No. Very few safe burglars carry a gun. They have no need for it. They are operating on the assumption that their plans have been made, that they are foolproof, and the gun would be excess weight—it could get you in trouble.

Q: What type of lighting do you use?

A: If we are operating in a darkened building, we would need light, which might be noticeable from outside. So we prefer a business that leaves night lights on.

Q: How do you cope with tear gas in a safe?

A: Most of the literature on safes indicates that tear gas is used, so we just assume it is in all of them, and go at it. You can work for a while before it bothers you. Occasionally, you can use an exhaust fan to draw it away.

Q: On occasion, the locking device and the tumblers from the safe have been found carefully laid out on the floor. What is the reason for that?

A: A new man will go with us, and we try to show him what makes those things work.

RESIDENTIAL BURGLARY

Earlier in this chapter it was noted that residential burglaries were primarily committed during the day, with the front door being the point of attack. Black homeowners are victimized at a higher rate than any other group.[23] The younger the head of a household is, the more likely that the residence will be burglarized.[24] As shown in Table 15–1, the losses associated with residential burglaries are not

Table 15-1
Home Burglary Victimizations by Amount of Loss

Amount of Loss	Percentage of Burglaries
No loss:	3.5%
Less than $50	16.0
$50–$99	9.2
$100–$249	16.3
$250–$499	11.2
$500–$999	10.0
$1,000 or more	19.9
Not known/not available	13.9

Source: Bureau of Justice Statistics, *Criminal Victimization in the United States–1994* (Washington, D.C.: U.S. Department of Justice, 1997) p. 75, table 83.

intrinsically significant. However, to many households even relatively small losses are devastating. Moreover, when you consider the residual feelings of the victims, there is another type of loss: they feel as though their privacy has been violated. They often struggle psychologically afterward to regain a sense of security in their own homes.

Many burglars are amateurs in the sense that even though they may commit the crime numerous times, they often act on impulse, driven by the need to have money:

Usually when I get in my car and drive around I'm thinking, I don't have any money, so what is my means for money? All of a sudden I'll just take a glance and say, there it is, there's the house! . . . Then I get the feelin', that very moment that I'm moving then.[25]

Some burglars report that "legitimate" financial emergencies are the only reason they resort to breaking in:

Usually what I'll do is a burglary [or a couple of them] if I have to . . . helps get me over the rough spot until I can get it straightened out. Once I get it straightened out, I just go with the flow until I hit a rough spot where I need the money again . . . The only time I would go and commit a burglary is if I needed money at that point in time. That would be strictly to pay light bill, gas bill, rent.[26]

While there are clearly such cases, burglaries are more often committed for other reasons:

I might find somebody with some good crack . . . while I'm high I say damn I want me some more of that good shit. Go knock a place off, make some more money, go buy some more dope.[27]

I use the burglary money for gifts for young ladies— flowers or negligee or somethin'. Some shoes . . . put them shoes on, them pumps . . . then watch 'em dance nude.[28]

See I go steal money and go buy me some clothes . . . See, I like to look good. I likes to dress . . . own only one pair of blue jeans 'cause I like to dress [well].[29]

Burglary is excitin' . . . it's just a thrill to going in undetected and walking out with all their shit . . . like going on a treasure hunt.[30]

From these vignettes, it can be seen that burglars tend to commit their crimes for four broad reasons: (1) keeping themselves and their families fed, clothed, and sheltered, (2) keeping the party going, (3) keeping up "appearances" so that they can look better off financially than they are, and (4) keeping adventure in their lives.[31]

While amateur burglars act on impulse, the more professional burglars are, the less likely they are to take such chances. They develop information on their own or pay tipsters for it. They may simply cruise well-to-do neighborhoods looking for opportunities or follow expensive cars to their homes. Once they have identified a preliminary target, they begin a "work-up," watching the house until they have become familiar with the people who live there, their daily routines, the absence or presence of alarms and dogs, views of possible attack points from other homes in the area, and frequency of private and public police patrols. One way of developing information on their own is simply to read the newspapers. Wedding announcements often reveal that a couple will honeymoon in another city or country and then reside in whatever community. With a little effort, burglars can often find out the actual address and burglarize the home, stealing wedding gifts and other items, while the victimized couple are blissfully enjoying their honeymoon. Other types of announcements that might provide similar opportunities include funeral arrangements and gala charity events or parties, which many wealthy people can be expected to attend. Butlers and maids can get lists of the people attending such events. Tipsters—sometimes called "spotters," "fingermen," "noses," or "setup people,"—are another source of information that can be used in selecting homes for burglaries. For example, insiders at cruise ship operations can provide passenger lists. Medical personnel know when patients will be in their offices for appointments. Many occupations enter numerous homes legitimately, such as telephone installers and flower delivery workers, and have the chance to size up opportunities. Coworkers know when their bosses are going on vacation. Insurance office personnel know which homes' contents have been heavily insured and which may have special riders attached for silverware or other valuables. Armed with such information, professional burglars reduce the risk of apprehension and increase the probability of "making a nice haul."

Homes are burglarized during the day because that's when the occupants are most likely to be gone—working, attending school, or running errands. The same generally holds true with many neighbors, who might otherwise witness the attack. Burglars do not want to attract attention to themselves, but they also do not want a confrontation with an occupant. If they have learned the home's telephone number, they will call to see if anyone is there. While an answering machine encourages some burglars, it makes others leery of going ahead, fearing that someone is home and using the machine to screen the calls. Alarms and deadbolt locks are a deterrent to amateur burglars but not to more professional ones. Residential burglars usually do not have to carry an assortment of tools because so many targets are "soft." Often they carry little other than workman's gloves and a large screwdriver or small prybar. If they cannot easily effect entry at the front door, they will try to enter through the garage—which is ideal because they are out of sight—or a rear window. Most home burglars go straight to the bedroom because that's where most people keep small valuables, such as jewelry, cash, furs, and guns. The master bathroom is also where most people keep their prescription drugs. As their experience builds up, burglars will begin to check the "clever" places

where people hide their valuables, including in freezer compartments and behind towels in linen closets. If they have an accomplice, they will call him or her to bring the vehicle into which televisions, VCRs, stereo systems, tools, and other valuables are loaded. Table 15–2 shows the seven types of property most commonly taken in burglaries.

TRACING AND RECOVERING STOLEN PROPERTY

Investigators attempt to recover stolen property through a variety of techniques. Once individual suspects are identified and arrested, legal searches pursuant to the arrest and/or a search warrant are carried out in the hope that property taken in a burglary may be found. Pawn shop records are monitored, flea markets are observed for visits of known and active burglars or for booths operated by them, and classified advertisements in newspapers are checked. As discussed more fully in the next chapter, efforts are made to identify the receivers of stolen property, or "fences," who act as go-betweens for the actual thieves and those who purchase the property. The police enjoy significant success in disrupting stolen-property markets and in identifying burglars and other types of thieves by going undercover and posing as illegal receivers of stolen property in "sting" operations. Additionally, the National Crime Information Center (NCIC) and complementary state and local computer systems provide a means of checking to see if property is stolen.

One of the principal difficulties police departments encounter when they seek the assistance of other police departments or merchants in recovering stolen jewelry is providing them with an accurate description of the stolen pieces. Members of one police department, investigating a burglary-homicide involving a female victim, faced such a problem. During their investigation of this crime, they learned from the victim's daughter that five pieces of jewelry could not be located in the house and were quite likely stolen by the murderer. The police department was given a verbal description of the jewelry by the victim's daughter and prepared a crime information bulletin for distribution to area

Table 15–2
Property Most Frequently Taken from Residences

Type of Property	Percent of Burglaries
Cash	6.8%
Purse, wallet, credit cards	2.3
Vehicles or parts (including bicycles)	5.5
Household furnishings	11.2
Portable electronics, photography gear, jewelry, clothing	27.3
Firearms	1.8
Tools, machinery	6.6
Total	61.5%

Source: Bureau of Justice Statistics, *Criminal Victimization in the United States–1994* (Washington, D.C.: U.S. Department of Justice, 1997) p. 77.

police departments, pawnshops, and jewelry stores. Prior to its distribution, there was general agreement among the detectives who were investigating this crime that the bulletin would be of limited value without sketches or photos of the stolen jewelry. With the cooperation of a large jewelry store in their area, they were able to locate a photograph of a piece of jewelry that was identical to one of the pieces stolen. In addition, with the assistance of the victim's daughter, an artist was able to sketch a color facsimile of the other stolen pieces. Color prints were then made of the original photograph provided by the jewelry store and the artist's color facsimiles; these were incorporated into the police bulletin. The bulletins were then distributed to area police departments, pawnshops, and jewelry stores.

Within 24 hours, the police recovered all of the jewelry and arrested and charged a suspect. The first break in the case came when the suspect pawned all the stolen pieces in four different pawnshops in two nearby cities. The pawnshop dealers had recognized the jewelry from the police department's bulletin.

The two cities in which these pawnshops were located had ordinances that required all persons pawning items to show identification. The suspect provided each pawnshop dealer with identification that gave his correct name and address. He was arrested several hours later after pawning jewelry and was charged with not only the murder of the victim in this case but also two other murders that had been committed in similar cases.

As a final note, one of the most vexing and troublesome issues in tracing and recovering stolen property has to do with the person who just may actually have been an innocent and unknowing purchaser of stolen goods. Among the indications of a lack of good faith by the purchaser are (1) buying at prices below a "good bargain"; (2) purchasing from people who are unknown to them and whom they "don't know how to reach"; (3) taking delivery of the merchandise under unusual conditions or at unusual times; (4) accepting the property without a sales receipt; (5) buying property when its identifying numbers have been removed or apparently altered or when there are unusual identifying stickers such as state inventory numbers; and (6) having a past history of receiving stolen goods.

THE INVESTIGATOR'S CRIME PREVENTION ROLE

While at the scene of a burglary, investigators should tell those victimized the precautions they can take to decrease the likelihood of their being "hit" again.

REDUCING THE RISK OF RESIDENTIAL BURGLARY

To protect their residences, occupants should do the following things when they are on vacation or otherwise away:

1. Stop delivery of mail and newspapers or arrange for a neighbor to pick them up daily.

2. Arrange for a special watch on their premises by patrol officers.

3. Use timers to turn on lights and radios at various times to make it look like the residence is occupied.

4. Ask reliable neighbors to immediately report any suspicious activity to the police.

5. Ask a trusted neighbor to come over occasionally and change the position of drapes, blinds, and other things.

6. Put up "Beware of Dog" signs, or if they really have a dog, ask someone to take care of it in the home whenever feasible.

For day-to-day security, occupants can take other actions that will help them avoid being a burglary victim or, if they are victimized, will help to reduce their losses:

1. Create an uninviting target: use motion-sensor lights, purchase an alarm system, use dead-bolt locks on solid doors mounted in steel frames; and place locks on windows.

2. If possible, avoid placing valuables where they can be seen through windows.

3. Cut plants around doors and windows low so that burglars can't conceal themselves while breaking in.

4. Grow thorny plants around places where someone might attempt to force an entry.

5. Don't leave ladders or tools laying around in the yard or clothes on an outside line—a thief who initially may have the thought of just taking them will see the greater opportunity they create.

6. Don't tell strangers about your comings and goings.

7. Don't allow strangers to use your telephone, and don't give your correct number to anyone who alleges calling by mistake; instead, ask caller who he or she was trying to reach at what number. Baby-sitters and children should be instructed to do the same thing.

8. Don't keep spare keys in the usual places—under the mat, over the door, and in flower pots. Burglars know these places.

9. Don't go out to run a quick errand without locking all doors, including garage doors.

10. Engrave valuables with special identifying numbers. Alternatively, mark them with small translucent decals that have your special identification data on them. These microdots are about the size of a speck of pepper and virtually invisible to the naked eye.

11. Keep strong control over your keys. It may be helpful to leave them for service workers or give them to maids, but at the cost of greater risk exposure.

12. Don't leave notes on the door saying where you have gone or when you will be back.

13. Get to know your neighbors; they'll be more likely to respond faithfully to requests to "watch my place while I'm gone."

14. When new snow is on the ground, back out of your driveway and pull back in several times; do the same walking in and out of your door. This makes it harder for burglars to figure out if you are home.

REDUCING THE RISK OF COMMERCIAL BURGLARY

Many of the suggestions for preventing residential burglaries also apply to businesses. Operators of businesses should be told to prevent easy access to their roofs by securing all vents and roof openings, to use security-providing locks, frames, and doors properly; to light the exterior of the building; to use, if feasible, an alarm system and surveillance camera; to use a money chest rather than a fire-resistant safe; and to set the safe in concrete in open view at a place that can be lighted at night. Completion of the office security checklist in Figure 15–21 will serve two purposes: it will provide the owners with useful information about how to improve their security, and it may provide important investigative leads, particularly if a surreptitious entry is involved.

Figure 15–21
Sample Office Security Checklist

	Yes	No
1. Do you restrict office keys to those who actually need them?	☐	☐
2. Do you keep complete, up-to-date records of the disposition of all office keys?	☐	☐
3. Do you have adequate procedures for collecting keys from terminated employees?	☐	☐
4. Do you restrict duplication of office keys, except for those specifically ordered by you in writing?	☐	☐
5. Do you require that all keys be marked "Do not duplicate" to prevent legitimate locksmiths from making copies without your knowledge?	☐	☐
6. Have you established a rule that keys must not be left unguarded on desks or cabinets, and do you enforce that rule?	☐	☐
7. Do you require that filing-cabinet keys be removed from locks and placed in a secure location after opening cabinets in the morning?	☐	☐
8. Do you have procedures which prevent unauthorized personnel from reporting a "lost key" and receiving a "replacement"?	☐	☐
9. Do you have some responsible person in charge of issuing all keys?	☐	☐
10. Are all keys systematically stored in a secured wall cabinet of either your own design or from a commercial key-control system?	☐	☐
11. Do you keep a record showing issuance and return of every key, including name of person, date, and time?	☐	☐
12. Do you use telephone locks or access codes to prevent unauthorized calls when the office is unattended?	☐	☐
13. Do you provide at least one lockable drawer in every secretary's desk to protect personal effects?	☐	☐
14. Do you have at least one filing cabinet secured with an auxiliary locking bar so that you can keep business secrets under better protection?	☐	☐
15. Do you leave a night light on?	☐	☐
16. Do you record all equipment serial numbers and file them in a safe place to maintain correct identification in the event of theft or destruction by fire?	☐	☐

(Courtesy Bolen Industries, Hackensack, New Jersey, with modification)

Questions

1. Describe the dimensions of the crime of burglary.
2. What is the profile of those arrested for burglary?
3. How are professional and amateur burglars distinguished?
4. What are the elements of the crime of burglary?
5. What considerations are important in approaching the scene of a burglary?
6. In the residential burglary section it is noted that black homeowners and younger people are victimized more frequently. What are some possible explanations for this?
7. How are fire-resistant safes and money chests differentiated?
8. What are "knob knocking" and the "drag"?
9. What special actions are required if there has been a "soup job"?
10. What is the method most likely to succeed when attacking a burglar-resistant safe?

Figure 15–21
Sample Office Security Checklist *(Continued)*

	Yes	No
17. Do you shred all important papers before discarding in wastebaskets?	☐	☐
18. Do you lock briefcases and attaché cases containing important papers in closets or lockers when not in use?	☐	☐
19. Do you insist on identification from repairmen who come to do work in your office?	☐	☐
20. Do you deposit incoming checks and cash each day so that you do not keep large sums in the office overnight?	☐	☐
21. Do you clear all desks of important papers every night and place them in locked fireproof safes or cabinets?	☐	☐
22. Do you frequently change the combination of your safe to prevent anyone from memorizing it or passing it on to a confederate?	☐	☐
23. When working alone in the office at night, do you set the front door lock to prevent anyone else from getting in?	☐	☐
24. Do you have the police and fire department telephone numbers posted and handy?	☐	☐
25. Do you check to see that no one remains in hiding behind you at night if you are the last to leave the office?	☐	☐
26. Are all windows, transoms, and ventilators properly protected?	☐	☐
27. Do you double check to see that all windows and doors are securely locked before you leave?	☐	☐
28. Are all doors leading to the office secured by heavy-duty, double cylinder, dead bolt locks?	☐	☐
29. If your office is equipped with a burglar alarm system or protected by a guard service, do you make sure the alarm equipment is set properly each night?	☐	☐
30. Do you have a periodic security review by a qualified security expert or locksmith?	☐	☐
31. Are computer access codes and/or selected files password protected on a need-to-know basis?	☐	☐
32. Are all computer disks and tapes containing sensitive, client, or secret information maintained under controlled conditions during the day and locked securely at night?	☐	☐

11. How do burglars get their information?

12. With respect to the possible illegal receiving of stolen property, what are some indicators of the absence of good-faith purchasing?

13. What measures can homeowners and business operators take to lessen their chances of being burglarized?

Notes

1. Federal Bureau of Investigation, *Crime in the United States, 1997* (Washington, D.C.: Government Printing Office, 1998), p. 6.

2. Ibid., p. 41.

3. Ibid.

4. Ibid.

5. Ibid.

6. Ibid., p. 44

7. Mildrade Cherfils, Associated Press, "Jury Convicts 'Spiderman,'" http://www.canoe.ca/TopStories/Spiderman_dec8.html, December 8, 1998.

8. Paulo Lima, staff writer, "The *Bergen Record* Online," http://www.bergen.com/bse/trainrob199811281.htm, November 28, 1998.

9. Richard A. Ballezza, "YACs Crime Groups," *FBI Law Enforcement Bulletin*, November 1998, Vol. 67, No. 11, pp. 7–12, is the source of information for this section on YACs.

10. Sandra Gonzales, "Ex-Cop Admits Burglary Charges," *San Jose Mercury News*, December 8, 1998.

11. Marvine Howe, "Anger Mixed with Sorrow for Organist Suspected in Church Burglaries," *New York Times*, January 6, 1992, p. B4.

12. FBI, *Crime in the United States*, p. 44.

13. Ibid., p. 44. For additional information on burglary offenders, see Richard T. Wright and Scott Decker, *Burglars on the Job* (Boston: Northeastern University Press, 1994).

14. " 'Masterpiece' Burglary Yields 'Mother Lode,'" *Dallas* (Texas) *Morning News*, March 12, 1980, p. 8A.

15. "Jewel Burglars Get $2 Million," *Atlanta Journal*, September 9, 1980, p. 7A.

16. Richard Perez-Pena, "3 Arrests Hit Burglary Ring in Manhattan," *New York Times*, November 14, 1992, pp. 21-22.

17. "Loot Jams Va. Home of Alleged Superthief," *Atlanta Constitution*, December 16, 1980, p. 20D.

18. Donald G. Webb, *Investigation of Safe and Money Chest Burglary* (Springfield, Ill.: Charles C. Thomas, 1975), p. 42.

19. Ibid.

20. Ibid., p. 62.

21. See Kentucky State Police, General Order OM-C-7, January 1, 1990.

22. Webb, *Investigation of Safe and Money Chest Burglary*, p. 58.

23. Bureau of Justice Statistics, *Criminal Victimization in the United States—1994* (Washington, D.C.: National Institute of Justice), p. 21, table 16.

24. Ibid., p. 22, table 19.

25. Wright and Decker, *Burglars on the Job*, p. 36.

26. Ibid., p. 37.

27. Ibid., p. 39.

28. Ibid., pp. 41–42.

29. Ibid., p. 43.

30. Ibid., p. 58.

31. Ibid., pp. 38, 58, with some restatement.

S I X T E E N

Larceny Offenses

CHAPTER OUTLINE

Investigative Procedure 424

Credit Card Fraud 425

Check Fraud 427

Cellular Phone Cloning 431

Receiving Stolen Property 434

Shoplifting 437

Confidence Games 440

White-Collar Crime 442

Fraudulent Use of Social Security Numbers 451

The Looting of Archaeolgical Sites 453

Questions 461

Notes 462

INTRODUCTION

The legal definition of *larceny* contains five essential elements: (1) taking and (2) carrying away (3) personal property (4) of another (5) with the intent to deprive permanently.[1] Many criminal offenses may be classified under the general heading of larceny.

In this chapter we discuss some of the most frequently encountered types of larceny: fraud by credit card and check; cellular phone cloning; buying, receiving, and distributing stolen property; shoplifting; and confidence games. The chapter also discusses Ponzi schemes, money laundering, the fraudulent use of Social Security numbers, and the looting of archaeological sites.

A look at the FBI Uniform Crime Reports quickly shows that the dollar loss suffered by the American public from larceny is enormous and makes up the largest volume of offenses reported by local law enforcement agencies to the FBI. Frequently, the dollar loss is directed back to consumers in the form of higher prices. Yet, except for cases that involve large sums of money or items of substantial value, larceny tends not to generate the same public interest as certain other crimes.

INVESTIGATIVE PROCEDURE

For theft to occur, two elements must be present: opportunity and desire. Investigative procedure depends on the facts of each case. Thus, the theft of an item from a home—possibly by a guest—would be handled differently from business thefts by employees. However, certain inquiries are common to most theft cases:

- At what time, as accurately as possible, did the theft occur? This information is valuable in identifying individuals who were in the area when it occurred and had the opportunity to commit the crime and in eliminating suspects.
- Who had access to the item, and, if the item was not readily visible, who knew its location?
- If the stolen item was not readily visible, did the perpetrator go directly to the item, or was a general search made of the area? Thieves who have prior knowledge of where an item is hidden because of a personal or professional relationship with the victim may intentionally disrupt drawers, closets, and so forth in order to convey the impression that the item was discovered during a general search and thereby cast suspicion away from themselves.
- Who discovered the theft? Is discovery by this person usual or unusual?
- Is anyone with access to the item having financial difficulties? Checks of credit and local pawnshop files might provide indications.
- Has anyone expressed a strong interest in the item lately?
- Is the stolen item likely to have been retained by a suspect, pawned, sold, or given to someone as a gift?
- Has the victim reported similar thefts to the police in the past?
- Was the item insured? If so, was the dollar amount of the policy sufficient to cover the total value of the item, or will the owner lose a considerable amount of money as a result of the theft?
- Do any circumstances about the case suggest that the victim is making a false or misleading report?

The following case illustrates one example of a suspected misleading report:

A coin dealer reported that he and his wife had been participating in a dealers' show at a local hotel. At the conclusion of the show the coin dealer placed his rare coins, valued at $5,000, in the trunk of his car and drove to a nearby supermarket. He told the police that he took the coins in an attaché case into the supermarket with him. His wife accompanied him into the supermarket.

When they returned to their car, they were confronted by three armed men. One ordered the coin dealer to surrender the attaché case, which he did. The three men then got into a vehicle parked nearby and sped away. The police were called and the coin dealer related what had happened.

The coins were insured for their full value, but a clause in the insurance policy nullified the coverage if the coins were stolen from an unattended vehicle. This information came to light only when the insurance policy was carefully reviewed by the investigator assigned to the case.

The supermarket cashier and the boy who bagged the groceries reported to the investigator that they were certain that neither the coin dealer nor his wife had been carrying an attaché case in the store. Therefore, there was reason to suspect that the coins had been left unattended in the car and were stolen from it—although there was no indication of forced entry into the vehicle—or that the coins had been stolen while unattended at some other location, or that the dealer had sold the coins, or that he was concealing them.

The coin dealer was requested to submit to a polygraph examination in order to corroborate his report. He refused. Upon his refusal, the initial pickup order on the three alleged suspects and the vehicle was canceled. A copy of the police report was forwarded to the insurance company.

There are many ramifications to a case like this one. The first consequence, of course, is that a police investigation and pickup order were sent in a completely erroneous direction, wasting time and presenting the specter of arresting innocent people. Criminal fraud also was attempted by the complainant, and so further investigation was required. Hence, if there is some serious doubt about the legitimacy of a complaint, every effort should be made to investigate thoroughly.

CREDIT CARD FRAUD

Companies issuing credit cards are secure from losses due to counterfeit account numbers because of a sophisticated electronic information system that provides approval of credit card transactions in advance of purchase. However, this system is defenseless if the card being used has a valid account number but was stolen.[2] Valid account numbers can be obtained in a variety of ways, but, according to MasterCard, "lost and stolen credit cards remain the biggest problems, accounting for 67 percent of the association's fraud."[3]

TYPES OF CREDIT CARD FRAUD

Credit card fraud can be classified in four categories: stolen cards, counterfeit cards, shave-and-paste schemes, and fraudulent applications.

Stolen Cards

Credit cards can be stolen in a variety of ways, such as muggings, purse snatchings, and office and health club thefts. However, one of the simplest ways to obtain bank card account information is through postal theft. Numerous Nigerian fraud rings run sophisticated theft operations throughout the eastern and southern regions of the United States. Having illegally obtained legitimate bank cards or account information, the group then creates portfolios of fictitious identification, including driver's licenses, Social Security cards, and other materials, to support the purchasing power behind those cards. At the direction of group leaders, "runners" purchase merchandise from a variety of sources until the legitimate owners report the cards stolen or confiscated.[4]

These organizations also take advantage of contacts within the various credit bureaus to obtain legitimate bank card account information for counterfeiting or telephone order purchasing. The groups commonly mail stolen cards and information via overnight courier to other factions located throughout the country. For this reason, the U.S. Postal Inspection Service has implemented the Express Mail Label Profiling Program to identify packages likely to contain contraband. The profile flags suspicious packages on the basis of mail quantity, delivery, delivery frequency, destination, label and packaging-material characteristics, and so on. The profile was developed intially to identify packages containing drugs. Postal inspectors in the drug unit forward profiles to the credit card fraud unit if they believe that nondrug criminal activity is occurring.[5]

Counterfeit Credit Cards

Counterfeit cards vary in quality from those made on embossing machines stolen from companies that produce cards to those of obviously poor quality. There are nine points merchants should check when examining credit cards:

1. Always check the credit card's expiration date to make sure the card has not expired. Expiration dates are frequently altered to give new life to an expired card.

2. Carefully feel the credit card. Does the card feel too heavy or too light? Does the card feel too lumpy or rough on the surface or edge? Any card possessing these abnormalities could be a counterfeit.

3. Examine the signature. Beware of any irregularities in the lettering or spacing of the name.

4. Be certain the printed and embossed issuing bank identification number (BIN) both match, and check to be certain the printed BIN above the embossed account number is not missing.

5. Examine the card for embossed characters that are uneven, faded, or have "ghost" images from a previously embossed number.

6. Look for crooked lines in the embossing or characters that do not line up with others on the same line of type.

7. Be alert for chipped or scratched printed surfaces.

8. Examine the card for silver or gold paint used to blend in the hologram or touch up the embossed numbers after they have been embossed.

9. Look for a missing, painted-on, or "blank" magnetic strip on the back of the card. Magnetic strips are occasionally erased accidentally, but counterfeit cards often omit the information entirely. When the strip is coded properly, the information contained there should match that on the front of the card exactly.[6] Figure 16–1 provides specific information on both VISA and MasterCard security features.

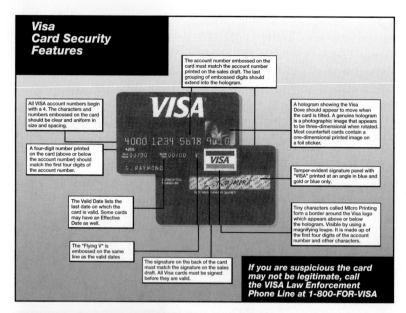

Figure 16–1
VISA and MasterCard
Security Features

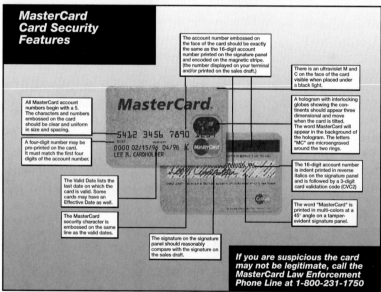

(Courtesy Federal Bureau of Investigation)

Shave-and-Paste Schemes

Account numbers are shaved off one or more legitimate credit cards and replaced by new numbers. The individuals using the altered card hope the forged account number will be a current, valid account number.

Fraudulent Application

Individuals apply to several credit card companies, hoping that one or more will issue them credit cards. The cards are then used as often as possible and as fast as possible. Information provided on the application is false.

Banks and credit card companies have attempted to counter the rise in credit card fraud in many ways. Some issue credit cards with the cardholder's photo on it. The banks use a computer imaging system to produce cards in-house.[7]

The biggest advance in the war on credit card fraud has been the development of the Issuers

Clearinghouse Service (ICS). The ICS helps to identify fraudulent applications by matching various information requested of the applicant with a large national database of consumer information. The service matches names, birth dates, addresses, telephone numbers, and Social Security numbers. If the information on the application does not match the information in the database, the application may well be fraudulent.[8]

PREVENTING CREDIT CARD FRAUD

Investigators are often asked how to prevent such fraud. They can make a number of suggestions. Merchants should be cautioned to follow the guidelines given above. Furthermore, certain types of behavior by the person presenting the card suggest a potential fraud.

Most stores set a limit on the amount of charge purchases a clerk may accept without authorization from a supervisor or manager. A purchase by credit card or check that is above the clerk's authorization limit must be brought to the attention of the manager. Therefore, the cardholder may split the purchase between charge cards to circumvent the need for authorization. The cardholder may attempt to explain this by saying that he or she is close to the credit limit and would prefer not to suffer the embarrassment of being turned down. A parallel tactic is for the cardholder to move through the store, making multiple charges for purchases with the credit card, but doing them separately so that they remain under the amount that requires authorization by the issuer.

The best way to avoid credit card fraud is for the individual consumer to protect his or her account number. Many merchants ask for two forms of identification when a customer pays with a check. Do not write your credit card account number on the back of a check, using it as a form of identification. Do not put your address and phone number on charge slips, even if requested to do so by the merchant. Do not write your account number on your checks when remitting payment, even if requested to do so by the credit card company.

The director of credit card fraud control at Citibank, MasterCard/Visa, discourages people from writing their account numbers on checks, "since that check goes through a lot of hands. With that information, someone could pose as you and contact your bank to get other information.[9] The director also advises against putting your telephone number and address on credit slips. A credit card fraud specialist of Visa USA, states that the practice is forbidden by major card issuers.[10] Moreover, according to The Bankcard Holders of America, writing your credit card number on a check serves no purpose because "Visa and MasterCard operating rules strictly prohibit merchants from charging a credit card to cover a bounced check."[11]

Finally, cardholders should not give their credit card account number to any individual who telephones them stating that they have won a valuable prize or trip and their credit card account number is required for verification. Old credit slips and carbons should be destroyed. Billing statements should be checked closely. Lost or stolen credit cards must be reported immediately to reduce the potential for loss. When consumers report a lost or stolen credit card before it is used, they are not liable for any unauthorized charges.

CHECK FRAUD

Prior to the 1980s, bank fraud schemes generally involved only a few transactions perpetrated by a single individual or small group. Losses averaged less than $100,000 to the victim institution, and law enforcement investigations were fairly routine in nature.[12]

Following the deregulation of the savings and loan industry in 1982 and the initiation of more speculative, risky ventures by those in charge of these institutions, a new wave of fraud emerged. During the late 1980s and early 1990s, large-scale frauds perpetrated by institution insiders and by persons held in trust within the banking industry became prevalent. Law enforcement agencies used massive, task-force-oriented investigations to calm the surge of these frauds. As a result, the banking industry as a whole has stabilized and continues to insulate itself from insider abuse.

Conversely, the number of frauds perpetrated by outsiders, especially organized ethnic groups, has risen dramatically in the last decade. Outsider fraud now accounts for more than 60 percent of all fraud against financial institutions.[13] The most prevalent problem in the industry, by far, centers on check fraud, but also involves other counterfeit negotiable instruments, such as traveler's checks, credit cards, certified bank checks, money orders, and currency.

CHECK FRAUD ORGANIZATIONS

Worldwide, 80 billion checks exchange hands annually; 60 billion of them are written in the United States.[14] As anyone who has mailed a check to a mortgage company three days before payday can attest, Americans have become enamored with writing checks and taking advantage of the "float" period, the time required for the check-clearing process. Criminal elements within numerous immigrant groups in the United States have analyzed American banking, noting the system's deficiencies and the fact that it affords opportunities for fraud. Presently, organized ethnic enterprises conduct a sizable portion of the annual check fraud activity throughout the country.

The Major Groups

The principal ethnic groups involved in illegal check fraud schemes include Nigerians, Asians (particulary Vietnamese), Russians, Armenians, and Mexicans. The majority of the Vietnamese, Armenian, and Mexican organizations base their operations in California, especially in the Orange County, San Francisco, and Sacramento areas. However, they have networked their operations throughout the country, with a number of connections in Chicago, Houston, and Washington, D.C.

The Nigerian and Russian groups, with bases in the northern and eastern areas of the country, exhibit more nomadic tendencies. They roam throughout the United States, stop to pass stolen or counterfeit checks, and then move on to new locations. The Russian groups initially established themselves in New York but have extended their activities to Chicago and the West Coast.

Nigerian groups often solicit legitimate identification and account information to further their check fraud schemes. Recently, law enforcement authorities have noted their interaction with Vietnamese organizations in the Chicago and Houston regions. In the Northeast, Nigerian rings have opened numerous investment accounts within various brokerage houses and deposited large sums of money using stolen and counterfeit corporate checks.

Most West Coast Asian gangs began to organize their bank fraud activities during the 1980s and have continued to expand and develop these sometimes-sophisticated operations. Many such groups originated in Taiwan, Hong Kong, and Vietnam, among them the Viet Ching, Big Circle Boys, V-Boyz, Wo Hop To, Wah Ching, and Red Door gangs.[15] Within the Asian gangs, known as triads, the group leader usually holds the title of "master" and oversees all organizational operations.

Current investigations indicate that some Asian groups have been dealing with Russian counterparts, especially to negotiate (deposit or cash) counterfeit currency through the banking system. Recently, members of the Russian Mafia obtained such currency, which was printed in Montreal, Canada, sold to several West Coast Vietnamese factions, and distributed throughout California.

Notably, each of these groups commits a myriad of white-collar, drug, and violent crimes. The groups perceive check fraud—unlike drug trafficking, extortion, or murder—as a "safe" crime, since it carries minimal penalties and a low risk of apprehension.

The Players

Regardless of ethnic origin, groups involved in check fraud maintain certain universal characteristics. Unlike traditional, tight-knit, organized criminal groups, such as La Cosa Nostra, these groups, which may embody several hundred members, usually are loosely organized. Members often network among several organizations. Despite the lack of a rigid hierarchy, members typically fall into one of several roles—leader, check procurer, counterfeiter, information broker, or check passer.

Leaders Leaders of an organization generally have an extensive criminal history and possess above-average intelligence. Often, they have a degree in business and/or law. These individuals provide the overall direction of the group, as well as expertise in understanding U.S. business and the banking system.

Check Procurers Check procurers obtain authentic checks, usually by stealing them while employed within a financial institution. Group members then sell or negotiate the stolen checks as is, or they duplicate the checks for future use.

Counterfeiters Counterfeiters duplicate corporate and payroll checks, traveler's checks, credit cards, certified bank checks, money orders, currency, and other negotiable instruments, as well as personal identification. They usually are well versed in the use of personal computers, especially in the field of desktop publishing.

Information Brokers Information broker gather personal and financial information on legitimate individuals. Using this credible information, associates open new bank accounts, pass counterfeit checks, and secure loans, which they fail to repay.

Check Passers Check passers actually negotiate stolen and counterfeit checks through the banking system and collect the proceeds to distribute to the group. They often travel throughout the country, opening new accounts and transporting their illicit proceeds. Typically, they negotiate only about 10 percent of a group's illicit checks; the group sells the rest of the checks to other individuals and organizations. Check passers maintain little contact or status within the hierarchy and often are the only members whose ethnic backgrounds differ from those of the core-group members.

Ethnic organizations tend to distrust anyone not of their own heritage, making it difficult for law enforcement to infiltrate them. Even though police frequently arrest check passers throughout the country, these street-level criminals generally possess little information concerning upper-echelon group members.

TYPES OF CHECK FRAUD SCHEMES

The variety of check fraud schemes perpetrated throughout the country ranges from depositing single stolen checks to counterfeiting thousands of negotiable instruments and processing them through hundreds of bank accounts. Although it is impossible to summarize all of the check fraud schemes currently operating, three schemes in particular— large-scale counterfeiting, identity assumption, and payroll-check fraud—typify frauds being tracked

by bank security officials and law enforcement authorities throughout the nation.

Large-Scale Counterfeiting

The most notorious groups engaged in large-scale counterfeiting operations are the Vietnamese triads operating out of Orange County, California. Members routinely get jobs within local financial institutions in order to collect master original bank checks, money orders, and corporate/payroll checks for counterfeiting. The triad masters, who often are counterfeit experts with a host of duplication devices, manage the group's criminal activities.

The groups exchange their counterfeit instruments for cash in a variety of ways. Check passers directly negotiate a portion of the counterfeit documents through financial institutions. They deposit the fraudulent checks, often into new accounts, and withdraw the funds before the bank can complete the check-clearing process and discover the fraud. The transient check passers open accounts in different institutions throughout the country; however, group members within the organizational hierarchy ultimately control their activities from a home base.

In order to minimize their exposure to law enforcement, the counterfeiters sell the majority of their phony goods to third parties for negotiation or further resale. They create most counterfeit checks in $2,000 to $5,000 increments and sell them to black-market customers at 5 to 25 percent of their face value, depending on quality and appearance.

Identity Assumption

Seen in various metropolitan areas, identity assumption schemes often involve Nigerian and Vietnamese criminal organizations. Group members obtain employment with or develop sources in local banks and credit agencies so that they can acquire otherwise-confidential information on bona fide bank customers. The groups then create counterfeit identification, including driver's licenses, Social Security cards, and credit cards, to assume the innocent persons' identities. Under the assumed identities, the criminals open new bank accounts, which they use to deposit fraudulent checks and subsequently withdraw the funds, as well as to secure personal loans and lines of credit.

Once bank accounts have been established, the financial institutons become vulnerable to a variety of frauds. Prior to depositing fraudulent checks and withdrawing the proceeds, the "customer" is likely to obtain a credit card account with a substantial credit line. The perpetrator withdraws funds against the credit line and distributes the money within the criminal organization, along with any bogus loan money he or she has procured. After withdrawing funds on the basis of deposit of fraudulent checks, the "customer" leaves town, and the bank sustains a substanial loss.

Such schemes hurt more than just the banks, however. The innocent people whose identities were assumed suffer from ruined credit histories, which may inhibit their future financial activity.

Payroll-Check Fraud

A variation of the identity assumption scheme involves placing group members within payroll-check processing companies. These firms compile and distribute payroll checks on behalf of their corporate clients.

The miscreant employees print duplicate payroll checks for various client recipients. They then steal the checks from the premises, and the group duplicates them for negotiation. Concurrently, the group obtains full background identifying data on the client's regular employees, which can be used in future schemes.

METHODS OF ALTERATION

New technologies give check fraud perpetrators a wide variety of schemes and devices for committing their crimes. Chemical techniques and computers provide the primary means by which criminals manipulate and counterfeit checks.

Chemical Techniques

Legitimate personal checks can be changed by chemical means. Similarily, someone well versed in manipulation techniques can modify corporate checks, traveler's checks, bank checks, and U.S. government checks with minimal effort.

Chemical alteration is commonly referred to as "check washing." Check washers use a variety of acid-based chemical solutions to erase amount and payee information while maintaining the integrity of the preprinted information. They then dry the check and inscribe a new payee and a significantly higher dollar amount before presenting it to a bank for payment.

One acid-based solution even allows criminals to revise a check and subsequently destroy the evidence. In this instance, the check washers must move quickly because the chemical solution causes the paper to disintegrate within 24 hours, leaving no supporting evidence of the transaction.

Technology

Today's computer technology makes it relatively simple to counterfeit checks. A counterfeiting operation requires only a laser scanner to capture the image of an original check, a personal computer to make changes, and a quality laser printer to produce the bogus check. The necessary equipment can be obtained for less than $5,000.

Once an original check has been scanned, its data can be manipulated and reprinted with ease. Still, the counterfeiter faces the tough challenges of matching the paper stock used by the check manufacturer; correlating complex color schemes, such as those used on U.S. government and traveler's checks; and overcoming some of the counterfeiting safeguards currently used by legitimate check printers.

Yet counterfeiters can overcome even these hurdles without much difficulty. A number of unscrupulous printers throughout the country offer preprinted checks containing whatever information the customer desires, without bank confirmation or concurrence. Further, today's computers can come very close to duplicating even the most complex color schemes and check safeguards. A counterfeiter's success hinges on knowing that most checks will not be scrutinized closely enough to detect the fraud until they have been cashed and cleared through the banking system.

CHECK-FRAUD PREVENTION

In order to prevent fraud, check-printing companies offer a variety of counterfeiting safeguards.[16] All such features make attempted alteration detectable in one way or another. Yet these enhancements are not foolproof and often prove cost-prohibitive to the purchaser. In response, financial institutions have begun to implement a type of biometric fingerprint identifier as a more cost-effective approach.

The Bank of America (BOA) in Las Vegas, Nevada, was the first financial institution to use fingerprinting technology to deter check fraud.[17] At

BOA, when customers who are not account holders present checks for payment, they must place an inkless fingerprint next to their endorsement. When bank officials identify an attempted fraud, the fingerprinting system provides law enforcement with evidence and background information never before attainable at the onset of an investigation. This pilot project has garnered impressive results. BOA officials report that the biometric identification system has nearly eliminated check fraud schemes perpetrated by outsiders. It also has reduced the bank's overall fraud problem by 40 percent.

BOA's success in Nevada spurred the Arizona Bankers Association to lead a campaign with member financial institutions to adopt a simiar program. A core group of Arizona-based banks implemented this technology in the fall of 1995. Moreover, BOA officials plan to extend fingerprinting operations to their branches in Texas and New Mexico. A number of financial institutions have expressed a desire to expand the program to new customer accounts, another hotbed for fraudulent checking activities.[18]

During this implementation process, the banks involved have become cognizant of the sociological and privacy concerns underlying such an identification system. Some customers fear the improper use of identifying information. Bank officials stress, however, that no central database of fingerprint information will be maintained and that fingerprint records will be furnished to law enforcement only in the event of suspected criminal conduct.

CELLULAR PHONE CLONING

Cloning is defined as the unauthorized and illegal programming of cellular phones with the access codes of legitimate cellular customers. It has allowed criminals to obtain cheap, mobile communications that are untraceable through traditional law enforcement methods. These crooks—or "bandits"—also have apparent anonymity in their communications and the ability to quickly migrate to a new number in a few minutes.[19]

But their calls can also help police build a solid case against them. Under federal law, Title 18 of the U.S. Code, Section 1029, it is a violation to possess, use, or traffic in altered cellular phones or devices used to alter phones, including computers, software, and scanners, with intent to defraud. Under Section 1029, the U.S. Secret Service has federal jurisdiction over cellular crimes. Most states have similar laws making it a felony to obtain telecommunications services through fraud. Applicable Canadian law is found under Sections 326 and 328 C.C.C., relating to theft of telecommunications service, as well as Section 380 C.C.C., relating to fraud, and Sections 362 and 403 C.C.C., dealing with false pretense/false statement and impersonation, respectively.

Investigators need to understand the logistics of cloning. To begin with, a cellular access code includes the customer's 10-digit phone number or mobile identification number (MIN) and the phone's electronic serial number (ESN). When a cellular phone places a call, it transmits the MIN and ESN so that the cellular system can verify whether the caller is a legitimate customer. As with credit card validation, the cellular system compares the transmitted MIN/ESN to a database of valid access codes. However, as in the case of the banking industry validation of counterfeit credit cards, the cellular validation system cannot differentiate between an access code transmitted by the true customer's phone and the same code transmitted by a counterfeit or clone phone.

The actual cloning process is completed using an IBM-compatible computer—usually a laptop—or a custom device called a cloning "black box" (see Figure 16–2). Both systems allow portable and easily concealed methods of illegal cloning operations. Such operations are run from homes, offices, or even moving cars. In each case, the MIN/ESN originally programmed into the phone is overwritten with a stolen MIN/ESN of a legitimate customer.

When a computer is used, the process requires specialized cables that are fabricated to plug into the phone, connecting it with a parallel port of the computer. Black-market cloning software, stored either on the computer's hard drive or on a diskette, runs the cloning process. The cloning software is "user-friendly," allowing an amateur to become a cloning expert in a matter of minutes. Programming a cloned MIN/ESN into a phone takes only about 5 minutes.

Figure 16–2
Cloning Box

A cloning box (also known as a "black box") with Motorola-brand "Flip and Brick"–style phones. This box can clone either of these types of Motorola phones.

(Courtesy *Police Magazine*)

Custom cloning computers, also known as black-boxes, are fabricated on the black market for sale to street-level cloning operators. They contain specialized computer chips, which store the cloning program. These chips are believed to be made in the Far East (Hong Kong, Taiwan) and smuggled into the United States and Canada, where the boxes are assembled. (See Figure 16–3.)

Once a cloner obtains cloning equipment, a source of MIN/ESN combinations is required in order to program the codes into customer phones. Until 1994, the most common source of MIN/ESN codes was insiders, persons working for a cellular carrier or the carrier's distribution chain. But the need for insiders is less common now, as cloners have become more self-sufficient through the use of ESN readers. An *ESN reader* is a radio scanner and decoder, which is able to monitor the radio signal of a cellular phone and intercept the phone's transmission of the MIN/ESN (see Figure 16–4). These devices were originally developed for use by cellular technicians as a testing unit for phones. However, a gray market has developed for the devices because of their ability to "suck MINs/ESNs out of the air."

The use of cloned service is proliferating rapidly—especially in metropolitan areas—because of the big profits and declining prices for equip-

ment and service. An average cloner may activate (or, in street jargon, "hook up," "air up," "chip" or "charge up") 20 to 40 phones per week, generating revenues of $1,500 to $5,000 weekly ($80,000 to

Figure 16–3
Cell Phone Cloning Box

This cellular phone cloning box accommodates programming of hexadecimal-format ESN transmissions.

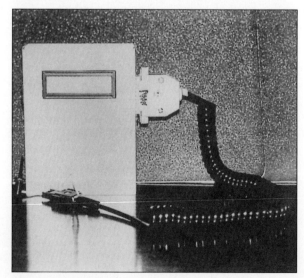

(Courtesy *Police Magazine*)

Figure 16–4
Cell Phone ESN Reader
This device is used by street criminals to scan MIN/ESN transmissions by cellular phones to obtain codes for cloning.

(Courtesy *Police Magazine*)

$260,000 annually). Cloning software and the necessary cables (to connect a computer to the cloned phone) currently sell for as little as $500 to $800. If a computer is included, the street price of a cloning package may be $2,500 to $3,000. Prices for cloning black boxes range from $3,000 to $6,000, depending on the city and the type of black box.

Street prices for cloned service range from $50 to $125 for 30 days' "guaranteed" service (assuming the customer provides his or her own phone). Lower prices apply in larger cities such as New York, Los Angeles, and Miami. If the cloner provides the phone, the price increases by $100 to $200. Cloners usually guarantee their service by

agreeing to reprogram the customer's phone with a new cloned number within 30 days. Cloners stimulate return business and maximize revenues by programming the same number into many customers' phones. The combined usage of a particular MIN/ESN usually generates enough fraudulant calls to guarantee that the carrier will detect the fraud and shut the number off within 30 days. When the number is shut off, each clone customer using that number must "resubscribe" for service. The multiple-clone approach also allows the cloner to activate many customers' phones—receiving activation fees from each—even if he or she has a limited supply of access codes (MIN/ESN combinations).

A POWERFUL INVESTIGATIVE TOOL

Cloning can provide law enforcement with a powerful investigative tool against major criminal enterprises. In the Los Angeles area, for instance, cellular cloning and major credit card fraud rings operate hand in hand.

Let us assume that a law enforcement agency is trying to arrest a major drug trafficker and that the individual's phone records are needed but there is no way of finding the cellular number. Often, the wanted person's pager number is known or can be determined through undercover sources or informants. In such cases the procedure that follows is the best course of action to be taken.

First, page the wanted person to a prearranged cold-line phone number. Second, record the data and time the call is returned. Finally, prepare a search warrant for each of the cellular carriers in your city requesting "automated message accounting (AMA) call records for any cellular telephone that placed a call to [your cold-line telephone number] on [date and time the page was returned]." Also, specify in the warrant that "the carrier must provide detailed call [AMA] records for any mobile number(s) identified by this search, together with the cell site and sector of origin for such calls for the following period: [insert time period of interest for crook's calling activity]." The carrier is also instructed to provide the investigating agency with "the address(es) of cell sites where such calls originate as requested by such agency."

If the wanted person does use a cell phone to return a call, the carrier should be able to identify the cellular number used (in response to the search warrant). As a result, the investigator will be able to obtain the cellular number by the wanted person, the person's call records, and an indicator of where the person is calling based on the cell site information requested in the warrant.

Cellular phones are commonly used by kidnappers, terrorists, and extremists to place ransom demands, make threats, or plan their intended actions. Each call generates an AMA call record, which identifies the cellular number used and the cell-site location from which the call originates. Cellular service also offers capabilities similar to those of land-line telephone service for establishing wire taps: call traps and dialed-number recorders.

A few other high-tech approaches are also available to law enforcement through the service of carrier personal or private consultants. These experts can assist with radio direction finding or other electronic and analytical measures to establish numbers being used by criminals. They also help to generate other evidence against suspects using cellular phones.

A strong rapport with local cellular carriers can be invaluable when their support is needed during an investigation. It is always a good idea to know which of the local carriers' personnel are responsible for fraud investigations and law enforcement support.

RECEIVING STOLEN PROPERTY

One of the most infrequently prosecuted criminals is the *receiver*, defined as one who knowingly purchases, sells, or otherwise traffics in stolen merchandise. A *fence* is a professional receiver who serves as a go-between by funneling stolen property purchased from thieves to various outlets, which sell the goods to the actual consumer.[20] If most theft of the items are for resale and not for personal consumption, it follows then that nearly every stolen item must be fenced—resold. Fencing is no small affair but an industry with sales running into the tens of billions of dollars annually.

The importance of the role of the fence and other receivers cannot be underestimated. For instance, the theft of car radios, cassettes, and compact disc players is epidemic in the United States. There must be a parallel distribution system to move the goods—which are almost impossible to identify as stolen—to consumers. "The thief goes to the used parts dealer, and they sell to the repair shops," says one senior FBI agent in Chicago. "The thief can get the radio out in minutes, and get $50 for it. The used parts dealers sell them for $200 or $300 and it is possible that the radio put in a car might be the same one that was stolen from it."[21]

The fence is crucial to the thief. In a 10-month investigation, the Special Operations Division of the Anaheim, California, Police Department received nearly $1.4 million in recovered stolen property. The division ran a sting operation in which the police were "fencing" goods from an Anaheim apartment. "Our goal was to get about $350,000 worth," said Sergeant Jim Flammini, who was in charge of the operation. "This wasn't police chasing crooks. This was crooks chasing fences, who were undercover officers in this case. They wanted our money. And we were happy to do that."[22]

Without fences and other receivers to play the pivotal role in the criminal system of distributing stolen goods, most incidents of burglary, hijacking, and pilfering would become unprofitable. The objective of most thieves is not the merchandise per se, but the cash for which the merchandise can be sold.

For example, several years ago law enforcement agencies in the Northeast broke a major "steal-to-order fraudulent check and stolen credit card ring" that was "responsible for bilking department stores between Washington, D.C., and New York of more than $12 billion" over a four-year period.[23] Almost all of the items stolen were ordered by fences regularly used by the ring, though some items did end up in flea markets, in boutiques, and with street vendors. This ring was sophisticated and professional. Its more than 200 members were provided with a training manual outlining which banks and merchants were the easiest targets for carrying out their crimes. The ring would obtain checks, credit cards, and associated IDs by muggings, purse snatchings, or office thefts. At that point, the members would go shopping with stolen credit cards and purchase items that fences had ordered or items the ring knew would move very easily.

A large part of the stolen-goods distribution network is through flea markets, pawnshops, and jewelers' rows. "Who goes to a flea market and asks whether a box of film or a package of razor blades is stolen?" asks one police officer. Adds a vehement Sergeant James Vucci of the Washington, D.C., police department: "All your pawnshops are just legalized fences."[24]

OPERATIONS OF RECEIVERS

Excerpts from testimony on fencing before the Select Committee on Small Business shed light on the scope, methods, and importance of fences and criminal receivers:[25]

Chairman: Now are there master fences in New York City? Chief fences, big fences, whatever you want to call them?

Witness: . . . Well, offhand, I know about four big fences that can come up with $100,000 in cash, no sweat.*

Chairman: Four big fences that can come up with $100,000 in cash?

Witness: Yes. On the okay level, without even seeing the stuff. Without even seeing it.†

Chairman: Now, who generally purchases the stolen property? . . .

Witness: Legit people. You know, stores.

Chairman: Stores do buy?

Witness: Yes. Then you got big stores, department stores, you got cut-rate stores.

The following statement, given to the committee by an assistant district attorney of an eastern city, is particularly enlightening:

"Mack," as we will refer to this fence, is a gnomelike man in his sixties who maintained three electrical outlet stores. . . . An analysis of Mack's books and records revealed that . . . Mack purchased stolen electrical construction materials valued at approximately $1 million, an amount which must be multiplied in terms of the loss to the construction industry in labor costs, delay, and replacement of the stolen property.

Mack's operation is typical because, as a fence, he would only deal in his specialty, that is, electrical construction materials. . . .

In addition, Mack was also typical in that he acted as a catalyst in causing certain materials to be stolen at certain times. When he was overstocked in certain materials, he would so advise thieves. . . . But when one of his clients needed particular materials, Mack would put out a contract for the theft of the particular items, and take great pains to see that his customers, who paid cash, would receive the property at the time requested.

Generally, there appears to be a hierarchy among fences. Some fences may deal directly with a thief and openly sell to a buyer. This type of fence . . . deals primarily with small amounts of property. He is the "neighborhood connection." . . .

Some fences may never see or touch the stolen property. . . . Their transactions are all consummated over the telephone. This type of fence is known as the "master fence." . . .

Organized crime figures will very often "stake" a fence with a large sum of money, if he will use his connections to move stolen property for them. This is usually the relationship that exists since a fence, especially a master fence, of necessity has the required legitimate contacts and travels in the highest business circles.[26]

Fences and other receivers deal in a vast array of merchandise: securities, steel, credit cards, forged or stolen identification documents, office equipment, meat, shavers, airline tickets, shoes, clothing, and appliances of all kinds, to name just a few. Some fences specialize in a particular type of merchandise:

Emeterio Marino Pijeira sold men's suits, thousands of them, from the living room of a duplex in a quiet Miami neighborhood. Top quality stuff: Hickey-Freeman, Oxford, and Austin Reed, and store labels such as Bloomingdale's, Dillard's, and Nordstrom. Unbeatable prices: $150 or less for a choice Hickey-Freeman suit that in other stores might cost $600–$800.

---

* The rule of thumb is that to earn $100,000 a fence would have to handle $750,000 to $1,000,000 in stolen merchandise.

† Master fences do not come into physical possession of goods or inspect them; they are "arrangers" for the distribution of the merchandise, not its handlers.

Pijeira's screaming bargains lured throngs of happy customers, including such civic leaders as the Dade County Manager, a county commissioner, a city commissioner, and a prosecuting attorney. Like Pijeira's other customers, they tried on the wares in the bathroom and paid with cash or with checks made out to "cash." No names or credit cards, please.

Police say records found in Pijeira's duplex show that he was supplied by thieves in 22 states, including crooks who would steal suits to order, by the single suit or by the vanload. Pijeira typically paid his "wholesalers" 10% of a suit's usual retail, then doubled the price to reach the standard retail markup of 50%. He paid little rent, collected and paid no state sales tax and, apparently, offered his son and one salesman only peanut wages. A dream business. Bargain prices and low overhead coupled with high profit margins.

Pijeira, police believe, cleared at least $500,000 in one year. His bonanza ended when a curious browser, himself a clothier, found on Pijeira's racks a designer-label suit stolen from his own store. Pijeira was convicted of racketeering but served no jail time. Now on probation, he runs another men's clothing store along Miami's Coral Way.[27]

Even children's bicycles and used cars are welcomed by fences. On the Miami River, small cargo boats loaded down with stolen bicycles are seen moving downriver and out to sea. The ships are bound for the Caribbean, where even a poor-quality bike can be worth between $30 and $50. Additionally, a "hot" car worth only $300 in the United States can be fenced in Central America for $15,000.[28]

Ethical businesspeople are doubly penalized. First, they suffer the loss of stolen goods and endure many consequent dislocations. Production and advertising schedules may suffer, sales may be lost or delayed, and insurance premiums and deductibles may increase. Second, their prices and terms have to compete with those of firms that achieve an illegal competitive edge by purchasing cut-rate goods from criminals.[29]

POSSIBLE INDICATORS OF FENCES AND OTHER RECEIVERS

The larceny investigator should talk to businesspeople or appear before their groups to educate them about fences and other receivers. They should be told about the possibility of unwittingly dealing with fences; the possibility that competitors are dealing with fences; and the possibility that company purchasing agents or buyers work directly with fences, if for no other reason than to impress management with their adroitness at obtaining favorable rates on merchandise.

Investigators should remind businesspeople that by setting unrealistically high performance standards for buyers and purchasing agents, they may pressure employees to deal with fences. Other indicators that businesspeople should examine carefully include offers to provide merchandise to the retailer at extremely low wholesale prices provided the sale is made in cash; reports that other retailers are buying or selling a product at abnormally low prices; and small neighborhood outlets that offer considerable savings to customers, do a large volume of business, and then suddenly close after a few weeks or months.

PREVENTIVE MEASURES

In the words of a former fence, the placement of identification numbers on products "would stop a lot of burglars from burglarizing, a lot of receivers from receiving." Indeed, the greatest problem confronting prosecutors and police in apprehending and convicting receivers is that stolen merchandise frequently cannot be identified by its owners. If businesspeople cannot distinguish between their goods that were legitimately and illegitimately marketed, their business presents a tempting target to criminals.[30]

Manufacturers play a vital role in devising methods by which identification numbers can be stamped on or otherwise affixed to products and merchandise. However, product identification achieves little if manufacturers, wholesalers, retailers, and consumers do not take the time and expense of recording them. Such numbers are invaluable to investigators, who can enter them into computerized criminal information systems, such as the NCIC's.

Company personnel—especially salespeople—can be instructed to remain alert for the sale of products at unusual discounts or through unusual channels. Other employees who have frequent external contacts could be given the serial numbers of items stolen from their firm. In one instance, a typewriter repairman noted that the serial number on the equipment he was servicing was on his employer's list of stolen equipment.

"Sellbacks"—in which victims of theft or their insurers are approached by receivers who offer the return of the stolen merchandise for a small percentage of its replacement value—are not infrequent. Occasionally people yield to such a temptation. But in addition to the legal hazards they risk, such action is hardly in their firm's best long-run interests. Perhaps most important of these is that the implied reciprocity compromises the business and offers the potential for coerced cooperation in other matters involving stolen merchandise.

Routine inspection by investigators of outlets that might traffic in stolen merchandise also may reveal problems. If certain types of outlets are commonly associated with selling stolen property, state or local governments should ban or at least regulate them. In one city, the police are charged with enforcing regulations of over 50 types of businesses, and some forms, such as flea markets, are banned altogether.

However, the public demonstrates little interest in preventing the fencing of stolen goods. So benign is the general public attitude toward property crimes that at least one criminal has rationalized himself into a public benefactor:

> I'm doing a public service. Say a guy buys a nice new Lincoln and he has an accident. The repair shop has to go out and find parts for the car. That's where I come in. I'll steal a comparable car and sell the front end to the repair shop. I'll take the doors off, rear end off and put it away for when someone else needs them.
>
> The insurance company pays less to have the whacked car fixed. The guy gets his car back, good as new, and he's happy. The stolen car gets paid off, and its owner is happy. He goes out and buys another Lincoln, so Ford Motor Company is happy. I get paid, I'm happy. As you can see, I'm really helping the economy.[31]

SHOPLIFTING

Who is the typical shoplifter? In an attempt to determine the profile of the average shoplifter, an as-

sessment was made of 10,000 adult shoplifting apprehensions in 40 large metropolitan areas, with the following results.[32]

Males	51%	Females	49%
Blacks	49	Whites	23
Hispanics	14	Other	14
Single	31	Married	41
Widowed	11	Divorced	10
Unknown	18		
18 to 30 years	55	30+ years	40
Unknown	5		

As one can see from looking at these statistics, there is no "typical" shoplifter. Store owners are best advised that the demographics of a typical shoplifter are the demographics of their particular customers.

Ironically, most shoplifters who are apprehended do not need to steal and have the means available to them to pay for the merchandise stolen. "There are many people . . . who don't need to steal. Eighty percent of the shoplifters who get caught have the cash or credit cards in their pocket to pay for what they stole.[33]

Shoplifters can be classified into two groups: *commercial shoplifters*, or "boosters," who steal merchandise for resale, and *pilferers*, who take merchandise for private use.

There are two patterns emerging in shoplifting: many more people are shoplifting, and the vast majority, as many as 92 percent, are amateurs. Many have no real personal need for the merchandise.[34]

As might be suspected, professional shoplifters are not only apprehended less frequently than amateurs but also steal more at each theft. Many professional shoplifters work in teams. For example, several years ago local, state, and federal officials arrested six men who were involved in a series of shoplifting thefts in the Alexandria, Virginia, area. These men were all part of what has been characterized by police as South American theft groups. The men had managed to steal $150,000 worth of merchandise from four northern Virginia malls in just a few days. These men were part of only one of a growing number of such operations around the country. Many of the shoplifting teams consisted of Central and South American immigrants.[35]

In addition, these Hispanic groups appear to be affiliated with a loose-knit organization based out of

New York, Los Angeles, California, and possibly Philadelphia, that fences the stolen property through makeshift apartment clothing "stores" or through flea-market-type setups in the Flushing and Corona areas of Queens, New York, and the "Bad Lands" and Franklin Mills sections of Philadelphia, Pennsylvania.

These particular groups' criminal activity involves the theft of large quantities of clothing from major malls and retail stores along the East Coast. The groups usually operate in teams of two to six people and generally follow the criminal pattern outlined here:

- The shoplifter uses a "booster bag" specifically designed and constructed to defeat electronic security sensor devices routinely placed on clothing in major retail stores as a loss prevention tool. These booster bags are always made of a large department store shopping bag lined with an inner bag made of tin foil and duct tape (see Figure 16–5). Several such bags have been recovered in Alexandria and Fairfax County, Virgina, and most recently in Nassau County, New York, and Howard County, Maryland, as a result of arrests and execution of search warrants. Also, specific tools are used to remove sensor devices (see Figure 16–6).

- The groups use the U.S. Mail, United Parcel Service (UPS), and/or Federal Express (FedEx) to ship the stolen clothing to specific addresses in New York, Los Angeles, and, during the initial phase of this investigation, Annandale, VA. Once the stolen property is received it is distributed through stores, set up specifically to market and sell the stolen merchandise; it is sold "on the street," or it is shipped back to specific countries in South America, particularly, Chili.

- The respective groups have been documented as routinely stealing between $25,000 and $40,000 worth of clothing (retail value) over a two- to three-day period, prior to shipping the stolen merchandise and moving on to their next target malls or stores. The groups particularly like to steal blue jeans, women's apparel and lingerie, and men's suits.

- Individual subjects routinely provide false information and identification at the time of

Figure 16–5
Shoplifting Booster Bag

Detective Irwin Ellman displays a shoplifting "booster bag" and other paraphernalia seized during a search warrant execution in Alexandria, Virginia.

(Courtesy of Detective Jospeh Morrash, Alexandria, Virginia, Police Department)

their arrests on local charges in any respective jurisdiction, and they are known to have an elaborate system in securing their release through the utilization of specific and apparently legitimate bonding companies that are backed by legitimate insurance companies based in Los Angeles, California, Miami, Florida, and Fairfax County, Virginia, among other places as yet unidentified.

- Subject groups routinely utilize local motels as a base of operation to inventory, store, and package stolen merchandise prior to shipping, (see Figure 16–7). A group usually rents one or several rooms in the same motel for periods of several days to a week.

Figure 16–6
Tools Used in Shoplifting
Tools seized in a raid that were used in removal of sensor devices.

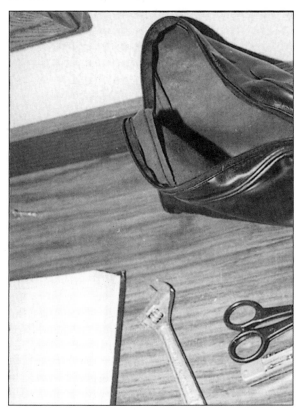

(Courtesy of Detective Jospeh Morrash, Alexandria, Virginia, Police Department)

Figure 16–7
Recovered Stolen Property
Stolen property piled up inside a motel room, found during a raid in Alexandria, Virginia.

(Courtesy of Detective Jospeh Morrash, Alexandria, Virginia, Police Department)

It is conservatively estimated that such groups, operating in the Washington, D.C., metropolitan area, are responsible for retail losses in excess of $1 million per month. Splinter groups, which have been documented to operate in the Washington metropolitan area and who arrive from Los Angeles, New York, and Philadelphia, are believed to account for conservatively estimated retail losses in excess of $10 million per month.

Additionally, it was originally documented that the group originating out of Los Angeles was also involved in travel agency burglaries throughout the country, several of which were confirmed in Fairfax County and Richmond, Virginia, respectively, as well as in Los Angeles, New York, Dallas, and Houston. During the commission of these burglaries, the group stole blank airline tickets and plates so as to manufacture, market, sell, and use the tickets throughout the United States and all over the world. Estimated losses to the airlines as a result of theft, manufacturing, and use of stolen and counterfeited airline tickets, as reported by the Airline Reporting Corporation and confirmed by the FBI's New York Division, is conservatively estimated at well in excess of $1 billion.

REDUCING SHOPLIFTING LOSSES

The retailing industry is increasingly taking steps to reduce shoplifting losses, with techniques running from the simple to the sophisticated. The new antishoplifting techniques are "designed to combine greater efficiency with unobtrusiveness."[36]

The Kroger food chain in Dallas, Texas, and Cub Foods in Colorado Springs, Colorado, have installed "scarecrooks" in high-theft areas of their stores. Six-foot cardboard cutouts of police officers in uniforms bear an apt slogan: "Shoplifting is a crime."[37]

In Denver, Colorado, a mannequin repairman has given birth to "Anne Droid," a female mannequin equipped with a video camera in her eye and a microphone in her nose—price: $1,150.[38] The camera has automatic iris control and automatic focus within a range of light and distance. The microphone has a range of about 10 feet, with quality of sound dependent on background noise levels.[39]

The Marshall Field Company has developed its Trojan Horse, "an enclosed structure covered with one-way glass that hides a lone detective."[40] The system can be moved from one location to another as needed, and it may or may not contain a security officer.

Electronic measures include the Sensormatic TellTag, a device that beeps whenever someone tampers with it or tries to walk out of the store with the tagged item. Knogo Corporation makes Chameleon, a micromagnetic thread that is hidden on the price label or bar-code sticker. Color-Tag, Inc., provides a tag that has a dye-filled capsule. When it is removed incorrectly, the capsule ruptures and releases a liquid staining agent, which stains the article as well as the individual.[41]

Customers are often recipients of subliminal messages while in a store or mall. The music broadcast in many stores subliminally says to the consumer: "I am an honest person; stealing is dishonest." Or the message may be merely a sound— the clanging of a prison door shutting.[42]

However well these devices work, many stores remain convinced that the greatest deterrent to shoplifting is a helpful, courteous, and watchful sales staff. "Shoplifters hate customer service."[43]

Local police usually become involved in shoplifting cases either to organize crime prevention programs for merchants or to respond to businesses that have been victimized or that have a violator in custody. The greatest security deterrents are often accomplished through security education programs for employees:

Staff should be trained to look for the incongruous—someone wearing a raincoat on a sunny day, a wheelchair shopper with worn soles on his or her sneakers, a baby stroller with too many blankets on it, people trying on clothes that is not their size. Salespeople [should] know about diversionary techniques—the heart attacks or marital squabbles faked by shoplifting teams.[44]

Other deterrents are the use of basic display controls relating to the type of merchandise displayed and its physical location, and the use of highly trained security personnel both in civilian clothes and in uniform.

Recently, merchants have gained another weapon to combat shoplifting. In order to help merchants recoup their losses from shoplifting, many states have legislated civil remedies for those who suffer at the hands of shoplifters. As of 1988, 30 states had enacted such legislation. Though the civil process and the amount of recoverable damages vary from state to state, the general procedures are common throughout.

The store calculates the damages it incurred due to the loss and mails the shoplifter a demand letter and a copy of the state's civil recoveries law. The shoplifter must pay the requested amount within a certain time. If payment is not received within the specified time, a second letter is sent to the shoplifter. This second letter informs the shoplifter that nonpayment may result in a civil court action. If the second letter is ignored, the merchant may seek redress of his or her grievance in civil court. Estimates of the recovery of damages by means of the two letters varies from 50 to 60 percent, both for in-house collection activities and for contract collection agencies.[45]

CONFIDENCE GAMES

The *confidence artist* is a recurring figure in history and in fiction, police annals, and the literature of criminology. The confidence artist steals by guile in a person-to-person relationship. Most confidence artists have insight into human nature and its frailties, not least among which is the desire to get something for nothing or for a bargain.

Many people who read the details of some of the confidence games below will find them hard to believe. How, they will ask, can anyone be so easily "conned"? But the police reports speak for themselves. The monetary loss and the number of confidence games very likely exceed the recorded figures because many victims are too embarrassed to make a police report.[46]

THE PIGEON DROP

This swindle is operated by two people. A lone victim, usually elderly, is approached on the street by one of the swindlers, who strikes up a conversation. A wallet, envelope, or other item that could contain cash is planted nearby. The second swindler walks past, picking up the wallet or envelope within full view of the pair. The swindler approaches the partner and victim, saying that he or she has found a large sum of money and is willing to divide it with them. But first the two must produce a large sum of money to show good faith. The victim is given no time to ponder and is urged to withdraw money from a savings account to show good faith. After withdrawing the money, the victim places it in an envelope provided by the first swindler. It is then shown to the second swindler who, by sleight of hand, switches envelopes, returning an identical envelope filled with paper slips to the victim. Both swindlers then depart. The victim does not become aware of the con until he or she goes to deposit the newfound "money."[47]

THE BANK EXAMINER SCHEME

The bank examiner scheme is one of the more sophisticated con games and requires knowing where targets bank. The con artist, usually a man, calls the victim—let us say an elderly woman—and introduces himself as a federal bank examiner, saying that there has been a computer breakdown at the bank and that he wants to verify when she last deposited or withdrew money and her current balance. If she replies, for example, that there should be a deposit of $8,000 in the account, then the caller indicates that the bank records show a deposit of some lesser amount, perhaps $2,000. The caller then suggests that a dishonest teller may be tampering with the account and asks for help in apprehending the teller. Once the victim agrees, the caller says that a cab will come and bring her to the bank. She is instructed that she should withdraw $7,000. One con man stays near the woman's house and observes her enter the cab. Another waits at the bank to verify the withdrawal and to be certain that bank officials or police are not alerted. After withdrawing the money, the woman gets back into the waiting cab and returns home. One of the con men then telephones her to discuss the next phase of the bank's "investigation." While she is still on the phone, the second man knocks on the door. The man at the front door identifies himself as a bank employee, the woman lets him in, and lets him talk to the "bank examiner" on the telephone. After a short conversation, the con man hands the phone back to the woman. The caller instructs her to give her money to the bank employee so that he can redeposit it with the suspected teller. Victim and money are soon parted—she may even be given a receipt.

INHERITANCE SCAM

In this scam, the victim's phone rings and, on the other end, a sweet-sounding person says, "You may be the recipient of a huge inheritance. But first some questions must be answered, such as birthday, birthplace, mother's maiden name, Social Security number"—all the information needed to withdraw money from the victim's bank account. When the victim answers the questions, the con artist says that he or she will deposit the inheritance in the victim's bank account. In the morning, a fraudulent check is deposited into the victim's account. In the afternoon, before the fraudulent check can be discovered, a withdrawal is made, and the victim has lost money.[48]

One variation of the inheritance scam involves a victim who pays an inheritance tax before the inheritance is paid. Sometimes the caller tells the victim to mail the inheritance tax. Sometimes a well-dressed, official-looking gentleman collects the inheritance tax in cash before awarding the victim a phony cashier's check.

THREE-CARD MONTE

This scam is similar to the traditional shell game. The crook, using three "marked" playing cards, shuffles the cards and coaxes the victim to pick the ace, queen of hearts, or whatever. In this case, the hands of the crook are usually quicker than the eyes of the victims. The cards are "marked"—sometimes by feel, such as folded edges—in some way that is recognizable to the shuffler. Initially permitted to win, thus receiving ego strokes, the victim is then cheated out of his or her money.

C.O.D. SCAM

The suspects usually pose as delivery employees. In an affluent neighborhood, the suspect spots an empty house and finds the resident's name. After writing a phony mailing label, the suspect goes next door and asks the neighbor to accept a perishable package for the absent neighbor and to pay cash for C.O.D. charges.

A variant carried out on weekends involves demanding that a naive teenage gas station attendant take cash register funds to pay for a package the owner supposedly ordered. Hoping to please the boss, who is off work for the weekend, the young employee pays the money. Of course, the boss ordered nothing, and the money is lost.

MONEY-MAKING-MACHINE SCAM

In this scam, a couple of con artists visit a local dice game to look for victims. They tell the victim that they have smuggled a secret formula out of Germany (or some other foreign country) that will bleach the ink on $1 bills. Then the blank paper can be pressed against a $100 bill to form another $100 bill. In one case reported in Philadelphia, a victim brought 150 hundred-dollar bills from his bank to a motel room, where the money was washed and stuck in between pieces of tissue paper with "bleached" dollar bills. While the victim went drinking with some of the con artists, one went back to the motel room and took the money. Another promised to look for the thieves and kept the victim from calling the police for a week. When the victim finally did call the police a week later, the suspects were long gone.

NIGERIAN OIL CON

In the Nigerian oil con, the suspects place an advertisement in a newspaper, claiming to have connections inside the Nigerian government. The price of oil that is quoted is usually just a few cents per barrel below the current market price. The victim's confidence in the "good deal" is raised when the suspects dispatch to the victim "a succession of convincing telexes and documents,"[49] some even originating from the oil-carrying vessel itself.

The key to the con is the bill of lading. However, bills of lading are easy to fake. There are few ways to check the authenticity of such documents, and the demand to see any additional papers will be of little concern to shipping con artists. "If it is only one document that stands in the way of making a deal, then they will ask you what color you want it in."[50]

Soon after the buyer begins negotiating for the cargo, typically worth millions of dollars, depending on the size of the oil tanker, the "supplier" will demand a cash advance of $250,000 to defray port costs and other expenses. After payment is made, that is usually the last time the buyer hears from the supplier.[51] Both purchasers, the true purchaser and the conned purchaser, often meet at the dock, awaiting the arrival of the same oil tanker.

WHITE-COLLAR CRIME

In 1949 a new type of crime was brought to the attention of law enforcement when Professor Edwin H. Sutherland defined *white-collar crime* as "a crime committed by a person of respectability and high social status in the course of his occupation."[52] The definition of white collar crime has since been expanded to include people of lower status. It is an illegal act or series of illegal acts committed by nonphysical means and by concealment or guile, to obtain money or property, to avoid the payment or loss of money or property, or to obtain business or personal advantage.[53]

For a successful prosecution, law enforcement officials must show that one or more criminal statutes have been violated. They must prove an illegal activity rather than concentrating on the offender.

It is important, therefore, for officers to understand how white collar crimes are committed. Knowing the identity of the perpetrator of a fraud is not enough. The law enforcement officer must be able to understand, explain, and show conclusively how and why the activities are illegal. In this section, we look at three types of white-collar crime and demonstrate their complexity and fraudulence: Ponzi, or pyramid, schemes; money laundering; and fraudulent use of Social Security numbers. These are only three examples of the briberies, kickbacks, payoffs, bankruptcy, credit card, check, consumer, and insurance frauds that occur each year.

PONZI, OR PYRAMID, SCHEMES

Pyramid sales schemes, otherwise known as "chain-referral schemes" or "Ponzi schemes," have mushroomed across the United States and may be operating in other countries. There is no way of calculating the exact amount of money lost by the victims, but it is estimated to be well over half a billion dollars in the United States alone. Some officials contend that pyramid sales schemes are the leading consumer fraud problem today. Despite the scope of the problem, many people still do not know what pyramids are.

A pyramid scheme is a marketing program by which people buy the right to sell others the right to sell a specified product. The promoters select a product, such as household items, cosmetics, or safety devices, and sell large inventories to distributors with the incentive of permitting the distributor to sell new distributorships. The real profit is earned as recruiters develop new recruits. In all of this activity, little or no real concern is given to the direct public sale of products or services. Consumer distribution is a sham.[54]

One of the earliest known examples of a pyramid scheme appeared in 1920, in Boston. Charles Ponzi, an Italian immigrant and financial wizard, established the Securities and Exchange Company. The corporation consisted of only Ponzi, who started his company with a few hundred dollars borrowed from two silent partners. The company promised investors substantial returns on their investments in Ponzi's company. Within 45 days investors were promised their original investment plus 50 percent interest; in 90 days, they would double their original investment. By June 1920 Ponzi claimed to be receiving $500,000 and paying out $200,000 a day.

Ponzi explained to doubters that knowing how to take advantage of the varying currency exchange rates in different parts of the world was how he made his profit. He started his company upon receiving a business letter from a conspirator in

Spain, who enclosed a reply coupon that, if exchanged at any U.S. Post Office, was worth $0.06. In Spain, the cost of the coupon to a buyer was only $0.01. Ponzi reasoned that by buying the coupon in Spain and redeeming it in the United States, he made a $0.05 profit. Thereafter, Ponzi began operations in nine different countries, with his agents traveling back and forth between these countries and the United States to take advantage of the disparity in currency value.

A *Boston Post* reporter was convinced that Ponzi had never purchased any coupons and that he was taking money from one investor to pay off another. This reporter turned up information that Ponzi, under his real name of Charles Bianchi, had been sentenced to prison in Canada for forgery several years earlier. At the end of 1920, Ponzi's world collapsed, and he was convicted in Massachusetts. Of the $15 million that Ponzi had taken in, there was no accounting for $8 million. Such schemes became known as Ponzi schemes.

In recent years, a pyramid scheme hit the United States in which one needed only a chart and $1,000 in cash (see Figure 16–8). With the $1,000, you could buy a slot on the bottom line. You gave $500 each to the investor above you (position 8) and in the 0 position. Pyramid success occurred when all the slots on the player's line were filled and the player progressed up the chart. When an investor finally moved into the zero position, he or she could begin collecting up to $16,000.

At the heart of each pyramid scheme was the expressed or implied representation that a new participant could recoup his or her original investment by simply inducing two or more prospects to make the same investment. Promoters failed to tell participants that this is mathematically impossible, because some people dropped out of the pyramid even before recouping their original investment, and others recouped their original investment and then dropped out. This misrepresentation constitutes the heart of the fraud. If each investor recruits two additional investors and no one drops out, everything works according to plan. If there are 15 investors at the meeting to start a pyramid and one person at the top level, the number of new members doubles each day thereafter until, at the end of two weeks, 262,143 people are involved and, at the end of three weeks, there are 33,554,431 participants. The whole scheme collapses before

Figure 16–8
The Pyramid Scheme

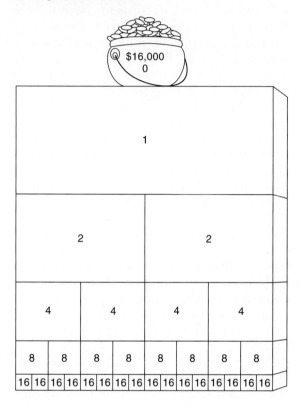

probable cause, they can obtain a search warrant and secure the relevant records.

Generally, in an investment fraud case, courts base the probable cause necessary to obtain a search warrant on multiple factors. Several individuals must have given money to a suspect for purposes of making an investment; these investors relied on the suspect's promise that their funds would be invested for a limited period of time; and the time period has since expired without repayment to the investors or a reasonable explanation from the suspect.

Investigators should be aware that because grand juries possess the authority to subpoena all information relevant to matters under their investigation, financial records may also be obtained through a grand jury subpoena duces tecum.[56] However, for a cash-flow analysis, securing a search warrant is generally preferable.

By securing a search warrant, investigators directly receive the relevant bank records, which can then be given to a forensic accountant. If the financial records are obtained through a grand jury subpoena duces tecum, auditors must complete the cash-flow analysis while the grand jury hears the case. This may prolong the time required to secure an indictment.

Step Two The second step for investigators in this process is to turn over all the financial records obtained through the search warrant or subpoena to a forensic accountant for the cash-flow analysis. The forensic accountant then analyzes the bank account records and prepares cash-flow compilations of these records in financial statement form. This statement shows all the known receipts of a particular bank account during a specified period of time. Accordingly, this report demonstrates the flow of funds into and out of a Ponzi artist's account.

When completed, the compilation also assists investigators in determining whether the suspect accurately represented the investments to contributors. If investigators determine that a crime may have been committed, the compilation can then be introduced at subsequent court proceedings as demonstrative evidence of theft. The cash-flow analysis compilation allows prosecutors to provide juries with a tangible record of how the suspect committed the crime and spent the victims' money.

this. Therefore, the earlier one gets in on the pyramid, the better the possibility to collect the $16,000. For everyone to win, an infinite number of investors would have to fill the chart.

Method of Cash-Flow Analysis

The method of cash-flow analysis in Ponzi schemes is a two-step process. The first step for investigators is to obtain all relevant records—such as checks, deposit slips, and monthly bank statements—from the financial institution(s) in which the suspect placed the victims' money. The second step involves turning over these financial records to a forensic accountant for the cash-flow analysis.[55]

Step One Since most victims make their investments by personal or cashier's check, the Ponzi artist usually deposits these funds (if only temporarily) into a bank account. This makes each investment a traceable transaction. After investigators become confident that they have amassed sufficient

Use of Forensic Accountants Investigators traditionally underuse forensic accountants in cases of white collar crime. This is an unfortunate and potentially damaging oversight. In other types of major crime cases, investigators employ such specialists as pathologists, serologists, psychiatrists, fingerprint and document examiners, and criminalists to aid in analyzing evidence. Similarly, in many major cases of white collar fraud, forensic accountants should be called on to apply their training and expertise to legal matters and to testify in court as expert witnesses.

Problems for Law Enforcement

When companies promote Ponzi schemes, auditing becomes difficult, expensive, and time consuming. The presence of many promoters in an area makes prosecution impractical. By the time police have all the information they need, most promotions have run their course.

The problem of establishing criminal liability is made more difficult by the need to separate victims from promoters. It is in the victim's best interest to become a promoter and transfer his or her loss to another. For this reason, useful victim testimony is limited. Only victims who invested in the pyramid for reasons other than participation in the chain referral provide useful testimony.

In a Ponzi scheme, investigators also face the arduous task of determining the validity of suspects' claims to victims regarding their investments. In addition, prosecutors must then demonstrate how offenders spent the victims' money. These two elements make Ponzi schemes especially difficult to investigate and prosecute, since Ponzi artists generally "cover their bases" well.

Often, in order to limit victims' inquiries, offenders represent investment opportunities as being highly technical and sophisticated in nature. Further, many victims of white-collar crime hesitate to cooperate with investigators, fearing that if the offender becomes aware of an investigation, they will not be repaid. Or victims may simply be embarrassed because they made a foolish investment.

While victim reluctance to cooperate hampers many investigative techniques used in white-collar crime, it has little effect on the method of cash-flow analysis. Because this approach traces suspected illegal activity through financial records, investigators and prosecutors do not have to base their cases predominately on the testimony of victims.

MONEY LAUNDERING

Al Capone, the infamous gangster of the 1920s, is said to have amassed a fortune of $20 million in 10 years through bootlegging and gambling. Yet when Capone was sentenced to 11 years in prison in 1931, it was for income tax evasion. The conviction of Capone taught other organized-crime members an important lesson: Money not reported on an income tax return is money that cannot be spent or invested without risk of detection and prosecution.

Because most money collected by organized crime is from illegal sources, such as loan-sharking, prostitution, gambling, and narcotics, criminals are reluctant to report the income or its sources on tax returns. Before spending or otherwise using these funds, they must give the money an aura of legality. This conversion is known as *laundering*. To combat organized crime successfully, law enforcement officials must understand how money is laundered.[57]

The Laundering of Money by Organized Crime

At the end of the 1800s, most money earned by the American underworld was gained through extortion, blackmail, and dock racketeering. By the 1920s, most came from bootlegging, and some believe that Prohibition supplied organized crime with the funds and skills to operate multimillion-dollar ventures. "Organized crime is an estimated $100 billion-a-year untaxed business operated by groups ranging from motorcycle gangs, to Asian drug triads, to the Italian Mafia."[58]

Domestic Laundries

Certain businesses lend themselves to laundering money. For example, the business must be capable of absorbing a large volume of cash income, because most illicit income is received as cash. The purpose of laundering funds is to commingle licit and illicit monies so that they cannot be separated and to prevent the discovery of the introduction of illegal money into the business. Because most checks and credit card receipts are traceable by law enforcement officials, businesses such as restaurants, bars, and massage parlors, which take in a high proportion of cash, tend to be more desirable as laundries than businesses that receive most of their income as checks or other traceable instruments.

Another favorable characteristic for a laundry is expenses that do not vary with sales volume. An example of such a business is a movie theater that shows pornographic films. The expenses of such a business (rent, electricity, wages) are almost constant, regardless of whether the theater is full. Illicit income can be introduced and camouflaged in this type of business quite easily, because the additional sales do not increase expenses. Law enforcement officials who examined the records of such a theater would have trouble proving that the legitimate income generated by the theater was lower than that recorded.

Businesses that experience a high rate of spoilage or other loss of goods may also be used to launder money. Groceries and restaurants are good examples. Money is introduced into the business and recorded in its general income accounts as if it had been received from customers. Fraudulent invoices for produce or other perishable items are issued to these businesses by companies acting as suppliers. The grocery or restaurant issues checks to these "suppliers" or records the transaction as a cash payment and charges it to an expense account, such as cost of goods sold. The undelivered produce or perishable items listed as spoiled and discarded are written off the books (see Figure 16–9). The grocery store or restaurant thus avoids tax liability, and the funds paid to "suppliers" seem legal and may be spent or invested with little risk of discovery. Within a week of the transaction, it is almost impossible for law enforcement officials to disprove the story of the grocer or restaurant owner.

The above techniques have been used to launder funds successfully for a number of years, and large

Figure 16–9
Laundering of Money from Illicit Sources

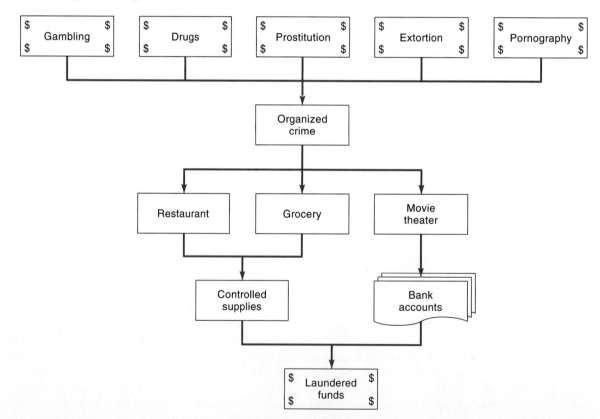

numbers of domestic businesses controlled by organized crime are still being used for this function. In recent years, however, law enforcement officials have adapted new methods, such as sampling, ratio analysis, and flow charting, to discover laundering operations and to prosecute the people involved in them.

Sampling is a statistical procedure in which the number of customers of an establishment is randomly counted, a conservative estimate made of the amount of money spent by each customer, and a projection made of how much money is actually received by an enterprise in the ordinary course of operation. If the projected income is materially smaller than that reported to taxing authorities, it is a good indication that the business is being used to launder funds.

Ratios to evaluate businesses have been used for many years by accountants, investors, and lending institutions. There are four basic types of ratios:

1. *Liquidity ratios*, which indicate the ability of an enterprise to satisfy its immediate (short-term) financial obligations.

2. *Operating ratios*, which indicate the efficiency of the business.

3. *Profitability ratios*, which indicate the effective use of assets and the return of the owner's investment in the business.

4. *Leverage ratios*, which indicate the extent to which the enterprise is financed by debt.

By using *ratio analysis*, an investigator can compare the past performance of a business with that of the industry in which the business operates. This comparison can be used to spot significant deviations from the norm, and these may indicate the existence of a laundering operation.

Another method used to uncover laundering involves researching the corporate and ownership structures of both the suspected business and all the companies with which it deals. The relationship between the various companies may be illustrated visually by the process of *flowcharting*, which allows investigators, prosecutors, and juries to grasp more easily the sometimes complex relationships that exist in laundering operations.

Although law enforcement agencies have been relatively successful in exposing domestic laundering operations, underworld leaders have perfected international laundering operations, which have traditionally been immune from exposure. Although international laundries vary greatly in form, organization, and complexity, their object is still to disguise the true nature and origin of illegal funds. International laundering schemes often involve the use of dummy corporations, numbered bank accounts, or financial instruments issued by banks (often referred to as *offshore banks*) located in countries where banking regulations are lax.

Foreign Laundries

Much of the money invested by organized crime in legitimate businesses in the United States is first routed through secret numbered bank accounts in countries such as Liechtenstein, Luxembourg, the Channel Islands, Panama, the Bahamas, the Netherlands Antilles, Antigua, Anguilla, Montserrat, the Grand Cayman Islands, Hong Kong, Dubai, the United Arab Emirates, Singapore, Nauru, Vanuatu, Uruguay, Austria, and Bulgaria.[59] This arrangement is ideal for the racketeer who wishes to clean large amounts of cash. Often it involves depositing illicit funds in a secret numbered account and then bringing them back into the United States as a loan from the foreign bank or from a dummy corporation set up under the laws of a foreign country. Not only are the illegal income and its sources hidden from the Internal Revenue Service and law enforcement agencies, but the interest on this supposed loan is often deducted as a business expense on the tax return of the racketeer.

In many cases, organized-crime members have not been content with merely using secret numbered accounts in foreign banks. As early as the 1960s, it was recognized that many banks in Switzerland and the Bahamas had been taken over by Americans known to be associated with organized-crime activities.[60] Not only did the American ownership protect the identity of bank customers and allow for the falsification of bank records, but it also enabled the racketeers to bring apparently legitimate money back into the United States in the form of various financial instruments issued by these banks and by foreign governments. Owners realized that controlled banks could also be used to generate illicit income by issuing fraudulent financial instruments that are used in this country as collateral for loans and in other fraud schemes. Enforcement agents working for the U.S. Comptroller of the Currency have estimated that the volume of phony financial instruments issued by offshore banks is in the hundreds of millions of dollars.[61]

Forensic Examination of Money-Laundering Records

Determining where suspects' cash originates and the means they use to conceal this cash can be exceedingly difficult for investigators, unless they have reliable informants, cooperating witnesses, or undercover agents. In addition, investigators may find it difficult to distinguish cash gained through legitimate businesses from cash gained through illegal means.[62]

For these reasons, circumstantial evidence becomes critical in money-laundering cases. It is often the only evidence available to provide a connection between the funds in question and their original source. In fact, it is this very link, the "specified unlawful activity" (SUA), that is a statutory requirement in federal money-laundering prosecutions.

Today, the Racketeering Records Analysis Unit (RRAU) of the FBI laboratory in Washington, D.C., can establish this necessary link by examining the records kept by criminals who launder money. Criminals, in order to provide proof to their superiors that they properly channeled all of the cash, document the collection and disbursement of all funds. Fortunately, these records also provide critical evidence for investigators, who must prove that the funds were acquired illegally.

This section provides information on the operations of the RRAU and how the unit can assist investigators and prosecutors in developing money-laundering cases. It also discusses some of the methods criminals commonly use to hide illegal proceeds. Although these methods vary greatly, experts can now identify characteristics unique to these types of organizations. And, while none of these methods are new, what *is* new is that law enforcement now recognizes the value of forensic examination of these records.

The RRAU uses the clandestine business documents confiscated from organizations believed to be laundering funds to trace the history of the alleged illicit businesses. These documents reveal valuable information as to the amount of money laundered and how the suspects packaged, transported, disguised, and hid these funds. By providing a more complete picture of the roles and behaviors of criminals and their illegal operations, the RRAU expands the scope of money-laundering investigations.

In addition, this information can aid prosecutors in gaining stiffer sentences for individuals found guilty of money laundering. The courts base suspects' sentences on the amounts they laundered, which are determined through their own business records. Current federal sentencing guidelines[63] allow for these sentence adjustments, and at least one federal appeals court has upheld the use of RRAU testimony in connection with related sentencing adjustments in drug matters.[64]

As previously discussed, individuals who launder money use a variety of techniques to avoid detection by law enforcement. Therefore, it is important that law enforcement personnel understand the various techniques and the proof needed to ensure successful prosecution of these cases.

Secreting Funds Criminals often hide illegally obtained funds until they can smuggle the money to another destination. Although hiding funds increases the risk of seizure by authorities or theft by other criminals, it eliminates the need for a professional money launderer, who typically charges a fee ranging from 3 to 5 percent to assist in transferring the money through legitimate financial institutions.

This technique was evident in a New York case in which authorities seized millions of dollars in currency, as well as business records, from an alleged furniture and appliance warehouse. Although officials had kept the warehouse under surveillance for several months, the evidence acquired during that time was largely circumstantial, consisting mainly of investigators' accounts of activity in and around the warehouse. In this case, investigators observed that the subjects frequently used telephone paging devices and made numerous attempts to elude, or otherwise mislead, surveillance units. Investigators also found cocaine residue on a piece of duct tape retrieved from a trash receptacle located outside the warehouse. Finally, they noted that although the warehouse moved little furniture, there still appeared to be a lot of activity inside the building.

When investigators raided the warehouse, they discovered a collection and storage point for drug proceeds, instead of the cocaine "stash house" that they had expected to find. And, although they did not confiscate drugs, they did confiscate approximately $18 million in U.S. currency, packaged in cardboard boxes and secreted in a concealed compartment of a truck. In addition, investigators also confiscated numerous handwritten documents from both the warehouse and other search locations, which they then submitted to the RRAU for analysis.

The initial review of the records indicated that they represented transactions involving millions of dollars in cash—recorded as it came into the warehouse—followed by confirmed totals counted by denomination. The suspects assigned the totals to at least 11 accounts before combining the cash into outgoing sums that were packaged in boxes and suitcases and placed in the truck. This method typifies how money launderers hide large sums of cash until they can transport it out of the country.

However, a more detailed analysis of the warehouse documents by the RRAU revealed more damaging evidence to be used at trial. Records showed that the organization had received, through at least 114 exchanges, over $44 million in cash during a three-month period. Individuals in the warehouse had listed the amount of cash received, the date of receipt, the account relating to each transfer of funds, the *alleged* amount at time of delivery, and the *confirmed* count of each amount. The listing of incoming and confirmed accounts, along with counts of the currency by denomination and coded account designations, characterize money-laundering records.

Of particular interest was an outgoing amount of nearly $7.5 million, listed on one page of the seized documents. The same amount appeared on another page of the documents as the sum of three smaller amounts of cash that the suspects placed in boxes and a suitcase. Further examination of the documents revealed a third page, which indicated that the individuals derived the smaller amounts of money by counting it by currency denominations, that is, $100s, $50s, $20s, and so on. The amount of money seized in the warehouse closely approximated that of the currency listed on an inventory recovered from one of the search locations. By comparing documents, examiners determined that the criminals sorted the cash according to denomination and boxed it for storage, most likely until

they could smuggle the money out of the country. Finally, the confiscated records revealed that the suspects had collected the nearly $7.5 million over a period of several days just prior to preparing it for shipment. This evidence served to further strengthen the case for prosecutors.

However, in order to prosecute the suspects under the federal money-laundering statutes, prosecutors needed to provide proof that the suspects had obtained the funds illegally. Therefore, an FBI examiner testified in court concerning notations on two seized documents. These notations showed the purchase/sale of 35 units, at prices of $13,500 and $14,000 each, between August 24 and October 4. The examiner further testified that there appeared to be a relationship between the units and their corresponding prices: the units were consistent with kilogram prices for cocaine. This type of bookkeeping—partial dates and an informal accounting flow—typifies drug records. It also provided another indication that the suspects had obtained the funds through an illicit drug trade.

It is important to note in this case that even though investigators found the drug documents in one location and the cash documents in another, RRAU experts were still able to establish a circumstantial relationship between the two sets of records. It is this type of evidence that can be so crucial to any such case.

Disguising the Source of Illicit Funds "Operation Polarcap," a joint investigation conducted by the FBI, the Drug Enforcement Administration (DEA), and the U.S. Customs Service, is an excellent example of how business records and paperwork provide critical evidence in money-laundering cases. By examining seized documents, examiners gained valuable insights into how the criminals had disguised the actual source of illegal funds. This undercover investigation, which involved months of surveillance, resulted in the seizure of thousands of documents, many of them found in trash receptacles at various businesses connected to the laundering scheme, including a jewelry store located in Los Angeles.

When RRAU examiners received the confiscated documents, their task was to show, based solely on an analysis of the documents, how the suspects received cash and circulated it through legitimate financial institutions in ways designed to conceal its true origin. Their analysis revealed a laundering network that acquired millions of dollars in cash from sources in New York, Los Angeles, and Houston. A large portion of this cash from these cities was delivered to the Los Angeles jewelry store.

RRAU examiners were able to show that when the suspects received the cash, they noted on bills of lading the total number of packages in a given shipment, as well as individual weights and total dollar values of each package. For example, one of the receipts indicated a delivery of five packages weighing 250 pounds and valued at $1,568,000. A handwritten entry in a seized ledger book showed that same dollar amount under the column heading "$ Received." Finally, a computerized summary of currency transaction reports (CTRs) filed by several Los Angeles area banks at which the jewelry store maintained accounts showed $1,568,000 deposited to an account at one of these banks. A comparison of all these documents confirmed that the numerical notations represented amounts of cash delivered from New York to Los Angeles.

Other evidence indicating that the suspects had attempted to disguise the illicit funds included a dated ledger entry showing that the jewelry store had received $2,800,000 on September 2. A scrap of paper bearing the same date showed that this figure was a combination of three smaller amounts labeled "L.A." One of these amounts was $1 million. Other scraps of paper found in the trash at the jewelry store indicated that the $1 million was counted by denomination on September 2. All this evidence pointed toward a possible money-laundering operation.

Fraudulent Documents   Money-laundering organizations also produce fraudulent documents, such as sales receipts, designed to conceal the true origin of a business's cash. For example, in the Los Angeles jewelry store case, investigators found a scrap of paper, dated August 10, 1988, which indicated two amounts of collected cash totaling $1,034,000 and designated "L.A." This corresponded with a cash deposit of $1,034,000 made on that date to an account of the business at another Los Angeles bank.

In addition, investigators recovered two consecutively numbered receipts from trash receptacles. These receipts revealed how the suspects broke down this total in an effort to portray the source of the money as cash proceeds from two sales of 24k gold to a gold refiner in the amounts of $693,000 and $341,000. Since cash sales that large would be highly unusual in any legitimate business, the suspects produced fraudulent documents designed to conceal the true origin of the business's cash. At trial, the RRAU examiner testified that these types of business practices are inconsistent with normal business activities. Instead, they are associated with money-laundering operations.

Of tremendous importance in this case was the seizure, on an almost daily basis, of many documents from trash discarded at the business. A critical lesson learned from this analysis is that the potential value of garbage in criminal investigations cannot be overestimated.

Structuring Financial Transactions   Another method for laundering money involves structuring financial transactions. This type of activity was evident in another case uncovered through a federal investigation in Brooklyn and Manhattan in 1990.

The case involved a residential setting—specifically, four apartments—where suspects collected, counted, and prepared drug funds for conversion to negotiable instruments, such as bank money orders. When investigators raided the apartments, they recovered $1,304,595 in cash, along with money orders worth approximately $73,000, all in amounts of less than $10,000. Investigators also seized hundreds of additional money order receipts and related handwritten documents, which they submitted for examination.

An RRAU analysis of the seized documents disclosed that the operation received cash totaling at least $13,503,441 in 26 deliveries from September 1989 to March 1990. After the suspects received the cash, they listed daily breakdowns that showed, through a series of deductions, how specific amounts were used to purchase money orders at area financial institutions. These purchases totaled a minimum of $11,022,141 during a six-month period, allowing authorities to convict the main defendant for laundering over $10 million in cash.

This evidence resulted in an increase of nine levels in the defendant's sentence under the federal sentencing guidelines. Based partly on a previously negotiated plea bargain, the defendant received a much longer prison sentence than would have resulted had the documents not been carefully examined.[65]

FRAUDULENT USE OF SOCIAL SECURITY NUMBERS

Almost every American has a Social Security number (SSN). This nine-digit number is becoming indispensable as a national identifier. The correct use of an SSN can help people get jobs, pay taxes, establish credit, open checking accounts, register firearms, and file for bankruptcy—among many other uses. Conversely, the use of a false SSN allows a criminal to assume a new identity and, in so doing, to victimize the unknowing legitimate holder of that SSN. The use of false SSNs has become a $24-billion-a-year crime. Criminals use false SSNs to fraudulently obtain things they cannot obtain using their own SSNs, including credit cards, real estate loans, and commercial credit. False SSNs also allow criminals to hide their criminal records, which would prevent them from buying firearms or allow them to be correctly identified when arrested.[66]

Victims of this crime are not confined to the financial institutions that are defrauded through the use of false SSNs. Often the real victim is the true SSN account holder, whose credit may be ruined by the abuser. In those cases in which false SSNs are used to file for bankruptcies, the true account holders will unknowingly have the bankruptcies charged against them. Unless they request a copy of their credit report, they may never know that bankruptcy proceedings took place.

The U.S. Department of Health and Human Services (DHHS) administers the Social Security Administration (SSA), which controls and manages the process by which Social Security numbers are issued. The Social Security Act was enacted in 1935 to provide Social Security payments to the aged, in the form of federal benefit payments. These payments are based on Social Security taxes paid through a person's employment. To administer this system of payments and benefits, the SSA created the Social Security numbering system. Under this system, each person who wants to gain employment applies for a number from the administration.

The SSA began issuing numbers in mid-November 1936, and by 1937, 40 million SSNs had been issued. Today, more than 325 million numbers have been assigned, of which 210 million are considered active. Originally, SSNs were assigned based on unsupported statements from the applicant about his or her identity. But as it became apparent that more and more applicants provided false information to fraudulently obtain additional numbers, and as the national importance of the SSN as an identifier grew, the SSA instituted stricter rules.

Beginning in 1978, applicants for SSNs had to offer documentary evidence to support their statements. The document most often used by applicants is their birth certificate. Also, all applicants over the age of 18 are personally interviewed, and all Americans are required to have a number by the age of 2. The first three digits (except for the 700 series) identify the geographic area of issuance. (see Table 16–1) The 700 series was reserved, until 1963, for people covered under the Railroad Retirement system. In 1963, newly hired railroad employees were issued regular SSNs, and new issuances in the 700 series were discontinued. To date, the 800 and 900 series have not been issued.

The second two numbers are known as group numbers, breaking geographic areas into groups. The last four numbers, called serial numbers, are a straight numerical progression from 0001 to 9999 within each group. It should be noted that SSA has never issued a 0000 serial number or a 00 group number.

There are 20 unique SSNs called "pocketbook numbers." These are SSNs that appeared on facsimile Social Security cards that wallet manufacturers sold with their wallets. Many people who bought these wallets assumed that this was a specific SSN assigned to them, and they used this number for employment or tax purposes. Below are some of the most common "pocketbook numbers":

022-28-1852	165-22-7999
042-10-3580	165-24-7999
062-36-0749	189-09-2294
078-05-1120	212-09-7694
095-07-3645	219-09-9999
128-03-6045	306-30-2348
135-01-6629	308-12-5070
141-18-6941	468-28-8779
165-16-7999	549-24-1889
165-18-7999	987-65-4320
165-20-7999	

Table 16–1
Designated Geographic Areas for Social Security Number Issuance

Numbers*	Area†	Number(s)*	Area†
001-003	New Hampshire	425-428, 587, 588‡	Mississippi
004-007	Maine	429-432, 676-679‡	Arkansas
008-009	Vermont	433-439, 659-665‡	Louisiana
010-034	Massachusetts	440-448	Oklahoma
035-039	Rhode Island	449-467, 627-645	Texas
040-049	Connecticut	468-477	Minnesota
050-134	New York	478-485	Iowa
135-158	New Jersey	486-400	Missouri
159-211	Pennsylvania	501-502	North Dakota
212-220	Maryland	503-504	South Dakota
221-222	Delaware	505-508	Nebraska
223-231, 691-699‡	Virginia	509-515	Kansas
232-236	West Virginia	516-517	Montana
232, 237-246	North Carolina	518-519	Idaho
247-251, 654-658‡	South Carolina	520	Wyoming
252-260, 667-675‡	Georgia	521-524, 650-653	Colorado
261-267, 589-595	Florida	525, 585, 648-649	New Mexico
268-302	Ohio	526-527	Arizona
303-317	Indiana	525-529, 646-647	Utah
318-361	Illinois	530, 680‡	Nevada
362-386	Michigan	531-539	Washington
387-399	Wisconsin	540-544	Oregon
400-407	Kentucky	545-573, 602-626	California
408-415, 756-763‡	Tennessee	574	Alaska
416-424	Alabama	575-576, 750-751	Hawaii
577-579	District of Columbia	586	American Samoa
580	Virgin Islands	586	Northern Mariana Islands
580-584, 596-599	Puerto Rico	586, 617	Philippine Islands
586	Guam	700-728§	Railroad Board

* Any number beginning with 000 will never be a valid Social Security number.

† When an area is shown more than once, either (1) certain numbers have been transferred from one state to another or (2) an area has been divided for use among certain geographic locations.

‡ New area allocated but not yet issued.

§ Issuance of these numbers to railroad employees was discontinued July 1, 1963.

Source: Investigator's Guide to Sources of Information, United States General Accounting Office, Office of Special Investigations. April 1997.

The DHHS Office of Inspector General (OIG) was established in 1978 to combat crimes committed against the department, including the misuse of SSNs.

Congress passed several laws in 1972 and 1976 making it a crime to obtain a Social Security card using false information or to knowingly use a false SSN. In 1982, Congress upgraded these crimes from misdemeanors to felonies. These laws come under Title 42 U.S.C., S408. The penalty for conviction under this section is a maximum of five years' imprisonment and/or a maximum fine of $5,000 for each count.

This law is becoming a favorite tool of some U.S. attorneys to combat a wide variety of white collar crimes. Assistant U.S. attorneys are increasingly using it because the law does not require proving intent to defraud. The only element of the crime is that the person using the false SSN had knowledge that this was a false number. Thus, this charge is often included in indictments in which credit card or bank loan fraud is alleged.

The OIG investigates allegations involving the use of false SSNs. Special agents of the OIG obtain whatever documents exist on which the false SSN and the subject's signature appear. Then the OIG works on proving that the subject had knowledge that the number was false. Most often, this is proven by information provided to OIG criminal investigators through admissions by the subjects themselves.

The following are examples of recent cases the OIG has investigated:

- A Georgia woman was sentenced to four years in prison and ordered to make restitution of $13,700 for having used a false SSN to fraudulently obtain unemployment benefits.
- A California man received a five-year sentence for using false SSNs in a complex real estate fraud scheme. In addition, the court ordered the subject to pay $230,000 in penalties to the Internal Revenue Service for not reporting his profits from the scheme.
- In North Carolina, a Nigerian national was sentenced to six years' imprisonment for using a false SSN to obtain fraudulent credit. He had defrauded several department stores of over $47,000.

In addition to individual cases, the OIG has initiated many projects across the country to increase the detection and investigation of—and prosecution for—misuse of Social Security numbers. These projects include the following:

- *Project Passport:* The objective is to obtain criminal convictions of individuals who attempt to obtain passports and visas through the State Department using false SSNs.
- *Project Credit Card:* The objective is to obtain criminal convictions of persons using false SSNs to evade a bad credit history and thereby obtain fraudulent bank loans and credit cards.
- *Project Bankruptcy:* The objective is to obtain criminal convictions of persons using false SSNs under which they file for bankruptcy.

Many states have laws (similar to the federal law) that make it a crime to use a false SSN. In California, for example, misuse of Social Security numbers can be prosecuted under California Penal Code Section 532(a) (False Financial Documents). This law provides that anyone knowingly using a false SSN, driver's license, or employment information on a financial document is guilty of a felony. A financial document is defined as any document from which the person receives financial gain. The OIG assists many local law enforcement agencies in California in prosecuting this crime. OIG reviews the documents in question to determine the validity of the SSN used. In cases in which the misuse of an SSN is determined, OIG special agents will provide documentary evidence and testimony in court regarding the false use of the SSN in question.

Unfortunately, many prosecutors and law enforcement agencies—at all government levels—are unfamiliar with the DHHS's OIG and are thus unaware of the invaluable assistance the OIG can provide in any case in which it is suspected that a person has used a false SSN for any reason. The OIG's assistance can be invaluable in the investigation of many financial fraud schemes. Prosecutors and law enforcement personnel are encouraged to call their nearest office of the U.S. Department of Health and Human Service's Office of Inspector General, Office of Investigations.

THE LOOTING OF ARCHAEOLOGICAL SITES

One type of larceny that has existed for centuries is increasingly an issue in this country. Unfortunately, many enforcement agencies lack awareness of its importance—or even its existence. "Archaeological looting is defined as illegal unscientific removal of archaeological resources."[67] This nationwide problem has been studied primarily as it relates to public and tribal lands, but looting also takes place on private land when objects are removed without the permission of the landowner. On federal land (e.g., national parks, areas under the direction of the Bureau of Land Management, and national forests) there were 1,720 documented violations of laws protecting archaeological resources between 1985 and 1987.[68] Because of the difficulty of even detecting the crimes in some areas, it is believed that this figure represents only 25 percent of the actual number of looting cases.[69] The looting of archaeological resources is related to the widespread fascination with our past; the interest of individuals in collecting archaeological materials; the high dollar value for which some archaeological works can be sold; the right to buy, possess, and sell legally obtained specimens; and the frequent difficulty of proving that the archaeological materials were illegally obtained.[70]

Archaeological resources are nonrenewable: when they are looted or vandalized, the information they contain is lost forever. The looting of archaeological sites in the United States is happening on a vast scale. Stated bluntly, part of our history has been, and continues to be, stolen. In the process, thieves have damaged and destroyed the archaeological sites that are the only way to learn about most of the 12,000-year history of humans in North America (see Figure 16–10). Such looting also means that some private collectors can withhold from the public precious and beautiful objects that they or others have stolen.

This problem is not isolated in one region of the country. It is occurring on public and private lands, in battlefield parks, and in historic cemeteries. Although a certain amount of the looting is done by individuals seeking to enhance their own collections, there is also significant illegal commercial trafficking in artifacts for personal profit.[71] Persons bent on profiting are not the only offenders responsible for the loss of artifacts; the so-called casual looters and vandals also contribute significantly to the problem.[72] Vandalism may be intentional—as in the case of defacement of ancient rock art by graffiti or target shooting—or unintentional, as in accidental site damage from off-road vehicles.[73]

There is a substantial market for Native American artifacts in this country, as well as in Germany, Japan, and other countries: an ancient pot from the Southwest was sold for $250,000 in Paris; a Mississippi stone ax was offered for sale for $150,000 in

Figure 16–10
Looted Grave at Chavez Pass, Pueblo, Arizona

(Courtesy National Park Service)

New Orleans; and a single rare arrowhead has an appraised value of $20,000.[74] In the Four Corners area alone (the point where Arizona, Colorado, New Mexico, and Utah meet), more than 44,000 known sites have been looted or vandalized in recent years.[75] On the Navajo Reservation, the number of archaeological sites victimized increased 900 percent between 1980 and 1987.[76] One of the most spectacular Native American sites is the famous Cliff Palace in Mesa Verde National Park, Colorado. This stone structure was built by the Anasazi (a Navajo word meaning "Ancient Ones") as home for 400 people nearly 900 years ago.[77] The Anasazi were the ancestors of the Pueblo, Hopi, Zuñi, and other tribes. The intricate designs of their pottery and woven baskets are stunning.[78] Today, an unbroken Anasazi mug or bowl crafted or painted not particularly well is worth $150 to $200, a piece of midrange quality is worth $500 to $800, and even a specimen that is just "pretty good" will bring several thousand dollars and up (see Figure 16–11).[79] In Oregon's Deschutes National Forest, a looter was apprehended with a trailer containing 3,000 artifacts, digging equipment, and site maps coded to where artifacts were most plentiful.[80] Other public lands that have suffered losses due to vandalism and theft of Native American artifacts include Pisgah National Forest in North Carolina, Chippewa

Figure 16–11
Anasazi Artifacts
Anasazi-Mesa Verde black-on-white bowl (*left*) and mug (*right*) from the Yellow Jacket area, southwestern Colorado.

(Courtesy University of Colorado Museum, photograph by Earl Bolton)

National Forest in Minnesota, Tongass National Forest in Alaska, and Ocala National Forest in Florida, as well as sites such as Metichawon, an area in New Milford, Connecticut, and Shawnee National Forest, Illinois.

It is not only prehistoric Native American artifacts that are being stolen; another target is historic Euro-American sites such as some of our national parks. In Virginia, park rangers spotted three men entering the Richmond National Battlefield Park at 1:30 A.M.[81] With the assistance of local deputy sheriffs, a stakeout was established. Four hours later, as the defendants left the park, they were arrested and charged with federal offenses. In their possession were state-of-the-art metal detectors and Civil War artifacts, including a bayonet, minnie balls, grapeshot, a button, and other associated items (see Figure 16–12). Physical evidence was gathered that connected the three men and the artifacts to freshly dug holes in the park's historic earthworks. A similar incident involving a different defendant occurred in the Fredericksburg and Spotsylvania National Military Park.[82] In Uncompahgre National Forest, Colorado, portions of a wooden cabin that was built around 1879 were taken for use as firewood; investigation of the case led to the execution of a search warrant and recovery of portions of the cabin.[83] California's Channel Islands Marine Sanctuary was the scene of underwater looting by scuba divers; the divers took hundreds of relics from the wreck sites of the *Winfield Scott* and the *Golden Horn*, fast sail transport ships that sank in the 1800s.[84]

LEGAL CONSIDERATIONS

Federal Provisions

Federal preservation laws date from the late nineteenth century; at that time the primary intent was to document information, to set aside land areas as monuments, and to collect items of importance related to national public figures, historic military events, and ancient cultures.[85] Federal policy to preserve historic and prehistoric sites on federal land was first embodied in the Antiquities Act of 1906.[86] This act authorized a permit system for investigation of archaeological sites on federal and Native American lands and gave the president the power to establish national monuments on federal

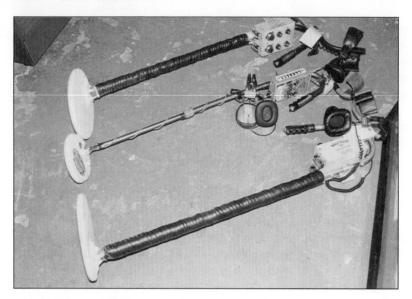

Figure 16–12
Metal Detectors used by Looters
Metal detectors seized from looters who entered Richmond National Battlefield Park and located and removed a bayonet, bullets, and other objects.

(Courtesy National Park Service)

lands to protect historic landmarks, historic and prehistoric structures, and other objects of historical and scientific interest.[87] This federal law has misdemeanor (but no felony) provisions, and fines of up to $500 and/or 90 days' imprisonment can be imposed on those "who shall appropriate, excavate, injure, or destroy any historic or prehistoric ruin or monument or any object of antiquity situated on lands owned or controlled" by the federal government unless they have been issued a permit.[88] Between 1906 and 1979, the overall enforcement impact of the Antiquities Act was very small, totaling only 18 convictions and two 90-day jail sentences.[89] It is important, however, to note that the federal management of prehistoric and historic resources on national and Native American lands has always included the responsibility to protect the resources from violators. A great deal of good was accomplished through this responsibility, although it is not reflected in enforcement statistics.

The federal government passed other legislation related to historic sites in the years following 1906, but from an enforcement standpoint, the most far-reaching law was the Archaeological Resources Protection Act (ARPA) of 1979, as amended in 1988.[90] Both felony and misdemeanor charges can be made against persons who violate ARPA, as listed in the following provisions:

1. No person may excavate, remove, damage, or otherwise alter or deface or attempt to excavate, remove, damage, or otherwise alter or deface any archaeological resource located on public lands or Native American lands (without a permit, unless the resource is specifically exempt under law);

2. No person may sell, purchase, exchange, transport, receive, or offer to sell, purchase, or exchange any archaeological resource (in violation of ARPA or any other federal law);

3. No person may sell, purchase, exchange, transport, receive, or offer to sell, purchase, or exchange, in interstate or foreign commerce, any archaeological resource excavated, removed, sold, purchased, exchanged, transported, or received in violation of any provision, rule, regulation, ordinance, or permit in effect under state or local law; and

4. Any person who knowingly violates, or counsels, procures, solicits, or employs any other person to violate any prohibition of the above shall be held accountable under the law.[91]

Archaeological resources that are protected include pottery, basketry, bottles, weapons, weapon projectiles, tools, structures, pit houses, rock paintings and carvings, graves, skeletal materials, organic waste, by-products from manufacture, rock shelters, apparel, shipwrecks, or any part of such items.[92] If the value of the damage to the archaeological resource or the value of the artifact(s) stolen is $500 or more, then the act is a felony and conviction carries a fine of up to $100,000 and/or a term of imprisonment not to exceed five years. Offenders may also be required to pay restitution, which is calculated on the basis of the actual archaeological damage done and is often used to restore the site.[93] When a defendant has a prior ARPA conviction, whether for a misdemeanor or felony, all second and subsequent ARPA violations are treated as felonies regardless of the actual dollar damage or loss.[94]

In contrast to traditional federal criminal legislation, ARPA is part of land use and conservation legislation and also contains a provision for the forfeiture of equipment, vehicles, and tools used in the attempted or actual taking of protected archaeological resources.[95] Protected resources can be characterized broadly as material remains of past human existence, of archaeological interest, that are over 100 years old.[96] ARPA has several exemptions: paleontological resources (fossils) not located within an archaeological site, arrowheads found on the surface of the ground, and the collection of rocks, bullets, coins, and minerals for private purposes. However, a "savings clause" in ARPA provides that items not protected by ARPA are still subject to protection under other federal laws.[97] In short, materials on federal lands remain federal property and may not be removed without permission.[98] ARPA and the regulations under which it is implemented defer to Native American tribal self-government and require close coordination with any tribe(s) affected when an excavation of potential tribal religious significance is contemplated outside of formal Native American lands.[99] A basic provision for permits to excavate on tribal lands is that the applicant must obtain the consent of the Native American tribe owning, or having jurisdiction over, those lands.

State Laws

As of mid-1990, none of the states had a unified law comprising all statutes protecting archaeological resources.[100] Instead, states tend to categorize laws related to archaeological resources under a variety of headings. These individual statutes may address such subjects as disturbance of marked and un-

marked burial sites, the forging of antiquities, vandalism to cemeteries, and grave robbing. As seen in Figure 16–13, about two-thirds of the states have laws—resembling to some extent the federal ARPA—that protect archaeological resources on state property.[101] Eleven states have passed legislation to discourage activities that damage archaeological resources on private land.[102] In addition, several states have statutes providing protection to specific types of areas, such as underwater salvage sites (10 states), caves (4 states), forts (two states), and ghost towns (Colorado only).[103] States also have statutes that provide for state archaeologists, registers of historic places, requirements for the issuance of permits to conduct field investigations, obligations to report discoveries that may have historic or prehistoric significance, and protection of the confidentiality of site locations.

Under federal law there is no regulation of archaeological resources on private land, and under most state laws, the types of "archaeological" activities conducted on private land by landowners or with their permission is largely uncontrolled. Perhaps the most noteworthy example of this issue occurred at the Slack Farm in western Kentucky.[104] Ten "artifact miners" paid the new owner of the farm $10,000 for the right to dig up and remove archaeological resources. It was long known that a Late Mississippian village, dating from around 1450-1650, was located on the farm, but it had enjoyed protection from exploitation by the previous owner.[105] This site was of special significance because it covered a period of centuries related to the first European contact with the "New World."[106] Legally empowered by the new owner, the artifact miners rented a tractor and began plowing through the village midden (the term archaeologists use for a refuse heap) and dwellings to get to graves to locate pottery, stone tools, and weapons.[107] The result was the large-scale destruction of an important site, the loss of invaluable information, and the littering of the field with more than 450 craters, exposed bones, and soft-drink and beer cans.[108] In response, the Kentucky legislature made such treatment of buried remains a felony:

> A person is guilty of desecration of venerated objects in the first degree when, other than authorized by law, he intentionally excavates or disinters human remains for the purpose of

Figure 16–13
State Archaeological Protection Laws

(Courtesy State Historical Society of Iowa)

commercial sale or exploitation of the remains themselves or of objects buried contemporaneously with the remains.[109]

Note that this Kentucky criminal statute does not distinguish between acts committed on public and private lands. Also, while some state statutes regarding desecration of graves have been interpreted to apply to historic, but not prehistoric sites, the Kentucky law covers both types.

CONDUCTING ENFORCEMENT INVESTIGATIONS

Archaeological resources protection investigations pose a number of challenges. Different laws apply when the violation occurs on federal land as opposed to state land, and there are relatively few laws applicable to private lands as opposed to the more heavily protected public lands. Moreover,

some historic areas are divided in such a manner that one portion is under federal jurisdiction while another section is on state and/or private land. As mentioned earlier, many offenses go undetected for long periods of time because of the difficulty in monitoring sites, which are numerous and often very remote, such as Alaska, with over 150,000 archaeological sites. Because of this delay, opportunities to gather crucial physical evidence, which can associate the crime scene with the offenders, may be lost. Moreover, an offender may leave his or her vehicle outside the boundaries of a protected area and claim to be transporting the collection from one point to another or transporting artifacts gathered on private land. Although a law enforcement officer in such circumstances may have some reasonable suspicion, if the subject was not observed entering or leaving the protected area, it is not likely to rise to the level of probable cause. Additional indicators may be found in several areas:

Would a claim that a person is transporting his or her personal collection be consistent with artifacts that appear to be freshly dug up? Does the subject claim to have been on private land but have maps of protected lands with site markings on them? Have digging tools been camouflaged to avoid reflecting light? How close was the subject's vehicle stopped in relationship to protected public lands? Does the subject seem unusually nervous? Can the subject's story of being on private land be verified by the owner? Is the subject's version credible if this occurs at 3 A.M.? Are there two or more subjects carrying two-way radios and scanners? Are the subjects known to have committed previous violations of archaeological resource protection or related laws? It is from the totality of the circumstances that reasonable suspicion may rise to the level of probable cause.

Being able to recognize the tools commonly employed by looters is essential. Looters typically have shovels and metal rods up to 5 feet long with a T handle, which they use to probe for human remains, artifacts, and changes in soil density that suggest good places to examine. Offenders often carry pieces of screen through which they sift dirt, leaving artifacts on the screen, or the screen may have a wooden edge built around it for added strength. Other equipment includes trowels, small brushes to clean artifacts, a small hand-held metal "claw" to break the soil and with which to dig, lanterns and head lamps (for night work), backpacks in which to carry the stolen artifacts, and motorcycles and all-terrain vehicles (ATVs).[110] In historic battlefield parks, suspects often carry metal detectors. Some small-time looters will appear innocent enough, walking along with a stick or staff in their hand, turning over apparent surface debris. The stick or staff is referred to as a "flipper," and as the subjects find articles of value, they pick them up and keep them.

Initial information about looting comes from a variety of sources. Hikers, farmers, campers, hunters, ranchers, and fishermen who see acts of vandalism or looting in progress or discover sites that have been victimized may contact a government agency with the information they have. Routine patrols by employees of the agency that manages the public land also may uncover crimes in progress, as well as those that have been completed. If there is evidence of fresh digging, the site or sites may be placed under surveillance. In examining a site that has been looted, one factor to consider is whether there is any evidence suggesting that the perpetrators may return. For example, has a supply of digging tools and screens been left behind, hidden in some way? Although subjects might have simply left the tools to avoid being seen leaving with them, if there are other significant sites in the immediate area that have not been disturbed, it is likely that the looters are planning to return.

Offenders conduct their looting operations using a variety of techniques. They may have someone drop them off and then pick them up there or at another location at a specified time. Looters frequently operate at night or on holidays, when they are unlikely to encounter other people and enforcement staffing levels are traditionally low, and they may use snow or heavy rain as a cover. In the Four Corners area, one violator used a jet boat to get into and away from a site in the mistaken belief that the method and speed of the approach would make apprehension almost impossible. Offenders may also have dogs with them to warn them when someone approaches.

CRIME SCENE AND FOLLOW-UP INVESTIGATION

Investigators occasionally come across looting operations in progress. In such situations investigators may let the operation go on so surveillance photographs of the crime, which make powerful evidence in court, can be taken. Or investigators may approach the subjects and halt the process to prevent large-scale destruction or to prevent a particularly important site from experiencing further damage. In either case, before acting the investigator must observe long enough to be able to evaluate the situation. How many subjects are there? Where are any lookouts located? What are the probable means and direction of flight if the subjects are approached? Are the subjects armed? Do some offenders in that region have a history of violently resisting arrest? How far away is assistance to the investigator? What law enforcement assets can be prepositioned along roads that the suspects must travel as they leave the area?

The principles discussed in Chapter 3, The Crime Scene and Its Associated Procedures, and Chapter 4, Physical Evidence, apply to crime scene investigations in looting cases. There are, however, some differences in approach and emphasis that deserve attention here. Violations of federal and state laws related to the protection of archaeological resources should be pursued, beginning with the crime scene investigation, by an archaeologist and an investigator.[111] Because a crime has been committed, the investigator is in charge of the process. However, the archaeologist makes a unique contribution by conducting the damage assessment, without which there is no ARPA case. The archaeologist must demonstrate that there has been damage, determine how the damage was caused, and fix the dollar amount of damage, which if $500 or more moves the offense from being a misdemeanor to a felony. In addition, the archaeologist's considerable contributions include taking the crime scene photographs, making the crime scene sketch, and identifying, collecting, marking, and preserving physical evidence.[112] The archaeologist can also offer tentative conclusions about the types of tools used by the suspects if they are not recovered at the scene, the amount of time the offenders spent on the site, the level of skill and knowledge of the perpetrators based on the type and amount of damage done to the site and the kinds of artifacts left behind (see Figure 16–14), the number of suspects involved, and whether the act was an opportunistic crime, an amateur's raid, or the work of commercial looters or serious private collectors. Both the archaeologist and the investigator must be alert to the possibility that the offenders were unable to transport all the artifacts and are planning to return later to collect artifacts hidden nearby.

Soil evidence is of particular importance in looting offenses. Although soil is class characteristic evidence, in some looting cases it has achieved the status of individual characteristic evidence. A number of factors may interact to allow soil evidence to achieve individual characteristic status, including layers of soil in unusual combinations, pollen content, pottery shards (fragments) that are unique to particular locations, and the inclusion of material that allows for carbon dating. The careful collection of soil evidence will permit meaningful comparison with samples collected from suspects' clothes, from under their fingernails, from their tools, from artifacts found in their possession, and from the floorboards, trunks, tires, and undersides of their vehicles. Because vegetation can also be highly unusual alone or in combinations and may also be located only in particular areas or elevations, the investigator should also take samples of vegetation found at the scene.

(Courtesy U.S. Forest Service)

Figure 16–14
"Rejects" Left Behind by Looters

Bold looters simply left their "rejects," a trowel, and an empty beer can, at one site in Uwharie National Forest, North Carolina.

To some extent, where stolen artifacts end up depends upon who took them and what was taken. Some people may take an arrowhead from the surface to keep as a memento. The offenders using flippers usually know they are on sites and have personal collections to which they want to add. Commercial looters steal artifacts to sell and may use a variety of channels, including dealer shows, auctions, and middlemen, or they may sell directly to collectors.

In the follow-up investigation the archaeologist can be of particular assistance to the investigator in estimating the amount of time a commercial looter would need to turn artifacts into salable items and in speculating about the markets in which they might appear.[113] Also, when an application for a search warrant is being prepared, archaeologists can be extremely helpful in specifying the shape, types, colors, raw materials from which made, and characteristic production process and appearance of artifacts that are normally associated with the site that has been looted. In this regard, they can make very useful diagrams.

It is essential for investigators to realize that although artifacts are typically stolen from remote, rural, or urban fringe sites, many of them will ultimately be sold in cities. Therefore, there is a considerable need for cooperation with, and coordination among many types of agencies.

Questions

1. What two elements must be present for a larceny to occur?
2. What are the ways in which a counterfeit credit card may be recognized?
3. Which groups constitute the principal ethnic enterprise involved in illegal check fraud schemes, and where are their bases of operation?
4. What is cellular phone cloning?
5. Discuss the possible signs that people are acting as fences and other receivers.
6. The greatest deterrent to shoplifting can be a security education program for employees. What were some of the suggestions made for such a program?
7. Describe the techniques employed in the "pigeon drop" and "bank examiner" schemes.
8. Describe a pyramid sales scheme.
9. The method of cash-flow analysis in Ponzi schemes is a two-step process. What are these two steps?
10. What is the purpose of laundering money?
11. Why are groceries and restaurants considered good businesses for laundering money?
12. What type of service can the Racketeering Records Analysis Unit (RRAU) provide in examining money-laundering records?
13. In what ways might criminals use fraudulently obtained Social Security numbers?
14. Which agency controls and manages the process by which Social Security numbers are issued?
15. Beginning in 1978, applicants for Social Security numbers had to offer documentary evidence to support their statements regarding their eligibility for a Social Security card. What document and other verification are necessary?
16. How is archaeological looting defined?
17. What are the major provisions of ARPA?
18. Summarize state laws pertaining to the protection of archaeological resources.
19. Describe the respective roles of the investigator and the archaeologist in crime scene and follow-up investigation.

Notes

1. Neil C. Chamelin and Kenneth R. Evans, *Criminal Law for Policemen*, 5th ed. (Englewood Cliffs, N.J.: Prentice-Hall, 1991), p. 153.

2. William T. Neumann, "Busting Credit Card Crime Is Tough," *American Banker,* September 18, 1989, Vol. 154, p. 26.

3. Ellen Memmelaar, "MasterCard Saw Fraud Drop in '89," *American Banker,* July 17, 1990, Vol. 155, p. 14.

4. Keith Slotter, "Plastic Payment—Trends in Credit Card Fraud," *FBI Law Enforcement Bulletin*, June 1997, pp. 2–3.

5. *Credit Card Mail Theft Newsletter* (U.S. Postal Inspection Service, Office of Criminal Investigations), November 1995, Vol. 4, No. 1 p. 3; see also Mark T. Langan and Gerald Vajgert, "Profiling Postal Packages," *FBI Law Enforcement Bulletin*, February–March 1996, pp. 17–21.

6. Timothy M. Dees, "Countering Credit Card Fraud," *Police,* March 1994, p. 46.

7. Ellen Braitman, "More Focus on Cards with Photos," *American Banker,* November 1, 1990, Vol. 155, p. 6.

8. Neumann, "Busting Credit Card Crime Is Tough," p. 26.

9. Ellen E. Schultz, "Plastic Explosives: Ways to Defuse Credit-Card Fraud," *Wall Street Journal,* November 16, 1990, p. C1.

10. Ibid.

11. John W. Merline, "Check Fraud," *Consumers' Research Magazine,* December 1989, Vol. 72, p. 2.

12. Keith Slotter, "Check Fraud—A Sophisticated Criminal Enterprise," *FBI Law Enforcement Bulletin*, August 1996, pp. 1–7.

13. "FBI Financial Institution Fraud Criminal Referral Statistics for Fiscal Year 1995," September 30, 1995.

14. Frank W. Abagnale, *Document Verification and Currency Transactions Manual* (Abagnale & Associates, 1994).

15. "Asian Gangs Involved in Credit Card Fraud," *Intelligence Operations Bulletin* (Office of the Attorney General, California Department of Justice), December 1994, Vol. 47.

16. Among the safeguards are embossing, artifical watermarks, laid lines, chemical voiding features, warning bands, high-resolution printing, dual-image numbering, and security number fonts.

17. Steven Marjanovic, "Arizona Group Pushes Fingerprinting as a Ploy to Deter Check Fraud," *American Banker,* July 6, 1995, p. 10.

18. Robert Bird, vice president, Bank of America, San Francisco, California, remarks at meeting of the Bank Fraud Working Group Subgroup on Check and Credit Card Fraud, Washington, D.C., July 19, 1995.

19. Todd H. Young, "Wireless Bandits," *Police*, May 1995, pp. 33–35. Todd Young, a nationally recognized expert in cellular fraud, is the director of consulting services for the Guidry Group, which specializes in telecommunication security. For more information on cellular technology and investigative methods or cellular training for law enforcement, contact Todd Young at (206) 836-0699.

20. Chamber of Commerce of the United States, *White Collar Crime* (Washington, D.C.: Chamber of Commerce, 1974), pp. 45–48.

21. Steve Weiner and John Harris, "Hot Retailing," *Forbes,* August 7, 1989, p. 106.

22. Nancy Wride, "57 Arrested in Anaheim Fencing Sting," *Los Angeles Times,* March 25, 1989, p. 19.

23. Rich Wilner, "Steal-to-Order Check, Credit Card Ring Is Broken," *Women's Wear Daily,* August 2, 1989, p. 23.

24. Weiner and Harris, "Hot Retailing," p. 106.

25. Chamber of Commerce, *White Collar Crime,* pp. 45–46.

26. Ibid.

27. Weiner and Harris, "Hot Retailing," pp. 105–106.

28. James N. Baker and Peter Katel, "Rolling on the Miami River: Police Crack Down on a Stolen-Goods Pipeline," *Newsweek,* June 11, 1990, p. 31.

29. Chamber of Commerce, *White Collar Crime,* pp. 46, 47. Additional details about fences and other receivers are capsuled in *Cargo Theft and Organized Crime* (Washington, D.C.: Government Printing Office, 1972). Also see *Criminal Redistribution Systems and Their Economic Impact on Small Business, Part I* (hearings before the Senate Select Committee on Small Business, May 1–2, 1973) (Washington, D.C.: Government Printing Office, 1973).

30. Ibid., pp. 80–82.

31. Weiner and Harris, "Hot Retailing."

32. Leonard A. Sipes, Jr., "And the Answer Is . . . ," *Security Management Review,* May 1989, Vol. 33, p. 71.

33. "Shoplifting: Bess Myerson's Arrest Highlights a Multibillion-Dollar Problem That Many Stores Won't Talk About," *Life,* August 1988, Vol. 11, p. 34.

34. Ibid., p. 35.

35. This information on South American theft groups was provided by Detective Joseph Moorash, Alexandria, Virginia, Police Department.

36. Dody Tsiantar, "Big Brother at the Mall, Retailers Go High Tech in the War on Shoplifters," *Newsweek,* July 3, 1989, Vol. 114, p. 44.

37. "American Notes: Police Presence," *Time,* January 8, 1990, Vol. 135, p. 53.

38. Tsiantar, "Big Brother at the Mall," p. 44.

39. Hassell Bradley, "Meet Miss Annie Droid, the Shoplifter's Nemesis," *Women's Wear Daily,* February 27, 1989, p. 18.

40. "Shoplifting: Bess Myerson's Arrest Highlights a Multi-billion-Dollar Problem," p. 34.

41. Tsiantar, "Big Brother at the Mall," p. 44.

42. "Shoplifting: Bess Myerson's Arrest Highlights a Multi-billion-Dollar Problem," p. 36.

43. Jack Acken Smith, "Shoplifters Hate Customer Service," *Gifts and Decorative Accessories,* October 1989, Vol. 90, p. 56.

44. "Shoplifting: Bess Myerson's Arrest Highlights a Multi-billion-Dollar Problem," p. 36.

45. Delaney J. Stinson, "Attention, Retailers: Civil Law Provides Tonic," *Security Management Review,* September 1988, Vol. 32, pp. 131, 132.

46. "Con Men—A Sucker's Sampler of the Games People Play," *Miami Herald,* April 21, 1977, p. 15.

47. Ottie Adkins, "Crime against the Elderly," *The Police Chief,* January 1975, Vol. 42, No. 1, p. 40.

48. R. Griffin, "Bunko Schemes—The Art of Flim Flam," *The National Centurion,* October 1983. The remainder of this discussion of confidence games, exclusive of telemarketing scams, was obtained from this source, pp. 38–42.

49. Len Baldassano, *American Shipper,* February 1990, Vol. 32, p. 96.

50. Ibid.

51. Ibid.

52. Edwin H. Sutherland, *White Collar Crime* (New York: Dryden Press, 1949), p. 9.

53. U.S. Department of Justice, LEAA, *The Nature, Impact, and Prosecution of White-Collar Crime* (Washington, D.C.: Government Printing Office, 1970), pp. 4–6.

54. Vincent P. Doherty and Monte E. Smith, "Ponzi Schemes and Laundering—How Illicit Funds Are Acquired and Concealed," *FBI Law Enforcement Bulletin,* November 1981, pp. 5–11. This discussion was taken from this source.

55. Tom L. Kitchens, "The Cash Flow Analysis Method: Following the Paper Trail in Ponzi Schemes," *FBI Law Enforcement Bulletin,* August 1993, pp. 10–13. This discussion of methods of cash-flow analysis was obtained, with modification, from this source.

56. This is a writ that requires a party summoned to appear in court to bring along a document or other piece of evidence for examination by the court.

57. Wayne Moquin and Charles Van Doren, *The American Way of Crime—A Documentary History* (New York: Praeger, 1976), p. 68.

58. Richard Behar, "The Underworld Is Their Oyster," *Time,* September 3, 1990, Vol. 136, p. 54.

59. Jonathan Beaty and Richard Hornik, "A Torrent of Dirty Dollars," *Time,* December 18, 1989, Vol. 134, p. 51.

60. James Cook, "The Invisible Enterprise," *Forbes,* October 13, 1980, p. 125.

61. Jim Drinkhall, "Con Men Are Raking in Millions by Setting Up Own Caribbean Banks," *The Wall Street Journal,* March 23, 1981, p. 1.

62. James O. Beasley II, "Forensic Examination of Money Laundering Records," *FBI Law Enforcement Bulletin,* March 1993, pp. 13–17. This discussion of forensic examination of money-laundering records was taken with minor modifications from this source.

63. *Federal Sentencing Guidelines Manual, 1992* (St. Paul, Minn.: West Publishing Co., 1991).

64. See *United States* v. *Harris,* 903 F. 2d 770 (10th Cir. 1990).

65. The following are some guidelines for handling and submitting evidence: submit original evidence (photocopies and facsimiles may be reviewed under limited circumstances, but examiners prefer to use the original documents when preparing a written forensic report); submit evidence as soon as possible following its acquisition; submit all documentary evidence relating to the seizure; contact an RRAU examiner in advance to resolve potential problems regarding large volumes of evidence (in some cases, a field examination may be in order); advise the RRAU of any requested examinations that may necessitate special handling, such as those involving handwriting or latent fingerprint comparisons; and indicate in a brief cover letter the subject's name, the exact place and date of seizure, any trial date or other reason for expeditious handling, and the name and telephone number of the submitter.

66. Steven M. Lack, "The New Numbers Game: The Use of Social Security Numbers in Committing and Combating White-Collar Crime," *The Police Chief,* July 1993, Vol. 60, No. 7, pp. 22, 23. This discussion was taken with permission from this source.

67. Sherry Hutt, Elwood Jones, and Martin McAllister, *Archeological Resource Protection* (Washington, D.C.: Government Printing Office, 1991), pp. 6–7.

68. National Park Service, *Listing of Outlaw Treachery: Loot Clearinghouse,* on file, Archeological Assistance Division, 1990.

69. Bennie Keel, Francis P. McManamon, and George S. Smith, *Federal Archeology: The Current Program* (Washington, D.C.: National Park Service, 1989), pp. 30–31.

70. Hutt, Jones, and McAllister, *Archeological Resource Protection*, p. 5.

71. The information in this paragraph is drawn, with restatement, from National Park Service, *Looting America's Archeological Heritage: An Update* (Washington, D.C.: U.S. Department of Interior, 1989), p. 1.

72. Robert K. Landers, "Is America Allowing Its Past to Be Stolen?" In *Congressional Quarterly's Editorial Research Reports,* Marcus D. Rosenbaum (ed.), January 18, 1991, p. 35.

73. Hutt, Jones, and McAllister, *Archeological Resource Protection*, p. 6.

74. Landers, "Is America Allowing Its Past to Be Stolen?" pp. 35, 37.

75. Hutt, Jones, and McAllister, *Archeological Resource Protection*, p. 2.

76. Landers, "Is America Allowing Its Past to Be Stolen?" p. 37.

77. Ibid.

78. Ibid.

79. Ibid.

80. National Park Service, *Looting America's Archeological Heritage: An Update,* p. 1.

81. National Park Service, *Summary of Archeological Looting Cases* (Washington, D.C.: U.S. Department of the Interior, 1989); prepared for the Society for American Archeological Anti-Looting Working Conference, Taos, New Mexico, May 7–12, 1989, manuscript unnumbered, but apparently p. 111.

82. Ibid., p. 150.

83. Ibid., p. 70.

84. Ibid., p. 100.

85. Christopher J. Duerksen, *A Handbook of Historic Preservation Law* (Washington, D.C.: The National Center for Preservation Law, 1983), p. 193.

86. National Park Service, *Archaeological Assistance Technical Brief No. 11: The Legal Background of Archeological Resources Protection, 1991* (Washington, D.C.: U.S. Department of the Interior, p. 2).

87. Ibid.

88. Ibid.

89. Hutt, Jones, and McAllister, *Archeological Resource Protection*, p. 20.

90. National Park Service, *Archeological Assistance Program Technical Brief No. 11,* pp. 3–4.

91. Hutt, Jones, and McAllister, *Archeological Resource Protection*, pp. 32–33.

92. Ibid., pp. 26, 28, 42, 48.

93. Ibid., p. 48.

94. Ibid.

95. Ibid., p. 42.

96. Ibid., p. 28.

97. Ibid.

98. Ibid.

99. Ibid., p. 26.

100. National Park Service, *Archeological Assistance Program Technical Brief No. 11,* p. 7.

101. Landers, "Is America Allowing Its Past to Be Stolen?" p. 41.

102. National Park Service, *Archeological Assistance Program Technical Brief No. 11,* p. 7.

103. Ibid.

104. This example is from Landers, "Is America Allowing Its Past to Be Stolen?" p. 44.

105. Ibid.

106. Ibid.

107. Ibid.

108. Ibid.

109. Criminal Law of Kentucky, 525.105.

110. Hutt, Jones, and McAllister, *Archeological Resource Protection*, p. 63.

111. Ibid., p. 59.

112. Ibid., p. 60.

113. Ibid., p. 93.

SEVENTEEN

Vehicle Thefts and Related Offenses

CHAPTER OUTLINE

Auto Theft 466

Theft of Heavy Equipment and
   Farm Equipment 473

Investigative Tools and Techniques 474

Prevention Programs 497

Odometer Fraud 501

Marine Theft 502

Aircraft and Avionics Theft 506

Questions 509

Notes 509

INTRODUCTION

Motor vehicles—cars, trucks, motorcycles, motor homes, construction equipment, agricultural equipment, and commercial trailers—are extremely valuable and costly items to the individual or business owner. Boats, motors, and personal watercraft are also highly valued, as are privately owned aircraft. It is an unfortunate fact that items so highly prized by owners are also items attractive to thieves. Theft, however, may take many forms and may be committed by a stranger or by the very person who is the owner of the property.

AUTO THEFT

The number of motor vehicle thefts in the United States surpassed the 1.3 million mark in 1997, with an estimated national loss of over $7 billion. Seventy-seven percent of the total thefts were of automobiles. Although a large percentage of the vehicles are later recovered, only 14 percent of the cases are cleared by law enforcement agencies.

If the reader is impressed with statistics, here are some more for 1997: There was one theft every 20 seconds. The average value of vehicles stolen was $5,416. The number of reported thefts fell by 3 percent from the previous year.[1]

It is important to note that any small reductions in numbers are not significant and could be caused by changes in reporting procedures, changes in crime classifications at local levels, fewer agencies reporting their statistics for central processing, or a variety of other reasons. In fact, auto theft remains a problem of national concern.

MISCELLANEOUS STATISTICS AND NOTES

- Motorcycle theft is on the increase. It has been estimated that approximately 2 percent of reported thefts are of motorcycles. A substantial portion of the increase has been directed at Harley-Davidsons.

- National and international rings operate, particularly in cities near ports, to export vehicles to countries all over the developing world where they can be sold for three or more times the price for which they are sold in the United States.

- Since the collapse of communism in eastern Europe, the theft of motor vehicles has skyrocketed. More than 2 million vehicles are stolen annually in Europe. Many are illegally exported to developing countries, particularly in the Middle East.

- The theft of airbags and the resale of stolen salvaged airbags is becoming epidemic. It is estimated that one insurance company that insures about 20 percent of the cars in the United States will pay out $10 million in 1998 for stolen airbags. Several states have enacted legislation that is largely ineffective because

there is not yet a national system in place to identify and respond to this problem. Since 1997, the National Insurance Crime Bureau (NICB) has been spearheading a drive to develop strategies for attacking this problem.

- Heavy-truck and tractor-trailer thefts are on the increase. At the same time, cargo theft is also increasing. Unfortunately, no one is yet keeping accurate figures on cargo theft, but it is estimated that losses exceed $10 million annually. Often, low-tech electrical equipment, jewelry, food, and fragrances are targets of cargo theft. The insurance industry paid out $17.9 million in 1997 on commercial vehicle theft, excluding cargo losses. California and Florida have the highest number of tractors stolen, and California, Texas, and Florida are ranked as the top three for trailer theft.

Auto Theft—Myths

- Auto theft happens to other people, not to me.
- Auto theft is a victimless crime. Insurance companies pay the costs.
- Most of the vehicles stolen are new models, so I don't need to worry if my car is a couple of years old.
- Most stolen vehicles disappear forever because they are either exported or cut up into pieces.
- When an auto thief is caught, punishment is severe.

Auto Theft—Facts

- It is estimated that in 20 to 30 percent of auto thefts, the operator has left the keys in the car.
- Everyone with comprehensive insurance pays for auto theft and fraud through increased premiums, even if they never have a vehicle stolen.
- An estimated 85 percent of stolen vehicles are recovered, indicating that a large percentage of those stolen are probably the object of temporary theft.
- Punishment for auto theft is not swift and sure.
- The theft of older-model cars is prevalent. Year after year, the overwhelming majority of cars stolen are between two and seven years old.
- Everyone's tax dollars pay the cost of fighting auto theft, including the costs of components of the criminal justice system.

- As to auto theft being a victimless crime, insurance does not pay for the victim's insurance deductible, work loss, inconvenience, emotional trauma, and time loss (estimated to average more than 40 hours, covering making telephone calls; filling out police reports; purchasing a replacement vehicle; completing insurance claim forms; and dealing with licensing and registration problems, vehicle inspection, and repairs, which may take many weeks if parts have to be ordered).[2]

TYPES OF THEFT

Motor vehicle thefts generally fall into one of four categories: temporary theft, joyriding, professional theft, or fraud.

Temporary Theft
The term *temporary theft* is used not to imply that the crime is not serious but, rather, to distinguish joyriding from something more ominous. Of growing concern are the thefts of vehicles specifically for use in the commission of other crimes such as robberies or drive-by shootings, after which the vehicles are abandoned. These thefts are on the increase and, when reported, are often recorded only as the underlying crime rather than also as a motor vehicle theft, thereby skewing the actual theft figures.

Joyriding
Joyriders are most often teenagers—15 to 19 years old—who steal a car simply to drive and then abandon it. Among the reasons most often cited for the thefts by joyriding teenagers are to feel important, powerful, and accepted among peers; it's fun and exciting; on a dare; it relieves boredom and gives an adrenaline rush; don't feel like walking; want to impress girls; to make money by stripping cars and selling the parts; get even with parents or escape family problems; it's addictive; part of a gang membership or initiation. Since many youngsters are not professionals, they frequently target vehicles that are easy to steal and generally lack any antitheft devices. Perhaps the large number of apprehensions in this age category is accounted for by the arrests of joyriders. (Twenty-one percent of the nationwide motor vehicle theft clearance rate is made up of persons under 18 years of age. Of the estimated 167,600 arrests for motor vehicle theft in 1997, al-

most 69 percent were of persons under 25 years of age, and 40 percent of the arrest total consisted of youths under 18 years of age.) Eighty-five percent of those arrested were male. Fifty-eight percent of those arrested were white, 39 percent black, and the remaining 3 percent of other races.[3] Nevertheless, no definitive statement is offered that joyriding is the foundation crime for these arrests, for, in fact, many of the thefts committed by or in support of the activities of professional vehicle thieves are accomplished by young people.

Professional Theft
The professional car thief is motivated by very high profits and generally low risk. The profits to be gained are second only to those for drugs. Anyone who has ever purchased a replacement part for a car is aware that the cost of replacing all the parts of a vehicle is much higher than the original cost of the entire vehicle. The professional can often sell the parts of a stolen car for up to five times the original assembled value. Considering what the thief "paid" for the vehicle, the profit margin is substantial.

However, professionals do have costs in operating their "businesses." It is not infrequent for professional thieves to employ and train youths to steal cars. Often a youth is paid a set amount, several hundred to several thousand dollars, for each theft. The amount varies depending on the make, model, and year of the vehicle. There are even "training schools" in some areas of the country where juveniles and young adults are taught how to steal cars, trucks, motorcycles, and other vehicles.

The professional thief can break into a locked, high-priced car, start it, and drive it away in as little as 20 seconds.

Fraud
Although certain types of theft involve fraud perpetrated on innocent purchasers, the major category of vehicle fraud as described here does not actually involve the theft of vehicles by professionals or even strangers. These various types of crimes are generally committed by the owner or someone acting on behalf of the owner, and the underlying purpose is to profit at the expense of an insurance company.

The NICB estimates that anywhere from 15 to 25 percent of all reported vehicle thefts involve some type of fraud and that a vast majority of these involve fraudulent insurance claims. Insurance crime is an enormous problem, and its true magnitude is almost impossible to pinpoint.

In addition, some experts on the costs of insurance estimate that between 16 and 35 cents of every dollar in premiums paid by the public for motor vehicle insurance is used to pay fraudulent claims or to fight fraud. The NICB says that if the amount of insurance claim fraud and vehicle theft occurring in the United States represented a corporation, it would rank in the top 25 of the *Fortune* 500 and be called a growth industry. And insurance fraud is on the rise because it is an easy crime to successfully commit. Insurance companies, even those with highly qualified special investigation units whose function is to investigate suspected cases of fraud, must be concerned about potential liability resulting from lawsuits if someone is wrongly accused or a claim is wrongly denied. The fact that insurance companies are believed to have a great deal of money—deep pockets—makes these companies even more susceptible to civil suits and potential liability and, in turn, even more cautious.

METHODS OF OPERATION—THE PROFESSIONAL

To turn a profit, professional thieves use a variety of techniques to dispose of stolen motor vehicles. Among the most common are chop shops, salvage switches, and exportation.

Chop Shops

Very simply, a *chop shop* is a place where stolen vehicles are disassembled for resale of their parts. The operators and employees of chop shops cut stolen motor vehicles apart with torches, power saws, and other tools, sometimes in as little as 8 or 9 minutes, either alter or dispose of the parts that are potentially traceable, and sell the untraceable parts to repair shops or salvage yards. Sometimes the parts buyers are unsuspecting. Often, the salvage yard or repair shop operator is in collusion with the thief or the chop shop. In fact, a chop shop may well direct the theft of a specific type of motor vehicle in order to "fill an order" for a specific part needed by a repair shop or salvage yard (see Figures 17–1, 17–2, and 17–3).

A modification of the typical chop shop operation is illustrated by the following: thieves steal a

Figure 17–1
Interior of a Chop Shop

(Courtesy National Insurance Crime Bureau)

car, disassemble it carefully so that the parts are not damaged, have the remainder conveniently recovered and disposed of through a salvage sale, buy the salvage, reassemble the vehicle with all its original parts, and sell the vehicle, which has already been classed as a recovered theft and is no longer considered stolen.

Quick Strip

A vehicle is stolen and stripped mainly for valuable accessories such as seats, stereos, car phones, and tires. These items are attractive to thieves because they normally do not contain any identifying numbers, thus making them difficult to identify and easily disposed of.

Salvage Switch

Generally, a *salvage* vehicle is one that has been damaged or wrecked to such an extent that the cost of repairing it is beyond its fair market value. Thus, its primary value in the legitimate market is for the sale of its undamaged parts. To the criminal, however, the value of a salvaged vehicle is far greater than its parts. The real profit is made after the criminal buys the salvage, provided it is accompanied by the certificate of title and the vehicle identification number (VIN) plate. Often the offender does not even want the vehicle and will leave it with the salvage yard from which it is purchased or dispose of it elsewhere. The thief then steals a vehicle identical to the wreck, changes the VIN plate, and sells the stolen vehicle, with a matching title, to an innocent purchaser or to a purchaser who is

Figure 17–2
Storage of Stolen Engines in a Chop Shop

(Courtesy National Insurance Crime Bureau)

Figure 17–3
Frame "Graveyard"
Auto parts left after a chop shop has removed all salable parts.

(Courtesy National Insurance Crime Bureau)

offered such a "good" price that no questions are asked. Through the salvage switch, the thief is able to disguise and dispose of stolen vehicles in the legitimate market.

Export

Vehicles manufactured in the United States are extremely popular in other countries. The sale of American manufactured vehicles can also be highly profitable. Buyers in these areas often pay double the purchase price for quality cars. The NICB estimates that 13 percent of all vehicles stolen in the United States are illegally exported.[4] Mexico and Central and South American countries are among the most popular but certainly not the exclusive destinations for stolen U.S. manufactured vehicles. It has been estimated that as many as 20,000 stolen or embezzled cars, trucks, buses, motorcycles, and other vehicles are transported into Mexico each year. This amounts to between 6.6 and 10 percent of the estimated number of stolen vehicles exported each year.

Contributing to this problem are the limited, although effective, controls exercised by Mexican customs and the few effective controls exercised by the United States over southbound traffic entering Mexico. The volume of traffic going into Mexico makes it almost impossible to inspect and investigate all vehicles. Many stolen vehicles are also taken to Canada. Some are resold, but many are exported to their final destinations. Exports are accounting for a growing percentage of the unrecovered stolen

vehicles, and the rate of growth of this problem is greater in port cities.

With the collapse of communism and the opening of free-market economies in eastern Europe, auto theft has grown to become an enormous problem. In 1997, Jacques De Remer, then president of the International Association of Auto Theft Investigators (IAATI), said:

> With this free market economy came a seemingly insatiable demand for goods that were previously unavailable, and automobiles were at the top of the list. The auto theft and trafficking problem in Europe is far more complex than it is in the United States, as Europe consists of more than forty separate countries, all of which have their own vehicle registration and titling systems, their own documents, their own language, and their own laws. The figures are staggering. In Poland alone, auto theft has gone up more than 400% in the past five years, from 14,691 to 63,527. Recoveries for 1995 were 8.4%, compared to around 50% in the U.S.
>
> Throughout Europe approximately two million cars are stolen each year, with most countries being categorized as "source countries" or "receiving countries." Put simply, the countries that have cars are losing them to the countries that don't.[5]

Fraud—In General

Fraudulent auto theft claims are not the only type of fraud to which the insurance industry is subjected, but it is a significant part. Fully 10 percent of all property and casualty claims are either inflated or outright fraud. Estimates are that fraudulent insurance claim payouts range between $18 billion and $50 billion annually. This amount fluctuates, since it is well recognized that fraud increases as the economy worsens.

FRAUDULENT THEFT SCHEMES

Fraudulent auto theft claim schemes fall into three major categories: false vehicle claims where no vehicle exists or the vehicle is not owned by the criminal, falsified theft losses, and inflated theft losses.

False-Vehicle Schemes

This scam is particularly prevalent where insurance companies are lax or have ineffective programs to verify the existence of a vehicle before issuing an insurance policy. As a general rule, this type of fraud is planned well in advance of obtaining insurance coverage. The criminal will purchase a policy that has a provision covering loss by theft. In fact, the vehicle does not exist, has already been salvaged, or does not belong to the person who buys the insurance. Most often, the vehicle insured is a recent model. Some time later (generally within three months, to hold down the cost of the insurance coverage purchase) a theft report will be filed with a law enforcement agency and a claim will be made to the insurance company.

Several modifications of the salvage switch, described earlier, are illustrative of false-vehicle schemes. Once a salvaged vehicle is purchased, insurance coverage will be obtained. After a short time, a theft loss claim will be filed for the vehicle, which, of course, was in "excellent condition."

In some jurisdictions a salvage title may be issued. This does not necessarily prevent false-theft claims on salvage; it merely channels the process in a different direction. One way the criminal avoids the problems associated with the issuance of salvage titles is to "wash," or "launder," the salvage title. This is done by fabricating the sale of the vehicle and transferring the title to an alleged purchaser in another state that does not issue salvage titles or does not carry forward a "brand" on the title issued by another state. The "buyer" then obtains a clean title in that state and transfers it back to the insured either directly or through several

other people or businesses to make it appear as a legitimate transaction. Then, with a clean title, the insured files a theft claim.

Another technique is for the salvage buyer to falsify the necessary support documentation to show that the salvage vehicle has been completely rebuilt or restored and thereby obtain a "clean," or regular, title. The thief may not even bother to get a clean title but, upon filing a claim for the alleged theft, may simply contend that the vehicle was rebuilt or restored but was stolen before the insured could file the necessary paperwork to obtain a nonsalvage title.

In still another version of the salvage switch, the VIN plate may be attached to a rented or borrowed car of the same make and model and, along with the certificate of title, may be presented to and inspected by an agent of the company from which coverage is sought. After the policy is issued, the salvage vehicle VIN plate is removed and the vehicle is returned to the person or company from which it was borrowed or rented.

Presenting a counterfeit or stolen certificate of title or manufacturer's certificate of origin (MCO) as the basis for having a policy issued on a "paper vehicle" or on a stolen vehicle with a concealed identity is another technique for defrauding insurance companies through the filing of false vehicle claims. A manufacturer's certificate of origin is the original identification document issued by a vehicle's manufacturer, somewhat like a birth certificate. It accompanies the vehicle through its delivery to a new car dealer until it is first sold to a retail purchaser, after which the MCO is surrendered to the jurisdiction issuing the first certificate of title in the name of the retail purchaser.

A variation on the counterfeit or blank title scheme is the altered title, whereby the criminal manages to conceal the existence of a lienholder who may have already repossessed the vehicle because of missed payments. A theft report is then filed along with the fraudulent insurance claim.

It is not uncommon to find the following scenario in a fraudulent claim on a false vehicle: Henry Johnson owns a late-model full-size car. The vehicle is paid for and Johnson has the title in his possession. Johnson decides to sell the car. After he has it advertised for a few days, he receives a satisfactory offer from a person who pays cash and takes the car to another state to have it titled and registered. Johnson signs the title over to the buyer, who takes possession of the vehicle and drives it to his own state of residence. The next day, Johnson, claiming he can't find his car title, applies for a duplicate title in his own state. The title is issued and is branded with the word "duplicate." Although it may take several weeks to receive the duplicate title, the process may still be faster than it takes for the buyer's home state to issue a new title to the buyer and send the original of Johnson's title back to his state for official cancellation. Upon obtaining the duplicate title, Johnson files a theft claim with his insurance company and surrenders the duplicate title to the company in exchange for the theft loss payment. After learning of the scam, the insurance company goes looking for Johnson and finds that all information he provided was false and he has now disappeared not only with the insurance money but with the money he made from selling the vehicle. Normally, the issuance of a duplicate title will render the original or any previously issued duplicate void, but this fact was unknown to the buyer of Johnson's car or to the buyer's home state, where he applied for a title in his own name.

False-Theft Schemes

As opposed to the many different fraudulent schemes where no vehicle exists, in the false-theft claim case, the vehicle does exist and is in fact owned by the person who has obtained the insurance policy. The primary reasons why an owner would file a phony theft loss are generally either to avoid liability for some conduct that resulted from the use of the vehicle or to reduce or avoid some financial loss. The specific motivation leading to the filing of the fraudulent claim may exist at the time the policy coverage is obtained or may result from circumstances that develop later.

Among the vast number of motivations—and there are as many motivations as there are false claims—for filing false-theft loss claims are the following:

- To cover or avoid personal responsibility for a hit-and-run accident, the owner will report the car stolen (before the police come to question him or her) and will subsequently file an insurance claim.
- To replace an old vehicle that just doesn't look good or drive smoothly any longer.

- To replace a "lemon" that can't be sold for a decent price.
- To obtain money for another vehicle that is in need of repair or replacement.
- To avoid loss of the vehicle without receiving any financial gain, for example, through repossession caused by a default of payments or in response to a court order to transfer title to a former spouse following a divorce.
- To end costly car payments or repair bills.
- To avoid the hassle of selling.
- To obtain a more favorable interest rate on a car loan.
- To break a restricting car lease.

As noted at the outset of this chapter, fraud may be committed by the insured acting alone or with another person or other persons. When a vehicle owner conspires with others, the fraud is often referred to as an "owner give-up." Examples of both solo and give-up false-theft schemes include the following:

- The vehicle is abandoned and later reported stolen.
- The vehicle, which may have been previously damaged or had some major mechanical defects, is reported stolen. Shortly afterward it is recovered, and the insured claims that the damage or defects were caused by the theft.
- The vehicle is sold to an out-of-state buyer, then a duplicate certificate of title is applied for and used to file the claim—just like the Johnson scenario reported earlier.
- The vehicle is not stolen but is hidden prior to the theft report and prior to the claim being filed. After the loss is paid, the vehicle can be returned to use, stripped, sold, chopped for parts, taken out of state, or otherwise disposed.
- The vehicle is dumped in water, a method of causing damage that is increasing in use. This is often referred to as "car dunking" or "vehicle dumping." Such vehicles generally cannot be repaired economically even if recovered.
- Vehicle burying is another way that owners dispose of unwanted vehicles. Consider the following: An employee at the Charlotte/ Douglas International Airport in North Carolina was charged with insurance fraud

after police unearthed his car from the ground at a remote, wooded edge of the airport. After his attempts to sell the car met with no success, the insured, who worked as a landscaper at the airport, decided to use a backhoe to dig a pit and bury his car inside. He then reported the car stolen in order to collect an insurance settlement.[6]

- Vehicle arson is another form of fraud that is planned beforehand and is motivated by a desire to collect on an insurance policy either to make a profit or to solve a financial problem. Vehicle arson will be covered in more detail later, but it should be noted that all vehicle fires, even though the numbers are increasing annually, are not necessarily arson cases. The first job of any investigator at the scene of a vehicle fire is to ascertain whether natural or accidental causes can be eliminated so that a full-fledged arson investigation can be undertaken. Although manufacturers have made it extremely difficult for vehicles to burn under normal circumstances,[7] it cannot be assumed that, because there was a fire, some accelerant was used and arson has occurred.

Inflated-Theft Loss Schemes

As distinguished from the preceding schemes, in the inflated-theft loss the vehicle actually exists, actually belongs to the insured, and actually is stolen. The fraud occurs when the insured makes a false claim concerning the physical or mechanical condition of the vehicle when it was stolen; actually causes some damage or removes some parts upon recovery of the vehicle but before it is inspected by the insurance company; claims there were expensive parts on or improvements made to the vehicle before it was stolen; or, if no follow-up inspection is conducted by the insurer, claims certain damage occurred that actually did not happen.

One frequently used scam has the insured enter into a conspiracy with a repair shop, after a stolen vehicle is recovered, to allege that damages were caused during the theft. The damages do not exist. The vehicle is immediately "repaired" before the insurance appraiser has the opportunity to inspect the vehicle, and the repair shop insists that the insurer accept the repair bill, possibly using a photo of a wrecked vehicle of the same make and condi-

tion as the vehicle "before repair." A spinoff of this basic scenario has the repair shop show the appraiser an actual wrecked vehicle in its possession of the same make and model as the insured's car.

The inflated-theft loss claim also extends to vehicle contents. The claimant alleges the vehicle contained valuable clothes, cameras, golf clubs, and other "new" items of considerable value when it was stolen.

Defrauding the Owner and Insurer

There are times when the owner is not involved in the fraud and both the owner and the insurer become victims, as illustrated in the following example. An individual leases a vehicle from a rental company, and, during the rental period, reports the vehicle stolen to both the police and the rental company. Shortly after, the renter again calls the police and reports the vehicle was recovered, using some excuse like his coworker took it to the store or he forgot where he parked it the night before because he had had too much to drink. Consequently, the police never enter the "stolen" report into the National Crime Information Center (NCIC). Conveniently, the renter fails to notify the rental company, which still assumes that the law enforcement agency entered the theft into NCIC. The thief may have several days' or longer use of the vehicle before the victims can put the whole story together.

Some vehicles are exported by owners for the purpose of filing and collecting on fraudulent theft claims.

Another type of export fraud occurs when a vehicle owner makes multiple copies of proof-of-ownership documents to present to U.S. Customs officials and exports his or her vehicle. After the vehicle arrives at its foreign destination, the VIN plate is removed and mailed back to the owner, who steals a car of the same make and model, switches the VIN plate, and, using the additional copies of ownership documents, exports the stolen vehicle.

As illustrated by the examples in the previous paragraphs, "insurance thieves are getting smarter each day. As law enforcement agencies put an end to one scheme, criminals conceive another. For example, after the insurance industry established mechanisms to thwart large claims fraud, criminals learned to file multiple small claims to avoid triggering automatic auditing systems."

THEFT OF HEAVY EQUIPMENT AND FARM EQUIPMENT

Heavy construction equipment and farm equipment are commonly referred to as "off-road" equipment. During the first half of 1997, 836 pieces of construction equipment and 1,340 pieces of farm equipment (not including lawn tractors and other lawn equipment) were reported stolen. The top theft states were California, Texas, Florida, Georgia, North Carolina, and Tennessee.[8] Only 5 to 10 percent of heavy equipment, including construction, farm, and lawn equipment, is recoverd.[9] Lawn and garden equipment accounts for 50 percent of John Deere Insurance Company losses, while construction equipment and farm equipment each account for 25 percent of the losses.[10]

It takes experienced tractor thieves approximately 4 minutes to invade a farm, start and load a tractor, and drive away, according to an informant who worked with a theft ring.[11] For pull-type equipment that does not have to be started, the amount of time required for the average theft is less than 2 minutes. Farm and construction equipment thefts are frequently committed by professional operatives who steal for profit. They may steal on order, for stripping, or for export. One offender was caught with a notebook filled with photographs he had taken of machinery on various farms; when interrogated he stated he had roamed the countryside obtaining the photographs in the notebook. The note-book was then used as a "sales catalog" when meeting with prospective buyers and as a means of instructing thieves working with him as to exactly what equipment from a particular location was to be taken. This arrangement made it possible for the equipment to be consigned or sold before it was even stolen, minimizing the amount of time that the equipment was in the thieves' hands and therefore their risk.

The theft of off-road equipment and the investigation of those thefts cause numerous problems for owners, manufacturers, and law enforcement agencies. Title or registration generally is not required for such equipment, and owners have traditionally resisted such requirements for several reasons. They fear that the title and registration records could be used to levy taxes on expensive items of property and that such a financial burden would have to be passed on to their consumers. Further, they believe that registration requirements would impede their ability to move the equipment rapidly and freely around the country.

Owners are also victimized by the problem of inventory control. Construction equipment is often spread over several miles of job site or over several job sites and may be left idle for days or weeks at a time in isolated areas. Thus, when the professional thief is overcome by the irresistible temptation, it is often days before the theft is noticed and reported to the police.

Compounding the issue is the fact that off-road equipment, unlike conventional motor vehicles, has no standard, permanently affixed identification number. Historically, each manufacturer has used its own numbering system, which varies from as few as 4 to as many as 15 characters. These parts identification numbers (PINs) vary in location, size, and composition. Professional thieves can easily remove an identification plate and replace it with a counterfeit plate. Some off-road equipment has identification plates for each separate component piece of the machinery, thus creating confusion for or misleading the inexperienced investigator.

Heavy equipment is also easily stolen; a single key may be used to start all models produced by a particular manufacturer, and where key locks are in place, the machinery can be jumped by placing a pocket knife or screwdriver across the electrical posts on the starter. Although manufacturers offer antitheft devices, they are costly items that add substantially to the base price of the equipment.

The unfamiliarity of most law enforcement officers with the nature, identity, and terminology of construction and farm equipment is among the principal problems faced by law enforcement. Few agencies have anyone with the expertise to identify specific machines or to locate and interpret identification numbers (see Figures 17–4 and 17–5).

Figure 17–4
Glossary of Terms

A.E.D. — Associated Equipment Distributors.

A.G.C. — Associated General Contractors.

AIR COMPRESSOR — A portable devise used to compress air for operating jack hammers, compactors, and other tools and equipment.

ARTICULATED — A means of connecting the front and rear section of a machine together to provide a steering action by hinging left to right.

AUGER — A rotating screw threaded drill which carries materials away from the face of the surface.

BACKHOE — A tractor attachment which does shovel or hoe work and is available in different sizes.

BELT CONVEYOR — An endless belt supported on rollers which transports materials on its upper surface.

BLADE — An elongated piece of metal used to push or move materials.

BOOM — An extension section hinged to the main frame of a crane or backhoe.

BUCKET — A device attached to backhoes and loaders used to pick up materials.

BUSH HOG — A heavy mower attachment for a tractor which is used to cut or mow brush.

CAB — An enclosure to protect a machine operator from the elements.

C.I.M.A. — Construction Industry Manufacturers Association.

CIRCLE — The rotary table on a motorgrader that supports and regulates the blade.

COMBINE — A machine to harvest corn, wheat, beans, etc.

COMPACTOR — A machine used to compact materials.

COTTON PICKER — A machine that picks or strips cotton, available in two, three, or four row models.

CRANE — a device used to lift materials.

CRAWLER — A unit mounted on tracks.

DOZER — A blade used to move materials by pushing. May be track or wheel mounted.

EXCAVATOR — A machine capable of simultaneous propulsion and digging or trenching in a 360 degree radius.

FACE OF SHOE — Part of track contacting the ground.

FORKLIFT — A machine with forks used to lift and/or transport materials.
Types: Rough Terrain
           Warehouse

HYDROSTATIC DRIVE — Working off hydraulic pumps and eliminating the use of gears, clutch plates, etc.

LOADER — A machine with a bucket mounted on the front to move materials.

LOWBOY or LOWBED — A trailer with a low deck used in transporting equipment.

MOTOR GRADER— A rubber tired machine used in road grading, sloping and finishing. Also called maintainers, motor patrols, and blades.

MOWER — An attachment to a tractor for mowing right-of-way, golf courses, and fields. May be rotary or reel type and is available in widths from 5 feet to 25 feet.

MOULDBOARD — A blade attached to a motorgrader for cutting or leveling.

OUTRIGGER — Leg type extensions used on the front or rear of machinery to improve its stability.

RIPPER — Fingerlike bars used to slice open the materials it is pulled through.
Types: Hinged
           Single shank
           Multishank

PIN — Product Identification Number.

PIN PLATE — A plate or sticker upon which the Product Identification Number has been embossed or stamped, and is attached to the unit with nail drive rivets, pop rivets, or adhesive.

P.T.O. — Power Take Off Unit on a tractor used to power implements such as mowers, bush hogs, augers, plows, etc.

R.O.P.S. — (Roll-Over Protection Struction) A frame or cab surrounding the operator area to prevent injury if machine turns over.

SCRAPER — A machine used to scrape, level, or move materials. May be single or twin engined.
Types: Elevating Scraper
           Nonelevating Scraper

TRACTOR — A gasoline or diesel powered machine to which may be attached farm or construction equipment.

TRENCHER — A machine used to dig trenches.
Types: Wheel type
           Ladder type

WHEEL UNIT — A machine that moves on wheels.

WINCH — A drum that rotates winding cable in or out.

Source: National Automobile Theft Bureau (now NIBC), *Commercial Vehicle and Off-Road Equipment Identification Manual*, 5th ed. (Palos Hills, Ill.: NATB, 1990), pp. 133–134.

INVESTIGATIVE TOOLS AND TECHNIQUES

Vehicle theft investigation is a fairly technical and sophisticated specialty. An effective investigator needs experience and expertise. Despite the fact that vehicle theft may not be among those offenses receiving the highest priority for the allocation of limited resources by a law enforcement agency, there are thousands of specialists in this country and elsewhere whose expertise is available to any investigator needing assistance; often, these resources are just a telephone call away.

As in any specialized investigative field, one is not born an expert and cannot become an expert without extensive training and experience. So it is with vehicle thefts and related crimes. Those who possess the expertise, such as highly skilled investigators, cannot assume that uniformed officers with general policing responsibilities have any knowledge about the field beyond their limited exposure in an academy setting. Thus, if investigators are anxious for patrol officers to perform some initial investigative tasks, the investigators should offer to teach those officers how to perform the desired tasks.

Figure 17–5
Illustrations of Heavy Construction Equipment

BACKHOE, CRAWLER MOUNTED
(HYDRAULIC)

BACKHOE/LOADER — WHEEL MOUNTED

CRANES, LIFTING

Crawler Mounted (Mechanical)

CRANES, LIFTING

Self-Propelled (Hydraulic)

Truck Mounted (Mechanical)

Truck Mounted (Hydraulic)

Figure 17–5 *(continued)*

DOZER, CRAWLER MOUNTED

GRADERS, MOTOR — SELF-PROPELLED

LOADER, CRAWLER MOUNTED

LOADER, WHEEL MOUNTED

ROLLER, RUBBER TIRED

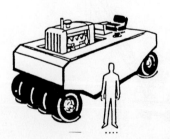

Figure 17–5 *(continued)*

ROLLER, SELF-PROPELLED PRIME MOVER
(WITH SHEEPSFOOT)

ROLLER, STEEL WHEEL — TANDEM

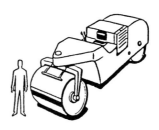

SCRAPER, MOTOR

Scraper, Elevating

Scraper, Standard

TRENCHER, CRAWLER MOUNTED
LADDER TYPE

MAJOR INVESTIGATIVE RESOURCES

National Insurance Crime Bureau

The NICB is not a law enforcement agency that investigates auto thefts and arrests offenders in the traditional sense. Rather, the NICB is an information-gathering and dissemination body and a law enforcement assistance agency. In this regard, its special agents do investigate professional theft rings and other auto theft cases in conjunction with local, state, and federal law enforcement agencies.

Beginning in 1912 with the efforts of a few individuals, representing different insurance companies, joining forces to disseminate information on stolen motor vehicles, the cooperation gradually spread and evolved into several independent regionalized and, later, national groups. This growth limited communication and interaction. Duplication of efforts and costs, along with the creation of considerable confusion among law enforcement officials in deciding whom to contact for information, led to the initial consolidation of all existing auto theft information agencies and organizations into the National Automobile Theft Bureau (NATB) in 1927. In 1965 the NATB was completely nationalized and centralized.

Late in 1991 a merger took place between the NATB and the Insurance Crime Prevention Institute (ICPI); on January 1, 1992, the National Insurance Crime Bureau (NICB) was formed. The NICB now has 200 investigative field agents coordinating with another 800 fraud investigators who work for individual insurance companies.

The NICB is not a government organization. It is a nonprofit organization operated by, funded by, affiliated with, and serving approximately 1,000 associated insurance companies nationwide. It conducts and supports engineering and other research and experiments aimed at reducing vehicle theft and fraud and is a recognized national voice for law enforcement and the insurance industry on legislative matters.

The NICB assists in the identification of vehicles and helps educate law enforcement officers in investigative techniques of vehicle identification, fraud, and theft.

In addition to the expertise of its field personnel, the computerized records developed and established by the NICB, now maintained and administered by the International Service Organization, a private company, are invaluable investigative aids. These database services include the following:

- *Theft file:* More than 1000 insurance companies report stolen vehicles. Theft records from the Canadian Automobile Theft Bureau (CATB) and most European countries are also maintained and include all types of vehicles, off-road machinery, boats, parts, and accessories. The records contain full ownership and insurance information.

- *Salvage file:* Salvage vehicle reports are received from insurance companies on vehicles where there has been a loss settlement and the company has taken title. These vehicles are generally sold through salvage pools or to salvage buyers. The file contains information on both sellers and buyers of salvage.

- *Export file:* The U.S. Customs Service and others send copies of export declarations for entry into the system. The information aids in the detection of illegal exports and fraudulent theft reports on exported vehicles where a subsequent stolen vehicle report is filed.

- *NCIC purge file:* Vehicle theft records purged from NCIC since 1972 for a variety of reasons are provided to NICB on a daily basis and are entered into the system as a permanent record. The file is an important and time-saving tool for law enforcement.

- *Information wanted file:* When a purchaser skips out on payments to a finance company that has purchased physical-damage insurance on the vehicle from one of the NICB sponsoring member companies, the information is made available to law enforcement agencies investigating the vehicle as a suspected stolen unit.

- *Inquiry file:* When a law enforcement agency makes an inquiry on a vehicle for an investigation, any subsequent information received or any inquiry on the same vehicle from another person or agency will be passed on to the original inquirer.

- *Shipping and assembly file:* This file holds the shipping and assembly records for most automobiles; light-, medium-, and heavy-duty trucks; semitrailers; motorcycles; and snowmobiles.
- *Impound file:* An increasing number of states are now collecting and reporting impound records to NICB for entry into this file. The file helps to clear many stolen records and is a valuable investigative tool.
- *VINASSIST*: This NICB program edits, evaluates, and corrects vehicle identification numbers, a process that greatly aids law enforcement in positively identifying specific recovered motor vehicles.
- The International Service Organization (ISO) also maintains an All-Claims Database, which allows claims filed against participating member insurance companies to be compared to detect possible fraudulent claims, including auto theft–related insurance fraud.

The NICB has eastern (Atlanta) and western (Glendora, California) divisions serving the United States and an International Division, headquarterd in Dallas. The bureau's headquarters office is located outside Chicago in Palos Hills, Illinois. Their web site address is www.nicb.org.

The International Division directs its efforts toward locating and repatriating vehicles stolen from the United States and now located in foreign countries. Vehicles are located through the investigative efforts of agents of NICB and other federal agencies, with assistance from law enforcement and other government officials in foreign countries. In addition, much of the work is in support of attempts by the State Department to negotiate treaties and other agreements for the return of vehicles.

Since 1929, the NICB and its predecessor, the NATB, have annually published the *Passenger Vehicle Identification Manual,* which contains the following:

- NICB directory.
- Summary of motor vehicle laws of the states.
- Information on federal motor vehicle marking standards.
- Information on vehicle identification numbers.
- Domestic and imported vehicle information.[13]

Every five years the NICB also publishes the *Commercial Vehicle and Off-Road Equipment Identification Manual,* which contains the following:

- World manufacturer identification codes.
- Model year identifier.
- Truck-tractor identification.
- Commercial trailer identification.
- Off-road equipment identification.
- Motorcycle identification.[14]

Canadian Insurance Crime Prevention Bureau

The Canadian Insurance Crime Prevention Bureau (ICPB) has been functioning since 1923 but became an independent division within the Insurance Council of Canada on January 1, 1998. It is to Canada what NICB is to the United States. Supported by over 90 percent of private-property and casualty insurers, ICPB employs 130 people, 86 of whom are investigators. Within the organizational structure of ICPB are found the Canadian Automobile Theft Bureau (CATB) and the Canadian Police Information System, the sister organization of NCIC. ICPB is headquartered in Toronto, Ontario.

International Association of Auto Theft Investigators

Another resource available to the investigator is the International Association of Auto Theft Investigators (IAATI) and its regional affiliated chapters. With a current membership in excess of 1,500, IAATI was formed in 1952 for the purpose of formulating new methods to attack and control vehicle theft and fraud. Its members represent law enforcement agencies, state registration and titling agencies, insurance companies, car rental companies, the automobile manufacturing industry, and other interested groups. International and regional training seminars are held throughout the year.

State Organizations

Many states have organizations comprised of auto theft investigators who meet regularly to exchange intelligence information and learn new methods of combating the problems of theft and fraud.

National Crime Information Center

Another valuable resource to the investigator is NCIC. On-line inquiries can be made into the vehicle or license plate files to check on records for stolen vehicles, vehicles wanted in conjunction with felonies, stolen component parts, and stolen license plates. In addition, a request can be made for an off-line search, which is a tool designed to assist an investigator by providing lead information. For example, an investigator attempting to track a stolen vehicle that is known to be traveling across the country can request an off-line search to see if any stolen inquiries had been made within a specific time frame on that vehicle. A hit would identify the time and location from which the inquiry was made, thus providing a lead to locating the vehicle.

As much as the NCIC system now holds in its more than 40 million records in 17 databases, the system is 30 years old. The system handles more than 1.7 million transactions a day. *NCIC 2000*, the updated version being developed for implementation in the latter part of 1999, will be able to send and receive pictures and single fingerprints to and from the IAFIS; allow law enforcement agencies to automatically check on stolen vehicles recovered within the previous five days; automatically check a stolen car inquiry against other files of property stolen in the vehicle; automatically link with the Canadian system; automatically search the records of the federal prison system to check an offender's history or determine whether an offender is still in the system; and automatically notify an entering agency of any inquiries. The system will also include an Immigration and Naturalization Service (INS) deported-persons file and probation and parole information.

Special Investigative Units

In the mid-1970s, Kemper Insurance Company created the first special investigative unit (SIU) for insurance companies. Its primary purpose was to investigate potentially fraudulent auto theft claims. There are more than 800 SIU investigators employed in the insurance industry working fraud claims. Approximately 80 percent of the insurance companies now have SIUs. The agents and units work with and train insurance adjusters to detect oddities and "red flags" indicating potential fraud. The SIUs also work closely with law enforcement by lending assistance in investigations—providing computer information, claims histories, and statements of insureds made under oath.

AAMVANET

This computerized communication network links state and provincial agencies on matters of highway usage and highway safety. The system was initiated by and for the American Association of Motor Vehicle Administrators (AAMVA). AAMVANET, a system as well as a subsidiary corporation of AAMVA, is coordinating the effort to create a National Motor Vehicle Title Information System (NMVTIS), being developed in cooperation with NICB and the R. L. Polk Company. Through NMVTIS any inquiry will receive a complete and up-to-the-minute history of a vehicle, including whether it was reported stolen, salvaged, or exported or is otherwise incapable of being the subject of a new transfer. In addition to inquiry capability, the system will prevent the laundering of titles between states for the purpose of removing brands such as those that appear on salvage, flood-damaged, rebuilt, or unrepairable vehicles. The program is being developed with the help of five pilot states. An ultimate goal of the developers is to provide a system whereby a potential purchaser of a used vehicle will be able to inquire about the status of the vehicle before making a final commitment to purchase.

Government Agencies

In virtually all state governments, organizations or entities exist that possess information of value to investigators. Specifically, motor vehicle and driver's license offices, insurance fraud investigative units, and fire and arson investigative units may provide valuable information or assistance.

Manufacturers

Manufacturers are one of the most important resources an investigator can cultivate and turn to for assistance, particularly as it relates to the content and location of numbers on vehicles or parts. Domestic and foreign automobile manufacturers are generally most supportive of an investigator's inquiries, as are the Harley-Davidson Motorcycle Company and the John Deere, Case, and Caterpillar companies, which manufacture construction and farm equipment. This list is not meant to be exhaustive. Help will generally be given by any manufacturer when requested.

North American Export Committee

In an effort to stem the tide of stolen vehicles being exported from the country, the NICB, U.S. and Canadian Customs, Royal Canadian Mounted Police, Insurance Crime Prevention Council in Canada, and Miami-Dade Police Department in Florida, along with participation from other law enforcement agencies, the insurance industry, and other interested parties, established the North American Export Committee in 1993 to investigate ways in which the exporting of stolen vehicles could be slowed without impeding commerce at port facilities.

Shipments of vehicles occur in two ways—some vehicles are rolled on and then rolled off and some are shipped in containers. These are quite different concepts requiring entirely different approaches. U.S. Customs is charged with the responsibility of checking the paperwork on vehicles to be exported, and the paperwork must be received by Customs three days before a vehicle can be shipped. Only limited resources are devoted to this responsibility, however, because Customs is more concerned about property coming into the country and about commodities, other than vehicles, being exported. Nevertheless, Customs, sometimes with the assistance and support of local law enforcement, checks the paperwork, physically examines as many of the vehicles as possible, and enters the VINs into a computer that transmits all those checked to NICB. Overnight, the list is run against the export, stolen, salvage, and VIN verification files. The next morning, an exceptions report is available to the submitting agencies so that the "trouble messages" (problems) can be checked out before the vehicle is shipped. At the Port of Miami, trouble messages occur on approximately 20 percent of the exports.

Containerized vehicles present a different set of problems. There are over 8 million containers exported from the United States in a year. No manifest is going to acknowledge that a container has one or more stolen vehicles. Checking a container, even if it meets a predetermined set of conditions called a *profile*, is hot, sweaty work—the unloading and reloading take hours—and it interferes with commerce. Stolen vehicles are usually found in the front or middle of a container, with goods packed all around them. To make enforcement more productive, an efficient, effective, and economic method of looking inside containers had to be found. X-ray equipment works but it is expensive and poses danger to workers subject to prolonged exposure. And it, too, slows down commerce because the container has to be stopped while the X-ray is taken, thus limiting the number of containers to about 30 that can be checked in one day at one location. Using gasoline-sniffing dogs and drilling holes in containers to insert a hydrocarbon "sniffer" or a camera on a pole have also been tried, with less than satisfactory results.

Science Applications International Corporation has developed a device that examines and photographs the contents of a container as it is passing through a gamma ray. In mid-1998, the corporation, in cooperation with the Dade County Multi-Agency Auto Theft Task Force and on behalf of the North American Export Committee, tested this equipment for a 90-day period at the Port of Miami in what was called the "Stolen Auto Recovery (STAR) System." Before the 90 days were up, more than 7700 containers were scanned in less than 6 seconds each while they continued to move. A total of 630 vehicles were identified and 6 stolen vehicles were recovered, valued at $217,000. There were no false identifications, and the flow of commerce was not impeded. The units cost around $270,000, are very transportable, and are easily installed in one day, and the gamma-ray scan preserves a video image of the contents of the container (see Figures 17–6 and 17–7).

LOCATING AND HANDLING VEHICLES

In recent years investigators have gotten seriously ill performing their jobs. Locating and handling the recovery of vehicles and parts can be very dangerous. Often, an investigator will climb or crawl around, through and over wrecks, in a remote area of a salvage yard in order to locate or identify a vehicle part. Not only is the physical work dangerous, but, unknowingly, the investigator may be exposed to toxic hazardous waste, which can cause permanent physical damage. Gloves should be worn at all times, along with protective clothing and a mask or breathing device, when encountering the unknown. Similarly, when investigating a vehicle fire, investigators must take precautions as toxic

Figure 17–6
Gamma-Ray Scan Showing Three Cars (two on ramps)

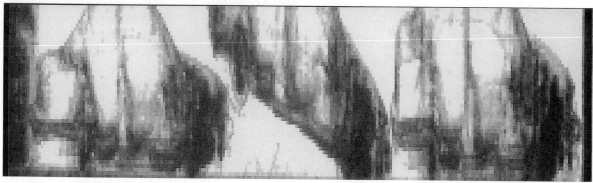

(Courtesy Miami-Dade Police Department)

chemicals may be around that can cause serious long-term illness due to exposure.

VEHICLE IDENTIFICATION

Often the most difficult and time-consuming task facing an investigator is the identification of a recovered vehicle. Although there are a number of ways by which motor vehicles can be identified, including a description by year, make and model, or license number, these items are easily generalized or alterable. For the investigator, identification is made by numbers affixed to or inscribed on the vehicle.

Since 1954 American automobile manufacturers have used a vehicle identification number instead of an engine number as the primary means of iden-

tification. However, before 1968, VINs, although usually inscribed on metal plates, were not uniformly located on vehicles, nor was there any standard method for attaching a VIN plate to a vehicle. On varying makes and models, VIN plates were affixed with screws or rivets or were spot-welded on doors, doorposts, or dashes. Since 1968 VIN plates on almost all domestic and foreign cars have been attached to the left side of the dash on the instrument panel in such a fashion as to be visible through the windshield. Corvettes, prior to 1984, had the VIN plate attached to the left side windshield post. Tractor and semitrailer manufacturers still lack consistency in the placement of VIN plates, as do construction and farm equipment manufacturers in the placement of product identification numbers (PINs).

Figure 17–7
Gamma-Ray Scan Showing Two Utility Vehicles

(Courtesy Miami-Dade Police Department)

VIN plates still are attached by a variety of methods. Several foreign manufacturers use a round-head "pop" rivet made of aluminum, stainless steel, or some plastic material. A six-petal "rosette" rivet made of aluminum or stainless steel has been used on General Motors products since 1966, on Chrysler-manufactured vehicles since 1968, and on Ford units since 1970. Sheet-metal screws are still occasionally used on some imports (see Figure 17–8).

The use of a public VIN is designed to provide a positive, individualized means of identifying a motor vehicle. The 1981 adoption of a standardized 17-character VIN for all cars manufactured in or sold in the United States was certainly a forceful step in that direction. Previously, General Motors used a 13-digit VIN, Ford and Chrysler each used 11 characters, and imports used a host of other lengths. The standardized 17-character configuration is required of all imports manufactured for sale in the

Figure 17–8
VIN Plate Attachment

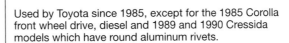

VIN PLATE ATTACHMENT

ROUND HEAD "POP" RIVET
ALUMINUM, STAINLESS STEEL OR PLASTIC

Used on early General Motors vehicles prior to 1965 after departure from "spot weld" method of attaching VIN plates. Still used by most foreign manufacturers.

Note: Most European rivets have a smaller center hole than the American version.

"ROSETTE" TYPE RIVET
6 PETALS ALUMINUM OR STAINLESS STEEL

Used by General Motors Corp. since 1965, Chrysler Corp. since 1966, and Ford Motor Co. since 1970. There have been instances when round head rivets were used at some assembly plants but only on very rare occasions.

"ROSETTE" TYPE RIVET
5 PETALS ALUMINUM

Used by Toyota since 1985, except for the 1985 Corolla front wheel drive, diesel and 1989 and 1990 Cressida models which have round aluminum rivets.

SHEET METAL SCREWS

Screws are occasionally used to attach VIN plates on some imported vehicles.

Note: In 1974 thru the present some manufacturers are using VIN plates with both concealed and exposed rivets.

Source: National Insurance Crime Bureau, *1994 Passenger Vehicle Identification Manual* (Palos Hills, Ill.: NICB, 1994), p. 41. Used with permission of NICB.

United States. The first 11 characters of the standardized VIN identify the country of origin, manufacturer, make, restraint system, model, body style, engine type, year, assembly plant, and a mathematically computed check digit that is used to verify all of the other characters in the VIN. The last six characters are the sequential production number of the vehicle (see Figures 17–9 and 17–10). The letters I, O, Q, U, and Z are not used so as to avoid confusion with similar-looking numbers.

Under the standardized 17-character system, the check digit is always the ninth character in the VIN and is calculated using the formula process illustrated on the worksheet depicted in Figure 17–11. By assigning specified numerical values to each letter and number, then multiplying and dividing, the appropriate check digit can be determined and matched with the check digit on the VIN in question to ascertain whether there are any flaws in the construction of the VIN such as altered or transposed characters.

The tenth character of the VIN represents the year of manufacture or vehicle model year. The letter A was used to designate 1980, B for 1981, and so on. Without the letters I, O, Q, U, and Z, the remaining 20 letters, followed by the use of numbers 1 to 9, establish a 30-year cycle before the possibility of an exactly duplicated VIN could result from the normal manufacturing process (see Figure 17–12).

VIN plates on some newer vehicles also have a bar code that contains all of the information represented by the alphanumeric characters of the VIN (see Figure 17–13). This makes attempted alteration of the VIN plate less effective because a reader can detect the true information in a second. Other manufacturers put a separate sticker on the door or doorpost that bears the VIN and bar code (see Figure 17–14).

Gray-Market Vehicles

When the U.S. dollar is strong overseas, it becomes economically feasible for individuals to purchase motor vehicles in other countries and have them shipped to the United States for sale, resale, or personal use. This effort can be profitable even though it may cost up to several thousand dollars apiece to "legalize" the vehicles for use in the United States. Since such vehicles are not manufactured for sale in this country, they are not constructed to meet U.S. emission control or safety standards, nor do they have a 17-character standardized VIN. If gray-market vehicles are brought into this country legally, a bond for each must be posted with U.S. Customs until such time as the appropriate modifications have been made to bring the vehicle into compliance with the U.S. Environmental Protection Agency (EPA) emission control requirements and the safety standards promulgated by the U.S. Department of Transportation (DOT). When these steps have been accomplished and the modifications approved, the federal government will issue a replacement VIN plate that conforms with the 17-character standard.

Many vehicles are found operating on the streets and highways of this nation prior to or without conforming to the legal conversion requirements for gray-market vehicles. The operation of these vehicles is unlawful, and they are subject to seizure by U.S. Customs. The frequency of such seizures and the ability to ensure compliance with the EPA and DOT regulations are, of course, a direct function of the resources devoted to the programs and the priorities established. Not unlike state and local agencies, federal law enforcement programs also suffer from limited resources. In some years, gray-market imports have approached 100,000 vehicles.

The nonconforming VIN on a gray-market vehicle is sometimes nothing more than a Dymo-

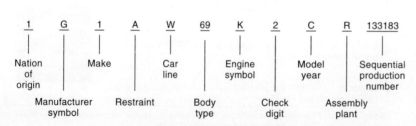

Figure 17–9
Example of 17-Digit VIN System

Figure 17–10

World Manufacturer Identification Codes

Code	Manufacturer	Code	Manufacturer
JH4	ACURA	1LN	LINCOLN
ZAR	ALFA ROMEO	SCC	LOTUS
1AM	AMERICAN MOTORS	ZAM	MASERATI
SCF	ASTON MARTIN	JM1	MAZDA
WAU	AUDI	WDB	MERCEDES BENZ
12A	AVANTI	1ME	MERCURY
ZBB	BERTONE	WF1	MERKUR
WBA	BMW	JA3	MITSUBISHI
1G4	BUICK	JN1	NISSAN
1G6	CADILLAC	1G3	OLDSMOBILE
1G1	CHEVROLET	VF3	PEUGEOT
1C3	CHRYSLER	ZFR	PININFARINA
2E3	EAGLE PREMIER	1P3	PLYMOUTH
JE3	EAGLE SUMMIT	1G2	PONTIAC
VF1	EAGLE MEDALLION	WPO	PORSCHE
SCE	DELOREAN	VF1	RENAULT
1B3	DODGE	SCA	ROLLS ROYCE
ZFF	FERRARI	YS3	SAAB
ZFA	FIAT	SAX	STERLING
1FA	FORD	JF1	SUBARU
KMH	HYUNDAI	JS3	SUZUKI
JHM	HONDA	JT2	TOYOTA
JAB	ISUZU	WVW	VOLKSWAGEN
SAJ	JAGUAR	YV1	VOLVO
1JC	JEEP		

(Courtesy NICB, Palos Hills, Ill.)

tape label stuck on the left side dash and visible through the windshield. Often such a VIN is on a plate riveted in the appropriate place, but its construction will not satisfy the accepted format requirements. Learning the proper appearance and configuration of the accepted VIN format will aid investigators not only in identifying gray-market vehicles but also in the detection of altered VINs.

Attempts to Conceal the Identity of Vehicles

The methods used to change the identity of a motor vehicle discussed earlier in this chapter include doing a salvage switch and altering genuine or counterfeiting ownership documents. Numbers can be intentionally transposed on documents, VIN plates can be counterfeited or removed, and other identifying numbers can be completely obliterated, altered, or defaced in an attempt to thwart any effort to accurately identify a vehicle.

Why is concealing a vehicle's identity so important? Simply, if a vehicle cannot be positively identified, it cannot be proved that the vehicle was stolen, when it was stolen, or from whom it was stolen. Thus, one who is in possession of such a vehicle cannot be prosecuted as a thief.

Even the most careful thief has extreme difficulty totally concealing the identity of a stolen vehicle. Although it does happen, total inability to identify a vehicle is rare if the investigator doesn't hesitate to call on his or her own or others' knowledge, training, and experience. Knowing how and when to call on outside resources is important to the successful investigation. NICB special agents and other highly qualified law enforcement officers know how and where to look for clues to a vehicle's identity.

Figure 17–11
Check Digit Calculation Formula

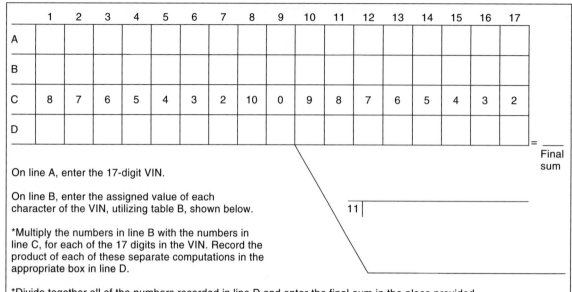

	1	2	3	4	5	6	7	8	9	10	11	12	13	14	15	16	17
A																	
B																	
C	8	7	6	5	4	3	2	10	0	9	8	7	6	5	4	3	2
D																	

= ____
Final sum

On line A, enter the 17-digit VIN.

On line B, enter the assigned value of each character of the VIN, utilizing table B, shown below.

*Multiply the numbers in line B with the numbers in line C, for each of the 17 digits in the VIN. Record the product of each of these separate computations in the appropriate box in line D.

11 |

*Divide together all of the numbers recorded in line D and enter the final sum in the place provided.

*Divide the final sum by the number 11. The remainder of this division is the "check digit" (the ninth character of the 17- digit VIN). If the remainder of this division is a single-digit number, then it should match the check digit in the VIN exactly; if the remainder is the number 10, then the check digit is the letter X.

Table B

A-1	J-1	T-3	1-1	6-6
B-2	K-2	U-4	2-2	7-7
C-3	L-3	V-5	3-3	8-8
D-4	M-4	W-6	4-4	9-9
E-5	N-5	X-7	5-5	0-0
F-6	P-7	Y-8		
G-7	R-9	Z-9		
H-8	S-2			

Assign to each number in the VIN its actual value and record that value in the appropriate box in line B.

The letters I, O and Q are never used in the new 17-digit VIN's.

To determine the year of manufacture from the 17-digit VIN (character 10 of the VIN) use the listed table.

1980-A   1981-B   1982-C   1983-D   1984-E   1985-F   1986-G   1987-H

– –

The decoding chart, shown above, may be photocopied to provide multiple blank work sheets for computing the check digits of the new 17-digit VIN's.

Example: 1981 Ford Mustang 1FABP12A4BR101093, final sum = 246

$$\begin{array}{r} 22 \\ 11\overline{)246} \\ 22 \\ \hline 26 \\ 22 \\ \hline 4 \end{array}$$

Check digit ⟶

Figure 17–12
Vehicle Model Year

1980	A	1995	S	2010	A
1981	B	1996	T	2011	B
1982	C	1997	V	2012	C
1983	D	1998	W		
1984	E	1999	X		
1985	F	2000	Y		
1986	G	2001	1		
1987	H	2002	2		
1988	J	2003	3		
1989	K	2004	4		
1990	L	2005	5		
1991	M	2006	6		
1992	N	2007	7		
1993	P	2008	8		
1994	R	2009	9		

The public VIN on the dash is not the only number that identifies a specific vehicle. The VIN may be stamped in several different places on the vehicle's body, frame, or component parts. The location of some of these secondary numbers is not a big secret, but others, referred to as *confidential numbers*, are stamped into frames or bodies in places supposedly known only to the manufacturer and to law enforcement agencies and officers who are specialists in vehicle identification and auto theft investigation, such as NICB special agents. Various other parts such as engines and transmissions will be given an identification number when manufactured, but, because they are distinct component parts, often manufactured in different locales from the final assembly plant, the numbers may be totally different from the VIN. However, documents created and maintained by the manufacturer, and perhaps already in the databanks of the NICB computer system, can be checked to determine the VIN of the vehicle in which the part was installed.

Other parts or components of a vehicle manufactured or subassembled elsewhere may be designed to fit a specific vehicle. In such cases, the part may have a serial number that is related to but not identical to the VIN. It may have a number that is a derivative of the VIN or formed from parts of the VIN, as where a T-top may need to be matched to a vehicle of a specific body type denoted by the sixth and seventh characters of the VIN and the six-digit sequential number. Numerous combinations are possible and plausible; again, this is where the manufacturer's records become indispensable.

The numbers often used to match parts so as to foster accurate assembly of a vehicle may be written on components with pen, pencil, chalk, marking pen, or crayon. It does not matter what they are written with, as long as there are numbers that can lead an investigator to the end result of positively identifying a vehicle. Frequently, the various components subassembled elsewhere in the same plant or shipped from other plants will be accompanied by production order forms or written orders containing the VIN or a derivative number, which matches the parts for assembly. After the parts are matched and assembled, the production form has no use and may be left in some nook, cranny, or crevice of the assembly. If the investigator knows where to look, such a document may often be found and thus lead to vehicle identification.

Federal Safety Certification Label

All cars distributed in the United States since 1970 must have a federal safety certification label. This sticker, in addition to the required certification statements, also contains the vehicle's VIN. If the sticker is removed, it leaves behind a "footprint" that often shows the word "void." Obviously, if the correct sticker is in place and the correct public VIN shows through the windshield, the VINs should match.

Shape and size of the labels, as well as the materials from which they are constructed, will

Figure 17–13
General Motors VIN Plate with Bar Code

Source: IAATI-SE newsletter, 1997.

Figure 17–14
Federal Safety Certification Label with Bar Code

MFD.BY HONDA OF AMERICA MFG.,INC.   2/92
GVWR 3945LBS GAWR F 2140LBS R 1885LBS
THIS VEHICLE CONFORMS TO ALL APPLICABLE
FEDERAL MOTOR VEHICLE SAFETY,BUMPER,
AND THEFT PREVENTION STANDARDS IN EFFECT
ON THE DATE OF MANUFACTURE SHOWN ABOVE:

V.I.N. 1HGCB7572NA107771

PASSENGER CAR   MADE IN U.S.A.

Source: IAATI-SE newsletter, 1997.

vary among manufacturers. More common among domestic manufacturers is a paper label covered with a clear Mylar-type plastic. The label is bonded to the vehicle with a mastic compound. Construction is such that the label should destruct if removal is attempted. Some foreign manufacturers construct the certifying label out of thin metal and attach it with rivets. In either case, security against removal and replacement is not absolute. However, investigators are encouraged not to use the VIN on the safety certification label as absolute proof of vehicle identification. The federal safety sticker will be located on the driver's door or on the doorpost.

Federal Legislation

In an effort to reduce auto theft by easing the process of vehicle identification, Congress enacted the Motor Vehicle Theft Law Enforcement Act of 1984. Title I of the law requires manufacturers to provide additional permanent identification numbers placed on up to 14 major parts of certain car lines. The car lines are selected each year for each manufacturer by the National Highway Traffic Safety Administration (NHTSA), the federal agency charged with setting the standards for the administration of the law. The car lines chosen each year are those designated as high-theft lines. The parts requiring the additional identification are those major parts that are normally most sought in a chop-shop operation and include the following (see Figure 17–15):

- Engine
- Transmission
- Both front fenders
- Hood
- Both front doors
- Front and rear bumpers
- Both rear quarter panels
- Decklid, tailgate, or hatchback (whichever is applicable)
- Both rear doors (if present)

The numbers must either be inscribed on the designated parts or printed on labels attached to the parts; labels must tear into pieces if removed, and if completely removed, they must leave a "footprint," which is visible using certain investigative techniques such as an ultraviolet light. The standards apply to the major parts of the designated new car lines and to replacement parts for those same car lines. The new-part labels must have the manufacturer's logo or other identifier printed and must use the full 17-character VIN for identification (see Figure 17–16); if, however, a VIN derivative of at least eight characters was being used to identify the engine and transmission on a particular covered line on the effective date of the law, that practice may continue. The identifier on covered replacement parts must carry the manufacturer's trademark, logo, or other distinguishing symbol, the letter R to reflect replacement, and the letters DOT (see Figure 17–16). The labels are to be

Figure 17–15
Components Requiring Marking

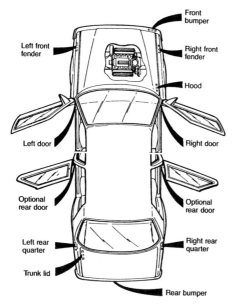

(Courtesy 3M Corporation)

Figure 17–16
Original and Replacement Parts Labels for Selected Manufacturers

AUTO MANUFACTURERS NAME	VIN LABEL	RDOT LABEL
Ford/US		R Ford DOT
Audi		OOOO R DOT
Ford/Germany		R Ford DOT
Mercedes Benz		R DOT
Porsche		R DOT
VW		VW R DOT
Renault		R DOT
Ferrari		R DOT
Maserati		R DOT

AUTO MANUFACTURERS NAME	VIN LABEL	RDOT LABEL
Saab		R SAAB DOT
Nummi/US		UNITED MOTOR R DOT
Honda		R H DOT
Isuzu		R DOT
Mazda		mazda R DOT
Mitsubishi		R DOT
Subaru		R DOT
Toyota		TOYOTA R DOT

(Courtesy 3M Corporation)

affixed to the part on a surface that is not normally exposed to damage when the part is installed, adjusted, or removed or damaged in an accident. When the part is removed from the vehicle, the label or inscription must be visible without the disassembling of the part.

The law limits the application of the requirements to no more than 14 production car lines for any one manufacturer, and the costs to the manufacturer for compliance cannot exceed $15 per vehicle, excluding the costs of marking the engine and transmission.

There is an exemption in the law, called a "black-box" exemption, which allows NHTSA to exempt from compliance with the standards up to two car lines per year for any single manufacturer if the vehicle line is equipped by the manufacturer with a standard equipment antitheft device determined by NHTSA to be as effective in deterring and reducing vehicle theft as would be compliance with the parts-marking requirements of the theft prevention standard.

The purpose and intent underlying the passage of the law, the promulgation of standards, and the marking of original and replacement parts was to reduce auto theft by ostensibly making it more difficult for the thief to conceal the identity of major parts, by providing fewer significant parts that would be untraceable, and by making it easier for law enforcement investigators to identify stolen parts.

Having determined that the parts-marking program initiated in 1984 has been effective, Congress passed the Anti-Car Theft Act of 1992, which continued and extended the program. The 1992 legislation also called for the U.S. attorney general to conduct an initial evaluation, in 1997, of the effectiveness of the program in inhibiting chop-shop operations and deterring motor vehicle theft with the objective of extending the parts-marking program to all lines (makes and models) by the end of 1997. The study recommended continuance of the program. The act also requires a long-range review of the program in 1999. In addition to evaluating whether chop-shop operations have been impacted and if theft has been deterred, the study will determine whether the black-box exemptions are an effective substitute for parts marking in substanially reducing motor vehicle theft.

The act also requires repair shops to check the VIN on all parts against a national file. Previously, this was the NCIC stolen-vehicle file, but the FBI, by direction of the act, established the National Stolen Parts Motor Vehicle Information System (NSPMVIS). Other provisions of the law include making armed carjacking a federal crime; doubling the maximum penalty for importing, exporting, transporting, selling, or receiving a stolen vehicle; and directing U.S. Customs to spot-check vehicles and containers leaving the country.

VIN Editing and Reconstruction

In any investigation, even where it appears that the VIN has not been altered or defaced, it is incumbent on the investigator to check the validity of the identifying numbers. Using the worksheet in Figure 17–11 will only verify the correctness of the check digit as compared with and calculated from the other 16 characters. A VIN edit computer program available at many law enforcement agencies and state motor vehicle regulatory offices can readily determine if the entered VIN is "good." If the VIN is invalid, there are now computer programs that can analyze the available information and at least narrow the valid possibilities of a correct VIN. Such programs replace what formerly was a long drawn-out manual process accomplished by checking manufacturers' records. VINASSIST, available from NICB, is one such program and is currently

being used by 7,000 insurers and law enforcement agencies. As noted earlier, the program edits, evaluates, and corrects vehicle identification numbers.

VIN Restoration

The restoration of manufacturers' serial numbers altered or obliterated from metal is a process that can be performed by an investigator with the proper material at hand. There is no mystery involved in number restoration as long as the investigator is willing to do the necessary preparation and has the patience to await results that are often slow in developing.

When a die is struck on metal, the molecules beneath the die are compressed and it is on these compressed molecules that the restoration processes are applied. The type of metal surface will dictate which of the three primary methods of restoration—heat, acid, or acid and electricity—should be applied. In the heat process an oxygen-acetylene torch is used on cast iron only. An electrolytic process in which 5 to 6 volts of electricity at 2 to 3 amps is used in conjunction with a solution of hydrochloric acid is generally used on steel. For the etching of aluminum, one solution of potassium hydroxide and a second solution of hydrochloric acid and mercuric chloride are applied using a cotton or fiberglass swab.

Regardless of which type of surface is involved and which restoration process is used, the surface must be painstakingly prepared. All paint, oil, grease, or other foreign matter must first be removed by using any solution that will work, including paint remover or acetone. But the surface is not to be scraped with a wire brush, knife, or any other tool, since one major purpose of preparation is to eliminate scratches and grind marks. Depending on how badly the surface is defaced, it may need to be polished with emery paper, a mill file, or by a high-speed sanding or polishing disk to remove scratches or gouges. Polishing the surface to a mirrorlike finish is desirable. Sometimes careful preparation of the surface will make all or some of the numbers visible.

Documenting the surface before beginning the restoration process is advisable. This can be done by photographing the area to be restored, dulling the shine with the use of fingerprint powder or carbon paper, and then taking a tape lift of the area (similar to lifting a fingerprint from a metal surface) and/or making a large-scale drawing of the area. It is always advisable to check with the manufacturer to ascertain the structure of the numbers used on a factory identification number if it is not already known. For example, the investigator should ask whether O's are rounded or squared and if 3's have rounded or flat tops. Such information can assist the investigator in determining whether visible numbers are valid.

If the heat process is to be used on cast iron, the ignited torch should be slowly moved back and forth over the area to be processed and gradually brought closer to the surface in a manner that will not crack the block. When the top of the blue cone of the flame is being moved back and forth about half an inch above the surface, the surface will soon reach a cherry-red color. When that happens, the torch should gradually be drawn away from the surface until it is about 6 inches away, all the while being slowly moved back and forth. After the surface has cooled, it should be very lightly polished with emery paper to remove the carbon deposits. The restored numbers should show up as a lighter color than the surrounding metal. If no numbers appear, either too much of the metal was removed and restoration will not produce results or the surface was not heated to a high-enough temperature, in which case the process should be repeated.

In the electrolytic process of restoring numbers on steel, two pieces of number 12 or 14 braided wire, 18 to 24 inches in length with alligator clips attached to the ends, along with a 6- or 12-volt battery, are needed. D.C. current may be used if a battery is not convenient. One wire should be connected to the positive pole with the other end grounded somewhere near the area to be restored. The other wire, connected to the negative pole, should have a swab dipped in acid solution attached to the other end; the swab should be moved one way only over the surface until any numbers are restored. The acid, speeded by the electricity, eats the surrounding metal surface until the numbers (if not totally destroyed) are revealed. In this and all acid processing techniques, drawings or sketches should be made as individual numbers or letters are revealed because they may fade before more heavily ground characters are restored. Once the process is completed, the surface should be neutralized with water, dried, and coated with oil to prevent rust. In using any acid, good ventilation is imperative.

Good ventilation is also necessary in the acid restoration of numbers on aluminum. Using potassium hydroxide solution and a swab, the surface area should be brushed in one direction for about 1 minute. The surface should be dried and brushed with a solution of hydrochloric acid and mercuric chloride in the same direction for 2 minutes. The surface should be dried again. This process constitutes one application. Often results will appear after two to four applications, but repeated applications may be made as often as necessary.[15]

STOLEN-VEHICLE INDICATORS

The thorough investigator will become suspicious enough from the presence of the indicators listed below to pursue an investigation to determine if auto theft has occurred.

Condition of Vehicle

Conditions such as the following may indicate that a vehicle is stolen:

- Missing or damaged ignition locks.
- Damaged doors, glove compartments, and trunks.
- Broken or missing door glass, particularly vent glass.
- Vehicle operated without lights at night.
- Vehicle being pushed or towed at night.
- Pry marks around windows, doors, glove compartment, or trunk.
- Vehicle parked or hidden in remote area.
- Missing parts, such as wheels, engine, or transmission.
- Missing accessories, such as radio, spare tire, or airbag.
- Vehicle illegally parked or abandoned long enough to accumulate dirt or debris under the wheels.
- Vehicle contains bullet holes.
- Vehicle used in other crimes.
- Windows open in inclement weather.
- Components such as four-speed transmission, bucket seats, or high-performance engine from a late-model vehicle on an older model.

- Vehicle showing evidence of having been lived in.
- Vehicle abandoned at the scene of an accident.
- Vehicle parked with engine running and no one around it.
- Vehicle with a new or used car lot identification number or sticker on it.
- Vehicle with license plates bent down, covered, fastened with wire, new bolts on old plates, or vice versa.
- Vehicle with nonmatching front and rear plates.
- Impacted insects on rear license plates.
- Out-of-state plates attached with a local dealer's license plate holder.
- Loose VIN plate or one showing evidence of tampering, such as scratches or different-style letters or numbers.
- VIN plate held by rivets that are loose or of the wrong type.
- Repainted VIN plate.
- Loose dashboard or loose ignition switch.
- Keys not original factory issue.
- Chisel or pull marks on ignition switch.
- Federal certification label tampered with or missing, or the VIN on the label does not match the plate on the dash.

Suspicious Driver Behavior

Any of the following suspicious acts by a driver may be indications that a vehicle is stolen:

- The driver seems extremely nervous or attempts to avoid police vehicles.
- The driver appears unfamiliar with the operation of the vehicle.
- The driver is wearing gloves in warm weather.
- The driver leaves a service station without paying for gasoline.
- The driver has little or no regard for the property of others or for the vehicle.
- The driver does not fit the vehicle. Usually a vehicle reflects its owner's economic status and his or her personal characteristics.
- The driver attempts to escape from minor traffic violations.

INVESTIGATION OF FRAUD CASES

The investigation of fraud cases is not unlike the investigation of other types of offenses. In the fraud case, the investigator should consider working very closely with any special investigative unit personnel available through an insurance company that may be involved in the case. Generally, the investigation of a motor vehicle fraudulent insurance claim case will center around questions involving the insured, the insurance policy, identification information on the vehicle, the police report, the status of the certificate of title, the condition of the vehicle, and any unusual conditions surrounding the claim.

The investigator should obtain all information and supporting documents regarding the purchase and possession of the vehicle and all the circumstances surrounding the alleged loss. It is important to determine whether the VIN on the stolen vehicle is consistent with the make and model and whether the VIN is, in fact, one that has been assigned to a manufactured vehicle. To determine the existence of and the condition of vehicles reported stolen, it is important that the investigator contact prior owners, lienholders, and insurers to verify information received on the reported loss. When information on a reported loss is supplied to a law enforcement agency, is any of the information inconsistent with the facts determined in the investigation? If the investigation centers on a possibly inflated theft loss, questions asked of people potentially having information should be directed to the condition of the vehicle immediately prior to the reported loss.

With only slight modification or expansion, the list of vehicle theft fraud indicators below can apply equally to accident and damage fraud cases, commercial vehicle theft fraud, false vehicle claims, inflated theft loss frauds, and even some vehicle arson cases. At the very least, the profile indicators can serve as an excellent foundation for beginning an investigation.

Indicators of Fraud Concerning the Insured

- Insured has lived at current address less than six months.
- Insured has been with current employer less than six months.
- Insured's address is a post office box or mail drop.

- Insured does not have a telephone.
- Insured's listed number is a mobile/cellular phone.
- Insured is difficult to contact.
- Insured frequently changes address and/or phone number.
- Insured's place of contact is a hotel, tavern, or other place that is neither his or her place of employment nor his or her place of residence.
- Insured conducts all business in person, does not use mails.
- Insured is unemployed.
- Insured claims to be self-employed but is vague about the business and actual responsibilities.
- Insured has recent or current marital and/or financial problems.
- Insured has a temporary, recently issued, or out-of-state driver's license.
- Insured's driver's license has recently been suspended.
- Insured recently called to confirm and/or increase coverage.
- Insured has an accumulation of parking tickets on vehicle.
- Insured is unusually aggressive and pressures for quick settlement.
- Insured is very knowledgeable of claims process and insurance terminology.
- Insured's income is not compatible with value of insured vehicle.
- Insured is behind in loan payments on vehicle and/or other financial obligations.
- Insured avoids meetings with investigators.
- Insured cancels scheduled appointments for statements and/or examination under oath.
- Insured has a previous history of vehicle theft claims.

Indicators of Fraud Related to the Vehicle

- Vehicle was purchased for cash with no bill of sale or proof of ownership.
- Vehicle is a new or late model with no lienholder.
- Vehicle was very recently purchased.
- Vehicle was not seen for an extended period of time prior to the reported theft.

- Vehicle was purchased out of state.
- Vehicle has a history of mechanical problems.
- Vehicle is a "gas guzzler."
- Vehicle is customized, classic, and/or antique.
- Vehicle displayed "For Sale" signs prior to theft.
- Vehicle was recovered clinically/carefully stripped.
- Vehicle is parked on street although garage is available.
- Vehicle was recovered stripped, but insured wants to retain salvage and repair appears to be impractical.
- Vehicle is recovered by the insured or a friend.
- Vehicle purchase price was exceptionally high or low.
- Vehicle was recovered with old or recent damage and coverage was high deductible or no collision coverage.
- Vehicle has an incorrect VIN (e.g., not originally manufactured, inconsistent with model).
- Vehicle VIN is different from VIN appearing on the title.
- Vehicle VIN provided to police is incorrect.
- Federal vehicle safety certification label is altered or missing.
- Federal vehicle safety certification label displays different VIN than is displayed on vehicle.
- Vehicle has theft and/or salvage history.
- Vehicle is recovered with no ignition or steering lock damage.
- Vehicle was previously involved in a major collision.
- Vehicle is late model with extremely high mileage (exceptions: taxi, police, utility vehicles).
- Vehicle is older model with exceptionally low mileage (i.e., odometer rollover/rollback).
- Vehicle is older or inexpensive model and insured indicates it was equipped with expensive accessories that cannot be substantiated with receipts.
- Vehicle is recovered stripped, burned, or sustained severe collision damage within a short time after loss allegedly occurred.

- Vehicle is a leased vehicle with excessive mileage for which the insured would have been liable under the mileage limitation agreement.

Indicators of Fraud Related to Coverage

- Loss occurs within one month of issue or expiration of the policy.
- Loss occurs after cancellation notice was sent to insured.
- Insurance premium was paid in cash.
- Coverage is for minimum liability with full comprehensive coverage on late model and/or expensive vehicle.
- Coverage was recently increased.

Indicators of Fraud Related to Reporting

- Police report has not been made by insured or has been delayed.
- No report or claim is made to insurance carrier within one week after theft.
- Neighbors, friends, and family are not aware of loss.
- Title is junk, salvage, out-of-state, photocopied, or duplicated.
- Title history shows nonexistent addresses.
- Repair bills are consecutively numbered or dates show work accomplished on weekends or holidays.
- An individual, rather than a bank or financial institution, is named as the lienholder.

Other General Indicators of Vehicle Theft Fraud

- Vehicle is towed to isolated yard at owner's request.
- Salvage yard or repair garage takes unusual interest in claim.
- Information concerning prior owner is unavailable.
- Prior owner cannot be located.
- Vehicle is recovered totally burned after theft.
- Fire damage is inconsistent with loss description.
- VINs were removed prior to fire.

- Vehicle is alleged to have been stolen prior to titling and registration, and insured presents an assigned title that is still in the name of the previous owner as his or her proof of ownership.
- Appraiser had difficulty getting into body shop to view and estimate damage.
- Insurance agent did not view the vehicle before or at the time of issuing the policy.
- The last-known driver of a commercial vehicle is no longer employed by the owner, and the owner is unable to provide the driver's job application or any other identification.
- The history of a commercial vehicle shows many sale-ownership transactions that reflect low purchase prices compared to the stated value of the vehicle.
- Loss (theft) of a commercial vehicle occurred in an area not frequently traveled by the owner/driver or outside the scheduled route.
- The odometer on a recovered vehicle has been smashed to conceal high mileage.
- The insured/claimant is reluctant to provide the name of a previous insurance carrier.
- The insured/claimant does not call the police to the scene of a major accident but, rather, goes to the police station and makes an over-the-counter report.
- The insured is overly enthusiastic or candid about taking the blame for an accident.
- A phantom (not identified) vehicle caused the accident.
- Insured's/claimant's vehicle is not repaired locally but is driven or shipped out of state for repair.
- Reported accident occurred on private property near the residence(s) of those involved.[16]

INVESTIGATION OF VEHICLE FIRES

Along with the general increase in crimes in the United States has come an increase in automobile fires. Many of the criminal fires occur when stolen vehicles have been stripped of valuable parts and the rest burnt to destroy the evidence (see

Figure 17–17). However, as in other fire investigations, the investigator first must eliminate natural and accidental causes of fire. Investigators who make unsubstantiated remarks about the origin of fires can damage their own and possible suspects' reputations.

Inspection of Salvage

Before beginning the physical investigation of a vehicle fire scene, the investigator must understand that the crime scene examination includes both the vehicle and the area in which it was burned. Hence, the investigation must follow established principles by first recording the scene. Photographs should be taken immediately, before there is any disturbance of the crime scene. Measurements must be taken to establish the exact location of the vehicle in relationship to fixed objects, crossroads, houses, and so on. A description should be recorded of the terrain, nearby roadways, and weather conditions, including prevailing wind directions.

A thorough search should be made of the area for tire tread marks, footprints, cans, bottles, other containers, unusual residue or materials, old tires, matches, or any other item that may be related to the case. Samples should be taken of soil, which may contain evidence of flammable liquids. When found, each item should be photographed before being moved, and then properly packaged and marked as evidence.

The successful investigation of automobile fire losses originates with basic lines of inquiry. First an inspection of the salvage must be completed for information on the origin and possible motive for the fire; second, an investigation must be made of the car owner for evidence of intent, motive, and opportunity; third, witnesses who might have information must be questioned; and last, the owner must be questioned to establish his or her knowledge of the fire and to verify information.

Generally investigators inspect the burnt automobile before contacting the owner, and the inspection is made as soon after the fire as possible. The inspection starts where the fire apparently originated. In accidental fires, this will normally be that part of the vehicle which is the most badly damaged from the intensity of the heat. Accidental fires usually spread in diminishing degree from the

Figure 17–17
Vehicle Burned to Destroy Evidence
(*Top*) Front and (*below*) rear view of a totally burned vehicle.

(Courtesy National Insurance Crime Bureau)

point of origin according to prevailing conditions. Conditions include direction and velocity of wind and/or materials on which flames feed, such as gasoline in the tank, woodwork, or other similarly flammable parts of the vehicle. When there are significant variations in these patterns, arson emerges as a possibility. Arson fires started with flammable materials usually show intense heat in more than one place. The investigator should carefully note the extent of the fire and its path. This information may prove valuable in the later questioning of the owner or witnesses.

The car also should be inspected for the removal of equipment such as stereo, heater, air horns, fog lights, and so forth. Notice should also be made of other irregularities such as old tires on new cars or missing spare tires.

Inspection of the Fuel System

The Gas Tank   The investigator should determine whether the cap to the gas tank was in place at the time of the fire. Sometimes gasoline to start the fire is siphoned from the tank and the cap is carelessly left off. If the cap is blown off, it will show effects of an explosion. The drain plug in the bottom of the tank should be checked. In addition, if it was removed or loosened before the fire, there might be evidence of fresh tool marks, especially pliers marks, on it.

The Gas Lines   The gas lines should be examined for breaks between the tank and the fuel pump. Breaks should be examined for tool marks. Some arsonists disconnect the line below the tank to obtain gasoline to start the fire and fail to replace the line.

The Fuel Pump   Gasoline to start the fire is sometimes obtained by disconnecting the line from the fuel pump and running the starter. If the fuel pump is melted, there should be evidence of fire on the sidepans. If the fuel pump was disconnected to allow the gasoline to run out and then set on fire, there may be carbon deposits inside the gas line at the fuel pump.

The investigator should establish whether parts of the fuel pump are missing. If key parts of the fuel system are missing and the owner says that the vehicle was running at the time of the fire, then there is strong reason to suspect arson.

Inspection of the Electrical System

A short circuit in the electric wiring is the most common excuse offered for automobile fires. The chances of a modern automobile's burning up from a short in the wiring are negligible. Engineers have virtually eliminated this hazard. If a fire in fact did start from malfunctions in the electrical system, there generally is enough evidence to substantiate it.

The wires near where the fire started should be inspected. If the wires are not melted completely, a short can be located. A short melts the strands of wire apart and causes small beads of melted wire to form on the ends. Wires that are burnt in two have sharp points. If the fire started in an electrical system, the system must be close to a flammable substance for the fire to spread. If a fire started from a short while the motor was running, the distributor points will be stuck or fused.

Inspection of the Motor, Radiator, and Parts under and near the Hood

The only possible place for an accidental fire to start at this location is around the fuel pump or carburetor and at the wiring. Any evidence of a fire on the front lower part of the motor not attributable to these parts indicates the use of flammables. If lead is melted from any lower or outside seams of the radiator, it is strong evidence of flammables. The fan belt does not usually burn in an accidental fire.

Gasoline on the motor sometimes causes the rubber cushions for the front of the motor to show evidence of fire. This evidence does not occur in accidental fires.

The radiator should also be checked. A badly burnt lower right corner indicates that the gas line from the fuel pump to the carburetor was disconnected, the starter run to pump out gasoline through the fuel pump, and then the gasoline set on fire.

Inspection of the Body

The body of the car is usually so badly burnt as to afford little evidence. However, signs of the intensity of heat sometimes point to the use of an inflammable. An excessive amount of flammable material may run through the floor of the car and burn underneath, causing oil or gasoline soot to form on the underside of the car. An examination should be made for this soot. If the hood was raised during the fire, the paint on the top panels may be blistered but not be burnt off where the two panels touched. If the wind was blowing from the rear of the car to the front, the paint should be burnt for almost the length of the hood; the radiator core will be burnt; but there will not have been enough fire at the rear of the car to do much damage to the gasoline tank. If the paint on the hood is burnt only an inch or so from the rear toward the front, this would indicate that the wind was blowing from the front of the car toward the rear, in which case the gasoline tank may be badly damaged but the radiator will be intact.

CONTACT WITH OWNERS

Before interviewing the owner of the car, the investigator should determine as completely as possible the character of the owner. This information may prove quite useful during the interview. The importance of preplanning the interview cannot be overemphasized. The more facts the investigator has available, the greater the probability of a successful clearance or later conviction.

Information should be obtained from the owner about the details of the purchase, such as date, cost, trade-in, down payment, amount of mortgage due, payments past due, name of salesperson, and so forth. The investigator should also inquire about the general condition of the car at the time of the fire and ask about defects, mileage, presence or absence of unusual equipment, and recent repairs.[17]

PREVENTION PROGRAMS

Each year new and innovative approaches to the prevention and detection of crime and the apprehension of offenders are developed. Some of these are related to investigative techniques, whereas others are high-tech equipment developments that are designed to reduce the vehicle theft problem or assist law enforcement officers in their efforts. Other strategies are available to reduce the incidence of fraud.

AUTO THEFT

Law enforcement officers and agencies in a number of jurisdictions now rely on integrated communications and computer networks of the FBI, state, and local police to identify and locate stolen vehicles. One unique system uses a small device called a *micromaster*, which is installed at random in a vehicle's electrical system. The micromaster is a microprocessor-controlled transceiver with its own unique code.

If a vehicle is stolen, the owner reports the theft to the local police in the usual way. The owner also tells the police that the vehicle is equipped with a micromaster. The police then announce through normal channels and the National Crime Information Center that a micromaster-equipped vehicle has been stolen. A computer then activates a transmitter that sends a signal with the stolen vehicle's own code. (The present system can manage up to 8 billion discrete micromaster codes.) The signal activates the micromaster's transceiver; it starts sending a signal identifying it as a stolen vehicle. The

activation and tracking of the micromaster signal is under the control of law enforcement authorities. They have a homing device that gives them information about the location of the car. The system also allows police officers to identify micromaster signals and determine whether the stolen car has been involved in a crime.[18] Some of these tracking systems rely on signal relay towers, while others use a satellite-enhanced global positioning system (GPS) method of tracking. The law enforcement vehicles are equipped with tracking computers that bring up street maps which pinpoint location and direction of travel within very close proximity.

Many vehicles are now being manufactured with antitheft locks, starter disengagement systems (called *ignition kill switches*), and various other devices in an attempt to reduce the attractiveness of a particular model to the thief. Some of these are models that qualify for the black-box exemption to the labeling standards established under the guidelines of the Motor Vehicle Theft Law Enforcement Act of 1984.

In recent years, a number of private concerns have begun marketing antitheft devices that can be used effectively on older vehicles. It should be noted at the outset that no device can absolutely prevent motor vehicle theft, and one should look askance at any product or brand of product that is represented to be an absolute theft preventative.

Theft deterrent devices are of two types—passive or active. A *passive* system requires no driver interaction to activate the system but may require that the driver do something to deactivate the system. An *active* system requires that the operator do something every time the vehicle is driven or parked.

Audible alarm systems may be either passive or active and may be effective if anyone pays attention when an alarm is activated. Because some systems activate easily when someone passes the vehicle, a strong wind blows, or lightning strikes half a mile away, many people pay little attention, beyond a passing glance, to a vehicle with an alarm blaring. Escape from the vicinity of the noise is more important than determining if a theft is occurring. The alarms are treated more as an annoyance than as a theft deterrent.

A *boot* is an active device installed under a front tire that prohibits the vehicle from being moved until the boot is removed.

"Collars," which are usually constructed of steel or an alloy, deter penetration of the steering column bowl associated with the General Motors and Chrysler "Saginaw steering column" (see Figure 17–18). Passive collars are generally recommended over those that require driver interaction.

Many communities have instituted decal "alert" programs that provide decals for vehicles registered with the local law enforcement agency and authorize any law enforcement officer to stop the vehicle and question the driver if the vehicle is observed on the streets during certain hours (such as 2 A.M. to 6 A.M.).

A fuel shut-off device, which blocks the fuel line, may be activated by removal of the ignition key or by the throwing of a switch.

A case-hardened steering-column ignition lock that cannot be removed using a conventional slide hammer or lock puller can be effective, as can a case-hardened steel protective cap that fits over the ignition lock to prevent extraction of the ignition lock cylinder. The cap fastens to a steel collar that fits around the steering post and over the ignition lock. The ignition key fits through a slot in the cap.

Several manufacturers install a microchip or transponder in the igition key that must be electronically read when inserted into the ignition in order for the vehicle to start. Early versions of some of these systems had only a few combinations, which could easily be defeated if a thief could procure a set of masters with all the combinations. However, General Motors' PASS-KEY III and Ford's Passive Anti-Theft System (PATS), as well as the newer systems on many other domestic and foreign-made brands, use much more advanced and sophisticated electronic systems that are deterring theft.

A steel or alloy post, rod, or collar may attach to the steering wheel, which can be extended and locked in place. Such a device prevents the steering wheel from making full rotations. Such an active device can be an effective deterrent to theft if used properly, but it is ineffective if the operator of the vehicle forgets or considers it an inconvenience to install it each time the vehicle is left unattended.

VIN etching is a process that helps identify vehicles recovered by the police after a theft has occurred. As noted earlier, thieves often attempt to conceal the identity of stolen vehicles by grinding numbers. When the VIN is permanently etched on all of the vehicle's windows using acid, that identification method will often be overlooked by the thief or require the thief to remove all the window glass to prevent identification, a major task a thief may not be willing to undertake.

Figure 17–18
A Collar Affixed to a Steering Column

(Courtesy Citizens for Auto-theft Responsibility–C.A.R., Inc.)

Some programs focus on the responsibilities of vehicle owners to do their part in preventing vehicle theft. The Michigan affiliate of the American Automobile Association implements a law providing that if a car is stolen and the keys are anywhere in the passenger compartment, the owner, in addition to absorbing his or her insurance deductible, also absorbs an additional $500 plus 10 percent of the value of the vehicle. The total amount is deducted from the amount of insurance payment made on the theft loss claim. The responsibilities of owners are also reflected in a survey initiated by the NICB that consists of scoring answers to some questions and taking necessary preventive actions on the basis of the total score. This is called a *layered approach* to theft deterrence (see Figure 17–19).

Some other prevention techniques include the following:

- If a lighter receptacle is used for a radio, telephone, or radar detector, remove the item when leaving the vehicle and reinsert the lighter. Thieves look for empty receptacles.
- Always lock the vehicle and remove the keys.

- Lock valuables in the trunk. Do not leave personal identification or credit cards in the vehicle.
- Do not leave a vehicle running while unattended.
- Photocopy registration and insurance papers and carry them on your person, not in the glove compartment.
- Park in a garage or in a well-lighted, heavily traveled area.
- When parking at a curb, turn the wheels toward the curb and use the emergency brake. This makes the vehicle harder to steal.
- Do not hide spare keys in or on vehicle.
- Write the name of the owner and the VIN in crayon under the hood and in the trunk.
- Drop business cards down window channels into door interiors. This will make later identification easier.

Theft of vehicles from new- and used-car dealers is not a new phenomenon. Sometimes the dealership knows a vehicle is missing, such as when a vehicle taken on a test drive is not returned. Other

Figure 17–19
The Layered Approach

❶ LOCATION

City population	Points
Over 250,000	8
250,000 to 100,001	6
100,000 to 50,001	4
50,000 to 10,000	2
Under 10,000	0

❷ VEHICLE STYLE

Vehicle owned	Points
Sports car	5
Luxury car	4
Sport-utility	4
Sedan	3
Passenger van	1
Station wagon	0

❸ VEHICLE AGE

Age of vehicle	Points
0 to five years	1
Six to eight years	2
Nine-plus years	0

❹ BONUS POINT

Add 1 point to your score if you live near an international port or border.

Your score tells how many layers of protection your vehicle needs. For example, if your vehicle scored a 4, the chance of theft is considered low and it should have a first layer of protection. If your vehicle scored a 12, it should have first, second and third layers. The scores:

Layer 1 (0 to 4 points)

Common sense Remove keys from the ignition, lock the doors, close all windows, park in lighted areas.

Layer 2 (5 to 10 points)

Visible or audible deterrent Steering wheel locks, steering column collars, theft-deterrent decals, tire locks, window etching.

Layer 3 (11 to 14 points)

Visible immobilizer Smart keys, fuse cutoffs, kill switches, and starter, ignition or fuel disablers.

Layer 4 (15 to 16 points)

Tracking systems

Source: National Insurance Crime Bureau.

times, if an inventory is large, a vehicle may be stolen overnight and not missed for several days. Key control is an essential crime prevention practice for a dealership. Keys should be kept in a locked cabinet with only a few people having access. Keys that are out for demonstration or sales purposes must be monitored. Customers should never be allowed to test-drive a vehicle without a salesperson going along. Display lots should be well lighted, and barriers should be erected that permit access and good observation from outside but are sufficient to deter theft at night and when the dealership is closed. Officers who are familiar with the concepts of crime prevention through environmental design should be consulted.

CAR RENTALS

Car rental companies are generally knowledgeable about motor vehicle theft and techniques of prevention, but an investigator would be wise to understand some basics. In daily rental, the company is handing over the keys of a car to a person no one in the company has seen before or knows anything about. The rental agreement should be completely filled out, and the picture and information on the renter's driver's license should be carefully checked to make sure it matches the description of the person to whom the vehicle is being rented.

Rental companies generally require a credit card even for a cash rental. This not only serves as a good indication that the customer is a responsible person but also helps ensure that the contract will be paid. The employee of the rental company should make sure the credit card is current and check it against the driver's license to make sure the same name is on both documents.

Theft of rental vehicles generally occurs when a vehicle is not returned after it has been rented. At least one national rental company is in the process of installing tracking systems, as described earlier, which are traceable using radio-wave or GPS systems.

HEAVY EQUIPMENT AND FARM EQUIPMENT

Tiny transponders that act as identification devices are now available. The device can be glued anywhere on the vehicle. Some agencies are experimenting with injecting the transponder into tires of construction or farm equipment. If attempts are made to completely conceal or alter a stolen vehicle's identity, a receiver can accurately distinguish the vehicle from all others.

Owners of construction and farm equipment are also encouraged to take the following actions:

- Use security devices such as ignition locks, stabilizer arm locks, and fuel shut-off valves.
- Record all product identification numbers (PINs) and participate in equipment identification programs.
- Photograph all equipment, paying particular attention to unique features such as dents, decals, and scratches, to aid in later identification.
- Leave equipment in well-lighted and fenced areas at job sites and equipment yards. Lock farm equipment in a secure building or an enclosed area that is kept locked.
- Know the location of all construction and farm equipment at all times.
- Keep law enforcement informed about where equipment is located and how long it will be maintained in a particular location.
- Take extra precaution on weekends. Most equipment thefts occur between 6 P.M. on Friday and 6 A.M. on Monday.
- Do not leave keys in any equipment that uses keys and lock all machines that can be locked when not in use.
- Immediately report suspicious activity, such as a stranger taking photographs of equipment, to law enforcement officials.

Other methods of reducing or preventing theft of off-road equipment are available. Programs are available through private enterprise whereby heavy equipment can be registered, with each piece being assigned its own identification number. The equipment is "decaled" with its own number welded on at several locations. Should a law enforcement officer become suspicious, the dispatcher can call a toll-free number and remain on the line as the company calls the owner to verify the location of the equipment.

FRAUD

The prevention of fraud can best be accomplished by knowing some things about the insured and about the vehicle. "Know your insured" is always sound advice for an insurance agent. Getting good identification on the person, learning why the person selected a particular agent or agency, and finding out how the insured learned of the agent or agency can all be useful in helping to determine whether the act of insuring is legitimate. Knowing about the insured vehicle is equally important in the fight against fraud.

Perhaps the most profound fraud prevention effort ever initiated is the preinsurance inspection program, particularly when photographs are required. Deceptively simple in concept and application, it is amazing that fewer than half a dozen states have even considered, much less adopted, mandatory legislation. The concept requires that before a vehicle can be insured, it must be physically inspected by a representative or an agent acting on behalf of the insurer.

A simple inspection requirement can immediately eliminate or substantially reduce two of the most prolific tactics in committing insurance fraud. First, it virtually eliminates the false vehicle theft, which is normally based on insuring a "paper," or "phantom," car—in other words, a vehicle that does not exist—and subsequently reporting it stolen in order to file against and recover on an insurance policy. Second, a well-written preinsurance report can substantially reduce fraudulent claims about theft of expensive equipment on a vehicle or claims that damage actually present prior to issuance of the policy occurred when the substandard vehicle either was involved in a reported accident or was stolen.

Photographs supporting an inspection report make the program particularly effective, and color photographs are even more revealing. Photographs can show the exact condition of a vehicle at the time a policy was issued so as to dispel fraudulent damage claims filed later. It is recommended that at least two photographs be taken from diagonal corners so that one picture shows the front and one side of the vehicle and the other photo shows the rear and other side. These two photos will eliminate false damage claims, but there remains a question of proving that the photos are of the insured vehicle and not simply one of the same year, make, and model. To resolve this concern, a few of the jurisdictions having inspection programs require that a third photograph be taken of the federal motor vehicle safety certification label (often called the *EPA label*), which is usually found on the left door. This label contains, among other information, the vehicle identification number, which, as noted earlier, is the specific identifier for that vehicle as distinguished from all other vehicles; this reverifies the number contained in the written report, thus avoiding or explaining inadvertent omissions or accidental transposition of numbers.

An inexpensive instant developing camera and film can be used for the program. In 1977, New York became the first state to enact legislation mandating photographic inspection prior to the issuance of insurance policies. The program initially required that two photographs be taken from a 180-degree angle, but the law was amended in 1986 to require the third photo of the federal motor vehicle safety certification label. Massachusetts was the next state to adopt a preinsurance inspection program. Legislation followed thereafter in New Jersey and Florida, although not all of these states have equally effective legislatively mandated programs. In addition to these states, two insurance companies have their own photographic inspection programs. Neither GEICO nor State Farm will insure a noninspected vehicle.

Is the program effective? Although it is difficult to measure how much crime (insurance fraud) is deterred by a photo inspection program, it has been estimated that in the state of New York, reduction in costs and in insurance fraud claims has saved well over $100 million, and these savings have been passed on to insurance buyers through premium reductions. Although insurance premiums have not actually been reduced in New York, the overall increase in premiums in that state has amounted to less than half of the national average.[19]

ODOMETER FRAUD

One of the most costly consumer frauds of modern times is odometer fraud, also known by various other names including *odometer tampering, rollbacks,* and *clocking*. The National Highway Traffic Safety Administration estimates that over 3 million cars are clocked each year and that the cost of this fraud to American consumers surpasses $3 billion annually.

The most susceptible vehicles to odometer tampering are those that are relatively new with exceptionally high mileage. Of the total number of passenger cars sold in the United States each year, approximately half are sold to car rental or leasing companies or to others for business use. Each year, at least 4 million of these late-model high-mileage cars are replaced. Those that are taken off lease or are no longer used for business purposes find their way into the used-car market.

The reason for odometer rollbacks is to increase the value of used vehicles on the market. Obviously, a car with fewer miles should bring a higher price than one with high mileage. It has been conservatively estimated that on a small or intermediate-size car, the sale value increases $50 for each 1,000 miles the odometer is set back; in larger vehicles, the value increases to around $65 per 1,000 miles the odometer reading is reduced. Thus, a late-model car that is clocked from 70,000 miles to 30,000 miles can increase its value to the seller by $2,000 to $2,600. This amounts to a nice additional profit for those inclined to indulge in such deceitful conduct.

Besides the obvious profits to the seller of clocked vehicles, the costs to the purchaser can be even greater in the form of potential unanticipated safety problems and increased repair costs. Since cars are generally the largest purchase made by people after the cost of a home, the condition of a car and the anticipated costs for repair and maintenance figure prominently in the decision of whether to buy a particular car. But when the odometer has been clipped, mileage is not a dependable guide for estimating potential maintenance costs, since such a vehicle will be more costly to maintain and more likely to need expensive repairs. If the purchaser-owner is unable to afford the higher costs, the quality of maintenance and repairs may suffer, along with the safety and roadworthiness of the vehicle.

Because of the proliferation of this fraud, most states have created some type of investigative unit to deal with odometer tampering by accepting complaints from citizens and determining if there is any basis for enforcement action. When examining a late-model low-mileage vehicle that is suspected of being clocked, the investigator should check for extensive wear on the brake pedal, the driver's seat, and the seals around the trunk. Does the extent of wear conform with the claimed mileage? A check should be made for service stickers on the door, on the doorpost, and under the hood. If present, a date and odometer reading may be present; missing stickers may suggest tampering. The odometer wheels should be in alignment, should not rotate freely, and should not be scratched or nicked. Any of these conditions may be indicative of a rollback and warrant further inquiry. The investigator should order a vehicle history file through the state's motor vehicle titling agency and then check with each successive owner (including individuals, dealers, and auctioneers), obtain all odometer disclosure statements, piece together an odometer history, and attempt to determine if there has been a rollback. If a rollback seems likely, the investigator should determine the possessor of the vehicle when it was clocked. Standard investigative techniques should then be applied.

Title fraud is as big a part of the odometer rollback problem as is the act of clocking. Title alteration, discarding of title reassignment forms to complicate the tracing of ownership, manufacturing of false reassignments, and title laundering are criminal acts that violators often engage in to support and cover up odometer rollbacks.

To mandate better record keeping, reduce the opportunity for odometer tampering, and assist law enforcement in the investigation of cases, Congress enacted the Truth in Mileage Act in 1986. This act, along with amendments made in several subsequent years, attempts to improve the paper trail of odometer readings by requiring more tightly controlled documentation and recording of odometer readings each time ownership of a vehicle changes. The law attempts to close loopholes that permit the inception of fraudulent title schemes and to reduce the incidence of title washing between jurisdictions by requiring all states to adhere to strict record-keeping criteria, thus avoiding schemes to create confusing paper trails that intentionally avoid jurisdictional boundaries of courts and law enforcement agencies.

MARINE THEFT

SCOPE OF THE PROBLEM

Marine theft is a serious problem to the boating community. It includes the theft of boats, boat trailers, outboard motors, jet skis, and all equipment associated with boating or water activities. Marine theft is a "shadow crime." It is real but difficult to define because of the lack of accurate statistical information. The main reporting mechanism, the Uniform Crime Reports (UCR), compiled and reported annually by the Federal Bureau of Investigation, enters the theft of an outboard motor in the burglary index, the theft of a boat trailer in the vehicle file, and other related thefts in different categories. As a result, the magnitude of the marine theft problem is hidden in other crime indexes. Marine insurance theft data are similarly disjointed because there are many types of policies—homeowners', business, inland marine, yacht—that provide coverage for marine equipment. Nevertheless, it is estimated that nationwide losses resulting from marine theft exceed $250 million annually.

The majority of thefts occur from homes, businesses, or dry storage facilities. A boat and outboard motor on a boat trailer can be stolen in a matter of seconds by a thief who simply backs up to the trailer, hooks up, and drives away. Although locking mechanisms are available for boat trailers and may deter the amateur thief, such devices are easily overcome by the professional.

Theft by water is accomplished simply by towing the boat away with another boat or by starting the motor and driving away. Boats powered by outboard motors, under 25 horsepower, usually do not have keyed ignition switches. However, even on larger boats, a dozen master keys will start virtually any marine motor, whether outboard or inboard.

Approximately 87 percent of all boats stolen are under 20 feet in length. Of these, boats of 16 feet and less constitute 65 percent of the thefts. The National Crime Information Center reports over 27,000 boat thefts entered into the computer system. Law enforcement experts agree that most thefts are not investigated thoroughly (if at all) because of the difficulty investigators experience understanding marine equipment identification numbers and the lack of available ownership information.

Because of the absence of accurate statistical data, law enforcement is somewhat hampered in its efforts to address the problem. Consequently, there is a general lack of knowledge about marine theft and a resulting lack of commitment of resources to address the problems. In many agencies,

marine theft reports are assigned to the auto theft or burglary unit and are treated as low-priority items.

Why are boats stolen? The number-one reason is profit. Marine theft is a high-profit, low-risk crime. Most often a boat, motor, and trailer are stolen and sold as a package at a fair market value. To reduce the possibility of identification, some organized theft rings operate a chop shop, switching stolen motors, trailers, and boats or selling them separately.

There is also a lucrative market for the exportation of stolen outboard motors. In Central and South America, a used outboard motor will sell for more than a new motor in the United States. In addition, as in auto theft, insurance fraud may be involved in 25 percent or more of the reported marine thefts.

The increase in marine theft has often been linked by the media to drug trafficking. Experts tend to disagree. If, in fact, 87 percent of the boats stolen are under 20 feet in length, it is unlikely that these are being used for drug trafficking. Boats 30 feet and longer could very well be involved in drug trafficking, but such thefts constitute only 3 percent of the problem. Of course, larger boats are also targets for professional thieves because of their high value. On the other hand, there may be some legitimate linkage between the theft of outboard motors and the drug problem. A 300-horsepower outboard motor, which retails for over $15,000, can be sold without any ownership documents.

Most small boats are stolen not by professionals but for the personal use of the thief or, occasionally, for joyrides. This is particularly true in the theft of personal watercraft. Approximately 20 percent of all boat thefts are personal watercraft stolen by juveniles for their own use. Only occasionally are boats stolen to be used as transportation in other crimes, such as burglary of a waterfront home or business.

HULL IDENTIFICATION

Effective November 1, 1972, the Federal Boating Safety Act of 1971 required boats to have a 12-character hull identification number (HIN). Prior to this, boat manufacturers assigned whatever numbers were needed for their own production records. The HIN was subsequently codified by federal regulation. The promotion of boating safety was the original purpose for the HIN. It enabled the United States Coast Guard to identify "batches" of boats produced by a manufacturer that failed to meet certain production standards. This consumer protection function soon became secondary after titling and registering authorities began using the HIN assigned to a boat to identify ownership in much the same manner as the VIN is used on a motor vehicle.

Although manufacturers are required to affix each HIN to the outside of the boat's transom in a "permanent manner" so that any alteration or removal will be evident, in reality this is rarely enforced. Many manufacturers attach the HIN using plastic plates pop-riveted to the transom. These can be easily removed and replaced with false HINs. Some manufacturers of fiberglass boats place the HIN on the outer layer of the gelcoat using a "dyno label"-type device during the molding process. However, this can easily be scraped or gouged out by a thief with a screwdriver or knife. A professional thief will replace the removed HIN with automotive body filler that often matches the color of the gelcoat. Then, by stamping a false HIN into the body filler, it appears that the HIN was affixed by the manufacturer and the alteration often goes undetected. An additional problem occurs when the Coast Guard allows a manufacturer to alter a HIN on any boat that remains in inventory by changing the production dates or model year to reflect a newer model year. Even for an experienced marine investigator, it is difficult to recognize whether a HIN was altered to cover a theft or modified by a manufacturer to reflect a newer model year.

Figure 17–20 shows the three different HIN formats approved by the Coast Guard. The "straight-year" and "model-year" formats were used from November 1, 1972, until August 1, 1984, when the "new" format replaced them. The only differences between the three formats are the last four characters. In the straight-year format, the last four characters reflect the calendar month and year of production. In the model-year format, the ninth character is always the letter M followed by the model year and a letter indicating the month of production. The new format, optional on January 1, 1984, and mandatory as of August 1, 1984, uses the ninth and tenth characters to reflect the calendar

month and year of production and the eleventh and twelfth characters to represent the model year.

The first three characters of the HIN are the manufacturer's identification code (MIC), assigned to each manufacturer by the Coast Guard. Since 1972, over 13,000 MICs have been assigned. Many codes have been reassigned after the original company went out of business. Because of this, it is very difficult even for the most experienced marine investigator to remain familiar with all the manufacturer's codes. In addition, large conglomerates such as Mercury Marine and Outboard Motor Corporation have purchased many boat manufacturers and used manufacturer's identification codes assigned to the parent corporation for multiple boat lines.

The middle five characters of the HIN are used as production numbers or serial numbers assigned by the manufacturer. Although the letters I, O, and Q cannot be used, any other letter can be used in combination with numbers. These "production" numbers can and often are repeated on a monthly basis for an entire year. Whereas the automobile VIN has a 30-year uniqueness and a check digit to avoid unintentional or deliberate omission of numbers and intentional or unintentional transposition of numbers, the HIN does not yet have this feature.

TITLE AND REGISTRATION ISSUES

There are approximately 12 million pleasure boats in the United States. Roughly 160,000 of these are federally registered by the Coast Guard and are referred to as "documented." Ownership and financial disputes over "documented" vessels can be resolved in the federal courts. The remainder of pleasure boats are registered and/or titled by each state, except Alaska, in which registration issues are regulated by the Coast Guard.

Over 30 states require that boats be titled, but only a few states require the titling of outboard motors. Even in titling states, many boats are exempted by being less than a specified length or powered by less than a specified horsepower of motor. More than half of the titling programs are administered by wildlife or natural resource agencies. The remainder are operated by motor vehicle agencies.

**Figure 17–20
Hull Identification Number
Formats**

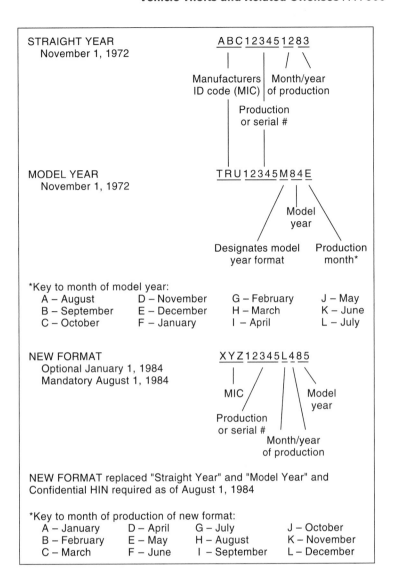

Many jurisdictions that title boats do not have computerized ownership records or do not retain the information for more than one year. The boat registration/title files in only a few states can be accessed using the National Law Enforcement Telecommunications System (NLETS). The inability of an investigator to obtain ownership information in a timely and efficient manner makes boat theft investigation very difficult.

NCIC BOAT FILE

As noted earlier, over 27,000 stolen boats are included in the NCIC system under the title "Boat File." The Boat File, one of the 13 NCIC files, records information on stolen boats, boat trailers, and boat parts. Information in the file is retrievable on an on-line basis by entering the registration or document number, the hull identification number, or the assigned NCIC number. Unless otherwise removed or located, information in the Boat File is maintained for the balance of the year of entry, plus four years. The exception to this is records that have no boat hull identification number or other number assigned by the owner that can be used for identification purposes. These remain in the file for only 90 days after entry.

The boat theft problem may be much greater than what the NCIC statistics display. There is no mandate requiring boat thefts to be entered into NCIC and, because of the difficulty of reporting, many thefts are not entered. According to marine theft experts, new edits installed in the NCIC Boat File in late 1993 contained errors, causing valid entries to be rejected and further discouraging the entry of stolen boat information by law enforcement agencies. Another major flaw in the system is that NCIC does not enter all of the Coast Guard-assigned manufacturer's identification codes and, in some cases, has assigned codes that are not those recognized by the Coast Guard.

INVESTIGATIVE RESOURCES

Marine theft investigations are often complex and time consuming. With the difficulty in obtaining ownership information, the tens of thousands of boat manufacturers, and the lack of computerized theft information, the success of an investigation is often predicated not on what the investigator knows but on whom he or she knows to contact for assistance. A major resource is the International Association of Marine Investigators. This organization has over 900 members who network with other law enforcement officers and agencies and insurance investigators throughout the United States, Canada, Europe, the Caribbean, and Central and South America. The organization holds an annual training seminar on marine theft issues.

PREVENTIVE METHODS

There are several ways a boat owner can lessen the possibility of marine theft. For example, one individual who used to make his living by stealing boats and reselling them recommended that any boat with an electric starter should have a toggle switch that shuts off the electrical system when in the off position. The switch can be located under the dash or behind a panel. Typically, when a thief attempts to start the boat and cannot, the thief assumes that it is malfunctioning and gives up the effort to steal it.

To discourage theft a boat owner may wish to remove a vital engine part when the boat is left unattended. Trailered boats are more easily stolen than boats in the water. The best way to protect boats on trailers is to keep them out of the sight of thieves.

They should be parked behind a house or behind a garage or inside a garage where they cannot be seen from the street.

Owners should never leave boats where they will tempt a potential thief. If a boat appears difficult to steal, the thief will seek an easier victim. The owner should never leave the keys or the registration on board when the vessel is not attended. Outboard motors should be bolted through the hull and secured with clamping locks. If the owner is to be away from the place where the boat is stored for an extended period of time, the engine should be disabled or one or more wheels should be removed from the trailer.

AIRCRAFT AND AVIONICS THEFT

SCOPE OF THE PROBLEM

With approximately 225,000 general-aviation aircraft in the United States, the theft of aircraft and burglary leading to the theft of avionics are certainly not as prevalent as motor vehicle theft. Nonetheless, these are significant criminal problems that law enforcement investigators may encounter.[20]

In 1997, 42 aircraft worth $5.55 million were stolen: 20 in California, 9 in Mexico, 3 in Arizona, 2 from New York, and 1 each from Florida, Texas, and Oklahoma. Of these aircraft, 31 were manufactured by Cessna, and 3 each by Beech and Piper, 3 were homebuilt, and 1 was a Gates Lear.

The theft of electronic equipment aboard aircraft (avionics) can be a highly lucrative enterprise for thieves. *Avionics* include all of the electronic radio and navigation equipment on board an aircraft—easily valued at over $10,000 in even the smallest aircraft. Many pieces of avionics look similar and can be accurately identified only by referring to the model number and/or name. Part of the difficulty encountered by many law enforcement officers is their unfamiliarity with such pieces of equipment. There were 106 burglaries in 1997 with 376 pieces of avionics stolen, valued at just over $895,000.

There are many reasons why equipment burglaries are so numerous. One of the prime reasons is the lack of security at airports and the indifference on the part of many sales outlets regarding the identification and sources of used equipment. In addition, although most avionics contain stickers and plates identifying the manufacturer, model number, part number, and even the serial number, these are often easily removed and in some cases are just stick-on labels.

Most modern avionics are designed to be easily removed from the panel of aircraft to allow frequent removal for repair and maintenance of the equipment. Stolen avionics are often resold through the used-parts market or to those who need the equipment and are willing to overlook the source of such reasonably priced equipment.

Much of the stolen avionics equipment is exported to other countries. Some is resold using counterfeited VIN labels and VIN plates. Other equipment is switched so that the stolen equipment is never discovered, as illustrated by the following example: A thief will identify the type of equipment desired in a specific aircraft at a specific airport. The thief or thieves will then locate the same type of equipment in another aircraft at another airport. At the time of theft, the electronic equipment will be removed from the first aircraft and placed in the second aircraft after the second aircraft's equipment has been removed. The equipment from the second aircraft is then sold on the market; normally, the owner of the second aircraft doesn't even know the equipment is missing because the same material, stolen from the first aircraft, has been installed in his craft. The theft of equipment from the first aircraft is reported, but it is never recovered because it is already comfortably installed in aircraft number two.

RESOURCES

An investigator who is unfamiliar with aircraft and aircraft thefts should not hesitate to obtain assistance from those who have the necessary expertise. It is advised that before undertaking a significant investigation, an investigator should visit a local airport, contact airport management, aircraft companies, flight schools, and so forth, to learn basic information about aircraft, avionics, and the theft of both. The Aviation and Crime Prevention Institute located in Hagerstown, Maryland, is an excellent source of assistance and support for law enforcement officers involved

in the investigation of aviation theft.[*] The mission of the institute is to reduce aviation-related crime through information gathering, communication with law enforcement and the public, and education programs in theft prevention and security awareness.

THEFT TECHNIQUES

The techniques thieves use to steal aircraft and burglarize aircraft for the avionics equipment are not that much different from and most frequently parallel to those used for stealing automobiles. Of course, if theft of the aircraft is the objective, it is unlikely that the thief will gain access by smashing a window. Indeed, smashing a window is generally not necessary. Perhaps the weakest security point of any aircraft is its locks. Most aircraft manufacturers use a limited number of key combinations, and a single key may open many aircraft of the same make. Occasionally, one manufacturer's key will open an aircraft of a different manufacturer.

Both door locks and ignition locks can easily be picked and generally there are no antitheft devices on aircraft. Many of the more expensive aircraft don't even use ignition keys, so the only requirement for the thief is to enter the cabin.

Many of the techniques used to cover the theft of aircraft are similar to the processes used to conceal the theft of motor vehicles. For example, the following illustrates a salvage switch involving aircraft. A thief decides on the type of aircraft desired and then purchases a total wreck of a similar aircraft from a junkyard. Rather than the certificate of title and VIN plate that come with a motor vehicle, the wrecked aircraft comes with its VIN plate and log book (a document required by the Federal Aviation Administration [FAA] that records the aircraft's history and repair record). The thief then steals (or has stolen) an aircraft of the same year, make, and model; switches the VIN plate; and installs the log book. After the thief adapts the registration

---

*The address of the Aviation Crime Prevention Institute, Inc., is Post Office Box 30, Hagerstown, Maryland 21741-0030. Robert J. Collins, president of the institute, invites and welcomes inquiries and requests for assistance from law enforcement agencies and officers. Telephone numbers for the institute are 800-969-5473 and 301-791-9791. The web site is www.acpi.org.

markings and ensures that colors match the wrecked aircraft, the salvage switch is complete.

Thefts of aircraft are most likely to occur at airports that have poor lighting and are unattended at night, especially if they have little or no security, no control tower, and perhaps are not even fenced.

AIRCRAFT IDENTIFICATION

Aircraft have the same basic identification information as do motor vehicles. The major difference is that aircraft are regulated under a federal licensing system, whereas motor vehicles are regulated under state licensing systems. All aircraft are identified by a registration number, which is similar to a license plate number; a VIN; and make and model. The U.S. registration numbering system is part of a worldwide system under which each country has a letter and/or number code. The United States code begins with the letter N. Consequently, all U.S.-registered aircraft display an N number.

Most registered aircraft receive their N number when they are manufactured. It is possible for the purchaser of a used aircraft or of an aircraft currently being built to request a special N number. Such requests are processed by the FAA.

The N number is found on each side of the aircraft or on the vertical tail in large or small letter and numeral combinations. In some cases, such as on older aircraft, the N number may be displayed on the underside of one wing and the topside of the opposite wing. Helicopters have the N number displayed under the nose or undercarriage.

Most aircraft have a small plate on the instrument panel with the plane's N number on it. An investigator can look at the plate and determine whether the plate number matches the N number displayed on the exterior of the aircraft. If the plate is missing, further investigation is warranted.

Although each aircraft has a VIN, manufacturers design their own numbering systems, and the location of a VIN plate varies depending on the make. For example, on Cessna aircraft the VIN plate is found on the door jamb. The door must be open to see the plate. The VIN plate on most single-engine and small twin-engine Beechcraft can be found on the right side above the wing flap. Large Beechcraft have the VIN plate inside the main cabin entry doorframe. On Piper aircraft the VIN plate is usually found on the lower side of the tail on the aircraft's body.

As in any attempt to identify a vehicle, vessel, or aircraft, the investigator should understand the construction process well enough to know whether and where to look for identifiers. When aircraft are built, many of the parts are subassembled elsewhere in the plant, and such subassemblies are marked with the VIN number in Magic Marker or pencil so the aircraft can later come together at the main assembly point. If the plate is missing, the investigator should look under seats, under carpeted areas, in inspection panels, and elsewhere for ID numbers relating to the VIN.

When trying to locate a VIN plate in aircraft other than those previously mentioned, the investigator should look in some of the most common locations, such as on the doorjamb on either side of the plane, on the lower tail section on either side of the plane, on the body where the main wing is attached, near the nose wheel, or on the lower body. In other words, when in doubt, the dedicated investigator will look over the entire aircraft in an attempt to find the attached plate, which will provide make, model, and VIN information.

THEFT PREVENTION TECHNIQUES

Following is a brief list of some of the theft deterrent devices available and some actions an aircraft owner can follow, some without cost, to reduce the chance of theft of the aircraft or the avionics:

- There are a number of alarm systems on the market, and some even have a pain generator, a second piercing alarm inside the cockpit that is most aggravating to the human ear.

- Ignition kills, which require entry of a security code into the control panel in the cockpit, are available. If the pilot fails to get the code right after a specific number of tries, the engine-starting circuits are disabled and, in some cases, a siren will sound.

- There should be a prearranged password known only to crew members and the airport operator. Thus a person who calls and directs that the plane be prepared for flight must know the password in order to get the plane. This technique has prevented the theft of many aircraft.

- A wheel-locking device, or "boot," prevents the plane from being towed or moving under its own power.
- More secure locks can be installed.
- Airplanes should be parked at night at airports that are well lighted, fenced, and otherwise provided with security. Window covers should be used to conceal avionics.
- Avionics equipment should be checked to ensure that it is the manufacturer-installed equipment. Each piece should then be marked with a dot, paint, engraving, or scratch, and a

detailed inventory should be made and recorded.

- Propeller chains and locks are available.
- Instrument panels can be equipped with a locking bar or locking cover.
- Flight operations personnel at airports should be given a list and identification of each crew member and others authorized to be around the plane or to authorize service over the phone.
- Airport authorities should have a central point of contact available 24 hours a day.
- Vital aircraft records should not be kept in the aircraft.

Questions

1. Describe a chop-shop operation.
2. How does a salvage switch work?
3. Distinguish false vehicle schemes, false theft schemes, and inflated theft loss schemes.
4. What is a "paper" vehicle?
5. How is a certificate of title "washed"?
6. What are some of the factors contributing to the theft of off-road equipment?
7. What are the two major types of off-road equipment?
8. What is the National Insurance Crime Bureau, and what functions does it perform for law enforcement?
9. Why is vehicle identification the most difficult and time-consuming task faced by an investigator in an auto theft case?
10. Why do vehicles have a standardized identification numbering system?
11. What was the purpose behind passage of the Motor Vehicle Theft Law Enforcement Act of 1984?
12. Describe the three basic methods for restoring vehicle identification numbers.
13. What are some observable indicators that should lead to further investigation of a possible stolen car?
14. Describe some of the principal investigative steps in determining whether a vehicle fire is accidental or arson.
15. Describe the workings and benefits of a photographic preinsurance inspection program.
16. What is odometer fraud, and why is it a significant offense?
17. Discuss the nature and seriousness of marine theft.
18. What are avionics, and why is avionics theft prevalent?

Notes

1. Federal Bureau of Investigation, *Crime in the United States, Uniform Crime Reports, 1997* (Washington, D.C.: Government Printing Office, 1998), pp. 51–54.
2. Citizens for Auto-Theft Responsibility, *CAR Newsletter,* Autumn 1992 (a quarterly publication of the not-

for-profit public awareness and victim support organization, P.O. Box 3131, Palm Beach, FL 33480).
3. FBI, *Crime in the United States,* p. 52.
4. "NICB Goes Globe Trotting to Bring Back Stolen Cars." *APB* (official publication of the International As-

sociation of Auto Theft Investigators), November 1996, p. 63.

5. Jacques DeRemer, Conference Report, "United Nations Addresses International Auto Theft in Warsaw, Poland," *APB* (official publication of the International Association of Auto Theft Investigators), July 1997, p. 9.

6. National Automobile Theft Bureau, 1990 Annual Report, p. 15.

7. National Insurance Crime Bureau, *Fire Investigation Handbook* (Palos Hills, Ill.: NICB, 1995), p. 31.

8. Compiled by Henry H. Brune, Sergeant, Motor Vehicle Theft Services, San Antonio, Texas Police Department.

9. Presentation by Wes Eller, John Deere Company, at the International Association of Auto Theft Investigators conference, Tulsa, Oklahoma, July 1998.

10. Ibid.

11. John Green, "Gone in Four Minutes," *Implement and Tractor*, June 21, 1977, Vol. 92, No. 14, p. 48.

12. National Automobile Theft Bureau, *NATB: 75th Anniversary 1912–1987* (Palos Hills, Ill.: NATB, 1987).

13. National Insurance Crime Bureau, *1998 Passenger Vehicle Identification Manual* (Palos Hills, Ill.: NICB, 1998).

14. National Automobile Theft Bureau, *Commercial Vehicle and Off-Road Equipment Identification Manual* 5th ed. (Palos Hills, Ill.: NATB, 1990).

15. "Restoration of Altered or Obliterated Numbers," training bulletin, Alabama Department of Public Safety.

16. Most of the material in these lists is taken from handout materials produced by the National Insurance Crime Bureau.

17. National Insurance Crime Bureau, *Fire Investigation Handbook*, pp. 31–67.

18. This information has been provided by the LoJack Corporation of Boston, Massachusetts.

19. Much of the material on this topic is drawn from Phillip J. Crapeau, "Photo Inspection Helps Deter Auto Theft," *National Underwriter*, September 18, 1990.

20. Most of the material in this section is drawn from Aviation Crime Prevention Institute, Inc., *Aviation Identification and Information Manual for Police Officers* (Frederick, Md.: Aviation Crime Prevention Institute and the Aviation Insurance Industry, 1987), and from *Alert Bulletin*, a quarterly publication of ACPI.

EIGHTEEN

Computer Crime

Robert W. Taylor[*]
University of North Texas

CHAPTER OUTLINE

Types of Computer Crime 512

The Hacker Profile 526

The Insider Profile 528

Investigating Computer Crime 529

Preventing Computer Crime 531

Questions 534

Notes 534

INTRODUCTION

Mainframe computers have been used for many years. During roughly the last 25 years there has been a proliferation of personal computers (PCs). Together, mainframe and personal computers have affected our lives to a degree far beyond that of any other technological development from the same period. Students can register for classes and go through drop-add in real time at terminals or by using their PCs and a modem. We can withdraw money from our bank accounts at any time by using automatic teller machines (ATMs). Stock quotes, flight schedules, travelers' advisers, reference libraries, electronic malls, classified ads, the latest news and weather reports, and miscellaneous bulletin boards can all be instantly accessed with a few clicks of the mouse on our personal computers. When sick, we can use the information on a CD-ROM, including narration and still or moving pictures, to give us information about possible causes and appropriate action to take.

Being "connected" is now less about politics and more about being on-line to the "information superhighway" a global network of computers, through service providers such as America On-Line (AOL) and CompuServe or through a number of local, national, and international Internet service providers (ISPs), which provide access to amazing arrays of information and databases.

[*] Special appreciation is given to Ms. Deanne Carp, who worked tirelessly as a research assistant on this project.

TYPES OF COMPUTER CRIME

The virtual explosion of the World Wide Web has dramatically increased communication between people, and the web has become a viable new conduit for business transaction. Consider that in 1989, fewer than 90,000 people were on-line. By 1998, the number grew to 51 million in the United States alone, with 100 million expected by 2003.[1] Business-to-business commerce via the Internet will reach $327 billion by 2002, in an industry that did not exist 10 years ago.[2] As is the case of many exciting developments, there is a dark side to the cyberspace age—computer abuse and computer crime.

Computer abuse covers a range of intentional acts that may not be covered by criminal laws. Any intentional act involving knowledge of computer use or technology is computer abuse if the perpetrator could have made some gain and the victim could have experienced loss.[3] By contrast, *computer crime* refers to any illegal act for which knowledge of computer technology is used to commit the offense.[4]

Due to the rapid increase in and increasingly serious nature of these crimes, several federal agencies have formed units that deal exclusively with computer crimes. These units include the FBI's National Computer Crime Squad and the U.S. Department of Justice's Computer Crime Unit. The U.S. Secret Service and the Department of Defense (as well as special units with the Army, Air Force, and Navy) also have experts responsible for computer crime investigations, as do many other federal, state, and local agencies. The first computer crime unit at the local level was developed in the early 1980s at the Maricopa County Sheriff's Office, Phoenix, Arizona. Since that time, most large police departments have special units that focus on computer-related crimes. A number of nongovernment organizations have also been developed that perform varied tasks, including investigating computer crimes, providing computer security training and alerts, and acting as clearinghouses for both general and specific information regarding the technicalities of computer crime. These organizations are often called upon as sources of experts who may be needed to assist law enforcement personnel conducting computer crime investigations. Two of the most prominent nongovernment organizations are the Computer Emergency Response Team (CERT) at Carnegie Mellon University and the worldwide Forum of Incident Response and Security Teams (FIRST).[5]

Today the opportunities for computer crime are greater than ever due to two basic facts: There are more computers, and they are increasingly connected (on-line) with the information superhighway, or World Wide Web. To illustrate, unwary investors are in danger today of being "taken for a ride" on the information superhighway. State securities regulators around the United States are concerned about the explosion in illicit investment schemes now flourishing on commercial bulletin board services operated by on-line service providers. In a Texas case, a retiree sent a total of $10,000 to an out-of-state man who promoted himself on a major computer bulletin board as a skilled money manager. In fact, the man was not a licensed stockbroker or investment adviser, the mutual fund in which the retiree had "invested" did not actually exist, and it appears that the money went "directly into the promoter's pocket."[6]

As Chapter 12, Crimes against Children, explains, even our children are not safe from exploitation and victimization on the web. A young teenage girl began visiting on-line with someone she believed to be a young teenage boy. She gave him her telephone number. However, the person actually turned out to be a 51-year-old man who made a series of obscene calls to her before he was stopped.[7] In another case, a 27-year-old man enticed a 14-year-old boy into meeting him after on-line conversations. The boy was blindfolded, handcuffed, shackled, and sexually abused by the man.

Other examples of computer crimes on the information superhighway include those committed by hackers, who may steal credit card numbers and use or sell them; alter, erase, and destroy records or steal confidential documents (one company believes it lost a $900 million bid to another corporation, which is believed to have hacked into the first company's computer and obtained information which gave it the advantage in winning the bid); sell and distribute child and other pornographic material; and place offers for illegal services, such as one made on a Colorado computer bulletin board that promised to help people avoid television cable bills for a fee of $15. Unfortunately, not all computer crimes are as restricted in their effects. Hackers have successfully changed government

World Wide Web sites, forcing sites to be shut down for days until the damage could be repaired. Other hackers have launched denial-of-service attacks on corporations or ISPs, shutting them down for hours or days at a time. Government studies have shown that many corporations, government agencies, and utility companies are highly vulnerable to attacks from outsiders, who in some cases may be able to seriously affect large segments of the population through a single organization's computer system. While a winter ice storm in 1998 cut electrical power to millions of customers, it is possible that computer hackers might be able to accomplish the same thing from a home computer.

Not all computer crimes take place on the information superhighway. As shown in Figure 18–1, the National Institute of Justice recognizes six ma-

jor categories of computer crime, many of which do not involve networked computers.[8] There are many other ways of categorizing computer abuse and crime. One way is in terms of vulnerabilities; hardware, software, networks, physical structures and buildings, information/data, and computer-controlled devices (such as phone switches, electric power, and airplanes being directed by air traffic controllers and their computers or automated equipment) are all vulnerable to electronic and physical attacks.

Another way to categorize computer crimes is in terms of the source of the threat: insiders or outsiders. *Inside computer crimes* are committed by persons who are employed by the targeted organization or have permission to be accessing its computer system. *Outsider computer crimes* are

Figure 18–1
Categories of Computer Fraud

Internal Computer Crimes
► Trojan horses
► Packet sniffers
► Salami techniques
► Back doors
► Logic bombs
► Viruses

Telecommunication Crimes
► Hacking
► Illegal bulletin boards
► Misuse of telephone systems

Computer Manipulation Crimes
► Embezzlement and fraud

Support of Criminal Enterprises
► Databases to support drug distributions
► Databases to keep records of client transactions
► Gambling and prostitution
► Money laundering

Hardware and Software Thefts
► Software piracy
► Thefts of computers
► Thefts of microprocessor chips
► Thefts of trade secrets

Invasion of Privacy and Related Issues
► Sexually explicit material
► Cookies

Source: Modified from C. H. Conely and J. T. McEwen. "Computer Crime," *NIJ Report*, January/February 1990, p. 3.

committed by persons from outside the organization. While these individuals may sometimes have legitimate access to part of the system for specific tasks (such as surfing an organization's web site), often they do not. Many of the same types of crimes, such as hardware theft and destruction of data, can be done by both insiders and outsiders.

INTERNAL COMPUTER CRIMES

Internal computer crimes are typically alterations to computer programs that result in the performance of unauthorized functions, such as deletion or manipulation of data in a computer program. Because these are unauthorized functions that have often been around for years, many have acquired colorful names like "Trojan Horse," "packet sniffer," "salami technique," "back door," and "logic bomb."

Trojan Horses

These malicious programs masquerade as legitimate programs. The most common Trojan horse involves replacing the normal password-verifying software with software that will capture user passwords and make them available to the criminal. The software might work in conjunction with the actual password software, so that users are allowed access to their computer accounts, or it may not. In one case, a hacker replaced the password program on a computer with a program that would give users the normal "login: password:" prompt. When a user entered his or her login ID and password, a message told the user he or she had incorrectly entered the password. The users would then enter it again and this time be given access to the system. In reality, the first entry of the information was to the Trojan horse program, and the information went directly to a database file that the hacker would come and get once a day. The second entry of information was to the legitimate password program, which had been called up by the Trojan horse after it had done its work. In another case, in New York City in 1993, Panix Public Access—an on-line service—had to shut down operations for three days when a Trojan horse program was found recording user's passwords in a secret file.[9]

Packet Sniffers

These are programs that sit in a computer on a network and monitor everything that goes over it, usually selectively keeping records of sensitive information such as passwords and credit card numbers. In most computer networks, as information passes from its origin to its destination, it must pass through many computers along the way. Normally, these computers simply pass along the information, sometimes logging that it went through the system. It is possible to install software on a computer, however, so that not only does it pass on the information but it also keeps a copy of it, undetected. Passwords, credit card numbers, and other sensitive information have been gathered this way by sniffers located on government networks, on corporate networks, and through on-line and Internet service provider networks. In one case, a major ISP in California had a sniffer sitting on its network for several weeks, taking in all password and credit card information that went across the network.

Salami Techniques

Typically, the salami technique is a money crime; it is an automated means of stealing assets from a large number of accounts. In the round-down salami technique, the program rounds down to the nearest dollar or other amount in many accounts and transfers this amount to an account controlled by the suspect.

Back Doors

In the development of large programs and operating systems, programmers often use debugging aids that provide breaks in the code called *back doors* (see Figure 18–2). Most of the time, these breaks are removed before the software is released for general use. However, their removal may be overlooked, or they may be left in to provide easy maintenance of the program in the future. Unfortunately, once hackers or other unscrupulous programmers find a back door, they have the means to commit internal computer crimes with little likelihood of detection. Further, unscrupulous programmers will often deliberately create programs with back doors or add back doors to existing software or systems, thus providing themselves with later access to the software or system. Although errors in software, known as "bugs," can sometimes provide similar opportunities for internal computer crimes, they should be differentiated from back doors as they are unintentional errors in the program. Bugs may be exploited by unscrupulous individuals, just as back doors may be.

Figure 18–2
Example of a Trap Door
Program

In this COBOL program, designed to print hospital staff activities by date, the programmer has developed a hidden line of code. Note that the highlighted line (line 9) is different in the two exhibits. Exhibit A represents the correct line of code. In Exhibit B, all of the "S" characters are changed to a "5" and all of the "5" characters are changed to an "S." In this manner, a hidden batch program is executed that bypasses system security. To the untrained eye, these types of trap doors are very difficult to detect and pose a significant problem for computer crime investigators.

```
                                   EXHIBIT A

 1.  03-A100-PACTSFT.
 2.    MOVE '03–A100–PACTSTF' TO 600–ABORT–MESSAGE
 3.    DISPLAY 'PRINT ACTIVITY FOR STAFF BY DATE'.
 4.    PERFORM 03–B100–INIT
 5.    PERFORM 03–B200–PROCESS–STAFF
 6.
 7.  03-B100-INIT.
 8.    MOVE '03–B100–INIT' TO 600–ABORT–MESSAGE
 9.    MOVE 510–STAFF TO 200–CLINIC–STAFF
10.    PERFORM 99–U180–OBTAIN–STAFF
11.
12.  03-B200-PROCESS-STAFF.
13.    MOVE '03–B200–PROCESS–STAFF' TO 600–ABORT–MESSAGE
14.    DISPLAY' '.
15.    IF DB–REC–NOT–FOUND
16.    DISPLAY'  ***** RECORD NOT FOUND   *****'
17.      ELSE
18.          DISPLAY ' STAFF NO.: ', 200–CLINIC–STAFF
19.          PERFORM 99–U190–CONVERT–DATES
20.          PERFORM 99–U200–OBTAIN–STAFF–DATE
21.          PERFORM 03–C100–PROCESS–STAFF–DATE
22.          UNTIL DB–END–OF–SET
          OR    222–DATE>620–END–4DATE.
```

```
                                   EXHIBIT B

 1.  03-A100-PACTSFT.
 2.    MOVE '03–A100–PACTSTF' TO 600–ABORT–MESSAGE
 3.    DISPLAY 'PRINT ACTIVITY FOR STAFF BY DATE'.
 4.    PERFORM 03–B100–INIT
 5.    PERFORM 03–B200–PROCESS–STAFF
 6.
 7.  03-B100-INIT.
 8.    MOVE '03–B100–INIT' TO 600–ABORT–MESSAGE
 9.    MOVE S10–5TAFF TO 200–CLINIC–5TAFF
10.    PERFORM 99–U180–OBTAIN–STAFF
11.
12.  03-B200-PROCESS-STAFF.
13.    MOVE '03–B200–PROCESS–STAFF' TO 600–ABORT–MESSAGE
14.    DISPLAY' '.
15.    IF DB–REC–NOT–FOUND
16.    DISPLAY'  ***** RECORD NOT FOUND   *****'
17.      ELSE
18.          DISPLAY ' STAFF NO.: ', 200–CLINIC–STAFF
19.          PERFORM 99–U190–CONVERT–DATES
20.          PERFORM 99–U200–OBTAIN–STAFF–DATE
21.          PERFORM 03–C100–PROCESS–STAFF–DATE
22.          UNTIL DB–END–OF–SET
          OR    222–DATE>620–END–4DATE.
```

Logic Bombs

Logic bombs are illegal program instructions that operate at a specific time or periodically. A logic bomb may be executed based on a specific date, time, or other instructions. For example, if a specific Social Security number is entered, all records pertaining to that person are erased.

Viruses

A *computer virus* is a rogue program that is secretly inserted into a normal software program or into the computer's operating system. The impact of such programs, which are typically short in length, runs from annoying messages to more serious problems such as interfering with the computer's normal operating procedures, printing errors, the deletion of data, and extended run times. In 1994, according to the National Computer Security Association, virus infections caused a loss of $2.7 billion in the United States due to such factors as the need to reconstruct files and lost productivity.[10] In 1997, the Computer Security Institute studied over 500 U.S. corporations and found that computer viruses continued to be a major problem.[11] Financial losses from computer crime for half of the companies surveyed (249) totaled over $100 million for one year, with over $12.5 million a direct result of computer viruses.[12] This is important data as companies are very reluctant to give accurate accounts of losses due to the fear of potential reputational damage and loss of investment capital.

A virus has two distinct objectives: propagation and destruction. Virus programs are usually created by a malicious computer programmer intent on causing electronic confusion. These programs are often designed to be "invisible" or "opaque," meaning they are extremely difficult, if not impossible, for the average user to detect. Many times these programs are implanted into useful and seemingly harmless programs. However, a malicious programmer can add a Trojan horse program with a virus to such programs. A user's computer becomes infected with the virus when the user downloads the useful—but maliciously altered—program from a bulletin board or network onto his or her own computer or uses infected floppy diskettes (see Figure 18–3). When first introduced into a computer, during the propagation stage, the computer performs normally while the virus reproduces or copies itself onto other programs or onto storage devices, such as hard drives. During the destructive stage, the virus program is awakened by a "trigger," such as a certain date or the touching of a specific key. The virus often shows itself by producing a message or some other form of symbology such as "Gotcha" or a bouncing Ping-Pong ball that grows as it travels across the screen.

In 1986, the U.S. Computer Fraud and Abuse Act was adopted. Two years later, a Cornell University graduate student was convicted of violating this law, sentenced to three years' probation, and fined $10,000 as a result of a virus that attacked more than 8,000 computers on a network. This case is important because it was the first major prosecution under the then-new federal law, because of the extent of the damage caused by the virus, and because it clearly demonstrated the vulnerability of networks to virus infections. Some viruses produce messages without destroying data, as exemplified by the 1988 "Universal Message of Peace" virus that infected CompuServe. This virus turned out to be particularly pernicious: the Aldus Corporation of Seattle, Washington, announced that the "World Peace" virus had found its way into its Freehand Graphics program. This event became an important milestone in the chronology of virus production, signifying the first known infection of a commercial program.

Viruses can also be used as a tool to extort money from a corporation. In one case, a large corporation was the target. One of its employees, who had been the system administrator for over a year and therefore had access to all of the corporation's computers, created a computer virus that would be triggered on a specific date unless it was deactivated. Over a period of several months, the individual placed the virus on all of the company's computers, including all backup tapes. Ten days before the virus was set to execute, he resigned and informed the company of the virus. He demanded $1.5 million in direct payment and immunity for all potential criminal charges against him. If his demands were not met, the virus program would activate and subsequently destroy all critical data relating to accounts payable and receivable. He informed the company of the location of one virus copy and showed the firm that it could not remove all of the copies in time. The company paid the money, and did not press charges; the virus was deactivated, and then slowly removed from the system.

**Figure 18–3
How Viruses Are
Spread**

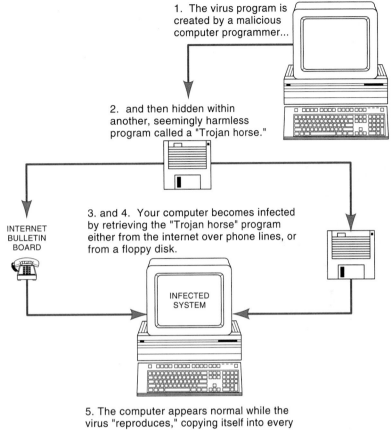

1. The virus program is created by a malicious computer programmer...

2. and then hidden within another, seemingly harmless program called a "Trojan horse."

INTERNET
BULLETIN
BOARD

3. and 4. Your computer becomes infected by retrieving the "Trojan horse" program either from the internet over phone lines, or from a floppy disk.

INFECTED
SYSTEM

5. The computer appears normal while the virus "reproduces," copying itself into every program or disk used on that computer.

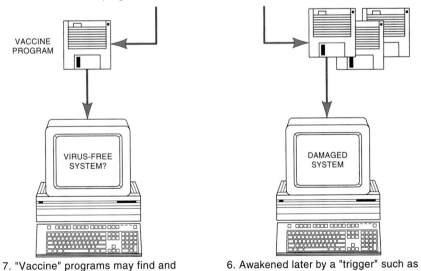

VACCINE
PROGRAM

VIRUS-FREE
SYSTEM?

DAMAGED
SYSTEM

7. "Vaccine" programs may find and remove the virus, preventing further damage, but they are not foolproof.

6. Awakened later by a "trigger" such as a certain date, the virus shows itself by producing a harmless message ("Gotcha!") or by destroying data and software.

Source: *Houston Chronicle,* August 8, 1988, p. 88. Modified, 1998.

There are a number of commercially available software programs to protect network and individual computers from viruses, including Symantec's Norton AntiVirus and McAfee's VirusScan. Some antivirus programs are available as free downloads from the Internet, while others must be purchased. These programs can detect known viruses as well as general indications of the presence of entirely new viruses.

As computer viruses become more complex, and virus makers are successful at staying one step ahead of antivirus scanning software, the ability to safeguard systems from viruses becomes even more complex. As Figure 18–4 details, a few simple procedures can help safeguard systems from the more common viruses: regular scanning of a system's hard disk drive and memory, scanning all removable disks that have been used in another system before using them in one's own system, scanning all files that are downloaded from the Internet before executing them, and scanning all word-processing files before they are opened for the first time.

TELECOMMUNICATION CRIMES

As shown in Figure 18–1, the major types of crime in this category are hacking, illegal bulletin boards, and misuse of telephone systems. The loss due to the combination of cellular fraud, toll fraud, cable TV fraud, PBX and voice-mail fraud, and fraudulent access to computers and data systems is estimated to be more than $9 billion per year and is projected to increase approximately 15 percent per year.[13]

Hacking

Hacking is the unauthorized entry into a computer system. For perhaps 99 percent of those who do it, the "hack," or getting in, is the thrill. The remaining 1 percent do things that range from mild pranks to the destruction or theft of data. To be able to hack, you have to get a password. People are often careless with their passwords, writing them down and leaving them in obvious places in their offices. Passwords can also be generated by using a special software program called a "hacker's dictionary." A common hacker's tool, the dictionary generates millions of combinations of letters and numbers until it finds a combination that matches a password—and the hacker is in. The prime targets for hackers are secure sites found on independent bulletin board systems and the Internet. Because of its massive size and its connection to international systems, the Internet offers seemingly endless possibilities for the hacker.

Packet sniffers and Trojan horse programs can also be used to attack telecommunication systems. These "tools" are much more difficult to detect and hence pose a greater security risk to targets such as banks, brokerage houses, defense contractors, and other institutions using bulletin board systems and/or the Internet. Reported hackings have skyrocketed in recent years. Such reports now appear routinely in newspapers throughout the world, yet they represent only the tip of the iceburg—as few as 3 percent of all hackings are ever discovered.[14] Even our most secure systems appear to be vulnerable to such attacks. In August 1996, the U.S. Department of Justice fell victim to hackers as its official web site was altered to read "United States Department of Injustice" accompanied by a red, black, and white flag bearing a swastika. The site also included criticism of current communication laws and a variety of obscene pictures.[15] Upon discovery, the site was immediately closed and repaired, costing little more than the time necessary to redesign the web page. However, in other cases, the losses may be much more extensive, "shutting down" entire global communication and computer systems:

> Brazen hackers repeatedly broke into the Stanford Linear Accelerator Center's computer system last week, prompting alarmed officials to take the unusual step of shutting down computer access to the outside world for a week.
>
> In what is believed to be the facility's worst computer security breach ever, a group of sophisticated hackers "sniffed"—or intercepted—a password to SLAC over the Internet and used it to gain access to more than 30 of the federal research facility's most important Unix servers, officials confirmed Tuesday.
>
> The shutdown of Internet services—which lasted until Tuesday—brought chaos for hundreds of international researchers, cutting them off from collaborators around the world.
>
> Scientists at SLAC comb through huge files on a daily basis, said spokeswoman P. A. Moore, who called the lost time on experiments an "incalculable" setback that would put people

Figure 18–4
Preventive Medicine

What do you do if you think you have computer crud? Stay calm and get expert advice before acting. But is that geek-in-law an expert? What about the nerds who sold you the box in the first place? Unfortunately, they probalby are not virus authorities.

In the absence of a local expert, a good place to stop for detailed information on computer viruses is the *alt.comp.cirus* Usenet newsgroup. There you will find advice from the world's top antivirus jockeys, along with plenty of others hoping to learn what they can—for good or evil.

Don't just wander in and start posting, though; lurk and learn. And be sure to read the frequently asked questions (FAQ) files (available at *www.webworlds. net/dharley/*) before announcing yourself or asking for help.

In an ideal world, if you use an on-access antivirus scanner (which checks files before loading or executing them) and keep it updated, you won't need the following list of ways to avoid data disaster. This, however, is the real world.

• Check all software and computers for viruses when you first bring them into your work environment.

• Make regular backups so you can recover as much data as possible.

• Keep floppies write-protected except when being written to.

• Change the boot sequence on your PC to skip the floppy drive.

• Reading e-mail messages is safe, but take special care with any item attached to an e-mail message or located in your download directories—and don't set your software to load or run e-mail attachments automatically.

• Don't install Microsoft Word as your default e-mail reader.

• When opening unfamiliar Microsoft Office documents (Word, Excel, etc.), use file viewers that don't support macros.

• If you don't know where a file came from or what it does, don't click it until you scan it with an antivirus program.

For the World Wide Web, one good appraoch is to set up your Web browser with middle- or high-level security options, selectively allowing scripts and controls to function on trusted websites. With up-to-date antivirus software scanning constantly in the background, Internet activity should be safe—in terms of computer viruses, anyway.

If you want to try out an antivirus software program—available online free for limited-term evaluation—these are among the best:

• Dr. Solomon's FindVirus (*www.drsolomon.com/download/findvirus.html*)

• Data Fellows F-Secure Anti-Virus (*www.datafellows.com/gallery/f-prot/download2.htm*)

• KAMI Ltd. AntiViral Toolkit Pro, distributed in North America by Central Command (*www.command-hq.com/html/body_downloads.html*)

• Data Fellows F-MACRO, free scanner and disinfector for Microsoft Word/Excel document macro viruses (*www.Europe.Datafellows.com/gallery/anti-virus/f-macro.htm*)

• Network Associates VirusScan (*www.nai.com/download/eval/eval.asp*)

• Disinfectant by John Norstad, Macintosh freeware (*www.host.ots.utexas.edu/mac/pub-mac-virus.html*)

For competent independent reviews of antivirus software, Bruce P. Burrell, head of the University of Michigan Antivirus Team, recommends the following websites:

• Virus Bulletin (*www.virusbtn.com/*)

• Secure Computing (*www.westcoast.com/*)

• Virus Research Unit, University of Tampere (*www.uta.fi/laitokeset/virus/*)

• Virus Test Center, University of Hamburg Computer Science Department (*agn-www.informatik.uni-hamburg.de/vtc/naveng.htm*)

• Dr. Solomon's Virus Alert Internet mailing list can inform you by e-mail when new viruses appear. For subscription information, visit *www.drsolomon.com/vircen/vamail.html*.

If you prefer a good book, look into *Robert Slade's Guide to Computer Viruses* (Springer-Verlag, $34.95). The book is a good resource and includes a computer disk of related material, including software.

To find out more about hoaxes, check the Web for the latest information. Along with the Virus Busters website (*www.umich.edu/~wwwitd/virus-busters/*) and Rob Rosenberger's Computer Virus Myths Homepage (*kumite.com/myths*), Burrell recommends the following sites:

• Data Fellows Hoax Warnings Page (*www.DataFellows.com/news/hoax.htm*)

• Dr. Solomon's Virus Central (*www.drsolomon.com/vircen/*)

• Network Associates Services—Support, Virus Info Library (*www.nai.com/services/support/hoax/hoax.asp*)

Source: J. Blake Lambert, "Attack of the Killer E-Mail," *Sky Magazine*, April 1998, p. 100.

behind in their work by at least several weeks. But she said it appears no permanent damage was done to data or programs at the facility, which does unclassified research.

SLAC researchers explore the structure of matter at the atomic scale by running experiments on the facility's giant colliders, including a two-mile-long linear accelerator. The laboratory—one of half a dozen high-energy particle generators in the United States—is operated by Stanford University under a contract from the U.S. Department of Energy. It has a staff of 1,300 and an additional 1,600 international researchers working there at any given time.

At Stanford's main campus, hackers have broken into the computer system before using "sniffers"—or networked computers with special software—and gone undetected for months. Such hackers, often teenagers who have easy access to sniffer kits, increasingly are causing problems for universities, research centers and companies, said Stanford computer security officer Stephen Hansen. At Stanford alone, there is about one incident a month involving sniffers, but security officials have never shut down the entire university's access to the Internet to address the problem.

Computer security officer Bob Cowles told employees in a letter that the extreme measure was taken at SLAC to protect the lab's computing infrastructure.

If hackers weren't stopped, the compromised SLAC servers could potentially have been used as a staging ground for attacks on other government facilities and research centers—one reason SLAC closed itself off from the outside world, one Stanford computer security official said.

The hackers gained unauthorized access to the highest-privilege "root" accounts on the Unix systems, giving them a kind of super-user access that allowed them to enter every account on each system without a password, modify the system and create hidden "back doors" that would allow them to conceal their presence and re-enter the system undetected.

And, unlike most hackers, who disappear when detected, these bold intruders were persistent and continued to create new breaches even as computer security personnel were plugging the old ones.

"My impression is the hackers were trying to put more holes in as quickly as they [security personnel] were trying to take them out," Hansen said.

SLAC officials are still assessing possible damage, but so far, they said, they believe no computer files or software were damaged. Stanford officials said more than one person was involved.

SLAC has long been vulnerable to a clever hacker, Moore said. It has operated under an "aura of trust" among scientists who use its computers, she said.

The break-in, she said, has prompted a soul-searching debate within the scientific community about how much it should tighten security—and limit freedom.

For example, until now a SLAC researcher working at a lab in France could log onto SLAC systems remotely.

Since France doesn't allow encryption, the password and user name typed in by the researcher were transparent to anyone and easily could be captured by a "sniffer" on its way to SLAC. In fact, this break-in could have occurred under a very similar scenario.

Now, SLAC scientists are debating whether to require researchers to take the cumbersome and hugely expensive step of paying for long-distance phone calls from abroad to transmit large volumes of data.

"We now have to access the trade-offs of an open community vs. a more Internet-secure community," Moore said. "It's a debate that's taking place heatedly among different scientists."[16]

A 1994 case involving the U.S. National Weather Service's network of more than 120 computers demonstrates how hackers operate.[17] The computer manager for the weather system located in Camp Springs, Maryland, saw signs that hackers were at work. These signs included the attempted use of passwords for former employees, passwords being changed without authorization, and mysterious slowdowns. The intrusions were tracked to a Massachusetts Institute of Technology (MIT) computer on the Internet. Aware of the problem, the computer manager began tracking the progress of the intruders and trying to find out who they were. Fortunately, the hackers stumbled and left their dictionary in one of the National Weather Service's computers. From this dictionary, it was learned that while only 30 files belonging to the National Weather Service had been entered, the hackers had been into numerous other networks on the Internet and were using passwords stolen from South America and Europe. After continued investigation, police in Denmark arrested the seven hackers, who used such cyberspace nicknames as "Dixie" and "Zepher." (Hackers also use less benign names such as "The Black Baron," "Major Theft," "The Plague," and "Killerette.") The stake in catching these hackers was substantial, as they were creeping closer to controlling the system used to make national weather forecasts. Without such forecasts there are no airline flights, and millions of dollars or more would have been lost.

Illegal Bulletin Boards

Computer bulletin boards, which store information on them for retrieval by someone dialing into the system, represent another vehicle for advancing illegal schemes. There are approximately 16,000 bulletin boards in this country, roughly 10 percent of which are involved in illegal activities.[18] Examples of these illegal activities include the unlicensed distribution and/or sale of copyrighted software, the distribution of stolen telephone calling numbers and credit card numbers, the distribution of pornographic material, and the exchange of sexually explicit messages.

An international ring of hackers operating out of Majorca, Spain, stole 140,000 telephone credit card numbers and sold them to bulletin boards in Europe and the United States.[19] Those acquiring the numbers made $140 million worth of long-distance calls. This loss was shared by MCI, AT&T, GTE, and Bell Atlantic, among others. *Playboy* magazine sued half a dozen bulletin boards in two years in the early 1990s for unauthorized use of its pictures.

Although clearly a reputable business, CompuServe was sued by 140 musical publishers for allegedly allowing subscribers to download popular songs, which takes only a few moments for a single. As digital music becomes increasingly popular and as digital transmission technology improves, the vulnerability of music publishers may increase because people will be able to download entire musical albums in seconds.

A variation on using illegal bulletin boards, hackers "park" illegal materials within computer systems used for legitimate purposes. A vast amount of hackers' "loot" was found in Florida State University's computer system, including proprietary software, test versions of new software that had not yet been released to the public, and a variety of hacker programs. Officials of the Lawrence Livermore National Laboratory in California pulled one of its public-access computers off-line when they discovered that a hacker had placed 1,000 pictures of naked women in the system and the lab was unwittingly distributing them.[20] The administrators of a server used for anonymous Internet access for sexual abuse survivors had to shut down their system for two days when a hacker started distributing pirated software through their machine. The subsequent investigation led to the hackers' being expelled from the university they had been attending, whose systems they had been using to reach the survivors' server.

Misuse of Telephone Systems

Telephone "phreakers" are people who trick telephone systems into believing that long-distance and air time are being legitimately purchased. In 1994, 1,000 hackers and phreakers gathered in the Hackers on Planet Earth Conference in New York City to attend seminars and exchange tips on their "hobby."[21] The interest of phreakers also extends to collateral areas, such as trying to break the code on magnetic subway cards for free rides and to decode the magnetic strips that are found on the back of some states' driver's licenses.[22]

In one phreaker case, a company employee figured out how to avoid the internal tracking system for long-distance charges and then sold time cheaply to friends to make telephone calls, which resulted in a $108,000 loss.[23] Cellular telephones are also subject to attack by phreakers. This is done by using one of two common counterfeit/cloning fraud methods: cloning and tumbling.[24] Cellular telephones have two numbers: a mobile identification number (MIN) and an electronic serial number (ESN). Every time a call is made, the microchip in a cellular phone transmits both numbers to the local switching office for verification and billing. *Cloning* involves using a personal computer to change the microchip in one cellular phone so that it matches a legitimate MIN and ESN from numbers "hacked" from a phone company, bought from a telephone company insider, acquired from a cellular phone whose theft will not be quickly discovered, or "plucked" from the airways by a portable device—about the size of a notebook—that can be plugged into a car's lighter receptacle. The user with the cloned numbers can simply use them until service is cut off and then change the MIN and ESN and start all over again. The use of cellular phones with cloned numbers is popular with criminals, particularly those dealing in drugs, who may lease them for up to $750 per day. In a related scam, a person leases a cloned cellular phone for a day and then sells international call time cheaply to immigrants or illegal aliens. *Tumbling* requires the use of a personal computer to alter a cellular phone's microchip so that its MIN and ESN numbers change after each call, making detection more difficult. One of the newest trends in cellular phone fraud is to use a combination *tumbler-clone*, which affords the fraudulent user the untraceability of a tumbled phone with the free service of a cloned phone. There are two other types of cellular telephone fraud: *subscription fraud*, in which free service is obtained through theft or forgery of subscriber information or through employee collusion, and *network fraud*, in which weaknesses in the cellular network's technology are exploited to defaud the cellular service provider.

COMPUTER MANIPULATION CRIMES

These types of crime involve changing data or creating electronic records in a system for the specific purpose of advancing another crime, typically fraud or embezzlement. The simplest, safest, and most common form of computer crime—data diddling—falls within this category. In its most basic form, payroll records are changed so that a person is paid for more hours than he or she worked or paid at a higher rate. However, there is a great deal of variety in computer manipulation crimes.

For example, the price of a stock can be manipulated on the information superhighway. Stock shares in one little-known Canadian company, Wye Resources, Inc., were traded outside of an established exchange. The value of the stock more than tripled after the company was hyped on messages posted on commercial bulletin board services and on the Internet.[25] The company reportedly owned a Zaire diamond mine where a major strike had been made. After the favorable on-line publicity had "pumped" up the stock's price, it was then "dumped," or sold for profit, by those in the know, and the stock collapsed.

According to the National Consumers League, the number of reported Internet frauds has tripled, from an average of 32 per month in 1996 to nearly 100 per month in 1997.[26] The scams threaten the development of commerce on the Internet, as consumers need to feel confident that purchases are safe and secure. While many state and federal laws governing deceptive sales practices apply to on-line promotions, the Federal Trade Commission's Telemarketing Sales Rule does not. Efforts are under way to expand the rule to the Internet, thereby allowing regulators to crack down on promoters who offer phony services.[27] Frauds on the Internet are usually based on a traditional methodology of offering goods and services that are never provided or are of very poor quality for the price paid. Figure 18–5 outlines a number of common Internet scams.

The advance of computerization has also opened new mechanisms for fraud. For instance, the Secret Service and FBI warned Congress in 1997 that a thriving new "point and click" counterfeiting scheme had been discoverd using high-quality scanners to capture an original check, a personal computer to alter the data, and a quality laser printer to develop the counterfeit instrument.[28] Total cost for equipment used in such cases has averaged less than $5,000, providing criminals with the ability to pass phony checks which look "exactly" like the originals. The Federal Reserve placed the cost of this type of check fraud to banks at $615 million in 1995, more than 10 times the $59 million attributed to bank robbery.[29] More alarming than the total amount of loss is the rapid growth and expansion of this type of crime. According to the FBI, counterfeit check schemes are the acts not just of lone, white-collar criminals but also of well-organized gangs and groups. A significant number of the cases discovered in 1997 were committed by organized ethnic enterprises, including Nigerians, Vietnamese, Russians, Armenians, and Mexicans. Some of these gangs were also heavily involved in the trafficking of guns and narcotics, extortion, and large-scale fencing of stolen property.[30]

Figure 18–5
Common Internet Scams

Common Internet Scams

According to the Internet Fraud Watch, these were the top 10 rip-offs on the Internet in 1997:

▶ Web auctions: Items bid for but never delivered by the sellers, value of items inflated, shills suspected of driving up bids, prices increased after highest bids accepted

▶ Internet services: Charges for services that were supposedly free, payment for on-line and Internet services that were never provided or falsely represented.

▶ General merchandise: From toys to clothes, goods never delivered or not as advertised.

▶ Computer equipment and software: Sales of computer products that were never delivered or were misrepresented.

▶ Pyramids and multilevel marketing: Schemes in which profits were made only from recruiting others, not from sales of goods or services to the end users.

▶ Business opportunities and franchises; empty promises of big profits with little or no work by investing in prepackaged businesses or franchise operations.

▶ Work-at-home plans: Materials and equipment sold with false promises of payment for piecework performed at home.

▶ Easy credit cards: False promises of credit cards to people with bad credit histories upon payment of up-front fees.

▶ Prizes and sweepstakes: Requests for up-front fees to claim winnings that were never awarded.

▶ Book sales: Genealogies, self-help improvement books and other publications that were never delivered or were misrepresented.

Source: *Dallas Morning News*, February, 16, 1998, p. 2D.

Even the federal government is not exempt from computer manipulation crimes. Fraudulent Internal Revenue Service tax filings cost the federal government $5 billion a year. A multimillion-dollar portion of this was due to bogus electronic tax filings. Thieves would obtain or prepare false supporting documentation to justify a refund, such as W-2s. Then they would go to a tax preparer who completed a return based on this information and filed it electronically. Within 48 hours, the IRS would confirm that the return had been accepted and that the person was eligible for a refund anticipation loan (RAL). This confirmation came in the form of a direct deposit indicator (DDI). In effect, the IRS served as credit reference, guaranteeing that the money would actually be forthcoming. With this information, the "filer" would obtain a loan from a bank, finance company, or the tax preparer and vanish. In 1994, the IRS announced new procedures for handling electronic filings to reduce such fraud.[31]

SUPPORT OF CRIMINAL ENTERPRISES

Computers appeal to criminal enterprises or businesses for many of the same reasons they appeal to others: they are quick, very reliable, accurate, and perform many business-type tasks far faster than if done manually. Thus they are used to support many different types of criminal enterprises, including loan-sharking and drug rings. A number of prostitution rings have been found using computers to keep track of customers and payroll.

Chapter 12, Crimes against Children, details the use of the Internet in luring unsuspecting children to pedophiles and in distributing child pornography. In the latter area, the Internet has been the key communication medium for the sale and exchange of child pornography on both an international and a domestic basis. In September 1998, the largest single child pronography sting operation in history occurred resulting in the arrest of over 200 people in 21 countries.[32] Code named "Operation Cathedral," British police coordinated raids in Europe, Australia, and the United States, confiscating more than 100,000 indecent images of children. Most of the images were being traded between child pornographers over the Internet. While most of those arrested were men, some were women who also belonged to exclusive child pornography clubs throughout the world. One U.S.-based club, called "Wonderland," had images for sale depicting children as young as 2 years of age. The sheer size of the pornography network shocked the police as well as the general public. The United Nations called for a worldwide offensive to curb the exchange of pedophilia on the Internet, a very difficult task considering the vast number of jurisdictions and judicial systems present in the international community.[33]

HARDWARE AND SOFTWARE THEFTS

The theft of desktop and laptop computers, monitors, printers, scanners, modems, and other equipment continues to be a major problem. In 1997, more than $1 billion worth of stolen laptop claims were filed by companies insured by just one insurance company in Ohio, a rise of 28 percent from 1996.[34] The full extent of computer theft is unknown because many thefts go unreported and because many police departments consider theft of computer hardware as just another stolen-property crime. According to Asset Software International, theft of computer components "totaled more than $5 billion in 1995 and its yearly growth rate is expected to exceed 30 percent by the year 2000."[35]

Apples, IBMs, "clones," and computer peripherals are available in many locations, are easily carried away, and can quickly be sold or "scavanged" for parts. Valuable internal components can be used to build a system or to enhance an existing system. Most stolen computer components are removed from the country within hours or days of the theft.[36] Increasingly, laptop computers are being stolen for the information contained on the hard drive, such as documents and passwords, and not for the hardware itself. This is particularly true as the cost of new laptops drops significantly. Some computer owners do not even know what they own and therefore cannot provide the police with an accurate description, let alone serial numbers. This is a problem compounded by the inability of some police offiers to accurately differentiate among computer equipment and peripherals. The following story details such a case: A major telecommunications company had two server memory chips stolen from a card-access-only storage room, each worth about $1,200. When local police detectives searched the home of one of the suspects, they had to ask the suspect what the chips looked like, how big they were, and what type of machine they would fit. Fortunately, the suspect was very cooperative and pointed out the stolen chips being used in a personal system.

The Business Software Alliance (BSA) is the principal software industry, antipiracy resource. The BSA estimates that in 1994, losses to the industry due to worldwide software piracy exceeded $15.2 billion for applications software products.[37] Refer to Figure 18–6, which provides a three-year, escalating graph of the problem. It is important to note that this figure does not account for losses due to operating system piracy. In Canada alone, it is estimated that 58 percent of the business software programs in use were illegal, pirated copies, resulting in an estimated loss to the Canadian software industry of over $345 million.[38] Even if software companies "tweaked" the figures somewhat to

Figure 18–6
The Cost of Software
Piracy in 1992-1994
(billions of dollars)

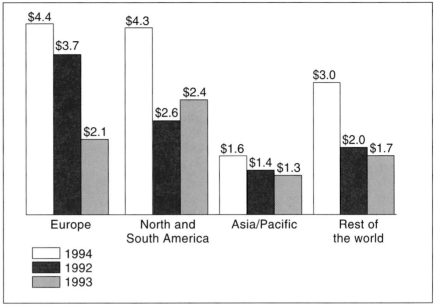

Source: Software Publishers Association, Washington. Modified 1998.

further heighten the attention drawn to the problem, this loss of revenue hurts not just the software industry but the national economy as well.

Large-scale software piracy began in Asia. The Software Business Association reports that just one person selling unauthorized copies of some 40 different popular programs in Singapore may have made several million dollars even though he charged as little as $15 for copies of programs that retailed for as much as $600.[39] Violations of American copyright laws in China—particularly piracy of software, videotaped entertainment, and compact discs—led the United States in early 1995 to announce that it would place a 100 percent tariff on all products entering this country from China unless the Chinese government took action to eliminate such violations.

Extensive software piracy now exists in Europe, where new organizations have also begun to sell high-quality imitations of Microsoft's DOS and Windows programs under the Microsoft label but without any license to do so.[40] In other instances, copyrighted programs have been placed on computer bulletin boards, and users have been allowed to download these to their own PCs for a modest fee. The operator of the "Davey Jones Locker" bulletin board was arrested on charges that he had illegally distributed a variety of copyrighted software

programs to paying subscribers in 36 states and 11 foreign countries.[41]

In 1994, "Jenny's" software pirates in the Pacific Northwest electronically raided the LucasArts Entertainment Company of San Rafael, California.[42] The prize was TIE Fighter, based on the three *Star Wars* movies. Intended for sale at about $60, the software had not yet been released. For $300, a LucasArts employee attached a cellular modem to the back of his computer—so there would be no company record of the call—and sent TIE Fighter to "Jenny's" computer. The program was then sent by Internet to Moscow, where "Skipjack," a person with excellent programming skills, cracked TIE Fighter's copyright protection code. It was sent back to Seattle, where it landed on a bulletin board called "Wave of Warez" and was made available to people throughout the world.

INVASION OF PRIVACY AND RELATED ISSUES

Sexually Explicit Material

Nothing seems to spur more controversy than debate concerning regulation of the Internet. While several attempts have been made to limit access to unwanted material available on the web, no set standards have yet been approved as law.

One side of the debate typically focuses on the vast amount of pornographic and obscene material easily accessible via the Internet. This includes sites that not only depict partially clothed and nude individuals but also venture into the world of sexual perversion, including sadomasochism, bestiality, and on-line voyeurism. Proponents for regulation contend that the web should be treated like any other medium (i.e., radio, television, print material) and thus be required, through internet service providers, to technically "ban" access to such material. This is a particularly strong argument when placed in the context of guarding minors from obtaining, receiving, and/or sending such material. Nowhere was this debate more intense than in the 1997 Supreme Court case involving the proposed Communications Decency Act of 1996.[43] The Court ruled that the act was much too broad and nonspecific. Further, the Court found that the requirement to limit such access was too burdensome and would essentially limit the free-speech clause of the First Amendment of the Constitution.[44] The Court added that parents and schools could use commercially available software that blocks sex-oriented sites to safeguard children from such material. Finally, it argued that significant federal statutes already existed that allowed authorities to act against obscenity—that is, hard-core pornography. Transmission of such material, especially that involving the depiction of children in a sexual venue, is *not* constitutionally protected and is a felony in the United States.[45]

The decision has had far-reaching effects. Adult sites continue to proliferate on the web. In fact, an adult web site (amateurs.com) is the second-most-visited site on the entire Internet, just behind microsoft.com. And adult sites continue to be top money-making ventures on the web. There appears to be no end to the pornographic explosion as technology now allows interactive, live sex shows via the Internet. While the Communications Decency Act had a short, but eventful, life, its impact may well limit the government's ability to impose other controls on Internet content, such as restrictions on commodity trading, stock advice sites, and electronic junk mail.

Cookies

Debate over the Communications Decency Act sparked interest in maintaining personal privacy while on the web. New discussions concerning the potential for clandestine "spying" and invasion of personal privacy have reached national agendas. Much of the debate centers on "cookies," which are small files planted by web pages on a visiting computer.[46] These files are stored within your browser (Netscape Navigator) or a separate file (Microsoft Explorer). They are used by a web server to identify past users. They can pass short bits of information, such as user name, from the web server back to itself the next time a visit occurs. Popular rumors about cookies describe them as evil programs that can scan your hard drive and gather information about you, including passwords, credit card numbers and lists of software on your computer. This information is simply not true. Cookies cannot gather and transmit information from your hard drive and cannot plant viruses.[47] Figure 18–7 provides more detailed information on cookies and tips for Internet privacy. However, computer and security experts agree on one simple guideline for governing all Internet activity: Assume that nothing is absolutely private or safe!

THE HACKER PROFILE

The computers that hackers use are typically far less sophisticated than those used by the systems they attack. Their weapon of choice is a fast computer with a large hard disk, a modem, and a telephone line through which they can access the information superhighway.

Hackers can spring from any group, as illustrated by cases involving an airline pilot and a homemaker. However, such instances are somewhat unusual and do not meet the more typical hacker profile (see Figure 18–8). Based on interviews with approximately 100 convicted hackers, most of them are relatively young, white males from middle-class environments.[48] Generally, they range from 14 to 25 years of age. They are not socially integrated and tend to be loners, except when communicating by computer. They tend not to associate with their peer group or become actively involved in peer group behavior such as dating or participating in school activities. They take on the air of self-assurance only when they are with fellow phreakers, talking about their computers.

Figure 18–7
Tips on Internet Privacy

Cookies:	A cookie is a small piece of information that is sent to a user's web browser by a particular web site's server. The information is saved on the user's hard drive in a file and has a set expiration date, which may be so far into the future that the cookie will effectively never expire. Each subsequent time that the user visits the site, the server requests the information that it put in the cookie file. These transactions are usually conducted transparently and without the user's knowledge. The vast majority of net users are unaware of cookie files.
	A cookie keeps track of what sites a computer has visited by providing users with unique identifiers. Cookies can be helpful, as they allow a web server to "remember" specific information about a user. Cookies can allow web site personalization, quicker access to user-ID and password-protected web sites, and the ability to return to the last actions at a specific site. Cookies can also be used by law enforcement during a computer crime investigation to view a history of potentially illicit activity while the suspect was on the Internet. They have been important tools in linking suspects to child molesting, pornography, terrorist organizations, and fraud crimes.
	For more information on cookies, visit the following web sites:
	www.cookiecentral.com www.luckman.com/products/anoncookie/index.html www8.zdnet.com/pcmag/features/cookies/_open.htm www.webattack.com/shareware/security/swcookie.html www.anu.edu.au/people/Roger.Clarke/II/Cookies.html#Appl www.gc.maricopa.edu/2dts000/cis133/modules/m20a.htm www.pcug.org.au/~amikkels/cookies.html
Usenet news groups:	Remember the "Mom rule": Don't include anything you wouldn't want your mother to read.
Chat rooms:	Even if you chat under an anonymous name, anyone can capture and rebroadcast the dialogue. With the "WHOIS" command, your real e-mail address and those of others who conversed with you can be revealed.
E-mail:	Messages are routed through possibly dozens of computers across the Internet. Any truly private information should be encrypted.
Anonymous remailers:	They let whistleblowers send untraceable messages. Unfortunately, they are also available to junk mailers and harassers.
Credit cards:	Credit card transactions on the Internet are as safe as phone and fax transactions as long as they occur on web pages with secure, encrypted connections.

Sources: Cookie information prepared by Matt Taylor, Texas Tech University, August 1998; and Pete Slover, "Cyber Eyes," *Dallas Morning News,* June 30, 1998, pp. 1F, 6F.

One convicted teenager reported that "hacking is like cocaine . . . it's a rush you can't forget."[49] Most hackers are thrill seekers; the challenge of entering a secure databank is exciting, just as mountain climbing is for people who climb mountains. To penetrate multiple levels of a computer system's security to get at the programs and files has been described as "orgasmic." One young man stated that "hacking is the next best thing to sex."[50] Often, these attacks cause little if any physical damage as the hacker "browses" through files looking for innocuous games to play.

- White males

- 14 to 25 years of age

- From families of medium to high socioeconomic status

- Highly intelligent individuals, yet underachievers in school

- Self-descriptions include feelings of boredom and apathy

- Favorite activities include computer games and/or other games emphasizing a fantasy world (e.g., Dungeons and Dragons)

- Membership in a "thrill-seeking" subculture group of computer hackers, often taking on the name of a fantasy world character (e.g., Zod, Captain Zap, The Wizard)

Figure 18–8
The Hacker Subculture
Demographic profile of the hacker subculture based on interviews and empirical observations of more than 100 convicted hackers.

Hackers' parents rarely suspect problems because they appear to be "model" young adults. As one investigator pointed out, "They [hackers] don't race cars, chase girls, drink beer, or get into trouble." Although hackers are smart, they tend to be underachievers in school. They stay in their rooms, working on their computers.

These are the kids of *War Games, Ferris Bueller's Day Off,* and other hit movies that romanticize the merry pranksters as young Robin Hoods. However, "kids" known as the "414 Gang"—named after their Milwaukee, Wisconsin, area code—penetrated a dozen computers in the United States and Canada, including those of a bank in Los Angeles and the nuclear weapons laboratory in Los Alamos, New Mexico. This same outfit broke into a computer in a Manhattan hospital, which controlled radiation and X-ray treatments given to cancer patients.[51] For young adults playing these "games," it is harmless fun. For the people whose businesses and lives depend on computers, it isn't.

Hackers use underground bulletin boards to trade merchandise, which is usually computer-related. The "swaps" are conducted just like the exchanges in used bookstores, that is, two for one. The merchandise ranges from pirated software and programs to lists of network access codes. Underground bulletin board "SYSOPS" (systems operators) may also sell information on prostitution, pornography, recipes for explosives, and stolen goods. Hackers even have their own magazines, such as *TAP* and *2001.*

THE INSIDER PROFILE

The most likely suspects in insider computer crime are programmers and system operators. Any other personnel who have inordinate amounts of autonomy, overlapping areas of responsibility, and freedom of movement within the electronic data processing (EDP) function of a business are also prime suspects. No one person should ever be allowed to control all—or overlapping—aspects of EDP operations. Within the government, computer criminals generally were found to be:

> young, good employees of a federal agency or a state, local, or private agency administering federal programs . . . their median age was thirty. Three-quarters had spent at least some time in college. They had been with their respective agencies for an average of five years before they committed their crimes. . . . Nearly three-quarters had been promoted and two-thirds reported receiving at least an above average performance rating. In fact, a quarter of the perpetrators told us they had received performance awards.[52]

When investigating what appears to be an insider computer crime, the investigator should consider the following factors:[53]

Opportunities

- Familiarity with operations (including cover-up capabilities).

- Position of trust.
- Close associations with suppliers and other key people.

Situational Pressures—Financial

- High personal debts.
- Severe illness in family.
- Inadequate income and/or living beyond means.
- Extensive stock market speculation.
- Loan shark involvement.
- Excessive gambling.
- Heavy expenses incurred from extramarital involvement.
- Undue family, peer, company, or community expectations.
- Excessive use of alcohol or drugs.

Situational Pressures—Revenge

- Perceived inequities (e.g., low pay or poor job assignment).
- Resentment of superiors.
- Frustration, usually with job.

Personality Traits

- Lacks personal moral honesty.
- No well-defined code of personal ethics.
- A wheeler-dealer, that is, someone who enjoys feelings of power, influence, social status, and excitement associated with rapid financial transactions involving large sums of money.
- Neurotic, manic depressive, or emotionally unstable.
- Arrogant or egocentric.
- Psychopathic.
- Low self-esteem.
- Personally challenged to subvert a system of controls.

Investigators should also construct a "personal demography" on suspects. This consists of three factors: (1) criminal history, (2) list of associates, and (3) references.[54]

Another activity that should raise suspicion involves employees who work late (after hours) and refuse promotions and/or transfers. Any scams they may be working will be more lucrative than the promotions. Other suspects might be persons who show remarkable curiosity toward aspects of EDP outside of their job requirements.

INVESTIGATING COMPUTER CRIME

Among the many problems confronting investigators is that some victims—such as financial institutions, consulting firms, and corporations —may not report the fraud or prosecute the offender because of the adverse publicity involved. They simply do not want depositors, potential clients, and shareholders to think them incapable of managing their affairs. Although no one wants bad publicity, this practice allows known violators to go free. Additionally, because many crimes go unreported, the police, prosecutors, and the legislative bodies that enact legislation have only a partial understanding of the true scope of the problem.

Because computer crime is difficult to detect, the trail is often cold, records may be at a minimum, key people to interview may have gone on to other jobs, and investigators may not recognize key evidence or know what to ask for due to a lack of training and experience.

The hackers who attacked the National Weather Service computers from Denmark used methods that were virtually antique, yet they got fairly far into the system. If those hackers were difficult for a computer expert to catch, consider how much harder it would be to investigate a crime committed by any of the 50 or so superelite hackers who use cutting-edge methods. However, investigators have a number of sources to which they can turn for information, training, and assistance when investigating computer crime. Federal Law Enforcement Training Centers in Georgia and Arizona offer excellent training courses on computer crime investigation that state and local police officers can attend. Both the FBI and the Secret Service have some jurisdiction in the area of computer crime, and both provide training and investigative assistance to nonfederal agencies. It is estimated that 30 percent of the Secret Service's computer crime effort is spent supporting state and local agencies. Many state police and state investigative agencies also provide training and assistance in investigating computer crime. Throughout the country there are also local or substate regional groups that have been formed to provide training, information, and mutual assistance. One example is the Law Enforcement Electronic Technology Assistance Committee in Florida's 18th judicial circuit. This group consists of prosecutors, police officers, and representatives from industry and the military who provide some training, as well as exchanging information and assistance on an as-needed basis.

Frequently, computer crime evidence will be seized by the execution of a search warrant.[55] This warrant should include information about the computer, data storage devices (including internal and external hard drives), floppy disks, tape backups, modems, programs, software manuals, user notes, hard-copy output, and any peripherals that may be of concern to investigators, such as scanners. When the warrant is served, a high priority is removing noninvestigative personnel from computers and terminals whenever feasible so as to prevent the possible deliberate destruction of electronic evidence.

A computer expert—either an investigator specializing in this field or a civilian with the necessary expertise—should be consulted for assistance in specifying what is to be searched for by the warrant and also in seizing it. The computer and related equipment and material should not be touched or moved until thoroughly documented by photography or videotaping. In particular, the screen needs to be photographed immediately in order to secure the information on it. More than one criminal case has been won because an investigating officer noticed incriminating evidence on the screen and photographed it before the screen changed. It is also important that all connections and wires be photographed and portrayed. The keyboard should not be used in a premature attempt to locate evidence. After the system has been photographed, the first step is to unplug the computer; do not use the on/off switch. All wiring connections should be tagged with notes indicating where they were connected. If there is a modem, disconnect it by unplugging the connecting cable from the wall jack. The serial numbers for all equipment should be recorded. The hard disk should be secured for transportation to prevent damage. Before actually moving the computer, check the outer perimeter of the room in which the computer is located to make sure that there is no magnetic force that would erase evidence of the crime on storage devices. All computer evidence should be stored in an area free from dust, heat, dampness, and magnetic fields.

Seized computers should be examined only by trained technicians who either are law enforcement officers or have appropriate training in search-and-seizure laws and procedures. The U.S. Department of Justice has published extensive documentation on federal guidelines for searching and seizing computers.[56] These should be consulted before computer equipment is likely to be seized or searched. There should never be just one investigator examining a seized computer, as additional observers may be able to provide the only supporting testimony regarding evidence seen on the computer screen. Seized computers should never initally be rebooted using their own disks; safe predesignated, preformatted floppies should be used for rebooting. Ideally, seized hard disks should be removed from their original computer and placed in a designated law enforcement computer as a second drive. The new, known-safe system can then be booted off of the law enforcement drive, and the seized drive can be examined. Only rarely should seized disks be booted, and even then booting should be done only when absolutely necessary and when it has been ascertained that there are no detectable traps that could lead to the loss of evidence.

Not following these safeguards can have devastating consequences for a criminal investigation, either before or after law enforcement officers are involved in the case. In 1997, an employee of the information systems department of a large telecommunications company was fired due to negligence of duty. The individual was escorted out of the company and not given access to his company computer. The computer had been powered down by the terminated employee the night before, as he normally did before leaving for the evening. A few days later, a supervisor discovered e-mail that suggested that the employee possessed child pornography on the company computer. A cursory search of the employee's computer found several files of pornographic pictures of children. Within a couple of minutes of the files' being discovered, a coincidental power failure caused the computer to reboot. Once the computer had rebooted, the supervisor looked for the incriminating files in order to record their location for investigative purposes. The files and e-mail were missing. The supervisor then started to determine what had happened to the files. It quickly became apparent that the employee had installed a trap on the machine. The trap was a custom-written software program that was automatically run whenever the machine was booted. The trap program looked for specific trap files, and if those files were not present, the program would delete the pornography files, e-mail, and other incriminating data. Before shutting down his computer, the employee would manually run a program that he had written that would create several specifically titled trap files. When the computer was then rebooted, the trap program would look for those files, and if they were present, it would delete them but do nothing else. If the computer was later powered down without the manual file-creation program being run, as occurred when the power failed, the needed trap files would not be created and therefore would not be found when the trap program automatically ran on reboot. The incriminating files would then be deleted by the trap program, as they were when the computer rebooted after the power failure. Since the supervisor was the only witness to the event, and because the files were no longer present on the system, criminal charges were not filed against the ex-employee. While this case occurred before police investigators were involved, similar losses of evidence have occurred from seized computers when insufficiently trained law enforcement officials tried to access data stored on computers. When examining a seized computer, do not save anything to the hard disk or floppies seized, as this alters it and is likely to make it inadmissible in court. Investigators should also remember that all equipment and software seized are the property of someone else. Damage done by the investigator to the equipment or programs or the erasure of or damage to data can open police agencies to legal action.

Finally, it is important to note that what may initially look like a computer crime may not actually prove to be an intentional or malicious act. Software bugs, hardware failures, and other noncriminal events can appear to be evidence that a crime has taken place. A failing modem may repeatedly try to dial a number, making it appear that someone is trying to break into a computer system. A software bug may inadvertently alter or delete data records. Poor communication within an organization may lead to the conclusion that hardware has been stolen when it was merely relocated. The complexity of computer crimes dictates that properly trained and technically competent individuals conduct the investigation or be consulted.

PREVENTING COMPUTER CRIME

There is a great deal going on in the area of computer crime prevention. The Software Business Association (SBA) is working internationally to combat software piracy. Some companies, such as Microsoft, donate to SBA 50 percent of whatever they recover in software piracy settlement cases to strengthen that effort, with the balance going to train unemployed information technology professionals.[57] At Pittsburgh's Carnegie Mellon University, the Computer Emergency Response Team was set up, with federal funding, to monitor the security of the Internet and other national computer networks, especially those operated by the government and the military.

While historically the focus of computer crime prevention has been on protecting software, hardware, and connected devices, the rapid growth of the information age has meant that *information* is the increasing focus of computer crime prevention. While a hard drive can be replaced, the information contained on that hard drive may be irreplacable, and its loss may be catastrophic to a corporation. The increase in laptop computer thefts may be not for the potential resale of the machine but for the invaluable information contained on the hard drive. Imagine the value to a competitor of the next five years' marketing plans for a major corporation, contained on a senior executive's laptop that was stolen as he went through airport security. Protecting information, largely by making it inaccessible to unauthorized users, is a key element of preventing computer crimes.

One way organizations protect their computer networks is by using *firewalls*, which are computers that stand as a single checkpoint between a company or government network, the Internet, and other computer systems.[58] A firewall checks all data coming in and going out. If the data do not fit strict criteria, they do not go through. In the past, firewalls were not widely used, since they severely reduced access from the protected network to the outside world. Firewalls have since improved greatly and are now able to provide better access to the outside world while providing a higher level of protection to the network. Software development, combined with rapidly increasing computer-based crime occurring through interconnected networks, has led to the widespread use of firewalls.

The single greatest problem in computer security is password protection. Although there are some basic dos and don'ts (see Figure 18–9), there are also sophisticated software programs that address this issue. Several approaches have been taken in an attempt to solve the problem of password protection, including password-creation software programs, one-time password generators, and user-authentication systems. Other tools, such as encryption, are used to protect passwords and the passage of highly sensitive information. Such programs "scramble" passwords and data files. This

makes them difficult to unscramble unless the person seeking to do so uses the same key.

There are a variety of software programs that system administrators can use in order to improve password security. Some programs force users to change their password on a regular basis, perhaps every month or few months, or even every week. Other programs automatically create random pronounceable passwords for users, such as "jrk^wud" which is pronounced "jerk wood." The user remembers that the ^ character is between the two words. Such pronounceable passwords are not subject to dictionary attacks by hackers, are easily remembered by users, and do not relate to user information (such as a child's first name) that might be easily determined by an outside attacker.

SecurID, from Security Dynamics Technologies, Inc. (see Figure 18–10), is perhaps the most popular one-time password generator, with over 3 million users in 5,000 organizations worldwide. SecurID identifies and authenticates each individual user on the basis of two factors: (1) something secret that the

---

1. Don't use words found in an English or other dictionary because hackers' programs test different words very quickly.

2. The longer a password is, the more difficult it is to guess it.

3. Use a mixture of number, letters, and special characters if possible. Also, some passwords are case sensitive–they can distinguish between lower and uppercase letters. This feature should be used if available. To illustrate, "K2jw&#69" is harder to guess than "Super Ace."

4. Don't use obvious or guessable passwords; don't use your child's name, birth date, car license number, Social Security number, or favorite sports team.

5. Don't write your password down where people can find it. Don't write it on the underside of your desk blotter or leave it in your wallet.

6. Change passwords as frequently as possible.

7. Don't disclose or lend your password to other people.

8. Don't allow people to watch what you type when you log on. Relatedly, when using your telephone calling card number in public places, be aware of people watching you. Credit card and other numbers have been stolen by people using video cameras and telescopes.

9. Don't tell your password to anyone over the telephone.

10. Promptly report any unusual log on experiences to your network administrator, as well as any suspicion that your password has been compromised.

Figure 18–9
Guidelines for Password Protection

Source: Peter H. Lewis, "Some Password Do's and Don'ts," *New York Times*, February 13, 1994, p. 9, with modification and additions.

Figure 18–10
SecurID Card

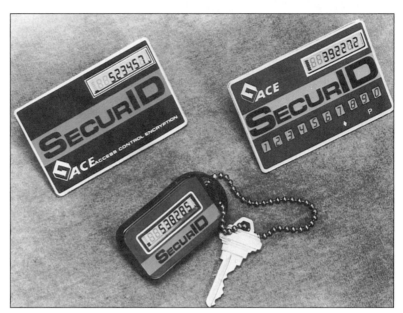

(Courtesy Security Dynamics Technologies, Inc., Bedford, Massachusetts)

user knows—a memorized personal identification number (PIN)—and (2) something unique that the user has—the SecurID card. Under this system, a computer user logging on first types in his or her PIN. Then the user types in the number currently displayed on his or her SecurID card, which changes every 60 seconds. Each individual SecurID card is synchronized with either hardware or software on the computer system that the user is attempting to access. The result is a unique access code that is valid only for a particular user during a 60-second period.

Kerberos is a program developed at MIT by the Athena Project. It is a leading network and data encryption system. Cygnus Support, a Mountain View, California, company, has developed Kerberos-based user-authentication software—Cygnus Network Security (CNS)—that eliminates the need to use clear, unencrypted text passwords on a network. In this system, an individual user is given an encryption key to encrypt and decrypt Kerberos passwords, log ins, and other computer system transactions. When this individual wants to access the network, he or she will send a message to the Kerberos server. This computer sends back an encrypted package that can be read only with that user's secret key. This package also includes a temporary encryption key good for only that session on the computer. To prove his or her identity, the user then sends a message coded in the temporary encryption key back to the computer. The Kerberos computer then acknowledges the user's identity by sending a second encrypted message to the user, which can be decoded only by using the temporary encryption key previously sent to the user. In 1994, CNS was posted on the Internet, available without charge to any American or Canadian network that wants it. Cygnus Support does, however, charge for support services it provides for CNS adopters.

Kerberos is just one program that utilizes encryption. Many other programs, such as SecureShell (SSH), also create encrypted sessions between the user's computer and the destination computer, thus protecting passwords and other sensitive information from hackers using tools like packet sniffers. All that the hackers are able to retrieve are indecipherable streams of encrypted data. Other programs use encryption to safeguard e-mail or files. Some can even encrypt the entire contents of a hard drive or floppy disk. The advent of widely available strong encryption products such as Pretty Good Privacy (PGP) has led the government and some law enforcement officials to grow concerned about the possible misuse of encryption by criminals. Terrorists, for example, could use encrypted e-mail to develop plans for a bombing in secrecy. While some officials have proposed that software developers build trap doors for the government into their encryption programs, civil liberty advocates have strongly opposed such measures, noting that such trap doors could be abused by the government. Strict export regulations on strong encryption products restrict the legal export of such software from the United States. However, these regulations have not stopped the illegal smuggling of such software.

New technologies are altering the face of user identification. The use of tools such as digital fingerprint identification, retinal identification, and palm biometric identification greatly increases the accuracy of user identification, sometimes eliminating the need for passwords. One system re-leased by Compaq (in 1998) allows computers to be hooked up to a small digital fingerprint scanner.[59] The user inserts a finger into the device, the fingerprint is scanned, and the user is uniquely identified. The computer looks the user up in a password database and will accept only the password listed in the database for that person. The person enters the password and gains entry to the system. Thus, a fingerprint is tied to a user ID, which, in turn, is linked to a specific password, providing greater accuracy in user authentication.[60] The future of computer security will continue to link users' unique physical attributes (those that do not change and cannot be easily altered) to known passwords, as experts focus on voice recognition and more secure transaction methodologies.

Questions

1. What are computer abuse and computer crime?
2. Can you identify and define the six major categories of computer crime?
3. Describe Trojan horse, salami, back door, and logic bomb programs.
4. What is a computer virus, and how does it operate?
5. Why is the Internet a favorite target for hackers?
6. How do cloning and tumbling work?
7. Give three case examples of computer manipulation crimes.
8. What are some indicators that software piracy is a problem worldwide?
9. Can you describe the "typical" hacker on the basis of seven different factors?
10. With respect to insider computer crime, what are financial situational pressures and revenge situational pressures?
11. Identify a one-time password generator system, and describe how it works.

Notes

1. "Internet World Projections," Forrester Reseach (Cambridge, Mass., 1998).

2. Ibid.

3. Donn B. Parker, *Computer Crime: Criminal Justice Resource Manual* (Washington, D.C.: National Institute of Justice, 1989), p. I-3.

4. Catherine H. Conly and J. Thomas McEwen, "Computer Crime," *NIJ Reports*, January–February 1990, No. 218, p. 3.

5. CERT and FIRST have extensive on-line services that provide detailed information on most computer crime units within federal, state, and local agencies. For more information, see *http://www.cert.org* and *http:// www.first.org*.

6. "On-Line Investment Schemes: Fraud in Cyberspace," *Consumers' Research Magazine*, August 1994, Vol. 77, p. 20.

7. Sandy Rovner, "Molesting Our Children by Computer," *Washington Post*, August 2, 1994, p. 15.

8. Five of the six categories are identified in Catherine H. Conly and J. Thomas McEwen, "Computer Crime," pp. 2–7. The material in this chapter retains these basic categories and extends them considerably with current research.

9. John Markoff, "A Dose of Computer Insecurity; Intruders Set Snares on Data Highway," *New York Times*, p. C1.

10. Cindy Hall, "USA Snapshots: Contaminated Computers," *USA Today*, October 31, 1994, p. B1.

11. Adrain Croft, "Security Group Sounds Alarm about Computer Crime," March 10, 1999, http://www.infowar.com/SURVEY/ survey–_____2.html-ssi.

12. Ibid.

13. Telecommunication Advisors, Inc., *Toll Fraud and Tele-Abuse* (Richardson, Tex.: AT&T Wireless Services, 1998), chap. 2.

14. J. Blake Lambert, "Attack of the Killer E-Mail," *Sky Magazine*, April 1998, pp. 96–102.

15. "Hackers Hit Justice Department Web Site," *Dallas Morning News*, August 18, 1996, p. 9A.

16. Michelle Levander, "Hackers Breach Stanford Computer Security," *Mercury News*, June 10, 1998.

17. This account is taken from John J. Fialka, "The Latest Flurries at Weather Bureau: Scattered Hacking," *The Wall Street Journal*, October 10, 1995, pp. A1, A17.

18. Michael Meyer with Anne Underwood, "Crimes of the Net," *Newsweek*, November 14, 1994, p. 47.

19. The information in this paragraph is drawn from Ibid.

20. Charles Burress, "Online Nudes Exposed at Livermore Lab," *San Francisco Chronicle*, July 12, 1994, p. A3.

21. Jennifer Steinhauer, "'Phreakers' Take a Swipe at Turnstiles and Nynex," *New York Times*, August 15, 1994, p. B3.

22. Ibid.

23. Conly and McEwen, "Computer Crime," p. 3.

24. The information on cellular phones is taken from William G. Flanagan and Brigid McMenamin, "Why Cybercrooks Love Cellular," *Forbes*, December 21, 1992, Vol. 150, No. 14, p. 189.

25. Ibid., p. 19.

26. "Consumers' Group Wants Telemarketing Rules Expanded to Net," *Dallas Morning News*, February 16, 1998, p. 2D.

27. Ibid.

28. "Congress Warned of New Fraud: Computers Simplify, Reduce Cost of Check Counterfeiting," *Dallas Morning News*, May 2, 1997, p. 5A.

29. Ibid.

30. Ibid.

31. Aaron Nathans, "IRS Moves to Block 'Rapid Refund' Scam Artists," *Los Angeles Times*, October 27, 1994, p. A24.

32. Jill Serjeant, "Police Raid Global Internet Child Porn Club," *Reuters Ltd.*, September 2, 1998.

33. Ibid.

34. Kim S. Nash, "Laptop Computer Thieves Running Rampant," *Computer World*, August 6, 1998, http://cnn.com/TECH/computing/9806/06/laptheif.idg/index. html

35. Royal Canadian Mounted Police, *Technological Crime Bulletin*, http://www.rcmp-grc.gc.ca/html/tcb3-3d.htm.

36. Ibid.

37. Microsoft Canada, "Anti-Piracy: Just the Facts. Questions and Answers," http://microsoft.com/canada/piracy/Q&A.htm

38. Ibid.

39. "Stalking Asian Software Pirates," *Technology Review*, February–March 1992, Vol. 95, No. 2, p. 15.

40. Cara A. Cunningham, "Microsoft Tries to Quash European Software Piracy," *Computerworld*, April 25, 1994, Vol. 28, No. 17, p. 41.

41. Barbara Carton, "Man Charged in Software Piracy Cases," *Boston Globe*, September 1, 1994, p. 41.

42. Adam Bauman, "The Pirates of the Internet," *Los Angeles Times*, November 3, 1994, p. A1.

43. David A. Price, "1st Amendment and the Internet," *Investor's Business Daily*, June 27, 1997, pp. A1, A24.

44. Ibid.

45. Ibid.

46. Pet Slover, "Cyber Eyes," *Dallas Morning News*, June 30, 1998, pp. 1F, 6F.

47. Ibid.

48. See R. W. Taylor, "Hackers, Phone Phreakers, and Virus Makers," paper presented at the Second Annual Conference on Computer Viruses, London, England, June 1990.

49. Ibid.

50. Ibid.

51. See "Playing Games," *Time*, August 22, 1983, p. 14; "The 414 Gang Strikes Again," *Time*, August 29, 1983, p. 75.

52. R. P. Kusserow, "An Inside Look at Federal Computer Crime," *Security Management*, May 1986, p. 75.

53. R. K. Elliot and J. J. Willingham, *Management Fraud: Detection and Deterrence* (New York: Petrocelli Books, 1980), pp. 223–226.

54. Ibid.

55. The information covering the search and seizure of computer crime evidence is drawn from an undated publication, *Crime Scene Computer Factsheet* (Washington, D.C.: National Institute of Justice), p. 1. Relatedly, an excellent training aid is the *Crime Scene Computer Video*, available from NIJ by calling (800) 851-3420 or, if in Maryland or metropolitan Washington, (301) 251-5500.

56. U.S. Department of Justice, Criminal Division, Office of Professional Development and Training, *Federal Guidelines for Searching and Seizing Computers*, July 1994, http://www.usdoj.gov/criminal/cybercrime/search _docs/search.htm; U.S. Department of Justice, Criminal Division, Computer Crime and Intellectual Property Section, *Supplement to Federal Guidelines for Searching and Seizing Computers*, October 1997, http://www.usdoj.gov/criminal/cybercrime/supplement/ssgsup.htm.

57. Cunningham, "Microsoft Tries to Quash European Software Piracy," p. 41.

58. See Peter H. Lewis, "How to Keep Bandits from 'Snarfing' Your Passwords," *New York Times*, February 13, 1993, Sec. 3, p. 9; Laurent Belsie, "Firewalls Help Protect Internet from Attack of the Hackers," *Christian Science Monitor*, April 29, 1994, p. 4.

59. Kristi Essick, "Compaq to Launch Fingerprint ID Module for PCs," *Infoworld*, July 1, 1998, http://www.cnn. com/TECH/computing/9807/01fingerprint.idg//index. html.

60. Ibid.

NINETEEN

Agricultural, Wildlife, and Environmental Crimes

CHAPTER OUTLINE

Agricultural Crime and Its City Connection 538

Some Dimensions of Agricultural, Wildlife, and Environmental Crimes 538

Timber Theft 539

Theft of Agrichemicals 540

Livestock and Tack Theft 541

Livestock Identification 546

Physical Evidence 547

Crime Prevention Measures 549

Wildlife Crimes 550

Environmental Crime 553

Questions 561

Notes 561

INTRODUCTION

Conventional wisdom says that crime is fundamentally, if not almost exclusively, an urban phenomenon. Yet, like most matters, some aspects of crime do not immediately meet the eye. Seventeen percent of our nation's farms—or roughly one in every five—are located within Metropolitan Statistical Areas (MSAs), and thus crime on and against them contributes to the magnitude of reported crime in urban areas.[1] Additionally, some crimes committed against wildlife have significant economic value, and single instances of them may yield more profit to the offender than do single episodes of conventional crimes such as burglary, robbery, or larceny. Environmental crimes, such as those involving the illegal treatment, storage, transportation, and disposal of hazardous waste, are a significant threat to the public health, the quality of outdoor recreation, and wildlife. The purpose of this chapter is to call attention to the nature and extent of crimes against agriculture, wildlife, and the environment and to provide information regarding their investigation.

AGRICULTURAL CRIME AND ITS CITY CONNECTION

There is a natural but mistaken view that crimes against agriculture are of little overall economic consequence and are not within the sphere of interest for urban police officers. Although these themes are examined in detail from various perspectives in subsequent portions of this chapter, a few observations are warranted here. Estimates of the economic impact of rural and agricultural crime are as high as $5 billion annually.[2] This figure may be low when the size of the agricultural enterprise is considered. National membership in the American Farm Bureau Federation exceeds 4 million people.[3] By almost every estimate, farm products nationally are worth more than $1,000 billion annually. Just in San Diego County, California, agriculture ranks as the fourth-largest industry, with an economic impact of $3.9 billion annully.[4]

There is also evidence that urban-based criminals and criminal groups are involved as both planners and perpetrators of crimes in rural areas and on farms. In some instances these crimes are raidlike actions in which city-dwelling street gang members enter the rural setting, commit their crimes, and return to their familiar urban habitat swiftly on the interstate highways that are so conveniently positioned. In California and surrounding states, thieves are stealing cattle to support their drug addictions. Currently, it is estimated that drug-related incidents account for about 30 to 40 percent of all cattle stolen in California. One reason for this development is that rustlers can get full market value for their "stolen goods." A weaned calf, depending on its size and market conditions, will bring at least $375; quality steers and heifers can command prices of $700 to $900. Urban centers are also conduits for the disposal of some property stolen in rural areas; some portion of the extensive amount of farm machinery and equipment that is stolen is rapidly passed through big-city ports and shipped for sale in foreign countries, particularly those located in South America. Illegal "killer plants" or slaughterhouses have also been located in some cities and are used as part of a distribution system for stolen animals that are processed and sold as meat.

Another direct connection between rural crime and city dwellers results from the changing composition of labor used by farmers. There was a time when the principal source of farm labor was provided by the immediate family of the farm owner, neighbors, or laborers who lived in the vicinity of the farms. With the growth of large conglomerate farms and huge citrus orchards, the reliance on labor has by necessity shifted more and more to both migrants and city-based labor. When workers from the cities are employed, they will typically travel to the farms or orchards on a daily basis and return to their homes in the cities at night. In some cases, these workers have returned to the farming areas for the purpose of committing crimes and have also, for a fee, tipped active criminals as to specific opportunities there.

Altogether, such illustrations provide substantial evidence that rural and agricultural crimes are economically significant and of concern to both rural and urban police agencies.

SOME DIMENSIONS OF AGRICULTURAL, WILDLIFE, AND ENVIRONMENTAL CRIMES

We really don't know what agricultural, wildlife, and environmental crimes cost us. The information that is available is fragmented and often based on estimates or extrapolations from small data sets. However, from that information, it is reasonable to conclude that these problems are widespread and costly.

Ranchers, farmers, and others living in rural places are often the victims of thefts, including those of livestock, tack, pesticides, tractors, dirt bikes, all-terrain vehicles, drip lines, stock trailers, plants and timber, tools, hay, grains and citrus, irrigation pipes, and sprinkler heads. Often when the prices of crops and cattle increase, thefts of them may increase 20 percent or more. For example when freezes kill oranges or droughts kill avocados—90 percent of which are grown in California[5]—prices rise on the remaining crops because there are less of them. The result is that thieves looking for an easy buck steal them. In the case of California avocados, thieves steal some $10 million worth annually, or about

5 percent of the total value of avocados statewide. A lone "night picker" can invade a grove and easily pick $300 to $500 worth of avocados and disappear. Or a worker commuting to a job beyond a grove might stop and tell a legal picker to "leave two burlap bags filled with avocados over there and I'll leave you $40 when I pick them up." The worker can get $200 for the two bags, pocketing a quick $160 in profit.[6]

Nationally, rustlers steal about 20,000 cattle worth $12.1 million.[7] Moreover, pigs, sheep, emu, and goats are also stolen. In a single year, Texas emu ranchers lost $600,000 to thieves.[8] In a three-county area of North Carolina, hog rustlers made off with 300 pigs valued at $50,000 in less than 90 days.[9] Because livestock theft is at least 50 percent underreported, the total national loss due to rustling of all types of animals is at least double the known figure.

With dinosaur skeletons selling for $500,000 or more, private and public lands are being invaded by "bone rustlers."[10] The theft of bull semen from dairy farms has become a criminal enterprise.[11] The bull semen is essential to the operation of dairies because cows must be either pregnant or nursing to produce milk. A full tank of bull semen can be worth $10,000 and is easy to dispose of. In central Florida, two men who were arrested for breaking the leg of a thoroughbred horse may be part of a nationwide ring that injured horses in order to collect on insurance policies.[12] Radical environmentalists in Washington are using guerrilla tactics to halt the cutting of trees.[13] For example, spikes are driven into trees still in the forest, causing chain saws to shatter when an attempt is made to cut the tree down. Although when such tactics are used notices are often posted to warn loggers of the danger, serious injuries have resulted. Our national parklands are also victimized by plant poachers. Ginseng roots are prized by Asians as an aphrodisiac and as a treatment for infection, lack of vigor, and inflammation.[14] A dried pound of ginseng root can bring its harvester as much as $300. In the Great Smokies National Park, rangers seized two separate loads of illegally picked ginseng roots, each of which weighed 1,600 pounds. In the Northwest each fall, hundreds of people sweep through places like Crater Lake National Park in Oregon picking mushrooms. The prize is the matsutake, which is sold in Japan for up to $200 per pound. Local harvesters—who may pick as much as 50 pounds per day—sell their finds to roadside buy-ers, who give them a few hundred dollars and then sell them to Japanese outlets for considerably more. Although both ginseng and matsutake may be legally gathered, people often do so at illegal times or go onto lands where their permit is not valid. Saguaro cactus is being stolen from ranches and public lands in New Mexico, Arizona, and Nevada. The saguaros can be sold for about $50 for each foot of height, plus $100 for each arm on the cactus. The saguaro cactus can be dug up, loaded onto a truck, and removed from the scene in 15 to 25 minutes.[15]

It must be observed that persons who live in rural areas and on farms, groves, vineyards, and ranches are not only crime victims but are themselves occasional offenders. For example, false reports of livestock or equipment theft are made to obtain insurance money, and the nature of crops may be misrepresented. In California when demand for wine outstrips the supply of grapes, prices increase dramatically. French colombard grapes, which usually sell for $150 per ton, have been sold as chardonnay grapes—at $1,500 per ton.[16]

TIMBER THEFT

The U.S. Forest Service concedes that it doesn't know how much timber is stolen from national forests but that it may be as much as $100 million worth annually and amount to about 1 in every 10 trees cut down.[17] In East Texas, timber is the number-one ranking agricultural commodity, with 500,000 acres a year being harvested, producing a revenue of $900 million; at least another $20 million is lost annually to "tree rustlers."[18] Winter is the prime season for hunting burls, the huge gnarly root at the base of walnut trees. Burls, used to make fine clocks, wood trim in expensive sports cars, and fancy rifle stocks, can command up to $20,000 on the black market.[19] Burl thieves sneak into a walnut grove at night looking for a prime specimen. They dig a large hole to expose the burl, which may weigh up to 2,000 pounds. Then they place the soil loosely back into the hole and return the next night. They can easily shovel away the soil, cut the burl loose quickly with a chain saw, and leave as soon as they get it into a truck.[20]

"Tippers" in Maine are people who harvest the tips of balsam tree branches. These branches are ultimately made into Christmas wreaths. Many tippers operate legitimately on their own land or purchase the right to work someone else's under a permit. However, there are also tippers who operate illegally and are referred to as "branch rustlers."[21] This type of rustler goes onto land illegally and may steal the choice tips that someone else has a permit to harvest, causing economic loss to legitimate tippers and an occasional violent confrontation. Other tippers purchase a permit to harvest on a particular section of land but then gather their branches from a more desirable tract of land. In a single day or night a tipper or branch rustler may earn $300, but the rustlers' profit is generally higher because they operate without the expense of the permit from the landowner.

Investigations into the illegal cutting of timber involve a full range of investigative techniques. Examination of crime scenes continues to result in the discovery of evidence of paint transfers and tool marks on wood debris left behind by suspects. These marks and paint transfers result from the use of axes, wedges, and splitting mauls and serve to tie a suspect to a crime. Examination of tool marks on wood is based on established principles that it is possible to identify a suspect tool with the mark it leaves on a surface. In several cases, containers left at the scene of a timber theft have been processed and fingerprints developed. These fingerprints have been useful in identifying and placing suspects at the scene. In addition, casts of both shoe and tire impressions that were later identified as belonging to a particular suspect and vehicle have been found at some crime scenes.

Although the crime scene examinations at the site of timber thefts are important, they are supplemented by the long and tedious process of interviewing potential witnesses to the crime, conducting investigations to develop witnesses in resort-type areas where thefts have occurred, and checking possible outlets where forest products might be sold. In order to conduct investigations concerning timber sales, law enforcement officers must become familiar with the variety of terms and techniques pertaining to a timber sale, from its inception to the eventual purchase.

THEFT OF AGRICHEMICALS

Agrichemical is a broad term whose meaning encompasses a variety of products used on farms including pesticides, fertilizers, and herbicides. As a rule of thumb, fertilizers are not a target of theft because of their bulk and relatively low cost. In contrast, pesticides and herbicides can be costly; even a small pickup truck's load can be worth thousands of dollars. Although the theft of agrichemicals is a multimillion-dollar-per-year problem nationally, the exact type of agrichemical taken varies by geographic region, depending on what the predominant crop is.

In general, manufacturers do not have a theft problem because they can maintain tight security. As the product moves from the manufacturer to the distributor to the dealer to the ultimate consumer, the farmer, the problem increases. Distributors in particular have been vulnerable to the hijacking of trucks carrying agrichemicals, with resulting losses of $200,000 or more per incident. Dealers typically have been victimized by burglaries. One crime prevention tactic that is recommended to farmers is buying agrichemicals only in quantities that can be immediately used. While some farmers have adopted this practice, many have found it to be impractical given the time, inconvenience, and cost of repeated trips to make purchases.

Because the theft of agrichemicals may take the form of any of several different criminally chargeable acts, it would be possible for investigators in different parts of the same agency to be working on various activities by the same ring without knowing it. For example, the hijacking of a truck might be worked on by robbery investigators, the burglary of a dealership by the property section or burglary investigators, while personnel assigned to the ranch and grove unit might be working on the theft of pesticides from a local farmer. Although one ring might not exhibit a wide range of criminally chargeable behaviors, they may be sufficiently different to cause the fragmentation of investigative information.

To be effective in the investigation of agrichemical thefts, the investigator must become familiar with the legal supply channels and the principal agrichemicals that are used in his or her region. In particular it is important to know that the same basic chemical or formulation may be sold by several different manufacturers under different product names. For example, atrazine is manufactured and sold by Ciba-Geigy as AAtrex; it is used as a corn herbicide. Imagine the difficulty created for an investigation if a victim reports the theft of "50 gallons of atrazine" and it is entered into police records that way, when the victim was using *atrazine* as a synonym for *AAtrex.* Another aspect of agrichemicals that requires a specialized knowledge is awareness of various security measures that have been taken by manufacturers, such as coded lot numbers and ultraviolet and chemical coding.

Finally, because of their precarious economic situation, some farmers will engage in the theft of agrichemicals or will readily purchase such commodities at "bargain prices." Because farmers are the end users of many agrichemicals, they know that a multigallon plastic jug of agrichemicals can be emptied in less than a minute, the jug readily and totally burned due to its high density, and the product immediately applied, making detection difficult. One method of identifying farmers who are possible illegal receivers of agrichemicals is to determine those whose purchasing patterns through legal supply channels are inconsistent with their crop needs.

LIVESTOCK AND TACK THEFT

It is sometimes difficult to comprehend that a society that can land people on the moon and safely return them still has a serious rustling problem. Yet rustling did not disappear with the closing of the American frontier in 1890. While new and often sophisticated methods of theft are now used, the object of attack—livestock—remains the same, as do the motivations: profit or food.

Cattle, horses, sheep, goats, hogs, mules, and jackasses are illustrative of species falling within the meaning of *livestock.* *Tack* refers to saddles, bridles, harnesses, and related equipment. Certain generalizations can be made with respect to livestock and tack thefts:

1. Most livestock thefts are committed by persons who have been or are currently employed in some aspect of a livestock business. One significant exception to this broad observation is that in economically hard times rural areas adjacent to urban centers experience more thefts in which the physical

evidence suggests that the motivation was food rather than profit. Such so-called freezer crimes typically involve only one or a few head of cattle, and when they are butchered at the scene, it is often in a manner that reflects only a crude understanding of the process.[22]

2. It is common for livestock to be stolen, transported, and disposed of before the theft is discovered. While the theft of horses may be discovered in a day to two weeks, theft of range cattle may go undetected for months.

3. Except for small roadside slaughters committed as freezer crimes, livestock is stolen to be sold for economic gain. The excellent interstate systems that cross the country lend themselves—like the famous trails of frontier days—to transporting the stolen livestock rapidly for sale in states other than the one in which the crime took place.

4. Because horse owners are typically very attached to their animals, such thefts are often very emotional situations.

5. Horse thieves also tend to be tack thieves; statistically, for every stolen horse there are approximately 20 cases of tack theft.

As awareness of the livestock theft problem develops, law enforcement agencies have created specialized investigative units or designated a particular individual as the agency's specialist in such matters.[23] Regardless of whether the investigator works out of a specialized unit or as the sole specialist, he or she must have or develop an expertise in the various aspects of livestock identification, including breeds, markings, blemishes, scars, marks, tattoos, and brands. In short, the investigator must be able to speak "livestock" in order to be effective.

The heaviest burden in livestock investigation often falls on the uniformed officer who takes the original offense report; this is true because such officers may have no knowledge, or only a rudimentary knowledge, of livestock and the applicable special laws.[24] One way in which police agencies can help compensate for this is to adopt forms similar to those depicted in Figures 19–1 and 19–2 and to provide training in their use. When such forms are not used, a good guide to follow is that an

Figure 19–1
Cattle Identification Form

LOS ANGELES COUNTY SHERIFF'S DEPARTMENT
CATTLE IDENTIFICATION FORM

Classification Lost ( ) Found ( ) Theft ( ) Other ( )

File No._____

Date & Time_____ Location_____

Victim ( )
Informant ( )

Suspect_____ Address City Phone

DBO_____ Sex____ Name Race_____ Address Age____ Hair City Eyes____ Ht.____ Phone Wt.____

Vehicle Year____ Make_____ Body_____ Color_____ Lic.____

Trailer Horse_____ Stock Rig_____ Make____ Color____ # Axles____ Gooseneck____

ON THE DRAWING INDICATE EAR MARKS, BLEMISHES, ODDITIES, DEFORMITIES, OR ANY INJURY THAT MAY BE USED TO IDENTIFY THIS ANIMAL. IF THE ANIMAL HAS DEWLAP OR WATTLE MARKINGS, SHOW TYPE AND LOCATION. ALSO HORNS CAN BE INDICATED.

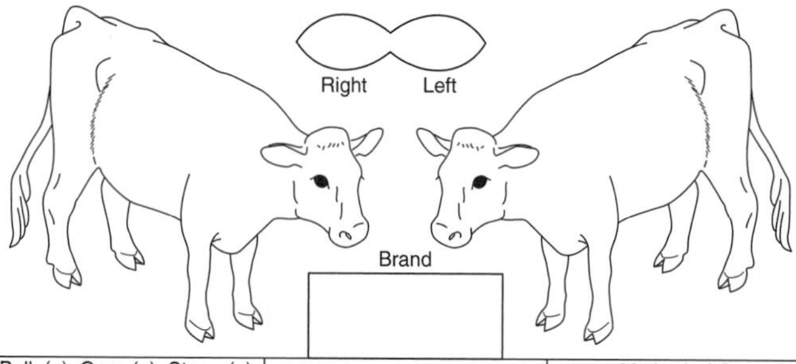

Right   Left

Brand

Sex Bull ( ) Cow ( ) Steer ( ) Calf ( ) Heifer ( )	Also indicate Location on Animal & any other Brands. Type of Brand.	Method of Operation Check all that apply
Breed	Hot Iron_____ ( )	Trailered ( ) Driven ( ).
Age____ Wt_____ Color	Chemical_____ ( )	Pasture ( ) Range ( )
Polled_____ Horned_____	Freeze_____ ( ) Hair Brand_____ ( )	Barn ( ) Dairy ( ) Corral ( ) Feed, Auction or Sale Yard ( )
Ear Tag ( ) No.____ Color	Horn Brand_____ ( )	Residential ( ) Other ( )

Field Slaughter
Items used   Gun ( ) Knife ( ) Axe ( ) Rope ( ) Hoist ( ) Chainsaw ( ) Other ( )

Carcass
Removed entire Carcass ( ) Hind Quarters ( ) Other ( )

Left at Scene   Feet ( ) Head ( ) Hide ( ) Waste ( ) Other ( )

To move Animal   used Horses ( ) On Foot ( ) Dogs ( ) Motorcycle ( ) Lead ( ) Other ( )

Remarks_____

Officer Reporting	Agency	Date

Source: Los Angeles County, California, Sheriff's Department.

animal is property and can be described like any other type of property, although the language may be unfamiliar to the investigator. In such situations, the frank acknowledgment of a lack of familiarity or expertise will elicit a more systematic and detailed description from the owner than would otherwise be obtained. Subsequent to the taking of the original offense report, the progress of an investigation often hinges on the mutual assistance, cooperation, and free exchange of information that is given by ranchers, feedlot operators, stock auctions, farm-

ers, sale yards, slaughterhouses, livestock associations, and other public agencies.

CATTLE RUSTLING

The majority of these thefts are committed by one or two people who take the animal for their own use (see Figure 19–3).[25] The usual method of operation is to drive to an isolated area, locate an animal, shoot it, and either butcher it there or load the carcass in a vehicle and butcher it at home.

**Figure 19–2
Horse Identification Form**

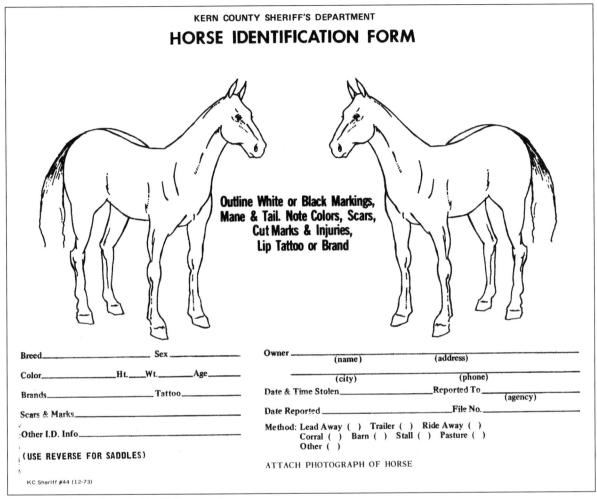

KERN COUNTY SHERIFF'S DEPARTMENT

HORSE IDENTIFICATION FORM

Outline White or Black Markings,
Mane & Tail. Note Colors, Scars,
Cut Marks & Injuries,
Lip Tattoo or Brand

Breed_____ Sex _____

Color_____Ht.____Wt._____Age_____

Brands_____ Tattoo_____

Scars & Marks_____

Other I.D. Info_____

(USE REVERSE FOR SADDLES)

KC Sheriff #44 (12-73)

Owner _____
　　　　　　　　(name)　　　　　　　　(address)
　　　_____
　　　　　　　　(city)　　　　　　　　(phone)
Date & Time Stolen_____Reported To _____
　　　　　　　　　　　　　　　　　　　　(agency)
Date Reported _____File No. _____
Method: Lead Away ( ) Trailer ( ) Ride Away ( )
　　　　Corral ( ) Barn ( ) Stall ( ) Pasture ( )
　　　　Other ( )

ATTACH PHOTOGRAPH OF HORSE

(Courtesy Kern County, California, Sheriff's Department)

Butchering the animal at the scene means the thieves must spend more time there, but it avoids the problem of having to dispose of unused remains later. At times the thieves will shoot the animal and then drive to a place where they can watch to see if anyone comes to investigate. If not, they then butcher the animal. As these incidents often occur at night, they can see the headlights of approaching vehicles for some distance, giving them ample time to depart from the area. Freezer-crime rustlers are difficult to apprehend because they must be caught in the act or while they are transporting the carcass or meat. Surveillances that work well in urban areas are usually dif-

ficult to execute in rural areas. Their success depends on:

- The topography of the area.
- The availability of cover for concealment.
- The number and position of access roads.
- The size of the area containing the cattle.

One proven method for successful surveillances is for investigators to choose the area of the theft themselves.[26] This is accomplished by picking an area that maximizes the considerations important to investigators and then having the rancher move the cattle into this area. The rancher must not allow employees or other persons to learn that an

Figure 19–3
Cattle Theft in Process

(Courtesy Southwestern Cattle Raisers' Association)

operation is being set up. If others are involved in moving the cattle to the area selected, they should be given some reason for the change of pasture, such as a tally, brand check, or veterinary inspection.

Vehicles coming out of isolated areas should routinely be visually inspected for signs of blood on the rear bumper or trunk areas.[27] Because rustlers are invariably armed with some type of firearm, extreme caution must be used when approaching suspicious vehicles. Panicky suspects, who might not otherwise think of assaulting a peace officer, may do so impulsively. In addition to firearms, this type of rustler will also often be carrying butcher knives and ropes.

In contrast to the modest equipment usually employed by the freezer thief, professional rustlers use more sophisticated means to commit their crimes, such as light planes or helicopters to spot vulnerable herds and watch for patrolling officers. The thieves coordinate their movements with walkie-talkies, and "dirt-bike cowboys" herd the cattle to where they will be killed and butchered, often by the use of chain saws. Refrigerated trucks with meat-processing equipment inside quickly transform the rough butchered cattle into salable products.[28] Professionals may also have a full array of forged documents, such as a forged bill of sale, and counterfeit U.S. Department of Agriculture inspection stamps. The professional rustling operation can be very profitable. Thirty head of cattle can be taken from the range, loaded onto a truck, and butchered in the truck; the waste dumped off the road, and the 60 sides of beef illegally stamped and delivered to the city at approximately $350 per side—a profit of $21,000 for a night's work.[29]

As a general matter, peace officers have a right to stop any conveyance transporting livestock on any public thoroughfare and the right to impound any animal, carcass, hide, or portion of a carcass in the possession of any person who they have reasonable cause to believe is not the legal owner or entitled to possession.[30] To transport cattle legally, certain written documents may be required, such as:

- Bill of sale
- Certificate of consignment
- Brand inspector's certificate
- Shipping or transportation permit[31]

Because these provisions vary by state, it is essential that every investigator know:

- What documentation is required for lawful transportation.
- What the investigator's precise authority is in such matters.
- How to handle violations of law.[32]

Equipped with such knowledge, the investigator is better prepared to deal with issues related to transportation violation or a possible theft. Although the applicable state law may permit the officer to impound livestock or meat, there are several less drastic alternatives short of it. Under unusual conditions or where only slight suspicion exists, investigators may elect to get a full description and identifying information of the driver and the rig and its contents. Other information essential for a useful follow-up inquiry is the origin and destination of the trip. Where suspicion is more pronounced, specialists may be requested to come to the scene of the stop. Such specialists may come from the investigator's own agency, another local department, the state police or state investigative agency, or the Marks and Brands Unit of the state's department of agriculture. If the investigator is sufficiently confident that a shipping violation or theft exists, the arrest can be made and

the load impounded. Live animals can be delivered to the nearest feedlot or sales yard and meat can be placed in refrigeration storage. Such situations require that officers in the field have a basic working knowledge of the applicable laws and exercise sound judgment. They are not required to be experts in such matters, and their general investigative experience is a substantial asset in making an evaluation of the situation.

HORSE RUSTLING

More than 50,000 horses are stolen each year[33] as compared to about 20,000 cattle.[34] About 60 percent of the stolen horses will end up in slaughter plants, where they will be processed and sold as meat for human consumption in Europe and Japan.[35] America is the world's leading exporter of horsemeat—which abroad commands a greater price than filet mignon.[36] Many of the slaughtered horses are bought at auction and are lame, unwanted, or just worn out. "Killer buyers" get them for a few hundred dollars a head and take them to the plants. Because some horse rustlers are not knowledgeable judges of livestock, a few very expensive horses end up being slaughtered too. In a Texas case, two unemployed men and a woman decided to "go into the rustling business." They loaded three horses worth $100,000 in a trailer and sold them to a buyer who promptly had them slaughtered.

There is not a great deal of variation in the way in which horse rustlers operate. If the horse is in a corral, the thief will park a vehicle and trailer nearby, walk up and take the horse, load it in the trailer, and drive off.[37] As most of these thefts occur during the hours of darkness, the rustler can be several hundred miles away before the theft is discovered. When horses are in pasture, the task of stealing them is only slightly more difficult. The thief walks into the pasture with a bucket of grain. One or more of the horses will usually approach him, and because they are herd animals, if one approaches, the others are also likely to follow along. The theft then proceeds in the same fashion as a corral theft. One tactic commonly used by horse rustlers is to knock down the corral or pasture fence after loading up the trailer with horses and chase any remaining horses down the road. The owner will think that the horses have gotten out on their own, and it may be several days before he or she realizes some horses have been stolen. Thus, even if there is not clear evidence of a theft, the investigator should not assume that the horse has strayed off. As a minimum action, a lost report should be initiated. If the horse is later discovered to have been stolen, the incident can be reclassified.

TACK THEFT

Simply stated, *tack* is equipment that is used with horses; the most common items are saddles, bridles, and horse blankets.[38] Of all stolen tack, approximately 80 percent is saddles—which often have base prices in excess of $2,000—and it is generally believed that 85 to 90 percent of all tack is unmarked for identification, making tracing a very difficult proposition. In order to help reduce tack thefts, particularly saddles, and to improve the low recovery rate, property-marking programs have been undertaken and specialized reporting forms, as depicted in Figure 19–4, adopted. These have been favorable developments, but tack theft remains a serious problem for several reasons: many owners prefer not to mark their equipment, feeling that even if the numbers are hidden, the tack, particularly saddles, is disfigured; owners think that the numbers can be altered or removed entirely from the tack with ease; and there is a ready market for the sale of tack, which is sufficiently diffuse to make detection a limited possibility in many situations. Some owners are now having microchips embedded in saddles to facilitate their recovery if stolen.[39]

LIVESTOCK IDENTIFICATION

In any livestock theft case one key to a successful prosecution is the positive identification of a specific animal as belonging to a particular owner. It

Figure 19–4
Saddle Identification Form

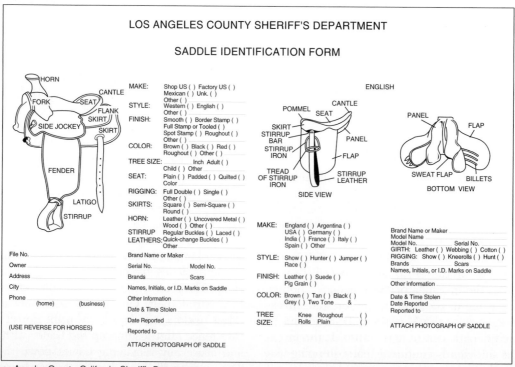

Source: Los Angeles County, California, Sheriff's Department.

is therefore essential that investigators have a basic knowledge of methods used to identify livestock. Among these methods of identification are brands, ear marks, tattoos, and freeze marking.[40]

BRANDS

There are a very large number of brands; just in Utah alone there are 26,000 different ones, some of which date back to 1847.[41] A brand is a mark that is permanently impressed on the hide of an animal by using a hot iron or chemicals. Brands may be located in several different places, as suggested by the following designations:

RS	right shoulder
LS	left shoulder
RR	right rib
LR	left rib
RH	right hip
LH	left hip

Brands are combinations of letters, numbers, and symbols that are read in one of three different ways: left to right (2—X denotes the Two Bar X); top to bottom (Two Bar X may also appear as $\underline{2}$); and outside to inside (Ⓐ is read as the Circle A).
$\overline{X}$

For various types of communication, an understanding of how brand locations and brands are combined is critical; thus, if the investigator receives a teletype about stolen cattle and a portion of that teletype reads " $\overline{M}$ RH," it can be understood they are branded Bar M on the right hip. The most commonly used brand terms and characters are shown in Figure 19–5. Horse owners resist the idea of branding their animals because they fear that it will hurt and disfigure them. Their acceptance of branding their horses is roughly comparable to that of urban persons who have been advised to brand their dogs for identification purposes.

EAR MARKS

Ear marks are used in conjunction with the brand for identification and are rarely used on horses. Commonly used earmark patterns are shown in Figure 19–6; when read or designated in writing, the correct method is to designate them from the animal's viewpoint. Therefore, as the investigator faces the animal, the right ear will be to the inves-

tigator's left. An example of how brands and ear marks may be combined for identification purposes is " $\overline{M}$ RH R-crop L-split."

TATTOOS

Tattoos have been in use for years at race tracks, and more recently they have found increasing popularity among other owners. The tattoo is placed on the inside of the horse's upper lip with a marking device that resembles a pair of wide-mouth pliers. The numbers or letters are a series of needles along one part of the plier-type device that is dipped into indelible ink. The upper lip is then squeezed in the "pliers," causing the needles to penetrate the lip and cause the tattoo.

FREEZE MARKING

Freeze marking is often used with horses because it does not hurt the animal or mark the hide. A mixture of dry ice and alcohol is placed into a Styrofoam container, and a device similar to a branding iron is placed in the solution until it is sufficiently cold. It is then applied to the area to be marked, often the neck, which must be shaved in preparation. An application of approximately 26 seconds causes the extreme cold to kill the color-producing cells in the treated area. When the hair regrows, the desired mark will appear in white.

Each of the methods of marking livestock for identification has certain disadvantages. Brands can be altered, ear marks are disfiguring, tattoos cannot be applied to horses until after they are two years old because growth can distort them if applied prior to that age, and freeze markings may be too apparent for some owners. Investigators should be somewhat cautious when asked which method of identification they recommend; as a general matter it would be a sound practice to summarize what the applicable requirements provided for by state law are and then note that the owner should determine what practices, beyond those officially sanctioned, best meet his or her needs.

PHYSICAL EVIDENCE

The processing of a crime scene where an agricultural-related theft has occurred is in many respects

Figure 19–5
Commonly Employed Brand Characters

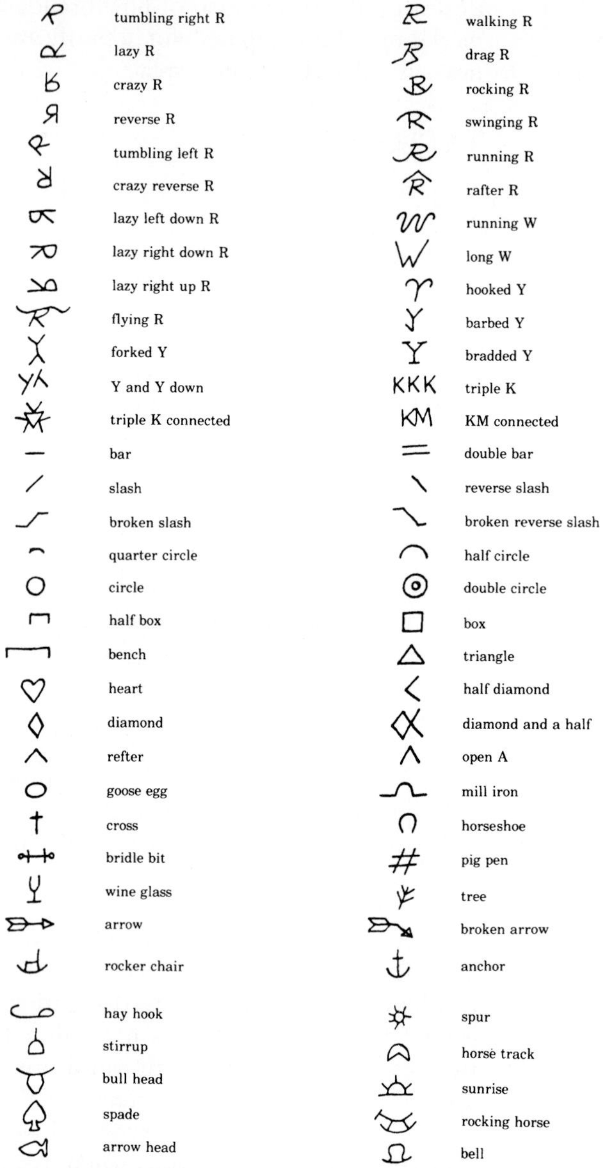

ℛ	tumbling right R	ℛ	walking R
α	lazy R	ℛ	drag R
ƅ	crazy R	ℬ	rocking R
я	reverse R	ℛ	swinging R
ᴚ	tumbling left R	ℛ	running R
ᴚ	crazy reverse R	ℛ	rafter R
ᴚ	lazy left down R	𝓦	running W
𝓡	lazy right down R	𝒲	long W
ᴚ	lazy right up R	𝒴	hooked Y
ᴚ	flying R	Y	barbed Y
Y	forked Y	Y	bradded Y
Y⅄	Y and Y down	KKK	triple K
✻	triple K connected	KM	KM connected
—	bar	=	double bar
/	slash	\	reverse slash
⌐	broken slash	⌐	broken reverse slash
⌒	quarter circle	⌒	half circle
○	circle	⊙	double circle
⊓	half box	□	box
⌐┐	bench	△	triangle
♡	heart	<	half diamond
◊	diamond	⋈	diamond and a half
∧	refter	∧	open A
○	goose egg	⌣	mill iron
†	cross	∩	horseshoe
⊷	bridle bit	#	pig pen
Y	wine glass	ᴪ	tree
⊐⟩	arrow	⟼	broken arrow
⊣	rocker chair	⚓	anchor
⌣	hay hook	✳	spur
◇	stirrup	⌒	horse track
∀	bull head	⌣	sunrise
♠	spade	⌣	rocking horse
⌣	arrow head	Ω	bell

(Courtesy Los Angeles County, California, Sheriff's Department)

no different from the processing of any other crime scene. For example, when cattle rustling occurs, the perpetrators frequently cut the barbed wire or locks securing a grazing area. The cut wire and lock will have tool marks left on them from the cutting tool. In addition, if the suspect's clothing came into contact with any of the barbed wire at the scene, pieces of fiber may be found adhering to the barbs. Shoe or tire impressions found at the crime scene may later be linked to a specific suspect and vehi-cle. Soil samples collected at the crime scene may also prove to be valuable, linking evidence to a suspect with similar soil on his or her shoes or clothes, or on the vehicle used to transport the cattle. There is increasing movement toward the use of DNA evidence in livestock theft cases. The types of evidence discussed in Chapter 4, Physical Evidence, can often be readily found and will be of great value to law enforcement officers in the investigation of agricultural crimes.

Figure 19–6
Basic Ear Mark Patterns

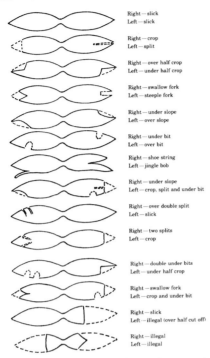

Right—slick
Left—slick

Right—crop
Left—split

Right—over half crop
Left—under half crop

Right—swallow fork
Left—steeple fork

Right—under slope
Left—over slope

Right—under bit
Left—over bit

Right—shoe string
Left—jingle bob

Right—under slope
Left—crop, split and under bit

Right—over double split
Left—slick

Right—two splits
Left—crop

Right—double under bits
Left—under half crop

Right—swallow fork
Left—crop and under bit

Right—slick
Left—illegal (over half cut off)

Right—illegal
Left—illegal

(Courtesy Los Angeles County, California, Sheriff's Department)

When their livestock has been stolen, farmers and ranchers will often move equipment into the area of a theft and make immediate repairs to corrals, fences, outbuildings, or as otherwise needed. The predictable and unfortunate result is that physical evidence is either hopelessly contaminated or lost altogether. This contributes to a recovery rate for stolen livestock of only 20 percent.

CRIME PREVENTION MEASURES

Information about how to prevent rural and agricultural crimes can be obtained from a variety of sources, including sheriff's departments, county police, state investigative agencies, state departments of agriculture, county extension agents, and various associations. Although some techniques developed in urban areas can be readily applied to the farm, others would create costs disproportionate to the benefits that could reasonably be expected to accrue to the farmer. Consequently, the technology in this area is sometimes familiar, sometimes takes advantage of unique aspects of the rural environment, and is continuously in the process of changing and developing. The suggestions that follow are organized around the object of attack; in general they are specialized and can be supplemented as may be appropriate by more conventional strategies, such as the use of case-hardened padlocks.

Farm Equipment Theft

- Participate in equipment identification programs.

- Do not leave unattended equipment in remote fields for hours at a time or overnight; if it is necessary to do so for some reason, disable the engine by taking a vital part and use logging chains to secure other equipment. Even if such precautions are taken, equipment in remote areas should be hidden from view from roadways.

- Equipment is best protected, in reducing order of preference, by positioning it as follows: secured in a locked building near the main house or an inhabited house; secured in a gated area that is kept locked and is close to the main or an inhabited house; secured in one or more ways and not visible from commonly traveled roads.

- Immediately report all suspicious activity, such as strangers taking photographs of equipment, to local enforcement officials.

Timber Theft

- Post the property.
- Check periodically to determine if any timber has been cut.
- Promptly report all losses.

Agrichemical Theft

- End users, whenever feasible, should buy only in quantities that they can readily use.
- If quantity purchases cannot be avoided, they should be stored in a locked, lighted building very close to the main house or an inhabited house; if available, place a few geese or guinea hens inside as watch animals.

- Rural dealers should employ security personnel during the months when they have large inventories.
- Be suspicious of people offering unusually good buys on agrichemicals; the absence of a market helps deter thefts.

Livestock and Tack Theft

- All livestock should be marked for identification; maximum deterrence is obtained when marks are readily visible.[42]
- A daily tally or count should be taken.
- Do not follow a set routine, such as going to the movies every Friday night, which would give a thief an advantage.
- Enter into cooperative arrangements with trusted neighbors to help watch one another's places.
- Avoid leaving animals in remote pastures or on faraway ranges whenever practical.
- Mark tack and keep it in a room that lends itself to security measures.
- Do not use "set guns" or "booby traps"; they are often illegal, frequently injure innocent people or animals, and surviving thieves have won damage suits because of the injuries that resulted.

Investigators interested in obtaining more detailed information can contact any of the sources mentioned earlier if their departments do not have active prevention programs. These sources are typically generous with the materials they send and often will give permission for them to be reproduced for use with the public.

WILDLIFE CRIMES

The transition from the topic of agricultural crimes to wildlife crimes is a natural one because of some overlaps. For example, in many states wildlife officers may be called on to assist local police officers in cases of livestock theft or slaughter because the basic physical evidence closely resembles the types of evidence that wildlife officers process in poaching cases. Within the respective states, the responsibility for enforcing game and fish laws is primarily that of a state-level agency.

Wildlife officers require much of the knowledge used by other peace officers because they operate under the same laws pertaining to arrest, search and seizure, and interrogation. They must also be able to recognize, collect, mark, and preserve many of the same types of physical evidence. Illustratively, hairs collected from the beds of pickup trucks or trunks of cars can be used to determine the species involved in suspected incidents of poaching. In addition, wildlife officers must also master the specialized laws, knowledge, and investigative techniques that apply to game and fish violations. For example, they must be able to determine the sex of game birds and the sex and age of mammals. Patrolling alone, often in remote areas, requires wildlife officers to exercise good judgment and appropriate caution. Beyond encountering those who may have violated game and fish laws, wildlife officers find evidence of conventional crimes such as murder, observe major narcotics violations, and meet heavily armed extremist paramilitary groups conducting training exercises.

MAJOR THREATS TO WILDLIFE

There are a number of major threats to our wildlife. As urban areas continue their sprawl outward from the core city, more construction occurs, destroying habitats. The accidental release of chemicals, illegal dumping, land erosion, and oil spills produce the same effect. The illegal taking or possession of game, fish, and other wildlife—*poaching*—is the major threat that the next portion of this chapter addresses.

Poaching reduces the amount of wildlife that would otherwise be available. It makes "camera safaris" less meaningful, has the potential to reduce tourism, hampers the reestablishment of game species, and constitutes a significant threat to endangered species. Although the actual cost of poaching is not known, it is very substantial. Worldwide, there may be as much as a $10 billion market[43] for trafficking in animal parts, with as much as 40 percent of it based on poaching.[44]

POACHERS AND POACHING

Poachers can be categorized into two types: situational poachers and professional poachers.

The largest number of poachers are *situational*, some being motivated by opportunity and others by circumstances. A normally law-abiding man or woman is driving home at night and suddenly sees an elk on the road frozen by the car's headlights. Impulsively, or after a quick deliberation, the person shoots the elk out of season, becoming a situational poacher. Others become situational poachers to feed their families because of economic circumstances. A few opportunistic poachers kill simply for the thrill of it.

Although fewer in numbers, *professional poachers* take much more game than do situational poachers because the more they take, the more they profit. Thus, while a situational poacher may take an elk or deer now and then, the professional will kill a half dozen or more in a single evening. It is estimated that for every incident in which a poacher is caught, there are another 30 to 50 incidents that go undetected or for which there will be no arrest made.[45]

Some trophy hunters pay to be taken into areas closed to hunters, to hunt out of season, or to have their guides use illegal hunting methods to ensure their success. One Alaskan admitted that every one of the 37 grizzlies that he had helped hunters bag— each of which was placed in the Boone and Crockett Club's record book—was illegally herded toward the hunters by use of an airplane.[46] Other "hunters" do not inconvenience themselves with actually going into the field; they just want the trophy to hang on the wall. They buy ready-to-mount bighorn sheep for $20,000[47] and grizzlies for $25,000.[48]

Poachers also shoot polar bears for the $4,000[49] they can get for the skin and the additional $2,000 or more for the gall bladder, valued by Asians for medical and aphrodisiac uses. About 65 days after they begin growing new antlers, elk and similar animals have the maximum amount of velvet on them; this velvet is a covering of blood vessels that nourish the antlers. Also believed to have medical and aphrodisiac qualities, this velvet sells for $85 to $135 per pound. A mature elk may have produced as much as 35 pounds of velvet, and even the velvet from small deer can bring $1,000. The market for velvet has resulted in legal elk farms to supply it, but it has also increased the incentive to illegally trap elk for breeding purposes in order to avoid paying the $4,000 to $16,000 or more for a legally raised elk (see Figure 19–7).

INVESTIGATIONS

Wildlife officers generally spend only about 20 percent of their time in law enforcement activities. The balance is spent in such activities as teaching hunting, boating, and snowmobile safety courses for the public, staffing exhibits at state and local fairs or other functions, participating in multiagency mock-disaster drills as part of emergency preparedness training, conducting various surveys for state and federal government, including counts of raccoon, deer, and midwinter waterfowl, as well as other censuses conducted on a one-time-only basis. When conducting law enforcement activities, wildlife officers use many of the same investigative techniques used by other types of peace officers.

Information
Information is an essential commodity in combating poachers. With it, more investigative successes are experienced. In some states, 80 percent of all poacher arrests come from leads from citizens. To assist wildlife officers in getting information, a number of states have established special programs. In some states, these efforts are referred to as Citizens Against Poachers (CAP) programs and in other states as Turn in a Poacher (TIP) programs.

Uniformed Patrol
Uniformed wildlife officers patrol in boats and cars to see if game is being taken out of season or by illegal means. They visit various sites to observe, to check licenses, and to examine each sportsman's daily take. As a supplement to patrolling by car, airplanes can be used during the day to locate hunters, trappers, and camps in remote areas. At night, aircraft can also be useful in pinpointing places where it appears artificial light is being used by poachers to take game, a tactic known as "jacklighting." In both day and night uses of aircraft, the pilot/spotter will relay information to ground units so they can take appropriate action. In some instances aircraft keep poachers leaving an area under surveillance and direct wildlife officers in cars on a course to intercept the poachers.

Intensive Hunting Patrols
Wildlife officers also employ intensive hunting patrols, especially during the opening weekends for various types of game such as pheasant, wild turkey, waterfowl, grouse, and deer. Intensive patrols tend

Figure 19–7
Poached Elk
Three elk in velvet, which were poached out of season near Wheatland, Wyoming.

(Courtesy Wyoming Game and Fish Department)

to be concentrated in areas of high public use, especially those with a history of excessive violations.

Vehicle Check Stops

Vehicle check stops are strategically set up on carefully selected roads to check vehicles for bag limits, unplugged shotguns, and licenses and to determine whether necessary special stamps (for ducks, for example) have been acquired (see Figure 19–8).

Fishing Patrols

Fishing patrols check for licenses among sportspersons in the field, for their compliance with keeping only fish that meet or exceed the minimal length, and their keeping only the daily allowed limit. Fishing patrols also check for illegal commercial fishing devices such as basket traps, trotlines, and seines. Computerized sonar is used to locate illegally set fish nets that take protected sport fish (see Figure 19–9).

Resident License Verifications

In a common wildlife violation, nonresidents of a state claim residency so that they can be issued less expensive hunting or fishing licenses. Periodically, wildlife officers go through copies of licenses to determine whether a purchaser may in fact have been a nonresident. The wildlife officer has many avenues to pursue in determining the actual legal residence of the license purchaser. Local utility companies are contacted for information concerning service by the individual, telephone books are checked, and driver's license records are examined, as are voter registration files. Once the information indicates that the purchase is not by a resident of a state, the wildlife officer contacts the individual to attempt a personal interview. Once confronted, the subjects will often make an admission.

Figure 19–8
Vehicle Check Stop
Wardens conducting an inspection at a vehicle check stop.

(Courtesy Tom Carbone, Maine Department of Inland Fisheries and Wildlife)

Covert Investigations

Covert investigations vary in their complexity. At the simplest, a wildlife officer who could not approach an area without being plainly visible for some distance may dress as a trout fisher and work his way along a stream watching for violations.

ENVIRONMENTAL CRIME

This planet—which we will pass on to our children—suffers from what the inhabitants do to it. Rain forests are being chopped down for their timber. The entry of raw (untreated) sewage into water systems threatens fish populations. Worldwide, smokestack industries pour carbon dioxide into the air, polluting it and further exacerbating our efforts to combat the greenhouse effect and its rising temperatures. Nuclear accidents render portions of countries uninhabitable. Swamps and marshes are disappearing at an alarming rate, along with their rich ecosystems. While not all of these events constitute environmental crimes, they do suggest our planet is in some distress. Therefore, it is incumbent on us to do what we can professionally: know, investigate, and enforce environmental laws.

Figure 19–9
Checking for Illegal Nets
Oregon State Police game officer using night-vision goggles to check for illegal nets on the Columbia River.

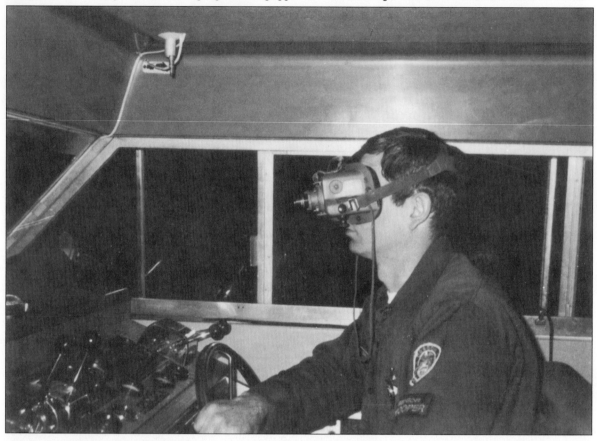

THE LEGAL AND ENFORCEMENT FRAMEWORK

There are roughly 15 federal and numerous parallel state laws with which environmental investigators must be familiar—these laws cover clean air, oil pollutants, pollution prevention, safe drinking water, toxic substances control, clean water, and endangered species. Additionally, some cities and countries are very aggressive in combating environmental crime and have enacted their own laws. From this maze of laws, three enforcement patterns emerge:

1. Only the federal government has jurisdiction.
2. There is concurrent federal and state jurisdiction.
3. There is only state or local jurisdiction.

Formerly, environmental crimes were punishable only by civil fines; the more recent trend in dealing with such crimes is the use of criminal fines for both individuals and businesses. Other sanctions that may also apply are losing the right to sell services and goods to the government, becoming ineligible for government grants, and having licenses and permits revoked.

Many state laws are substantially similar to the federal Resource Conservation and Recovery Act (RCRA) of 1976 and regulate handling of hazardous waste. *Hazardous waste* is solid waste or a combination of solid wastes (such as garbage, refuse, sludge, and other discarded material in a solid, liquid, semisolid, or gaseous state) that—because of its quantity, concentration, or physical, chemical, or infectious characteristics—may produce serious or incapacitating irreversible illness or pose a substantial or present threat to human life or the environment when improperly stored, treated, transported, or disposed of or when otherwise improperly managed. Hazardous waste may have any of the following characteristics: ignitability, corrosivity, reactivity, and toxicity. Most state RCRA laws have the following provisions:

1. An identification and listing of hazardous wastes. Typically, state laws give themselves some flexibility by noting that hazardous wastes include, but are not limited to, those that they specifically identify.
2. The establishment of permit and license systems regarding various types of hazardous waste, including their T/S/D.
3. A manifest or shipping-paper system that tracks hazardous waste from its cradle to its grave.
4. The identification of responsibilities of the generators and transporters of hazardous waste.
5. Requirements for hazardous-waste management facilities, such as proof of financial reliability.
6. Compliance evaluation programs that grant warrant-free access or right of entry to inspectors.
7. Designation of enforcement authority and criminal penalties.

Hazardous-waste crime charges typically involve charges against one or more individuals and/or corporations involved in any combination of the three major components of the waste cycle:

• *Generating*: Among the companies engaging in activities that involve hazardous waste are chemical companies, which produce it as a by-product of their legal activity; furniture and wood manufacturing companies working with various solvents and ignitable waste, which must periodically be disposed of; and vehicle maintenance operations, which involve lead-acid batteries, solvents, and heavy metal and inorganic wastes.

• *Transporation*: This component involves the hauling away of hazardous waste from industrial sites. False manifests may be prepared to make the loads look less harmful, thereby allowing for inexpensive disposal of the waste. Tankers in poor condition may leak hazardous waste as they are driven along

highways, and illegal disposal of hazardous waste also occurs when tankers deliberately discharge the waste in small amounts onto the road.

• *Treatment, storage, and disposal:* T/S/D crimes are committed by companies that treat hazardous waste without a permit or treat it inadequately, store it without a permit to do so, improperly identify the nature of the waste or store it under inadequate conditions (see Figure 19–10), discharge it into sewers, simply abandon it, mix it with regular waste for cheaper disposal, and store incompatible chemicals or amounts of chemicals beyond their permitted level.

The most frequent violators of hazardous-waste regulations and laws are the small to midsize generating firms. Companies in this group violate hazardous-waste laws to maintain their profitability by avoiding the cost of legal disposal. However, large companies or their employees who have violated

Figure 19–10
Storage of Hazardous Waste under Inadequate Conditions
Properly identified hazardous waste stored in a deteriorated drum.

(Courtesy Environmental Protection Agency)

state RCRAs or various federal environmental laws include such well known businesses as Texaco, Ocean Spray Cranberries, Fleischmann's, Ashland Oil, B.F. Goodrich, and Kaiser Steel.

Investigators must be alert to the fact that traditional crimes are also involved in acts that constitute environmental crimes. Examples of these include falsification of records and forgery—typically involving manifests and T/S/D records and bribery of public officials, such as regulation inspectors and landfill operators, who accept money to certify that the hazardous waste was properly disposed of when it actually ends up being illegally dumped or abandoned somewhere else.

INVESTIGATIVE METHODS

Initiation of Complaints

Investigators should proactively look for signs which suggest that illegal dumping of hazardous waste is occurring, including:

1. Dead vegetation along creeks, rivers, and channels that flow through manufacturing, chemical, or other businesses.
2. Reports of large fish kills.
3. Abnormally discolored water.
4. Unusual truck activity at odd hours and locations, such as abandoned buildings (see Figure 19–11).
5. New reports of persistent chemical odors.
6. Tankers discharging their contents into ravines, water systems, or alongside roads.
7. Secretive activity, including bulldozers operating at night.
8. Smells that burn the eyes, nose, mouth, or skin.[50]

Officers investigating potential environmental crime sites must exercise caution and should review their training in this area periodically. If approaching a potential hazardous-waste spill, officers should stay upwind and uphill; use binoculars to check the scene; isolate the area; and relay information quickly and accurately.[51]

Despite the need to be proactive, the fact is that most investigations are reactive and based on information from a current or former employee of a business committing environmental law violations. Information may also be provided by residents

neighboring the business, who complain of odors or report things that they have seen, such as large numbers of rusting barrels in a field. Less frequently, residents or visitors to more remote areas will observe illegal hazardous-waste dumping activity or its results. On a few occasions, a legitimate competitor will come forward with information.[52]

Other ways in which investigative leads are developed are from incidents reported by news media, such as the washing ashore of syringes, scalpels, and other medical waste on public beaches; from published work by investigative reporters; from firefighters who have to respond to fires generated by improperly stored chemicals or discover it in the course of conducting fire prevention surveys; from union officials concerned with worker safety; and from other people.[53] Given that both federal and state RCRAs allow regulatory inspections without warrants to check compliance with laws, it is natural to expect that inspectors would provide a great deal of information. Although generally this does happen, there are situations in which their information may not be reliable. Inspectors may be under orders to ignore all but the most severe violations; occasionally an inspector will be "on the take"; inspectors may be inadequately trained or inexperienced; they may simply rely on assurances by management, as opposed to thoroughly checking; they may be allotted insufficient time to conduct proper inspections; or they may fear the economic consequences to the community, friends, or relatives if a plant is shut down.

Investigative Considerations

On receipt of a possible hazardous-waste violation complaint, investigators should ask the following questions:

- How reliable is the complaint?
- Is there an immediate and substantial danger to health, human life, and the environment?
- Are there public records—such as those recording real estate transactions, identifying corporate officers, and vehicle registrations—that would provide investigative leads?
- Who in the particular business would know the most but be the least involved (e.g., secretaries who can confirm office visits and business

Figure 19–11
Improper Disposal of Hazardous Waste
Hazardous waste that was "disposed" of by being hidden under a warehouse floor.

(Courtesy Environmental Protection Agency)

relationships and would have seen and typed correspondence, manifests, and bills)?

- Who are the ultimate investigative targets?
- What are the expected charges that will grow out of this investigation and the elements for proof for each of them?
- What amount of time and resources will be required?
- What is the best way to initiate the investigation (e.g., documenting sites by aerial photography or physical surveillance of T/S/D sites)?
- What investigative obstacles are anticipated?
- What legal obstacles may arise (e.g., proving the substance involved falls within the legal definition of "hazardous waste")?[54]

Investigative Practices

The types of investigative practices used will depend on the nature and complexity of the practices alleged to constitute a hazardous waste crime. Illegal dumping often—but not exclusively—occurs at night. If the disposal site is not known, the hauler must be kept under surveillance. However, if the site to which the hauler is going is known already, it is kept under surveillance by investigators equipped with appropriate photography equipment for taking pictures at night, as discussed in Chapter 7, Follow-Up Investigation. Other types of surveillance that may be used to establish probable cause for search and/or arrest warrants include electronic and aerial photography. Of particular use to investigators is the EPA's ability to provide aerial photographs taken over a period of time as well as taken on demand.[55]

Generators are allowed to store hazardous waste on site for 90 days in order to avoid the cost of moving many small loads. After 90 days, however, generators are considered a storage facility and must meet additional standards, including having the appropriate permit. Aerial photographs can be used to establish that a generator that has no permit for storage is exceeding the 90-day storage limitation. They can also be used when looking for specific things, such as drums floating in a river, illegal dump sites, or evidence of midnight dumping along a railroad track (see Figure 19–12). When wider-area aerial photographs are necessary, the EPA works with other federal agencies to procure them. When the EPA inventoried Pennsylvania for potential hazardous-waste violations, aerial photographs covering the entire state kept analysts busy for a year.

When a complaint is sufficiently corroborated to justify applying for a search warrant, considerable thought must be put into the affidavit that supports the warrant and how it will be executed. This point of the investigative process further reveals the most fundamental aspect of hazardous-waste investigations: a number of technical noninvestigative skills are required of the investigative team. If the search is to be conducted outdoors, then a topographical map—which provides details about the surface terrain of the area to be searched—must be prepared. Specific authority must be obtained to drill for samples, to excavate trenches (see Figure 19–13), to dismantle plumbing and machinery, and to perform similar functions in order to locate and seize

Figure 19-12
Aerial Photograph

Aerial photograph of a New Hampshire business that cleaned out used toxic-waste barrels and recycled them, and crushed and disposed of drums that were unsalvageable. In the cleaning process, chemicals were washed into local groundwater and recreational lakes nearby, creating serious pollution problems. This photograph was important in refuting the defendant's claim in a sworn deposition that, as of a certain date, there were only 300 to 400 barrels on site. Analysts counted more than 3,000 barrels.

(Courtesy Environmental Protection Agency)

evidence. Trained operators and special equipment such as backhoes may be needed to support the search. It may be necessary to perform hydrological studies to demonstrate that toxic waste has moved from a particular location into waterways. The appropriate protective clothing and evidence containers must be gathered together to support the operation. To scientifically monitor conditions, the investigative team must include a safety officer, who may require the searching team to move from the initial level of protective clothing to more ex-

tensive measures, including the so-called moon suit with its own respiratory system. These same principles apply when all or a portion of the search is conducted inside of buildings. Whether the search is conducted indoors or outside, in many instances an engineer must also be consulted as to the specific machinery, equipment, and areas—pipelines, sewers, drums, holding ponds, tanks, and so on— most likely to provide evidence, to suggest proper sampling procedures, and to identify the anticipated level of safety risk to the search team. Regu-

Figure 19–13
Trench Excavation
Excavation of a trench to locate hazardous-waste tanks that were illegally buried.

(Courtesy Environmental Protection Agency)

latory inspectors can often be particularly helpful to the phase of the investigation leading to the search by identifying insiders who will provide detailed information. Safety lines around certain hazardous-waste sites (HWSs) must also be planned (see Figure 19–14), and decontamination areas and procedures must be specified. Other factors that may affect logistical planning for the search include the size of the facility and the weather.

When entering the facility to be searched, many environmental investigative teams prefer not to display weapons unless they may be immediately needed. The searching team must determine whether to allow the facility to operate or to suspend operations during the search. The termination of operations may be necessary for search team safety, but continued operation may also be required for a successful execution of the warrant. Continued operation offers two advantages: (1) somewhat more cooperation and (2) any statements made by defendants are voluntary and, therefore, not custodial statements subject to *Miranda* warnings. Unless conditions require other action, it is best to announce that no one is under arrest; everyone is free to come, to go, and to continue to operate as long as they do not obstruct the search, move items specified in the search warrant, or attempt to adversely affect the search team's safety.

Although the purpose of a search is to obtain evidence that can be used to support a prosecution, at all times this objective is secondary to

Figure 19–14
Physical Evidence Collection
Investigators collecting physical evidence inside of the safety line. In this case personnel who are not fully equipped with "moon suits" would be excluded from coming inside the area established by the tape banner.

(Courtesy Environmental Protection Agency)

the search team's safety. While the investigation leading to the search will have provided a great deal of information, investigators cannot assume that they fully know the risks involved in conducting the search. Therefore, investigators and other members of the search team must maintain a high level of alertness. Spills must be approached with great caution. Every effort must be made to determine what type of material is being encountered. Potentially helpful sources include witnesses, labels on nearby drums, U.S. Department of Transportation identification numbers on drums, and knowledge of the type of industry and the associated operations and chemicals in use. At all times the first responsibility of investigators must be their own safety.

During the search, the person normally in charge of the facility should regulate access to the extent that it does not hamper search operations or violate the safety lines established. As the physical search progresses, other team members should conduct as many interviews as possible, being careful to document their noncustodial nature, that is, the freedom to come and go, nonconfinement to one particular area, and the unrestricted ability to make telephone calls. Such interviews are ordinarily a rich source of information, particularly

if employees believe that management has lied to them with respect to the health hazard that the facility's operation posed to them.

The collection and handling of HWS evidence incorporates many of the same basic principles used in handling physical evidence from traditional crimes, such as avoiding cross-contamination of samples, proper packaging and marking, and maintaining the chain of custody (see Figure 19–15). It is more specialized because of the safety hazards posed by the very nature of the evidence involved, the requirements to keep certain types of samples widely separated, the need for specific containers and packing materials, the potential hazard created by transporting the evidence to a laboratory, the need for special storage arrangements, including ventilation, and the requirement to meet regulations established by the U.S. Department of Transportation when a nongovernment vehicle is used to remove the evidence from the HWS. The specifics of these peculiarities of HWS evidence are important, but it is sufficient for present purposes that traditional crime investigators be aware of the existence of such uniqueness and appreciate the high level of skill that their counterparts in environmental crime also must possess.

Figure 19–15
Soil Samples
Soil samples are collected in clear glass containers; a photographic record of all samples is maintained.

(Courtesy Environmental Protection Agency)

Questions

1. In what ways are the cities and agricultural crime linked?

2. What specialized knowledge is required by the investigator with respect to the theft of agri-chemicals?

3. What five generalizations can be made about livestock and tack theft?

4. What are four concerns with respect to conducting stakeouts in rural areas?

5. The legal provisions for transporting cattle vary by state; at a general level what three things must investigators know regarding such matters?

6. What does $\overline{M}$ RH R-crop L-split mean?

7. State and briefly describe four different methods of marking livestock for identification.

8. What are the two major categories of poachers, and how are they different?

9. Identify and briefly discuss seven different investigative programs or techniques used by wildlife officers.

10. Identify and describe the three major components of the waste cycle.

11. What does T/S/D mean?

12. Identify the provisions of a typical RCRA state law.

13. Discuss the role of planning when executing a search warrant at a hazardous-waste site.

14. What steps can investigators take to show that interviews conducted in the course of serving a search warrant at a hazardous-waste site were voluntarily made?

Notes

1. For an extension of this and related propositions, see Charles Swanson, "Rural and Agricultural Crime," *Journal of Criminal Justice,* 1981, Vol. 9, No. 1, pp. 19–27.

2. Charles Swanson and Leonard Territo, "Agricultural Crime: Its Extent, Prevention and Control," *FBI Law Enforcement Bulletin,* 1980, Vol. 49, No. 5, p. 10. We originally estimated $3 billion annually. The figure in the text is based on an assumption of an annual 3 percent increase in losses over the past 20 years.

3. San Diego County Farm Bureau, November 11, 1998, http://www.sdfarmbureau.org/index.html.

4. Ibid.

5. Jerome Weeks, "California Story: Avocado vs. 'Night-time Pickers'; One Year Theft Losses Amounted to 10 Million Dollars," *St. Louis Post-Dispatch,* September 21, 1997.

6. Ibid.

7. E.N. Smith, *The Seattle Times,* "Modern Rustlers Steal Livestock Via the Highway," June 7, 1998.

8. S. K. Bardwell, "New West-Style Rustlers Target Big Birds, Not Cattle," *Houston Post,* September 17, 1992.

9. Craig Whitlock, "Police Strive to Lasso Hog Rustlers," The (Raleigh, N.C.) *News and Observer,* May 22, 1997.

10. James Coates, "Rustlers Finding Gold in Dinosaur Bones," *Chicago Tribune,* November 10, 1991, Section 1, p. 25.

11. Mark Arax, "Rural Cops Battle Rising Crime in the Cropland," *Los Angeles Times,* March 2, 1998, p. 1.

12. "Horses Killed for Insurance Money? Investigators Think So," *Columbus* (Georgia) *Ledger-Enquirer,* February 5, 1991, p. B1.

13. Jack Anderson and Dale Van Atta, "Tree Spiking: 'An Eco-Terrorist' Tactic," *Washington Post,* March 5, 1990, p. C20.

14. Yvette La Pierre, "Poached Parklands," *American Horticulturist,* October 1994, Vol. 73, No. 10, p. 22. Our discussion of poached parklands is drawn from this source.

15. See Jerry Kammer, "Year in Prison for Cactus Thief," *The Arizona Republic,* October 31, 1998 and Frank J. Prial, "Feds Getting Tough on Outlaws Rustling Cactus," *Houston Post,* March 4, 1990.

16. Frank J. Prial, "California Brings Grape-Fraud Suits," *New York Times,* June 28, 1990, p. C1.

17. Brad Knickerbocker, "U.S. Fight against Timber Thieves," *The Christian Science Monitor,* March 23, 1998, internet edition.

18. Kate Thomas, "Illegal Logging Cases Sprout up over US: Increase in Rustling Due to Rise in Prices," The *Journal of Commerce*, March 10, 1997, internet edition.

19. Arax, "Rural Cops Battle Rising Crime in Cropland," p. 2.

20. Ibid.

21. Clarke Canfield, "Wreath Boom Triggers Theft of Tree Branches," (Portland) *Maine Sunday Telegraph*, November 25, 1990.

22. These points are drawn from Sgt. William Bacon, *Livestock Theft Investigation*, Los Angeles County Sheriff's Department, undated, p. 2, and with modifications made by the coauthors.

23. Ibid., p. 2, which is the source for the information in this paragraph.

24. Ibid.

25. Some of the information in this paragraph is drawn from ibid., pp. 5–6.

26. Ibid., p. 5.

27. Ibid.

28. E. N. Smith, "Modern Rustlers Steal Livestock via the Highway," *Seattle Times Com*, June 7, 1998, p. 1.

29. Ibid., p. 6, but recomputed in 1999 dollars.

30. Ibid.

31. Ibid., p. 12.

32. Ibid.

33. Alex Kershaw, "Return of the Rustler," *The Guardian* (London, England), September 12, 1998.

34. Staff and Wire Reports, "Cattle Rustling Nowadays Uses Pickups, Not Ponies," *Columbus* (Ohio) *Dispatch*, July 14, 1998.

35. Kershaw, "Return of the Rustler."

36. Ibid.

37. Bacon, *Livestock Theft Investigation*, p. 16, from which this paragraph was obtained with restatement.

38. Ibid., p. 24.

39. St. Tammany Bureau, "Saddle Microchips Offered," *The Times-Picayune*, October 25, 1997.

40. Unless otherwise indicated, the information in this section is derived from ibid., pp. 7-11 and 18.

41. See *Utah Livestock Brand Book*, Utah Department of Agriculture, 1996.

42. Several of these points were taken from Bacon, *Livestock Theft Investigation*, p. 17.

43. National Fish and Wildlife Service Forensics Laboratory, September 1997, http:/toltecs.lab.rl.fws.gov/lab/hpstory/cag/feature/9-97/index.html.

44. Jeff Bernard, "Beauty Threatens Survival of Many Species," *Los Angeles Times*, January 1, 1995.

45. David Van Biema, "The Killing Fields," *Time*, August 22, 1994, Vol. 144, No. 8, p. 37.

46. "Poachers Enlisted to Save Big Game," *New York Times*, December 26, 1990, p. A28.

47. Telephone interview, Fran Marcoux, Colorado Division of Wildlife, March 3, 1995.

48. Van Biema, "The Killing Fields," p. 37.

49. Constance J. Poten, "A Shameful Harvest," *National Geographic*, September 1991, Vol. 180, No. 3, pp. 110, 131.

50. Wayne Brewer, "Traditional Policing and Environmental Enforcement," *FBI Law Enforcement Bulletin*, May 1995, Vol. 65, No. 4, pp. 6–11, with some restatement.

51. Ibid., p. 10.

52. Donald Rebovich, Northeast Hazardous Waste Project Offender Profile Report—1988, p. 12 (mimeo).

53. Ibid., p. 20.

54. Michael M. Mustokoff, *Hazardous Waste Violations: A Guide to Their Detection, Investigation, and Prosecution* (Elgin, Ill.: Midwest Environmental Enforcement Association, 1990), p. 54.

55. Some of the information in this section is drawn from Susan Tejada, "On Camera for EPA," *EPA Journal*, March 1986, pp. 2–4.

TWENTY

Arson and Explosives Investigations

CHAPTER OUTLINE

Preliminary Investigation 564

Where and How Did the Fire Start? 564

Burn Indicators 567

Fire Setting and Related Mechanisms 568

Arson for Profit 573

Other Motives for Arson 579

Detection and Recovery of Fire-Accelerant
    Residues 583

Scientific Methods in Arson Investigation 585

Interviews 588

The Arson Suspect 591

Photographing the Arson Scene 592

Explosives Investigation 592

Bomb Threats 597

Suspicious Packages and Letters 600

Questions 601

Notes 602

INTRODUCTION

The crime of arson has increased dramatically in recent years. It is estimated that more than 1,000 lives are lost each year due to arson fires. Another 10,000 injuries are sustained each year as a result of these arson fires. Conservative estimates show that approximately $2 billion in property damage is caused each year by arsonists. This $2 billion is the tip of the iceberg when it comes to the total amount of money lost as a result of arson each year. The cost of fire services increases by at least an additional $10 billion. Law enforcement spends additional time and money trying to bring arsonists to trial. The judicial system then must spend its time and many personnel hours to try the case. In the event of conviction, the penal system must house and feed the convicted arsonists. Even greater than these additional costs to governmental bodies are the costs to the person in the street. Untold thousands of jobs are lost when factories are burned for profit. Thousands of homes are lost each year, forcing homeowners and tenants to relocate, with higher rent and higher house payments.[1]

Arson is an inherently difficult crime to detect and prosecute, and it falls between police and fire department responsibility, an area that is too often not effectively covered. Both the police and fire services can legitimately claim authority in arson cases, but each also may rationalize that the responsibility belongs to the other. Unfortunately, in most jurisdictions neither is prepared to devote the resources needed to achieve identification, arrest, and conviction rates commensurate with other crimes. Arson investigators need cooperation and better training. Administrative officials also need to help, but in order to help they need to give the problem a greater share of their attention. Probably the most urgent step in controlling arson rates is for top fire and police officials and local, state, and national government officials to recognize the magnitude of the problem and then provide the necessary resources to combat it.[2]

PRELIMINARY INVESTIGATION

Arson investigations entail several exceptions to fire service training. For example, the fire service has taught firefighters that fire loss is less and public relations better if they clean premises of debris, water, and so forth. However, if arson is suspected, firefighters should not disarrange the premises, especially at the point of origin. Moving debris, even window glass, may destroy valuable physical evidence.[3]

In nearly all cases, there is little additional loss if the area encompassing the point of origin is not cleaned out, because this area is usually the most heavily damaged by the fire, with little salvage possible. Often it is necessary during overhauling to move large quantities of acoustical tile, plasterboard, canned goods, cartons, and other items. If this material is beyond salvage, it is natural to throw it into the worst burned area of the building. But this is probably the area the investigator will want to examine carefully, and such discards will have to be moved again. In the confusion, the fire cause is likely to remain in doubt.

One effective way to determine fire causes is to determine the point of origin. Neighbors', on-lookers', or others' ideas about the cause sometimes lead investigators astray. When the exact point of origin is established, the cause usually becomes obvious. For instance, a point of origin in the middle of a bare concrete basement floor probably eliminates defective heating appliances or wiring.

Points of origin sometimes are established by reconstructing furniture and walls, replacing loose boards and doors. Neighbors and occupants can help describe how things were before the fire. The direction of heat flow then can be followed by checks for deepest charring, indications of highest temperature, and duration of heat. Temperatures are indicated by the condition of metal, glass, wood, plastics, and other materials. Because heat rises, a general rule is to look for the lowest point of deep char as the point of origin. This rule, however, has many exceptions.

After the area of origin has been established, the investigator should check for the level of origin by examining the bottoms of shelves, ledges, moldings, and furniture and all sides of the legs, arms, and framework of reconstructed furniture. The investigator also should clean the floor carefully at the point of origin, examining and moving all objects to one side. After this is done, the floor or rugs should be swept as clean as possible for examination of burn patterns.

The floor and lower areas of the room produce the most clues to the cause of the fire, because they are the living area. Most equipment and contents are near floor level, actions of occupants are conducted near floor level, and most materials drop there during a fire.

WHERE AND HOW DID THE FIRE START?

Once the fire is out, the primary task is to begin examining what is left of the building for physical evidence that may indicate how the fire began (see Figure 20–1). The point of origin can be a clue to possible arson. For example, if two or more distinct points of origin are found, two or more separate

Figure 20–1
Arson Investigators at Work
A team of arson investigators searching the scene of a suspected arson.

(Courtesy Thomas Evans, Pinellas County, Florida, Sheriff's Office)

fires probably were deliberately set. Also, if the fires started in the middle of a large room or in a closet, then the index of suspicion should go up sharply.[4]

TWO FACTORS NEEDED TO CAUSE FIRE

During the investigation, it should be borne in mind that a fire always has two causes: a source of heat and material ignited.

In checking for the fire cause at the point of origin, it is usually an advantage to use the *layer-checking technique*. Before any material is moved

or shoveled out, the investigator should make notes and carefully examine the strata while working through to the floor. These layers often contain wood ash, plaster, melted aluminum, window glass, charred drapery fabric, and charred newspapers. They may give a picture of the sequence of burning. If, for example, charred newspapers were found beneath charred drapery fabric, this could indicate a set fire, particularly if papers would not usually be in the area or if they were of different types of dates. Aluminum and similar alloys melt fairly early in a fire (at about 1,150°F), often splash or run over other material near floor level, solidify, and protect the material from further damage.

Draperies and heavy curtains may burn free and drop on flammable liquid, preventing it from being completely consumed, especially if the liquid is heavy or less volatile.[5]

ACCIDENTAL FIRES

Once the point of origin has been discovered, the next step is to determine how the fire started. Even though arson may be suspected, the investigator must first investigate and rule out all possible accidental or natural causes. Many courts have held that this elimination of accidental causes is a firm basis for an arson charge. Also, if the investigator is put on the witness stand, it is likely that a question will be raised about the possibility of accidental causes. A failure to eliminate accidental causes could substantially weaken the prosecution's case.

Some of the more common accidental or natural causes of fire fall into the following categories:

- *The electric system:* Fuses in which pennies have been inserted; broken or rotted insulation; overloaded circuits; defective switches; and improperly installed wiring.
- *Electrical appliances and equipment:* Defective electrical units with short circuits; overheated irons; and light bulbs covered by paper shades.
- *Gas:* Leaks in gas pipes; defective stoves and heating units.
- *Heating units:* Overheated stoves or steam pipes; clothing being dried too close to fireplaces or open flames; faulty chimneys; explosions from kerosene stoves; and overturned space heaters.
- *Sunlight:* The concentration of sun rays on bubbles in glasses, windowpanes, or convex shaving mirrors placed near combustible materials such as paper or rags.
- *Matches:* Children playing with matches, especially in enclosed areas such as closets or utility rooms.
- *Smoking:* The careless disposal of cigars, cigarettes, pipe ashes, and other lighted devices into trash cans in the home; individuals who fall asleep while smoking in bed or in a chair.

Indications of cigarettes in furniture or mattresses are heavy charring of the unit and the floor; a char-pattern on furniture frames, heaviest on the inside; heavy staining and blackening of mirrors and window glass in the area, indicating a long, slow fire; a burning time of from 1½ to 3 or 4 hours; collapsing of part or all of the core springs. Lying flat on a padded surface, cigarettes usually char a small hole and burn out. If the cigarette is partially covered at the sides or bottom, a fire usually results in an hour or so. Cigarettes ignite foam rubber padding to about the same degree as other padding. With foam rubber padding, fire occurs a little faster because smoldering rubber reaches an ignition temperature faster and burns with greater intensity.[6]

SPONTANEOUS HEATING AND IGNITION

There are a few fundamental causes of spontaneous heating, but the conditions under which these factors may operate are numerous. Nearly all organic materials and many metals are subject to oxidation, fermentation, or both and, therefore, have some potential for spontaneous heating.

Spontaneous heating is produced in three major ways: chemical action, fermentation, and oxidation (the most common way). For example, *chemical actions* occur when unslaked lime and water or when sodium and water are combined. *Fermentation* heating is caused by bacterial action. Here, moisture is a prime factor. The most dangerous materials are those subject to combinations, such as fermentation and oxidation with drying. Fresh sawdust over 10 feet deep is subject to fermentation heating but rarely reaches ignition temperature. In oxidation heating, rapid oxidation must take place in the presence of a good insulating factor and an oxygen supply. *Oxidation* takes place in oils containing carbon, hydrogen, and oxygen. This combination is mostly found in vegetable and fish oils and, to some extent, in animal oils.

The susceptibility to spontaneous heating is usually determined by drying time. Unadulterated hydrocarbons, such as mineral and petroleum oils, are not considered subject to spontaneous ignition.

Spontaneous ignition is rare in residences and small businesses. It is considerably accelerated by external heat such as sunshine, steampipes, hot air ducts, or friction from wind or vibration. Spontaneous ignition is rather mysterious because of many unknowns. Therefore, it is often used as a catch-all explanation.

The usual time required to produce spontaneous ignition by oxidation or fermentation runs from several hours to several days or months. This form of ignition is characterized by internal charring of a mass of combustibles, and some of the remains of this material usually are found at the point of origin (if the firefighters have been careful and especially if fog was used), because it normally takes a considerable mass—several inches of fairly dense material—to create the factors necessary for spontaneous heating. Sometimes when material of the appropriate type is suspected and found to be deeply charred all the way through, investigators must satisfy themselves that external heat was not responsible. When not heated internally, sacks of meals, flour, and the like usually survive fire with only an inch or two of charring on the exposed surface.

Dust and polishing mops have often been accused of causing spontaneous ignition and probably have in some rare cases. Most fires originating near a mop in a closet or on a back porch are caused by a child playing with matches.[7] It is debatable whether the average mop would have enough bulk to provide the necessary insulation to raise the temperature to the ignition point, although with favorable conditions—such as a large mop, saturated with fast-drying oils, pressed in a corner with other brooms, and receiving outside heat from a steampipe or the sun's rays through a window—ignition could occur. During the several hours required for the material to ignite, it gives off very acrid odors. Linseed and similar oils are especially odorous. People in the area during that time usually would be aware of these odors.

BURN INDICATORS

Burn indicators are the effects of heat or partial burning that indicate a fire's rate of development, points of origin, temperature, duration, time of occurrence, and the presence of flammable liquids. Interpretation of burn indicators is a principal means for determining the causes of fires, especially arson. Some of the burn indicators used are the following:[8]

- *Alligatoring:* Checking of charred wood, giving it the appearance of alligator skin. Large, rolling blisters indicate rapid, intense heat; small, flat alligatoring indicates long, low heat.

- *Crazed and fractured glass:* "Crazing" refers to the cracking of glass into smaller segments or subdivisions in an irregular pattern. The extent to which a glass item (e.g., windowpane) will crack or craze is related to the type of glass involved, the thickness of the glass, the temperature range to which it was exposed, and its distance from the point of origin.[9] Crazing into small segments or pieces suggests that the item was subjected to a rapid and intense heat buildup. It also suggests that the item may be located at or close to the point of origin. On the other hand, a glass item that exhibits a larger crazing pattern implies that it may be located in an area some distance away from the point of origin.

- *Depth of char:* This is the depth of burning of wood—used to determine length of burn and thereby locate the point of origin of the fire (see Figure 20–2).

- *Distorted light bulbs:* Incandescent light bulbs can sometimes show the direction of heat impingement. As the side of the bulb facing the

Figure 20-2
Line of Demarcation in a Wood Section

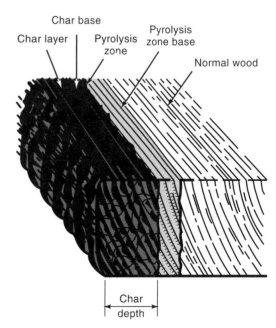

Source: Factory Mutual Engineering Corporation, Norwood, Massachusetts. Reprinted with permission.

source of heat is heated and softened, the gases inside a bulb greater than 25 watts can begin to expand and bubble out of the softened glass. This has traditionally been called a "pulled" light bulb, although the action is really a response to internal pressure rather than pulling. The bulge, or pulled portion of the bulb, will be in the direction of the source of heating[10] (see Figure 20–3).

- *Line of demarcation:* Boundary between charred and uncharred material. On floors or rugs, a puddle-shaped line of demarcation is believed to indicate a liquid fire accelerant. In a cross section of wood, a sharp, distinct line of demarcation indicates a rapid, intense fire (see Figure 20-2).
- *Sagged furniture springs:* Because of the heat required for furniture springs to collapse from their own weight (1,150°F) and because of the insulating effect of the upholstery, sagged springs are believed to be possible only in either a fire originating inside the cushions (as from a cigarette rolling between the cushions) or an external fire intensified by a fire accelerant.
- *Spalling: Spalling* is a condition ordinarily associated with masonry and cement (concrete) building materials. It may appear as a distinctive discoloration of brick or concrete; in some cases, the surface of these building materials may be pitted and rough. This is because an intense fire may cause the moisture inside the brick or masonry element to convert to steam. As they expand, these steam pockets may burst through the surface of the cement or brick floor or wall, leaving the surface pitted or pock-marked.[11]
- *Freezing of leaves:* Drying of leaves in a forest fire into their position at the time of the fire. Because leaves turn during the day to face the sun, their position indicates the time of day the fire occurred.

Although burn indicators are widely used to establish the causes of fires, they have received little or no scientific testing. In reference to freezing of leaves, one expert states, some persons are inclined to regard this evidence as unreliable because of insufficient clinical and research confirmation and the influence of the fire wind.[12] Another authority cautions that puddle-shaped lines of demarcation may have nothing to do with flammable liquids; that depth of char is strongly affected by factors other than burning time, such as temperature and species of wood; and that much greater care must be taken in its interpretation than is usual.[13]

FIRE SETTING AND RELATED MECHANISMS

It is the duty of an arson investigator to search the debris of a suspicious fire, particularly around the point of origin, to gather evidence pointing to the mechanism used by the fire setter in the arson effort.[14]

Figure 20–3
A "Pulled" Light Bulb
A typical "pulled" light bulb, showing that the heating was from the right side.

Source: Reprinted with permission from *NFPA 921 Guide for Fire and Explosion Investigations.* Copyright 1992, National Fire Protection Association, Quincy, Massachusetts 02269.

An arsonist may use the simplest of methods, a match and some paper, or elaborate mechanical or chemical methods. An incendiary mechanism may be mechanical or chemical. It consists of an ignition device, possibly a timing device, one or more "plants" to feed or accelerate the initial flame, and frequently "trailers" to spread the fire about the building or from plant to plant.

IGNITION DEVICES

Matches

Only juvenile arsonists and pyromaniacs seem to favor striking matches. Other fire setters want some delay, so they adapt the ordinary match to some timing mechanism.

Several matches may be affixed to a lighted cigarette with a rubber band or tape, the heads of the matches set about halfway down the cigarette from its glowing end (see Figure 20–4). In some cases, matches are laid alongside a cigarette. Books of paper matches are also popular. Because cigarettes will continue to burn when laid on their sides, they are effective ignition devices; the slow-burning cigarette allows the fire setter a few minutes to get away from the scene before the fire makes any headway.

Figure 20–4
Arson Device
Kitchen matches are placed around a cigarette and secured with a rubber band.

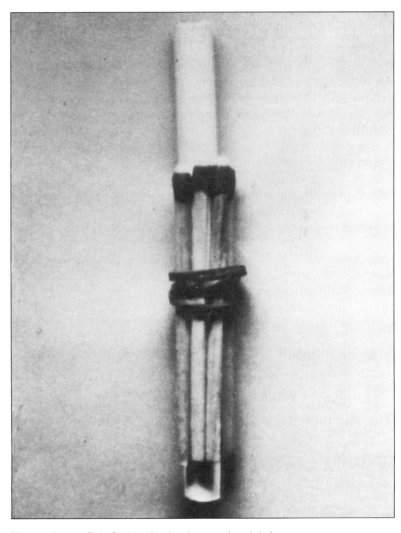

(Courtesy Property Claim Services, American Insurance Association)

Matches are also used in conjunction with mechanical devices. One arsonist strapped matches to the ringing mechanism of a telephone in a wall box and inserted a piece of abrasive board in place of the bell. He thought he could set a fire from miles away by calling his home. But his estranged wife came home unexpectedly and noticed a wisp of smoke from a pile of old clothing on the floor in the living room. Frightened, she called the fire department. The ignition device had been activated but had fizzled out. The firefighters carefully preserved the rags (wet with lighter fluid), the matches, and an abrasive board. These were later used in the prosecution of the husband.

Unburnt or partially burnt matches found around the point of origin should be carefully preserved. A suspect may have similar matches in his or her pocket.

Candles

As a timed ignition device, candles have been in use by arsonists for over a century. Candles burn at various rates, depending on their composition and size. Thick candles burn slowly, long candles longer than short candles.

Some years ago, Dr. Richard Steinmetz established a table of the burning time of candles of various compositions and sizes. A summary of this table is presented in Table 20–1.

Arson investigators sometimes work on a rule of thumb of an hour's burning time for each inch of candle of the diameters shown. Of course, this is only guesswork and investigators will arrive at a more definite time only after completing their own experiments. Once the arsonists know the average burning time of the candle, they can adjust to a desired time lag merely by cutting the candle to the desired length. The candle is therefore not only an ignition unit but also a device that can be adjusted

Table 20–1
Burning Time of Candles

Composition	Diameter	Time to Burn 1 Inch
Tallow	¾ in.	61 min.
Wax	⅞ in.	57 min.
Paraffin	¹³/₁₆ in.	63 min.

within certain limits to set a fire hours after the arsonist has departed from the scene of the crime.

Candles are mostly used in conjunction with containers of easily combustible materials, which are sometimes set within, or close to, other containers of inflammable liquids or in an area sprinkled with such accelerants. However, many candles leave a deposit of wax as their telltale sign. Wax may have soaked into the wood of a floor, or it may be found in a pool at the low point of a floor or table top. Another sign is the protection afforded the floor or table top by such wax—the spot on which the candle rested will show less charring than the surrounding area. In many cases a part of the candle, and possibly the container in which the candle was placed, may be found in a search of the fire scene.

Chemicals

Various chemical combustions have been used to set fires. Saboteurs have used such means for years. Units that provide for an acid to be released upon some combination of chemicals are a favorite device, with the acid releasing itself by eating its way through the cork or even the metal of its container. The time lag from setting to ignition can be estimated with some certainty by an arsonist with a little knowledge of chemistry.

Various rubber receptacles, such as hot water and ice bags or contraceptives, have been used for a phosphorus and water ignition device. A pinhole is made in the rubber container, allowing the water to seep out. Once it drains below the level of the phosphorus, ignition takes place. As this chemical ignites upon contact with air, a time lag is secured by controlling the amount of water and the size of the hole in the container.

Even the ordinary fire setter sometimes uses a chemical that ignites upon contact with water. The device is activated by rain. Holes in a roof or a connection to the building's gutter system have been used to trigger these devices. Another device is to divert the sewage line in a building. It is set up at night to trigger the next morning when the toilet is flushed for the first time.

Most chemical ignition units leave some residue, have a distinctive odor, or both. Debris must be analyzed at a laboratory when it is suspected that chemicals have been used as ignition devices. Fortunately, most arsonists do not know enough to use chemical ignition or timing devices, and the machinery and tools necessary for the construction of some of these devices are not always readily available. The devices usually are fairly simple. Most complex devices usually are used only in time of war by enemy agents.

Gas

Although not commonly encountered, the combination of gas and the pilot light on the kitchen stoves of many residences is always a possibility. Illuminating gas rises to the ceiling, being lighter than air, and then slowly moves to floor level as it continues to escape. When it reaches a combustion buildup, it is close to the pilot light level. An explosion, usually followed by fire, takes place. A candle placed in a room adjoining the kitchen has also been used as a means of ignition. Therefore, arson investigators must remember that although such explosions usually follow suicide attempts or accidents, arsonists may use an ordinary gas range as a tool.

In such cases, investigators should get help from an engineer at the local public utility. The time lag between the initial release of the gas and the explosion can be estimated from the size of the room involved, number of openings, type of gas, and related data. For example, a kitchen 10 by 15 feet with a ceiling 9 feet high equals a total volume of 1,350 cubic feet. When 71 cubic feet of gas are introduced into the room, the lowest limit of explosive range will have been reached. In a well-ventilated room, it is almost impossible to build up to this limit, but an arsonist seals off the room so that the gas builds up. In a fairly well sealed room, a single burner left open on a kitchen gas stove will deliver enough gas to explode in about 5 hours. The oven jets will build up the same volume in 2 hours; an oven plus four burners, 30 minutes to 1 hour.

The widespread use of gas as an arson tool has been thwarted because of its smell. Neighbors usually detect the smell, call the police or the fire department, or break in themselves, ruining a carefully planned arson attempt.

Electrical Systems

Any wiring system, including doorbell and telephone circuits, can be used as a fire-setting tool. Ignition devices hooked to the wiring systems of buildings have been used throughout the country by arsonists. The time can be established by a study of the habits of those using the premises. Possibly a security guard switches on the light every hour while inspecting the various portions of the building, or employees turn on the lights at opening time, and so on.

Although a doorbell system also can be used to trigger an ignition device, the bell may be rung by some chance visitor and the plans of the fire setter thwarted. Telephone timing devices have the same fault. A wrong number or an unexpected call and the fire is under way, possibly days ahead of schedule.

Figure 20–5 depicts an electric timer, appliance cord, matches, and shredded paper used as an ignition device. Once the paper catches on fire, it ignites the clothing.

Electrical appliances have also been used to set off fires. An open heater is placed close to a flimsy set of curtains, and an apparently accidental fire results. An electrical circuit is deliberately overloaded with several appliances until it heats up. Sometimes an accelerant such as kerosene is dropped into a switch box. In a few cases, a length of normal wiring is removed and lighter wire substituted so that it will overheat and, without blowing the fuses, serve as an ignition device. Figure 20–6 depicts the use of a toaster with a paper trailer leading to an accelerant in the overhung kitchen cabinet. After the toaster is activated, the heat ignites the trailer, travels to the accelerant, and causes it to ignite.

Investigators generally discover physical traces of electrical ignition devices after a fire.

Mechanical Devices

Alarm clocks were once a favored weapon of arsonists. With a simple alarm clock, some wire, and a small battery, a fire setter was "in business." But a search of the fire debris usually sent the arsonist to prison. Some arsonists used the lead hammer in the clock to break a glass tube that fed flammable matter to a fixed flame. This action pushed one container of chemicals into another, closing an electrical circuit. Some arsonists attached matches to the hammer, where they were pressed against an abrasive surface to ignite flammable material. The clock was activated by setting the alarm for a certain time. The weights in a grandfather's clock have been used in a similar manner.

Figure 20–5
Arson Device
An electric timer used in conjunction with an appliance cord, matches, and shredded paper.

(Courtesy Property Claim Services, American Insurance Association)

Some mechanical devices are childish, some are worthy of master craftsmen, and others are truly fiendish. Unfortunately for many of these ingenious incendiaries, their machines do not burn and can later be used in their prosecution.

PLANTS

A *plant* is the material placed around the ignition device to feed the flame. Newspapers, wood shav- ings, rags, clothing, curtains, blankets, and cotton waste are some plants. Newspapers are the most fre- quently used; cotton waste is used extensively in fac- tory or industrial fires.

Accelerants, or "boosters," to speed the progress of the fire are also part of the plant. Kerosene and gasoline are favored boosters; alcohol, lighter fluid, paint thinners, and other solvents are also popular. However, any flammable fluid or compound may be used to accelerate the blaze.

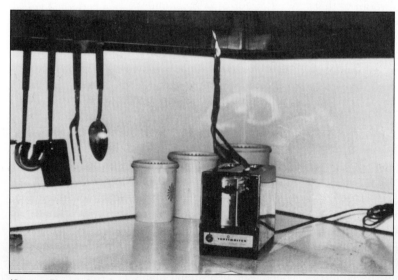

Figure 20–6
Arson Device
A toaster with a paper trailer leading to an accelerant in overhung kitchen cabinets.

(Courtesy Property Claim Services, American Insurance Association)

TRAILERS

Trailers are used to spread the fire. A trailer is ignited by the blaze from the plant. It carries the fire to other parts of a room or building. Usually a trailer ends in a second plant, another pile of papers, or excelsior sprinkled with gasoline, kerosene, or other booster. From the primary plant, the fire setter may lay four trailers to four secondary plants. Four separate fires thus result from one ignition device.

Rope or toilet paper soaked in alcohol or similar fluid, motion picture film, dynamite fuses, gunpowder, and other such substances have been used as trailers. Sometimes rags or newspapers are soaked in some fire accelerant and twisted into rope. Some arsonists use a fluid fire accelerant such as kerosene as a trailer by pouring a liberal quantity on the floor in a desired path. Figure 20–7 depicts shredded paper as a trailer leading into a clothes closet containing a plastic bowl filled with a liquid accelerant.

INCENDIARY FIRES

When any fire-setting device, ignition and timing units, plants, or trailers are found near a suspicious fire, it should be classified as an incendiary fire.

When kerosene, gasoline, candles, and like substances are discovered around the point of origin of a suspicious fire, it is evidence of arson. If investigators can prove such material had no right to be in such premises, then they have established the corpus delicti; that is, they have overcome the presumption of accident as established by law and have proved the body of the crime.

MISSING ITEMS

Sometimes items that are missing from the fire scene can prove valuable. For example, does it appear that much of the building contents, especially furniture, clothing, or valuable items were removed prior to the fire? Have house pets been removed? Moving a pet to a kennel or the home of friends just before a fire should raise the suspicions of the investigator.

ARSON FOR PROFIT

Understanding the motives of the arsonist is extremely important if the investigation is to be successful. There are several common motivations for arsonists to set fires.

The motive for committing arson for profit is economic gain, whether it be the enormous gain from inflating insurance coverage beyond the building's value or limited economic gain derived from cutting one's losses before oncoming financial disaster.[15]

To decide where and how to begin the investigation, the investigator needs to determine whether the arson in question was due primarily to financial stress, to a fraud scheme (without much stress), or to a combination of some stress and the profitability of fraud.

FINANCIAL STRESS AS THE PRIMARY CAUSE

The homeowner or business owner who decides to arrange an arson fraud may do so out of submission to financial stress. In general, two primary factors influence the insured person's decision to commit arson fraud: (1) the desire for financial relief, and (2) greed—the desire for easily obtained financial assistance. One way to conceive of an arson-fraud scheme is to view it as the result of the interplay between these two factors. Experience in cases where

Figure 20–7
Arson Device
A shredded paper trailer leading to a liquid accelerant in a plastic bowl located in a clothes closet.

(Courtesy Property Claim Services, American Insurance Association)

owners have been caught in arson-fraud schemes indicates that the more extreme and immediately pressing the financial stress, the more desperate the insured becomes. Certainly, the number of insureds who are not persuaded to commit arson—no matter how severe their financial stress—is great, and the swelling bankruptcy court dockets reflect the prevailing honesty of most citizens. However, a rapidly developing situation of financial stress can place the insured in a position where he or she desperately examines all kinds of options both legal and illegal.

Perhaps we can understand the arson-fraud motive of a homeowner who has just been fired or who faces mortgage foreclosure and burns a home or business. It is important to conduct a search for evidence for those forms of stress. The investigator is likely to find a great deal about such matters in court papers associated with divorces, foreclosures, bankruptcies, and liens. Although it is not fully accepted as a rule of thumb, the more severe the financial stress of an insured, the more likely the person is to either personally set the fire or involve a minimum number of people—usually a professional arsonist—in the crime.

Investigators often view real estate arson schemes as purely the result of the fraudulent motives of the owners. Actually, the motives for committing real estate arson split between those that are pure scams (discussed later) and those that result from the owner's or landlord's deteriorating financial position. Financial stress in the latter instance can result from any number of factors: strong net migration out of the neighborhood, a long and expensive backlog of code violation citations and fines, or steady deterioration in the quality of the housing—sometimes by design of the landlords. Whatever the specific reasons, housing that no longer produces net income for the owner or landlord can help place the person (and perhaps the coinvestors) in a financially precarious position. The clues to determining whether the financial condition of a building or real estate corporation would make arson-fraud attractive lie in the financial records of investment, income, and tax depreciation.

Short-Term Business Problem

The businessperson on the brink of insolvency faces financial stress that is more severe than the one who faces a short-term problem, such as a slack period in a seasonal business or an unforeseen problem of cash flow. Because of the regularity with which insurance settlements occur (when claims are not denied), the businessperson who selects arson can be fairly sure of having much of the money or all of it in hand within a short period of time. One reason to suspect that a short-term business problem, rather than a more serious one, led to the arson is the absence of creditors threatening to force the owner into bankruptcy, and thus the absence of a bankruptcy filing. An examination of the business's books will enable the investigator (or accountant) to infer better whether the cash flow problem was the likely motive for arson.

Desire to Relocate or Remodel   Arsons do occur in businesses that are subject to quickly shifting consumer tastes, and this type of arson-fraud scheme may be motivated by the desire of the owner to secure enough money to remodel or move. In this way, the insured feels able to keep up with changing tastes or to move to a more fashionable location with better market potential. Examples of businesses vulnerable to these trends are beauty salons, "theme" restaurants, and furniture stores. Frequently, such owners arrange for the arson because they realize that shifting tastes have caught them unprepared. However, an owner may also sense the onset of a new trend in its early stages and try to avoid financial distress and arrange for the arson to occur early enough to remodel or move by using the insurance proceeds. In cases where an inventory no longer sells because of shifting tastes, a variety of internal business and supplier records can help to establish whether this was the motive. In this type of arson for profit, as in many other types, the actual discomfort of financial distress may not be the motive as much as the perception that the insured will soon be in such distress—unless he or she acts immediately.

Buildup of Slow-Moving Inventory   A short-term cash-flow problem can be caused by an unusually large buildup of slow-moving inventory. While the inventory problem may not appear to the investigator to be a logical motive for the arson, this issue may be easier to understand if the investigator becomes familiar with what are normal or abnormal levels of inventory for a particular type of business, for certain periods of the year. If an inventory problem led to the arson, it is likely that the insured has filed a full and possibly even inflated claim to recoup the value of the allegedly destroyed inventory. For this reason, such documentation may point toward the motive but in itself be insufficient to establish the motive. The investigator should look also for multiple points of fire origin and the attempt to destroy all inventory.

Outmoded Technology   Several years ago, two of the largest arson-for-profit cases prosecuted in this country involved companies that failed to keep pace with the technological progress of their competitors. The arson frauds involving the Sponge Rubber Products Company and the Artistic Wire Products Company originated partly because the technologies for making the respective products had changed to more efficient, profitable forms. For whatever reasons, the owners had not kept pace. Where an industrial concern may be destroyed because of these technological problems, telltale signs of arson for profit are usually present. First, professional arsonists, even good ones, can rarely destroy a large industrial facility simply by burning it. Incendiary devices, sometimes involving explosives, may be required. Remnants and residues of these can often point to a "professional" arson job. Second, books and business records of the companies will often reveal financial stress in ways such as corporate debt reorganizations as well as documented searches for new capital or drastic changes in marketing strategies prior to the arson. Third, since an owner involved in an industrial arson may claim that a labor-management grievance led to it, investigators should search for documentation on formally filed labor grievances, both with the local union and state and federal regulatory bodies, in order to confirm or deny the validity of such a claim.

Satisfaction of a Legal or Illegal Debt

The businessperson or homeowner whose property is destroyed by fire does not always broadcast clear signals of financial stress. One reason for this is that the source of the stress may not be apparent. It may not show up in the books of a business or in other indicators such as divorce or bankruptcy records. For example, if the owner incurred an illegal loan-sharking debt that the lender has called in, the tremendous pressure and threats of violence can make an incendiary fire an acceptable risk to the business owner. On many occasions,

the owner either sets the fire or arranges for it to be set. In others, however, the loan shark sets it or has it set, knowing that the businessperson has fire and perhaps other (e.g., business interruption) insurance in force.

Evidence of an illegal debt will be difficult to locate if the investigator follows only the "paper trail" from the insured to his or her business and personal records of transactions. Where arson to satisfy an illegal debt is suspected, it is important for the investigator to seek out information on the owner's actions that led to the indebtedness, for example, a recent gambling junket, heavy betting during the sports season, or borrowing from a loan shark for a highly speculative venture that initially appeared to have enormous profit potential but later went sour. When the trail leads to an illegal debt involving the insured, but that person's denial of any involvement is convincing, the investigator should examine the possibility that the loan shark arranged the fire without the insured's knowledge or consent.

PURELY FRAUD SCHEMES AS THE PRIMARY MOTIVE

Many types of arson occur because of the actual or anticipated problem of financial stress; others result from schemes where there was not and probably would not be any financial problem. These types of arson-fraud schemes result from the planning and plotting of professional fraud schemers and their associates. Their objective is to defraud insurance companies, as well as banks and even creditors, of as much money as possible. Some of the common types of frauds encountered by investigators follow.

Redevelopment

In cases where a defined tract has been designated for receipt of federal redevelopment funds, owners and investors may stand to make more money if existing buildings on the tract are razed at no cost to themselves. Arson is a convenient vehicle, for although it may not destroy the building, the city or redevelopment authority will usually raze the remains at no cost to the owner, especially if the building is a safety hazard. Investigators who study tracts designated for redevelopment can often plot which blocks and even which buildings may burn as a result of redevelopment fraud schemes. Owners who decide to arrange this type of arson realize that if the building is only partly damaged, the adjusted insurance settlement may pay for repairs (which they do not want) but not for rebuilding. Therefore, in the interest of ensuring maximum destruction, professional arsonists are likely to be called upon for their expertise.

Building Rehabilitation

In order to improve the condition of old or run-down dwellings, a variety of federal and state loan and loan insurance programs are available for housing rehabilitation. Certain unscrupulous owners, contractors, and others who know the "rehab" business realize that they stand to reap huge profits by obtaining funds to make repairs and then claiming that fire destroyed the rehabilitated unit. In most cases, the claimed repairs were not made, or they were only partially completed, or they were done with inferior (cheaper) materials. Therefore, in addition to reaping a profit from that portion of the loan that was not used to buy materials and pay laborers, this type of arsonist often files insurance claims for the full amount of the allegedly completed work. In addition to arson and insurance fraud, such persons commit a variety of frauds against the federal or state government that provides the rehabilitation program assistance. Financial records should indicate the cost of the work actually done.

Real Estate Schemes

In many core urban areas, the most common form of arson for profit involves the destruction of dilapidated multifamily housing. While such housing is usually in an advanced state of disrepair, there may be little if any financial stress facing the owners. This is so because either the owner recouped the investment through depreciation of the building and through rent gouging or the owner recently purchased the building for a small fraction of the amount for which it was insured. The typical MO involves an owner purchasing the housing for a small cash down payment, often accompanied by a large, unconventional mortgage. The owner then sells the building to another speculator (usually an associate) for an inflated amount, again with little money down and a large mortgage. Often the building is insured not only for the inflated, artificial value of the second sale but for the replacement value of that building, which is even greater.

Then the building burns, the policyholder is almost routinely paid, and the speculating schemers split the proceeds according to a preset formula.

To reap the maximum profit from this type of scheme, the speculators often involve one or more kinds of specialists:

- Several arsonists, so that one arsonist will not know all the plans or be easily recognized because of repeated trips to the neighborhood.
- A public insurance adjuster to help inflate the claim on the building.
- A realtor who scouts around for "bargain" properties to buy.
- An insurance agent who may be corrupted and who is helpful in insuring buildings far beyond what normal, reasonable underwriting standards would permit.

This type of real estate–arson scheme is very lucrative, and its perpetrators realize that the greater the number of buildings burned, the greater the profits. Soon another speculator, perhaps in league with a contractor or realtor, sees how "well" the first speculator is doing, and out of greed the latter begins the same type of arson scheme, creating a chain reaction. The idea spreads to still other speculators, and shortly an entire city can find itself in the midst of a real estate arson-for-profit epidemic.

Planned Bankruptcy

Although this variation of arson for profit is not encountered often, its incidence does seem to be growing. In a typical bankruptcy fraud, the owner establishes a business and buys quantities of goods on credit. The owner pays the first few creditors quickly and in cash in order to increase the volume of merchandise he or she can then buy on credit. The inventory is then sold, often surreptitiously through another company or to a fence, and then the business declares bankruptcy. Often the creditors are left with large numbers of unpaid bills. One way to satisfy them is by paying them off with insurance proceeds obtained after a "mysterious" fire in the business. Additional money is generated from such a fraud scheme because the owner represents in the fire insurance claim that substantial amounts of inventory were destroyed, when in fact merchandise was purposely moved out prior to the fire. Occasionally, a cheaper grade of merchandise is substituted in its place. Because the creditors are paid, their incentive to complain or report the probable fraud is reduced. Because the destroyed records of such inventory are hard to reconstruct, it is difficult to determine exactly what was destroyed in the fire, and hence its value. Also, since bankruptcy fraud fires always seem to destroy the office and files where the books are kept, it is difficult for the investigator to reconstruct the flow of money into and out of the business, as well as the flow of merchandise.

ARSON GENERATED BY THIRD PARTIES

This is another broad category of arson for profit, where the beneficiary of the fire is not the owner-insured but a third party who arranges for the fire out of some economic motive. Because the insured is really the major victim here, rather than the culprit, it is important for the investigator to determine whether a third-party arson for profit did occur in order to avoid targeting the wrong individual. The following are some examples of major forms of third-party arson.

Elimination of Business Competition

This type of scheme is motivated by someone who seeks to create a business monopoly, or at least to maintain a competitive edge. Businesses most prone to this type of arson are those that stand to suffer from too great a concentration of similar businesses in a limited geographic area. Examples include restaurants, taverns, and sex-oriented establishments (e.g., topless bars, adult bookstores, and massage parlors), which need to generate a large volume of business in order to make a profit. Increased competition can pose an economic problem to similar businesses in a limited area, which can cause some or all of them a degree of financial distress. Consequently, the financial records of a burned business may indicate the existence of financial problems that could lead the investigator to the mistaken assumption that the owner arranged the fire in order to obtain relief from that condition. Actually, in this example, a competitor is more likely to set the arson in order to improve his or her business situation.

The following case illustrates the type of arson in this category:

A brand-new nightclub had recently been opened in fairly close proximity to an older nightclub. The new nightclub was highly successful and started to draw business away from the old nighclub. Two employees of the old nightclub thought they would take matters into their own hands and "torch" the new nightclub one night after it closed, in hopes that this would help get back some of the old club's customers. Sometime during the early morning hours these two individuals broke into the new nightclub and set out eight 2 ½ gallon cans of gasoline at strategic locations throughout the business. Three 12-inch pipe bombs were then inserted into three of the cans of gasoline (see Figure 20–8). The fuses were lit and the individuals quickly fled the business and drove away. Unbeknownst to the would-be arsonists was the fact that the gasoline-soaked black powder could not be ignited. Thus, when the fuse finally made contact with the black powder, nothing happened (see Figure 20–9). The following morning, when the business was reopened, the unexploded devices and cans of gasoline were found.

During the initial investigation, it was suspected that at least one of the possible motives for this attempted arson was to eliminate competition with the older nightclub. Thus, the investigators focused their efforts on the owners and employees associated with the older nightclub. Several days after the attempted arson, an investigative inquiry was made at the nightclub and it was determined that two employees had recently left town and were working in a companion business of the old club 260 miles away. Not surprisingly, the sudden departure of these individuals caused them to emerge as major suspects. Their fingerprints, which were on file, were compared with fingerprints found on the gasoline cans and a positive fingerprint identification was made of both suspects. The suspects has assumed that any fingerprints they left on the cans would be destroyed once the cans were ignited, so they failed to take any precautions to ensure that their fingerprints were not left on the cans. They were subsequently arrested and convicted of attempted arson. An interesting sidelight to this was the presence of a handwritten number on one of the pipes (see Figure 20–10). After checking with several local hardware stores in the general area of both businesses, the investigators determined that the number was actually the price of the pipe and had been handwritten on the pipe by one of the hardware store employees. The employee who had written the number on the pipe was not able to make an identification of the individuals who had purchased it, but the possibility of an identifcation had to be considered by the investigators in their investigative process.

Although this was not considered to be an organized-crime-related attempted arson, the same category of arson is fairly common when an organized-crime figure maintains a financial interest in this type of business and either seeks a monopoly or offers to hire out his or her services to create the monopoly for a client or associates in that business. In either case it is important to involve investigators who are familiar with organized-crime intelligence gathering and investigation when elimination of business competition is suspected as a motive pattern behind arson.

Extraction of Extortion Payments

The identity of the criminal who drives out competitors by burning them out may not be known to the victim. On the other hand, offenders who demand extortion payments to let someone remain in business will necessarily identify themselves (if only through their collectors) in order to effect timely

Figure 20–8
Pipe Bomb and Gasoline

A pipe bomb intended to be used in conjunction with a can of gasoline. A hole was cut out of the top of the gasoline can between the handle and the lid to allow the bomb to be inserted into the can. The pipe bomb was immersed into the can. It was at this point the gasoline saturated the inner workings and got the gunpowder wet, therefore making it impossible to ignite.

(Courtesy Michael M. Gonzalez, Chief of Fire Investigations, Tampa Fire Department, Tampa, Florida)

payment. In this motive pattern, the arson may be a warning signal to a businessperson to "pay up or else," or it may be a signal to other businesspersons in that type of business to pay or wind up like the "example" of the burned-out victim. This pattern is similar to that found in the elimination of business competition, in that an organized-crime figure or someone who wants to appear to victims as such a figure (e.g., a juvenile gang leader) is often behind this type of scheme. Investigators who suspect this motive should examine the possibility of extortion payments being demanded of similar businesses in the locality.

Labor-Management Grievances

Arsons in business establishments may be the result of an unresolved labor-management grievance for which the perpetrator felt there was insufficient redress or resolution. Investigators should be careful to distinguish whether this type of arson is part of a more regularized pattern of violent activity in that industry or whether it could have resulted from a lone disgruntled employee. It is important to approach the possibility of this motive pattern carefully, for it can occur in an industry that is feeling the effects of an economic downturn and where the management may logically be reluctant to accede to labor demands because of their cost. Therefore, the financial records of that business, as well as of that entire industry, may signal financial stress. In reality the arson may have been caused by an employee unsympathetic to that economic condition. Investigators who suspect this motive pattern should examine the history of labor-management grievances in that business by reviewing records of complaints filed with state and federal labor regulatory agencies.

PEOPLE AND PAPER EVIDENCE IN ARSON-FOR-PROFIT INVESTIGATIONS

Figure 20–11 briefly summarizes the people and documents that are most likely to provide information on motive. The presence of certain documents is a good, direct indicator of fraud, economic stress, or combined fraud-stress motive. Other people and documents are more remote indicators and provide only a glimpse of a possible motive. The chart is intended merely as a guide to assist the investigator in determining motive.

Figure 20-9
Internal view of Pipe Bomb
A pipe bomb with the cap removed. When the burning fuse reached the gasoline-soaked gunpowder, it failed to ignite.

(Courtesy Michael M. Gonzalez, Chief of Fire Investigations, Tampa Fire Department, Tampa, Florida)

OTHER MOTIVES FOR ARSON

REVENGE, SPITE, JEALOUSY

This category includes jilted lovers, feuding neighbors, disgruntled employees, quarreling spouses, people getting even after being cheated or abused, and people motivated by racial or religious hostility. Lovers' disputes and domestic squabbles are the greatest contributors to this category (see Figure 20–12). In some parts of the country, particularly in rural areas, disagreements result in the burning of homes or barns. Many arsonists drink alcohol before this kind of fire.[16]

Figure 20-10
Pipe Bomb with Handwritten Price on it at Time of Sale
Handwritten on the pipe bomb was "519," which represented the price of the item when it was sold. Investigators were able to trace the pipe to a nearby hardware store and the clerk who had written the price on the pipe, which was $5.19. The clerk was able to confirm that the number was written by him.

(Courtesy Michael M. Gonzalez, Chief of Fire Investigations, Tampa Fire Department, Tampa, Florida)

Figure 20–11
Establishing Arson-for-Profit Motive
The roles of people and paper in arson-for-profit enforcement.

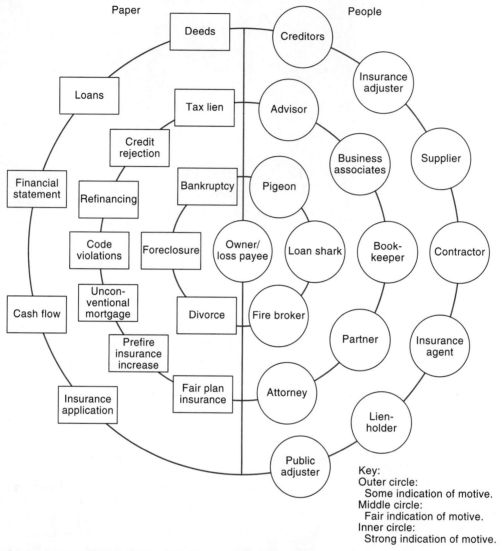

Source: C. L. Karchmer, M. E. Walsh, and J. Greenfield, *Enforcement Manual: Approaches for Combating Arson-for-Profit Schemes* (Washington, D.C.: U.S. Department of Justice, 1979), p. 31.

VANDALISM, MALICIOUS MISCHIEF

Vandals set fires for excitement and have no other motive. Many fires in vacant buildings, so common in recent years, are set by vandals. Vandals also set fires in abandoned cars, garbage cans, and so on; junk fires are also started as a protest to local conditions and for "instant urban renewal." Vagrants and drug users sometimes set fires. Vandalism fires seem to be increasing at a fairly rapid rate.[17]

CRIME CONCEALMENT, DIVERSIONARY TACTICS

Criminals sometimes set fires to obliterate the evidence of burglaries, larcenies, and murders. The

Figure 20–12
Revenge Arson
A female victim's car was set on fire by her boyfriend after she jilted him for another man.

(Courtesy Michael M. Gonzalez, Chief of Fire Investigations, Tampa Fire Department, Tampa, Florida)

fire may destroy evidence that a crime was committed, may obscure evidence connecting the perpetrator to the crime, or may make visual identification of a murder victim impossible or difficult. (For a further discussion of fire deaths, see Chapter 10, Injury and Death Investigation.) People set fires to destroy records that contain evidence of embezzlement, forgery, or fraud. Arson has also been used to divert attention while the perpetrator burglarizes another building and to cover attempted escapes from jails, prisons, and state hospitals.

The following case falls into this category:

An individual went to a local U-Haul sales office and set fire to one of the trucks on the property in order to draw employees outside the business so that the individual could remove money from the cash register. The tactic worked and all the employees left, but one employee returned sooner than expected and observed the individual removing the contents from the cash register. Other employees were summoned, and the individual was held by the employees and turned over to the police. (see Figure 20-13).

PSYCHIATRIC AFFLICTIONS— THE PYROMANIAC AND SCHIZOPHRENIC FIRE SETTER

Pyromaniacs differ characteristically from other arsonists in that they lack conscious motivation for their fire setting. In fact, they are considered by many to be motiveless. They may derive sensual satisfaction from setting fires. Pyromaniacs have been described as setting their fires for no particular reason and no material profit. In one study, the pyromaniac represented 60 percent of the sample population. Of this number, 241 expressed receiving some sort of satisfaction from the fire. The remaining 447 offenders offered no special reason or persistent interest beyond the fact that something within them forced them to set fires.[18]

The urge to set fires has been referred to as an irresistible impulse. However, authorities should be cautioned against accepting this explanation. Some researchers have postulated that pyromania releases sexual tension; others reject that as a major motive. In another study of pyromania, only a small percentage of subjects claimed to receive sexual gratification from fire setting.[19]

Psychosis is generally defined as a severe form of personality disorganization characterized by

Figure 20–13
Arson Fire Set as a Diversion
A truck set on fire at a U-Haul sales office in an effort to draw employees outside of the business so that the fire setter could remove money from the cash register.

(Courtesy Michael M. Gonzalez, Chief of Fire Investigations, Tampa Fire Department, Tampa, Florida)

marked impairment of contact with reality and personal and social functioning. Delusions, hallucinations, emotional blunting, and bizarre behavior may also be present in varying degrees. The most serious of all psychotic disorders is *schizophrenia*, which has been defined as "a group of psychotic disorders characterized by gross distortions of reality, withdrawal from social interaction, and disorganization and fragmentation of perception, thought, and emotion."[20]

In one study of 1,145 male fire setters, 13.4 percent could be classified as psychotic. These fire setters seemed distinct from others in that their fires were set for suicidal purposes, or their motives were delusional in character, or they manifested bizarre behavior during or immediately after the fire setting. Nonetheless, psychotic fire setters also fell into other categories, such as those of revenge fire setter and pyromaniac.[21]

VANITY, HERO FIRES

On occasion the person who "discovers" a fire turns out to be the one who started it and did so to be a hero:

In a recent case, a private guard company hired extra personnel and soon promoted one to sergeant. After a while, the company decided that the extra guards were not needed and discussed reducing the force. This reduction would have resulted in a demotion for the sergeant. Shortly thereafter, a fire was "discovered" by the sergeant. His quick action meant that the fire was confined, although it did cause thousands of dollars worth of damage. A polygraph examination showed reactions indicative of deception, and the sergeant confessed to a police lieutenant that he had in fact set the fire. His criminal record revealed that he had recently been released from a mental institution in another state and that he had been sent there in lieu of being sent to state prison.

The fire investigator must look for any overlap among types of fires, such as pathological, profit for employment, and vanity.

The setting of fires by police officers and firefighters, although relatively rare, does occur. Although sometimes volunteer firefighters might set a fire with a profit motive, those who are paid on an hourly or individual basis most often do so because they like to fight fires and there is no activity in the neighborhood. They might also like to save people and property and be called heroes. Baby-sitters sometimes find a need to be "recognized"; they may start fires where they are working, discover the fire, and "save the child."[22]

THE TYPICAL FEMALE FIRE SETTER

The female arsonist usually burns her own property, rarely that of an employer or neighbor. Her motives may be similar to those of male fire setters, but she seems to have more self-destructive tendencies. In one study of 201 female fire setters, most were found mentally defective. One third were psychotic, primarily schizophrenic. They were described generally as older women who were lonely, unhappy, and in despair.[23]

THE CHILD FIRE SETTER

Authorities on fire setting behavior believe that repetitive or chronic fire setting by children represents a severe behavior symptom or psychological disturbance. For the disturbed child, fire setting becomes an outlet for vengeful, hostile reactions, resentment, and defiance of authority.

In one study of 60 child fire setters, 60 percent were between 6 and 8 years of age and had the following characteristics:

- They set fires with fantasies of burning a member of the family who had withheld love or was a serious rival for parental attention.
- Most fires were started in or near their homes.
- The fires usually were symbolic, caused little damage, and were extinguished by the child.
- Prior to the fire setting, the child often had anxious dreams and fantasies of devils and ghosts.
- They suffered acute anxiety over their dreams, fantasies, and sexual preoccupations. All experienced sexual conflicts. Most actively masturbated; some participated in mutual masturbation, sodomy, and fellatio.
- Many of the boys who were bed-wetters were also passive.
- Many had learning disabilities.

- Some had physical handicaps.
- They also demonstrated other forms of asocial behavior, including truancy, stealing, running away, and aggressive behavior.
- Some were orphans and institutionalized.
- Their home environments were pathological or broken. Many had absent or ineffective fathers.
- They lacked a sense of security, love, and attention.

THE ADOLESCENT FIRE SETTER

There have been extensive studies on adolescent fire setting. One study of adolescent male fire setters showed that home-centered fire setting diminished as the age of the fire setter increased. Scenes of fires shifted to schools, churches, factories, and homes of strangers. These targets were preferred by adolescents aged 12 to 16. The highest incidence of fire setting at schools involved 12- to 14-year-olds. Fires directed at schools were generally associated with adolescents who had school problems and were motivated by revenge. These fires often were preceded by theft, vandalism, and harassment of teachers. Defective intelligence was not found to be a factor in adolescent fire setting until perpetrators reached the age of 16.[24]

Common characteristics of adolescent fire setters include a history of delinquency, disruptive home environment, pathological personality development, sexual immaturity, aggressive or destructive behavior, poor social adjustment, emotional disturbance, and poor academic achievement. Some researchers have suggested that adolescents set fires for excitement.

Whatever the motive, vandalism fires appear to represent 80 percent of adolescent fire setting. Adolescent fire setters generally work in pairs or groups, in which one boy assumes a dominant role and the others assume a submissive role.

DETECTION AND RECOVERY OF FIRE-ACCELERANT RESIDUES

Because flammable liquids flow to the lowest level, heat travels from this level up, and the charring on the bottom of the furniture, ledges, and shelves will be as deep as, or deeper than, the charring on the top.[25]

After a fire has been extinguished, the floor should be carefully cleaned. Many signs may be found there, such as charred, inkblotlike outlines of flammable liquids. A rug that appears charred all over may, when dried out and swept with a stiff broom, show a distinct pattern of the flammable liquid. This pattern occurs because the liquid is absorbed into the nap of the rug and burns more heavily. Flammable liquid usually soaks into the joints of wooden flooring, and as a result the joints will be heavily burned (see Figure 20–14).

The baseboards and sills should be checked, because flammable liquid often runs under and chars them on the bottom. Corners of the rooms should also be checked, because few floors are perfectly level, and flammable liquid often runs into and burns out the corners. In most common household fires, the corners at floor level are least damaged. The depth of charring in the floor and ceiling should be compared. If the floor is charred as much or more than the ceiling, it indicates a flammable material directly at floor level. In the aver-age fire, the floor temperature is only about one third that of the ceiling.

When gasoline or similar material is suspected to have been thrown on porches or buildings without basements, especially those with single constructed flooring, the soil beneath the burned area should be checked. The investigator should dig 1 or 2 inches into the earth and smell for the odor of flammable liquids. A vapor tester is better for this purpose, because flammables like alcohol have little or no odor in cold, wet earth.

If recovered material is suspected of containing flammable liquids, it should be sealed in an uncoated metal paint can, not in plastic bags or plastic containers. Uncoated metal paint cans can be purchased at auto supply houses. Plastic can give off hydrocarbons that contaminate the material. The container should be tightly sealed to minimize evaporation or contamination. Evidence tape should be used to assure integrity of the chain of evidence. The container may also be marked for identification purposes with permanent ink (see Figure 20–15).

Figure 20-14
Unusual Burn Patterns

Unusual burn patterns on wood floors should be closely examined. Flooring that was saturated with flammable liquid, like this, has deeply pronounced char. Burning between floorboards indicates that flammable liquid seeped down into the cracks. The area beneath the floor should also be examined for evidence of burning, and a sample of the burned floor should be sent to a laboratory for analysis.

(Courtesy Fire and Fraud Section, Aetna Casualty Surety Company)

Figure 20–15
Storage Containers

Samples of evidence found at the fire scene should be collected, placed in clean containers such as those shown here, and sent to a laboratory for professional analysis.

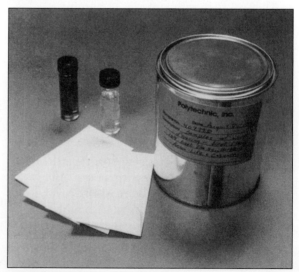

(Courtesy Fire and Fraud Section, Aetna Casualty Surety Company)

Before they can be analyzed, accelerant residues must first be separated from the ashes, wood, carpeting, or other material in which they are found. This extraction is usually accomplished by simple, steam, or vacuum distillation. These are listed in increasing order of efficiency, particularly for petroleum products, and increasing complexity of apparatus. Steam and vacuum distillation are capable of extracting 65 percent of any gasoline from debris; for fuel oil the efficiencies are 30 percent and 90 percent, respectively.[26]

SCIENTIFIC METHODS IN ARSON INVESTIGATION

The presence of flammable liquids may establish arson and sometimes link a suspect to the fire.[27] The objection is sometimes raised that identifiable amounts of liquid fire accelerants rarely survive a fire, and efforts to detect them would be largely wasted. But arson investigators often find accelerant residues and accelerants can survive fires. One expert, for example, performed the following experiment: He poured 2½ gallons of kerosene over furniture and rugs in one room of a wooden building, 1 gallon of gasoline over straw in another room, and left a trail of gasoline as a fuse. The building was allowed to burn freely and completely. He was able to extract identifiable amounts (more than 1 milliliter*) of both kerosene and gasoline from the debris.[28]

The areas most likely to contain residues of liquid fire accelerants—floors, carpets, and soil—are likely to have the lowest temperatures during the fire and may have insufficient oxygen to support the complete combustion of accelerant. Porous or cracked floors may allow accelerants to seep through to underlying earth. Numerous instances have been recounted of the excellent retention properties of soil for flammable liquid.[29] Another place where accelerants may be discovered is on the clothes and shoes of a suspect.

Because each method of accelerant detection (including the human nose) has a threshold of sensitivity, another question that arises is the vapor concentration that is produced by accelerant

residues. Some idea of the order of magnitude can be obtained from the experiment of two experts. They burned small (2-milliliter) samples of various accelerants for 30 seconds and then measured vapor concentrations ranging upward from 60 parts vapor per million of air—within the range of detection of currently available portable detectors and generally, but not always, well above readings produced by hydrocarbons from such things as burnt wood and burnt mattresses.[30]

Another way of looking at the potential vapor concentration is to consider the following hypothetical case: Suppose that a gallon of gasoline is used to accelerate a fire in a 15- by 15- by 8-foot room and that 1 percent (39 milliliters) survives the fire in cracks in the floor. (The residue would consist of higher boiling point components, such as naphthalene.) The subsequent evaporation of 1 milliliter (3 percent) of the residue would produce an average vapor concentration of 2.7 parts per million throughout the entire room. Such a concentration can be detected with available equipment. Ventilation of the room, of course, dissipates the vapor and generally causes the vapor concentration to be highest at the points where the residues are located, a situation that can be used to advantage in locating evidence samples to be preserved for laboratory analysis.

DETECTION OF FIRE ACCELERANTS

Several types of portable equipment are available to the arson investigator for detecting residues of flammable liquids at fire scenes. Some of these use chemical color tests, catalytic combustion, flame ionization, gas liquid chromatographs, and infrared spectrophotometers and ultraviolet fluorescence. The sensitivities, limitations, advantages, and disadvantages of each of these are discussed in the following sections.

Olfactory Detection
The sensitivity of the human nose to gasoline vapor is about 1 part per 10 million. Gasoline is a complex mixture of chemical compounds, the proportions of which vary with the source of the crude oil and the type of process used in its manufacture. Benzene and other aromatic hydrocarbons, for example, may constitute from 0.1 to 40 percent of the mixture.

---

*There are approximately 30 milliliters in 1 fluid ounce.

Although no conclusive data on the sensitivity of the nose to gasoline are available, the sensitivity of the nose to benzene vapor is 0.015 part per million. Assuming that 15 percent (or more) of gasoline vapor consists of aromatic hydrocarbons to which the nose is as sensitive as it is to benzene, then the sensitivity to gasoline is 1 part in 10 million (or greater). Thus, the nose is as sensitive as any of the currently available detecting equipment. But there are flammable liquids to which the nose is not sensitive. Another problem is the tendency of the nose to lose its sensitivity to an odor after prolonged or intense exposure to it. Further, the odor of fire accelerants may be masked by another strong odor such as that of burnt debris. In fact, in one case an arsonist attempted to camouflage gasoline by mixing it with vanilla.[31] Finally, it may be impractical or impossible to search with the nose for accelerant odors along floors or in recessed areas.[32]

Increasingly, agencies are using specially trained canines for the detection of accelerants. They have proved to be quite effective. On occasion such dogs are even brought to the scene of the arson while the fire is occurring in the hopes that the dogs will be able to detect accelerants on individuals who may have set the fire and are in the crowd watching the fire. (see Figure 20–16).

Chemical Color Test Detectors

Chemical color tests may be used to detect both liquid accelerant residues and their vapors. Certain dyes indicate the presence of hydrocarbons by turning red. Dyes are less sensitive and less specific to flammable liquids than other available methods. Dyes also may interfere with laboratory identification of the accelerant. Hydrocarbon vapors can be detected by pumping a suspected sample through a glass container of reagent that changes color in the presence of hydrocarbons. The reported sensitivity of this method is on the order of 1 part per 1,000. Again, the method is less sensitive and less specific (reacting to hydrocarbons that are not fire accelerants) than others available. Its main advantages are low cost (approximately $100 for the vapor detector) and simplicity (see Figure 20–17).[33]

Catalytic Combustion Detector

The most common flammable vapor detector operates on the catalytic combustion principle and is popularly known as a *sniffer, combustible-gas indicator, explosimeter*, or *vapor detector*. They are portable, moderate in cost, and fairly simple to operate. Vapor samples are pumped over a heated, platinum-plated coil of wire that causes any combustible gas present to oxidize. The heat from the oxidation raises the electrical resistance of the coil,

Figure 20–16
Accelerant Detecting Canine
An ATF-certified accelerant-detecting canine from the Salt Lake City Sheriff's Office, working the scene of a warehouse arson in Utah.

(Courtesy U.S. Department of the Treasury Bureau of Alcohol, Tobacco and Firearms)

Figure 20–17
Hydrocarbon Vapor Detector
Arson investigator using a
hydrocarbon vapor detector in testing
for the presence of accelerants at the
scene of a suspected arson.

(Courtesy Thomas Evans, Pinellas County, Florida, Sheriff's Office)

and this change in resistance is measured electronically. A sensitivity (to hexane vapor) on the order of a few parts per million can be achieved with this method. Because oxygen is required for the operation of the detector, its sensitivity is reduced in oxygen-deficient areas, but these are unlikely to occur in arson investigations. (An internal source of oxygen could be fitted to a detector if required.) Another problem is the gradual loss of sensitivity when this type of detector is exposed to gasoline containing lead. Lead deposits form on the platinum catalyst and interfere with its operation.[34]

Flame Ionization Detector

In the flame ionization detector, the sample gas is mixed with hydrogen and the mixture is burned. Ionized molecules are produced in the flame in proportion to the amount of combustible organic gases in the sample. (Pure hydrogen, air, and water vapor produce little ionization.) The degree of ionization is then measured by electrometer. The sensitivity of this method (to methane) is on the order of 1 part in 10 million. It is thus more sensitive but more complex and expensive than the catalytic combustion method.

Gas Liquid Chromatograph

The portable gas liquid chromatograph (GLC) adapted for field use, sometimes called the *arson chromatograph*, is one of the most common detectors in arson investigations. The sample gas is first separated into components based on the speed with which they travel through a tube filled with packing material. The amounts of each component are then measured by either a catalytic combustion or flame ionization detector. The sensitivity ranges from a few hundredths of a part per million to a few parts per million, depending on the type of detector used. The main advantage is specificity because of the preliminary separation process. The main disadvantages are its size, weight, and cost. Also, the time required for the analysis of each sample is about ½ hour, a disadvantage in some situations. In addition, there is a setup time of about 1 hour. The operation of the gas chromatograph requires a certain amount of technical training.

Infrared Spectrophotometer

Infrared spectrophotometers can achieve high specificity to flammable liquids and high sensitivity (on the order of hundredths of a part per million).

Infrared light of varying wavelengths is directed through the sample, and the amount of light passing through is plotted on a pen recorder. The recording is compared with those of known compounds to determine the identity of the sample. Because the chemical bonds in a compound determine how it absorbs infrared radiation, these recordings (called *spectrograms*) are unique for different compounds. However, evidence mixed with impurities must be purified before it can be successfully identified. In particular, since water vapor absorbs infrared light, it interferes with the identification of flammable vapors. This is a disadvantage in arson investigation, where water is commonly present. A final disadvantage is the high cost of this type of detector.

Ultraviolet Fluorescence

This procedure consists of illuminating the darkened fire scene with an ultraviolet lamp. Certain substances, including constituents of gasoline and its residue, absorb the ultraviolet light and release it as visible light. They appear to glow against the darkened background. The color of the glow is affected by exposure to heat, and so the method also can be used to locate the point of origin of a fire. The only equipment required is an ultraviolet lamp and a portable power supply. The sensitivity of the method appears comparable to that of other methods of detection. The main disadvantage of the method is that it requires extensive testing, particularly to identify those fire accelerants to which it does not respond.[35]

INTERVIEWS

To establish possible motives and develop suspects, the arson investigator must interview people who might know about the fire and how it started. The following kinds of different people may provide information.[36]

POSSIBLE WITNESSES

Prospective witnesses include tenants of buildings; tenants of surrounding buildings; businesspeople in surrounding buildings; customers of businesses in buildings; customers of businesses in surrounding buildings; and passers-by, including bus drivers, taxi drivers, delivery people, garbage collectors, police patrols, and people waiting for buses and taxis.

Questions to Ask

Did you observe the fire? At what time did you first observe the fire? In what part of the building did you observe the fire? What called your attention to the building? Did you see any people entering or leaving the building before the fire? Did you recognize them? Can you describe them? Did you observe any vehicles in the area of the fire? Can you describe them? Can you describe the smoke and the color of the flame? How quickly did the fire spread? Was the building burning in more than one place? Did you detect any unusual odors? Did you observe anything else?

FIREFIGHTERS AT THE SCENE

Firefighters can be an invaluable source of information to arson investigators because of their technical knowledge and because of what they observed at a fire.

Questions to Ask

What time was the alarm received? What time did you arrive at the scene of the fire? Was your route to the scene blocked? What was the extent of burning when you arrived? Were doors and windows locked? Were the entrances or passageways blocked? What kind of fire was it? What was the spread speed of the fire? In what area(s) did the fire start? How near was the fire to the roof? Was there evidence of the use of an accelerant? Was any evidence of arson recovered? Did the building have a fire alarm system? Was it operating? Was there any evidence of tampering with the alarm system? Did the building have a sprinkler system? Did it operate? Was there any evidence of tampering with the sprinkler system? Was there anyone present in the building when you arrived? Who was the person in the building? Did that person say anything to you? Were there any people present at the scene when you arrived? Who were they? Did you observe any vehicles at or leaving the scene when you arrived? Can you describe them? Were there contents in the building? Was there evidence that contents had been removed? Was the owner present? Did the owner make a statement? What did the owner say? What is the fire history of the building? What is the fire history of the area?

INSURANCE PERSONNEL

The profit in many arson-for-profit cases is an insurance payment. Three people may be interviewed to determine if the profit centers around an insurance claim: the insurance agent or broker, the insurance adjuster, and the insurance investigator.

There may be restrictions on the amount of information insurance personnel can turn over without a subpoena, but the investigator should be able to determine enough to indicate whether a subpoena or search warrant would prove fruitful.

Questions to Ask the Agent or Broker

Who is the insured? Is there more than one person insured? Is the insured the beneficiary? What type of policy was issued? What is the amount of the policy? When was it issued? When does it expire? What is the premium? Are payments up to date? Have there been any increases in the amount of coverage? What amount? When did the increase take effect? What was the reason for the increase? Are there any special provisions in the policy (e.g., interruption of business or rental income)? What are they, and when did they take effect? Does the insured have any other policies? Were there previous losses at the location of the fire? Were there losses at other locations owned by the insured?

Questions to Ask the Insurance Claims Adjuster

Did you take a sworn statement from the insured? Did the insured submit documents regarding proof of loss, value of contents, bills of lading, value of building, and the like? Did you inspect the fire scene? Did you inspect the fire scene with a public insurance adjuster? Did you and the public adjuster agree on the cost of the loss? Have you dealt with this public adjuster before? Has he or she represented this owner before? Has the insured had any other losses with this company? If so, get details.

Questions to Ask the Insurance Investigator

Were you able to determine the cause of the fire? Did you collect any evidence? Who analyzed the evidence? What were the results of the analysis? Was the cause of the fire inconsistent with the state of the building as known through underwriting examination? Have you investigated past fires at the location? Have you investigated past fires involving the insured? What were the results of the investigations? Have you had prior investigations involving the public adjuster? Have you had prior investigations involving buildings handled by the same insurance agent or broker? What were the results of these investigations? Does this fire fit into a pattern of fires of recent origin in this area? What are the similarities? What are the differences? Have you taken any statements in connection with this burning? Whose statements did you take? What do they reveal?

OTHER WITNESSES CONCERNING FINANCES OF INSURED

A number of other people may have information on the finances of the owner, including business associates, creditors, and competitors. This information may indicate how the owner stood to profit from the burning.

Questions to Ask

How long have you known the owner/insured? What is the nature of your relationship with the owner/insured? Do you have any information on the financial position of the business? Is the owner/insured competitive with similar businesses? Have there been recent technological advances that would threaten the owner/insured's competitive position? Has there been a recent increase in competition that would affect the owner/insured's position? Have changes in the economy affected the owner/insured's position? Has the owner/insured had recent difficulty in paying creditors? Has the owner/insured's amount of debt increased recently? Has the owner/insured lost key employees lately? Has the location where the owner/insured does business changed for the worse recently? Has the owner/insured increased the mortgage or taken out a second or third mortgage? Has the owner/insured had difficulty making mortgage payments? Do you have any other information about the owner/ insured's financial position?

NEWS MEDIA PERSONNEL

This category includes both the print and electronic media. Individuals affiliated with these groups may have noticed something of value to the investigator or perhaps have films of the fire and fire scene. For example, if the arsonist remained in the area after the fire and mingled with spectators, his or her presence may be captured on film and prove quite valuable in an investigation.

THE MEDICAL EXAMINER

The autopsy should reveal whether any victim found dead in the fire was dead or alive before the fire started and what the cause of death was. It is not uncommon for a person to be murdered and the scene made to appear as if the person had been killed by fire. See Chapter 10, Injury and Death Investigation, for more detailed discussion of fire deaths.

INTERVIEWING A SUSPECT

The following is based on the assumption that the person to be interviewed is involved in arson for profit, that the investigator has enough evidence for an arrest or enough to convince the subject that he or she is liable to arrest, and that the subject is more valuable to the investigation in a cooperative role than as a defendant.

Questions to Ask the Subject

Are you willing to cooperate in this investigation? How many other people are involved in the arson-for-profit scheme? How are they involved? What role does each person play in the scheme? Explain (in detail) how the scheme works. How did you first become involved in the scheme? How did you meet the other participants? Where did you meet the other participants? Are you still in contact with the other participants? How often do you see them? Where do you see them? What do you talk about when you meet with them? Would you be able to record your conversations with them? Are you willing to record your conversations with them? Would you be willing to introduce an undercover investigator into the group? Could you introduce an undercover investigator into the group without their becoming suspicious? How far in advance of an arson are you told about it? What role do you play in connection with the arson (torch, driver, pigeon, fence, and so forth)? Are you willing to swear to an affidavit for a search warrant? Are you willing to testify before a grand jury? Are you willing to testify at trial? Do you have information on other arson-for-profit schemes?

Questions to Ask the Torch, Specifically

What method(s) was (were) used to accomplish the arson? Specify whether it was an incendiary device, gasoline or other inflammable fluid, or other. If an incendiary device was used, be specific as to the type of device. Where did you obtain the incendiary device? If it was improvised, who made it? How much did it cost? Who paid for the incendiary device? Was it paid for by cash or check? If gasoline or other flammable fluid was used, where was it obtained? How much was obtained and used? Are any special techniques used in setting a fire or causing an explosion to avoid detection?

INTERVIEWING THE OWNER/TARGET

The target of the investigation may be an owner, landlord, fire broker, or the like. The interview should take place after obtaining the background information on the fire and after interviewing the individuals previously listed.

Questions to Ask the Target

Tell me in your own words what you know about this fire. When did you first hear of the arson? Who told you? Where were you, and what were you doing before, during, and after the arson? Who was with you? Do you know who committed the arson? Do you have any knowledge of any previous fire at the building? Do you have any knowledge of any previous incidents of any kind and at any location owned or rented by the owner/occupant of the building? Do you know of any recent changes in insurance coverage? Do you know the owner of the arson property? Describe your relationship to the owner. Do you have any financial interest in the burned property?

Questions to Ask the Owner

Tell me in your own words what you know about this fire. How long have you owned the burned property? What was the purchase price? What was the total amount of the mortgage? Who is your insurance company? agent? broker? public adjuster? How much insurance do you carry? Is there more than one policy on this property? on its contents? on rental or business interruption? Have you increased your insurance coverage on the property in the past year? If so, why and at whose suggestion? Have you ever received an insurance cancellation notice on this property? Where were you at the time of the fire? When did you first hear of the arson? Who told you? When were you last in the building? Was the building secured? If so, in what manner? Who else has access to or keys to the building? Who was the last person to leave the building? Do you have any knowledge that the sprinkler system or burglar alarm system was on and working? Indicate the name and address of all lienholders. What is the amount of each lien? What was the value of the inventory on hand immediately prior to the fire? Can you provide documentation for this value? Was any inventory removed from the premises prior to the fire? If yes, by whom and for what purposes? Where did it go, and why was it removed? Was any inventory removed from the premises after the fire? If yes, by whom and for what purpose? List the inventory removed and its value. Did you set the fire or cause it to be set? Do you know who set it?

INTERVIEWING A POTENTIAL INFORMANT WHO IS NOT A SUSPECT

Before interviewing a potential informant who is not a suspect, investigative efforts should be made to determine if the informant has any police record and, if so, if it could have any bearing on the reliability of the information provided. For example, if a potential informant has previously been convicted of arson and perjury, then the investigator should be cautious in acting on his or her information.

Questions to Ask a Potential Informant

How are you currently supporting yourself? Do you have any pending prosecutions against you? Where? What are you charged with? Do you have any information about arson for profit in this city, county, state? How did you acquire this information? Do you know anyone engaged in arson for

profit? What roles does that person play in the scheme? How do you know this? What is your relationship with this person or persons—loan shark, bookmaker, fence, or the like? Where does this person live, frequent? Who are his or her associates? Do you know them? Are they part of the scheme? Have you been asked to involve yourself in the scheme? In what way? Have any of these people talked freely to you about their activities? Have they talked in your presence? What was said? Can you engage them in conversation about past arsons? future arsons? Would they be suspicious of you? Could you wear a concealed recorder during conversation? Could you introduce an undercover officer into the group? Would you be willing to testify before a grand jury? Would you be willing to testify at trial? Would you be willing to swear to an affidavit for a search warrant? Would you be willing to swear to an eavesdropping warrant? What do you expect in return for your help?

THE ARSON SUSPECT

In some arson investigations, a single prime suspect may emerge and investigative efforts will be focused accordingly. However, in most cases, a number of suspects emerge, and merely establishing that one or more of them had a motive to set the fire is not proof enough for an arrest and conviction. The investigator must also determine which of the suspects had the opportunity and the means to commit the crime. This determination must be related to the background, personal characteristics, past activities, and financial status of each of the suspects. For example, 10 people may have had a chance to set the fire, but only 4 or 5 may have had a motive, and of this number, perhaps only 1 or 2 would risk an arson conviction for the expected profit or satisfaction.

In probing an arson fire, seldom does direct evidence link a suspect with a fire. Because arsonists tend to take elaborate precautions not to be seen near the fire, they are seldom caught in the act. It may be best for the investigator to concentrate on gathering circumstantial evidence and some provable facts from which valid conclusions can be drawn. For example, let us assume that the fire which occurred in a warehouse was ignited by a timing device—a slow-burning candle attached to some flammable material triggered 2 hours before the fire actually started. The owner, who is also a prime suspect, is identified but can prove his whereabouts at the time of the fire. However, he cannot prove where he was 2 hours before the fire. In addition, the structure was locked when the fire department arrived to fight the fire, and the owner is the only one with a set of keys. The owner also took a large insurance policy out on the warehouse a short time ago.

Although far more evidence would likely be needed to arrest and convict the owner, there is sufficient justification for focusing a considerable amount of the investigation in his direction. If some other evidence is found to link him more directly to the fire (say, candles and flammable material found in the trunk of his car), then the circumstantial evidence becomes significant.

PHOTOGRAPHING THE ARSON SCENE

STILL PHOTOGRAPHY

Photographing a fire scene can be a challenge. Adverse conditions—poor lighting, time constraints, inconvenient angles, and so forth—necessitate the use of camera equipment that is reliable and quick because there rarely is time to adjust the focus on every shot or arrange perfect lighting. Therefore, the ideal still camera is one that is fully automatic, such as a 35-millimeter camera with a good-grade film. This type of camera is more than adequate for taking interior as well as exterior photos. The adjustable setting on a 35-millimeter camera allows close-up photos at approximately 3 feet. In cases where the crime scene photographer wants more detail, photos can be enlarged.

The photo session should take at least as long as the physical examination; however, it is not necessary to photograph every step. The investigator should follow the same path in photographing the structure as is followed in the physical examination—following the burn trail from least to greatest amount of damage. The photos are as important as the written report because they show what happened rather than merely telling what happened.

Ideally the investigator should be concerned with photographing the areas that show, in detail, what happened. For example, if there are severely darkened ventilation patterns out of a window or a door, the investigator should photograph them. Other areas to be photographed are burn patterns at lower levels and those that show distinct lines of demarcation, melted or stained glass, areas where explosions occurred, broken locks, and areas where the electrical service enters the building. If the investigator does not know what happened, detailed photos will help in assessing what took place.

In some cases it is necessary to compile a panoramic view. This can be accomplished with a composite of several photos that are taped together to create a much larger overview. The area of the fire's origin should be photographed twice, first before the rubble is disturbed and then after the debris has been removed. Severe burn patterns should be documented, especially patterns that show how the fire burned. Burn patterns at the base of doors and underneath door moldings are a strong indication that flammable liquids were used. This is because a fire spreading of its own accord burns upward, not downward.

If clocks are present, the investigator should always photograph the faces of the clocks showing the times they stopped. Fires often cause interruptions in electricity, which means electrical clocks will usually stop within 10 minutes to ½ hour after the time the fire started. Knowing when the fire started is crucial to the case.

VIDEOTAPE

Another form of visual documentation is videotaping, discussed in Chapter 3, The Crime Scene and Its Associated Procedures. While the average fire investigation does not require videotaping, it should be done if the investigator reasonably believes that the case will involve litigation.[37]

EXPLOSIVES INVESTIGATION

Under the fire and explosion investigation definition, an *explosion* is a physical reaction characterized by the presence of four major elements: high-pressure gas, confinement or restriction of the pressure, rapid production or release of that pressure, and change or damage to the confining (restricting) structure, container, or vessel that is caused by the pressure release. Although an explosion is almost always accompanied by the production of a loud noise, the noise itself is not an essential element of an explosion.[38] The generation and vilent escape of gasses are the primary criteria of an explosion.

TYPES OF EXPLOSIONS

There are two major types of explosions: mechanical and chemical. These types are differentiated by the source or mechanism by which the explosive pressures are produced.

Mechanical Explosions

In *mechanical explosions*, the high-pressure gas is produced by purely physical reactions. None of the reactions involves changes in the basic chemical nature of the substances. The most commonly used example of a mechanical explosion is the bursting of a steam boiler. The source of overpressure is the steam created by heating and vaporizing water. When the pressure of the steam can no longer be confined by the boiler, the vessel fails and an explosion results.

Chemical Explosions

In *chemical explosions*, the generation of high-pressure gas is the result of reactions in which the fundamental chemical nature of the fuel is changed. The most common chemical explosions are those caused by the burning of combustible hydrocarbon fuels such as natural gas, liquified petroleum gas, gasoline, kerosene, and lubricating oils.

An example of a chemical explosion is the one that destroyed the Alfred P. Murah Federal Building in Oklahoma City several years ago. In this case the convicted bomber, Timothy McVeigh, loaded a van with 4,000 pounds of ammonium nitrate (commonly used as a fertilizer) that had been soaked in fuel oil and detonated with high explosives. The explosion killed 167 people.[39] As depicted in Figure 20–18, the destructive force of such a device is enormous.

INVESTIGATING THE EXPLOSION SCENE

The objectives of the explosion scene investigation are no different from those for a regular fire inves-

Figure 20–18
Damage Resulting from a Chemical Explosion
The effects of a chemical explosion that destroyed the Alfred P. Murah Federal Building in Oklahoma City.

(Courtesy UPI/Corbis-Bettman)

tigation: to determine the origin, identify the fuel and ignition sources, determine the cause, and establish the responsibility for the incident. A systematic approach to the scene examination is just as important in an explosion investigation as in a fire investigation—or even more—because explosion scenes are often larger and more disturbed than fire scenes. Without a preplanned, systematic approach, explosion investigations become more difficult or even impossible to conduct effectively.[40]

The first duty of the investigator is to secure the scene of the explosion. First responders to the explosion should establish and maintain physical control of the structure and surrounding areas. Unauthorized persons should be prevented from entering the scene or touching blast debris remote from the scene itself because the critical evidence from an explosion (whether accidental or criminal) may be very small and may be easily disturbed or moved by people passing through. Evidence is also easily picked up on shoes and tracked out. Properly securing the scene also tends to prevent additional injuries to unathorized and/or curious persons who may attempt to enter an unsafe area. As a general rule the outer perimeter of the incident scene should be established at one and a half times the distance of the farthest piece of debris found. Significant pieces of blast debris can be propelled great distances or into nearby buildings or vehicles, and these areas should be included in the scene perimeter (see Figure 20–19). If additional pieces of debris are found, the scene perimeter should be widened.

The investigator should establish a scene pattern. Investigation team members should search the scene from the outer perimeter inward toward the area of greatest damage. The final determination of the location of the explosion's epicenter should be made only after all of the scene has been examined. The seach pattern itself may be grid, zone, or spiral shaped. (See Chapter 3, The Crime Scene and Its Associated Procedures, for a more detailed description of these search patterns.) Often the particular circumstances of the scene will dictate the nature of the pattern. In any case, the assigned area of the

Figure 20–19
Damage from a Metal Pipe Bomb
Photograph shows the devastation that occurs when a metal pipe bomb is placed in the front seat of a vehicle and detonated. Explosive filler in the pipe bomb was 1.5 pounds of smokeless powder.

(Courtesy Jack H. Adkins, Bomb Squad Commander, Big Bend Bomb Disposal Team, Tallahassee, Florida)

search pattern should overlap so that no evidence will be lost at the edge of any search area.

It is often useful to search areas more than once. When this is done, a different searcher should be used on each search to help ensure that evidence is not overlooked. The number of actual searchers will depend upon the physical size and complexity of the scene. The investigator in charge should keep in mind, however, that too many searchers can often be as counterproductive as too few. Searchers should be briefed as to the proper procedures for identifying, logging, photographing, marking, and mapping the location of evidence. The location of evidence may be marked with chalk marks, spray paint, flags, stakes, or other marking means. After being photographed, the evidence may be tagged, moved, and secured (see Figure 20–20).

Structures that have suffered explosions are often more structurally damaged than those burned in a fire. The possibility that a floor, wall, ceiling, roof, or entire building will collapse is much greater and should always be considered. Explosion scenes that involve bombings or explosives have added dangers. Investigators should be on the lookout for additional devices and undetonated explosives. The modus operandi (MO) of some bomber-arsonists includes using secondary explosive devices specifically targeted for the law enforcement or fire service personnel who will be responding to the bombing

incident. For example, several years ago bomb blasts an hour apart rocked a building containing an abortion clinic in Atlanta, Georgia, injuring six people who had rushed to the scene of the first explosion, including federal agents, rescue workers, and TV cameramen (see Figure 20–21). The second explosion was clearly designed to maim and hurt those who were coming to assist.

A thorough search of the scene should be conducted for any secondary devices prior to the initiation of the postblast investigation. If undetonated explosive devices or explosives are found, it is imperative that they not be moved or touched. The area should be evacuated and isolated, and explosives disposal authorities summoned. (This will be discussed in greater detail later in this chapter.)

LOCATING AND IDENTIFYING ARTICLES OF EVIDENCE

Investigators should locate, identify, note, log, photograph, and map any of the many and varied articles of physical evidence. Because of the propelling nature of explosions, the investigator should keep in mind that significant pieces of evidence may be found in a wide variety of locations, including outside the exploded structure, embedded in the walls or other structural members of the exploded structure, in nearby vegetation, inside adjacent

Figure 20–20
Debris from a Bombing Being Examined
Special Agents of the Department of the Treasury/Bureau of Alcohol, Tobacco and Firearms inspecting debris from the scene of a bombing.

(Courtesy U.S. Department of Treasury/Bureau of Alcohol, Tobacco, and Firearms)

Figure 20–21
Explosion at an Abortion Clinic
Bystanders protect themselves seconds after a second explosion (*left*) detonated outside the Atlanta Northside Family Planning Services building in Atlanta, Georgia. Two explosions rocked the building containing an abortion clinic and police said it appeared the clinic was targeted.

(Courtesy AP Photo/Alan Mothner)

structures or vehicles, or embedded in adjacent structures. In the case of bombing incidents or incidents involving the explosion of tanks, appliances, or equipment, significant pieces of evidence debris may have pierced the bodies of victims or be contained in their clothing.

The clothing of anyone injured in an explosion should be obtained for examination and possible analysis. The investigator should ensure that photographs are taken of the injuries and that any material removed from a victim during medical treatment or surgery is preserved. This is true whether the person survives or not. Investors should note the condition and position of any damaged and displaced structural components such as walls, ceiling, floors, roofs, foundations, support columns, doors, windows, sidewalks, driveways, and patios. Investigators should also note the condition and position of any damaged and displaced building contents such as furnishings, appliances, heating or cooking equipment, manufacturing equipment, victim's clothing, and personal effects. Investigators should note the condition and position of any damaged and displaced utility equipment such as fuel gas meters and regulators, fuel gas piping and tanks, electrical boxes and meters, electrical conduits and conductors, heating-oil tanks, parts of explosive devices, or fuel vessels.

Investigators should identify, diagram, photograph, and note pieces of debris that indicate the

direction and relative force of the explosion. They should keep in mind that the force necessary to shatter a wall is more than that necessary to merely dislodge or displace it and that the force necessary to shatter a window is less than that necessary to displace a wall but more than that necessary to blow out a window intact. The greater the force, the farther pieces of debris will be thrown from the epicenter.

Investigators should log, diagram, and photograph varying missile distances and directions of travel for similar debris, such as window glass. Larger, more massive missiles should be measured and weighed for comparison of the forces necessary to propel them. The distance as well as the direction of significant pieces of evidence from the apparent epicenter of the explosion may be critical. The location of all significant pieces should be completely documented on the explosion scene diagram, along with notes as to both distance and direction. This enables investigators to reconstruct the trajectories of various components.

ANALYZING THE FUEL SOURCE

Once the origin, or epicenter, of the explosion has been identified, the investigator should determine what type of fuel was employed. This is done by comparing the nature and type of damage to the known available fuels at the scene.

The available fuel sources must be considered and eliminated until one fuel is identified as meeting all of the physical damage criteria. For example, if the epicenter of the explosion is identified as a 6-foot crater of pulverized concrete in the center of the floor, escaping natural gas can be eliminated as the fuel. Chemical analysis of debris, soot, soil, or air samples can be helpful in identifying the fuel. With explosives or liquid fuels, gas chromatography, mass spectrography, or other chemical tests of properly collected samples may be able to identify their presence. (See Chapter 9, The Crime Laboratory and the Criminal Investigation Process, for a more detailed discussion of instrumental analysis).

Air samples taken in the vicinity of the area of origin can be used in identifying gases or the vapors of liquid fuels. For example, commerical "natural gas" is a mixture of methane, ethane, propane, nitrogen, and butane. The presence of ethane in an air sample may show that commercial natural gas was there rather than naturally occurring "swamp," "marsh," or "sewer" gas, which are all methane.

Once a fuel is identified, the investigator should determine its source. For example, if the fuel is identified as a lighter-than-air gas and the structure is serviced by natural gas, the investigator should locate the source of gas that will most likely be at or below the epicenter, possibly a leaking service line or malfunctioning gas appliance. All gas piping—including that from the street mains or LP-gas storage tanks, up to and through the service regulator and meter, to and including all appliances—should be examined and leak-tested if possible.

Odorant verification should be part of any explosion investigation involving, or potentially involving, flammable gas, especially if there are indicators that there were no signs of leaking gas detected by people present. Its presence should be verified.

BOMB THREATS

Bomb threats are numerous and occur for a number of reasons. Since relatively few reported threats actually result in the finding of a bomb or explosive device, law enforcement officers may consider following the procedures discussed below.

RESPONDING TO THREATS

Telephone Call
There are generally several explanations for why someone would telephone to report that a bomb is about to go off in a particular location. First, the person may have definite knowledge or may believe that an explosive device has been or will be placed and may want to minimize the potential personal injury or property damage. Second, the caller may want to create an atmosphere of fear and/or panic, which will, in turn, possibly result in the disruption of normal activities.[41]

When a telephone bomb threat is made, the caller should be kept on the line as long as possible. The call should be taped or monitored on an extension telephone whenever possible. The person answering the call should determine the following:

- The time the call was recieved.
- The sex and age of the caller (based on the caller's voice). Voice characteristics of the caller, such as accent, calm, stutter, giggling, stressed, disguised, slow, deep, nasal, sincere, crying, loud, angry, lisp, squeaky, slurred, broken, rapid, excited, normal.
- Background noices.

In addition, the person answering the call should ask questions designed to elicit:

- The location of the bomb.
- The caller's reason for placing the bomb.
- When the bomb is going to explode.
- What the bomb looks like.
- What kind of bomb it is.
- What will cause it to explode.
- Whether the caller placed the bomb.

Evacuation
The decision to evacuate the premises should be made by the responsible party at the scene. If the responsibile party decides to evacuate, law enforcement officers will generally recommend that the evacuation be completed, including all searchers, at least 15 minutes prior to the time designated by the suspect as the blast time and remain in effect for at least 15 minutes after the designated time. The officers should assist with the evacuation and crowd control if requested. If officers have reason

to believe that an extreme emergency exists, they should take whatever action is necessary to save lives, including an order to evacuate the building.

Industrial Plants, Shopping Centers, and the Like

When a bomb threat is reported at an industrial plant, office building, shopping center, or apartment complex, the assigned officer should contact the owner or manager of the scene and advise the responsible party that search procedures, evacuations, and so forth, are the responsibility of the building owner or person in charge. The law enforcement officer responding should request any specific equipment necessary (fire, utility, etc.). Employees of the business should be briefed on what to look for (e.g., unusual or out-of-place items) and cautioned that suspicious items should not be touched if located.

Private Homes and Small Businesses

If it is necessary to search a private home or small business and there are no responsible persons present to do a search, officers should conduct the search themselves. Canine teams and/or bomb detail personnel may be contacted for assistance.

Police and Public Safety Buildings

If a bomb threat is received against a police or public safety building by a civilian employee, the employee should refer the threats to a sworn officer and the chief of police should be notified. Usually, the chief will make arrangements to have a systematic search done of the facility. If a possible explosive device is located, the bomb detail should be notified and will then take charge.[42]

SEARCHING FOR CONCEALED EXPLOSIVES

Search procedures should always stress measures for protecting life and property. To help detect anything suspicious or out of the ordinary, search procedures should include interviews with persons familar with the buildings or structures to be searched. Such people include maintenance or security personnel, janitorial staff, and personnel in charge of specific areas. It is important to eliminate some areas in order to focus attention on others that are potentially more dangerous.[43] Search personnel must be cautioned not to move, jar, or touch any suspicious object.

In general, the following search techniques should be employed to ensure an orderly and systematic search: The suspected area should be cordoned off on all sides (by at least 300 feet, if possible). In multistory buildings, at least the floors directly above and below the suspected area should be evacuated. The doors and windows should be left open. All electrical equipment should be disconnected. However, the building's main power source should not be shut down. Entry and exit to the building should be controlled by management with police assistance. Traffic should be directed away from the scene. Radio and cellular phone transmissions are prohibited in the area of a possible explosive device, that is, within 1,000 feet of a suspected area. Search team members should be selected from volunteer personnel who are most familiar with the building or area to be searched. Areas accessible to the general public should be searched first, unless there is reason to suspect some other location. Searchers should look for items that are foreign or out of place. The search area should be divided equally among search team personnel. A recommended technique is to stand still with eyes closed and listen for the sound of a mechanical timer. An attempt should be made to locate and determine the source of all noise. The search sweep should be systematic, left to right, ground to waist level, waist to eye level, and eye level to the highest level that can be searched. Each area should be marked and controlled upon completion of the search to avoid duplication and later contamination. Whenever a suspicious object is located, all search operations should be suspended within a radius of 300 feet. The object should be left untouched until the bomb technician determines that it is safe (see Figures 20–22 and 20–23).

WHAT NOT TO DO

- Do not ignore bomb threats.
- Do not touch suspected explosives.
- Do not touch suspected bombs.
- Do not move suspected bombs.
- Do not move things if you do not know what they are.
- Do not open things if you do not know what they are.

Figure 20–22
Bomb Squad Officers
Officer in a bomb suit preparing to respond to a bomb threat call.

(Courtesy of Jack H. Adkins, Bomb Squad Commander, Big Bend Bomb Disposal Team, Tallahassee, Florida)

- Do not place in water.
- Do not shake.
- Do not turn any suspicious objects.
- Do not cut wires.
- Do not pull wires.
- Do not cut any strings.
- Do not pull any fuses.

- Do not stamp out fuses.
- Do not undo glued packages.
- Do not pass metallic tools near suspected bomb.
- Do not move switches.
- Do not release hooks.
- Do not smoke near suspected bombs.

Figure 20–23
Robot Used in Handling Suspicious Objects
MAX TR 2000 Enhanced Technical Robot System. Configured with a Benelli 90 shotgun that is fired remotely, this device can be used to detonate a suspicious object or can remove it from its existing location to a safer area.

(Courtesy HDE Robotics Group, Inc., Fort Worth, Texas)

- Do not carry the bomb outside.
- Do not carry the bomb, period.
- Do not place near heat.
- Do not place near vital equipment.
- Do not use insulating materials (bomb blankets or sandbags) unless you know how the bomb works.
- Do not move the bomb away from people— move the people away from the bomb.
- Do not get near bombs.
- Do not transmit on radios. Turn beepers and all other transmitters *off*.[44]

POTENTIAL CONCEALMENT AREAS FOR BOMBS

Buildings and Structures

- Elevator wells and shafts, including nooks, closets, storage rooms, false panels, walk areas, counterweights, motors, cables, and trash in shaft.
- All ceiling areas.
- Restrooms.
- Access doors.
- Crawl space in restrooms and areas used as access to plumbing fixtures.
- Electrical fixtures.
- Utility and other closet areas.
- Space under stairwells.
- Boiler (furnace) rooms.
- Flammable storage areas.
- Main switches and valves.
- Indoor trash receptacles, including covered ashtrays.
- Storage areas, including record-storage areas.
- Mailrooms.
- Ceiling lights with easily removable panels.
- Firehose racks and fire extinguishers.
- Basements.
- Around windows hidden by drapes or shades.
- Inside desks.
- Inside storage cabinets and containers.
- Under tables and chairs.

Auditoriums and Theaters

- Under each seat and into cut seat cushions.
- Stage area.
- Microphones, cameras, and radios.

- Speaker platform.
- Crawlways.
- Tunnels.
- Trapdoors.
- Dressing rooms.
- Restrooms.
- Storage areas.
- Ceilings.
- Props.
- Hanging decorations.
- Lighting fixtures.
- Sound system.
- Air-conditioning system.
- Roof.
- Heating system.
- Projection booths.
- Offices, including personal articles such as purses and briefcases.

Outside Areas

- Street drainage systems.
- Manholes in street and sidewalk.
- Trash receptacles.
- Garbage cans.
- Dumpsters.
- Incinerators.
- Mailboxes.
- Parked cars, trucks, and carts and outside storage areas.[45]

SUSPICIOUS PACKAGES AND LETTERS

It must be rememberd that items do not have to be delivered by a carrier. Most bombers set and deliver the bombs themselves. The following are precautions that should be followed when encountering a suspicious package or letter:

- If deliverd by carrier, inspect for lumps, bulges, or protrusions, without applying pressure.
- If delivered by carrier, balance-check to determine if it is lopsided or heavy-sided.
- If there is a handwritten address or label from a company, check to see if the company exists and if it sent the package or letter.[46]

Any of the following characteristics could denote a suspicious package or letter (see Figure 20–24):

Figure 20–24
Warning! Suspect Letter and Package Indicators

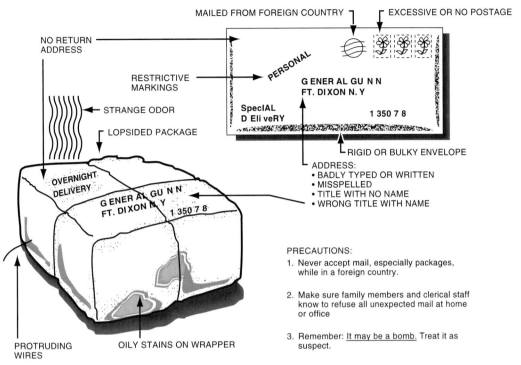

(Courtesy U.S. Department of the Treasury, Bureau of Alcohol, Tobacco and Firearms)

- Packages wrapped in string, as modern packaging materials have eliminated the need for twine or string.
- Excess postage on small packages or letters, which indicates that the object was not weighed at a post office.
- Any foreign writing, address, or postage.
- Handwritten notes, such as "To Be Opened in the Privacy of. . .", "Confidential," "Your Lucky Day Is Here," and "Prize Enclosed."
- Improper spelling of common names, places, or titles.
- Generic or incorrect titles.
- Leaks, stains, or protuding wires, string, tape, etc.
- Hand delivery or a "drop-off for a friend."
- No return address or a nonsensical return address.
- Delivery before or after a phone call from an unknown person asking if the item was received.[47]

Questions

1. If arson is suspected, why should firefighters not disarrange the premises, such as by mopping up or overhauling the scene of the fire, especially at the point of origin?

2. What two factors are needed to cause a fire?

3. What is the layer-checking technique, and how can it assist in determining the cause and origin of a fire?

4. What are some of the more common causes for accidental or natural fires?

5. What types of burn indication can be examined by the arson investigator to assist in determining whether a fire is accidental or incendiary in nature?

6. What are some of the most commonly used ignition and timing devices employed in the commission of arsons?

7. Why can items missing from the fire scene be as valuable as things remaining at the scene?

8. What are some of the most common motives for arson?

9. What are the major characteristics of the child fire setter?

10. Why should uncoated metal paint cans (or similar containers), not plastic bags or containers, be used for the storage of material suspected of containing flammable liquids?

11. What are some of the advantages and disadvantages of olfactory detection in determining the presence of fire accelerants at the scene of a fire?

12. What types of individuals might be able to provide information relevant to the fire?

13. There are basically two types of explosions. What are they, and briefly describe each type.

14. The objectives of an explosion scene investigation are not different from those of a regular investigation. What are the principal objectives?

15. What is the first duty of the investigator at the scene of an explosion?

16. Once the origin, or epicenter, of the explosion has been identified, the investigator should determine what type of fuel has been employed. How is this typically done?

17. In general, certain search techniques should be employed to ensure an orderly and systematic search for explosive devices. What are they?

Notes

1. This information was obtained from "Stop Arson Now," a brochure published by the Florida Advisory Committee on Arson Prevention.

2. K. D. Moll, *Arson, Vandalism, and Violence: Law Enforcement Problems Affecting Fire Departments* (Washington, D.C.: Government Printing Office, 1977), pp. 20–21.

3. C. W. Stickney, "Recognizing Where Arson Exists," *Fireman Magazine*, September–December 1960, p. 3.

4. *Touched Off by Human Hands,* 1979. This booklet was originally published by the Illinois Advisory Committee on Arson Prevention in Cooperation with the Illinois Chapter of the International Association of Arson Investigation and was reprinted for distribution by the State Farm Fire and Casualty Company, Bloomington, Ill. Much of the information in this section was taken from this source, pp. 7–11.

5. Stickney, "Recognizing Where Arson Exists," p. 4.

6. Ibid., p. 8.

7. Ibid.

8. C. W. Stickney, "Recognizing Where Arson Exists," *Fire and Arson Investigator,* October–December 1970; W. A. Derr, "Wildland Fire Investigation: Information from Objects," paper presented at the 18th Annual Fire and Arson Investigators Seminar, Palm Springs, Calif., June 14–18, 1971.

9. John J. O'Conner, *Practical Fire and Arson Investigation* (Boca Raton, Fla.: CRC Press, 1993), p. 94.

10. *NFPA 921 Guide for Fire and Explosion Investigations* (Quincy, Mass.: National Fire Protection Association, 1992), pp. 921–942.

11. O'Conner, *Practical Fire and Arson Investigation,* p. 89.

12. Derr, "Wildland Fire Investigation."

13. P. L. Kirk, *Fire Investigation* (New York: Wiley, 1969), p. 75.

14. B. P. Battle and P. B. Weston, *Arson: A Handbook of Detection and Investigation* (New York: Arco Publishing, 1972), pp. 19–28. Much of the information in this section was taken with permission from this source.

15. C. L. Karchmer, M. E. Walsh, and J. Greenfield, *Enforcement Manual: Approaches for Combating Arson for Profit Schemes* (Washington, D.C.: Department of Justice, 1981), pp. 15–31. This discussion was adapted from this source.

16. B. S. Huron, *Elements of Arson Investigation* (New York: Reuben Donnelley, 1972), Chap. 1; Battle and Weston, *Arson: A Handbook of Detection and Investigation,* pp. 34–39.

17. J. A. Inciardi, "The Adult Firesetter, A Typology," *Criminology,* August 1970, pp. 145–155.

18. Anthony O. Rider, "The Firesetter—A Psychological Profile (Part 2)," *FBI Law Enforcement Bulletin,* July

1980, p. 12 (much of this discussion and accompanying references have been adapted with permission from this source, pp. 7–17); Nolan D. C. Lewis and Helen Yarnell, "Pathological Firesetting (Pyromania)," *Nervous and Mental Disease Monographs,* No. 82 (New York: Coolidge Foundation, 1951), pp. 228–242.

19. Louis H. Gold, "Psychiatric Profile of the Firesetter," *Journal of Forensic Science,* October 1962, p. 407; Lewis and Yarnell, "Pathological Firesetting," p. 118.

20. James C. Coleman et al., *Abnormal Psychology and Modern Life,* 6th ed. (Glenview, Ill.: Scott, Foresman & Co., 1980), p. 395.

21. Lewis and Yarnell, "Pathological Firesetting," pp. 376–377, 428.

22. E. B. Bates, *Elements of Fire and Arson Investigation* (Santa Cruz, Calif.: Davis Publishing, 1975), pp. 43–44.

23. Rider, "The Firesetter—A Psychological Profile," pp. 12–13.

24. Lewis and Yarnell, "Pathological Firesetting," pp. 286–287, 311–345.

25. Stickney, "Recognizing Where Arson Exists," 1960, pp. 11–12.

26. B. B. Caldwell, "The Examination of Exhibits in Suspected Arson Cases," *Royal Canadian Mounted Police Quarterly,* 1957, Vol. 22, pp. 103–108.

27. J. F. Bordeau, Q. Y. Kwan, W. E. Faragker, and G. C. Senault, *Arson and Arson Investigation* (Washington, D.C.: Government Printing Office, 1974), pp. 77–83. Much of the information in this section was taken from this source.

28. J. D. Nicol, "Recovery of Flammable Liquids from a Burned Structure," *Fire Engineering,* 1961, Vol. 114, p. 550.

29. D. Q. Burd, "Detection of Traces of Combustible Fluids in Arson Cases," *Journal of Criminal Law, Criminology, and Police Science,* 1960, Vol. 51, pp. 263–264; P. Rajeswaran and P. L. Dirk, "Identification of Gasoline, Waves, Greases, and Asphalts by Evaporation Chromatography," *Microchemical Journal,* 1962, Vol. 6, pp. 21–29.

30. R. Milliard and C. Thomas, "The Combustible Gas Detector (Souffer), An Evaluation," *Fire and Arson Investigator,* January–March 1976, pp. 48–50.

31. D. M. Lucas, "The Identification of Petroleum Products in Forensic Science by Gas Chromatography," *Journal of Forensic Sciences,* 1960, Vol. 5, No. 2, pp. 236–243.

32. Kirk, *Fire Investigation,* pp. 43–44; E. C. Crocker and L. B. Sjostrom, "Odor Detection and Thresholds," *Chemical Engineering News,* 1949, Vol. 27, pp. 1922–1931; H. Zwaardemaber, "Camera Inoorata," *Perfumery and Essential Oil Record,* 1921, Vol. 12, pp. 243–244.

33. P. L. Kirk, *Crime Investigation, Physical Evidence, and the Police Laboratory* (New York: Interscience, 1966), p. 717; H. P. Wonderling, "Arsonists—Their Methods and the Evidence," *International Association of Arson Investigators Newsletter,* October–December 1953; reprinted in *Selected Articles for Fire and Arson Investigators*, International Association of Arson Investigators, 1975; K. Ol'Khosvsbaya, "Colormetric Determination of Hydrocarbons, Gasoline, Kerosene and White Spent in the Air of Industrial Installations," *Gigiena Truda i Professional'nye Zabolevaniza,* 1971, Vol. 15, No. 11, pp. 57–58.

34. J. W. Girth, A. Jones, and T. A. Jones, "The Principle of Detection of Flammable Atmospheres by Catalytic Devices," *Combustion and Flame,* 1973, Vol. 21, pp. 303–312.

35. C. M. Lane, "Ultra-Violet Light . . . Gem or Junk," *Fire and Arson Investigator,* December 1975, Vol. 26, No. 2, pp. 40–42.

36. Clifford L. Karchmer and James Greenfield, *Enforcement Manual: Approaches for Combatting Arson-for-Profit Schemes* (Washington, D.C.: Government Printing Office, 1981), pp. 249–252.

37. John Barracato, *Burning: A Guide to Fire Investigation* (Stamford, Conn.: Aetna Casualty and Surety Co., 1986), pp. 14–16.

38. *Guide for Fire and Explosion Investigations* (Quincy, Mass.): National Fire Protection Association, 1992), pp. 921-94 to 921-100).

39. George Buck, *Preparing for Terrorism* (Albany, N.Y.: Delmar, 1998), pp. XI–XII.

40. Guide for Fire and Explosion Investigations, pp. 921-103 to 921-107).

41. *Public Safety News,* December 1996, No. 34.

42. City of Phoenix Police Department, "Operations Order D-5, Explosives and Bomb Threat 495," p. 3.

43. Honolulu Police Department, "Procedure: Bomb Threat," November 18, 1996.

44. Lesson plan prepared by the New Orleans Police Department, "Bombs and Hazardous Devices," October 21, 1996, p. 8.

45. Ibid., p. 11. *Note:* Law enforcement and fire personnel should use the information in this chapter only within the framework of their training and departmental guidelines and policies. The departments having guidelines and police will always take precedence over the information discussed herein.

46. This checklist was provided by the U.S. Department of the Treasury, Bureau of Alcohol, Tobacco and Firearms, 1999.

47. Ibid.

TWENTY-ONE

Recognition, Control, and Investigation of Drug Abuse

CHAPTER OUTLINE

The Opium Poppy 606
Synthetic Narcotics 608
Recognizing an Addict 609
Stimulants 610
Depressants 619
Speedballing 622
Hallucinogens 622
Field Testing for Controlled Substances 628
Investigative Procedures 628

Drug Informants: Motives, Methods, and Management 629
The Investigator's Prevention Responsibility 633
Drug Abuse by Practitioners 634
Clandestine Drug Laboratories 635
Search Warrants and Probable Cause 638
Evidence Handling and Security Problems 639
Questions 641
Notes 641
Drug Glossary 643

INTRODUCTION

Currently, every major police department in this country has assigned—with ample justification—the control of drug abuse and related offenses a top priority. However, the illegal importation, manufacture, sale, and use of drugs have increased more rapidly than the resources to combat them.

Explanations for the phenomenal growth of drug abuse abound in the literature on this subject. Many cite variables associated with certain socioeconomic and political conditions. Many of the explanations are well founded, reasoned, and articulated. But police must deal with the violation itself, not the motivations and human conditions that produce it.

In this chapter we will focus on the following categories of drugs, which are most commonly encountered by law enforcement officers in their enforcement activities: opium-derived drugs, synthetic narcotics, stimulants, depressants, and hallucinogens. We will also discuss procedures involved in narcotics investigations, clandestine laboratories, and search warrants.

THE OPIUM POPPY
(Papaver somniferum)

Several drugs are derived from the opium poppy, including opium, morphine, heroin, codeine, and others less well known.

OPIUM

One of the first drugs of abuse was opium. Its pleasurable effects were known to many ancient civilizations, including the Egyptians, as early as 1500 B.C. During the Renaissance in Europe, opium was employed in the treatment of hysteria, making it one of the early therapeutic agents in treating mental disorders.

In the seventeenth century, opium smoking spread throughout China, and opium dependence was recognized as a problem. Opium eating was known in the United States and England during the Revolutionary War. Opium was used by eighteenth-century doctors to treat venereal disease, cancer, gallstones, and diarrhea and to relieve pain at childbirth.

Opium comes from the poppy plant. Its bulb is carefully cut to allow a milky white fluid to ooze onto the surface of the bulb. There, after it air-dries into tan beads, it is carefully scraped by hand (see Figure 21–1) and allowed to further air-dry, after which it turns a blackish brown color. Raw opium has a pungent odor and may be smoked. The user appears sleepy and relaxed. Prolonged use creates both physical and psychological dependence. Raw opium is the source of morphine, heroin, and codeine.

MORPHINE

Morphine is obtained from raw opium; 10 pounds of raw opium yield 1 pound of morphine. A German named Sertürner first isolated the substance in 1804 and a few years later named it *morphine* after the Greek god of sleep, Morpheus. The drug was first used in medicine in 1825 as a painkiller and is still used as such today.

The use of morphine increased considerably with the invention of the hypodermic syringe by an Englishman around 1843. The hypodermic syringe was introduced into this country about 1853 and was used extensively for wounded Union troops during the American Civil War. Some developed physical and psychological dependence, for doctors did not clearly understand the addictive nature of opiates until around 1870.

Morphine appears in tablet, capsule, and liquid forms. It has no distinguishing color and provides the medical standards by which other narcotics are evaluated. Morphine is usually administered by injection. The drug creates both physical and psychological dependence in the user, who feels euphoric and seems sleepy or relaxed. The pupils of the eyes may constrict.[1]

HEROIN (DIACETYLMORPHINE)

Heroin was developed in England in 1874, but it evoked little interest until about 1890, when it was found to be considerably stronger than morphine. Commercial production of heroin began in 1898 in Germany by the Bayer Company. Heroin was advertised as a cure for morphine dependence, but it was soon learned that heroin dependence was even more difficult to cure.

Heroin is an odorless, crystalline, white powder. It is usually sold in glassine paper packets, aluminum foil, or capsules. The darker the color, the more impurities it contains. Being about four to five times stronger than morphine, heroin is the principal drug of addiction among the opium derivatives. It is generally injected.

Figure 21–1
Traditional Method of Gathering Opium

(Courtesy Drug Enforcement Administration)

By the time the heroin reaches the addict, it often has been diluted considerably. Heroin reaching this country is perhaps 20 to 80 percent pure. (See Figures 21–2 to 21–5.) Deaths from overdoses are not uncommon and ordinarily occur because a dose was more pure than that to which the addict's body was accustomed. Addicts may also have a fatal allergic reaction to the drug or some substance used to "cut," or reduce, the purity level of the drug, such as powdered milk, sugar, or quinine. The fatal overdose is not always accidental. On occasion, addicts suspected of being police informers have been given "hot shots"—pure heroin—to eliminate them.

In addition to facing the perils of the law, withdrawal, and other aspects of addiction, the drug addict also faces the serious health problems associated with dirty needles. Many suffer venereal disease and serum hepatitis. Because both are transmitted diseases, those sharing needles with other drug abusers run the risk of injecting themselves with traces of blood from a disease carrier.[2]

Drug users who administer their drugs through intravenous injections and share their needles with others face the additional danger of contracting the almost always fatal acquired immune deficiency syndrome (AIDS).

It should be noted that Colombia has become a major source of heroin production; the DEA estimates that as much as 5 percent of the heroin in this country comes from Colombia. Although this percentage may not seem to be high in comparison to the amount of heroin imported from other countries, it should be noted that the rate of importation has grown enormously since the early 1990s. Seizures of Colombian heroin by the DEA indicate that it is 80 to 99 percent pure. It is usually a light brown or tan powder. The poppies are being grown in the mountains of the Cauca Province around Popayan. It is anticipated that within the next several years Colombia will be the major source of heroin in the United States because the existing cocaine cartels have well-established routes from Colombia.

Figure 21–2
Heroin Trafficking Patterns

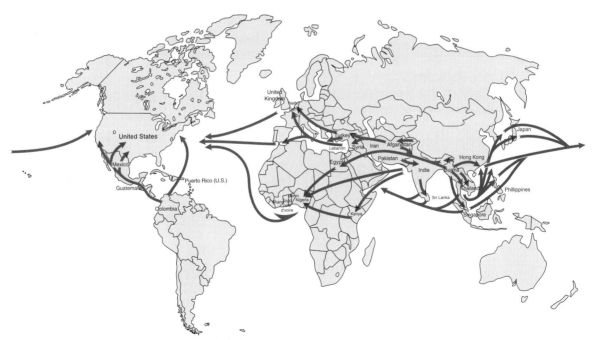

Source: Bureau of Justice Statistics, U.S. Department of Justice.

Figure 21–3
Mexican Brown Heroin and
Southeast Asian Heroin

(Courtesy Drug Enforcement Administration)

CODEINE

The alkaloid codeine is found in raw opium in concentrations from 0.7 to 2.5 percent. It was first isolated in 1832 as an impurity in a batch of morphine. Compared to morphine, codeine produces less analgesia, sedation, and respiratory depression. It is widely distributed in products of two general types. Codeine to relieve moderate pain may consist of

Figure 21–4
Heroin-Filled Latex Balloons
In another method of smuggling heroin, couriers swallow heroin-filled latex balloons before boarding commercial airlines.

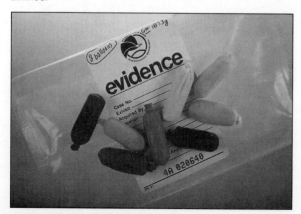

(Courtesy Drug Enforcement Administration)

tablets or be combined with other products such as aspirin. Liquid codeine preparations for the relief of coughs (antitussives) include Robitussin AC, Cheracol, and terpin hydrate with codeine. Codeine is also manufactured in injectable form for pain relief.

OTHER OPIUM DERIVATIVES

Other opium derivatives abused and stolen from pharmacies, hospitals, and physicians are Dilaudid, Papaverine, and Pantopon.

SYNTHETIC NARCOTICS

Synthetic narcotics, though chemically related to the opium alkaloids, are produced entirely within the laboratory. A continuing search for a drug that kills pain but does not create tolerance and dependence has yet to yield a drug that is not susceptible to abuse. Two synthetic opiates are meperidine and methadone.

MEPERIDINE (PETHIDINE)

The commercial name for meperidine is Demerol, and it was the first synthetic narcotic. Next to morphine, it is probably the most widely used drug for the relief of intense pain. It is available in pure

Figure 21–5
Heroin Pressed into Bricks
Heroin pressed into bricks for bulk shipment to destination countries.

(Courtesy Drug Enforcement Administration)

form and in combination products. The drug is administered by mouth or by injection; the latter is the more common method of abuse.[3]

METHADONE

Methadone is known by the commercial names Dolophine Hydrochloride and Methadone HCl Diskets. A heroin-dependent person can be treated with doses of methadone as a replacement for heroin. Methadone is manufactured in a solid form and administered orally. Methadone is a "maintenance drug." The drug is used to maintain a heroin addict at a stable level of opiate use and to remove the addict from the incidental dangers of heroin use.

The beneficial properties of methadone are that it is longer acting than most opiates and addicts do not build up tolerance. Also, oral administration is less potentially hazardous than injection, since it significantly reduces the addict's risk for diseases such as hepatitis and AIDS. As a rule of thumb, it takes about three weeks on methadone before a heroin addict completes the withdrawal stage and moves to the maintenance stage. However, it must be noted that the simultaneous use of methadone and heroin will not totally negate the physiological effect of the heroin on the user.

There is considerable controversy over the adoption of methadone maintenance programs. Critics argue that drug dependence is not cured. Proponents argue that it presents a cheaper way of supporting drug dependence and gets abusers out of crime and back to a conventional life. Proponents recognize that the programs need to include the appropriate psychiatric help for the psychological dependence.[4]

RECOGNIZING AN ADDICT

Drug abuse often falls into one of four categories: experimental, recreational, circumstantial, and compulsive or addictive.[5] The following list may be useful in identifying an individual who is addicted to natural or synthetic opiates:[6]

- The possession of addicting drugs without adequate medical explanation.
- A tendency on the part of the suspect to hide or conceal these drugs.
- The presence of needle marks in the form of black or blue spots resembling tattooing.
- The presence of elongated scars over the veins, especially those of the forearms and lower legs.
- The presence of boil-like abscesses over the veins or near where veins approach the surface.
- An appearance of drowsiness, sleepiness, or lethargy, especially if accompanied by a tendency to scratch the body, which sometimes indicates a slight overdose.
- Wide fluctuations in the size of the pupils of the eyes, with maximum constriction immediately after the suspect takes an injection.
- Possession of equipment for smoking opium.
- A tendency to wear long sleeves or other concealing clothing, even in hot weather, to cover needle marks.
- A tendency for the suspect to isolate himself or herself at regular intervals in order to take hypodermic injections.
- An obvious discrepancy between the amount of money the suspect earns and the amount he or she spends.
- The tendency of a person who has previously been reliable to resort to thievery,

embezzlement, forgery, prostitution, and so forth.

- The tendency to develop withdrawal symptoms. The withdrawal symptoms from the denial of opium-derived drugs and synthetic opiates are quite similar: nervousness, anxiety, and sleeplessness; yawning, running eyes and nose, hoarseness, and perspiring; enlargement of the pupils of the eyes, goose flesh, muscle twitching; severe aches of the back and legs; hot and cold flashes; vomiting, diarrhea, and stomach cramps; increase in breathing rate, blood pressure, and body temperature; a feeling of desperation and an obsessive desire to secure more of the drug.

- Typically, the onset of symptoms occurs about 8 to 12 hours following the last dose. Symptoms increase for 72 hours, gradually diminish over the next 5 to 10 days, and usually disappear entirely within 10 to 14 days; weakness, insomnia, nervousness, and muscle aches may persist for weeks.

STIMULANTS

Drugs falling into this group directly stimulate the central nervous system, producing excitation, alertness, wakefulness, and, in some cases, a temporary rise in blood pressure and respiration rate. The major stimulants abused are cocaine, amphetamines, phenmetrazine, and methylphenidate. The effects of an overdose are agitation, increase in body temperature, hallucinations, convulsions, and possibly death. The withdrawal symptoms are apathy, long periods of sleep, irritability, depression, and disorientation.[7]

COCAINE

Cocaine is a naturally occurring stimulant that is extracted from the leaves of the coca plant (*Erythroxylon coca*). The leaves of this western South American shrub have been chewed by Colombian, Bolivian, and Peruvian Indians since antiquity for religious, medicinal, and other reasons (see Figure 21–6). Allegedly, the chewing of coca leaves has enabled the Indians to work in high altitudes and on inadequate diets. This chewing of the coca leaf,

Figure 21–6
Powdered Cocaine

(Courtesy Drug Enforcement Administration)

which continues to the present day, should not be confused with the use of the extracted drug, cocaine (see Figure 21–7). Coca leaves contain only about ½ to 1 percent cocaine; the cocaine contained within them is released more slowly, and the route of administration (oral) is different from that in most cocaine use.[8]

Because reports of native coca use generated considerable interest in Europe, efforts were made in the nineteenth century to isolate the purified psychoactive ingredient in coca leaves. When success was achieved in the 1880s, cocaine's potential value as a tonic, its general stimulant properties, its possible value for specific ailments, and its local anesthetic properties were explored. Its use as an anesthetic was particularly important because it could be used in eye surgery, where no previous drug had been suitable. Cocaine also constricted blood vessels and limited bleeding in the anesthetized area. This property made it valuable for surgery of the nose and throat, areas that are richly supplied with blood. Although many of cocaine's uses as a therapeutic drug have been abandoned, it continues to be used as a local anesthetic.

Illicit cocaine is sold as a white, translucent, crystalline powder, frequently adulterated to about half its volume. The most common adulterants are sugars (especially lactose and glucose) and local

Figure 21-7
Cocaine Trafficking Patterns

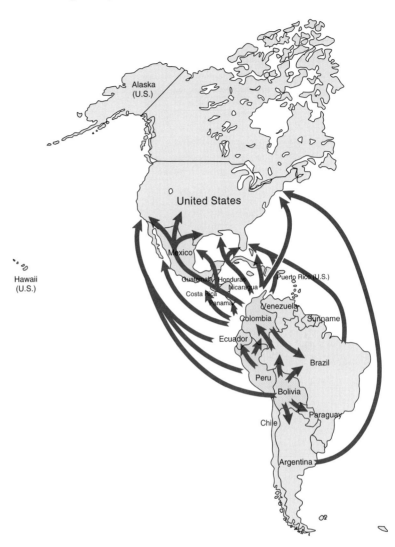

Source: Bureau of Justice Statistics, U.S. Department of Justice.

anesthetics (Lidocaine, Procaine, and Tetracaine) similar in appearance and taste to cocaine. Amphetamines, other drugs with stimulant properties, are also used. Given the high cost of the drug, the temptation to adulterate at each level of sale is great (see Figure 21–8). The combination of high price and the exotic properties attributed to it have contributed to cocaine's street reputation as *the* status drug.

How Is It Used?

Cocaine is most commonly inhaled, or snorted, through the nose. It is deposited on the mucous linings of the nose, from which it is readily ab-

sorbed into the bloodstream. Repeated use often results in irritation to the nostrils and nasal mucous membranes. Symptoms may resemble those of a common cold, that is, congestion or a runny nose. Users therefore often resort to cold remedies, such as nasal sprays, to relieve their chronic nasal congestion. They may be unable to breathe comfortably without habitually using a spray.

A less common route of administration for cocaine is intravenous injection. The solution injected may be cocaine or a combination of heroin and cocaine. This route of administration carries the dangers of any intravenous use. Furthermore, intravenous injection introduces unknown quantities

Figure 21–8
Coca Leaves and Cocaine
Coca leaves and what cocaine looks like after being processed in a clandestine lab.

coca leaves and cocaine

(Courtesy Drug Enforcement Administration)

of cocaine or cocaine and heroin directly and suddenly into the bloodstream, leaving body organs wholly unprotected from the toxic effects of the drug. Cocaine deaths from intravenous injection are more numerous than from snorting, despite the greater prevalence of the latter method.

Acute and Chronic Effects

Cocaine, like other drugs of abuse, has both fascinated and repelled people throughout history. It is little wonder, then, that a bewildering array of "effects," which may have little to do with the pharmacological action of the drug itself, have been attributed to it. Reassertion of often repeated fictions does not, however, make them well-verified facts. Our need for certainty is not necessarily matched by equally adequate evidence to allay our doubts. Unfortunately, a lack of adequate information is sometimes interpreted as indicating that a

drug is "safe" when it would be more accurate to admit that our knowledge is simply inadequate to specify the parameters of risk. Moreover, a substance that poses few hazards when used under conditions of relatively infrequent, low dosage may present quite a different picture when widely available and regularly used in larger amounts.

An important verified effect, when used medically, is cocaine's local anesthetic action as well as its ability to constrict blood vessels in the area to which it is applied. One consequence of this property when cocaine is used illicitly and snorted repeatedly is a tendency to cause a chronic inflammation of the nasal membranes, ulceration, and local tissue death. While perforation of the nasal septum (the wall dividing the two halves of the nose) is often mentioned, it is noteworthy that in the United States, at least, this consequence appears to be rare.

There is good evidence that cocaine in moderate doses (10 to 25 milligrams intravenously and 100 milligrams intranasally) significantly increases both heart rate and blood pressure. Increases following lower doses occur more rapidly when the drug is administered directly into the vein rather than when snorted. Heart rate increases from about 30 to 50 percent above normal nondrug levels. Increases in blood pressure when the heart is in its contracting phase (systolic pressure) are on the order of 10 to 15 percent.

In addition to the street reputation of the drug and historical accounts, even under conditions of carefully controlled laboratory administration, a sense of well-being—euphoria— subjectively characterizes cocaine use. Interestingly enough, however, when the drug is administered intravenously under laboratory conditions, the subjective effects are not easily distinguished from those of amphetamines (synthetic stimulants having more prolonged activity). A feeling of calmness and relaxation is described by most of the subjects who have participated in controlled laboratory studies; they also report diminished appetite. The observed and reported effects of several laboratory studies are generally consistent with accounts based on street use. However, there is much street lore and some clinical evidence emphasizing other effects that have not been systematically verified by controlled experimentation.

Clinical reports dating back to the 1800s have described a range of responses to heavier, more prolonged use of cocaine. Early reports by Freud and others also emphasized that there was wide individual variation in physiological and psychological responses to cocaine. Von Fleischl, who was encouraged to use cocaine by Freud to alleviate symptoms of nerve pain, rapidly progressed to heavy intravenous use (up to a gram per day). With heavier use, Fleischl's condition deteriorated into chronic intoxication, characterized by hallucinations of white snakes and insects creeping over and under his skin. A cocaine psychosis similar to paranoid schizophrenia has been described in the scientific literature. Tactile hallucinations similar to those experienced by Fleischl are a common aspect of this disorder. The hallucinations have been described as so real to the victims that they injure their skin in an attempt to remove the imagined parasites. Other paranoid delusions include fear of imaginary police and the belief that one is being watched.

Cocaine Fatality

There is little question that cocaine can kill. By 1891 some 13 deaths had been attributed to the drug, and in 1924 a report was published of 26 cocaine deaths. These deaths were results of medical errors. They were virtually always rapid in onset and characterized by respiratory depression and cardiovascular collapse. In recent years, an increasing number of cocaine-related deaths among individuals who had snorted the substance have been reported. These deaths would seem to dispel the street wisdom and myth that snorting is completely safe.

Freebasing

The practice of *freebasing* cocaine involves the dissolving of cocaine in a base solution, usually distilled water and calcium carbonate or lactose. The mixture is then shaken so the cocaine is dissolved completely. Several drops of ether are then added, and the mixture is shaken again. The cocaine is attracted to the ether while the other additives are attracted to the base solution.

The ether-cocaine solution separates from the base (like oil and water), with the ether rising to the surface. An eyedropper is commonly used to suction off the ether-cocaine solution, which is then placed on an evaporating dish or crucible and allowed to evaporate naturally. This process can be accelerated by the use of a flame; however, this practice is extremely dangerous since the ether is highly flammable.

The cocaine crystals are then scraped off the dish with a metal spatula, placed in a glass pipe or bong (water pipe), and smoked (see Figure 21–9).

The resultant high is alleged to be greater than that from simple snorting, although users remark that injection of the drug provides a more intense high than even freebasing.

The pleasant effects of freebasing begin to decrease in duration as usage increases, and users display changes in moods and irritability if a high cannot be maintained. As freebasing usage becomes chronic, a person can experience the same symptoms as a chronic nonfreebasing abuser of cocaine.

Rock Cocaine (Crack)

A relatively inexpensive form of cocaine called *rock cocaine* or *crack* has grown tremendously in popularity among cocaine users (see Figure 21–10). The drug is made by mixing ordinary cocaine with baking soda and water and heating the solution in a pot. The material, which is somewhat purer and more concentrated than regular cocaine, is dried and broken into tiny chunks that dealers sell as crack rocks. These little pellets are usually smoked in glass pipes and are frequently sold in tiny plastic vials. It is 5 to 10 times more potent than powdered cocaine; the high lasts about 5 minutes and leaves the user wanting more. According to mental health specialists, crack users are more likely to show

Figure 21–9
Glass Pipe Used for Smoking Freebase Cocaine

(Courtesy Fair Oaks Hospital, Del Ray Beach, Florida)

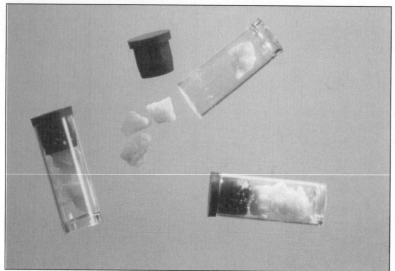

Figure 21–10
Rock Cocaine/Crack
Crack, the smokable form of cocaine, provides an immediate "rush."

(Courtesy Drug Enforcement Administration)

serious psychiatric consequences, including intense paranoia, extreme depression, and often suicidal and even violent behavior. Part of the attraction to the dealer is the enormous profit that can be made by the sale of crack. For example, in Los Angeles an ounce of cocaine can sell for $1,000 to $1,500. Since each ounce contains 28 grams and each gram can produce up to six rocks selling for $25 each, the dealer can realize a profit of around $2,700.

Profiling and Tracing Cocaine

The prosecution of cocaine conspiracy cases—usually among the most difficult criminal cases to prove—can be made much easier if samples from several street-level dealers can be traced back to a single source. This task, no small feat in itself, is now more readily achieved, thanks to a sophisticated technique known as chromatographic impurity signature profile analysis (CISPA), developed by the North Carolina State Bureau of Investigation (SBI).[9]

Suspects in cocaine conspiracy cases are usually linked through telephone toll-call records, hotel receipts, surveillance of suspects, and co-conspirator testimony. One of the nagging problems in drug enforcement has been the lack of a technique to match cocaine samples believed to have originated from the same source. Quite often, those at the top levels of a cocaine distribution ring are insulated from

street-level dealing by several layers of intermediate buyers and sellers. Without proof that cocaine samples found in several different places all came from the same original source, it was very difficult to prosecute the heads of these rings.

The problem of cocaine analysis was made exasperatingly complex by the nature of cocaine distribution. Although large amounts of the drug may be imported in single batches, the lower-level dealers almost invariably adulterate, or "cut," the cocaine before resale (see Figures 21–11 and 21–12). This is accomplished manually, by adding materials ranging from vitamin B_{12} to Italian baby laxative. Because lower-level dealers do this on their own, the resulting street cocaine is composed of the original source cocaine plus whatever "cut" is added. Thus, although the cocaine from several street-level dealers may have originated in the same source batch, the composition of each dealer's supply is different due to their manually diluting their personal stock.

The processing of certain types of forensic evidence, such as drugs, is typically accomplished by visually comparing chromatographic signature patterns of the trace evidence with the signature pattern of a known reference. Because of the widely varying quantities and types of cut used with cocaine, this was both time consuming and inaccurate.

The challenge of CISPA, therefore, was to develop a system that could "see through" the adulterants and still distinguish between source

Figure 21–11
Kilo Packages of Cocaine
Kilo packages of cocaine. Confiscated by the Drug Enforcement Administration from a warehouse in Guatemala.

(Courtesy Drug Enforcement Administration)

groups of cocaine with a high degree of accuracy. The key to doing this is identifying impurities created during the original cocaine manufacturing process, as opposed to impurities added later as adulterants.

Because of the imprecise nature of the clandestine labs producing cocaine, the impurities created during manufacture vary too much between samples to provide for accurate identification even between samples manufactured using the same technique. The addition of other substances as cuts later on does not change the impurity signature of the underlying cocaine, which can still be identified as belonging to the same source batch.

Even knowing this, however, the job was far from done. Before impurity analysis could begin, the North Carolina SBI's forensic laboratory had to develop a reference signature of cocaine against which impurities could be measured. To learn more about the nature of cocaine, an SBI forensic chemist synthesized pure cocaine in the laboratory and developed a reference signature for it.

The chemist then spent several months synthesizing pure forms of 16 different impurities created by the various processes for cocaine manufacture and refinement. Once the impurities were identified, analyzed, and cataloged, it was possible to distinguish between source groups of cocaine by identifying both the type and quantity of individual impurities in each sample.

However, the visual comparison of samples remained very time consuming. The volume of cocaine imported into the country meant that the system needed to be able to pick out an original source from hundreds or even thousands of possible batches—and do so with almost no chance of error.

Cutting-edge computer technology and the Automated Fingerprint Identification System (AFIS) provided the answer. SBI chemists now had a good profile of pure cocaine and the impurities that could differentiate between batches, but they needed a means of rapidly identifying the batch.

Since a cocaine signature is in many ways analogous to a fingerprint, in that it is a unique pattern that can be digitized and stored in a computer, the AFIS system provided a good model. However, AFIS requires a large mainframe computer and many support systems and the funds were simply not available for a similar system for CISPA. Working with the Research Triangle Institute, the SBI developed a lower-cost system using one of the newest techniques in artificial intelligence: neural networks.

Figure 21–12
Drugs Concealed in Vehicle
The floorboard of this vehicle was cut out and used to conceal these kilo-sized packages of cocaine.

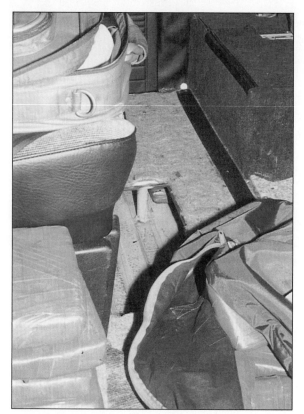

(Courtesy Drug Enforcement Administration)

Neural nets are interlocked computing nodes that have the capability of "learning" to recognize patterns. Once the network learns a pattern, it has no problem identifying other patterns as being either similar or dissimilar to the known pattern. It can also identify a pattern as being similar to a certain degree, represented as a percent figure. This allows a human operator to analyze only those patterns most similar to the sample in question, vastly cutting down on search time and costs.

CISPA, which was developed with the help of a $127,000 Federal Drug Control and System Improvement grant, has been used by local law enforcement agencies and prosecutors hundreds of times since it was developed. The speed and accuracy of CISPA allows it to be used on cases ranging from major distribution rings to the street-level dealer who denies that the 1-gram vial in his pocket came from the same

source as the 1-ounce bag found in the street next to him.

Using the combination of "wet chemistry" in the lab and the world's newest computer techniques, the North Carolina SBI and the Research Institute have provided a significant and promising breakthrough in linking—and successfully prosecuting—cocaine distribution rings.

AMPHETAMINES

Amphetamine, dextroamphetamine, and methamphetamine are so closely related chemically that they can be differentiated from one another only in the laboratory.[10] These compounds resemble the natural body hormones of epinephrine and norepinephrine. As a result of this similarity, they can act directly, by mimicking the natural hormones in their effects on nerve endings, and/or indirectly, by causing increased release of the natural hormones (see Figure 21–13). In either case, the

Figure 21–13
Amphetamine Tablets and Capsules

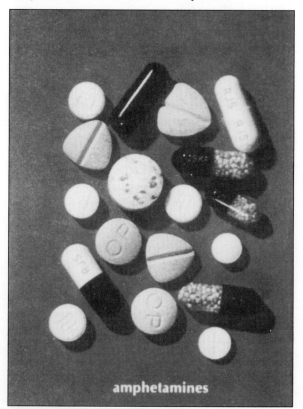

amphetamines

(Courtesy Drug Enforcement Administration)

amphetamines stimulate certain areas of the nervous system that control blood pressure, heart rate, and respiratory and metabolic rates, all of which are increased. Appetite is markedly decreased, and the senses are hyperalert. The body is in a general state of stress, as if it were extremely threatened or expecting a violent fight. This group of drugs artificially intensifies and prolongs such stimulation, keeping the body in a state of tension for prolonged periods of time.[11] Many different classes of people employ amphetamines in abusive quantities, including middle-aged businesspeople, housewives, students, athletes, and truck drivers. Government studies indicate that young people are the greatest abusers. Drivers take them to stay awake on long trips; students take them while cramming for exams; and athletes take them for extra energy and stamina.[12] When the drug is prescribed, the dose frequently ranges between 2.5 and 15 milligrams per day. Abusers have been known to inject as much as 1,000 milligrams every 2 or 3 hours. Medical use of amphetamines is now limited to control of narcolepsy, appetite control, and control of hyperactivity in children.

PHENMETRAZINE (PRELUDIN), METHYLPHENIDATE (RITALIN), AND PEMOLINE (CYLERT)

Phenmetrazine is related chemically to the amphetamines, and its abuse produces similar effects. Like phenmetrazine, methylphenidate is related chemically to amphetamines. It is prescribed for treatment of mild depression in adults and attention deficit disorder in children. Pemoline, like amphetamines, is a stimulant. It was developed early in 1975 and was approved for marketing as a drug to be used in the treatment of hyperactive children.

CHRYSTILIZED METHAMPHETAMINE

"Chrystilized" methamphetamine, better known as "chrystal meth" and "speed" during the 1960s and 1970s, was originally taken as pills or injected. A new, smokable version, known as "ice," has now appeared on the drug market. In Hawaii, where ice first appeared in 1989, it was sold in $50 cellophane packets that contained about 1/10 gram, good for one or two smokes. Ice owes its special appeal to several factors:

- A puff of crack cocaine buoys its user for approximately 20 minutes, but the high from smoking ice endures for 12 to 24 hours. It does, however, share crack's addictive properties, and it produces similar bouts of severe depression and paranoia as well as convulsions.

- Ice can be manufactured in clandestine speed labs, whereas cocaine must be extracted from the leaf of the coca plant, refined, and imported by smugglers at considerable risk.

- Because it is odorless, ice can be smoked in public virtually without detection.

In its solid form the drug resembles rock candy or a chip of ice (see Figure 21–14). When lighted in a glass pipe, the crystals turn to liquid and produce a potent vapor that enters the bloodstream directly through the lungs. Ice reverts to its solid state when it cools, thus becoming reusable and highly transportable.[13]

Ice has already become the number-one drug problem in Hawaii, where it is smuggled in from illegal labs in South Korea and the Philippines. Methamphetamine produced in California, Oregon, and Texas is making serious inroads across the United States. Drug enforcement officers have concluded that if an effort to stop the cocaine flow from Latin America makes crack hard to get, users will simply shift to easily available speed.[14]

METHCATHINONE

Methcathinone,[15] called "cat" or "goob," is a psychomotor stimulant with a chemical structure similar to methamphetamine. Originally patented in Germany in 1928 and later used in the Soviet Union in the late 1930s and 1940s for the treatment of depression, methcathinone was all but unknown in the United States until 1957, when an American pharmaceutical firm received a patent for it and began animal studies to determine its potential as an appetite suppressant.

Because initial testing revealed that methcathinone was approximately one and a half times as potent as methamphetamine, clinical trials were never initiated and testing was discontinued. The formula for methcathinone languished in the archives of the pharmaceutical firm until 1989,

(Courtesy Drug Enforcement Administration)

Figure 21–14
"Ice"

"Ice," so-named because of its appearance, is a smokable form of methamphetamine.

when it was rediscovered and "liberated" by a college intern working for the firm. He shared the formula, and in 1990 a close friend set up a clandestine laboratory on the campus of Northern Michigan University (NMU) and attempted to develop a market for cat.

Although cat use did not take hold among the students at NMU, it rapidly found acceptance among the local population of Michigan's upper peninsula (UP). The relative ease with which cat is manufactured made it readily available, and its use and abuse rapidly spread throughout the UP and northern Wisconsin.

Methcathinone first came to the attention of law enforcement in the winter of 1990, when the Michigan State Police in the UP purchased a sample of what was purported to be a "new" drug more powerful than crack. The substance was analyzed to be methcathinone, closely related to but more powerful than methamphetamine. In January 1991, the Michigan State Police seized the first clandestine methcathinone lab ever discovered in the United States in a college dormitory room in Marquette, Michigan. Six months later, the DEA seized a methcathinone lab in Ann Arbor, Michigan. However, much to the surprise of law enforcement authorities, methcathinone was not a controlled substance under either Michigan state law or federal statute.

Since that time, 33 cat laboratories have been seized in Michigan, Wisconsin, Indiana, Illinois, and Colorado. Cat samples have been purchased or seized in several other states, including Illinois, Missouri, and Washington.

On May 1, 1992, under the DEA's emergency scheduling authority, methcathinone was placed in Schedule 1 of the Controlled Substances Act. After a scientific and medical evaluation, this classification was made permanent on October 7, 1993.

The effects of methcathinone on the human body are very similar to those of methamphetamine. Cat is reported by users to induce feelings of omnipotence and euphoria, marked by increased energy. Other reported effects include relief from fatigue, increased self-assurance, acute alertness, hyperactivity, talkativeness, a sense of invincibility, confidence, and increased sexual stimulation.

Cat is usually a white or off-white powdered substance, very similar in appearance to methamphetamine. It is usually sold in gram quantities for $75 to $100 and snorted in lines ranging from $\frac{1}{10}$ to $\frac{1}{4}$ of a gram. Because cat is usually sold in pure form, it reportedly can produce an immediate "rush," with a high that lasts 4 to 6 hours or more. There is typically a delay of 1 to 2 hours between dosages.

Users rapidly develop a tolerance for cat, requiring them to use larger amounts more frequently.

Because cat destroys the sinus membranes, causing chronic nosebleeds and sinusitis, users may eventually resort to intravenous injection or oral ingestion.

Chronic cat use is characterized by binging. Addicts often go for up to eight days without sleep—eating very little, if at all—until they finally collapse. The onset of the "crash" occurs 4 to 6 hours after the last instance of use. Users often sleep for several days before beginning the cycle again.

Undesirable side effects reported by users include loss of appetite, weight loss, dehydration, stomachaches, profuse sweating, temporary blindness, deterioration of the nasal membranes, dry mouth, and an increased heart rate. Other side effects include anxiety, nervousness, depression, and hallucinations. The most consistently reported side effect—one with a serious implication for law enforcement officers—is extreme paranoia. In one case a cat abuser killed himself when he thought he was about to be arrested.

Symptoms of methcathinone intoxication can include profuse sweating, sweaty palms, increased heart rate, restlessness, increased body temperature, and uncontrollable shaking. Officers encountering suspected cat users should be particularly aware of withdrawal symptoms, which include irritability and argumentativeness. Other withdrawal symptoms include convulsions, hallucinations, and severe depression.

DEPRESSANTS (SEDATIVES)

These drugs depress the central nervous system and are prescribed in small doses to reduce restlessness and emotional tension and to induce sleep (see Figure 21–15). The drugs most frequently abused are barbiturates, glutethimide, methaqualone, and meprobamate. Chronic use produces slurring of speech, staggering, loss of balance and falling, faulty judgment, quick temper, and quarrelsomeness. Overdoses, particularly in conjunction with alcohol, result in unconsciousness and death unless proper medical treatment is administered. Therapeutic doses cause minimal amounts of psychological dependence; chronic excessive doses result in both physical and psychological dependence. Abrupt withdrawal, particularly from barbiturates, can produce convulsions and death. Barbiturates are frequently nicknamed after the color of the capsule or tablet or the name of the manufacturer. The barbiturates most frequently abused are secobarbital and amobarbital.[16] These are among the short- and intermediate-acting barbiturates. The onset time is from 15 to 40 minutes, and the effects last for up to 6 hours.

GLUTETHIMIDE (DORIDEN)

When introduced in 1954, glutethimide was wrongly believed to be a nonaddictive barbiturate substitute. The sedative effects of glutethimide begin about 30 minutes after oral administration and last 4 to 8 hours. Because the effects of this drug last for a long time, it is exceptionally difficult to reverse overdoses, and many result in death.

Figure 21–15
Barbiturates
These are among the most frequently prescribed drugs to induce sedation and sleep by physicians and veterinarians. Barbiturates are classified as ultrashort-, immediate-, and long-lasting.

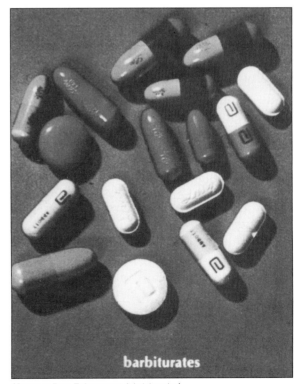

barbiturates

(Courtesy Drug Enforcement Administration)

Glutethimide used with 16-milligram codeine tablets is one of the most popular pill combinations on the black market today. This combination gives a heroinlike effect and is known as "dors and 4's" or "D's and C's." It is commonly taken by oral ingestion.

METHAQUALONE

Methaqualone was at one time very popular in the United States but has since been removed from the market. The drug was widely abused because it was mistakenly thought to be safe and nonaddictive and to have aphrodisiac qualities. Methaqualone caused many cases of serious poisoning. When administered orally, large doses produce a coma that may be accompanied by thrashing or convulsions. It was marketed in the United States under various names, including Quaalude, Parest, Optimil, Somnafac, and Soper. Most methaqualones found on the streets today are counterfeit and usually test as diazepam (Valium).

MEPROBAMATE

First synthesized in 1960 as a mild tranquilizer, it is distributed in the United States under the generic name as well as under brand names such as Miltown, Equanil, and Deprol. This drug is prescribed primarily for relief of anxiety, tension, and associated muscle spasms. The onset and duration of action are like those of intermediate-acting barbiturates, but this drug differs in that it is a muscle relaxant, does not produce sleep at therapeutic doses, and is less toxic. Excessive use, however, can result in psychological and physical dependence.[17]

ROHYPNOL

Rohypnol, known as the drug flunitrazepam, belongs to a class of drugs called benzodiazepines. It produces a spectrum of effects similar to that of other benzodiazepines such as diazepam (Valium). These effects include skeletal muscle relaxation, sedation, and reductions in anxiety. Of these effects, the sedative/hypnotic effects are most important. Flunitrazepam is considered to be approximately 8 to 10 times more potent than Valium. The effect or "high" may last from 7 to 12 hours, with residual effects lasting up to 24 hours or more after the last dose. With pills or "hits" readily available for prices ranging from $2 to $5, Rohypnol is extremely sought after. Street names include "roofies," "R-2's," "roach-2's," "Rophs," "trip & fall," and "mind erasers." (See Figures 21–16 and 21–17.)

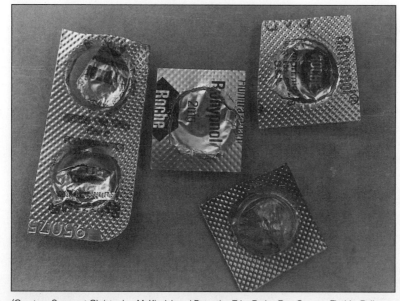

**Figure 21–16
Rohypnol Packaging**

(Courtesy Sergeant Christopher McKissick and Detective Tyler Parks, Port Orange, Florida, Police Department)

Figure 21–17
Rohypnol

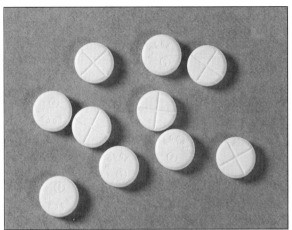

(Courtesy Sergeant Christopher McKissick and Detective Tyler Parks, Port Orange, Florida, Police Department)

Adverse effects include drowsiness, light headedness, dizziness, confusion, vertigo, gastrointestinal disturbances, and urinary retention. It is most important to note that the adverse effects substantially increase with the use of other depressants, such as alcohol.

Abuse seems concentrated among high school teenagers and college students who use Rohypnol to potentiate and prolong the intoxicating effects of alcohol. For this reason, Rohypnol has quickly become known as the "date-rape drug." Rohypnol also causes substantial memory loss in its victims, making it a "drug of choice" among sexual party predators.[18]

The following case, which occurred in Prince William County, Virginia, several years ago, illustrates this point:

Two 15-year-old girls were forcibly raped after unknowingly ingesting Rohypnol. During the trial, prosecutors dubbed this drug the "New Stealth Weapon" on the basis of its odorless and tasteless properties. Commonly known as the "date-rape drug." it dissolves rapidly when placed in a carbonated drink, making it virtually impossible for unsuspecting victims to detect. Once in the victim's system, it quickly produces physical as well as mental incapacitation. Ten times stronger than Valium, Rohypnol's sedative effect occurs 20 to 30 minutes after ingestion. The main side effect is amnesia, but it also produces an intoxicated appearance, impaired judgment, impaired motor skills, drowsiness, dizziness, and confusion.

The Prince William County's investigation revealed that in the late afternoon, the two young girls were taken willingly to an adult's apartment, having been reassured they would be returned home after they saw the apartment. Once at the apartment, they were offered a soft drink. They both drank a Mountain Dew and started to feel "weird," as one victim put it, within about 30 minutes. Neither victim could remember what occurred over the next 9 hours.

The first victim woke up, disoriented, on the couch in the early morning hours. She went to the bathroom and noticed "hickeys" on her neck that had not been present the day before. She could not remember having sexual contact with anyone. She then went to look for the second victim, whom she found asleep on a pull-out bed. Once awakened, she too was disoriented. The second victim noticed a "hickey" on her inner thigh but did not remember engaging in any sexual contact. During subsequent interviews, the men present in the apartment admitted having sexual intercourse with the victims but said it was consensual.

Three white tablets, marked "RH," were recovered from one of the men. These tested positive for Rohypnol. Both victims were seen by a sexual assault nurse examiner. The internal genital findings were consistent with nonconsensual sexual assault.

After a jury trial, the defendant was found guilty of rape, distribution of a Schedule IV drug to a minor, and contributing to the delinquency of a minor. The codefendant was found guilty of contributing to the delinquency of a minor.[19]

When confronted with an incident whose circumstances suggest that Rohypnol might be involved, investigators should treat it as both a sex and a drug case. Identifying physical evidence, locating the drug on the scene, and acting quickly to detect it in the victim's body are imperative. All items relevant to a sex case must be recovered, including victim and suspect physical evidence, recovery kits, clothing, hair and fiber evidence, linen materials, and the presence of biological fluids. (For a detailed discussion of collecting evidence from sexual assault victims, see Chapter 11, Sex-Related Offenses.) Efforts can then be turned toward items relevant to a drug case, including drug paraphernalia, containers, bottles, and cans.

The most challenging evidence to find and secure is the Rohypnol in the victim's body. Although detection can be made through a urine screen, the drug dissipates rapidly.

Produced by the Hoffman-La Roche pharmaceutical company, Rohypnol is illegal in the United States. It can, however, be brought into this country legally from Europe or Mexico with a prescription and has been legitimately used for insomnia and presurgical procedures.[20]

SPEEDBALLING

Speedballing is a slang term to describe the simultaneous ingestion, usually through injection, of heroin (a depressant) and cocaine (a stimulant). The cocaine provides the user with a tremendous euphoric "rush"; after the initial euphoria, the heroin provides a drowsy or depressing effect. An overdose of either drug can produce convulsions and death. Combined use greatly increases this risk.

HALLUCINOGENS

The *hallucinogenic drugs*, natural or synthetic, distort perception of objective reality. In large doses, they cause hallucinations. Most of these drugs are processed in clandestine laboratories and have yet to be proved medically valuable. The effects experienced after taking hallucinogens are not solely related to the drug. They are modified by the mood, mental attitude, and environment of the user. The unpredictability of their effects is the greatest danger to the user. Users may develop psychological dependence but not physical dependence, so far as is known. The most commonly abused hallucinogens are PCP (phencyclidine), LSD 25 (lysergic acid diethylamide), mescaline (peyote), psilocybin, and psilocyn.

PCP (PHENCYCLIDINE)

Phencyclidine, commonly called *PCP*, in pharmaceutically pure form is a solid white powder. Because the hydrochloride salt readily dissolves in water and as a street drug is often adulterated or misrepresented as other drugs, its appearance is highly variable. It is sold in powder form and in tablets, both in many colors. Often it is placed on parsley or on other leaf mixtures to be smoked as cigarettes (joints) (see Figure 21–18).[21]

When misrepresented, PCP is commonly sold as THC (the main psychoactive ingredient in marijuana, which in reality is rarely available on the street). But phencyclidine has also been sold as cannabinol (another marijuana constituent), mescaline, psilocybin, LSD, and even as amphetamine or cocaine. Because of the variability in street names and appearance, and because PCP is sometimes found in combination with barbiturates, heroin, cocaine, amphetamine, methaqualone, LSD, and mescaline, users may be mistaken about its true identity.

Depending on how carefully PCP is synthesized, it may contain impurities, including potassium cyanide. The mixture of marijuana and PCP has been thought to be common, but it has rarely been reported by street-drug analysis laboratories. At least one major laboratory on the West Coast that does such drug analysis has never encountered the combination.

Significantly adding to the risk of PCP use, especially when it is taken orally, is the wide variability in purity of the street drug. Even when PCP is not misrepresented, the percentage of PCP has

Figure 21–18
PCP

PCP is most commonly sold as a powder (*left*), or liquid (*center*), and is applied to a leafy material such as oregano (*right*), which is then smoked.

(Courtesy Drug Enforcement Administration)

been found to be quite variable. Generally, samples represented as "crystal" or "angel dust" tend to be purer than those sold under other names or misrepresented as other drugs.

In addition to phencyclidine, over 30 chemical analogues, some of which are capable of producing similar psychic effects, can also be synthesized and may appear on the street. Thus the problems of identifying and tracking the use of PCP and related drugs is unusually difficult.

THC is sometimes misrepresented as PCP. Unlike THC, PCP can be synthesized rather easily. The starting chemicals are widely available. Media accounts have sometimes exaggerated the ease with which phencyclidine can be made, but it is not particularly difficult for individuals with only modest technical training or elaborate equipment to make it.

Phencyclidine is used legally in veterinary medicine to immobilize primates. Although it was originally developed as an anesthetic for humans, it was later abandoned because it produced psychological disturbances and agitation in some patients. PCP made its first illicit appearance in the United States in 1965 on the West Coast. At that time it rapidly developed a bad street reputation and had only limited popularity. But in recent years use has markedly increased.

Because of its great variation in appearance, PCP is difficult to identify by sight. It is found in powder and tablet forms, but also on parsley, mint, oregano, or other leafy material, as a liquid, and in 1-gram "rock" crystals. When PCP is sold as a granular powder ("angel dust"), it may consist of 50 to 100 percent phencyclidine. Sold under other names and in other guises, the purity is from 10 to 30 percent; leafy mixtures contain still smaller amounts of the drug.

How Is It Used?

PCP is most commonly smoked or snorted. By smoking a leafy mixture on which the drug has been sprinkled, users can better regulate the dose. Because of the longer period before the drug takes effect and the greater purity, overdoses are probably worse when the drug has been taken orally.

Clinical Aspects

The best known effects of PCP would seem so unpleasant that many have wondered how it could possibly prove popular. For example, medical students volunteering for an experiment involving several hallucinogens and PCP were uniformly unwilling to return after having smoked moderate amounts of PCP. The drug made them feel weightless, smaller, out of touch with the immediate environment, and dying or dead. Common signs of PCP use include flushing, profuse sweating, involuntary eye movements, muscular uncoordination, double vision, dizziness, nausea, and vomiting. Police officers have reported that individuals under the influence of PCP can be extremely violent and almost superhumanly strong.

Many PCP users do not knowingly take it again. Yet others use it chronically.

Clinical Test for PCP

A 1-minute test to identify PCP was introduced by the Syva Company. The Emit[R] PCP semiquantitative urine assay is similar to Emit drug-abuse assays and can be performed with existing laboratory equipment. It can be used in hospital emergency rooms and in parole, probation, and work-release programs.[22]

MDMA

MDMA, a derivative of oil of sassafras or oil of nutmeg, is known chemically as 3,4-methylenedioxymethamphetamine. It was synthesized in 1914 by a chemist who mistakenly thought that it might be useful as an appetite suppressant. MDMA is best known to users and enforcement officers as "ecstasy" (see Figure 21-19). Medical authorities disagree about its therapeutic benefits. Proponents claim that it delivers a gentle 2- to 4-hour journey that dissolves anxieties and leaves the user relaxed and emotionally open, without the bad trips or addictive problems associated with other psychoactive drugs. A small group of psychiatrists, psychologists, and scientists contend that MDMA has enormous therapeutic potential and cite case histories in which MDMA has neutralized emotional defenses.

The DEA has concluded that MDMA is an uncontrolled and rapidly spreading recreational drug that can cause psychosis and perhaps brain damage. It banned the manufacture and distribution of MDMA under the Controlled Substance Act of 1984. Manufacturers and sellers of the drug are subject to fines of $125,000 and 15-year prison

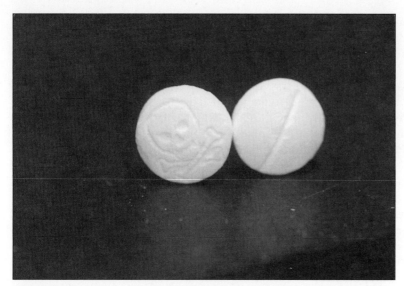

Figure 21–19
Ecstacy Pills
These pills are street named "pirates" because of the skull and crossbones that are sometimes imprinted on them.

(Courtesy Sergeant Christopher McKissick and Detective Tyler Parks, Port Orange, Florida, Police Department)

sentences. Possession is a misdemeanor. The DEA reports that thousands of MDMA capsules are sold on the streets each month for $8 to $20, particularly to college students and young professionals in at least 20 states, including California, Texas, and Florida.[23] The DEA also reports that in recent years this drug has become increasingly popular among juveniles and is commonly used as a recreational drug at large parties called "raves."

LSD 25 (LYSERGIC ACID DIETHYLAMIDE)

LSD is a semisynthetic compound produced from lysergic acid, a natural substance found in ergot fungus, a disease which affects rye and wheat. An average dose of 30 to 50 micrograms—about the size of a pinpoint—will take the user on a "trip" lasting 10 to 12 hours. Drops of the solution are taken on a lump of sugar or on blotted paper. Along with experiencing mental changes, the user may have dilated pupils, lowered temperature, nausea, goose bumps, profuse perspiration, increased blood sugar, and rapid heart rate. Flashbacks are not uncommon.

Before 1972 there was no way to detect LSD in the body chemically. However, scientists of Collaborative Research, Inc., Waltham, Massachusetts, developed a means to detect it in small amounts in human blood and urine and to measure the amount present. This discovery made it possible to study the distribution of LSD in the bodies of animals to determine the residual effect of the drug.[24] The DEA reports that LSD is making a comeback with juvenile circles and is also used frequently at "raves."

MESCALINE (PEYOTE)

The primary active ingredient of the peyote cactus is the hallucinogen mescaline, which is derived from the buttons of the plant (see Figure 21–20). Mescaline has been used by the Indians of Central America and the southwestern United States for centuries in religious rites. Generally ground into a powder, it is taken orally. A dose of 350 to 500 milligrams of mescaline produces illusions and hallucinations for 5 to 12 hours. Like LSD, mescaline is not likely to produce physical dependence but may produce psychological dependence.

PSILOCYBIN AND PSILOCYN

Psilocybin and psilocyn are obtained from mushrooms generally grown in Mexico (see Figure 21–21). Like mescaline, they have historically been used in Indian rites. They are taken orally, and their effect is similar to mescaline's, except that a smaller

Figure 21–20
Mescaline (Peyote)

(Courtesy Drug Enforcement Administration)

dose—4 to 8 milligrams—produces effects for about 6 hours.

MARIJUANA (*CANNABIS SATIVA L.*)

Marijuana is found in the sensimilla, the flowering tops and leaves of the unpollinated female Indian hemp plant. The leaves of the plant always grow in odd numbers. The plant grows in mild climates around the world, but the principal sources of import into the United States are Colombia, Mexico, and Jamaica (see Figure 21–22). Its most common nicknames are "pot," "reefer," "tea," "grass," "weed," "Maryjane," and "joint." Marijuana is made by crushing or chopping the dried leaves and flowers of the plant into small pieces. The cleaned or

Figure 21–21
Psilocybe Mushroom

Psilocybin and psilocyn do not produce physical dependence, although users have been known to develop a tolerance for them.

(Courtesy Drug Enforcement Administration)

manicured leaves are then rolled into a cigarette, smoked otherwise, or mixed with food and eaten (see Figure 21–23). The principal psychoactive substance is thought to be delta-9-tetrahydro-cannabinol (THC), a chemical found nowhere else in nature. Low doses of the drug tend to produce initial restfulness and well-being, followed by a dreamy, carefree state of relaxation and an alteration of sensory perceptions, including an illusory expansion of time and space.

Figure 21–22
Sources of Marijuana

Domestic
16%

Mexico
30%

Jamaica
12%

Colombia
30%

All others
12%

Source: U.S. General Accounting Office.

Figure 21–23
Manicured Marijuana and Seeds
Note smaller size of marijuana cigarette when compared to a regular cigarette on the left.

(Courtesy Drug Enforcement Administration)

Indoor Marijuana Operations

The move indoors has turned into a match of wits, pitting knowledgeable growers against seasoned narcotics agents.[25]

The outdoor marijuana growing season typically spans April to October. Not only do indoor growers hope to elude police by going inside; they are also able to control the climate, temperature, light, and soil conditions, thus being able to grow up to four crops a year. By controlling the crops, growers are also able to produce cannabis with a higher level of tetrahydrocannabinol (THC), the chemical found in the plant's flower tops that produces the mind-altering effects desired by marijuana smokers (see Figure 21–24).[26]

The move to indoor grow operations, a trend seen on a nationwide scale, is a direct result of both police pressure and the ability to grow better marijuana. Growers are trying to hide their illicit crop more effectively from police because of the pressure from aerial surveillance (see Figure 21–25).[27]

Another new trend is the growing of marijuana plants through *hydroponics*, which uses a growth medium other than soil. Unusually large purchases of hydroponic equipment are being more closely monitored these days.[28]

Domestic marijuana has come a long way in this country. The DEA reports that the marijuana smoked in the 1960s had a THC level of about 2 percent. Today it is common to find marijuana in the United States with a THC level of 5 to 7 percent.[29]

HASHISH

A drug-rich resinous secretion from the flowers of the cannabis plant, hashish is processed by drying to produce a drug several times as potent as

(Courtesy Drug Enforcement Administration)

Figure 21–24
Marijuana Plants
Marijuana plants being grown indoors.

Figure 21-25
Marajuana Concealment
Kilo packages of marijuana—first compressed, then put in vacuum-sealed bags, then concealed inside this piano.

(Courtesy Drug Enforcement Administration)

marijuana. The resin from the flowers is richer in cannabinols than the leaves and tops; the THC content ranges from 5 to 12 percent. (The leaves range from 0.27 to 4 percent in THC content.) Hashish is most commonly smoked in a small "hash pipe."

HASHISH OIL

The Middle East is the main source of hashish entering this country.[30] Liquid hashish is produced by concentrating THC. The liquid hashish so far discovered has varied between 20 and 65 percent THC. There is reason to suspect that methods are now being employed to make an even more powerful concentrate. The purity of the final product depends on the sophistication of the apparatus used.

Like other forms of the drug, liquid hashish can be used several ways. Because of its extraordinary potency, one drop of the material can produce a high. A drop may be placed on a regular cigarette, used in cooking, in wine, and even smeared on bread. When smoked, a small drop of hashish oil is smeared inside the glass bowl of a special pipe with a flattened side. The user exhales deeply, tilts the bowl, and holds the flame from a match under the oil. In one inhalation, the smoker draws slowly on the pipe as the oil begins to bubble, continuing as it chars and burns (see Figure 21–26).

There are many ways to produce hashish oil, but most clandestine operations use a basket filled with ground or chopped marijuana suspended inside a larger container, at the bottom of which is contained a solvent, such as alcohol, hexane, chloroform, or petroleum ether. Copper tubing or similar material is arranged at the top, and cold water circulates through it. The solvent is heated, the vapors rise to the top, they condense, and then they fall into the basket of marijuana. As the solvent seeps through the plant materials, the THC and other soluble chemicals are dissolved, and the solution drops back to the bottom of the container. Continued heating causes the process to recur. The solution becomes increasingly stronger until the plant material is exhausted of its THC.

KETAMINE

Ketamine hydrochloride is a synthetic drug that was developed in the mid-1960s and is an anesthetic agent that has legitimate uses, mostly in veterinary medicine. Ketamine was used extensively in the Vietnam War because it is fast-acting and has a relatively short duration, making it a drug of choice for "battlefield medicine." However, it soon became obvious that many humans who were anesthetized with ketamine often became agitated and suffered hallucinations when they awoke. It has since been replaced as an anesthetic for humans by other, more efficient agents with fewer side effects.

Ironically, the side effects that made ketamine unpopular and unsafe as a legitimate medical drug have spawned its use in the illegitimate market. On

Figure 21–26
Hash Pipe
The paraphernalia of cannabis abuse, including a glass apparatus for smoking hashish oil, pipes for smoking hashish and marijuana, and a variety of "roach holders" used to hold marijuana cigarettes when they burn low.

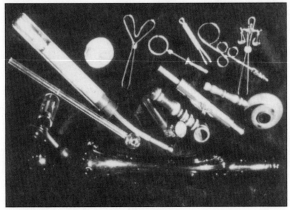

(Courtesy Drug Enforcement Administration)

the street, ketamine is called "vitamin K," "kat," "kit," "special K," or "K." It has been closely associated with the all-night party phenomenons known as "raves," where large crowds of young people listen to music and reportedly dance for 6 to 8 hours at a time. Ketamine causes hallucinations, excitement, and delirium similar to the drugs phencyclidine (PCP) and LSD; however, the effects are not as pronounced or as long in duration. Hallucinations caused by ketamine may last only an hour or two, but the intoxicationlike effects of the drug may be noticeable for several hours. Because ketamine is an anesthetic, it may temporarily mask the feeling of pain. Users of ketamine can injure themselves and not know it.

Because ketamine is so difficult to produce, it is not manufactured in clandestine laboratories. Most of the ketamine abused today comes from stolen veterinary stock, and is known by brand names such as Ketalar and Ketaset (see Figure 21–27). The legitimate drug is usually supplied in vials of liquid, although it can be in the form of white powder or pills.

In liquid form, ketamine may be injected into a large muscle. This route allows for a slower absorption and longer duration than the intravenous route. In powder form, ketamine is usually snorted in the same manner as cocaine. Both powder and liquid can be sprayed or sprinkled on vegetable matter and smoked or mixed with a drink. While it is not known if a person can become physically dependent upon ketamine, tolerance and psychological dependence are distinct possibilities with frequent use.

The average street dose of ketamine ranges from 0.2 to 0.5 gram. The size and weight of the abuser, the desired effects, and the presence of other drugs in the abuser's system determine the ultimate effect. A vial of liquid ketamine is equivalent to approximately 1 gram of powder and sells for $100 to $200. A 0.2-gram dose of powder, or a "bump," commonly sells for $20. Ketamine may be packaged for sale in small plastic bags, aluminum foil, paper folds, or gelatin capsules. Obviously, an abuser must also possess hypodermic syringes and needles to abuse the drug by injection.

Ketamine is not a federally scheduled controlled dangerous substance. On the state level, it is controlled only in California, Connecticut, New Mexico, and Oaklahoma. The DEA is presently collecting data on ketamine and may reevaluate the drug's nonscheduled status in the future.[31]

FIELD TESTING FOR CONTROLLED SUBSTANCES

Chemical field tests, using reagents and test kits, give valuable clues about the identity of samples. Field tests are easy to perform. They are, however, only presumptive because they may produce false positives. Any drug that will be used as evidence must be positively identified by a qualified chemist. Additionally, a negative test does not preclude the possibility that another similar drug may be present.[32]

INVESTIGATIVE PROCEDURES

Most of the techniques used in investigating dangerous drugs and in narcotics investigations are the same as those used in other cases; however, there are certain unique procedures.[33]

Figure 21–27
Ketamine

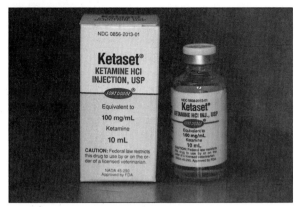

(Courtesy Sergeant Christopher McKissick and Detective Tyler Parks, Port Orange, Florida, Police Depatment)

THE PURCHASE

One important aspect is identification of the source. This is accomplished through review of completed reports of investigation, from other information received from an informant, or from surveillance and direct efforts to purchase drugs. It is desirable to make more than one direct purchase from a seller, if possible. This procedure gives investigators more opportunity to locate the peddler's cache of narcotics or source of supply. It also serves to identify other customers and to establish that the seller is not a one-time or opportunistic dealer. As a seller's sources of supply and customers are identified, the possibility of identifying key people in the network increases.

If an arrest is to be made immediately after a purchase, the currency used to make the buy should be dusted with fluorescent powder. The serial numbers of the currency should always be recorded for comparison with that recovered from other defendants, for it may suggest an unsuspected link among traffickers and thus a conspiracy. Recovered currency should be treated as evidence.

If a peddler will sell only to an informant and not to an undercover investigator, the informant must be searched before the sale to make sure that he or she has no narcotics. Any money found on the informant should be removed. Informants should be searched immediately after the sale. At this time, money should be returned. Between the two

searches, the informants must be kept under constant surveillance so that their testimony can be corroborated. Evidence obtained through "informant buys" is admissible in court, but the testimony of the informant may be required.

THE APPREHENSION

All arrests should be as unobtrusive as possible to prevent them from becoming common knowledge on the street. This practice preserves the usefulness of the information the arrested party provides.

When approaching a drug suspect, the investigator must be particularly observant of the suspect's hands. The suspect may attempt to drop, throw, flush, eat, or otherwise dispose of drugs. If drugs are found on the ground or some distance away from the suspect, it may be extremely difficult, if not impossible, to connect the drug with the suspect. Because addicts can be dangerous, unpredictable, and uncooperative, investigators must exercise caution. Addicts may use a weapon or suddenly attack the unwary investigator. As soon as possible after apprehension, suspects should be required to place their hands directly in the air or behind their heads to preclude further disposal of evidence.

The investigator must ensure that drugs taken from the custody of persons suspected of a narcotics offense have not been prescribed. If certain seized drugs are necessary for a suspect's health, a physician's opinion should be sought on administering the drug.

Immediately after the apprehension or as soon as possible thereafter, a thorough search should be made of the suspect's person, clothing, and area of immediate control. The possession of even the minutest of drug particles may be sufficient to establish a connection.[34] Because the quantity of the drug may be small, hiding places are almost limitless. The law enforcement officer should use the full range of skills and imagination to search for them.

DRUG INFORMANTS: MOTIVES, METHODS, AND MANAGEMENT

Informants in drug enforcement are unique among criminal informants and perhaps the most difficult to manage. However, investigators who know what motivates individuals to become informants can manage them more effectively.[35]

INFORMANTS: MOTIVATIONS AND TYPES

Like most people, informants need motivation to produce. The more motivated they are, the more likely they are to apply themselves to the task at hand and remain committed to achieving success. Therefore, by identifying an informant's true motives, an investigator greatly enhances the potential success of an investigation. Initially, informants commonly voice a specific motive for providing assistance. However, as a case proceeds and a relationship with an investigator develops, other reasons may surface. Some of the more common motivational factors encountered by drug enforcement investigators are fear, revenge, money, repentance, and altruism.

The most frequently encountered motivational factor may be the confidential informant's (CI's) fear of punishment for criminal acts. Severe criminal penalties tend to increase the number of persons wishing to cooperate with drug enforcement authorities. Informants may also fear their criminal associates. Individuals wrongly accused by drug dealers of being informants may then become informants for self-preservation, money, or both.

Next, informants frequently cooperate with the government to seek revenge against their enemies. Jealousy may also prompt these acts of vengeance.

In addition, some individuals provide information or services for money. These money-motivated informants, known as mercenaries, are usually the most willing to follow the directions of their handlers. Mercenaries frequently possess other motives as well.

Furthermore, repentance can be a motivating factor. Informants often claim they cooperate in order to repent for past crimes. However, this is seldom their only motive for cooperating.

Finally, some individuals are motivated by a sense of altruism. People with professional obligations or feelings of responsibility frequently provide information to the police. Examples of altruistic informants include airline ticket agents and private mail-service carriers.

Problem Informants

Some informants have personalities that make them difficult, if not impossible, to manage. These individuals may also have questionable motives for offering their services to a law enforcement agency. Investigators who misjudge the true motives of informants experience tremendous control problems. This can create safety problems and place department resources and personnel in jeopardy. Therefore investigators should avoid recruiting certain types of individuals, if possible.

Egotistical Informants

These informants, who are encountered frequently, may not have received positive reinforcement from their parents or schoolmates when growing up. Consequently, they seek positive feedback from their handlers as their primary reward. Investigators who provide this positive reinforcement motivate egotistical informants to continue supplying information. Unfortunately, these informants are often the hardest to handle because their egos prevent them from relinquishing control of the investigation entirely to their handlers.

Informants with the "James Bond Syndrome"

Some persons see their roles as informants as a way to have their lives imitate art. While working as informants, they imagine themselves in a police or spy drama. Sometimes they even attempt to orchestrate events to parallel a scene from a movie or novel. Frequently hard to handle, these informants often exaggerate their knowledge of criminal activity to enhance the likelihood of their becoming informants.

"Wannabe" Informants

Wannabe informants are people who, for whatever reason, failed to qualify for a law enforcement position and now seek to become involved in law enforcement as informants. Because they lack criminal associates, these individuals usually cannot provide specific information about drug dealing. Therefore they do not make good informants.

Perversely Motivated Informants

The most dangerous and disruptive informants in drug law enforcement are perversely motivated CIs. They offer their services in order to identify undercover agents; learn the department's methods, targets, and intelligence; or eliminate their own competition in drug sales. Sometimes criminal organizations instruct these individuals to infiltrate departments and learn whatever they can to assist the traffickers. These individuals may even provide genuine information about specific events as a decoy to divert resources from more significant trafficking activity.

Therefore investigators must question all walk-in and call-in informants (i.e., individuals who volunteer their services without prompting) because they may be, or have the potential to be, perversely motivated. After completing a thorough background investigation of CIs, investigators must constantly guard against providing more information than informants furnish in return. Furthermore, investigators should not discuss with informants specific details of methods and techniques used during drug investigations.

Restricted-Use Informants

In addition to problem informants,[36] certain other informants, by virtue of their criminal background or other status, pose special management challenges to both investigators and supervisors. Department managers should carefully scrutinize these individuals prior to using them as CIs. Examples include juveniles, individuals on probation or parole, individuals currently or formerly addicted to drugs, felons with multiple convictions, and individuals known to be unreliable.

Investigators should not use these individuals as informants until a supervisor approves them. In fact, because these informants require special scrutiny, only senior investigators should handle them. Furthermore, investigators must constantly reevaluate the motives of these individuals.

DEPARTMENT POLICY

Agencies should not leave the management of drug informants exclusively to investigators. Formulating a written policy ensures consistency in the use and management of CIs and serves as a guide for inexperienced investigators.

The policy should indicate which investigators may maintain informants, as well as who will supervise these CIs. In addition, the policy should clearly establish that informants are assets of the department, not of individual investigators. In this regard,

management should both authorize and encourage investigators to share informants. Also, checks and balances must be in place to ensure that the policy is followed.

Policy concerning the management of confidential informants should establish procedures in several areas. These include creating and documenting informant files, debriefing and interacting with informants, and determining methods and amounts of payments for services rendered.

The Informant File

Investigators should formally establish files for CIs who regularly furnish information to investigators, as well as for those who expect compensation for information they supply. Informant files document the investigator's interaction with them. In fact, investigators should not use any source that cannot be documented.

Although investigators should document their contacts with CIs, not everyone in the department needs to know an informant's identity or have access to informant files. Access should be on a need-to-know basis, including only those investigators and their supervisors who deal directly with the informant.

To further protect informants' identities, investigators should use code numbers in lieu of informants' names in investigative reports. Informants should keep the same number throughout their working relationships with the department.

The informant file should include information pertaining to the CI's vital statistics, such as physical description, work and home addresses, vehicles driven, contact telephone numbers, next of kin, and so forth. National Crime Information Center searches, performed before the informant is used and then systematically thereafter, ensure that the informant has no outstanding warrants. These records should be kept in the informant's file, along with the CI's photograph, fingerprints, and FBI and state "rap" sheets.

Establishing an informant file sends a not-so-subtle message to CIs that investigators document every encounter and verify all information that CIs supply. Such documentation may also deter a perversely motivated informant. In addition, informant files enhance the credibility of the department in the eyes of the court and the public, who view CIs as inherently unreliable and who may believe that the agency fabricated information. Therefore, every time the informant provides information concerning an actual or potential criminal matter, the agency should include a written report detailing this information in the file. The original report should remain in the CI's file, and a copy should be maintained in the case file.

The department must also document what steps it takes to corroborate information provided by the CI. This is especially important when informants act unilaterally. As a matter of policy, all CI information should be verified regardless of the CI's past reliability.

Informant Debriefings

Each time investigators initiate investigations based on information received from a CI, the designated handler should interview and debrief the CI in order to ascertain the informant's motive(s) and to advise the informant of the department's rules. For example, informants should know that they carry no official status with the department, that the department will not tolerate their breaking the law or entrapping suspects, and that the department cannot guarantee that they will not be called as witnesses in court.

At the end of the interview, the investigator should put this information in writing in an "informant agreement." This agreement should be signed by the informant, witnessed by the handler, and placed in the informant's file. Investigators should debrief their informants on a regular basis—for example, every 30, 60, or 90 days—to keep them active or, if necessary, to terminate their association with the department due to lack of productivity.

Investigator-Informant Contact Procedures

The department must establish investigator-informant contact procedures and train employees in their use. For example, the handler should meet with the informant in private, if possible, but always in the presence of another investigator. In fact, the department should either strongly discourage or prohibit investigators from contacting informants alone, especially if the officer plans to pay the informant. Meeting with or paying a drug informant alone leaves the officer and the department vulnerable to allegations of wrongdoing.

Although informant handlers often develop special working relationships with their informants, department policies should preclude contact with informants outside the scope of official business. Investigators must keep their relationships with CIs strictly professional. This is particularly important when the informant and the investigator are not of the same sex. Policies should also expressly prohibit such contact as socializing with informants and/or their families, becoming romantically involved with or conducting nonpolice business with them, and accepting gifts or gratuities from them.[37]

To ensure adherence to department policy, supervisors should review informant files regularly. In addition, they need to attend debriefings periodically to oversee the entire informant management process.

Finally, department administrators must establish procedures for investigating alleged policy violations by investigators or informants. Thorough investigations of this type maintain the integrity of the department by dispelling any notion that the department does not enforce its own policies.

Informant Payments

CI payments can be divided into two distinct categories—awards and rewards. Awards take a monetary form. They are based on a percentage of the net value of assets seized during a drug investigation as a result of information provided by a CI. Advising the informant of the exact amount of the percentage at the beginning of the case provides incentive for the CI to seek out hidden assets that might otherwise go undetected. However, because payments based on seized assets are not universally accepted in the courts, the investigator should consult the case prosecutor before promising a specific amount to the informant.

Rewards, on the other hand, do not represent a percentage of the value of the seized assets. Amounts are usually determined by the type and quantity of drugs seized, the quality of the case produced, the number of defendants indicted, the amount of time and effort the CI exerted, and the danger faced by the CI during the course of the investigation. Unlike awards, rewards come directly from an agency's budget.

While an informant might receive money as a reward, many informants cooperate with law enforcement agencies to receive a reduced sentence for a pending criminal matter. Regardless of the form of compensation, the department's policy must address the circumstances under which an informant qualifies for an award and/or reward, who can authorize such payments, and the conditions under which payments will be granted.

Although many informants receive substantial *awards* when they locate the assets of drug dealers, agency budgets may limit the dollar amount of *rewards* paid to informants. For this reason, investigators should exercise caution when explaining the payment policy to informants. They should avoid mentioning a specific dollar amount the informant will receive. Otherwise, the informant may try to hold the department to that amount, regardless of future budgetary constraints.

In addition to providing awards and rewards, departments can reimburse informants for expenses incurred during an investigation. In fact, the department may wish to reimburse the CI with small amounts of money beyond actual expenses as added incentives to continue working.

It is highly recommended that informants be paid only in the presence of witnesses, with the final payment made after all court proceedings have been completed to help ensure the informant's presence at the trial. Once a payment is made, a record documenting the date, exact amount, and who made the payment must be included in the CI file in anticipation of future court inquiries.

THE INVESTIGATOR'S PREVENTION RESPONSIBILITY

Investigators can often reduce the possibility that a physician or pharmacist will be victimized or help reduce the magnitude of the loss. Ordinarily, investigators talk with these professionals during the investigation of an offense, while obtaining information not directly related to an offense, or in the context of speaking before civic or professional groups. Physicians and pharmacists should be made aware of the following precautions:

Physicians Should Not:

- Leave unattended prescription pads in the open.
- Forget that prescriptions must be written in ink or indelible pencil or on a typewriter.
- Carry a large stock of narcotics in their medical bags.
- Store narcotics where patients can obtain easy access (near sinks or lavatories).
- Issue a narcotics prescription without seeing the patient.
- Write prescriptions for large quantities of narcotics unless absolutely necessary.
- Prescribe a narcotic because a patient says that another physician has been doing it.
- Leave signed blank prescriptions in the office for nurses to complete.
- Treat an ambulatory case of addiction.
- Dispense narcotics without making the necessary records.
- Purchase narcotics for office use with prescription blanks; the law requires an official order form.
- Act resentful if a pharmacist calls to confirm a prescription for narcotics (the pharmacist can be held responsible for filling forged prescriptions).
- Hesitate to call the local police department to obtain or give information.

Pharmacists Should Not:

- Leave or display narcotics near the cash register.
- Fail to scrutinize prescriptions written in a way that makes alterations possible; for example,

  Morph. HT ½ #X

  or

  Morph. HT ¼ #10

  In this illustration several "X" marks or zeros could be added to increase quantities. Physicians should be advised to spell out the prescription completely or to use brackets.
- Carry a large stock of narcotics; a three-month supply is advisable.
- Leave a key in the lock of the narcotics cabinet, which is locked at all times.
- Fail to keep all excess drugs in a safe, if possible
- Place narcotics stock where it is accessible to others.
- Leave the prescription area unattended, if possible.

- Forget that a request for rapid filling of a prescription may be a ploy to distract them from checking a forged prescription.
- Fill telephone orders for narcotic drugs unless assured that a prescription will be available upon delivery.
- Be taken in by a person wearing a white uniform who presents a narcotics prescription.
- Refill narcotics prescriptions.
- Fill prescriptions for unusual quantities without checking with the physician.
- Hesitate to call a physician if the validity of a prescription is questioned.
- Supply a doctor's office needs from a prescription.
- Accept a narcotics prescription written in pencil.
- Leave prescription pads in accessible areas.

DRUG ABUSE BY PRACTITIONERS

It has always been perplexing to investigators that a professional would become involved with drugs. But doctors do succumb to addiction. They have ready access to drugs and may turn to them out of fatigue, stress, or pain. Those who succumb may be only marginally adjusted to their environment.

They may function reasonably well at the onset of their addiction. An injection of Demerol, a tablet of codeine with aspirin, or a bottle of cough medicine may offer temporary euphoria and an escape from the pressure of living. Once the drug is used habitually, the doctor's ability to discern right from wrong falters. The doctor begins to rationalize, lie, connive, steal, and sometimes beg to perpetuate the habit. Physically, morally, and mentally, addiction becomes complete. The spouse may be initiated into the habit, whether for commiseration or to avoid censure.

Regardless of previous social or professional position, the addicted doctor becomes unreliable. Each day is governed by the need to "get right," and maintenance of a routine is more and more difficult. Functioning by reflex works for a time, but discriminating judgments become increasingly less possible.

Well-meaning colleagues may become aware of the problem and try to assist. But the addict requires extensive assistance, usually beyond a colleague's "outpatient" approach. Discounting the criminal aspect, an adequate approach is hospitalization in a narcotics-free environment with extensive follow-up psychological treatment. The absence of responsible action may lead to tragedy.

Among the most common indications that a physician may be unlawfully diverting drugs are:

- A physician places excessively frequent orders for narcotics.
- A physician picks up and pays for filled narcotics prescriptions from a pharmacy.
- A physician places an emergency call for a narcotic medication to a pharmacy and requests delivery. The deliverer is met by the physician and given a prescription for the drugs. In some instances, no patient exists, or if one does exist the narcotics are retained by the physician and other medication substituted.
- A narcotics prescription is issued to a patient by a physician with instructions to have it filled and to return with the drug for administration. Substitute medication is then given to the patient.
- In narcotics records, a physician uses fictitious or deceased people's names and addresses.
- The physician frequently requests that a prescription for an alleged patient be taken to the pharmacy by a nurse, a receptionist, or a member of the family and be returned to the doctor personally.
- While other physicians are in the operating room or making hospital rounds, the addict-physician searches their vehicles or medical bags for narcotics.
- A physician obtains a key to the narcotics locker in a hospital and has a duplicate made.
- A physician may place an order for a patient in a hospital; when the drug is prepared by a nurse, the doctor takes it over and either uses a substitute syringe containing a placebo or administers only a small portion of the drug.

If a case for prosecution is indicated against an addicted physician, an investigator must interview pharmacists, review prescriptions, and take statements from patients who allegedly received drugs prescribed by the doctor. The evidence thus obtained is used to secure an indictment.[38]

CLANDESTINE DRUG LABORATORIES

Clandestine laboratories throughout the United States produce a variety of illegal drugs for sale and distribution. The processes used in production of these drugs range in their degree of sophistication from primitive to advanced. By the same token, those who operate such laboratories may range in expertise from the novice experimenter to the professional chemist. These factors alone can have a serious impact on the safety of the general public and on police and fire department personnel who may deal with these laboratories in enforcement and emergency situations.[39]

Raids conducted on clandestine drug laboratories are inherently dangerous, irrespective of the dangers associated with taking suspects into custody. The degree of danger is based largely on the types of chemicals that are typically used and the chemical processes employed. These dangers may be heightened by the operator's lack of expertise and experience and by the physical limitations and restrictions of the facility being used, as well as by weather conditions and other factors. Such dangers cannot be overemphasized. Major accidents resulting in loss of life have occurred during raids conducted on such facilities by those who are untrained, inexperienced, or careless in the dismantling, handling, transportation, storage, or disposal of the involved chemicals.

Normally, direct physical involvement with drug laboratories takes place during the execution of a search warrant on a suspect property. Under these circumstances, there is generally enough information to forewarn police officers about the nature of the operations and the types of chemicals that are most likely involved. Adequate safety precautions can thus be developed and employed. However, police officers may inadvertently encounter a laboratory operation while conducting other enforcement or investigatory operations. In such instances, unless there is imminent danger of loss of life, police officers and civilians alike should be restricted from entering laboratory premises. Clandestine laboratories typically employ processes using chemicals that are toxic, corrosive, caustic, and flammable. The laboratory environment may pose explosive toxic or carcinogenic risks that should be dealt with only by specially trained and equipped personnel.

IDENTIFYING LABORATORY OPERATIONS

Clandestine laboratory operations are typically identified in one of four ways. In some instances, fire departments responding to the scene of a fire or explosion will find evidence of laboratory operations. Positive determinations, however, depend on the ability of emergency service personnel to recognize the type of substances and equipment typically used in such operations. It is important, therefore, that these personnel be trained in identification of clandestine lab operations. Since fire departments should be close at hand during police raids of drug laboratories, it is important that responsible personnel from both agencies develop a working relationship in dealing with problems that may arise from these types of operations.

Evidence of drug laboratory operations may also be generated through informants. Laboratory operators who are attempting to establish operations in a new community often need to determine sources for the purchase of specific chemicals. Plans for development of a lab and related involvement of suppliers or distributors frequently are revealed by confidential informants and intelligence gathered from arrestees.

The community at large may also provide valuable tips on laboratory operations based on observations of unusual activities or circumstances. Many drug labs operate in urban or suburban residential communities where citizens who are alerted to the common signs of laboratory operations can provide valuable information to the police. These indicators include the following:

- A residence where one or more individuals visit but where no one lives. Laboratory operators are generally cautious about the risks of fire, explosion, or contamination and attempt to limit their exposure and risk.
- Residences or other buildings that have sealed doors and windows, although they are not abandoned facilities.

- The presence of ventilating fans that operate irrespective of weather conditions.
- Strong ammonia or related odor.
- An unfurnished "residence."
- A "resident" who frequently goes outside for a cigarette or to get some air.

Although these circumstances do not prove the existence of an illegal drug manufacturing operation, several of these factors together may be suggestive enough to warrant establishment of low-profile police surveillance.

METH LABS

One of the fastest-growing types of clandestine laboratories is the methamphetamine lab. Such labs have been around since the 1960s, when they were organized and operated by outlaw motorcycle gangs. To stop the spread of "clan labs," chemicals such as ether and ephedrine were restricted by the Chemical Diversion and Trafficking Act of 1988. Rogue chemical companies that sold to clan-lab precursors were prosecuted and put out of business by the DEA and other local, state, and federal law enforcement agencies.[40]

In the late 1980s and early 1990s, the biker manufacturers began to be edged out of the market by new and very violent methamphetamine manufacturers—the Mexican national methamphetamine organizations. Today, they dominate the meth manufacturing market. Their industrial-size labs are producing methamphetamine in mass quantities for distribution across the United States. This is evidenced by recent DEA operations that resulted in methamphetamine arrests in California, Texas, and North Carolina, as well as the seizure of three methamphetamine labs (see Figure 21–28).

With the restriction of methamphetamine manufacturing chemicals, lab seizures started to decline in the late 1980s. Since then, however, the trend has been reversed with a vengeance, and lab seizures have started to skyrocket. One of the reasons for this increase is the Internet. Now all a methamphetamine manufacturer has to do is turn on his or her computer, point and click to find a recipe, and point and click again to find the chemicals. If the "meth cook" has any questions during the manufacturing process, he or she can simply visit one of the methamphetamine manufacturing

Figure 21–28
Meth Lab

Paraphernalia used in the production of methamphetamine discovered in a laboratory raided by special agents of the Drug Enforcement Administration.

(Courtesy Drug Enforcement Administration)

chat pages. These small "tweeker"-type labs are capable of making anywhere from ounce to pound quantities of methamphetamine. Size does not matter when it comes to clan labs; these small labs are just as dangerous for law enforcement officers as are the biker and Mexican national labs.

Meth labs can be broken down into different styles:

- Biker or traditional
- Mexican national
- Cold-cook
- Pressure cooker
- Hydrogenation
- "Tweeker"

Chemicals used to manufacture methamphetamine are easily obtainable, even with chemical restrictions. Laboratory equipment used to manufacture methamphetamine runs the full spectrum from the scientific to the yard-sale purchase. Heating mantles, condensers, vacuum pumps, buchner funnels, and 22-liter reaction vessels are regularly seized at clandestine labs. Not wanting to attract attention of law enforcement, clandestine laboratory equipment manufacturers are turning to other types of clan-lab equipment. They now use pressure cookers, hot plates, mason jars, sun tea dispensers, nhalgene containers, homemade compressed-gas cylinders, Pyrex bowls, sports bottles, microwave ovens, and other such material.[41]

SEIZURE AND FORFEITURE

Laboratory operators may be arrested under a wide variety of circumstances, only the most typical of which are discussed here. Most laboratory operations are closed as the result of police raids following intensive investigative work.

On occasion, police officers will inadvertently discover a clandestine lab operation while responding to other public safety situations. It is essential that officers take only those steps necessary to protect their lives or the lives of bystanders and to make arrests only if entry into the laboratory is not required. Normally, if the officer's presence has not been detected, this involves relaying information to supervisory personnel and/or other appropriate personnel in the department who have received specialized training in handling clandestine laboratories.

Once the scene is secure, it may be possible to interview neighbors in order to determine information on occupancy. Officers should also make note of all vehicles parked in the immediate area of the laboratory.

Another means of interdiction involves the civil forfeiture of illicit chemicals and drug manufacturing paraphernalia. This procedure, which pertains to individual laboratory operators as well as chemical suppliers, allows federal agents to seize anything used or intended for use to illegally manufacture, deliver, or import drugs. Most states have similar prohibitions, and officers should be familiar with the provisions and limitations of these laws. Use of these forfeiture statutes may be a reasonable alternative to attempts to establish a criminal case, particularly where staffing constraints limit surveillance and other operations, when suspects' discovery of surveillance may necessitate terminating the investigation, or when it is feared that the laboratory operation is preparing to relocate quickly. It should be noted that often the circumstances that justify a civil seizure will lead thereafter to successful prosecution under criminal statutes relating to conspiracy or the attempt to manufacture controlled substances.

When making a decision concerning civil seizure of illegal drugs and manufacturing materials, offi-cers should contact their local prosecuting attorney for advice. Evidence not sufficient to support criminal prosecution may be adequate for a civil seizure. Normally, successful seizure requires that officers demonstrate the suspect's probable intent to manufacture a controlled substance. This can be accomplished by reference to the type and combination of chemicals and paraphernalia on hand, furtive activity, use of subterfuge, or other questionable practices.

Those who supply materials to clandestine laboratories with knowledge of their use are also subject to civil and criminal penalties under various federal and state laws. Chemical companies or supply houses may knowingly sell chemicals to laboratory operators without reporting those sales to the police, disguise sales records, assist buyers in using the chemicals, or otherwise assist in the preparation or merchandising process. It is normally possible to apply seizure and forfeiture actions to such merchants if investigation can establish any factor that shows the suppliers' "guilty knowledge" of the illegal uses of their merchandise.

An undercover purchase of chemicals from suspected suppliers is the most typical means of developing criminal cases against them. In addition, chemicals seized at drug laboratories may display manufacturers' labels, including lot numbers, and equipment may have manufacturers' plates and serial numbers that can be used to trace their sales or transfers.

Under proper circumstances, therefore, civil seizure may be an acceptable, if not preferred, approach to termination of illegal drug manufacturing operations. Additionally, once such actions are taken, perpetrators will often cooperate with the police and provide intelligence that will assist in additional enforcement operations.

CONDUCTING A LABORATORY RAID

Conducting a raid on an occupied laboratory requires careful planning. Normally, a planning meeting involves the police tactical unit, bomb squad, hazardous-material or chemical-waste disposal personnel, a chemist, and fire department representatives—all of whom are specially trained. The nature of the operation from initial entry to dismantling should be reviewed with particular attention to the types of chemicals most likely being used, the nature of the suspects involved, and contingency plans for emergency services should a fire, explosion, or toxic reaction take place.

The initial entry team should be outfitted with Nomex clothing, body armor, and goggles. Nomex will provide short-term protection from fire, and goggles will protect one's eyes from airborne fumes and thrown chemicals. The tactical unit is responsible only for securing the suspects and exiting the laboratory as quickly as possible and with the minimum amount of force.

It should be noted that to avoid unduly restricted movements, the tactical team should wear the minimum amount of protective clothing necessary. It is important, therefore, that the team's exposure to the laboratory environment be extremely limited. The team should make a mental note of the laboratory environment and report its findings to the assessment team members who will follow. Laboratory operators, in anticipation of possible raids, sometimes booby trap the facility in order to destroy evidence. The ability to recognize traps and other potential hazards depends on the training and experience of team members, a factor that underscores the importance of special training for such operations. After leaving the facility, the tactical team should undergo decontamination.

After the site is secured, the assessment team is free to enter. Team members should wear Nomex clothing covered with disposable protective suits, as well as chemical-resistant gloves and boots covered with disposable gloves and boots. All seams of the suits should be taped with nonporous adhesive tape and each team member should be equipped with a self-contained breathing apparatus. The team should be outfitted with two air-monitoring devices—a combustible-gas indicator and indicator tubes.

The combustible-gas indicator is an essential air-monitoring device that tests for oxygen levels, airborne gas particle levels, and the combustibility of the environment. The indicator tubes test for the presence and quantity of specific types of chemical vapors. A pump is used to force air through the individual tubes.

Assessment team members test the lab environment at several locations and make notes of instrument readings. They should also make a diagram of the interior, noting any dangers or problems that may be encountered. When their work is completed, the assessment team should leave the facility, decontaminate, and give their report to the dismantling team.

The dismantling team should wear the same type of protective clothing as the assessment team. Even though dangerous substances may not have been found, there is always the possibility of spills and damage during dismantling, which could create a hazardous situation. A chemist trained in laboratory dismantling should be on hand to take samples of chemicals present and products being manufactured so that informed judgments can be made on safety in packaging, transportation, storage, disposal, and handling of evidence samples.

Crime scene personnel, under the close supervision of the dismantling team supervisor, should conduct standard crime scene processing procedures, including photographs and searching for latent fingerprints. Videotaping of laboratory operations is also helpful for evidentiary purposes and for court presentation.

The chemist can direct the proper packaging of chemical substances. Care must always be taken that only compatible chemicals are packaged together. Typically, chemicals are placed in drums filled with vermiculite or a similar absorbant, nonflammable substance. A waste disposal company approved by the Environmental Protection Agency (EPA) can be of great value in the packaging process.

Chemicals that are not being used in court because of potential hazards, together with contaminated clothing and equipment, must be packaged, transported, and stored or disposed of according to EPA guidelines.

SEARCH WARRANTS AND PROBABLE CAUSE

Officers engaged in drug enforcement must understand the legal elements necessary to constitute probable cause for obtaining search warrants. The criteria for ascertaining probable cause vary somewhat even within judicial districts.

The vast majority of drug information provided to law enforcement officers comes from confidential informants. Therefore, it is particularly significant that certain guidelines be followed carefully by those responsible for drafting search warrants.

LAW ENFORCEMENT BACKGROUND OF THE APPLICANT

Some factors to be considered in assessing the background of the law enforcement officer seeking the warrant are length of time employed by the agency, present position, familiarity with the offense in question, the number of previous arrests made by the applicant for this type of offense, and, if applicable, familiarity with any paraphernalia used in connection with the offense.

PAST RELIABILITY OF THE CONFIDENTIAL INFORMANT

The past reliability of the confidential informant is of considerable importance, especially when the effort to determine probable cause to obtain a search warrant is based exclusively on such information. One should consider the length of time the applicant has known the informant and the number of occasions on which reliable information was supplied. For example, how many times before did the confidential informant's information result in the seizure of contraband or paraphernalia on persons, on premises, or in vehicles, and how many of these offenses resulted in a conviction? To confirm that the confidential informant has been reliable, the officer should be prepared to cite specific instances of reliable information. Other considerations are the informant's familiarity with the type of offense involved in the affidavit and familiarity with paraphernalia used in connection with the offense.

INFORMATION SUPPLIED BY THE INFORMANT

Information to be considered in this area includes the date, time, and place of the meeting between police and the informant; the substance and content of the information; and the date, time, and place that the information was obtained.

The law enforcement officer should try to elicit from the informant as many facts as possible that can be corroborated, for example, the telephone number and address of the suspect's residence, a physical description of the suspect, the occupation of the suspect, vehicles owned or operated by the suspect, a description of the vehicle and the tag number, and the time at which the suspect may be observed at the premises or within the described vehicle.

CORROBORATION OF THE INFORMATION SUPPLIED

All efforts should be made to corroborate information supplied by a confidential informant. In some instances, corroboration is a simple check of the accuracy of portions of the information, such as the suspect's address, associates, vehicle, hangouts, patterns of behavior, and criminal record. When information is corroborated, careful records should be kept, including the date, time, and method of corroboration. Some jurisdictions have found it useful to attach a mug shot of the suspect and a photograph, diagram, or sketch of the property, vehicle, store, or other place to be searched.[42]

EVIDENCE HANDLING AND SECURITY PROBLEMS

Aside from the burglaries, larcenies, and other crimes committed because of narcotics, there are additional related problems sprouting from the drug culture vine. Some of these growths entwine the individual police officer and the overall police function. One offshoot, the handling and securing of narcotics and dangerous drugs after they are collected and seized, has emerged as an area of growing concern to police administrators for a number of reasons.

Once seized by the police, narcotic and dangerous-drug evidence requires protection in order that it may be preserved in its original state until it is brought before a court or destroyed through legal process. It is during this period that the greatest demands are placed on personnel of the law enforcement agency concerned. Narcotic and dangerous-drug evidence must be protected not only against loss and outside threats of incursion, but, unfortunately, sometimes from internal intrusions as well.

Although relatively uncommon, there have been occasions when narcotic and dangerous-drug evidence has disappeared from a "secure" area under the control and within the confines of a police agency. The following methods for handling drug evidence will go far in addressing these concerns and minimizing their happening.

There are two recognized methods for introducing narcotic and dangerous-drug evidence into the processing sequence immediately after it is seized and marked. Neither method omits any of the processing steps; the difference is found in the manner in which the sequential steps are arranged.[43]

The first method (the laboratory-first method) requires that all seized evidence (after it is field tested, marked, photographed, weighed, and initially inventoried) be transported immediately to the laboratory for analysis. Drop boxes are provided in the laboratory for the deposit of evidence during periods when the facility is not operational. All seized narcotic and dangerous-drug evidence is taken directly to a room in the vicinity of the laboratory. This room, known as an inventory or display room, is specially equipped for inventorying narcotic and dangerous-drug evidence and is not used for any other purpose. Weighing scales, camera, film holders, lighting equipment, evidence seals, evidence containers, appropriate forms, desk, typewriter, table or counter, and necessary administrative supplies are maintained in the room. When not in use, the room is locked and the keys (two) are retained in a secure location (normally, one key is kept in the laboratory and the other is controlled by the watch supervisor or desk officer). In order to achieve even greater control over inventory rooms, departments that have a high volume of narcotic evidence are employing more sophisticated entry-control systems, including "entry" or "swipe" cards on a system that records the cardholder's identity and time of entry and departure. Video cameras may also be used to record all behavior in the inventory room.

After seizure of the evidence and while en route to police headquarters, the seizing officer requests a witnessing officer of supervisory grade (at least one grade above that held by the seizing officer) and a member of the laboratory staff (technician on duty) or a technician from the mobile laboratory unit, if available to meet with him or her at the narcotic and dangerous-drug inventory room. When the supervisory official arrives at the inventory room, the seizing officer displays the material seized (the witnessing officer does not handle any of the evidence). After the evidence package has been marked and displayed in the manner best suited for a photographic inventory, the laboratory technician photographs the evidence (the photographer does not handle any of the evidence). When photographs of the evidence have been taken, the evidence is weighed and inventoried under the direct supervision of the supervisory officer. Appropriate forms are then completed and witnessed, and the evidence is sealed in containers or envelopes provided for that purpose.

After these steps have been accomplished, in company with the witnessing officer and the laboratory technician, the seizing officer carries the evidence to the laboratory drop box and deposits it therein. If the drop box cannot accommodate the evidence package, the laboratory evidence room custodian or an alternate is requested to come to the laboratory, assume custody of the evidence, and store it in the laboratory evidence room. If the evidence is taken to the laboratory during normal operational hours, the drop box is not used; the evidence is turned over directly to the laboratory evidence custodian or alternate.

On completion of the analytical process by the laboratory, the evidence is delivered to the narcotic and dangerous-drug evidence room in the property room. Here, the evidence custodian assumes control of the evidence and provides for its preservation and subsequent processing as required.

In the second method (the evidence room-first method), seized narcotic and dangerous-drug evidence, after being field tested, marked, photographed, weighed, and inventoried, is sealed in an appropriate container and deposited in a drop box or delivered directly to the evidence room in the property room. There are variations to the procedure; in some cases certain intermediate steps (photographing the evidence, for example) are omitted or the initial processing (weighing, photographing, and inventorying) may be accomplished in the property room or evidence room. The single difference between the two methods is that in one the evidence is analyzed before it is stored whereas in the other the evidence is taken directly to the narcotic and dangerous-drug evidence room (or to an adjunct depository), receipted, and then removed to the laboratory for analysis.

Of the two methods used for introducing narcotic and dangerous-drug evidence into the processing sequence, the laboratory-first procedure is preferred and should be followed whenever possible. The main advantage of this method is that it reduces actual handling of the evidence and decreases the number of custody transfer points. By first delivering the evidence to the laboratory, the evidence must undergo only one journey to the narcotic and dangerous-drug evidence room, that is, after analysis, not before and after. Consequently, the exposure of the evidence to various loss hazards is reduced and its security is enhanced.

It must be recognized, however, that establishment of the laboratory-first method depends on the existence of certain features that are not available to many law enforcement agencies. The laboratory-first method requires that a mobile laboratory unit or laboratory technician be on call for around-the-clock operation. Second, this method requires an easily accessible laboratory—preferably located in the same building housing the headquarters of the police agency itself.

Questions

1. What major drugs of abuse are derived from opium?
2. What role does the drug methadone play in treating heroin addicts?
3. What factors may indicate that a person is addicted to opium-derived drugs or synthetic opiates?
4. What are the acute and chronic effects of cocaine use?
5. What is freebasing?
6. How is the chromatographic impurity signature profile analysis (CISPA) used in the investigation of drug distribution?
7. What is methcathinone?
8. What are the effects of the drug Rohypnol?
9. What is speedballing?
10. What are some of the known side effects of PCP?
11. What are the positive and negative arguments for the use of MDMA?
12. Why has the indoor growing of marijuana become so popular in the past few years?
13. A number of categories of drug-related confidential informants were discussed in the text. What were these categories?
14. What types of drug theft preventive measures may physicians and pharmacists take to reduce the likelihood of being victimized?
15. What are the most common indications that a physician is unlawfully diverting drugs for his or her own use?
16. How are clandestine drug laboratory operations typically identified?
17. Which major factors should be considered when attempting to secure a search warrant based solely on information supplied by a confidential informant?
18. There are two recognized methods for introducing narcotics and dangerous drugs into the processing sequence immediately after they are seized and marked. What are these two methods?

Notes

1. U.S. Department of the Army, *Field Manual—Military Police Criminal Investigation* (Washington, D.C.: U.S. Department of Defense, 1971), p. 28-5.
2. Ibid., pp. 28-5, 28-7.
3. John H. Langer et al., "Drugs of Abuse: Narcotics," in *Drugs of Abuse* (Washington, D.C.: Drug Enforcement Administration, 1975), pp. 10–13.
4. U.S. Department of the Army, *Field Manual*, p. 28-8.

5. Ian R. Tebbet, "A Pharmacist's Guide to Drugs of Abuse," *Drug Topics*, September 3, 1990, Vol. 134, p. 58, with modification.

6. Malachi L. Harney and John C. Cross, *The Narcotics Officer's Notebook* (Springfield, Ill.: Charles C. Thomas, 1961), pp. 96–98.

7. Smith Kline and French Laboratories, *Drug Abuse* (Philadelphia, 1971), p. 10.

8. Robert C. Petersen, "Cocaine: An Overview," in *Drug Enforcement* (Washington, D.C.: Government Printing Office, 1977), pp. 9–12.

9. Keith Sarji and Jose Rosch, "Now Cocaine, Too, Can Be Profiled & Traced," *Law Enforcement News*, April 30, 1993, Vol. 19, No. 379, p. 9. This discussion of profiling and tracing cocaine was obtained with permission from this source.

10. Langer et al., "Drugs of Abuse," p. 19.

11. John B. Williams, *Narcotics and Drug Dependence* (Encino, Calif.: Glencoe, 1974), p. 273.

12. U.S. Department of Health, Education, and Welfare, *Students and Drugs* (Washington, D.C.: Government Printing Office, 1969), pp. 8–9.

13. "Hawaii's Problems with 'Ice,'" *Police*, October 1989, p. 14.

14. Adapted from "The Menace of Ice," *Time*, September 18, 1989, p. 28.

15. James McGiveny, "'Made in America': The New and Potent Methcathinone," *Police Chief*, April 1994, pp. 20–21 (this discussion was adapted with permission from this source). Methcathinone is also known as 2-methylamino-1-phenylpropan-1-one, n-methcathinone, monomethylproprion, and ephedrone; street names include "go," "goob," "sniff," "crank," "star," "wonder star," "bathtub speed," "gaggers," "wildcat," and "cat."

16. Drug Enforcement Administration, *Fact Sheets* (Washington, D.C.: Government Printing Office, 1973), p. 43.

17. Langer et al., "Drugs of Abuse," p. 16.

18. Chris McKissick, "Rohypnol: The New Date Rape Party Drug of the 1990's," *Narc Officer*, July–August 1996, p. 12.

19. A. G. Gardiner, Jr., "Rohypnol: The New 'Stealth' Weapon," *Police Chief*, April 1998, p. 37.

20. Ibid.

21. Robert C. Petersen and Richard C. Stillman, "Phencyclidine Abuse," in *Drug Enforcement* (Washington, D.C.: Government Printing Office, 1978), pp. 19–20.

22. "Angel Dust—Abuse Diagnostic Test Introduced," *Police Chief*, November 1979, Vol. 46, No. 11, p. 12.

23. Anastasia Toufexis and Patricia Delaney, "A Crackdown on 'Ecstasy,'" *Time*, June 10, 1985, p. 64.

24. "Way Found to Detect LSD in Humans," *Tampa Tribune*, September 8, 1972.

25. Loukia Louka, "Cropping Up Indoors," *Police*, November 1993, Vol. 17, No. 11, p. 38.

26. Ibid.

27. Ibid.

28. Ibid., p. 39.

29. Ibid., p. 90.

30. Drug Enforcement Administration, *Drugs of Abuse* (Washington, D.C.: Government Printing Office, 1988), p. 45.

31. John S. Farrell, "An Overview of Ketamine Abuse," *Police Chief*, February 1998, p. 47.

32. Drug Enforcement Administration, "Field Testing for Controlled Substances" (Washington, D.C.: National Training Institute, U.S. Department of Justice, 1973), pp. 1–6.

33. U.S. Department of the Army, *Field Manual*, pp. 28-16, 28-17.

34. Ibid., 28-18.

35. Gregory D. Lee, "Drug Informants, Motives, and Management," *FBI Law Enforcement Bulletin*, September 1993, pp. 10-15. This information was obtained with some modifications from this article.

36. Drug Enforcement Administration, *Agents Manual*, Appendix B, "Domestic Operations Guidelines," sec. B.

37. *DEA Integrity Assurances Notes*, August 1991, Vol. I, No. 1.

38. Drug Enforcement Administration, "Addict Practitioners," handout material provided by the U.S. Department of Justice, Drug Enforcement Administration, National Training Institute, Washington, D.C.

39. Reprinted from Training Key 388, *Clandestine Laboratories* by L. Ray Brett. Copyright held by the International Association of Chiefs of Police, Inc., 1110 North Glebe Road, Suite 200, Arlington, Virginia 22201, U.S.A. Further reproduction without the express written permission from IACP is strictly prohibited.

40. Michael Cashman, "Meth Labs: Toxic Timebombs," *Police Chief*, February 1998, p. 44.

41. Ibid., pp. 44–45.

42. E. J. Salcines, "Checklist of Elements Constituting Probable Cause in Search Warrant Affidavits." Prepared by the State Attorney's Office, Hillsborough County, Tampa, Fla., 1974.

43. *Guidelines for Narcotic and Dangerous Drug Evidence Handling and Security Procedures* (Washington, D.C.: Drug Enforcement Administration, U.S. Department of Justice and Field Operation Division, International Association of Chiefs of Police, 1976). This discussion on the identification and recording of drug evidence was adapted from this source (pp. 42–54).

Drug Glossary

Acapulco Gold: High grade of marijuana

Acid: LSD, LSD 25 (lysergic acid diethylamide)

Acidhead: Regular user of LSD

Acid Test: Party at which LSD has been added to the punch, food, etc.

Agonies: Withdrawal symptoms

All Lit Up: Under the influence

Amphetamine: Stimulant drug that increases the activity of the central nervous system

Angel Dust: Phencyclidine (PCP on parsley)

Artillery: Equipment for injecting drugs; the works; the needle, eyedropper, spoon, bottle cap, cotton, and cloth, string, or belt for a tourniquet

Baghead: Someone involved in glue sniffing

Bagman: Supplier; person holding drugs for supplier

Balloon: A balloon containing approximately two doses of heroin

Bang: Injection of drugs

Barbs: Barbiturates

Barrels: LSD tablets

Bathtub Speed: Methcathinone, a psychomotor stimulant with chemical structure similar to methamphetamine

Bennies: Benzedrine, an amphetamine

Bindle: Packet of narcotics

Black Beauties: Amphetamines

Blanks: Extremely low-grade narcotics

Blast: Strong effect from a drug

Blue Acid: LSD

Blue Angels: Barbiturates (amytal and amobarbital)

Blue Birds: Barbiturates (amytal and amobarbital)

Blue Devils: Barbiturates (amytal and amobarbital)

Blue Heavens: Barbiturates (amytal and amobarbital)

Blue Velvet: Paregoric (camphorated tincture of opium) and pyribenzamine (an antihistamine) mixed and injected

Bombed Out: High on marijuana

Bombita: Amphetamine injection, sometimes taken with heroin

Brown: Mexican heroin; usually of lower quality than white heroin

Burn, Burned: To cheat; to be cheated out of money or drugs; to have identity disclosed

Burned Out: Collapse of the veins from repeated injections

Busted: Arrested

Buttons: The sections of the peyote cactus

Candy Man: Drug seller; one who deals in a variety of pills, tablets, and capsules of various shapes and colors

Cannabinol: Tetrahydrocannabinol (THC), active ingredient of cannabis

Cartwheels: Amphetamine powder (round, white, double-scored tablets)

Cat: Methcathinone

China Death: Heroin containing strychnine or cyanide

China White: An illicitly synthesized derivative of fentanyl (a designer drug); high-grade heroin from Southeast Asia

Chipping: Taking narcotics occasionally

Clean: Out of drugs; not using drugs

Coke: Cocaine

Cold Turkey: Abrupt withdrawal from drugs, without medication; skin resembles the texture of a cold plucked turkey

Come Down: End of a trip; drug effect wearing off

Connection: Source of supply

Cooker: Spoon or bottle cap for heating heroin and water

Cop Out: Quit, take off, confess, inform, be defeated

Cotton Shot: Drug-saturated cotton to which water is added to get whatever heroin is left

Crack: Also known as rock cocaine, it is purer and more concentrated than regular cocaine

Crack House: Room, apartment building, or residence in which crack is sold and/or smoked

Crank: Street name for methamphetamine or methcathinone

Crash: To collapse from exhaustion after continuous use of amphetamines; enjoyable sleep after smoking marijuana; to come down from an LSD trip

Crash Pad: Place where the user withdraws from amphetamines

Cut: Dilute drugs by adding milk, sugar, or another inert substance

Dealer: Drug supplier

Deck: Packet of narcotics

Dexies: Dexedrine, an amphetamine

Dime Bag: $10 package of narcotics

Dirty: Possessing drugs; liable to be arrested if searched

Doper: Person who uses drugs regularly

Downers: Depressant drugs; barbiturates

Dried Out: Cured of drug dependence (usually cold turkey)

Ecstasy: MDMA

Feed Bag: Container of narcotics or other drugs

Feed Store: Place where drugs can be purchased

Fifteen Cents: $15; a packet of drugs selling for $15

Fire Up: Take a drug intravenously

Fix: Injection of narcotics

Flash: First euphoric sensation after taking a drug

Flashback: Unpredictable recurrence of an LSD trip long after the last trip was taken with drugs; may occur weeks or months after the last drug-induced trip

Flip: Become psychotic

Floating: Under the influence of drugs

Freakout: Bad experience with psychedelics; also, a chemical high

Freebasing: Chemical process used to increase the strength of cocaine

Garbage: Low-grade drug; no drug content

Go: Methcathinone

Goob: Methcathinone

Good Trip: Happy experience with psychedelics

Goofballs: Barbiturates

Grass: Marijuana

H: Heroin

H and C: Mixture of heroin and cocaine (speedball)

Hard Narcotics: Opiates, such as heroin and morphine

Hard Stuff: Heroin

Hash: Hashish, the resin of cannabis

Hearts: Dexedrine tablets (from the shape)

Heavenly Blues: Type of morning-glory seeds

Heroin: The most potent narcotic drug derived from morphine

High: Euphoric; under the influence of a drug

Hit: Make a purchase; the effect of drugs; to steal drugs, money, or merchandise; to inject

Holding: Having drugs in one's possession

Hooked: Addicted

Horse: Heroin

Hot Load, Hot Shot: Overdose; lethal drug dose; usually refers to drugs given deliberately to eliminate a troublesome customer, such as an informer; pure heroin or a heroin mixture containing a poison such as strychnine or cyanide

Hustle: Activities involved in obtaining money to buy heroin

Hustler: Prostitute

Joint: Marijuana cigarette

Joy Pop: Occasional injection of narcotics (usually under the skin rather than in a vein)

Junkie: Narcotics addict who injects drugs

K: Ketamine hydrochloride

Kat: Ketamine hydrochloride

Key: One kilogram (2.2 pounds)

Kicking: Withdrawal process

Kicking Cold: Ceasing drug use without medical support

Kicking the Gong: Usually refers to smoking marijuana or hashish

Kilo: Kilogram (2.2 pounds)

Kit: Equipment for injecting drugs; the works: (2) ketamine hydrochloride

Loaded: High on marijuana

Loco Weed: Marijuana

Ludes: Quaaludes (methaqualone)

M: Morphine

Mainline: Inject drugs into a vein

Maintaining: Keeping at a certain level of drug effect

Make: To identify a police officer who is working undercover

Make a Reader: Have a doctor write a prescription

(The) Man: Can be either the police or one's main supplier of drugs

Manicure: Remove the dirt, seeds, and stems from marijuana

Mary Jane: Marijuana

Mesc: Mescaline, the alkaloid in peyote

Meth: Methamphetamine

Methhead: Habitual user of methamphetamine

Mind Erasers: Street name for Rohypnol

Monkey: Drug habit; physical dependence

Mule: Transporter of drugs

Nailed: Arrested

Narc: Narcotics detective

Nembies: Nembutal (a barbiturate); pentobarbital

Nickel Bag: $5 bag of drugs

Nod: The sleep and relaxation after a shot of heroin (on the nod)

Nose Candy: Cocaine

O.D.: Overdose of narcotics

On a Trip: Under the influence of a hallucinogen

On the Nod: Sleepy from narcotics

Oranges: Amphetamines (orange colored, heart shaped); Dexedrine

Paper: Small quantity of drugs; prescription for drugs

Peaches: Amphetamines (Benzedrine)

Pep Pills: Amphetamines

Persian White: Fentanyls (designer drugs)

Peyote: Hallucinogen from peyote cactus

Pink Hearts or Pinks: Dexedrine tablets

Pirates: Ecstacy pills

Pop: Inject beneath the skin

Pot: Marijuana

Pothead: Heavy user of marijuana

Powder: Heroin

Pure: Very good grade of heroin
Purple Hearts: Dexamyl, a combination of Dexedrine and Amytal (from the shape and color)
Pusher: Drug peddler

Rainbows: Tuinal (Amytal and Seconal), a barbiturate combination in a blue and red capsule
Red Birds, Red Bullets, Red Devils, Reds: A barbiturate (Seconal)
Reentry: Return from a trip
Roach: Marijuana cigarette
Roach 2's: Street name for Rohypnol
Rocks: High-grade cocaine
Roofies: Street name for Rohypnol
Rophs: Street name for Rohypnol
R-2's: Street name for Rohypnol

Satch Cotton: Cotton used to strain drugs before injection; may be used again if supplies are gone
Score: Make a purchase of drugs
Scrip, Script: Prescription for drugs; money
Script Writer: Sympathetic doctor; prescription forger
Seccies, Seccy: Seconal
Shit: Drugs in general; heroin
Shoot, Shoot Up: Inject
Shooting Gallery: Place where addicts inject drugs
Shot Down: Under the influence of drugs
Sick: Going through drug withdrawal, usually from heroin
Skin Popping: Injecting drugs under the skin
Smack: Heroin
Snorting: Inhaling drugs
Snow: Cocaine
Special K: Ketamine hydrochloride
Speed: Methamphetamine
Speedball: An injection of a stimulant and a depressant, originally heroin and cocaine
Speedfreak: Habitual user of speed
Stash: Supply of drugs in a secure place
Step-on: Dilution of a drug, typically heroin or cocaine, with some other substance

Stomach Addict: An addict who eats heroin
Stoned: Under the influence of drugs
Stoolie: Informer
STP: Hallucinogen (stands for Serenity, Tranquility, and Peace) related to mescaline and amphetamines
Strung Out: Addicted

Tea: Marijuana
Tea Pad: Place where marijuana is bought and smoked
Tea Party: Get-together of marijuana smokers
THC: Tetrahydrocannabinol; purified resin extract from the hemp plant, also synthetically produced; said to be the substance responsible for the mind-altering effects of cannabis
Tooies: Tuinal
Tools: Equipment for injecting drugs
Tracks: Scars along veins after many injections
Tripping Out: High on psychedelics
Turkey Trots: Marks or scars from repeated injections
Turned On: Under the influence of drugs
Turps: Elixir of terpin hydrate and codeine, a cough syrup
25: LSD (from its original designation, LSD 25)

Uppers: Stimulants, cocaine, and psychedelics

Vitamin K: Ketamine hydrochloride

Weed: Marijuana
Whites: Stimulants, generally amphetamines
Works: Equipment for injecting drugs

Yellow Jackets: Nembutal, a barbiturate
Yen Shee: Ashes of opium
Yen Shee Suey: Opium mixed with wine or other beverages
Yen Sleep: A drowsy, restless state during the withdrawal period

Zonked: Heavily addicted; under the extreme influence of drugs

TWENTY-TWO

The Decision to Initiate the Criminal Process

CHAPTER OUTLINE

Arrest Defined 648
Arrest Procedures 649
The Arrest Warrant 650
The Probable-Cause Requirement 651
Evaluating the Case 653
Questions 655
Notes 655

INTRODUCTION

At some point during the fruitful investigation of any criminal offense, officers must make a number of decisions that invoke the formal processes of the justice system. When an arrest is to be made and formal charges brought against a suspect or when the investigator brings an uncharged suspect in for interrogation, he or she must know the legal requirements.

ARREST DEFINED

There are a number of definitions of the term "arrest." They range from "any interference with a person which, if not privileged, would constitute false imprisonment," to "interfering with the freedom of a person who is suspected of criminal conduct to the extent of taking him to the police station for some purpose," to "the taking of custody upon sufficient and proper evidence for the purpose of prosecution."[1] Each of these definitions is valid and depends on context. For example, what may appear to be a simple street stop or field interrogation may, in fact, constitute an arrest according to the first definition. Taking a person to the police station for interrogation may fit the second definition. When an investigator intends to incarcerate and charge a person with a crime, the third definition applies.

INGREDIENTS

There are three essential ingredients to an arrest:

1. Intention.
2. Authority.
3. Custody.

The officer must have the intention of taking the suspect into custody. This factor distinguishes an arrest from a lesser form of detention, but actual or expressed intention is not always the controlling factor. The intention may be inferred by a court if its estimate of all the conduct and circumstances indicates that an arrest occurred, despite any contrary intent on the part of the police officer.

The officer must have real or assumed legal authority for taking the person into custody. The officer must have the actual authority to make a legal arrest or at least believe this to be the case. For example, an investigator may make an arrest under a defective warrant but not know about the defect. The third ingredient is that the person arrested must come within the custody and control of the law. This element can be satisfied either by physical restraint (see Figure 22–1) or by voluntary submission of the arrestee to the custody and control of the arresting officer.

ARREST DISTINGUISHED FROM DETENTION

Detention is a temporary and limited interference with the freedom of a person for investigative purposes. Sometimes called *investigative detention*, it is also commonly referred to by police as a "street stop" or "field interrogation." In this instance, police are justified in employing "stop and frisk" measures—patting down the outer clothing—if they suspect that the person being questioned may be armed and their safety is in jeopardy.[2]

There is a fine line between detention and arrest. Because an officer does interfere with the freedom of the individual stopped, even for only a few minutes, some theorists view any such action as constituting arrest. Most people and most courts recognize the validity of street stops and uphold them as not being arrests if conducted properly.

A valid detention must be brief and made for good reason. The officer must limit questioning and investigation and must then either release the subject or decide to arrest. Detention for an undue length of time could be construed as an arrest if later challenged in court.

ARREST DISTINGUISHED FROM CHARGING

As noted earlier, one definition of arrest is to interfere with the freedom of a person suspected of involvement in a crime to the extent that the person is taken to the police station. But investigators do not always intend to prosecute or have the ability to prosecute at that time. Formally *charging* a suspect with a crime does not automatically flow from an arrest. Charging follows a decision to prosecute. This decision may be made by the police, by the prosecutor, or by both. But they may also decide not to bring charges. For example, the evidence that justified the arrest may not be sufficient to warrant charges, or additional information may come to light after the arrest. Some arrests are made following improper procedures or based on insufficient evidence. Charges are not brought following faulty arrests such as these.

Figure 22–1
An Arrest
A suspect restrained by handcuffs and under the close control of officers.

(Courtesy Los Angeles County Sheriff's Department)

ARREST PROCEDURES

The laws of most jurisdictions permit an arrest in at least three types of situations:

1. When a crime is committed in the presence of an arresting officer.
2. When a warrant has been issued.
3. When an officer has probable cause to believe that the suspect being arrested has committed a felony.

Any offense committed in the presence of an officer, whether felony or misdemeanor, can be the basis of arrest without a warrant. The in-presence requirement is usually thought of in the narrow context of sight. However, to satisfy the legal requirements, perception of some or all of the elements of an offense as they occur, through the use of any or all of the five senses—sight, hearing, taste, touch, or smell—can justify a warrantless arrest.

The most preferred method of effecting an arrest is under the authority of a warrant. In fact, if one were to read the constitutional requirements in their strictest sense, arrests can be justified only if made with a warrant. Of course, the courts have chosen to be more liberal in their interpretation so that warrantless arrests can be made in certain situations. But there are sound reasons for both the warrant requirements and the exceptions created by judicial case law. In our constitutional system, the functions of government—executive, legislative, and judicial—are each the responsibility of a separate branch. The police function is an executive one, while the judicial responsibility obviously belongs to the courts. Although the mechanism of arrest is an executive function, it is subject to judicial scrutiny and review. This position is supported by the very wording of the Fourth Amendment to the United States Constitution:

> and no warrant shall issue but upon probable cause, supported by oath or affirmation, particularly describing the . . . persons . . . to be seized.

The two major benefits derived from securing prior judicial approval for arrests through the warrant process are that it relieves the police of the burden of proving the legality of the arrest—so that officers need not fear charges of false arrest, malicious prosecution, or other civil suits—and it provides for an independent evaluation of the evidence.

Even the most objective, well-trained, and well-intentioned investigators sometimes become so involved in a case that it may affect their ability to evaluate its merits objectively. Presenting the case before a qualified judge has the benefits of allowing for an independent third party, with no emotional involvement in the investigation and with the knowledge of legal standards that must be met, to assist the investigator in determining whether those standards have been achieved. It is also logical to assume that the validity of an arrest made following this review and the issuance of a warrant is more likely to be upheld if later challenged in court than an arrest based solely on an officer's own determination of the sufficiency of the evidence. The wise police officer recognizes the value of obtaining a warrant whenever practical. The word "practical" has significance with regard to the propriety of securing an arrest warrant. The law recognizes that the innumerable situations encountered by police officers in daily activities and the variety of conditions inherent in the nature of the police function make it impossible and unrealistic to expect an officer to obtain a warrant in every situation before effecting an arrest; hence, the exceptions to the warrant requirement. One of those exceptions, the

in-presence commission, has already been discussed; another, probable cause, is discussed in a subsequent section of this chapter.

The procedure required for obtaining a warrant is often time consuming and inconvenient. Frequently, the process in major felony cases requires the investigator to seek out the prosecutor; present the facts, which will be reduced to paper in affidavit form; find a judge who is authorized to issue warrants; present the case again for a determination of the sufficiency of the grounds for arrest; and then wait for the warrant to be typed up and signed. In many cases the procedure can take many hours, even during the normal workday. On weekends and late at night it may take even longer, as the prosecutor, judge, or both are located or roused from bed. As a consequence, officers sometimes tend to take the easy way out by making a warrantless arrest, hoping they are right and believing they have sufficient grounds to act. By conducting themselves in this manner, they neglect the basic rule of thumb—get a warrant—and its underlying rationale. But the warrantless arrest is not always a shortcut. As clear as the law may appear to be on the need for warrants, each case must rest on its own facts. There are relatively few cases in which it is obvious that an arrest may be made without a warrant. Similarly, those clear-cut instances when a warrant is absolutely needed are relatively few. The majority of cases fall within that vast plane requiring evaluation of the merits of each case. An arrest without a warrant, however, does not save time. In reality an officer will spend as much or more time justifying this decision in motion hearings demanded by the defense attorney than it would have taken to get a warrant in the first place. The potential consequence is that the case may be dismissed for want of a valid arrest, or that important evidence, seized as a result of the arrest, may be suppressed.

THE ARREST WARRANT

The investigator is not relieved of all responsibility for the legality of the arrest simply because a warrant was obtained. The investigator must be aware of what constitutes a valid warrant to ensure that the one in possession permits a legal arrest. An *arrest warrant* is a judicial order commanding the person to whom it is issued or some other person to arrest a particular individual and to bring that person promptly before a court to answer a criminal charge.

The arrest warrant generally must be written. By legislation, some jurisdictions allow for verbal authorization supported by written authorization in warrant form that is issued later.

In most cases, particularly major felonies, the warrant must be issued by a judge who personally reviews the facts to determine the existence of reasonable grounds as required by the Constitution. The warrant must be supported by an *affidavit*—a written statement of the information on which the officer seeks issuance of the warrant. In major cases, the requirements vary on whether the warrant must be issued in the county in which the offense occurred, but once issued, major case warrants can be served anywhere in the state.

The contents of a warrant are fairly standard and incorporate constitutional as well as statutory requirements. Most modern warrants, samples of which appear in Figures 22–2, 22–3, and 22–4, simply require that blanks be filled in. The form and contents usually include:

1. The authority under which the warrant is issued (the name of the state).
2. The person who is to execute the warrant (generally addressed to any peace officer of the state).
3. The identity of the person to be arrested.
4. The designation of the offense.
5. The date, time, and place of the occurrence.
6. The name of the victim.
7. A description of the offense and how it occurred.

Blank warrants are not constitutionally valid. Before a warrant can be issued, the identity of the perpetrator must be known. The mere fact that a crime has been committed by someone unknown will not support a warrant's issuance. The Constitution requires that the warrant contain a particular description of the suspect. This description must be specific enough to permit an officer not acquainted with the case to identify the person to be arrested with reasonable certainty. Aliases may be used. If the suspect's name is not known, "John Doe" may be used provided there are other methods of particularly describing the person to be arrested, such as place of residence, occupation, and a physical description.

THE PROBABLE-CAUSE REQUIREMENT

The third and final major category in which a lawful arrest is generally permitted involves offenses not committed in the officer's presence and for which a warrant has not been issued. The law allows an officer to make warrantless arrests in felony cases provided reasonable grounds or probable cause exist to make the arrest. (As previously noted, probable cause also must be shown in an affidavit to support the issuance of a warrant.)

"Probable cause" is a difficult term to define because in no two instances are circumstances identical. One acceptable definition of *probable cause* is that it is more than suspicion but less than actual knowledge. It is suspicion plus facts and circumstances that would lead a reasonable person exercising ordinary caution to believe that a crime has been, is being, or is about to be committed. Probable cause may be based on a number of sources of information, not all of which have to be the kind of evidence admissible at trial. However, if prosecution is an aim of the arrest, there must also be sufficient evidence to take the case to court. In addition, the probable cause must exist at the time the arrest is made and may not be developed by subsequently acquired evidence.

Mere suspicion is not enough to justify an arrest; there must be supporting facts and circumstances. Certain factors may help to decide the existence of probable cause. The most common is the personal knowledge of the investigator. Information obtained from informants also may be of value, although that information may not be admissible at a subsequent hearing or trial. The investigator must be able to establish the reliability of the information and the informant by indicating the length of time the investigator has known or dealt with the informant, the general character and reputation of the informant, the number of tips received from the informant in the past, the accuracy of previous information, whether the

Figure 22–2
Front of Arrest Warrant

National Graphics Corp., Cols., O.
Form No. M86-12

THE STATE OF OHIO

```
------------------------------------          ------------------------------- Municipal Court
              vs                              ------------------------------- County, Ohio
                                               (City)   (Name of County)
------------------------------------
  Name                                         No. ----------------
------------------------------------
  Address                                      WARRANT ON COMPLAINT
                                                      (Rule 4)
```

****

FORM VII

TO _____
                    (officer authorized to execute a warrant)

A complaint, a copy of which is attached hereto, has been filed in this court charging

_____
(describe the offense and state the numerical designation of the applicable statute or ordinance)

_____

_____

You are ordered to arrest _____ and bring (him)(her) before this
                                    (defendant)

court without unnecessary delay.

You (may) (may not) issue summons in lieu of arrest under Rule 4(A)(2) or issue summons

after arrest under Rule 4(F) because _____
                                     (state specific reasons if issuance of summons restricted)

_____

Special instructions to executing officer:

                            Judge—Officer designated by Judge(s)
                            Clerk—Deputy Clerk—Municipal Court

****

SUMMONS ENDORSEMENT
Use only in appropriate case

This warrant was executed / by arrest and / by issuing the following summons:

TO _____
                         (defendant)

You are hereby summoned and ordered to appear at _____ o'clock _____ M.,

_____, _____, 19 _____, at the above captioned Court.
      (day)   (month)   (date)
If you fail to appear at the time and place stated above you may be arrested.

                            Issuing Officer, Title
                            See Rule 4(A)(2) Rule 4(F) and Return Forms

NOTICE TO DEFENDANT: For information regarding your duty to appear call _____
                                                              (fill in telephone number(s))
The address of the Court is: _____

(Courtesy Geauga County, Ohio, Sheriff's Department)

informant is paid for the information, and the informant's motives for volunteering the information.

Other sources of probable cause include information from a police department or from other law enforcement agencies, such as notice of outstanding warrants, the past criminal record of the suspect, physical evidence found at the scene of the crime, other evidence detected in the follow-up investigation, crime laboratory analyses, and reports of victims and eyewitnesses.

Figure 22–3
Return of Executed Warrant

RECEIPT OF WARRANT BY EXECUTING AUTHORITY

First Receipt

Received this warrant on _____, 19____,

at _____o'clock____m.

Officer
By_____
Title

Subsequent Receipt

Received this (alias) (warrant) on _____,

19____, at _____o'clock____m.

Officer
By_____
Title

RETURN OF EXECUTED WARRANT

Fees

Mileage $_____

_____

_____

_____

_____

Total $_____

1. **Execution By Arrest**

I received this warrant on _____, 19____, at

_____o'clock____m. On _____, 19____, I

arrested_____and gave / him/her / a copy of this warrant with

complaint attached and brought / him/her / to_____
state the place

_____
Arresting Officer, Title

Fees

Mileage $_____

_____

_____

_____

_____

Total $_____

2. **Execution By Issuance Of Summons Under Rule 4(A)(2) By Executing Officer**

I received this warrant on _____, 19____, at

_____o'clock____m. On _____, 19____, I

executed this warrant by issuing_____a summons by / personal

service / residence service / which ordered him/her to appear at_____
time

_____at the captioned Court. The sum-
day   date   room

mons was endorsed upon the warrant and accompanied by a copy of the complaint.

_____
Issuing Officer, Title

Fees

Mileage $_____

_____

_____

_____

_____

Total $_____

3. **Execution By Arrest And Issuance Of Summons Under Rule 4(F) By Arresting Officer**

I received this warrant on _____, 19____, at

_____o'clock____m. On _____, 19____, I

arrested_____and after arrest I issued him/her a summons by

personal service which ordered him/her to appear at captioned Court at_____
time

_____. The sum-
day, date, room

mons was endorsed upon the warrant and accompanied by a copy of the complaint.

_____
Arresting-Issuing Officer, Title

4. **Execution By Arrest And Issuance Of Summons Under Rule 4(F) By Superior Of Arresting Officer**

On _____, 19____, _____was arrested by_____
name of arresting officer

and I issued_____a summons by personal service which ordered / him/her / to appear at

_____
time, day, date, room

at the captioned Court. The summons was endorsed upon the warrant and accompanied by a copy of the complaint.

_____
Issuing Officer, Title

RETURN OF UNEXECUTED WARRANT

Fees

Mileage $_____

_____

_____

_____

_____

Total $_____

I received this warrant on _____, 19____, at

_____o'clock____m. On _____, 19____, I

attempted to execute this warrant but was unable to do so because_____

_____
state specific reason or reasons and

_____
additional information regarding defendant's whereabouts

_____
Executing Officer, Title

RETURN OF UNEXECUTED WARRANT

Fees

Mileage $_____

_____

_____

_____

_____

Total $_____

I received this warrant on _____, 19____, at

_____o'clock____m. On _____, 19____, I

attempted to execute this warrant but was unable to do so because_____

_____
state specific reason or reasons and

_____
additional information regarding defendant's whereabouts

_____
Executing Officer, Title

(Courtesy Geauga County, Ohio, Sheriff's Department)

EVALUATING THE CASE

The decisions investigators must make involve a great deal of discretion. Investigators must consider what may be termed risk factors. As suggested by Figure 22–5, the fact that probable cause exists does not require that the arrest be made at the moment, nor does it mean that the investigation is complete.

APPLICATION FOR COMPLAINT NUMBER

Trial Court of Massachusetts
Boston Municipal Court Department

Boston Municipal Court
Criminal Division, Room 411 —
Fourth Floor, New Court House
Boston, MA 02108

☐ ARREST ☐ HEARING ☐ SUMMONS ☐ WARRANT

The within named complainant requests that a complaint issue against the within named defendant, charging said defendant with the offense(s) listed below.

DATE OF APPLICATION	DATE OF OFFENSE	PLACE OF OFFENSE

NAME, ADDRESS AND ZIP CODE OF COMPLAINANT

NAME, ADDRESS AND ZIP CODE OF DEFENDANT

NO.	OFFENSE	G.L. Ch. and Sec.
1.		
2.		
3.		
4.		

IF ADDITIONAL OFFENSES CHECK HERE. ☐ AND ATTACH.

DEFENDANT IDENTIFICATION INFORMATION — Complete data below if known.

C.C. #	DATE OF BIRTH	SEX	RACE	HEIGHT	WEIGHT	EYES	HAIR	SOCIAL SECURITY NUMBER

COURT USE ONLY → A hearing upon this complaint application will be held at the Boston Municipal Court, Rm. 411 on DATE OF HEARING AT TIME OF HEARING ← COURT USE ONLY

CASE PARTICULARS — BE SPECIFIC

NO.	NAME OF VICTIM Owner of property, person assaulted, etc.	DESCRIPTION OF PROPERTY Goods stolen, what destroyed, etc.	VALUE OF PROPERTY Over or under $100.	TYPE OF CONTROLLED SUBSTANCE OR WEAPON Marijuana, gun, etc.
1				
2				
3				
4				

OTHER REMARKS:

X ____________________
SIGNATURE OF COMPLAINANT

IF PROCESS IS ORDERED, THIS APPLICATION MUST BE PRESENTED AT ONCE TO PLEADING CLERK AT ROOM 411

NAMES OF WITNESSES	Recog. to S.C.	Give place of business or employment, if in Boston, otherwise, residence	ST. NO.

State if defendant is arrested ____________ Date of Arrest ____________

COMPLAINANT'S COPY

BMC-CR-2 (5/85) **FOR ADDITIONAL REMARKS OR WITNESSES-USE REVERSE OF ORIGINAL AND CHECK HERE** ☐

(Courtesy Boston Police Department)

Figure 22-4
Application for Complaint

Certain disadvantages may result from a premature arrest, even one that is valid. In Figure 22-5, B^1 through B^7 represent the alternative times when arrest may take place between the establishment of probable cause and the existence of certainty requiring arrest as a prerequisite to prosecution. (The spacing and numbering are arbitrary and are intended for graphic purposes only.)

One prime consideration is whether the suspect is likely to flee if allowed to remain free. If there is a high risk of this, the investigator should make an arrest as soon as probable cause can be established and complete the investigation while the suspect is in custody. In evaluating the likelihood of flight, the investigator will consider such factors as the nature and seriousness of the offense, whether the suspect is a transient or an established member of the community, the suspect's occupation and income, and whether the suspect has a family to support.

Another risk that must be considered by the investigator deals with the potential danger posed to others if the suspect is allowed to remain free. Again, the nature of the offense along with any past criminal record or history of the suspect must be carefully evaluated. If the case under investigation involves a violent crime or one that tends to reveal violent propensities on the part of the suspect, early arrest is most probably the wisest course of action.

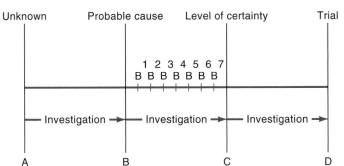

Case Evaluations

Figure 22–5
Case Evaluations

The investigator should also consider the hardships imposed on the suspect by early incarceration. Although this is often overlooked, it is one additional portion of the investigator's responsibility in evaluating the case.

Questions

1. Define *arrest*.
2. Distinguish arrest from detention.
3. Distinguish arrest from charging.
4. What are the benefits to a police officer and the case if an arrest is made under the authority of a warrant?
5. Is a "John Doe" arrest warrant valid under any circumstances? Explain.
6. Define and describe *probable cause*.
7. During an ongoing criminal investigation, what factors must the criminal investigator consider in deciding whether to make an arrest and when to make it?

Notes

1. Wayne R. LaFave, *Arrest: The Decision to Take a Suspect into Custody* (Boston: Little, Brown and Company, 1965), pp. 3-4.

2. *Terry* v. *Ohio*, 392 U.S. 1 (1968).

TWENTY-THREE

The Rules of Evidence

CHAPTER OUTLINE

Evidentiary Concepts 658
Judicial Notice 662
Types of Evidence 663
The Hearsay Rule 665
Evidentiary Privileges 667
Witnesses 668
Questions 668

INTRODUCTION

Every police officer must have a working knowledge of the rules of evidence. This requirement is particularly true for the criminal investigator, on whose shoulders falls the responsibility to collect and preserve evidence that will be useful to the prosecutor in presenting the state's case in court. Therefore, the investigator also must be able to distinguish between factual material that is admissible in court and that which is worthless as evidence.

EVIDENTIARY CONCEPTS

The language and terminology used in the field of law are quite different from those that most of us are accustomed to using. In the rules of evidence, many terms have specific meanings that investigators must know and understand. Many of these are set forth in this chapter.

EVIDENCE

Evidence can be defined as anything that tends logically to prove or disprove a fact at issue in a judicial case or controversy. Simply put, anything that might have the slightest bearing on the outcome of a case can be broadly classified as evidence, provided it has a logical tendency to relate to the outcome of the case. In a criminal case, if the matter has a bearing on the guilt or innocence of the defendant, it is evidence. The word "anything" should be emphasized because, in its broadest sense, *anything* can be evidence.

THE FIRST RULE OF EVIDENCE

The rules of evidence are designed primarily to keep a jury from hearing or seeing improper evidence, and the first rule of evidence is designed to set parameters on the above definition of evidence. Because evidence can be anything having a bearing on the outcome of the case, the first rule of evidence provides that anything is admissible as evidence unless there is some rule that prohibits its admissibility. Thus this first rule provides that all the other rules of evidence may limit those things that a jury is entitled to hear, see, and decide on. From this it can be surmised that most of the rules are stated in negative form.

PROOF

Many people confuse proof with evidence. They are separate but related elements of the judicial process. As noted, evidence consists of individual facts submitted to the jury for its consideration. *Proof* may be defined as the combination of all of those facts—of all the evidence—in determining the guilt or innocence of one accused of a crime. Thus, in referring to Figure 23–1, one can see that

the entire pie might constitute proof of guilt, while slices of the pie are matters of evidence.

TESTIMONY

Although testimony and evidence often are considered to be interchangeable, they are distinct. *Testimony* is simply evidence given in oral form. It consists of spoken facts of which witnesses have knowledge. Although the gun found at the scene, fingerprints, and tire treads are evidence, they require testimony to explain their significance to the case. In Figure 23–1, it is apparent that all six segments of the pie constitute evidence. But only segments 2, 3, and 5 are testimonial evidence.

ADMISSIBILITY

Admissibility is the essence of the rules of evidence. The rules of admissibility protect the trier of fact, generally a jury, from hearing improper evidence that may be unreliable or untrustworthy and that may prejudice the case unjustifiably against the defendant. The majority of the rules of evidence deal with what is admissible. Questions of admissibility are decided by the judge, and these decisions are made out of the hearing of the jury.

RELEVANCE

One of the rules governing the admissibility of evidence requires that the evidence be *relevant*. The evidence must have a bearing on the issues in the case being tried. The relevance of a particular piece of evidence can easily be determined by the answer to this question: "Does this piece of evidence have probative value?" Alternatively stated, "Will it aid in proving or disproving a particular point that the jury should consider in determining the guilt or innocence of the defendant?" If it cannot throw some light on the case, it is irrelevant.

MATERIALITY

Admissibility is also governed by the test of materiality. Even assuming that a particular piece of evidence is relevant, if it is such an insignificant and unimportant point that its admissibility will not affect the outcome of the case, it may be ruled

Figure 23–1
The Relation of Evidence and Proof

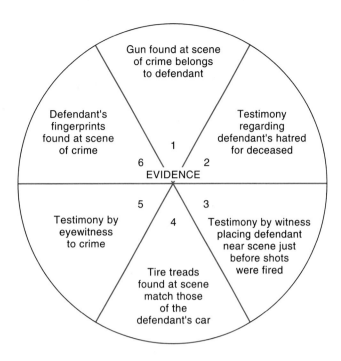

inadmissible. Admissibility may be denied on the basis of immateriality. Thus, *materiality* deals with the importance of the item of evidence in question.

COMPETENCE OF EVIDENCE

The test of *competence of evidence* relates to its legal significance to the case. Because of certain statutory requirements or other rules of evidence, a particular item of evidence may not be admissible. For example, there is a rule of evidence to the effect that the defendant's character cannot be attacked by the prosecution unless and until the defendant tries to show that he or she is of good character. Hence, unless the defendant did proceed in this direction, any attempt by the prosecution to introduce evidence of the defendant's character would be inadmissible on the grounds of incompetence.

The competence of physical evidence must also be established as a condition of admissibility. This is done through a process known as *laying a foundation*. For instance, the admissibility of a tape-recorded conversation would have to be prefaced by testimony about the date, time, place, and circumstances under which the recording was made; the

satisfaction of legal requirements in the making of the recording; proper identification of the voices on the tape; assertions about the functioning of recorder and tape at the time of recordings; and assurances about the absence of editing or modification of the tape.

COMPETENCE OF WITNESSES

Regardless of their knowledge of the facts of a case, certain individuals are not permitted by law to testify for or against a defendant in a criminal case. For example, the rules of evidence generally prohibit people who have been declared legally insane from testifying in a criminal case. A child "of tender years" may or may not be declared a competent witness. A person intoxicated by alcohol or drugs at the time of testifying will not be permitted to relate his or her knowledge in court. In some circumstances, a witness may be competent to testify regarding particular aspects but be held incompetent to testify regarding other matters. One spouse may be competent to testify for or against the other spouse on certain matters but not others. This aspect of competence of witnesses is discussed in greater detail later in the chapter.

WEIGHT OF EVIDENCE

Once evidence has been admitted into the trial, it must be weighed by the jury. The object of the attorneys for both sides in a case is to persuade the jury to believe their side's view of the facts at issue and the responsibility of the defendant. The jury must then weigh all the evidence and determine which is the more believable. Guilt or innocence then is determined. *Weight*, then, deals with the elements of persuasion and believability. Within certain guidelines, discussed below, the jury is free to give whatever weight it desires to the evidence presented to it. In essence, the entire judicial system in the United States is directed toward persuading the jury to weigh one side more favorably than the other.

PRESUMPTIONS

Among the guidelines that the jury is required to follow in weighing and applying evidence are those regarding presumptions. There are two types of presumptions: conclusive and rebuttable. A *conclusive presumption* is one that the jury must follow without alternatives. For example, when the prosecution creates a reasonable belief in guilt, and the defense does not contradict any of the prosecution's case, the jury must follow a conclusive presumption that guilt has been established and must find the defendant guilty. A *rebuttable presumption* requires that a specific conclusion be drawn unless that conclusion has been dispelled or rebutted by evidence presented to the jury for its consideration. The presumption that one is innocent until proven guilty is an example of a rebuttable presumption. Another presumption of this type is that all persons are presumed sane at the time they commit criminal acts. This presumption can be rebutted by the introduction of evidence to the contrary indicating insanity.

INFERENCES

An inference is similar to a presumption but differs in that the jury has more latitude in accepting or rejecting an inference. Thus an *inference* is a permissible deduction that the jury may make. An inference is a natural conclusion arrived at by deduction, in logical sequence, from given facts. For example, if fact A—the gun found at the scene of the crime belongs to the defendant—and fact B—testimony by a witness placing the defendant near the scene just before the shots were fired—are all known facts, it is not conclusive proof that the defendant committed the crime. However, based on these known facts, the jury may logically infer that the defendant did in fact commit the crime. But it is equally free to reject that inference if it feels that the evidence is not sufficient for that conclusion.

BURDEN OF PROOF

In each criminal case, the prosecution has the responsibility of affirmatively proving the allegations on which it has based its accusation. This is known as the *burden of proof*. The burden of proof is on the prosecution and never shifts to the defense. The defendant is never required to prove innocence. Innocence is presumed. The state must prove guilt. Assuming that both the prosecution and the defense present evidence in the trial in support of their theories of the case, the prosecution must establish proof beyond and to the exclusion of every reasonable doubt. The jurors must be convinced that the prosecution has proved the defendant guilty beyond any doubt to which they can attach a reason. Often only the defendant knows positively whether he or she is guilty or innocent. Because juries are composed of human beings, they are subject to some doubt in every case and must rely on testimony and physical evidence in reaching their decision. However, if the prosecution so thoroughly convinces the jurors of the defendant's guilt that they cannot give a reasonable explanation of why they doubt that guilt, then the burden of proof has been satisfied beyond and to the exclusion of every reasonable doubt. The word "reasonable" is included to separate human fallibility from the alleged infallibility of machines.

There is one exception to the requirement that the state prove its case beyond reasonable doubt. When the prosecution shows sufficient facts to indicate that the defendant more likely did commit the crime than not, it has a prima facie case. The prosecution has satisfied its burden of proof if it presents a prima facie case, *provided that there is no contradiction by the defense.* Figure 23–2 illustrates these relationships.

Figure 23–2
Relations among Burden of Proof, Burden of Going Forward, and Preponderance of Evidence

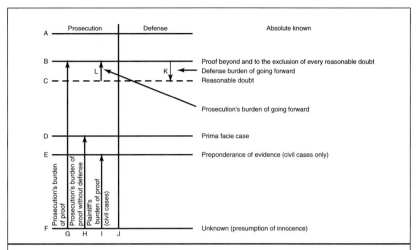

Line A	Represents truth generally known only to the defendant.
Line B	Level of proof needed to convict. Area between lines A and B represents human doubt but not reasonable doubt.
Line C	Can be anywhere below Line B and represents reasonable doubt.
Line D	Represents prima facie case (level of proof needed to convict if no defense is offered).
Line E	Level of proof needed for decision in civil case.
Line F	Starting point–presumption of innocence.
Arrow G	Represents prosecution's burden of proof.
Arrow H	Represents prosecution's burden of proof necessary to convict if no defense is offered.
Arrow I	Plaintiff's burden of proof in civil cases.
Line J	Represents the continuum between unknown and absolute known.
Arrow K	Defense burden of going forward with evidence to create a reasonable doubt (line C).
Arrow L	Prosecution's burden of going forward with evidence to overcome reasonable doubt created by defense, thereby elevating level of proof (pushing line C up to overlie line B).

BURDEN OF GOING FORWARD

The requirements concerning burden of proof do not mean that a defendant has no responsibility for convincing the jury of his or her innocence. The defense carries a *burden of going forward* with evidence. That responsibility is a great deal less than the burden of proof carried by the prosecution. The burden of going forward with evidence is placed on the defense so that it will present evidence that creates a reasonable doubt of guilt. In other words, the defense need present only enough evidence to overcome the prosecution's contentions and create a reasonable doubt of guilt in the minds of the jurors. When a unanimous decision by the jury is necessary to find the defendant guilty, the burden is even lighter, for the defense need create that reasonable doubt in the mind of only one juror to avoid a verdict of guilty.

This explanation sounds as though every benefit is being given to the defendant, and it is. The very essence of our entire criminal justice system is to place the heaviest responsibility on the accuser—the prosecution.

The prosecution also has a burden of going forward with evidence. If the prosecution presents a prima facie case that is contradicted by evidence presented on behalf of the defendant, the state must then erase the reasonable doubt by presenting evidence that contradicts that offered by the defense.

PREPONDERANCE OF EVIDENCE

In a civil case, the party allegedly wronged is called the *plaintiff*. The plaintiff may be an individual, a group, a business, or a representative of some other private concern. The plaintiff in a civil action is not required to prove allegations beyond and to the exclusion of every reasonable doubt. All that is required is that the evidence the plaintiff presents be considered weightier by the jury than the contrary evidence presented by the defendant. Thus if the civil jury believes that the plaintiff's story offers a higher probability of being true than does the defendant's contention, the plaintiff will win the case. But the defendant wins if the jury gives greater credibility to the defense. In nonlegal terms, if evidence had to be weighed on a 100-point scale of probability, 51 percent believability would win.

ORDER OF PROOF

Court procedures generally require that the prosecuting attorney prove the existence of the corpus delicti at trial before attempting to show the guilt of the defendant. The *corpus delicti* is the combination of all the elements of the crime. It is, of course, only logical that the prosecution be required to show that a crime has been committed before it can begin proving the defendant's guilt. Trial judges rarely exercise their discretionary power to allow evidence to be submitted to prove a point out of order. The judge has the prerogative of allowing the introduction of evidence to establish the guilt of the defendant prior to the prosecution's showing the existence of all the elements of the crime. However, this is done only on rare occasions, when to maintain the order of proof might be a major inconvenience to a particular witness. Permission is given only on the condition that the prosecution guarantee it will later establish the corpus delicti. If the guarantee is made and the prosecution later cannot show the corpus delicti, grounds exist for a mistrial or a directed verdict of innocence.

JUDICIAL NOTICE

The doctrine of judicial notice is an evidentiary shortcut. Judicial notice is designed to speed up the trial and eliminate the necessity of formally proving the truth of a particular matter when that truth is not in dispute. *Judicial notice*, then, is proof without evidence and may be taken in three situations:

1. *Judicial notice may be taken of matters of common knowledge that are uniformly settled and about which there is no dispute.* If the fact is known to most reasonably informed people in the community where the trial is being held, judicial notice may be taken of that fact. For example, the fact that a particular intersection, located in a city where an accident occurred, is a business district might well be a matter of common knowledge of which judicial notice could be taken if the trial is held in that city. Since most reasonably informed people in a community would know that a particular intersection was a business area, the court would accept that as a given fact without requiring formal proof.

2. *Judicial notice may be taken of laws.* A state court, for example, is required to take judicial notice of the state statutes of the jurisdiction in which the court operates; a municipal court takes judicial notice of municipal ordinances.

3. *Judicial notice may be taken of matters that may be ascertained as true by referring to common authoritative sources such as books or official agencies.* Included in this category are scientific facts, medical facts, historical facts, and meanings of words, phrases, and abbreviations. Examples would include the official time of sunset on a particular date by reference to a weather bureau; the fact that the abbreviation M.D. following a name stands for medical doctor; that the hair and blood types of human beings differ from

those of animals; and that no two individuals have identical fingerprints.

Judicial notice must be distinguished from judicial *knowledge*. The latter refers to knowledge possessed by a judge. The fact that the judge may know a fact is not material in applying the doctrine of judicial notice. Personal knowledge may not be substituted for common knowledge in the community or for facts capable of being ascertained.

Judicial notice may be taken only on a collateral or minor point of fact in a case. Judicial notice may never be used to prove a fact that the jury is required to decide in determining the proper charge and verdict. For example, in the case of a defendant on trial for stealing a car, the court may not take judicial notice of the value of the car if that value will determine the seriousness of the charge against the defendant. Even if it is a matter of common knowledge that a brand new Cadillac El Dorado is worth more than $100, judicial notice may not be taken, because the value is an important element that the prosecution must prove to assure the propriety of the charge placed against the defendant.

TYPES OF EVIDENCE

There are many ways of classifying evidence. Not all authorities agree on the classifications, but the differences are immaterial as long as the principles are understood. Five types of evidence are defined next.

DIRECT EVIDENCE

Direct evidence usually refers to the testimony of witnesses that ties the defendant directly to the commission of the crime, such as the testimony of an eyewitness who can positively state that the defendant committed the crime. It is based on the firsthand knowledge of the witness regarding the guilt of the defendant.

REAL EVIDENCE

Sometimes referred to as "physical evidence", *real evidence* is connected with the commission of the crime and can be produced in court. Items of physical evidence found at a crime scene, such as a weapon used to commit a homicide, a crowbar used to pry open a window, and fingerprints, all constitute real evidence that can be observed by the jury (see Figure 23–3).

DEMONSTRATIVE EVIDENCE

Demonstrative, or *illustrative*, *evidence* is not identical to real evidence even though the items introduced are tangible. It refers to maps, diagrams, sketches, photographs, tape recordings, videotapes, X-rays, and visual tests and demonstrations produced to assist witnesses in explaining their testimony. When testimony alone would be inadequate to describe a victim or crime scene, photographs taken by police officers are used to help the jury understand the conditions that existed.

The use of demonstrative evidence is governed by some complex and highly restrictive rules to ensure that the jury is not prejudiced against the defendant.

CIRCUMSTANTIAL EVIDENCE

It is a myth that one cannot be convicted of a crime solely on circumstantial evidence. The broad definition of *circumstantial evidence* encompasses all evidence other than direct evidence, provided that it logically relates the defendant to the crime. Circumstantial evidence is sometimes referred to as "indirect evidence" for this reason. Circumstantial evidence is used in a criminal case by inferring from a series of known facts the existence of an unknown fact. In other words, by the process of deductive reasoning, inferences are logically drawn from a series of known facts, and a conclusion is reached. For example, the fact that the defendant's fingerprints are detected on a weapon found at the scene of a homicide does not necessarily mean that the defendant committed the crime. The fingerprints tie the defendant to the gun, and finding the gun at the scene of the crime may be a circumstance relating the gun to the commission of the crime. Likewise, testimony that the defendant was seen near the scene of the crime shortly after its commission does not necessarily constitute guilt; but again, it may lead the jury to infer guilt.

Figure 23–3
The Introduction of Real Evidence at Trial

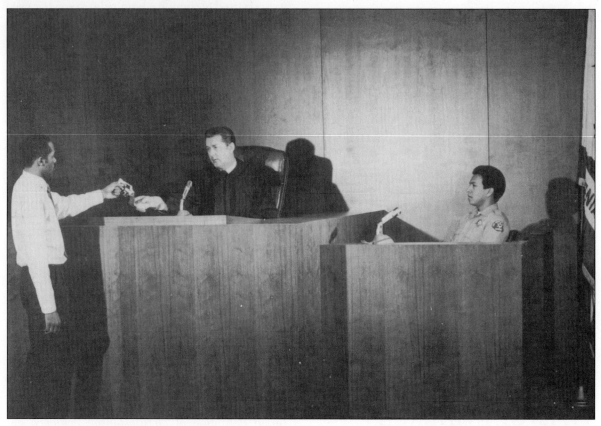

(Courtesy Los Angeles County Sheriff's Department)

It is possible that an accumulation of circumstantial evidence may be nothing more than a series of unfortunate coincidences for which the defendant may have a logical and truthful explanation. How much circumstantial evidence is required for a jury to convict someone of a crime varies from case to case and depends largely on the composition of the jury.

Circumstantial evidence can be considered analogous to links in a chain. Each link might be an unfortunate coincidence, but the greater the number of links, the more a jury is likely to infer guilt by joining the links into a chain of overwhelming circumstantial evidence.

OPINION EVIDENCE

Witnesses ordinarily are not permitted to give their opinions or draw conclusions on matters about which they are testifying. Their function is to present the facts about which they have firsthand knowledge. It is within the province of the jury to determine the truthfulness of those facts and to draw whatever conclusions it believes are necessary. However, there are a few exceptions to that general rule. Everything a human being perceives through the senses is generally expressed in the form of a conclusion. It is difficult, if not impossible, to describe something perceived as an absolute fact without expressing it in the form of a conclusion. The only situation in which a nonexpert may give an opinion is on matters of description in which fact and opinion are so interwoven that they cannot be separated without losing most of their probative value. Matters of description in which a nonexpert may give an opinion include color, size, shape, speed, mental condition, identity, race, and language.

An *expert* is someone with special skills or knowledge not ordinarily possessed by others. The skills or knowledge may be acquired through experience, study, observation, or education. To be an expert witness, one need not necessarily have a formal education. The expert witness is permitted to interpret facts and give opinions about their significance; the lay witness may present only facts that are a matter of firsthand knowledge. The expert witness is called on to assist the jurors in understanding facts that they are ordinarily not sufficiently trained to understand, such as the results of medical examinations, chemical analyses, ballistics reports, and findings from questioned documents. Results of DNA analysis, for example, would certainly require the supporting testimony of an expert witness.

THE HEARSAY RULE

HEARSAY EVIDENCE

Most people have heard a story from several different sources and recognized how different the versions sound. Whether these alterations are caused by poor memory or deliberate attempts to spice up the truth is immaterial in a legal context. The fact that stories tend to be changed when they are repeated makes their reliability and truthfulness questionable. For this reason, the hearsay rule was created. *Hearsay* is derived from "heard say." Testimony in court that repeats what others were heard to say means testifying to a second version of what actually happened. The witness has no personal knowledge of the facts in question. Thus, the truth of the testimony depends on the truthfulness and the competence of the person from whom the information was heard rather than of the person testifying. For these reasons the hearsay rule is perhaps one of the most important yet most confusing rules of evidence.

Inaccuracy, unreliability, and untrustworthiness are only some of the reasons why hearsay evidence is excluded. The inability of the judge and jury to observe the demeanor or conduct of the person who actually has firsthand knowledge of the information is another.

Other reasons for generally excluding hearsay rely on protections guaranteed in the Constitution.

The Sixth Amendment guarantees a defendant the right to be confronted by the witnesses against him or her and the right to cross-examine those witnesses. Because the person with firsthand knowledge is not present in court, that person cannot be confronted or cross-examined by the defendant.

Hearsay is a version of the truth repeated in court by one who does not know whether the assertion is true. People may assert things lightly and casually out of court without being overly concerned about the truth; but they would likely be more careful about speaking truthfully in court, when an individual's life or liberty may be at stake and when they are testifying under oath.

The hearsay rule also excludes written statements by people not in the courtroom to testify. Because the writer's personal knowledge is in his or her head, writing that knowledge makes it secondhand information.

If the out-of-court assertion is not being offered as evidence to prove the truth of a matter but only to show that it was said, it is not hearsay and thus may be admissible. This is one of the rare occasions in which the hearsay rule would not be applicable. For example, a homicide victim may have made threats against the defendant. These threats can be repeated in court to show the defendant's state of mind when he or she killed the victim and to support a claim of self-defense. The truth or falsity of the threats is not the issue.

A second exception deals with reputation. The reputation of a defendant or a witness in a trial may be questionable. A third party may testify about what he or she has heard concerning another's reputation. Because an individual's reputation is not representative of actual character, but rather what other people think of that person, the truth of the reputation is immaterial. But the fact that such a reputation exists is admissible. For example, if the defendant presents evidence in a trial for assault that he or she is a calm individual, a witness may testify to having heard that the defendant is extremely short-tempered.

In these situations, evidence is offered only to show that the statements were made, not that they are true. Because the witness has personal knowledge, it is not hearsay, and because the statements are not offered for the truth of their contents, they are admissible.

The hearsay rule is based on the recognition that human beings have human weaknesses, and the testimony of human witnesses provides the majority of evidence presented to juries in modern trials. Because we will continue to rely on the testimony of human beings as the principal source of information for trying cases, the law must continue to impose standards to assure the most accurate and reliable testimony possible. Unequivocal application of the hearsay rule to all situations does, however, present certain injustices in our modern judicial system. For this reason, a number of specific exceptions to the hearsay rule have developed.

EXCEPTIONS TO THE HEARSAY RULE

The sheer number of exceptions often creates doubt about whether the hearsay rule has any merit. Among the many reasons for the existence of the hearsay rule, two stand out as the most critical: the unreliability and the untrustworthiness of declarations repeated under oath in court. The exceptions to the rule can be justified only if these two major drawbacks can be overcome. If the circumstances surrounding the hearsay evidence can ensure a high degree of trustworthiness and reliability, that evidence is admissible as an exception to the rule in order to minimize any injustice. Thus, each exception must meet many tests to satisfy the criteria of reliability and trustworthiness before it is admissible. Several decisions by the courts have eliminated the concern over the constitutional issues involved. These decisions, in effect, have held that allowing the admissibility of the exceptions does not violate the Sixth Amendment guarantees of confrontation and cross-examination, nor does it violate the due process guarantees of the Fourteenth Amendment. Some exceptions apply in both civil *and* criminal cases; others apply only to civil *or* criminal cases. The following paragraphs discuss several exceptions applicable in criminal cases.

Confessions

A *confession* is an acknowledgment by a person accused of a crime that he or she is guilty of that crime. To constitute a confession, the admission of guilt must apply to all the elements of the crime and exclude any reasonable doubt about the possibility of innocence. Confessions are generally of two types. A judicial confession is an in-court confession made before a judge. A judicial confession can also take the form of a guilty plea. Judicial confessions do not fall within the hearsay rule, because they are *in-court* assertions of the truth of the matter asserted by the person directly involved.

Confessions made out of court fall within the hearsay rule. For such confessions to be admissible, they must meet the tests of admissibility and overcome the assumptions of unreliability and untrustworthiness.

The admissibility of a confession usually raises questions about constitutionality. First, it must be shown that the confession satisfies constitutional requirements of voluntariness. A confession that is obtained involuntarily certainly would not be admissible under modern law. Second, courts admit confessions as an exception to the hearsay rule on the theory that it is highly unlikely that a person will say something against his or her own interest unless it is true. Therefore, a confession tends to establish the reliability and trustworthiness of the truth of the matter asserted. People do not often deliberately make statements that jeopardize their own life or liberty unless those statements are true. Based on this assumption, the major objections to admitting confessions, as hearsay, are overcome.

Admissions

One who makes an *admission* does not acknowledge all the facts surrounding the crime necessary to constitute guilt but does admit to certain facts or circumstances from which guilt may be inferred by the jury. For example, without confessing to the crime, an accused may admit having been at or near the scene of the crime at the time it occurred, having a motive to commit the crime against the victim, possessing the gun used in the crime, having foot impressions that match those found outside the window of the victim's house, and leaving town the day after the crime was committed. These admissions may be introduced in the trial by a witness who overheard the accused make these statements or in the form of a written document repeating these statements. They may be introduced for basically the same reasons as confessions are admissible. The contents of the admissions are certainly against the interest and welfare of the defendant and, like confessions, must have been made voluntarily to be admissible. If these factors exist, it is unlikely that a defendant would make such admissions unless they were true. Therefore, the courts allow the admissions on the basis that the principal objections to the hearsay rule—unreliability and untrustworthiness—have been overcome.

Spontaneous and Excited Utterances

Human nature is such that speaking the truth is an instinctive reaction. Therefore, if one makes a spontaneous or excited utterance after something startling or unusual has happened, the utterance may be admissible as an exception to the hearsay rule when testified to by one who heard it made. It may be offered to prove the truth of the matter asserted. The spontaneity of the utterance and its declaration under startling and unusual circumstances lend credence to its reliability and trustworthiness. To illustrate, a 5-year-old girl, observing a playmate struck at a railroad crossing, was heard by a passer-by to scream, "The engine runned over Billy!" The passer-by was permitted to testify in court about what he had heard the girl say.

Dying Declarations

A declaration concerning the facts and circumstances of the fatal injury made by the victim of a homicide who is about to die, expects to die, and does not hope to recover is admissible as an exception to the hearsay rule. The theory is that a person about to die has no reason to lie. Statements admissible under this exception must concern the injury inflicted to the declarant and are admissible only in the trial of the person charged with the declarant's death.

Former Testimony

Written or oral testimony in a hearing or trial falls within the hearsay rule if that testimony is sought to be introduced in a later judicial proceeding. For example, if a witness testifies against the defendant in a preliminary hearing to determine probable cause to hold the defendant for trial, the court record is not admissible in the later trial unless it meets the tests of the former-testimony exception to the hearsay rule. Because the testimony was given in a court under oath, it is presumed reliable and trustworthy and is admissible, provided the two judicial proceedings involve the same defendant, charged with committing the same act, under the same circumstances. In addition, the witness who originally testified at the former hearing must be unavailable for testimony before the transcript of

the hearing is admissible and, to show that constitutional requirements have been satisfied, it must be proved that the defendant had the right to cross-examine the witness in the former hearing or trial.

EVIDENTIARY PRIVILEGES

Defendants and other witnesses have a right to have certain matters of communication barred from disclosure in court—for example, confidential communications between husband and wife, confidential communications between attorney and client, and grand jury proceedings that are confidential by requirements of law are barred.

The evidentiary privileges may vary from state to state. Some are universally recognized as necessary and have existed since the early days of common law. Others exist only if the state legislature has created the privilege by statute. Some of the more common evidentiary privileges fall into four basic categories. The first might be called *professional privileges* and includes those that exist between attorney and client, physician and patient, priest and penitent, and journalist and informant. Government communications and information, state secrets, and matters of diplomacy are classified as *political privileges*. The third category is *social privileges* and includes confidential communications between husband and wife or between a guidance counselor and a child. Finally, *judicial privileges* include grand jury proceedings, communications among jurors deliberating a verdict, and the privilege against self-incrimination guaranteed by the Fifth Amendment.

All of these privileges can be waived by the person against whom the evidence is to be used or who would suffer from its disclosure. Thus an attorney cannot disclose evidence of a confidential communication between attorney and client unless so directed by the client. Likewise, a spouse cannot testify against a mate without the latter's express permission, unless the spouse is the victim of the mate's crime.

Although only confidential communications are excluded by the privilege, it is the relationship, not the communication, that is privileged. The theory underlying evidentiary privileges creates a balance between the disclosure of truth and the welfare of society. The assumption is that the public benefits more by protecting these relationships than it does by requiring disclosure of the truth to seek to convict one defendant.

WITNESSES

Until a few hundred years ago, witnesses appeared at a trial voluntarily. There were no legal means to compel attendance. With the advent of the rules of evidence, procedures had to be established for requiring the presence of people who possessed knowledge of the facts of the case. The *subpoena* is used for this purpose. It is a written order commanding the person named to appear in court at a specified date and time to testify, under oath, before a judicial tribunal, to facts within the witness's personal knowledge that are pertinent to the case. A *subpoena duces tecum* commands the individual to bring certain records or documents in his or her possession. Refusal to obey subjects the individual to punishment for contempt. Likewise, refusal to testify or answer specific questions may be grounds for contempt unless valid grounds exist, such as the self-incrimination protections guaranteed in the Constitution. People who possess firsthand knowledge have a duty, not a right, to appear in court.

In early common law, defendants had no right to call witnesses on their behalf. Therefore, the prosecution was required to call all witnesses having knowledge of facts, regardless of which side those facts favored. Today, the defense has an equal right to compel the attendance of witnesses. Hence, the state may use only those witnesses it chooses. Witnesses may also be called by the judge, but this power is rarely exercised.

Once in court, the witness's competence to testify must be ascertained. Competence of witnesses was discussed previously in this chapter. If the witness is not insane, intoxicated, or excluded for other reasons, and if the testimony will not fall within any of the evidentiary privileges, he or she will be presumed competent to testify, though this must first be asserted by taking an oath or affirmation.

In common law, taking an oath was a process by which individuals swore to tell the truth based on their sacred belief in a supreme being. Today, of course, the oath is still a recognized means of establishing a witness's competence, but it is no longer the only method. The affirmation is also used for people who refuse, for personal reasons, to take the oath. Because they are otherwise competent to testify, some guarantee that they will tell the truth is necessary. A witness may be declared competent if he or she understands and undertakes the obligation of an oath. This obligation is to tell the truth with a realization of the penalties for perjury. As long as the witness understands and undertakes the obligation, even without swearing to a supreme being, the witness is considered competent to testify. This process is called *affirmation*.

A declaration of a witness's competence in no way guarantees the credibility of the testimony. Credibility deals with believability, which, like the weight of any other evidence, is determined by the jury. Attitude, personality, appearance, hygiene, and general demeanor all affect a witness's credibility, along with the substance of the testimony.

Questions

1. Why must a criminal investigator know the rules of evidence?
2. Define the following concepts:
   (a) Evidence
   (b) Proof
   (c) Testimony
   (d) Admissibility
   (e) Relevancy
   (f) Materiality
   (g) Competency of evidence
   (h) Competency of witnesses
   (i) Weight
3. Distinguish between burden of proof and burden of going forward with evidence.
4. What is the purpose of judicial notice?
5. Describe the manner in which circumstantial evidence is used in a criminal prosecution.
6. Why does the opinion rule of evidence exist?
7. What is the hearsay rule and why does it exist?
8. What is the philosophy under which exceptions to the hearsay rule have evolved?
9. Describe the philosophy underlying the existence of evidentiary privileges.

TWENTY-FOUR

The Investigator as Witness

CHAPTER OUTLINE

The Role of the Police Witness 670
Credibility 670
Characteristics of a Good Witness 670
Understanding the Jury 671
Appearance and Demeanor 671
Trial Process 671

Taking the Witness Stand 672
Answering Questions 673
Cross-Examination 674
Use of Notes on the Stand 675
Leaving the Witness Stand 676
Questions 677

INTRODUCTION

The success or failure of a criminal investigation is often ultimately measured in terms of the quality and effectiveness of an officer's presentation of evidence to court and jury. Because one aim of the entire process of criminal investigation is to bring about the apprehension and prosecution of violators of the criminal laws, the presentation of the case in court must be of paramount concern to the investigator from the moment of arrival at the crime scene. Inability to understand and appreciate this crucial role in the judicial process not only adversely affects the investigator's performance as a witness but reflects on the investigator's overall professional effectiveness.

Every police witness, whether a uniformed officer or criminal investigator, must become skilled at testifying on the witness stand. Preparation should include a knowledge of the rules of evidence so that the officer not only can perform in the field more effectively but also can have a better understanding of courtroom procedures and the functions of the prosecution and the defense. To prepare a case adequately, the investigator must understand the rules of admissibility and the relevance of evidence collected. The best witnesses are those who have an understanding and appreciation of their role in the courtroom and their relationship to other participants in the judicial process.

THE ROLE OF THE POLICE WITNESS

The function of any witness in the courtroom, including the investigator, is to present firsthand knowledge of facts to the jury for its consideration. The investigator must inform the jury of the matters investigated in the case and present this information so that the jury understands the sequence of events and their significance. But the investigator may not offer personal conclusions.

To understand his or her role in the courtroom completely, the witness must also understand the functions of the other participants in the criminal process. Specifically, the witness must understand the functions of the judge and the jury in relation to the role of a witness.

As seen in the previous chapter, the function of any witness is to present facts from firsthand knowledge. The jury's function is to weigh the facts presented by witnesses from both prosecution and defense and to interpret these facts, giving appropriate weight and credibility to the evidence and to the witnesses for the purpose of reaching a decision regarding the guilt or innocence of the defendant. The responsibility of the judge is twofold. The judge functions as a referee to ensure compliance with the rules of evidence and interprets the law as applicable to the facts of a case.

CREDIBILITY

A police officer is not entitled to any more credibility in the courtroom than any other witness. The officer has an equal responsibility, through presentation, appearance, demeanor, and the substance of testimony, to persuade the jury to believe those facts being related.

The issue of credibility is of special concern to the police witness. Few people from the general population ever view a criminal offense or act as witnesses in court. It is likely that the trauma of such an event would be so vivid for them that remembering it would not be difficult. However, police officers regularly deal with criminal cases and investigate some with striking similarities. Thus, for officers, the frequency and similarities of, and the time lag between investigations and court appearances may create difficulties in the presentation of testimony.

A related area that may affect the credibility of the police witness stems from public expectations and perceptions of the police role. Many citizens expect nothing less than perfection from police officers in both the performance of their duties and their presentation of testimony in court. They often lose sight of the fact that police officers are subject to human frailties. An officer's credibility may suffer if his or her recall is less than perfect.

Another issue in the investigator's credibility relates to the perceptions of the jurors. Some individuals regard as suspect any statements made by police officers. The predisposition of jurors with this attitude may be reinforced by defense attorneys who, on cross-examination, seek to discredit the testimony of the officer on the basis of his or her occupation.

The police witness can overcome all of these barriers by preparing meticulously for testimony and by giving straightforward, unemotional responses.

CHARACTERISTICS OF A GOOD WITNESS

The successful testimony of the investigator is based on adequate preparation of the case, familiarity with the rules of evidence and with how juries think and react, knowledge of trial processes, and maintenance of proper appearance and conduct at all times.

Preparation for testimony, as has already been indicated, is of extreme importance and cannot be overemphasized. For the police witness the first step in preparation is to ensure that a complete investigation was conducted, that all leads were followed and all avenues explored. It must be remembered that the prime responsibility of the investigator is not to convict but to ascertain the facts objectively. The investigator must also prepare complete and accurate notes on information obtained and evidence gathered. Before appearing in court, investigators must review all notes; on the stand, they must recall events in as much detail as possible with minimal referral to notes. In addition to reviewing notes, it is critical that investigators thoroughly review all written re-ports, all evidence, and any deposition that may have been given prior to trial to ensure that their memory is complete and accurate.

The investigator should review the case with prosecuting officials so that they will know the testimony the investigator can offer and the evidence available. This review also gives the investigator a chance to learn the nature of the questions that might be asked on direct examination. Admittedly investigators rarely can spend much time with the prosecutor before a trial. The demands on prosecu-tors' time and the case loads that most prosecutors carry make in-depth preparation with each witness a virtual impossibility. But even a short time spent in preparation is valuable.

UNDERSTANDING THE JURY

The jury's task is unique. In theory, it is constrained in what it may consider by rules of evidence and other procedural requirements. In practice, juries are composed of human beings who are subject to influences other than those that might appear in written rules and regulations. The study of jury psy-chology is fascinating, for it points out the flexibility and fallibility of the human mind and, in turn, the absurdity of some of the procedural requirements imposed on the jury. The good police witness will, at the very least, understand and appreciate the fact that juries do not make their determination of guilt or innocence solely on the substance of testi-mony and evidence offered. The appearance and demeanor of the defendant, attorneys, and wit-nesses; the manner in which witnesses make their presentations and answer questions; the profes-sionalism displayed by police officers while in the courtroom; and the way in which witnesses respond to cross-examination all bear on the reactions of in-dividual jurors. A good witness is conscious of these factors at all times.

APPEARANCE AND DEMEANOR

Law enforcement authorities disagree as to whether police officers should wear uniforms or civilian clothes to court. Some believe that a police officer should always wear a uniform when testify-ing in court for immediate identification by the ju-rors. Others contend that civilian clothing is proper dress because the uniform presents an authoritar-ian appearance that may be offensive to the jury. A third group takes the view that the officer should wear the type of dress—that is, uniform or civilian clothes—worn at the time of the arrest. Often this decision is largely a matter of departmental policy. In any event, dress should be clean and neat. If civilian clothes are worn, a degree of formality is appropriate. Conservative clothes are less likely to offend members of the jury than are wild, flashy outfits, even though neat. Identify-ing items such as jewelry representing a specific occupation or association membership should be avoided. Lapel pins from specific civic clubs or tie tacks with emblems of handcuffs or service re-volvers should not be worn. Although these are extremely small points, one can never predict who might be offended. Additionally, all the fundamen-tals pertaining to personal hygiene should be scrupulously observed.

Police witnesses should be conscious of their de-meanor from the time they arrive at the courthouse. Prior to trial or during recesses, jurors may be stand-ing around the courthouse. If an officer makes a bad impression through his or her appearance or ac-tions, this may be remembered by a juror when the officer takes the stand and may adversely affect the credibility of the officer in that juror's mind. Conse-quently, any actions that could be offensive to jurors are to be avoided. The police officer should avoid talking to the prosecutor, court clerks, or judges and refrain from acting overly friendly to anyone in-volved in the trial. Although there is nothing inher-ently wrong with idle talk or friendliness, jurors may perceive it as collusion.

TRIAL PROCESS

Some police officers and criminal investigators are not fully aware of the order in which a trial is con-ducted because time often prohibits them from attending a complete trial from beginning to end. Also, witnesses are often sequestered from the courtroom before and after giving testimony. This very common practice is used to minimize the possibility that a witness's testimony might be affected by other witnesses' testimony.

The courtroom process begins with the selection and swearing in of the jury. Then the trial begins with the prosecutor's and defense attorney's opening statements. These statements acquaint the jury with the allegations in the case. The prosecutor tells the jury how he or she will attempt to prove that a crime was committed and that it was committed by the defendant. The defense tells how it will attempt to convince the jury that either no crime was committed or it was not committed by this defendant.

Then the prosecution presents its case, calling witnesses and introducing evidence to establish that a crime was committed and that it was committed by the defendant. While the prosecution is presenting its case, the questioning of witnesses it calls to testify on behalf of the prosecution is called *direct examination*. When that same witness is questioned by the defense attorney, the process is called *cross-examination*. In most jurisdictions, the scope of cross-examination is limited to matters brought up during direct examination. If on cross-examination the defense attorney manages to confuse a point raised on direct examination, the prosecutor has the opportunity to conduct a *redirect examination* after the defense attorney has completed cross-examination, and likewise the defense later has an opportunity to re-cross-examine each witness.

When the prosecution finishes introducing all its evidence and presenting all its witnesses, the defense attorney usually moves to dismiss the charge on the grounds that the state failed to prove that a crime was committed or that the defendant committed it. This is a normal procedural response to the state's case by the defense attorney. If, in fact, the judge is convinced that the prosecution did substantially fail to establish that a crime was committed or that the defendant is guilty, charges are dismissed, and the trial ends. But if the judge feels that the jury could reasonably decide that the defendant is guilty after hearing the defense case, the motion is denied and the defense attorney is permitted to present the case for the defendant.

The presentation of the defense case follows the same pattern as that for the state. Evidence is introduced at the appropriate time and witnesses called. Witnesses called by the defense are directly examined by the defense attorney and cross-examined by the prosecutor. The procedures for redirect and re-cross-examination are applicable.

After the defense rests its case, the prosecution has an opportunity for *rebuttal*. New evidence may be presented, or witnesses may be reexamined to clarify or rehabilitate earlier testimony. If the prosecutor uses the opportunity to present rebuttal evidence, then the defense is given equal opportunity to rebut this, through the process called *surrebuttal*.

After the introduction of all evidence by both sides, each attorney may make a closing argument. They summarize for the jury the evidence they have presented. The prosecutor attempts to show the jury that sufficient evidence has been presented to indicate that the defendant is guilty of the particular crime charged, that it should find guilt, and it should punish accordingly. The defense attorney attempts to persuade the jury that the prosecution has failed to prove its case against the defendant and that the jury should acquit.

Once closing statements are completed, the judge has the responsibility for instructing the jury on the law applicable to the case and of advising the jury of its responsibilities: to weigh the testimony of witnesses and the evidence presented. The judge also tells the jury the various decisions it may reach in terms of guilt or innocence and the elements of the crimes—including lesser offenses—of which they may find the defendant guilty. The judge advises the jurors of the degree to which they must be convinced of guilt or acquit the defendant.

TAKING THE WITNESS STAND

From the moment the police witness enters the courtroom, people are forming opinions. The officer should walk naturally when approaching the witness stand, not look at or speak to the prosecutor, and not frown at the defendant. If the jury sees these expressions, it interprets them as signs of partiality. The police witness should stand erect while being sworn in (see Figure 24–1) and, when permitted to be seated, should sit erect, facing the jury. The investigator should not continually cross his or her legs or fidget uncomfortably. Hands should be

Figure 24–1
An Officer Being Sworn in as a Witness

(Courtesy Miami-Dade County Police Department, Florida)

kept comfortably in the lap or on the arms of the chair.

Nervousness is natural for anyone who appears as a witness. Usually it disappears with experience. However, if the police witness is properly prepared and answers all questions accurately and truthfully to the best of his or her knowledge, nervousness is minimized.

Eye contact and speaking voice are extremely important. Many authorities contend that the witness should maintain eye contact with the jury while answering questions rather than watching the prosecutor or defense attorney. But this skill must be developed. It is difficult for most people to look at the jury when responding to a question from an attorney who may be standing on the opposite side of the courtroom. If the jury cannot hear or understand what the witness is saying, the testimony is worthless. Witnesses should speak loudly enough for people in the back of the courtroom to hear clearly and understand what they are saying. Then they can be sure that the jury, the attorneys, and the judge also can hear them.

ANSWERING QUESTIONS

The ability to answer questions under direct and cross-examination is usually developed through experience. The police witness must answer without emotion or partiality. Sarcasm, witty remarks, or an attitude of "I'm out to get the defendant" must be avoided at all times. The good police witness must be positive and firm in answering all questions and should readily admit not knowing an answer, if this is the case. The witness who constructs an answer to avoid embarrassment jeopardizes the case for the prosecution. Even the slightest fabrication of testimony is perjury and is likely to be discovered on cross-examination. It should be remembered that to err is human. It is not impossible for police witnesses to make mistakes in their testimony. Although it is slightly embarrassing, the witness should not hesitate to admit having made a mistake. This acknowledgment should be accompanied by an explanation. Even if the mistake is not discovered until after testimony is complete, the witness should immediately advise the prosecutor of the mistake so that the prosecutor will have the opportunity to correct it before the conclusion of the trial.

The requirement of being positive and firm in responding to questions also means that the witness must avoid the use of such expressions as "I think," "I believe," or "as I recall." It is difficult to avoid using expressions such as these because they are part of everyday usage of the English language, but in court they can raise questions as to the definitiveness of the officer's testimony and can be a factor in the degree of credibility given to the testimony by the jury.

There are two basic methods by which witnesses are examined. The *narrative technique* allows the witness to tell the facts in his or her own words as they are known to be, in response to a question such as, "Now tell us what you found at 1234 Elm Street." This technique is used if the examiner knows the witness well and has confidence that the witness will relate only relevant, unobjectionable matters. The advantage of the narrative technique is that it permits the witness to relate details chronologically and make them clearer to the jury. The obvious disadvantage is that an inexperienced witness may ramble, give objectionable or irrelevant testimony, or expose the jury to tainted evidence, potentially causing a mistrial. Hence, prosecutors use this technique sparingly.

Usually attorneys use the *question-and-answer technique* for examining witnesses. They ask a single, pointed question and receive an answer to it. When the question-and-answer technique is used, the police witness should hesitate momentarily before answering. This allows time for the opposing attorney to raise any objections. It also allows the witness an opportunity to digest the question to make sure it has been clearly understood. If not, the witness should ask that the question be

repeated as many times as necessary. If the question does not make any sense after several repetitions, the witness may ask that the question be phrased in different terms. The witness should not volunteer information.

Courtesy and respect are important qualities of an effective witness. The judge should always be addressed as "Your Honor." The witness's language should be intelligible and understandable to the jury. Police witnesses should deliberately avoid the use of slang and words unique to the police service, for these may not be understood by the jury. Profanity should not be used in the courtroom unless the witness is repeating a direct quote. If such is the case, the officer should have no hesitation in using the exact words that were used during the investigation.

Occasionally a yes or no answer may be demanded of a witness, particularly on cross-examination. Sometimes such an answer is not an appropriate response to the question. If this occasion arises, the witness should not be pressured into an inaccurate response for the sake of brevity. The witness is always permitted to qualify answers and should persist in this right, if necessary asking the judge for permission to qualify the answer. But if the question can be accurately answered with a simple yes or no, the witness should respond accordingly.

CROSS-EXAMINATION

The purpose of cross-examination is to ensure that testimony given under direct examination has been accurate and truthful. Through cross-examination the attorney attempts to impeach witnesses called by the opposing side. *Impeachment* is the process of discrediting or contradicting the testimony of the witness to show that the witness is unworthy of belief. It is designed to weaken or destroy the effect of the testimony presented under direct examination and thus to destroy the credibility of the witness in the eyes of the jury. Cross-examination tests the reliability of the witness by attempting to detect whether testimony was intentionally slanted or whether an error or misstatement was made.

The five basic methods for attacking the credibility of a witness are:

1. Showing that the witness's previous statements, personal conduct, or conduct of the investigation is inconsistent with the witness's testimony in court.

2. Showing that the witness is biased or prejudiced for or against the state or the defendant, because of a close relationship, personal interest in the outcome of the case, hostility toward the opposing party, or similar biases.

3. Attacking the character of the witness—revealing prior criminal convictions or other irrefutable characteristics that would render testimony unworthy of belief.

4. Showing the witness's incapacity to observe, recollect, or recount due to mental weakness, a physical defect, influence of drugs or alcohol, or the like.

5. Showing that the witness is in error, that the facts are otherwise than as testified.

Cross-examination tactics used by attorneys vary widely, but they fall into two basic categories. Browbeating or belligerent cross-examination is designed to put the witness under pressure to provoke an unprofessional reaction. The attorney may ask a series of questions rapidly in an attempt to confuse the witness and force inconsistent responses. The attorney may try to reverse the witness's words or may continually repeat the same questions in an attempt to elicit inconsistent or conflicting answers.

The cross-examiner who assumes a friendly, condescending role attempts to lull the witness into a false sense of security to bring about less caution in listening to and answering questions. Once the witness's guard is down, the cross-examiner often resorts to leading questions. Leading questions suggest the answer desired. Although leading questions are not permitted in direct examination, they are permitted in cross-examination.

Another danger that should be avoided in cross-examination involves questions regarding whether the officer has talked with anyone about the case. Police witnesses often have the impression that this kind of question is designed to attack their integrity by attempting to show that they discussed the details of the case with the press or others in an attempt to create prejudice toward the defendant. In

fact, discussing the case with the prosecutor before the trial is perfectly permissible. If the officer answers no to the question, and this later turns out to be false, his or her credibility suffers. Likewise, if the witness responds no to the question, "Did the prosecutor tell you how to testify?" the answer is only partly complete. Obviously, the prosecutor generally has instructed the witness to testify to firsthand knowledge of facts and to tell the truth. But the question is designed in such a manner as to imply that an affirmative response means the prosecutor told the witness exactly how to answer each question. The best way of handling this type of situation is to respond, "Yes, I talked with the prosecutor about the case. The prosecutor advised me to relate the facts about which I had firsthand knowledge."

USE OF NOTES ON THE STAND

It is permissible for witnesses to use notes to help refresh their memory while testifying; the human mind can retain only so much information. The witness is not and cannot be expected to remember minute details such as dates and numbers that are of lesser importance than the major facts of the case (see Figure 24–2). However, the witness should constantly be aware of the proper use of notes and the ramifications of their use.

There are two reasons why a witness may refer to notes. The first is a need to remember a particular fact in question. In this case, the officer does remember the case and is permitted to use the notes to help recall minor details. This use of notes is perfectly permissible. On the other hand, if the officer's references to the notes are necessitated by an inability to remember anything about the events preceding the trial, the consequences of referring to notes are entirely different.

In the rules of evidence, using notes simply to refresh the memory is referred to as past recollection refreshed. As indicated, this is permissible but should be used with restraint, for it may indicate a lack of pretrial preparation. When notes are used by a police officer in direct examination, the defense attorney has an absolute right to examine those

Figure 24–2
An Officer Uses Notes on the Witness Stand

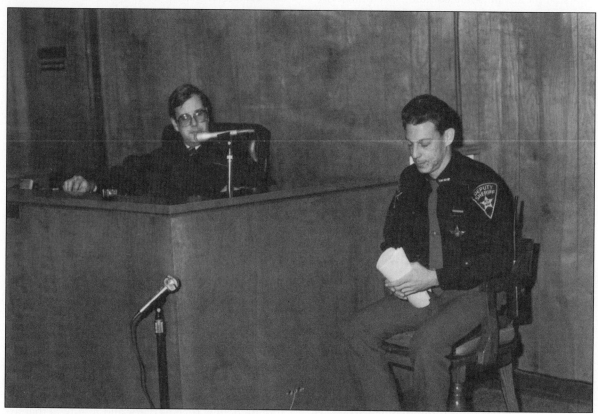

(Courtesy Geauga County, Ohio, Sheriff's Department)

notes and test the witness's memory before allowing the witness to continue testifying under direct examination. This is done to ensure that the witness is, in fact, testifying from memory.

In the event that the witness cannot remember the facts of the case but uses the notes as the sole basis of testimony without any independent recall, the term applied is *past recollection recorded*. In this instance the oral testimony of the police officer becomes worthless, as the knowledge is entirely based on the notes. Should this occur, the prosecutor most likely will, at the insistence of the defense attorney, dismiss the police officer as a witness and introduce the notes as evidence in the trial. If the notes are meaningless to everybody but the police officer who took them, the entire substance of the knowledge will be excluded from evidence.

For the various reasons described above, it is highly recommended that police officers use loose-leaf notebooks during their investigations. In this way, materials not relevant to the particular case at hand can be removed prior to trial and only those notes that are pertinent will be brought into the courtroom. If this is not done, the defense attorney may question the officer on any irrelevant part of the contents of the notebook and perhaps, by embarrassment, decrease the officer's credibility with the jury.

LEAVING THE WITNESS STAND

How witnesses leave the witness stand is just as important as how they enter, because the eyes of the jury follow them. It is improper for the witness to rise and leave the witness stand on completion of cross-examination. The prosecutor may conduct a redirect examination, or the defense attorney may think of a last-minute question. During this time, the witness should be careful not to be caught off guard. A common tactic in cross-examination is to ask a last-minute question while the witness is preparing to leave the stand, in hopes of catching the witness in an error after the pressure of testifying seems over. The witness should wait to be excused by the judge and should leave the courtroom without smiling, speaking, or glaring at anyone.

Questions

1. What is the role of the investigator as a witness?
2. What factors affect the credibility of the investigator as a witness?
3. What are the characteristics of a good witness?
4. How important are a witness's appearance and demeanor to credibility?
5. Describe the trial process step by step.
6. What is the function of cross-examination?
7. When and how may a witness use notes on the witness stand?

Index

ABFO scale, 95, 98
Active neglect, 356–357
Addicts; *see also* Drug abuse
  heroin, 607
  recognizing, 609–610
Admissibility, 201–203
  of crime lab results, 211
  of confessions, 666
  definition, 658
Admissions
  admissibility
    delay-in-arraignment rule,
      202–203
    free-and-voluntary rule, 202
  definition, 201
  exception to hearsay rule,
    666–667
Aging process
  hearing loss, 355–356
  vision changes, 354–355
Agrichemical theft, 540–541
  preventing, 549–550
Agricultural crime
  city connection, 538
  dimensions of, 538–539
  physical evidence, 547–549
  prevention measures, 549–550
  theft of chemicals, 540–541
AIDS, 607
  disinfectants used for, 43
  high-risk groups, 42
  protection from exposure to,
    41–46
  unauthorized disclosure, 45–46
Aircraft/avionics theft
  investigations, 507
  prevention of, 508–509
  scope of problem, 506–507
  techniques, 507–508
Alcohol
  death by, 265
  in fire death victims, 275
Allen, David, 121n
Alligatoring, 567
Alpert, Geoffrey P., 390n
Altered handwriting, 117
Ambush, 370
American Association of Motor
  Vehicle Administrators, 480
American Association of Retired
  Persons, 363
American Automobile
  Association, 499
American Farm Bureau, 538
American Psychiatric Association,
  *Diagnostic and Statistical
  Manual of Mental
  Disorders*, 282
American Society of Crime
  Laboratories, 206
Americans with Disabilities Act,
  46–47
America On-Line, 511
Ammonia, 267
  in fire death victims, 275
Amphetamines, 616–617
Anaheim Police Department
  Special Operations
  Division, 434
Anthropometry, 11–13
Archaeological looting, 453–461
  crime scene, 459–461

Archaeological looting—*Cont.*
  follow-up investigation,
    459–461
  investigation of, 458–461
  legal considerations, 455–458
Archaeological Resources
  Protection Act,
    456–457, 460
Arrest
  compared to charging, 648
  compared to detention, 648
  definition, 648
  for felony, 22–23
  legal, 22
  probabilities in robbery cases,
    375–376
  probable-cause requirement,
    651–652
Arrest warrants
  benefits of having, 649–650
  definition and contents,
    650–651, 652, 653
Arson
  damage caused by, 563
  detection difficulties,
    563–564
  fire-setting mechanisms,
    568–573
  generated by third parties
    elimination of competition,
      577–578
    extortion, 578
    labor-management
      grievances, 578
  preliminary investigation, 564
Arson for profit; *see also* Arson
  motives
    building rehabilitation, 576
    desire to relocate/remodel, 574
    destroying outmoded
      technology, 575
    financial stress, 573–575
    indicators, 578, 580
    planned bankruptcy, 576–577
    real estate schemes, 576
    redevelopment schemes,
      575–576
    satisfaction of debt, 575
    short-term business problems,
      574–575
    slow-moving inventory, 574–575
Arson investigation
  detection of accelerants,
    585–588
  fire accelerant residues,
    583–585
  interviews, 588–591
  origin and cause, 564–567
  preliminary, 564
Arson motives; *see also* Arson for
  profit
    adolescent fire-setters, 582
    child fire-setters, 583
    to conceal a crime, 580–581
    female fire-setters, 583
    pyromaniacs, 581–582
    revenge, spite, or jealousy, 579
    schizophrenics, 581–582
    vandalism/malicious
      mischief, 580
    vanity/hero fires, 582–583
Arson suspect, 590, 591–592

Ashworth, Dawn, 15
Autoerotic death, 306–310
Automated Fingerprint
  Identification System,
    91–92, 213–215, 615
  Unsolved Latent Fingerprint
    File, 213–214
Automated message accounting call
  records, 433–434
Automatic teller machines
  burglaries, 393
  robberies, 371, 374
Automobile paint, 74–75
Automobile theft
  car rentals, 500
  facts, 466–467
  fraudulent schemes
    defrauding owner and
      insurer, 472
    false-theft schemes,
      471–482
    false-vehicle schemes,
      470–471
    inflated loss schemes, 472
  involving fraud, 467–468
  methods of operation
    chop shops, 468
    exporting stolen cars, 469
    insurance fraud, 470
    quick strip, 468
    salvage switch, 468
  myths, 466
  prevention programs,
    497–500
  statistics, 466–467
  types of
    joyriding, 467
    professional, 467
    temporary, 467
Autopsy, 229–230
  psychological, 310
  sudden infant death
    syndrome, 344

Balthazard, Prof., 17
Baltimore, first police department,
  3–4
Bank fraud schemes, 427–431
Barker, Ma, 8
Baseline sketching, 57–58
Basu, Pamela, 372
Beckwith v. United States, 183
Be on lookout, 28–29
Berkman v. McCarty, 185, 186
Bertillon, Alphonse, 11–12, 15
Blood evidence, 28, 99–104
  handling, 102–104
  investigator questions,
    99–100
  locating, 100–102
  parent and wave cast-off
    patterns, 103
Bodies
  developing latent prints from,
    90–91
  estimating time of death,
    239–246
  hair evidence from, 98
  identification of, 230–233
  search for burial sites, 233–239
  submerged, 245–246

Bodies—*Cont.*
  unidentified, 231–233
Bomb threats
  concealed explosives, 598
  concealment areas, 600
  evacuation, 597–598
  locations, 598
  packages and letters, 600–601
  telephone call response, 597
  what not to do, 598–600
Bonnie and Clyde, 8, 372
Booth, John Wilkes, 93
Botanists, 236–237
Bow Street Runners, 2, 3
Brands, 547, 548
British Medical Journal, 353
Browbeating, 675
Brown v. Mississippi, 202
Bundy, Ted, 93
Bureau of Alcohol, Tobacco, and
  Firearms
  ceasefire system, 216
  crime lab, 206
  forensic science laboratories,
    219–220
Bureau of Narcotics and Dangerous
  Drugs, 9
Burglars, 392–395
Burglary
  of elderly, 358
  forcible entry, 391–392
  frequency and impact, 391
  loiding, 399
  offenders, 392–395
  reducing risk of, 418–419
  residential, 414–416
  of safes, 401–414
Burglary-in-progress calls,
  396–397
Burglary investigation
  at crime scene, 397–398
  fraudulent and distorted
    complaint, 400
  recognition of tools, 398–399
  safe insulation evidence,
    408–409
  surreptitious entries, 399–400
  time factors, 400–401
  tracing and recovering stolen
    property, 416–417
Burns, 167
  accidental/nonaccidental,
    318–319
  classifications, 315, 316
  immersion, 317
  spill/splash injuries, 315–316

California Bureau of Criminal
  Identification, 8
California v. Beheler, 184
Canadian Automobile Theft
  Bureau, 478, 479
Can't-miss investments, 359–360
Capone, Al, 445
Carbon monoxide, 267, 275
Carboxyemoglobin, 275
Cardiopulmonary resuscitation, 45
Caregivers, elderly abuse by, 357
Cargo Criminal Apprehension
  Team, 375
Carjacking, 371–373

Carp, Deanne, 511
Case evaluation, 653–654
Case-hardened steering column
    ignition lock, 498
Cassidy, Butch (Robert Parker), 5–6
Catalytic combustion detector,
    586–587
Cat (drug), 617–619
Cattle rustling, 539, 542–543
Ceasefire system, 215–216
Cellular phone cloning, 431–434
    by hackers, 521–522
    as investigator tool,
        433–434
    losses due to, 432–433
Check fraud, 427–431
    as computer crime, 522
    methods of alteration, 430
    prevention of, 430–431
    types of schemes, 430
        identity assumption,
            429–430
        large-scale counterfeiting,
            429
        pay-roll check fraud, 430
Check fraud organizations
    major groups, 428
    players
        check passers, 428
        check procurers, 428–429
        counterfeiters, 428
        information brokers, 428
        leaders, 428
Chemicals
    for developing latent prints,
        87–89
    in fire death victims, 275
Chicago, first police department, 3
Child abductors
    general characteristics, 346
    motivation, 346–347
    planning by, 347
Child abuse
    burn injuries, 314–317
    Munchausen syndrome by
        proxy, 321–323
    role of physician, 320–321
    shaken-baby syndrome,
        319–321
Child molestation
    preferential molestation,
        325–326
    risk of false allegations, 334–335
    situational molesters, 323–325
Child pornography
    commercial, 336
    on computers, 338–339
    definition, 336
    homemade, 336–337
    on Internet, 524
    use of collection, 337–338
Child Protection Act of 1984, 337
Children
    assaults against, 314
    burn injuries, 314–317
    interviewing victims of
        molestation, 326–333
    reaction to victimization,
        333–334
    search for, 348–349
Child sex ring, 326
Chop shops, 468
Chromatographic impurity
    signature profile analysis,
        614–616

Chrystal meth, 617
Cincinnati, first police
    department, 3
Circumstantial evidence, 663–664
Citizens Against Poachers, 551
Civil War artifacts, 455
Clandestine drug labs, 635–638
Clan laboratories, 636
*Classification and Use of
    Fingerprints* (Henry), 14
Cloning, 521–522
    cell phones, 431
Clothing, in fire death
    identification, 273
Coatman, John, 19n
COBOL program, 515
Cocaine, 610–616
    acute and chronic effects,
        612–613
    crack, 613–614
    freebasing, 613
    policy and tracing, 614–616
    use of, 611–612
Cocaine fatality, 613
Cognitive interviewing technique,
    134–135
Coleoptera, 244
Collaborative Research Inc., 624
Colombia, heroin production, 607
Colquhoun, Patrick, 2
Combined DNA Index System, 212
Combustible-gas indicator,
    586, 638
Commercial burglary
    reducing risk of, 418–419
    safe burglaries, 411–414
Commercial child
    pornography, 336
Commercial shoplifters, 437
*Commercial Vehicle and Off-Road
    Equipment Identification
    Manual* (NCIB), 479
Competence
    of evidence, 659
    of witnesses, 125, 659
Compusketch, 37, 382
Computer crime
    categories of, 513
    cookies, 526
    definition, 512
    hacker profile, 526–528
    hardware and software thefts,
        524–525
    insider profile, 528–529
    internal, 514–518
    invasion of privacy, 525–526
    opportunities, 512–513
    prevention of, 531–534
    preventive medicine, 519
    sexually explicit material,
        525–526
    software piracy, 524–525
    source of threat, 513–514
    support of criminal enterprises,
        524
    telecommunications crimes,
        518–522
    types of, 512–514
    vulnerabilities, 513
Computerized fingerprint
    identification, 214–215
Computerized lie-detector scoring,
    170–171
Computer manipulation crimes,
    522–523

Computer printer evidence,
    117–118
Computers; *see also* Personal
    computers
    age-progression technology,
        348–349
    and child pornography,
        338–339
Computer viruses, 516–518
Concealed explosives, 598, 600
Condom trace evidence, 304–306
    exchangeable traces, 305
    guidelines for collecting,
        305–306
    value of, 305
Confessions, 162
    admissibility
        delay-in-arraignment rule,
            202–203
        free-and-voluntary rule,
            202
    definition, 201
    exception to hearsay rule, 666
    methods of documenting, 200
    reasons for, 188
Confidence games, 440–442
    bank examiner scheme, 441
    C. O. D. scam, 442
    inheritance scam, 441
    money-making machine, 442
    Nigerian oil, 442
    pigeon drop, 441
    three-card Monte, 441–442
Confidential communications,
    667–668
Confidential informants, 630
    debriefing, 632
    past reliability, 639
    payments to, 632–633
    perversely motivated,
        630–631
    rules for, 631–632
Contact burns, 315, 318–319
Control
    of crime scene, 36–38
    of evidence, 52–53
Controlled Substance Act,
    618, 623
Coordinate sketching method,
    57–58
Copper sulfate, 267
Corbone, Richard, 128
Cord, 79–81
Corpus delecti, 47
    condom trace evidence,
        305–306
    in rules of evidence, 662
Counsel, suspect request for, 181
Counterfeiting
    check fraud, 429
    by computer, 522
    technology for, 430
Covert investigations, 553
Cowles, Bob, 520
Crack cocaine, 613–614
Credibility
    attack on, 674–675
    of police witness, 670
    of witnesses, 125–126, 668
Credit card fraud
    fraudulent application, 426–427
    by hackers, 521
    prevention of, 427
    shave-and-paste schemes, 426
    types of, 425

Credit card security features,
    425–426
Crick Francis, 15
Crime analysis
    basic functions, 160–161
    data collection, 161–162
    definition, 159
    dissemination of data, 164
    external data sources, 161–162
    feedback, 164
    and tactical crime analysis,
        162–164
Crime-concealment, arson for,
    580–581
Crime Investigation (Kirk), 18
Crime laboratories
    Bureau of Alcohol, Tobacco,
        and Firearms,
        219–220
    expectations about, 207
    Federal Bureau of
        Investigation, 8–9,
        220–222
    Florida locations, 210
    handling evidence
        human factors, 217
        instrumental analysis,
            217–219
    measures of effectiveness,
        207–211
        admissibility of results, 211
        proximity, 208–209
        quality, 208
        timeliness, 209–210
    morgues, 207
    programs and personnel,
        206–207
    submission of evidence to,
        60–63
    scientific staff, 208
    technologies
        ceasefire and drugfire
            systems, 215–216
        DNA analysis, 211–213
        fingerprint identification
            system, 213–215
        toxicology reports, 266
        unified state systems, 209
Crime prevention, 161
    by surveillance, 168–169
Crime(s), 22; *see also* specific types
    categories of, 209
    impact of, 21
    national clearance rates, 30
    types of evidence, 47–48
Crime scene
    archaeological looting,
        459–461
    burglaries, 397–398
    in criminal investigation
        analysis, 283
    definition, 33–34
    description in reports, 149
    homicide, 227–229
    of infant abduction, 347–348
    presence of news media, 36–38
    robbery
        action stereotyping, 377
        forensic photographic
            analysis, 385
        physical stereotyping, 377
        situational stereotyping,
            378
        tactical situations, 378–379
    types of evidence, 47–48

Crime scene investigators, 34–36, 36–47
  cautions, 41
  conceptualization, 38–41
  documentation, 47
  inclusiveness rule, 41
  maintenance of control, 36–38
  protection from infection, 41–47
  questions about blood, 99–100
  questions on firearms evidence, 106–109
  search process, 47–52
  visual documentation, 53–60
Crime scene search
  boundary determination, 48
  choice of search pattern, 48–49
  coordination of, 50
  instruction of personnel, 49–50
  patterns of, 48–49
  termination of, 50–52
Criminal Identification Bureau, Chicago, 7
Criminal investigation, evolution of
  agricultural revolution, 2
  American initiatives, 3–10
  Bow Street Runners, 2
  industrial revolution, 2
  Metropolitan Police Act of 1829, 2–3
Criminal Investigation (Gross), 10
Criminal investigation analysis, 282–284
Criminal Investigation Department, London, 3
Criminalistics, 206
  historical contributors to, 18
  milestones in
    firearms identification, 17–18
    personal identification methods, 10–16
  origins of, 10
Cross-examination, 672, 673–675
Cross-projection sketching, 58–60
Custody
  definition, 183–187
  of evidence, 52–53
Cyancrylate, 89
Cyanide, 267
Cyclert, 617
Cystoscope, 405
Czolgosz, Leon, 8

Dactitoscopic Comparanda (Vucetich), 13
Dactylography; *see also* Fingerprints
  Automated Fingerprint Identification System, 213–215
  early discoveries, 13
  Faurot's work, 14
  Galton's system, 13
  Henry-Faulds controversy, 13
  Henry system, 13–14
  rivalry of systems, 15
  Vucetich's system, 13
  West case, 14
Darwin, Charles, 13
Data
  dissemination of feedback, 164
  at National Crime Information Center, 164

Databases
  National Crime Information Center, 480
  National Insurance Crime Bureau, 478–479
Data collection
  external sources, 161–162
  internal sources, 162
Deception
  body language, 193–197
  recognizing and coping with, 193–197
  verbal signals, 193
Decision models, 156–158
Decomposition, 242–243
Deductive reasoning, 23, 663–664
Dental comparison, 95–97
Dental evidence
  bite marks, 95–97
  in fire death identification, 272
  and forensic dentistry, 92
  in history, 93
  identification, 94
Dental records, 94
Department of Justice
  Bureau of Narcotics and Dangerous Drugs, 9
  Computer Crime Unit, 516
  guidelines for seizing computers, 530
Depressants/sedatives
  effects, 619
  glutethimide, 619–620
  meprobamate, 620
  methaqualone, 620
  rohypnol, 620–622
Deprol, 620
Dermal nitrate test, 252
Detective forces
  Bow Street Runners, 2
  earliest, 6–7
  London, 3
DFO chemical, 88
Diagnostic and Statistical Manual of Mental Disorders, 282
Dilaudiel, 608
Dillinger, John, 8
DiMaiao, Dominic J., 256, 257, 270, 285n
DiMaiao, Vincent J. M., 256, 257, 270, 285n
Direct examination, 672, 673–674
Disguises, 381
Distorted light bulbs, 567–568
DNA, 211–212
DNA analysis, 16, 210
  of blood evidence, 99, 103–104
  at crime labs, 211–213
  forensic identity test, 213
  human excretions/secretions, 104–105
DNA printing in fire death identification, 272–273
DNA typing
  DNA analysis, 16
  DNA as fingerprints, 15
  Orlando cases, 15–16
  from semen and hair, 301
Doctrine of judicial notice, 662–663
Documentation, 29
  of arson scene, 592
  of crime scene, 47, 53–60
    photographing, 55–56
    sketching, 56–60
    videotaping, 54–55

Documentation—*Cont.*
  of interrogations, 199–202
  of interviews, 135–136
Document examination
  age of documents, 226
  altered or obliterated handwriting, 117
  burned or charred paper, 116
  computer printers, 117–118
  handwriting/handprinting, 113–116
  mechanical-impression examination, 117
  paper examination, 226
  photocopiers, 116
  typewriting, 117
Documents
  forgeries, 114–115
  questioned, 113–118
Doe v. Borough of Barrington, 46
Domestic money laundering, 445–447
Dot-matrix printers, 117–118
Dreyfus, Alfred, 12
Drug abuse
  growth of, 605
  by physicians, 634–635
Drug Enforcement Administration, 9, 607, 636
  Operation Polycarp, 449–450
Drug enforcement agencies
  drug investigations, 628–629
  evidence handling, 639–641
  policy on informants, 631–633
  prevention responsibilities, 633–634
  proper clothing for raids, 638
  raids in laboratories, 637–638
  search warrant/probable cause, 638–639
  security problems, 639–641
  use of informants, 629–633
Drug investigations, 628–629
  informants, 629–633
  use of informants, 629–633
Drug laboratories
  clandestine, 635–638
  identifying, 635–636
  meth labs, 636–637
  raids in, 637–638
  seizure and forfeiture, 637
Drugs
  in fire death victims, 275
  glossary of terms, 643–645
  inventory display room, 640
  pharmacist responsibilities, 633–634
  physician responsibilities, 633
Duckworth v. Eagen, 182
Due process revolution, 9–10
Duval County Sheriff's Office, Florida, 161

Ear marks, 547, 549
Eckert, William G., 65n, 101, 102, 103, 120n
Edwards v. Arizona, 181
Egotistical informants, 630
Eighteenth Amendment, 8
Elderly
  crimes affecting
    burglary, 358
    financial abuse, 360–362
    robbery, 358

Elderly—*Cont.*
  crimes affecting—*Cont.*
    telemarketing frauds, 359–360
    vandalism, 358
  police officer communication with, 355–356
  quality of life, 353
  triads to protect, 362–363
Elderly abuse
  categories of mistreatment, 356–358
  extent of problem, 353
  signs and symptoms, 357–358
Electronic serial number, 431–433, 521–522
Embezzlement, 522
Encryption, 533–534
Enderby, England, 15
Enderby cases, 15
England, 2–3
Entomologists, in homicide investigation, 243–245
Entrance wound, 250–251
Environmental crime, 538, 553–559
  dimensions of, 538–539
  investigative procedures, 556–560
  legal and enforcement framework, 554–556
Environmentalists, radical, 539
Environmental Protection Agency, 484, 501, 557, 638
Escharatomy, 274
Escobedo v. Illinois, 10, 179
ESN reader, 432, 433
Ether-cocaine solution, 613
Ethnic gangs, 393–394
  in check fraud, 428, 429
  computer fraud, 522
  in shoplifting, 437–439
Evacuation for bomb threats, 597–598
Evans, Thomas, 587
Evidence; *see also* Physical evidence
  admissibility, 658
  admissibility of photographs, 56
  collection and care of, 52–53
  competence of, 659
  in computer crime, 530
  crime scene search, 47–52
  definition, 658
  handling in crime labs, 217–219
  from hypnosis, 129
  inclusiveness rule, 41
  locating and examining, 38–40
  materiality, 658–659
  needed by crime laboratory, 60–62
  needed by profilers, 283
  Ockham's razor rule, 283–284
  in Ponzi schemes, 444–445, 447
  proper sealing of, 63
  related to proof, 659
  relevance, 658
  in reports, 147–149
  submission to crime laboratory, 60–63
  transmission to police station, 29–30
  types and uses, 47–48
  types of, 663–665
  weight of, 660
Excavation of burial site, 234–235
Excusable homicide, 226

Executions by hanging, 261–262
Exit wound, 247, 252
Explosions, 592–593
   bomb threats, 597–600
   chemical, 593
   mechanical, 593
Explosion scene
   analysis of fuel source, 596–597
   investigating, 593–595
   locating and identifying
      evidence, 595–596
Explosives
   for blasting safes, 405
   packages and letters, 600–601
   pipe bomb, 578, 579
Explosives investigation, 592–597
   searching for concealed
      explosives, 598
Eye
   movements, 194–195
   petechial hemorrhaging, 263
Eyewitnesses
   evaluating credibility of,
      125–126
   mistaken identification by, 128
   reliability of identification,
      126–128

Facial expressions, 194–195
Fairfax County Police Department,
   Virginia, 260
False allegations
   of child molestation, 334–335
   of rape, 298–300
Family/domestic violence
   investigation of, 276–278
   stalking, 278–279
Farm-equipment theft, 473–477
   prevention, 500, 549
Faulds, Henry, 13
Faurot, Joseph, 14
Fay, John, 180, 190, 204n
Federal Aviation Administration,
   507, 508
Federal Boating Safety Act,
   503–504
Federal Bureau of Investigation,
   214, 497, 529
   on carjacking, 373
   on computer check fraud, 522
   crime laboratory, 8–9, 206,
      220–222
   DNA analysis, 16
   Drugfire system, 216
   Hazardous Materials Response
      Unit, 221
   National Academy, 9
   National Automotive Paint
      Files, 74–75
   National Center for the Analysis
      of Violent Crime,
      280–281, 346
   National Computer Crime
      Squad, 512
   National Crime Information
      Center, 164
   National Stolen-Parts Motor
      Vehicle Information
      system, 490
   Operation Polycarp, 449–450
   origin of, 8
   Racketeering Records Analysis
      Unit, 448–450
   reference files, 222

Federal Bureau of Investigation—
      Cont.
   Uniform Crime Reports, 209,
      423, 503
Federal Drug Control System
   Improvement, 615–616
Federal government, early police
   agencies, 7–9
Federal Law Enforcement Training
   Center, 529
Federal safety certification label,
   487–488
Federal Trade Commission, 522
Felony arrests, 22–23
Fences, 416, 434
   indicators of, 436
Fielding, Henry, 2
Fielding, John, 2
Field notes, 140–141
Field reports, 146, 147
Fifth Amendment, 171, 179, 667
Financial abuse of elderly, 360–362
Fingerprints, 12, 13–15; see also
      Dactylography
   Automated Fingerprint
      Identification System,
      213–215
   basis of identification, 83–84
   biometric identification system,
      431
   categories of latent prints, 83
   collecting and preserving latent
      prints, 91–92
   conditions affecting quality,
      84–85
   developing latent prints, 86–90
   elimination prints, 41
   in fire death identification, 272
   Henry classification system, 214
   latent prints on bodies, 90–91
   locating latent prints, 85–86
   major patterns of, 85
   marking and identifying print
      lifts, 90
   as physical evidence, 81–92
   as universal characteristic, 81–83
Finger Prints (Galton), 13
Fire accelerant detection
   catalytic combustion detector,
      586–587
   chemical color test, 586
   flame ionization detector, 587
   gas liquid chromatograph, 587
   infrared spectrophotometer,
      587–588
   olfactory detection, 585–586
   ultraviolet fluorescence, 588
Firearms
   ceasefire and drugfire systems,
      215–216
   discharged at close range, 251
   handguns, 151
   long guns, 152
   in suicides, 259–261
Firearms evidence
   collecting, 109
   investigator questions, 106–109
   marking, 109–110
Firearm wounds, 246–253
   close and distance shots,
      247–249
   contusion ring, 246
   residues, 252–253
   shotguns, 249–252
   smudge ring, 246

Fire deaths
   coordination and cooperation in
      investigating, 272
   degrees of burning, 272
   external body examination
      blistering/splitting skin, 273
      noncranial fractures, 274
      pugilistic body attitude, 274
      signs of trauma, 273
      skull fractures, 273
   flash fires, 275
   histological examination, 275
   identification of remains,
      272–273
   internal body examination,
      274–275
   motives, 275–276
   recording the scene, 276
   scene considerations, 273
   toxicological examination, 275
Fires
   accidental, 566
   burn indicators, 567–568
   common causes, 566
   factors needed to cause,
      565–566
   incendiary, 573
   missing items, 573
Fire-setting mechanisms
   ignition devices, 569–572
   plants, 572
   trailers, 473
   used by arsonists, 568–569
Fire-setting personalities,
   581–583
First Amendment, 526
Fisher, John, 18
Florida
   crime lab locations, 210
   Department of Law
      Enforcement, 213–214
Floyd, "Pretty Boy," 8
Flunitrezepan, 620–622
Fluorescent fingerprint powders,
   87–88
Follow-up investigation, 30
   archaeological looting, 459–461
   decision to initiate
      decision models, 156
      good leads, 159–160
      investigative solvability
         factors, 156
      named suspects, 159
      recontacting victims,
         156–159
   informants, 165–167
   lie detection, 169–171
   lineups, 172–173
   neighborhood canvas, 165
   relationships with victims and
      witnesses, 171–172
   reports on, 149–154
   of robbery, 382–385
   surveillance, 167–169
Force, in robbery, 367–368
Forensic accountants
   for money-laundering records,
      448–450
   for Ponzi schemes, 445
Forensic pathologists, 207, 229
   estimating time of death,
      239–246
   in search of buried bodies, 233,
      235–236
Fourteenth Amendment, 10, 666

Fourth Amendment, 650
Fracture match tool, 111, 112
Fraud schemes
   arson for profit, 575–577
   auto theft, 467–468
Fraudulent and distorted burglary
   complaint, 400
Fraudulent auto theft schemes
   investigation of, 492–494
   prevention of, 500–501
Fraudulent credit card application,
   426–427
Freud, Sigmund, 613
Frye v. United States, 211

Gainer v. State of Alabama, 362
Galton, Francis, 13
General Motors, 483, 498
   PASS-KEY II, 498
   VIN Plate and barcode, 487
Gideon v. Wainwright, 10
Glass evidence
   fracture match, 76
   radial/concentric fractures, 77
Goddard, Henry, 17
Gonzalez, Michael M., 578, 579,
   581, 582
Gravelle, Phillip, 18
Greenberg, Bernard, 243
Greenfield, James, 580, 602n, 603n
Grew, Nehemiah, 13
Grid search pattern, 49, 51
Gunpowder residue, 247–249
Gunshot residue, 252–253
Gunshot wounds, in suicides,
   259–261

Hackers
   credit card fraud, 521
   crimes by, 512–513
   illegal bulletin boards, 521
   National Weather Service
      break-in, 520–521
   profile of, 526–528
   Stanford Linear Accelerator
      Center break-in,
      518–520
   telephone misuse, 521–523
Hallucinogens
   effects of, 622
   hashish, 626–627
   hashish oil, 627
   ketamine, 627–628
   LSD 25, 624
   marijuana, 625–626
   MDMA, 623–624
   mescaline, 624
   PCP, 622–623
   psilocyclin, 624–625
   psilocyn, 624–625
Hammer-spur impressions, 260, 261
Handprinting examination, 113–116
Handwriting
   altered or obliterated, 117
   examination, 113–116
   samples, 115–116
Harding, Tonya, 279
Harrison Act, 9
Hashish, 626–627
Hazardous waste, 554–555
   improper disposal, 557, 558
   investigation of, 556–560
Hearing loss, 355–356

Hearsay evidence, 665–666
Hearsay rule
  basis of, 666–667
  exceptions to, 666–667
  hearsay evidence, 665–666
Heat-sealed clear plastic envelopes, 52, 53
Heavy equipment
  glossary of terms, 474
  illustrations of, 475–477
Heavy-equipment theft, 466, 473–477
  prevention of, 500
Henry, Edward, 13–14, 15
Henry fingerprint classification system, 214
Hepatitis B virus, 46
Hero fires, 582–583
Heroin, 606–607
Herschel, William, 13
Herschel-Faulds controversy, 13
Hitler, Adolf, 282
Hit-run accidents, 270–271
HIV
  disinfectants used for, 43
  protection from exposure to, 41–46
Hoffman-LaRoche, 622
Home invasion robberies, 373–374
Homemade child pornography, 336–337
Homicide
  dying declarations, 667
  fire deaths, 272–276
  law on, 226
  motivational models, 226–227
  and rape, 294–295
  serial murder, 280–282
  sudden infant death syndrome, 345–346
  variety of poisons used, 265–266
  vehicular, 270–271
Homicide investigation
  autopsy, 229–230
  chain of custody, 228–229
  estimating time of death
    body cooling, 239–240
    cadaveric spasm, 242
    decomposition, 242–243
    helpful observations, 239–246
    livor mortis, 240–242
    by means of carrion insects, 243–245
    rigor mortis, 240
    using aquatic insects, 245–246
  evidence from wounds
    defense wounds, 255–256
    firearm wounds, 246–253
    incised and stab wounds, 253
    lacerations, 254–255
    puncture wounds, 254
    strangulation, 256–258
  identification of body, 230–233
  medico-legal examination, 229
  personality reconstruction from unidentified remains, 231–233
  search for buried bodies
    discovery, 233–234
    examination of body, 235–236

Homicide investigation—Cont.
  search for buried bodies—Cont.
    excavation, 234–235
    identification of site, 236–238
    preplanning, 233
    use of cadaver dogs, 238–239
  tools and equipment, 229
Homicide investigations
  suicides, 259–270
  uncooperative victims, 258
Homicide scene
  arrival at
    agency representatives, 228
    confirming death, 228
    initial procedures, 227
    scene safety, 227–228
    scene walk-through, 228
  responding to, 227
Hoover, J. Edgar, 8, 9
Human excretions/secretions, 104–105
Hydrocarbon vapors, 586
Hydrochloric acid, 267
Hydrogenation laboratories, 636
Hydrogen cyanide, 275
Hydrogen sulfide, 275

Identification
  of body at homicide, 230–233
  of burial site, 236–238
  limiting factors, 127
Ignition devices
  candles, 570
  electrical systems, 571
  gas, 571
  matches, 569–570
  mechanical, 571–572
Illinois v. Perkins, 185
Incest, 339–340
  definition, 339
  mother's role in, 342–343
  police officer role, 342–343
Incestuous fathers, 340–342
Indirect evidence, 663–664
Individual characteristics of evidence, 68–69
Infant abduction
  investigative strategies, 348–349
  method, 348
  profile of abductor, 346–347
  scene of crime, 347–348
Informants; see also Confidential informants
  at arson investigation, 591
  awards/rewards, 633
  dealing with, 166–167
  department policy on, 631–633
  in drug cases, 629–633, 639
  establishing reliability of, 168
  in follow-up investigation, 165–167
  motives and types, 630–631
  payments to, 632–633
  providing protection for, 168
  types of, 166
Information
  data collection, 161–162

Information—Cont.
  for examining physician, 301–302
  focus on computer crime protection, 531
  from informants, 165–167
  from original investigation, 149
  provided by eyewitnesses, 126–128
  provided by juveniles, 125
Infrared spectrophotometer, 218, 587–588
Insects
  aquatic, 245–246
  carrion, 243–245
Instrumental analysis of evidence, 217–219
Insurance fraud
  auto theft, 467–468, 469–470
  false auto theft, 471–472
  inflated auto loss claims, 472
  vehicle theft investigation, 492–494
Intelligence-gathering
  on illegal group activities, 169
  on individual premises, 169
Internal computer crime
  back doors, 514
  definition, 513
  insider profile, 528–529
  logic bombs, 516
  packet sniffers, 514
  salami techniques, 514
  Trojan horses, 514
  viruses, 516–518
Internal Revenue Service, 9, 400
  fraudulent tax filings, 523
International Association of Auto Theft Investigators, 469
International Association of Chiefs of Police, 363
International Service Organization, 479
Internet pornography, 524, 526; see also Child pornography
Interrogation
  beginning, 192–193
  compared to interviewing, 178, 180
  composing and asking questions, 193
  court rulings, 179–188
  documenting, 199–202
  importance of listening, 198–199
  in-custody, 183–188
  legal definition, 187–188
  objectives, 178
  planning for
    interrogation room, 190–192
    interrogator, 188–190
    reasons for confessions, 188
  recognizing and coping with deception, 193–197
  requirements prior to, 179–183
  statement analysis, 197
  techniques and approaches, 197–198
Interrogator
  knowledge of suspect, 190
  knowledge of victim, 189
  knowledge of offense, 189
  objectives on interrogations, 178

Interrogator—Cont.
  preparation, 189–190
  qualifications, 188–189
Interviewing
  barriers to, 125
  cognitive technique, 134–135
  compared to interrogation, 178, 180
  importance of listening, 135
  interviewing molested children, 326–333
  neighborhood canvas, 165
  post-interview checklist, 136
  process and techniques, 142–135
  purpose of, 123–124
  time, place, and setting, 130–132
Interviews
  in arson investigation, 588–591
  comparison of documenting methods, 136
  documenting, 135–136
  leading questions to children, 332–333
  of rape victim, 295
  report format, 149
  in sex-related investigation, 295–298
Investigation; see also Follow-up investigation; specific types of investigation
  cocaine trafficking, 614–616
  of computer crime, 529–531
  dangerous drugs, 628–629
  of environmental crime, 556–560
  of explosion scene, 593–595
  of fire deaths, 272
  follow-up, 30, 149–154
  importance of, 22–23
  of infant abduction, 348–349
  information from original, 149
  of larceny, 424
  Munchausen syndrome by proxy, 323
  neighborhood canvas, 165
  preliminary, 25–30
  purpose of, 22
  of shaken-baby syndrome, 320
  of sudden infant death syndrome, 344–345
  terminology, 22
  qualities of investigators, 23–24
  uncooperative victims, 258
  use of cell phone cloning for, 433–434
  use of hypnosis, 128–130
  of wildlife crimes, 551–553
Investigator, 22
  emotional reactions to pedophiles, 335–336
  essential qualities of, 23–24
  evaluating credibility of witnesses, 126
  evaluation of case, 653–654
  fathering/evaluating information, 123–124
  follow-up, 30
  at homicide scene, 227–229
  as interviewers, 124
  proximity of crime labs, 208–209
  qualification for wildlife crimes, 550

Investigator—*Cont.*
  relationships with victims and
    witnesses, 171–172
  tools needed by, 229
  as witness, 670–677

"James Bond" syndrome, 630
Jeffreys, Alec, 15
Jury
  and police witness, 671
  rules of evidence, 658–669
Juveniles
  data collection on, 161–162
  interviewing, 131–132
  as witnesses, 125

Kansas City Police Department,
  79–81
Karchmer, Clifford L., 580, 602n,
  603n
Karpis, Alvin, 9
Kerberos program, 533
Kerrigan, Nancy, 279
Ketalar, 628
Ketamine, 627–628
Ketaset, 628

Lacassagne, Prof., 17
Laceration wounds, 254–255
Lambert, J. Blake, 519, 535n
Langer, William, 282
Lanning, Kenneth V., 326, 336,
  350n, 351n
Larceny
  archaeological looting,
    453–461
  bull semen thefts, 539
  cattle rustling, 539
  cellular phone cloning, 431–434
  check fraud, 427–431
  confidence scams, 440–442
  credit card fraud, 425–427
  essential elements, 423
  fraudulent use of Social
    Security numbers,
    451–453
  frequency and types of, 423
  hardware and software thefts,
    524–525
  investigative procedures, 424
  livestock/tack theft, 541–546
  receiving stolen property,
    434–437
  shoplifting, 437–440
  theft of agrichemicals, 540–541
  timber theft, 539–540
  white-collar crime, 442–450
Larceny investigation
  archaeological looting, 458–461
  of fences and receivers, 436
  money laundering, 447–450
  Ponzi schemes, 444–445
  procedures, 424
Larson, John, 18
Lasers, 39
  for visualizing latent prints,
    89–90, 91
Latent fingerprints
  from bodies, 90–91
  categories of, 83
  collecting and preserving,
    91–92

Latent fingerprints—*Cont.*
  conditions affecting quality,
    84–85
  locating, 85–86
  marking and identifying, 90
  methods for developing
    chemicals, 87–88
    cyanocrylate, 89
    fluorescent powders, 87
    superglue fuming, 89
    traditional powders, 86–87
    visualizing under
      laser/alternative
      lights, 89–90
  Unidentified Latent
    Fingerprint File,
    213–214
Lattes, Leone, 18
Law
  on archaeological looting,
    455–458
  on burglary, 395–396
  on cloning cell phones, 431
  on confessions/admissions,
    202–203
  on environmental crime,
    554–556
  on homicide, 226
  on interrogation, 187–188
  on lie detection, 171
  on rape/sexual assault, 294
  on rights of suspects, 179–187
  on Social Security numbers, 453
  on stalking, 278
  on vehicle identification,
    488–490
Letter bombs, 600–601
Lie detection
  computerized scoring, 170–171
  legal considerations, 171
  polygraph, 169–171
  psychological stress evaluator,
    170
Listening
  at interrogations, 198–199
  by interviewers, 135
Livestock crime, 541–546
  cattle rustling, 542–543
  horse rustling, 545–546
  physical evidence, 547–549
  preventing, 550
  prevention measures, 549–550
Livor mortis, 240–242
  after suicide by hanging, 263
LSD 25, 622, 624
LSD (lysergic acid), 622, 625
Luma Lite, 39–40
  for visualizing latent prints,
    89–90

Mallory v. United States, 203
Mapping
  of burial site, 233, 235
  programs, 163–164
Mapp v. Ohio, 10
Marine theft
  hull identification number,
    503–504
  investigation, 506
  prevention of, 506
  scope of problem, 502–503
  title and registration issues,
    504–505
Mathis v. United States, 184–185
McNabb v. United States, 202–203

Men, suicide rates, 269
Mental disorders, 282
Meperidine, 608–609
Meprobamate, 620
Mercury poisoning, 267
Metcathinone, 617–619
Methadone, 609
Methamphetamine labs,
  636–637
Methqualone, 620
Methyl alcohol, 267
Methylphenidate, 617
Metropolitan Police Act of 1829,
  England, 2–3
Metzger, Herb, 169
Michigan State Police, 618
Michigan v. Mosely, 181
Miltown, 620
Minnick v. Mississippi, 181
Miranda, Ernest, 179
Miranda v. Arizona, 10, 179–180,
  182, 183–189, 202
Misadventure, 226
Misdemeanors, 22
Missing children, 348–349
Mitochondrial DNA, 212
Mobile identification number,
  431–433, 521–522
Modern Criminal Investigation
  (Soderman &
  O'Connell), 18
Modus operandi, 161
  bomber-arsonists, 595
Molested children, interviews of,
  326–333
Money laundering
  domestic laundries, 445–447
  foreign laundries, 447–450
  fraudulent documents, 450
  by organized crime, 445–450
  structuring financial
    transactions, 450
Moore, P. A., 518
Moralse, George, 128
Morgues, 207
Morphine, 606
Motives
  for child abduction, 346–347
  for fire deaths, 275–276
  of witnesses, 124–126
Mulberry Street Morning Parade,
  7–9
Munchausen syndrome by proxy,
  321–323, 345
Murder, 226; *see also* Homicide

Narcotics, 606–608
  handling and security problems,
    639–641
  synthetic, 608–609
National Bureau of Standards
  automated fingerprint
    identification process, 214
National Center for Missing and
  Exploited Children, 347,
  348
National Center for the Analysis of
  Violent Crime, 280–281,
  346
National Computer Crime Squad,
  512
National Computer Security
  Association, 516

National Consumers League, 522
National Crime Information
  Center, 9, 416, 436, 472,
  490, 497, 503
  boat file, 505–506
  description, 164
  functions of, 480
  purpose, 478
National Forensic Science
  Technology Center, 206
National Fraudulent Check File,
  222
National Highway Safety
  Administration, 501
National Highway Traffic Safety
  Administration, 488, 489
National Institute for Occupational
  Safety and Health, 374
National Institute of Justice, 513
National Insurance Crime Bureau,
  466, 467–468, 469, 480,
  485, 487, 499
  database services, 478–479
  International Division, 479
  resources and functions,
    478–479
National Institute of Justice, 278
National Law Enforcement
  Telecommunication
  System, 505
National Motor Vehicle Certificate
  of Title File, 222
National Stolen-Parts Motor
  Vehicle Information
  system, 490
National Vehicle Identification
  Number Standard File, 222
National Violence Against Women
  survey, 278, 280
National Weather Service break-in,
  520, 529
Newark, New Jersey, first police
  department, 3–4
*New England Journal of
  Medicine*, 344
New Orleans, first police
  department, 3
Newport Beach Police
  Department, 92
New York Police Department,
  rogues' gallery, 6–7
New York v. Quarles, 185
Nicolosi, Rosemary, 427
Nigerian gangs, 428
Ninhydrin, 88
Nitric acid, 267
Nitrous oxide, 275
Nolan, Daniel, 14
Nontraditional interrogation
  room, 191
Nonverbal signals, 193–197
North American Export
  Committee, 481
North American Man-Boy Love
  Association, 338
North Carolina State Bureau of
  Investigation, 614, 615,
  616
Northern Michigan University, 617

Ockham's razor rule, 283–284
O'Connell, John, 18
Offenders
  in burglaries, 392–395

Offenders—*Cont.*
in robbery, 368–371
Offense
categories of, 209
exceptionally cleared, 154
investigator knowledge of, 189
unfounded, 154
Omnichrome, 39, 89–90
Ontario Provincial Police
Department, 90
Operating ratios, 447
Operation Cathedral, 524
Operation Polycarp, 449–450
Opium, 606
Optimil, 620
Oregon v. Mathaison, 183, 184
Organized crime
and agricultural crime, 538
burglary, 393–394
and computers, 524
domestic money laundering,
445–447
foreign money laundering,
447–450
fraudulent documents, 450
infiltrating police departments,
631
secreting funds, 448–449
sources of illicit funds, 449–450
Orlando, Florida, 15–16
Orozco v. Texas, 184
Osborn, Albert, 18
Outlaw groups, 169

Paraffin test, 252
Parks, Tyler, 621, 624, 629
*Passenger Vehicle Identification
Manual* (NICB), 479
Patterson v. Illinois, 181
PCP (phenylcylidine), 622–623
Pedophiles
and child pornography, 337
computers and child porn,
338–339
investigator reactions to,
335–336
Peel, Robert, 2, 3
Peel, the, 403–404
Pennsylvania State Police, 8
Pennsylvania v. Bruder, 186
Pennypacker, Samuel, 8
Perception
by eyewitnesses, 127
of witnesses, 124–126
Perkinje, John, 13
Personal computers, 511; *see also*
Computer crime
theft of, 524
Personal identification methods
anthropometry, 11–13
dactylography, 13–15
DNA typing, 15–16
kinds of, 10–11
Person description, 149, 150
in reports, 145
Petechial hemorrhaging, 263
Pethidine, 608–609
Peyote, 624
Phenmetrazine, 617
Philadelphia police ordinance, 3
Phosphorous, 267
Photographs
admissibility of evidence, 56
arson scene, 592

Photographs—*Cont.*
of burial site, 233–234
of crime scene, 55–56
of fire death scene, 276
forensic photography analysis,
385
of impressions in snow, 74
of shoe impatiens, 72, 73
Physical evidence, 33, 38–39, 663;
see also Evidence
agricultural crime, 547–549
archaeological looting,
458–461
assuring integrity of, 228–229
blood, 99–104
burglary scene, 397–398
class versus individual
characteristics, 68–69
collection and care of, 52–53
common errors in collecting,
303
condom trace evidence,
304–306
crime lab admissibility, 211
crime scene search, 47–52
defense wounds, 255–256
dental, 97
DNA analysis, 211–213
in drug cases, 639–641
examination in BATF labs,
219–220
examination in Federal Bureau
of Investigation labs,
220–222
explosion scene, 595–596
fibers, cloth
fragments/impressions,
77–79
fingerprints, 81–92
fire accelerant residues,
583–585
from firearms, 106–110
firearm wounds, 246–253
in fire deaths, 272–276
glass, 75–77
hair, 97–99
hazardous waste crime, 560
human excretions/secretions,
104–105
incised/stab wounds, 253
instrumental analysis of,
217–219
laceration wounds, 254–255
lipstick/lip-print, 105–106
paint, 74–75
puncture wounds, 254
questioned documents,
113–118
rape victim's clothing, 302–303
request for examination of, 62
safe insulation, 408–409
sex offenses, 300–304
soil, 69–74
strangulation wounds, 256–258
string, cord, and rope, 79–81
submission to crime laboratory,
60–63
in suicides, 259–269
tool marks, 111–113
vehicle homicide, 270–271
Physicians
drug abuse by, 634–635
and drug availability, 633
Pijeira, Emetrio Marino, 435–436
Pinkerton, Allan, 4–5

Pinkerton National Detective
Agency, 4–6
Poison
suicide by, 265–267
types and symptoms, 267
Police departments
adoption of uniforms, 4
computer crime units, 512
drug investigations, 628–629
first American departments, 3–4
infiltrated by crime, 631
in London, 2–3
news-release policies, 37–38
policy on informants, 631–633
relationships with victims and
witnesses, 171–172
and rights of suspects,
179–188
and US Supreme Court, 9–10
Police officer; *see also* Investigators
arrest procedures, 649–650
burglary-in-progress calls,
396–397
communicating with elderly,
355–356
incest cases, 342–343
Police witness
appearance and demeanor, 671
characteristics of good witness,
670–671
credibility, 670
cross-examination, 674–675
direct and cross-examination,
673–674
leaving witness stand, 676–677
role, 670
in trial process, 671–672
understanding jury, 671
use of notes on stand, 675–676
on witness stand, 672–676
Ponzi, Charles, 443
Ponzi schemes, 443–445
cash flow analysis, 444–445
problems for law enforcement,
445
Popay, Sergeant, 3
Preinterrogation requirements
legal, 179–180
suspect's response, 180–183
Preliminary investigation, 25–30
for arson, 564
key elements, 25, 28–30
Preludin, 617
Probable cause, 168
drug enforcement, 638–639
requirement, 651–652
Professional Criminals in America
(Byrnes), 7
Proof; *see also* Evidence; Physical
evidence
definition, 658
related to evidence, 659

Questioned Documents
(Osborne), 18
Questions
for arson firefighters, 588–589
for arson informants, 591
for arson insurance personnel,
589
for arson suspects, 590
for arson target, 590–591
for arson witnesses, 588–589
at interrogation, 193

Rape
anger rape, 290–293
autoerotic death, 306–310
delayed reporting of, 298
false allegations, 298–300
as legal term, 294
power rape, 289–290
reasons for not reporting, 298
theft during, 297–298
type and sequence of, 296
typology of, 288–289
Rape victim, 295
collecting clothing of, 302–303
instructions to, 301
record of injuries, 306
verbal activity, 297
Rapists
change in attitude, 297
verbal activity, 296
Receivers, 434
indicators of, 436
operations of, 435–436
Receiving stolen property,
434–437
indicators of fences/receivers,
436
operations of receivers, 435–436
preventive measures, 436–437
Reliability
of eyewitness identification,
126–128
of hypnosis, 129
Report format
evidence, 147–149
interviews, 149
suspects, 146–147
witnesses, 147
Reports
checklist for person description,
150
common elements, 144–146
on follow-up investigation,
149–154
importance of using, 141–143
rules for writing, 143–144
suspects named in, 159
Residential burglary, 414–416
reducing risk of, 417–418
Rhode Island v. Innis, 187–188
Robbery
anticipatory measures, 387–388
arrest probabilities, 375–376
automatic teller machines, 374
carjacking, 371–373
of convenience stores, 374
definition, 365
of elderly, 358
elements of, 366–368
home invasion, 373–374
intraracial crime, 369
preventive measures, 386–387
reactive measures, 388
taxi-cab, 374
three-strikes law, 385
truck-hijacking, 374–375
victims and offenders, 368–371
visible street robberies, 371
Robbery investigation
follow-up, 382–385
original investigation, 379–382
responding to scene, 376–378
tactical situations at scene,
378–379
Robbery investigators, educative
responsibilities, 386–387

Rules of evidence
  crime lab results, 211
  doctrine of judicial notice,
    662–663
  evidentiary concepts, 658–662
  evidentiary privileges, 667–668
  hearsay rule, 665–667
  types of evidence, 663–665
  use of witnesses, 126
  witnesses, 668
Rustlers, 538
  of cattle, 539, 542–543
  of horses, 545–546

Safes
  attack methods
    blasting, 405
    burning, 406–408
    carry-off, 408
    drilling, 405–406
    manipulation of
      combination, 408
    the peel, 403–404
    the pry, 408
    pulling, 403
    the punch, 401–403
    the rip, 405
    types of, 401
Search warrant, 168, 169
  drug enforcement, 638–639
Semen, 105
  as evidence, 301
Serial murder, 280–282
Sex offenses
  autoerotic death, 306–310
  child molestation, 323–326
  child pornography, 336–339
  child pornography on Internet,
    524
  common errors in collecting
    evidence, 303
  false allegations, 298–300
  incest, 339–343
  information for examining
    physician, 301–302
  Internet pornography, 526
  mutual-consent, 288
  nuisance, 288
  semen and hair evidence, 301
  serious, 288
  typology of rape, 288–293
  victim and physical evidence,
    300–304
Sex-related investigation, 294–298
  condom trace evidence,
    304–306
  incest, 342–343
  interviewing molested children,
    326–333
  interviews, 295–298
  interview of victim, 295
  record of injuries, 306
Shaken-baby syndrome
  indicators and symptoms, 320
  investigative guidelines, 320
  mechanics of injury, 319–320
  role of physician, 320–321
Shoe impressions, 70
  preserving, 71–72
  in soil, 72–74
  in vehicle suicide, 268
Shoplifters
  boosters and pilferers, 437
  profiles of, 437

Shoplifting, 437–440
  reducing losses, 439–440
  tools used in, 439
Shotgun wounds, 249–252
  entrance wound, 250–251
  lack of exit wound, 252
  range determination,
    251–252
  wad, 251
Sketching, 47
  basic equipment, 58
  general considerations, 57
  information included in, 57
Sketching methods
  baseline, 57–58
  coordinate, 57–58
  cross-projection, 58–60
  rough and smooth sketches, 60
  triangulation, 58, 59
Smith and Wesson
  Identi-Kit, 381–382
  manual Identification Kit, 381
Social Security numbers
  fraudulent use of, 451–453
  geographic area designations,
    452
  pocketbook numbers, 451
Software
  mapping programs, 163
  for sketching, 60
  theft of, 524
Soil evidence
  class characteristics, 69
  locating and handling, 69–71
  preserving shoe prints, 71–72
  preserving shoe prints, 72–74
Stalking
  categories of stalkers, 278–279
  legal definitions, 278
  protective orders, 279–280
  psychological/social
    consequences, 280
  threat management, 279
States
  early police agencies, 7–9
  laws on archaeological sites,
    457–458
  Marks and Brands units, 545
Stimulants
  amphetamines, 616–617
  cocaine, 610–616
  crystallized
    methamphetamine, 617
  kemoline, 617
  methcathinone, 617–619
  methylphenidate, 617
  phenmetrazine, 617
Stolen property
  receiving, 434–437
  recovering, 439
  tracing and recovering,
    416–417
Stolen-vehicle indicators; see also
    Automobile theft; Vehicle
    theft
  condition of vehicle, 491–492
  suspicious driver behavior, 492
Strangulation wounds
  ligature strangulation, 256–257
  manual, 257–258
Sudden infant death syndrome
  as homicide, 345–346
  misconceptions about, 344
  police officer role, 344–345
  research on, 344

Suicide
  common methods, 259
  by cutting/piercing
    instruments, 265
  by drowning, 264–265
  by gas, 267
  by hanging, 261–263
  insurance schemes, 269–270
  jumping from high places, 267
  main factors in investigation,
    260
  methods and evidence of
    gunshot wounds,
    259–261
  by poisons, 265–267
  reasons for, 259
  by sleeping pills, 264
  vehicular, 267–269
Surveillance
  definition and terminology, 167
  objectives, 167–169
  uses of, 167
Suspects
  arrest of, 648–653
  arson cases, 590, 591–592
  at arson investigation, 590
  charging, 648
  court rulings on, 179–188
  investigator knowledge of, 190
  likelihood of flight, 654
  named in report, 159
  probable-cause requirement,
    651–652
  in rape cases, 306
  in reports, 146–147
  request for counsel, 181
  response to police, 180–183
  right to remain silent, 181
  waiver of rights, 181

Tatoos
  in fire death identification, 273
  livestock identification, 547
Telecommunications crime
  hacking, 518–521
  illegal bulletin boards, 521
  telephone misuse, 521–523
Terry v. Ohio, 185–186
Theft, 424; *see also* Burglary;
    Larceny; Robbery
  during rape, 297–298
Trials
  evidentiary concepts,
    658–662
  police witnesses, 670–677
  rules of evidence, 658–668

Ultraviolet light, 40
  for fluorescent powders, 87
  for visualizing latent prints,
    89–90
Uniform Crime Reports, 209, 423,
    503
United States
  early state/federal police
    agencies, 7–9
  emergence of municipal
    detectives, 6–7
  evolution of criminal
    investigation, 3–10
  first police departments, 2–3
  Pinkerton agency, 4–6
United States Coast Guard, 504

United States Comptroller of the
    Currency, 447–448
United States Customs Service,
    478, 484
United States Forest Service, 539
United States Immigration and
    Naturalization Service, 480
United States Postal Inspection
    Service, 425
United States Secret Service, 8,
    168, 528
  cell phone crime
    jurisdiction, 431
United States Supreme Court,
    206, 211
  and Internet pornography, 526
  on rights of suspects, 179,
    181–188, 202–203
United States v. Dockery, 184
United States v. J. H. H., 186–187
United States v. Lee, 184

Vandalism, 358
  and arson, 580
Vehicle
  odometer tampering, 501–502
  preinsurance inspection, 501
Vehicle fires, 494–496
  electrical system
    inspection, 496
  fuel system inspection, 496
  inspection of body, 496
  inspection of motor and
    radiator, 496
  inspection of salvage, 495–496
Vehicle homicide
  hit-run, 270–271
  search for vehicle, 271
Vehicle identification, 482–491
  attempts to conceal, 485–488
  black-box exemption, 498
  check digit calculation
    formula, 486
  components requiring
    marking, 489
  federal legislation, 488–490
  federal safety certification label,
    487–488
  gray-market vehicles,
    484–485
  model year, 487
Vehicle identification number, 222,
    468, 482–491
  aircraft, 507, 508
  boats, 507
  editing and reconstruction, 490
  restoration, 490–491
Vehicle identification number
  etching, 498
Vehicle theft; *see also*
    Aircraft/avionics theft;
    Marine theft
  automobile theft, 466–472
  farm equipment, 473–477
  glossary of terms, 474
  heavy equipment, 473–477
  prevention programs,
    497–500
  types of vehicles, 465
Vehicle theft investigation
  contact with owners, 496–497
  fraud cases, 492–494
  locating and handling vehicles,
    481–482

Vehicle theft investigation—*Cont.*
   major investigative resources,
     478–481
   stolen-vehicle indicators,
     491–492
   tools and techniques, 474–477
   vehicle fires, 494–496
   vehicle identification, 482–491
Verbal activity
   of rape victim, 297
   of rapist, 296
Victim
   in criminal investigation
     analysis, 283
   dying declarations, 667
   investigator knowledge of, 189
   investigator relationships with,
     171–172
   recontacting, 156–159

Victim—*Cont.*
   of robbery, 368–371
   sex offenses, 300–304
   of sudden infant death
     syndrome, 344
Videotaping
   arson scene, 592
   of crime scene, 54–55
   at interrogations, 199–200
Violation, 22
   establishing existence of,
     167–168
Violators; *see also* Suspects
   apprehending, 168
   identifying associates of, 168
   illegal groups, 169
Violent criminal apprehension
   program; *see* VI-CAP
     Crime Report

White collar crime, 442–450
   money laundering, 445–450
   Ponzi/pyramid schemes,
     443–445
Wildlife crimes, 538
   dimensions of, 538–539
   investigation of, 551–553
   investigator qualifications, 550
   major threats, 550
   poaching and poachers,
     550–551
Witness
   abstract concepts, 125
   at arson scene, 588
   attacking credibility of, 674–675
   barriers to interviewing, 125
   competence of, 125, 659, 668
   impeaching, 674
   information from, 124

Witness—*Cont.*
   investigator relationships with,
     171–172
   juvenile, 125
   motivation and perceptions,
     124–126
   reinterviewing, 132
   in reports, 147
   requirements for, 124
   rules of evidence, 668
   testimony, 672
   time, place, and setting,
     130–132
   traits, 124
   use of hypnosis, 128–130
Women
   reasons for not reporting
     rape, 298
   suicide rates, 269